The Life of Muḥammad

Al-Wāqidī's Kitāb al-Maghāzī

Muḥammad b. ʿUmar al-Wāqidī was a Muslim scholar, born in Medina in the Second Century hijra. Of his several writings the most significant is the Kitāb al-Maghāzī, one of the earliest standard histories of the life of the Prophet.

Rizwi Faizer brings this key text, translated into English for the first time, to a new, English-speaking audience. It includes an "Introduction," authored jointly by Rizwi Faizer and Andrew Rippin, and a carefully prepared index. The book deals with the events of the Prophet's life from the time of his emigration from Mecca to his death, and is generally considered to be biographical. Bringing together events in the Prophet's life with appropriate passages of Qur'ān in a considered sequence, the author presents an interpretation of Islam that existed in his times. It includes citations from the Qur'ān, as well as poetry that appears to have been inspired by activities during his life.

This English translation of a seminal text on the life of Muḥammad is an invaluable addition to the existing literature, and will be of great significance to students and scholars in the field of Islamic studies, Islamic history, Medieval history and Arabic literature.

Rizwi Faizer is an independent scholar, residing in Cornwall, Ontario, Canada. Having obtained her B.A. at the University of Peradeniya, Sri Lanka, she went on to work at the Asia Council for Law and Development in Colombo. In 1984 she obtained her M.A. at the University of New Brunswick, Fredricton, and then obtained her Ph.D. at the McGill University in 1995.

Routledge studies in classical Islam
Series editor: Andrew Rippin
University of Victoria, Canada

The nature of the historical period in which the emergence of Islamic civilization occurred has produced vigorous scholarly debate. While the general impact of the newly formed Arab empire on pre-existing cultures is evident to historians, establishing the varied trajectories of the transition from pre-Islamic times to the period in which the establishment of an Islamic social, political, administrative and cultural order took place is a matter of significant discussion. *Routledge Studies in Classical Islam* is dedicated to the best scholarship on that period, revealing the difficulties and the complexities in establishing the history of the time. Focusing on the Arab and Persian worlds up to the tenth century, the series includes original textual sources in translation, modern scholarly works not previously available in English, and newly commissioned works dedicated to examining the period critically in light of the evidence that is available to historians today. Every work in this series focuses on the question of "how do we know" when it comes to establishing the history of this controversial period, producing a persuasive body of insightful scholarship as conducted in the academic community today.

1. The Biography of Muhammed
Nature and authenticity
Gregor Schoeler, translated by Uwe Vagelpohl, edited by James E. Montgomery

2. The Life of Muḥammad
Al-Wāqidī's Kitāb al-Maghāzī
Edited by Rizwi Faizer

The Life of Muḥammad

Al-Wāqidī's Kitāb al-Maghāzī

Edited by Rizwi Faizer

Translated by Rizwi Faizer, Amal Ismail and AbdulKader Tayob
With an introduction by Rizwi Faizer and Andrew Rippin

Routledge
Taylor & Francis Group
LONDON AND NEW YORK

First published 2011
by Routledge
2 Park Square, Milton Park, Abingdon, Oxon, OX14 4RN

Simultaneously published in the USA and Canada
by Routledge
711 Third Avenue, New York, NY 10017

Routledge is an imprint of the Taylor and Francis Group, an informa business

First issued in paperback 2013

Typeset in Times New Roman by
RefineCatch Limited, Bungay, Suffolk

British Library Cataloguing in Publication Data
A catalogue record for this book is available from the British Library

Library of Congress Cataloging-in-Publication Data
A catalog record has been requested for this book

ISBN: 978–0–415–57434–1 (hbk)
ISBN: 978–0–415–86485–5 (pbk)
ISBN: 978–0–203–84458–8 (ebk)

Contents

Preface

This translation of al-Wāqidī's *Kitāb al-Maghāzī*, based on manuscripts edited by Marsden Jones,[1] began while I was working on my Ph.D. dissertation, "Ibn Isḥāq and al-Wāqidī Revisited: A case Study of Muhammad and the Jews in Biographical Literature" (McGill University 1995). Needless to say, I focused on those chapters that involved the Jews, such as the chapters on the Banū Qaynuqāʿ, Khandaq, the Murder of Ibn al-Ashraf, Khaybar and so forth. As a Sri Lankan who entered McGill with a limited knowledge of Arabic, I found the Medieval Arabic text extremely challenging, and the help of generous fellow students from Jordan and Sudan, who had enjoyed an Arabic education and were, for their own part, intrigued by the relatively unknown work of al-Wāqidī, was greatly appreciated.

The translation of al-Wāqidī's entire *Kitāb al-Maghāzī* that is presented here, has been to a large extent a matter of sheer perseverance, but also the result of the good fortune of having met the right people at the right time. There was firstly Abdul Kader Tayob, who I met at a conference in Denver, Colorado, and who very willingly agreed to take the journey with me as I struggled through the text, dictionary[2] in hand. Tayob lives in South Africa, and since I myself had just become a resident of Cornwall, Ontario, Canada, we were fortunate to have the connectivity provided by the internet, which was, by this time, a well-understood feat of technology. E-mail played a huge part in enabling our communication and this translation; that truly was quite the opportunity. Of course, it was also a very slow process. When Tayob finally became too busy with his own lecturing and writing to stay with the translation, however, Amal Ismail appeared practically at my door-step. Her family had decided to immigrate to Canada from Egypt and they had purchased a home in my very neighbourhood. Besides being an engineer who has qualified in Egypt, Amal is deeply involved in the study of Islam as a personal quest, and, when I told her of my interest in al-Waqidī, she happily became an enthusiastic participant in the translation, and helped me complete the work despite all the other neighbourhood distractions.

For an introduction to this work I have turned to Andrew Rippin, who I first came to know as an author of very fine textbooks on Islam while lecturing at Carleton University, Ottawa. Since then I have met him, read many more of his writings and come to respect his unorthodox views on the rise of Islam.

Essentially the overall translation has been my responsibility, and I am accountable for the mistakes that occur. I have used other translated material to guide me especially in two particular areas. Within the work, al-Wāqidī does include several passages from the Qur'ān and in translating these passages I have been guided by the published translations of Yusuf Ali[3] and A. J. Arberry.[4] Al-Wāqidī also cites many verses of poetry which are familiar because they also appear in ʿAbdul Malik Ibn Hishām's (d. 218 AH) edition of the work of Ibn Isḥāq known as *Sīrat Rasūl Allāh*.[5] I have used the translation of Alfred Guillaume[6] wherever possible for these passages as I felt this was necessary, but also unavoidable if one was to indicate that this poetry was either taken from Ibn Isḥāq without acknowledgment, or a well known feature of the time.

In order to maintain the flow of translation, annotation has been avoided; instead, glosses have tended to be incorporated into the text. Consistency of translation of technical terms has been considered highly important. It is also my hope that the index to the book will serve to provide some level of overall coherence and cross-referencing that may be useful. Ultimately, the goal has simply been to make this text accessible to a greater range of readers than it currently is so as to popularize the study of it and incorporate it more fully into the resources available for the study of the life of Muḥammad. Those needing access to more detailed analysis of the text would best be served by accessing the Arabic original.

Last but by no means least, I would like to thank my husband and three sons but particularly Iqbal, for their patience, kindness and tolerance. I dedicate this work to my mother, Noor Rahmaniya Kaleel, nee Marikar Bawa whose very beautiful recitation of the Qur'ān and love for the Prophet, peace be upon him, were what brought me to this venture.

Rizwi Faizer, January 2010

Introduction

Rizwi Faizer and Andrew Rippin

Abū ʿAbdullāh Muḥammad b. ʿUmar al-Wāqidī was born in Medina around the year 130/747, towards the end of the Umayyad caliphate during the reign of Marwān b. Muḥammad, and died at the age of 78 around 207/823: he was buried in the cemetery of Khaizurān in Baghdad[7]. Occupied in the sale of wheat,[8] al-Wāqidī nevertheless spent much of his time collecting information and traditions about the Prophet Muḥammad. He made a point of meeting with those who had been acquainted with either a companion of the Prophet or one of their descendants, and visiting the places to which the Prophet had been. When the ʿAbbasid caliph Hārūn al-Rashīd visited Medina with his friend Yaḥyā b. Khālid al-Barmakī, after performing the hajj pilgrimage in 170 AH, it was al-Wāqidī who was their tour guide through Medina, told them about the significant places associated with the Prophet, and indicated to them the graves of the many martyrs who had died for his cause.[9]

Al-Wāqidī's meeting with the caliph led to his moving with his family to Baghdad in the year 180/796. According to some sources, Hārūn al-Rashīd appointed al-Wāqidī judge over the eastern side of Baghdad while other accounts suggest that this position was granted later by al-Maʾmūn, Hārūn al-Rashīd's son.[10] That such an appointment was warranted was indicated by his knowledge of the traditions concerning early Islam and the Prophet, and of the genealogy of the Prophet's companions. Additionally it was deserved for his ability to cite recognized exegetes such as Sufyān al-Thawrī (716–78) and Mujāhid (647–722), and explain numerous passages from the Qur'ān as demonstrated in his *Kitāb al-Maghāzī.*

Al-Wāqidī is also said to have amassed a considerable library and with the help his student and amanuensis, Ibn Saʿd (d. 230/845), authored several books[11] concerning the Prophet, his companions and the early Islamic period. Indeed, al-Wāqidī is one of the main sources for later historians covering this period, including Ibn Saʿd, in his "Book of Classes" (*Kitāb al-ṭabaqāt*) and al-Ṭabarī (d. 310/923), who in his now famous "History of Prophets and Kings" (*Taʾrīkh al-rusul wa l-mulūk*) presents the transmissions of Ibn Isḥāq and al-Wāqidī, one after the other, probably indicating his recognition of the fact that they offered two different strains of information on the life of the Prophet.

Tradition has it that it was the Caliph al-Manṣūr (d. 158/775) who first understood the need for Muslims to have a biographical account of their Prophet. While the Biblical Testaments of both Jews and Christians explain the circumstances in which their prophets speak and act, the Qur'ān barely mentions Muḥammad and provides no such context for its message. It was thus, at the Caliph's behest, that Ibn Isḥāq (d. 150/767) put together a two-part compilation – Mabʿath and Maghāzī – that told of

Muḥammad's birth, prophethood, and struggles.[12] Essentially, it was a compilation of traditions that Muslims had been passing down orally for generations. Still, it differed from the usual collections of the *Muhaddithūn*, who categorized their traditions on the basis of their pertinence to ritual and legal information. Ibn Isḥāq laid out, instead, a chronological sequence to provide a narrative of the Arab prophet's life in his 7th century milieu. Included as well were Qur'ānic citations that complemented and helped Muslim interpretation of their scripture, and poetry that reflected the tribal environment.

Al-Wāqidī's *Kitāb al-Maghāzī* maintains the broad narrative outline provided by Ibn Isḥāq. It describes for us a leader who is very much a part of his community; he shares in the people's hunger and pain, insists on their charity for the needy, participates in their toil and labor, and incessantly reminds them of a just, but forgiving Lord, who is on his (Muḥammad's) side, helping him win battles and perform miracles as only a prophet can. Like Ibn Isḥāq, al-Wāqidī is driven by a focus on the narrative itself. After listing a series of transmitters, he often mixes each one's disparate accounts into a combined narrative to convey a more interesting 'tale' of what the Prophet did on a certain occasion. Contained, as well, are communications from persons who are either unrecognized or lacking in credibility, after which, al-Wāqidī sometimes conveys his scepticism.

The knitting together of these materials required considerable skill, and compilers competed with each other to produce what they hoped would be the most artful and plausible representation of the Muslim Prophet. The *Maghāzī* compilation by al-Wāqidī was probably an attempt to challenge that of his older contemporary, Ibn Isḥāq. With this in mind he tries to differentiate his work, most obviously, by moving the focus of his compilation directly to those traditions regarding the Prophet's life in Yathrib (known as the 'City of the Prophet,' Medinat al-Nabī, and called "Medina," for short), the chosen home, to which he immigrated in 622 C.E. and where he died and was buried. It was from here that he captured the sanctuary of the Kaʿba from the polytheistic Meccans to finally establish the Arab version of monotheism that was Islam. As well, al-Wāqidī entitles only those expeditions in which the Prophet actively participated as *ghazwa* (those in which the Prophet did not participate are differentiated as *sariyya*). He then extends the term to incorporate all the key negotiations of Muḥammad, including the Peace of Ḥudaybiyya and several defensive battles, and thus brings together what may be viewed as the Prophet's achievements under the title *Maghāzī*.

To fully comprehend al-Wāqidī's originality, however, one must understand the 9th century political environment in which he writes. Despite the overturn of the Umayyad caliphate by a largely Shiʿite leadership, the 'Abbāsids had cleverly manipulated a restoration of Sunni authority. The caliphates of Abū Bakr and 'Umar, momentarily challenged by the Shiʿites, were acknowledged as legitimate once more. In describing the life of Muḥammad in Medina, al-Wāqidī thus makes it a point of presenting both Abū Bakr and 'Umar as noteworthy companions of the Prophet to whom he turns frequently for advice. Perhaps more interesting is his rendering of al-'Abbās (the eponym of the 'Abbāsids) as a caring uncle of the Prophet even though he does not convert in the first years of Muḥammad's prophethood. Thus, though al-'Abbās continues to live in Mecca after the Prophet's immigration to Medina, he is not seen to participate in the battle against him at Badr. Moreover, just previous to the battle of Uḥud, he sends secret messages to the Prophet warning him of the impending attack by the Meccans. Interestingly, the primary theme that runs through al-Wāqidī's *Maghāzī* is that Muḥammad's battles were always defensive. Even his attack on Khaybar is justified in this manner.

However successful al-Wāqidī may have been, it is generally agreed that the compilation by Ibn Isḥāq was the more popular in its time.[13] Today it is available to us in various editions and in English translation. Yet, this so-called Ibn Isḥāq compilation is, in fact, Ibn Hishām's (d. 218/833) edition of it, under the title *Sirat rasūl Allah*, which Ibn Hishām admits to having modified – abridging the text in some places and adding information of his own in others. Consequently, it is difficult to determine the exact nature of Ibn Isḥāq's contribution. Since Ibn Hishām was a younger contemporary of al-Wāqidī, it means that al-Wāqidī's relatively unknown *Kitāb al-Maghāzī* is, in fact, the earliest 'composition' on the Prophet's life that has come down to us in its entirety. Al-Wāqidī's *Kitāb al-Maghāzī* is his only extant work. Of all the other books recorded in classical biographical and bibliographical works that he is said to have authored, a few others had been thought to exist. However, these are now understood to be false ascriptions; this is notably the case in a series of works describing the Arab conquests of various regions (the *futūḥ* literature). The attribution of these works to al-Wāqidī should be taken simply as indicative of his renown as a historian of the early period.[14] Even the existence of *Kitāb al-Maghāzī* may be thought to be one of luck and some happy circumstances of history. What is here presented as the *Kitāb al-Maghāzī* by al-Wāqidī has in fact come down to us through the transmissions of a series of scholars, as indicated by the introductory chain of authority (*isnād*), who are in order of priority: Muḥammad b. Shujāʿ al-Thaljī (d. 266/879), who specialized in law and the recitation of Qur'ān and *ḥadīth*, and was appointed judge by the caliph al-Mutawakkil (d. 247/861); Abū l-Qāsim ʿAbd al-Wahhāb b. Abī Ḥayya (d. 319/931) who was the librarian of al-Jāḥiz (d. 255/869); Abū ʿUmar Muḥammad b. al-ʿAbbās b. Zakariyā b. Ḥayawayhi (d. 382/992), who specialized in *ḥadīth and maghāzī* and was a transmitter of both al-Wāqidī and Ibn Saʿd; and Abū Muḥammad al-Ḥasan b. ʿAlī al-Jawhari (d. 454 A.H.) who was one of the *ʿulama* of the Iraqi school and later judge of Medina.[15]

Today, the work exists in three main manuscripts: British Library Or. 1617, the sole complete copy discovered so far (dated 564 *hijrī* [1169 CE]), one that is error-ridden and a significant challenge to use; British Library Add. 20737, a good manuscript but one that contains only the first half of the text; and Vienna 881, containing about one-third of the overall text in a somewhat fragmentary state. These three manuscripts served as the basis for the edition by Marsden Jones[16] upon which this translation is based (and for which the page numbers are indicated within the translated text). Citations of al-Wāqidī's work also appear in a variety of later sources that were used by Jones to establish his critical edition, but none of those sources come close to providing a full version. Jones's edition of al-Wāqidī's compilation was not the first one accomplished: that was published by Alfred Kramer as *The History of Mohammed's Campaigns by Aboo ʿAbdollah Mohammad bin ʿOmar al-Wakidy* in Calcutta in 1856. Kramer's edition was based on the Vienna manuscript and thus was far from complete.[17] Julius Wellhausen's German translation, *Muhammed in Medina. Das ist Vakidi's Kitab alMaghazi in verkürzter deutscher Wiedergabe* (Berlin: G. Reimer, 1882), is based upon the British Museum Or. 1617 manuscript but is an abbreviated translation, one that suffers because of the challenges of the manuscript source itself. Kramer and Wellhausen's works served as the basis for some of the major academic work done on the text in the 19th and early 20th centuries, notably that of Joseph Horowitz who published his

Berlin dissertation in 1898 with the Latin title *De Wāqidii libro qui Kitāb al Maġāzī inscribitur*.

Scholarly interest in al-Wāqidī's *Kitāb al-Maghāzī* has tended to focus on some very specific issues. There have been no recent exhaustive studies that have been devoted to considering the work's overall contribution and value to history. Certainly the book has been tapped for its particular views on certain subjects of prominence during the Medinan period of Muḥammad's life, especially the relationship with the Jewish communities.[18] However, two major historical considerations have been of particular interest and they have tended to dominate academic discussions. One is the emergence of the entire genre of literature concerning the life of Muḥammad and the various names attached to that genre. The focus has been on *maghāzī*, as in the title of al-Wāqidī's work, and *sīra*, the title that has become attached to the work of Ibn Isḥāq in the recension of Ibn Hishām. While the term *sīra* has become the generic term for the narrative biography of Muḥammad, the term *maghāzī* appears to have been used earlier, specifically being attached to the narrative that tells of Muḥammad's life after his immigration to Medina.[19] Why this word became applied to this genre is the crux of the problem. *Maghāzī*, the plural of *ghazwa*, means "raids," yet there is a lot more to these accounts of Muḥammad's life than simply raids. That the term had two senses (and certainly it came to have multiple meanings over time, as some consideration of the use of the term in works of *ḥadīth* has pointed out[20]) is one way of resolving the issue. However, another resolution that has been proposed suggests that the word had an overarching meaning of "achieving goals," a sense that is broad enough to cover all its uses.

The other main scholarly issue which has been discussed concerns the relationship of al-Wāqidī's work to its predecessors, especially that written by Ibn Isḥāq, and the accusation of plagiarism made against al-Wāqidī by modern European scholars. While it may be pointed out that it is anachronistic to speak of "plagiarism" as such, that is, nevertheless, the way the issue has tended to be framed.[21] Fundamentally, what is being questioned concerns the determination of al-Wāqidī's sources, what his original contribution was in the narrative he provided[22] (or what material he had access to that others did not), and what it means for him to apparently not have disclosed the commonality of his material with that found in Ibn Isḥāq.

The concern about al-Wāqidī's sources is apparent to the student of this literature who sees that the poetry found in al-Wāqidī was previously cited by Ibn Isḥāq, and that many of the traditions found in al-Wāqidī are also provided by Ibn Isḥāq. Yet al-Wāqidī never cites Ibn Isḥāq as an authority. Al-Wāqidī, it seems, either came by his information through other transmitters of the same material, or he was dishonest and obscured his source, Ibn Isḥāq. On the other hand, al-Wāqidī does commend Ibn Isḥāq's compilation and, indeed, his own narrative broadly follows the sequence provided by Ibn Isḥāq. It is possible that the answer to this dilemma lies in the intense rivalry that existed between competing scholars. Despite the popularity of Ibn Ishāq's recitals, there were those who challenged his credibility, and, in fact, preferred the transmission of his rival, Mūsā b. ʿUqba of whose *Maghāzi* we have discovered but a few pages, Importantly, al-Wāqidī does transmit several traditions from Mūsā b. ʿUqba, who significantly, is never cited by Ibn Isḥāq.[23]

This question has a deeper and more significant historiographical dimension than this stark way of putting things suggests. Al-Wāqidī has a style that pays particular attention to detail and it has been observed most trenchantly by Michael Lecker[24] that

Kitāb al-Maghāzī might be a good example of the general theory of growth in historical traditions (following the theories of Joseph Schacht in the development of *ḥadīth* reports) and the tendency of information to "improve" through time. However, Lecker's conclusion is that this is not actually so. He suggests that, while al-Wāqidī and Ibn Isḥāq had a common source, they did not, for their own reasons, include some of the information that might have been available and thus the details of their narrations do not overlap fully. Al-Wāqidī's material, according to Lecker, does not "improve" in its historical accuracy over time; he merely used earlier sources that Ibn Isḥāq either did not have access to or did not choose to use.

These two questions—that of defining the genre and of determining the sources—also come together in scholarly discussions. Much attention has been directed to understanding the historical nature of this material. Can one actually understand al-Wāqidī's compilation, the *Kitāb al-Maghāzī*, as an account of the Prophet's life in Medina? Is al-Wāqidī's description of the Battle of Badr a historical account? Or, has the story emerged from an attempt to understand a particular detail from the Qur'ān, as suggested by Crone.[25]

However one chooses to answer the above question, modern scholars such as Lecker contend that, as far as al-Wāqidī is concerned, the traditions that he provides are always cited from an earlier transmission; al-Wāqidī himself is not the author of this information. If information that cannot be reconciled with earlier transmissions should appear in his compilation, this is probably due to some copy-error on al-Wāqidī's part. It is in such a manner that Lecker dismisses al-Wāqidī's description of the Medinan Jews as allies, rather than clients, of the polytheistic Arabs. Faizer challenges this interpretation to explain that, in fact, al-Wāqidī is very cleverly manipulating the material to portray exactly what he intends. Thus, al-Wāqidī repeatedly portrays the Jews as having very close, 'foster' relations with the Arabs as the same 'mother' customarily nursed infants of both communities. Thus, Faizer argues, according to al-Wāqidī, the Jews were clearly allies of the Arabs.[26]

Indeed, al-Wāqidī's desire to shape this material is clearly indicated by the way he lays out, in his introduction, an unbelievably detailed chronology of the events that marked the life of the Prophet during his stay in Medina. These events span the very first expedition that took place in the seventh month after the *hijra* led by Ḥamza b. ʿAbd al-Muṭṭalib, an uncle of the Prophet, to Muḥammad's death ten years later.[27] Nor can one discount al-Wāqidī using Ibn Isḥāq's transmission as a tool of reference. As ridiculous as it may seem, the simple act of borrowing what the Muslim public had so favorably received enabled an easier retention of the narrative, which was coming to be recognized as what could have been the life of Muḥammad. To enable his memory, Ibn Isḥāq had used all kinds of mnemonics to facilitate the retelling of what he had compiled. The mnemonic of "three," for instance, reminds performers that there were three crucial battles against the Meccans, each followed by hostility towards three distinguished groups of Medinan Jews. Other points of reference are the *hijra*, the implementation of the *hijāb*, the various expeditions and battles; and the pilgrimages to Mecca. Al-Wāqidī wisely retains these patterns, perhaps not obviously, enabling not only the retelling of his own compilation but also, to a considerable degree, validating and therefore rendering more plausible a tale that had earlier not been so familiar.

Importantly, al-Wāqidī was clearly endowed with a considerable scepticism towards the sources and keenly aware of the subjective nature of these traditions. Despite the chain of authority which links the information to either a companion of the Prophet (who would have been a witness to the incident), or to a close relative of that companion, the compiler did not necessarily view these traditions as "facts," but understood them as reports tainted either by the prejudices of the transmitter, whether political or religious, or the ambiguity of his memory. With al-Wāqidī, this authorial scepticism towards the sources is seen, for one, in the way he provides different transmissions of a single incident, one after the other, and then concludes his presentation by informing his audience of which one of the traditions he prefers. It is also seen in the way he repeats certain events in the midst of different circumstances. The attack on some Jews by the Prophet's aunt Ṣafīya from the fortress of Farī is first narrated in the midst of the Raid of Uḥud, for instance, and then repeated in the context of al-Khandaq. Al-Wāqidī seems to be indicating that one really could not say when exactly the incident happened, though Ibn Isḥāq had indicated the tale in the context of al-Khandaq.[28]

Finally, these compilers were aware, that to make their audiences believe that Muḥammad was indeed chosen by God as His messenger it was important to portray him as an extraordinary man, whose close links to God would not only bring angels to his side when he fights the more numerous forces of the enemy; but also enable him to repeatedly heal the wounded, feed the hungry and predict what will come to be. And yet al-Wāqidī never allows us to forget that essentially Muḥammad was but a man: irritable, fearful, sometimes even doubting that God was watching over him, and – as a typical Arab of his times – yearning for a son to preserve his legacy.

Such an understanding of al-Wāqidī's technique brings us to appreciate al-Wāqidī not as a plagiarist who has concealed the pre-existing source material from which he has derived his compilation. Rather, we see a far more artful interaction with the sources being used. Each narrative becomes a unique selection and composition where the focus is not so much on the details of history as it is on bringing information forward that suits the stylistic and ideological goals of the author.

In the end, these academic discussions bring us back to the contents of the work. For many scholars the notion of establishing the historical details of the life of Muḥammad on the basis of any of these early narrative sources is virtually impossible.[24] When one combines the variations in dating of events, the divergences among the accounts and the difficulties in the reliability of the manuscript sources, the problems of establishing history must be recognized to be immense. It then becomes clear that answering other types of questions, ones not related to re-establishing the history of Muḥammad, is more likely to be profitable when dealing with a source such as al-Wāqidī. Such questions must revolve around establishing the goal of the writing of the accounts to begin with. Here we can see that *Kitāb al-Maghāzī* is a work designed to show the role of Muḥammad as the chosen messenger of God whose work led to the fulfillment of the will of God in establishing His community of Islam. It portrays the Prophet within the ideals of the time, establishing his image as a prophet and his status as a statesman. It provides a basis for establishing the general outlines of Muslim behavior modeled on the example of Muḥammad.[29] It also works within typical models of story-telling devoted to continuing and enhancing cultural notions of heroes and legends. Of course, some of this material is "embarrassing" by modern standards, speaking of the cruel realities of a daily life to which we no longer respond positively. Fighting, slavery and the harsh treatment of women[30] are all enmeshed in the narrative. Such are the challenges to our modern sensibilities when we study historical works. The core message of Islam is clearly conveyed, however: the unity of God and the devotion to His Prophet are the resounding themes, even if they are, for the most part, implicit simply in the act of writing the narrative. What was understood—or, better, argued for—in the composition of a work such as *Kitāb al-Maghāzī* is the picture of Islam as being fully existent during the time and life of its prophet. Into that framework then flows the Qur'ān, creatively given a historical context through which the scripture can (and must) be interpreted, grounding the word of God in the day-to-day encounters of Muḥammad with his compatriots. That is the message that we should take from al-Wāqidī's *Kitāb al-Maghāzī*.

Notes To The Preface and Introduction

1 Al-Wāqidī, *The Kitāb al-Maghāzī*, edited by Marsden Jones, London: OUP, 1966.
2 E. W. Lane, Arabic-English Lexicon. 2 Volumes. Islamic Texts Society: Cambridge, 1984.
3 A. Yusuf Ali, *The Holy Quran: Text, Translation and Commentary*, Leicester: The Islamic Foundation, 1975.
4 A. J. Arberry, *The Koran Interpreted*, New York: The Macmillan Company, 1967.
5 Muhammad b. Ishāk, *Das Leben Muhammad's*, abridged by Abd al-Malik Ibn Hischam. Edited by Ferdinand Wüstenfeld, 3 vols. Göttingen, Dietrichsche Universitäts-Buchhandlung, 1859.
6 Alfred Guillaume, *The Life of Muhammad. A Translation of Ibn Isḥāq's Sīrat Rasūl Allah*, Karachi: Oxford University Press, 1955.
7 Ibn Saʿd, *Kitāb al-Tabaqāt al-Kabīr*, edited by Eduard Sachau, Leiden: E. J. Brill, 1940, vol. 5, pp. 314–21.
8 Marsden Jones citing Khaṭīb al-Baghdādi in his "*Muqaddima al-taḥqīq*," p. 7, in al-Wāqidī, *Kitāb al-Maghāzī*, 1966.
9 Marsden Jones, "*Muqaddima al-taḥqīq*," p. 6.
10 See Josef Horowitz, *The Earliest Biographies of the Prophet and their Authors*, ed. Lawrence I. Conrad (Princeton: Darwin Press, 2002), 107.
11 See the list and discussion in Horowitz, and Jones, "*Muqaddima*," pp. 10–11.
12 R. Sellheim, 'Prophet Chalif und Geshichte,' *Oriens* 18–19 (1967): 3.
13 See Johann Fück, "Muhammad b. Isḥāq: Literarhistorische Untersachungen," (Ph.D. dissertation, Frankfurt am Main, 1925), p. 44.
14 See Rudi Paret, "Die Legendäre Futūḥ-Literature," in *La poesia epica e la sua formazione* (Rome, 1970), 735–49, English translation, "The Legendary *Futūḥ* Literature," in *The Expansion of the Early Islamic State*, ed. Fred M. Donner (Aldershot: Ashagte Variorum, 2008), 163–75.
15 Marsden Jones, "Preface" to the *Kitāb al-Mghāzī*, London: Oxford University Press, 1966, p. v.
16 Ibid.
17 See A. Sprenger "Notes on *Alfred von Kremer's* edition of Wakidy's Campaigns," *Journal of the Asiatic Society of Bengal* 25/1 (1856), 53–74 this article is primarily an analysis of the contents but with some interesting comments on the transmission of the manuscript source itself. (Our thanks to H. Berg for providing access to this article). For the scholarly background to this edition, see Conrad's "Editor's Introduction," to Horowitz, *The Earliest Biographies*, p. xvi.
18 Rizwi S. Faizer, "Muhammad and the Medinan Jews: A Comparison of the Texts of Ibn Ishaq's *Kitāb Sīrat Rasūl Allāh* with Al-Waqidi's *Kitāb al-Maghazī*," *International Journal of Middle East Studies* 28 (1996), 463–89; Michael Lecker, "Wāqidī's Account on the Status of the Jews of Medina: a Study of a Combined Report," *Journal of Near Eastern Studies*, 54(1995), 15–32; reprinted in *The Life of Muḥammad*, ed. Uri Rubin (Aldershot: Ashgate Variorum, 1998), 23–40—Lecker's interest here is also focused on determining whether sources prior to Ibn Isḥāq and al-Wāqidī can be uncovered; on that point also see Ella Landau-Tasseron, "Processes of Redaction: the Case of the Tamīmite Delegation to the Prophet Muḥammad," *Bulletin of the School of Oriental and African Studies* 49(1986),

253–70, and Gregor Schoeler, *The Biography of Muhammad: Nature and Authenticity*, trans. U. Vagelpohl, ed. J. E. Montgomery (London: Routledge, 2010).

19 See Martin Hinds, " 'Maghāzī' and 'Sīra' in Early Islamic Scholarship," in *La vie du Prophète Mahomet: Colloque de Strasbourg, Octobre 1980* (Paris: PUF, 1983), 57–66, reprinted in *The Life of Muḥammad*, ed. Uri Rubin (Aldershot: Ashgate Variorum, 1998), 1–10.

20 See Muhammad Qasim Zaman, "*Maghāzī* and the *Muḥaddithūn*: Reconsidering the Treatment of 'Historical' Materials in the Early Collection of Hadith," *International Journal of Middle East Studies* 28 (1996), 1–18.

21 For a summary see Rizwi S. Faizer, "The Issue of Authenticity Regarding the Traditions of al-Wāqidī as Established in his Kitāb al-Maghāzī," *Journal of Near Eastern Studies*, 58(1999), 97–106; also see J. M. B. Jones, "Ibn Isḥāq and al-Wāqidī: the Dream of ʿĀtika and the Raid to Nakhla in Relation to the Charge of Plagiarism," *Bulletin of the School of Oriental and African Studies*, 22 (1959), 41–51, reprinted in *The Life of Muḥammad*, ed. Uri Rubin (Aldershot: Ashgate Variorum, 1998), 11–21.

22 This is particularly the focus of Donald P. Little, "Narrative Themes and Devices in Al-Wāqidī's *Kitāb al-Maghāzī*," in *Reason and Inspiration in Islam: Theology, Philosophy and Mysticism in Muslim Thought: Essays in Honour of Hermann Landolt*, ed. Todd Lawson (London: I. B. Tauris, 2005), 34–45.

23 See Guillaume, "Introduction" in *The Life of Muhammad*, p. xvi.

24 See, for example, Michael Lecker, "The Death of the Prophet Muḥammad's Father: Did Wāqidī Invent some of the Evidence?" *Zeitschrift der Deutschen Morgenländischen Gesellschaft* 145(1995), 9–27.

25 Patricia Crone, *Meccan Trade and the Rise of Islam* (New Jersey: Princeton University Press, 1987).

26 See Faizer, "The Issue of Authenticity."

27 On the issue of the chronological framework, see J. M. B. Jones, "The Chronology of the *Maghāzī*—a Textual Survey," *Bulletin of the School of Oriental and African Studies*, 19 (1957), 245–80, reprinted in *The Life of Muḥammad*, ed. Uri Rubin (Aldershot: Ashgate Variorum, 1998), 193–228; see also Fred M. Donner, *Narratives of Islamic Origins: The Beginnings of Islamic Historical Writings* (Princeton: Darwin Press, 1998), 245–8 (al-Wāqidī is "one of the major chronological systematizers of the early Islamic historiographical tradition").

28 It is unlikely that the attitude reflected in Marsden Jones's work would be expressed quite as plainly today; see his "The *Maghāzī* literature," in *The Cambridge History of Arabic Literature: Arabic Literature to the end of the Umayyad Period*, ed. A. F. L. Beeston et al (Cambridge: Cambridge University Press, 1983), 344–51, in which he states that al-Wāqidī is "the most important source on the development, both social and political, of the early Islamic community". Compare J. N. Mattock, "History and Fiction," *Occasional Papers of the School of Abbasid Studies*, 1 (1986), 80–97.

29 Gordon D. Newby, "Imitating Muhammad in Two Genres: Mimesis and Problems of Genre in Sīrah and Sunnah," *Medieval Encounters* 3 (21997), 266–83, while based primarily on Ibn Isḥāq's work, has some relevant insights on this theme.

30 Bärbel Köhler, "Die Frauen in al-Wāqidīs Kitābal-Maġāzī," *Zeitschrift der Deutschen Morgenländischen Gesellschaft* 147 (1997), 303–53.

The Life of Muhammad

[VOLUME 1 Page 1] **INTRODUCTION**

In the name of God, the Merciful, the Compassionate.

Abū Muḥammad al-Ḥasan b. ʿAlī b. (ibn, son of) Muḥammad al-Jawharī informed us of what Abū ʿUmar Muḥammad b. al-ʿAbbās b. Muḥammad b. Zakariyya b. Ḥayawayh related to us, word for word. He said: It was read from the book of Abū l-Qāsim ʿAbd al-Wahhāb b. Abī Ḥayya, while I listened, and he confirmed it, on Saturday morning, in the house of Abū ʿAbdullah al-Warrāq, in the district of Shabīb, at the gate of al-Shām, by the Gate of Gold in the Alley of Balkh, in the month of Jamādā l-Ākhira in the year 318 AH. He said: Abū ʿAbdullah Muḥammad b. Shujāʿ al-Thaljī related to us saying: Muḥammad b. ʿUmar al-Wāqidī related to me that ʿUmar b. ʿUthmān b. ʿAbd al-Raḥmān b. Saʿīd b. Yarbūʿ al-Makhzūmī, Mūsā b. Muḥammad b. Ibrāhīm b. al-Ḥārith al-Taymī, Muḥammad b. ʿAbdullah b. Muslim, Mūsā b. Yaʿqūb b. ʿAbdullah b. Wahb b. Zamaʿa, ʿAbdullah b. Jaʿfar b. ʿAbd al-Raḥmān b. al-Miswar b. Makhrama, Abū Bakr b. ʿAbdullah b. Muḥammad b. Abī Sabra, Saʿīd b. ʿUthmān b. ʿAbd al-Raḥmān b. ʿAbdullah al-Taymī, Yūnus b. Muḥammad al-Ẓafarī, ʿĀʾidh b. Yaḥyā, Muḥammad b. ʿAmr, Muʿādh b. Muḥammad al-Anṣārī, Yaḥyā b. ʿAbdullah b. Abī Qatāda, ʿAbd al-Raḥmān b. ʿAbd al-ʿAzīz b. ʿAbdullah b. ʿUthmān b. Ḥunayf, Ibn Abī Ḥabība, Muḥammad b. Yaḥyā b. Sahl b. Abī Ḥathma, ʿAbd al-Ḥamīd b. Jaʿfar, Muḥammad b. Ṣāliḥ b. Dīnār, ʿAbd al-Raḥmān b. Muḥammad b. Abī Bakr, Yaʿqūb b. Muḥammad b. Abī Ṣaʿṣaʿa, ʿAbd al-Raḥmān b. Abī l-Zinād, Abū Maʿshar, [Page 2] Mālik b. Abī l-Rijjāl, Ismāʿīl b. Ibrāhīm b. ʿUqba, ʿAbd al-Ḥamīd b. ʿImrān b. Abī Anas, and ʿAbd al-Ḥamīd b. Abī ʿAbs, all related to me about this in portions, and some of them were more reliable than others regarding their traditions. Others also related to me, and I wrote down all that was related to me.

They said: The Messenger of God, may peace be upon him, arrived in Medina on Monday, the twelfth of Rabīʿ al-Awwal—some say the second of Rabīʿ al-Awwal—but the twelfth is confirmed. The Messenger of God entrusted the first flag to Ḥamza b. ʿAbd al-Muṭṭalib, may God be satisfied with him, in the month of Ramaḍān, the seventh month after the emigration (*hijra*) of the Prophet from Mecca, to confront the caravan of the Quraysh. Then he awarded the flag to ʿUbayda b. al-Ḥārith in the month of Shawwāl, eight months after the *hijra* (AH), to go to Rābigh, ten miles from Juḥfa on the way to Qudayd. The expedition (*sariyya*) led by Saʿd b. Abī Waqqāṣ to al-Kharrār followed in Dhū l-Qaʿda, the ninth month AH. Then the Messenger of God marched (*ghazā*) in Ṣafar, the eleventh month AH, until he reached al-Abwā, and then returned. There was no fighting. He was gone for fifteen nights. The Prophet marched to Buwāṭ, which is close to Juḥfa, in Rabīʿ al-Awwal, the thirteenth month AH, obstructed the caravan of the Quraysh, in which were Umayya b. Khalaf and a hundred men from the Quraysh with two thousand five hundred camels, and returned. There was no fighting. Next, seeking Kurz b. Jābir al-Fihrī, the Prophet marched in Rabīʿ al-Awwal, the thirteenth month AH, until he reached Badr, and returned. He raided again in Jamādā l-Ākhira, the sixteenth month AH—known as the raid of Dhū l-ʿUshayra—obstructing the caravans of the Quraysh as they began their journey to al-Shām, and returned. The Prophet sent ʿAbdullah b. Jaḥsh to Nakhla, in Rajab, the seventeenth month AH. Then he marched (*ghazā*) to the Battle of Badr on the morning of Friday, the seventeenth of Ramaḍān, the nineteenth month AH. The expedition (*sariyya*) to ʿAṣmā bt (bint-daughter of) Marwān followed; she was killed by ʿUmayr b. ʿAdī [Page 3] b. Kharasha. ʿAbdullah b. al-Ḥārith b. al-Faḍl told me, from his father, that he said that Ibn Kharasha killed her five nights before the end of Ramaḍān, the nineteenth month AH.

The expedition (*sariyya*) of Sālim b. ʿUmayr to kill Abū ʿAfak took place in Shawwāl, the twentieth month AH. The raid of the Banū Qaynuqāʿ took place in the middle of Shawwāl. The Messenger of God marched to the raid of al-Sawīq in Dhū l-Ḥijja, the twenty-second month AH. He raided the Banū Sulaym at al-Kudr in al-Muḥarram, the twenty-third month AH. The expedition (*sariyya*) for the murder of Ibn al-Ashraf took place in Rabīʿ al-Awwal, the twenty-fifth month AH. The raid of the Ghatafān at Najd, in Dhū Amarr, followed in Rabīʿ al-Awwal, the twenty-fifth month AH. Then it was the expedition (*sariyya*) led by ʿAbdullah b. Unays to Sufyān b. Khālid b. Nubayḥ al-Hudhalī. ʿAbdullah said: "I went out from Medina on Monday, the fifth of Muḥarram, the thirty-fifth month AH. I was gone for eighteen nights and returned on Saturday, with seven days left to the month of Muḥarram." The Prophet raided the Banū Sulaym at Buḥrān, in Jamādā l-Ūlā, the twenty-seventh month AH. The expedition to al-Qarada led by Zayd b. Ḥāritha followed in Jumādā l-Ākhira, the twenty-eighth month AH; Abū Sufyān b. Ḥarb was there.

The Prophet raided Uḥud in Shawwāl, the thirty-second month AH, and then Ḥamrā' al-Asad, also in Shawwāl. An expedition (*sariyya*) led by Abū Salamā b. ʿAbd al-Asad to Qaṭan against the Banū Asad took place in Muḥarram, the thirty-fifth month AH, and was followed by one to Bi'r Maʿūna led by [Page 4] al-Mundhir b. ʿAmr, in Ṣafar, the thirty-sixth month AH. The raid (*ghazwa*) of al-Rajīʿ, commanded by Marthad, was also in Ṣafar. The Prophet raided the Banū Naḍīr in Rabīʿ al-Awwal, the thirty-seventh month AH. Then he marched for his appointment to Badr in Dhū l-Qaʿda, the forty-fifth month AH. The expedition led by Ibn ʿAtīk to Sallām b. Abī l-Ḥuqayq took place in Dhū l-Ḥijja. When Sallām b. Abī l-Ḥuqayq was killed, the Jews fled to Sallām b. Mishkam in Khaybar, but he refused to lead them. Usayr b. Zārim, however, supported their war. The Prophet raided Dhāt al-Riqāʿ in Muḥarram, the forty-seventh month AH, and then attacked Dūmat al-Jandal in Rabīʿ al-Awwal, the forty-ninth month AH.

The Prophet marched to al-Muraysīʿ in Shaʿbān in year five AH. In the same year he fought at al-Khandaq in Dhū l-Qaʿda, and raided the Banū Qurayẓa during some nights of Dhū l-Qaʿda and Dhū l-Ḥijja.

In the year six AH, in Muḥarram, Ibn Unays led an expedition to Sufyān b. Khālid b. Nubayḥ, and Muḥammad b. Maslama led another to al-Qurṭā'. The Prophet raided the Banū Liḥyān at al-Ghāba in Rabīʿ al-Awwal. In Rabīʿ al-Ākhir four expeditions (*sariyya*) were carried out: one was led by ʿUkkāsha b. Miḥṣan to al-Ghamr, the second, by Muḥammad b. Maslama to Dhū l-Qaṣṣa, the third, by Abū ʿUbayda b. al-Jarrāḥ to Dhū l-Qaṣṣa, [Page 5] and the fourth, by Zayd b. Ḥāritha against the Banū Sulaym at al-Jamūm (which lies between Baṭn Nakhl and al-Naqra). The last two raids took place in the same month. Zayd led an expedition to al-ʿĪṣ in Jumādā l-Ūla, and then to al-Ṭaraf (which lies thirty-six miles from Medina) and Ḥismā (which lies behind Wādī al-Qurā) in Jamādā l-Ākhira. Zayd led another expedition to Wādī al-Qurā in Rajab. ʿAbd al-Raḥmān b. ʿAwf commanded a march to Dūmat al-Jandal in Shaʿbān. The raid [*ghazwa*] led by ʿAlī to Fadak followed in the same month. The raid led by Zayd b. Ḥāritha to Umm Qirfa (which lies beside Wādī al-Qurā) took place in Ramaḍān. The expedition led by Ibn Rawāḥa to Uṣayr b. Zārim, as well as that led by Kurz b. Jābir to al-ʿUraniyyīn followed in Shawwāl. In Dhū l-Qaʿda the Prophet traveled to perform the ʿUmrat al-Ḥudaybiyya.

In the year seven AH, the Prophet raided Khaybar in Jamādā l-Ūlā. He turned from Khaybar to Wādī al-Qurā in Jamādā l-Ākhira, and fought there. Then ʿUmar b. al-Khaṭṭāb led an expedition to Turba, which lies six nights from Mecca, in Shaʿbān. Abū Bakr b. Quḥāfa led an expedition to the Najd, and Bashīr b. Saʿd led another to Fadak, also in Shaʿbān. The expedition led by Ghālib b. ʿAbdullah to Mayfaʿa (Mayfaʿa is near Najd) followed in Ramaḍān, [Page 6] and another led by Bashīr b. Saʿd to al-Jināb followed in Shawwāl. The Prophet performed the ʿUmrat al-Qaḍiyya in Dhū l-Qaʿda. The raid of Ibn Abī l-ʿAwjāʾ al-Sulamī took place in Dhū l-Ḥijja.

In the year eight AH, Ghālib b. ʿAbdullah led an expedition to al-Kadayd (which lies behind Qudayd), in Ṣafar. The expedition led by Shujāʿ b. Wahb against Banū ʿĀmir b. Mulawwaḥ, and that led by Kaʿb b. ʿUmayr al-Ghifārī at Dhāt Aṭlāḥ (which is in the direction of Shām about a night's journey from al-Balqāʾ) followed in Rabīʿ al-Awwal. In the same year, Zayd b. Ḥāritha led an expedition to Muʾta. Then ʿAmr b. al-ʿĀṣ led one to Dhāt al-Salāsil in Jamādā l-Ākira and Abū ʿUbayda b. al-Jarraḥ led another to al-Khabaṭ, in Rajab. In Shaʿbān, Abū Qatāda led an expedition to Khaḍira (which lies in the direction of Najd about twenty miles from the garden of Ibn ʿĀmir). In Ramaḍān, Abū Qatāda led an expedition against Iḍam. On the thirteenth of Ramaḍān, the Prophet marched to the Conquest of Mecca. Five nights before the end of Ramaḍān al-ʿUzzā was destroyed by Khālid b. al-Walīd; Suwāʿ and Manāt were also destroyed in Ramaḍān by ʿAmr b. al-ʿĀṣ and Saʿd b. Zayd al-Ashhalī, respectively. Khālid b. al-Walīd led the raid against the Banū Jazima in Shawwāl while the Prophet marched to Ḥunayn and then to al-Ṭāʾif. Later, the people went on the *Ḥajj* pilgrimage. Some say that the Prophet appointed ʿAttāb b. Asīd over that pilgrimage; others, that the pilgrimage of the people was divided and without a leader.

In the year nine AH, the expedition led by [Page 7] ʿUyayna b. Ḥiṣn against the Banū Tamīm took place in Muḥarram. The expedition led by Quṭba b. ʿĀmir to Khathʿam followed in Ṣafar, and the march of the Banū Kilāb commanded by Daḥḥāk b. Sufyān followed in Rabīʿ al-Awwal. The expeditions led by ʿAlqama b. Mujazziz to Ḥabasha and ʿAlī to al-Fuls were in Rabīʿ al-Ākhir. The Prophet raided Tabūk, and Khālid b. al-Walīd attacked al-Ukaydir, in Rajab. The destruction of Dhū l-Kaffayn, the idol of ʿAmr b. Ḥumama al-Dawsī followed. The people, including Abū Bakr, performed the *Ḥajj* pilgrimage in the year nine AH.

In the year ten AH, the expedition led by Khālid b. al-Walīd to the Banū ʿAbd al-Madān, and the march of ʿAlī to Yemen took place in Rabīʿ al-Awwal. Some say there were two expeditions to Yemen, and that one of them was in Ramaḍān of the year ten. Then the Prophet went on pilgrimage with the people; when he returned from Mecca he was sick for ten nights. He dispatched Usāma b. Zayd during his sickness to al-Shām. When the Messenger of God died, Usāma did not return until Abū Bakr sent for him. The Prophet died on Monday, the twelfth of Rabīʿ al-Awwal in the year eleven AH.

The Prophet actively participated in twenty-seven raids. He fought in nine of them: Badr, Uḥud, al-Muraysīʿ, al-Khandaq, Qurayẓa, Khaybar, the Conquest of Mecca, Ḥunayn and al-Ṭāʾif. He directed forty-seven expeditions and performed three *ʿUmra*s [pilgrimage to the Meccan Kaʿba undertaken before or after the annual *Ḥajj* ritual]. Some say that he fought the Banū Naḍīr, but God made it a special booty for him. He also fought in the raid of Wādī al-Qurā on his return from Khaybar, when some of his companions were killed. Then he fought in al-Ghāba until Muḥriz b. Naḍla and six of the enemy were killed.

They said: The Messenger of God appointed several companions to take his place in Medina during his raids. During the raid of Waddān he appointed Saʿd b. ʿUbāda;

during the raid of Buwāṭ, Saʿd b. Muʿādh; during the search for Kurz b. Jābir al-Fihrī, Zayd b. Ḥāritha; during the raid of Dhū l-ʿUshayra, Abū Salama b. ʿAbd al-Asad [Page 8] al-Makhzūmī; during the raid of the Battle of Badr and the raid of al-Sawīq, Abū Lubāba b. ʿAbd al-Mundhir al-ʿAmrī. During the raid on al-Kudr, Ibn Umm Maktūm al-Maʿayṣī; during the raid of Dhū Amarr, ʿUthmān b. ʿAffān; during the raid of Buḥrān, Ibn Umm Maktūm; during the raid of Uḥud, Ibn Umm Maktūm; during the raid of Ḥamrāʾ al-Asad, Ibn Umm Maktūm; during the raid of the Banū Naḍīr, Ibn Umm Maktūm; during the raid of Badr al-Mawʿid, ʿAbdullah b. Rawāḥa; during the raid of Dhāt al-Riqāʿ, ʿUthmān b. ʿAffān; during the raid of Dūmat al-Jandal, Sibāʿ b. ʿUrfuṭa; during the raid of Muraysīʿ, Zayd b. Ḥāritha; during the raid of al-Khandaq, Ibn Umm Maktūm; during the raid of the Banū Qurayẓa, Ibn Umm Maktūm; during the raid of the Banū Liḥyān, Ibn Umm Maktūm; during the raid of al-Ghāba, Ibn Umm Maktūm; during the raid of al-Ḥudaybiyya, Ibn Umm Maktūm; during the raid of Khaybar, Sibāʿ b. ʿUrfuṭa al-Ghifārī; during the raid of ʿUmrat al-Qaḍīya, Abū Ruhm al-Ghifārī; during the raid of al-Fatḥ and Ḥunayn and al-Ṭāʾif, Ibn Umm Maktūm; during the raid of Tabūk, Ibn Umm Maktūm—some said it was Muḥammad b. Maslama al-Ashhalī; during the *Ḥajj* of the Prophet, Ibn Umm Maktūm.

The code words of the Messenger of God during battle were: In Badr, "Yā Manṣūr, kill." Some said that the battle cry of the Muhājirūn was "Banū ʿAbd al-Raḥmān," that of the Khazraj was "Banū ʿAbdullah;" and that of the Aws was "Banū ʿUbaydullah." During Uḥud, the raid of the Banū Naḍīr and the raid of Muraysīʿ the codewords were "Kill, kill;" and during al-Khandaq: "Hā Mīm they will not be victorious!" During the raid on the Banū Qurayẓa and al-Ghāba, none was stated. During Ḥunayn the code was "Yā Manṣūr kill;" during al-Fatḥ the battle cry of the Muhājirūn was "Banū ʿAbd al-Raḥmān;" that of the Khazraj, "Banū ʿAbdullah;" and of the Aws, "Banū ʿUbaydullah." During Khaybar, the call of the Muhājirūn was "Banū ʿAbd al-Raḥmān," that of the Khazraj, "Banū ʿAbdullah;" and that of the Aws, "Banū ʿUbaydullah." During al-Ṭāʾif there were no codewords used.

[Page 9] **THE EXPEDITION (SARIYYA) OF ḤAMZA B. ʿABD AL-MUṬṬALIB**

The expedition of Ḥamza b. ʿAbd al-Muṭṭalib occurred in Ramaḍān, the seventh month AH.

They said: The Prophet granted the first banner, after he arrived in Medina, to Ḥamza b. ʿAbd al-Muṭṭalib. He sent him with thirty riders from two groups, fifteen from the Muhājirūn and fifteen from the Anṣār. Among the Muhājirūn were Abū ʿUbāda b. Jarraḥ, Abū Ḥudhayfa b. ʿUtba b. Rabīʿa, Sālim the *mawlā* of Abū Ḥudhayfa, ʿĀmir b. Rabīʿa, ʿAmr b. Surāqa, Zayd b. Ḥāritha, Kannāz b. Ḥuṣayn, his son Marthad b. Kannāz, Anasa the *mawlā* of the Prophet, and other men. From the Anṣār: Ubayy b. Kaʿb, ʿUmāra b. Ḥazm, ʿUbāda b. al-Ṣāmit, ʿUbayd b. Aws, Aws b. Khawlī, Abū Dujāna, al-Mundhir b. ʿAmr, Rāfiʿ b. Mālik, ʿAbdullāh b. ʿAmr b. Ḥarām, Quṭba b. ʿĀmir b. Ḥadīda, as well as men who have not been named to us.

They reached Sīf al-Baḥr, and Ḥamza advanced towards the caravan of the Quraysh that was traveling from al-Shām towards Mecca. In it were Abū Jahl and three hundred riders from the people of Mecca. When they encountered each other and lined up for battle, Majdī b. ʿAmr, an ally of both parties, came between them and did not cease to negotiate between the two groups until the people turned away. Ḥamza turned back, returning to Medina with his companions, while Abū Jahl continued towards Mecca with his caravan and his companions. There was no fighting between them. [Page 10] When Ḥamza returned to the Prophet he informed him of how Majdī (b. ʿAmr) intervened between them, and that they had seen justice from him. When a group from Majdī arrived before the Prophet he clothed them and was good to them. Mentioning Majdī b. ʿAmr the Prophet said, "Indeed he has a winning disposition and finds a blessed result," or "righteous deeds."

ʿAbd al-Raḥmān b. ʿAyyāsh from ʿAbd al-Malik b. ʿUbayd from Ibn al-Musayyib, and ʿAbd al-Raḥmān b. Saʿīd b. Yarbūʿ both related to me that the Messenger of God did not send anyone from the Anṣār until he himself raided at Badr because he thought that they would not support him except in their homeland (Medina). This tradition is confirmed.

THE EXPEDITION (*SARIYYA*) OF ʿUBAYDA B. AL-ḤĀRITH TO RĀBIGH

The Prophet gave the flag to ʿUbayda b. al-Ḥārith, in Shawwāl, the eighth month AH, to march to Rābigh (Rābigh lies ten miles from Juḥfa in the direction of Qudayd).

ʿUbayda went out with sixty riders. He met Abū Sufyān b. Ḥarb at the water known as Aḥyāʾ in the valley of Rābigh. Abū Sufyān was at that time with two hundred men. Saʿd b. Abī Waqqāṣ was the first who aimed an arrow for Islam. He scattered his quiver-full before his companions, while his companions shielded him. He said: He aimed with what was in his quiver until he emptied it. There was not an arrow aimed except he injured someone with it. It was said: There were twenty arrows in the quiver, that they all injured either a man or an animal, and that there was no other arrow at that time. They did not draw swords nor stand in line for battle other than for this shooting and skirmish. Then each group turned back towards its garrison. Saʿd b. Abī Waqqās used to say concerning what Ibn Abī Sabra related to me from al-Muhājir b. Mismār, that there were, in all, sixty from the Quraysh. Saʿd said: I said to ʿUbayda, "If we follow them we will overpower them for surely they have turned away in fear." [Page 11] But he didn't agree with me, so we turned back towards Medina.

THE EXPEDITION OF SAʿD B. ABĪ WAQQĀṢ TO AL-KHARRĀR

The Prophet gave the flag to Saʿd b. Abī Waqqāṣ to march to al-Kharrār (al-Kharrār is in Juḥfa near Khum) in Dhū l-Qaʿda, the ninth month AH. Abū Bakr b. Ismāʿīl b. Muḥammad related to me from his father, from ʿĀmir b. Saʿd, from his father, who said: The Prophet said, "Go, O Saʿd, until you reach al-Kharrār for surely a caravan of the Quraysh will pass by." I left with twenty or twenty-one men on foot. We were hiding by day and traveling by night, until we arrived there on the morning of the fifth day, but we found that the caravan had passed by the day before. The Prophet had made me promise that I would not go beyond al-Kharrār and if not for that I would have surely followed.

It was said that the Prophet did not send anyone from the Anṣār until he raided with them at Badr. This was because they had promised that they would protect him in their land alone. ʿAbd al-Raḥmān b. ʿAyyāsh al-Makhzūmī related this to me from ʿAbd al-Malik b. ʿUbayd b. Saʿīd b. Yarbūʿ, from Saʿīd b. al-Musayyib and ʿAbd al-Raḥmān b. Saʿīd b. Yarbūʿ.

THE RAID OF AL-ABWĀʾ

The Prophet set out in the month of Ṣafar, eleven months after his emigration, [Page 12] until he reached al-Abwāʾ and advanced to the caravan of the Quraysh. There was no fighting. In this raid he made an agreement with the Banū Ḍamra of Kināna that they would not increase forces or help any one against him. The Prophet wrote a document between them and himself and then returned. He was gone for fifteen nights.

THE RAID OF BUWĀṬ

The Prophet raided Buwāṭ (Buwāṭ lies opposite Ḍabba from the direction of Dhū Khushub)—between Buwāṭ and Medina are three postal stations—in Rabīʿ al-Awwal, the thirteenth month AH. He advanced to the caravan of the Quraysh that carried Umayya b. Khalaf, a hundred Quraysh and two thousand five hundred camels. Then he returned. There was no fighting.

THE RAID OF THE FIRST BADR

The Prophet marched in Rabīʿ al-Awwal, the thirteenth month AH, seeking Kurz b. Jābir al-Fihrī who raided the pasturing cattle of Medina (that used to graze at al-Jammāʾ and around the region), until he reached Badr. He did not reach Kurz.

THE RAID OF DHŪ L-ʿUSHAYRA

The Prophet marched to Dhū l-ʿUshayra in Jamādā l-Ākhira, the sixteenth month AH. He advanced to the caravans of the Quraysh as they started off to Syria. He selected his companions and went out with a hundred and fifty, and some say two hundred, men. News of the departure of the caravan, in which the Quraysh had collected their wealth, from Mecca to al-Shām had come to the Prophet. [Page 13] They traveled through a gorge, Naqb Banū Dīnār to Buyūt al-Suqyā. This was the raid of Dhū l-ʿUshayra.

THE EXPEDITION TO NAKHLA

The expedition to Nakhla commanded by ʿAbdullah b. Jaḥsh (Nakhla is a valley in Bustān Ibn ʿĀmir) took place in the month of Rajab, the seventeenth month AH.

They said: ʿAbdullah b. Jaḥsh said: The Prophet called me when he prayed ʿIshā, and said, "Come to me at dawn with your weapons, for I would send you on a mission!" He said: So I approached at dawn with my sword, my bow, my quiver and my shield. The Prophet prayed Subḥ with the people, and then he left and found me—I had preceded him—standing at his door. I found myself with a group of Quraysh. The Prophet called Ubayy b. Kaʿb, and commanded him to write a document. Then he called me and giving me the sheet of leather from Khawlān, said, "I have appointed you over this group. Proceed until you have traveled for two nights, then unfold my letter and do as it says." I said, "O Messenger of God, in which direction?" He replied, "Go towards Najdiyya until you reach a small well."

He said: ʿAbdullah b. Jaḥsh hurried, until he was at the well of Ibn Ḍumayra, opened the letter and read it. It said: Go, in the name of God and with His blessings, until you come to the valley of Nakhla, but do not force any one of your companions to go with you. Proceed according to my commands with whoever follows you, until you reach the valley of Nakhla and observe the caravan of the Quraysh from there.

[Page 14] After he read the letter to them, ʿAbdullah said, "I do not compel any one of you, so let whoever desires to be witness to and follow the Prophet's command, proceed, and let whoever desires to return, do so immediately." They responded altogether, "We hear and obey God and his Prophet, and you. We will go, by the grace of God, where you wish."

So he went until he came to Nakhla and found a caravan of the Quraysh with ʿAmr b. al-Ḥaḍramī, al-Ḥakam b. Kaysān al-Makhzūmī, ʿUthmān b. ʿAbdullah b. al-Mughīra al-Makhzūmī, and Nawfal b. ʿAbdullah al-Makhzūmī. When the companions of the caravan saw them, they feared them and were uncertain of their intentions. ʿUkkāsha shaved his head immediately and came forward and the people were calmed.

ʿĀmir b. Rabīʿa said: I shaved the head of ʿUkkāsha with my own hand—Wāqid b. ʿAbdullah and ʿUkkāsha thought that they could overpower them—and so he says to them, "We are pilgrims! We are in the month of protection!" ʿUkkāsha rose into view, and the polytheists said to one another, "It is no matter. The people are pilgrims." They felt secure and they tied their animals and let them graze while they prepared their food.

The companions of the Prophet consulted with their commander. It was the last day of Rajab, and some say it was the first day of Shaʿbān. They said, "If you delay about them today, they will enter the sanctuary and will be protected, and if you attack them now, it is in the sacred month." Someone said, "We do not know whether this day is in the protected month or not." Another said, "We do not know this day except that it is in the protected month, and we do not think that you should violate it for what you desire." But those who desired the things of the world emerged victorious.

The group was encouraged and they attacked the Meccans. [Page 15] Wāqid b. ʿAbdullah set out leading the group. He twanged his bow, aimed his arrow, and shot at ʿAmr b. al-Ḥaḍramī—he never missed his mark—and his arrow killed al-Ḥaḍramī. The group attacked the Meccans, and ʿUthmān b. ʿAbdullah b. al-Mughīra and al-Ḥakam b. Kaysān surrendered; Nawfal b. ʿAbdullah b. al-Mughīra escaped. They captured the caravan.

Muḥammad related to us saying: ʿAlī b. Yazīd b. ʿAbdullah b. Wahb b. Zamaʿa al-Asadī related to me from his father, from his paternal aunt, from her mother, Karīma bt. al-Miqdād, from al-Miqdād b. ʿAmr, who said: I captured al-Ḥakam b. Kaysān, and our commander wanted to execute him. I said, "Let us hand him to the Prophet." So we took him to the Prophet and he invited him to Islam and spoke to him for a long time. ʿUmar b. al-Khaṭṭāb said, "Do you speak to this man, O Messenger of God? By God, he will not convert even if it were the end of the world. Give him to me and I will cut off his head and lead him to his destiny." But the Prophet did not pay any attention to ʿUmar until he had converted al-Ḥakam. ʿUmar said: When I saw he had converted to

Islam, what happened earlier and how it was settled took a hold of me. I said. "How could I dare rebut the Prophet on a matter about which he is more knowledgeable than I?" Then I said, "Indeed, I desired only the advice of God and his Messenger about that!" ʿUmar said: He converted, and, by God, he was the best of converts. He strove in the way of God until he was martyred on the day of Biʾr Maʿūna. The Prophet was satisfied that he entered Paradise.

Muḥammad related to us that al-Wāqidī related to us that: Muḥammad b. ʿAbdullah related to me from al-Zuhrī, who said: Al-Ḥakam said, "What is Islam?" Muḥammad said, "You worship God alone, attributing no partners to him, and witness that Muḥammad is his servant and messenger." He said, "I have converted." The Prophet turned around [Page 16] to his companions and said, "Had I obeyed you and killed him in anger, he would now be in hell."

They said: They drove the caravan containing wine, skin/leather and raisins from al-Ṭāʾif, and brought it to the Prophet. The Quraysh said, "Muḥammad has profaned the protected month. He has taken blood and wealth though that month has been declared sacrosanct and great importance is attached to it." Those who rebutted them said, "Rather, you were struck in the night of Shaʿbān." The group approached with the caravan, and when they arrived before the Messenger of God, the Messenger of God stopped the caravan and did not take anything from it. Then he put away the captives, saying to his companions, "I did not command you to fight in the protected month." Ibn Abī Sabra related to me from Sulaymān b. Suḥaym saying: The Messenger of God did not order fighting either in the sacred month, or in the unprotected months. Rather, he commanded them to seek information about the Quraysh.

They said: The people were bewildered. They thought that especially those who led the attack would be destroyed. They treated them severely and blamed them. Medina heated up like a boiling kettle. The Jews said: Wāqid b. ʿAbdullah al-Tamīmī killed ʿAmr b. al-Haḍramī. ʿAmr meant the war thrived; al-Haḍramī indicated that war is present. And Wāqid meant the war is fuelled. Ibn Wāqid said: They regarded it as an omen. That was something from God to the Jewish people.

They said: The Quraysh sent the Prophet the ransom for their companions. The Prophet said, "We will never accept their ransom until they arrive with our companions," referring to Saʿd b. Abī Waqqāṣ and ʿUtba b. Ghazwān.

Abū Bakr b. Ismāʿīl b. Muḥammad related to me from his father, saying: Saʿd b. Abī Waqqāṣ said: We went out raiding with ʿAbdullah b. Jaḥsh until we alighted at Buḥrān [Page 17] (Buḥrān is close to Maʿadin Banū Sulaym), where we slackened the rope of our camels. We were twelve men. Every two of us sat one behind the other on a camel. I was the companion of ʿUtba b. Ghazwān, and the camel was his. But our camel strayed from the route and we spent two days looking for it. Our companions departed and we set out on their tracks, but we erred, and they arrived in Medina days before us, so we did not witness Nakhla. We proceeded to the Messenger of God while they thought that we were captured. We had become very hungry during our journey for we had left from al-Mulayḥa—and between Mulayḥa and Medina are six mail posts, and between Medina and Maʿadin is one night, i.e. Maʿadin Banū Sulaym and Medina.

He said: We left from al-Mulayḥa in a group. We had no food with us until we reached Medina. Someone said, "O Abū Isḥāq how many days is it from there to Medina?" He replied, "Three days." When we were attacked by hunger we ate the *ʿĪḍāh* (a shrub) and drank water. When we arrived in Medina, we found a group of Quraysh that had arrived with ransom for their companions. The Prophet had refused their ransom. He said, "I fear for my companions." When we arrived the Messenger of God accepted their ransom.

They said: There is from the sayings of Muḥammad to them: If you kill my companion I will kill two of yours. Their ransom was forty ounces of silver for each one; an ounce was forty dirhams.

ʿUmar b. ʿUthmān al-Jaḥshī related to me from his father from Muḥammad b. ʿAbdullah b. Jaḥsh, who said: In *jāhiliyya* one-fourth of the plunder was the share of the leader, but when ʿAbdullah b. Jaḥsh returned from Nakhla it was made a fifth of what was plundered. He apportioned the rest among his companions. [Page 18] The first fifth was apportioned in Islam after the words *Know that one fifth of whatever you capture belongs to God* (Q. 8:41), was revealed.

Muḥammad b. Yaḥyā b. Sahl related to me from Muḥammad b. Sahl b. Abī Ḥathma from Rāfiʿ b. Khadīj from Abū Burda b. Niyār, who said: The Prophet put away the plunder of the people of Nakhla and proceeded to Badr. When he returned from Badr he apportioned it together with the plunder from the people of Badr, and gave all the people their rightful share.

They said: The Qurʾān revealed: *They ask you about the protected month* (Q. 2:217). *God related to them in His book: Fighting in the protected month was just as it was. But those who seize unlawfully from the Muslims and, more than that, hinder them from the way of God until they hurt them and imprison them so that they emigrate to the Prophet; and those who disbelieve in God and hinder the Muslims from the Masjid al-Ḥaram during the Ḥajj and ʿUmra, theirs is the sedition according to the law*. God says: *Sedition is worse than fighting* (Q. 2:219). He said: This was in reference to the idols Isāf and Nāʾila.

Maʿmar related to me from al-Zuhrī from ʿUrwa saying: The Messenger of God paid the blood money for ʿAmr b. al-Ḥaḍramī. He observed the protected month as it was until God revealed *Barāʾa*. Abū Bakr b. Abī Sabra related to me from ʿAbd al-Majīd b. Sahl from Kurayb, who said: I asked Ibn ʿAbbās, "Did the Messenger of God pay the blood money for [Page 19] Ibn al-Ḥaḍramī?" He replied, "No." Ibn Wāqid said: We are agreed that he did not pay the blood money. Abū Maʿshar told me that ʿAbdullah b. Jaḥsh was named the Commander of the Believers for that expedition (*sariyya*).

THOSE WHO WENT OUT WITH ʿABDULLAH B. JAḤSH ON HIS EXPEDITION

There were eight individuals. ʿAbdullah b. Jaḥsh, Abū Ḥudhayfa b. ʿUtba b. Rabīʿa, ʿĀmir b. Rabīʿa, Wāqid b. ʿAbdullah b. Tamīmī, ʿUkkāsha b. Miḥṣan, Khālid b. Abī Bukayr, Saʿd b. Abī Waqqāṣ, and ʿUtba b. Ghazwān. The last two did not witness the event. Some said there were twelve and others that there were thirteen, but eight is confirmed among us.

THE BATTLE OF BADR

The Prophet watched for the caravan returning from al-Shām, and assigned his companions to it. The Prophet sent Ṭalḥa b. ʿUbaydullah and Saʿīd b. Zayd, ten nights before he went out himself from Medina, to seek information about the caravan. When they alighted before Kashad al-Juhanī in al-Nakhbār at Ḥawrāʾ—al-Nakhbār is behind

Dhū l-Marwa along the coast—Kashad protected the two of them and made them alight. They continued to stay with him in a tent until the caravan passed, and then, Ṭalḥa and Saʿīd ascended the hill and looked at the people, and at what the caravan carried. The people of the caravan inquired, "O Kashad, [Page 20] did you see any of Muḥammad's men?" Kashad says, "God forbid. How are there spies of Muḥammad in al-Nakhbār?" When the caravan left, the two Muslims rested the night, rose in the morning and left, and Kashad went with them, for protection, until he brought them to Dhū l-Marwa. Meanwhile the caravan sped along the coast. They traveled by night and day fearful of being discovered.

Ṭalḥa b. ʿUbaydullah and Saʿīd b. Zayd arrived in Medina on the day the Prophet was to meet them in Badr, so they set out in the direction of the Prophet and met him in Turbān—Turbān is between Malal and al-Sayyāla—at al-Maḥja, in the house of Ibn Udhayna the poet. Kashad arrived after that and informed the Messenger of God that both Saʿīd and Ṭalḥa had sought his protection. The Messenger of God greeted him and was generous to him saying, "Shall I apportion some land for you at Yanbuʿ?" He replied, "I am old, and my life is coming to an end, but apportion it to my brother's son." So the Prophet apportioned some land to Kashad's nephew.

They said: The Prophet encouraged the Muslims saying, "This caravan of the Quraysh holds their wealth, and perhaps God will grant it to you as plunder," so whoever was swift, hastened. Some men were even prepared to draw lots against their fathers. Among those who drew lots about going out to Badr were Saʿd b. Khaythama and his father. Saʿd said to his father, "If it was other than Paradise, I would prefer it for you. Indeed, I hope this is the way to martyrdom." Khaythama said, "Prefer me, and stay with your women," but Saʿd refused. Khaythama said, "Indeed it is inevitable that one of us stays." They drew lots and the arrowhead went to Saʿd. He was killed at Badr.

Many of the Prophet's companions held him back. [Page 21] They hated his going out raiding and there were many words of dispute about it. Those who stayed behind were not censured because a battle had not been intended. Indeed, they had set out for the caravan. The people who stayed behind were from families of resolve and discernment and if they thought that it would be a battle they would not have stayed behind. Among those who stayed behind was Usayd b. Ḥuḍayr. When the Prophet arrived, Usayd said to him, "Praise be to God who gladdens you and gives you victory over your enemies. By Him who sends you with the truth, I did not stay away from you desiring for myself above you. I did not think that you will meet the enemy; I thought that it was only for the caravan." The Messenger of God said to him, "You speak the truth." It was the first raid in which God strengthened Islam and humbled the disbelievers.

The Messenger of God went out with those who were with him until they reached Naqb Banī Dīnār. He alighted at al-Buqʿ, i.e. Buyūt al-Suqyā—al-Buqʿ of Naqb Banī Dīnār is in Medina and al-Suqyā adjoins the houses of Medina—on Sunday the twelfth of Ramaḍan. The army set up its tents there, and he reviewed the combatants. ʿAbdullah b. ʿUmar, Usāma b. Zayd, Rāfiʿ b. Khadīj, Barāʾ b. ʿĀzib, Usayd b. Ẓuhayr, Zayd b. Arqam, and Zayd b. Thābit appeared before him, and he rejected them and did not permit them to fight.

Abū Bakr b. Ismāʿīl related to me from his father from ʿĀmir b. Saʿd from his father, saying: I saw my brother, ʿUmayr b. Abī Waqqāṣ, hiding, before the Prophet reviewed us, and I said, "What is the matter with you, O my brother?" He replied, "I fear the Prophet will see me and consider me too young and reject me. I want to go out raiding, so that God might bless me with martyrdom." He said: He was looked over by the

Messenger of God and considered too young. The Messenger of God said, “Return!” But ʿUmayr cried, and so the Messenger of God permitted him. He said: Saʿd used to say, “I had tied the shoulder belt of his sword for him since he was little.” He was killed at Badr at the age of sixteen.

[Page 22] Abū Bakr b. ʿAbdullah related to me saying: ʿAyyāsh b. ʿAbd al-Raḥmān al-Ashjaʿī related to me that, at that time, the Prophet commanded his companions to draw water from their well. The Messenger of God drank the water from their well. ʿAbd al-ʿAzīz b. Muḥammad related to me from ʿAmr b. Abī ʿAmr that the Prophet was the first who drank from their well that day. ʿAbd al-ʿAzīz b. Muḥammad related to me, from Hishām b. ʿUrwa from his father from ʿĀʾisha that after that, the Messenger of God sought the sweet water from Buyūt al-Suqyā.

Ibn Abī Dhiʾb related to me from al-Maqburī from ʿAbdullah b. Abī Qatāda from his father that the Messenger of God prayed at Buyūt al-Suqyā. He prayed for the people of Medina, at that time, saying, “O God, surely Ibrahīm, your servant, your friend and your prophet, prayed for the people of Mecca. So I, Muḥammad, your servant and your Prophet, pray for the people of Medina; that you bless their measures, their provisions and property. Make us love Medina, and transfer its pestilential air to Khumm. O Lord, I have declared sacrosanct that which is between its two tracts just as Abraham your friend protected Mecca.” Khumm is about two miles from al-Juḥfa.

They said: The Prophet dispatched ʿAdī b. Abī l-Zaghbāʾ and Basbas from Buyūt al-Suqyā. They said: ʿAbdullah b. ʿAmr b. Ḥarām came to the Messenger of God at that time, and said, [Page 23] “O Messenger of God, it gladdens me, this place of yours, and I believe it is suitable for the scrutiny of your companions. Indeed this place of ours, Banū Salama, is where there took place between us and the Banū Husayka what occurred—Husayka is on al-Dhubbāb—and al-Dhubbāb is a mountain in the direction of Medina. There were Jews in Husayka and they had many houses there. We scrutinized our companions there. We permitted fighting to those who had mastery of the weapons and prevented the young from carrying weapons. Then we marched to the Jews of Husayka, and they were the mightiest of the Jews at that time. We fought them as we wished, and have to this day kept the rest of the Jews humble. I hope, O Messenger of God, that we will meet, we and the Quraysh, and that God grants you satisfaction over them.”

Khallād b. ʿAmr b. al-Jamūḥ said that when it was daylight, he returned to his people in Khurbā, and his father said to him, “I thought that you had gone.” He replied, “The Messenger of God is scrutinizing the people at al-Buqʿ.” ʿAmr said, “It is a good omen. By God, I hope that you plunder and are successful against the disbelieving Quraysh. Indeed this was our station the day we marched to Ḥusayka.” He [Khallād] said that the Messenger of God had changed its name to al-Suqyā. He said: I wanted to purchase it, but Saʿd b. Abī Waqqāṣ bought it for the price of two young camels—some said for seven ounces of gold. He added: It was mentioned to the Prophet that Saʿd bought it, and he said, “A profitable sale!”

They said: The Prophet left Buyūt al-Suqyā on Sunday, the evening of the twelfth of Ramaḍān. Three hundred and five Muslims went with him. Eight stayed behind but he granted them their share and their reward. There were seventy camels [Page 24] and they sat one behind the other on the camels, two, three and four. The Prophet, ʿAlī, and Marthad—some say Zayd b. Ḥāritha instead of Marthad—sat on one camel. Ḥamza b. ʿAbd al-Muṭṭalib, Zayd b. Ḥāritha, Abū Kabsha and Anasa, the freedman (mawlā) of the Prophet, sat on one camel; ʿUbayda b. al-Ḥārith, al-Ṭufayl and al-Ḥuṣayn, the two sons of al-Ḥārith, and Misṭaḥ b. Uthātha sat on a watering camel belonging to ʿUbayda b. al-Ḥārith who bought it from Ibn Abī Dāwud al-Māzanī. Muʿādh, ʿAwf, and Muʿawwidh, the sons of ʿAfrāʾ and their freedman Abū l-Ḥamrā shared a camel. Ubayy b. Kaʿb, ʿUmāra b. Ḥazm and Ḥāritha b. Nuʿmān shared a camel; Khirāsh b. al-Ṣimma, Quṭba b. ʿĀmir b. Ḥadīda and ʿAbdullāh b. ʿAmr b. Ḥarām, one camel; ʿUtba b. Ghazwān and Ṭulayb b. ʿUmayr shared a camel belonging to ʿUtba b. Ghazwān—which they named al-ʿUbays. Muṣʿab b. ʿUmayr, Suwaybiṭ b. Ḥarmala and Masʿūd b. Rabīʿ shared a camel belonging to Muṣʿab; ʿAmmār b. Yāsir and Ibn Masʿūd shared a camel; ʿAbdullah b. Kaʿb, Abū Dāwud al-Māzanī, and Salīṭ b. Qays shared a camel belonging to ʿAbdullah b. Kaʿb. ʿUthmān, Qudāma, ʿAbdullah b. Maẓʿūn and al-Sāʾib b. ʿUthmān shared a camel. Abū Bakr, ʿUmar, and ʿAbd al-Raḥmān b. ʿAwf, shared a camel; Saʿd b. Muʿādh, his brother, his nephew al-Ḥārith b. Aws and al-Ḥārith b. Anas, shared a watering camel belonging to Saʿd b. Muʿādh named al-Dhayyāl; Saʿd b. Zayd, Salama b. Salāma, ʿAbbād b. Bishr, Rāfīʿ b. Yazīd and al-Ḥārith b. Khazama shared a watering camel belonging to Saʿd b. Zayd. Each was supplied with only one measure of dates.

[Page 25] ʿUbayd b. Yaḥyā related to me from Muʿādh b. Rifāʿa, from his father, saying: I went raiding with the Prophet to Badr. Every three of us sat one behind the other on a camel. I and my brother, Khallād b. Rāfiʿ, rode on a camel of ours with ʿUbayd b. Zayd b. ʿĀmir. We went along until we reached al-Rawḥā. Our camel was fatigued and standing still, and its legs folded on us, and it became disabled. My brother said, "O God, indeed I give You a solemn pledge that if You take us back to Medina I will sacrifice this camel." He said: The Prophet passed by us while we were in that situation, and we said, "O Messenger of God, our camel is fatigued." The Messenger of God asked for water, and gargled his mouth with it while performing ablution in a vessel. Then he said, "Open its mouth," and we did. Then he poured the water into its mouth, on its head, neck, withers, hump, back, and tail. Then he said, "ride!" and the Messenger of God went on his way. We caught up with him at the bottom of al-Munṣarif, for indeed our camel was running with us, until, when we reached al-Muṣalla, it collapsed. My brother sacrificed it and divided its meat as *ṣadaqa* (alms).

Yaḥyā b. ʿAbd al-ʿAzīz b. Saʿīd b. Saʿd b. ʿUbāda related to me from his father, saying: Saʿd b. ʿUbāda provided twenty camels in Badr. Abū Bakr b. Ismāʿīl related to me from his father from Saʿd b. Abī Waqqāṣ [Page 26], who said: We set out with the Prophet to Badr taking seventy camels with us. They sat one behind the other, three, four and two on a camel. I was among the most favored of the companions of the Prophet, free from want, the spriest pedestrian, and the best shot with an arrow, and I did not ride a step either going or coming.

The Messenger of God said, when he left from Buyūt al-Suqyā, "O God, surely they are bare footed, so provide them with beasts to ride on; and naked, so clothe them; and hungry, so feed them, and dependent, so provide for them by Your grace!" He said: Not one among them desiring to ride returned, except he found a ride: for one man a camel or two; clothed were those who were naked; they took food from their provisions and ransom from the prisoners and enriched the needy. The Messenger of God appointed Qays b. Abī Ṣaʿṣaʿa—and his name was ʿAmr b. Zayd b. ʿAwf b. Mabdhūl—over the pedestrians, and ordered him, when he left Buyūt al-Suqyā, to count the Muslims. Ibn Abī Ṣaʿṣaʿa stopped at the well of Abū ʿInaba, and counted them, and informed the Prophet.

The Messenger of God set out from Buyūt al-Suqyā until he came to Baṭn al-ʿAqīq;

then he took the road to al-Muktamin until he reached the plain of Ibn Azhar, where he alighted under a tree. Abū Bakr brought some stones and built a mosque under that tree. The Messenger of God prayed in it. Monday dawned when the Prophet was here, and he appeared in Malal and Turbān between al-Ḥafīra and Malal.

Saʿd b. Abī Waqqāṣ said: When we were in Turbān, the Messenger of God said to me, "O Saʿd, look at the gazelle." He said: I aimed an arrow at it. [Page 27] The Messenger of God stood and placed his chin between my shoulder and my ear; then he said, "Shoot, and may God guide your shot." My arrow did not err from its neck. He said: The Prophet smiled. He said: I went running, and found it at its last breath, so I slaughtered it, and we carried it until we alighted close by. The Prophet commanded that it be divided between his companions. Muḥammad b. Bijād related to me about that, from his father, from Saʿd.

They said: They had two horses with them; the horse belonging to Marthad b. Abī Marthad al-Ghanawī, and the horse belonging to al-Miqdād b. ʿAmr al-Bahrānī, the ally of the Banū Zuhra. Some said that one of the horses belonged to al-Zubayr. But there were only two horses, and there is no dispute among us that one horse belonged to Miqdād. Mūsā b. Yaʿqūb related to me from his aunt, from her father, from Ḍubāʿa bt. Zubayr, from al-Miqdād b. ʿAmr, who said: On the day of Badr I had a horse called Sabḥa. Saʿd b. Mālik al-Ghanawī related to me from his ancestors that Marthad b. Abī Marthad al-Ghanawī was seen at that time on a horse of his named al-Sayl.

They said: The Quraysh entered al-Shām in their caravan. It was a caravan of a thousand camels. It contained significant wealth, for there was not a man or woman from the Quraysh in Mecca who had some wealth accruing, but it was sent in the caravan. Even the woman who had a paltry sum sent it. Some said that it contained fifty thousand dinar, though others said there was less. It was said that much of what was in it came from the property of the family of Saʿīd b. al-ʿĀṣ—Abū Uḥayḥa—either the wealth belonged to them, or to those who borrowed against half the profits to be made, and most of the caravan belonged to them. Some said that it belonged to the Banū Makhzūm who owned two hundred camels and five or four thousand pieces of gold. Others, that Ḥārith b. ʿĀmir b. Nawfal owned a thousand pieces of gold and Umayya b. Khalaf, two thousand pieces of gold. [Page 28] Hishām b. ʿUmāra b. Abī l-Ḥuwayrith related to me, saying: There were 10,000 gold pieces belonging to the Banū ʿAbdManāf in the caravan. Their merchandise was going to Ghazza from al-Shām and there were several small caravans that the Quraysh concealed in it—i.e. in the large caravan.

ʿAbdullah b. Jaʿfar related to me from Abū ʿAwn, the *mawlā* of al-Miswar, from Makhrama b. Nawfal, who said: When we entered al-Shām a man from Judham caught up with us and informed us that Muḥammad had been observing our caravan ever since we started our journey; he had left him conscientiously awaiting our return and had become an ally and made an agreement against us with the people on the road. Makhrama said: We set out cautiously fearing an ambush, and sent Ḍamḍam b. ʿAmr, when we left al-Shām.

ʿAmr b. al-ʿĀṣ used to relate, saying: When we were in Zarqāʾ (which is in al-Shām in the direction of Maʿān, about two *mirhal* from Adhriʿāt when descending to Mecca), we met a man from Judhām, who said, "Muḥammad and his companions have been observing you since you started your journey." We said that we did not know. He said, "But indeed, he stayed a month then returned to Yathrib. On the day Muḥammad approaches you, you must be quick for he is now well prepared to obstruct you. Surely he has computed for you the number of days, so be careful of your caravan and consider your decision. By God, I do not see the numbers, or the camels, or the weapons."

They made a joint decision and sent Ḍamḍam who was in the caravan. The Quraysh had passed by him while he was on the coast with two camels of his. They paid him twenty pieces of gold and Abū Sufyān commanded him to inform the Quraysh that Muḥammad was observing their caravan. He ordered him to cut his camel's ears when he entered, and to turn his saddle around: to tear his shirt both in front and behind and shout, help! help! Some say: Rather, they sent him from Tabūk. There were thirty men from the Quraysh in the caravan and with them were ʿAmr b. al-ʿĀṣ and Makhrama b. Nawfal.

[Page 29] They said: ʿĀtika bt. ʿAbd al-Muṭṭalib saw a dream that frightened her, before Ḍamḍam b. ʿAmr arrived, and she was distressed in her heart. She sent a message to her brother al-ʿAbbās saying, "O my brother, by God, I had a dream at night and I was distressed by it. I fear that a great evil will come upon your people. Keep it secret and I will relate it to you." She said, "I saw a rider approach on a camel until he stopped at al-Abṭaḥ, then he screamed at the top of his voice, 'O family of Ghudar, disperse to your slaughtering place in three days.' He shouted it three times. The people saw and gathered to him. Then he entered the sanctuary (*masjid*)and the people followed him, and lo and behold, the camel ascended with him to the top of the Kaʿba and he shouted three times as before. Then the camel ascended with him to the head of Abū Qubays and he shouted again, as before, three times. Then he took a stone from Abū Qubays and threw it, and it arrived falling to the bottom of the hill. There did not remain a house (*bayt*) nor a room (*dār*) in Mecca but a piece of the stone had entered it." ʿAmr b. al-ʿĀṣ used to relate saying, "Surely I saw all this, and I saw a splitting from the rock which had been broken off from Abū Qubays, and surely that was a warning. But God did not desire that we convert at that time for He delayed our conversion until He desired."

They said: Nothing from that rock entered a house or room from the houses of Banū Hāshim or Banū Zuhra. They said: Her brother said, "Surely, this is but a dream!" He went out distressed until he met al-Walīd b. ʿUtba b. Rabīʿa, who was his friend. He mentioned it and asked that he keep it a secret, but he spread the news among the people. Al-ʿAbbās said: I left in the morning and circumambulated the house. Abū Jahl was seated with a group [Page 30] of Quraysh, talking about the dream of ʿĀtika. He said, "What ʿĀtika saw was this!" And I said: "What is that?" And he replied, "O Banū ʿAbd al-Muṭṭalib, does it not satisfy you that your men prophecy, but that even your women must prophecy? ʿĀtika claims that she saw in her sleep whatever she saw and we will wait three days until it happens. If it happens that what she said is true, it will be. But if three days pass and it does not happen, we will write of you that you are the worst liars of any family (*ahl bayt*) with the Arabs." He (al-ʿAbbās) responded, "O you of the yellow buttocks, you are the first of the liars and more vile than us!"

Abū Jahl said, "Indeed we have competed for greatness with you. You said, 'With us is the distribution of water (*siqāya*)'. We said, 'No matter, you shall quench the thirsty pilgrims.' Then you said, 'With us is the office of gate keeper (*ḥijāba*).' And we said, 'No matter, you shall watch over the house.' Then you said, 'With us is the council (*nadwā*).' And we said, 'No matter you will prepare the food and feed the people.' Then you said, 'With us is support for the weak (*rafāda*).' And we said, 'No matter, you will gather what is needed for the weak.' And when we fed the people, you fed them. The travelers gathered, and we competed for greatness; we were like two race horses.

But now you say, 'From us is a prophet.' Then you say, 'From us is a prophetess!' No, by al-Lāt and al-ʿUzza, this will never be!"

Al-ʿAbbās said: I could do nothing but deny that. I denied that ʿĀtika saw something. In the evening every mother who had given birth from the Banū ʿAbd al-Muṭṭalib came to me. They said, "Are you satisfied with this sinful, evil, person (Abū Jahl) who falls upon your men and now attacks your women while you listen? Have you no shame?" Al-ʿAbbās said, "By God, I have only done insignificant deeds. By God, surely I will go to him tomorrow, and if he repeats himself I will satisfy you about him." When the next day, from that day in which ʿĀtika saw what she saw, dawned, Abū Jahl said, "This is one day." On the next, he said, "These are two days." And when it was the third day Abū Jahl said, "This is the third day, nothing more remains."

[Page 31] Al-ʿAbbās said: I rose early, on the morning of the third day, and I was sharp with anger. I saw the matter had escaped me and I desired to grasp it. I remembered how the women had made me angry about it and what they had said to me. By God, I was walking towards him (Abū Jahl)—a thin man, with a sharp face; sharp of tongue and sharp of sight—when all of a sudden he set out towards the gate of Banū Sahm with urgency. I asked myself: What's in his mind . . . may God curse him! Is all this from fear that I would scold him? But he had heard the voice of Ḍamḍam b. ʿAmr saying, "O you Quraysh, O family of Luʾāyy b. Ghālib, the young weaned camels (*laṭīma*). Muḥammad approaches them with his companions. Help! Help! By God, I do not think that you will reach them." Ḍamḍam shouted about that in Batn al-Wadi. He had cut off the ears of his camel and torn his shirt in front and behind, and turned his saddle around (back to front). He used to say: Surely, I remember, before I even entered Mecca, and indeed, I saw in my sleep—while I was on my saddle, as though the valley of Mecca was dripping blood from top to bottom. I awoke with fear and alarm, and I feared for the Quraysh, for I was convinced that it would be a disaster for them.

It was said: Surely it was Satan who called out at that time. He took the shape of Surāqa b. Juʿsham, went ahead of Ḍamḍam, and made them rush to their caravan. Ḍamḍam arrived after him. ʿUmayr b. Wahb used to say, "I never saw an affair more astonishing than the affair of Ḍamḍam." It was Satan alone who screamed in his voice. Indeed, he did not let us take control of our affairs, urging us, until we all set out whether in difficulty or ease. Ḥakīm b. Ḥizām used to say, "It was not a man that incited us to the caravan. Indeed, it was Satan." It was said, "How was that, O Abū Khālid?" He replied, "Indeed I was astonished about it. We could not take control of our affairs."

They said: The people made preparations and were distracted from each other. There were only two kinds of men: Those who wanted to go out and those who wanted to send another instead. The Quraysh inclined towards the dream of ʿĀtika, and the Banū Hāshim were content. One of them said: Indeed, you claimed that we lied and that ʿĀtika lied. The Quraysh were mobilized in three days, and some said two. They went out armed [Page 32] and bought weapons. The powerful among them helped the weak. Suhayl b. ʿAmr stood up in the midst of the Quraysh, saying, "O you Quraysh, this is Muḥammad; the youths with him are from your youth and from the people of Yathrib. They observe your caravan and the camels of the Quraysh, the young weaned camels, the *laṭīma*—and the *laṭīma* is the merchandise." Abū Zinād said, "The young camels (*laṭīma*) are all that is carried by the camels as merchandise." Others said, "The fragrant *laṭīma* are special—for those who desired a mount this was a mount; for those who desired power, this was power." Zamaʿa b. al-Aswad stood up and said, "By al-Lāt and al-ʿUzzā, a matter of greater importance than this has not come down to you. Surely,

Muḥammad and the people of Yathrib observe your caravan and desire the property in it on which you depend for your living. So stir yourselves. Not one of you shall stay behind. Those who have no strength, this is his strength. By God, if Muḥammad attacks it, he will not alarm you until he has taken you completely." Ṭuʿayma b. ʿAdī said, "O Qurayshī people, by God, a matter has not come down to you that was more significant than this: that your caravan, containing your property and your living and the camels of the Quraysh, is taken. By God, I do not know a man or a woman from the Banū ʿAbdManāf who owns but twenty dirham or more, but it is in this caravan. For those who have no strength, we have strength, and we will bring then our strength."

He provided twenty camels, and strengthened them and followed them with their families in Maʿūna. Ḥanẓala b. Abī Sufyān and ʿAmr b. Abī Sufyān stood up and incited the people to go out, but they offered neither power nor beasts. It was said to them, "Will you two not offer what your people offer of beasts of burden?" They both replied, "By God, we do not have wealth. Only Abū Sufyān has wealth." Nawfal b. Muʿāwiya al-Dīlī walked up to the more powerful families among [Page 33] the Quraysh and spoke to them about granting money and camels to those going out. He spoke to ʿAbdullah b. Abī Rabīʿa, who said, "Here are five hundred dinars. Put it where you think fit." He spoke to Ḥuwayṭib b. ʿAbd al-ʿUzzā and took two or three hundred dinars from him and purchased weapons and animals to ride on.

They said: None of the Quraysh stayed behind unless he sent someone else in his place. The Quraysh went to Abū Lahab and said, "Surely you are one of the lords of the Quraysh, and if you stay behind, the rest of your people will follow your example. So either leave yourself, or send someone." He replied, "By al-Lāt and al-ʿUzza, I will not go out, nor will I send someone." Abū Jahl came to him and said, "Rise, Abū ʿUtba, for by God, we do not go out except for the protection of your religion and the religion of your forefathers." Abū Jahl feared that Abū Lahab would convert to Islam. Abū Lahab was silent but he did not go out, nor did he send any one for apprehension regarding the dream of ʿĀtika. Indeed he used to say that the dream of ʿĀtika helped him stand by his decision. Some said that he sent al-ʿĀṣ b. Hishām b. al-Mughīra, for the latter was indebted to him. He said, "Go and your debt is paid!" So Ibn Mughīra went out for him.

They said: ʿUtba and Shayba (the sons of Rabīʿa) went out in their coats of mail. ʿAddās (their slave) saw them restoring their coats of mail, and their tools of battle, and said, "What do you intend?" They replied, "Did you not see the man to whom we sent you with grapes from our grape vine in al-Ṭāʾif?" He said, "Yes." They both said, "We will go out and fight him." ʿAddās cried out, "Do not go out, for by God, he is surely a prophet." But they rejected him, and went out. ʿAddās went out with them and was killed in Badr with them.

They said: The Quraysh drew lots before Hubal for going out. Umayya b. Khalaf, ʿUtba and Shayba drew lots before Hubal for commanding or forbidding, and drew out the forbidding arrowhead for going out. They gathered at the place until Abū Jahl disturbed them and said, "I shall not cast lots, nor shall we [Page 34] stay away from our caravan." When Zamaʿa b. Aswad decided to go out, he was in Dhū Ṭuwā. He drew lots about it. He drew out one forbidding his going out, and felt anger. He tried a second time and drew out one similar to the one before, so he broke it. He said, "I have not seen such a day when an arrowhead was more false than this!" Suhayl b. ʿAmr passed by him while he was in that situation and said, "How is it that I see you angry, O Abū Ḥukayma?" Zamaʿa informed him, and he said, "Keep it from you, O man. What is more false than these arrowheads! ʿUmayr b. Wahb has informed me similar to what you inform me, that the forbidding arrowhead met him." Then they both left, according to this tradition.

Muḥammad related to us that al-Wāqidī related to us, saying: Mūsā b. Ḍamra b. Saʿīd related to me from his father, who said: Abū Sufyān b. Ḥarb said to Ḍamḍam, "When you arrive before the Quraysh say to them: Do not cast lots with arrow heads."

Muḥammad b. ʿAbdullah related to me from al-Zuhrī from Abū Bakr b. Sulaymān b. Abī Ḥathma, saying: I heard Ḥakīm b. Ḥizām say, "I did not ever take a position more hateful to me than my march to Badr. I have never seen anything similar to what I saw before I set out on this trip." Then he says: Ḍamḍam approached, and he called out the troops to battle. I cast lots with the arrowheads detesting all that came out. Then I set out in spite of that until we alighted at Marr al-Ẓahrān. Ibn Ḥanẓaliyya (i.e. Abū Jahl) slaughtered the camels. But one of the camels was still alive, and there did not remain a tent among the soldiers' tents, but it was spattered with its blood. This was a clear sign. For that reason I was on the verge of returning, when I remembered Ibn Ḥanẓaliyya and his misfortune. The memory caused me to change my mind and set me on my course.

[Page 35] Ḥakīm used to say: Indeed you saw us when we reached al-Thaniyyat al-Bayḍāʾ (which brings you down to Fakh if you are approaching from Medina). There was ʿAddās, seated, and people were passing by, and the two sons of Rabīʿa passed by him. ʿAddās jumped at them and grabbed their legs as he lunged at them. He said, "By my father and mother, you two, surely he is the Messenger of God. Do not conscript for it will be your death!" Tears fell from his eyes onto his cheeks. I desired to return, as well, so I left, and al-ʿĀṣ b. Munabbih b. al-Ḥajjāj passed by and he stopped before him when ʿUtba and Shayba left. Al-ʿĀṣ said, "What makes you cry?" He replied, "My lords and the lord of the Ahl al-Wādī make me cry. They are leaving to their deaths. They will fight the Messenger of God." Al-ʿĀṣ said, "Muḥammad is the Messenger of God?" Al-ʿAddās rose in protest, and he had goose flesh. He cried out, saying: "By God, he is indeed the Messenger of God to all the people." He said: Al-ʿĀṣ b. Munabbih converted, but continued to be doubtful until he was killed with the disbelievers in doubt and suspicion. Some say that ʿAddās returned and did not witness Badr. Others, that he witnessed Badr and was killed at that time. The first saying is confirmed among us.

They said: Saʿd b. Muʿādh went out to *ʿUmra* before Badr and alighted with Umayya b. Khalaf. Abū Jahl came to Umayya and said, "Do you lodge this enemy? He has sheltered Muḥammad and he notifies us of war." Saʿd b. Muʿādh said, "Say what you wish, is not the route of your caravan before us." Umayya b. Khalaf said, "Be careful! Do not say this to Abū l-Ḥakam. Indeed, he is the lord of the Ahl al-Wādī." Saʿd b. Muʿādh said, "You say that, O Umayya, did I not, by God, hear Muḥammad say, 'I will kill Umayya b. Khalaf.'" Umayya said, "You heard him?" He said: I said, "Yes." [Page 36] He said: He took it to heart, and when the troops came, Umayya refused to go out with them to Badr. So ʿUqba b. Abī Muʿayṭ and Abū Jahl came to him (Umayya), and ʿUqba held a censer with perfume; and Abū Jahl held a *koḥl* container and an application stick (*mirwad*). ʿUqba placed the censer under his nose and said, "Perfume yourself, for surely you are a woman!" And Abū Jahl said, "Pencil your eyes, for indeed you are a woman!" Then Umayya said, "Buy me the best camel in the Wādī." They bought him a stallion for 300 dirhams from the livestock of the Banū Qushayr. The Muslims claimed it as booty on the day of Badr. It was included in the portion of Khubayb b. Yasāf.

They said: None among those who went out to the caravan detested it more than al-Ḥārith b. ʿĀmir. He said, "I wish the Quraysh had decided to sit it out and that my property in the caravan was destroyed, and the property of the Banū ʿAbd Manāf also." It was said, "Surely you are the Lord of Lords. Did you not stop them from going out?" He replied, "Indeed, I thought that the Quraysh had decided to go out. I did not think that one who had the strength should stay behind unless for a reason and I detested opposing them. I do not like the Quraysh to learn what I say now, but though Ibn Ḥanẓaliyya (i.e. Abū Jahl) is a man of ill omen for his community, I know only that he protects his community from the people of Yathrib. Indeed, he has apportioned some of his properties to his son for he is convinced that he will not return to Mecca." Ḍamḍam b. ʿAmr came to al-Ḥārith, for he was indebted to him, and said, "Abū ʿĀmir, I had a dream which I detested. I was awake on my riding beast and I saw your Meccan valley drip blood from its lowest to its highest part." Al-Ḥārith said, "One did not go out in a direction more hateful to him than this direction of mine." He said: Ḍamḍam says to him, "By God, I think that you should stay." Al-Ḥārith replied, "If I had heard this from you [Page 37] before I set out I would not have taken a single step. Hide this news from the Quraysh, for indeed they accuse all those who desired to stay away from the march." Ḍamḍam mentioned this news to al-Ḥārith in the valley of Yaʾjaj.

They said: The Quraysh—i.e. the people of opinion among them—hated the march. They consulted each other. Among those who held back from the march were al-Ḥārith b. ʿĀmir, Umayya b. Khalaf, ʿUtba and Shayba the sons of Rabīʿa, Ḥakīm b. Ḥizām, Abū l-Bakhtarī, ʿAlī b. Umayya b. Khalaf, and al-ʿĀṣ b. Munabbih; until Abū Jahl accused them of being cowards. ʿUqba b. Abī Muʿayṭ and Naḍr b. al-Ḥārith b. Kalada supported his going out. They said: This is the act of women, and they came together for the march. The Quraysh said: Do not leave any of your enemies behind.

Among the proofs for al-Ḥārith b. ʿĀmir, ʿUtba, and Shayba hating to go out was that none of them offered a means of transport (beasts), nor did they carry one of the people. If the man was coming to them as an ally or to give assistance and did not have the ability to do so, and requested a camel from them, they said, "If you have wealth and you want to go out, then do so, but if not, stay," until even the Quraysh learned of it.

When the Quraysh gathered for the march, they remembered the hostility that existed between them and the Banū Bakr. They feared the Banū Bakr would attack those who stayed behind (the women and children). ʿUtba b. Rabīʿa had the greatest fear for them. He said, "O people of the Quraysh, even if you achieve what you desire, surely we [Page 38] are not protecting those who stay behind, and it is the women and children who have no power who stay behind. So consider your decisions!" Then Satan took on the form of Surāqa b. Juʿshum al-Mudlijī and said, "O Qurayshī people, you know my nobility and place among my people. I am your protector who will ensure that Kināna will not bring you something you detest," and ʿUtba was content. Abū Jahl said, "What more do you want? This is the lord of the Kināna who will protect those who stay behind." ʿUtba said, "Nothing. I am leaving."

Concerning that which was between the Banū Kināna and the Quraysh, Yazīd b. Firās al-Laythī related to me from Sharīk b. Abī Namir, from ʿAṭāʾ b. Zayd al-Laythī, that a son of Ḥafṣ b. al-Akhyaf, one of the sons of Maʿīṣ b. ʿĀmir b. Luʾayy, set out looking for a missing camel. He was a youth with a head of flowing hair, wearing a suit of clothes, a radiant youth. He passed by ʿĀmir b. Yazīd b. ʿĀmir b. al-Mulawwaḥ b. Yaʿmar, in Ḍajnān, who said, "Who are you, O youth?" He replied, "A son of Ḥafṣ b.

al-Akhyaf." ʿĀmir said, "O Banū Bakr, is there not blood between you and the Quraysh?" They said, "Yes." He said, "A man who will kill this youth in revenge for one of his own men will surely find fulfillment." So a man from the Banū Bakr followed him and killed him for the blood that was his due from the Quraysh. The Quraysh discussed it. ʿĀmir b. Yazīd said, "You owed us a blood debt, so what do you want? If you want to discharge money for what you owe us, we will discharge that the debt which is with us. If you wish, let it be blood, man for man. But if you wish to overlook that which we owe you, we will overlook what you owe us." The youth was of no significance to the Quraysh, so they said, "Fulfill, man for man!" And they neglected to demand his blood price.

Meanwhile, his brother Mikraz b. Ḥafṣ was in Marr al-Ẓahrān. All of a sudden he saw ʿĀmir b. Yazīd, lord of the Banū Bakr, on a camel. When he saw him, he said to himself: I will not seek a shadow and let what is before me escape! [Page 39] He knelt his camel, drew his sword and struck ʿĀmir with it until he killed him. Then he went to Mecca by night, and hung up the sword of ʿĀmir b. Yazīd, whom he had killed, under the curtain of the Kaʿba. In the morning the Quraysh saw the sword of ʿĀmir b. Yazīd and knew that Mikraz b. Ḥafṣ had killed him. A poem about this from Mikraz was heard. The Banū Bakr grieved about the killing of their lord. The revenge they sought was to kill two or three lords from the Quraysh.

The troops arrived while they were in this predicament. They instilled fear in them regarding their children who stayed behind in Mecca. When Surāqa said what he said, when he was speaking with the tongue of Satan, the people became emboldened, and the Quraysh went out swiftly. They left with their songstresses and their tambourines. Sara, the slave girl of ʿAmr b. Hāshim b. al-Muṭṭalib, ʿAzza the slave girl of al-Aswad b. al-Muṭṭalib, and the slave girl of Umayya b. Khalaf sang in every drinking place. They killed the slaughter-camel. They went out as soldiers throwing spears at each other in war. They left with nine hundred and fifty warriors. They led a hundred horses, proud, and to be seen by men, just as God mentions in His book: *Be not like those who started from their homes insolently and to be seen of men . . .* (Q. 8:47) to the end of the verse. Abū Jahl said, "Does Muḥammad think that he can take from us what his companions took at Nakhla? He will know whether we protect our caravan or not!" The people of power among them had horses. The Banū Makhzum had thirty horses with them, and there were seven hundred camels. The people on horses were all clad in armor—and there were a hundred—as were those on foot.

They said: Abū Sufyān approached with the caravan. As they came closer to Medina they became very afraid and lingered waiting for Ḍamḍam and the troops. On the night following the morning they spent at Māʾ Badr [Page 40] the caravan approached Māʾ Badr. They spent the last part of the night behind Badr in order that they enter Badr by morning if they were not attacked. They did not settle the caravan until they tied it with rope, although some of them praised the use of two ropes. The groans of the camels reminded them of the water of Badr, though there was no need for water among them for surely they had drunk the day before. The people of the caravan began to say, "Indeed this is something that the camels have not done since we set out." They said: darkness concealed us that night until we could not recognize a thing.

Basbas b. ʿAmr and ʿAdī b. Abī l-Zaghbāʾ came to Majdī at Badr in search of information. When they alighted at Māʾ Badr they knelt their camels close to the water, then, took their water bags and filled them from the water. They heard two slave girls from the slaves of Juhayna. One of them, Barza, owed her companion a dirham. Her companion was saying, "Surely the caravan will be here tomorrow or the day after. It has alighted at al-Rawhā'." Majdī b. ʿAmr heard her and said, "You speak the truth!" When Basbas and ʿAdī heard that, they set off on their return to the Prophet. They met him at ʿIrq al-Ẓabya and informed him of the news. Muḥammad informed us that al-Wāqidī related to us, saying: Kuthayr b. ʿAbdullah b. ʿAmr b. ʿAwf al-Muzannī related to us from his father, from his grandfather, who was one of the weepers, that the Messenger of God said, "Moses, the prophet, on whom be peace, went through Fajja al-Rawḥā' with 70,000 of the Banū Isrā'īl." They prayed in the Masjid in ʿIrq al-Ẓabya, which is about two miles towards Medina from al-Rawḥā' if you go to the left.

[Page 41] That night Abū Sufyān rose in Badr and went ahead of the caravan fearful of being observed. He said, "O Majdī, did you see anyone? You know, by God, that there is not a man or a woman in Mecca with one *nashshun* or more—one *nashshun* is half an *awqiyya*, weighing twenty dirhams—but he has sent it with us. If, indeed, you keep secret from us a matter concerning our enemies no man from the Quraysh will settle with you for a very long time." Majdī replied, "By God I have not seen anyone whom I do not like for there is not an enemy between you and Yathrib. And if there was an enemy between you and Yathrib, he would not be hidden from us and I would not conceal it from you; except that I saw two riders coming to this place," and he pointed to the place where ʿAdī and Basbas alighted. "They knelt their camels, drew water for their water bags and then turned back." Abū Sufyān came to where the riders had alighted and took a dropping from their camels; he crumbled it and found there were date stones in it. He said, "This, by God, is the fodder of Yathrib. They are spies of Muḥammad and his companions. I believe they must be near." Abū Sufyan directed his caravan to take the coast, and leaving Badr on his left, departed swiftly.

The Quraysh approached from Mecca alighting at every watering place, feeding those who came to them, and slaughtering their sacrificial camels. While the Quraysh were thus on their journey ʿUtba and Shayba lagged behind, chatting to each other. One of them said to his companion, "Did you not consider the dream of ʿĀtika bt. ʿAbd al-Muṭṭalib? I was surely afraid of it." The other said, "Recall it." He was recollecting it when Abū Jahl came up to them and asked, "What are you talking about?" They said, "We were recollecting the dream of ʿĀtika." He said, "O how remarkable of the Banū ʿAbd al-Muṭṭalib! Are you not satisfied that their men should prophecy for us, but even their women should be prophets among us? By God, if indeed we return to Mecca we shall surely do with them what we will do with them!" ʿUtba said, "Indeed they have a kinship and a close relationship." One of them said to his companion, "Do you want to return?" Abū Jahl said, "Will you return after the distance you have traveled, and leave your people in the lurch and separate from them after you saw your blood avenged with your own eyes? Do you two doubt that Muḥammad and his companions [Page 42] will confront you? By God, I have with me, among my group 180 from my family. They will disperse when I disperse; they will ride when I ride, so return if you wish." They both said, "By God you are destroyed and you destroy your people with you!" ʿUtba said to his brother Shayba, "This man is unlucky—meaning Abū Jahl. Indeed he is not affected by his relationship to Muḥammad as we are, although Muḥammad has the offspring with him. Return with us and leave what he says." Shayba said, "By God, it will be a disgrace for us, O Abū l-Walīd, if we return now after going out!" So they went.

They reached al-Juḥfa, at *ʿI*shā', where Juhaym b. al-Ṣalt b. Makhrama b. al-Muṭṭalib b. ʿAbdManāf was sleeping. He said, "I believe I was between sleep and waking looking at a man approaching on horseback and leading a camel. He stopped before me and said, ʿUtba b. Rabīʿa, Shayba b. Rabīʿa, Zamaʿa b. al-Aswad, Umayya b. Khalaf, Abū l-Bakhtarī, Abū Ḥakam, Nawfal b. Khuwaylid, as well as others from the nobility of the Quraysh are killed. Suhayl b. ʿAmr is taken prisoner. Ḥārith b. Hisham has run away from his brother.' " He said: One of them said, "I thought that you were among those going out to your graves!" He said: Then I saw him slash the neck of his camel and send it into the camp. And there was not a tent from the camp, but it was spattered with its blood. This was mentioned to Abū Jahl.

The dream spread throughout the camp. Abū Jahl said, "This is another prophet from the Banū al-Muṭṭalib, and you will know tomorrow who was killed, us or Muḥammad and his companions." The Quraysh said to Juhaym, "Surely Satan jokes with you in your sleep, for tomorrow you will see the dissimilarity from what you saw in your sleep. The noble companions of Muḥammad will be taken captive and killed." He said: ʿUtba turned to his brother and said, "Would you return? This is a dream like the dream of ʿĀtika and the words of ʿAddās, and by God, ʿAddās did not lie to us. By my life, if Muḥammad is a liar then there are among the Arabs those who will protect us from him (Muḥammad) [Page 43] and if he is truthful, then we will be the happiest of Arabs with him. We are certainly his kinsmen." Shayba said, "He is as you say, so shall we return from among the people of the camp, in full view of them?" Abū Jahl arrived while they were discussing it. He said, "What do you wish?" They said, "The return. Do you not consider the dream of ʿĀtika, the dream of Juhaym b. al-Ṣalt and the sayings of ʿAddās to us?" He [Abū Jahl] said, "You will desert your people and separate yourselves from them?" They replied, "You are finished and you will destroy your people with you," and they left with that.

When Abū Sufyān escaped with the caravan, he thought he had saved it. He sent Qays b. Imrā' l-Qays—who was with the companions of the caravan he went out with from Mecca—to command them to turn back to Mecca. He says, "Your caravan has been saved, so do not give yourselves up to be killed by the people of al-Yathrib. There is no need for you to pursue them. You went out to protect your caravan and your property, and God has saved them. If they refuse you they will not refuse a single target, and they will destroy the songstresses. Indeed, war when it devours, deters."

He took pains to persuade the Quraysh, but they refused to return. They said: As for the singers, we will surely return them and they returned them from al-Juḥfa. The messenger caught up with Abū Sufyān at al-Hadda (Hadda is seven miles from al-ʿAqaba ʿUsfān and thirty-nine miles from Mecca). He informed him of the Quraysh going forward. Abū Sufyān said, "O my people! This is the work of ʿAmr b. Hishām [Abū Jahl]. He hates to return because he has become the leader of the people. He has unjust desires, despicable and shameful. If the companions of Muḥammad overpower the troops, Muḥammad will humiliate us until he enters Mecca." The singers were Sara the slave girl of ʿAmr b. Hishām, the slave girls of Umayya b. Khalaf, and the slave girl called ʿIzza belonging to al-Aswad b. al-Muṭṭalib. Abū Jahl said, "No, by God, we will not return [Page 44] until we appear at Badr—and Badr is the place of the festivities of *jāhiliyya* where the Arabs gather, for there is a market in it. The Arabs will hear of us, and of our marching out. We will stay for three days at Badr, where we will slaughter the camels, supply food, and drink wine. The singers will sing for us, and the Arabs will fear us forever."

The Quraysh sent al-Furāt b. Ḥayyān al-ʿIjlī, when they dispersed from Mecca, to Abū Sufyān b. Ḥarb informing him of their marching and departure, and where they had gathered. But he missed Abū Sufyān, i.e. to say Abū Sufyān stayed close to the sea, and Furāt took al-Maḥajja and showed up before the polytheists at al-Juḥfa where he heard the words of Abū Jahl who was saying, "We will not return!" He said, "They have no desires against you. Surely he who returns after he sees his revenge at hand is weak!" So he went with the Quraysh and left Abū Sufyān. He was wounded on the day of Badr, and ran away, saying, "I have not seen so painful an affair as this day. Indeed Ibn Ḥanẓaliyya is not blessed."

ʿAbd al-Malik b. Jaʿfar related to me from Umm Bakr bt. al-Miswar from her father, who said: Akhnas b. Sharīq, also named Ubayy, who was an ally of the Banū Zuhra, said, "O Banū Zuhra, God saved your caravan, your property, and your companion Makhrama b. Nawfal. Indeed, you went out to protect the caravan and what was in it. Muḥammad is a man from among you, the son of your sister. If he is a prophet, you are lucky with him. If he is a liar, it is better that another kills him than that you kill the son of your sister. So return, and let me take the blame. There is no need for you to go out when there is no profit to be made. This man (Abū Jahl) will not do what he says, for indeed he is the destroyer of his people, swift in corrupting them." So they obeyed him, and his prayers for them were answered. They found in him [Page 45] a good omen. They asked, "How shall we return if we return." Al-Akhnas said, "We will go out with the people, and when it is the evening, I will fall, and you will say, al-Akhnas is bitten. And when they say, 'Proceed,' you shall say, 'No, we will not be parted from our companion until we know whether he lives or dies so we may bury him.' And when they leave, we will return." The Banū Zuḥra did so. In the morning when they were in al-Abwāʾ returning, it was clear to the people that the Banū Zuhra had gone back. Not one of the Banū Zuhra witnessed Badr. They said: They numbered a hundred or less than a hundred, and this is most likely. Another said that they were three hundred. ʿAdī b. Abī l-Zaghbāʾ from Muḥammad's party while descending to Medina from Badr, informed the riders around him saying:

> Stand up to them, O Basbas,
> Indeed, the riding beasts of the people should not be stopped.
> Forcing them on the road is smarter
> Allah granted victory and Akhnas fled.

Muḥammad b. Shujāʿ al-Thaljī told us that Muḥammad b. ʿUmar al-Wāqidi said: Abū Bakr b. ʿAbdullah related to me from Abū Bakr b. ʿUmar b. ʿAbd al-Raḥmān b. ʿAbdullah b. ʿUmar b. al-Khaṭṭāb, who said: The Banū ʿAdī went out with a group until they were in Thaniyyat-Laft. When they were in al-Saḥr they turned away from the coast and departed to Mecca. Abū Sufyān unexpectedly came across them, and said, "O Banū ʿAdī, how is it that you return without a caravan and troops?" They said, "You sent to the Quraysh to return, so whoever desired to return, returned." Not one of the Banū ʿAdī witnessed Badr. Some said that Abū Sufyān said those words when he met them at Marr al-Ẓahrān. Muḥammad b. ʿUmar al-Wāqidī said: The Zuhra returned through al-Juḥfa; as for the Banū ʿAdī, they returned from the road, some say, from Marr al-Ẓahran.

[Page 46] The Messenger of God left and, on the morning of the fourteenth of Ramaḍān, he was in ʿIrq al-Ẓabya. A Bedouin arrived approaching from Tihāma. A companion of the Messenger of God said to him, "Do you have information on Abū Sufyān b. Harb?" He replied, "I do not have information on Abū Sufyān." They said, "Come, greet the Messenger of God." He said, "Is the Messenger of God with you?"

They said, "Yes." He said, "Which of you is the Messenger of God?" They said, "This." He said, "Are you the Messenger of God?" The Messenger of God said, "Yes." The Bedouin said, "If what you say is true, tell me what is in the belly of my camel?" Salama b. Salāma b. Waqash replied, "You had sexual intercourse with it and it has been impregnated by you!" The Prophet hated his words and he turned away from him. The Prophet continued on his journey until he reached al-Rawḥāʾ on the night of Wednesday, in the middle of the month of Ramaḍān. He prayed at Biʾr Rawḥāʾ.

Muḥammad b. Shujāʿ al-Thaljī related to me that: Muḥammad b. ʿUmar al-Wāqidī told us: ʿAbd al-Malik b. ʿAbd al-ʿAzīz related to me from Abān b. Ṣāliḥ, from Saʿīd b. al-Musayyib, that the Messenger of God, when he raised his head from the last prostration (*rakʿa*) of his night prayer (*witr*), cursed the disbelievers and said, "O God do not release Abū Jahl, the pharoah of this community. O God, do not let Zamʿa b. al-Aswad escape; O God, make hot the eyes of Abū Zamaʿa b. Zamaʿa. O God blind him. O God, do not release Suhayl. O God, save Salama b. Hishām and Ayyāsh b. Abī Rabīʿa and the weak among the believers." al-Walīd b. al-Walīd was not included in his list at that time. He was captured at Badr, but he converted when he returned from Mecca after Badr. He desired to leave for Medina and was captured. The Prophet prayed for him after that. The Messenger of God said to his companions at al-Rawḥāʾ, "This is *Sajāsij* (winds which are neither hot nor cold)," [Page 47] referring to Wādī al-Rawḥāʾ. "This is the best valley of the Arabs."

They said: Khubayb b. Yasāf was a brave man. He refused Islam. When the Prophet went out to Badr, he and Qays b. Muḥarrith went out, but they followed the religion of their people. They caught up with the Prophet in al-ʿAqīq. Khuybayb was wearing iron armor, but the Messenger of God recognized him from under his helmet. The Messenger of God wheeled around towards Saʿd b. Muʿādh who was coming to his side, and said, "Is it not Khubayb b. Yasāf?" He replied, "Of course." He said: Khubayb approached until he took the girth of the camel of the Prophet. The Prophet said to Qays b. Muḥarrith—who was also called Qays b. al-Miḥrath and Qays b. al-Ḥārith—"What is it that brings you two out with us?" They said, "You were the son of our brother and our neighbor. We are coming out with our people for the plunder." The Messenger of God said, "A man does not come out with us without accepting our faith." Khubayb said, "My people know that I have great ability in war, and am strong in offense. I will fight with you for plunder but I will not convert." The Messenger of God said, "No; but convert, then fight." Then he met him again at al-Rawḥāʾ and he said, "I submit to God the Lord of the worlds, and I witness that you are the Messenger of God." The Prophet was happy about that. He said, "Go forth!" He was of great use both in and out of Badr. Qays b. Muḥarrith refused to convert, so he returned to Medina. But when the Messenger of God arrived from Badr, he converted. Then he witnessed Uḥud and was killed.

They said: The Messenger of God, while fasting, went out for a day or two. Then he returned and his herald called out, "O people of disobedience, indeed I am breaking my fast, so break your fast!" This was because [Page 48] he had said to them before, "Break your fast," and they had not broken their fast.

They said: The Messenger of God went out until he was at a place below Badr, and news came to him about the Quraysh marching. The Messenger of God informed the people about their march and consulted them. Abū Bakr stood up and said nice words. Then ʿUmar got up and he said some nice words. Then he added, "O Messenger of God, they are the Quraysh, and they have power, and, by God, they are not humble since they are powerful, and, by God, they are not protected since they are disbelievers. By God, they will never surrender their power. They will surely fight you. Be ready therefore for war and make your preparations." Then al-Miqdād b. ʿAmr stood up and said, "O Messenger of God, go to the affair of God and we will come with you. By God, we will not say to you as the Banū Isrāʾīl said to their prophet, 'Go you and your Lord and fight, while we sit here,' but go you and your Lord and fight and we will fight with you. By Him who sent you with the truth, if you go with us to Birk al-Ghimād surely we will go with you"—Birk al-Ghimād is beyond Mecca by five nights' journey towards the coast that follows the sea; it lies eight nights from Yemen on the way from Mecca. The Messenger of God said kind words to him, and prayed for his happiness. Then the Messenger of God said, "Advise me, O people!" But the Messenger of God meant the Anṣār, for he thought that the Anṣār would help him in their land alone. That was because they stipulated to him that they would protect him from that which they protected their women and children.

The Messenger of God said, "Advise me." Saʿd b. Muʿādh stood up and said, "I will answer for the Anṣār for it appears to me that you are referring to us." He said, "Yes, indeed." Saʿdsaid, "Perhaps you have gone out of an affair because another was revealed to you. But surely we already believe in you and trust you, and we testify that all of what you bring us is true and we give you our agreement and our promise that are based on 'we hear and obey.' So go, O Prophet of God, for by Him who [Page 49] sent you with the truth, if you consider this a sea and go through it, we will go with you, for there is not a man among us who will stay behind. Take whoever you wish and leave behind whoever you wish. And take from our property what you wish, for what you take from it is dearer to us than what you leave. By Him who holds my soul in His hands, I have not taken this path before, and have no knowledge of it. But we do not hate to meet our enemy tomorrow. Surely, we are patient in war and trustworthy at the meeting. Perhaps God will show you what will endear us to you."

Muḥammad related to us that al-Wāqidī related to us, saying: Muḥammad b. Ṣāliḥ related to me from ʿĀṣim b. ʿUmar b. Qatāda from Maḥmūd b. Labīd, that Saʿd said, "O Messenger of God, surely we have left behind among our people, a people whose love for you is as strong as ours. Nor are we more obedient than them. They have a desire for *jihād* and an intention. If they had thought that you were going to meet an enemy they would not have stayed away. But they thought that it was the caravan.

We will build a booth for you, and watch over you and your riding animals. Then we will meet our enemy, and if God strengthens us he will grant us victory and that is what we desire. But if it is otherwise, you will sit on your camel and meet those who are behind us." The Prophet spoke kind words to him. He said, "O Saʿd, may God grant something better than this." They said: When Saʿd concluded his advice, the Messenger of God said, "Go, by the grace of God, for He has promised me one of the two parties. By God, it looks to me as if I see the places where the people fall." The Messenger of God showed us the places of death at that time. This is the site of so and so; and not one of them was killed away from his prescribed place. The people knew that they were joining the battle, and that the caravan had escaped. They hoped for victory in accordance with the words of the Prophet.

Muḥammad related to us, he said: Al-Wāqidī related to us, he said: Abū Ismāʿīl b. ʿAbdullah b. ʿAṭiyya b. ʿAbdullah b. Unays, from his father, said: [Page 50] The Prophet gave out the flags, at that time, and there were three, and he displayed the weapons. He had set out from Medina without an established flag.

The Messenger of God went out from al-Rawḥā' and he took the road to al-Maḍīq. Then he went to Khabīratayn, and he prayed between the two cities. Then he turned right, and then left, in the valley until he passed Khayf al-Muʿtariḍa and went past Thanniyat al-Muʿtariḍa until they came to al-Tayya. Here they met Sufyān al-Ḍamrī. The Messenger of God was hurrying along with Qatāda b. al-Nuʿmān al-Ẓafarī—and some say ʿAbdullah b. Kaʿb al-Māzanī, while others say Muʿādh b. Jabal—and he met Sufyān al-Ḍamrī at al-Tayyā. The Messenger of God said, "Who is this man?" He said, "Ḍamrī; and who are you?" The Messenger of God said, "Tell us, and we will tell you." Al-Ḍamrī said, "This for that?" The Prophet said, "Yes." Al-Ḍamrī said, "Ask about what you wish!" The Prophet said, "Tell us about the Quraysh." Al-Ḍamrī said, "It has reached me that they set out on such and such a day from Mecca, and if he who informed me was telling the truth, they will now be by the side of this valley." The Messenger of God said, "Inform us about Muḥammad and his companions?" He said, "I was informed that they went out from Yathrib on such and such a day, and, if he who informed me was truthful, they will be by this valley." Al-Ḍamrī said, "Who are you?" The Prophet said, "We are from Mā'," and he pointed with his hand towards al-ʿIrāq. Al-Ḍamrī said, "From Mā' of al-ʿIrāq!" Then the Messenger of God turned to his companions. Not one of the two parties knew about the situation of the other. Between them was a mound of sand.

[Page 51] They prayed at al-Daba; then they prayed at Sayar, at Dhāt al-Ajdāl, at Khayf ʿAyn al-ʿAlā', and then at al-Khabīratayn. The Messenger of God looked at the two mountains and said, "What are the names of these two mountains?" They said, "Musliḥ and Mukhrī." He asked, "Who lives on them?" They said, "The Banū Nār and Banū Ḥurāq." The Messenger of God turned from Khabīratayn and continued until he crossed al-Khuyūf. Then he made them take the left route until they came to Muʿtariḍa, where Basbas and ʿAdi b. Abī l-Zaghbā' joined him and informed him of the news.

The Prophet alighted at the valley of Badr on the eve of Friday, the seventeenth of Ramaḍān. He sent ʿAlī, al-Zubayr, Saʿd b. Abī Waqqāṣ, and Basbas b. ʿAmr to look for water. He pointed towards al-Ẓurayb and said: I hope that you will find news at this well near al-Ẓurayb: the well is a water-hole whose source is in al-Ẓurayb—al-Ẓurayb is a small hill. They pushed on until they reached al-Ẓurayb and found at that well, which the Prophet mentioned, the watering camels of the Quraysh and their water carriers. The Muslims encountered the Quraysh, but most of them slipped away.

Among those known to have escaped was ʿUjayr. He was the first who came to the Quraysh with news of the Messenger of God. He called out: O family of Ghālib, this son of Abū Kabshā and his companions took your water-carriers. The soldiers became agitated for they hated the news.

[Page 52] Ḥakīm b. Ḥizām said: We were in a tent of ours, around a slaughtered camel roasting its flesh, when all of a sudden we heard the news, and could no longer digest our food. We started to meet with each other. ʿUtba b. Rabīʿa met me and said: "O Abū Khālid, I do not know of any expedition more strange than ours. Indeed, our caravan has been saved, yet we come to a people in their land wishing them harm." ʿUtba said of the momentous affair, "There is no decision for one who is not obeyed. This is the misfortune of Ibn Ḥanẓaliyya (Abū Jahl)! O Abū Khālid, do you not fear that the people will attack us at night?" I said, "I do not feel safe about that." He said, "And what is the decision, O Abū Khālid?" I said, "We will keep watch until morning when you will see who is behind you." ʿUtba said, "This is the decision!" He said: So we kept watch until dawn. Abū Jahl said, "What is this? This is from the command of ʿUtba who hates fighting Muḥammad and his companions! Surely this is strange. Do you doubt that Muḥammad and his companions will confront your gathering? By God, I shall move aside with my people where no one is guarding us." He turned aside, and the heavens rained down upon him. ʿUtba says, "This is, indeed, an unhappy diversion. They have taken your water carriers."

That night, Yasār, the slave of ʿUbayda b. Saʿīd b. al-ʿĀṣ, and Aslam the slave of Munabbih b. al-Ḥajjāj and Abū Rāfiʿ the slave of Umayya b. Khalaf were taken, and brought to the Prophet while he was standing in prayer. They said; "We are the water carriers of the Quraysh who sent us to fill their bags with water." The community hated their news. They had hoped that they belonged to Abū Sufyān and the companions of the caravan, so they struck them. Once they had unsettled them with their strokes the slaves said, "We belong to Abū Sufyān and we are with the caravan. This caravan is in this sand hill." So they kept away from them.

The Prophet freed himself from his prayer. He said: [Page 53] "If they tell you the truth, you strike them, and if they lie to you, you leave them!" The companions of the Prophet said: "They informed us, O Messenger of God, that the Quraysh have come." The Messenger of God said: "They told you the truth. The Quraysh have set out to protect their caravan. They fear you will take it." Then the Messenger of God approached the water carriers and said: "Where are the Quraysh?" They said: "Behind this sand dune." He said: "How many are they?" They said: "Many." He said: "How many do they number?" They said: "We do not know their numbers." He said: "How many camels did they slaughter?" They replied: "Some days ten, and on others, nine." He said: "The people number between one thousand and nine hundred." The Messenger of God said to the water carriers: "Who went out from Mecca?" They said: "There was not one who had a belly (courage) but he went out." The Messenger of God approached the people and said: "This is Mecca. It has thrown out to you its liver (most dear)." Then he asked them: "Did any of them go back?" They said, "Ibn Abī Shurayq of the Banū Zuhra returned." The Messenger of God said, "He has guided them rightly, even though, as you know, he is an enemy of God and His book." He said: "Anyone else?" They said: "The Banū ʿAdī b. Kaʿb."

Then the Messenger of God said to his companions: "Advise me about the campsite." al-Ḥubab b. al-Mundhir said: "O Messenger of God, have you considered this site? Is it a site that God revealed to you, for then it is not for us to encourage you in it or hold you back from it. Or is it a decision and a strategy of war?" The Prophet replied, "Rather, it is the decision and strategy of war." He said: "Surely, this is not a good site. Let us go until we are near the water of the people. Indeed I know it and its wells; in it is a well, I know, with sweet water; the water is plentiful and it is not far. Then we will build above it a cistern, and throw in it our vessels, and we will drink and we will fight and we will spoil the other wells." [Page 54] Muḥammad related to us that al-Wāqidī related to us that: Ibn Abī Ḥabība related to me from Dāwud b. al-Ḥuṣayn from ʿIkrima from Ibn ʿAbbās, who said: Gabriel revealed to the Messenger of God, saying, "The counsel is as al-Ḥubāb indicated." The Messenger of God said: "O Ḥubāb, you indicated the right advice." The Messenger of God endorsed and acted on it.

Muḥammad related to us, that al-Wāqidī related to us that: ʿUbayd b. Yaḥyā related to me from Muʿādh b. Rifāʿa, from his father, who said: "God sent rain from the heavens and the valley was *Dahsan—Dahsan* means sandy. The muddy earth was difficult but it did not prevent us from marching. It hurt the Quraysh such that they were unable to ride, for between them were mounds of sand. They said: Sleep overcame the Muslims that night. Neither rain nor harm overtook them. al-Zubayr b. al-Awwām said: Sleep ruled over us that night until even I could not resist. The earth had covered me and I was capable of only that. The Messenger of God and his companions were in that same situation. Saʿd b. Abī Waqqāṣ said, "I remember having my beard between my hands, and I did not feel a thing until I fell on my side." Rifāʿa b. Rāfiʿ b. Mālik said: Sleep overcame me, and I had wet dreams until I washed late at night.

They said: When the Prophet withdrew to his camp after he took the water carriers. He sent ʿAmmār b. Yāsir and Ibn Masʿūd and they both went among the people and returned to the Prophet and said, "O Messenger of God, the people are alarmed and frightened. Indeed when a horse wants to whinny they strike its face." The heavens rained down on them. When they arose, Nubayh b. al-Ḥajjāj—and he was a man who recognized tracks—said, [Page 55] "These are the signs of Ibn Sumayya and Ibn Umm ʿAbd. I know them. Muḥammad has come with our foolish, and the foolish from Yathrib." Then he said: "Hunger does not let us shelter for the night; it is inevitable that we die or cause death."

Abū ʿAbdullah said: I mentioned the words of Nubayh b. al-Ḥajjāj, "Hunger does not let us shelter," to Muḥammad b. Yaḥya b. Sahl b. Ḥathma: and he said: By my life, they were surely satisfied! Indeed my father informed me that he heard Nawfal b. Muʿāwiya say: That night we slaughtered ten camels. We were in one of their tents roasting the hump and the liver and the delicious meat, fearful of a sudden attack from the enemy, and keeping watch until the light of dawn. I heard a warner say after the glow of dawn, "These are the signs of Ibn Sumayya and Ibn Masʿūd!" And I heard him say, "Fear does not let us take shelter in the night: It is inevitable that we die or cause death. O people of the Quraysh, observe tomorrow. If we encounter Muḥammad and his companions, stay with those kinsmen of yours and attack the people of Yathrib. Indeed, if we return with them to Mecca, they will recognize their error and will not part from the faith of their forefathers."

Muḥammad related to us, that al-Wāqidī related to us that: Muḥammad b. Ṣāliḥ related to me from ʿĀṣim b. ʿUmar from Maḥmūd b. Labīd, who said: When Muḥammad alighted at the well, a resting place of palm branches was built for him. Saʿd b. Muʿādh stood at the door of the booth wearing his sword on a belt. Then the Prophet, he and Abū Bakr entered.

Yaḥya b. ʿAbdullāh b. Abī Qatāda related to me from ʿAbdullah b. Abī Bakr [Page 56] b. Ḥazm, who said: The Messenger of God arranged his companions in rows before the Quraysh appeared. When the Quraysh appeared, the Prophet was still arranging them in rows. They had filled a basin before dawn and thrown their vessels in it. The Messenger of God gave the flag to Muṣʿab b. ʿUmayr, and Musʿab approached the place where the Prophet wanted him to place it. The Messenger of God stopped and looked at the lines. He turned to face the West and put the sun behind him. The polytheists approached and faced the sun. The Messenger of God alighted on the side of al-Shām while they alighted on the side of Yemen—ʿUdwat al-nahr or ʿUdwat al-wādī means the two sides. One of his companions said, "O Messenger of God, if this came from you according to an inspiration, then go to it. If not, I think I see you go above the valley, for I think I see a wind has risen from above it; Indeed, I think it was sent to help you. The Messenger of God said: I have arranged my rows and I have placed my flag, and I will not change that. Then the Messenger of God asked his Lord, and Gabriel came down to him with this verse: *When you implored the assistance of your*

Lord, He answered you, "I will assist you with a thousand angels rank upon rank (Q. 8:9)," i.e. a group of angels immediately following an earlier group.

Muḥammad related to us that al-Wāqidī related to us saying: Muʿāwiya b. ʿAbd al-Raḥmān related to me from Yazīd b. Rūmān from ʿUrwa b. al-Zubayr that the Prophet arranged the lines at that time. Sawād b. Ghaziyya appeared and stood in front of the rows, and the Prophet pushed his arrowhead into his stomach, saying to him, "Stand in line, O Sawād." Sawād said, "You have hurt me. [Page 57] By Him who sent you with the truth as Prophet, let me retaliate!" The Messenger of God uncovered his stomach and said, "Retaliate!" Instead, Sawād embraced and kissed him. The Prophet said to him, "What changed you regarding what I did?" He replied, "What you see is one who attends to the affairs of God. I fear the battle and hope it will be my last time with you, so I embraced you." They said: The Messenger of God straightened out the lines at that time as though he were arranging arrowheads.

Muḥammad related to us that al-Wāqidī related to us saying: Mūsā b. Yaʿqūb related to me from Abū l-Ḥuwayrith, from Muḥammad b. Jubayr b. Muṭʿim from a man from the Banū Awd, who said: I heard ʿAlī say, when he was speaking in al-Kūfa: While I was drawing water at the well of Badr—*amīḥ* means to draw water and he who draws the bucket, and *al-matḥ* is also used—a wind came, and I have not seen one so strong. Then it went and another wind came, and I had not seen one like it except for that which came before. Then it went and another wind came, and I had not seen one like it except for that which came before. The first was Gabriel with a thousand angels with the Messenger of God, and the second was Mikāʾīl with a thousand from the right of the Messenger of God and Abū Bakr, and the third was Isrāfīl with a thousand, who alighted from the left side of the Messenger of God and I was on the left. When God most high defeated his enemies, the Messenger of God carried me on his horse, and when it trotted I fell on its neck and called out, "My Lord," and the Prophet held me until I was stable, for what had I to do with horses; surely [Page 58] I was but a shepherd! When I was firmly seated, these hands of mine pierced the enemy until this—meaning his armpit—was reddened with my blood.

They said: Abū Bakr, who was at that time on the right, and Zamaʿa b. al-Aswad commanded the cavalry of the polytheists. Yaḥyā b. al-Mughīra b. ʿAbd al-Raḥmān related to me from his father, who said that al-Ḥārith b. Hishām was commander of the cavalry of the polytheists, and on the right was Hubayra b. Abī Wahb, while on the left was Zamʿa b. al-Aswad. Another said that on the right was al-Ḥārith b. ʿĀmir, and on the left was ʿAmr b. ʿAbdWadd.

Muḥammad related to us that, al-Wāqidī related to us saying: Muḥammad b. Ṣāliḥ related to me from from Yazīd b. Rūmān; and Ibn Abī Ḥabība related to me from Dāwud b. al-Ḥuṣayn: they both said that neither the one on the right—that is of the Messenger of God—on the day of Badr, nor the one on his left, was named. Likewise, we have no names for those on the right or left of the polytheists. Ibn Wāqid said: This is confirmed with us.

Muḥammad related to us that al-Wāqidī related to us saying: Muḥammad b. Qudāma related to me from ʿUmar b. Ḥusayn, who said: The flag of the Messenger of God was at that time the biggest. The flag of the Muhājirūn was with Muṣʿab b. ʿUmayr; the flag of the Khazraj, with al-Ḥubāb b. Mundhir; and the flag of Aws, with Saʿd b. Muʿādh. The Quraysh had three flags: there was a flag with Abū ʿAzīz, a flag with al-Naḍr b. al-Ḥārith, and a flag with Ṭalḥa b. Abī Ṭalḥa.

They said: The Messenger of God spoke at that time. He praised God and commended

Him. Then he said, while he was commanding them and urging them and increasing their desire regarding the reward that was to come, "As for that which is after, indeed I urge you to what God urges you, and I forbid you from what God forbids you. Surely God is great in His affairs, commanding the right and loving the truth. He gives His people happiness according to their position with Him. With Him do they seek remembrance and with Him do they seek precedence in excellence. Surely, you have awakened in one [Page 59] of the places of righteousness. God receives in it only those who desire His face. Indeed, patience in places of difficulty is one of the means by which God releases one's grief and saves one from distress, and brings one to deliverance in the next world. With you is the Prophet of God who will warn you and command you. Be humble today that God most high will overlook something of your affair that He detests you for. Indeed God says: *greater was the aversion of God to you than your aversion of yourselves* (Q. 40:10). Observe that which He commands you from His Book and shows you of His signs, for He has strengthened you after lowliness. Cling to it so that your Lord will be satisfied with you. Perform repeatedly for your Lord in these situations as decreed, so you will deserve that which He promised you in it from His graciousness and His forgiveness. Indeed His promise is true, His word, trustworthy, and His punishment, severe. Indeed you and I are with God everlasting. He is our refuge, and to Him do we cling. In God do we trust. With Him is our destiny. May God forgive me and the Muslims."

Muḥammad related to us that al-Wāqidī related to us saying, Muḥammad b. ʿAbdullah related to me from al-Zuhrī according to ʿUrwa b. al-Zubayr and Muḥammad b. Ṣāliḥ; and from ʿĀṣim b. ʿUmar according to Yazīd b. Rūmān who both said that when the Messenger of God saw the Quraysh coming down the valley—the first who appeared was Zamaʿa b. al-Aswad upon a horse of his, followed by his son—he turned around with his horse desiring to prepare a stop for the people. The Messenger of God said, "O God, surely You revealed the Book to me, You commanded me to fight, and You promised me one of the two factions. You will not betray your promise! O God, these Quraysh have arrived with their horses and their glory. They challenge You and lie about Your messenger. O God, You promised me Your help. O God, destroy them this morning!" ʿUtba b. Rabīʿa appeared [Page 60] on a red camel, and the Messenger of God said, "If there is a good man in this group he will be the master of that red camel. If they obey him they will be rightly guided."

Muḥammad related to us that al-Wāqidī related to us saying, Muḥammad b. ʿAbdullah related to me from al-Zuhrī, from ʿAbdullah b. Mālik, who said: Īmāʾ b. Raḥḍa sent a son of his with ten slaughtering camels to the Quraysh, when they passed by him. He gifted them to the Quraysh and said, "If you want, we can provide you weapons and men—we are prepared for that and ready—we will act." And they sent a reply saying, "You are closely related, and have fulfilled your responsibility. By my life, if we are fighting people we are not weak compared to them. But if we are fighting God, as Muḥammad claims, surely there is none with the power of God."

Muḥammad related to us that al-Wāqidī related to us saying, ʿAbd al-Raḥmān b. al-Ḥārith related to me from his grandfather, ʿUbayd b. Abī ʿUbayd, from Khufāf b. Īmāʾ b. Raḥḍa, who said: Nothing was more desirable to my father than peace among his people. He was the keeper of that peace. When the Quraysh passed by he sent me with ten slaughtering camels as a gift for them. I approached driving them and my father followed behind. I gave them to the Quraysh and they accepted them and delivered them to the tribes. My father passed by ʿUtba b. Rabīʿa—and he was the lord of the people at that time—and my father said, "O Abū l-Walīd, what is this march?" He replied, "By God I do not know, I have been over ruled." My father said, "But you are the lord of the tribe. What prevents you returning with the people and assuming the blood of your ally, and bringing the caravan that they captured at Nakhla and delivering it to your people? By God, what do you seek of the power of Muḥammad other than this? By God, O Abū l-Walīd, you only kill yourselves through Muḥammad and his companions."

Ibn Abī l-Zinād related to me from his father, who said: We have not heard that anyone was lord without [Page 61] wealth except ʿUtba b. Rabīʿa. Muḥammad related to us that al-Wāqidī related to us saying, Mūsā b. Yaʿqūb related to me from Abū Ḥuwayrith from Muḥammad b. Jubayr b. Mutʿim, who said: When the people descended, the Messenger of God sent ʿUmar b. al-Khaṭṭāb to the Quraysh saying, "Return! I would have preferred it if someone other than you had come to take control of this affair, and I would rather that I take control of the affair from other than you." And Ḥakīm b. Ḥizām said, "He proposes justice, so accept it. By God, you will not be victorious over him after what he proposes of justice."

He said: Abū Jahl said, "By God, we will not return now that God has made it possible to get them. We will not run after a shadow after we have seen the source. Our caravan will not be intercepted after this, ever." They said: A group of Quraysh approached until they arrived at al-Ḥawḍ. Among them was Ḥakīm b. Ḥizām. The Muslims desired to oust them i.e. to drive them away. The Prophet said, "Leave them!" They arrived and drank the water, and not one from among them drank but he was killed, except for Ḥakīm b. Ḥizām.

Abū Isḥāq related to me from ʿAbd al-Raḥmān b. Muḥammad b. ʿAbd from Saʿīd b. al-Musayyib, who said: Ḥakīm was saved from fate twice for what God desired with him of good. The Messenger of God went out against a group of polytheists. They were seated and waiting for him, and he read Yā Sīn and left sand on their heads. And there was not one among them present but he was killed except for Ḥakīm. He arrived at al-Ḥawḍ on the day of Badr. None arrived at al-Ḥawḍ, at that time, but he was killed except for Ḥakīm.

[Page 62] They said: When the people became calm they sent ʿUmayr b. Wahb al-Jumaḥī who was the master of the divining arrows. They said: Evaluate Muḥammad and his companions for us. So, he went around the campsite with his horse towards the wadi, and ascended it, saying, may be they have assistance or have prepared an ambush. But he returned and said: "They have neither assistance nor ambush. They have three hundred people or a little more with seventy camels and two horses." Then he said: "O people of the Quraysh, the catastrophe brings death. The camels of Yathrib carry poisonous death. The people do not have the power of resistance or refuge other than their swords. Do you not see them dumb and not speaking. They put forth their evil tongues like serpents. By God, I do not see that a man among them will be killed until he kills a man from us. If they kill among you as many as their number, there will be no goodness in life after that. So consider your decision."

Muḥammad related to us, that al-Wāqidī related to us saying: Yūnus b. Muḥammad al-Ẓafarī related to me from his father, who said: When Umayr b. Wahb said these words to them, they sent Abū Usāma al-Jushamī—he was a rider—He went around the Prophet and his companions, then returned to them and they said to him: "What did you see?" He said: "By God, I did not see toughness, or numbers or weapons or quivers. But, by God, I saw a people who did not desire to return with their families; a people desiring death. They did not have the power of resistance nor refuge except their swords. Blue eyed, they were like pebbles under the shield." Then he said that he [I] feared that they would have an ambush or assistance, so he went towards the wadi and ascended. Then he returned to them and said. "There is neither ambush nor assistance. Consider your decision!"

Muḥammad related to us saying, al-Wāqidī related to us that Muḥammad b. ʿAbdullah related to us from al-Zuhrī from [Page 63] ʿUrwa; and Muḥammad b. Ṣāliḥ from ʿĀṣim b. ʿUmar and Ibn Rūmān, who said: That when Ḥakīm b. Ḥizām heard what ʿUmayr b. Wahb said, he walked with the people to ʿUtba b. Rabīʿa and said, "O Abū l-Walīd, you are an elder of the Quraysh and their Lord, and command their obedience. What is there for you except to continue doing happily, among them, until the end of time, what you did on the day of ʿUkkāẓ!" ʿUtba at that time was the leader of the people. He said, "What is that, O Abū l-Khālid?" He replied, "Return with the people and assume the blood of your confederate and what Muḥammad captured of that caravan in the valley of Nakhla. Surely you do not seek from Muḥammad anything other than this blood and the caravan?" ʿUtba said, "I shall do so or you can testify against me about that." He said: Then ʿUtba sat on his camel and went among the polytheists of the Quraysh saying: "O people, obey me and do not fight this man and his companions. Bind this affair on my head and blame it on my cowardice. Indeed among them are men whose relationship is close. The man among you will not stop looking at the killer of his father and his brother. Hatred and malice will be bequeathed among you. You will never be able to finish them off without them killing the same number among you. Moreover there is no guarantee that you will have success. You seek only the blood of this man and the caravan that was taken. I will carry that and take it upon myself! O people, if Muḥammad is false to you, the jackals of the Arabs will take care of him—the jackal of the Arabs is the most destitute of the Arabs; but if he will be your king, you will eat in the kingdom of the son of your brother; and if he will be your prophet you will be the happiest of men with him! O people, do not reject my advice or consider my opinion light witted!" He said: Abū Jahl was envious of ʿUtba when he heard his speech, and he said to himself that if the people responded to [Page 64] ʿUtba's speech, he would be the lord of the community.

ʿUtba was the most outspoken among the people, and his language was most beautiful. He said, "I implore you, by God, make these directions, that are like lanterns, replace those directions that compare to serpents!" When ʿUtba completed his words, Abū Jahl said, "Surely ʿUtba points you in this direction because his son is with Muḥammad, and Muḥammad is the son of his uncle. He detests the fact that his son and the son of his uncle will be killed. Filled, by God, were your lungs, O ʿUtba, yet were you fearful of when the two armies met. (The two rings of the belly girth met)! Now you abandon us and command us to return? No, by God, we will not return until God judges between Muḥammad and us." He said: ʿUtba was angry, and he replied, "O you with the yellow buttocks, you will learn which of us is a coward and low. The Quraysh will learn who is the corrupt coward for his people!" He recited:

> Was it cowardice, when I commanded my commands?
> I will make my announcement of bereavement to the mother of ʿAmr.

Then Abū Jahl wen to ʿĀmir b. al-Ḥaḍramī the brother of the man who was killed at Nakhla, and said, "This is your ally, ʿUtba, and he desires to return with the people after you have seen your revenge. He weakens the people and takes upon himself the blood of your brother, and claims that you accepted the blood money. Are you not ashamed to accept the blood money when you have power over the killer of your brother? Stand up and plead for your rights." ʿĀmir b. Ḥaḍramī stood up and was revealed. He scattered dust on his head, [Page 65] then shouted, "Woe is his life!" ʿUtba was insulted by that because he (ʿUtba) was his ally from the Quraysh. ʿĀmir had spoiled for the people the opinion to which ʿUtba had invited them. He vowed that he would not return until he killed one of the companions of Muḥammad. He said to ʿUmayr b. Wahb, "Incite the people!" ʿUmayr attacked the Muslims in order to destroy the lines, but the Muslims stood firm and adhered to their rows. Ibn Ḥaḍramī came forward and exerted pressure on the people and war broke out.

Muḥammad related to us, that al-Wāqidī related to us that: ʿĀʾidh b. Yaḥyā related to me from Abū l-Ḥuwayrith from Nāfiʿ b. Jubayr from Ḥakīm b. Ḥizām, who said: When Abū Jahl corrupted the opinion of the people ʿĀmir b. al-Ḥaḍramī instigated them and pushed in with his horse. Mihjaʿ, the *mawlā* of ʿUmar, was the first who went out to oppose him, and ʿĀmir killed him. Ḥāritha b. Surāqa was the first to fall in battle and be killed among the Anṣār. Ḥibbān b. al-ʿAriqa killed him; but some said it was ʿUmayr b. al-Ḥumām, and that Khālid b. al-Aʿlam al-ʿUqaylī killed him. Muḥammad related to us saying al-Wāqidī related to us that all the Meccans say it was none other than Ḥibbān b. al-ʿAriqa.

They said: ʿUmar b. al-Khaṭṭāb said in the council of his guardianship, "O ʿUmayr b. Wahb, you appraised us for the polytheists on the day of Badr. You ascended to the valley and then you came down such that I saw your horse under you, and you informed the polytheists that we had no ambush or assistance." He said, "By God, O commander of the faithful!" Another said, "It was I, by God, who instigated the people at that time; but God came with Islam and guided us to it. The polytheism within us was not greater than that." ʿUmar said, "You speak the truth!"

They said: ʿUtba spoke to Ḥakīm b. Ḥizām and said; "There is no disagreement with anyone but [Page 66] Ibn al-Ḥanẓaliyya. Go and say to him: Surely ʿUtba will take the blood of his confederate and the responsibility for the caravan." Ḥakīm said: I visited Abū Jahl and he was applying perfume, and his coat of mail was in his hands. I said to him: ʿUtba sent me to you. He approached me angrily and said: Could ʿUtba not find anyone other than you to send? I replied: If it was other than him, I would not, by God, do this; but I come to ameliorate between the people, for Abū l-Walīd is the lord of the tribe. Abū Jahl became angry again and said: You say also the lord of the tribe? I said: I say it, and all of the Quraysh say it! So Abū Jahl commanded ʿĀmir to shout out his protection and be revealed. He said, "Indeed ʿUtba is hungry, so satisfy him with barley." The polytheists began to say, "Indeed ʿUtba is hungry, so satisfy him with barley." Abū Jahl was delighted by what the polytheists did with ʿUtba.

Ḥakīm said: I went to Munabbih b. al-Ḥajjāj and said what I said to Abū Jahl, and found him better than Abū Jahl. He said, "Blessed is what you come with, and what ʿUtba invites us to." I returned to ʿUtba and found him angry over the words of the Quraysh. He alighted from his camel and walked among them in the camp and commanded them to stop fighting, but they refused. So, seething with rage he put on his coat of mail. They searched for a helmet for him, but could not find one among the soldiers to fit his head because his skull was so large. When he saw that, he draped a turban and appeared between his brother Shayba and his son al-Walīd b. ʿUtba. Meanwhile Abū Jahl was in line on a female horse. ʿUtba came beside him and drew his sword. It was said: By God, he will kill him! ʿUtba struck the tendon of Abū Jahl's horse and the horse collapsed. I said, "I have not seen such a day!" They said: ʿUtba said, "Get down. This day is not [Page 67] a day of riding. Not all your people are mounted." Abū Jahl got down and ʿUtba says, "You will learn which of us is more corrupting of his tribe this morning!" Then ʿUtba called for a duel.

The Messenger of God was in the booth and his companions were lined up. While lying down, sleep had overcome the Prophet. He said, "Do not fight until I command you. If they draw near, aim at them with arrows but do not draw your swords until they overpower you." Abū Bakr said, "O Prophet, the people draw near and they attack us." Now, the Prophet awoke for God had shown them to him a little in his sleep. Some of it appeared little in the eyes of others. The Prophet became fearful and raised his hands and begged God for the help He had promised him, saying, "O God, if this group perseveres over me, polytheism will prevail and your religion will not stand." Abū Bakr says, "God will surely help you and bring you happiness." Ibn Rawāḥa said, "O Messenger of God, I will counsel you. The Messenger of God is more wise and knowledgeable about God than he who advises him. Indeed God is most exalted and most knowledgeable about that which you implore Him and His promise." The Messenger of God said, "O Ibn Rawāḥa, did I not beseech God for His promise? Surely God will not fail in His promise."

ʿUtba approached intending to fight. Ḥakīm b. Ḥizām said to him, "Abū l-Walīd, hold back, hold back. You have forbidden something and you are the first to it!" Khufāf b. Īmāʾ said: I saw the companions of the Prophet on the day of Badr. The people marched in close rank. I saw that the companions of the Prophet did not draw the sword, but strummed the bow. Some of them shielded others with rows arranged so close that there was no gap between them. Still others drew their swords when they appeared. I marveled at that and I asked a man from the Muhajirūn about that later. He said: The Messenger of God commanded us not to draw our [Page 68] swords until we were overwhelmed.

They said: When the people of the two armies came closer to each other, al-Aswad b. ʿAbd al-Asad al-Makhzūmī said, when he drew near to the cistern, "By God, I promise, I shall drink from their cistern or destroy it, or I shall die in the attempt." Aswad b. ʿAbd al-Asad ran until he was close to the cistern, and Ḥamza b. ʿAbd al-Muṭṭalib approached him and struck him and cut his foot. When he fell, al-Aswad crawled until he fell into the cistern, broke it with his healthy foot, and drank from it. Ḥamza followed him and struck him in the cistern and killed him. The polytheists observing their lines thought that they were victorious. Some of the people approached others for a duel. ʿUtba, Shayba and al-Walīd went out until they were separated from the line. Then they called for a duel. Three youths from the Anṣār went out to them; they were the sons of ʿAfrāʾ: Muʿādh, Muʿawwidh and ʿAwf, the Banū al-Ḥārith—though some say the third was ʿAbdullah b. Rawāḥa. It is confirmed with us that they were the sons of ʿAfrāʾ.

The Messenger of God was ashamed of that. He hated that the first battle in which the Muslims met the polytheists was with the Anṣār. He wanted the affective force to be from the sons of his uncle and his people. He commanded them and they returned to their lines. He said to them, "Well done!" Then a herald from the polytheists called out, "O Muḥammad, send our equals from our people out to us." The Messenger of God said to them, "O Banū Hāshim, stand and fight for the rights that God sent with your prophet for they have brought their evil to extinguish the light of God." Ḥamza b. ʿAbd al-Muṭṭalib, ʿAlī b. Abī Ṭālib and ʿUbayda b. al-Ḥārith b. ʿAbd al-Muṭṭalib b. ʿAbdManāf stood up, and walked up to them. ʿUtba said, "Speak that we may recognize you—for they were wearing helmets that hid their faces—and if you are a match we will fight you." Ḥamza said, "I am Ḥamza b. ʿAbd al-Muṭṭalib, the lion of God and the lion of His Prophet." ʿUtba said, "A gracious match." Then ʿUtba said, "I am the lion of the confederates/forest. And who are these with you?" Hamza said, [Page 69] "ʿĀlī b. Abī Ṭālib, and ʿUbayda b. al-Ḥārith." He responded, "Two gracious equals."

Ibn Abī l-Zinād said from his father: I have not heard a word from ʿUtba so feeble as his words, "I am the lion of the forest," for *al-Ḥalfā* means the confederates/forest. Then ʿUtba said to his son, "Stand, O Walīd," and al-Walīd stood up. And ʿAlī stood up to him. Walīd was the youngest of the group and ʿAlī killed him. Then ʿUtba came forward, and Ḥamza stood up to him. The two of them exchanged blows and Ḥamza killed him. Then Shayba stood up, and ʿUbayda b. al-Ḥārith stood up to him—he was at that time the oldest companion of the Prophet—and Shayba struck ʿUbayda with the edge of his sword. Then he reached out to the muscles of his leg and cut them. Ḥamza and ʿAlī turned upon Shayba and killed him. They carried ʿUbayda and returned him to the line. The marrow of his leg oozed out, and ʿUbayda said, "O Messenger of God, am I not a martyr?" He replied, "But of course." ʿUbayda said, "By God, if Abū Ṭālib were alive he will know that I am more trustworthy about what he said about it," He said:

> [Page 70] You lied, by the house of God, when you said: We will give Muḥammad up without a thrust in his defense.
> We are committed to him until we lie dead around him, unmindful of our children and wives.

A Qurʾān verse was revealed: *These two antagonists dispute about their lord* (Q. 22:19).

Ḥamza was older than the Prophet by four years, and al-ʿAbbās was older than the Prophet by three years. They said: When ʿUtba b. Rabīʿa called for the duel, his son came up to him and challenged him. The Messenger of God said to him, "Sit down!" When the group stood up to him Abū Ḥudhayfa b. ʿUtba helped with blows against his father. Muḥammad related to us that al-Wāqidī related to us that: Ibn Abī Zinād related to us from his father that: Shayba was older than ʿUtba by three years.

Muḥammad related to us saying, al-Wāqidī related to us that: Maʿmar b. Rāshid related to me from al-Zuhrī, from ʿAbdullah b. Thaʿlaba b. Ṣuʿayr, who said: Abū Jahl implored God for victory on the day of Badr. He said, "O God, he cut us off from our relatives, and brought us the unknown. So destroy him today." God revealed in his graciousness. *If you ask your lord for victory the conquest comes to you. If you desist (from wrong) it is better for you* (Q. 8:19).

ʿUmar b. ʿUqba related to me from Shuʿba, the *mawlā* of Ibn ʿAbbās, saying: I heard Ibn ʿAbbās say: When the people stood up, the Prophet fell down in a faint for an hour. Then he was lifted from it and he proclaimed to the believers that Gabriel was with an army of angels to the right of the [Page 71] people, Mīkāʾīl was with an army on the left of the Messenger of God, and Isrāfīl was with another army of a thousand.

Satan, who had taken the form of Surāqa b. Juʿsham al-Mudlijī, incited the polytheists informing them that none of the people could defeat them. When the enemy of God perceived the angels, he retreated. He said: Indeed I am free of you, for I saw what you did not see. Ḥārith b. Hishām stayed with him for he thought that it was Surāqa because of what he heard him say. But he struck al-Ḥārith in the chest and al-Ḥārith fell. Then Satan rushed away and was not seen until he fell into the sea, and raised his two hands crying, "O lord, keep the appointment that you promised me."

Abū Jahl approached his companions and urged them to fight, saying, "Do not be deceived by the withdrawal of Surāqa b. Juʿshum. Indeed, he was on an appointment with Muḥammad and his companions. He will learn when we return to Qudayd what we will do to his people. Do not be disturbed by the death of ʿUtba and Shayba and al-Walīd. Surely they were hasty and reckless when they went to battle. I swear by God, we will not return today until we bind Muḥammad and his companions with ropes. Not one among you shall kill one of them, but rather, take them captive. We will teach them a lesson for their withdrawal from your religion and their detestation of what your fathers' worshipped."

Muḥammad related to us that al-Wāqidī said: Ibn Abī Ḥabība related to me from Dāwud b. al-Ḥuṣayn from ʿUrwa from ʿĀʾisha, who said: The Prophet made a secret code "O Banū ʿAbd al-Raḥmān," for the Muhajirūn on the day of Badr. The secret code for the Khazraj was "O Banū ʿAbdullah." And the secret code for the Aws was "O Banū ʿUbaydullāh." Muḥammad related to us that al-Wāqidī related to us that: ʿAbdullah b. [Page 72] Muḥammad b. ʿUmar b. ʿAlī related to me from Isḥāq b. Sālim from Zayd b. ʿAlī that the code of the Prophet on the day of Badr was "O Manṣūr, kill!"

They said: Seven youths from the Quraysh converted, so their fathers detained them. Those who went out with them to Badr in a state of doubt and indecision were: Qays b. al-Walīd b. al-Mughīra, Abū Qays b. al-Fākih b. al-Mughīra, al-Ḥārith b. Zamaʿa, ʿAlī b. Umayya b. Khalaf, and al-ʿĀṣ b. Munabbih b. al-Ḥajjāj. When they arrived in Badr and saw the small number of the companions of the Prophet, they said: Their religion has misled these. God most high says: *Who puts his trust in God, surely God is most exalted in might* (Q. 8:49). And they are killed now. God most high says: *When the Hypocrites say those who in their hearts have a disease, those misled by their religion* (Q. 8:49). Then God mentions those who disbelieve with an evil mentioning, saying: *For the worst of beasts in the sight of God are those who reject Him and will not believe. They are those with whom you did make a covenant every time, and they have not the fear of God* (Q. 8:55–56) . . . until His saying: *Disperse with them, those who follow them, that they may remember* (Q. 8:57). He says: He will approach to punish those who are behind them from the Arabs, all of them. *And if the enemy incline towards peace do thou incline also towards peace and trust in God, for He is the one who hears and knows all things* (Q. 8:61). He says: If they said, "We have converted," aloud, then accept it from them. *And if they desire (in their hearts) to deceive you, verily God is sufficient for you. He it is that has strengthened you with his aid and with the company of the believers. And moreover He has put affection between their hearts* (Q. 8:62–63). They say he placed affection between their hearts in accordance with Islam. *Not if you had spent all that is in the earth, could you have produced that affection, but God has done it, for he is exalted in might, wise* (Q. 8:63).

[Page 73] Muḥammad related to us that al-Wāqidī related to us that: ʿAbd al-Raḥmān b. Muḥammad b. Abī l-Rijjāl related to me from ʿAmr b. ʿAbdullah, from Muḥammad b. Kaʿb al-Quraẓī, who said: God put power in the hands of the believers on the day of Badr such that twenty, if they were forbearing, could conquer two hundred. He bestowed on them two thousand Angels, and when he knew that they were weak he relieved them. God most high revealed the return of His Prophet from Badr. With those who were taken in Badr were those who claimed to be Muslims, but were doubting, and were killed with the polytheists at that time.

There were seven individuals whom their fathers detained, as in the tradition of Ibn Abī Ḥabība—with them was al-Walīd b. ʿUtba b. Rabīʿa who was among those who stayed in Mecca and were not able to go out. He said: *Those whose lives the angels take [while] in a state of wrong-doing to their own souls* (Q. 16:28), to the last three verses. He said: The Muhājirūn wrote about this to those who were Muslims in Mecca. Jundub b. Ḍamra al-Junduʿiyyu said, "I have no excuse or justification for my stay in Mecca." But he was sick, and he said to his family, "Leave with me and perhaps I will find a change." They said, "Which direction is most desirable to you?" He replied, "Towards al-Tanʿīm." He said: They went out with him to al-Tanʿīm: between al-Tanʿīm and Mecca are four miles on the Medinan road. He said: O God, I am coming out to you an emigrant! God most high revealed about it: *He who forsakes his home in the way of God and His Messenger* . . . to the end of the verse (Q. 4:100). When those who were in Mecca among those who were able to leave saw that, they too went out. But Abū Sufyān and men from the polytheists went in search of them and brought them back and imprisoned them. The people were tempted and left Islam. There were those who were tempted when they were tortured. God most high revealed: [Page 74] *And among people are such as say: We believe in God; but when they suffer affliction in the cause of God, they treat men's oppression as if it were the wrath of God* . . . to the end of the verse, and the two verses after (Q. 29:10). The Muḥājirūn wrote about it to those who were Muslims in Mecca, and when the Book came to them about what was revealed about them, they said: O God surely you are watching over us and if we escape we will turn to you alone! They went out a second time. Abū Sufyān and the polytheists looked for them again, but they escaped them by fleeing into the mountains until they arrived in Medina.

The trial was severe against those Muslims who were returned. They hit them and molested them. They compelled them to leave Islam. Ibn Abī Sarḥ returned and said to the Quraysh: It was only Ibn Qammaṭa, the Christian slave, who informed Muḥammad. I used to write for him [Muḥammad] and I changed whatever I wished. God most high revealed about that: *We know indeed that they say that it is a man that teaches him. The tongue of him they wickedly point to is notably foreign, while this is Arabic pure and clear* (Q. 16:103). God revealed about those whom Abū Sufyān and his companions returned from those who were tortured. *Except under compulsion his heart remaining firm in faith* (Q. 16:106), and three verses after. And among those whose hearts were opened to disbelief was Ibn Abī Sarḥ. Then God most high revealed about those who fled from Abū Sufyān to the Prophet, who were patient about the pain after the temptation: *But verily thy Lord—to those who leave their homes after trials and persecutions* (Q. 16:110), to the end of the verse.

Abū l-Qāsim ʿAbd al-Wahāb b. Abī Ḥayya, informed us saying: Muḥammad b. Shujāʿ al-Thaljī related to us that: Muḥammad b. ʿUmar al-Wāqidī related to us, saying: Abū Isḥāq b. Muḥammad related to me from Isḥāq b. ʿAbdullah from ʿUmar b. al-Ḥakam, who said: At that time Nawfal b. Khuwaylid b. al-ʿAdawiyya called out: O People of the Quraysh, [Page 75] indeed you knew Surāqa and his people and their desertion of you in every place, so advance boldly and strike the people. Indeed, I know that the two sons of Rabīʿa rushed to duel their (duelling) opponents.

Al-Wāqidī informed us saying: ʿUbayd b. Yaḥyā informed me from Muʿādh b. Rifāʿa b. Rāfiʿ from his father, who said: Indeed we heard Satan moo, calling for destruction and affliction. He took the form of Surāqa b. Juʿshum until he fled and plunged into the sea, with his hands raised and extended, saying, "O Lord, grant me what you promised me!" The Quraysh used to reproach Surāqa about what he did at that time, and he replied, "By God, I did not do any of it."

Muḥammad related to us that, al-Wāqidī related to us saying: Abū Isḥāq al-Aslamī related to me from al-Ḥasan b. ʿUbaydullah b. Ḥunayn, freedman of the Banū ʿAbbās, from ʿUmāra b. Ukayma al-Laythī, who said: An old man of ʿArrāk related to me—ʿArrāk means a fisherman from the clan—he was at that time on the coast looking down at the sea, and he said: I heard a shout, "Woe unto me!" It filled the valley. "O what sorrow!" So I looked, and lo and behold, it was Surāqa b. Juʿshum. I went close to him and said, "Would I not ransom my father and mother for you?" He did not reply. Then I saw him plunge into the sea, his hands outstretched, saying: "O Lord, did you not promise me!" I said to myself, "By the house of God, Surāqa has gone mad!" That was when the sun declined from the meridian. That was with their defeat on the day of Badr.

They said: The mark of the angels was turbans that dropped to their shoulders, green, yellow, and red, of light. The wool was in the forelocks of their horses. Muḥammad related to us that al-Wāqidī related to us saying: Muḥammad b. ʿAlī related to me from ʿĀṣim b. ʿUmar from Maḥmūd b. Labīd, who said: The Messenger of God said, "Indeed the angels were marked. The wool in their helmets and their headgear distinguished them."

Al-Wāqidī informed us that: Mūsā b. Muḥammad informed me from his father, who said: Four companions of the Prophet were distinguished in the march: Ḥamza b. ʿAbd al-Muṭṭalib was marked on the day of Badr by an Ostrich feather; ʿAlī, by white wool; al-Zubayr, by a yellow head cloth—al-Zubayr related that the angels alighted on the day of Badr riding dappled horses, and wearing yellow turbans—and, Abū Dujāna, by a red band.

Al-Wāqidi related to us that ʿAbdullah b. Mūsā b. Umayya b. ʿAbdullah b. Abī Umayya related to me from Muṣʿab b. ʿAbdullah from the freedman of Suhayl, who said: I heard Suhayl b. ʿAmr say, "On the day of Badr, I saw white men on dappled horses between the heavens and the earth. They were distinguished, killing and taking prisoners." Abū Usayd al-Sāʿidī said after his sight had left him, "If I was with you now, at Badr, and I had my sight, I would show you the mountain path al-Malṣ—a specific place—which the angels left from." I did not doubt it nor contest it. He used to relate from a man from the Banū Ghifār who related to him, saying: I, and the son of my uncle went forward, on the day of Badr, until we ascended a mountain. We were two polytheists on one of two sand hills at Badr, the sand hill of al-Shām and the sand hill of Raml. We waited to fall on those whose turn it was in order to plunder with those who were plundering, when all of a sudden I saw the clouds draw near us, and I heard, in them, the sounds of horses and their iron bits. I heard someone say, [Page 77] "Advance, O Ḥayzūm!" As for my cousin, the veil from his heart was lifted and he died of fear. As for myself, I was almost destroyed. I held myself together and followed with my eyes where the cloud went. It went to the Prophet and his companions. Then it [the cloud] returned and I heard nothing from it.

Muḥammad related to us that al-Wāqidī said: Khārija b. Ibrāhīm b. Muḥammad b. Thābit b. Qays b. Shammās related to me, from his father, who said: The Messenger of God asked Gabriel, "Who was it, who said on the day of Badr, 'Advance, O Ḥayzūm!' " Gabriel replied, "O Muḥammad, I do not know all the people of the heavens."

He said: ʿAbd al-Raḥmān b. al-Ḥārith related to me from his father from his grand father ʿUbayd b. Abī ʿUbayd from Abū Ruhm al-Ghifārī from the son of an uncle of his, who said: While I and the son of my uncle were at Mā' Badr, we saw how few were with Muḥammad and how many were with the Quraysh and we said, "When the two factions meet we will aim for the army of the Prophet and his companions," and we departed towards the left wing of the companions of Muḥammad. We were saying, "These are a quarter of the Quraysh!" while we walked on the left side, when a cloud came and overwhelmed us. We raised our eyes to it and we heard the sounds of men and weapons. We heard a man say to his horse, "Advance, O Ḥayzūm!" And we heard them say, "Slow down, wait for those behind you." They alighted on the right side of the Messenger of God. Then another like that arrived. It stayed with the Prophet. We saw the Prophet and his companions and all of a sudden they were double the number of Quraysh. My cousin died. As for myself, I remained calm and informed the Prophet." Later he converted and his Islam was beautiful.

They said: The Messenger of God said: Satan was not seen on any day to be smaller, more despicable or as hateful as he was on the day of ʿArafa. And that was only because of what he saw of the coming down of compassion. God overlooked the great sins except what he saw on the day of Badr. It was said: What did he see on the day of Badr? He said: Did he not see Gabriel direct the angels? They said: The Messenger of God said at that time, "This is Gabriel driving the wind as Dihya al-Kalbī. Indeed I was helped by the East wind just as the ʿĀd was destroyed by the West wind."

Muḥammad related to us that al-Wāqidī related to us: Abū Isḥāq b. Abī ʿAbdullah related to me from ʿAbd al-Wāḥid b. Abī ʿAwn from Ṣāliḥ b. Ibrāhīm, who said: ʿAbd al-Raḥmān b. ʿAwf says: I saw two men on the day of Badr: One of them was on the right side of the Prophet, and the other on the left side of the Prophet. The two of them fought the strongest battle. Then a third appeared behind him and a fourth, in front of him.

Muḥammad related to us that al-Wāqidī related to us saying: Abū Isḥāq b. Abī ʿAbdullah related to me from ʿAbd al-Wāḥid b. Abī ʿAwn from Ziyād, *mawlā* of Saʿd, from Saʿd, who said: I saw two men on the day of Badr, fighting with the Messenger of God, one on his right and the other on his left. I saw him look once at one and once at the other, happy for the assistance that God most high granted him.

Muḥammad related to us that al-Wāqidī related to us that Isḥāq b. Yaḥyā related to me from Ḥamza b. Ṣuhayb from his father, who said: I do not know how many cut hands and deep strokes I saw that did not bleed on the day of Badr. Muḥammad related to us that al-Waqidī related to us: Muḥammad b. Yahyā related to me from Abū ʿUfayr from Rāfiʿ b. Khadīj from Abū Burda b. Niyār, who said: I came [Page 79] on the day of Badr with three heads and placed them before the Messenger of God, and said, "O, Messenger of God, I killed two heads. As for the third, I saw a tall white man strike it and it rolled before him, and I picked it up." The Messenger of God said, "That was one of the angels." Ibn ʿAbbas used to say: The angels fought only on the day of Badr.

Ibn Abī Ḥabība related to me from Dāwud b. al-Ḥuṣayn from ʿIkrima from Ibn ʿAbbās, who said: The angels took the form of those known among the people to motivate them. He said: Indeed I went close to them [the people] and I heard them say, "If they attack us we will not stay. They are nothing." That is the saying of God most high: *When thy Lord inspired the angels that I am with you to give firmness to the Believers* . . . (Q. 8:12) to the end of the verse.

Mūsā b. Muḥammad related to me from his father, who said: Sā'ib b. Abī Hubaysh al-Asad used to say during the caliphate of ʿUmar b. al-Khaṭṭāb, "By God, no human ever captured me." Someone said: "Then who did?" He replied, "When the Quraysh were defeated I was defeated with them. A tall white man overtook me riding a piebald horse between the heaven and the earth, and he tied me with a rope. ʿAbd al-Raḥmān came and found me tied. He called out to his soldiers, 'Who captured this man?' There was not one who claimed that he captured me. He took me to the Messenger of God. The Messenger of God said, 'O Ibn Abī Ḥubaysh who captured you?' I said, 'I do not know.' I hated to inform him about what I saw. The Messenger of God said, 'One of the gracious angels captured him. Go, O Ibn ʿAwf, with your prisoner!' And ʿAbd al-Raḥmān went with me." [Page 80] Al-Sā'ib said: I kept remembering these words. My conversion was delayed until finally I became a Muslim.

Muḥammad related to us that al-Wāqidī related to us that ʿĀ'idh b. Yahyā related to me from Abū l-Ḥuwayrith from ʿUmāra b. Ukayma al-Laythī from Ḥakīm b. Ḥizām, who said: You saw us on the day of Badr when smoke came down from the sky in Wādī Khalṣ and clogged up the horizon—Wādī Khalṣ is in the direction of al-Ruwaytha—and all of a sudden the Wādī was flowing with ants. I realized that this thing from the sky was a help to Muḥammad, for there was nothing but defeat. They were angels.

They said: The Prophet forbade the killing of al-Bakhtarī. He had put on his weapons one day in Mecca concerning some harm that had reached the Prophet. He said: One will not obstruct Muḥammad except he will find my weapon in him. The Prophet was grateful about that. Abū Dāwud al-Māzani said; and I followed him and I said, "Indeed the Prophet has forbidden your killing if you give yourself up." He said, "What do you want from me? If he has forbidden my killing, indeed, I shall test that; as for giving myself up, by al-Lāt and al-ʿUzzā, surely the women of Mecca know that I will not give myself up. And I know that you will not leave me. So do what you desire." Abū Dāwud aimed an arrow at him. He said, "Praised be your arrow. Abū Bakhtari is your slave, so put it in a vulnerable spot." Abū Bakhtarī was in armor. The arrow ripped the armor and killed him. Some say al-Mujadhdhar b. Dhiyād killed Abū Bakhtarī, not knowing him. al-Mujadhdhar declared in his poem that he killed him.

The Prophet forbade the [Page 81] killing of Ḥārith b. ʿĀmir b. Nawfal. He said, "Take him prisoner but do not kill him. He hated to go out to Badr." Khubayb b. Yasāf met him and killed him without knowing who he was. The news reached the Prophet, who said: If I had found him before you killed him I would have left him for his women. The Prophet forbade the killing of Zamaʿa b. al-Aswad, as well; Thābit b. al-Jadhʿa killed him without knowing him.

They said: When the battle intensified the Messenger of God raised his hands and asked God most high to help him as He had promised. "O God, if this band is defeated polytheism will appear and your religion will never prevail." Abū Bakr said, "By God, God will surely help you and vindicate you." God brought down a thousand angels and placed them in the midst of the enemy. The Messenger of God said, "O Abū Bakr, rejoice. This is Gabriel appearing in a yellow turban, taking the reign of his horse between heaven and earth." When he alighted on earth he was hidden from me for a while, and then he appeared, dust upon his teeth, saying: God gave you help when you asked Him.

They said: The Messenger of God ordered, and taking a handful of pebbles, aimed them at the enemy. He said, "The faces are ugly! O God, terrify their hearts and let their steps stumble." The enemies of God fled and they did not turn around for anything. The Muslims were killing and taking prisoners. There did not remain one among them, but his face and eyes were full of pebbles and he could not tell from his eyes where he was going. The angels and the believers killed them.

ʿAdī b. Abī l-Zaghbāʾ recited on the day of Badr: I am ʿAdī and I walk in *al-saḥl*, the walk of a stallion. The Prophet said, "Who is ʿAdī?" And one [Page 82] of the people said, "I am ʿAdī, O Messenger of God." The Prophet said, "And what else?" He replied, "The son of so and so." The Prophet said, "You are not ʿAdī!" And ʿAdī b. Abī l-Zaghbāʾ said, "I am ʿAdī, O Messenger of God." The Prophet repeated, "And what else?" He replied, "And I walk in al-Saḥl, the walk of a stallion." The Prophet said, "And what is al-Saḥl?" He replied, "The armor." The Prophet said, "That is the best of ʿAdīs, ʿAdī b. Abī l-Zaghbāʾ!"

Meanwhile ʿUqba b. Abī Muʿayṭ was in Mecca and Muḥammad was an emigree to Medina, and he [ʿUqba] used to say:

> O emmigrant on the she-camel al-Qaṣwāʾ,
> Soon you will see me, the rider of a horse,
> And I will thrust my weapon in you, then drink it,
> And the sword will take from you all uncertainty.

Ibn Abī Zinād transmitted it to me. When the saying reached him the Prophet said, "O God, direct his nose to the ground and destroy him." He said: ʿUqba's horse ran away with him on the day of Badr and ʿAbdullah b. Salama took him captive. The Prophet commanded ʿĀsim b. Thābit b. Abī l-Aqlaḥ to execute him.

ʿAbd al-Raḥmān b. ʿAwf used to say: I was collecting armor for myself on the day of Badr after the people left, when all of a sudden Umayya b. Khalaf, who was a friend during *jāhiliyya*, appeared. I used to call myself ʿAbdʿAmr, and when Islam arrived I called myself ʿAbd al-Raḥmān. But he called out to me saying ʿAbdʿAmr, so I would not reply. So he says, "Indeed, I do not call you ʿAbd al-Raḥmān, for surely Musaylima in Yamāma is named al-Raḥmān and I will not call you by it." So he used to call me ʿAbd al-Ilah. When it was the day of Badr I saw him on a dusky white camel, and with him was his son ʿAlī. [Page 83] He called out to me, "O ʿAbdʿAmr," and I refused to reply. Then he called, "O ʿAbd al-Ilah," and I answered him. "Do you not need some milk? We are better for you than this armor of yours." I replied, "Go!" and I began to drive them before me. Umayya saw that he had some security, and he said to me, "I saw a man with you today marked by the feather of an ostrich on his chest, who is he?" I replied, "Ḥamza b. ʿAbd al-Muṭṭalib." He said, "That was he who did much to us." Then he added: "And who was the short man, fat and active. Well known for his red scarf?" He said: I replied, "That is a man from the Anṣār named Simāk b. Kharasha (Abū Dujāna)." He said, "By that man also, O ʿAbd al-Ilah, today we were slaughtered by you!" He said: While he was with me—and I was leading him before me, together with his son—all of a sudden Bilāl recognized him, and he was making dough for himself. And he left the dough and began to scrub the dough off his hands vigorously. Then he called out, "O People of the Anṣār, Umayya b. Khalaf, the chief of the disbelievers is here. I will not live if he lives."

ʿAbd al-Raḥmān said: They approached like women yearning for their children, when Umayya flung himself on his back and I prostrated myself over him. Al-Ḥubāb b. al-Mundhir approached and drawing his sword, cut off the tip of his nose. When Umayya lost his nose, he said, "Go ahead. Free this space between me and them." ʿAbd al-Raḥmān said: I remember the words of Ḥassān about that amputated nose.

Khubayb b. Yasāf approached him and struck him until he killed him. Umayya struck Khubayb until he cut his arm at his shoulder. The Prophet returned it and it joined and was healed. Later Khubayb married the daughter of Umayya b. Khalaf. When she saw the cut she said, [Page 84] "God do not wither the hand of this man!" Khubayb said: And I, by God, had brought her father death.

Khubayb used to relate saying: I struck him above the shoulders, and I cut his shoulder until I reached the covering of armor over him. I said, "Take this. I am the son of Yasāf." I took his weapon and his cut armor. Then ʿAlī b. Umayya approached and al-Hubāb blocked him and cut his leg. He screamed a scream, in sorrow, the like of which I have never heard. Then, ʿAmmār reached him and struck him a blow that killed him. It is said by some that ʿAmmār met him before the blow and that they exchanged blows and he killed him. The first saying, that he struck him after his leg was cut, is more reliable. But we have heard other things about the killing of Umayya.

Al-Wāqidī related to us saying, ʿUbayd b. Yaḥyā related to me from Muʿādh b. Rifāʿa b. Rāfiʿ from his father, saying, "When it was the day of Badr we surrounded Umayya b. Khalaf who had a position with the Quraysh. I had my spear and he had his spear and we spontaneously went at each other until our spears fell; then we took to the swords and we struck with them until they were broken at the edge. Then I saw a slit in his armor under his armpit, and I pierced my sword in him until I killed him. The sword came out with fat on it." But we have heard another version.

Muḥammad b. Qudāma b. Mūsa related to me from his father, from ʿĀʾisha bt. Qudāma, who said: Ṣafwān b. Umayya b. Khalaf said to Qudāma b. Maẓʿūn, "O Qudāma, did you destroy my father the day he roused the people?" Qudāma replied, "No, by God, I did not. And if I did I would not be ashamed of killing the polytheist." Safwān said, "Then who, O Qudāma, destroyed him the day he roused the people?" [Page 85] He said, "I saw youths from the Anṣār approach him. With them was Maʿmar b. Ḥabīb b. ʿUbayd b. al-Ḥārith, and he raised his sword and placed it in him." Ṣafwān says, "Abū Qird [the father of the monkey]!" for Maʿmar was an ugly man. Al-Ḥārith b. Ḥāṭib heard of that and was angered by it. He visited the mother of Ṣafwān, Karīma bt. Maʿmar b. Ḥabīb, and said, "Ṣafwān has not stopped hurting us in *jāhiliyya* and Islam." She said, "What is that?" So he informed her of Ṣafwān's words for Maʿmar when he called him Abū Qird. Ṣafwān's mother said, "O Ṣafwān, do you insult Maʿmar b. Ḥabīb, one of the people of Badr? By God, I will not accept a gift from you for a year." Ṣafwān said, "O Mother, by God I will never repeat it again. I spoke a word without thinking."

Muḥammad informed us that al-Wāqidī related to him saying: Muḥammad b. Qudāma related to me from his father, from ʿĀʾisha bt. Qudāma, who said: It was said to Umm Ṣafwān b. Umayya, while she observed al-Ḥubāb b. al-Mundhir in Mecca, "This is he who cut the leg of ʿAlī b. Umayya on the day of Badr." She replied, "Stop reminding us of who was killed among the polytheists. God humiliated ʿAlī b. Umayya with the blows of al-Ḥubāb b. Mundhir, and was gracious to al-Ḥubāb with his blows against ʿAlī. He was of Islam when he left from here, but died a non-Muslim."

They said: al-Zubayr b. al-Awwām said: At that time I met ʿUbayda b. Saʿīd b. al-ʿĀṣ upon a horse, and he was wearing a head covering which was complete so that one could only see his eyes. He says, while carrying a little girl who had a swollen tummy and was seriously ill, "I am the father of she who has a swollen tummy!" He said: In my hand was a little spear, [Page 86] and I pierced him in his eyes, and he fell. Then I placed my foot upon his cheek until I drew out the spear from his eye, and I drew out his eye.

The Messenger of God took the spear and it was held between his hands and those of Abū Bakr, ʿUmar, and ʿUthmān, may peace be upon them.

When the Muslims went out, wandering, they mixed with each other, and ʿĀṣim b. Abī ʿAwf b. Ṣubayra al-Sahmī appeared, like a wolf, saying, "O Qurayshī people, aim for Muḥammad the divider of the community who comes with the unknown! I will not live if he lives." Abū Dujāna opposed him. They exchanged blows, and Abū Dujāna struck and killed him. He reached out to take the plunder, but ʿUmar b. al-Khaṭṭāb passed by, at that moment, and said, "Leave the plunder until the enemy has been weakened, and I will testify for you about it." Maʿbad b. Wahb approached and he struck Abū Dujāna a blow, and Abū Dujāna knelt like a camel and then rose to fight. Abū Dujāna struck him twice, but his sword did not do anything. Then Maʿbad not seeing a hole in front of him fell in it, and Abū Dujāna knelt over him and killed him and took his booty.

They said: When, at that time, the Banū Makhzūm saw the killing of those who had died, they said: Abū l-Ḥakam should not be reached. Indeed, the two sons of Rabīʿa had rushed and been reckless, and their people did not rally to them. The Banū Makhzūm gathered and surrounded him [al-Ḥakam/Abū Jahl] and placed him within what was like a dense forest. They gathered to place the head cover of Abū Jahl upon a man among them. And they put it on ʿAbdullah b. al-Mundhir b. Abī Rifāʿa. ʿAlī charged at him and killed him, thinking it was Abū Jahl, then went his way, saying, "Take it, and I am from the sons of ʿAbd al-Muṭṭalib." Then they put the head cover on Abū Qays b. al-Fākih b. al-Mughīra, and Ḥamza charged at him thinking he was Abū Jahl, and struck [Page 87] and killed him. And he says, "Take it and I am the son of ʿAbd al-Muṭṭalib." Then they put it on Ḥarmala b. ʿAmr, and ʿAlī charged at him and killed him. But Abū Jahl was with his companions. Then they desired to put it on Khālid b. al-Aʿlam, and he refused to wear it at that time. Muʿādh b. ʿAmr b. al-Jamūḥ said, "I observed Abū Jahl confined in what was like a thicket, and they were saying, 'Abū l-Ḥakam should not be reached,' and I knew that it was he. I said to myself, by God, I will reach him or die in the attempt. I charged at him until when there was the slightest possibility I reached him. I struck him a blow and I took his leg from his thigh that looked like a date seed crushed by a nutcracker. Then his son ʿIkrima came at me and struck me on my shoulder, and removed my arm from my shoulder leaving only some skin. I withdrew my hand with its skin behind me. But when it hurt me, I placed my foot upon it and stretched myself until I cut it. Then I met ʿIkrima while he sought refuge at every shelter, and if I had my hand with me I would have hoped to take him." Muʿādh died during the caliphate of ʿUthmān.

Muḥammad related to us that al-Wāqidī said: Abū Marwān told me from Isḥāq b. ʿAbdullah from ʿĀmir b. ʿUthmān, from Jābir b. ʿAbdullah, who said: ʿAbd al-Raḥmān b. ʿAwf informed me that the Prophet gave Muʿādh b. ʿAmr b. Jamūḥ the sword of Abū Jahl. It is with the family of Muʿādh b. ʿAmr to this day, and has a dent. Later, the Prophet sent for ʿIkrima b. Abī Jahl and asked him, "Who killed your father?" He replied: He whose arm I cut off. The Prophet pushed him towards Muʿādh b. ʿAmr, for ʿIkrima had cut his arm on the day of Badr. Thābit b. Qays related to me from Nāfiʿ b. Jubayr b. Muṭʿim that he heard him say: the Banū Mughīra did not doubt that the sword of Abū l-Ḥakam went to Muʿādh b. ʿAmr b. [Page 88] Jamūḥ, for it was he who killed him on the day of Badr.

Muḥammad b. Shujāʿ related to us that al-Wāqidī related saying: Abū Isḥāq related to me from Yūnus b. Yūsuf, who said: Muʿādh b. ʿAmr related to me that the Prophet left him the possessions of Abū Jahl. He said, “I took his armor and his sword. Later I sold his sword.” But I have heard other tales of how he was killed, and his possessions plundered.

ʿAbd al-Ḥamīd b. Jaʿfar related to me from ʿUmar b. al-Ḥakam b. Thawbān from ʿAbd al-Raḥmān b. ʿAwf. He said: The Prophet mobilized us by night, arranging us in rows. As we lined up the next morning in the same rows, suddenly, two youths appeared, each of them wearing his sword on a rope around his neck. One of them turned to me and said, “O uncle, which of them is Abū Jahl?” He said: I replied, “What will you do with him, O son of my brother?” He said, “It has reached me that he insults the Messenger of God, and I swear I will kill him or die in the attempt.” So I pointed out Abū Jahl to him. Then the other said similar words to me. So I pointed out Abū Jahl to him as well and said, “Who are you two?” They said, “The two sons of al-Ḥārith.” He said: And they did not take their eyes off Abū Jahl until the battle was completed and they had all killed each other.

Muḥammad related to us that al-Wāqidī related to us saying: Muḥammad b. ʿAwf related to me from the son of Muʿawwidh b. ʿAfrāʾ from Ibrāhīm b. Yaḥyā b. Zayd b. Thābit, who said: At that time ʿAbd al-Raḥmān said, and he saw them from his right and his left, “I wish there was one at my side who is stronger than these two youths.” ʿAwf did not hesitate to turn to me, and ask, which of them is Abū Jahl. I replied, “That is where you see him.” He went running to him like a lion and his brother reached him as well, and I saw them clash with their swords. [Page 89] Then I saw the Messenger of God pass by, and they were among the dead at Abū Jahl’s side.

Muḥammad related to us that al-Wāqidī related to us that Muḥammad b. Rifāʿa b. Thaʿlaba b. Abī Mālik said: I heard my father deny what the people say about the younger of the two sons of ʿAfrāʾ. He says, “On the day of Badr the younger son was thirty-five years of age, and this still tied the scabbard of his sword?” The first saying is more reliable.

Muḥammad related to us saying: Al-Wāqidī related to us saying: ʿAbd al-Ḥamīd b. Jaʿfar and ʿAbdullah b. Abī ʿUbayd related to me from Abū ʿUbayda b. Muḥammad b. ʿAmmār b. Yāsir from Rubayyiʿ bt. Muʿawwidh, who said: I joined with the wives of the Anṣār to visit Asmāʾ bt. Mukharriba, the mother of Abū Jahl, during the time of ʿUmar b. al-Khaṭṭāb. Her son ʿAbdullah b. Abī Rabīʿa sent her perfume from Yemen, and she would sell it to anyone who offered for it. We used to buy from her, and when she put some for me in a *Qawariri* container, and weighed for me just as she weighed for my companions, she said, “Write your claim for me.” I said, “Yes,” and I wrote for her ‘Rubayyiʿ bt. Muʿawwidh.’ Asmāʾ said, “Unhappy woman! Surely you are not the daughter of he who killed his lord.” I replied, “No; but I am the daughter of he who killed his slave.” She said, “By God, I will never sell you anything.” I replied, “By God I will never buy anything from you! And by God, it is neither agreeable nor fragrant!” By God, my son, I had never smelled a perfume that was better, but, my son, I was angry!

They said: When the war put down its burdens, Muḥammad commanded that Abū Jahl be sought out. Ibn Masʿūd said: I found him on the verge of death, and I placed my leg [Page 90] upon his neck and said, “Praise be to God who humiliates you.” He replied, “Indeed God humiliates the slave of the son of the mother of a slave! Surely you have made a difficult ascent, little shepherd. Whose turn is it?” I said, “Of God and His prophet.” Ibn Masʿūd continued: I pulled out his helmet from the back of his head and I said, “Indeed, I shall kill you Abū Jahl.” He replied, “And you are not the first slave to kill his master. It is indeed the hardest that I encounter in my heart, today, that you should kill me. Would that my death was undertaken by the al-Aḥlāf or the al-Mutayyibūn!"

ʿAbdullah struck him a blow and his head fell before him. Then he plundered him, and when he looked at his body, he looked around it as though it were scourged. He took his weapons, his armor, and his helmet and placed them before the Prophet saying, "Rejoice, O Prophet, for the killing of Abū Jahl, the enemy of God." The Messenger of God said, "Is it true, O ʿAbdullah? By Him who holds my soul in His hands surely it is more desirable to me than the most excellent of camels," or something like it. He said: I mentioned to the Prophet the marks that were on him. He replied, "That is from the beating of the angels." The Prophet said that a scratch marked Abū Jahl from a push he had received during the banquet of Ibn Judʿān, when his knee was scratched. So they searched him and they found that mark. He says: Indeed, Abū Salama was with the Prophet at that time. He was angry with himself, and went to Ibn Masʿūd and said, "Did you kill him?" He said, "Yes, God killed him." Abū Salama said, "Did you, by God, kill him?" He said, "Yes." He said, "If Abū Jahl wished, he could put you in his sleeve!" Ibn Masʿūd replied, "By God, I killed him and I stripped him." Abū Salama b. ʿAbd al-Asad al-Makhzūmī said, "What were the marks on him?" He said, "A black birthmark in the middle of his right thigh." Abū Salama knew of this characteristic; he said, [Page 91] "You stripped him! No other Qurayshī was stripped but him." Ibn Masʿūd said, "Indeed he was not with the Quraysh, and there was not one among their allies who was a greater enemy of God or His messenger than he. And I am not ashamed of anything that I did to him." Abū Salama was silent. Later, Abū Salama was heard seeking forgiveness for his words regarding Abū Jahl.

The Prophet rejoiced over the killing of Abū Jahl. He said, "O God, You have done as You promised me. So fulfill upon me Your blessings." The family of Ibn Masʿūd says: The sword of Abū Jahl, ornamented in silver, is with us. ʿAbdullah b. Masʿūd plundered it at that time. Our companions have brought together the saying that Muʿādh b. ʿAmr and the two sons of ʿAfrāʾ confirmed. Ibn Masʿūd cut off his head when he was at the end of his tether. All of them had participated in killing him.

They said: The Prophet stood before the sons of ʿAfrāʾ on the battle ground and said, "May God have mercy on the two sons of ʿAfrāʾ for surely they participated in killing the pharaoh of this community, and the leader of the community of disbelief." It was said: "O Messenger of God, who else joined in killing him?" He said, "The angels; and Ibn Masʿūd finished him off. All joined in killing him."

Muḥammad related to us that al-Wāqidī related to us saying: Maʿmar related to me from al-Zuhrī, who said: The Messenger of God said, "O God, seek out Nawfal b. Khuwaylid." And Nawfal approached at that time and he was terrified. He had seen the killing of his companion, and he was with the first of those the Muslims met, shouting in his *zajal* voice, "O people of the Quraysh, indeed this day is a day of high rank." But when he saw that the Quraysh had been destroyed he began to shout at the Anṣār, "What is your need for our blood? Do you not see how many you have killed? Do you not need some milk?" Jabbār b. Ṣakhr took him captive and drove him before him.

[Page 92] Nawfal began to say to Jabbār: for he saw ʿAlī approach him, "O brother of the Anṣār, who is this? By al-Lāt and al-ʿUzzā, surely I see a man who desires me." He replied, "This is ʿAlī b. Abī Ṭālib." He said, "I have not seen on such a day a man more swift with his people than he." ʿAlī confronted him, and struck him, and he attacked the sword of ʿAlī and opposed him for a while. Then ʿAlī disarmed him and struck his thighs, and his armor buckled and ʿAlī cut both of them. Then ʿAlī strove against him and killed him. The Messenger of God said, "Who possesses knowledge of Nawfal b. Khuwaylid?" ʿAlī replied, "I killed him." He said: The Prophet proclaimed *takbīr* and said, "Praise be to God who answered my prayer concerning him."

Al-ʿĀṣ b. Saʿīd approached, goading to battle, and ʿAlī encountered him and killed him. ʿUmar b. al-Khaṭṭāb said to his son, Saʿīd b. al-ʿĀṣ, "I saw you turn away; you think that I killed your father. I am not ashamed of killing a polytheist, for surely I killed my uncle, al-ʿĀṣ b. Hishām b. Mughīra, with my own hands." Saʿīd said, "If you killed him surely he was wrong, and you were right." He said, "The Quraysh are the greatest people in wisdom, and the greatest in honesty. One does not oppress or disable them, but God puts him down."

ʿAlī used to say: Indeed I was at that time in broad daylight, and we and the polytheists had confused our rows and their rows. I went out on the tracks of one of them, when lo and behold, there was a man from the polytheists and Saʿd b. Khaythama upon a sand dune. They fought [Page 93] each other until the polytheist killed Saʿd b. Khaythama. The polytheist was masked in iron, and on a horse. He came down from his horse, and recognized me. He was knowledgeable, but I did not recognize him. He called out, "Come, Ibn Abī Ṭālib, to a duel." He said: I turned to him and he descended towards me. I am a short man, so I backed off in order to make him come down to me. I hated that he was above me with a sword. He said, "O Ibn Abī Ṭālib, are you fleeing?" I replied, "Only to return like Ibn Shatara, the highwayman!" He said: When I established myself on my feet, he approached. When he was close to me, he struck me, but I protected myself with my shield, and his sword fell to the ground and stayed there. I struck him on his shoulder and it was armed. He trembled, for my sword pierced his armor. I thought that my sword would kill him, when all of a sudden a sword glistened from behind me. I bowed my head, and the sword fell, and the skull of his head clanged in the helmet, and he says, "Take this, and I am Ibn ʿAbd al-Muṭṭalib." I turned around, and lo and behold, there was Ḥamza b. ʿAbd al-Muṭṭalib.

Muḥammad related to us that al-Wāqidī related to us saying: ʿUmar b. ʿUthmān al-Jaḥshī from his father related to me from his paternal aunt, who said: ʿUkkāsha b. Miḥṣan said, "I broke my sword on the day of Badr, and the Messenger of God gave me a rod. And lo and behold, it was a sword bright and long. I fought with it until God defeated the polytheists." It stayed with him until his death. Muḥammad related to us that al-Wāqidī related to us saying: Usāma b. Zayd related to me from Dāwud b. al-Ḥuṣayn from a number of men from the Banū ʿAbd al-Ashhal, who said: The sword of Salama b. Aslam b. Ḥarīsh broke on the day of Badr and he remained unarmed and without a weapon until [Page 94] the Messenger of God gave him a rod, which was in his hand, from the date palms of Ibn Ṭāb. He said, "Strike with it!" And lo and behold, it was an excellent sword. He continued with it until he was killed on the day of the Bridge of Abū ʿUbayd.

He said: While Ḥāritha b. Surāqa was sipping water from a cistern, an arrow came to him, from no one knows where, and became lodged in his throat. He fell in the stream, and surely, by the end of the day the people had drunk his blood. It reached his mother and his sister who were in Medina when he died. His mother said, "By God I will not cry for him until the Prophet arrives; I will ask him, and if my son is in heaven I will not cry for him. But if my son is in hell, I will cry for him, by the everlasting God, and mourn him." When the Messenger of God arrived from Badr, his mother came to the Messenger of God and said, "You know of the situation of Ḥāritha from my heart and

I want to cry for him, but I said, I will not act until I ask the Messenger of God, and if he is in Paradise I will not cry for him, but if he is in hell I will cry for him and mourn him." The Prophet said, "Bereaved one, do you think there is only one Paradise? Indeed there are many gardens. By Him who holds my soul in His hands, he is in the highest Paradise." She said, "I will not cry for him ever!" The Prophet asked for a container of water, dipped his hand in it and washed his mouth. He presented it to the mother of Ḥāritha and she drank it. Then she presented some to her daughter and she drank it. Then he commanded them to splash it on their chests. They did so and returned from the home of the Prophet. There have not been in Medina two women more content or more joyful than them.

They said: Hubayra b. Abī Wahb, when he saw the defeat, was helpless; his back was wounded and he [Page 95] could not stand. Abū Usāma, his ally, came following him and cut his armor from him and carried him. Others said: Abū Dāwud al-Māzinī struck Hubayra with his sword and cut his armor, and he fell on his face and remained on the ground, and Abū Dāwud walked away. The sons of Zuhayr al-Jushamī, Abū Usāma and Mālik recognized him, and they were his allies. They defended him until they saved him. Abū Usāma carried him and protected him, and Mālik defended him. The Prophet said, "His two dogs protected him." The friendship of such as Abū Usāma is like a palm tree, for the palm of the date is tall. Some said: Indeed he who struck him was al-Mujadhdhar b. Dhiyād.

Muḥammad related that al-Wāqidī related to us saying: Mūsā b. Yaʿqūb related to me from his uncle, who said: I heard Abū Bakr b. Sulaymān b. Abī Ḥathma say: I heard Marwān b. al-Ḥakam ask Ḥakīm b. Ḥizām about the battle of Badr. The old man tried to avoid that until he was urged to it. Ḥakīm said, "We met and we fought. I heard a sound of something falling from the sky to the ground like pebbles falling in a tub. The Prophet grabbed a hand full and threw it and defeated us."

Muḥammad related to us that al-Wāqidī related to us saying: Abū Isḥāq b. Muḥammad related to me from ʿAbd al-Raḥmān b. Muḥammad b. ʿAbd, from ʿAbdullāh b. Thaʿlaba b. Ṣuʿayr, who said: I heard Nawfal b. Muʿāwiya b. al-Dīlī say, "We were defeated on the day of Badr when we heard what seemed like pebbles falling in a tub in front of us and behind us, and that was what frightened us the most."

Ḥakīm b. Ḥizām used to say: We were defeated on the day of Badr, but I kept going forward saying, "May God battle Ibn al-Ḥanẓaliyya!" He claimed that the day was done. And. by God, the day was as it was. Ḥakīm said: There was only a longing that night would come and shorten for us the search for Muḥammad's community. ʿUbaydullāh and ʿAbd al-Raḥmān the sons of al-ʿAwwām overtook Ḥakīm on a camel of theirs. ʿAbd al-Raḥmān said [Page 96] to his brother, "Get down and carry Abū Khālid." ʿUbaydullāh was lame and did not have the strength to walk, so he said, "I have not the strength to walk, as you see." ʿAbd al-Raḥmān said, "By God, if it is necessary, shall we not carry a man who, if we die, shall be sufficient for us and for those who follow us among our dependants; and if we live will carry our burden?" So, ʿAbd al-Rahmān and his brother, who was lame, alighted, and carried him, and took turns on the camel. When they were close to Mecca, in Marr al-Ẓahrān, he (Abū Khālid) said, "By God, I saw over there an affair, and one who possesses an opinion does not go out against the likes of it, but it was the bad luck of Ibn al-Ḥanẓalīya! Indeed a camel was slaughtered over there, and there did not remain a tent, but it was touched by its blood." They both replied, "We saw that. But we saw you and our people depart for battle, and we departed with you. We did not have a choice."

In the name of God, most gracious and merciful. It was recited according to Abū l-Qāsim b. Abī Ḥayya, who said: Abū ʿAbdullah Muḥammad b. Shujāʿ related to us, saying: Muḥammad b. ʿUmar al-Wāqidī said: ʿAbd al-Raḥmān b. al-Ḥārith related to me from Makhlad b. Khufāf from his father saying: There were many coats of mail with the Quraysh. When they were defeated they began to discard them. The Muslims followed them and picked up what they discarded. At that time I picked up three coats of mail and brought them to my family. They have been with us since. A man from the Quraysh declared, when he saw one of the coats of mail with us, that he recognized it. He said: This is the armor of al-Ḥārith b. Hishām.

Al-Wāqidī said: Muḥammad b. Abī Ḥumayd related to me from ʿAbdullah b. ʿAmr b. Umayya, who said: I heard my father, ʿAmr b. Umayya, saying: Inform me who revealed defeat, at that time? Indeed he was saying to himself, "I have not seen such a day of flight except with women."

[Page 97] They said: Qubāth b. Ashyam al-Kinānā used to say: I witnessed Badr with the polytheists. I observed the small number of the companions of Muḥammad and the larger number of camels and men among us. Yet I was among those defeated. Indeed, I saw and observed the Polytheists fleeing in every direction. I said to myself: I have not seen such an affair of fleeing except with women. My companion was a man and while he was walking with me we met those who were behind us. I said to my companion, "Would you hurry up?" He replied, "No, by God I cannot." He said: He slowed down while I hastened and I arrived in Ghayqa—which is to the left of al-Suqyā and a night from al-Furʿ, and eight posts from Medina—before the sun. I knew the road so I did not take it, for I feared being found and I avoided it. In Ghayqa a man from my tribe met me. He said, "What brings you?" I replied, "Nothing. We were killed and taken prisoner and defeated. Do you have a riding beast?" He said, "I will take you on my camel." He supplied me with provisions until I came to the road to al-Juḥfa. Then I departed until I arrived at Mecca. I saw al-Ḥaysumān b. Ḥābis al-Khuzāʿī in al-Ghamīm. I knew he was arriving to announce the death of the Quraysh in Mecca. If I desired to overtake him I would have surely overtaken him, but I held back until he preceded me by a part of the day. When I arrived, news of their death had finally reached Mecca, and they were cursing al-Khuzāʿī and saying: He never brought us good news. I lingered on in Mecca. But when it was after al-Khandaq I said: If I arrived in Medina I shall observe what Muḥammad says, for surely Islam had come into my heart. When I arrived in Medina and asked about the Messenger of God [Page 98] they said, "He is that man in the shade of the Mosque with all of his companions." So I came to him and I did not know him from among them, and I greeted him. He replied, "O Qubāth b. Ashyam, you are the one, who said on the day of Badr, 'I have not seen such an affair of fleeing except from women.'" I responded, "I testify that you are the Messenger of God. Surely this affair never went out from me to any one. I did not speak of it, for it was something that I said to myself. If you were not a prophet, God would not have acquainted you of it. Come, that I may pledge my allegiance." He offered Islam to me, and I converted.

They said: When the disbelievers and the Muslims had been arranged in rows, the Messenger of God said, "For he who made a killing, to him is thus and thus; for he who captured a prisoner, to him is thus and thus." When they were defeated the people were in three groups. One group stood at the tent of the Prophet—Abū Bakr was with the Prophet in the tent. The second group went for the plunder; and the third group sought out the enemy and took prisoners and spoils. Saʿd b. Muʿādh spoke, and he was with those who stood at the tent of the Prophet. He said, "O Messenger of God, what prevents us seeking the enemy is not moderation in recompense, nor cowardice about the enemy, but fear that your station will be unprotected and some riders from their men will attack and separate you. The lords of the people from the Muhajirūn and the Anṣār stand at your tent, and one will not be isolated from them. But the people are many, O Messenger of God, and once you have given those who attack, nothing will be left for your companions. The prisoners and the dead are many, but the plunder is little." They disputed. And God most high revealed: *They ask you about the booty. Say the booty is for God and His Messenger* (Q. 8:1). So the people returned, for there was nothing for them from the plunder. Then God most High revealed: *Know that from what you plunder of anything, to God and His prophet belongs a fifth* (Q. 8:41). The Messenger of God apportioned it among them.

[Page 99] Yaʿqūb b. Mujāhid Abū Ḥazra from ʿUbāda b. al-Walīd b. ʿUbāda from his father, from his grandfather ʿUbāda b. al-Ṣāmit, who said: We submitted the booty to God and his Messenger. The Messenger of God did not take a fifth at Badr. Later, it was revealed: *Know that from what you plunder of anything, to God belongs a fifth*. The Messenger of God received the fifth from the first plunder of Badr. ʿAbd al-Muhaymin b. ʿAbbās b. Sahl from his father from Abū Usayd al-Sāʿidī informed me similarly.

Abū Bakr b. ʿAbdullāh b. Muḥammad b. Abī Sabra from Sulaymān b. Suḥaym from ʿIkrima related to us saying: The people quarreled about the plunder on the day of Badr. Regarding the booty, the Prophet commanded that the portions be returned to him, and every bit of it was returned. The brave thought that the Messenger of God would prefer them to the rest of the weak. However, the Messenger of God commanded that it be apportioned among them equally. Saʿd said, "O Messenger of God did you give the horsemen who defended them in battle the same as what you gave the weak?" The Prophet replied, "Your mother grieves for you, would you be victorious without the weak?"

ʿAbd al-Ḥamīd b. Jaʿfar related to me saying: I asked Mūsā b. Saʿd b. Zayd b. Thābit: What did the Prophet do, on the day of Badr, with the prisoners and the looting and the booty? He replied: A herald called out at that time, "Whoever killed a man, to him belongs his booty; whoever takes a prisoner, keeps him." And whoever killed an enemy was given his booty. He commanded concerning what was found in the camp and what was taken without battle, and he apportioned it among them quickly (within the time between the milking of two camels). I said to ʿAbd al-Ḥamīd b. Jaʿfar: Who was given the booty of Abū Jahl? He replied: There is disagreement among us [Page 100] about it. Someone said: Muʿādh b. ʿAmr b. al-Jamūḥ took it. Another said: He gave it to Ibn Masʿūd. I said to ʿAbd al-Ḥamīd, "Who informed you?" He replied, "As for he, who said he gave it to Muʿādh b. ʿAmr, Khārija b. ʿAbdullah b. Kaʿb informed me of it. And as for he, who said it was Ibn Masʿūd, indeed Saʿīd b. Khālid al-Qāriẓī informed me of it." They said: ʿAlī took the armor of al-Walīd b. ʿUtba, his helmet and head-guard; Ḥamza took the weapons of ʿUtba; and ʿUbayda b. al-Ḥārith took the armor of Shayba b. Rabīʿa and it went to his heirs.

Muḥammad b. Yaḥyā b. Sahl informed me from his uncle Muḥammad b. Sahl b. Abī Ḥathma saying: The Messenger of God commanded that the prisoners and the spoils and what was taken of the booty be returned. He commanded them to draw lots about the prisoners. He apportioned the spoils that the man had taken freely for himself in a duel, and what was taken in the camps, and he apportioned it among them quickly. We have confirmed that whatever he promised them he submitted to them, and what he did not promise, he apportioned among them. The plunder was collected and the Messenger of God employed ʿAbdullah b. Kaʿb b. ʿAmr al-Māzinī over it. Muḥammad b. Yaḥyā b. Sahl b. Abī Ḥathma told me about it, from his father, from his grandfather, from the Prophet. He apportioned it in Sayar. Sayar is a pass in Maḍīq al-Safrāʾ. Others said that the Prophet employed Khabbāb b. al-Aratta over it.

Ibn Abī Sabra related to me from al-Miswar b. Rifāʿa from ʿAbdullah b. Muknif al-Ḥārithī from Ḥāritha al-Anṣār, who said: When the plunder was collected, there were camels, leather mats, and clothing included. The man in charge apportioned it. He gave one man a camel and some old clothes, to another two camels and to another, leather mats. There were 317 portions [Page 101] and 313 men. But there were two riders and they were entitled to four shares.

Eight individuals did not attend, but the Prophet apportioned their shares and rewarded them. All of them were entitled in Badr. Three were from the Muhājirūn, and there was no dispute about them with us. There was ʿUthmān b. ʿAffān; the Prophet left him behind with his daughter Ruqayya. She died the day Zayd b. Ḥāritha arrived. The other two were Talha b. ʿUbaydullah and Saʿīd b. Zayd b. ʿAmr b. Nufayl; the Messenger of God had sent the two of them to locate the caravan. They reached al-Ḥawrāʾ—which is behind Dhū l-Marwa. Between these two is two nights' journey along the coast, and between Dhū l-Marwa and Medina are roughly eight postal stations. From the Ansār were: Abū Lubāba b. ʿAbd al-Mundhir—he was appointed over Medina; ʿĀṣim b. ʿAdī, who was appointed over Qubāʾ and the people of al-ʿĀliya; al-Ḥārith b. Ḥāṭib, who was appointed as commander over the Banū ʿAmr b. ʿAwf; Khawwāt b. Jubayr and al-Ḥārith b. al-Ṣimma had stayed behind in al-Rawḥāʾ, and there was no dispute among us concerning these persons.

It was related that the Prophet fixed a share for Saʿd b. ʿUbāda and rewarded him. He said, at the end of the battle of Badr, that although Saʿd b. ʿUbāda did not witness it, he had wanted to. This was because when the Prophet prepared for battle, Saʿd went to the homes of the Anṣār and spurred them to go out to battle. However, he was bitten by something at that place and that prevented him from going out. So the Prophet made a portion for him and rewarded him. He also apportioned for Saʿd b. Mālik al-Sāʿidī and rewarded him. Saʿd had prepared for Badr but fallen sick in Medina and died. He appointed the Prophet as the executor of his will. The Prophet also apportioned to a man from the Anṣār and to another man. These four had no agreement like the agreement for the eight.

[Page 102] Ibn Abī Sabra related to me from Yaʿqūb b. Zayd from his father that the Messenger of God apportioned for those who died at Badr. Fourteen men were killed at Badr. Zayd b. Ṭalḥa said: ʿAbdullah b. Saʿd b. Khaythama related to me saying, "We took the portion of my father that the Prophet apportioned for him from the plunder. ʿUwaym b. Sāʿida brought it to us."

Ibn Abī Sabra related to me from al-Miswar b. Rifāʿa from ʿAbdullah b. Muknif, who said: I heard al-Sāʾib b. Abī Lubāba report that the Messenger of God apportioned to Mubashshir b. ʿAbd al-Mundhir and Maʿan b. ʿAdī brought his portion to us.

They acquired 150 camels, at that time. They had much leather that they carried for the merchants, and the Muslims plundered it. At that time, there was with what they had taken, red velvet. Some of them said: Why do we not see the velvet? We think the Messenger of God alone took it. God most high revealed: *It is not for a Prophet to be unfaithful* (Q. 3:161) to the end of the verse. A man came to the Messenger of God and said, "O Messenger of God, so-and-so has misappropriated the velvet." The Messenger of God asked the man, and he said, "I did not do it, O Messenger of God!" The guide said, "Dig over there." The Messenger of God commanded, and they dug, and the velvet was discovered. Someone said, "O Messenger of God, ask forgiveness for so-and-so, twice or several times." The Messenger of God said, "Keep us from one who commits a crime." There were two horses. A horse of al-Miqdād, which he named Sabḥa, and a horse of al-Zubayr—some said it was Marthad's horse. al-Miqdād used to say: The Messenger of God apportioned, at that time, a portion for me and a portion for my horse. Another said: [Page 103] The Prophet apportioned two portions, at that time, one for the horse and one for its master.

ʿAbd al-Majīd b. Abī ʿAbs related to me from Abū ʿUfayr Muḥammad b. Sahl, who said: Abū Burda b. Niyār returned with a horse he captured (as booty) on the day of Badr, and the horse went to Zamaʿa b. al-Aswad; it came with his portion. The Muslims captured ten horses from the enemy. They took weapons and rides for themselves. There was a camel belonging to Abū Jahl with them, at that time. The Prophet took it as booty and kept it for himself. He placed it with his camels and raided with it until he dispatched it as a sacrificial animal to Ḥudaybiyya. The polytheists asked him, at that time, to return the camel in exchange for a hundred camels. He replied, "If we had not named it as a sacrificial animal we would do so." The first choice from the booty, before anything was apportioned from it, was for the Messenger of God.

ʿAbd al-Raḥmān b. ʿAbdullah b. Dhakwān related to me from his father from ʿUbaydullah b. ʿAbdullah b. ʿUtba from Ibn ʿAbbās, and from Muḥammad b. ʿAbdullah from al-Zuhrī from Saʿīd b. al-Musayyib, who both said: The Prophet obtained the sword Dhū l-Faqār, which had belonged to Munabbih b. al-Ḥajjāj, as spoil. The Prophet raided Badr with a sword gifted to him by Saʿd b. ʿUbāda, called al-ʿAḍb, and his armor, Dhāt al-Fuḍūl. I heard Ibn Abī Sabra say: I heard Ṣāliḥ b. Kaysān say: The Messenger of God went out on the day of Badr without a sword. The first sword that he acquired was the sword of Munabbih b. al-Ḥajjāj. He captured it on the day of Badr as spoil.

Abū Usayd al-Sāʿidī used to talk about what ʿAbd al-Muhaymin b. ʿAbbās b. Sahl related to him from his father from Abū Usayd who, when Arqam b. Abī l-Arqam was mentioned, said, [Page 104] "My misery from al-Arqam is not one!" Someone said, "What is it?" He replied, "The Messenger of God commanded the Muslims to return what was in their hands from the booty they had taken. So I returned the sword of Ibn ʿĀ'idh al-Makhzūmī. The name of the sword was Marzubān. It was valuable and strong and I desired that he give it to me. But he [Arqam] spoke to the Messenger of God about it. The Prophet did not hold back anything that was asked of him, so he gave Arqam the sword. Again, a young son of mine, Yafaʿa, set out, and a demon took off with him, carrying him on her back." Someone said to Abū Usayd, "There were demons at that time?" He replied, "Yes, but they have been destroyed. My son met Ibn al-Arqam, and he ran to him seeking his protection. He said, 'Who are you?' And my son informed him. But the demon said, 'I have embraced him,' and he was turned away from him. The youth accused her of lying, but Arqam did not stop for him. And again, a horse of mine went out from my house for it had cut its halter. Al-Arqam came across it, at al-Ghāba, and rode it until he came to Medina, where it escaped from him. He apologized to me that it had escaped him, but I have not yet been able to find it."

Abū Bakr b. Ismāʿīl b. Muḥammad related to me from his father from ʿĀmir b. Saʿd from his father, who said: I asked the Messenger of God for the sword of al-ʿĀṣ b. Munabbih on the day of Badr and he gave it to me. It was revealed about me: *They will ask you about the booty* (Q. 8:1).

They said: The Messenger of God granted spoil to the slaves who attended Badr, but he did not [Page 105] apportion for them. The three slaves were: The slave of Ḥāṭib b. Abī Baltaʿa, the slave of ʿAbd al-Raḥmān b. ʿAwf, and the slave of Saʿd b. Muʿādh. Shuqrān the slave of the Prophet was employed to watch over the captives. They gave him from each prisoner what he would have obtained of what was divided, if he were free.

Abū Bakr b. Ismāʿīl related to me from his father from ʿĀmir b. Saʿd from his father, who said: On the day of Badr I aimed at Suhayl b. ʿAmr and cut his vein. Then I followed the traces of his blood until I found him. Mālik b. al-Dukhshum had taken him. He was holding him by his forelock, when I said, "He is my captive, I shot him!" Mālik said, "He is my captive, I took him." So they both came to the Messenger of God and he took Suhayl from both of them. But Suhayl escaped in al-Rawḥā' from Mālik b. Dukhshum. Mālik shouted about it to the people, and went out in search of him. The Messenger of God said, "Whoever finds him, kill him!" But the Prophet found him and did not kill him.

ʿĪsā b. Ḥafṣ b. ʿĀṣim related to me from his father, who said: Abū Burda b. Niyār took a prisoner from the polytheists named Maʿbad b. Wahb, of the Banū Saʿd b. Layth. ʿUmar b. al-Khaṭṭāb met him. He used to urge the killing of prisoners. He did not see anyone who held a prisoner except he commanded him to kill him. That was before the people dispersed and Maʿbad met him. And he was a captive of Abū Burda. Maʿbad said, "Do you think, O ʿUmar, that you have taken control?" "No, by al-Lāt and al-ʿUzza!" ʿUmar replied, "By the worship of the God of the Muslims! Do you speak, and you are a prisoner in our hands?" Then he took him from Abū Burda and cut off his head. Some said that Abū Burda killed him.

Abū Bakr b. Ismāʿīl related to me from his father from ʿĀmir b. Saʿd, who said: [Page 106] The Messenger of God said, "Do not inform Saʿd about the killing of his brother for he will kill all the prisoners in your hands."

Khālid b. al-Haytham, a *mawlā* of the Banū Hāshim, related to me from Yaḥyā b. Abī Kuthayr, who said: The Messenger of God said, "Not one of you will take a prisoner from his brother and kill him." When the prisoners were brought Saʿd b. Muʿādh hated it. The Messenger of God said, "O Abū ʿAmr it seems the prisoners we have taken trouble you." He replied, "Yes, O Messenger of God, it is the first time we encounter the polytheists. I would like to overpower them, by God, and massacre them in battle."

Al-Naḍr b. al-Ḥārith was captured by al-Miqdād at that time. When the Messenger of God went out from Badr to al-Uthayl, the prisoners were displayed and he looked at al-Naḍr b. al-Ḥārith with a prolonged glance. Al-Naḍr said to a man at his side, "By God, Muḥammad will kill me, indeed, he looked at me with death in his eyes!" The man at his side said, "By God, what is this from you but fear." Al-Naḍr said to Muṣʿab b. ʿUmayr, "O Muṣʿab, you are the closest relative to me here. Speak to your companion to make me as a man among my companions." Muṣʿab replied, "Surely, you said thus and thus about the Book of God." He said, "O Muṣʿab let him treat me as he would treat one of my companions. If they are killed then I shall be killed. But if he is benevolent to them, let him be benevolent to me." Muṣʿab said, "Surely, you tortured his companions." He said, "By God, if the Quraysh capture you, you will never be killed as long as I live." Muṣʿab said, "By God, I see you speak the truth, [Page 107] but I am not like you. Islam has canceled my previous commitment." Miqdād said, "My prisoner!" The Prophet said, "Cut off his head. O God, reward al-Miqdād by your grace." ʿAlī b. Abī Ṭālib executed al-Naḍr at al-Uthayl.

When Suhayl b. ʿAmr was captured, ʿUmar said, "O Messenger of God, remove his incisors so that his tongue will hang out and he will not stand before you to speak ever." The Messenger of God said, "I will not mutilate him for God would then mutilate me even if I am a prophet. Perhaps he will stand at a place and you will not hate it." And when news of the death of the Prophet came to ʿUmar, Suhayl b. ʿAmr stood in Mecca with the speech of Abū Bakr given in Medina, as though he were listening to it. When the words of Suhayl reached ʿUmar, he said, "I witness that you are indeed the Messenger of God." He was referring to the words of the Prophet: "Perhaps he will stand at a place and you will not hate it."

ʿAlī used to relate saying; Gabriel came to the Prophet on the day of Badr, and gave him the choice, regarding the prisoners, of cutting off their heads, or taking a ransom for them, "on condition that there will be martyred among you the same number as those ransomed." The Messenger of God invited his companions and said: This is Gabriel and he gives you a choice regarding the captives: between cutting of their heads or taking a ransom from them on the condition that there will be martyred among you the same number as those ransomed." They said: Rather we will take the ransom and make use of it, and there will be martyrs among us and we will enter Paradise. So they received from them the ransom and the same number as those ransomed were killed among the Muslims at Uḥud.

They said: When the prisoners were captured in Badr, Shuqrān was employed to watch over them. The Muslims had cast lots regarding them, but the prisoners wanted to live. They said, "Let us send for Abū Bakr, for indeed he is the closest relative to the Quraysh. We do not know one who is more favored by Muḥammad than he. So they sent for Abū Bakr. [Page 108] When he came to them, they said, "O Abū Bakr, with us are your fathers, sons, brothers, uncles, and sons of uncles. The farthest of us is a relative to you. Speak to your companion so that he will be kind to us and permit the payment of our ransom." He replied, "Yes, if God wills, I will stop at nothing for your good." Then he turned back to the Prophet. They said, "Send to ʿUmar b. al-Khaṭṭāb, for indeed it is he whom you have known. We cannot guarantee that he will not spoil your plan. Perhaps he will abstain from you." So they sent for him, and he came to them and they said to him as they said to Abū Bakr, and he replied, "I will never desist from harming you." Then he turned to the Prophet, and he found Abū Bakr and the people around him. Abū Bakr was appeasing him, saying, "O Messenger of God you are both father and mother to me. Your people have with them fathers, sons, uncles, brothers, and the sons of our uncles. The most distant of them is a close relative of yours. Be kind to them, and God will be kind to you. Or leave them, God will save them with you from the fire, and you will take from them, as ransom, what will empower the Muslims. Perhaps God will bring their hearts to you." Then he stood up and turned aside. The Prophet was silent and he did not answer him. Then ʿUmar came and he sat on the seat of Abū Bakr. ʿUmar said, "O Messenger of God they are the enemy of God. They did not believe in you and they fought you and expelled you. Cut off their heads. They are the leaders of the polytheists and the guides of the false. God most high will put them down with Islam, and humiliate the people of polytheism." The Prophet was silent and did not answer him. Abū Bakr returned to his seat, and said, "O Messenger of God, you are my father and mother. Your people have with them our fathers, sons, uncles, brothers, and the sons of uncles. The most distant of them is a close relative. Be kind to them and take their ransom. They are your community and family. Do not be the first to destroy them. God will guide them, and that is better than you destroying them." The Prophet was silent and did not answer him. And Abū Bakr turned aside. Then

ʿUmar got up and sat in his seat and said, "O Messenger of God, what are you waiting for? Cut off their heads and God will put them down with Islam, and humiliate the people of polytheism. They are the enemies [Page 109] of God. They did not believe in you, and they fought you and exiled you! O Messenger of God, heal the hearts of the believers. If they had similar power over us they would not release us, ever." The Messenger of God was silent and he did not answer him. So ʿUmar stood up and sat aside. And Abū Bakr came forward and spoke words similar to what he had said before. And the Prophet did not reply. And he sat aside. Then ʿUmar stood up and spoke words similar to what he had said before. The Prophet did not answer him. He stood up and entered his tent, and he stayed there a while.

The Prophet came out, and the people were engrossed in their affair, some of them saying the words that Abū Bakr said and others saying what ʿUmar said. When the Messenger of God came out he said, "What do you say about these two companions of yours? Recall their parallels, for surely they have a parallel. The parallel of Abū Bakr is Mīkā'īll who revealed the satisfaction of God and His forgiveness of his servants. He compared him with prophets, such as Ibrahīm, who was gentler than honey to his people, yet his people ignited a fire for him and threw him in it. He did not say more than this: *Woe unto you, why do you worship other than God? Have you no sense* (Q. 21:67)? And he said: *Who follows me is of me, and who disobeys me, but indeed Thou art oft forgiving, most merciful* (Q. 14:36). And he compared him to Jesus when he says: *If You hurt them, surely they are Your slaves; if You forgive them surely You are the most mighty, most wise* (Q. 5:118).

The Messenger of God compared ʿUmar with angels such as Gabriel who reveals about the displeasure of God and the revenge against the enemies of God. He compared ʿUmar with prophets such as Noah who emphasized to his people about the stones when he says: He was firmer than stones against his people. O my lord, *leave not of the unbelievers a single one on earth* (Q.16:26). He prayed against them a prayer, and God flooded the earth, all of it. And he compared ʿUmar to Moses when he says: *O Lord, destroy their wealth and harden their hearts for they will not believe until they see grievous pain* (Q. 11:88). Surely you are needy. A man from among these shall not escape except with a ransom or the cutting off of his head.

[Page 110] ʿAbdullah b. Masʿūd said, "O Messenger of God, except for Suhayl b. Bayḍā' (Ibn Wāqid says that this is an error; Suhayl b. Bayḍā' was among those who emigrated to Abyssinia, he did not witness Badr. Rather it was a brother of his named Sahl), for I saw him proclaim Islam in Mecca." The Prophet was silent and did not answer him. ʿAbdullah said: Never did an hour pass by me that was more terrible than that hour. I began to look at the heavens fearing that the stones would fall upon me, for the words I put forward before God and His Messenger. The Messenger of God raised his head and said, "Except for Suhayl b. Bayḍā'!" He said: And an hour that gave me greater pleasure has not passed by me since the Messenger of God said that. Then the Messenger of God said, "Surely God most High is capable of strengthening the heart until it will be stronger than the stones. And indeed He is able to melt hearts until it will be the softest of butter." The Prophet accepted ransom from them. The Messenger of God said, "If punishment were brought down on the day of Badr, no one would escape it except ʿUmar." He used to say, "Kill and do not take a ransom." Saʿd b. Muʿādh used to say the same.

Maʿmar related to me from al-Zuhrī from Muḥammad b. Jubayr b. Muṭʿim from his father, who said: The Messenger of God said on the day of Badr; "If Muṭʿim b. ʿAdī is living I would gift him these rotten Quraysh". Muṭʿim b. ʿAdī had a protection from the Prophet when he returned from al-Ṭāʾif.

Muḥammad b. ʿAbdullah related to me from al-Zuhrī from Saʿīd b. al-Musayyib, who said: Among the prisoners to whom the Messenger of God granted protection on the day of Badr was Abū ʿAzza ʿAmr b. ʿAbdullah b. ʿUmayr al-Jumahī. He was a poet. The Messenger of God set him free. [Page 111] He said, "I have five daughters who have nothing. Grant me life and be charitable to them, O Muḥammad." The Messenger of God did so. Abū ʿAzza said, "I give you my word that I will not fight you nor increase against you ever." The Messenger of God sent him back. But when the Quraysh went out to Uḥud, Ṣafwān b. Umayya came to him saying, "Come out with us" He replied, "I have given a promise to Muḥammad that I will not fight him nor increase against him ever. He was kind to me, and he was not kind to any other but rather killed him or took ransom from him." Ṣafwān guaranteed that he would keep his daughters with his own daughters if he were killed. And if he lived he would give him so much wealth that his debt would not consume it. So Abū ʿAzza went out calling the Arabs together. Then he went out with the Quraysh on the day of Uḥud. He was taken captive, and no other Qurayshī was taken captive. He said, "O Muḥammad, surely I went out, hating it. I have daughters and I am their guarantor." The Messenger of God said, "Where is what you gave me of promise and trust. No, by God, you will not wipe your two cheeks in Mecca to say, 'I made fun of Muḥammad a second time'"

Isḥāq b. Ḥāzm from Rabīʿa b. Yazīd from al-Zuhrī from Saʿīd b. al-Musayyib related to me saying; the Messenger of God said, "The believers will not be deceived twice. O ʿĀṣim b. Thābit send him ahead to his execution." So ʿĀṣim sent him ahead to be executed.

They said: On the day of Badr, the Prophet commanded that the graves be prepared; then he commanded that the dead be thrown in, all of them, except Umayya b. Khalaf for he was fat, swollen from his battle. When they tried to throw his body in, it disintegrated. The Prophet said, "Leave it." The Prophet looked at ʿUtba, a huge man with traces of small pox on his face, being dragged to the well, and he saw the face of ʿUtba's son, Abū Ḥudhayfa, change. [Page 112] The Prophet said, "O Abū Hudhayfa, are you saddened by what your father has reached?" He replied, "No, by God. But, Messenger of God, I saw that my father had an intellect and nobility. I hoped that God would guide him to Islam. And when that eluded him and I saw he did not take it, it irritated me." Abū Bakr said, "By God, O Messenger of God, he had a greater desire to stay than the others of the tribe; he detested going out. But it is destiny and the end of evil." The Messenger of God said, "Praise be to God who makes Abū Jahl low, and puts him down and saves us from him." When they were all in the grave, the Messenger of God went around them and they were on the ground. Abū Bakr informed him about them man by man. The Messenger of God praised God and thanked Him saying, "Praise be to God who fulfilled what He promised me. He promised me one of the two factions."

He said: Then the Messenger of God stopped before the people of the hole and called out to them man by man, "O ʿUtba b. Rabīʿa, O Shayba b. Rabīʿa, O Umayya b. Khalaf, O Abū Jahl b. Hishām, did your Lord give you what he promised you? Truly, I have found what my Lord promised me. Evil were your people and you to your prophet: You called me a liar, but my people trusted me. You exiled me, but my people protected me; you fought against me, but my people helped me." They said, "O Messenger of God, you are calling to a people who have died." The Messenger of God replied, "They knew that in truth their lord did not promise them."

They said: The defeat of the people took place after noon. The Messenger of God stayed at Badr and commanded ʿAbdullah b. Kaʿb to take the plunder and transport it. The Messenger of God commanded a group of his companions to help him. [Page 113] He prayed. ʿAsr in Badr then traveled through al-Uthayl (which is a valley that extends for a distance of three miles, and between Uthayl and Badr is a distance of two miles such that he spent the night four miles from Badr). He alighted there before sunset. He spent the night with his companions who had wounds, though not many.

He said to his companions, "Is there a man who will watch over us this night?" The people were silent. Then a man stood up. The Prophet said, "Who are you?" He replied, "Dhakwān b. ʿAbdQays." He said, "Be seated," and the Prophet repeated his words. A man stood up. And the Prophet asked, "Who are you?" He replied, "Ibn ʿAbdQays." The Prophet said, "Be seated." Then he stayed a while, and a man stood up. The Prophet said, "Who are you?" He replied, "Abū Sabūʿ." The Prophet stayed awhile and then said, "Stand up the three of you." Dhakwān b. Qays alone stood up. The Prophet asked, "Where are your companions?" He replied, "O Prophet, I am he who answered you this night." The Messenger of God said, "May God protect you." So Dhakwān watched over the Muslims until the end of the night; then he departed.

He said: It was said: The Prophet prayed ʿAsr in al-Uthayl, and when he prayed a bowing he smiled. When he said the greeting he was asked about the smile. He replied; "Mikāʾīl passed by me and there was dust on his wings. He smiled at me and said, 'Indeed I was in search of the people'." Gabriel came to him, at the end of his fighting the people of Badr, upon a female horse with knotted forelock and dust on its front teeth, saying, "O Muḥammad, my Lord sent me to you and He commanded me not to leave you until you are satisfied. Are you satisfied?" The Messenger of God replied, "Yes."

The Messenger of God approached with the prisoners until he was in ʿIrq [Page 114] al-Ẓabya, he commanded ʿĀṣim b. Thābit b. Abū l-Aqlaḥ to cut off the head of ʿUqba b. Abī Muʿayṭ. ʿAbdullah b. Salama al-ʿAjlānī had taken him prisoner. ʿUqba began to say, "O woe is me, for what reason will I be killed, O people of the Quraysh, among those who are over here?" The Messenger of God said, "For your enmity to God and His Prophet." He said, "O Muḥammad, grant me your favor and do for me as you would to one of my people. If you kill them, kill me, and if you are kind to them, be kind to me, and if you take ransom from them, let me be one of those. O Muḥammad, who will take care of the youth?" The Messenger of God said, "Fire. Lead him, O ʿĀṣim, and cut off his head." ʿĀṣim did so. The Messenger of God said, "Miserable is the man that you were, and by God, I do not know one who rejects God and His Messenger, and His Book, and was more harmful to his Prophet. I praise God who kills you and establishes my satisfaction over you." When they embarked at Sayar, a pass at al-Ṣafrāʾ, the Messenger of God apportioned what was captured from them among his companions. This was related to me by Muḥammad b. Yaḥyā b. Sahl b. Abī Ḥathma from his father, from his grandfather.

The Messenger of God sent Zayd b. Ḥāritha and ʿAbdullah b. Rawāḥa ahead of him from al-Uthayl. They arrived on Sunday before noon. Then ʿAbdullah departed from Zayd to al-ʿAqīq. ʿAbdullah began to call out from atop his riding beast, "O people of the Anṣār, rejoice in the peace of the Prophet and the death of the polytheists and his capture of them. The two sons of Rabīʿa, the two sons of al-Ḥajjāj and Abū Jahl are killed. Zamaʿa b. al-Aswad and Umayya b. Khalaf are killed. Suhayl b. ʿAmr, possessor of the old camels, is captured with many prisoners. ʿĀṣim b. ʿAdī said: I stood up and went to him and said, "Is it true what you say, O Ibn Rawāḥa?" He replied, "Indeed, and by God, tomorrow the Prophet will arrive, God willing, with the prisoners, chained to each other." Then he continued on to the land of the Anṣār at al-ʿĀliya [Page 115]—at al-ʿĀliya are houses of the Banū ʿAmr b. ʿAwf, the Khaṭma and the Wāʾil—and proclaimed the good news to them, house by house. The youths hastened with him saying, "Abū Jahl the corrupt one is dead!" until they finally reached the Banū Umayya b. Zayd."

Zayd b. Ḥāritha arrived on the camel of the Prophet, al-Qaswāʾ and announced the good news to the people of Medina. When he arrived at al-Musallā he shouted from his riding beast, "ʿUtba and Shayba the sons of Rabīʿa, the sons of al-Ḥajjāj, Abū Jahl, Abū l-Bakhtarī, Zamaʿa b. al-Aswad and Umayya b. Khalaf are killed. Suhayl b. ʿAmr, the owner of the old she-camels has been taken prisoner along with many prisoners." The people did not believe Zayd b. Ḥaritha. They were saying: Zayd did not arrive except as one who is defeated! Until the Muslims became angry, and they were afraid.

Zayd arrived as they grieved, having buried the daughter of the Prophet, Ruqayya, in the ground of al-Baqīʿ. One of the Hypocrites said to Usāma b. Zayd, "Your companion and those who were with him are killed." Another from the Hypocrites said to Abū Lubāba b. ʿAbd al-Mundhir "Your companions have dispersed such that you will never meet them again. Muḥammad and the more prominent of his companions are killed, and this is his camel and we know it. This Zayd does not know what he says for fear. He comes defeated." Abū Lubāba said, "God will refute your words." The Jews said, "Zayd did not come except in defeat."

Usāma b. Zayd said: I approached until I was alone with my father and I said, "O Father is it true what you say?" He replied, "Indeed, and by God it is true, my dear son." I became strong in my heart and returned to that hypocrite and said, "You spread falsehood about the Messenger of God and the Muslims. The Messenger of God will surely approach you when he arrives and behead you." He replied, "O Abū Muḥammad, surely it is something I heard the people say."

Shuqrān arrived with the prisoners, watching over them. There were forty-nine men whom I counted, and they were [Page 116] seventy in the beginning. All confirmed it, and there was no doubt about it. Shuqrān the slave of the Prophet was employed over them. He had witnessed Badr and he was not free at that time. The people met him and congratulated him about the conquest of God. The nobility of the Khazraj met him. Salama b. Salāma b. Waqash said, "What is it that you are congratulating us about. By God, we only killed bald old men." The Prophet smiled. He said, "O son of my brother, those were the elite; if you had seen them you would have feared them; if they had ordered you, you would have followed them; if you had compared your acts with theirs you would consider them unworthy. Miserable are people who do that to their Prophet." Salama said, "I seek refuge from God against His anger and the anger of His Prophet. Surely, you, O Prophet of God, keep turning away from me since we were in al-Rawḥāʾ in our beginning." The Messenger of God said, "As for what you said to the Bedouin—'You fell upon your camel and it is impregnated by you'—you are shameless and you speak of what you do not know. As for what you said about the people, surely you undertook to excel from God's goodness, and you have been miserly about it." Salama apologized to the Prophet, and the Prophet accepted his apology. Salama was among the chosen of the Prophet's companions.

Muḥammad b. ʿAbdullah related to me from al-Zuhrī, saying: Abū Hind al-Bayāḍī, the *mawlā* of Farwa b. ʿAmr, met him and he had a receptacle full of a date-sweet. The

Messenger of God said, "Surely Abū Hind is a man from the Anṣār, so give him in marriage." So they gave him in marriage.

Ibn Abī Sabra related to me from ʿAbdullah b. Abī Sufyān, who said; Usayd b. Ḥuḍayr met him and he said, "O Messenger of God, praise be to God who grants you victory, and gladdens you. By God, O Messenger of God, I did not stay behind from Badr thinking that you would meet the enemy. [Page 117] I thought that it was the caravan. If I thought it was an enemy I would not have stayed behind". The Messenger of God said, "You speak the truth." ʿAbdullah b. Nūḥ related to me from Khubayb b. ʿAbd al-Raḥmān, who said: ʿAbdullah b. Unays met him in Turbān, and he said, "O Messenger of God, praise be to God and peace upon you. What success He has granted you! I, O Messenger of God, was attacked by fever on the night you departed. It did not leave me until yesterday, and I came to you." He said, "May God reward you!"

When Suhayl b. ʿAmr was in Shanūka—and it is between al-Suqyā and Malal—he was with Mālik b. al-Dukhshum (who had captured him). He said, "Set me free that I may excrete. So he stood up with him and Suhayl said, "I am embarrassed, so stay away from me." So he stayed away from him, and he let Suhayl move away. Suhayl pulled his hand away from the chain and escaped. When Suhayl delayed to return, Mālik came forward and shouted to the people, "Go out in search of Suhayl." The Prophet went out seeking him. He said, "Whoever finds him, kill him." The Messenger of God found him. He had concealed himself between some Samura trees. He commanded that his hands be tied to his neck. Then he bound him to his riding beast. But he did not ride a step until Usāma b. Zayd arrived in Medina.

Isḥāq b. Ḥāzm related to me from ʿAbdullah b. Muqsam from Jābir b. ʿAbdullah, who said: [Page 118] The Messenger of God met Usāma b. Zayd while the Messenger of God was on his camel al-Qaṣwāʾ. He seated Usāma in front of him, while Suhayl was at his side his hands tied to his neck. When Usāma looked at Suhayl he said, "O Messenger of God, it is Abū Yazīd." The Prophet said, "Yes, this is he who used to serve the bread in Mecca."

ʿAbd al-Raḥmān b. ʿAbd al-ʿAzīz related to me from ʿAbdullah b. Abī Bakr b. Ḥazm from Yaḥyā b. ʿAbdullah from ʿAbd al-Raḥmān b. Saʿd b. Zurāra, who said: When the Messenger of God arrived in Medina, he arrived with the prisoners. Sawda bt. Zamaʿa was with the family of ʿAfrāʾ, lamenting over ʿAwf and Muʿawwidh. That was before the veil was established. Sawda said: He came to us, and said, "Those are the prisoners, I have brought them." I went out to my house and the Messenger of God was in it. And lo and behold, Abū Yazīd was also assembled, his hands tied to his neck, near my house. And by God, I was so deeply affected when I saw him there, his hands tied to his neck, that I said, "Abū Yazīd: You gave with your two hands! Will you not die nobly?" And by God, I was taken aback by the words of the Prophet from the house, "O Sawda, are you against God and His Prophet?" I said, "O Prophet of God, by Him who sent you with the truth, you are a prophet. I forgot myself when I saw Abū Yazīd bound, with his hands tied to his neck, that I said what I did."

Khālid b. Ilyās related to me saying: Abū Bakr b. ʿAbdullah b. Abī Jahm related to me saying: Khālid b. Hishām b. al-Mughīra and Umayya b. Abī Ḥudhayfa b. al-Mughīra entered the house of Umm Salama, and Umm Salama was lamenting the family of ʿAfrāʾ when it was said to her, "The prisoners are come." So she went out and entered upon them, but she did not speak to them until after she returned. She found the Messenger of God [Page 119] in the house of ʿĀʾisha, and she said, "O Messenger of God, surely the sons of my uncle seek to visit me, and I to receive them. I would anoint their heads, and restore them to good condition. But I do not like to do that until I have sought your permission." The Messenger of God said, "I do not disapprove of any of that, do what you think is best."

Muḥammad b. ʿAbdullah informed me from al-Zuhrī saying: the Messenger of God said, "Be good to the prisoners." Abū l-ʿĀṣ b. al-Rabīʿ said, "I was with a group of the Anṣār, may God reward them, and when we were eating dinner or breakfast they preferred the bread for me while they ate the dates—they had less bread and more dates with them. Even if the man found a fragment in his hand he pushed it to me. Al-Walīd b. al-Walīd b. al-Mughīra used to say similar to that and more. They used to carry us on the rides while they walked. Muḥammad b. ʿAbdullah related to me from al-Zuhrī, who said that the prisoners arrived one day before the Prophet. Some said that they arrived at the end of the day on which the Prophet arrived.

They said: When the polytheists directed themselves to Badr there were two youths who stayed behind from them chatting through the night. They talked in Dhū Ṭuwan in the moonlight until the night was gone. They sang poetry while they talked. They were thus by night until they heard a voice close to them, but they did not see the speaker who raised his voice, singing:

> The Hanīfiyyūn brought Misfortune to Badr
> That will demolish the pillars of Kisra and Caesar
> The solid mountains observed it
> The tribes between al-Watīr and Khaybar were frightened.
> [Page 120] It crossed the two Mountains of Akhshab
> And the free women were exposed striking their bare breasts.

ʿAbdullah b. Abī ʿUbayda informed me from Muḥammad b. ʿAmmār b. Yāsir, who said: They listened to the voice but could not see anyone. They went out in search of it but did not see anyone. They went out fearful until they crossed the Ḥijr and found a group of elders and among them were excellent conversationalists. They informed them of the news and they said to them, "If what you say is true, surely Muḥammad and his companions are named Ḥanīfiyya," and they did not know the name Ḥanīfiyya at that time. One did not remain among the two youths in Dhū Ṭuwan unless he fell sick.

They had only stayed two or three nights when al-Ḥaysumān b. Ḥābis al-Khuzāʿī arrived with news about the people of Badr and those who were killed among them. He informed them of the death of ʿUtba and Shayba the sons of Rabīʿa and the two sons of al-Ḥajjāj, and Abū l-Bakhtarī and Zamaʿa b. al-Aswad. He said: Ṣafwān b. Umayya was seated in al-Ḥijr and saying, "He does not know what he is talking about. Ask him about me." They said, "Ṣafwān b. Umayya, do you have information about him?" He replied, "Yes, that man is in al-Ḥijr. Surely I saw his father and his brother killed." He said, "I saw Suhayl b. ʿAmr and Naḍr b. al-Ḥārith taken captive." They said, "How did you know that?" He said, "I saw them linked together with ropes."

They said: The killing of the Quraysh of Mecca and how God gave victory to His Prophet reached al-Najjāshī. So he went out with two white garments, sat on the ground, then called for Jaʿfar b. Abī Ṭālib and his companions and said, "Which of you knows Badr?" So they informed him. Al-Najjāshī (the Negus) said, "I am acquainted with it. [Page 121] I used to graze sheep at its side. It is a part of a day's journey from the coast. But I desire to confirm my information with you. God gave victory to His

Prophet at Badr. I praise God about that." Baṭāriq said to him, "May God restore the king! Surely this is something you should not do, putting on two garments and sitting on the ground!" Najjāshi said, "Indeed, I am from a people who when God establishes goodness for them are more humbled." It was said that he said that whenever good news was conveyed to ʿĪsā son of Maryam, he became more humble.

When the Quraysh returned to Mecca, Abū Sufyān b. Ḥarb stood before them and said, "O people of the Quraysh, do not cry over your dead; mourners, do not lament over them; poets, do not weep over them. Appear patient and composed, for if you lament and cry over them with poetry, that anger of yours will leave, and the enmity against Muḥammad and his companions will be blunted, and if your mourning reached Muḥammad and his companions they would rejoice in your misfortune. The greatest pain will give them joy. Perhaps you will achieve your revenge. Oil and my women are forbidden to me until I have raided Muḥammad." The Quraysh waited a month, and poets did not cry nor mourners lament over them.

When the prisoners arrived, God humbled the disbelievers, the Hypocrites and the Jews. There did not remain a Jew or a hypocrite in Medina but he had submitted because of the battle of Badr. ʿAbdullah b. Nabtal said: I wish that we had gone with him and won spoils of war. God separated in their dawn disbelief from faith. The Jews among them said to each other: This is what is described in the Torah. By God, a flag will not be raised for him after this day but it will be victorious. Kaʿb b. al-Ashraf said, "Today, the bowels of the earth are better than the earth above. Those are the nobles of the people, and their lords, the kings of the Arabs, the people of sanctuary and protection. They have been taken." He went out to Mecca and alighted on Abū [Page 122] Wadāʿa b. Ḍubayra, and began to dispatch the insults of the Muslims to the heirs of the dead among the Quraysh. dead of Badr from the Quraysh. He sent these verses saying:

Badr's mill ground out the blood of its people
At events like Badr you should weep and cry.
The best of the people were slain around its cisterns,
Don't think it strange that the Kings are being killed.
Some people whose anger humiliates me say
Kaʿb b. al-Ashraf is utterly afraid.
They speak the truth. O that the earth when they were killed
Had split asunder and engulfed its people.
I was told that Ḥārith b. Ḥishām
Is doing well and gathering troops
To visit Yathrib with armies
For only that noble handsome man protects the ancient reputation.

Al-Wāqidī said: ʿAbdullah b. Jaʿfar, Muḥammad b. Ṣāliḥ, and Ibn Abī Zinād recited it to me. They said: The Messenger of God invited Ḥassān b. Thābit al-Anṣārī and informed him of Kaʿb's stay in the home of Abū Wadāʿa. He insulted those who stayed with him until Kaʿb returned to Medina. When he sent these verses the people took them from him and publicized the dirge. He made those whom he met among the youth and slaves recite these verses in Mecca. The Quraysh mourned over their dead with that poetry until there did not remain a house in Mecca but there was mourning in it. The women cut their hair, and the camel or horse of one of the men would be brought and they would lament around it. The women went out to the streets and put curtains in the alleys and the roads to set aside areas for mourning and crying. They believed the dream of ʿĀtika and Juhaym b. al-Ṣalt.

Al-Aswad b. al-Muṭṭalib had lost his sight and he was distressed about who was killed [Page 123] from among his sons. He wanted to cry over his son, but the Quraysh would not let him. He used to say to his slave, every other day, "Carry some wine and take me to the pass which Abū Ḥukayma took." So he took him on the road to Fajj, and there he drank until he was intoxicated, then he cried over Abū Ḥukayma and his brothers. Then he scattered dust on his head saying to his slave, "Woe unto you, conceal what you know of me from the Quraysh. Indeed I do not see them gather to cry over their dead."

Muṣʿab b. Thābit related to me from ʿĪsā b. Maʿmar from ʿAbbād b. ʿAbdullah b. Zubayr, from ʿĀʾisha, who said: The Quraysh said, when they returned after the people of Badr were killed to Mecca, "Do not cry over your dead for it will reach Muḥammad and his companions and they will rejoice over your misfortune. Do not send for your prisoners for the people will be hard on you; and stop crying."

ʿĀʾisha said: al-Aswad b. al-Muṭṭalib lost three of his sons, Zamaʿa, ʿAqīl and al-Ḥārith b. Zamaʿa and he wanted to mourn their death. While he was thus, he heard a lament from the night, and he said to his slave, for he had lost his sight, "Do the Quraysh cry over their dead? Perhaps I will cry over Abū Ḥukayma, meaning Zamaʿa. Indeed, my stomach burns." His slave went and returned to him and said, "Surely it is a woman crying over her camel that she has lost." That was when he said:

Does she weep because she lost her camel?
And does this keep her awake all night?
Weep not over a young camel.
But over Badr where cheeks were servile.
Weep, if you must weep, over Aqīl
Weep for Ḥārith the lion of lions
[Page 124] Weep for all of them and never get bored
For Abū Ḥakīma who had no peer.
Over Badr the finest sons of Ḥuṣayṣ
And Makhzūm and the clan of Abū l-Walīd.
Did not men become lords after them? If not for
The day of Badr they (Muḥammad and his companions) would not be lords.

Ibn Abī l-Zinād informed me saying: I heard my father recite: The cheeks were servile. He does not deny the use of "the ancestors" in place of "the cheeks," however.

They said: The women of the Quraysh walked to Hind bt. ʿUtba and said, "Will you not cry over your father and your brothers and your uncles and the people of your house?" She replied, "May God afflict your throat! Shall I cry over them so it will reach Muḥammad and his companions and the women of the Khazraj, so they will rejoice over our misfortune? No, by God, not until I am revenged of Muḥammad and his companions. Oil is forbidden to me, even if my Lord enters, until we raid Muḥammad. By God, if I knew that the sorrow would leave my heart I would cry. But it will not leave unless I see my revenge before me for the death of the beloved ones." She stayed in that condition and oil was not brought near her nor did she go to the bed of Abū Sufyān from the day she took her oath until the battle of Uḥud.

It reached Nawfal b. Muʿāwiya al-Dīlī while he was with his family, and he had witnessed Badr with them, that the Quraysh wept over their dead. When he arrived he said, "O people of the Quraysh, surely your forbearance has decreased, your decision was stupid and you obey your women. Do the likes of your dead deserve to be mourned? They deserve more than tears. Moreover, tears will make your anger depart from your enmity against Muḥammad and his companions. Your anger should not leave you unless your revenge reaches your enemy." Abū Sufyān b. Ḥarb heard his words and said, "O Abū Muʿāwiya, by God, you are defeated. Women of the Banū ʿAbdShams have not wept over the dead until today. A poet does not make them weep [Page 125] for I forbid it until our revenge reaches Muḥammad and his companions. Indeed, I am the furious wronged by the loss of sons and relatives. My son Ḥanzala and the lords of this valley have been killed, and this valley trembles for their loss."

Muʿādh b. Muḥammad al-Anṣārī informed me from ʿĀṣim b. ʿUmar b. Qatāda saying: When the polytheists returned to Mecca and their brave ones and nobility were dead, ʿUmayr b. Wahb b. ʿUmayr al-Jumaḥī approached and sat down with Ṣafwān b. Umayya in the Ḥijr. Ṣafwān b. Umayya said, "God has disfigured life after the battle of Badr." ʿUmayr b. Wahb replied, "Yes indeed! By God, there is no goodness in life after this. If I had no debt to settle, and no family for which I should put away something, I would ride to Muḥammad and kill him if I would recognize him. It has reached me that he is going around the markets, and indeed, a son of mine is with them. I will say, 'I have come for my son, this prisoner.'" Ṣafwān laughed about his saying that. He said, "O Abū Umayya will we see you act?" He replied, "Indeed, by the Lord of this building." Ṣafwān said, "Then to me is your debt repaid. Your family is like my family; and you know that there is not a man more generous to his family, in Mecca, than I." ʿUmayr replied, "I know about that O Abū Wahb." Ṣafwān said, "And surely your family will be with my family; I will share all that I get with them. And your debt is mine." Ṣafwān gave him a camel and prepared him; and he did for ʿUmayr's family as he did for his own.

ʿUmayr ordered that his sword be sharpened and touched with poison. Then he went out to Medina, saying to Ṣafwān, "Be silent about me for some days until I reach Medina." He went away, and Ṣafwān did not mention it. ʿUmayr arrived in Medina, alighted at the gate of the Mosque, and tied his beast. He took his sword and girded it. Then he went towards the Prophet. ʿUmar b. al-Khaṭṭāb who was with a group of his companions conversing and mentioning the kindness of God towards them at Badr, saw ʿUmayr wearing his sword, [Page 126] and was alarmed by it. He said to his companions, "Take this dog! This is the enemy of God who incited against us on the day of Badr. He evaluated us for the people, he observed us and aimed. He informed the Quraysh that we were few and powerless." So the Muslims went up to him and held him, while ʿUmar rushed to the Prophet saying, "O Messenger of God, this is ʿUmayr b. Wahb who enters the mosque wearing weapons. He is treacherous and disgusting and one who is not to be trusted about anything!" The Prophet said, "Bring him to me." ʿUmar went out; he took the girder of his sword and placed his hand upon it, and with his other hand he held the hilt of the sword. Then he brought ʿUmayr before the Prophet. When the Messenger of God saw him he said, "O ʿUmar, stay away from him." When ʿUmayr came close to the Prophet, he said, "Good Morning!" The Prophet replied, "God honored us with a better greeting. He made our greeting 'Peace.' It is the greeting of the people of Paradise." ʿUmayr replied, "Surely your tradition is new." The Prophet said to him, "God will compensate us with the good from it. But what brought you, O ʿUmayr?" He said, "I came for the prisoner with you, if you will deal with us about him. Surely you are of the same tribe and people." The Prophet said,

"What about the sword?" He replied, "May God make it the ugliest of swords. Has it enriched us with anything? Indeed I forgot it when I alighted, and it was around my neck. By my life I have other concerns apart from the sword!" The Messenger of God said to him, "Speak the truth. For what did you arrive?" He replied, "I approach only for the prisoner." The Messenger of God said, "Did you not make some stipulations to Ṣafwān b. Umayya in the Ḥijr?" ʿUmayr was alarmed. He said, "What did I stipulate to him?" He said, "You agreed to kill me to fulfill your debt while he supports your family, but God stood between me and you," ʿUmayr replied, "I testify that you are the Messenger of God and that you speak the truth; and I testify that there is no God but Allah. We did not believe you, O Messenger of God, about your [Page 127] inspiration and what came to you from the heavens. But surely this was a conversation between me and Ṣafwān, just as you describe, and no one knew of it other than myself and he. I ordered him to be silent about me and my journey, but God has informed you about it. I believe in God and His Messenger. I witness that you come with the truth. Praise God who drove me to this point."

The Muslims were happy when they heard of God's guidance to ʿUmayr. ʿUmar b. al-Khaṭṭab said, "Surely I preferred the pig to him, when he appeared, but in this hour he is more preferable to me than some of my children." The Prophet said, "Inform your brother of the Qur'ān and release his prisoner for him." ʿUmayr said, "O Messenger of God, indeed I was striving to extinguish the light of God, to Whom be praise that He guided me and permits me to meet with the Quraysh and invite them to God and Islam. Perhaps God will guide them and deliver them from destruction." So the Messenger of God permitted him, and ʿUmayr went out and arrived in Mecca.

Ṣafwān asked every rider approaching from Medina about ʿUmayr saying, "Is there any news from Medina?" And he says to the Quraysh, "Rejoice in a time when you will forget the battle of Badr." A man approached from Medina and Ṣafwān asked him about ʿUmayr and he replied, "He converted." And Ṣafwān cursed him, and the polytheists in Mecca cursed him saying, "ʿUmayr has converted!" Ṣafwān swore that he would never speak to him, and that he would be useless to him. He rejected ʿUmayr's family. ʿUmayr approached them in that situation and invited them to Islam. He informed them of the honesty of the Prophet, and many people converted with him.

Muḥammad b. Abī Ḥumayd from ʿAbdullah b. ʿAmr b. Umayya related to me saying: When ʿUmayr b. Wahb arrived, he alighted with his family and he did not approach Ṣafwān b. Umayya, but practiced Islam and invited people to it. It reached Ṣafwān and he said, "I knew when he did not begin with me before he went to his house; for surely he departed from my home. Indeed, he has suffered a set back. I will not speak to him intentionally ever. I will not be useful to him or his family with support ever. ʿUmayr went up to him while [Page 128] he was in the Ḥijr and said, "Abū Wahb!" But he turned away from him. ʿUmayr said, "You who are the lord of our lords, did you consider that we are worshiping stones and sacrificing to stones? Is this religion? I witness that there is no God but Allah and that Muḥammad is his servant and His messenger." Ṣafwān did not answer him a word.

THE PROVIDERS OF THE POLYTHEISTS AT BADR

The Providers from the ʿAbdManāf were: al-Ḥārith b. ʿĀmir b. Nawfal, Shayba and ʿUtba b. Rabīʿa. From the Banū Asad: Zamaʿa b. al-Aswad b. al-Muṭṭalib b. Asad, and Nawfal b. Khuwaylid b. al-ʿAdawiyya. From the Banū Makhzūm: Abū Jahl. From the Banū Jumaḥ: Umayya b. Khalaf. And from the Banū Sahm: Nubayh and Munabbih, the two sons of al-Ḥajjāj. He said: Saʿīd b. al-Musayyib used to say, "Everyone that I fed at Badr was killed." He said, "We disputed among us about them." This is confirmed with us. They mentioned a number of them including Suhayl, Abū l-Bakhtarī and others of them.

Hishām b. ʿUmāra related to me from ʿUthmān b. Abī Sulaymān from Nāfiʿ b. Jubayr b. Muṭʿim from his father, who said: I had approached the Prophet about the ransom of the prisoners, and I was lying down in the Mosque after ʿAṣar, when sleep overtook me. The prayer of Maghrib woke me, and I rose moved by the recitation of the Prophet during *Maghrib* (*wa l-Ṭūr*). I heard him reciting it until I left the mosque. It was the first time that Islam entered into my heart.

ʿAbdullah b. ʿUthmān b. Abī Sulaymān related to me from his father, saying: [Page 129] fourteen men from the Quraysh arrived with ransom for their companions. Shuʿayb b. ʿUbāda related to me from Bashīr b. Muḥammad b. ʿAbdullah b. Zayd, who said: Fifteen men arrived, and the first of them was al-Muṭṭalib b. Abī Wadāʿa, then the others arrived after him three nights later. Muḥammad b. Ṣāliḥ related to me from ʿĀṣim b. ʿUmar b. Qatāda from Yazīd b. al-Nuʿmān b. Bashīr from his father, who said: The Prophet of God made the ransom for the Battle of Badr four thousand for every man. Isḥāq b. Yaḥyā related to me saying, I asked Nāfiʿ b. Jubayr: How much was the ransom? He replied, "From the highest of them four thousand, to three thousand, to two thousand, to one thousand, to nothing for the people who had no money. The Prophet was kind to them."

The Messenger of God said concerning Abū Wadāʿa, "Surely he has an elegant son in Mecca who has money, and he will exceed his ransom." He provided a ransom of four thousand, and he was the first prisoner to be ransomed. The Quraysh said to his son al-Muṭṭalib, when they saw him prepare to go out to his father, "Do not hurry. Indeed we fear that you will spoil our chances with those of us he has imprisoned. Muḥammad will see how much we desire 'our prisoners' and increase the ransom against us. Indeed, you will find that all your people will not find the wealth that you find." He replied, "I will not go out until you go out." But he deceived them, and when they were heedless, he went out at night, eastwards, on his beast. He traveled for four nights to Medina, and he ransomed his father with four thousand.

The Quraysh blamed him about that. He said, "I could not leave my father a prisoner in the hands of the people while you sleep." Abū Sufyān b. Ḥarb said, "Indeed, this boy is young [Page 130] and opinionated. He has spoilt your chances. Indeed I, by God, have no ransom for ʿAmr b. Abī Sufyān, and either he stays a year, or Muḥammad will release him. By God, I am not the most needy among you, but I detest that what happens to me should affect you such that it will be hard for you. ʿAmr will be an example for you."

THE NAMES OF THOSE WHO APPROACHED ABOUT THE PRISONERS

From the Banū ʿAbdShams: al-Walīd b. ʿUqba b. Abī Muʿayṭ and ʿAmr b. al-Rabīʿ brother of Abū l-ʿĀṣ. From the Banū Naufal b. ʿAbdManāf: Jubayr b. Muṭʿim. From the ʿAbd al-Dār: Ṭalḥa b. Abī Ṭalḥa. From the Banū Asad: ʿUthmān b. Abī Hubaysh.

From the Banū Makhzūm: ʿAbdullah b. Abī Rabīʿa, Khālid b. al-Walīd, Hishām b. al-Walīd b. al-Mughīra, Farwa b. al-Sāʾib, and ʿIkrima b. Abī Jahl. From the Banū Jumaḥ: Ubayy b. Khalaf and ʿUmayr b. Wahb. From the Banū Sahm: al-Muṭṭalib b. Abī Wadāʿa and ʿAmr b. Qays. And from the Banū Mālik b. Ḥisl: Mikraz b. Ḥafṣ b. al-Akhyaf.

Al-Mundhir b. Saʿd related to me from ʿĪsā b. Maʿmar, from ʿAbbād b. ʿAbdullah from ʿĀʾisha, who said: When the people of Mecca sent the ransom for their prisoners, Zaynab, the daughter of the Prophet, sent the ransom for her husband, Abū l-ʿĀṣ b. al-Rabīʿ. She included with it a necklace of hers, which had belonged to Khadīja. It was said that it was made of Onyx of al-Ẓafār. Khadīja bt. Khuwaylid had given it to Zaynab when Abū l-ʿĀṣ consumated his marriage with her. When the Prophet saw the necklace, he recognized it and felt pity for her. [Page 131] He mentioned Khadija and asked God's blessings for her. He said, "If you deem it appropriate to release Zaynab's prisoner for her, and return her goods to her, you will do so." They said, "Yes, O Messenger of God." They released Abū l-ʿĀṣ b. al-Rabīʿ, and returned Zaynab's goods to her. The Prophet made Abū l-ʿĀṣ promise that he would set her free, and he promised.

ʿAmr b. al-Rabīʿ arrived with ransom for his brother. ʿAbdullah b. Jubayr b. al-Nuʿmān and his brother Khawwāt b. Jubayr were those who captured him.

THE MENTIONING OF THE QURĀN CHAPTER *AL-ANFĀL*

They ask you about the booty—He said: When the Messenger of God captured booty on the day of Badr, they disagreed. Each faction maintained that they had a better claim to it. This verse was revealed about it, and the blessed Lord says: *Surely, the believers are those who, when God is mentioned, are fearful in their hearts, and, when his verses are recited to them, their faith is strengthened*—He means: Their certainty is strengthened. According to His words: *They are the true believers*—He says: When your Lord commands you to go out to Badr, it is obligatory. Ibn Jurayj informed me from Muḥammad b. ʿAbbād b. Jaʿfar al-Makhzūmī about His words: *From your house*—He means: from Medina. And about His saying: *Indeed a faction of believers hated (to go out) and argued with you about the truth after what was made clear, as if they were driven to their death and they were observing*—People from his companions hated to go out with the Messenger of God to Badr. They said: We are few and it is not in our interests to go out, until there was a great dispute about that. Including His words: *Behold, God promised one of the two factions for you*—when the Messenger of God was outside Badr, the angel Gabriel alighted upon him and informed him of the march of the Quraysh. He desired their caravan. God promised him either their caravan or that he will meet with the Quraysh and take them. [Page 132] When they were in Badr, they met the water carriers and asked them about the caravan, and they informed them about the Quraysh. The Muslims did not desire that because of the fighting. They desired the caravan. And about His words: *God desired to confirm the truth with His words*—He says: He demonstrated faith. *He destroyed the disbelievers*—meaning those who were killed at Badr from among the Quraysh. *To confirm the truth*—meaning to demonstrate the truth. *Prove false the falsehood* that they came with. *If the guilty hated it*—meaning the Quraysh. *When you implored of your Lord for assistance, and He answered you, I will assist you with a thousand angels rank on rank*—meaning some of them follow some.

God made it only joyous—meaning the number of angels that God informed them (the believers) about, so that they would learn that God would help them. *When he covered you with drowsiness and gave you calmness from Himself*—He says he made you sleepy to make you feel secure. He flung it (drowsiness) in your hearts. *And there came down upon them rain from the heavens and you were cleansed with it*—referring to some who had become impure from wet dreams. *The filth of Satan was gone from you*—He says, one could pray without taking ablutions! *He strengthened your hearts*—with serenity. *And you planted your feet firmly*—It was a muddy place, but God made it firm. *When your Lord inspired the angels that I (God) am with you, and affirmed those who believed*—The angels took the form of the man who says: Be firm for they are nothing. *And the hearts of those who disbelieve were met with fear*—their hearts were pounding for they were beating like the pebbles that were thrown in the tub. *Strike above the necks*—meaning the necks. *Strike them in every fingertip*—hand and leg. *That is because they are hostile to God and His prophet*—He says they disbelieved in God and repudiated His prophet. And about His saying: *Thus you will taste it*—meaning the killing at Badr. *To the disbelievers is the torment of fire, when you meet those who disbelieve marching (against you)*, to His saying, *Miserable will be the outcome*—on the day of Badr especially. *And you will not kill them but God will kill them*—concerning the saying of a man from the companions of the Prophet: "I killed so and so."

[Page 133] *You did not aim when you aimed, but God aimed*—When the Prophet aimed with a handful of dust. *He tested the believers with a gracious trial*—meaning He helped them on the day of Badr. *If you pray for victory, victory will come to you*—referring to the words of Abū Jahl: "O God, he has cut off from the family/tribe and brings us what we do not know. So destroy him." *And if you desist*—for who remained among the Quraysh. *It will be good for you*—meaning to convert to Islam. *And if you return*—that is, to the battle, *so shall we*—that is, to kill you. *Not the least good will your forces be for you*—they said: we have a group in Mecca we shall raid him and the raid will take him. *O you, who believe, obey God and His Prophet and turn not away from Him when you hear Him*—meaning the call. This verse was revealed during the battle of Uḥud: God blamed them for it. *Betray not the trust in you nor misappropriate what is entrusted to you.* He says: Do not pretend, and return all of what has been entrusted to you. *Know that your wealth and your children are but a trial*—He says: when his wealth increases his trial is greater, for he may go beyond the limit with his wealth. If he has many children he thinks that he is respectable. And in His saying: *He makes for you a proof*: meaning an escape. *And remember those who disbelieved who plotted against you to convict you or kill you*: this was in Mecca before the *hijra*, when he [Muḥammad] desired to go out to Medina. *When you read to them Our verses they say, We have heard, if we wish we could say . . .* to the end of the verse. *Remember how they said, O God! If this is indeed the truth from You, rain down on us a shower of stones from the sky or send us a grievous penalty*: He said, that this speaker was Naḍr b. al-Ḥārith. God most High revealed about him, *Do they wish to hasten Our punishment? But when it descends into the open space, evil will be the morning for those who were warned*: the day of Badr. *But God was not for hurting them while you were with them*: meaning the people of Mecca. *Nor would he hurt them if they would ask for pardon*: meaning they are praying. Then he returned and he said, *But what plea do they have that God should not punish them*: meaning the defeat and the slaughter. And about His saying, *Taste the penalty for your disbelief*: referring to the day of Badr.

Surely those who disbelieve spend their wealth [Page 134] *to turn away from the path of*

God . . . to His saying, *Then they will be overcome*: Since they go out to Badr with regret and remorse. *Then they will be overcome*: they were killed at Badr. He says, *They will be gathered in hell. Say to those who disbelieve, if they desist (from unbelief) their past would be forgiven them*: God says, if they submit, their past actions would be forgiven them, and if they return, you will see who is killed at Badr. *Fight them until there is no more discord*: meaning there will be no disbelief. *And there will prevail faith in Allah*: meaning, Isāf and Nā'ila will not be mentioned. *And know that of that which you plunder of anything, to God and His Messenger, to those who are relatives, orphans, the needy, and the wayfarer is a fifth*: He says, that which is for God is for His Messenger, and that which is for relatives, is for the relatives of the Prophet of God. *And the revelation which we sent down to our servant on the day of testing, on the day of the meeting of the two forces*: meaning the day of Badr, he distinguished between the true and the false. *Remember you were on the nearer side*: meaning the companions of the Prophet, when they came down to Badr, and the disbelievers who were on the farther side, between them was a ditch of sand, and the escort, the escort of Abū Sufyān clung to the sea which was lower south than Badr. *If you had made a mutual appointment to meet, you would have failed in that appointment*: Clearly, a group would arrive before the other group, and they would not meet. *But God will accomplish a matter already enacted*: referring to the death of those who were killed at Badr. *For those who would perish would perish after a clear sign*: He says, he who was killed was killed for a clear reason, and he lives who lives among them for a clear reason. *Remember, God showed them in your dream as a few*: He said, the Prophet slept at that time, and they seemed few in his eyes. *If He had shown them to you as many you would have surely been discouraged*: He said, You would have been afraid. *You would have disputed*: He says you would have disagreed. *But God saved you*—meaning from a disagreement among you. *He knows the secrets of all hearts well*: meaning the weakness in your hearts. *O you who Believe, when you meet a foe be firm and remember God often*: meaning stay together, and do not flee or proclaim the *takbīr. And do not dispute lest you become discouraged and your power leaves you, and be patient*: meaning with the sword. He says: mention God in your hearts but do not proclaim aloud the *takbīr*. Indeed to proclaim during the battle is a sign of weakness.

[Page 135] *Be not like those who left from their homes with insolence and seen of men, while turning (men) from the way of God*: meaning the Quraysh who went out to Badr. *Remember Satan made their (sinful) acts seem alluring to them, and said: No one among men can overcome you this day* (Q. 8:48): these are the words of Surāqa b. Juʿsham who says about what they saw that Satan took his form at that time. *When the two forces came in sight*: meaning the Prophet and the Quraysh, Satan withdrew when he saw the angels kill and take prisoners. He said, *indeed I am clear of you; indeed I see what you do not see*: He saw the angels. *The Hypocrites and those in whose hearts is a sickness say that their religion has misled these people* (Q. 8:49): referring to a group who accepted Islam. So when the companions of the Prophet were reduced in their eyes, they fled. They said those words, and they were killed, disbelieving. *They strike their faces and their backs*: meaning their buttocks, but this was a figure of speech; al-Thawrī informed us about that from Abū Hāshim from Mujāhid from Usāma b. Zayd, from his father. *After the manner of the people of the Pharoah* (Q. 8:52): meaning, he acted like the people of the Pharoah. About his saying: *For the worst of beasts in the sight of God are those who reject him* (Q. 8:55) until his saying, *They have no fear (of God)* (Q. 8:56): meaning the Qaynuqāʿ, the Banū Naḍīr and the Qurayẓa. *If you gain mastery over them in war, disperse with them*: Kill them. *If you fear treachery from any group . . .* (Q. 8:58) to the end of the verse: This was revealed about the Banū Qaynuqāʿ. The Prophet marched to them with this verse. *Make ready your strength to the utmost of your power* (Q. 8:60): He said: Aim. *Including steeds of war*: He says, Take the horses that neigh and that you see. *And others besides, whom you may not know but whom God knows*—meaning Khaybar. *But if the enemy incline towards peace, do you incline to peace* (Q. 8:61), to the end of the verse: meaning the Qurayẓa. *Should they intend to deceive you, surely God is sufficient for you. It is He who strengthened you with His help*: meaning the Qurayẓa and the Naḍīr when they said we submit and will follow you. *O Apostle, God and those who follow you among the believers are sufficient for you* (Q. 8:64): about the battle. *If there were twenty among you who were patient* (Q. 8:65): [Page 136] This was revealed about Badr; then His words were abrogated. *For now, God has lightened for you (your task) for He knows that in you is a weakness and if there will be among you a hundred who are patient, they will overcome two hundred.* (Q. 8:66): The man came to defeat two men. *It is not fitting that an apostle have prisoners of war until he has thoroughly subdued the land* (Q. 8:67): meaning the capture of prisoners by Muslims on the day of Badr. *You desire the temporal goods* (Q. 8:67): He means the ransom. *But God desires the hereafter*: He desires that they be killed. If not for a Book (what was predetermined) from God a severe penalty would have reached you (Q. 8:68): He says that it anticipated the legality of plunder. *But now enjoy the lawful and good things that you took in war* (Q. 8:69): He said that plunder is lawful. *Those who believed and emigrated and fought for their faith with their property, and their persons in the cause of God as well as those who gave them asylum and help* (Q. 8:72): referring to the Quraysh who emigrated before Badr, and the Anṣār who gave them refuge and help. Does He not say, *As for those who believed but did not emigrate, you owe no duty of protection to them until they come into exile*: He says that there is not between you and them any inheritance until they emigrate. *But if they seek your aid in religion, it is your duty to help them except against a people with whom you have a mutual alliance.* (Q. 8:72): meaning a period and an agreement. *The unbelievers are protectors one of another; unless you do this there will be tumult and oppression on earth, and great mischief*: He says do not befriend one of the disbelievers, for some of them are friends of others. Then he abrogated the verse of inheritance. *But kindred by blood have prior rights against each other in the Book of God, verily God is acquainted with every thing.*

About His words: *We shall seize you with a mighty onslaught* (Q. 44:16): Refers to the day of Badr. *And it (the punishment) will be inevitable* (Q. 25:77): referring to the battle of Badr. *Or it will come to them, the penalty of a day of disaster* (Q. 22:55): the day of Badr. *Until we open on them a gate leading to severe punishment* (Q. 23:77): the day of Badr. *Their multitude will be put to flight and they will show their backs* (Q. 54:45) [Page 137]: the day of Badr. *It may well be that their term is drawing to an end* (Q. 7:185): It was only a little before the hour of Badr. *And leave me (alone to deal with) those in possession of the good things in life, who (yet) deny the truth, and bear with them for a little while* (Q. 73:11): It was revealed only a little before the time of Badr. *And grant me from Your presence an authority to help me* (Q.17:80): the day of Badr. *Be patient until God decides, for He is the best to decide* (Q.10:109): From before the day of Badr. *And if any do turn his back at that time* (Q. 8:16): He said that the day of Badr is special, it was determined for them that when twenty Muslims meet two hundred disbelievers, they must not flee. For, indeed, if they did not flee, they would conquer. Then God lightened it for them and said, *If there will be among you a hundred, patient, they will overcome two hundred* (Q. 8:66): the first was abrogated. Ibn ʿAbbās used to say, "Whoever fled from two, he is a deserter, but whoever fled from three, he is not a deserter." And this was about His saying, *Hast thou not turned thy vision to those who have changed the favor of God to blasphemy and caused their people to descend to the House of Perdition?* (Q.14:28): meaning the Quraysh on the day of Badr. About His words, *Until when we seize in punishment those of them who received the good things* (Q. 23:64): He said, with the swords on the day of Badr. *And we will make them taste of the penalty of this (life) prior to the supreme penalty* (Q. 32:21): He says: The sword on the day of Badr. Muḥammad b. Hilāl related to me from his father from Abū Hurayra about God's words, *We receive in punishment those who received the good things*: He said the day of Badr. Al-Thawrī related to us from ʿAlqama b. Marthad, from Mujāhid, saying: About the swords on the day of Badr. [Page 138] ʿUmar b. ʿUthmān al-Makhzūmī from ʿAbd al-Malik b. ʿUbayd from Mujāhid from Ubayy b. Kaʿb related to us about His words: *Or there comes to them the penalty of a day of disaster*: He said, The day of Badr.

A RECORD OF THOSE TAKEN CAPTIVE FROM THE POLYTHEISTS

Mūsā b. Muḥammad b. Ibrāhīm related to me from his father, who said, Muḥammad b. Ṣāliḥ related to me from ʿĀṣim b. ʿUmar b. Qatāda, and from Maḥmūd b. Labīd who both said: From the Banū Hāshim, ʿAqīl b. Abī Ṭālib was taken prisoner. Maḥmūd said, ʿUbayd b. Aws al-Ẓafarī took him prisoner. Jabbār b. Ṣakhr captured both Nawfal b. al-Ḥārith and ʿUtba of the Banū Fihr who were allies of the Banū Hāshim.

ʿĀ'idh b. Yaḥyā related to me from Abū Ḥuwayrith, saying: Two men were taken from the Banū al-Muṭṭalib b. ʿAbdManāf: al-Sā'ib b. ʿUbayd and ʿUbayd b. ʿAmr b. ʿAlqama. They were both taken by Salama b. Aslam b. Ḥarīsh al-Ashhalī. Ibn Abī Ḥabība related to me about that from ʿAbd al-Raḥmān b. ʿAbd al-Raḥmān al-Anṣārī. No one came for them, nor did they own any property. The Messenger of God released both of them without any ransom.

From the Banū ʿAbdShams b. ʿAbdManāf, ʿUqba b. Abī Muʿayṭ, who was executed at Ṣafrā. ʿĀṣim b. Thābit b. Abī l-Aqlaḥ killed him on the order of the Prophet. ʿAbdullah b. Salama al-ʿAjlānī took him prisoner. And, al-Ḥārith b. Abī [Page 139] Wajza. Saʿd b. Abī Waqqāṣ took him prisoner. Al-Walīd b. ʿUqba b. Abī Muʿayṭ arrived with his ransom. He ransomed him for four thousand dirhams. Muḥammad b. Yaḥyā b. Sahl related to me from Abū ʿUfayr, that when the Prophet commanded the return of the prisoners, Saʿd b. Abī Waqqāṣ returned him. Saʿd took him prisoner the first time, then they cast lots about him and he came to Saʿd, as well. ʿAmr b. Abī Sufyān came with the arrow of the Prophet in casting lots. ʿAlī had taken him prisoner. The Prophet set him free, without a ransom, in exchange for Saʿd b. al-Nuʿmān b. Akkāl of the Banū Muʿāwiya, who had set out for *ʿUmra* but was imprisoned in Mecca. And, Abū l-ʿĀṣ b. al-Rabīʿ who was captured by Khirāsh b. Ṣimma. Isḥāq b. Khārij b. ʿAbdullah related to me about it from his father. He said: ʿAmr b. al-Rabīʿ approached with the ransom for his brother, and an ally of theirs called Abū Rīsha also came for him. Amr b. Rabīʿ paid the ransom. ʿAmr b. al-Azraq who had come in fulfillment of the portion of Mawlā Khirāsh b. al-Ṣimma was also redeemed by ʿAmr b. al-Rabīʿ. Then there was ʿUqba b. al-Ḥārith al-Haḍramī, who was captured by ʿUmāra b. Ḥazm. ʿUqba came as the portion of Ubayy b. Kaʿb. ʿAmr b. Sufyān b. Umayya paid his ransom. Abū l-ʿĀṣ b. Nawfal b. ʿAbdShams who was captured by ʿAmmār b. Yāsir; his cousin arrived with his ransom.

And from the Banū Nawfal b. ʿAbdManāf: ʿAdī b. al-Khiyār, who was captured by Khirash b. al-Ṣimma—Ayyūb b. Nuʿmān told me about that; ʿUthmān b. ʿAbdShams the nephew of ʿUtba b. Ghazwān an ally of Banū Nawfal who was captured by Ḥārith b. al-Nuʿmān; and Abū Thaur. Abū Marthad al-Ghanawī took him prisoner—Jubayr b. Muṭʿim paid their ransom. A total of three.

[Page 140] From the ʿAbd al-Dār b. Quṣayy: Abū ʿAzīz b. ʿUmayr. Abū l-Yasar took him prisoner, but then when lots were cast he went to Muḥriz b. Naḍla. Abū ʿAzīz, the brother of Muṣʿab b. ʿUmayr, who was ransomed by his parents. Muṣʿab said to Muḥriz, strengthen your hand with him for indeed, his mother has much wealth in Mecca. Abū ʿAzīz said to Muṣʿab, "Is this how you take care of me, my brother?" Muṣʿab replied, "Indeed, leaving you aside, he is my true brother in Islam." His mother sent four thousand dirhams for him. That was after she said: Declare what the Quraysh would pay for him, and it was said to her, four thousand. And, al-Aswad b. ʿĀmir b. al-Ḥārith b. al-Sabbāq. Ḥamza b. ʿAbd al-Muṭṭalib took him prisoner. Ṭalḥa b. Abī Ṭalḥa arrived with their ransom. A total of three.

From the Banū Asad b. ʿAbd al-ʿUzza: al-Sāʾib b. Abī Ḥubaysh b. Muṭṭalib b. Asad was captured by ʿAbd al-Raḥmān b. ʿAwf; al-Ḥārith b. ʿĀʾidh b. Asad was captured by Ḥāṭib b. Abū Baltaʿa; and Sālim b. Shammākh was captured by Saʿd b. Abī Waqqāṣ. ʿUthmān b. Abī Ḥubaysh ransomed them with four thousand for all three men.

From the Banū Taym, Mālik b. ʿAbdullah b. ʿUthmān was captured by Quṭba b. ʿĀmir b. Ḥadīda. He died in Medina in captivity.

From the Banū Makhzūm: Khālid b. Hishām b. al-Mughīra was captured by Sawād b. Ghaziyya; Umayya b. Abī Ḥudhayfa b. al-Mughīra was taken by Bilāl; and ʿUthmān b. ʿAbdullah b. al-Mughīra who was released on the day of Nakhla, but was re-taken captive by Wāqid b. ʿAbdullah al-Tamīmī on the day of Badr. Wāqid said, "Praise God who made it possible for me concerning you. You were set free the first time on the day of Nakhla." ʿAbdullah b. Abī Rabīʿa arrived with their ransom, and he ransomed every man among them for four thousand.

Al-Walīd b. al-Walīd b. al-Mughīra was captured by ʿAbdullah b. Jaḥsh. His brothers Khālid b. al-Walīd and Hishām b. al-Walīd arrived with his ransom. ʿAbdullah b. Jaḥsh declined it [Page 141] until he released him for four thousand. Hishām wanted to pay only three thousand. But Khālid said to Hishām, "Is he not the son of your mother? By God, if he refuses it, unless thus and thus, surely I must do so." They left with al-Walīd but when they reached Dhū l-Ḥulayfa he escaped and came to the Prophet, and submitted. The Prophet said to him, "Why did not you convert before you were ransomed?" He replied, "I detested that I convert until I was ransomed with a ransom similar to that of my people." And he converted. Yaḥyā b. al-Mughīra related something similar to me from his father, except he said that Salīṭ b. Qays al-Māzanī captured him. Qays b. Sāʾib was taken by ʿAbda b. al-Ḥasḥās who imprisoned him for a while, for he thought that he had money. His brother Farwa b. al-Sāʾib arrived with his ransom, and he also stayed for some time. Then he ransomed him for four thousand dirhams, including some goods.

From the Banū Abī Rifāʿa: Ṣayfī b. Abī Rifāʿa b. ʿĀbid b. ʿAbdullāh b. ʿAmr b. Makhzūm. But he had no money. One of the Muslims captured him and he stayed with them, and was later released; Abū l-Mundhir b. Abū Rifāʿa was ransomed for two thousand; and ʿAbdullah, named Abū ʿAṭā b. al-Sāʾib b. ʿĀbid b. ʿAbdullah, who was taken captive by Saʿd b. Abī Waqqāṣ was ransomed for a thousand dirhams. Al-Muṭṭalib b. Ḥanṭab b. al-Ḥārith b. ʿUbayd b. ʿUmar b. Makhzūm, who was taken captive by Abū Ayyūb al-Anṣārī, did not have any money and was released after a while. And Khālid b. al-Aʿlam, an ally of theirs from the ʿUqaylī, who used to say: [Page 142] We did not sit on our heels with wounds bleeding but stood on our feet, dripping blood. ʿIkrima b. Abī Jahl arrived with his ransom. Ḥubāb b. al-Mundhir b. Jamūḥ took him captive. They were a total of eight.

From the Banū Jumaḥ: ʿAbdullah b. Ubayy b. Khalaf who was captured by Farwa b. ʿAmr al-Bayāḍī. His father Ubayy b. Khalaf arrived with his ransom. Farwa resisted him for a while. Abū ʿAzza ʿAmr b. ʿAbdullah b. Wahb. The Prophet was kind to him and he promised that he would not encourage anyone against him. The Prophet released him without a ransom, but he was captured on the day of Uḥud and executed. And Wahb b. ʿUmayr b. Wahb b. Khalaf. His father ʿUmayr b. Wahb b. Khalaf arrived with his ransom and Ṣafwān sent him to the Prophet, but he converted, so the Prophet released his son without a ransom. Rifāʿa b. Rāfiʿ al-Zuraqī took him prisoner; Rabīʿa b. Darrāj b. al-ʿAnbas b. Wahbān b. Wahb b. Ḥudhāfa b. Jumaḥ. He had no money so they took something from him and released him. And al-Fākih, the freedman of Umayya b. Khalaf. Saʿd b. Abī Waqqāṣ took him prisoner. They were a total of four.

From the Banū Sahm b. ʿAmr: Abū Wadāʿa b. Ḍubayra. He was the first of the prisoners who was ransomed. His son, al-Muṭṭalib, arrived with his ransom, and ransomed him for four thousand. Farwa b. Khunays b. Ḥudhāfa b. Saʿīd b. Saʿd b. Sahm. Thābit b. Aqram captured him. ʿAmr b. Qays arrived with his ransom, and he paid four thousand; Ḥanẓala b. Qabīṣa b. Ḥudhayfa b. Saʿīd b. Saʿd b. Sahm. ʿUthmān b. Maẓʿūn took him captive; Ḥajjāj b. al-Ḥārith b. Saʿd: ʿAbd al-Raḥmān b. ʿAwf captured him. Then he escaped and Abū Dāwud al-Māzanī took him captive. A total of four.

[Page 143] From the Banū Mālik b. Ḥisl: Suhayl b. ʿAmr b. ʿAbdShams b. ʿAbdWudd b. Naṣr b. Mālik. Mikraz b. Ḥafṣ b. al-Akhīf arrived with his ransom. Mālik b. al-Dukhshum took him captive. Mālik said:

> I captured Suhayl and I would not exchange him
> For a prisoner from any other people.
> Khindif knows that its hero is Suhayl
> When they are oppressed.
> I struck with my keen sword until it bent
> I forced myself to fight this hare-lipped man.

When Mikraz arrived, he finally satisfied them regarding Suhayl and agreed to pay the ransom of four thousand. They said, "Bring us our money." He said, "Yes." They paid with a man in place of a man, and set him on his way. ʿAbdullah b. Jaʿfar used to say, "A man for a man!" So they set Suhayl free and imprisoned Mikraz b. Ḥafṣ, and Suhayl sent money for Mikraz from Mecca.

ʿAbd b. Zamaʿa b. Qays b. Naṣr b. Mālik was taken by ʿUmayr b. ʿAwf, the *mawlā* of Suhayl b. ʿAmr and ʿAbd al-ʿUzza b. Mashnūʾ b. Waqdān b. Qays b. ʿAbdShams b. ʿAbdWudd. The Messenger of God named him ʿAbd al-Raḥmān; al-Nuʿmān b. Mālik had taken him. A total of three.

From the Banū Fihr: al-Ṭufayl b. Abī Qunayʿ and Ibn Jaḥdam.

Muḥammad b. ʿAmr related to me from Muḥammad b. Yaḥyā b. Ḥibbān, saying: [Page 144] The captives who were imprisoned numbered forty-nine. ʿUmar b. ʿUthmān related to me, from ʿAbd al-Malik b. ʿUbayd from Ibn al-Musayyib, saying: The prisoners were seventy and those killed were seventy. Ḥamza b. ʿAbd al-Wāḥid related to me from ʿAmr b. Abī ʿAmr, from Abū ʿIkrima from Ibn ʿAbbās, similarly. Muḥammad related to me from al-Zuhrī saying: The Prisoners exceeded seventy, and those killed exceeded seventy. Yaʿqūb b. Muḥammad b. Abī Ṣaʿṣaʿa related to me from ʿAbd al-Raḥmān b. ʿAbdullah b. Abī Ṣaʿṣaʿa, who said; Seventy-four men were taken on the day of Badr.

THE NAMES OF THE PROVIDERS ON THE ROAD TO BADR AMONG THE POLYTHEISTS

ʿAbdullah b. Jaʿfar related to me from Muḥammad b. ʿUthmān al-Yarbūʿ from ʿAbd al-Raḥmān b. Saʿīd b. Yarbūʿ, who said: The providers in Badr numbered nine. From the ʿAbdManāf there were three: al-Ḥārith b. ʿĀmir b. Nawfal b. ʿAbdManāf, and Shayba and ʿUtba the two sons of Rabīʿa; From Banū Asad: Zamaʿa b. al-Aswad b. Muṭṭalib b. Asad and Nawfal b. Khuwaylid b. al-ʿAdawiyya—two. And from the Banū Makhzūm: Abū Jahl b. Hishām—one. From Banū Jumaḥ: Umayya b. Khalaf—one; from Banū Sahm: Nubayh and Munabbih the two sons of al-Ḥajjaj—two men.

Ismāʿīl b. Ibrāhīm related to me from Mūsā b. ʿUqba saying, the first of those who slaughtered their animals for them was Abū Jahl in Marr al-Ẓahrān, and he slaughtered ten; then Umayya b. Khalaf slaughtered nine in ʿUsfān; and Suhayl b. ʿAmr, ten in Qudayd. They went to the waters from the direction of the sea, and lost their way, [Page 145] so they stopped there for a day, and Shayba b. Rabīʿa slaughtered nine. Then they arrived at al-Juḥfa and ʿUtba b. Rabīʿa slaughtered ten; then they arrived in al-Abwāʾ and Qays al-Jumaḥī slaughtered nine; another slaughtered ten; and al-Ḥārith b. ʿĀmir slaughtered nine. Then, at the waters of Badr, Abū l-Bakhtarī slaughtered and Miqyas slaughtered nine. The war preoccupied them so they ate what was in their provisions. Ibn Abī Zinād said: By God, I did not think that Miqyas had the ability to slaughter even one. Al-Wāqidī did not know Qays al-Jumaḥī. ʿAbdullah b. Jaʿfar related to me from Umm Bakr bt. al-Miswar, from her father, saying, they shared in the slaughter for food. This tradition was traced to one man, and he was silent about the rest of them.

THE NAMES OF THOSE MUSLIMS WHO WERE MARTYRED AT BADR

ʿAbdullah b. Jaʿfar related to me saying: I asked al-Zuhrī: How many were martyred from the Muslims at Badr? He replied fourteen men. Then he enumerated them for me. Muḥammad b. Ṣāliḥ related to me from ʿĀṣim b. ʿAmr b. Rūmān, similarly. There were six from the Muhājirūn and eight from the Anṣār. From the Banū Muṭṭalib b. ʿAbdManāf: ʿUbayda b. al-Ḥārith who was killed by Shayba b. Rabīʿa. The Prophet buried him at al-Ṣafrāʾ. From the Banū Zuhra: ʿUmayr b. Abī Waqqāṣ, killed by ʿAmr b. ʿAbd. Abū Bakr b. Ismāʿīl b. Muḥammad related this to me from his father. ʿUmayr b. ʿAbdʿAmr, master of the two factions was killed by Abū Usāma al-Jushamī. From the Banū ʿAdī b. Kaʿb, ʿĀqil b. Abī l-Bukayr an ally of theirs from the Banū Saʿd b. Bakr was killed by Mālik b. Zuhayr al-Jushamī.

[Page 146] ʿĀmir b. al-Ḥaḍramī killed Mihjaʿ the mawlā of ʿUmar b. al-Khaṭṭāb. Ibn Abī Ḥabība informed me about it from Dāwud b. al-Ḥuṣayn, who said: Muḥammad b. ʿAbdullah related to me from al-Zuhrī that it was said that he was the first to be killed from the Muhājirūn. And from the Banū al-Ḥarith b. Fihr: Ṣafwān b. Bayḍāʾ was killed by Ṭuʿayma b. ʿAdī. Muḥriz b. Jaʿfar b. ʿAmr related to me about that from Jaʿfar b. ʿAmr.

From the Anṣār: from the Banū ʿAmr b. ʿAwf, Mubashshir b. ʿAbd al-Mundhir who was killed by Abū Thawr. Saʿd b. Khaythama who was killed by ʿAmr b. ʿAbd—though others say Ṭuʿayma b. ʿAdī killed him.

From the Banū ʿAdī b. Najjār: Ḥāritha b. Surāqa. Ḥibbān b. al-ʿAriqa aimed an arrow at him, which took his throat and killed him. (Al-Wāqidī says, "I heard the Meccans say Ibn al-ʿAriqa.")

From the Banū Mālik b. Najjār: ʿAwf and Muʿawwidh the two sons of ʿAfrāʾ, were killed by Abū Jahl.

From the Banū Salama b. Ḥarām: ʿUmayr b. al-Ḥumām b. al-Jamūḥ was killed by Khālid b. Aʿlam. Muḥammad b. Ṣāliḥ related to me saying: The first who was killed from among the Anṣār in Islam was ʿUmayr b. al-Ḥumām; Khālid b. Aʿlam killed him. Others say, Ḥāritha b. Surāqa killed him, and Ḥibbān b. al-ʿAriqa aimed at him.

From the Banū Zurayq: Rāfiʿ b. al-Muʿallā was killed by ʿIkrima b. Aī Jahl.

From the Banū Ḥārith b. al-Khazraj: Yazīd b. al-Ḥārith b. Fusḥum was killed by Nawfal b. Muʿāwiya al-Dīlī.

Ibn Abī Ḥabība related to me from Dāwud b. al-Ḥuṣayn, from ʿIkrima from Ibn ʿAbbās that: Anasa the freedman of the Prophet was killed at Badr.

Al-Thawrī related to me from al-Zubayr b. ʿAdī, from ʿAṭāʾ that the Prophet prayed for those who died at Badr. ʿAbd Rabbih b. ʿAbdullah related similarly to me [Page 147] from ʿAṭāʾ from Ibn ʿAbbās.

Yūnus b. Muḥammad al-Ẓafarī related to me saying, "My father showed me four graves in Sayar—a pass in the straights of al-Ṣafrā—saying: These are among the martyrs of Badr from the Muslims; and another three in al-Dabba, below the spring of Mustaʿjila. He showed me the grave of ʿUbayda b. al-Ḥārith in Dhāt Ajdāl at the pass below al-Jadwal. Yūnus b. Muḥammad related to me from Muʿādh b. Rifāʿa that Muʿādh b. Māʿiṣ was wounded at Badr and died of his wounds in Medina. ʿUbayd b. al-Sakan also suffered and died when he arrived in Medina.

Yaḥyā b. ʿAbd al-ʿAzīz related to me from Saʿīd b. ʿAmr, who said: The first of he Anṣār who was killed in Islam was ʿĀṣim b. Thābit b. Abī l-Aqlaḥ. ʿĀmir b. al-Ḥaḍramī killed him at Badr.

The first who was killed from the Muslims of the Muhājirūn was Mihjaʿ. ʿĀmir b. al-Ḥaḍramī killed him, and from the Anṣār, ʿUmayr b. al-Ḥumām. Khālid b. al-Aʿlam killed him. Others said the first of them was Ḥāritha b. Surāqa. Ḥibbān b. al-ʿAriqa killed him. He aimed at him with an arrow.

THE NAMES OF THE POLYTHEISTS WHO WERE KILLED AT BADR

From the Banū ʿAbdShams b. ʿAbdManāf: Ḥanẓala b. Abī Sufyān b. Ḥarb was killed by ʿAlī b. Abī Ṭālib. Mūsā b. Muḥammad related to me from his father about that; and Yūnus b. Muḥammad related to me from his father similarly. He said: Ibn Abī Habība related it to me from Dāwud b. al-Ḥuṣayn. Al-Ḥārith b. Ḥaḍramī was killed by ʿAmmār b. Yāsir; and, ʿĀmir b. al-Ḥaḍramī was killed by ʿĀṣim b. Thābit b. Abī l-Aqlaḥ. ʿAbdullāh b. Jaʿfar related to me about that from Ibn Abī ʿAwn as well as ʿUmayr b. Abī ʿUmayr [Page 148], his son. And two freedmen (*mawlā*) of theirs: Sālim the freedman of Abū Ḥudhayfa, killed ʿUmayr b. Abī ʿUmayr. ʿUbayda b. Saʿīd b. al-ʿĀṣ was killed by al-Zubayr b. al-Awwām. Abū Ḥamza ʿAbd al-Wāḥid b. Maymūn related to me about that from ʿUrwa b. al-Zubayr (Ibn Ḥayyawayh said, "I saw in an old transcript: Abū Ḥamza ʿAbd al-Malik b. Maymūn"), and Muḥammad b. Ṣāliḥ related about it from ʿĀṣim b. ʿUmar b. Qatāda. Al-ʿĀṣ b. Saʿīd was killed by ʿAlī b. Abī Ṭālib; Muḥammad b. Ṣāliḥ related to me about that from ʿĀṣim b. ʿAmr b. Rūmān, and Mūsā b. Muḥammad related a similar story from his father. And ʿUqba b. Abī Muʿayṭ was executed by ʿĀṣim b. Thābit, on the command of the Prophet at al-Ṣafrāʾ, with his sword. ʿUtba b. Rabīʿa was killed by Ḥamza b. ʿAbd al-Muṭṭalib; Shayba b. Rabīʿa was killed by ʿUbayda b. al-Ḥārith and dispatched by Ḥamza and ʿAlī. Al-Walīd b. ʿUtba b. Rabīʿa was killed by ʿAlī b. Abī Ṭālib, ʿĀmir b. ʿAbdullah, an ally of theirs from Anmār, was killed by ʿAlī b. Abī Ṭālib; But Ibn Abī Ḥabība related to me from Dāwud b. al-Ḥuṣayn that Saʿd b. Muʿādh killed him. A total of twelve.

From the Banū Nawfal b. ʿAbdManāf: Al-Ḥārith b. ʿĀmir b. Nawfal was killed by Khubayb b. Yasāf. Ṭuʿayma b. ʿAdī was killed by Ḥamza b. ʿAbd al-Muṭṭalib. That is two in all.

From the Banū Asad: Rabīʿa b. al-Aswad was killed by Abū Dujāna: ʿAbdullah b. Jaʿfar informed me about it from Ibn Abī ʿAwn. But ʿAbdullah b. Jaʿfar related to me from Jaʿfar b. ʿAmr saying: Thābit b. al-Jadhʿ killed him. Al-Ḥārith b. Rabīʿa was killed by ʿAlī b. Abī Ṭālib. ʿAqīl b. al-Aswad b. al-Muṭṭalib was killed by both Ḥamza and ʿAlī [Page 149] who joined in killing him. Abū Maʿshar related to me saying ʿAlī, alone, killed him. Abū l-Bakhtarī who is al-ʿĀṣ b. Hishām was killed by al-Mujadhdhar b. Dhiyād. Saʿīd b. Muḥammad related to me about that from ʿUmāra b. Ghazīyya from Muḥammad b. Yaḥyā b. Ḥibbān. And Saʿīd b. Muḥammad related to me from ʿUmāra b. Ghaziyya from ʿAbbād b. Tamīm, who said: Abū Dāwud al-Māzanī killed him. Yaʿqūb b. Muḥammad b. Abī Ṣaʿṣaʿa related to me from Ayyūb b. ʿAbd al-Raḥmān b. Abī Ṣaʿṣaʿa that Abū Dāwud al-Māzanī killed him. But Ayyūb b. al-Nuʿmān related to me from his father saying Abū l-Yasar killed him. And, Nawfal b. Khuwaylid b. Asad, who was Ibn al-ʿAdawīyya was killed by ʿAlī b. Abī Ṭālib. Muḥammad b. Ṣāliḥ related to me about that from ʿĀṣim b. ʿAmr b. Rūmān saying, Ibn Abī Ḥabība related to me from Dāwud b. al-Ḥuṣayn, who said, ʿUmar b. Abī ʿĀtika related it to me from Abū l-Aswad. A total of five.

From the Banū ʿAbd al-Dār b. Quṣay: Al-Naḍr b. al-Ḥārith b. al-Kalada was executed by the sword of ʿAlī b. Abī Ṭālib in al-Uthayl on the order of the Prophet. Zayd b. Mulayṣ, *mawlā* of ʿUmayr b. Hāshim b. ʿAbdManāf b. ʿAbd al-Dār, was killed by ʿAlī b. Abī Ṭālib. Ayyūb b. al-Nuʿmān related to me about that from ʿIkrima b. Muṣʿab al-ʿAbadī. But ʿAbdullah b. Jaʿfar related to me from Yaʿqūb b. ʿUtba that Bilāl killed him.

From the Banū Taym b. Murra: ʿUmayr b. ʿUthmān b. ʿAmr b. Kaʿb b. Saʿd b. Taym was killed by ʿAlī b. Abī Ṭālib. Mūsā b. Muḥammad related to me about that from his father. And ʿUthmān b. Mālik b. ʿUbaydullah b. ʿUthmān was killed by Ṣuhayb: Mūsā b. Muḥammad related to me about that from his father. Two in all.

From the Banū Makhzūm b. Yaqẓa; there was from the Banū al-Mughīra b. ʿAbdullah b. ʿUmar b. Makhzūm: Abū Jahl. Muʿādh b. ʿAmr b. al-Jamūḥ as well as Muʿawwidh and ʿAwf the two sons of [Page 150] ʿAfrāʾ struck him, and ʿAbdullah b. Masʿūd dispatched him. Al-ʿĀṣ b. Hishām b. al-Mughīra was killed by ʿUmar b. al-Khaṭṭāb. Ibrāhīm b. Saʿd related to me about it from Muḥammad b. ʿIkrima b. ʿAbd al-Raḥmān b. al-Ḥārith b. Hishām, from Nāfiʿ. Jubayr, and Muḥammad b. Ṣāliḥ from ʿĀṣim b. ʿAmr b. Rūmān, similarly. Yazīd b. Tamīm al-Tamīmī an ally of theirs was killed by ʿAmmār b. Yāsir. ʿAbdullah b. Abī ʿUbayda related it to me from his father. Others say that ʿAlī killed him. Abū Musāfiʿ al-Ashʿarī, an ally of theirs, was killed by Abū Dujāna and Ḥarmala b. ʿAmr b. Abī ʿUtba. All our companions related about that.

From the Banū Walīd b. al-Mughīra: Abū Qays b. al-Walīd was killed by ʿAlī: ʿAbdullah b. Jaʿfar informed me about that from Jaʿfar b. ʿAmr.

From the Banū al-Fakih b. al-Mughīra: Abū Qays b. al-Fākih b. al-Mughīra was killed by Ḥamza b. ʿAbd al-Muṭṭalib. But, Isḥāq b. Khārija told me that Ḥubāb b. ʿAmr b. al-Mundhir killed him.

From the Banū Umayya b. al-Mughīra: Masʿūd b. Abī Umayya was killed byʿAlīb. Abī Ṭālib. From the Banū ʿĀbid b. ʿAbdullāh b. ʿUmar b. Makhzūm, then from the Banū Rifāʿa, the Umayya b. ʿĀbid: Rifāʿa b. Abī Rifāʿa was killed by Saʿd b. al-Rabīʿ. Abū l-Mundhir b. Abī Rifāʿa was killed by Maʿan b. ʿAdī al-ʿAjlānī. ʿAbdullah b. Abī Rifāʿa was killed by ʿAlī b. Abī Ṭālib. Zuhayr b. Abī Rifāʿa was killed by Abū Usayd al-Sāʿidī: Ubayy b. al-ʿAbbās b. Sahl related that to me from his father. And al-Sāʾib b. Abī Rifāʿa was killed by ʿAbd al-Raḥmān b. ʿAwf.

[Page 151] From the Banū Abī l-Sāʾib, then the Ṣayfī b. ʿĀbid b. ʿAbdullah b. ʿUmar b. Makhzūm: al-Sāʾib b. Abī Sāʾib was killed by al-Zubayr b. al-Awwām. Al-Aswad b. ʿAbd al-Asad b. Hilāl b. ʿAbdullah b. ʿUmar b. Makhzūm was killed by Ḥamza b. ʿAbd al-Muṭṭalib. All our companions informed us about that. Of their two allies from Ṭayī, ʿAmr b. Sufyān was killed by Yazīd b. Ruqaysh; and his brother Jabbār b. Sufyān was killed by Abū Burda b. Niyār.

From the Banū ʿImrān b. Makhzūm: Ḥājiz b. al-Sāʾib b. Uwaymir b. ʿĀʾidh was killed by ʿAlī b. Abī Ṭālib. ʿUwaymir b. ʿĀʾidh b. ʿImrān b. Makhzūm was killed by al-Nuʿmān b. Abī Mālik. Nineteen.

From the Banū Jumaḥ b. ʿAmr b. Huṣayṣ: Umayya b. Khalaf was killed by Khubayb b. Yasāf and Bilāl. Ibn Abī Ṭuwāla informed me of this from Khubayb b. ʿAbd al-Raḥmān, and Muḥammad b. Ṣāliḥ from ʿĀṣim b. ʿUmar and Yazīd b. Rūmān. ʿUbayd b. Yaḥyā related to me from Muʿādh b. Rifāʿa b. Rāfiʿ saying that Rifāʿa b. Rāfiʿ b. Mālik killed him.

ʿAlī b. Umayya b. Khalaf was killed by ʿAmmār b. Yāsir. And Aws b. al-Miʿyar b. Laudhān was killed by both ʿUthmān b. Maẓʿūn and ʿAlī b. Abī Ṭālib, together. Qudāma b. Mūsa related to me from ʿĀʾisha bt. Qudāma, who said, ʿUthmān b. Maẓʿūn killed him. Munabbih b. al-Ḥajjāj was killed by Abū l-Yasar; others said ʿAlī. Some said Abū Usayd al-Sāʿidī. Ubayy b. ʿAbbās related to me from his father from Abū Usayd, who said, "I killed Munabbih b. al-Ḥajjāj. [Page 152] But Nubayy b. al-Ḥajjāj was killed by ʿAlī b. Abī Ṭālib." Al-ʿĀṣ b. Munabbih was killed by ʿAlī b. Abī Ṭālib. Abūl-ʿĀṣ b. Qays b. ʿAdī b. Saʿd b. Sahm was killed by Abū Dujāna. However, Abū Maʿshar related to me from his companions that ʿAlī killed him, and Ḥafṣ b. ʿUmar b. ʿAbdullah b. Jubayr, the *mawlā* of ʿAlī, also informed me about that. ʿĀṣim b. Abī ʿAwf b. Ḍubayra b. Saʿīd b. Saʿdwas killed by Abū Dujāna. There were seven.

From the Banū ʿĀmir b. Luʾayy then from the Banū Mālik b. Ḥisl: Muʿāwiya b. ʿAbdQays an ally of theirs was killed by ʿUkkāsha b. Miḥṣan. Maʿbad b. Wahb, an ally of theirs from the Kalb, was killed by Abū Dujāna. Ibn Abī Sabra related to me about that from Saʿd b. Saʿīd, the brother of Yaḥyā. ʿAbdullah b. Jaʿfar related it to me from

Yaʿqūb b. ʿUtba, and Muḥammad b. Ṣāliḥ related to me from ʿĀṣim, as well, that Abū Dujāna killed him. Altogether forty-nine men were listed dead. (Among those who were killed, the Commander of the believers, ʿAlī, killed or participated in killing twenty-two men.)

THOSE FROM THE QURAYSH AND THE ANṢĀR WHO WITNESSED BADR

For those who were martyred in battle and those who fought, the Prophet assigned a portion for each in his absence; there were three hundred and thirteen men.

Muḥammad b. ʿAbdullah related to me from al-Zuhrī from ʿUrwa, who said: Ibn Abī Ḥabība related to me from Dāwud b. al-Ḥuṣayn from ʿIkrima; and Muḥammad b. Ṣāliḥ related to me from Āṣim b. ʿUmar and Yazīd b. Rūmān; [Page 153] and Mūsa b. Muḥammad related to me from his father that the Prophet assigned portions for eight groups and rewarded them.

Sulaymān b. Bilāl related to me from ʿAmr b. Abī ʿAmr from ʿIkrima from Ibn ʿAbbās, who said: Among the Mawālī, twenty men witnessed Badr. ʿAbdullah b. Jaʿfar related to me saying, I heard ʿAbdullah b. Ḥasan say, "Only the Quraysh, the Anṣār, their allies and their *mawālī* witnessed Badr."

From the Banū Hāshim: Muḥammad, the Messenger of God, the good and the blessed, Ḥamza b. ʿAbd al-Muṭṭalib, ʿAlī b. Abī Ṭālib, Zayd b. Ḥāritha, Abū MarthadKannāz b. Ḥuṣayn al-Ghanawī and Marthad b. Abī Marthad, the two allies of Ḥamza and Anasa the *mawlā* of the Prophet, Abū Kabsha, the *mawlā* of the Prophet and Shuqrān witnessed it. Shuqrān was a slave of the Prophet, and nothing was apportioned to him. His conduct was exemplary over the prisoners. All the men assigned to him were prisoners. Not a man among the people achieved more than what he did. It took eight to equal Shuqrān.

ʿAbd al-ʿAzīz b. Muḥammad related to me from Jaʿfar b. Muḥammad from his father that the Prophet apportioned a portion to Jaʿfar b. Abī Ṭālib as his reward. But our companions do not mention it and his name is not in the sources.

From the Banū Muṭṭalib b. ʿAbdManāf: ʿUbayda b. al-Ḥārith b. ʿAbd al-Muṭṭalib b. ʿAbd Manāf, al-Ḥusayn b. al-Ḥārith b. ʿAbd al-Muṭṭālib b. ʿAbdManāf, al-Ṭufayl b. al-Ḥārith b. ʿAbd al-Muṭṭalib b. ʿAbdManāf and Misṭaḥ b. Uthātha b. ʿAbbād b. ʿAbd al-Muṭṭalib b. ʿAbdManāf—four.

From the Banū ʿAbdShams b. ʿAbdManāf: ʿUthmān b. ʿAffān b. Abī l-ʿĀṣ b. [Page 154] Umayya b. ʿAbdShams. He did not attend but stayed behind with the daughter of the Prophet, Ruqayya. The Prophet apportioned to him and rewarded him, and all the people mention it; Abū Ḥudhayfa b. ʿUtba b. Rabīʿa, and Sālim the *mawlā* of Abū Ḥudhayfa. From their allies among the Banū Ghanm b. Dūdān: ʿAbdullah b. Jaḥsh b. Riāb, ʿUkkāsha b. Miḥṣan, Abū Sinān b. Miḥsan, Sinān b. Abī Sinān b. Miḥsan, Shujāʿ b. Wahb, ʿUtba b. Wahb, Rabīʿa b. Aktham, Yazīd b. Ruqaysh, and Muḥriz b. Naḍla b. ʿAbdullah. From their allies from the Banū Sulaym: Mālik b. ʿAmr, Midlāj b. ʿAmr, and Thaqāf b. ʿAmr. And an ally of theirs from the Ṭayyiʾ, Suwayd b. Makhshī. Abū Maʿshar and Ibn Abī Ḥabība related to me about it from Dāwud b. al-Ḥuṣayn, who said: ʿAbdullah b. Jaʿfar al-Zuhrī claimed that he was Arbid b. Ḥumayra and that his *kunya* was Abū Makhshī, and that he was from the Banū Asad b. Khuzayma who were on their own. Some of our companions informed us that Ṣubayḥ, the *mawlā* of al-ʿĀṣ prepared for battle and fell sick. So he was carried on the camel of Abū Salama b. ʿAbd al-Asad. He witnessed with the Prophet the places where all the martyrs had died. Without Ṣubayḥ there were sixteen.

From the Banū Nawfal b. ʿAbdManāf: ʿUtba b. Ghazwān b. Jābir b. Uhayb b. Nusayb b. Mālik b. al-Ḥārith b. Māzin b. Manṣūr b. ʿIkrima; and his brother Sulaym. And from the Banū Māzin: Ḥubāb, the *mawlā* of ʿUtba b. Ghazwān. A total of two.

From the Banū Asad b. ʿAbd al-ʿUzza: al-Zubayr b. al-ʿAwwām, Ḥāṭib b. Abī Baltaʿa, an ally of theirs and Saʿd, the *mawlā* of Ḥāṭib. A total of three.

From the Banū ʿAbd b. Quṣay: Ṭulayb b ʿUmayr b. Wahb. ʿAbdullaḥ b. Jaʿfar related to me about that from Ismāʿīl b. Muḥammad, and Muḥammad b. ʿAbdullah b. ʿAmr; and, Qudāma b. Mūsā related to me about it from ʿĀʾisha bt. Qudāma.

[Page 155] From the Banū ʿAbd al-Dar b. Quṣay: Muṣʿab b. ʿUmayr and Suwaybiṭ b. Ḥarmala b. Mālik b. ʿUmayla b. al-Sabbāq b. ʿAbd al-Dār b. Quṣay. Two in all.

From the Banū Zuhra b. Kilāb: ʿAbd al-Raḥmān b. ʿAwf b. ʿAbd al-Ḥārith b. Zuhra, Saʿd b. Abī Waqqāṣ b. Uhayb b. ʿAbdManāf b. Zuhra and his brother ʿUmayr b. Abī Waqqāṣ. And from their confederates: ʿAbdullah b. Masʿūd al-Hudhalī, al-Miqdād b. ʿAmr b. Thaʿlaba b. Mālik b. Rabīʿa b. Thumāma b. Maṭrūd b. Zuhayr b. Thaʿlaba b. Mālik b. al-Sharīd b. Faʾs b. Dhuraym b. al-Qayn b. Ahwad b. Bahrāʾ, he who was called al-Miqdād b. al-Aswad b. ʿAbdYaghūth b. ʿAbd b. al-Ḥārith b. Zuhrā, and Khabbāb b. al-Aratta b. Jandala b. Saʿd b. Khuzayma b. Kaʿb b. Saʿd, *mawlā* of Umm Sibāʿ bt. Anmār. Mūsā b. Yaʿqūb b. ʿAbdullāh b. Wahb b. Zamaʿa informed me of the genealogy of Khabbāb from Abū l-Aswad Muḥammad b. ʿAbd al-Raḥmān b. Nawfal b. Asad b. ʿAbd al-ʿUzzā, the orphan of ʿUrwa; as well as Masʿūd b. al-Rabīʿ from al-Qāra, and the ambidextrous ʿUmayr b. ʿAbdʿAmr b. Naḍla b. Ghubshān b. Sulaym b. Mālik b. Aqṣā from the Khuzāʿa. Eight in all.

From the Banū Taym: Abū Bakr al-Ṣiddīq (whose name was ʿAbdullah b. ʿUthmān b. ʿĀmir b. ʿAmr b. Kaʿb b. Saʿd b. Taym), Ṭalḥa b. ʿUbaydullah (the Prophet apportioned to him and rewarded him), Bilāl b. Rabāḥ, ʿĀmir b. Fuhayra, the *mawlā* of Abū Bakr, and Ṣuhayb b. Sinān. Five.

From the Banū Makhzūm b. Yaqẓa: Abū Salama b. ʿAbd al-Asad b. Hilāl b. ʿAbdullah b. ʿUmar b. Makhzūm, Shammās b. ʿUthmān b. al-Sharūd, Arqam b. Abū l-Arqam, ʿAmmār b. Yāsir, and Muʿattib b. ʿAwf b. al-Ḥamrāʾ an ally of theirs from the Khuzāʿa. Five.

[Page 156] From the Banū ʿAdī b. Kaʿb: ʿUmar b. al-Khaṭṭāb b. Nufayl b. ʿAbd al-ʿUzza b. Riyāḥ, Zayd b. al-Khaṭṭāb, and Saʿīd b. Zayd b. ʿAmr b. Nufayl. The Prophet had sent him with Ṭalḥa to find out about the caravan so he apportioned a portion for him and rewarded him. ʿAmr b. Surāqa b. al-Muʿtamir b. Anas b. Adhā b. Riyāḥ. From their confederates among the Banū Saʿd b. Layth: ʿĀqil b. Abī l-Bukayr who was killed at Badr; and Khālid b. Abī l-Bukayr who was killed on the day of al-Rajīʿ; Iyās b. Abī l-Bukayr, ʿĀmir b. Abī l-Bukayr, Mihjaʿ, the *mawlā* of ʿUmar from Yemen, and Khawlī and his son, two allies of theirs. ʿĀmir b. Rabīʿa al-ʿAnzī—ʿAnz is the valley of Rabīʿa—an ally of theirs, and Wāqid b. ʿAbdullah al-Tamīmī, an ally of theirs. Thirteen in all.

From the Banū Jumaḥ b. ʿAmr: ʿUthmān b. Maẓʿūn, Qudāma b. Maẓʿūn, ʿAbdullah b. Maẓʿūn, Sāʾib b. ʿUthmān b. Maẓʿūn, and Maʿmar b. al-Ḥārith. Five in all.

From the Banū Sahm b. ʿAmr: Khunays b. Ḥudhāfa b. Qays. From the Banū Mālik b. Ḥisl: ʿAbdullah b. Makhrama b. ʿAbd al-ʿUzza, ʿAbdullah b. Suhayl b. ʿAmr who arrived with the polytheists but joined with the Muslims, and Wahb b. Saʿd b. Abī Sarḥ.

Muḥammad b. ʿAbdullah related to me about it from al-Zuhrī, who said: Ibn Abī Ḥabība related to me from Dāwud b. al-Ḥuṣayn from ʿIkrima, who said, ʿAbdullah b. Jaʿfar related to me from Ismāʿīl b. Muḥammad. There were also Abū Sabra b. Abī Ruhm, ʿUmayr b. ʿAwf—*mawlā* of Suhayl b. ʿAmr, Saʿd b. Khawla, an ally of theirs from Yemen and Ḥāṭib b. ʿAmr b. ʿAbdShams b. ʿAbdWudda. [Page 157] ʿAbdullah b. Jaʿfar related to me about it from ʿAbdRabbih b. Saʿīd from Muḥammad b. ʿAmr b. ʿAṭāʾ; they were six without Ḥāṭib.

ʿAṭā b. Muḥammad b. ʿAmr b. ʿAṭā related to me from his father, who said, ʿAbdullah b. Suhayl came out with his father who funded him. When he came out, his father did not doubt that he was of his religion. When they arrived, he withdrew until he came to the Prophet before the battle: that angered his father. Later, Suhayl said, "God provided me and him with that blessing."

From the Banū al-Ḥārith b. Fihr: Abū ʿUbayda (his name was ʿĀmir b. ʿAbdullah b. al-Jarraḥ), Ṣafwān b. Bayḍā, Suhayl b. Bayḍā, ʿIyāḍ b. Zuhayr; Maʿmar b. Abī Sarḥ, and ʿAmr b. Abī ʿAmr. They were from the Banū Ḍabba. They numbered six in all.

Nāfiʿ b. Abī Nāfiʿ Abū l-Ḥuṣayb and Ibn Abī Sabra related to me from Hishām b. ʿUrwa from his father, who said: the portions of the Quraysh were a hundred portions. Mūsā b. Muḥammad related to me from his father, who said: The Quraysh were eighty-six men and the Anṣār were two hundred and twenty-seven men. ʿAbd al-Raḥmān b. ʿAbd al-ʿAzīz related to me from Abū l-Ḥuwayrith from Muḥammad b. Jubayr, who said: The Quraysh numbered seventy-three men and the Anṣār, two hundred and forty men.

From the Anṣār, from the Banū ʿAbd al-Ashhal: Saʿd b. Muʿādh b. al-Nuʿmān b. Imrā l-Qays b. Zayd b. ʿAbd al-Ashhal; ʿAmr b. Muʿādh b. al-Nuʿmān; Al-Ḥārith b. Aws b. Musʿādh b. al-Nuʿmān; And al-Ḥārith b. Anas b. Rāfiʿ b. Imrā l-Qays.

From the Banū ʿAbd b. Kaʿb b. ʿAbd al-Ashhal Banū Zaʿūrā: Saʿd b. Mālik [Page 158] b. ʿAbd b. Kaʿb, Salama b. Salāma b. Waqash, ʿAbbād b. Bishr b. Waqash, Salama b. Thābit b. Waqash, Rāfiʿ b. Yazīd b. Kurz b. Sakan b. Zaʿūrā b. ʿAbd al-Ashhal, al-Ḥārith b. Khazama b. ʿAdī b. Abī Ghanm b. Sālim b. ʿAwf b. ʿAmr b. ʿAwf who was an ally of theirs from the Banū Ḥārith of the Qawāqila, and lived with them. Muḥammad b. Maslama b. Khālid b. ʿAdī b. Majdaʿa b. Ḥāritha b. al-Ḥārith of the Banū Ḥāritha; Salama b. Aslam b. Ḥarīsh b. ʿAdī b. Majdaʿa who was killed at the battle of the Bridge by Abū ʿUbayd in 14 AH. Abū l-Haytham b. al-Tayyihān and ʿUbayd b. al-Tayyihān, two allies of theirs from Baliyy, and ʿAbdullah b. Sahl. Fifteen men.

From the Banū Ḥāritha b. al-Ḥārith b. al-Khazraj b. ʿAmr b. Mālik b. al-Aws: Masʿūd b. ʿAbdSaʿd b. ʿĀmir b. ʿAdī b. Jusham b. Majdaʿa b. Ḥāritha, and Abū ʿAbs b. Jabr b. ʿAmr b. Zayd b. Jusham b. Ḥāritha. From their allies there was Abū Burda b. Niyār of the Baliyy. They were three. ʿAbd al-Majīd b. Abī ʿAbs related this to me from his father, and Muḥammad b. Ṣāliḥ, from ʿĀṣim b. ʿUmar from Maḥmūd b. Labīd; and ʿAbd al-Majīd b. Abī ʿAbs b. Muḥammad b. Abī ʿAbs b. Jabr also related similar information to me.

From the Banū Ẓafar, from the Banū Sawād b. Kaʿb: Qatāda b. al-Nuʿmān b. Zayd, and ʿUbayd b. Aws b. Mālik b. Sawād.

From the Banū Rizāḥ b. Kaʿb: Naṣr b. al-Ḥārith b. ʿAbdRizāḥ b. Ẓafar b. Kaʿb, and from their two allies, two men from Baliyy, ʿAbdullah b. Ṭāriq b. Mālik b. [Page 159] Taym b. Shuʿba b. Saʿd Allah b. Farān b. Baliyy b. ʿAmr b. al-Ḥāf b. Quḍāʿa, who was killed in al-Rajīʿ; and his brother through his mother, Muʿattib b. ʿUbayd b. Unās b. Taym b. Shuʿba b. SaʿdAllah b. Farān b. Baliyy b. ʿAmr b. al-Ḥāf b. Quḍāʿa. Eight.

ʿAbd al-Majīd b. Abī ʿAbs related to me about that from his father and Muḥammad b. Ṣāliḥ from ʿĀṣim b. ʿUmar from Maḥmūd b. Labīd. Ibn Abī Ḥabība related a similar tradition to me from Dāwud b. al-Ḥuṣayn.

From the Banū Umayya b. Zayd b. Mālik b. ʿAwf: Mubashshir b. ʿAbd al-Mundhir b. Zanbar who was killed at Badr, Rifāʿa b. ʿAbd al-Mundhir, Saʿd b. ʿUbayd b. al-Nuʿmān b. Qays b. ʿAmr b. Umayya b. Zayd b. Umayya, ʿUwaym b. Sāʿida, Rāfiʿ b. ʿAnjada—his mother's name was Anjada—ʿUbayd b. Abī ʿUbayd, Thaʿlaba b. Ḥāṭib, Abū Lubāba b. ʿAbd al-Mundhir; the Prophet returned him from al-Rawhāʾ and appointed him over Medina, and apportioned for him a portion and rewarded him. And al-Ḥārith b. Ḥāṭib also returned from al-Rawhāʾ, and the Prophet apportioned for him and rewarded him.

From the Banū Ḍubayʿa b. Zayd b. Mālik b. ʿAwf b. ʿAmr b. ʿAwf: ʿAṣim b. Thābit b. Qays and Qays is Abū l-Aqlaḥ; his kunya was Ibn ʿIṣma b. Mālik b. Umayya b. Ḍubayʿa. He was killed at al-Rajīʿ, and al-Aḥwaṣ his son, the poet, was also killed. Muʿattib b. Qushayr b. Mulayl b. Zayd b. al-ʿAṭṭāf, Abū Mulayl b. al-Azʿar b. Zayd b. al-ʿAṭṭāf-who had no heirs, ʿUmayr b. Maʿbad b. al-Azʿar, who had no heirs, and Sahl b. Ḥunayf b. Wāhib b. ʿUkaym b. al-Ḥārith b. Thaʿlaba. A total of five.

[Page 160] From the Banū ʿUbayd b. Zayd b. Mālik b. ʿAmr b. ʿAwf: Unays b. Qatāda b. Rabīʿa b. Khālid b. al-Ḥārith b. ʿUbayd b. Zayd, who was killed on the day of Uḥud. He was married to Khansāʾ daughter of Khidhām, and had no heirs. And from their allies: Maʿan b. ʿAdī b. al-Jadd b. al-ʿAjlān who was killed on the day of al-Yamāma, Ribʿī b. Rāfiʿ, Thābit b. Aqram, killed on the day of Ṭulayḥa, ʿAbdullah b. Salama b. Mālik b. al-Ḥārith b. ʿAdī b. al-Jadd b. al-ʿAjlān, Zayd b. Aslam b. Thaʿlaba b. ʿAdī b. al-Jadd b. al-ʿAjlān, who had no heirs; and ʿAṣim b. ʿAdī b. al-Jadd b. al-ʿAjlān who went out to the masjid al-Ḍirār for something that had reached him about them, and the Prophet brought him back and apportioned for him and rewarded him. Sālim—the *mawlā* of Thubayta bt. Yaʿār—who was killed on the day of Yamāma. Aflaḥ b. Saʿīd related to me from Saʿīd b. ʿAbd al-Raḥmān b. Ruqaysh from Abū l-Badāḥ b. ʿĀṣim about that. A total of eight.

From the Banū Thaʿlaba b. ʿAmr b. ʿAwf: ʿAbdullah b. Jubayr b. al-Nuʿmān who was killed on the day of Uḥud, and was the commander of the Prophet on the day of Uḥud over the hurlers (marksmen). ʿĀṣim b. Qays, Abū Ḍayyāḥ b. Thābit, Abū Ḥanna—who did not participate in Badr—Sālim b. ʿUmayr, one of the Weepers, al-Ḥārith b. al-Nuʿmān b. Abī Khadhma, Khawwāt b. Jubayr b. al-Nuʿmān, who was defeated in al-Rawḥāʾ. ʿAbd al-Malik b. Sulaymān related it to me from Khawwāt b. Ṣāliḥ from his father. A total of eight.

From the Banū Jaḥjabā b. Kulfa b. ʿAwf b. ʿAmr b. ʿAwf: Al-Mundhir b. Muḥammad b. ʿUqba b. Uḥayḥa b. Julāḥ b. Ḥarīsh b. Jaḥjaba b. Kulfa, whose *kunya* was Abū ʿAbda, and who did not have an heir. But Uḥayḥa had other heirs. [Page 161] And from their allies of the Banū Unayf: Abū ʿAqīl b. ʿAbdullah b. Thaʿlaba b. Bayḥān, whose name was Abū ʿAqīl ʿAbd al-ʿUzzā, whom the Messenger of God named ʿAbd al-Raḥmān, the enemy of the idols. He was killed in Yamāma. He was Abū ʿAqīl b. ʿAbdullah b. Thaʿlaba b. Bayḥān b. ʿĀmir b. Unayf b. Jusham b. ʿAbdullah b. Taym b. Yarāsh b. ʿĀmir b. ʿUbayla b. Qasmīl b. Farān b. Balī b. ʿAmr b. al-Ḥāf b. Quḍāʿa. That was two.

From the Banū Ghanm b. al-Salm b. Imrā l-Qays b. Mālik b. al-Aws b. Ḥāritha: Saʿd b. Khaythama who was killed at Badr, al-Mundhir b. Qudāma, Mālik b. Qudāma, Ibn ʿArfaja, and Tamīm, *mawlā* to the Banū Ghanm b. al-Salm. That was five. These were the Aws.

From the Banū Muʿāwiya b. Mālik b. ʿAwf b. ʿAmr b. ʿAwf: Jābir b. ʿAtīk b. al-Ḥārith b. Qays b. Haysha b. al-Ḥārith b. Muʿāwiya, Mālik b. Thābit b. Numayla an ally from the Muzayna, Nuʿmān b. ʿAṣar, an ally from Baliyy, and al-Ḥārith b. Qays b. Haisha b. al-Ḥārith b. Umayya, who is not confirmed.

From the Banū Mālik b. al-Najjār b. ʿAmr b. al-Khazraj, there is the Banū Ghanm b. Mālik. There is from the Banū Thaʿlaba b. ʿAbdʿAwf b. Ghanm: Abū Ayyūb, and his name was Khālid b. Zayd b. Kulayb b. Thaʿlaba. He died in the land of the Byzantines during the time of Muʿāwiya.

From the Banū ʿUsayra b. ʿAbdʿAwf: Thābit b. Khālid b. al-Nuʿmān b. Khansāʾ b. ʿUsayra. [Page 162] From the Banū ʿAmr b. ʿAbdʿAwf: ʿUmāra b. Ḥazm b. Zayd, and Surāqa b. Kaʿb b. ʿAbd al-ʿUzzā b. Ghaziyya b. ʿAmr b. ʿAbd.

From the Banū ʿUbayd b. Thaʿlaba b. Ghanm b. Mālik: Ḥāritha b. al-Nuʿmān and Sulaym b. Qays b. Qahd. Qahd was named Khālid b. Qays b. Thaʿlaba b. ʿUbayd b. Thaʿlaba b. Ghanm.

From the Banū ʿĀʾidh b. Thaʿlaba b. Ghanm: Suhayl b. Rāfiʿ b. Abī ʿAmr b. ʿĀʾidh b. Thaʿlaba b. Ghanm and ʿAdī b. Abī l-Zaghbāʾ—the name of Abī l-Zaghbāʾ was Sinān b. Subayʿ b. Thaʿlaba b. Rabīʿa b. Budayl b. Saʿd b. ʿAdī b. Naṣr b. Kāhil b. Naṣr b. Mālik b. Ghatafān b. Qays b. Juhayna. That is eight in all.

From the Banū Zayd b. Thaʿlaba b. Ghanm: Masʿūd b. Aws b. Zayd, Abū Khuzayma b. Aws b. Aṣram b. Zayd b. Thaʿlaba, and Rāfiʿ b. al-Ḥārith b. Sawād b. Zayd b. Thaʿlaba. Three.

From the Banū Sawād b. Mālik b. Ghanm b. ʿAwf: ʿAwf and Muʿawwid and Muʿādh, the sons of al-Ḥārith b. Rifāʿa b. Sawād, and ʿAfrāʾ—she was the daughter of ʿUbayd b. Thaʿlaba; Nuʿaymān b. ʿAmr b. Rifāʿa b. al-Ḥārith b. Sawād; ʿĀmir b. Mukhallad b. Sawād; ʿAbdullah b. Qays b. Khalid b. Khalada b. al-Ḥārith b. Sawād; ʿAmr b. Qays b. Sawād, Qays b. ʿAmr b. Qays b. Zayd b. Sawād, Thābit b. ʿAmr b. Zayd b. ʿAdī b. Sawād; ʿUṣayma an ally of theirs; a man from the Juhayna called Wadīʿa b. ʿAmr b. Jurād b. Yarbūʿ b. Ṭuḥayl b. ʿAmr b. Ghanm b. al-Rabaʿa b. Rushdān b. Qays b. Juhayna. ʿAbdullah b. Abī ʿUbayda related to me from his father saying: I heard Rubayyiʿ daughter of Muʿawwidh b. ʿAfrāʾ say, "Abū l-Ḥamrā, the *mawlā* of al-Ḥārith b. Rifāʿa, witnessed Badr." [Page 163] He said: Ibn Abī Ḥabība related something similar to me from Dāwud b. al-Ḥuṣayn. They numbered twelve with Abū l-Ḥamrā. But the total, of those who witnessed from among the Banū Ghanm b. Mālik b. Najjār including Abū l-Ḥamrāʾ, was twenty-three.

From the Banū ʿĀmir b. Mālik b. al-Najjār, then from the Banū ʿAmr b. Mabdhūl, and the Banū ʿAtīk b. ʿAmr b. Mabdhūl: Thaʿlaba b. ʿAmr b. Miḥṣan b. ʿAmr b. ʿAtīk; Sahl b. ʿAtīk b. al-Nuʿmān b. ʿAmr b. ʿAtīk; al-Ḥārith b. al-Ṣimma b. ʿAmr b. ʿAtīk, who was defeated at al-Rawḥāʾ. The Prophet apportioned for him and rewarded him, and all our companions related about it to me. He was killed on the day of Biʾr Maʿūna. They were a total of three.

From the Banū ʿAmr b. Mālik, and they were the Banū Ḥudayla, and the Banū Qays b. ʿUbayd b. Zayd b. Rifāʿa b. Muʿāwiyā b. ʿAmr b. Mālik: Ubayy b. Kaʿb b. Qays b. ʿUbayd, and Anas b. Muʿādh b. Anas b. Qays b. ʿUbayd. They were two.

From the Banū ʿAdī b. ʿAmr b. Mālik b. Najjār: Aws b. Thābit b. al-Mundhir b. Ḥarām the brother of Ḥassān b. Thābit, and Abū Shaykh whose name was Ubayy b. Thābit b. al-Mundhir b. Ḥarām b. ʿAmr; and Abū Ṭalḥa, whose name was Zayd b. Sahl b. al-Aswad b. Ḥarām. Three.

From the Banū ʿAdī b. al-Najjār: Ḥāritha b. Surāqa b. al-Ḥārith b. ʿAdī b. Mālik (who was killed in the battle of Badr), ʿAmr b. Thaʿlaba b. Wahb b. ʿAdī b. Mālik b. ʿAdī (ʿAmr's *kunya* was Abū Ḥakīma), Salīṭ b. Qays b. ʿAmr b. ʿUbayd b. Mālik b. ʿAdī b. ʿĀmir, Abū Salīṭ, whose name was Usayra b. ʿAmr b. ʿĀmir b. Mālik (who was killed in the battle of Uḥud), ʿAmr was the *kunya* of Abū Khārija b. Qays b. Mālik b. ʿAdī b. ʿĀmir b. Khansāʾ b. ʿAmr b. Mālik b. ʿAdī b. ʿĀmir, [Page 164] ʿĀmir b. Umayya b. Zayd b. al-Ḥashās b. Mālik b. ʿAdī b. ʿĀmir; Muḥriz b. ʿĀmir b. Mālik b. ʿĀdī b. ʿĀmir b. Ghanm b. ʿAdī; Thābit b. Khansā b. ʿAmr b. Mālik b. ʿAdī b. ʿĀmir (who was killed on the day of Uḥud), and Sawād b. Ghaziyya b. Uhayb, an ally of theirs from the Baliyy. Eight.

From the Banū Ḥarām b. Jundub b. ʿĀmir b. Ghanm b. ʿAdī b. al-Najjār: Qays b. al-Sakan b. Qays b. Zayd b. Ḥarām (his *kunya* was Qays Abū Zayd), Abū l-Aʿwar, Kaʿb b. al-Ḥārith b. Jundub b. Ẓālim b. ʿAbs b. Ḥarām b. Jundub, Sulaym b. Milḥān, and Ḥarām b. Milḥān b. Khālid b. Zayd b. Ḥarām. Five in all.

From Banū Māzin b. al-Najjār, then from the Banū ʿAwf b. ʿAmr b. ʿAwf b. Mabdhūl b. ʿAmr b. ʿAwf b. Ghanm b. Māzin: Qays b. Abī Ṣaʿṣaʿa who was named ʿAmr b. Zayd b. ʿAwf b. Mabdhūl. Yaʿqūb b. Muḥammad related to me from ʿAbdullah b. ʿAbd al-Raḥmān that the Prophet employed him over the infantry. ʿAbdullah b. Kaʿb b. ʿAmr b. ʿAwf b. Mabdhūl b. Ghanm b. Māzin was appointed by the Prophet over the booty on the day of Badr. ʿUṣaym was an ally of theirs from the Banū Asad. Three.

From the Banū Khansāʾ b. Mabdhūl b. ʿAmr b. Ghanm b. Māzin: ʿUmayr whose *kunya* was Abū Dāwud b. ʿĀmir b. Mālik b. Khansā and Surāqa b. ʿAmr b. ʿAṭiyya b. Khansā b. Mabdhūl. Two.

From the Banū Thaʿlaba b. Māzin: Qays b. Mukhallad b. Thaʿlaba b. Ṣakhr b. Ḥabīb b. al-Ḥārith b. Thaʿlaba b. Māzin.

From the Banū Dīnār b. al-Najjār, there was the Banū Masʿūd b. ʿAbd al-Ashhal b. Ḥāritha b. Dīnār: al-Nuʿmān b. ʿAbdʿAmr b. Masʿūd b. ʿAbd al-Ashhal, and al-Ḍaḥḥāk [Page 165] b. ʿAbdʿAmr b. Masʿūd b. ʿAbd al-Ashhal, Sulaym b. al-Ḥārith b. Thaʿlaba, who is the brother to al-Nuʿmān, and al-Ḍaḥḥāk the sons of ʿAbdʿAmr through their mother; Kaʿb b. Zayd who was killed on the day of al-Khandaq, and wounded on the day of Biʾr Maʿūna was carried out with the dead, Jābir b. Khālid b. ʿAbd al-Ashhal b. Ḥāritha, and Saʿīd b. Suhayl b. ʿAbd al-Ashhal b. Ḥāritha b. Dīnār. From the Banū Qays b. Mālik b. Kaʿb b. Ḥāritha b. Dīnār: Kaʿb b. Zayd b. Mālik, and Bujayr b. Abī Bujayr, an ally of theirs. They were eight.

From the Banū al-Ḥārith b. al-Khazraj, then from the Banū Imrāʾl-Qays b. Thaʿlaba: Saʿd b. Rabīʿ b. ʿAmr b. Abī Zuhayr b. Mālik b. Imrāʾ l-Qays, who was killed at Uḥud; ʿAbdullah b. Rawāḥa b. Thaʿlaba b. Imrāʾl-Qays, killed on the day of Muʾta; Khallād b. Suwayd b. Thaʿlaba b. ʿAmr b. Ḥāritha b. Imrāʾl-Qays, killed on the day of the Banū Qurayẓa; Khārija b. Zayd b. Abī Zuhayr b. Mālik—related by marriage to Abū Bakr (the daughter of Khārija was the wife of Abū Bakr), killed on the day of Uḥud. Four.

From the Banū Zayd b. Mālik b. Thaʿlaba b. Kaʿb b. al-Khazraj b. al-Ḥārith b. al-Khazraj: Bashīr b. Saʿd b. Thaʿlaba b. Julās who was killed in the battle of ʿAyn al-Tamr with Khālid b. al-Walīd, Subayʿ b. Qays b. ʿAysha b. Umayya b. ʿĀmir b. ʿAdī b. Kaʿb b. al-Khazraj, ʿUbāda b. Qays b. Mālik, Simāk b. Saʿd, ʿAbdullah b. ʿUmayr, Yazīd b. al-Ḥārith b. Qays b. Mālik b. Aḥmar b. Ḥāritha b. Thaʿlaba b. Kaʿb b. al-Khazraj whom they called Fusḥum. Six.

From the Banū Jusham [Page 166] b. al-Ḥārith b. al-Khazraj, from the son of his brother and his brother Zayd b. al-Ḥārith b. al-Khazraj who were twins: Khubayb b. Yasāf b. ʿInba b. ʿAmr b. Khadīj b. ʿĀmir b. Jusham, ʿAbdullah b. Zayd b. Thaʿlaba

b. ʿAbdRabbih b. Zayd b. al-Khazraj b. al-Ḥārith who dreamed of the call to prayer, and his brother Ḥurayth b. Zayd. Shuʿayb b. ʿUbāda related it to me from Bashīr b. Muḥammad from his father, and our companions related to me that Ḥurayth participated in the Battle of Badr. And Sufyān b. Bishr. Five.

From the Banū Judāra b. ʿAwf b. al-Ḥārith b. al-Khazraj: Tamīm b. Yaʿār b. Qays b. ʿAdī b. Umayya b. Judāra, ʿAbdullah b. ʿUmayr of the Banū Judāra, Yazīd b. al-Muzayyan, and ʿAbdullah b. ʿUrfuṭa. Four.

From the Banū al-Abjar b. ʿAwf b. al-Ḥārith b. al-Khazraj: ʿAbdullah b. al-Rabīʿ b. Qays b. ʿAbbād b. al-Abjar. One.

From the Banū ʿAwf b. al-Khazraj, there was from the Banū ʿUbayd b. Mālik b. Sālim b. Ghanm b. al-Khazraj, and they were the Banū l-Ḥublā, and indeed Sālim had a big stomach and was named al-Ḥublā, the pregnant one. ʿAbdullah b. ʿAbdullah b. Ubayy b. Mālik b. al-Ḥārith b. ʿUbayd b. Mālik (Ibn Salūl). Indeed, al-Salūl is a woman and the mother of Ubayy, and Aws b. Khawlī b. ʿAbdullah b. al-Ḥārith b. ʿUbayd b. Mālik. Two.

From the Banū Jaz b. ʿAdī b. Mālik b. Sālim b. Ghanm: Zayd b. Wadīʿa b. ʿAmr b. Qays b. Jaz, Rifāʿa b. ʿAmr b. Zayd b. ʿAmr b. Thaʿlaba b. Mālik b. Sālim b. Ghanm, ʿĀmir b. Salama b. ʿĀmir b. ʿAbdullah, an ally [Page 167] of theirs from the people of Yemen, ʿUqba b. Wahb b. Kalada an ally of theirs from the Banū ʿAbdullah b. Ghaṭafān, Maʿbad b. ʿAbbād b. Qashʿar b. Qadm b. Sālim b. Ghanm, and his *kunya* was Abū Khamīṣa, and ʿĀṣim b. al-ʿUkayr, an ally of theirs. Six.

From the Banū Sālim b. ʿAmr b. ʿAwf b. al-Khazraj, there is from the Banū ʿAjlān b. Ghanm b. Sālim: Nawfal b. ʿAbdullah b. Naḍla b. Mālik b. al-ʿAjlān, Ghassān b. Mālik b. Thaʿlaba b. ʿAmr b. al-ʿAjlān, Mulayl b. Wabra b. Khālid b. al-ʿAjlān, and ʿIṣma b. al-Ḥuṣayn b. Wabra b. Khālid b. al-ʿAjlān. Four.

From the Banū ʿAṣram b. Fihr b. Ghanm b. Sālim: ʿUbāda b. al-Ṣāmit b. Aṣram and his brother Aws b. al-Ṣāmit.

From the Banū Daʿd b. Fihr b. Ghanm: al-Nuʿmān b. Mālik b. Thaʿlaba b. Daʿd who was named Qawqalan. Al-Wāqidī says: He was called Qawqalan because when a man sought protection from him, he said to him, "Wander (Qawqil) in upper Yathrib and under it you will be safe," so he was named Qawqal. From the Banū Quryūsh b. Ghanm b. Sālim: Umayya b. Lawdhān b. Sālim b. Thābit b. Hazzāl b. ʿAmr b. Quryūsh b. Ghanm. From the Banū Daʿd: two men.

From the Banū Marḍakha b. Ghanm b. Mālik: Mālik b. al-Dakhshum. One.

From the Banū Lawdhān b. Ghanm: Rabīʿ b. Iyās and his brother Waraqa b. Iyās b. ʿAmr b. Ghanm, ʿAmr b. Iyās, an ally of theirs from the people of Yemen, and their allies from the Baliyy. Then from the Banū Ghuṣayna: al-Mujadhdhar b. Dhiyād b. ʿAmr b. Zamara b. ʿAmr b. [Page 168] ʿAmmāra, ʿAbda b. al-Ḥasḥās b. ʿAmr b. Zamara, Baḥḥāth b. Thaʿlaba b. Khazma b. Aṣram b. ʿAmr b. ʿAmmāra, and his brother ʿAbdullah b. Thaʿlaba b. Khazma b. Aṣram and an ally of theirs from Bahrāʾ, named ʿUtba b. Rabīʿa b. Khalaf b. Muʿāwiya. Shuʿayb b. ʿUbāda related to me from Bashīr b. Muḥammad from his father about that. He said: All our companions confirmed the ally. There were eight.

From the Banū Sāʿida b. Kaʿb b. al-Khazraj, then the Banū Zayd b. Thaʿlaba b. al-Khazraj: Abū Dujāna, who was called Simāk b. Kharasha b. Lawdhān b. ʿAbdWudd b. Thaʿlaba. He was killed on the day of Yamāma. Al-Mundhir b. ʿAmr, who was appointed commander over the people by the Prophet, was killed on the day of Biʾr Maʿūna. Two.

From the Banū Sāʿida, from the Banū al-Badiyy b. ʿĀmir b. ʿAwf: Abū Usayd al-Sāʿidī, whose name was Mālik b. Rabīʿa b. al-Badiyy, Mālik b. Masʿūd, and those are the Banū l-Badiyy. Ubayy b. al-ʿAbbās b. Sahl related to me from his father from his grandfather, who said, Saʿd b. Mālik prepared to go out to Badr but fell sick and died. The place of his grave is in the land of Ibn Fāriṭ. The Prophet apportioned for him and rewarded him. ʿAbd al-Muhaymin related to me from his father from his grandfather, who said that he died in Rawḥāʾ. The Prophet apportioned for him, and he was from the Banū al-Badiyy.

From the Banū Ṭarīf b. al-Khazraj b. Sāʾida: ʿAbdRabbih b. Ḥaqq b. Aws, Ibn Qaysb. Thaʿlaba b. Ṭarīf, and Kaʿb b. Jammāz b. Mālik b. Thaʿlaba, an ally of theirs from Ghassān; Ḍamra b. ʿAmr b. Kaʿb b. ʿAdī b. ʿĀmir b. Rifāʿa b. Kulayb b. Mardagha b. ʿAdī b. Ghanm b. al-Rabaʿa b. Rushdān b. [Page 169] Qays b. Juhayna, Basbas b. ʿAmr b. Thaʿlaba b. Kharasha b. Zayd b. ʿAmr b. Saʿīd b. Dhubyān b. Rushdān b. Qays b. Juhayna. Five.

From the Banū Jusham b. al-Khazraj, there is from the Banū Salima b. Saʿd b. ʿAlī b. Asad b. Sārida b. Tazīd b. Jusham, from the Banū Ḥarām b. Kaʿb b. Ghanm b. Kaʿb b. Salima: Khirāsh b. al-Ṣimma b. ʿAmr b. al-Jamūḥ b. Ḥarām, ʿUmayr b. Ḥarām, Tamīm, *mawlā* of Khirāsh b. al-Ṣimma, ʿUmayr b. al-Ḥumām b. al-Jamūḥ—who was killed at Badr, Muʿādh b. al-Jamūḥ, Muʿawwidh b. ʿAmr b. al-Jamūḥ b. Zayd b. Ḥarām, ʿAbdullah b. ʿAmr b. Ḥarām b. Thaʿlaba who was killed at Uḥud (he was Abū Jābir). Ḥubāb b. al-Mundhir b. al-Jamūḥ b. Zayd b. Ḥarām b. Kaʿb, Khallād b. ʿAmr b. al-Jamūḥ b. Zayd b. Ḥarām, ʿUqba b. ʿĀmir b. Nābā b. Zayd b. Ḥarām, Ḥabīb b. al-Aswad, a *mawlā* of theirs, Thābit b. Thaʿlaba b. Zayd b. Thaʿlaba—who was called al-Jizʿ—and ʿUmayr b. al-Ḥārith b. Thaʿlaba b. Ḥarām. A total of eleven men.

ʿAbd al-ʿAzīz b. Muḥammad related to me from Yaḥya b. Usāma from the two sons of Jābir from their father that Muʾādh b. al-Ṣimma b. ʿAmr b. al-Jamūḥ witnessed Badr. But there is no agreement about this.

From the Banū ʿUbayd b. ʿAdī b. Ghanm b. Kaʿb b. Salima, then from the Banū Khansāʾ b. Sinān b. ʿUbayd: Bishr b. al-Barāʾ b. Maʿrūr b. Ṣakhr b. Sinān b. Ṣayfī b. Ṣakhr b. Khansāʾ, ʿAbdullah b. al-Jadd b. Qays b. Ṣakhr b. Khansāʾ, Sinān b. Ṣayfī b. Ṣakhr b. Khansāʾ, ʿUtba b. ʿAbdullah b. Ṣakhr b. Khansāʾ, Ḥamza b. al-Ḥumayyir, who said: I heard that Khārija b. al-Ḥumayyir and ʿAbdullah b. al-Ḥumayyir were allies of theirs from the Ashjaʿ of the Banū Duhmān.

[Page 170] From the Banū Nuʿmān b. Sinān b. ʿUbayd b. ʿAbd b. ʿAdī b. Ghanm: ʿAbdullah b. ʿAbdManāf b. al-Nuʿmān b. Sinān, Nuʿmān b. Sinān, a *mawlā* of theirs, Jābir b. ʿAbdullah b. Riāb b. al-Nuʿmān, Khulayda b. Qays b. al-Nuʿmān b. Sinān. Others said Labda b. Qays. Four.

From the Banū Khunās b. Sinān b. ʿUbayd b. ʿAdī: Yazīd b. al-Mundhir b. Sarḥ b. Khunās, his brother Maʿqil b. al-Mundhir b. Sarḥ b. Khunās, and ʿAbdullah b. al-Nuʿmān b. Baldhama b. Khunās. Three.

From the Banū Khansā b. ʿUbayd: Jabbār b. Ṣakhr b. Umayya b. Khansāʾ b. ʿUbayd. One.

From the Banū Thaʿlaba b. ʿUbayd: al-Ḍaḥḥāk b. Ḥāritha b. Thaʿlaba b. ʿUbayd, and Sawād b. Zayd b. Thaʿlaba b. ʿUbayd.

From the Banū ʿAdī b. Ghanm b. Kaʿb b. Salima: ʿAbdullah b. Qays b. Ṣakhr b. Ḥarām b. Rabīʿa b. ʿAdī b. Ghanm, and his brother Maʿbad b. Qays b. Ṣakhr b. Ḥarām b. Rabīʿa b. ʿAdī b. Ghanm.

From the Banū Sawād b. Ghanm b. Kaʿb b. Salima, then from the Banū Ḥadīda: Yazīd b. ʿĀmir b. Ḥadīda (Yazīd's *kunya* was Abū al-Mundhir), Sulaym b. ʿAmr b. Ḥadīda, Quṭba b. ʿĀmir b. Ḥadīda, ʿAntara, the *mawlā* of Sulaym b. ʿAmr b. Ḥadīda.

From the Banū ʿAdī b. Nābā b. ʿAmr b. Sawād: ʿAbs b. ʿĀmir b. ʿAdī b. Thaʿlaba b. Ghanama b. ʿAdī, Thaʿlaba b. Ghanama, Abū l-Yasar whose name was Kaʿb b. ʿAmr b. ʿAbbād b. ʿAmr b. Sawād, Sahl b. Qays b. Abī Kaʿb b. al-Qayn, who was killed at Uḥud, Muʿādh b. Jabal b. ʿĀʾidh b. ʿAdī b. Kaʿb, and Thaʿlaba and ʿAbdullah the two sons of Unays who broke the idols of the Banū Salima.

[Page 171] From the Banū Zurayq b. ʿĀmir b. ʿAbd Ḥāritha b. Mālik b. Ghaḍb b. Jusham b. al-Khazraj, then from the Banū Mukhallad b. ʿĀmir b. Zurayq: Qays b. Miḥṣan b. Khālid b. Mukhallad, al-Ḥārith b. Qays b. Khālid b. Mukhallad, Jubayr b. Iyās b. Khālid b. Mukhallad, Saʿīd b. ʿUthmān b. Khālid b. Mukhallad (his *kunya* was Abū ʿUbāda), ʿUqba b. ʿUthmān b. Khālid, Dhakwān b. ʿAbdQays b. Khālid b. Mukhallad, and Masʿūd b. Khalada b. ʿĀmir b. Mukhallad. Seven.

From the Banū Khālid b. ʿĀmir b. Zurayq: ʿAbbād b. Qays b. ʿĀmir b. Khālid b. ʿĀmir b. Zurayq. One.

From the Banū Khalada b. ʿĀmir b. Zurayq: Asʿad b. Yazīd b. al-Fākih b. Zayd b. Khalada b. ʿĀmir, al-Fākih b. Bishr b. al-Fākih b. Zayd b. Khalada, Muʿādh b. Māʿiṣ b. Qays b. Khalada, and his brother ʿĀʾidh b. Māʿiṣ, Masʿūd b. Saʿd b. Qays b. Khalada, who was killed on the day of Biʾr Maʿūna. Five.

From the Banū al-ʿAjlān b. ʿAmr b. ʿĀmir b. Zurayq: Rifāʿa b. Rāfiʿ b. Mālik b. al-ʿAjlān, Khallād b. Rāfiʿ b. Mālik b. al-ʿAjlān, and ʿUbayd b. Zayd b. ʿĀmir b. al-ʿAjlān. Three.

From the Banū Ḥabīb b. ʿAbd Ḥāritha b. Mālik b. Ghaḍb b. Jusham b. al-Khazraj: Rāfiʿ b. al-Muʿallā b. Lawdhān b. Ḥāritha b. Zayd b. Ḥāritha b. Thaʿlaba b. ʿAdī b. Mālik and his brother Hilāl b. al-Muʿallā, who was killed at Badr. Two.

From the Banū Bayāḍa b. ʿĀmir b. Zurayq b. ʿĀmir b. ʿAbd Ḥāritha: Ziyād b. Labīd b. Thaʿlaba b. Sinān b. ʿĀmir b. ʿAdī b. Umayya b. Bayāḍa, Farwa b. ʿAmr b. Wadhfa b. ʿUbayd b. ʿĀmir, Khālid b. Qays b. Mālik b. al-ʿAjlān b. [Page 172] ʿAlī b. ʿĀmir b. Bayāḍa, and Ruḥayla b. Thaʿlaba b. Khālid b. Thaʿlaba b. Bayāḍa. Four.

From the Banū Umayya b. Bayāḍa: Ḥulayfa b. ʿAdī b. ʿAmr b. Mālik b. ʿĀmir b. Fuhayra b. ʿĀmir b. Bayāḍa, Ghannām b. Aws b. Ghannām b. Aws b. ʿAmr b. Mālik b. ʿĀmir b. Bayāḍa, and ʿAṭiyya b. Nuwayra b. ʿĀmir b. ʿAṭiyya b. ʿĀmir b. Bayāḍa. Khālid b. al-Qāsim related to me about that from Zurʿa b. ʿAbdullah b. Ziyād b. Labīd that the two men are confirmed. Al-Wāqidī said: There is no agreement about the two of them.

THE EXPEDITION TO KILL ʿAṢMĀʾ BT. MARWĀN

ʿAbdullah b. al-Ḥārith related to me from his father that ʿAṣmāʾ bt. Marwān of the Banū Umayya b. Zayd, who was married to Yazīd b. Zayd b. Ḥiṣn al-Khaṭmī, insulted the Prophet, vilified Islam and incited the people against the Prophet with poetry:

> I despise the Banū Mālik and al-Nabīt and ʿAwf and I despise the Banū l-Khazraj
> You obey a stranger who is from other than you; not from Murād or Madhḥij,
> Do you have hopes of him even after the killing of your chiefs
> Like one who awaits a well-cooked broth?

When her provocative words reached ʿUmayr b. ʿAdī b. Kharasha b. Umayya al-Khaṭmī, [Page 173] he said, "O God, indeed I promise that if you return the Messenger of God to Medina, I will surely kill her," for the Messenger of God was at that time in Badr. When the Messenger of God returned from Badr, ʿUmayr b. ʿAdī went looking for her in the middle of the night, and entered her home. Her children were sleeping around her, and one suckled at her breast. He touched her with his hand, and discovering the suckling babe pushed it from her. He placed his sword upon her heart and pierced her until it came out from behind her. Then he returned to pray the dawn prayer with the Prophet in Medina. When the Prophet turned and saw ʿUmayr he said, "Did you kill the daughter of Marwān?" He replied, "Yes, for you are dearer to me than my father, O Messenger of God." But ʿUmayr feared that he had undermined the Prophet by killing her. He said, "Do you fault me for that, O Messenger of God?" The Prophet replied, "Two goats will not thrust about her." And surely this was the first time such words were heard from the Prophet. ʿUmayr said: The Prophet then turned towards those who were around him and said, "If you desire to look at a man who secretly helped God and his Messenger, look at ʿUmayr b. ʿAdī." ʿUmar b. al-Khaṭṭāb said, "Look at this blind one who is relentless in his obedience to God." He [the Prophet] said, "Do not say blind one, but rather, the one with vision!"

When ʿUmayr returned from the Prophet he found all ʿAṣmā's children burying her. They approached him when they saw him coming from Medina, and said, "O ʿUmayr, did you kill her?" He replied, "Yes; and do me any harm and you will see what happens to you! By Him who holds my soul in His hands, if you, all of you together, say what she said, I will surely strike you with my sword until I kill you, or die in the attempt."

At that time Islam appeared with the [Page 174] Banū Khaṭma. There were among them men who concealed Islam for fear of their people. Ḥassān b. Thābit praised ʿUmayr b. ʿAdī, and ʿAbdullah b. al-Ḥārith recited to us:

> Banū Wāʾil and Banū Wāqif and Khaṭma are inferior to the Banū al-Khazraj.
> When your sister called her woes with her lament, and death approached,
> She stirred up a man of glorious origin, noble in his coming in and going out
> He colored her in the redness of blood
> Shortly before dawn, and he felt no guilt.
> God will convey you to soothing Paradise,
> Rejoicing in the blessing of the entry.

ʿAbdullah b. al-Ḥārith related to me from his father that the death of ʿAṣmāʾ took place in the last five nights of Ramaḍān. The return of the Prophet from Badr was in the nineteenth month AH.

THE EXPEDITION TO KILL ABŪ ʿAFAK

Saʿīd b. Muḥammad related to us from ʿUmāra b. Ghāzīyya, and Abū Muṣʿab related to us from Ismāʿīl b. Muṣʿab b. Ismāʿīl b. Zayd b. Thābit from his elders, who said: There was a sheikh of the Banū ʿAmr b. ʿAwf, called Abū ʿAfak. He was an old man who had reached one hundred and twenty years when the Prophet arrived in Medina. He provoked the enmity of the Prophet and did not enter Islam. When the Messenger of God went out to Badr and returned, and God granted him victory, Abū ʿAfak envied him and [Page 175] opposed him saying:

Long have I lived but never have I seen
An assembly or collection of people,
More minds that came to a commitment swiftly when called.
A rider dispossessed them of their affairs
Splitting them into forbidden and permitted.
If it was kingship that you believed in
You would have followed Tubbaʿ.

Sālim b. ʿUmayr said—and he was one of the weepers of the Banū Najjār—"I vowed that I would kill Abū ʿAfak or die in the attempt. I waited for a heedless moment." Then, one Summer's night, as Abū ʿAfak slept in the courtyard with the Banū ʿAmr b. ʿAwf, Sālim b. ʿUmayr approached, and pressed the sword upon his liver until it entered his bed. The enemy of God screamed. Those among the people who heard his words returned to him. They entered his place and buried him. They said, "Who killed him? By God, if we learn who killed him we will surely kill him for it." Al-Nahdiyya, a Muslim woman, said these verses about that:

You lied about the religion of God and the man Aḥmad
By the life of he who produced you, miserable is what he produced.
A Ḥanīf gave you, at the end of the night, a thrust.
Abū ʿAfak, take it inspite of your age.
Indeed if I knew who killed you in the dead of night
Whether man or Jinn, I would not say.

Maʿan b. ʿUmar related to me saying: Ibn Ruqaysh informed me that Abū ʿAfak was killed in Shawwāl, the twentieth month AH.

[Page 176] THE RAID OF THE BANŪ QAYNUQĀʿ

The raid of the Qaynuqāʿ began on Saturday in the middle of Shawwāl, the twentieth month AH. The Prophet besieged them until the first day of the month of Dhū l-Qaʿda.

ʿAbdullāh b. Jaʿfar related to me from al-Ḥārith b. al-Fuḍayl from Ibn Kaʿb al-Quraẓī, saying: When the Messenger of God arrived in Medina, the Jews, all of them, were reconciled with him, and he wrote an agreement between him and them. The Prophet attached every tribe with its confederates and established a protection between himself and them. He stipulated conditions to them, among which it was stipulated that they would not help an enemy against him.

When the Prophet overcame the companions of Badr and arrived in Medina, the Jews acted wrongfully and destroyed the agreement that was between them and the Messenger of God. The Prophet sent for them and having gathered them together, said, "O Jewish people, submit, for, by God, you surely know that I am the Messenger of God, before God inflicts upon you the like of what he inflicted on the Quraysh." The Jews said, "O Muḥammad, let not those whom you met deceive you. Surely you have defeated a people who have no experience in war. But we are, by God, the masters of war, and if you fight us you will learn that you have not fought with the likes of us."

While they were thus showing enmity and breach of the agreement, a woman from the Bedouin married to a man from the Anṣār came to the market of the Banū Qaynuqāʿ. She sat down at a Goldsmith's with a trinket of hers. A Jew of the Banū Qaynuqāʿ came and sat behind her, and without her knowledge fixed her outer garment to her back with a pin. When the woman stood up her pudenda showed and they laughed at her. [Page 177] A man from the Muslims stood up and followed the Jew and killed him. The Banū Qaynuqāʿ gathered and surrounded and killed the Muslim. They abandoned the agreement with the Prophet and opposed him, fortifying themselves in their fortress. The Prophet went to them and besieged them. They were the first of those to whom the Prophet marched. The Jews of Qaynuqāʿ were driven away. They were the first of the Jews who fought the Prophet.

Muḥammad b. ʿAbdullāh from al-Zuhrī from ʿUrwa told me: When this verse was revealed, *if thou fearest treachery from any group, throw back (their covenant) to them, (so as to be) on equal terms: for God loves not the treacherous* (Q. 8:58), the Prophet marched to the Banū Qaynuqāʿ on the basis of this verse. They said: He besieged them in their fortress for fifteen nights most vigorously until God put fear in their hearts. The Jews said, "May we surrender and leave?" The Prophet said, "No, except upon my judgment." The Jews surrendered unconditionally to the Prophet and he ordered that they be tied up.

He said: "They were fettered with shackles." They said: The Prophet employed al-Mundhir b. Qudāma al-Sālimī to fetter them. Muḥammad b. ʿAbdullāh said: Ibn Ubayy passed by them and he said, "Set them free!" And al-Mundhir said, "Will you set free a people whom the Prophet has tied up? By God, a man will not set them free but I will cut off his head." Ibn Ubayy rushed to the Prophet, thrust his hand into the Prophet's coat of mail from behind him, and said, "O Muḥammad, deal kindly with my clients." The Prophet turned to him angrily, his face changed, and said, "Woe unto you, release me!" But Ibn Ubayy said, "I will not release you unless you deal kindly with my clients. Four hundred men in mail, and three hundred without mail protected me on the day of Ḥadāʾiq and Buʿath from all my enemies, and you desire to mow them down [Page 178] in one morning? O Muḥammad, I am a man who fears consequences." The Prophet said, "Set them free, and may God curse them and curse him with them!" When Ibn Ubayy spoke for them the Prophet refrained from killing them, and commanded that they be exiled from Medina.

Ibn Ubayy came with his confederates who were prepared to leave. He desired to speak to the Prophet about settling them in their houses. Ibn Ubayy found ʿUwaym b. Sāʾida at the door of the Prophet when he went to enter, and ʿUwaym turned him back, saying, "Do not enter until the Prophet notifies you." Ibn Ubayy pushed him, and ʿUwaym treated him harshly until the wall scratched Ibn Ubayy's face and blood flowed. His Jewish confederates shouted, "Abū l-Ḥubāb, we will never stay in a home/land wherein your face suffered this, and we are not able to change it." Ibn Ubayy began to shout to them while he wiped the blood from his face, saying, "Woe unto you! Stand firm, stay!" But they began to shout together, "We will never live in a home/land in which your face suffered such as this, and we are not in a position to change it!" They were surely the bravest of the Jews, and Ibn Ubayy had ordered them to enter their fortress, claiming that he would enter with them, but he forsook them and did not enter with them. They remained in their fortress and did not shoot an arrow nor fight until they surrendered to the peace and judgment of the Messenger of God with their possessions for him.

When they came out and opened their fortress, it was Muḥammad b. Maslama who expelled them and seized their possessions. The Prophet took from their weapons three bows: one bow named al-Katūm, which was broken at Uḥud, another bow named al-Rawhā', and another named al-Bayḍā'. He took two coats of mail from their weapons: one, which was called al-Ṣaghdiyya and another, Fiḍḍa. And three swords: a Qala'ī sword, a sword named Battār, and [Page 179] another sword; and three spears. He said: They found many weapons and tools for gold smithery in their fortresses, for they were goldsmiths.

Muḥammad b. Maslama said: The Messenger of God gave me one of their coats of mail. To Saʿd b. Muʿādh he gave a coat of mail, which is famous, called al-Saḥl. They did not possess land or plantations (meaning fields). The Messenger of God took one fifth (*khums*) from whatever was captured from them (booty), and apportioned what remained among his companions. The Messenger of God commanded ʿUbāda b. al-Ṣāmit to expel them. The Qaynuqāʿ began to say, "O Abū l-Walīd, from among the Aws and the Khazraj we are your confederates, and you do this to us?" ʿUbāda said to them, "When you fought, I came to the Prophet and said, 'O Prophet, I exonerate myself to you from them and from my alliance with them.'" Ibn Ubayy and ʿUbāda b. al-Ṣāmit were in the same position with them, in alliance. ʿAbdullāh b. Ubayy said, "Did you free yourself from your alliance with your confederates? How is this which is in their hands with you!" And he reminded him of some cases in which they had stood the test. ʿUbāda said, "Abū l-Ḥubāb, hearts have changed and Islam has erased the agreements. On the other hand, by God, surely you are involved in an affair whose end you will see tomorrow."

The Qaynuqāʿ said, "O Muḥammad, some people owe us a debt." The Messenger of God said, "Hasten and settle it." ʿUbāda imposed departure and exile upon them. They asked for time, but he told them there would not be an hour exceeding three days for them. "This is the command of the Messenger of God; if it were I, I would not have given you a moment." When three days passed he set out on their trail until they were on their way to al-Shām. He says, "The most distant and furthest honor is the furthest." When he reached Khalf Dhubāb [Page 180] he turned back. They settled in Adhriʿāt. Regarding their expulsion when they breached the pact, we heard a report other than that of Ibn Kaʿb.

Muḥammad [b. ʿAbdullah] related to me from al-Zuhrī from ʿUrwa, saying: Surely when the Prophet returned from Badr, they (the Jews) were envious and displayed deceit. Jibrīl revealed this verse to him: *If you fear treachery from any group, throw back (their covenant) to them (so as to be) on equal terms, for God loves not the treacherous* (Q. 8:58). He said: When Jibrīl had finished, the Messenger of God said to him, "I fear them." The Prophet marched to them on the basis of this verse until they yielded to his judgment. The Prophet got their possessions, and they kept their children and their women.

Muḥammad b. al-Qāsim related to me from his father from al-Rabīʿ b. Sabra from his father. He said: I was between the two Faljās coming from al-Shām when I met the Banū Qaynuqāʿ carrying their children and women on camels while they themselves walked. I questioned them and they said, "Muḥammad expelled us and he took our possessions." I said, "Where are you going?" They said, "Al-Shām." Sabra said: When they alighted at Wādī al-Qurā they remained for a month. The Jews of Wādī al-Qurā gave mounts to those who were on foot and fed them. They went to Adhriʿāt and stayed there, and theirs was such a short stay.

Yaḥyā b. ʿAbdullāh b. Abī Qatāda related to me from ʿAbdullāh b. Abī Bakr b. Ḥazm, saying: The Prophet appointed Abū Lubāba b. ʿAbd al-Mundhir to represent him at Medina on three occasions: The battle of Badr, the raid on the Banū Qaynuqāʿ, and the raid of al-Sawīq.

[Page 181] THE RAID OF AL-SAWĪQ

The raid of al-Sawīq was in Dhū l-Ḥijja, the twenty-second month AH. The Prophet went out on Sunday, the fifth of Dhū l-ḥijja. He was absent for five days.

Muḥammad b. ʿAbdullah related to me from al-Zuhrī, and Isḥāq b. Ḥāzm from Muḥammad b. Kaʿb. They both said: When the polytheists returned to Mecca from Badr, Abū Sufyān forbade oil for himself until he took his revenge on Muḥammad and his companions for those whom they had taken from his people. He went out with two hundred riders, according to al-Zuhrī, but according to the traditions of Ibn Kaʿb with four hundred riders, and took the road to al-Najd. They came to the Banū Naḍīr by night and knocked at Ḥuyayy b. Akhṭab's and inquired of news of Muḥammad and his companions. Ḥuyayy refused to open to them so they knocked on Sallām b. Mishkam's door, and he opened his doors for them and was hospitable to them. He gave Abū Sufyān to drink and news of Muḥammad and his companions. At daybreak Abū Sufyān left, passing through al-ʿUrayḍ. Finding a man from the Anṣār with an employee of his in his fields, he killed them and burned their homes at al-ʿUrayḍ and burned their field. He believed that he was released from his vows. Then he went swiftly, fearing to be found.

This reached Muḥammad and he selected his companions and they went out in Abū Sufyān's tracks. Abū Sufyān and his companions tried to relieve themselves by throwing off the sacks of barley, which was their provision, and the Muslims who were passing by [Page 182] picked them up. For this reason the raid was named the raid of al-Sawīq. Finally the Messenger of God reached Medina. Abū Sufyān, according to a tradition of al-Zuhrī, said these verses about that:

> Salllām b. Mishkam gave me to drink and quenched my thirst with the wines of Kumayta and Mudīma.
> Abū ʿAmr is generous. His house in Yathrib, a residence for every nobleman, a place of plenty.

Al-Zuhrī called him Abū ʿAmr, but the people called him Abū l-Ḥakam. The Messenger of God appointed Abū Lubāba ʿAbd al-Mundhir to take his place over Medina. Muḥammad related to me from al-Zuhrī saying: This took place in Dhū l-Ḥijja, the twenty-second month AH.

THE RAID OF QARĀRA AL-KUDR

The Prophet marched to the Banū Sulaym and Ghaṭafān in the middle of Muḥarram, the twenty-third month AH. He was absent for fifteen nights.

ʿAbdullah b. Jaʿfar related to me from Ibn Abī ʿAwn from Yaʿqūb b. ʿUtba saying: The Prophet went out from Medina to Qarara al-Kudr, and what motivated him was that it had reached him that those from the Ghaṭafān and the Sulaym had gathered there. So the Prophet marched to them. He took them on the road until he arrived where he saw traces of cattle at their watering place. But he did not find anyone in the fields. The Prophet sent a group of his companions to the valley above, while he confronted them at the valley of the wadi. [Page 183] Here, he found shepherds, and with them a youth named Yasār. He asked them about the people and Yasār said, "I have no information about them. Indeed, they come to water for five days and this is the fourth day." The people had rushed to the water, and we were far from home grazing cattle. The Prophet turned and took the cattle with him. He descended towards Medina until when he prayed the Ṣubḥ prayer, lo and behold, it was Yasār and he saw him praying. He commanded the people to apportion their spoils. The people said, "O Messenger of God, we will be stronger if we drive the cattle together. Indeed with us are those who are weak from carrying his portion." The Messenger of God said, "Apportion!" They said, "O Messenger of God, if you would rather that the praying slave be with you, then we will give him to you with your portion." The Messenger of God said, "Would you be content?" They said, "Yes." The Messenger of God accepted the youth and set him free. The people departed and the Messenger of God arrived in Medina. They apportioned their plunder, and every man among them obtained seven camels. There were two hundred people.

ʿAbd al-Ṣamad b. Muḥammad al-Saʿdī, related to me from Ḥafṣ b. ʿUmar b. Abī Ṭalḥa from one who informed him, from Abū Arwā al-Dawsī, who said: I was with the expedition, among those who drove the cattle. When we were in Ṣirār, i.e. three miles from Medina, the cattle were divided into five portions; the cattle were five hundred camels. The Prophet took out his fifth and apportioned four-fifths to the Muslims. They received two camels each.

ʿAbdullah b. Nūḥ related to me from Abū ʿUfayr, who said: The Messenger of God appointed [Page 184] Ibn Umm Maktūm over Medina in his absence; he assembled them and spoke at the side of the *minbar*. He kept the *minbar* to the left of him.

THE KILLING OF KAʿB B. AL-ASHRAF

He was killed in Rabīʿ al-Awwal, the twenty-fifth month AH.

ʿAbd al-Ḥamīd b. Jaʿfar related to me from Yazīd b. Rūmān, and Maʿmar from al-Zuhrī from Ibn Kaʿb b. Mālik, and Ibrāhīm b. Jaʿfar from his father from Jābir b. ʿAbdullah. All of it was related to me in portions, and it is what was collected for us about it. They said: Ibn al-Ashraf was a poet who had insulted the Prophet and his companions with his poetry, and incited the disbelieving Quraysh against them.

The Prophet arrived in Medina, and its people were a mix—among them were the Muslims who had come together to the call of Islam. With them were the people of weapons and fortresses, and among them were the confederates of the two regions, the Aws and the Khazraj. When the Messenger of God arrived in Medina he desired to establish peace for them and he reconciled with all of them—the man would be a Muslim and his father a polytheist. The polytheists and Jews among the people of Medina hurt the Prophet and his companions grievously but God most high commanded His prophet and the Muslims to be patient and forgiving. About them it was revealed: *And you shall certainly hear much that will grieve you from those who received the Book* [Page 185] *before you and from those who worship many Gods. But if you persevere patiently and guard against evil, then that will be the determining factor in all affairs* (Q. 3:186). And about them God most high revealed: *Many from the People of the Book wished they could turn you back* (Q. 2:109).

When Ibn al-Ashraf refused to abstain from insulting the Prophet and the Muslims, he really affected them, and when Zayd b. Ḥāritha arrived with tidings from Badr about the killing of the polytheists and the capture of prisoners from them, and when he informed them that he saw the prisoners chained, Ibn al-Ashraf was dejected and made low, and he said to his people, "Woe unto you! By God, the bowels of the earth are better for you than its surface today! The best of these people have been killed and taken prisoner. What will you do?" They replied, "His enmity will last as long as we live." He said, "What are you? Has he not trampled his people, and taken them? But I will go out to the Quraysh and incite them, and I will mourn their dead so they will, perhaps, authorize me to go out with them." Kaʿb went out until he arrived in Mecca, placed his saddle with Abū Wadāʿa b. Ubayra al-Sahmi who was married to ʿĀtika bt. Asayd b. Abū l-ʿĪṣ. Then, he began to lament the Quraysh, saying:

Badr's mill churned out the blood of its people.
At events like Badr you should weep and cry.
The best of the people were slain round its cisterns,
Don't think it strange that the Kings were left lying.
Some people whose anger pleases me say
"Kaʿb b. al-Ashraf is utterly dejected."
They are right. O that the earth when they were killed
Had split asunder and engulfed its people!
How many noble handsome men, the refuge of the homeless, were slain,
[Page 186] Liberal when the stars gave no rain,
Who bore others' burdens, ruling and taking their due forth.
I was told that all the Banū al-Mughīra were humiliated
And brought low by the death of Abū l-Ḥakīm
And the two sons of Rabīʿa with him, and Munabbih
Was he destroyed in the manner of Tubbaʿ?

Ḥassān b. Thābit answered him saying:

Does Kaʿb weep for him incessantly
And live in humiliation hearing nothing?
In the vale of Badr I saw some of them, killed,
Eyes shedding tears for them.
Weep for you have made a sordid slave shed tears
Like a pup following a little bitch.
God has granted satisfaction to our leader
And put to shame and prostrated those who fought him.
Those whose hearts were torn with fear
Escaped and fled from them
Swiftly, the few defeated fugitives
Escaped and fled from them.

The Messenger of God called Ḥassān and he informed him about Kaʿb's coming down. Ḥassān said:

Did not a letter reach Asyad from me
Your uncle is an experienced slave of deceit
[Page 187] By your life, Asayd did not fulfill what was due to his neighbor,
Nor Khālid, nor the fat bellied Zaynab.
And ʿAttāb is a slave who gave no protection
A liar in the affairs of the head;
A schooled monkey who does as he is told.

When his insults reached ʿĀtika, she threw out his saddle and said: Why is this Jew with us? Have you not seen what Ḥassān does with us? So Ibn al-Ashraf moved, and whenever he moved from one group, the Messenger of God invited Ḥassān and said: Ibn al-Ashraf has descended upon so-and-so. Ibn al-Ashraf continued to insult them until his saddle was thrown out, and when he was not able to find shelter he arrived in Medina. When news of Ibn al-Ashraf's arrival reached the Prophet, he said, "O God, grant me satisfaction over Ibn al-Ashraf however you wish with regard to his evil pronouncements and words of poetry."

The Messenger of God said, "Who will bring me Ibn al-Ashraf, for he has harmed me?" Muḥammad b. Maslama answered, "I will do it, O Messenger of God, I will kill him." He replied, "Do so!" But Muḥammad b. Maslama stayed a few days without eating, so the Messenger of God called him and said, "O Muḥammad, you have kept away from food and drink?" He replied, "O Messenger of God, I have agreed to do something for you which I do not know that I can." The Messenger of God said, "Do your best." He added, "Consult with Saʿd b. Muʿādh about the matter." Muḥammad b. Maslama assembled a group of people including ʿAbbād b. Bishr, Abū Nāʾila Silkān b. Salāma, al-Ḥārith b. Aws, and Abū Abs b. Jabr, and they said, "O Messenger of God, we will kill him, but permit us to speak freely. Indeed, we have no alternative." He replied, "Say as you wish."

Abū Nāʾila went out to Kaʿb, and when Kaʿb saw him, he hated his affair. He was quite terrified. He feared he would be ambushed. [Page 188] Abū Nāʾila said, "We need you." Ibn al-Ashraf said, while he was in the company of his people and in their gathering, "Come closer to me and inform me of your need," and he changed color in fear. Abū Nāʾila and Ibn Maslama were his foster brothers, so they talked for an hour and exchanged poetry with each other. Then Kaʿb smiled and said, from time to time, "What is your need!" Abū Nāʾila was reciting poetry, and Abū Nāʾila used to say poetry—and Kaʿb said, "Your need is perhaps that you desire those who are with us to get up and leave?" And when the people heard that, they stood up. Abū Nāʾila said, "I hate the people hearing parts of our words so they have doubts! The arrival of this man (Muḥammad) upon us is a trial. The Arabs have fought us and aimed at us with a single bow. The roads are cut off from us. The people are exhausted and their dependants are frustrated. He takes charity from us and we do not find what we eat." Kaʿb said, "By God, did I not warn you, O Ibn Salama, that this authority will go to him (the Prophet)?"

Abū Nāʾila said, "My companions who hold a similar opinion to mine are with me. I would like to bring you to them and purchase food and dates from you. You will be good to us about that, and we will deposit what ever will give you confidence with you." Kaʿb said, "My shelves are filled with the dates of Ajwah in which one's tooth disappears.

O Abū Nāʾila, it is not that I like to see this privation in you. Indeed, you were among the most generous of people to me. You are my brother, and I competed with you for the nipple!" Silkān said, "Be silent about us and what I have told you about Muḥammad." Kaʿb said, "I will not mention a word of it." Then he said, "O Abū Nāʾila, O you who possess my heart, tell me the truth. What is it that you desire in this affair?" He replied, "To abandon him and withdraw from him." Kaʿb said, "Indeed, you make me happy, O Abū Nāʾila. And what will you deposit with me? Your sons and your women?" Abū Nāʾila replied, "Surely you seek to dishonor us and expose our affairs. But we will deposit coats of mail with you and what ever satisfies you." Kaʿb said, "Indeed in coats of mail is fulfillment." Surely, Silkān said this in order that they would not be denied when they arrived with weapons.

[Page 189] Abū Nāʾila went out from his home for the appointment. His companions came and gathered, and he ordered them to come to his appointment in the evening. They came to the Prophet at ʿIshāʾ and informed him, and the Prophet walked with them until he came to al-Baqiʿ, when he faced them and said, "Proceed, by the Grace of God, and with His help."

Others say that he directed them after they prayed ʿIshāʾ, on a moonlit night, which was like day, on the fourteenth of Rabīʿ al-Awwal, the twenty-fifth month AH.

He said: They went until they came to Ibn al-Ashraf. When they finally reached his fortress, Abū Nāʾila called out to him. Ibn al-Ashraf had recently contracted a marriage, but he jumped out of bed while his wife grabbed in the direction of his blanket saying, "Where are you going? Surely you are a fighting man and such a man does not go out at this hour?" He replied, "I have an appointment—Surely it is my brother Abū Nāʾila. By God, if he finds me sleeping he will not awaken me." He struck the blanket with his hand saying, "If a young man is invited for a challenge, he answers." Then he went down and greeted them.

They sat down and talked for an hour until he opened to them, and relaxed. They said to him: O Ibn al-Ashraf, would you like to walk to Sharj al-ʿAjūz, so we can talk about it for the rest of the night?" He said: They continued walking until they faced the direction of Sharj. Then Abū Nāʾila put his hand on the head of Kaʿb saying, "Woe unto you, how excellent is this perfume of yours, Ibn al-Ashraf," for Kaʿb had been anointed with youthful musk, water and ambergris, until Abū Nāʾila's hand was entangled in his temple, and it was a beautiful curl. Then he walked awhile and returned similarly, until Kaʿb was composed, while his two hands were knotted in his hair. Then he grasped the crown of his head and said to his companions, "Kill the enemy of God." They struck with their swords but the blades went by his sides and were useless. Some of them pushed away the others while he was stuck to Abū Naʾila.

Muḥammad b. Maslama said: I remembered a short knife of mine [Page 190] it was with my sword. I pulled it out and placed it in his navel. Then I pressed heavily on it and cut him until, finally, I reached his pubic region. The enemy of God shouted, and not a fortress of the Jews remained but it kindled a flame. Ibn Sunayna, one of the Jews of the Banū Ḥāritha said, and there were three miles between them: Indeed the air smelled of blood in Yathrib. Some of them (the attackers) struck al-Ḥārith b. Aws with the sword, while they were killing Kaʿb, and wounded him in his leg.

When they finished cutting off al-Ashraf's head they took it with them. They went out hurrying for they were fearful of a Jewish ambush. They took the path over the Banū Umayya b. Zayd, then above the Qurayẓa, where the fires in their fortresses were high. Then on to Buʿāth, until when they were in the district of al-ʿUrayd, al-Ḥārith, drained of blood, lagged behind. He called to them: Give the Messenger of God greetings from me. So they turned for him and carried him until they reached the Prophet. When they reached Baqīʿ al-Gharqad they proclaimed *takbīr*. The Messenger of God had stayed up that night praying. When he heard the *takbīr* proclaimed at al-Baqīʿ he knew that they had killed Kaʿb.

They ran until they found the Messenger of God standing at the door of the mosque. He said, "May your faces prosper!" They replied, "And your face too, O Messenger of God." They threw Ibn al-Ashraf's head before him, and he praised God for his death. Then they brought their companion al-Ḥārith to the Prophet. The Prophet spat in his wound and it no longer hurt him. ʿAbbād b. Bishr said about that:

> [Page 191] I called to him but he did not hasten to my voice
> But he appeared rising from above the castle
> So I called again, and he said: Who is this caller?
> I replied: Your brother ʿAbbād b. Bishr.
> Muḥammad said: Hurry to us.
> We have come for your thanks and hospitality
> And your support for us. Surely we have come in hunger
> With a half load of grain and dates
> and these our weapons as security/pledge, take them
> For a full month or a half.
> He said to himself, a people who are hungry and in need
> Surely they lack wealth but are without poverty.
> He approached us coming down swiftly
> And he said you have come for a matter
> But in our right hands are white swords
> Practiced in the slitting of the unbeliever.
> Ibn Maslama the one who struck embraced him
> Like a lion and smothered him.
> Strengthened by his sheathed sword upon him
> Abū Abs Ibn Jabr pierced him.
> I arrived with my companions and when
> We killed the infidel he was like a slaughtered animal.
> A noble took off his head.
> They were renowned for fidelity and piety
> And God was the sixth among us, and we
> Returned with mercy and blessings and a splendid victory.

Ibn Abī Ḥabība said: I saw the sayer of this poetry. Ibn Abī l-Zinād said: If it were not for the saying of Ibn Abī Ḥabība I would not regard it as confirmed.

They said: When the Messenger of God rose from the night in which Kaʿb was killed, he said, "Who ever from among you can get the better of men from among the Jews, kill him." The Jews became fearful. Not one of their leaders ventured out. They did not speak for they feared they would be sought out in their homes just as Ibn al-Ashraf was.

Ibn Sunayna was from the Jews of the Banū Ḥāritha, a confederate of Huwayyiṣa b. Masʿūd. [Page 192] Muhayyiṣa had converted, and he attacked Ibn Sunayna and killed him. Huwayyiṣa [his older brother] began to strike Muḥayyiṣa—saying, "O enemy of God, did you kill him? Many a piece of fat that is in your belly has come from his wealth." Muhayyisa replied, "By God, if he who commanded me to kill him, commanded me to kill you, I would kill you." Huwayyiṣa said, "By God, if Muḥammad had commanded you to kill me you would have killed me?" Muhayyiṣa replied, "Yes." Huwayyiṣa said, "By God, indeed a religion which reaches this is a wondrous faith," and Huwayyiṣa converted at that time. Muhayyiṣa said: It is true, and I did not see anyone force it upon him. It was said:

My mother's son blames me because if I were ordered to kill him
I would smite his nape with a sharp sword,
A blade white as salt, from polishing.
My downward stroke never misses its mark.
It would not please me to kill you voluntarily
If I owned all that lives between Busra and Maʿrib.

The Jews and the polytheists among them were alarmed. They came to the Prophet when it was morning and said, "Our companion, who was one of our lords, was knocked up at night and murdered treacherously with no crime or incident by him that we know of." The Messenger of God replied, "If he had remained as others of similar opinion remained he would not have been killed treacherously. But he hurt us and insulted us with poetry, and one does not do this among you, but he shall be put to the sword." The Messenger of God then invited them to write a document between them establishing what was in it. They wrote between them and him a document under the date palm in the house of Ramla bt. al-Ḥārith. The Jews became cautious and were fearful and humbled from the day Ibn al-Ashraf was murdered.

Ibrāhīm b. Jaʿfar related to me from his father saying: Marwān b. al-Ḥakam said, while he was at Medina and Ibn Yāmīn al-Naḍr was with him, "How was Ibn al-Ashraf murdered?" [Page 193] Ibn Yāmīn replied, "It was treachery." Muḥammad b. Maslama was an old sheikh, seated, and he said, "O Marwān, is the Messenger of God treacherous for you? By God, we did not kill him except under the command of the Messenger of God. By God, you and I will never be under the same roof other than in a mosque. As for you, O Ibn Yāmīn, by God who is above me, even if you are free, if I have the power over you, and in my hand a sword I will surely cut off your head."

Ibn Yāmīn did not come down with the Banū Quarayẓa until he sent him a message to see if Muḥammad b. Maslama was there. If he was in some other region of his, he alighted, fulfilled his need and left; if not, he did not come down. While Muḥammad b. Maslama was at a funeral, and Ibn Yāmīn was in al-Baqīʿ, Maslama saw a bier for a woman with young palm leaves on it. He came and untied the palms. And the people stood up and said, "O Abū ʿAbd al-Rahmān, what are you doing? We are sufficient for you." But he went up to Ibn Yāmīn and continued to hit him with palm after palm, until he broke that bunch of palms on his face and on his head, and a healthy palm was not left in it. Then he released Ibn Yāmīn and he had no strength left in him. Maslama said, "By God, if I could have a sword, I would cut you with it."

THE AFFAIR OF THE RAID OF THE GHATAFĀN IN DHŪ AMARR

It was in Rabīʿ al-Awwal, the twenty-fifth month AH. The Messenger of God went out on Thursday, the twelfth of Rabīʿ. He was absent for eleven days.

[Page 194] Muḥammad b. Ziyād b. Abī Hunayda related to me that Ibn Abī ʿAttāb related to us, and ʿUthmān b. al-Ḍaḥḥāk b. ʿUthmān and ʿAbd al-Raḥmān b. Muḥammad b. Abī Bakr from ʿAbdullah b. Abī Bakr, both related to me—and some had more on this tradition than others, and others have related to us, also, that: It reached the Messenger of God that a group of the Thaʿlaba and Muḥārib were at Dhū Amarr. They had rallied desiring to take from the borderlands of the Messenger of God. A man among them called Duʿthūr b. al-Ḥārith b. Muḥārib had assembled them. The Messenger of God selected the Muslims and they went out with four hundred and fifty men and their horses. They took the road to al-Munaqqā, and then the pass of al-Khubayt. Then he went to Dhū l-Qaṣṣa, where he captured a man among them called Jabbār, from the Banū Thaʿlaba. The Muslims asked him, "Where are you going?" He replied, "Yathrib." They said, "What is your purpose in Yathrib?" He replied, "I desire to explore for myself and see." The Muslims said, "Have you passed by a group, or has news come to you from your people?" He said, "No. But it has reached me that Duʿthūr b. al-Ḥārith including men from his people have left." They took him to the Messenger of God, and he invited him to Islam, and he converted. He said, "O Muḥammad, surely they will never confront you. If they hear about you marching, they will flee to the tops of the mountains. I will march with you and guide you to their weak spots." So the Prophet went with him and assigned him to Bilāl. He took a road descending from a sand dune, and the Bedouin fled [Page 195] to the top of the mountains. But before that they concealed their cattle and their offspring by dispersing them to the mountains. The Messenger of God did not encounter anyone except that he saw him or her on the mountaintops.

The Messenger of God alighted on Dhū Amarr, and the troops encamped. They received much rain, and the Messenger of God went for his purposes and the rain wet his clothes. The Messenger of God stopped where the wadi lay between him and his companions. Then he took off his clothes, and spread them out to dry, laying them on a tree, and he lay down under it. The Bedouin watched all that he was doing, and one of them said to Duʿthūr who was their master, and the bravest of them, "Muḥammad has made himself available to you for he has withdrawn from his companions to a place where if he cries for help they will not be able to come to his aid before you kill him."

Duʿthūr chose one of their swords, which was sharp, then he approached carrying the sword until he stood at the head of the Prophet with the reputed sword, and said, "O Muḥammad, who is protecting you from me today?" The Messenger of God said, "God." He said: And Gabriel pushed him in the chest, and his sword fell from his hand, and the Messenger of God took it, and he stood up with the sword at Duʿthūr's head and said, "And who is prohibiting you from me today?" He replied, "No one." Then he declared, "I testify that there is no God but God and that Muḥammad is his Prophet." He said, "By God, I will never gather a group against you." The Messenger of God gave him his sword, and then turned away from him. Then Duʿthūr approached him saying, "Are you not, by God, better than me?" The Messenger of God said, "I am more deserving about that than you."

Duʿthūr went back to his people and they said, "Where is what you were saying: he was available, and the sword was in your hand?" He said, "By God, it was so, but I looked at the noble tall man who pushed me in my chest so that I fell on my back, and I knew that he was an angel. I testified [Page 196] that there is no God but God and that Muḥammad is his Messenger, and by God, that I would not gather against him," and he began inviting his people to Islam. These verses were revealed about it. *O you who believe call to remembrance the favor of God unto you when certain men planned to stretch out their hands against you* (Q. 5:14).

The Prophet was absent for eleven nights. He appointed ʿUthmān b. ʿAffān over Medina during his absence.

THE RAID OF THE BANŪ SULAYM IN BUḤRĀN IN THE REGION OF AL-FURʿ

The raid took place on a night in Jumādā l-Ūla, the twenty-seventh month AH. The Prophet was absent for ten days.

Maʿmar b. Rāshid related to me from al-Zuhrī, who said: When it reached the Messenger of God that all of the Banū Sulaym—and there were many—were in Buḥrān, the Messenger of God prepared for that but he did not display his intent. He went out with three hundred men from his companions and they hurried along until they stood before Buḥrān by night. He met a man from the Banū Sulaym and he asked him for information about the people and about their group. The man informed them that they had split up the day before and returned to their waters. The Prophet commanded that he be imprisoned with a man from the Muslims. Then the Prophet marched until he arrived in Buḥrān. There was no one there. He stayed [Page 197] a day and then returned. There was no fighting. The Prophet released the man. He was gone for ten nights.

ʿAbdullah b. Nūḥ related to me from Muḥammad b. Sahl that the Messenger of God had appointed Ibn Umm Maktūm to take his place in Medina.

THE AFFAIR OF THE EXPEDITION TO AL-QARADA

Participating in the attack was Zayd b. Ḥāritha; it was the first raid in which he went out as a commander. He set out in Jamādā l-Ākhira, the twenty-seventh month AH.

Muḥammad b. al-Ḥasan b. Usāma b. Zayd related to me from his family saying: The Quraysh were cautious whenever they took the road to al-Shām. They feared the Messenger of God and his companions for they were a merchant people. As Ṣafwān b. Umayya said, "Indeed Muḥammad and his companions have made our trading difficult. We do not know how we will act with his companions. They do not leave the coast and the people of the coast have made an agreement with the Muslims. The majority has joined with them. We do not know which path we should take. If we stay, we eat up our capital while we are in this land of ours, and we do not have adequate support in it. Indeed, we go as traders to al-Shām in Summer, and to the land of al-Ḥabsha [Abyssinia] in Winter." Al-Aswad b. al-Muṭṭalib said, "Turn away from the coast and take the road to al-ʿIrāq." Ṣafwān replied, "I have no knowledge of it. Abū Zamaʿa said, "I will take you to the guide who is most informed about it. He can take that road with his eyes closed, God willing." He said, [Page 198] "Who is it?" He replied, "al-Furāt b. Ḥayyān al-ʿIjlī. He has mastered the road and he uses it." Ṣafwān said, "If that is so, by God, send for al-Furāt," and when al-Furāt arrived he said to him, "Indeed I desire to go to al-Shām but our caravan goes by Muḥammad and he blocks our way. So I want the road to al-ʿIrāq." al-Furāt replied, "I will travel with you on the road to al-ʿIrāq. Not one of Muḥammad's companions have set foot on it, for surely it is a land of plateaus and deserts." Ṣafwān said, "This is what I need—as for the deserts, we are in winter and today, our need for water is little." Ṣafwān b. Umayya made preparations, and he sent Abū Zamaʿa with al-Furāt and three hundred *mithqāl* of gold and coins of silver, and he also sent with him men from the Quraysh with goods. ʿAbdullah b. Rabīʿa and Ḥuwayṭib b. ʿAbd al-ʿUzzā including others from the Quraysh went out with him. Ṣafwān went with much wealth, coins of silver and vessels of silver weighing three thousand dirhams. They set out to Dhāt al-ʿIrq.

Nuʿaym b. Masʿūd al-Ashjaʿī arrived in Medina. He followed the religion of his people. He alighted on Kināna b. Abī l-Huqayq of the Banū al-Naḍīr and drank with him, and Salīṭ b. al-Nuʿmān b. Aslam also drank with him. Wine was not prohibited at that time, and he came to the Banū l-Naḍīr and had their drinks. Nuʿaym mentioned Ṣafwān going out with the caravan and the wealth that was with them. Salīṭ went out, after a while, to Muḥammad and informed him of it, and the Messenger of God sent Zayd b. Ḥāritha with a hundred men to block them and take their caravan.

The leaders of the people of the caravan fled, and they captured one or two men. They arrived with the caravan before the Prophet and he apportioned it into five parts. The value of every fifth at that time was twenty thousand dirhams. After taking his fifth he apportioned what remained to the people of the expedition. Included among the prisoners was al-Furāt b. Ḥayyān. He was brought before the Prophet and it was said to him, "Convert—if you convert, we will not kill you." So he converted and was not killed.

[Page 199] THE RAID OF UḤUD

The raid of Uḥud took place on Saturday, the seventh of Shawwāl, thirty-two months after the emigration of the Prophet. Ibn Umm Maktūm was appointed to take his place in Medina.

Muḥammad b. Shujāʿ related to us that Muḥammad b. ʿUmar al-Wāqidī related to us that: Muḥammad b. ʿAbdullah b. Muslim, Mūsā b. Muḥammad b. Ibrāhīm b. al-Ḥārith, ʿAbdullah b. Jaʿfar, Ibn Abī Sabra, Muḥammad b. Ṣāliḥ b. Dīnār, Muʿādh b. Muḥammad, Ibn Abī Ḥabība, Muḥammad b. Yaḥyā b. Sahl b. Abī Ḥathma, ʿAbd al-Raḥmān b. ʿAbd al-ʿAzīz, Yaḥya b. ʿAbdullah b. Abī Qatāda, Yūnus b. Muḥammad al-Ẓafarī, Maʿmar b. Rāshid, Abd al-Raḥmān b. Abī l-Zinād and Abū Maʿshar, as well as men who are not named have all related portions of this tradition to me, and some of the people are more reliable than others. I have collected all that was related to me.

They said: When those among the polytheists who attended Badr returned to Mecca, the caravan in which Abū Sufyān b. Ḥarb arrived from al-Shām was deposited at the Dar al-Nadwa as was customary, and Abū Sufyān did not move it or divide it because of the absence of the people of the caravan. The leaders of the Quraysh: Al-Aswad b. al-Muṭṭalib b. Asad, Jubayr b. Muṭʿim, Ṣafwān b. Umayya, ʿIkrima b. Abī Jahl, al-Ḥārith b. Hishām, ʿAbdullah b. Abī Rabīʿa, Ḥuwayṭib b. ʿAbd al-ʿUzzā, and Ḥujayr b. Abī Ihāb marched to Abū Sufyān b. Ḥarb and said, "O Abū Sufyān, observe this caravan in which you arrived and which you have detained. You know that it holds the wealth of the Meccans and the small weaned camels (*laṭīma*) of the Quraysh. They would willingly use this [Page 200] caravan to prepare a force against Muḥammad. You saw who was killed among our fathers and our sons and our tribes." Abū Sufyān said,

"Are the Quraysh willing to do that?" They said, "Yes." He said, "Then, I am the first to agree to that, and the Banū ʿAbdManāf with me. By God, I am the avenger whose beloved was killed. My son Ḥanẓala and the nobility of my people were killed at Badr." The caravan continued to be detained until they began preparations for Uḥud. Then they sold it for gold money that was kept with Abū Sufyān. Others said, "Rather, O Abū Sufyān, sell the caravan and put its profits aside." The caravan consisted of a thousand camels, and the wealth was fifty thousand dinars. They made a profit with their merchandise, dinar for dinar. Their place of trade was Ghazza in al-Shām and they never changed it.

Abū Sufyān had detained the caravan of Zuhra because they had turned back from the road to Badr. Yet he surrendered what belonged to Makhrama b. Nawfal, to the sons of his father, and to the sons of ʿAbdManāf b. Zuhra. Makhrama refused to accept the return of his caravan unless what belonged to the Banū Zuhra was returned at the same time. Al-Akhnas asked, "What does the caravan of the Banū Zuhra have that distinguishes it from the caravans of the Quraysh?" Abū Sufyan replied, "They turned away from the Quraysh." Al-Akhnas said, "You sent word to the Quraysh saying 'Return, for we have saved the caravan-so do not go out for no reason,' so we returned." The Zuhra took their caravan, and groups from the people of Mecca—weak people who belonged to no tribe and had no protection—each took its portion from the caravan. This makes it clear that the people had taken the profit from the caravan. About them it was revealed: *The unbelievers spend their wealth to hinder (men) from the path of God.* (Q. 8:3b)

When they gathered to the march they said: We will march by the Bedouin and seek their assistance. Surely, neither the ʿAbdManāt—our closest kin from the Bedouin—nor those who follow us from the Ahābīsh (a mix of Bedouin), will stay away from us.

[Page 201] They agreed to send four of the Quraysh to the Bedouin to seek their help. They sent ʿAmr b. al-ʿĀṣ, Hubayra b. Abī Wahb, Ibn al-Zibaʿrā and Abū ʿAzza al-Jumaḥī. The group agreed, but Abū ʿAzza refused to go. He said, "Muḥammad did a favor for me on the day of Badr, and he was not kind to any one else. I promised I would not help an enemy of his ever." Ṣafwān b. Umayya went to him and said, "Go!" But he refused him saying, "I promised Muḥammad on the day of Badr that I would not help an enemy of his ever, and I will be faithful to what I promised him. He was kind to me, and he was not kind to any one else, but killed him or took a ransom from him." Ṣafwān said to him, "Come out with me, and if you survive I will give you what ever you wish from the wealth, and if you are killed, your family will be with my family." But Abū ʿAzza continued to refuse until it was the next day and Ṣafwān b. ʿAmr turned away from him in despair.

The following day Ṣafwān and Jubayr b. Muṭʿim came to him. Ṣafwān spoke to him first, and he refused. Then Jubayr said, "I did not think that I would live to see the day when Abū Wahb comes to you about a matter and you refuse him." It upset Abū ʿAzza and he said, "I will go out!" He said: And Abū ʿAzza went out to gather the Bedouin saying:

O sons of ʿAbdManāt, the steadfast, you are protectors and your father too.
Do not abandon me, and Islam will not take root.
Do not promise me your help after the year.

He said: The group went out with him. They incited the Bedouin and gathered them, and they reached the Thaqīf who also gathered. When they met for the march, those who were with them from the Bedouin rallied and joined them. The Quraysh [Page 202] disputed about whether the women should go out with them.

Bukayr b. Mismār related to me from Ziyād, the *mawlā* of Saʿd, from Nisṭās, that Ṣafwān b. Umayya said, "Leave with the camel litters (carrying women), and I will be the first to do so. Indeed it is most appropriate that the women rouse you and remind you of those who were killed at Badr. The time is recent, and we are a reckless people who do not desire to return to our homes until we take our revenge or die in the attempt." ʿIkrima b. Abū Jahl said, "I am the first who answers to your call about that," and ʿAmr b. al-ʿĀṣ said similarly. Nawfal b. Muʿāwiya al-Dīlī, however, came forward and said, "O Quraysh, I do not agree that you should expose your women to your enemy. No, I fear that they will be victorious, and you will be disgraced along with your women." Ṣafwān b. Umayya said, "No, this will never be!" Nawfal came to Abū Sufyān and told him of his position, and Hind bt. ʿUtba shouted, "Indeed, you, by God, were safe on the day of Badr and you returned to your women. Yes, we will go out and witness the battle. The singers from al-Juḥfa were returned during their journey to Badr, and the beloved were killed at that time." Abū Sufyān said, "I will not dispute the Quraysh, I am one of them. I will do what they do." The women went out.

They said: Abū Sufyān b. Ḥarb went out with his two wives, Hind bt. ʿUtba and Umayma bt. Saʿd b. Wahb b. Ashyam b. Kināna. Ṣafwān b. Umayya went out with two wives, Barza bt. Masʿūd al-Thaqafī who was the mother of ʿAbdullah, the older, and al-Baghūm bt. al-Muʿadhdhil b. Kināna who was the mother of ʿAbdullah b. Ṣafwān, the younger. Ṭalḥa b. Abī Ṭalḥa went out with his wife Sulāfa bt. Saʿd b. Shuhayd, from al-Aws, who was the mother of his sons, Musāficʿ, al-Ḥārith, Kilāb and Julās. [Page 203] ʿIkrima b. Abī Jahl went out with his wife Umm Juhaym bt. al-Ḥārith b. Hishām. Al-Ḥārith b. Hishām went out with his wife Fāṭima bt. al-Walīd b. al-Mughīra. ʿAmr b. al-ʿĀṣ went out with his wife, Hind bt. Munabbih b. al-Ḥajjāj, the mother of ʿAbdullah b. ʿAmr b. al-ʿĀṣ. Khunās bt. Mālik b. al-Muḍarrib went out with her son Abū ʿAzīz b. ʿUmayr al-ʿAbdarī. Al-Ḥārith b. Sufyān b. ʿAbd al-Asad went out with his wife, Ramla bt. Ṭāriq b. ʿAlqama, Kināna b. ʿAlī b. Rabīʿa b. ʿAbd al-ʿUzzā went out with his wife Umm Ḥakīm bt. Ṭāriq, Sufyān b. ʿUwayf went out with his wife Qutayla bt. ʿAmr b. Hilāl. Al-Nuʿmān and Jābir the sons of Masak al-Dhi'b went out with their mother al-Dughanniyya. Ghurāb b. Sufyān b. Uwayf went out with his wife ʿAmra bt. al-Ḥārith b. ʿAlqama. It was she who raised the flag of the Quraysh, when it fell, in order that the Quraysh could retreat to their flag. They said: Sufyān b. ʿUwayf went out with ten of his sons, when the Banū Kināna mobilized. There were flags on the day they went out from Mecca, and three of them were established in the Dār al-Nadwa: a flag that Sufyān b. ʿUwayf carried, a flag with one of the *Ahābīsh*, and a flag that Ṭalḥa b. Abī Ṭalḥa carried. It was said, "The Quraysh set out with one flag wound up, and Ṭalḥa b. Abī Ṭalḥa was carrying it." Ibn Wāqid said, "This tradition is confirmed with us."

The Quraysh went out and there were three thousand in all, including those who joined them. Among them were a hundred men from the Thaqīf. They went out prepared and with many weapons. They led two hundred horses, and had seven hundred coats of mail and three thousand camels with them.

When they gathered to march, al-ʿAbbās b. ʿAbd al-Muṭṭalib wrote [Page 204] a letter and sealed it. He hired a man from the Banū Ghifār and stipulated to him that he travel for three days to the Messenger of God and inform him that "the Quraysh have gathered to march to you, so do what you must when they come to you. They are headed towards you, and number three thousand. They lead two hundred horses, and have seven hundred armor plates and three thousand camels, and they have collected all the weapons." Al-Ghifārī arrived in Medina and did not find the Messenger of God there, but found him in Qubā', at the door of the Mosque of Qubā' riding a donkey. He gave him the letter and Ubayy b. Kaʿb read it to him. The Messenger of God told Ubayy to keep quiet about the news, then, he entered the house of Saʿd b. al-Rabīʿ and said, "Is anyone home?" Saʿd replied, "No, so speak of your need." So the Prophet informed him of the letter of al-ʿAbbās b. ʿAbd al-Muṭṭalib. Saʿd said, "O Messenger of God, I hope that some good will come out of it. The Jews and the Hypocrites of Medina have spread lies. They say, "Muḥammad did not receive what he liked." The Messenger of God turned towards Medina and asked Saʿd to keep the news secret.

When the Messenger of God went out, the wife of Saʿd b. al-Rabīʿ came to Saʿd and said, "What did the Messenger of God say to you?" He replied, "What is it to you, you who have no mother?" She said, "I heard you," and she informed Saʿd of the news. Saʿd said, "From God do we come and to God do we return! I did not see you listening to us, and I told the Messenger of God to speak freely!" Then he began to reason with her, then he went out running with her until he reached the Messenger of God at the bridge, and she could not move for exhaustion, and he said, "O Messenger of God, [Page 205] my wife asked me about what you said, and I concealed it from her, but she said she heard the words of the Messenger of God, and she came out with all the news. I fear, O Messenger of God that you will think that I spread your secret." The Messenger of God said, "Let her go." And the news spread among the people that the Quraysh were marching.

ʿAmr b. Sālim al-Khuzāʿī arrived with a group of Khuzāʿa. They had marched from Mecca for four days. They had appeared before the Quraysh and had camped at Dhū Ṭuwā. They informed the Messenger of God of the news. Then they turned and the found the Quraysh in Baṭn Rābigh and they swerved away from the Quraysh. Rābigh is a nights' journey from Medina. ʿAbdullah b. ʿAmr b. Zuhayr related to me from ʿAbdullah b. ʿAmr b. Abī Ḥukayma al-Aslamī saying: When Abū Sufyān arose in al-Abwā' he was informed that ʿAmr b. Sālim and his companion had traveled by night to Mecca. Abū Sufyān said, "I swear by God they went to Muḥammad and informed him of our march. They have warned him and informed him about our numbers and they are now adhering to their fortifications. I don't think we will get anything in this outing." Ṣafwān said, "If they do not come out to us, we will approach the date palms of the Aws and the Khazraj and we will cut them and leave them, and there will be no wealth for them, and they will not be restored to them, ever. If they come out to us, our numbers are more than theirs, and our weapons are more than theirs, and we have horses while they have none, and while we fight, motivated by revenge, they have no desire for revenge against us."

Now, when the Prophet arrived in Medina, Abū ʿĀmir, the corrupt one, had gone out with fifty men from the Aws Allah until he arrived with them in Mecca and stayed with the Quraysh. He called his people and said, "Indeed Muḥammad is successful, so come out with us to a community that we will help." [Page 206] He went out to the Quraysh and instigated them and informed them that they were right, and that Muḥammad had come with what was false. When the Quraysh marched to Badr, he had not marched with them, but when the Quraysh set out to Uḥud he marched with them. He used to say to the Quraysh, "If I approached my people, no two men among them will dispute about you. Those who are with me are a group of my people, and there are fifty men." The Quraysh believed him and desired his support.

The women went out with their tambourines, and instigated the men and reminded them of the dead of Badr in every station. The Quraysh alighted in every watering place, slaughtered the animals that they had collected from the caravan and strengthened themselves during their march. They ate from the provisions they had collected with their wealth. When the Quraysh passed al-Abwāʾ they said, "Surely you have come out with your women, while we are fearful for ours. Go, open the grave of Muḥammad's mother for indeed women are a weak spot, and if one of your women is taken say, this is the corpse of your mother, and if he is as dutiful about his mother as is alleged, by my life, you will pay ransom with the corpse of his mother; and if he is not successful in taking one of your women, by my life, he will ransom the corpse of his mother for much money, if he is dutiful about her." Abū Sufyān sought the advice from the decision makers of the Quraysh about that, and they said, "Do not mention this thing, for if we do so the Banū Bakr and the Khuzāʿa will unearth our dead."

On Thursday the Quraysh were at Dhū l-Ḥulayfa in the morning, ten days since their leaving Mecca, on the fifth night of Shawwāl, thirty-two months after the Prophet's emigration. They had three thousand camels and two hundred horses. When they arose in Dhū l-Ḥulayfa two riders set out, and Abū Sufyān hosted them at al-Wiṭāʾ. The Prophet sent two spies of his, Anasan and Mu'nisan the sons of Faḍāla, on the fifth night. They met the Quraysh in al-Aqīq. They both marched with the Quraysh until they camped [Page 207] in al-Wiṭāʾ. Then they came to the Messenger of God and informed him.

The Muslims had planted from al-ʿIrḍ (the land was between al-Wiṭāʾ, in Uḥud, until al-Jurf) to al-ʿArṣa (named ʿArṣat al-Baqal today). Its people were the Banū Salima, the Ḥāritha, the Ẓafar and ʿAbd al-Ashhal. At that time, water in al-Jurf was freely available. The driver of the sprinklers stayed in one spot, while the camel encircled it for a short while; this continued until the water was gone from the springs of al-Ghāba which Muʿāwiya b. Abī Sufyān dug. They had brought the tools of cultivation on the night of Thursday to Medina.

The polytheists arrived upon their crops, and they let their camels and their horses graze on the crop, which had just been watered. Usayd b. Ḥuḍayr had twenty sprinklers in the field watering the barley. The Muslims were protecting their camels and their workers and their tilling tools. The polytheists tended their cattle on the Thursday until evening, and when it was evening they gathered the camels, harvested the barley and fed their horses. When they woke up on Friday, they grazed their camels and their horses on the fields until nothing green was left. When they alighted they untied the knot and were confident. The Messenger of God sent al-Ḥubāb b. al-Mundhir b. al-Jamūḥ to the community. Al-Ḥubāb entered with them and evaluated and looked at all that he desired. The Prophet had sent him secretly saying: "Do not inform me in front of the Muslims [Page 208] unless we are few." When Ḥubāb returned to the Prophet, he informed him in isolation, and the Messenger of God said to him, "What did you see?" He replied, "O Messenger of God, I saw many. I estimated them at roughly three thousand. The cattle included two hundred horses and I saw obvious coats of mail that I estimated at seven hundred." The Prophet asked, "Did you see women?" He replied, "I saw women and tambourines, and bigger,"—meaning drums. The Messenger of God said, "The women desire to instigate the community and remind them of the dead at Badr. News of them came to me. You will not mention even a word of this matter. God is sufficient for us, and the best protection. O God, with You is the strength and with You is the attack."

Salama b. Salāma b. Waqash went out on the Friday when suddenly ten horses came towards the field, the first signs of the animals of the polytheists. They rushed in his tracks and he stopped for them on the top of the rock, challenging them, once, with arrows and once with stones until they moved away from him. When they left, he came to his crop that was close to al-ʿIrd and drew out a sword and iron armor that were buried near his crop. Then he set out with them, running, until he came to the Banū ʿAbd al-Ashhal, and informed his people about what he met from the enemy. They had arrived on Thursday, the fifth of Shawwāl. The incident took place on Saturday, the seventh of Shawwāl. The nobility of the Aws and the Khazraj, Saʿd b. Muʿādh, Usayd b. Ḥuḍayr, and Saʿd b. ʿUbāda, including a number of others stayed up that Friday night in the mosque at the door of the Prophet, wearing weapons, fearful of a sudden attack by the polytheists. They guarded the city until morning. The Prophet had a dream that Friday night, and when he arose he gathered the Muslims and spoke.

[Page 209] Muḥammad b. Ṣāliḥ related to me from ʿĀṣim b. ʿUmar b. Qatāda from Maḥmūd b. Labīd that the Prophet appeared on the *minbar* and praised God and commended Him. Then he said, "O people, surely I had a dream. I was wearing invulnerable armor, and my sword, Dhū l-Fiqār, broke at the tip; I saw cows slaughtered, and I led a ram behind me." The people asked, "How do you explain it?" He replied, "The invulnerable armor is Medina," so stay in Medina. "The break at the tip of my sword is an injury to myself; as for the slaughtered cows they are the dead among my companions; the ram that I lead are the troops that we will kill, God willing."

ʿUmar b. ʿUqba related to me from Saʿīd, saying: I heard Ibn ʿAbbās say, that the Prophet said, "As for my broken sword it is for the death of a man from the family of my house." Muḥammad b. ʿAbdullah related to me from al-Zuhrī from ʿUrwa, from al-Miswar b. Makhrama, who said: The Prophet said, "I saw in my sword a notch and I hated it." It referred to the injuring of the face of the Prophet.

The Prophet said, "Advise me!" The Messenger of God thought that he would not go out of Medina because of his dream. The Messenger of God desired to stay in Medina because of what he dreamed and the way he interpreted it. ʿAbdullah b. Ubayy stood up and said, "O Messenger of God we fought in *jāhiliyya* and at that time we kept [Page 210] the women and children in this fortress, and we gave them stones. By God, may be the children took a month moving the stones and preparing for the enemy. We joined the buildings of Medina so that it was like a fortress from every direction. The women and the youths from above the lofty fortress would aim at the enemy, while we fought with our swords in the side streets. O Messenger of God, our city is a virgin and she will not be forced against us ever. We will never go out to an enemy unless the enemy takes us, and one did not enter upon us ever, except we captured him. So leave them, O Messenger of God, and indeed if they stay they stay in misery and imprisonment, and if they return, they return defeated and unsuccessful. They will not achieve a good result. Listen to me in this affair, for I know that I inherited this opinion from the elders of my people, and the decision makers among them, for they were the people of war and experience." The Messenger of God agreed with Ibn Ubayy, and it was the opinion of the elders of the companions of the Messenger of God from among the Muhājirūn and the Anṣār. So the Messenger of God said, "Stay in Medina, and keep the women and children in the lofty fortresses, and if they enter upon us, we will fight them in the alleys. We are more informed about it than they. Aim from above the fortresses, and join all the buildings of Medina from every direction so that it is like a fortress."

But, new youths who had not witnessed Badr said, "Ask the Messenger of God to go out to the enemy," for they desired martyrdom. They wanted to meet the enemy. Come out with us to our enemies! Men from the people of age and decision, among them Ḥamza b. ʿAbd al-Muṭṭalib, Saʿd b. ʿUbāda, al-Nuʿmān b. Mālik b. Thaʿlaba, as well as others from the Aws and the Khazraj said, "We fear, O Messenger of God, that our enemy thinks we hate going out to them for we are cowardly about meeting them, and that this will encourage them against us. On the day of Badr, you had only three hundred men [Page 211] and God gave you victory over them. Today, we are many and have every reason to hope, so let us ask God about it, for God has driven us in our battle field."

The Messenger of God hated to consider their solicitations. They had put on their weapons and brandished their swords, and they strutted like braggarts. Mālik b. Sinān the father of Abū Saʿīd al-Khudrī said, "O Messenger of God we stand between two good possibilities: if God grants us victory over them, this is what we desire, and if God humbles them for us, this will be an occasion like the occasion of Badr. There will not remain among them except vagabonds. The other, O Messenger of God, is that God grants us martyrdom. By God, O Messenger of God I do not care which of them it will be, for indeed both are good!"

We did not hear the Prophet reply, for he was silent. Ḥamza b. ʿAbd al-Muṭṭalib said, "By Him who revealed the Book to you, I will not eat today until I fight them with my sword going out from Medina." It was said that Ḥamza was fasting on Friday and on the Sabbath, and that he encountered the enemy while he was fasting. They said: al-Nuʿmān b. Mālik b. Thaʿlaba, brother of the Banū Sālim said, "O Messenger of God, I testify that the slaughtered cows are the killed among your companions and I was among them. Why do you deprive us of Paradise? I swear by the One God that I will enter it." The Messenger of God said, "How?" He replied, "I love God and His prophet and I will not flee on the day of the raid." The Messenger of God said, "You speak the truth." He was martyred at that time.

Iyās b. Aws b. ʿAtīk said, "O Messenger of God, we are the Banū ʿAbd al-Ashhal of the slaughtered cows [the dream]. We hope, [Page 212] O Messenger of God, that we will be slaughtered with the people and that they will be slaughtered with us. But we will achieve Paradise while they achieve the fire. And yet, O Messenger of God, I do not desire that the Quraysh return to their people and say, "We besieged Muḥammad in his castle, in Yathrib, with its towers!" This will be a bonus for the Quraysh. If they trampled our palm, and we did not defend our land, and we would not be able to cultivate it again. We were in *jāhiliyya* when the Bedouin used to come to us, but they could never desire this from us without us going out to them with our swords until we pushed them away. Today, we are more worthy since God helps us with you. We know our destiny, we will not besiege ourselves in our homes." Khaythama, the father of Saʿd b. Khaythama said, "O Messenger of God, surely the Quraysh have spent a year gathering a crowd and summoning the Bedouin in their valleys and whoever follows them from the *Aḥābīsh*. They will come to us leading their horses and riding their camels, until they alight in our fields and besiege us in our homes and our fortresses. Then they will return in abundance and unharmed. And that will encourage them to make repeated attacks against us. They will take our borders, and place spies and ambushes against us in what they make of our tilled land. The Bedouin around us will be emboldened and even encouraged against us if they see that we do not go out to them; but we will drive them from our neighborhood, and may be God will give us victory over them, for that is God's custom with us. Or it will be the other, and it is martyrdom. Indeed the occasion of Badr skipped me, and I was keen. And indeed, because of my greed I cast lots with my son about going out, but his arrow came out and he was granted martyrdom. I am greedy for martyrdom. Yesterday, I saw my son in my sleep, in good form roaming among the fruits and rivers of Paradise, saying, 'Join us, keep us company in Paradise. Surely [Page 213] I have found what my lord promised me to be true!' By God, O Messenger of God, I have come to yearn to be with my son in Paradise. I have grown old, and my bones tender. I desire to meet my Lord. Pray to God, O Messenger of God, to grant me martyrdom and the companionship of Saʿd in Paradise." The Prophet prayed for him about that, and he was martyred at Uḥud.

They said: Anas b. Qatāda said, "O Messenger of God, it is one of the two good results. Either martyrdom or plunder and victory in killing them." The Messenger of God said, "Indeed I fear defeat." They said: When the people insisted on going out, the Messenger of God prayed Jumʿa with them and appealed to them to be diligent and to strive. He told them that they would have victory if they would be patient. The people rejoiced when he informed them about their going out to the enemy. But many of the companions of the Prophet hated to go out. The Messenger of God commanded them to prepare for their enemies. Then he prayed ʿAṣar with the people. He gathered the people, and the families of al-ʿAwālī attended. They sent the women up to the towers. The Banū ʿAmr b. ʿAwf attended with their allies and they put on their weapons.

The Messenger of God entered his house, and Abū Bakr and ʿUmar entered with him. They dressed him and wrapped his turban for him. The people lined up to see him from his room to the *minbar*. They anticipated his going out. Saʿd b. Muʿadh and Usayd b. Ḥuḍayr came to them and said, "You have spoken to the Messenger of God and forced him to go out. But the orders come to him from heaven, so return the command to him, and do as he commands you. [Page 214] What ever he desires or thinks, obey him."

While the people were on that affair, some of the people said, "Saʿd is right." Some of them had the view to go out. Others hated to go out. When the Messenger of God came out, he put on his cuirass. He was wearing his armor and displaying it, and he tied around it a girdle of leather for carrying his sword, which was later with the family of Abū Rāfiʿ, the *mawlā* of the Messenger of God. The Prophet put on the turban and took up the sword. But when the Messenger of God went out, the people regretted what they did. Those who had pressured the Messenger of God said, "It was not for us to force the Messenger of God about a matter which he did not desire and ignore the people of opinion who advised staying." They said, "O Messenger of God it was not for us to disagree with you, so act according to your opinion." The Prophet replied, "I asked you about this, and you refused. It is not appropriate for a prophet once he puts on his cuirass to then put it down until God judges between him and his enemies." There were prophets before him, and when a prophet put on a cuirass he did not put it down until God judged between him and his enemies. Then the Messenger of God said: "Pay attention to my commands and follow them. Go, by the name of God, and victory will be yours if you are patient."

Yaʿqub b. Muḥammad al-Ẓafarī related to me from his father that Mālik b. ʿAmr al-Najjārī died on Jumʿa. The Prophet put on his cuirass before he went to the funeral and prayed for him. Then he asked for his riding beast and rode off to Uḥud. Usāma b. Zayd related to us from his father that Juʿāl b. Surāqa said to him, while he was on his way to Uḥud, "O Messenger of God, some say that you will be killed tomorrow!" and sighed sadly. [Page 215] The Prophet struck his chest with his hand and said, "Is not tomorrow the whole future?" Then the Messenger of God asked for three javelins and established three flags; he gave the flag of the Aws to Usayd b. Ḥuḍayr, the flag of the Khazraj to al-Ḥubāb b. Mundhir b. al-Jamūḥ -some say to Saʿd b. ʿUbāda; and he gave the flag of the Muhājirūn to ʿAlī b. Abī Ṭālib, and some say to Muṣʿab b. ʿUmayr. Then the Prophet called for his horse and rode it. The Prophet took a bow and a spear in his hand—the heads of the arrows were at that time of brass. The Muslims put on their weapons and displayed their armor, and they had a hundred armor plates.

When the Messenger of God went out, he went with the two Saʿds, Saʿd b. ʿUbāda and Saʿd b. Muʿādh, running ahead of him. Every one among them was in armor. The people were to his right and to his left until he came to al-Badāiʿ, and then Zaqāq al-Ḥisā until he came to Shaykhayn, (they were fortresses of *jāhiliyya*, in which a blind old man and a blind old woman were found talking together, and therefore the two towers were named al-Shaykhayn), until he finally reached the peak of the second tower. He turned around and saw a battalion of rough troops making a high-pitched sound behind him. He said, "What is this?" They replied, "O Messenger of God these are the Jewish confederates of Ibn Ubayy." The Messenger of God said, "We will not seek help from a people of polytheism against others of polytheism."

[Page 216] The Prophet marched until he came to al-Shaykhayn and camped there. Several youth came before him: ʿAbdullah b. ʿUmar, Zayd b. Thābit, Usāma b. Zayd, al-Nuʿmān b. Bashīr, Zayd b. Arqam, al-Barāʾ b. ʿĀzab, Usayd b. Ẓuhayr, ʿArāba b. Aws, Abū Saʿīd al-Khudrī, Samura b. Jundub, and Rāfiʿ b. Khadīj, and he rejected them. Rāfiʿ b. Khadīj said: Ẓuhayr b. Rāfiʿ said, "O Messenger of God, indeed he is a thrower!" And I made myself tall, and I wore my boots, so the Messenger of God permitted me. When he permitted me Samura b. Jundub said to his foster father Murayy b. Sinān al-Ḥārithī who was the husband of his mother, "O father, the prophet permitted Rāfiʿ b. Khadīj but he rejected me, and I can wrestle Rāfiʿ to the ground." So Murayy b. Sinān al-Ḥārithī said, "O Prophet, you returned my son and you permitted Rāfiʿ b. Khadīj, and my son can wrestle him to the ground." The Messenger of God said, "wrestle!" So Samurā wrestled Rāfiʿ to the ground and the Prophet permitted him as well. His mother was a woman from the Banū Asad.

Ibn Ubayy approached and alighted in the region of the encampment, and his confederates and those who were with him from the Hypocrites said repeatedly to Ibn Ubayy, "You indicated an opinion to him, you advised him and informed him that this is an opinion that went to your forefathers, yet that was his decision regarding your opinion: he refused to accept it. Instead, he obeyed those youth who are with him!" So they encountered hypocrisy and disloyalty from Ibn Ubayy.

The Messenger of God spent the night in al-Shaykhayn and Ibn Ubayy spent the night with his companions, and the Prophet concluded the examination of his companions. The sun set and Bilāl proclaimed the call to pray Maghrib, and the Prophet prayed with his companions.

[Page 217] Then the Messenger of God called for the ʿIshaʾ prayer and prayed with his companions. The Messenger of God stayed with the Banū Najjār. He employed Muḥammad b. Maslama with fifty men over the watch. They went around with the soldiers until the Messenger of God set out at nightfall.

The polytheists had seen the Messenger of God set out at nightfall and alight at Shaykhayn. They gathered their horses and rides, and employed ʿIkrima b. Abū Jahl over the watch with a horse from the polytheists. Their horses stayed up the night neighing, and would not calm down. Their vanguard drew near until it was attached to *al-ḥarra*, but did not ascend it until their horse returned. They feared the place of *al-ḥarra* and Muḥammad b. Maslama.

When he prayed ʿIsha', the Messenger of God said, "Who will protect us this night?" A man stood up and said, "I, O Messenger of God." The Messenger of God said, "Who are you?" The man replied, "Dhakwān b. ʿAbdQays." The Messenger of God said, "Sit down." Then the Messenger of God repeated, "Who is the man who will watch over us to-night?" A man stood up and said, "I." The Messenger of God asked, "Who are you?" and the man replied, "I am Abū Sabūʿ." The Messenger of God said, "Sit down." Then the Messenger of God said, again, "Who is the man who will protect us this night?" A man stood up and said, "I," and the Messenger of God said, "Who are you," and the man replied, "Ibn ʿAbdQays." The Messenger of God said, "Sit down." Then, the Messenger of God waited a while, and said, "Stand up the three of you," and Dhakwān b. ʿAbdQays stood up. The Messenger of God said, "Where are your companions?" Dhakwān replied, "I am he who is answering you this night." The Prophet said, "Go, and may God protect you!" He said: He put on his armor, took his shield and patrolled the camp that night. Some said that he was watching out for the Messenger of God that night, and that he did not part from him.

The Messenger of God slept until he set out before the break of dawn. At dawn, the Messenger of God said, "Where are the guides? Who is the man who will lead us on the road [Page 218] and take us out close to the enemy?" Abū Ḥathma al-Ḥārithī stood up and said, "I, O Messenger of God." Some say it was Aws b. Qayẓī, and others that it was Muḥayyiṣa, but Abū Ḥathma is confirmed with us.

He said: The Messenger of God went out riding his horse. He went with the guide to the Banū Ḥāritha, then through al-Amwāl until he passed the wall of Mirbaʿ b. Qayẓī, who was blind and a hypocrite. When the Messenger of God and his companions entered his property he stood up scattering dust in their faces, and saying, "If you are the Messenger of God do not enter my enclosure." Saʿd b. Zayd al-Ashhalī struck him with the bow that was in his hand, and injured his head, and it bled. Some of the Banū Ḥāritha were angered by it. He said: "It is your enemity, O Banū ʿAbd al-Ashhal. You will never let go of your enmity for us." Usayd b. Ḥuḍayr said, "No, by God, it is your hypocrisy. And by God, if I did not know that the Prophet would not approve, I would cut off his head, and the heads of others of similar opinion!" So they were silent.

The Prophet was on his way, when all of a sudden the horse of Abū Burda b. Niyār, which was chasing flies with its tail, struck the tack of Abū Burda's sword, and Abū Burda immediately drew his sword. The Messenger of God said, "O Master of the sword, sheath your blade. Indeed I anticipate that you will draw the sword and draw it often." The Messenger of God liked a good omen and hated a bad one.

[Page 219] From Shaykhayn, the Messenger of God put on a single armor until he reached Uḥud, where he put on another, as well as a head cover, over which he wore a helmet. When the Messenger of God rose from Shaykhayn, the polytheists crept forward in preparation until they reached the place which today is the land of Ibn ʿĀmir. When the Messenger of God reached Uḥud at the place that is today known as Qanṭara, it was the time of prayer and he saw the polytheists. He commanded Bilāl to proclaim the call to prayer and he stood and prayed the dawn prayer with his companions lined up. Ibn Ubayy departed from that place with his troops, like an Ostrich leading them. Following them ʿAbdullah b. ʿAmr b. Ḥarām said, "I remind you of God and your religion and your Prophet, and what you promised him that you would protect him from whatever you protect your children and your women." Ibn Ubayy replied, "I do not think there will be a battle between them. If you obey me, O Abū Jābir, you will surely return. Indeed the people of intellect and opinion have returned. We are the Prophet's helpers in our town. He disagreed with us and I advised him of my opinion. But he insists on following the opinion of the youth." When ʿAbdullah refused to return, and entered the alleys of Medina, Abū Jābir said to them, "May God curse you! Surely God will make the Prophet and the believers independent of your help." Ibn Ubayy turned and said, "He disobeys me, and obeys the children?" ʿAbdullah b. ʿAmr b. Ḥarām turned, running until he came to the Prophet who was straightening the lines. When the companions of the Prophet were taken, Ibn Ubayy was pleased and expressed joy. He said, "He disobeyed me and obeyed those who have no understanding of it."

The Messenger of God began to arrange his companions in rows. He made marksmen of fifty men at ʿAynayn, and appointed ʿAbdullah b. Jubayr over them—some say Saʿd [Page 220] b. Abī Waqqāṣ. Ibn Wāqid said: ʿAbdullah b. Jubayr is confirmed with us. The Messenger of God arranged his companions in rows. He placed Uḥud behind him, and faced Medina; he placed ʿAynayn to his left. The polytheists approached with their backs to Medina in the valley, while they faced Uḥud. Some said, "The Prophet kept ʿAynayn behind him, and turned his back on the sun, while it faced the disbelievers." The first saying is confirmed with us, that Uḥud was behind him while he faced Medina.

Yaʿqūb b. Muḥammad al-Ẓafarī related to me from Ḥuṣayn b. ʿAbd al-Raḥmān b. ʿAmr from Maḥmūd b. ʿAmr b. Yazīd b. al-Sakan that when the Messenger of God reached Uḥud, the people alighted at ʿAynayn, and he continued on until he had placed Uḥud behind him. He prohibited fighting until he commanded it. When ʿUmāra b. Yazīd b. al-Sakan heard about that, he asked, "Shall the crops of the Banū Qayla be taken without a fight?"

The polytheists approached; they were arranged in lines. Khālid b. al-Walīd was appointed over their right flank, and ʿIkrima b. Abī Jahl, over the left. In their two flanks they had a hundred horses. They placed Ṣafwān b. Umayya—some say ʿAmr b. al-ʿĀṣ—over their horses, and ʿAbdullah b. Abī Rabīʿa over their marksmen. There were a hundred Javelin throwers. They gave the flag to Ṭalḥa b. Abī Ṭalḥa. The name of Abī Ṭalḥa is ʿAbdullah b. ʿAbd al-ʿUzzā b. ʿUthmān b. ʿAbd al-Dār b. Quṣay. Abū Sufyān shouted at that time, "O Banū ʿAbd al-Dār, we know that you are [Page 221] more deserving of the flag than us. But surely we were overtaken on the day of Badr from the flag. Indeed the people were attacked at the flag. So keep to your flag and preserve it, and give us a free hand! Indeed we are a people reckless and unavenged. We seek the revenge of a recent time." Abū Sufyān said repeatedly, "If the flags are removed what would the people stand and support?" The Banū ʿAbd al-Dār were angered and said, "Shall we put down our flag? This will never be! As for preserving it, you shall see!" They supported their flag with their spears, and surrounded the flag and were rude to Abū Sufyān. Abū Sufyān said, "We will choose another flag." They said, "Yes, but only a man from the Banū ʿAbd al-Dār will carry it. It will never be otherwise!"

The Messenger of God began to walk to his men equalizing the rows and placing his companions in position to fight, saying, "Come forward, so-and-so, and go back, so-and-so." When he saw the shoulder of a man out of place he moved him back. He arranged them such that they were as straight as arrows. When the rows were equal, he asked, "Who will carry the flag of the polytheists?" Some one said, "The Banū ʿAbd al-Dār." The Prophet said, "We are more deserving of loyalty than them. Where is

Muṣʿab b. ʿUmayr?" He answered, "Here I am!" The Prophet said, "Take the flag," and Muṣʿab b. ʿUmayr took it and brought it before the Messenger of God.

The Messenger of God stood up and spoke to the people and said, "O people, let me advise you as God has advised me in His book: Do good works in obedience to Him, and abstain from His taboos. Then indeed he who remembers his duty and devotes himself to it with patience and certitude with effort and zeal shall have a place of reward and treasure. Fighting the enemy is hard. Strong is his distress, and few are those who are patient about it unless God decides to bring him to his senses. [Page 222] For surely God is with he who obeys Him, and indeed the devil is with he who resists Him. So conquer your works with patience and effort and what God has promised you will follow. Observe what He commands you. Indeed, I am hungry to guide you. The differences the controversy and the frustrations belong to the category of the weak and impotent and is not what God desires, and He will not grant it victory or success. Oh people, it has been restored in my heart that God alienates Himself from one who commits the forbidden; as for he who opposes it, God will forgive him his sins. And who prays for me, God and His angels will bless him ten times over. Whoever does good whether he be a Muslim or disbeliever, God will reward him in this world or the next. He who believes in God and the last day must gather for the Friday prayer, except the youth or the women or the sick or the possessed slave. He who dispenses with it, God will dispense with him, and to God are the riches and the praises. I do not know about the good works that endear you to God, except that I have ordered you to do them; and I do not know what actions take you closer to the fire except those that I have forbidden you from. The trustworthy spirit (Gabriel) has revealed to me that a soul will not die until all of its blessings are fulfilled. It will not be reduced from him even though it may be slow to arrive. Fear God, your Lord, and adorn yourselves in seeking God's blessings, and let not its delay lead you to disobey your Lord. For indeed there is no power over what God grants except by obeying Him. God has made clear to you what is permitted and what is forbidden. However between them is a similarity of matter, and many people do not recognize it [the forbidden] except he who is watchful. He who leaves it preserves his honor and his religion. He who falls in it is like a shepherd at the side of a sanctuary but on the verge of falling in it. And every king [Page 223] has a sanctuary. Indeed, is not the sanctuary of Allah sacrosanct? One of the believers is like the head of the body, and when he complains, the rest of the body commiserates. Peace upon you!"

Ibn Abī Sabra related to me from Khālid b. Rabāḥ from Muṭṭalib b. ʿAbdullah that the first of those who started the war among them was Abū ʿĀmir. He came up with fifty of his people including the slaves of the Quraysh. Abū ʿĀmir whose name was ʿAbdAmr called out, "O people of the Aws, I am Abū ʿĀmir." They said, "There is neither greeting nor welcome for you, O corrupt one!" And he said, "Surely evil has taken my people after I left!" With him were the slaves of the Meccans. They threw stones at the Muslims and the Muslims engaged them for a while until Abū ʿĀmir and his companions turned away. Ṭalḥa b. Abī Ṭalḥa invited them to a duel. It was said that the slaves did not fight, but they were ordered to guard the troops.

He said: Before the two groups met, the women of the polytheists led the rows of polytheists, striking their large drums and tambourines. When returning, the women were at the end of the row until all of a sudden they were close to us (Muslims). The women stayed back, standing behind the rows, and whenever a man turned away, they goaded him and reminded him of their dead at Badr.

Quzmān was among the Hypocrites. He had stayed away from Uḥud. When he arose the women of the Banū Ẓafar reproached him saying, "O Quzmān, the men have gone out and you have stayed! Are you not ashamed of what you do? What are you but a woman! Your people have gone out and you stay in the house!" They made him angry, so he entered his house and came out with his bow and quiver and sword, for he was known for his bravery.

[Page 224] He went out running until he came to the Messenger of God while he was arranging the lines of Muslims. He came from behind the lines until he reached the first, and he was in it. He was the first who aimed an arrow from the Muslims. He sent arrows as though they were spears, and they made a sound like the soft sound of the camel. Then he came to the sword and he performed feats, until at the end of that he killed himself. When this was mentioned, the Messenger of God said, "He is of the people of fire." When the Muslims were exposed he broke the scabbard of his sword, saying, "Death is better than fleeing! O families of the Aws, fight for honor, and do as I do!" He said: He entered with his sword into the middle of the polytheists until it was said that he was killed. Then he rose, saying, "I am the youth Ẓaffarī," and he killed seven of them. He died of the wounds, and there were many. Qatāda b. al-Nuʿmān passed by him and said, "Father of generosity!" And Quzmān said, "I am at your service!" Qatāda said, "Congratulations on your martyrdom!" He replied, "By God, I did not fight, O Abū ʿAmr, for religion. I fought only to prevent the Quraysh march to us and trample our palms." His wounds were mentioned to the Prophet, and he said, "He is of the people of fire." The wounds scarred him and he took his life. The Messenger of God said, "God supports this religion even with shameless men."

They said: The Prophet approached the marksmen and said, "Shield our backs, for we fear those who come from behind us, and stay in your places and do not leave them. Even if you see us put them to flight and enter their camps, do not withdraw from your places. If you see us being killed, do not come to help us or defend us. O God, I testify to You against them! [Page 225] Pelt their horses with arrows, for indeed, the horses would not come forward against the arrows!"

The polytheists had two flanks. On their right was Khālid b. al-Walīd, and on their left ʿIkrima b. Abī Jahl. They said the Messenger of God made a right wing and a left wing. He gave his great flag to Muṣʿab b. ʿUmayr, the flag of the Aws to Usayd b. Ḥuḍayr, and the flag of the Khazraj to Saʿd or Ḥubāb. The marksmen protected their backs. They pelted the horsemen of the polytheists with arrows and the horses turned and fled. Some of the marksmen said, "Surely I aimed with our arrows, and I did not see a single arrow that we aimed at their horses fall to the ground other than with a horse or a man."

They said: The people approached each other. They pushed the keeper of their flag Ṭalḥa b. Abī Ṭalḥa, to the front; they arranged themselves in rows while the women struck their drums and tambourines, standing behind the men, between their shoulders. Hind and her companions instigated and urged the men and reminded them of those wounded at Badr saying:

We are the daughters of Ṭāriq, and we proceed on saddle-pads.
If you advance, we will embrace you,
If you flee, we will turn away and leave you.
Leave no tender love.

Ṭalḥa b. Abī Ṭalḥa shouted, "Who is for a duel?" ʿAlī replied, "Are you prepared to duel?" Ṭalḥa said, "Yes." They appeared between the two rows, and the Messenger of God was seated under the banner in his two coats of mail, head cover and helmet. They encountered each other. [Page 226] ʿAlī rushed and struck him on the head. His sword passed until it broke Ṭalḥa's crown and reached his beard. Ṭalḥa fell and ʿAlī turned. Someone said to ʿAlī, "Did you not finish him off?" ʿAlī replied, "When he was thrown down his nakedness confronted me, and our relationship inclined me towards him. I knew that God had killed him. He was but a scapegoat for the troops." Some said that Ṭalḥa attacked him, but ʿAlī avoided him with his shield and did nothing with his sword. Then ʿAlī attacked Ṭalḥa. Ṭalḥa was wearing his armor tucked up, and ʿAlī struck him on his thighs and cut his legs. He wanted to finish him off but Ṭalḥa reminded him of their relationship and ʿAlī left him and did not finish him off. Then some Muslims passed by Ṭalḥa and finished him off. Others say that ʿAlī finished him off. When Ṭalḥa was killed, the Prophet was gladdened and proclaimed *takbīr*, and the Muslims proclaimed *takbīr*. Then the companions of the Prophet stood firm against the troops of the polytheists and began to-strike until their lines were destroyed. But only Ṭalḥa was killed.

After Ṭalḥa, ʿUthmān b. Abī Talḥa, i.e. Abū Shayba carried their flag. He stood in front of the women and proclaimed *rajaz* saying:

It is the duty of the people of the flag
To either dye the spear red with blood or destroy it.

Abū Shayba arrived with the banner, while the women prodded their troops on, beating the drums. Ḥamza b. ʿAbd al-Muṭṭalib attacked Abū Shayba and struck him with his sword on the nape of the neck, and cut his hand [Page 227] and his shoulder until he reached his covering (apron) and his lungs were exposed. Then he returned saying, "I am the son of he who quenches the thirst of the pilgrims!" Then Abū Saʿd b. Abī Ṭalḥa took the flag, and Saʿd b. Abī Waqqāṣ aimed at him, and the arrow grabbed his throat. He was wearing armor and a helmet but had no covering for his neck, so his neck was exposed. His tongue stuck out like that of a dog. It was said that when Abū Saʿd took the flag the women stood behind him saying:

Strike the Banū ʿAbd al-Dar,
Strike the protector of the rear
Strike as sharply as you can.

Saʿd b. Abī Waqqāṣ said: I struck him and I cut his right hand. He took the flag in his left hand, and I attacked his left hand and struck it and cut it. Then, he took the flag with both his fore arms and held it to his chest, and bent upon his back. Saʿd said: I placed the bend of my bow between his armor and his helmet, and I pulled out his helmet, and I threw it behind his back. Then I struck until I killed him. I began to take his armor but Subayʿ b. ʿAbdʿAwf and a group with him pounced upon me and prevented me from plundering him. His spoils were among the best of spoils from the polytheists, ample armor and helmet and an excellent sword. But I was kept away from them. This is the more authentic of the two sayings. Thus the consensus about it was that Saʿd killed him.

Then, Musāfiʿ b. Ṭalḥa b. Abī Ṭalḥa carried the banner, and ʿĀṣim b. Thābit b. Abī l-Aqlaḥ shot him. [Page 228] He said, "Take this and I am Ibn Abī l-Aqlaḥ!" He killed him, and the body was taken to his mother Sulāfa bt. Saʿd b. Shuhayd who was with the women. She said, "Who killed you?" He replied, "I do not know, but I heard him say, take this and I am Ibn Abī l-Aqlaḥ!" Sulāfa said, "Al-Aqlaḥī, by God! Indeed he is from my tribe." Some said that he said, "Take this and I am Ibn Kisra," in *jāhiliyya* they used to be called Kisra al-Dhahab. He said to his mother when she asked him, "Who killed you," I do not know, but I heard him say, "Take this and I am Ibn Kisra!" And Sulāfa said, "One of mine, by God, a Kisarī. Indeed he is a man from us." At that time she vowed that she would drink wine in the skull of ʿĀṣim b. Thābit, and she promised a hundred camels to whoever brings it to her.

Then Kilāb b. Ṭalḥa b. Abī Ṭalḥa carried the flag, and al-Zubayr b. al-ʿAwwām killed him; Then Julās b. Ṭalḥa b. Abī Ṭalḥa carried it, and Ṭalḥa b. ʿUbaydullah killed him. Then Arṭā b. Shuraḥbīl carried it and ʿAlī killed him. Then Shurayḥ b. Qāriẓ carried it, and we do not know who killed him. Then Ṣuāb a youth of theirs carried it and there is disagreement about who killed him. Someone said Saʿd b. Abī Waqqāṣ, and another said, ʿAlī, and yet another said, Quzmān. Quzmān is confirmed with us. He said: Quzmān reached him and attacked him and cut his right hand; so he transferred the flag to his left hand, and he cut the left. Then he clasped the flag with his upper arms and forearms, and bent on his back saying, "O Banū ʿAbd al-Dār, am I forgiven?" Quzmān attacked him and killed him.

[Page 229] They said: God never granted such a victory on a field to his Prophet as He granted him and his companions on the day of Uḥud, until they disobeyed the Prophet and disputed his command. Indeed, the masters of the banner were killed. The polytheists were revealed defeated, and they fled without looking back, while their women cursed, after having struck the drums and rejoiced when they encountered us. Al-Wāqidī said that many of the companions of the Prophet who witnessed Uḥud related that, every one of them said: By God, indeed I looked at Hind and her companions and they were fleeing. Nothing prevented their capture from those who desired that.

Whenever Khalid approached from the left of the Prophet in order that he could cross over and come from the foot of the mountain, he was repelled by the marksmen, and they did that many times. But now, the Muslims were reached from the direction of the marksmen. The Messenger of God had indicated to them and said, "Stay in your battle positions and protect our backs. If you see us capturing plunder do not join us, and if you see us being killed do not come to help us." But when the polytheists were defeated, the Muslims followed them, and placed the weapons that they held where they wished, in order to expel them from the camp, and they came down and pillaged the camp. Some of the marksmen said to the others, "Why do you stand over there without doing anything? God has defeated the enemy and those brothers of yours are pillaging their camp. So enter the camp of the polytheists and plunder with your brothers." Some of the Marksmen said to others, "Do you not know that the Messenger of God said to you 'Protect our backs and do not leave your places. If you see us being killed, do not come to our aid, and if you see us taking plunder do not join us, protect our backs?' " Others said, "The Prophet did not desire this. God has humiliated the polytheists and defeated them, so enter the camp and pillage with your brothers."

When they argued, their commander ʿAbdullah b. Jubayr [Page 230]—who was at that time recognized by his white garment—spoke to them: He praised God and commended Him, as was fit. Then he commanded obedience to God and His messenger, and that they not dispute the command of the Messenger of God. But they disobeyed and went off. Less than ten marksmen remained with the commander. Among them was al-Ḥārith b. Anas b. Rāfiʿ, who said, "O people, remember your Prophet's promise to you, and obey your commander."

He said: But they refused and went pillaging to the camp of the polytheists. They left the mountain and they began to pillage. The lines fell apart and the polytheists returned. The wind changed from the beginning of the day; until they returned, the wind had come from the East. Now, it became westward and the polytheists poured back attacking. Meanwhile the Muslims were busy with the spoils and the plunder.

Nisṭās the *mawlā* of Ṣafwān b. Umayya, whose Islam was the best Islam, said: I was a Mamluk and I was with those who stayed behind in the camp. At that time a Mamluk—except for Waḥshī and Ṣuāb the slave of Banū ʿAbd al-Dar—did not fight. Abū Sufyān said, "O people of the Quraysh, leave your slaves behind in order to protect your possessions. They will watch over your beasts." We gathered them together and tied the camels. The people set off in preparation to the right and to the left, and we put on the saddlecloths. The two sides came closer to each other and they fought for a while, when, all of a sudden, our masters were defeated, and the companions of Muḥammad entered our camp and we were in the dwelling. [Page 231] They encircled us, and I was among those who were taken captive. They pillaged the camp and it was the ugliest of pillages, until a man among them said, "Where is the wealth of Ṣafwān b. Umayya?" I replied, "He only brought sufficient for the expenses. It is in the saddlebag." He came out and drove me until I took it out from the purse—one hundred and fifty mithqāl. Our masters had turned away and we despaired about them. The women took fright and were in their rooms vulnerable for those who desired them. The men had plundered and we were on the verge of submission, when I looked at the mountain, and lo and behold, the riders were returning and entering the camp and there was no one to turn them back. The gap in which the marksmen had been placed was abandoned, for the marksmen had come to the camp and were plundering. I looked at them with their bows and quivers under their arms while every man among them held in his hands or in his embrace something he had taken. When our cavalry entered, they entered upon a people falsely secure, and they placed their swords in them and killed them swiftly. The Muslims dispersed in every direction leaving behind what they had pillaged and fled from our troops. We returned to our possessions later, for we had lost nothing. We set those captured among us free, and we found the gold in the battlefield. Indeed, I saw one of the Muslims, whom Ṣafwān b. Umayya approached with an embrace, and thought he would be dead until I overtook him and he was barely alive. I cut off his head with my dagger and he fell. I asked about him later and I was told that he was a man from the Banū Sāʾida. Later, God guided me to Islam.

Ibn Abī Sabra related to me from Isḥāq b. ʿAbdullah from ʿUmar b. al-Ḥakam, who said: We did not know anyone from the companions of the Prophet who [Page 232] attacked for plunder or land. They took what they took of the gold but, when the polytheists attacked, they (the Muslims) became confused, and only two men returned with the gold. One of them was ʿĀṣim b. Thābit b. Abī al-Aqlaḥ who brought a belt he had found at the camp with fifty dinars in it. He had fastened it over his loins under his clothes. While ʿAbbād b. Bishr arrived with a bundle of thirteen dinars. He dropped it in the pocket of his shirt, wore a coat of mail over his shirt, and tied a belt over it. They brought it to the Prophet at Uḥud, but the Prophet did not take a fifth of their plunder.

Rāfiʿ b. Khadīj said: When the marksmen turned around, and he remained who remained, Khālid b. al-Walīd looked at the emptiness of the mountain and the small number of its people, and he attacked with the cavalry. ʿIkrima followed in the cavalry, and they rushed towards some of the marksmen and attacked them. The people aimed until they were taken. ʿAbdullah b. Jubayr shot his arrows until they were used up. Then he thrust with the spear until it broke, then he broke the scabbard of his sword and fought until he was killed, may peace be upon him. Juʿāl b. Surāqa and Abū Burda b. Niyār approached. They had witnessed the death of ʿAbdullah b. Jubayr, and were the last of those who turned from the mountain when they met the enemy. The polytheists were on horseback and our lines had dispersed.

Satan, who had taken the form of Juʿāl b. Surāqa, called out, "Muḥammad has been killed," three times." Juʿāl b. Surāqa was afflicted with a great calamity when Satan took his form. Indeed, Juʿāl was fighting a strong battle against the Muslims, and at his side were Abū Burda b. Niyār and Khawwāt b. Jubayr. Indeed we did not see a turn of fortune more speedy than the turn of the polytheists over us. The Muslims came towards Juʿāl b. Surāqa desiring to kill him saying, "This is he who shouted that Muḥammad has been killed." Khawwāt b. Jubayr and Abū Burda b. Niyār witnessed that he was at their side when the scream was shouted, and that it was not his shout. Rāfiʿ said: I testified for him, later.

[Page 233] Rāfiʿ b. Khadīj said: We were attacked by the enemy from our side because we had disobeyed our Prophet. The Muslims were confused and some of them fought and struck each other, they did not recognize it for the haste and surprise. At that time, Usayd b. Ḥuḍayr was wounded twice; Abū Burda gave him one wound without knowing him, saying, "Take this and I am the slave of the Anṣār!" He said: Abū Zaʿna turned around and struck Abū Burda twice in the turmoil of the battle, not knowing. Indeed he says, "Take this and I am Abū Zaʿna!" until he recognized him later. Whenever he met him, Abū Burda would say, "Look at what you did to me." Abū Zaʿna replied, "You struck Usayd b. Ḥuḍayr and you did not know." But this wound was in the cause of God. He mentioned it to the Messenger of God, and the Messenger of God said, "It was in the cause of God, O Abū Burda, and for you is a reward exactly as if one of the polytheists struck you. And, whoever was killed, he is a martyr."

The Yamānī Ḥusayl b. Jābir and Rifāʿa b. Waqash were two old men who were put up in the fortress with the women. One of them said to his companion, "May you have no father! Why do we protect our lives, for by God, we stand only today or tomorrow? What remains of our lives is very little. If we take our swords and join the Prophet perhaps God will provide us martyrdom." He said: They joined the Prophet at Uḥud during the day. As for Rifāʿa, the polytheists killed him. As for Ḥusayl b. Jābir, the swords of the Muslims met him, for they did not recognize him when they mingled. Ḥudhayfa called out, "My father, my father!" until he was killed. Ḥudhayfa said, "May God—the most gracious and merciful—forgive you what you did!" It increased his favor with the Prophet. The Messenger of God commanded that his blood money be given to Ḥudhayfa. It was said that ʿUtba b. [Page 234] Masʿūd killed him. Ḥudhayfa gave his blood money to the Muslims, in charity. Al-Ḥubāb b. al-Mundhir b. al-Jamūḥ approached, at that time, shouting, "O family of Salima!" They approached as one group, "O caller of God, we are at your service! O caller of God we are at your service." And at that time he struck Jabbār b. Ṣakhr a heavy blow on his head for he did not recognize him until they proclaimed their battle slogan among them shouting, "Kill! kill!" so they refrained from each other.

Al-Zubayr b. Saʿd related to me from ʿAbdullah b. al-Faḍl that the Messenger of God gave Muṣʿab b. ʿUmayr the flag, and Muṣʿab was killed; but then, an angel in the form of Muṣʿab took it. The Prophet said to Muṣʿab, "It is the last day. Go forward, O Muṣʿab!" The angel looked at him and said, "I am not Muṣʿab," and the Messenger of God knew that he was an angel helping him. I heard Abū Maʿshar tell a similar story. ʿUbayda bt. Nāʾil related to me from ʿĀʾisha bt. Saʿd from her father Saʿd b. Abī Waqqāṣ, who said, "Surely I remember aiming with an arrow, at that time, which was returned to me by a man, white, with a beautiful face, whom I did not know; later, I thought he must be an angel." Ibrāhīm b. Saʿd related to me from his father from his grandfather, from Saʿd b. Abī Waqqāṣ, who said, "I saw two men in white garments, one of them on the right of the Messenger of God, the other on his left, fighting a hard battle; I did not see them before or after."

ʿAbd al-Malik b. Sulaym related to me from Qatan b. Wahb, from ʿUbayd b. [Page 235] ʿUmayr, who said: When the Quraysh returned from the battle of Uḥud they began to relate how they succeeded saying, "We did not see the piebald horses nor the white men that we saw on the day of Badr." ʿUbayd b. ʿUmayr said, "The angels did not fight on the day of Uḥud." Ibn Abī Sabra related to me from ʿAbd al-Ḥamīd b. Suhayl from ʿUmar b. al-Ḥakam that he said, "The Messenger of God was not helped by a single angel on the day of Uḥud, but rather on the day of Badr." Ibn Khadīj related to me from ʿAmr b. Dīnār from ʿIkrima, similarly. Maʿmar b. Rāshid related to me from Ibn Abī Luḥayḥ from Mujāhid, who said, "The angels were present at that time but they did not fight." Sufyān b. Saʿīd related to me from ʿAbdullah b. ʿUthmān from Mujāhid, who said, "The angels did not fight except on the day of Badr." Ibn Abī Sabra related to me from Thawr b. Zayd from Abū l-Ghayth, from Abū Hurayra, who said that God promised them that He would help them if they were patient. When the Muslims were exposed the angels did not fight at that time."

Yaʿqūb b. Muḥammad b. Abī Ṣaʿṣaʿa related to me from Mūsā b. Ḍamra b. Saʿīd from his father from Abū Bashīr al-Māzinī, who said: When Satan, Azabba al-Aqaba (this is Satan's name) shouted, "Indeed Muḥammad has been killed," for that was what God desired, the Muslims were at a loss and they scattered in every direction, and ascended the mountain. Kaʿb b. Mālik was the first who announced the good news that the Prophet was safe. Kaʿb said: [Page 236] I began to shout, and the Prophet indicated to me, with his finger on his mouth, to be silent. Mūsā b. Shayba b. ʿAmr b. ʿAbdullah b. Kaʿb b. Mālik, from ʿUmayra bt. ʿUbaydullah b. Kaʿb b. Mālik from her father, who said: When the people were exposed, I was the first to recognize the Messenger of God and proclaim the good news to the believers: that he lives and is well. Kaʿb said that he was in the pass, and the Messenger of God asked Kaʿb for his cuirass—it was yellow or something like it, and the Messenger of God put it on. Then, the Messenger of God pulled out his cuirass and Kaʿb put it on. Kaʿb fought, at that time, a strong battle until he had seventeen wounds. Maʿmar b. Rāshid related to me from al-Zuhrī from Ibn Kaʿb b. Mālik from his father, who said: I was the first to recognize the Messenger of God at that time. I recognized his eyes from under his helmet, so I called out, "O people of the Anṣār rejoice! This is the Messenger of God!" But the Prophet indicated to me to be silent.

Ibn Abī Sabra related to me from Khālid b. Rabāḥ from al-Aʿraj, who said: When Satan shouted, "Surely Muḥammad has been killed," Abū Sufyān b. Ḥarb said, "O people of the Quraysh, which of you killed Muḥammad?" Ibn Qamīʾa said, "I killed him." Abū Sufyān said, "We will decorate you with an iron band just as the Persians did with their braves." Abū Sufyān began to walk around with Abū ʿĀmir, the corrupt one, in the battlefield seeking Muḥammad among the dead. He passed Khārija b. Zayd b.

Abī Zuhayr, and Abū ʿĀmir said, "O Abū Sufyān, do you know who this killed one is?" Abū Sufyān replied, "No," and he said, "This is Khārija b. Zayd b. Abī Zuhayr al-Khazrajī, this is the lord of the [Page 237] Bal Ḥārith b. al-Khazraj." And he passed ʿAbbās b. ʿUbāda b. Naḍla at his side, and he said, "This is Ibn Qawqal, this is the lord of the noble house." Then he passed Dhakwān b. ʿAbdQays, and he said, "This is one of their lords." Then he passed his son Ḥanẓala, and Abū Sufyān said, "Who is this, O Ibn ʿĀmir?" And he replied, "This is the dearest of those who are here, to me, this is Ḥanẓala b. Abī ʿĀmir." Abū Sufyān said, "We do not see the body of Muḥammad, if he was killed surely we would see it. Ibn Qamīʾa lied." He met Khālid b. al-Walīd and said, "Is it clear to you that Muḥammad was killed?" Khālid said, "I saw him approach with a group of his companions ascending the mountain." Abū Sufyān said, "This is the truth! Ibn Qamīʾa lied. He claims that he killed him."

Ibn Abī Sabra related to me from Khālid b. Rabāḥ from Abū Sufyān the *mawlā* of Ibn Abī Aḥmad, who said: I heard Muḥammad b. Maslama say: My two ears heard and my two eyes saw the Messenger of God speak, at that time. The Muslims were exposed on the mountain, and they were not heeding him while he was saying, "Come to me, O so-and-so; come to me, O so-and-so, I am the Messenger of God." But neither of them stopped before him; they both left.

Ibn Abī Sabra related to me from Abū Bakr b. ʿAbdullah b. Abī Jahm whose name was Abū Jahm ʿUbayd, who said: Khālid b. al-Walīd used to relate, when he was in al-Shām, saying: Praise be to God who guided me to Islam. Surely you saw me, and you saw ʿUmar b. al-Khaṭṭāb when they were doing the rounds and suffering defeat on the day of Uḥud. There was no one with him, and I was with a troop of tough people, and not one among them knew him other than I, I kept away from him, for I feared that if I tempt my troops with him they would attack him, and I watched him move towards the pass.

Ibn Abī Sabra related to me from Isḥāq b. ʿAbdullah b. Abī Farwa from Abū l-Ḥuwayrith, from Nāfiʿ b. Jubayr, who said: I heard a man among the Muhājirūn say: [Page 238] I witnessed Uḥud and I saw arrows coming from every direction, and the Messenger of God was at the center of it, yet all of that was turned away from him. Indeed I saw ʿAbdullah b. Shihāb al-Zuhrī say, at that time, "Guide me to Muḥammad, for I will not live if he lives!" And indeed the Messenger of God was at his side, and no one was with him. Then he passed by him. ʿAbdullah b. Shihāb met Ṣafwān b. Umayya and Ṣafwān said, "May you suffer! Was it not possible for you to strike Muḥammad and cut off this sore, surely God made him available to you?" He (ʿAbdullah) said, "Did you see him?" He (Ṣafwān) said, "Yes, you were at his side." He (ʿAbdullah) said, "By God, I did not see him. I swear by God, that he is forbidden to us. Four of us went out and we promised each other and swore that we would kill him, but we were not able to achieve that."

Ibn Abī Sabra related to me from Khālid b. Rabāḥ from Yaʿqūb b. ʿUmar b. Qatāda from Namla b. Abī Namla (and the name of Abū Namla was ʿAbdullah b. Muʿādh, and his father was Muʿādh the brother of Barāʾ b. Maʿrūr through his mother), who said: When the Muslims were exposed that day, I looked at the Messenger of God and there was only a little group with him. His companions from the Muhājirūn and the Anṣār surrounded him, and they proceeded with him to the pass. The Muslims did not have a standing flag, there were no troops, and there was no gathering. Indeed the troops of the polytheists were attacking them coming and going in the valley, meeting and dispersing. They did not see any one of the Muslims pushing them back. I followed the Messenger of God with my eyes and saw him take precedence with his companions. Then the polytheists returned towards their camp and plotted about Medina and about seeking us out. The people were in disagreement. The Messenger of God appeared to his companions [Page 239] and it was as though nothing could harm them when they saw the Messenger of God safe.

Ibrāhīm b. Muḥammad b. Shuraḥbīl al-ʿAbdarī related to me from his father, who said: Muṣʿab carried the flag when the Muslims did their rounds, and he stuck to it. Ibn Qamīʾa approached him on his horse and struck his right hand and cut it, while Muṣʿab said, "*Muḥammad is no more than an Apostle; many were the Apostles who passed away before him* (Q. 3:144)." He took the flag in his left hand, and bent on it. When Ibn Qamīʾa cut his left hand, he bent over the flag with his upper arms at his chest and said, "*Muḥammad is no more than an Apostle, many were the Apostles who passed away before him.*" Then he attacked him for the third time and pierced him. Muṣʿab fell and the flag dropped. Two men from the Banū ʿAbd al-Dār, Suwaybiṭ b. Ḥarmala and Abū l-Rūm rushed to it. Abū l-Rūm picked it up and continued to hold it until he entered Medina, when the Muslims returned.

Mūsā b. Yaʿqūb related to me from his aunt, from her mother, from al-Miqdād, who said: When we lined up for battle, the Messenger of God sat under the banner of Muṣʿab b. ʿUmayr. When the masters of the flag were killed, the polytheists were defeated for the first time. The Muslims attacked their camp and plundered it. Then the disbelievers turned around and attacked the Muslims and they came from behind them, and the people dispersed. The Messenger of God called out to the masters of the banners. Muṣʿab b. ʿUmayr took the flag and was killed. Saʿd b. ʿUbāda took the banner of the Khazraj, and the Messenger of God stood under it, and his companions surrounded him. He gave the flag of the Muhājirūn to Abū l-Rūm al-ʿAbdarī, at the end of the day, and I saw the flag of the Aws with Usayd b. Ḥuḍayr, and they brushed against them for an hour, and fought over the confusion of the lines. The polytheists called out their battle cry, "O al-ʿUzzā, O al-Hubal!" By God, they caused pain and a massive killing among us. [Page 240] They took what they took from the Messenger of God. By Him who sent him with the truth, I did not see the Messenger of God move an inch; verily he was in the face of the enemy. A faction of his companions returned to him once and separated from him once, and sometimes I saw him standing, aiming from his bow or with a stone until they departed.

The Messenger of God was steadfast with a group that was patient with him. They were fourteen men, seven from the Muhajirun and seven from the Anṣār. Abū Bakr, ʿAbd al-Raḥmān b. ʿAwf, ʿAlī b. Abī Ṭālib, Saʿd b. Abī Waqqāṣ, Ṭalḥa b. ʿUbaydullah, Abū ʿUbayda b. al-Jarrāḥ, al-Zubayr b. al-Awwām; and from the Anṣār, al-Ḥubāb b. al-Mundhir, Abū Dujāna, ʿĀṣim b. Thābit, al-Ḥārith b. al-Ṣimma, Sahl b. Ḥunayf, Usayd b. Ḥuḍayr, and Saʿd b. Muʿādh. Some said, Saʿd b. ʿUbāda and Muḥammad b. Maslama were confirmed and they put them in the place of Usayd b. Ḥuḍayr and Saʿd b. Muʿādh. And at that time eight of them made an oath unto death, three from the Muhājirūn and five from the Anṣār. They were ʿAlī, al-Zubayr, and Ṭalḥa, Abū Dujāna, al-Ḥārith b. Ṣimma, Ḥubāb b. al-Mundhir, ʿĀṣim b. Thābit, Sahl b. Ḥunayf, and not one of them was killed. The Messenger of God was in their rear praying for them until they ended up at a place close to al-Mihrās.

ʿUtba b. Jabīra related to me from Yaʿqūb b. ʿUmar b. Qatāda, who said: Thirty men were confirmed at that time before him, all of them saying, "my direction is under your direction, my soul is under your soul, and upon you be peace forever."

They said: When the battle reached the Messenger of God [Page 241] Muṣʿab b. ʿUmayr and Abū Dujāna defended him until he had many wounds. The Prophet kept repeating, "Is there any man who offers himself for the hereafter?" A group of five Anṣār jumped up, among them ʿUmāra b. Ziyād b. al-Sakan, and he fought until he could not move. A group of Muslims returned and they fought until they aborted the enemies of God. The Messenger of God said to ʿUmāra b. Ziyād, "Come close to me, to me, to me!" The Prophet placed his foot as a cushion for him—and he had fourteen wounds—until he died. The Prophet made to chide the people at that time and incite them to battle.

Some of the polytheists, at that time, had disquieted the Muslims with arrows, and among them was Ḥibbān b. al-ʿAriqa and Abū Usāma al-Jushamī. The Prophet said to Saʿd b. Abī Waqqāṣ, "Shoot, and may my father and mother be your ransom!" Ḥibbān b. al-ʿAriqa shot an arrow that struck the hem of Umm Ayman who had come, at that time, to give water to the wounded. She tripped and was revealed and his laughter was loud. That grieved the Prophet, so he gave Saʿd b. Abī Waqqāṣ an arrow without an arrow head and said," Shoot!" The arrow fell in the gap of the chest of Ḥibbān and he fell down exposing his buttocks. Saʿd said, "I saw the Messenger of God laugh then, until his teeth could be seen." Then he said, "Saʿd retaliated for her. God answered your prayer and guided your arrow." At that time Mālik b. Zuhayr al-Jushamī—brother of Abū Usāma al-Jushamī—took aim. He and Ḥibbān b. al-ʿAriqa had attacked the companions of the Messenger of God and increased the killing among them with arrows while hiding in the rocks and aiming at the Muslims. And while they were at that, Saʿd b. Abī Waqqāṣ saw Mālik b. Zuhayr [Page 242] behind a rock. He had taken a shot, and his head was raised. Saʿd aimed at Mālik, and an arrow struck his eye and came out from the back of his head, sprang up in the sky, and then fell down. Thus did God most high kill him.

The Messenger of God aimed at that time with his bow until it became worn out. Qatāda b. al-Nuʿmān took it and kept it with him. An eye of Qatāda was injured then and it fell on his cheek. Qatāda b. al-Nuʿmān said: I came to the Prophet and said, "O Messenger of God, a young and beautiful woman is married to me, and I love her and she loves me, but I fear that the place of my eye is ugly." The Messenger of God took it and replaced it and his vision returned as it was before, and it did not let him down by night or day. He used to say after he grew old, "It is, by God, the stronger of my eyes." It was the better of the two.

The Messenger of God took part in the battle. He aimed with arrows until they dwindled, and the bend at the end of his bow broke. But, before that, he cut the string, and a piece remained in his hands from what had spanned the bend at the end of his bow. ʿUkkāsha b. Miḥṣan took the bow and strung it for him. He said, "O Messenger of God, the string will not reach." The Messenger of God said, "Pull it, and it will reach!" ʿUkkāsha said: By Him who sent him with the truth, I extended the string until it reached the end of the bow, and I strung it twice or thrice across its bend. Then the Messenger of God took his bow and continued to aim with it. Abū Ṭalḥa was in front of them, hiding him with his shield, until I looked at his bow, and it had disintegrated. Qatāda b. al-Nuʿmān took it.

[Page 243] On the day of Uḥud, Abū Ṭalḥa had scattered his quiver before the Prophet, and he was a strong voiced marksman. The Messenger of God said, "The voice of Abū Ṭalḥa with the soldiers is as good as that of forty men." There were fifty arrows in his quiver, and he scattered them before the Prophet, and began to shout, "O

Messenger of God, my soul instead of yours!" and he continued to aim arrow after arrow. The Messenger of God raised his head behind Abū Ṭalḥa, between his head and his shoulder, and saw to the placing of the arrows, until his arrows diminished. He said, "My throat for yours, make me, by God, your ransom!" Indeed, the Messenger of God took twigs from the earth and said, "Shoot, O Abū Ṭalḥa!" And he shot excellent arrows with them.

Marksmen from the companions of the Prophet are mentioned, among them: Saʿd b. Abī Waqqāṣ, al-Sā'ib b. ʿUthmān b. Maẓʿūn, Miqdād b. ʿAmr, Zayd b. Ḥāritha, Ḥāṭib b. Abī Baltaʿa, ʿUtba b. Ghazwān, Khirāsh b. al-Ṣimma, Quṭba b. ʿĀmir b. Ḥadīda, Bishr b. al-Barā' b. Maʿrūr, Abū Nā'ila Silkān b. Salāma, Abū Ṭalḥa, ʿĀṣim b. Thābit b. Abī l-Aqlāḥ, and Qatāda b. al-Nuʿmān. Abū Ruhm al-Ghifārī was shot at that time with an arrow that pierced his throat. He came to the Prophet, and the Prophet spat on his wound and it was healed. Abū Ruhm was named the slaughtered one.

Four of the Quraysh had promised and made an agreement to kill the Messenger of God. The polytheists recognized them as ʿAbdullah b. Shihāb, ʿUtba b. [Page 244] Abī Waqqāṣ, Ibn Qamī'a and Ibn Abī Khalaf. At that time, ʿUtba aimed four stones at the Messenger of God and broke his incisor splintering it from within at the lower right hand side; his two cheeks were cut until the ring of his helmet was hidden in his cheek, and his knees were wounded and grazed. There were pits that Abū ʿĀmir, the corrupt one, had dug which were like ditches for the Muslims. The Prophet was standing in front of one of these pits and did not know it. It is confirmed with us that he who aimed at the cheeks of the Messenger of God was Ibn Qamī'a, and he who aimed at his lips and took his tooth was ʿUtba b. Abī Waqqāṣ. Ibn Qamī'a approached saying, "Take me to Muḥammad, for by Him who everyone swears by, if I see him I will surely kill him!" and he stood above the Prophet with a sword, while ʿUtba b. Abī Waqqāṣ aimed at him and raised his sword. But the Messenger of God, who was wearing two armors, fell into the pit, which was before him, and grazed his knees. Ibn Qamī'a did not do anything but strike feebly with the weight of the sword, for the Messenger of God had fallen below. Ṭalḥa raised and carried the Messenger of God from behind, and ʿAlī held him in his arms until he was standing straight.

al-Ḍaḥḥāk b. ʿUthmān related to me from Ḍamra b. Saʿīd from Abū Bashīr al-Māzanī, who said: I attended the day of Uḥud, and I was a youth, and I saw Ibn Qamī'a above the Messenger of God with a sword. Then, I saw the Messenger of God fall on his knees and disappear into a hole in front of him. I began to shout, for I was a lad, until I saw the people [Page 245] return to him. He said: I saw Ṭalḥa b. ʿUbaydullah lift the Messenger of God in his embrace until he stood up. Some said that he who grazed the Messenger of God on his face was Ibn Shihāb; he who splintered his tooth and made his lips bleed was ʿUtba b. Abī Waqqāṣ, and he who aimed at his cheeks until the ring of his helmet pressed against them, was Ibn Qamī'a. The blood flowed from the wound on his face until it wet the beard of the Prophet. Sālim, the *mawlā* of Abū Ḥudhayf, washed the blood from his face. The Prophet said, "How will a people succeed if they do this to their prophet, while he invites them to God?" God most high revealed about that: *Not for you is the decision whether He turn in mercy to them . . .* (Q. 3:128) to the end of the verse.

Saʿd b. Abī Waqqāṣ said: I heard him say, "Severe is the anger of God upon a people who make the mouth of the Messenger of God bleed. Severe is the anger of God against a people who make the face of the Messenger of God bleed. Severe is the anger of God against a man who kills the Messenger of God!"

Saʿd said: Surely the prayer of the Messenger of God released me from ʿUtba, my brother. Indeed I desired to kill him more than any thing else. For as long as I knew him he was uncaring to his father and had an ill-mannered disposition. Indeed, I penetrated the lines of the polytheists twice, seeking my brother in order to kill him, but he eluded me with the elusiveness of a fox. When it was the third time, the Prophet said to me, "O ʿAbdullah, what do you desire? Do you want to kill yourself?" So I stopped, and the Messenger of God said, "O God, may the year not be complete for any one of them!" He said: And by God, it was not complete for any one of those who shot him or wounded him. ʿUtba died; and as for Ibn Qamīʾa, he died as well. Some say that Ibn Qamīʾa was killed at al-Maʿrak; others, that on the day of Uḥud he aimed [Page 246] an arrow, which wounded Muṣʿab b. ʿUmayr. He said, "Take this, and I am Ibn Qamīʾa," and killed Muṣʿab. The Messenger of God said, "May God humiliate him!" When Ibn Qamīʾa approached a sheep to milk it, it butted him with its horns while he was holding it, and it killed him. He was found dead among the mountains because of the prayer of the Messenger of God. The enemy of God returned to his companions and informed them that he had killed the Messenger of God. He was a man from the Banū al-Adram of the Banū Fihr.

ʿAbdullah b. Ḥumayd b. Zuhayr was approaching when he saw the Messenger of God in that condition. Galloping on his horse and veiled in iron, he says, "I am Ibn Zuhayr, lead me to Muḥammad, and by God, I will kill him or die in the attempt!" Abū Dujāna obstructed him and said, "Come to one who preserves the soul of Muḥammad with his own." Then he struck Ibn Zuhayr's horse on its tendon so that it fell down, and he was upon him with his sword saying, "Take this, and I am Ibn Kharasha!" The Messenger of God looked at him, saying, "O God may you be as pleased with Ibn Kharasha as I am!"

Isḥāq b. Yaḥyā b. Ṭalḥa related to me from ʿĪsā b. Ṭalḥa, from ʿĀʾisha, who said that she heard Abū Bakr say: On the day of Uḥud the Messenger of God was shot in his face until the two rings of his helmet entered his cheeks. I approached, walking, to the Prophet, and a man had come from the direction of the east, almost flying, and I said, "O God, let it be [Page 247] Ṭalḥa b. ʿUbaydullah," until we were before the Prophet, and, lo and behold, it was Abū ʿUbayda b. al-Jarrāḥ. He turned to me and said, "I ask you, by God, O Abū Bakr, let me remove it from the face of the Prophet." Abū Bakr said: I let him, and the Messenger of God said, "Peace to you and your companion," meaning Ṭalḥa b. ʿUbaydullah. Abū ʿUbayda took the ring of the helmet with his tooth and removed it. He fell on his back and the tooth of Abū ʿUbayda fell. Then he took the other ring with his other tooth. Thus Abū ʿUbayda became toothless among the people. It was also said, "Verily he who removed the rings from the face of the Prophet was ʿUqba b. Wahb b. Kalada." Others said, Abū l-Yasar. ʿUqba b. Wahb b. Kalada is confirmed with us.

Abū Saʿīd al-Khudrī used to relate that the Messenger of God was shot in his face on the day of Uḥud, and the two rings of the helmet entered his cheeks. When they were removed, blood began to flow as though from a water bag. Mālik b. Sinān began to suck the blood with his mouth and then swallow it. The Messenger of God said, "Whoever desires to see one who mixes his blood with mine, let him look at Mālik b. Sinān." It used to be said to Mālik, "You drank the blood?" He replied, "Yes, I drank the blood of the Messenger of God." The Messenger of God said, "Whoever touches his blood and my blood, the fire of hell will not wound him."

Abū Saʿīd said, "We were among those who returned from al-Shaykhayn; we had not participated with the warriors. On [Page 248] the day news concerning the wounds of the Prophet reached us, and the people dispersed from him, I arrived with two youths of the Banū Khudra. We approached the Prophet and observed that he was safe, and returned with the news to our people. We met the people who were turning away in Baṭn Qanāt. Our only desire was to see the Prophet. When the Prophet saw me, he said, "Saʿd b. Mālik?" I replied, "Yes, by my father and my mother!" I drew close to him and kissed his knee, for he was upon his horse. Then he said, "May God reward you in your father!" Then I looked at his face, and lo and behold, there was the mark of a dirham in each cheek; a fracture in his forehead at the root of his hair, his lower lip bled, and his central incisor on the right was broken, and on his wound was something black. I asked, "What is this on his face?" They said, "A burnt mat." I asked, "Who made his cheeks bleed?" Someone said, "Ibn Qamīʾa." I said, "Who fractured his forehead?" Someone said, "Ibn Shihāb," I said, "Who wounded his lip." Someone said, "ʿUtba." I made to run before the Messenger of God when he arrived at his door. He did not alight but was carried. I saw his wounded knees resting on the two Saʿds, Saʿd b. ʿUbāda and Saʿd b. Muʿādh, until he entered his house. When the sun set, Bilāl pronounced the call to prayer and the Messenger of God came out, as he went in, resting on the two Saʿds. Then he returned to his house. The people in the mosque lit fires and applied hot compresses on the wounds. Then Bilāl proclaimed the call to prayer for ʿIshāʾ when twilight set. But the Prophet did not come out, and Bilāl sat at his door until a third of the night had passed; then he called out to him, "The prayer, O Messenger of God." The Messenger of God came out, and he had been sleeping. He said, "I looked at him, and lo and behold, he was lighter in his walk than when he entered his house. I prayed ʿIshāʾ with him, and then he returned to his house.

The men had lined up [Page 249] for him, from his house up to the place of prayer. He walked alone until he entered. I returned to my family and informed them about the safety of the Prophet. They praised God for that and went to sleep. The faces of the Khazraj and the Aws were in the Mosque at the door of the Prophet watching over him, fearful that the Quraysh might return.

They said: Faṭima came out with the women. She saw what was in the face of the Prophet, embraced him and began to wipe the blood from his face, while the Messenger of God said, "Severe is the anger of God against a people who made the face of His messenger bleed." ʿAlī went and brought some water from al-Mihrās. He said to Fāṭima, "Keep this blameless sword for me." He brought water in his shield. The Messenger of God desired to drink from it, but he was not able for he found the stench of the water terrible. He said, "The water is brackish." He gurgled his mouth with it for there was blood in his mouth. Fāṭima washed the blood from her father. When the Prophet saw the sword of ʿAlī smeared with blood he said, "Indeed, you have fought very well." ʿĀṣim b. Thābit, al-Ḥārith b. al-Ṣimma and Sahl b. Ḥunayf were very good, too. And the sword of Abū Dujāna was blameless. But the Prophet could not bear to drink the brackish water. Muḥammad b. Maslama sought out the women bringing water.

Fourteen women had arrived, among them, Fāṭima the daughter of the Prophet, carrying food and drink on their backs. They quenched the thirst of the wounded and treated them. Kaʿb b. Mālik said, "I saw Umm Sulaym bt. Milhān and ʿĀʾisha carrying water bags upon their backs on the day of Uḥud. Ḥamna bt. Jaḥsh gave water to the thirsty [Page 250] and cared for the wounded. Umm Ayman was quenching the thirst of the wounded.

When Muḥammad b. Maslama did not find any water with them—the Messenger of God was extremely thirsty at that time—he went to the canal and filled his water skin from the rainwater that had collected there, where the castles of the Taimī stand today. He brought sweet water, and the Prophet drank, and he prayed for Muḥammad b. Maslama's good fortune. But the bleeding did not stop, and the Prophet began to say, "They will never obtain such as this from us again until you kiss the black stone." When Fāṭima saw that the blood did not stop flowing, she washed it—ʿAlī poured water on it with his shield—then, she took a piece of mat, burnt it until it became ash, and she placed it on the wound, and it absorbed the blood. Some said that she treated it with burnt wool. The Messenger of God later treated the wound that was on his face with whalebone until the traces disappeared. The Messenger of God continued to feel the effects of the blow of Ibn Qamīʾa on his shoulder for a month or more. He was treating the traces on his face with whalebone.

Muḥammad b. ʿAbdullah related to me from Zuhrī from Saʿīd b. al-Musayyib, who said: When it was the day of Uḥud, Ubayy b. Khalaf approached galloping on his horse until he was close to the Prophet, in order to kill him, so the companions of the Prophet obstructed him. But the Messenger of God said, "Keep away from him!" The Messenger of God stood, his lance in his hand, and aimed it between the lower part of Ubayy's helmet and his coat of mail, and pierced him there. Ubayy fell from his horse, breaking one of his ribs. They carried him until they turned back home. He died on the road, and it was revealed about him: *You did not shoot when you shot, but God shot* (Q. 8:17).

[Page 251] Yūnus b. Muḥammad al-Ẓafarī related to me from ʿĀṣim b. ʿUmar from ʿAbdullah b. Kaʿb b. Mālik from his father, who said: Ubayy b. Khalaf arrived with the ransom for his son who was taken prisoner on the day of Badr. He said, "O Muḥammad, I have a horse and I feed it a large portion of millet every day, I will kill you on it." Muḥammad replied, "Rather, I will kill you upon it, God willing." Some say that he said that in Mecca, and his words reached the Messenger of God in Medina, where he said, "I will kill him on it, God willing."

They said: The Messenger of God was in the battle not paying attention to what was behind him, and saying to his companions, I fear that Ubayy b. Khalaf will come from behind me, so if you see him inform me about him. And lo and behold, Ubayy came galloping upon his horse, and he saw the Messenger of God and recognized him. And he began to shout at the top of his voice, "O Muḥammad, I will not live if you live!" The people said, "O Messenger of God, what will you do when he descends on you and comes to you? If you wish some of us will attack him." The Messenger of God refused. When Ubayy drew near, he took the spear from al-Ḥārith b. al-Ṣimma, then shook off his companions and dispersed us away from him, just as the camel disperses flies. There was not one who resembled the Messenger of God when he concentrated. Then, the Messenger of God threw a spear; it grazed Ubayy on his throat as he rode his horse, and he began to moo like a mooing bull. Some of his companions said to him, "O Abū ʿĀmir, by God, there is nothing wrong with you! If what is with you was in the eye of one of us, it would not hurt him." [Page 252] He protested, "By al-Lāt and al-ʿUzzā, if that which is with me was with the people of Dhū l-Majāz, they would die together. Did he not say, 'I will kill you?'" They carried him, and that took them away from seeking the Prophet. The Messenger of God met the majority of his companions in the pass. Some say that he had obtained the spear from al-Zubayr b. al-Awwām.

Ibn ʿUmar said: Ubayy b. Khalaf died in Baṭn Rābigh. Indeed, I was walking in Baṭn Rābigh some hours into the night, when a fire was kindled, I feared it, and lo and behold a man came out of it with a chain, and he seized it, shouting, "The thirst!" A man says, "You will not quench his thirst. Indeed this is Ubayy b. Khalaf 'the killed of Muḥammad.' I said, "May he be destroyed!" Some said that he died in Sarif. Others said: When the Prophet grabbed the spear of al-Zubayr, Ubayy was coming to the Messenger of God to strike him. Muṣʿab b. ʿUmayr obstructed Ubayy to protect the Prophet, and struck his face. The Messenger of God saw a gap between the lower part of the helmet and armor of Ubayy, and pierced him there and he fell, mooing.

He said: ʿUthmān b. ʿAbdullah b. al-Mughīra al-Makhzūmī approached attending a piebald horse of his, desiring the Messenger of God. He wore a complete cuirass. The Messenger of God faced the pass and ʿUthmān was shouting, "I will not live if you live." The Messenger of God stopped, and the horse stumbled with him in some of what was dug by Abū ʿĀmir. The horse fell on its face and came out wounded, and the companions of the Messenger of God took it, and killed it. [Page 253] Al-Ḥārith b. al-Simma walked to ʿUthmān and they both fought for a while with their swords. Al-Ḥārith struck his leg, his armor was tucked up, and ʿUthmān knelt, and al-Ḥārith finished him off. At that time al-Ḥārith took his armor, his excellent helmet and sword, and one did not hear of any other who was plundered at that time. The Messenger of God saw them fighting and asked about the man. When he learned that it was ʿUthmān b. ʿAbdullah b. al-Mughīra, he said, "Praise be to God who wiped him off." ʿAbdullah b. Jaḥsh had taken him prisoner in Baṭn Nakhla, but when he arrived before the Prophet, he was ransomed and returned to the Quraysh until the raid of Uḥud, when he was killed. His death was seen by ʿUbayd b. Ḥājaz al-ʿĀmarī—i.e. ʿĀmir b. Lu'ayy—who approached running like a lion, and struck a blow at al-Ḥārith b. al-Ṣimma, wounding him on his shoulder. Al-Ḥārith fell wounded until his companions carried him. Abū Dujāna approached ʿUbayd and they fought for a part of the day, each fending off the other's sword with his shield. Finally, Abū Dujāna attacked him, clasping him in his arms, and pinned him to the ground, and slit him with his sword just as he slit sheep. Then he turned and met the Prophet.

They said: Indeed Sahl b. Ḥunayf began to sprinkle the arrows of the Messenger of God, and the Messenger of God said, "Offer arrows to Sahl, for indeed it is easy." The Messenger of God looked at Abū l-Dardā' and the people were fleeing in every direction. He said, "Blessed is the rider ʿUwaymir!" Al-Wāqidi says: Another said that ʿUwaymir did not witness Uḥud.

Al-Wāqidī said: Ibn Abī Sabra related to me from Muḥammad b. ʿAbdullah b. Abī Ṣaʿṣaʿa, from al-Ḥārith b. ʿAbdullah b. Kaʿb b. Mālik, who said: One who met Abū Usayra b. al-Ḥārith b. ʿAlqama related to me that Abū Usayra had met one of the Banū ʿAwf and they had argued and exchanged blows. [Page 254] Each of them dodged his companion. He said: He looked at them as though they were two wild lions. They stopped once and they fought once. Then they embraced, and one of them grabbed his companion and they fell to the ground. Abū Usayra was on top of his opponent and slit him with his sword just as he slit sheep, and then rose from him. At that moment Khālid b. al-Walīd appeared on a black horse with a blaze on its forehead and white feet. He drew a long spear and pierced Abū Usayra from behind. I observed the head of the spear come out of Abū Usayra's chest, as he fell dead. Then, Khālid turned, saying, "I am Abū Sulaymān!"

They said: Ṭalḥa b. ʿUbaydullah fought by the Prophet, at that time, and he fought bravely. Ṭalḥa used to say: Surely I saw the Messenger of God when his companions were defeated. The polytheists returned and surrounded the Prophet from every direction, and I did not know if I should stand in front of him or behind him or to his right or to his left. I kept them off with the sword from in front of him, once, and again from behind him, until they were removed. The Prophet said repeatedly to Ṭalḥa, at that time, "His time has come!" Saʿd b. Abī Waqqāṣ said that the Prophet mentioned Ṭalḥa and said, "May God bless him." Indeed he was the one most beneficial to the Messenger of God on the day of Uḥud! Someone inquired, "How, O Abū Isḥāq?" He replied, "He stayed attached to the Messenger of God, while we were dispersing and returning to him. Surely I saw him circling around the Prophet and shielding him with himself."

Ṭalḥa was asked: O Abū Muḥammad, what took your finger? He replied: Mālik b. Zuhayr al-Jushamī shot an arrow at the Prophet and there was no mistaking his shot, so I protected the face of the Messenger of God with my hand and the arrow took my little finger. His finger was pierced and became crippled. When he was shot, Ṭalḥa said, "Ḥassi!" for the pain. The Messenger of God said, "If he had said, 'In the name of God,' he would have surely entered Paradise as the people watched! Whoever desires to see [Page 255] a man from the people of Paradise who walks the earth, let him look on Ṭalḥa b. ʿUbaydullah. Ṭalḥa is among those who fulfilled his vows."

Ṭalḥa said: When the Muslims went out on patrol and then returned, a man from the Banū ʿĀmir b. Lu'ayy b. Mālik b. Muḍarrab approached, on a chestnut horse with a blaze on its forehead, armed in iron. Drawing out his spear, he shouted, "I am the father of Dhāt al-Wadaʿ (the possessor of sea shells). Guide me to Muḥammad!" So I struck the Achilles' tendon of his horse and it fell. Then I took his spear, and by God, I did not err from his pupil. He bellowed like a bull, and I did not leave him, but placed my foot upon his cheek until he died. Ṭalḥa had a cross-like injury upon his head. A man from the polytheists struck him twice: a blow in confrontation, and another as he turned from him, and he bled. Abū Bakr said: I came to the Prophet on the day of Uḥud and he said, "Go to the son of your uncle!" So I came to Ṭalḥa b. ʿUbaydullah, who had lost blood. I began to splash his face with water, for he had lost consciousness. Then he came to, and said, "How is the Prophet?" I said, "Well; he sent me to you." He said, "Praise be to God! Every misfortune is insignificant after him."

Ḍirār b. al-Khaṭṭāb al-Fihrī used to say: I observed Ṭalḥa b. ʿUbaydullah—he had shaved his head at al-Marwa during the *ʿUmra*—and I saw the cross-like scar on his head. Ḍirār said: By God, I gave him this blow. He confronted me and I struck him, and as he turned away I struck him again.

They said: At the Battle of the Camel, ʿAlī killed those who were killed among the people [Page 256] and entered al-Baṣra. A man from the Bedouin came to him and spoke badly of Ṭalḥa, in front of him. ʿAlī scolded him and said, "Surely, you did not witness the battle of Uḥud and his great beneficence to Islam because of his place by the Messenger of God," and ʿAlī put down the man, and he was silent. A man among the people said: Were his abilities and his trials on the day of Uḥud, by the grace of God? ʿAlī replied: Yes, may God bless him. Surely I saw him. He made a shield of himself for the Messenger of God. The swords and arrows surrounded him from every direction, and he was like a shield for the Messenger of God. Someone said: Though it was a day when the companions of the Messenger of God were killed and the Messenger of God was wounded? ʿAlī said: I testify that I heard the Messenger of God say, "Would that I was left with my companions at the root of the mountain." Ibn Abī l-Zinād said: "Root" means the bottom of the mountain. Then ʿAlī said: Surely, I remember how I gave chase to them in the region. Indeed, Abū Dujāna gave chase to a portion of them in another region; And Saʿd b. Abī Waqqāṣ chased a portion of them, until God dispersed all of them. I remember being alone among them, at that time, a rough group, including ʿIkrima b. Abī Jahl. I entered into the middle of it with a sword and struck with it, while they wrapped around me, until I got rid of the last of them. Then I attacked again, until I returned to where I came from. But the moment was delayed, and God fulfills an affair as He has prescribed.

Al-Wāqidī says: Jābir b. Sulaym related to me from ʿUthmān b. Ṣafwān from ʿUmāra b. Khuzayma, who said: One who saw Ḥubāb b. al-Mundhir b. al-Jamūḥ related to me that he rounded them up at that time as he rounded up sheep, and they wrapped around him until it was said that he was killed. [Page 257] But he appeared with the sword in his hand until they fled from him. He began to attack a group of them and they fled from him to another group. Ḥubāb came to the Prophet, at that time, marked by a green band on his helmet.

At that time, ʿAbd al-Raḥmān b. Abī Bakr appeared on his horse, covered, so that one only saw his eyes, and he said: Who is for a duel? I am. ʿAbd al-Raḥmān b. Atīq. Abū Bakr jumped to it, saying, "O Messenger of God, I will duel with him," and Abū Bakr drew his sword. The Mesenger of God said, "Sheath your sword, and return to your place, and reward us with your life."

The Messenger of God said, "The only comparison for Shammās b. ʿUthmān is a shield," referring to how he fought around the Messenger of God at that time. The Messenger of God did not shoot to the right or the left unless he saw Shammās, in that direction, giving chase with his sword. And when the Prophet was overwhelmed, Shammās shielded him with his body, until he was killed. A saying of the Prophet was, "I cannot find a comparison for Shammās other than the shield."

The first of the Muslims who approached, after they turned back, was Qays b. Muḥarrith with a group of the Anṣār. They reached the Banū Ḥāritha and then returned swiftly. They came upon the polytheists during their comeback attack, and entered their battle fray. Not a man among them escaped until they were killed. Qays b. Muḥarrith fought them and resisted them with his sword until he killed a group of them. They did not kill him except with the spear, and they planned it. Indeed fourteen stabs were found to have pierced him, [Page 258] and ten blows were on his body.

There were ʿAbbās b. ʿUbāda b. Naḍla, Khārija b. Zayd b. Abī Zuhayr, and Aws b. Arqam b. Zayd. ʿAbbās raised his voice saying, "O Muslims, by God and your Prophet, this is what you achieved by disobeying our Prophet. You were promised victory, but you were not patient." Then he removed his helmet from his head, and took off his armor, saying to Khārija b. Zayd, "Do you want my armor and helmet?" Khārija said, "No, I desire what you desire." The people were mixed together. ʿAbbās said, "Are we not responsible to our lord if our Prophet is taken and we live?" Kharija said, "There is no excuse for us with our lord, and there is no proof." As for ʿAbbās, Sufyān b. ʿAbdShams al-Sulamī killed him. Indeed, ʿAbbās struck him twice and wounded him grievously, and at that time he was reduced by an injury that did not heal for a year. Then he recovered. The spear killed Khārija b. Zayd who was wounded some ten times. Ṣafwān b. Umayya passed by him and recognized him. He said, "This is among the oldest companions of Muḥammad at his last breath," and he finished him off. Aws b. Arqam was also killed.

Ṣafwān b. Umayya inquired, "Has anyone seen Khubayb b. Yasāf?" He was seeking him and unable to find him. He mutilated Khārija, at that time, saying, "This was one of those who attacked my father at the battle of Badr"—referring to Umayya b. Khalaf.

"Now, I heal myself when I kill the exemplary among the companions of Muḥammad. I killed Ibn Qawqal, Ibn Abī Zuhayr, and Aws b. Arqam."

On the day of Uḥud, the Messenger of God said, "Who will take this sword [Page 259] in its proper manner?" They asked, "What is its proper manner?" He replied, "To strike the enemy with it." ʿUmar said, "I." But the Prophet turned away from him. Then the Prophet repeated the stipulation and al-Zubayr said, "I," and the Messenger of God turned away from him, so that ʿUmar and al-Zubayr were both hurt. Then he offered it a third time. Abū Dujāna said, "I, O Messenger of God, will take it in its proper manner." The Messenger of God gave it to him and believed in him. When he met the enemy, and gave the sword its due, one of the two men—either ʿUmar or Zubayr—said, "By God, I shall make this man to whom the Prophet gave the sword and prevented me from it, my concern. He said, "I will follow him." Later, he said: By God, I did not see one fight better than he fought. Indeed I saw him strike with the sword, until when he blunted it and feared it was not effective any more, he found his way to a stone and sharpened it. Then he struck with it at the enemy, until he returned, as though it were a scythe. When Abū Dujāna was given the sword, he walked between the lines with a pride in his walk. The Messenger of God said, when he saw him walk that walk, "Indeed, this is a walk odious to God except in such a situation."

Four of the companions in the army were distinguished. One of them was Abū Dujāna who had wrapped his head in a red head cloth. His people knew him when he fought the best of battles wearing it. ʿAlī was known for his white woolen garment. al-Zubayr was recognized by his yellow head cloth, and Ḥamza was known by his ostrich feather. Abū Dujāna said: I saw a woman at that time inciting the people in a dreadful manner. I raised the sword above her for I did not consider her to be other than a man. He said: I hated that I struck a woman with the sword of the Messenger of God. The woman was ʿAmra bt. al-Ḥārith.

[Page 260] Kaʿb b. Mālik used to say: When I was injured on the day of Uḥud, I saw the polytheists mutilating the dead Muslims badly. I stood up and avoiding the dead, moved away. I was thus, when Khālid b. al-Aʿlam al-ʿUqaylī approached gathering the cuirasses and driving the Muslims, saying, "Proceed as mangy sheep proceed." One heavily armed in iron was shouting, "O people of the Quraysh, do not kill Muḥammad. Take him prisoner so we may apprise him of what he has done." Quzmān stood up to him and struck him a blow on his shoulder with the sword, so that I could see his lungs. Then he took his sword and turned. Another polytheist appeared, and I could only see his eyes. He struck him a single blow until he cut him in two. He said: We said, "Who is he?" He replied, "Al-Walīd b. al-ʿĀṣ b. Hishām." Then Kaʿb said: I looked, at that time, and I said, "I have not seen a man so brave with his sword whose life ended thus." He says, "Who is he and how did his life end?" Kaʿb said, "He is of the people of the fire, he killed himself at that time."

Kaʿb said: Then, a man from the polytheists appeared collecting cuirasses and shouting, "Proceed together, just as the mangy proceed." There was a man from the Muslims wearing a cuirass, and I walked until I was behind him, and I stood up to see the Muslim and the disbeliever for myself. The disbeliever was the more prepared and better equipped of the two. I continued observing them until they clashed. The Muslim struck the disbeliever on [Page 261] the vein of his shoulder with the sword. The sword passed until it reached his thighs. The polytheist was divided into two. The Muslim revealed his face saying, "What do you see O Kaʿb? I am Abū Dujāna."

He said: Rushayd the Persian slave of the Banū Muʿāwiya met one of the polytheists from the Banū Kināna masked in iron and saying, "I am Ibn ʿUwaym!" Saʿd the *mawla* of Ḥāṭib obstructed him and struck him a blow cutting him in two. Rushayd was approaching him when Saʿd struck him on his shoulder and cut through the armor until he had cut him in two. He says, "Take this, for I am the Persian slave." The Messenger of God seeing that and hearing him, said, "Did he not say, 'Take this and I am a youth from the Anṣār?' " Then, his brother was before him, and he approached running like a dog saying, "I am Ibn ʿUwaym." Rushayd struck him on his head upon his helmet, and split his head saying, "Take this, and I am an Anṣārī youth!" The Prophet smiled and said, "You are the best, O Abū ʿAbdullah." The Messenger of God named Ibn ʿUwaym Abū ʿAbdullah although he did not have a son at the time.

Abū Namir al-Kinānī said: I approached on the day of Uḥud. The Muslims were exposed, and I was with the polytheists. I attended with ten of my brothers and four of them were killed. The wind was for the Muslims on our first encounter. I was there and we were exposed turning back. The companions of the Prophet approached to plunder the camp, when I reached al-Jammāʾ on foot. Then our cavalry attacked and we said, "By God, the cavalry does not attack except about a considered affair." We attacked on foot as though we were the cavalry when we found the people had taken some of them. They fought without lines. Some of them did not know who struck. There was no standing flag for the Muslims. Our flag was with a man from the Banū ʿAbd al-Dār. I heard the battle cry [Page 262] of the companions of Muḥammad among them, "Kill! Kill!" I was saying to myself: What is the meaning of "Kill!"? I looked at the Messenger of God and indeed his companions had surrounded him. The arrows passed to his right and left, they fell short before his hand and they went out from behind him. I aimed, at that time, fifty spears and took some of his companions with arrows. Later, God guided me to Islam.

ʿAmr b. Thābit b. Waqash had doubts about Islam. He spoke to his people about Islam saying, "If I knew that what they say is true I would not stay away from it!" until when it was the day of Uḥud, Islam became evident to him. The Messenger of God was in Uḥud, and he converted and took his sword and went out and joined the people, and fought until he was paralyzed. He was found among the killed, wounded and dying. They came close to him while he was at his last breath, and they said, "What brought you here, O ʿAmr?" He replied, "Islam; I believe in Allah and His messenger so I took my sword and I joined in the battle. God granted me martyrdom." He died in their hands. The Messenger of God said, "Indeed he is of the people of Paradise."

They said: Al-Wāqidī said: Khārija b. ʿAbdullah b. Sulaymān related to me from Dāwud b. al-Ḥuṣayn from Abū Sufyān, *mawlā* of Ibn Abī Aḥmad, who said: I heard Abū Hurayra say, while the people were around him, "Tell me about a man entering Paradise, who has not worshiped God with a bowing ever?" The people were silent, and Abū Hurayra says, "It is the brother of the Banū ʿAbd al-Ashhal, ʿAmr b. Thābit b. Waqash."

They said: Mukhayrīq was a Jew from among the learned. He said on the Sabath, [Page 263] while the Messenger of God was in Uḥud, "O Jewish people, by God you know that Muḥammad is a Prophet, and that you should help him." They said, "Today is the Sabbath." He said, "There is no Sabbath!" Then he took his weapon and he joined the Prophet and was killed. The Messenger of God said, "Mukhayrīq is the best of the Jews." When Mukhayrīq went out to Uḥud he had said, "If I am taken, my wealth is for Muḥammad. He may put it where God shows." It became a public charity of the Prophet.

Ḥāṭib b. Umayya was a hypocrite. His son was Yazīd b. Ḥāṭib, a man of truth. He witnessed Uḥud with the Prophet and was carried off, from the battlefield, wounded. His people returned with him to his home and his father said, as he and the people of his house looked and cried with him, "By God, you did this to him!" They said, "How?" He replied, "You seduced him from himself until he came out and was killed. Then you told him something else: you promised him that he will enter Paradise. Paradise is a delusion!" They said, "May God destroy you!" He said, "That is it!" He did not accept Islam.

They said: Quzmān was counted among the Banū Ẓafar, but he was not recognized by them. He was to them a loving wall. He was destitute, and without son or wife. But he was brave and recognized for his bravery in the wars that were fought among them. He witnessed Uḥud and fought a brave battle, killing six or seven. He was injured, and the Prophet was informed that Quzmān had been wounded and become a martyr. The Prophet said, "He is among the people of the fire." They came to Quzmān and said to him, "Congratulations, O father of bounty." He responded, "Why do you rejoice? By God, we did not fight except for prestige." They said, "We rejoice for you entering Paradise." He said, [Page 264] "The paradise of delusion—*Ḥarmal*. By God, we did not fight over Paradise or the fire. Rather we fought for our prestige." Then he took out an arrow from his quiver and pierced himself with it. When he found the arrow blade was slow, he took the sword and pierced himself until it came out from his back. That was mentioned to the Prophet and he said, "He is among the people of the fire."

ʿAmr b. al-Jamūḥ was lame. When it was the day of Uḥud—he had four sons who witnessed with the Prophet and observed like lions—his sons desired to confine their father, saying, "You are lame, you are not obligated, your sons will go with the Prophet." He said, "Bakh! They go to heaven and I sit with you!" Hind bt. ʿAmr b. Ḥizam, his wife, said, "As for me, I watched him leave. He took his shield saying, 'O God do not return me to my family in disgrace.' " He went out and his sons met him and spoke to him about staying. The Messenger of God arrived and he said, "O Messenger of God, my sons desire to keep me from going out with you. By God, I hope that I can step into Paradise with this limp." The Messenger of God replied, "As for you, God absolves you, and you are not required to fight." But he refused. So the Prophet said to his sons, "You have no right to stop him. Perhaps God will provide him with martyrdom." They let him go, and he was killed, at that time, a martyr.

Abū Ṭalḥa said: I saw ʿAmr b. al-Jamūḥ, at that time, when the Muslims were exposed. [Page 265] Then they returned and he was in the first squadron. I saw the bend in his leg and he was saying, "I, by God, am yearning for Paradise." Then I saw his son and he was running in his tracks until they were both killed.

ʿĀʾisha, the wife of the Prophet went out with the women rejoicing in the news—the *hijāb* had not been established at that time—until she reached the break in al-Ḥarra. As she descended from Banū Ḥāritha to the Wadi, she met Hind bt. ʿAmr b. Ḥarām the sister of ʿAbdullah b. ʿAmr b. Ḥarām driving her camel carrying her husband, ʿAmr b. al-Jamūḥ, her son, Khallād b. ʿAmr, and her brother, ʿAbdullah b. ʿAmr b. Ḥarām Abū Jabir. ʿĀʾisha said, "You have news. What is behind you?" Hind replied, "Good. The Messenger of God is well, and every misery after him is insignificant. God has taken martyrs from the believers." *God rejected those who disbelieve with their resentment and they did not obtain happiness. God is sufficient for the believers who fight. God is strong and wise* (Q. 33:25). ʿĀʾisha said, "Who are those?" She replied, "My brother, my son Khallād, and my husband ʿAmr b. al-Jamūḥ." ʿĀʾisha said, "Where are you going with them?" She replied, "To Medina. I will bury them there. Hal!" She restrained her camel, then her camel knelt and ʿĀʾisha said, "Is it because of what is on it!" She replied, "That is not it. Maybe it carries what two camels carry—but I think it is something else." She scolded it and it stood up. When she directed it to Medina it knelt. But when she directed it to return to Uḥud it hastened. She returned to the Prophet and informed him about that. He said, "Indeed the camel is charged. Did ʿAmr say anything?" She replied, "Indeed, ʿAmr, [Page 266] when he was going to Uḥud, faced the *qibla* and said, 'O God, do not return me to my people in disgrace, but provide me martyrdom.' " The Messenger of God said, "That is why the camel will not go. Indeed, O people of the Anṣār, among you are those who if they swear in the name of God, fulfill it, including ʿAmr b. al-Jamūḥ. O Hind, the angels will continue to shade your brother from the moment he was killed until the hour they observe where he is buried." Then the Prophet stayed until they were buried. Then he said, "O Hind, they travel together to Paradise: ʿAmr b. Jamūḥ, your son Khallād, and your brother ʿAbdullah." Hind said, "O Messenger of God, pray God, that it will be possible that I join them."

Jābir b. ʿAbdullah said: The people, including my father, drank wine on the day of Uḥud, but they were killed as martyrs. Jābir said: My father was the first of those killed among the Muslims on the day of Uḥud. Sufyān b. ʿAbd Shams the father of Abū l-Aʿwar al-Sulamī killed him. The Messenger of God prayed over him before the defeat. Jābir said: When my father was martyred, my aunt began to cry, and the Prophet asked, "Why is she crying? The angels will continue to shade him with their wings until he is buried."

ʿAbdullah b. ʿAmr b. Ḥarām said: Before the battle of Uḥud, I dreamed about the battle. I thought I saw Mubashshir b. ʿAbd al-Mundhir say, "You are coming to us in days." I said, "Where are you?" He said, "In Paradise where we may roam wherever we wish." I said to him, "Were you not killed on the day of Badr?" He replied, "Of course. But then I came alive." He mentioned that to the Messenger of God, who said, "This is martyrdom, O Abū Jābir."

The Messenger of God said on the day of Uḥud, "Bury ʿAbdullah b. ʿAmr b. Ḥarām and ʿAmr b. Jamūḥ in one grave." It was said: They were found mutilated in every way. [Page 267] Their limbs were cut, piece by piece; their torsos were not recognizable. The Prophet said, "Bury them together in one grave." It was said: Surely he commanded their burial in one grave because they had a good relationship. He said, "Bury the two who loved each other in this world in one grave." ʿAbdullah b. ʿAmr b. Ḥaram was ruddy and bald and not tall. ʿAmr b. Jamūḥ was tall. They were well known. A stream had entered upon them, so it was dug around them and there were two black and white striped coverings on them. ʿAbdullah had taken a wound on his face, and his hand was over his face. When his hand was drawn from his face, blood flowed, so it was returned to its place and the blood stopped flowing. Jābir said, "I saw my father in his grave as though he were sleeping. There was, more or less, no change in his condition." He was asked, "Did you see his shroud?" He replied, "Indeed, his face was wrapped in an excellent striped covering and on his legs were blossoms. And we found the covering, just like the blossoms on his legs, to be in excellent condition". And between then and the time of his burial forty-six years had passed. Jābir sought their advice about perfuming with musk. The companions of the Prophet refused that, saying, "Do not do anything new with them."

Indeed, when Muʿāwiya desired to dig the canal of al-Kaẓāma, a herald in Medina called out, "Whoever has a relative killed at Uḥud, come and witness!" So, the people went out to their dead and they found the bodies fresh and supple. [Page 268] A spade struck a man among them and blood flowed. Abū Saʿīd al-Khudrī said, "No one can ever deny this, after this." ʿAbdullah b. ʿAmr and ʿAmr b. al-Jamūḥ were found in a single grave, and Khārija b. Zayd b. Abī Zuhayr and Saʿd b. al-Rabīʿ were found in a single grave. As for the grave of ʿAbdullah and ʿAmr b. al-Jamūḥ it was displaced and that was because the canal had passed over their grave. As for the grave of Khārija and Saʿd b. al-Rabīʿ it was left. That was because their place was isolated. The sand was spread on them. They used to dig the sand, and whenever they dug a little in that sand, it smelled of musk.

They said: Indeed the Messenger of God said to Jābir, "O Jābir, do you not rejoice?" He replied, "But, of course, by my father and my mother!" The Messenger of God said, "Indeed, by God, your father lives." Then he spoke a few words to him saying, "You will be granted whatever you wish by your Lord." He said, "Grant that I return to battle with Your Prophet and be killed, and that I will live again and be killed with Your Prophet." He said: Indeed I have determined that they will not return.

They said Nusayba bt. Kaʿb was the mother of ʿUmāra, and the wife of Ghaziyya b. ʿAmr. She and her husband and her two sons witnessed Uḥud. She set out with her water bag on the first day desiring to quench the thirst of the wounded. She fought at that time and proved herself in battle, and received twelve wounds either pierced by a spear or cut by a sword.

Umm Saʿd the daughter of Saʿd b. Rabīʿ used to say: I visited her and I said to her, "O aunt, tell me your news." She said, "I set out on the Sunday to Uḥud, and I looked at what the people did. I had a water bag full of water so I went to the Messenger of God who was with his companions. [Page 269] The wind had turned for the Muslims, and the Muslims were defeated. I went down to the Messenger of God and began to attend to the battle. I protected the Prophet with the sword while shooting with the bow until I was wounded." I looked at her shoulder and she had a deep hollow wound. I said: O Umm ʿUmāra, who did this to you? She said: Ibn Qamīʾa approached, when the people had turned away from the Messenger of God, shouting, "Guide me to Muḥammad, for I will not live if he lives." Muṣʿab b. ʿUmayr and the people with him obstructed him, and I was with them. He struck me this blow, and indeed I struck him for that twice. But the enemy was wearing two armor plates. I said: Your hand, what happened to it? She said: It was wounded on the day of Yamāma when the Bedouin were defeated by the people. The Anṣār called out, "Save us," and the Anṣār were saved. I was with them until we reached the garden of the dead. We fought there for a while until Abū Dujāna was killed at the gate of the garden. I entered it desiring the enemy of God, Musaylima. One of their men obstructed me and struck my hand and cut it. By God, the outcome was not for me, nor did I stop over it until I stood over his dead body, and my son ʿAbdullah b. Zayd al-Māzanī was wiping his sword on his garment. I said, "You killed him?" He said, "Yes." I bowed in prayer thanking God.

Ḍamra b. Saʿīd used to relate from his grandmother who had witnessed Uḥud and provided water. She said: I heard the Prophet say, "The place of Nusayba bt. Kaʿb is better than so and so, and so and so!" He had seen her fight a strong battle at that time. She secured her garment around her waist until she was wounded with thirteen wounds. [Page 270] When death came to her I was with those who washed her. I counted her wounds wound by wound, and found thirteen. She used to say: Indeed I observed Ibn Qamīʾa. He had struck her on her shoulder, and it was her biggest wound. She had nursed it for a year. Then a herald of the Messenger of God called to go out to Ḥamrāʾ

al-Asad. She tightened her garment around her but she was unable to go from loss of blood. We stayed up the night and applied compresses on the wound until it was dawn. When the Prophet returned from Hamrā' he did not enter his house until he had sent ʿAbdullah b. Kaʿb al-Māzanī to inquire about her. ʿAbdullah returned to the Prophet and informed him of her well being and the Prophet was happy about that.

ʿAbd al-Jabbār b. ʿUmāra related to us from ʿUmāra b. Ghaziyya, who said: I was there when people withdrew from the Messenger of God, and only a small group of less than ten remained. I and my son and my husband stood in front of him and defended him, while the people passed by him fleeing. He saw me, and I did not have a shield, and he saw a man leaving with a shield and he said, "O possessor of the shield, give your shield to one who is fighting." The man put down his shield and I took it and shielded the Prophet with it. Indeed, the cavalry did much against us; if they had been on foot like us we could have hurt them, God willing! A man approached on a horse and to struck me. I put my shield before him and his sword did nothing, and he turned. I struck the tendon of his horse and it fell on its side. The Prophet began to shout, "O Son of Umm 'Umāra, your mother, your mother!' " She said: My son helped me against him until I transported him to the valley of death.

Ibn Abī Sabra related to me from ʿAmr b. Yaḥyā from his father from ʿAbdullah b. Zayd, who said: I was wounded at the time with a wound in my left upper arm. A man struck me as though he were a palm. [Page 271] He did not stop over me, but went away. The blood did not cease to flow and the Messenger of God said, "Bandage your wound." My mother came to me with a band from her girdle and she prepared it for the wound. She tied my wound while the Prophet stood watching. Then she said, "Rise, my little son and fight the people." The Prophet said repeatedly, "Who was capable of this, O Umm ʿUmāra?" She said, "The man who struck him approaches." The Prophet said, "This is the man who struck your son." She said: I obstructed him and I struck his leg and he knelt. I saw the Messenger of God smile until his teeth showed. He said, "You are zealous, O Umm ʿUmāra." Then we approached him and we were above him with the weapons until we overcame him. The Prophet said, "Praise God who granted your victory and made you happy with regard to your enemy, and showed you your revenge."

Yaʿqūb b. Muḥammad related to us from Mūsā b. Ḍamra b. Saʿīd from his father who said: ʿUmar b. al-Khaṭṭāb was brought silk wraps, and one wrap was wide and excellent. Some of them said: Indeed this wrap is costly and so on, if only you would send it to Ṣafiyya bt. Abī ʿUbayd, the wife of ʿAbdullah b. ʿUmar. That gossip reached Ibn ʿUmar and he said, "Send it to one who is more deserving than her—Umm ʿUmāra Nusayba bt. Kaʿb. I heard the Messenger of God say on the day of Uḥud, 'I did not turn right or left but I saw her fight for me.' "

[Page 272] Al-Wāqidī said: Saʿīd b. Abī Zayd related to me from Marwān b. Abī Saʿīd b. al-Muʿalla, who said: Some one asked Umm ʿUmāra: At that time, did the women of the Quraysh fight alongside their husbands? She replied: In the name of God, I did not see a woman among them aim with an arrow or stone, but I saw them strike tambourines and drums and remind the people of the dead at Badr. Moreover, they kept kohl and kohl sticks and whenever a man turned or withdrew from battle, one of them took a kohl stick to him and said, "Surely, you are a woman!" Indeed, I saw them turn back the defeated, rallying them. The cavalry did not pay attention to the women, and were saved on the backs of the horses. The women followed the men at the lead on foot. They began to fall on the road. Indeed, I saw Hind bt. ʿUtba who was a heavy woman for her frame, sitting with another woman, fearing the cavalry, and having no strength to walk;

until the people attacked us again and took what they took from us. God knows how much was taken from us at that time on account of the marksmen who did not listen to the Prophet.

Al-Wāqidī said: Ibn Abī Sabra related to me from ʿAbd al-Raḥmān b. ʿAbdullah b. Abī Ṣaʿṣaʿa from al-Ḥārith b. ʿAbdullah, who said: I heard ʿAbdullah b. Zayd b. ʿĀṣim say: I witnessed Uḥud with the Messenger of God, when the people dispersed from him, and my mother defended him. The Messenger of God said, "O son of Umm ʿUmāra!" I said, "Yes." He said, "Shoot/throw!" So, right in front of him, I aimed at a man on a horse from the polytheists with a stone. I struck the eye of the horse, and the horse became restless until its rider fell. I continued to attack him with stones—and I had piled up a heavy load against him—until its rider fell. The Prophet looked and smiled. Then he saw my mother wounded on her shoulder and said, "Your mother! Your mother! [Page 273] Bind her wound. God's blessings to you from the family of the Prophet! The place of your mother is better than the place of so and so, and so and so. And the place of your guardian—meaning the husband of my mother—is better than the place of so and so and so and so. And your place is better than so and so, and so and so. May God bless you and your family!" My mother said, "Ask God to let us be with you in Paradise." He said, "O God, make them my companions in Paradise!" And my mother said, "I do not care what takes me from this world."

They said: Jamīla bt. ʿAbdullah b. Ubayy b. Salūl, the wife of Ḥanẓala b. Abī ʿĀmir, came to her husband on the eve of the battle of Uḥud. So Ḥanẓala asked permission of the Messenger of God to spend the night with her and he permitted him. When he prayed the *Ṣubḥ* prayer the next morning he wanted to go to the Messenger of God, but Jamīla was attached to him so he returned and was with her. Then he decided to go out to battle, and he was in a state of ritual impurity. But before that, Jamīla testified before four of her people that he had had sexual relations with her. Later, she was asked, "Why did you testify about him?" She replied, "I saw as though the sky opened and Ḥanẓala entered in it and then it closed," and she said that this was martyrdom. She testified that he had sexual relations with her and that she was impregnated by ʿAbdullah b. Ḥanẓala. Later, Thābit b. Qays married her and she gave birth to Muḥammad b. Thābit b. Qays.

Ḥanẓala b. Abī ʿĀmir took his weapons and joined the Messenger of God as he straightened the lines at Uḥud. He said: When the polytheists were exposed, Ḥanẓala b. Abī ʿĀmir confronted Abū Sufyān b. Ḥarb and struck the Achilles' tendon of his horse, and the horse kicked, and Abū Sufyān fell to the ground. He began to shout, "O people of the Quraysh, I am Abū Sufyān b. Ḥarb," but his voice was heard by men who were too busy with the defeat. Ḥanẓala desired to kill him with his sword, when al-Aswad b. Shaʿūb saw Ḥanẓala and attacked him with the spear [Page 274] and pierced him. Then, Ḥanẓala, while pierced by the spear, walked to al-Aswad, struck him twice and killed him. Abū Sufyān fled, running on his feet and joined with some Quraysh, and Ḥanẓala alighted from his horse and followed behind Abū Sufyān—and those were the words of Abū Sufyān. When Ḥanẓala was killed, his father (Abū ʿĀmir) passed by him. He was killed at the side of Ḥamza b. ʿAbd al-Muṭṭalib and ʿAbdullah b. Jahsh. He (Abū ʿĀmir) said, "Indeed, I warned you of this man (Muḥammad) before this death. By God, you were dutiful to your father, noble in character during your life. Indeed, your place of death is with the path of your companions and their nobility. If God will reward this dead, referring to Ḥamza, or any of the companions of Muḥammad, then may God reward you too." Then he called, "O people of the Quraysh, do not mutilate Ḥanẓala even if he opposed me and you; he did not gain anything." The people mutilated the bodies of the dead Muslims, but Ḥanẓala's body was spared and not mutilated.

Hind was the first who mutilated the companions of the Prophet. She ordered the women to mutilate—the nose and ears were cut—and there did not remain a woman but she had two tree cutting knives, and other tools; and all the dead companions of the Prophet were mutilated by them, except for Ḥanẓala. The Messenger of God said, "Indeed, I saw angels wash Ḥanẓala b. Abī ʿĀmir between the heavens and the earth with water from the clouds in a bowl of silver." Abū ʿUsayd al-Sāʿidī said: We went and looked at him, and lo and behold, on his head were drops of water. Abū Usayd said: I returned to the Messenger of God and informed him, so he sent for Ḥanẓala's wife and questioned her and she informed him that he had set out in a state of ritual impurity.

Wahb b. Qābūs al-Muzannī and his nephew al-Ḥārith b. ʿUqba b. Qābūs approached [Page 275] with their cattle from Mount Muzayna. They found Medina empty so they asked, "Where are the people?" They said, "In Uḥud. The Messenger of God set out to fight the polytheists among the Quraysh." Qābūs and his nephew said, "We do not desire the trace instead of the source," and they set out until they reached the Messenger of God and found the people fighting. It was the turn of the Messenger of God and his companions, so they attacked with the Muslims for the plunder. Just then, the cavalry came from behind them including Khālid b. al-Walīd and ʿIkrima b. Abī Jahl, and they mingled. They fought the Muslims in a severe battle. A group of polytheists dispersed, and the Messenger of God said, "Who is for this division?" Wahb b. Qābūs al-Muzannī replied, "I, O Messenger of God." He stood and aimed arrows at them until they turned and Ibn Qābūs returned. Another group broke off, and the Messenger of God said, "Who is for this squadron?" Al-Muzannī replied, "I, O Messenger of God," and he chased them with the sword until they turned away and al-Muzannī returned. Then another squadron appeared and the Prophet said, "Who will stand for these?" Al-Muzannī said, "I, O Messenger of God, and the Messenger of God said, "Stand, and rejoice in Paradise." Al-Muzannī stood up happily, saying, "By God, I will not be removed, nor will I be excused." He began to move towards them striking with his sword, while the Messenger of God watched him and the Muslims, until he set out from the far end. The Messenger of God said, "O God, bless him!" Then he returned to them and he continued thus, until they surrounded him, and their swords and spears contained him and killed him. At that time, twenty spear stabs were on him and all of them were deadly, and he was mutilated in the ugliest manner. Then his nephew stood up and fought as he had fought, until he was killed. ʿUmar b. al-Khaṭṭāb used to say: Indeed I would like to die as al-Muzannī died.

[Page 276] Bilāl b. al-Ḥārith al-Muzannī used to relate saying: We witnessed al-Qādisiyya with Saʿd b. Abī Waqqāṣ. When God conquered for us, and our booty was apportioned among us, a youth from the family of Qābūs of Muzayna was omitted. When he had completed his sleep, Saʿd came and said, "Bilāl?" Bilāl said, "Yes, I am Bilāl!" He said, "Greetings to you; who is this with you?" Bilāl replied, "A man from my people from the family of Qābūs." Saʿdsaid, "Are you not from the family of al-Muzannī who was killed on the day of Uḥud?" Bilāl replied, "The son of his brother." Saʿd said, "Greetings and welcome. May the blessings of God and happiness be upon you. I testify that on the day of Uḥud, that man did what I have not seen any other do. Indeed, we were there, and the polytheists surrounded us from every direction. The Messenger of God was amidst us, and squadrons appeared from every direction. Indeed, the Messenger of God looked at the people, distinguishing them, and saying, 'Who is for this squadron?' and each time al-Muzannī said, 'I, O Messenger of God!' And each time he chased away the squadron. And I cannot forget the last time he stood up to fight them. The Messenger of God said, 'Stand and rejoice in Paradise.'" Saʿd said, "I stood in his tracks, and God knows that at that time I too desired martyrdom. We went through the enemy and returned a second time. Then, they killed him, may God bless him. I wanted, by God, to be taken with him, but my end was delayed." Then Bilāl asked Saʿd, immediately, about his portion and Saʿd gave it to him and was gracious to him saying, "Choose a place with us or return to your people." Bilāl said that he preferred to return, and we returned.

Saʿd said: I witnessed and I saw the Messenger of God stop before al-Muzannī when he was [Page 277] killed. He says, "May God be satisfied with you for indeed I am satisfied with you." Then I saw the Messenger of God stand up on his feet. The Messenger of God had a wound and indeed, I knew that standing before his grave—until he was placed in it and covered with a green flag—was difficult for him. The Messenger of God extended his cloak over his head, covered it, and wrapped him in it lengthwise. It reached to half the length of his legs. The Prophet commanded us to gather flowers, and we placed them at his feet while he lay in his grave. Then he turned away. There is no situation of death that I prefer than to meet God in the condition of al-Muzannī.

They said: When Satan shouted, "Indeed Muḥammad has been killed," the people dispersed, and among them were those who arrived at Medina. The first of those who arrived at Medina to convey that Muḥammad had been killed was Saʿd b. ʿUthmān, the father of ʿUbāda. Then men arrived after him until they stood before their wives. The women began to say, "Are you fleeing from the Messenger of God?"

He said: Ibn Umm Maktūm said, "Are you fleeing from the Messenger of God?" and he began to complain about them. The Messenger of God had appointed him over Medina. Then, he prayed with the people. He said, "Show me the road," meaning the road to Uḥud, and they put him on the road to Uḥud. He began to inquire from all whom he met about the road to Uḥud until he joined the people. He learned about the well being of the Prophet, and then returned. Among those whom he appointed to take his place were so and so, al-Ḥārith b. Ḥāṭib, Thaʿlaba b. Ḥāṭib, Sawād b. Ghaziyya, Saʿd b. ʿUthmān, ʿUqba [Page 278] b. ʿUthmān, and Khārija b. ʿĀmir. He reached Malal. Aws b. Qayẓī was with a group of the Banū Ḥāritha. They reached al-Shuqra, and Umm Ayman met them and threw dust in their faces, saying to some of them, "Take the spindle and spin with it, and give me your swords!" She went towards Uḥud with other women. Some who narrated traditions said: Indeed the Muslims did not run far from the mountain. They were at its foot. They did not go beyond it elsewhere. The Prophet was there.

It was said: Indeed there were words between ʿAbd al-Raḥmān and ʿUthmān. ʿAbd al-Raḥmān sent for al-Walīd b. ʿUqba and said to him, "Go to your brother and inform him, from me, what I say to you, for I do not know one who will inform him, other than you." Al-Walīd said, "I will do so." He said, "Say, ʿAbd al-Raḥmān says to you, "I witnessed Badr, and you did not; and I affirmed the day of Uḥud but you turned away from it. I witnessed the Pact of Riḍwān and you did not." So he came to ʿUthmān and informed him, and ʿUthmān said, "Your brother speaks the truth. I stayed behind from Badr for the daughter of the Messenger of God was sick and the Messenger of God gave me my portion and my reward was similar to those who attended in the house. I turned away on the day of Uḥud, but God forgave me about that. As for the Pact of

Riḍwān, indeed I went out to the people of Mecca. The Messenger of God sent me, for the Messenger of God said, [Page 279] "Indeed ʿUthmān is obedient to God and His messenger." And the Prophet made a pact, representing me with his left hand, and united the others before him, and the left hand of the Prophet is better than my right. And ʿAbd al-Raḥmān said, when al-Walīd b. ʿUqba came to him, "My brother spoke the truth."

ʿUmar b. al-Khaṭṭāb looked at ʿUthmān b. ʿAffān and said, "He is among those whom God forgave, and by God, God does not forgive something and then retract it. He turned away on the day the two factions met (Uḥud)." A man asked Ibn ʿUmar about ʿUthmān and he said, "Indeed he committed a great sin on the day of Uḥud, but God forgave him; he was among those who turned away on the day of Uḥud when the two factions met. But he committed a small mistake about you and you killed him."

ʿAlī said: When it was the day of Uḥud and the people were patroling the camp, Umayya b. Abī Ḥudhayfa b. al-Mughīra approached, and he was in armor and covered in iron, so that one could see only his eyes. He said, "A battle for the battle of Badr." So one of the Muslims confronted him, and Umayya killed him. ʿAlī said: I withstood him and struck him with my sword on the crown of his head, but he was wearing a helmet and under it a skull cap (*mighfar*) so my sword bounced off. I am a short man. Then he struck me with his sword but my shield protected me, and his sword was stuck. I struck him, and his armour was tucked up so I cut his legs. He fell and began to attend to his sword until he pulled it out of the shield and engaged me in a skirmish, but he was kneeling on his knees. When I saw a hole in his armpit I inserted my sword in it, and he caved over and died, and I turned away from him."

[Page 280] The Prophet said at that time, "I am the son of the three ʿĀtikas [the mother of ʿAbd Manāf b. Quṣāyy was ʿĀtika, the daughter of Hilal b. Fālij b. Dhakwān; the mother of Ḥashim b. ʿAbd Manāf was ʿĀtika, the daughter of Murra b. Hilāl b. Fālij b. Dhakwān; the mother of Wahb, the father of Āmina, the mother of the Prophet was ʿĀtika bt. al-Awqaṣ b. Murra b. Hilāl]." And he also said, "I am the Prophet, there is no lie about it, I am the son of ʿAbd al-Muṭṭalib!"

They said: ʿUmar b. al-Khaṭṭāb came across us sitting with a group of Muslims, and Anas b. al-Naḍr b. Ḍamḍam the uncle of Anas b. Mālik passed by them, and he said, "Why are you sitting?" They replied, "The Messenger of God is killed." He said, "So what will you do with life after him? Stand and die for what he died for!" Then he fought with his sword until he was killed. ʿUmar b. al-Khaṭṭāb said, "I hope that God raises him as an *umma* by himself on the day of resurrection." He was found with seventy blows in his face. He was not known until his sister recognized his beautiful fingers—some say his beautiful teeth.

They said: Mālik b. al-Dukhshum passed Khārija b. Zayd b. Abī Zuhayr seated on his cushion. He had thirteen wounds, all of which led to his death. He said, "Do you not know that Muḥammad has been killed?" Khārija said, "If he has been killed surely God lives, and He will not die. Muḥammad said, 'Fight for your religion!'" He passed Saʿd b. al-Rabīʿ who had twelve wounds and all of them resulted in his death. He said, "You know that Muḥammad has been killed?" Saʿd b. Rabīʿ said, "I witness that Muḥammad reported the message of his lord, 'Fight for your religion.' Indeed God lives and will not die!" A Hypocrite said, "Indeed the Messenger of God has been killed, so return to your people for they [the enemy] will enter your homes."

[Page 281] ʿAbdullah b. ʿAmmār related to me from al-Ḥārith b. al-Fuḍayl al-Khaṭmī, who said: At that time, Thābit b. al-Daḥdāḥa approached the Muslims who were scattered in groups, and he began to shout, "O people of the Anṣār come to me, come to me. I am Thābit b. Daḥdāḥa. If Muḥammad has been killed, yet, God lives and will not die. Fight for your religion! Indeed God will help you and give you victory." A group of the Anṣār joined him and he began to attack with the Muslims, when a squadron of tough men stopped before them led by Khālid b. al-Walīd, ʿAmr b. al-ʿĀṣ, ʿIkrima b. Abī Jahl, and Ḍirār b. al-Khaṭṭāb. There was a skirmish and Khālid b. al-Walīd pierced Thābit with a spear and he fell dead. Those Anṣār who were with him were killed. Some said that they were the last of those killed among the Muslims.

Meanwhile, the Messenger of God arrived with his companions at the ravine where there was no fighting. Before Uḥud, the Messenger of God had an orphan from the Anṣār dispute with Abū Lubāba about some grapes. The Messenger of God judged in favour of Abū Lubāba and the orphan was grieved. The Prophet asked Abū Lubāba to give the grapes to the orphan. Abū Lubāba refused and the Prophet said to him, "If you give it, you will have grapes in heaven." But Abū Lubāba still refused. Then Ibn Daḥdāḥa said, "O Messenger of God, if I gave the orphan grapes, what do you see for me?" The Messenger of God said, "Grapes in Paradise." Thābit b. Daḥdāḥa bought those grapes from Abū Lubāba for a garden of dates and handed the grapes to the orphaned youth. The Messenger of God said, "May the grapes hang low for Ibn Daḥdāḥa in Paradise." [Page 282] Martyrdom was expected for him because of the Prophet's words; he was killed at Uḥud.

Ḍirār b. al-Khaṭṭāb approached riding a horse. He drew a long spear and thrust it at ʿAmr b. Muʿādh and pierced him. ʿAmr walked to him until he was overpowered and fell on his face. Ḍirār said, "You will not miss a man who gives you in marriage to the virgins of Paradise." He added, "I have given ten of the Prophet's companions in marriage." Ibn Wāqid said, "I asked Ibn Jaʿfar whether he killed ten men, and he replied, "We only learned that he killed three." He had struck ʿUmar b. al-Khaṭṭāb, at the time when Muslims roamed with their spears. He said, "O Ibn al-Khaṭṭāb, indeed it was a praiseworthy blessing, and by God, I would not have killed you."

Ḍirār b. al-Khaṭṭāb related what happened at Uḥud. He mentioned the Anṣār adding, "May God have mercy on them." He mentioned their wealth, and their braves and their daring against death. Then he said, "When the nobility of my people were killed at Badr I asked repeatedly, "Who killed Abū l-Ḥakam?" Some said, "Ibn ʿAfrāʾ." Who killed Umayya b. Khalaf? Some said, "Khubayb b. Yasāf." Who killed ʿUqba b. Abī Muʿayṭ? They said, "ʿĀṣim b. Thābit b. Abī l-Aqlaḥ." Who killed so and so? And he was named to me. Who took Suhayl b. ʿAmr prisoner? They said, "Mālik b. al-Dukhshum."

When we went out to Uḥud I used to say, "If they stay in their fortress and it is well protected, there is no way for us to reach them. We will stay for several days and then turn back. If they come out to us from their fortress, however, we will injure them. Our numbers are larger than theirs, we are a people of revenge and we have our women to remind us of our dead at Badr. We have horses and they have none. And we have more weapons than they. It was prescribed for them to go out. We met. And by God, [Page 283] how we stood up to them until we were defeated and exposed, turning away. I said to myself, "This is worse than the fall of Badr!" I said repeatedly to Khālid b. al-Walīd, "Attack the Muslims." He replied, "Do you see a direction where we can attack?" I looked at the mountain where there had been marksmen, and it was, now, empty, and I said, "O Abū Sulaymān, look behind you!" He leaned on the bridle of his horse. He attacked, and we attacked with him. We finally reached the mountain but we did not find any one of significance. We found a little group and we took them, then we entered the camp. The people were negligent, plundering the camp. We pushed the horses at them and they fled in every direction. We placed the swords in them where we wished. I began to seek the elders of the Aws and the Khazraj, the killers of the loved ones, but I did not see one. They had fled.

It was a short time before the Anṣār summoned each other. They approached and intermingled with us but we were on horses, and they waited patiently for us. They sacrificed themselves until they stunned my horse and I was unhorsed. I killed ten of them, but I met poisonous death from a man among them when I found the smell of blood. He embraced me until spears came at him from every direction, and he fell. Praise be to God who blessed them by my hand and did not disgrace me by theirs.

They said: Surely the Messenger of God said on the day of Uḥud, "Who knows about Dhakwān b. ʿAbd Qays?" ʿAlī said, "O Messenger of God, I saw a rider galloping in his tracks until they met, and he says, 'I will not live if you live!' He attacked him from his horse, while Dhakwān was walking, and he struck him saying, 'Take this and I am Ibn ʿIlāj.' I hastened to him while he was riding and I struck his leg with the sword until I cut it from the middle of the thigh. Then I threw him from his horse and dispatched with him. And lo and behold, he was Abū l-Ḥakam b. al-Akhnas b. Sharīq b. ʿIlāj b. ʿAmr b. Wahb al-Thaqafī."

[Page 284] Ṣāliḥ b. Khawwāt related to me from Yazīd b. Rūmān saying: Khawwāt b. Jubayr said, "When the polytheists returned to attack and reached the mountain, it had been deserted by the Muslims. ʿAbdullah b. Jubayr had remained with a group of ten, and they were at Ra's ʿAynayn. When Khālid b. al-Walīd and ʿIkrima ascended with the cavalry, ʿAbdullah b. Jubayr said to his companion, "Spread out so that the enemy cannot pass," and they lined up facing the enemy. They faced the sun and they fought awhile until their commander ʿAbdullah b. Jubayr was killed, and the majority of them wounded. When ʿAbdullah fell, they stripped him and mutilated him in the ugliest manner. The spear was pointed at his stomach until it pierced what was between his navel and his hips down to his pubic region. A piece of him had come out from it. When the people came out I passed him in that condition. Indeed I laughed about a situation no one ever laughs about, I slept in a situation no one ever sleeps in, and I was miserly in a situation no one is ever miserly in. It was said: What is it? He said: I carried him and I took his two limbs while Abū Ḥanna took his two legs. I bandaged his wound with my turban. We took him and the polytheists in a direction until my turban fell from his wound and a piece of him came out. My companion became fearful and kept turning, looking behind him thinking that it was the enemy, while I laughed. A man pointed his spear at the base of my throat; then sleep overcame me, and the spear vanished.

I remember, when I was digging his grave, I had my bow. The mountain was rugged for us, and we descended with him into the valley. I dug with the curve of my bow and with it was the string, and I said, "I will not destroy [Page 285] the string!" I untied it and then dug with the bend of the bow until I was satisfied. We buried him and then returned. The polytheists were still there. We attacked each other, and it was not long before they turned away.

They said: Waḥshī was a slave of the daughter of al-Ḥārith b. ʿĀmir b. Nawfal. Some say he belonged to Jubayr b. Muṭʿim. The daughter of al-Ḥārith said, "Indeed my father was killed on the day of Badr, and if you kill one of three you shall be free: Muḥammad or Ḥamza b. ʿAbd al-Muṭṭalib or ʿAlī b. Abī Ṭālib, for indeed I do not see in the people an equal to my father other than them." Waḥshī said, "As for the Messenger of God you know that I have no power over him, and that his companions will not submit him. As for Ḥamza, by God, if I find him sleeping I will not wake him for fear. As for ʿAlī, I looked for him." He said, "I was with the people seeking ʿAlī until he appeared. He seemed to be a cautious and experienced man, who constantly turns around. I said to myself, this is not the companion whom I seek! Then, all of a sudden, I saw Ḥamza crushing the people completely. I hid at a rock and observed him attack the people with a roar. Sibāʾ b. Umm Anmār confronted him. His mother was a female circumciser in Mecca, the mawlat of Sharīf b. ʿIlāj b. ʿAmr b. Wahb al-Thaqafī. Sibāʾ was called Abū Niyār. Ḥamza said to him, "You too, O son of a female circumciser are among those who have increased against us. Come here." He lifted him until his legs did not support him any more, then threw him to the ground. He knelt upon him and struck him as though he were a sheep. Then he came towards me at the rock when he saw me. But when he reached the stream, he tread on a wet spot and his foot slipped. I brandished my lance [Page 286] until I was satisfied with it, then I struck with it at his waist until it came out from his bladder. A faction of his companions turned towards him and I heard them say, "Abū ʿUmāra!" But there was no reply. I said, "By God, the man has died." I remembered Hind and what she encountered in her father and her uncle and her brother. His companions left once they had ascertained his death, and they did not see me. Then I returned to him and split his stomach and took out his liver. I brought it to Hind bt. ʿUtba and said, "What will you give me if I say I killed the killer of your father?" She replied, "My booty." I said, "This is the liver of Ḥamza." She chewed it, and then spat it out, and I do not know if she disliked its taste or hated it. She removed her clothes and her jewelery and gave them to me. She said, "When you come to Mecca you shall have ten dinars." Then she said, "Show me the place of his death?" I showed her his death site. She removed his male parts. She cut off his nose and ears and made and wore two bracelets, armbands and anklets until she arrived with them in Mecca. She arrived with his liver.

ʿAbdullah b. Jaʿfar related to me from Ibn Abī ʿAwn from al-Zuhrī from ʿUrwa saying: ʿUbaydullah b. ʿAdī b. al-Khiyār related to us saying: We raided al-Shām in the time of ʿUthmān b. ʿAffān and we passed through Ḥimṣ after the ʿAṣar prayer, and we looked for Waḥshī. They said, "You will not be able to get him now, for he drinks wine until dawn." We stayed up the night on account of it, and indeed we were eighty men. After we prayed the Ṣubḥ prayer we went to his house, and there he was, a very old man. There was an old mat sufficient for him to sit on. We said to him, "Inform us about the death of Ḥamza and Musaylima." He hated it and turned from it. We said to him, "We did not spend the night here except for you." He said, "I was the slave of Jubayr b. Muṭʿim b. ʿAdī, and when the people went out to Uḥud he called me and said, 'You saw the death of Ṭuʿayma b. ʿAdī. Ḥamza b. ʿAbd al-Muṭṭalib killed him on the day of Badr, and our women continue to be very sad to this day. [Page 287] If you kill Ḥamza you are free.' I went out with the people and I had many spears. I passed Hind bt. ʿUtba and she said, 'O Abū Dasma, heal me and heal yourself.' When we arrived at Uḥud, I looked at Ḥamza approach the people and destroy them. He saw me, and I hid from him under a tree. He came towards me when Sibāʿ al-Khuzāʿī confronted him. He approached him saying, 'You, too, O son of the female circumciser are among those who attack us, come forward!'" He said, "Hamza approached and lifted him, until I saw his legs weaken, then he struck him to the ground and killed him. Then he came towards me, swiftly, until he stepped on a wet spot and fell, and I aimed my spear and it fell in his lower belly until it came out from between his legs, and I killed him. I passed by Hind bt. ʿUtba and she gave me her jewelery and her clothes."

"As for Musaylima, indeed we entered the garden of the dead. When I saw him I aimed my javeline at him, when a man from the Anṣār struck him with his sword, and your lord knows which of us killed him, but I heard a woman shout above the houses 'The Abyssinian slave killed him.'"

ʿUbaydullah said: I said, "Do you know me?" He said: He turned his eyes on me and said, "The son of ʿAdī and ʿĀtika bt. Abī l-ʿIṣ!" He said: I said, "Yes." He said, "By God, my last time with you was when I raised you to your mother in her sedan chair in which she suckled you. I remember your unsteady feet as though it were now. [Page 288] Hind gave me two anklets of onyx from Ẓafar, two clasps of silver and the rings of silver that she wore on her toes."

Ṣafiyya bt. ʿAbd al-Muṭṭalib used to say: We were taken up to the fortresses—and we had Ḥassān b. Thābit with us—and we were in Fāriʿ. A group of Jews charged the fortress. I said, "Your resistance, O Ibn al-Furayʿa!" He said, "No, by God, I cannot. It is what stops me going out with the Messenger of God to Uḥud!" A Jew was ascending the fortress, so I said, "Strengthen my hands with the sword and you will be acquitted." And he did. She said: I struck off the Jew's head and threw it at them. When they saw it they disappeared. She said: Indeed, the first day I was in Fāriʿ overlooking the fortress, I saw spears fly. I said, "Are there spears among their weapons? Maybe they killed my brother, and I did not know." She said: At the end of the day, I set out to meet the Messenger of God.

She used to relate saying: I knew of the exposure of the companions of the Messenger of God when I was at the fortress. Ḥassān would go to the furthest fortress. If he saw the turn was for the companions of the Messenger of God, he would approach until he stopped at the wall of the fortress. She said: I went out with the sword in my hand, until I was in Banū Ḥāritha and I reached a group of women. Umm Ayman was with them. We went steadily along until we reached the [Page 289] Messenger of God and his companions in groups. The first of those I met was ʿAlī, the son of my brother. He said, "Go back, O my aunt, for indeed the people are exposed." I said, "The Messenger of God?" He said, "He is secure, Praise God!" I said, "Guide me to him until I see him." He pointed him out to me counselling secretly about the polytheists. I reached him and he was wounded.

He said: The Messenger of God began to say, "What is my uncle doing? What is my uncle Ḥamza doing?" Al-Ḥārith b. al-Simma went out slowly. ʿAlī b. Abī Tālib went out saying a *rajaz* verse:

> O Lord, surely al-Ḥārith b. al-Simma was a companion and with us the keeper of his pledge.
> He strayed from his important task looking for heaven in what he completed.

Al-Wāqidī said: I heard this from al-Aṣbagh b. ʿAbd al-ʿAzīz, when I was a lad, and he was the same age as Abū l-Zinād. When he reached al-Ḥārith, and found Ḥamza killed, he informed the Prophet. The Prophet went out walking until he stopped before Ḥamza's body. He said, "I have never been so angry as in this place." Ṣafiyya rose and the Messenger of God said, "O al-Zubayr, take your mother from me, a grave has been dug for Ḥamza." al-Zubayr said, "O mother, indeed the people are exposed, so return!" She said, "I will not go until I see the Messenger of God." When she saw the Messenger of God she said, "O Messenger of God, where is the son of my mother, Ḥamza?" The Messenger of God said, "He is with the people." She said, "I will not return until I see him." Al-Zubayr said, "I continued to hold her to the ground until Ḥamza was buried." The Messenger of God said, "If our women were not saddened I would have left him for the lions and the birds, until he assembles on the day of resurrection from the stomachs of the lions and the crops of the birds."

[Page 290] Ṣafwān b. Umayya looked at Ḥamza at that time and he shocked the people saying, "Who is this?" They said, "Ḥamza b. ʿAbd al-Muṭṭalib." He said, "I have not seen such a day and a man so swift with his people." On that day he was marked by the feather of the Eagle. It was said: When Ḥamza was killed, Ṣafiyya bt. ʿAbd al-Muṭṭalib came looking for him. The Anṣār came between her and him. The Messenger of God said, "Leave her." So she sat with him and began to cry, and the Messenger of God began to cry, and then she began to sob and the Messenger of God began to sob. And Fāṭima the daughter of the Prophet began to cry. The Prophet said repeatedly, "Never has the likes of you been taken, ever!" Then the Messenger of God said, "Rejoice! Gabriel came to me and informed me that Ḥamza is destined with the people of the seventh Paradise." Ḥamza b. ʿAbd al-Muṭṭalib was the lion of God and the lion of the Messenger of God.

He said: The Messenger of God saw a great mutilation, and that mutilation saddened him. The Messenger of God said, "If I am victorious with the Quraysh, I shall mutilate thirty of them!" This verse was revealed about that: *If you punish then punish in the manner that you were afflicted; But if you endure patiently, verily it is better for the patient* (Q.16:126). The Messenger of God was patient and did not mutilate anyone.

Abū Qatāda wanted to punish the Quraysh for the sorrow of the Messenger of God because of the killing of Ḥamza and the mutilation of his body. All that the Prophet indicated to him was to sit down three times, for he was standing. The Messenger of God said, "Consider your position with God." Then the Messenger of God said, "O Abū Qatāda, surely the Quraysh are a people of trust; whoever desires their difficulty, God will prostrate him for it. Perhaps a time will come [Page 291] when you will despise your deed with theirs, and your actions with theirs. If the Quraysh would not reject the truth, I would inform them of what they would have with God." Abū Qatāda said, "By God, O Messenger of God, I am not angry except on behalf of God and his Messenger that they took what they took from him." The Messenger of God said, "You speak the truth." They were the worst of people to their Prophet.

ʿAbdullah b. Jaḥsh said, "O Messenger of God, indeed they have descended, as you see. So, I ask God most high and his messenger: "O God, I entreat you, that we meet the enemy tomorrow, and they kill me, split me open, and mutilate me; and that I meet You, killed, after this was done to me. You will say: Why was this done to you? I will say: For You! And I also ask you that you look after my heirs after me." The Messenger of God agreed. So ʿAbdullah went out and he fought until he was killed. He was mutilated with every mutilation, and buried. He and Ḥamza were buried in the same grave. The Prophet became guardian to his heirs and he purchased a property for ʿAbdullah's mother at Khaybar.

Ḥamna bt. Jaḥsh came forward, and she was ʿAbdullah's sister. The Prophet said to her, "O Ḥamna, expect a reward in the hereafter." She said, "Who is it, O Messenger of God?" He replied, "Your uncle Ḥamza." She said, "From God do we come and to God do we return. May God have mercy upon him and be gracious to him. May he enjoy Paradise." Again, he said, "Expect a reward in the hereafter." And she said, "Who, O Messenger of God?" He replied, "Your brother." She said, "From God do we come and to God do we return. May God have mercy upon him; may he enjoy martyrdom." Then he said once more, "Expect a reward in the hereafter." She said, "Who, O Messenger of God?" He replied, "Muṣʿab b. ʿUmayr." She said, "How grieved are we." And some say, she said, "What a loss!" The Messenger of God said, "Indeed a husband has a place with his wife that no one else shares." Then the Messenger of God said to her, "Why did you say this?" She replied, "O Messenger of God, [Page 292] I think of his orphaned children and it frightens me." The Messenger of God prayed for his children and that his heirs may be treated well. She married Ṭalḥa b. ʿUbaydullah and had a son by him named Muḥammad b. Ṭalḥa. He was most kind to Muṣʿab's children. Ḥamna had come out at that time to Uḥud with the women who provided water.

Al-Sumayrāʾ bt. Qays, one of the women of the Banū Dinār, came out, and her sons Nuʿmān b. ʿAbdʿAmr and Sulaym b. al-Ḥārith had been injured with the Prophet at Uḥud. When their death was announced to her, she said, "How is the Messenger of God?" They said, "Well! Praise be to God, he is as well as you desire." She said, "Show him to me, I will look at him." They indicated him to her, and she said, "All misery after you, O Messenger of God, is insignificant." She came out with her sons driving a camel returning to Medina. ʿĀʾisha met her and said, "What has happened to you?" Sumayra replied, "As for the Messenger of God, praise God, for he is well, not dead. God has taken martyrs from the believers." She said, "Who are those with you?" She said, "My sons. Ḥal!"

They said: The Messenger of God said, "Who will bring me news of Saʿd b. al-Rabīʿ? I saw him—and he indicated with his hand in the direction of the valley—and he was pierced with twelve spears." He said: Muḥammad b. Maslama went out—some say it was Ubayy b. Kaʿb—in that direction. He said: I was amidst the dead, identifying them, when all of a sudden I passed Saʿd b. al-Rabīʿ lying injured in the valley. I called out to him but he did not reply. Then I said, "Surely, the Messenger of God sent me to you." He heaved a deep sigh like the breath of the bellows, saying, [Page 293] "The Messenger of God lives?" I said, "Yes. He indicated to us that you were pierced with twelve spears." He said, "I was pierced by twelve spears. They all pierced my stomach. Go to your people, the peaceful Anṣār, and say to them, 'Hold to God, and to what you promised the Messenger of God on the night of al-Aqaba. By God, there is no excuse for you with God if your Prophet is taken, whilst among you is an eye that waters.'" I did not move from him until he died. He said: I returned to the Messenger of God and informed him. He said: I saw the Messenger of God face the *qibla* and raise his hands saying, "O God, meet Saʿd b. al-Rabīʿ and be satisfied with him."

They said: When the devil shouted, "Surely Muḥammad is killed," they were sad about that. They dispersed in every direction. People passed by the Prophet, but not one among them turned towards him. The Messenger of God invited them from the rear until they all reached al-Mihrās. The Messenger of God turned seeking his companions in the pass.

Mūsā b. Muḥammad b. Ibrāhīm related to me from his father saying: When the Messenger of God appeared to them, they were in a group. Al-Ḍaḥḥāk b. ʿUthmān related to me from Ḍamra b. Saʿīd saying: When the Messenger of God reached them, they were in a group. When he reached the ravine, his companions in the mountain had split up. They mentioned the death of those who were killed among them, and they mentioned what they had learned about the Messenger of God. Kaʿb said: I was the first who recognized him. He was [Page 294] wearing a helmet. I began to shout, "This is the Messenger of God," and I was in the ravine. The Messenger of God signalled to me with his hand over his mouth that I was to be silent. Then he asked for my cuirass and it was yellow or something, and he put it on, and he pulled out his cuirass. He said: The Messenger of God appeared above his companions in the ravine between the two Saʿds, Saʿd b. ʿUbāda and Saʿd b. Muʿādh, and he leaned forward as he walked in his armor. When the Prophet walked he leaned heavily—and some say that he rested on Ṭalḥa b. ʿUbaydullah—for the Messenger of God was wounded at that time. He prayed Ẓuhr while seated. He said: Ṭalḥa said, "O Messenger of God, indeed I am strong," and he carried him until he reached the rock on the road to Uḥud—on the way to Shiʿb al-Jazzārayn—and the Messenger of God did not go beyond it. Then Ṭalḥa carried him to the top of the rock. Then he went to his companions, for with the Prophet was a group that stayed with him. When the Muslims saw those with him, they began to turn away into the ravine for they thought they were from the polytheists. Then Abū Dujāna began to wave to them with the red turban from his head, and they recognized it and returned, or some of them did.

It is said that when the Messenger of God appeared with the group that remained with him, fourteen men—seven from the Muhājirūn and seven from the Anṣār—began to turn away into the mountain. The Messenger of God smiled at Abū Bakr, who was at his side, saying to him, "Wave to them!" Abū Bakr began to wave, but they did not return until Abū Dujāna removed the red turban on his head, approached the mountain and began to shout and wave. They waited until the Muslims joined them. Abū Burda b. Niyār placed an arrow in the center of his bow [Page 295] desiring to shoot at the people, but when they spoke and the Messenger of God called out to them, it was as if nothing could hurt them.

While they were thus and Satan appeared with his insinuations and his humiliation of them, they saw their enemy had dispersed from them. Rāfiʿ b. Khadīj said, "I was at the side of Abū Masʿūd al-Anṣārī," and he mentioned those killed from his people and asked about them. He was informed about the men, among them Saʿd b. al-Rabīʿ and Khārija b. Zuhayr, and he said, "From God do we come . . . and may God have mercy on them." Some of them asked others about close friends. And some of them informed others. While they were thus, God returned the polytheists in order that their sorrow leave them. A squadron of polytheists ran above them, and we forgot what we were talking about. The Messenger of God charged us and spurred us on to battle. I saw so and so, and so and so running as I glanced up at the mountain.

ʿUmar used to say: When Satan shouted, "Muḥammad is killed," I ascended the mountain like a female mountain goat. I reached the Prophet and he was saying: *Muḥammad is only a messenger who discloses the message from his heart* (Q. 3:144), to the end of the verse. Abū Sufyān was at the foot of the mountain. The Messenger of God said, "O God it is not for them to rise above us," and they were removed.

Abū Usayd al-Sāʿidī said: I remember how before sleep overcame us we were easily available for whoever desired us, for the sorrow that we felt. Then sleep overtook us and we slept until [Page 296] there was a clashing of shields and we were so alarmed it was as though we had not been tired before that disaster. Ṭalḥa b. ʿUbaydullah said: Sleep overcame us until the shields of the people clashed. al-Zubayr b. Awwām said: Sleep overtook us, and there was not a man among us but his chin was in his chest from sleep. I heard Muʿattib b. Qushayr say, "I am as a dreamer." God most high revealed about that: *If we had anything to do with this affair we should not have been in the slaughter here* (Q. 3:154). Abū l-Yasar said: I was at that time, with fourteen men from my people, at the side of the Prophet. Sleep overtook us and we were calmed by it. Everyone was immersed, snoring, until the shields clashed. Indeed, I saw the sword of

Bishr b. al-Barā' b. Maʿrūr fall from his hand and he did not know it. He took it after and it was blunted. And indeed the disbelievers were below us. Abū Ṭalḥa said: Sleep overtook us and even my sword fell from my hand. Sleep did not overcome the people of hypocrisy and doubt at that time. All the Hypocrites spoke of what was in their heart. Indeed sleep overtook only the people of conviction and faith.

They said: When they stopped fighting Abū Sufyān desired to depart. He approached marching on a horse of his, a dark red female that moaned and stopped before the companions of the Prophet in the middle of the mountain. He called out in a high voice, "Hubal above!" Then he shouted, "Where is Ibn Abī Kabsha (the Prophet was known as Ibn Abī Kabsha) Where is Ibn Abī Quḥāfa? Where is Ibn al-Khaṭṭāb? Today is for the day of Badr. Indeed, the [Page 297] days have reversed. Indeed, war is a contest. Ḥanẓala (Ibn Abī ʿĀmir) for Ḥanẓala (Ibn Abī Sufyān)." ʿUmar said, "O Messenger of God, shall I answer him?" The Messenger of God said, "Yes, of course, answer him!" Abū Sufyān said, "Praise to Hubal." And ʿUmar said, "Rather, Allah is more high and exalted!" Abū Sufyān said, "Indeed she is most gracious so keep away from her." Then he said, "Where is Ibn Abī Kabshā? Where is Ibn Abī Quḥāfa? Where is Ibn al-Khaṭṭāb?" ʿUmar said, "This is the Messenger of God, and this is Abū Bakr, and this is ʿUmar." Abū Sufyān said, "Today is for the day of Badr. Indeed the days have reversed! Indeed war is a contest." ʿUmar said, "It is not the same. Our dead are in Paradise, and your dead are in hell." Abū Sufyān said, "Indeed, you will say that. Indeed, we failed when we lost." Abū Sufyān said, "But we have al-ʿUzza, and you do not have al-ʿUzzā." ʿUmar replied, "Allah will protect us, and there is no protection for you." Abū Sufyan said, "Indeed she is gracious, O Ibn al-Khaṭṭāb, so stay away from her." Then he said, "Come before me, O al-Khaṭṭāb, I will speak with you." ʿUmar stood up and Abū Sufyān said, "I implore you by your religion, did we kill Muḥammad?" ʿUmar replied, "By God, no. Surely he hears your words now." He replied, "You are to me more trustworthy than Ibn Qamī'a"—for Ibn Qamī'a had informed them that he had killed Muḥammad.

Then Abū Sufyān said, raising his voice, "Indeed you will find corruption and mutilation with your dead that is not the result of an opinion from our elders." The zeal of al-Jahiliya overtook him, and he added, "However, when it happened, we did not detest it. We will meet you in Badr al-Ṣafrā' at the beginning of next year." ʿUmar stopped, awaiting the Prophet's words. The Prophet said, "Say, Yes." ʿUmar said, "Yes." Abū Sufyān turned [Page 298] to his companions and set off with his beasts.

The Messenger of God and the Muslims were gravely apprehensive about the polytheists raiding Medina and destroying the children and the women. The Messenger of God said to Saʿd, "Inform us with news of the polytheists. If they ride their camels and lead their horses it means departure. But if they ride their horses and lead their camels it means that they will raid Medina. By Him who holds my soul in his hand, if they march to Medina I shall go to them and attack them."

Saʿd said: I directed my walk and prepared my heart so that if anything frightened me I would return to the Prophet. I followed on foot in their tracks until all of a sudden they were in al-ʿAqīq. I was where I saw them and I watched carefully. They were riding camels and at their side were the horses. I said, "Surely they depart to their lands." They stopped and waited in al-ʿAqīq and deliberated about entering Medina. Ṣafwān b. Umayya said to them, "You have taken the people, so turn and do not enter upon them for you are tired. Victory is yours. Indeed, you do not know what overcomes you. You turned away on the day of Badr, and by God they did not follow you though victory was theirs." The Messenger of God said, "Ṣafwān has restrained them!' "

When Saʿd saw them on the point of departure and they had entered al-Mukhtamin, he returned to the Messenger of God, and was dejected. He said, "O Messenger of God, the People are directed towards Mecca. They have mounted their camels and lead their horses." The Prophet said, "What did you say?" And Saʿd repeated that. Saʿd said: Then the Prophet withdrew with me and said, "Is it true what you said?" I replied, "Yes, O Messenger of God." He said, "Why do I see you dejected?" He said: I said, "I hated to come to the Muslims [Page 299] rejoicing in their return to their land." The Messenger of God said, "Indeed, Saʿd is experienced!" Some said: Indeed, when Saʿd returned, he attempted to shout out that they were leading their horses and riding their camels, but the Prophet indicated to Saʿd, "lower your voice." He said: Then the Messenger of God said, "Indeed war is deception. Do not show people such joy about their return. Rather, God most high has returned them."

Al Wāqidī said: Ibn Abī Sabra informed me from Yaḥya b. Shibl from Abū Jaʿfar saying: The Messenger of God said, "If you see the people desiring Medina, inform me about the situation quietly and do not undermine the support of the Muslims." So he went and looked at them, and they were riding their camels; and when he returned, he could not control his shouting with joy about their return to Mecca.

According to the Quraysh, when Abū Sufyān arrived in Mecca, he did not go to his house until he went to Hubal and said, "You are most gracious, you have helped me and you have protected me from Muḥammad and his companions," and Abū Sufyān shaved his head.

It was said to ʿAmr b. al-ʿĀṣ, "How were the polytheists and the Muslims split up on the day of Uḥud?" He said, "Why do you want to know? God has brought Islam and expelled polytheism and its people." Then he said, "When we attacked them we took whom we took from them and they dispersed in every direction. A party of them returned later. The Quraysh deliberated and said: We have won, and if we turn, though it has reached us that Ibn Ubayy has turned back with a third of the people, and people from the Aws and Khazraj have stayed behind, we are not certain that they would not return to attack us. We were wounded and arrows had injured most of our horses. So we left. We had not reached al-Rawḥā' before a number of them attacked us, but we continued on."

[Page 300] **A RECORD OF THOSE KILLED AMONG THE MUSLIMS AT UḤUD**

Muḥammad b. Shujāʿ al-Thaljī related to us that al-Wāqidī related to us saying: Sulaymān b. Bilāl related to me from Yaḥyā b. Saʿīd from Saʿīd b. al-Musayyib, who said: Seventy from the Anṣār were killed at Uḥud. Ibn Abī Sabra related a similar tradition from Rubayḥ b. ʿAbd al-Raḥmān from Abū Saʿīd al-Khudrī; and so did ʿUmar b. ʿUthmān from ʿAbd al-Malik b. ʿUbayd from Mujāhid. Four of those killed were from the Quraysh and the rest were from the Anṣār; that is al-Muzannī, his nephew and the two sons of al-Habīt—a total of seventy-four. This is the consensus.

From the Banū Ḥāshim: Ḥamza b. ʿAbd al-Muṭṭalib was killed by Waḥshī. This is verified and there is no dispute about it with us.

From the Banū Umayya: ʿAbdullah b. Jaḥsh b. Ri'āb was killed by Abū l-Ḥakam b. al-Akhnas b. Sharīq.

Some say five from the Quraysh. From the Banū Asad: Saʿd, the *mawlā* of Ḥāṭib. From the Banū Makhzūm: Shammās b. ʿUthmān b. al-Sharīd was killed by Ubayy b. Khalaf. Some say that Abū Salama b. ʿAbd al-Asad was wounded at Uḥud, and his wound continued until he died. He was washed by Banū Umayya b. Zayd at al-ʿAliya between the two horns of the well, which belongs to ʿAbd al-Ṣamad b. ʿAlī today.

From the Banū ʿAbd al-Dār: Muṣʿab b. ʿUmayr was killed by Ibn Qamīʾa. From the Banū Saʿd b. Layth: ʿAbdullah and ʿAbd al-Raḥmān, the two sons of al-Habīt. [Page 301] From the Muzayna, two men were killed: Wahb b. Qābūs and his nephew al-Ḥārith b. ʿUqba b. Qābūs.

From the Anṣār: From the Banū ʿAbd al-Ashhal, twelve men: ʿAmr b. Muʿādh b. al-Nuʿmān (killed by Ḍirār b. al-Khaṭṭāb), al-Ḥārith b. Anas b. Rāfiʿ, ʿUmāra b. Ziyād b. al-Sakan, Salama b. Thābit b. Waqash (killed by Abū Sufyān b. Ḥarb), ʿAmr b. Thābit b. Waqash (killed by Ḍirār b. al-Khaṭṭāb), Rifāʿa b. Waqash (killed by Khālid b. al-Walīd), al-Yamān Abū Ḥudhayfa (mistakenly killed by the Muslims, and some say ʿUtba b. Masʿūd killed him by mistake), Ṣayfī b. Qayẓī (killed by Ḍirār b. al-Khaṭṭāb), al-Ḥubāb b. Qayẓī and ʿAbbād b. Sahl (killed by Ṣafwān b. Umayya).

From the people of Rātij—one of the fortresses of Medina—and they were at ʿAbd al-Ashhal: Iyās b. Aws b. ʿAtīk b. ʿAbd al-Aʿlam b. Zaʿwara b. Jusham was killed by Ḍirār b. al-Khaṭṭāb. ʿUbayd b. al-Tayyihān was killed by ʿIkrima b. Abī Jahl. And Ḥabīb b. Qayyim.

From the Banū ʿAmr b. ʿAwf: the Banū Ḍubayʿa b. Zayd: Abū Sufyān b. al-Ḥārith b. Qays b. Zayd b. Ḍubayʿa. He was the father of girls, who said to the Messenger of God, "I will fight and then return to my daughters." The Messenger of God said, "Trust in God most high."

From the Banū Umayya b. Zayd b. Ḍubayʿa: Ḥanẓala b. Abī ʿĀmir was killed by al-Aswad b. Shaʿūb. From the Banū ʿUbayd b. Zayd: Unays b. Qatāda was killed by Abū l-Ḥakam b. al-Akhnas b. Sharīq. ʿAbdullah b. Jubayr b. al-Nuʿmān, the commander of the marksmen of the Prophet [Page 302] was killed by ʿIkrima b. Abī Jahl.

From the Banū Ghanm b. al-Salm b. Mālik b. Aws: Khaythama Abū Saʿd was killed by Hubayra b. Abī Wahb. From the Banū al-ʿAjlān: ʿAbdullah b. Salama was killed by Ibn Zibaʿra. From the Banū Muʿāwiyā: Subayq b. Ḥāṭib b. al-Ḥārith b. Haysha was killed by Ḍirār b. al-Khaṭṭāb—eight.

From the BalḤārith b. al-Khazraj: Khārija b. Zayd b. Abī Zuhayr was killed by Ṣafwān b. Umayya. And Saʿd b. Rabīʿ; they were both buried in a single grave. And, Aws b. Arqam b. Zayd b. Qays b. al-Nuʿmān b. Thaʿlaba b. Kaʿb—three.

From the Banū al-Abjar: They were the sons of Khudra: Mālik b. Sinān b. al-Abjar; who was the father of Abū Saʿīd al-Khudrī—Ghurāb b. Sufyān killed him. Saʿd b. Suwayd b. Qays b. ʿĀmir b. ʿAmmār b. al-Abjar; and ʿUtba b. Rabīʿ b. Rāfiʿ b. Muʿāwiya b. ʿUbayd b. Thaʿlaba—three.

From the Banū Sāʿida: Thaʿlaba b. Saʿd b. Mālik b. Khālid b. Numayla, Ḥāritha b. ʿAmr, and Nafith b. Farwa b. al-Badī—three.

From the Banū Ṭarīf: ʿAbdullah b. Thaʿlaba, Qays b. Thaʿlaba; and Ṭarīf and Ḍamra, their two allies from Juhayna.

From the Banū ʿAwf b. al-Khazraj; from the Banū Sālim; then the Banū Mālik b. al-ʿAjlān b. Yazīd b. Ghanm b. Sālim: [Page 303] Nawfal b. ʿAbdullah was killed by Sufyān b. ʿUwayf. ʿAbbās b. ʿUbāda b. Naḍla was killed by Sufyān b. ʿAbdShams al-Sulamī. Al-Nuʿmān b. Mālik b. Thaʿlaba b. Ghanm was killed by Ṣafwān b. Umayya, and ʿAbda b. al-Ḥasḥās; they were both buried in a single grave. And Mujadhdhar b.

Dhiyād was killed by al-Ḥārith b. Suwayd. Al-Yamān b. Maʿan related to me from Abū Wajza saying: Three individuals were buried on the day of Uḥud in a single grave—al-Nuʿmān b. Mālik, Mujadhdhar b. Dhiyād, and ʿAbda b. al-Ḥasḥās.

There was the story of Mujadhdhar b. Dhiyād: Ḥuḍayr al-Katāʾib came to the Banū ʿAmr b. ʿAwf to speak to Suwayd b. al-Ṣāmit, Khawwāt b. Jubayr and Abū Lubāba b. ʿAbd al-Mundhir, and some say Sahl b. Ḥunayf. He said, "Visit and stay with me for a few days and I will feed you with drink and meat." They said, "We will come to you on such and such a day." When it was that day, they came to him and he slaughtered a camel for them and provided them with wine to drink, and they stayed with him for three days until the meat turned putrid. Suwayd was at that time an old man. When three days had passed, they said, "We did not consider except to return to our people." Ḥuḍayr said, "Whatever you desire! If you wish, stay! If you wish, return!" The two youths went out with Suwayd, carrying him on a hawdah because he was intoxicated. They passed very close to the Ḥarra until they came close to Banū Ghuṣayna, which was in the direction of the Banū Sālim towards the rising sun. Suwayd was seated and he was urinating, for he was quite intoxicated, and he was noticed by a man from the Khazraj. The man went out until he came to Mujadhdhar b. Dhiyād and said, "Would you have some cold plunder?" he said, "What is it?" He said, "Suwayd! Defenseless, carrying no weapons, and intoxicated!" He said: al-Mujadhdhar b. Dhiyād [Page 304] went out with sword drawn. When the two youths saw him, they fled. They were defenseless and carried no weapons, and moreover, there was enmity between the Aws and the Khazraj—so they left swiftly.

Al-Mujadhdhar jumped on the old man, but there was no motion in him. Al-Mujadhdhar stopped before him and said, "God has given you to me." He answered, "What do you desire with me?" He said, "To kill you." He said, "Go higher than the stomach and lower than the head, and when you return to your mother say, 'I killed Suwayd b. al-Ṣāmit.'" His killing stirred up the Battle of Buʿāth.

When the Messenger of God arrived in Medina, al-Ḥārith b. Suwayd b. al-Ṣāmit and al-Mujadhdhar b. Dhiyād converted to Islam. They witnessed Badr. Then, al-Ḥārith began seeking out al-Mujadhdhar to kill him for his father, but he was not able to do anything about it at that time. When it was the day of Uḥud and the Muslims had gone out on that patrol, al-Ḥārith came from behind Mujadhdhar and cut off his head. The Messenger of God returned to Medina and then set out for Hamrāʾ al-Asad. When he returned from Hamrāʾ al-Asad, Gabriel came to him and informed him that al-Ḥārith b. Suwayd killed al-Mujadhdhar by assassination and commanded the Prophet to kill him. The Messenger of God rode to Qubā on the same day that Gabriel informed him—it was a hot day—and it was a day on which he did not usually ride to Qubāʾ. Indeed, the Messenger of God would come to Qubā usually on the Sabbath and the Monday. When the Messenger of God entered the mosque of Qubā he prayed, as God wished him to pray, and the Anṣār heard and came to greet him. They did not know why he came in that hour and on that day. The Messenger of God sat and spoke and he arranged the people in lines until al-Ḥārith b. Suwayd appeared in a yellow blanket, and when the Messenger of God saw him [Page 305] he called ʿUwaym b. Sāʿida and said, "Deliver al-Ḥārith b. Suwayd at the door of the mosque and cut off his head for the killing of al-Mujadhdhar b. Dhiyād, for indeed he killed him on the day of Uḥud." So ʿUwaym took him captive. Al-Ḥārith said, "Leave me, and I will speak to the Messenger of God!" But ʿUwaym refused. So al-Ḥārith b. Suwayd pushed him aside to speak to the Messenger of God.

The Messenger of God rose desiring to ride. He called for his donkey at the door of the mosque; and al-Ḥārith began to say, "By God, indeed I killed him, O Messenger of God, but I did not kill him turning away from Islam nor apostatizing from it. It was the zeal of Satan and his command that took my soul. Indeed, I ask forgiveness from God and His messenger for what I did. I will pay his blood money; I will fast for two months consecutively, and I will manumit a slave and feed sixty poor. Indeed I ask pardon from God and His messenger." He began to grab the beast of the Messenger of God. The sons of al-Mujadhdhar were present, but the Messenger of God did not say anything to them until when he finished speaking he said, "Bring al-Ḥārith forward, O ʿUwaym, and cut off his head!" The Messenger of God rode away, and ʿUwaym preceded him to the gate of the Mosque, and cut off al-Ḥārith's head.

Another said, "Indeed Khubayb b. Yasāf saw al-Ḥārith when he cut off al-Mujadhdhar's head and came to the Prophet and informed him. The Messenger of God rode to them about this affair. While the Messenger of God was on his donkey, the angel Gabriel had alighted and informed him of it during his journey. The Messenger of God commanded ʿUwaym to cut off al-Ḥārith's head." Ḥassān b. Thābit said:

> O you, Ḥārī, in deep sleep;
> Woe unto you, were you unaware of Gabriel.

[Page 306] Mujammiʿ b. Yaʿqūb and their elders recited to me that Suwayd b. al-Ṣāmit said these verses at his death:

> Hand Julās and ʿAbdullah a message.

If you proclaim it you will not fail them, O Ḥārī Kill Jidāra. If you meet them, the precinct is for ʿAwf whether known or unknown.

From the Banū Salima: ʿAntara mawlā Banū Salima was killed by Nawfal b. Muʿāwiya al-Dīlī.

From the Bal Ḥubla: Rifāʿa b. ʿAmr. From the Banū Ḥarām: ʿAbdullah b. ʿAmr b. Ḥarām was killed by Sufyān b. ʿAbdShams. ʿAmr b. al-Jamūḥ, Khallād b. ʿAmr b. Jamūḥ was killed by al-Aswad b. Jaʿūna—three.

From the Banū Ḥabīb b. ʿAbdḤāritha: Al-Muʿallā b. Lawdhān b. Ḥāritha b. Rustum b. Thaʿlaba was killed by ʿIkrima b. Abī Jahl.

From the Banū Zurayq: Dhakwān b. ʿAbdQays was killed by Abū al-Ḥākam b. al-Akhnas b. Sharīq.

From the Banū Najjār from the Banū Sawād: ʿAmr b. Qays was killed by Nawfal b. Muʿāwiya al-Dīlī. And his son Qays b. ʿAmr, and Salīṭ b. ʿAmr and ʿĀmir b. Mukhallad were also killed.

From the Banū ʿAmr b. Mabdhūl: Abū Usayra b. al-Ḥārith b. ʿAlqama b. ʿAmr b. Mālik was killed by Khālid b. al-Walīd. And ʿAmr b. Muṭarrif b. ʿAlqama b. ʿAmr.

From the Banū ʿAmr b. Mālik, from the Banū Mughāla: Aws b. Ḥarām. [Page 307]

From the Banū ʿAdī b. al-Najjār: Anas b. al-Naḍr b. Ḍamḍam was killed by Sufyān b. ʿUwayf.

From the Banū Māzin b. Najjār: Qays b. Mukhallad, Kaysān their mawlā, and some say, a young slave of theirs.

From the Banū Dinār: Sulaym b. al-Ḥārith and al-Nuʿmān b. ʿAmr the sons of al-Sumayrā' bt. Qays. Twelve were martyred from the Banū Najjār.

THE NAMES OF THOSE KILLED AMONG THE POLYTHEISTS

From the Banū Asad: ʿAbdullah b. Ḥumayd b. Zuhayr b. al-Ḥārith was killed by Abū Dujāna.

From the Banū ʿAbd al-Dār: Ṭalḥa b. Abī Ṭalḥa who carried their flag was killed by ʿAlī b. Abī Ṭālib. ʿUthmān b. Ṭalḥa was killed by Ḥāmza b. ʿAbd al-Muṭṭalib. Abū Saʿīd b. Abī Ṭalḥa was killed by Saʿd b. Abī Waqqāṣ. Musāfiʿ b. Ṭalḥa b. Abī Ṭalḥa was killed by ʿĀṣim b. Thābit b. Abī l-Aqlaḥ. Al-Ḥārith b. Ṭalḥa was killed by ʿĀṣim b. Thābit. Kilāb b. Ṭalḥā was killed by al-Zubayr b. al-Awwām. Al-Julās b. Ṭalḥa was killed by Ṭalḥa b. ʿUbaydullah. Arṭā b. ʿAbdShuraḥbīl was killed by ʿAlī b. Abī Ṭālib. Qāsiṭ b. Shurayḥ [Page 308] b. ʿUthmān was attacked by Ṣuāb. Some say Quzmān killed him. Abū ʿAzīz b. ʿUmayr was killed by Quzmān.

From the Banū Zuhra: Abū l-Ḥakam b. al-Akhnas b. Sharīq was killed by ʿAlī b. Abī Ṭālib. Sibāʿ b. ʿAbd al-ʿUzzā al-Khuzāʿī was killed by Ḥamza b. ʿAbd al-Muṭṭalib. The name of ʿAbd al-ʿUzza was ʿAmr b. Naḍla b. ʿAbbās b. Sulaym. He was the son of Umm Anmār.

From the Banū Makhzūm: Hishām b. Abī Umayya b. al-Mughīra was killed by Quzmān. Al-Walīd b. al-ʿĀṣ b. Hishām was killed by Quzmān. Umayya b. Abī Ḥudhayfa b. al-Mughīra was killed by ʿAlī b. Abī Ṭālib. Khālid b. al-Aʿlam al-ʿUqaylī was killed by Quzmān. Yūnus b. Muḥammad al-Ẓafarī related to us from his father, who said: Quzmān approached, attacking the polytheists, and he encountered Khālid b. Aʿlam. Each one of them was on foot, and they struck each other with their swords. Khālid b. al-Walīd passed by them and he threw his spear at Quzmān. The spear was deflected from him, but Khalid went away, for he thought that he had killed him. While they were in that situation, ʿAmr b. al-ʿĀṣ struck him, and pierced him again, but he was not killed. They continued fighting each other until Quzmān killed Khālid b. al-Aʿlam. Quzmān died from his wounds of that time. ʿUthmān b. ʿAbdullah b. al-Mughīra was killed by al-Ḥārith b. al-Ṣimmma. Five.

From the Banū ʿĀmir b. Luʾayy: ʿUbayd b. Ḥājiz was killed by Abū Dujāna. Shayba b. Mālik b. al-Muḍarrib was killed by Ṭalḥa b. ʿUbaydullah.

From the Banū Jumaḥ: Ubayy b. Khalaf was killed by the hand of the Messenger of God. ʿAmr b. ʿAbdullah b. ʿUmayr b. Wahb b. Ḥudhāfa b. Jumaḥ, also known as [Page 309] Abū ʿAzza, was taken prisoner by the Messenger of God on the day of Uḥud, and the Messenger of God did not take any other prisoner during the battle of Uḥud. Abū ʿAzza said, "O Muḥammad, be kind to me!" The Messenger of God said, "Indeed, a believer will not be bitten from a snake hole twice. And you will never go back to Mecca to boast that you deceived Muḥammad twice." Then he commanded ʿĀṣim b. Thābit to cut off his head.

ʿAbdullah al-Wāqidī said: We also heard another story about his capture. Bukayr b. Mismār related to us that when the polytheists turned from Uḥud they alighted for a while in Hamrāʾ al-Asad during the first night. Then they rode off, leaving behind Abū ʿAzza, sleeping in his place. When day broke, the Muslims found him there in a state of confusion. He who took him prisoner was ʿĀṣim b. Thābit. The Prophet commanded ʿĀṣim to cut off Abū ʿAzza's head.

From the Banū ʿAbdManāt b. Kināna: Khālid b. Sufyān b. ʿUwayf, Abū Shaʿthāʾ b. Sufyān b. ʿUwayf, Abū al-Ḥamrāʾ b. Sufyān b. ʿUwayf and Ghurāb b. Sufyān b. ʿUwayf.

They said: When the polytheists turned away from Uḥud, the Muslims approached their dead. Ḥāmza b. ʿAbd al-Muṭṭalib was among those who were brought to the Prophet first. The Messenger of God prayed over him. Then the Messenger of God said: I saw the angels wash him, for Ḥamza was in a state of impurity that day. The Messenger of God did not wash the martyrs. He said, "Wrap them in their blood and their wounds. Indeed, one who is wounded in the service of God does not appear on the day of judgment except with his wounds. He is marked by the color of blood, and exudes the perfume of musk." Then the Messenger of God said, "Place them in their graves, and I will be witness over those on the day of judgment." Ḥāmza was the first over whom he proclaimed *takbīr* [Page 310] four times. Then the Prophet gathered the martyrs to him; whenever a martyr was brought he was placed at the side of Ḥamza and the Prophet prayed over him and the martyrs, until he had prayed seven times for there were seven martyrs. Some say nine were brought and that Ḥamza was the tenth, and he prayed over them; then he removed the nine while Ḥamza was in his place, and another nine were brought and placed at the side of Ḥamza, and he prayed over them, until he did that seven times. Others say he proclaimed *takbīr* over them nine, seven, and five times.

Ṭalḥa b. ʿUbaydullah, Ibn ʿAbbās and Jābir b. ʿAbdullah used to say: The Messenger of God prayed over the dead of Uḥud and said, "I am a witness over those." Abū Bakr said, "O Messenger of God, are they not our brothers? They converted just as we converted; they strove just as we strove." He replied, "But of course. But these did not enjoy anything of their reward, and I do not know what you will innovate after me." Abū Bakr wept and said, "Are we to live after you?"

Usāma b. Zayd related to me from al-Zuhrī from Anas b. Mālik, who said: The Messenger of God did not pray over them. ʿUmar b. al-ʿUthmān related to me from ʿAbd al-Malik b. ʿUbayd from Saʿīd b. al-Musayyib from the Prophet, similar to it.

The Messenger of God said to the Muslims at that time, "Dig, and widen and improve, and bury two and three in the grave, and place the one who had more of the Qurʾān in front. So the Muslims placed those who had memorized more of the Qurʾān at the front of the grave. Those known to be buried in one grave were: ʿAbdullah b. ʿAmr b. Ḥarām, ʿAmr b. al-Jamūḥ, Khārija b. Zayd, Saʿd b. al-Rabīʿ, al-Nuʿmān b. Mālik and ʿAbda b. al-Ḥasḥās. [Page 311]

When they buried Ḥamza b. ʿAbd al-Muṭṭalib the Messenger of God commanded that a cloak be spread over him. But when the cloak concealed his head, his legs were revealed, and when it covered his feet it exposed his face. The Messenger of God said, "Cover his face and place flowers on his feet." The Muslims wept at that time and said, "O Messenger of God, he is the uncle of the Messenger of God and we cannot find a covering for him!" The Prophet said, "Agricultural lands and towns will be opened to you, and you will send people to them, then they will send to their families. Surely you are in a land lacking trees. Yet, the town is better for them if only they knew. By Him who holds my soul in His hand, one will not be patient with its distress and affliction, but I will be a mediator for him on the Day of Judgment."

They said: ʿAbd al-Raḥmān brought some food. He said, "A shroud cannot be found for Ḥamza—or another man. Muṣʿab b. ʿUmayr was killed and a shroud could not be found for him except a cloak, and they were both better than me." The Messenger of God passed Muṣʿab b. ʿUmayr who was killed in a cloak. He said, "Surely, I saw you in

Mecca and there was none who was more finely dressed or better combed than you. And now, here you are with matted hair in a cloak." Then he commanded that he be buried. His brother, Abū l-Rūm, ʿĀmir b. Rabīʿa and Suwaybiṭ b. ʿAmr b. Ḥarmala alighted in his grave. ʿAlī alighted in the grave of Ḥamza, while al-Zubayr, Abū Bakr, ʿUmar and the Messenger of God sat by it.

[Page 312] The people, or most of them, carried their dead to Medina, and a number of them were buried in al-Baqīʿ at the house of Zayd b. Thābit, which today is in the market—the market of the camel (sūq al-Ẓahr). Some of them were buried with the Banū Salima. Mālik b. Sinān was buried in the place of the companions of ʿAbāʾ, which is in Dār Nakhla. Then the herald of the Messenger of God called out: Return the dead to the place where they fell! But the people had buried their dead, and not one was returned except a man whom the caller reached before he was buried. This was Shammās b. ʿUthmān b. al-Makhzūmī. He was carried to Medina barely alive and taken to the house of ʿĀʾisha, the wife of the Prophet. And, Umm Salama, another wife of the Prophet, said, "My cousin is taken to other than me!" The Messenger of God said, "Carry him to Umm Salama." He was taken to her and he died with her. The Messenger of God commanded us to return him to Uḥud. He was buried there, just as he was, in the garment in which he had died. He stayed a day and a night but he did not taste anything. The Messenger of God did not pray over him or wash him.

Those who were buried there among the Muslims were buried in the wadi. When Ṭalḥa b. ʿUbaydullah was asked about the community grave in Uḥud, he used to say: People from the Bedouin, in the time of the drought during the age of ʿUmar, were there, and they died in that grave of theirs. ʿAbbād b. Tamīm al-Māzanī used to deny that grave saying surely they were a people who died in the time of the drought. Ibn Abī Dhiʾb and ʿAbd al-ʿAzīz b. Muḥammad used to say: We do not know that collective grave. Indeed it is the grave of persons from the people of the desert.

One of the graves of the martyrs was lost. We do not know them in the wadi in Medina and the region, except for the grave of Ḥamza b. ʿAbd al-Muṭṭalib, the grave of [Page 313] Sahl b. Qays, and the grave of ʿAbdullah b. ʿAmr b. Ḥarām and ʿAmr b. Jamūḥ. The Messenger of God used to visit their graves every year. When he reached the pass, he raised his voice, saying, "Peace upon you, for your patience. How blessed is the final abode!" Later, Abū Bakr did similarly every year. Then ʿUmar b. al-Khaṭṭāb and then ʿUthmān, and Muʿāwiya, whenever they passed by while going for the *Ḥajj* or *ʿUmra*.

The Messenger of God used to say, "Would that I had departed with the companions of the mountain!" Fāṭima the daughter of the Messenger of God would go every two or three days, and cry and pray for them. Saʿd b. Abī Waqqāṣ when visiting his property in al-Ghāba, would come from behind the graves of the martyrs saying, "Peace upon you," thrice. Then he would approach his companions saying, "Will you not greet a people who return your greetings? One does not greet them but his greeting will be returned until the Day of Judgment." The Messenger of God passed by the grave of Muṣʿab b. ʿUmayr and stood over him and prayed and recited, "*Men who have been true to their covenant with God, of them some have completed their vow, and some wait: But they have never changed in the least* (Q 33:24). I shall testify that these are martyrs with God on the Day of Judgment; so come to them, visit them and greet them. By Him who holds my soul in His hands, one does not greet them until the Day of Judgment, but they will return it." Abū Saʿīd al-Khudrī used to stand at the grave of Ḥamza and pray and say to whoever was with him, "One does not greet them except they return his greetings, so do not stop greeting them and visiting [Page 314] them." Abū Sufyān, mawlā of Ibn Abī Aḥmad used to relate that he would go with Muḥammad b. Maslama and Salama b. Salāma b. Waqash every month to Uḥud. They gave greetings at the grave of Ḥamza whose grave was the first. They both stood at his grave and the grave of ʿAbdullah b. ʿAmr b. Ḥarām and the graves of whoever was there. Umm Salama, the wife of the Prophet, used to go and greet them every month and spend her day there. One day she came with her slave Nabahān and he did not give greetings, so she said, "Do you not give greetings? What depravity! By God, one does not greet them but they will return it until the day of Resurrection." Abū Hurayra would visit them frequently. When ʿAbdullah b. ʿAmr rode to al-Ghāba and reached Dhubāb, he turned towards the graves of the martyrs and greeted them. Then he returned to Dhubāb until he reached the road—the road to al-Ghāba—and he hated to use their graveyard as a road, so he avoided the road until he returned to his earlier road. Fāṭima al-Khuzāʿiyya who had reached maturity at that time used to say: I remember, the sun had set at the graves of the martyrs, and a sister of mine was with me, so I said to her, "Come, we will greet at the grave of Ḥamza and return." She agreed, so we stood at his grave and said, "Peace upon you, O Uncle of the Prophet." And we heard words returned to us, "And peace to you and God's blessings." The two said, "There was no one near us."

They said: When the Prophet finished burying his companions he called for his horse and rode it. The Muslims went out; most of those around the Prophet were wounded. There was no comparison to the Banū Salama or the Banū ʿAbd al-Ashhal. There were fourteen women with him. When they were at the bottom of the al-Ḥarra he said, "Get into rows and let us praise God." The men arranged themselves in two rows, the women behind them. Then the Messenger of God prayed and said, "O God, to you is due all praise. [Page 315] O God, there is no one to take what You have spread and no one to prevent what You have given. And there is no giver for what You have denied. There is no guide for whom You have led astray, and there is none to lead astray one You have guided. No one can bring close to God one whom You have abandoned, and there is no one who can distance one whom You have brought close. O God, I seek Your blessings, grace, Your generosity and Your forgiveness. O God, I seek Your significant blessings that never change or come to an end. O God, I seek Your protection on the day of fear, and riches on the day of poverty. Protection is with You, O God, from the worst of what You give us, and the evil that You keep from us. O God, cause us to die as Muslims. Endear faith to us, and beautify it in our hearts, and make disbelief and ignominy and sin detestable to us. Make us among the righteous. O God, punish the disbelievers among the people of the book who rejected Your messenger and obstructed Your path. O God, send upon them Your chastisement and punishment. God of truth, amen."

The Prophet approached until he alighted with the Banū Ḥāritha, on the right, in order to appear before the Banū ʿAbd al-Ashhal who were weeping over their dead. He said, "But no one weeps for Ḥamza." The women set out to observe the safety of the Messenger of God, and Umm ʿĀmir al-Ashhalī used to say: We were told that the Prophet had come while we were mourning our dead. We came out and looked at him, and he was wearing his armor plates just as they were. I looked at him and said, "Every misery after you is insignificant."

Umm Saʿd b. Muʿādh set out—and she was Kabsha bt. ʿUbayd b. Muʿāwiya b. BalḤārith b. al-Khazraj. She ran towards the Messenger of God, and the Messenger of God stopped on his horse, while Saʿd b. Muʿādh held it by its bridle. Saʿd said, "O Messenger of God, my mother!" The Messenger of God greeted her. She drew near in order to examine the Messenger of God and said, "If I did not [Page 316] see that you are safe, surely, the misery would be deadly." The Messenger of God gave her his condolences for her son ʿAmr b. Muʿādh. Then he said, "O Umm Saʿd, rejoice and inform their families that their dead have risen in Paradise together—they are twelve men—and they will intercede for their families." She said, "We are satisfied, O Messenger of God. Who will cry over them after this?" Then she said, "Pray, O Messenger of God, for those who remain." The Messenger of God said, "O God, remove the sadness from their hearts and restore them from their misery. Be good to the successors of those who are left behind."

Then the Messenger of God said, "Abū ʿAmr, let the animal loose." So he let loose the horse and the people followed it. The Messenger of God said, "O Abū ʿAmr, the wounded of your family are many. There is not with them one wounded but he will rise on the Day of Judgment and his wound will be a deep red, the color of blood and it will smell of the perfume of musk. He who is wounded must stay in his house and nurse his wounds. He should not accompany me to my house." Saʿd proclaimed about them: "The decision of the Messenger of God is that the wounded from the Banū ʿAbd al-Ashhal should not follow the Messenger of God." All the wounded stayed behind. They spent the night kindling the fires and helping the wounded. There were thirty wounded with them. Saʿd b. Muʿādh went with the Messenger of God to his house; then he returned to his women and dispatched them.

A woman did not remain except she was brought to the house of the Messenger of God and they wept between Maghrib and al-ʿIshā. The Messenger of God rose after sleeping for a third of the night. [Page 317] He heard the crying and asked, "What is this?" Someone said, "The women of the Anṣār weep over Ḥamza." The Messenger of God said, "May God satisfy them with their children," and he ordered them to return to their homes. She said: We returned to our homes after the night, with our men. A woman among us does not cry except she begins with Ḥamza, until this day of ours. It was said: Indeed Muʿādh b. Jabal came with women of the Banū Salima, and ʿAbdullah b. Rawāḥa came with women of BalḤārith b. al-Khazraj. The Messenger of God said, "I did not want this!" The next morning, he forbade them from deep mourning.

The Messenger of God prayed Maghrib in Medina. He had returned to Medina during the disaster that had taken his companions. The Messenger of God was wounded himself. Ibn Ubayy and the Hypocrites with him took malicious pleasure and laughed at what had happened to the Muslims; they put out the ugliest sayings about it. Most of the companions who returned were wounded.

ʿAbdullah, the son of ʿAbdullah b. Ubayy, returned and he too was wounded. He spent the night cauterizing the wounds with fire until the night was gone. Then his father began to say, "Your going out with him in this direction was not wise! Muḥammad resisted me, and obeyed the youth. By God, I was expecting this." His son replied, "What God did for His messenger and the Muslims was good." The Jews professed the same evil words and said, "Muḥammad is only seeking kingship. A Prophet is never wounded thus. His body was wounded and his companions were wounded as well!" The Hypocrites began to wean the Prophet's companions away from him. They ordered them to separate from the Messenger of God. The Hypocrites said to the companions of the Prophet, "If those who were killed among you were with us they would not have been killed," until ʿUmar b. al-Khaṭṭāb heard about that in many places. [Page 318] ʿUmar went to the Prophet and asked permission to kill those Jews and Hypocrites whom he heard it from. The Messenger of God said, "O ʿUmar, indeed God will elevate his religion and esteem his Prophet; But the Jews have a protection so I will not kill them." ʿUmar said, "And those Hypocrites, O Messenger of God?" The Messenger of God replied, "Did they not proclaim the *shahāda*—that there is no God but Allah and that I am His messenger?" He said, "But of course, O Messenger of God, but they only do it to take refuge from the sword. Their affair is clear now, and God has demonstrated their enmity with this disaster." The Messenger of God said, "I forbade the killing of those who say 'there is no God but Allah and Muḥammad is His messenger,' O Ibn al-Khaṭṭāb. Indeed the Quraysh will never take from us similar to this day until we kiss the Black stone of the Kaʿba."

They said: There was a place allotted to ʿAbdullah b. Ubayy every *Jumʿa*, a dignity granted to him that he did not want to let go. When the Messenger of God returned from Uḥud to Medina, Ibn Ubayy, who was seated on the *minbar* on the day of *Jumʿa*, stood up and said, "This is the Messenger of God amidst you. God is most generous to you through him. Help him and obey him." But when he (Ibn Ubayy) did in Uḥud what he did, and stood up to do the same on the following *jumʿa*, the Muslims came to him and said, "Sit! O enemy of God!" Abū Ayyūb and ʿUbāda b. al-Ṣāmit, the most harshly opposed to him among those present, went up to him—none of the Muhājirūn approached him—and Abū Ayyūb took his beard, while ʿUbāda b. al-Ṣāmit pushed him in the neck, and they both said to him, "You are not good enough for this place!" Ibn Ubayy went out after they dismissed him, stepping over the necks of the people, saying, "I did not speak insults but strengthened his command." Muʿawwidh b. ʿAfrāʾ met him and said, "What is your problem?" He said, "I stood at that place where I used to stand from the beginning. Men from the people came to me. ʿUbāda and Khālid b. Zayd were the strongest of them against me." Muʿawwid said to him, "Return, and the Messenger of God will ask forgiveness for you." He said, [Page 319] "By God, I do not desire that he seek forgiveness for me." So these verses were revealed: *When it is said to them, "Come, the Apostle of God will pray for your forgiveness,"* . . . (Q. 63:5) to the end of the verse. He said: I was looking at his son, seated with the people, avoiding looking at his father, who said, "Muḥammad expelled me from the enclosure of the two orphans Sahl and Suhayl."

WHAT WAS REVEALED OF THE QURʾĀN AT UḤUD

Al-Wāqidī said: ʿAbdullāh b. Jaʿfar related to me from Umm Bakr bt. al-Miswar b. Makhrama, who said: Abū Miswar b. Makhrama said to ʿAbdul Raḥmān b. ʿAwf, "Tell us about Uḥud!" He said, "O son of my brother, if you want to know about Uḥud, consider what came to us after verse 120 of *sūra* Āl ʿImrān: *Remember the morning when you left your household to post the faithful* (Q. 3:121)" . . . to the end of the verse. He said: This refers to the morning Muḥammad left for Uḥud and began to line up his companions such that they stood as straight as an arrow. If he saw a chest protruding he said, "Get back!" About God's words: *Remember two of your parties meditated cowardice* . . . (Q. 3:122) to the end of the verse. He said: They refer to the sons of Banū Salima and Banū al-Ḥāritha, who had decided not to go out with the Prophet to Uḥud. Then He determined for them and, they went out. *God helped you at Badr when you were a little force* . . . (Q. 3:123). He says "little," referring to the three hundred and some ten men. *Then trust in God; perhaps, you will show your gratitude* (Q. 3:123), referring to the victory He gave you in Badr. *Remember you said to the Faithful*—this was on the day of

Uḥud—*Is it not enough for you that God should help you with three thousand angels especially sent down?* [Page 320] *Rather, if you remain patient and God fearing . . .* (Q. 3:124) to the end of the verse. This was revealed to the Prophet before he went out to Uḥud: Indeed you could consider about three thousand angels came down: *Yes, if you remain patient, and act right, even if the enemy should rush here on you in hot haste, Your lord would help you with five thousand marked angels. Thus God made it a message of hope for you* (Q. 3:126). He said: But they were not patient and they were exposed, and not a single angel helped the Prophet on the day of Uḥud. His saying, "*marked*," meaning, the angels were distinguished by what they wore. God made it but a message of hope for you, for surely they will give them glad tidings and they will be assured by them. *That he might cut off a fringe of the unbelievers or expose them to infamy* (Q. 3:127). His saying: We will attack them as one, and they will turn back disappointed. *Not for you (but for God) is the decision whether He turn in mercy to them or punish them, for they are indeed wrongdoers* (Q. 3:128). He said: referring to those who were defeated on the day of Uḥud. But some say it was revealed about Ḥamza, when the Messenger of God saw how they had mutilated Ḥamza's body, and the Prophet said, "I will do the same to them!" So this verse was revealed. And some say it was revealed about the Prophet when he was shot on the day of Uḥud and he said repeatedly, "How can a people prosper when they do this to their prophet?"

O you who believe, devour not usury doubled and multiplied (Q. 3:130). He means the people of *jāhiliyya*, who, when the payment is due, and the debtor has not the ability to repay, would allow him time, but multiplies the debt for him. *Be quick in the race for forgiveness from your Lord* (Q. 3:133). He said: Be present at the first *takbīr* with the *Imām*. *For a garden whose width is that of the heavens and of the earth.* Some say Paradise is in the fourth heaven. *Those who spend freely whether in prosperity or in adversity* (Q. 3:134), refers to the ease of prosperity and the difficulty of austerity. *Who restrain anger . . .* meaning to be patient with those who hurt him. *And pardon all men*, what was brought to them. *And those who having done something to be ashamed of or wronged their souls, bring God to mind and ask for forgiveness for their sins, and are not obstinate in what they do* (Q. 3:135). It was said that there is no big sin when there is repentance, and it is no small sin if it is intentionally repeated. *Here is a plain statement to men* (Q. 3:138), meaning, you are no longer blind. *And a guidance*, so that you will not go astray. *And instruction to those who fear God, so lose not heart*, He says, in fighting the enemy. [Page 321] *Nor fall into despair* (Q. 3:139), over those who were overtaken among you in Uḥud from the killing and the wounds. *For you must gain mastery*: He says that on the day of Badr you had overwhelmed double what you overwhelmed in Uḥud. *If a wound has touched you* (Q. 3:140), meaning an injury. *Be sure a similar wound has touched the others*, referring to the wounds of the battle of Badr. *Such days we give to men*, meaning to them is a turn and to you is a turn, but the result/victory is for you. *That God may know those that believe.* He says about those who fight with the Prophet. *That He may take to Himself martyrs*, meaning those who were killed at Uḥud. *God purifies those who believe*, meaning he tests them—those who fought and stood firm. He destroys those who disbelieve, referring to the polytheists. *Did you think that you would enter heaven, and God not knowing who among you strove*, referring to those who were killed in Uḥud and performed well in it. *He knows the steadfast* (Q. 3:142), those who were patient at that time. *You did indeed wish for death before you met it, now you have seen it with your own eyes* (Q. 3:143). He said: The swords were in the hands of men. There were men among the companions of the Prophet who stayed away from Badr, but they were among those who implored the Prophet about going out to Uḥud, and they would take from the remuneration and the plunder. But when the day of Uḥud arrived, some of them turned away. It was said, this was revealed about a group that was speaking before the Prophet went out to Uḥud. They said, "Would that we meet a group of polytheists so that we may be victorious over them or be granted martyrdom." But when they saw death on the day of Uḥud they fled. *And what is Muḥammad if not a messenger, many were the messengers that passed away before him* (Q. 3:144) to the end of the verse. Indeed Satan took the form of Juʿāl b. Surāqa al-Thaʿlaba on the day of Uḥud, and called out, "Muḥammad has been killed!" and the people departed in every direction. ʿUmar said, "I will ascend the mountain like a mountain goat until I finally reach Muḥammad;" and it was revealed, *Muḥammad is no more than a messenger, many were the messengers that passed away before him* to the end of the verse. *And those who turn back on his heels . . .* He refers to those who run away.

[Page 322] *Nor can a soul die except by God's leave, the term being fixed by writing* (Q. 3:145). He says: It was not for him to die without a time. It is due to a saying of Ibn Ubayy when he returned with his companions, and whoever was killed was killed in Uḥud: *If they were with us they would not have died and they would not have been killed* (Q. 3:156). God informed him that there is a fixed time. *God most high says: If any desire a reward in this life we shall give it* (Q. 3:145) . . . He says: those who work for this world, We will give him from it what he wishes. *And if any desire a reward in the hereafter . . .* He says he who desires the after life, *We shall give it to him, and swiftly shall we reward those that serve us with gratitude. How many of the prophets fought in His way*. He says, a large group. *And with them fought large bands of those who did not weaken*. He says they were not destroyed in the way of God nor were their intentions weakened. *Nor did they give in*, He says: They were not subservient to their enemies. *For God loves the patient* (Q. 3:146). He is declaring that they were patient. All that they said was, "O God forgive us our sins," until His words, *the most excellent reward of the hereafter* (Q. 3:148). He says he gave them help and victory and promised them Paradise in the end.

O you who believe if you believe the unbelievers, they will drive you back on your heels and you will turn back (Q. 3:149). He says: If you obey the Jews and the Hypocrites about that which they are deserting you, and you withdraw from your religion . . . *For God is your protector* (Q. 3:150), meaning the believers. He says, He is your protector. *Soon shall We cast terror into the hearts of the unbelievers* (Q. 3:151), He said, the Messenger of God said, "I was helped by the fear a month in advance and a month after. *Surely God fulfilled His promise to you when you routed them with His permission, killing them* (Q. 3:152). He says: He informed you that if you are patient, your Lord will help you with five thousand angels. *Until you became faint-hearted and disagreed about the affair*, and you were weak about the enemy. You disagreed . . . meaning, the marksmen disputed, when the Messenger of God positioned them, and they disobeyed. The Prophet commanded you not to depart or leave your position: Even if you saw us fighting, do not come to help us; and even if you saw us plunder, do not join us. *After he had shown you what you longed for*, referring to the flight of the polytheists while you seized control of those in flight.

[Page 323] *Some of you desired the world* (Q. 3:152), meaning the camp and its plunder. *Some of you desired the hereafter*, meaning those marksmen who stood firm and did not plunder, such as ʿAbdullah b. Jubayr and those who stayed with him. Ibn Masʿūd said, "I did not think a companion of the Messenger of God desired this world until I heard this verse." He said: *Therefore he made you flee from them*—He says when it was your turn against them. *That He might try you*, for the polytheists returned to fight those who were killed among you, and wound those who were wounded among you.

Yet He has forgiven you, meaning those who, at that time, turned from you, and those who desired what they desired of plunder, *He forgives all of it. When you were ascending* (Q. 3:153), meaning the mountain on which you were fleeing, *and you paid no heed to anyone, and the Messenger called you from behind*, referring to when they were passing the defeated, ascending the mountain, and their Messenger called out to them, "O Muslim people, I am the Messenger of God, come to me, to me!" But not one of them turned to him and he forgave them that. *Therefore He rewarded you with grief for (his) grief*. The first grief was the wounded and the dead, the last grief was when they heard that the Messenger of God was killed. And the last grief, which overwhelmed them, made them forget the first grief, caused by the wounded and the dead. Some say the first grief was when they came to the mountain with their defeat and their leaving the Prophet, and the last grief was when the polytheists divided them. So He raised them from the section of the mountain and they forgot their first grief. *And some say grief after grief*, means trial after trial, *In order that you are not saddened by what you miss*. He says in order that you do not remember what you missed from the plunder of their goods. *Nor that which befell you* . . . those who were killed or wounded among you. *Then He sent down upon you a drowsy security, after* . . . until his saying, *we were not killed here*. al-Zubayr said: I heard these words from Muʿattib b. Qushayr, for indeed sleep overcame me [Page 324] and I was in a dream. I heard him say these words, and there is agreement that he said these words.

God said: *Even if you were in your houses, those for whom death was written would have gone forth to their places of rest* (Q. 3:154). God said: There could be no escape from going to their places of rest. *All this has happened so that Allah might try what is in our breasts, and purify what is in our hearts*. He says their malice and dishonesty will leave, for *God knows well the secrets of the breasts*: He says, they cannot conceal good advice or faithlessness. *Lo, those of you who fled on the day the two hosts met, it was Satan alone who caused them to backslide because of some of what they had done* (Q. 3:155): referring to those who were defeated on the day of Uḥud. He says that He overwhelmed them with some of their sins. *Allah has forgiven them*: referring to when they were exposed. *O you who believe! Be not as the disbelievers who say of their brothers* . . . until His words . . . *they would not have died or been killed* (Q. 3:156): He said that it was revealed about Ibn Ubayy: God most high says to the believers, Do not speak or say as Ibn Ubayy said. It is what God said about him. *Like the unbelievers. That Allah makes the pain in their hearts. And if you are killed or die in the way of God* . . . (Q. 3:158) until the end of the verse: He means those who were killed by the sword or died confronting the enemy or garrison, for it is better than what he gathers from this world. And His words, *It is unto Allah that you are gathered*: He says, you will come to Him together on the day of Resurrection. *It was by the God's mercy that you were lenient with them* (Q. 3:159), and his saying, *they dispersed from around you*: meaning his companions who fled at Uḥud. *So pardon them and ask forgiveness for them and consult with them about the affair*: He commanded him to consult them about the war, alone. The Prophet did not consult anyone except about war. *Then when you have taken a decision*, and you are certain, *put your trust in God. It is not for any prophet to deceive (mankind). Whoever deceives will bring his deceit with him on the day of Resurrection* (Q. 3:161): He said: This verse was revealed on the day of Badr. They had plundered red velvet and said: We thought that the Prophet had taken it, and this verse was revealed. *Is one who follows the pleasure of Allah like one who earned the condemnation of Allah* (Q. 3:162)? He said, Are those who believe in Allah comparable to those who disbelieve in Allah? Till His words *They are on varying levels with God* (Q. 3:163): He said, [Page 325] Their virtues are with God. His words, *Allah verily hath shown grace to the believers by sending them a messenger of their own*, meaning Muḥammad, *rehearsing to them the signs of God* . . . meaning the Qur'ān. *Sanctifying them and instructing them*: The Qur'ān, wisdom and reason in the words. *While previously they had been in obvious error*. His words, *And was it so when a misfortune hurt you, though you had hurt them with a misfortune twice as hard* . . . until the end of the verse: This is what overcame them on the day of Uḥud. Seventy were killed among the Muslims together with the wounded. *You said, How is this? Say, It is from yourselves*: Your disobedience of the Messenger, referring to the marksmen. His words, *You hurt them twice as hard*: On the day of Badr they killed seventy and captured seventy. *What you suffered on the day the two armies met*—the day of Uḥud—*was by permission of Allah, that He might know the true believers from the Hypocrites* (Q. 3:166): He knows those who were tested and fought and were killed, and he knows those who were Hypocrites. *It was said to them, Fight in the way of God, or defend yourselves. They said, If we knew how to fight we would follow you* (Q. 3:167): This is Ibn Ubayy. His words, *or defend yourselves*: He says they increased the large number of people. Some say, the prayers. Ibn Ubayy said, on the day of Uḥud: If we knew how to fight surely we would have followed you. God says, *They were that day nearer to unbelief than to faith* . . . was revealed about Ibn Ubayy. About His saying, *Those, who said of their brothers while they sat at home, if they had been guided by us they would not have been slain* (Q. 3:168): This is Ibn Ubayy. *Avert death from yourselves if you speak the truth* . . . was revealed about Ibn Ubayy. *Think not of those who are slain in God's way as dead*, until his words, *Allah does not waste the wage of the believers*: Ibn ʿAbbās said about it, "The Messenger of God said, Indeed your brothers when they were overcome, their souls were kept inside green birds. These birds will visit the rivers of Paradise and eat from its fruits; they will lodge under candelabra of gold under the shade of the throne. And when they experience the goodness of their drinks and food, and when they see the beauty of the final destiny, they say, "Would that our brothers knew of our lord's generosity to us, and of what we have, so they would not abstain from striving nor shrink from war." God most high said: I will inform them [Page 326] about you.

God revealed: *Think not of those who are slain in God's way as dead* (3:169), to the end of the verse: It reached us from the Messenger of God that the martyrs were at the glistening river in Paradise in a green dome, and their nourishment would come to them every morning and evening. Ibn Masʿūd used to say about this verse: Indeed the souls of the martyrs are with God like green birds, and they have chandeliers hanging by the throne. They roam in every heaven. Your Lord looked at them and said: Do you desire something more that I can give you? They said: Our Lord, do we not roam freely in Paradise as we wish? He looked at them a second time and said: Do you desire something more that I can give you? They said: Our Lord, return our souls to our bodies that we may fight in your way. And His saying, *Of those who answered the call of God and His apostle even after being wounded* (Q. 3:172) until the end of the verse, refers to those who raided at Ḥamrā' al-Asad.

ʿAbd al-Ḥamīd b. Jaʿfar related to us about his father saying: When it was Muḥarram, the night of the Sunday, ʿAbdullah b. ʿAmr b. ʿAwf al-Muzannī stood at the door of the Messenger of God. Bilāl, who was seated at the door of the Prophet, called out the call to prayer (*adhān*), and watched the departure of the Prophet until he went out. Then, Muzannī came to the Prophet and said, "O Messenger of God, I was coming from my people, when suddenly I found myself in Malal where the Quraysh had alighted. I said (to myself) I will enter with them and listen to their news. So I sat with them and I heard Abū Sufyān and his companions say, 'We have not done anything. You have destroyed the bravery of the people and their rage; so return and destroy those who remain.' But Ṣafwān refused that." The Messenger of God called Abū Bakr and ʿUmar and told them what al-Muzanni had told him. They said: Seek out the enemy, they will not attack the children (descendents). When the people were secure and refreshed, he commanded Bilāl to call out commanding the people to seek out [Page 327] the enemy. They said: When the Prophet rose in Medina on Sunday, he commanded them to seek out their enemy. So they went out with the wounded.

About His words: *Men said to them "A great army is gathering against you," and frightened them, but it only increased their faith* (Q. 3:173), until His words, *for they followed the good pleasure of God* (Q. 3:174): Abū Sufyān b. Ḥarb promised the Prophet, on the day of Uḥud, an appointment at Badr al-Ṣafrā' in the begining of the year. And it was said to Abū Sufyān, "Did not the Prophet die?" So he sent Nuʿaym b. Masʿūd al-Ashjaʿī to Medina to impede the Muslims, and promised him ten camels if he would send them back home. He said, They have gathered together to come to you in your homes, so do not go out to them. He had barely discouraged them or some of them, when it reached the Prophet, and he said, "By Him who holds my soul in His hands, if no one will go out with me, I will surely go out by myself, and clarify their understanding." So they went out with merchandise, and Badr was in festivity (there was a fair?). *They returned with grace and bounty from God* (Q. 3:174): About the trade, He says they made a profit. *No harm ever touched them* (Q. 3:174): They did not meet with battle. They waited eight days, then they returned. *It is only Satan who suggests to you the fear of his followers; do not fear them, but fear Me* (Q. 3:175): He said, Satan terrifies his friends and those who obey him. *Let not those who rush into unbelief cause you grief. They will do no harm to God* (Q. 3:176). *Those who purchase unbelief at the price of faith* (Q. 3:177): He says they love disbelief above faith. *Let not the unbelievers think that our respite to them is good for themselves* (Q. 3:178): He says, Their bodies are well, and He nourishes them and shows them their turn against their enemies. He says, I will prolong for them so as to increase disbelief. *God will not leave the believers in the state in which you are now, until he separates evil from good. Nor will He disclose to you the secrets of the unseen.* (Q. 3:179): meaning the misery of the people of Uḥud. *But God chooses of His apostles who He pleases* (Q. 3:179): Meaning He brings His messengers close.

About His words: *Let not those who are miserly,* [Page 328] *with what God gives them of his grace, think that it is good for them,* till His words . . . *On the Day of Judgment* (Q. 3:180): He said, He brings treasure that does not lead to his rights, like a snake around his neck grabbing for his throat. He said, I am your treasure. *God hears the taunt of those who say, Truly God is indigent and we are rich* (Q. 3:181): when these verses were revealed. *Who is he that will give God a beautiful loan* (Q. 2:245): He said that Finḥāṣ the Jew said, "God is poor and we are rich, for He seeks a loan from us." *And their slaying the prophets in defiance of right, and we shall say, Taste ye the penalty of the scorching fire.* (Q. 3:181) *This is because of what your hands sent* (Q. 3:182): referring to your disbelief and your killing of the prophets. *They said, God took our promise not to believe in an Apostle unless he showed us a sacrifice consumed by fire. And you shall certainly hear much that will grieve you from those who received the Book from before you*: meaning the

Jews. *From those who worshiped many Gods*: meaning the Arabs, to the end of the verse. *Remember God took a covenant from the People of the Book to make it known and clear to mankind* (Q. 3:187), till His words, *To them is a grievous penalty*: He said that He made a covenant with the Jews including the command about the description of the Prophet, that they shall not conceal it. *But they threw it away behind their backs* (Q. 3:187): they took the provision and changed his description. *Think not that those who exult in what they have brought about and love to be praised for what they have not done* (Q.3:188): He said that this was revealed about the people among the Hypocrites. The Messenger of God, when he raided, approached them. They said, "When you raid, we will go out with you," but when he raided they did not go out with him. It was said that they were the Jews. *Men who celebrate the praises of God, standing, sitting and lying down on their sides* (Q. 3:191): He said that they prayed, standing, sitting and on their sides, meaning they were reclining. *Our Lord, we have heard the call of one calling us to faith, "Believe in the Lord," and we have believed* (Q. 3:192): Referring to the Qur'ān. He said, all of them did not see the Prophet. His words: [Page 329] *Those who have left their homes or been driven out, or suffered harm in my cause, or fought, or been slain* (Q. 3:195): meaning the Muhājirūn who went out from Mecca. *Let not the wanderings of the unbelievers through the land deceive you* (Q. 3:196). *Little is it for enjoyment* (Q. 3:197): He means their merchandise and trade. *There are certainly among the People of the Book those who believe in God, in the revelation to you, and the revelation to them* (Q. 3:199): meaning ʿAbdullah b. Salām. *O you who believe, persevere in patience and constancy, and fear God* (Q. 3:200): He said that at the time of the Prophet there were no hospices (*ribāṭ*). Indeed, it meant one prayer after another.

Jābir b. ʿAbdullah said: When Saʿd b. al-Rabīʿ was killed, the Messenger of God returned to Medina and then marched to Ḥamrāʾ al-Asad. The brother of Saʿd b. al-Rabīʿ came and took the inheritance of Saʿd. But Saʿd had two daughters and his wife was pregnant. The Muslims used to inherit as they did during *jāhiliyya* until Saʿd b. al-Rabīʿ was killed. When their uncle grabbed the wealth, for the distributive shares had not been revealed, the wife of Saʿd, who was a determined woman, prepared food and invited the Prophet to some bread and meat, at the time, in al-Aswāf.

We had turned back to the Prophet at dawn, and while we were with him, seated, we mentioned the time of Uḥud, and those who were killed among the Muslims. We mentioned Saʿd b. al-Rabīʿ until the Messenger of God said, "Come with us!" So we went with him, and we were twenty men, until we finally reached al-Aswāf. The Messenger of God entered and we entered with him. We found that Saʿd's wife had sprinkled what was between two palm trees and thrown a mat of straw. Jābir b. ʿAbdullah said, "By God, there was no cushion or rug." We sat and the Messenger of God [Page 330] related to us about Saʿd b. al-Rabīʿ. He said, "May God have mercy upon him," adding, "Indeed I saw spears pierce him when he was killed." When they heard that, the women wept, and the Prophet's eyes were full of tears, and he did not forbid the women from weeping. Jābir said: Then the Prophet said, "A man from the people of Paradise is coming upon you." He said: We observed who was approaching, and Abū Bakr appeared. We stood and told him the good news that the Messenger of God had stated. Then he greeted, and they replied, and he sat down. Again, the Messenger of God said, "A man from the people of Paradise is coming to you." We observed who appeared from the gap in the palms. ʿUmar b. al-Khaṭṭāb appeared, and we stood and we informed him of the good news that the Messenger of God had informed us. Then he sat down. Then the Messenger of God said, again, "A man from the people of Paradise is coming upon you, and we observed the gap in the palms, and lo and behold it was ʿAlī who appeared. We stood and we told him of the good news regarding Paradise. He came and greeted and sat down. Then food was brought.

Jābir said: Food sufficient for one or two men was brought; the Messenger of God put his hand in it and said, "Take in the name of God!" We ate from it until we were full, and by God, it did not appear to us that we had touched a thing. Then they brought us ripe dates in a saucer from the first fruit or a little later, and the Messenger of God said: "In the name of God, eat!" He said: We ate until we were full, and I looked in the saucer and there remained approximately what was brought in it. *Ẓuhr* arrived and the Messenger of God prayed with us, and he did not perform ablutions. Then Messenger of God returned to his seat and conversed. Then ʿAṣar came, and the remainder of the food was brought and there was plenty of it to fill them up. The Messenger of God stood [Page 331] and prayed ʿAṣar, but he did not touch water.

Then the wife of Saʿd b. al-Rabīʿ stood up and said, "O Messenger of God, Saʿd b. Rabīʿ was killed at Uḥud, and his brother came and took what he left. But Saʿd left two daughters and there is no property for them. Surely, Messenger of God, women are married for their wealth?" The Messenger of God said, "God grant the best protection to his heirs; nothing is revealed to me about that. Come back to me when I return!" When the Messenger of God returned to his house he sat at his door and we sat with him. A convulsion seized him until we thought that he had a revelation about it. He regained his composure and sweat dripped from his brow like pearls. The Prophet said, "Bring me the wife of Saʿd!" He said: "Abū Masʿūd ʿUqba b. ʿAmr went and brought her." He said: She was a woman who was determined and tough. The Prophet said, "Where is the uncle of your children?" She said, "O Messenger of God, he is in his house." He said, "Call him to me!" Then the Messenger of God said, "Sit by me!" She sat, and he sent a man running to the uncle and he was with the BalḤārith b. Khazraj. He came and he was tired. The Prophet said, "Pay the daughters of your brother two-thirds of what your brother left." And his wife proclaimed *takbīr* and the people of the masjid heard her. "Pay the wife of your brother an eighth and the rest is for you."

The child in her womb did not inherit at that time. She was Umm Saʿd, daughter of Saʿd b. al-Rabīʿ, wife of Zayd b Thābit, and mother of Khārija b. Zayd. When ʿUmar b. al-Khaṭṭāb was appointed ruler, Zayd married Umm Saʿd bt. Saʿd and she was pregnant. He said, "If you have a need to speak about your inheritance from your father, the Amīr al-Mu'minīn has decreed that the fetus should receive a portion of the inheritance." On the day her father was killed Umm Saʿd was in the womb. She said, "I do not seek anything from my brother."

When the polytheists were defeated at Uḥud, the first of those who came with news of Uḥud and their defeat of [Page 332] the polytheists was ʿAbdullah b. Abī Umayya b. al-Mughīra. He hated to arrive in Mecca so he arrived at al-Ṭā'if and announced, "Indeed the companions of Muḥammad have won and defeated us. I am the first who comes to you!" That was when the first defeat was inflicted on the polytheists. Then the polytheists retreated after they took what they could. The first of those who informed the Quraysh of the death of the companions of Muḥammad and the victory of the Quraysh was Waḥshī.

Mūsā b. Shayba related to me from Qaṭar b. Wahb al-Laythī saying, "When Waḥshī arrived before the people of Mecca with the misery that had befallen the companions of the Messenger of God, he went on his camel for four days and finally reached al-Thanniya which rose above al-Ḥajūn. There, he called out at the top of his voice, "O people of the Quraysh!" several times. When the people returned to him—and they were fearful lest he brought them what they detested—and when he was satisfied about them, he said, "Rejoice! We have killed the companions of Muḥammad in a slaughtering that no other army has achieved. We wounded Muḥammad so that he cannot move, and I killed the leader of the squadron Ḥamza." The people left in every direction in malicious joy at the killing of the companions of Muḥammad, showing their joy. Jubayr b. Muṭʿim was alone with Waḥshī and he said, "Consider what you say." Waḥshī said, "By God, I spoke the truth." He said, "You killed Ḥamza?" He said, "I supplied him with a spear in his stomach until it protruded from between his legs. Then he was called but he did not reply. I took his liver and I have brought it to you for you to see." He said, "You have eliminated the sorrow of our women. You have cooled the heat in our hearts!" He commanded his women, at that time, to return to their pleasure and their paints, perfume and oil.

Muʿāwiya b. al-Mughīra b. Abī l-ʿĀṣ was defeated, at that time, so he went towards [Page 333] Medina and slept close to that city. In the morning he entered Medina and went to the house of ʿUthmān b. ʿAffān and knocked on his door. His wife Umm Kulthūm, the daughter of the Prophet, said, "He is not here. He is with the Messenger of God." He replied, "Send for him. Indeed, I have for him the price of a camel that I purchased a year ago. I come now with its price, otherwise I will go."

He said: She sent for ʿUthmān and he came, and when he saw Muʿāwiya he said, "Woe unto you, you have destroyed me and yourself. What brought you here?" He replied, "O son of my uncle, there is not anyone closer to me than you, nor more trustworthy." ʿUthmān took him towards the side of the house, then he went out to the Prophet desiring to give him protection. The Prophet had said before ʿUthmān came to him, "Surely Muʿāwiya will enter Medina in the morning, so seek him out." They looked for him but they could not find him. Some of them said, "Seek him in the house of ʿUthmān b. ʿAffān," so they entered the house of ʿUthmān and asked Umm Kulthūm. She pointed to him and they pulled him out from under a *Ḥimāra* (a support to hang a water bag), then, they rushed with him to the Prophet. When ʿUthmān saw him, he came with him and said, "By Him who sent you with the truth, I did not come to you except to ask you to protect him. Give him to me, O Messenger of God?" So the Prophet handed him to ʿUthmān, and ʿUthmān protected him, and postponed his destiny for three days, on condition that if he were found after that, he would be killed.

He said: ʿUthmān went out and bought him a camel, and prepared him. Then he said, "Ride!" And he rode. The Messenger of God went to Ḥamrāʾ al-Asad, and ʿUthmān went out with the Muslims to Ḥamrā al-Asad. Muʿāwiya stayed until three days had passed. Then he sat up on his horse and he went out until lo and behold he was in the heart of al-ʿAqīq. The Messenger of God said, "Muʿāwiya is close by, so find him." The people went out in search of him. Then Muʿāwiya mistook the road.

[Page 334] They followed in his tracks until they overtook him on the fourth day. Zayd b. Ḥāritha and ʿAmmār b. Yāsir had hastened in search of him. They overtook him in Jammāʾ where Zayd b. Ḥāritha struck him. ʿAmmār said, "Surely I have a right in him." So he aimed an arrow at him, and thus they killed him. They returned to the Prophet and informed him of it. It was also said: He was overtaken at Thanniyat al-Sharīd, eight miles from Medina. That was when he made a mistake on the route. They overtook him, and they continued to shoot arrows at him, treating him as a target until he died.

THE RAID OF ḤAMRĀ' AL-ASAD

The raid of Ḥamrā' al-Asad took place on Sunday, the eighth of Shawwāl, thirty-two months after the Prophet's emigration. The Prophet entered Medina on Friday and was absent for five days.

They said: When the Messenger of God prayed the *Ṣubḥ* prayer on Sunday, eminent members of the Aws and the Khazraj, who had spent the night at the mosque at his door, were with him, including Sa'd b. 'Ubāda, Ḥubāb b. al-Mundhir, Sa'd b. Mu'ādh, Aws b. Khawlī, Qatāda b. al-Nu'mān, 'Ubayd b. Aws, as well as a number of others. When the Messenger of God turned away from his prayer, he commanded Bilāl to call out, "The Messenger of God commands you to seek out your enemy; only those who witnessed the battle yesterday shall go out."

He said: Sa'd b. Mu'ādh returned to his home and ordered his people to march. He said: The wounds in the people were widespread. The majority of the Banū 'Abd al-Ashhal, in fact all of them, were wounded. Sa'd b. Mu'ādh came to them and said, "The Messenger of God commands that you seek out your enemy." [Page 335] He said: Usayd b. Ḥuḍayr, who had seven injuries and desired to treat them, said, "Hear and obey God and His Prophet!" and he took his weapons and did not turn back to treat his wounds, but joined the Messenger of God.

Sa'd b. 'Ubāda came to his people, the Banū Sā'ida, and ordered them to march; so they got dressed and joined them. Abū Qatāda came to his people, at Khurbā, who were treating their wounded, and said, "This call of the Messenger of God commands you to seek out your enemy." So they jumped to their weapons and did not stop for their wounds. Forty wounded went out from the Banū Salima: al-Tufayl b. al-Nu'mān had thirteen wounds; Khirāsh b. al-Ṣimma, ten wounds; Ka'b b. Mālik, more than ten wounds; Quṭba b. 'Āmir b. Ḥadīda, nine wounds. They joined the Prophet at Bi'r Abī 'Inaba at the beginning of al-Thanniya, which was the first road at the time. They had their weapons and were arranged in lines for the Messenger of God. When the Prophet looked at them and saw the spread of wounds among them, he said, "O God, bless the Banū Salima!"

Al-Wāqidī said: 'Utba b. Jabīra related to me from some of his men saying: Indeed 'Abdullah b. Sahl and Rāfi' b. Sahl b. 'Abd al-Ashhal returned from Uḥud with many injuries, though of the two of them 'Abdullahhad the more serious injuries. When they rose in the morning, Sa'd b. Mu'ādh came to them and informed them that the Messenger of God commanded them to seek out their enemy. One of them said to his companion, "By God, surely leaving the raid to the Messenger of God was cowardly. But, by God, we have no animal to ride on and we do not know what to do!" 'Abdullah said, "Come with us!" Rāfi' said, "No, by God, I have no strength to walk." His brother said, "Come with us and we will protect each other as we proceed." They went out slowly: Rāfi' was weak, so 'Abdullah would carry him on his back one turn, and then he would walk one turn, [Page 336] until they came to the Messenger of God, where they lit several fires, at 'Ishā'. The two wounded men were both brought to the Prophet, and 'Abbād b. Bishr, who was keeping watch that night, said, "What held you back?" They informed him of their weakness, so he prayed for their happiness and added, "If your life is extended may you have many mounts of horses and mules and camels. Wouldn't that be good for you!" 'Abd al-'Azīz b. Muḥammad from Ya'qūb b. 'Umar b. Qatāda said: These two are Anis and Mu'nis, and this is their story.

Jābir b. 'Abdullah said, "O Messenger of God, indeed a caller cried out that only one who had attended the battle yesterday may go out now. I wanted to attend but my father left me in charge of my sisters, saying, 'O my son, it is not correct for you and me to leave them. There is no man with them, and I fear they are weak women. I must go out with the Messenger of God for I hope that God will grant me martyrdom.' So I stayed behind, for God preferred him over me for martyrdom, though I desired it too. So, permit me now, O Messenger of God, to march with you." The Messenger of God permitted him. Jābir said: One who did not witness the battle the day before did not go out with the Prophet, except I. Men who had not attended sought his permission, but he refused them.

The Prophet asked for the banner, which was still knotted, and not put away since the day before, and handed it to ʿAlī. Some say he gave it to Abū Bakr. The Messenger of God went out while he was wounded. On his face were the traces of two links, and a cut on his forehead at the root of his hair. His tooth had splintered, his upper lip cut from within, his right shoulder weakened by the blow from Ibn Qamīʾa, [Page 337] and the two sides of his knees bruised. The Prophet entered the mosque and prayed two prostrations. The people had mobilized. The people of al-ʿAwālī came down when the call came to them. Then the Prophet prayed two prostrations and called for his horse at the gate of the mosque. He met Ṭalḥa who had heard the caller and come out to see when the Prophet desired to march. But the Messenger of God was already clad in armor and helmet so one could see only his eyes. He said, "O Ṭalḥa, your weapons!" Ṭalha said, "Soon."

Ṭalha said: I went out running and put on my armor, took my sword, and held my shield to my chest. Indeed, I had nine wounds, but I was more distressed about the wounds of the Messenger of God than I was about mine. The Prophet approached Ṭalḥa and said, "Do you see the people now?" Ṭalha said, "They are at al-Sayyāla." The Messenger of God said, "That is what I thought. Indeed, O Ṭalḥa, they shall never take from us as they did yesterday until God conquers Mecca for us."

The Messenger of God sent three individuals from the Aslam ahead in the tracks of the people: Salīt and Nuʿmān the two sons of Sufyān b. Khālid b. ʿAwf b. Dārim of the Banū Sahm. With them a third man from the Aslam from Banū ʿUwayr, who was not named for us. The third delayed them while they hurried on. The front strap of the shoe of one of them broke, and he said, "Give me your shoe." The other said, "No, by God, I will not." So the first struck the other in his chest with his foot, and when he fell on his back, took his shoe.

The people met at Ḥamrāʾ al-Asad. They heard a voice, while they were trying to return, but Ṣafwān prevented them from returning. Then, they saw two men and turned and attacked them. The Muslims reached the site of their death and set up camp, and buried the two dead in a single grave. Ibn ʿAbbās said, [Page 338] "This is the grave of the two from the village."

The Messenger of God went with his companions until they camped at Ḥamrāʾ al-Asad. Jābir said: Our main provision was dates. Saʿd b. ʿUbāda brought thirty camel loads when he arrived in al-Ḥamrāʾ. They drove the slaughtering animals and killed two or three in a day. During the day the Prophet commanded us to gather firewood, and when it was evening he commanded us to light fires. Every man lit a fire. That night we lit five hundred fires so that we could be seen from afar. Word of our camps and our fires traveled in every direction until God overwhelmed our enemy.

Maʿbad b. Abī Maʿbad al-Khuzāʿī arrived. At that time the Khuzāʿā were at peace with the Prophet, though Maʿbad remained a polytheist. He said, "O Muḥammad, indeed we were affected by what happened to you and your companions. We wished that God would increase your success, and that misfortune befalls the others." Then Maʿbad set out until he found Abū Sufyān and the Quraysh in al-Rawḥāʾ. They were saying, "You neither killed Muḥammad nor captured slave girls. Miserable is what you did!" And they agreed to return. One of them, referring to what happened among them, said, "We did not do anything. We attacked their nobility but then returned without destroying them completely, and they may flourish later." This speaker was ʿIkrima b. Abī Jahl. When Maʿbad came to Abū Sufyān, the latter said, "This is Maʿbad and he has news. What is behind you, O Maʿbad?" Maʿbad replied, "I left Muḥammad and his companions behind me burning for you like fires. Those who had stayed away from him yesterday among the Aws and the Khazraj have gathered to him, and they promise they will not return until they meet you and take their revenge. Indeed, their people are [Page 339] very angry about those you have killed from their nobility." They said, "Woe unto you, what are you saying?" ʿIkrima said, "By God, we do not think that we should leave until we meet the forelocks of the horses!" Then Maʿbad said: What I saw about them moved me such that I said these verses:

My mount almost fell from fright at the voices
When the ground flowed with troops of horse.
They ran with noble lion like warriors
Eager for the fray, firm in the saddle, fully armed.
I said: Alas for Ibn Ḥarb when he meets them
When the plain is surging with men.

One of the ways by which God most high returned Abū Sufyān and his companions to Mecca was the words of Ṣafwān b. Umayya before Maʿbad appeared, when Ṣafwān said, "O people, do not act, for indeed the people are saddened. I fear that those of the Khazraj who stayed behind will gather against you, so return home while you are victorious. Indeed I do not believe that if you meet again you will be successful." The Messenger of God said, "Ṣafwān guides them even while he is not guided. By Him who holds my soul in His hand, the stones have been marked for them. If they return they will be gone like yesterday."

The people (Quraysh) left swiftly fearing to look for them. A group of ʿAbd al-Qays passed by Abū Sufyān [Page 340] seeking Medina. Abū Sufyān said, "Will you inform Muḥammad and his companions of what I send, if I load your camels with raisins in ʿUkkaẓ tomorrow when you come to me?" They replied, "Yes." He said, "When you meet Muḥammad and his companions, inform them that we have gathered to return to them, for we are on their tracks," and Abū Sufyān departed.

The rider arrived before Muḥammad and his companions at Ḥamrāʾ. They informed them of what Abū Sufyān had commanded them. They said, "God is sufficient for us." About that God most high revealed: *Those who answered the call of God and His Apostle even after being wounded*, and His words: Men said, "*A great army is gathering against you* (Q. 3:172,173)." Maʿbad sent a man from the Khuzāʿa to the Messenger of God informing him that Abū Sufyān and his companions had turned back, and left fearfully. The Messenger of God returned to Medina.

THE EXPEDITION LED BY ABŪ SALAMA B. ʿABD AL-ASAD TO QAṬAN, TO THE BANŪ ASAD

Al-Wāqidī said: ʿUmar b. ʿUthmān b. ʿAbd al-Raḥmān b. Saʿīd b. Yarbūʿ from Salama b. ʿAbdullah b. ʿUmar b. Abī Salama b. ʿAbd al-Asad, and others as well, have related this tradition about the expedition to me. The pillar of the tradition is from ʿUmar b. ʿUthmān from Salama. They said: Abū Salama b. ʿAbd al-Asad had witnessed Uḥud and alighted with the Banū Umayya b. Zayd in the high lands when departing from Qubāʾ. His wife Umm Salama bt. Abī Umayya was with him. He was wounded on his upper arm at Uḥud and had returned to his home, when news came to him that the Messenger of God was marching to Ḥamrāʾ al-Asad. [Page 341] He did as the Messenger of God did, and set out on a donkey until he joined the Messenger of God as he was descending from al-ʿAṣba in al-ʿAqīq. Then he proceeded with the Prophet to Ḥamrāʾ al-Asad. When the Prophet returned to Medina, Abū Salama turned back with the Muslims and returned from al-ʿAṣba. He stayed a month and treated his wounds until he believed he had recovered. But the wound had closed hiding some infection, and he did not know it.

When it was the month of Muḥarram, thirty-five months after the *hijra*, the Messenger of God called Abū Salama and said, "Go out on this raid for I appoint you its commander." He then handed him the banner and said, "Go until you reach the land of the Banū Asad and attack them before they gather together and confront you," and he urged him, by the power of God, to take care of those Muslims who were with him. A hundred and fifty went out with Abū Salama on that march, among them were Abū Sabra b. Abī Ruhm who was the brother of Abū Salama—for they had the same mother, Barra bt. ʿAbd al-Muṭṭalib—ʿAbdullah b. Suhayl b. ʿAmr, and ʿAbdullah b. Makhrama al-ʿĀmirī, and from the Banū Makhzūm: Muʿattib b. al-Faḍl b. Ḥamrāʾ al-Khuzāʿī an ally of theirs, Arqam b. Abī l-Arqam and others of them. From the Banū Fihr: Abū ʿUbayda b. al-Jarrāḥ and Suhayl b. Bayḍāʾ; from the Anṣār: Usayd b. al-Ḥuḍayr, ʿAbbād b. Bishr, Abū Nāʾila, Abū ʿAbs, Qatāda b. al-Numān, Naḍr b. Ḥārith al-Ẓafarī, Abū Qatāda, Abū ʿAyyāsh al-Zuraqī, ʿAbdullah b. Zayd, Khubayb b. Yasāf, and some who are not named for us.

What angered the Prophet was that a man from the Tayyiʾ—who had arrived in Medina desiring to meet a woman from Tayyiʾ who was related to him, but married to one of the companions of the Prophet—had alighted at the house of that companion of the Prophet and informed him that Ṭulayḥa and Salama, the two sons of Khuwaylid, had left with their people and those who obeyed them inviting them to fight the Messenger of God, [Page 342] and intending to draw near to Medina. They said, "We will march to Muḥammad within his very home, and attack the outermost fringe of it." Indeed they possessed land for grazing by the side of Medina. "We will go out on the backs of horses for indeed they have grazed in the Spring, and we will go out on the most excellent camel, so that when we capture booty we will not be overtaken. If we encounter a group of them, we will be ready for war as we have horses and they have none with them, and we have the best camels that are as good as horses. The people (Muslims) are wounded, for the Quraysh attacked them recently, so they cannot fight for long, and a group will not return for them." A man among them named Qays b. al-Ḥārith b. ʿUmayr stood up with them and said, "O people, by God, this is not a considered decision. We have no desire for revenge against them. They are not an easy prey. Indeed our land is far from Yathrib, and we do not have a group like the group of

Quraysh who remained for a period of time marching amidst the Bedouin seeking their help. They desired revenge. Then they marched riding camels and leading the horses carrying a great number of weapons—three thousand warriors and their followers—and indeed, you strive to go out with three hundred men if they can be found. You deceive yourselves going out from your land, for I do not believe that it will be your turn." These words almost stopped their going out. They were still in this situation when the man who was the companion of the Prophet went with him to the Prophet and told him of what the man had informed him.

The Messenger of God sent Abū Salama. Abū Salama set out in haste with his companions, and taking the Ṭāʾī guide with him. He turned away from the road, taking the side road and traveled with them by night and day. They went ahead of the news, and they reached the closest point to Qaṭan—at the water from the streams of Banū Asad. They found grazing cattle and they raided and captured them. They captured their shepherds [Page 343] and three of their slaves. The rest of them fled to their community and informed them of the news and warned all of them of Abū Salama, exaggerating their fear, so that they dispersed in every direction. When Abū Salama arrived at the water and found that all had dispersed, he camped and sent his companions in search of the cattle and sheep. He divided them into three groups. One group stayed with him while the other two went raiding in different directions. He indicated to them that they were not to go far in their search and that they should not spend the night except with him if they were secure. He ordered them not to disperse, and he appointed a worker among them over each group. They all returned to him safely. They had taken camels and sheep and not met anyone. Abū Salama descended with all of it to Medina on his return, and the Ṭāʾī returned with him. When they went at night Abū Salama said, "Apportion your plunder." Abū Salama gave the Ṭāʾī guide his fill of plunder. Then he sent out the leader's choice, a slave, to the Messenger of God. Then he sent the fifth. Then he apportioned what remained between his companions, and they knew their portions. Then they proceeded with the cattle and sheep, driving them until they entered Medina.

ʿUmar b. ʿUthmān said: ʿAbd al-Malik b. ʿUmayr related to me from ʿAbd al-Raḥmān b. Saʿīd b. Yarbūʿ from ʿUmar b. Abī Salama, who said: Abū Usāma al-Jushamī was he who wounded Abū Salama by aiming an arrowhead at his upper arm on the day of Uḥud. He spent a month nursing it and we thought it was healed. The Messenger of God then sent him in Muḥarram, the thirty-fifth month AH, to Qaṭan, and he was away for more than ten days. When he arrived back in Medina, the wound re-opened, and he died with three nights remaining in Jamādā l-Ākhira. He was washed from Yusayra the well of the Banū Umayya (between the two horns. In *jāhiliyya* they called it al-ʿAbīr and the Prophet named it Yusayra). Then he was carried from the Banū Umayya and buried in Medina.

[Page 344] ʿUmar b. Abī Salama said: My mother was in *ʿidda* until four months and ten days passed. Then the Messenger of God married her and consummated his marriage with her on the last day of the month of Shawwāl. My mother used to say: There is nothing wrong with a wedding in Shawwal. The Prophet married me in Shawwal and stayed with me during Shawwal. Umm Salama died in Dhū l-Qaʿda in 750 AH.

Abū Abdullah al-Wāqidī said: I related to ʿUmar b. ʿUthmān al-Jaḥshī, and he knew of the raid and the going out of Abū Salama to Qaṭan. He said, "Did he not name the Ṭayyī for you?" I said, "No." He said, "He was al-Walīd b. Zuhayr b. Ṭarīf the uncle of Zaynab the Ṭā'ī woman who was married to Ṭulayb b. ʿUmayr; the Ṭā'ī had stayed with him and informed him. Ṭulayb had gone with him to the Messenger of God and informed him of the news of the Banū Asad, and what was among their worries about the march. The Ṭā'ī went with them as a guide, for he was experienced. He traveled with them for four days to Qaṭan. He took them through a different route in order to fool the people. When the Muslims came to the people who were grazing their cattle, they found the people had been warned and were fearful of them and prepared. They fought, were wounded, and dispersed. After that, the Ṭā'ī raided against the Banū Asad, and there were the wounded among them as well, and captured cattle and sheep. They did not release anything from them until they converted.

Al-Wāqidī said: Our companions say: Abū Salama was among the martyrs of Uḥud, for the wound he received on the day of Uḥud became infected later. Similarly, Abū Khālid al-Zuraqī from the people of al-ʿAqaba was wounded at Yamāma, but the wound became infected later during the Khilāfat of ʿUmar [Page 345] and he died of it. ʿUmar prayed for him and said: He is among the martyrs of Yamāma because he was wounded in Yamāma.

Al-Wāqidī said: I related to Yaʿqūb b. Muḥammad b. Abī Ṣaʿṣaʿa all of the tradition of Abū Salama. He said: Ayyūb b. ʿAbd al-Raḥmān b. Abī Ṣaʿṣaʿa informed me that the Messenger of God sent Abū Salama in Muḥarram, the thirty-fourth month AH, with a hundred and twenty-five men including Saʿd b. Abī Waqqāṣ, Abū Ḥudhayfa b. ʿUtba and Sālim, the *mawlā* of Abū Ḥudhayfa. They were marching by night and hiding by day until they arrived at Qaṭan and found the people had come together. Abū Salama surrounded them in the darkness of the dawn. He admonished the people and commanded them to fear God. He incited them to *jihād* and urged them about it. He advised them to be careful in their search, and brought together every two men. The settlement was aware, before the people attacked them, and had prepared its weapons; or some of them took their weapons. They were arranged in line for battle.

Saʿd b. Abī Waqqāṣ attacked one of their men. He struck him and severed his leg and then finished him off. A man from the Bedouin attacked Masʿūd b. ʿUrwa, and he attacked him with a spear and killed him. The Muslims feared that he would be deprived of his garments so they gathered him to themselves. Then Saʿd shouted, "Do not delay!" and Abū Salama attacked, and the polytheists were exposed in their garrison. The Muslims followed them and the polytheists dispersed in every direction. Abū Salama desisted from the search and they returned to the camp. They buried their companion and took the lighter utensils of the people. There were no children in the camp. Then they turned back towards Medina until when they were one night from the water, they lost their way. They captured some cattle and sheep of theirs. Then they changed the path, and drove the cattle and sheep; there were seven camels in their plunder.

Ibn Abī Sabra related to me from al-Ḥārith b. al-Fuḍayl saying: Saʿd [Page 346] b. Abī Waqqāṣ said: When we mistook the road, we employed a Bedouin as guide and he showed us the road. He said, "If I capture some cattle with you, what will you give me from it?" They replied, "A fifth." He said: He guided them to the cattle and he took a fifth.

THE RAID OF BI'R MAʿŪNA

The Raid of Bi'r Maʿūna took place in the month of Ṣafar, thirty-six months after the Prophet's emigration.

Muḥammad b. ʿAbdullah, ʿAbd al-Raḥmān b. ʿAbd al-ʿAzīz, Maʿmar b. Rāshid, Aflaḥ b. Saʿīd, Ibn Abī Sabra, Abū Maʿshar, and ʿAbdullah b. Jaʿfar—as well as those who have not been named—all informed me of some portion of this tradition, and some of the people were more reliable than others. I collected all that was related to me. They said: ʿĀmir b. Mālik b. Jaʿfar Abū l-Barā' Mulāʿib al-Asinna arrived before the Prophet and gave him two horses and two riding camels. The Messenger of God said, "I do not accept gifts from polytheists!" The Messenger of God proposed Islam to him, but he did not convert. However, he did not go away, either. He said, "O Muḥammad, indeed I consider this affair of yours an excellent affair. My people are behind me, and, if you send a group of your companions with me I hope that they will answer your call and follow your command. If they follow you how excellent will be your affair." The Messenger of God replied, "Indeed I fear the people of Najd will attack my companions." ʿĀmir said, "Do not fear for them. I will be security for them, and not one of the people of Najd will obstruct them."

[Page 347] There were among the Anṣār seventy young men who were called al-Qurrā'. When it was evening they would gather on a side of Medina, studying together and praying, until it was dawn. They would gather fresh water and firewood and bring it to the rooms of the Messenger of God. Their families thought that they were in the mosque, while the people in the mosque thought that they were with their families. The Messenger of God sent them to Bi'r Maʿūna and they went there only to be killed. The Messenger of God prayed against those who killed them for fifteen nights. Abū Saʿīd al-Khudrī said that they numbered seventy. Others, that they were forty. I believe that forty is confirmed.

The Messenger of God wrote a document with them. He gave authority to his companion al-Mundhir b. ʿAmr al-Sāʿidī. They went out until they were in Bi'r Maʿūna. Bi'r Maʿūna is one of the waters of the Banū Sulaym. It lay between the land of the Banū ʿĀmir and the Banū Sulaym; both lands were provided by it.

Muṣʿab b. Thābit related to me from Abū l-Aswad from ʿUrwa saying: Al-Mundhir went out with a guide from the Banū Sulaym called al-Muṭṭalib. When they alighted upon Bi'r Maʿūna they camped there, and dispatched their camels to graze under the care of al-Ḥārith b. al-Ṣimma and ʿAmr b. Umayya. Then, they dispatched Ḥarām b. Milḥān with the letter of the Prophet to ʿĀmir b. al-Ṭufayl and men of the Banū ʿĀmir. When Ḥarām reached them, they did not read the letter, but ʿĀmir b. Ṭufayl grabbed Ḥarām and killed him. Ḥarām had called to the Banū ʿĀmir for help, but they refused help.

ʿĀmir b. Mālik Abū l-Barā' had gone out before the people towards Najd. He informed them that he had granted protection to the companions of Muḥammad, and that they should not attack them. They said that the protection of Abū Barā' is never broken. ʿĀmir refused to join with ʿĀmir b. al-Ṭufayl, and when the Banū ʿĀmir refused him, he asked the tribes of the Sulaym, the ʿUṣayya and Riʿl for help. They joined with him, and appointed [Page 348] him their leader.

ʿĀmir b. al-Ṭufayl said, "I swear by God this man did not come alone." They followed in his tracks and found the people who had waited for their companion and approached in his tracks. They (Ṭufayl and his men) met the Muslims and al-Mundhir was with them. The Banū ʿĀmir surrounded them and outnumbered them. The people fought until the companions of the Prophet were killed and only al-Mundhir remained. They said, "If you wish we will protect you." He replied, "I will never submit nor accept your protection unless you bring me to the place of Ḥarām's killing and then free me from your protection."

They protected him until they brought him to the place of Ḥarām's death, and then released him from their protection, and he fought them until he was killed. That was who the Prophet meant by his saying, "The quick to seek death."

Al-Ḥārith b. al-Ṣimma and ʿAmr b. Umayya approached the grazing field. They became suspicious because of the activity of the birds above their camp, or close to their camp. They said: By God, our companions are killed. Only the people of Najd could have killed them. They appeared on a mound of earth, and beheld their companions, killed, and their horses standing by. Al-Ḥārith b. Ṣimma said to ʿAmr b. Umayya, "What do you think?" He replied, "I think that I will join the Messenger of God and inform him of the news." Al-Ḥārith said, "I will not delay from the place where al-Mundhir was killed." They both approached the people and al-Ḥārith fought them and killed two of them. But they captured both him and ʿAmr b. Umayya. They said to al-Ḥārith, "What do you want us to do with you for, indeed, we do not desire to kill you?" He said, "Take me to the death site of al-Mundhir and Ḥarām, and then release me from your protection." They said: We will do so. Then they took him there and released him. He fought them and killed two of them. Then he was killed. They did not kill him until they aimed a spear at him and pierced him with it. ʿĀmir b. al-Ṭufayl said to ʿAmr b. Umayya who was a prisoner in their hands and would not fight, "Indeed, there was the debt of a soul upon my mother, and you are free on account of it," and he cut off his forelock.

ʿĀmir b. al-Ṭufayl said to [Page 349] ʿAmr b. Umayya, "Did you know your companions?" He said: I said, "Yes." He said: He walked around them asking him questions about their lineage. He said, "Do you miss anyone?" He said: "I miss a *mawlā* of Abū Bakr named ʿĀmir b. Fuhayra." He said, "How was he with you?" He said: I said, "He was among the most excellent of us and among the first companions of the Prophet." He said, "Did I not inform you about him?" and he pointed to a man and said, "This pierced him with his spear. Then he pulled out the spear and the man was taken high in the sky, until by God, I saw him not." ʿAmr said: I said, "That was ʿĀmir b. Fuhayra!" He who killed him was a man from the Banū Kilāb named Jabbār b. Salmā. He mentioned that when he was pierced, he said, "I have won, by God!" He said, "I said to myself, why does he say I have won?" He said, "So I came to Ḍaḥḥāk b. Sufyān al-Kilābī and I informed him of what happened and asked him about his words, 'I have won.'" He said, "He meant Paradise." He said, "He proposed Islam to me and I submitted. What I saw of ʿĀmir b. Fuhayra's death and his ascension to the heavens, attracted me to Islam." He said, "Ḍaḥḥāk wrote to the Messenger of God and informed him of my conversion because of what I saw of the death of ʿĀmir b. Fuhayra." The Messenger of God said, "Indeed the angels have concealed his dead body! He has alighted in the uppermost heaven."

When news of Biʾr Maʿūna came to the Messenger of God, there arrived in the same night news of their wounded and the wound of Marthad b Abī Marthad and the mission of Muḥammad b. Maslama. The Prophet said repeatedly, "This is the work of Abū l-Barāʾ. I had feared this." He prayed against their killers after the first prostration of the *Ṣubḥ* prayer, in the morning of that night on which the news arrived, when he said *samiʿ Allahu liman Ḥamida*! He said, "O God, strengthen your oppression of the

Muḍar. O God, protect me from the Banū Liḥyan, Zi'b, Ri'l, Dhakwān and 'Uṣayya. Indeed, they disobey God and His messenger. [Page 350] O God, protect me from the Banū Liḥyān and 'Aḍal and al-Qāra; O God, save al-Walīd b. al-Walīd and Salama b. Hishām and 'Ayyāsh b. Abī Rabī'a, and the Muslims who are deemed weak. O God, forgive the Ghifār. May Allah keep them safe." Then he prostrated. He kept saying this for fifteen, and some say forty days until these verses were revealed: *Not for thee is the decision whether he turn in mercy to them* (Q. 3:128), until the end of the verse. Anas b. Mālik used to say: O Lord, seventy of the Anṣār on the day of Bi'r Ma'ūna. Abū Sa'īd al-Khudrī used to say: From the Anṣār, groups of seventy were killed in various places: on the day of Uḥud seventy; on the day of Bi'r Ma'ūna seventy, on the day of Yamāma seventy, on the day of the Bridge of (Jasr) Abū 'Ubayda seventy. The Messenger of God did not find for the killed as he found for the dead of Bi'r Ma'ūna. Anas b. Mālik used to say: God revealed a Qur'ān about them. We recited it until it was abrogated. *They conveyed to our people that we joined our Lord, and He was satisfied with us and we were satisfied with Him.*

They said: Abū l-Barā' approached walking and he was a very old, senile man. He sent, from al-'Īṣ, the son of his brother Labīd b. Rabī'a with the gift of a horse. The Prophet returned it saying, "I cannot accept gifts from a polytheist." Labīd said, "I did not think that any one from the Muḍar would return a gift from Abū l-Barā'." The Prophet said, "If I accepted gifts from polytheists, I would certainly accept the gift of Abū Barā'." He said, "He seeks with it a cure from pain from you." He had tonsillitis. The Prophet took a clod of earth and spat upon it. Then he handed it and said, "Heat it with water and give it to him." Barā' did so. Some say [Page 351] that the Prophet sent him honey in a leather bowl into which he continued to dip his finger and lick, until he was healed.

Abū l-Barā' was at that time traveling with his people to the land of Baliyy. He passed al-'Īṣ and he sent his son Rabī'a with Labīd carrying food. The Messenger of God said to Rabī'a, "What does the protection of your father mean? Rabī'a said, "The blow of a sword or prick of a spear destroys it." The Messenger of God said, "Yes." Ibn Abī Barā' went out and informed his father. He grieved about what 'Āmir b. al-Ṭufayl did and what happened to the Companions of the Prophet. But he was unable to move from old age and weakness. So he said, "The son of my brother from the Banū 'Āmir let me down." He proceeded until they were at the waters of al-Baliyy—some call it al-Hadm. Rabī'a rode a horse of his and he was met by 'Āmir on a camel. He pierced him with a spear, but it was not deadly. The people shouted and 'Āmir b. al-Ṭufayl said, "Indeed it did not harm me, it did not harm me. The protection of Abū Barā' was fulfilled. 'Āmir b. Ṭufayl said, "I forgive my uncle. This is his doing!" The Prophet said, "O God, bring down the Banū 'Āmir and grant me protection from 'Āmir b. al-Ṭufayl."

'Amr b. Umayya was going to meet the Prophet. He traveled on foot for four days and, when he was in the heart of the Qanāt, he was joined by two men from the Banū Kilāb. They had already met the Prophet who had clothed them and granted them a protection. 'Amr did not know about that. When they lay down for a nap and fell asleep, he pounced on them and killed them for what the Banū 'Āmir did to the companions at Bi'r Ma'ūna. Then he arrived before the Prophet [Page 352] and informed him about the killing of the companions at Bi'r Ma'ūna. He said, "You are from them!" Some said that Sa'd b. Abī Waqqāṣ returned with 'Amr b. Umayya, and the Prophet said, "Whenever I send you, you return to me from your companions." And others said that he was not with them and that only the Anṣār were with the raid. This is confirmed with us.

ʿAmr informed the Prophet about the killing of the two ʿĀmirs. The Prophet said, "Miserable is what you did. You killed two men who had a promise of protection from me. Now, I am in their debt." ʿĀmir b. al-Ṭufayl wrote to him and sent a group of his companions to inform him saying, "Indeed, one of your companions killed two men from our companions while they had a promise of protection from you." The Messenger of God took out their blood money to the value of two free Muslims, and sent it to them.

Musʿab related to me from Abū l-Aswad from ʿUrwa saying: The polytheists desired to protect ʿUrwa b. al-Ṣalt but he refused, for he had a friendship with ʿĀmir. Although his people, the Banū Sulaym, desired that, he refused saying, "I will not accept a protection from you, nor do I desire to stay away from the death site of my companions." They said, when he was surrounded by them, "O God, we have not found one who will convey greetings to your messenger other than you. So please greet him for us." The angel Gabriel informed him of that.

THE NAMES OF THOSE WHO WERE MARTYRED AMONG THE QURAYSH

From the Banū Taym: ʿĀmir b. Fuhayra. From the Banū Makhzūm: al-Ḥakam b. Kaysān, an ally of theirs. From the Banū Sahm: Nāfiʿ of Budayl b. Warqāʾ. From the Anṣār: al-Mundhir b. ʿAmr, the commander of the people. From the Banū Zurayq: Muʿādh b. Māʿiṣ. From the Banū Najjār: Ḥarām and Sulaym, the two sons of Milḥān. From the Banū ʿAmr b. Mabdhūl: al-Ḥārith b. al-[Page 353] Ṣimma, Sahl b. ʿĀmir b. Saʿd b. ʿAmr, and al-Ṭufayl b. Saʿīd. And from the Banū ʿAmr b. Mālik: Anas b. Muʿāwiya b. Anas, Abū Shaykh Ubayy b. Thābit b. al-Mundhir. From the Banū Dīnār b. Najjār: ʿAṭiyya b. ʿAbdʿAmr. But he was confused about the death of Kaʿb b. Zayd b. Qays, who was killed on the day of al-Khandaq. From the Banū ʿAmr b. ʿAuf: ʿUrwa b. al-Ṣalt, their ally from the Banū Sulaym, and from al-Nabīt: Mālik b. Thābit and Sufyān b. Thābit. The total of those who were deemed martyrs and whose names were preserved was sixteen men.

ʿAbdullah b. Rawāḥa said that Nāfiʿ b. Budayl was mourned. I heard our companions recite:

> God bless Nāfiʿ b. Budayl with the blessing of one who seeks the reward of *jihād*.
> Enduring, truthful at confrontation, who, where people said too much, said the appropriate words

Anas b. ʿAbbās al-Sulamī said, and he was the uncle of Ṭuʿayma b. ʿAdī and the kunya of Ṭuʿaym was Abū l-Rayyān: He went out on the day of Biʾr Maʿūna instigating the people seeking the blood of his nephew, until he killed Nāfiʿ b. Budayl b. Warqāʾ. He said:

> I left Ibn Warqāʾ al-Khuzāʿī dead on the ground,
> With the dust blowing over him.
> I remembered Abū Rayyān when I recognized him.
> I ascertained that I was achieving my revenge.
> I heard our companions confirm it.
> Ḥassān b. Thābit mourned Mundhir b. ʿAmr:

God decreed upon Ibn ʿAmr the truth that was most appropriate.
They said to him, "Choose between two affairs."
So he chose the affair that was gentler.
Ibn Jaʿfar related the poem of Ḥassān to me. "He wept a lot."

[Page 354] THE RAID OF AL-RAJĪʿ

Musa b. Yaʿqūb related to me from Abū l-Aswad from ʿUrwa that the Messenger of God sent the companions of al-Rajīʿ as spies to Mecca to inform him of the Quraysh. They went towards al-Najdiyya until they reached al-Rajīʿ where the Banū Liḥyān confronted them.

Muḥammad b. ʿAbdullah, Maʿmar b. Rāshid, ʿAbd al-Raḥmān b. ʿAbd al-ʿAzīz, ʿAbdullah b. Jaʿfar, Muḥammad b. Ṣāliḥ, Muḥammad b. Yaḥyā b. Sahl b. Abī Hathma, Muʿādh b. Muḥammad, and men who have not been named, have all informed me of some of this tradition. Some of the people were more reliable than others. I have brought together all that was related to me.

They said: When Sufyān b. Khālid b. Nubayḥ al-Hudhalī was killed, the Banū Liḥyan went to ʿAḍal and Qāra, and promised them a share if they would go to the Messenger of God and speak to him, so that he would send them a group of his companions to invite them to Islam. "We shall kill whoever killed our companion, and we shall take the rest of them to the Quraysh in Mecca and exchange them for money, for the Quraysh desired nothing more than to have one of the companions of Muḥammad to mutilate and kill for those who were killed among them at Badr." Thus, seven individuals from ʿAdal and al-Qāra who belonged to the Khuzayma arrived to accept Islam. They said to the Messenger of God, "Indeed, Islam is spreading among us, so send a group of your companions with us to teach the Qurʾān and instruct us in Islam."

[Page 355] The Prophet sent seven individuals with them: Marthad b. Abī Marthad al-Ghanawī, Khālid b. Abī l-Bukayr, ʿAbdullah b. Ṭāriq al-Balawī—an ally of the Banū Ẓafar—and his maternal brother, Muʿattib b. ʿUbayd—an ally of the Banū Ẓafar, as well—Khubayb b. ʿAdī b. Balḥārith b. al-Khazraj, Zayd b. al-Dathinna of the Banū Bayāḍa, and ʿAṣim b. Thābit b. Abī l-Aqlaḥ. Some say there were ten, and their commander was Marthad b. Abī Marthad. Others say their commander was ʿĀṣim b. Thābit b. Abī l-Aqlaḥ. They went out until they were at the waters of Hudhayl. It was called al-Rajīʿ and it lay close to al-Hadda. The group of ʿAdal and al-Qāra went out and called their companions who were sent by the Banū Lihyān to attack the Muslims. The companions of the Prophet were surprised by the people, a hundred marksmen with swords in their hands. The companions of Muḥammad unsheathed their swords and stood up. The enemy said, "We do not desire to fight you. We only desire to take you to the people of Mecca for a price. We give you a promise by God, that we will not kill you." Khubayb b. ʿAdī, Zayd b. al-Dathinna, and ʿAbdullah b. Ṭāriq, surrendered. Khubayb said, "Indeed, the Quraysh owe me a debt." ʿĀṣim b. Thābit, Marthad, Khālid b. Abī Bukayr, and Muʿattib b. ʿUbayd, refused to accept their protection and their security. ʿĀṣim b. Thābit said, "I swear that I will never accept the protection of a polytheist." ʿĀṣim began to fight them while saying:

No weakling I, an archer bold, my bow is thick and strong
From its surface the arrow blades flow

Death is certain and life a falsehood.
What God decrees men shall behold, and we all shall return to Him.
If I do not fight you, my mother will be childless.

[Page 356] Al-Wāqidī said: I did not see one of our companions urge him. He said: He aimed at them with arrows until he finished the arrows. Then he pierced them with the spear until his spear broke. His sword remained. He said, "O God, I defended your religion from the first light, so protect my flesh at the end of the day." They stripped all of those who were killed among his companions. They said: He broke the sheath of his sword, then he fought until he was killed. He wounded two men, and killed one. ʿĀṣim said as he fought:

I am Abū Sulayman the model marksman.
I inherited nobility from a noble people.
I wounded Marthad and Khālid standing up.

They aimed spearheads at ʿĀṣim until they killed him. Sulāfa was the daughter of Saʿd b. al-Shuhayd. Her husband and four sons had been killed. ʿĀṣim had killed two of them, al-Ḥārith and Musāfaʿ. She vowed that if God made it possible, she would drink wine from the skull of ʿĀṣim's head, and promised, to whoever came with the head of ʿĀṣim, a hundred she-camels. She had informed the Bedouin and the Banū Liḥyān, so they wished to cut off the head of ʿĀṣim and take it to Sulāfa in exchange for the camels. But God sent a swarm of wasps and stopped it, for one could not approach him but his face would be stung. A swarm of wasps had come among them and one had no power over it.

They said leave it until night, for when night comes the wasps would have gone from him. But when night came, God sent a torrential stream, though we had not seen a cloud anywhere in the sky. The stream carried his body away, and they could not reach him. ʿUmar b. al-Khaṭṭāb said while he was mentioning ʿĀṣim, "ʿĀṣim vowed that he would never touch a polytheist for the polytheist is dirty, nor would a polytheist touch him." ʿUmar said, "Indeed God most high protects the believers. He prevented them [Page 357] touching ʿĀṣim after his death just as He prevented it during his life."

Muʿattib fought until he wounded them, then they got to him and killed him. The Banū Lihyān set out with Khubayb, ʿAbdullah b. Ṭāriq and Zayd b. al-Dathinna, who were tied up with the string of their bows until they reached Marr al-Dhahrān. ʿAbdullah b. Ṭāriq said, "This is the first treachery. By God, I will not accompany you. Indeed, for me in these is an example, referring to the dead. They pleaded with him but he refused. He removed his hand from its string and took his sword. They withdrew from him and increased their distance from him, and aimed stones at him until they killed him. His grave is in Marr al-Dhahrān.

Khubayb b. ʿAdī went out with Zayd b. al-Dathinna until they arrived in Mecca. Ḥujayr b. Abī Ihāb bought Khubayb for eighty weights of gold. Some said that he was bought for fifty camels. Some say that the daughter of al-Ḥārith b. ʿĀmir b. Nawfal bought him for a hundred camels. Ḥujayr bought him to give to the son of his brother ʿUqba b. al-Ḥarith b. ʿĀmir to kill him for his father who was killed on the day of Badr. As for Zayd b. al-Dathinna, Ṣafwān b. Umayya bought him for fifty camels and killed him for his father. Some say that people from the Quraysh participated in his killing. He entered with them in the sacred month of Dhū l-Qaʿda.

Hujayr imprisoned Khubayb b. ʿAdī in a house of a woman named Māwiyya, the freed woman (*mawlat*) of the Banū ʿAbd al-Manāf. Ṣafwān b. Umayya imprisoned Zayd b. Dathinna with a group from the Banū Jumaḥ. Some say with Nisṭās. Māwiyya converted to Islam later, and hers was the best Islam. She used to say: By God I do not see any one better than Khubayb b. ʿAdī. By God, indeed I looked at him through the crack of the door, and he was in iron shackles, and I knew that there was nothing to be eaten on the ground, not even one little grape. And, yet, in his hand was a bunch of grapes as big as the head of a man and he was eating from it. There was no nourishment for him but God gave it to him."

Khubayb used to stay awake at night reciting the Qur'ān. [Page 358] The women heard him and they wept and felt pity for him. She said: I said to him, "O Khubayb, what do you need?" He replied, "Nothing, but that you give me some fresh water, and do not feed me with what is slaughtered before an idol. Inform me when they desire my death." She said: When the sanctified months had passed they gathered to kill him, and I came to him and informed him. By God, I do not think that distressed him. He said, "Send me a blade that I might be fitting for it." She said: I sent him a razor with my son Abū Ḥusayn, and when the lad turned I said, "By God, the man will overpower you and kill you. What have I done? I sent this lad with this sharp blade, and he will kill him and say a man for a man." When my son came to him with the blade he took it from him and said jokingly to him, "By your father, you are indeed reckless! Did your mother not fear treachery when she sent a blade with you, while you desire my death?" Māwiyya said, I heard that and I said, "O Khubayb, I trusted you with God's trust. I did not give it to you to kill my son." Khubayb replied, "I would not kill him. In our religion, treachery is not lawful." Then I informed him that they were going out the following day to kill him.

He said: They took him out shackled, until they reached al-Tanʿīm. Women, youths and slaves went out with him gathering from the people of Mecca. No one stayed behind. Those who desired blood revenge desired to be fulfilled by the sight of blood revenge. Those who did not desire blood revenge were against Islam and its people. When they reached Tanʿīm with him, and Zayd b. al-Dathinna was with him, they ordered a long piece of wood and it had holes, and they took Khubayb to the wood. He said, "Will you allow me to pray two prostrations?" They said, "Yes." He prayed two prostrations without prolonging them.

Maʿmar informed me from al-Zuhrī from ʿAmr b. Abī Sufyān b. Usayd b. al-ʿAlā'i, from Abū Hurayra that the first who established the two prostrations at death was Khubayb. [Page 359] They said: Then he said, "If I feared death, as you believe, then I would have extended my prayer, but I did not extend my prayer." Then he said, "O God enumerate them by number and kill them one by one. Do not leave even one of them."

Muʿāwiya b. Abī Sufyān said: His prayer was fulfilled, and I remember when Abū Sufyān threw me to the ground in fear of Khubayb's prayer. Indeed Abū Sufyān repelled me at that time with a push, I fell right on my bottom, and I continued to suffer from this fall for a long time. Ḥuwayṭib b. ʿAbd al-ʿUzzā said: Indeed I remember that, I put my fingers in my ears and ran, fleeing, terrified that I would hear his prayer. Ḥakīm b. Ḥizām said: I remember that! I concealed myself in a tree fearful of Khubayb's prayer. ʿAbdullah b. Yazīd said Saʿīd b. ʿAmr related to me saying that he had heard Jubayr b. Muṭʿim say: "Indeed, I remember hiding behind the men fearful that I would be exposed to his prayer." Al-Ḥārith b. Barṣā' said: By God, I did not think that Khubayb's prayer would miss any one of them.

ʿAbdullah b. Jaʿfar related to me from ʿUthmān b. Muḥammad al-Akhnasī saying: ʿUmar b. al-Khaṭṭāb appointed Saʿīd b. ʿĀmir over Ḥimṣ. He used to have a fainting spell when he was in the midst of his companions. This was mentioned to ʿUmar, and ʿUmar asked him during a visit when he arrived before him from Ḥimṣ, "O Saʿīd, [Page 360] what is it that overpowers you? Is there a madness in you?" He replied, "No, by God, O Amīr al-Muʾminīn, but I was with those who attended Khubayb when he was killed, and I heard his curse. By God, I do not remember it when I am in a council, but a fainting-spell comes over me." He said that it endeared him to ʿUmar.

Qudāma b. Mūsā related to me from ʿAbd al-ʿAzīz b. Rummāna, from ʿUrwa b. al-Zubayr, from Nawfal b. Muʿāwiya al-Dīlī, who said: I was present at the time of Khubayb's prayer, and I did not see any one of those who attended escape it. Indeed I was standing, and I leaned to the ground terrified of his prayer. The Quraysh stayed a month or more, and all they talked of in their councils was the prayer of Khubayb.

They said: When he had prayed two prostrations, they took him to the piece of wood, then faced him towards Medina and fastened him with fetters. Then they said: "Return from Islam, and we will set you free!" He replied, "No, by God, I will not leave Islam even if all that is on earth were mine!" They said, "Do you not wish that Muḥammad were in your place and that you were seated in your house?" He said, "By God, I do not desire that Muḥammad were pierced with prongs while I am seated in my house." They repeated, "Return, O Khubayb!" He replied, "I will never return!" They said, "By al-Lāt and al-ʿUzzā, if you will not do so we will kill you." He said, "My death in the path of God is little." When he refused them they attempted to direct him towards where he came from, He said, "Regarding your turning my face away from the *qibla* (Q 2:115), indeed God says: Wherever you turn is God." Then he said, "O God, I do not see except the face of an enemy. O God, there is not one here who will take your Messenger greetings from me, so please convey my greetings to him."

Usāma b. Zayd related to me from his father that the Messenger of God was seated with his companions, when a faint overcame him just as when he is inspired by a revelation. [Page 361] He said, "Then we heard him say, 'And peace unto him and God's blessings.' Then he said, 'This is Gabriel who brings me greetings from Khubayb.' "

Then the Quraysh called for the sons of those who were killed at Badr and found there were forty youths. They gave every youth a spear and said, "This is he who killed your fathers," So they pierced him with their spears a light prick. He moved on the wood and turned with his face towards the Kaʿba. He said, "Praise God who directed my face to the *qibla* that satisfies Him, His prophet and the believers."

Those who brought death to Khubayb were: ʿIkrima b. Abī Jahl, Saʿīd b. ʿAbdullah b. Qays, al-Akhnas b. Sharīq, ʿUbayda b. Ḥakīm b. Umayya b. al-Awqaṣ al-Sulamī. ʿUqba b. al-Ḥārith b. ʿĀmir who was also among those present used to say: I did not kill Khubayb, as I was only a small boy at the time. But a man from the sons of ʿAbd al-Dār named Abū Maysara of ʿAwf b. Sabbāq took my hand and placed it on a spear. Then he held my hand and began to pierce him with his hand until he died. While he pierced him with the spear I slipped away, and they shouted: O Abū Sarwaʿa, miserable is the manner in which Abū Maysara pierced him. So Abū Sarwaʿa pierced him until the spear came out from behind him. He stayed awhile proclaiming the oneness of God, and bore witness that Muḥammad was His messenger. Al-Akhnas b. Sharīq used to say: If there was a circumstance under which he would stop mentioning Muḥammad, surely this was it. We have never seen a father as fond of his son as the companions of Muḥammad were fond of Muḥammad.

They said Zayd b. al-Dathinna was kept in iron chains with the family of Ṣafwān b. Umayya. He stayed up the night praying and fasted by day and would not eat anything that was brought to him that had been slaughtered. That was unbearable to Ṣafwān, for they were good to him. Ṣafwān sent him a message: What food will you eat? He replied: I will not eat that which is slaughtered other than before Allah. But I will drink milk. He used to fast. Ṣafwān ordered a bowl of milk for him [Page 362] with his breakfast and he would drink all of it as though he were a child just born. When he was brought out with Khubayb on the same day they met, with each one of them was a group of people. Each of them was attached to his companion, and each one of them decreed patience to his companion about what had happened. Then they dispersed.

The one who was appointed to kill Zayd was Nisṭās, the slave of Ṣafwān. He went out with him to Tanʿīm and they raised a pole for him. He said; I will pray two bowings. He prayed two bowings and then they carried him on the wood. Then they began to say to Zayd, "Return from your recent religion and follow our religion, and we will release you." He said, "No, I will not leave my religion ever." They said, "Would you be happy if Muḥammad were in our hands instead of you and you were in your house?" He replied, "I would not be happy if Muḥammad was attacked by you with a prong while I was in my house." He said: Abū Sufyān b. Ḥarb says, "No, we have never seen the companions of a man that possess a greater love for him than the companions of Muḥammad for Muḥammad." Ḥassān b. Thābit used to say, "I heard it correctly, from Yūnus b. Muḥammad al-Ẓafarī."

> Would that Khubayb had not been deceived by your trustworthiness.
> Would that he had known what people he was dealing with.
> Zuhayr b. al-Agharri and Jāmiʿ sold him,
> Both of them committing foul crimes.
> You promised him protection and having done so betrayed him.
> In the region of al-Rajīʿ you were as weaklings.

Ḥassān said: It was confirmed a long time ago.

> [Page 363] If there was in the land a noble,
> The protector of truth whose uncle is Anas,
> Then Khubayb you would be free, in a spacious place,
> And the shackles and the guards would not bind you.
> They would not take you to Tanʿīm,
> A group of people in which ʿUdas had no part.
> Be patient, Khubayb, indeed being killed is an honour,
> For the soul will return to Paradise.
> They deceived you with treachery.
> They are people of deceit and you were a guest in their home imprisoned.

THE RAID OF THE BANŪ NAḌĪR

The raid of the Banū Naḍīr took place in Rabīʿ al-Awwal, thirty-seven months after the emigration of the Prophet.

Muḥammad b. ʿAbdullah, ʿAbdullah b. Jaʿfar, Muḥammad b. Ṣāliḥ, Muḥammad b.

Yaḥyā b. Sahl, Ibn Abī Ḥabība, and Maʿmar b. Rāshid, among men whom I have not named, related to me, and each one has related to me about some of this tradition, though some of the people were more reliable than others, and I have combined all of what they related to me.

They said: ʿAmr b. Umayya approached Biʾr Maʿūna until he was at a canal, where he met two men from Banū ʿĀmir, and he asked them about their genealogies, and they narrated them. He compared notes with them, until when they slept, he pounced on them and killed them. Then he left and [Page 364] arrived before the Prophet in about the time it takes to milk an ewe. When he informed him about these two men, the Prophet said, "What you have done is unfortunate. The two of them had a protection and an agreement from us!" ʿAmr said, "I did not know. I saw them in their polytheism, their people taking what they took from us by deceit." When he brought what he had plundered from them, the Messenger of God commanded that their plunder be set aside until he sent it with their blood money, because ʿĀmir b. al-Ṭufayl had sent a message to the Messenger of God stating: Surely a man from your companions has killed two men from my tribe who had a protection and an agreement from you. So send their blood money to us.

The Messenger of God went to the Banū Naḍīr seeking help with the payment of the blood money, because the Banū Naḍīr were confederates of the B. ʿĀmir. The Messenger of God left on Saturday, and he prayed in the mosque of Qubāʾ with a group of Muhājirūn and Anṣār who were with him. Then he arrived at the Banū Naḍīr and found them at their meeting place. The Messenger of God and his companions sat, and the Messenger of God asked them to help him with the blood money for the two Kilābīs whom ʿAmr b. Umayya had killed. They said, "O Abū l-Qāsim, we will do whatever you desire. It is about time that you visited us, so come to us. Be seated until we bring you food!" While the Messenger of God was leaning against one of their houses, some of them withdrew and whispered to each other. Ḥuyayy b. Akhṭab said, "O community of Jews, Muḥammad has come to you with less than ten of his companions, including Abū Bakr, ʿUmar, ʿAlī, al-Zubayr, Ṭalḥa, Saʿd b. Muʿādh, Usayd b. Ḥuḍayr, and Saʿd b. ʿUbāda. Throw a stone upon him from above this house, which he is under, and kill him, for you will never find him with less companions than he has with him now. It is certain that if he is killed, his companions will split up, and those from the Quraysh will go back to their sanctuary while the Aws and the Khazraj who remain over here are your confederates. The time for that which you had desired to do some day is now!" ʿAmr b. Jiḥāsh said, "I will ascend atop the house [Page 365] and throw a stone upon him."

Sallām b. Mishkam said, "Obey me this once, my people, and you may disagree with me forever after, for by God, if you do this (throw a stone on Muḥammad) he will surely be informed that we are acting treacherously against him. Surely this is the violation of the agreement, which is between us and him, so do not do it! By God, if you do what you intend, this religion will surely stay among them until the Day of Judgment. He will destroy the Jews and his religion will triumph."

ʿAmr had prepared to let go the stone and drop it on the Messenger of God, when news came to the Prophet from the heavens about what they planned for him. The Prophet rose swiftly as though he had a need and went toward Medina. His companions sat talking among themselves, thinking that he had gone to fulfill a need. When they became distressed about that, Abū Bakr said, "There is no reason for us to stay when the Prophet must have left for some matter," and they stood up. Ḥuyayy said,

"Abū l-Qāsim has hurried away when we desired to fulfill his need and feed him." The Jews regretted what they did.

Kinānah b. Ṣuwayrā' said to them, "Did you know why Muḥammad got up?" They said, "No, by God, we do not know, and you do not know!" He said, "But certainly, by the Torah, I do know! Muḥammad was informed about the treachery you planned against him. Do not deceive yourselves. By God, he is surely the Messenger of God, for he would not have stood up except that he was informed about what you planned against him. Surely he is the last of the prophets. You desire him to be from the Banū Hārūn, but God has placed him as He pleases. Surely our books and what we studied of the Torah that were not changed and altered, state that his birth is in Mecca and the land of his emigration is Yathrib. His exact description does not disagree by a letter from what is in our book. What he brings you is better than his fighting you. But it appears to me as if I see you departing. Your children scream, for you have left your homes [Page 366] and your possessions that are the basis of your nobility behind. So obey me in two things, for the third has no virtue in it." They said, "What are the two?" He said, "Convert and enter with Muḥammad, and secure your possessions and children. Thus, you will be among the highest of his companions, and your possessions will remain in your hands, for you will not leave from your homes." They said, "We will not depart from the Torah and the covenant of Moses."

Ibn Suwayrā' said, "Surely he will send to you to 'Leave from my land.' Say, 'Yes,' and then surely he will not deem your blood and money lawful, and your possessions will remain. If you wish you may sell it, and if you wish you may keep it." They said, "As for this, yes." He said, "By God, surely the other is the best of them for me." He said, "By God, would it not have disgraced you, I would have converted to Islam, but by God, Sha'thā' shall never be reproached for my conversion, so I will share your fate". His daughter was Sha'thā' whom Ḥassān used to flirt with. Sallām b. Mishkam said, "I disliked what you did. He will send a message to us to 'Leave from my land.' O Ḥuyayy, do not comment on his words; agree to leave and depart from his land!" He said, "I will leave."

When the Prophet returned to Medina his companions followed him. They met a man leaving Medina and they asked him, "Did you meet the Messenger of God?" He said, "I met him entering the bridge." When his companions finally reached him, they found he had sent for Muḥammad b. Maslama. Abū Bakr said, "O Messenger of God, you left without our knowing!" He (the Messenger of God) said, "The Jews plotted treachery against me, and God informed me about it, so I left." Muḥammad b. Maslama came and the Prophet said to him, "Go to the Jews of the Banū Naḍīr and say to them, the Messenger of God sent me to you to tell you to leave his homeland."

When he came to them he said, "The Messenger of God has sent me to you with a message, but I will not tell it to you until I inform you of something you know." [Page 367] He said, "I adjure you by the Torah, which God revealed to Moses, you know that I came to you before the sending of Muḥammad's mission, and between you was the Torah. You said to me in this same assembly of yours, 'O Ibn Maslama, if you wish us to feed you, we will feed you, and if you wish us to convert you to Judaism, we will convert you.' And I said to you, 'Feed me, but do not convert me, for by God, I will never become a Jew!' You gave me food in a bowl of yours, and it looked to me as if it were left over milk. You said to me, 'Nothing forbids you from our religion, except that it is the Jewish religion. It is as though you desire the Ḥanafīya, which you have heard about. Is it not what Abū 'Āmir deplored and would not follow? The leader of it will be one who is constantly laughing, yet deadly, and will come to you with reddened eyes from the direction of Yemen, riding a camel, wearing a shamlah/cloak, and is content with a small piece of bread, his sword upon his shoulder. He has no miracle, but speaks with wisdom, as if he had a close relationship with you. By God, there will surely be in your village, plundering and killing and mutilation.' They said, 'By God, yes, we have said that to you, but he is not the expected one.' "

He said, "I have finished. The Messenger of God sent me to you to say to you, 'you have broken the agreement which I have made for you with what treachery you planned against me,' " and he informed them about what they had planned: the appearance of ʿAmr b. Jiḥāsh atop the house to throw the rock. They were silent and did not say a word. The Prophet says, "Leave from my land. I have granted you a period of ten days. Whoever is seen after that, his head will be cut off!" They said: "O Muḥammad, we did not think that a man from the Aws would come with this message." Muḥammad b. Maslama said, "Hearts have changed."

They stayed thus some days in preparation. They sent for camels for them from Dhū l-Jadr and brought them together, and they rounded up from the people of Ashjaʿ [Page 368] a herd of camels, and they began the preparation to leave. While they were thus, the messengers of Ibn Ubayy, Suwayd and Dāʿis came to them saying, "ʿAbdullah b. Ubayy says, 'Do not leave your homes and your possessions. Remain in your fortress for I have two thousand of my tribe and others from the Arabs who will enter with you into your fortress, and they will die to the last one of them before Muḥammad reaches you. You will be helped by the Qurayẓa, for surely they will never disappoint you, and you will be helped by your confederates among the Ghaṭafān.' " Ibn Ubayy then sent to Kaʿb b. Asad and told him to help his companions. But Kaʿb refused, saying, "Not a single man from the Banū Qurayẓa would break the agreement."

Ibn Ubayy despaired of the Banū Qurayẓa and he desired to test what was between the Banū Naḍīr and the Messenger of God. He continued to send to Ḥuyayy until Ḥuyayy said, "I will send to Muḥammad informing him that we will not leave from our homes and our possessions and he must do whatever is best." Ḥuyayy had hopes for what Ibn Ubayy said, stating, "We will repair our fortress, and bring in our cattle; we will enter our streets and move stones to our fortresses. We have sufficient food for a year, and the source of water in our fortress is continuous—we do not fear it will be cut. Do you think that Muḥammad will besiege us for a year? We do not."

Sallām b. Mishkam said, "By God, your soul has deceived you, O Huyayy, with what is futile! By God, were it not for the fact that your opinion would be discredited and you belittled, I would surely withdraw from you with whoever obeys me from among the Jews. Do not do it, O Ḥuyayy, for by God you know and we know that he is the Messenger of God, and that we have his description with us. Indeed, we did not follow him, but envied him when prophecy left the Banū Hārūn. So come let us accept the protection he offers us and leave [Page 369] from his land. I know that you disagreed with me about the treachery against him. And when it is the time for the ripening fruit we would come, or some from among us would, to the fruit/dates, sell them or do what is seen fit to be done, and then return to us. So it would be as though we did not go away from our lands because our property will be in our hands. Indeed, we have been ennobled over our people with our possessions and our actions. But if our wealth goes from our hands, we would be like the rest of the Jews in lowness and deprivation. If Muḥammad marches to us and besieges us in this fortress for a single day and we then propose to him that we do what he has already ordered us to do, he would not agree: he would refuse us."

Ḥuyayy said, "Surely Muḥammad will not besiege us unless he found an opportunity; if not, he will leave. Ibn Ubayy promised me what you have seen." Sallām said, "Ibn Ubayy's word is meaningless. Ibn Ubayy only wanted to put you in danger so that you would fight Muḥammad. Then he will sit in his house and abandon you. He desired help from Kaʿb b. Asad, but Kaʿb b. Asad refused and said, 'Not a single man from the Banū Qurayẓa will destroy the agreement while I am alive.' Did not Ibn Ubayy promise his confederates among the Banū Qaynuqāʿ, the same as what he promises you, until they fought, breaking the agreement, and fortified themselves in their fortresses, awaiting Ibn Ubayy's help? But he sat in his house, while Muḥammad went and besieged them until they submitted to his judgment."

"Ibn Ubayy does not help his confederates or those who used to protect him from the people. We joined the Aws and continued to fight him with our swords in all their wars until Muḥammad arrived and stopped them. Ibn Ubayy is not a Jew according to the religion of Judaism, nor is he of the religion of Muḥammad or the religion of his tribe. So how do you accept anything he says?" Ḥuyayy said, "My soul rejects everything except opposing and fighting Muḥammad." Sallām said, "By God, he exiles us from our land, and our wealth and our nobility will be lost; but otherwise our children will be imprisoned and our warriors killed." Huyayy insisted on fighting the Messenger of God. Sārūk Ibn Abī l-Ḥuqayq said to him—and they regarded him as feeble minded [Page 370] as though he were possessed—"O Ḥuyayy, you are a man of ill omen, you will destroy the Banū Naḍīr." Ḥuyayy became angry and said, "All the Banū Naḍīr have spoken to me, even this maniac." His brothers struck Sārūk and said to Ḥuyayy, "Our fate follows yours. We will not oppose you."

Ḥuyayy sent his brother Judayy b. Akhṭab to the Messenger of God saying, "We will not leave from our homes and our possessions. You can do whatever you want." He commanded him to go to Ibn Ubayy and inform him of his letter to Muḥammad, demanding that he expedite the help he had promised him. Judayy b. Akhṭab went to the Messenger of God with what Ḥuyayy sent him, reaching him while he was seated with his companions, and informed him. The Messenger of God proclaimed *takbīr* and the Muslims magnified it. He said, "The Jews have chosen war!"

Then, Judayy continued on his way until he reached Ibn Ubayy who was seated in his house with a small group of his confederates. The herald of the Messenger of God had called out, commanding them (his companions) to march to the Banū Naḍīr. ʿAbdullah b. ʿAbdullah b. Ubayy entered the place of ʿAbdullah, his father, and the group that was with him—including Judayy b. Akhṭab—and put on his armor, took his sword and left at a run. Judayy said, "When I saw Ibn Ubayy seated in his house while his son put on his weapons, I gave up all hope of his help and left at a run to Ḥuyayy." He said, "What is behind you?" I said, "Evil! As soon as I informed Muḥammad about the message you sent him, he proclaimed *takbīr*, and said, "The Jews have chosen war!" Huyayy said, "This is a trick of his." Judayy said, "I came to Ibn Ubayy and informed him, while Muḥammad's herald proclaimed the march on the Banū Naḍīr." Huyayy said, "And how did Ibn Ubayy answer you?" Judayy said, "I saw no good from him. He said, 'I will send a messenger to my confederates and they will join you.'"

The Messenger of God marched with his companions and prayed ʿAsar in the yard of the Banū Naḍīr who, when they saw them, stood up on the walls of their fortresses with arrows and stones. The Qurayẓa kept away from them and did not help them [Page 371] with weapons or men, and did not come near them. They began to shoot that day with arrows and stones until darkness was upon them. The companions of the

Messenger of God began to arrive—there were those who had stayed behind for some reason—until they all gathered at the time of the evening prayer. When the Messenger of God had prayed ʿIshā, he returned to his house with ten of his companions, wearing armor and riding a horse. He left ʿAlī in charge of the army, but some say it was Abū Bakr. The Muslims spent the night besieging them, and shouting *takbīr* until dawn. Then, Bilāl called out the call to prayer in Medina.

The Messenger of God rose with those companions who were with him. He prayed with the people on the yard of the Banū Khaṭma, having appointed Ibn Umm Maktūm to take his place in Medina. A tent of leather was carried with the Prophet. Yaḥyā b. ʿAbd al-ʿAzīz related to me that the tent was of *gharab*, and was covered with hair. Saʿd b. ʿUbāda had sent it, and he ordered Bilāl to pitch it at the site of the small mosque in the yard of the Banū Khaṭma. The Messenger of God entered the tent. A Jew named ʿAzwak, who was a left handed marksman, shot an arrow which reached the tent, so the Prophet commanded that it to be moved to the masjid al-Faḍīkh, out of arrow range.

By evening Ibn Ubayy and his confederates had not come near them; he sat in his house. The Banū Naḍīr gave up hope of help. Sallām b. Mishkam and Kināna b. Suwayrāʾ were saying to Ḥuyayy, "Where is the help you claimed Ibn Ubayy would bring us?" Ḥuyayy said, "What can I do? [Page 372] It is the trial that was written for us." The Messenger of God spent the night in armor as he continued to besiege them.

One night, ʿAlī b. Abī Ṭālib went missing around ʿIshā. People said, "We do not see ʿAlī, O Messenger of God." He replied, "Leave him, for surely he is in some affair of yours!" Soon ʿAlī arrived with the head of ʿAzwak, which he threw before the Prophet, saying, "Surely I waited in ambush for this rogue, and I saw a brave man. I said, how brave of him to leave, when evening falls upon us, seeking to take us by surprise. He drew near with his sword unsheathed amid a group of Jews. I overpowered and killed him. His companions ran away and did not stay. If you send me with a group, I hope to catch them." The Prophet sent ten of his companions with Abū Dujāna and Sahl b. Ḥunayf. They reached the group of Jews before they entered their fortress. They killed them, and returned with their heads. The Messenger of God commanded that their heads be thrown in one of the wells of the Banū Khaṭma.

Saʿd b. ʿUbādah was carrying dates to the Muslims. The Jews remained in their fortress, and the Prophet commanded that the date-palms be cut and burnt, appointing two of his companions, Abū Laylā al-Māzinī and ʿAbdullāh b. Salām, to cut them. Abū Laylā was cutting the dates (*ʿajwa*), ʿAbdullah b. Salām was cutting the palms (*al-lwn*). When they were asked about that, Abū Laylā said: Cutting the ʿAjwa hurt them most. Ibn Salām said: I knew that God would award him their possessions as booty, and the ʿAjwa were the best of their possessions. The following verse was revealed in approval of what we did together. *What you cut off the Līna*, a kind of date palm, referring to what Ibn Salām did, *or you left them standing on their roots*, meaning the ʿAjwa, *it was by leave of God.* Abū Layla cut the ʿAjwa—*to shame the transgressors* (Q. 59:5), meaning the Banū Naḍīr, [Page 373] referring to God's satisfaction with what the two factions did together. When the ʿAjwa was cut, the women tore their dresses, struck their cheeks, crying out in affliction. The Messenger of God said, "What is wrong with them?" It was said, "They are saddened by the cutting of the ʿAjwa." The Messenger of God said, "Is the like of ʿAjwa grieved over?" Then he added, "The mellowed ʿAjwa, and the dry—the male with which the female date palm is pollinated—are the date palms of Paradise. The ʿAjwa are a cure for poison." And when the women shouted, Abū Rāfiʿ Sallām shouted to them, "If the ʿAjwa are cut over here, we have ʿAjwa in Khaybar." An old woman among them said, "Khaybar will see the same fate!" Abū Rāfiʿ replied, "May God break your jaw! Surely my confederates at Khaybar are ten thousand warriors."

When this reached the Messenger of God, he smiled. Their anguish over the cutting of the ʿAjwa induced Sallām b. Mishkam to say, "O Ḥuyayy the cluster (*ʿAzq*) is better than the *ʿAjwa*. They are planted and not fed or cut for thirty years." Ḥuyayy sent to the Messenger of God, "O Muḥammad, surely you used to forbid wrong doing. Why are you cutting the date palms? We will give you what you ask. We will leave your land." The Messenger of God said, "I will not accept that now. But leave from here, and to you is that which a camel can carry, excluding weapons."

Sallām said (to Ḥuyayy): "Accept, woe unto you, before you have to accept worse than this." Ḥuyayy said, "What can be worse?" Sallām said, "The enslavement of children and the killing of your warriors in addition to the loss of our possessions. Wealth today is worthless among us if we are to meet this order of killing and enslavement." Ḥuyayy refused to accept itfor a day or two. When Yāmīn b. ʿUmayr and Abū Saʿd b. Wahb saw that, one of them said to the other, "Surely you know that he is the Messenger of God, so why wait? Let us convert and secure our blood and possessions." They descended by night and converted, thereby saving their blood and possessions.

[Page 374] Then the Jews submitted on condition that they could take what the camels could carry other than weapons. Having expelled them, the Messenger of God said to Ibn Yāmīn, "Did you not see how your cousin ʿAmr b. Jiḥāsh, plotted to kill me?" The latter was the husband of Ibn Yāmīn's sister, al-Ruwāʿ bt. ʿUmayr, married to ʿAmr b. Jiḥāsh. Ibn Yāmīn said, "I will protect you from him, O Messenger of God." He gave ten dinars to a man from the Qays to kill ʿAmr b. Jiḥāsh; and some say five loads of dates. So he sought out and killed him. Then Ibn Yāmīn came to the Prophet and informed him of the killing and the Prophet was pleased.

The Messenger of God besieged them for fifteen days. He drove them away from Medina appointing Muḥammad b. Maslama to expel them. They said, "We have debts from the people that are due at different times." The Messenger of God said, "Hurry and settle." Usayd b. Ḥuḍayr owed Abū Rāfiʿ Sallām b. Abī l-Ḥuqayq a hundred and twenty dinars which were due in a year, so he agreed to take his capital of eighty dinars, canceling the remainder. While they were besieged, the Jews were destroying their own homes that were on their side, and the Muslims were destroying what was on their side, until peace was settled. They loaded, and they carried the wood and the lintels of the doors. The Messenger of God said to Safiyya bt. Ḥuyayy, "You should have seen me lash the saddle of your uncle Baḥrī b. ʿAmr and drive him away from there." They gave their women and children beasts upon which to ride. They left BalḤārith b. Khazraj, then Jabalīya, then went over the bridge until they passed Bal Muṣallā, and then crossed the market of Medina. The women in the howdas were dressed in their silks and brocade and green and red velvets. The people lined up for them. They proceeded, one camel train in the tracks of another. They were carried on six hundred camels.

[Page 375] The Messenger of God said, "These are among their people like the Banū Mughīra among the Quraysh." Ḥassān b. Thābit, seeing them with their chiefs on their saddles, said, "By God, surely it is with you that one who seeks favor will find it, the hospitality prepared for the guests, water for the thirsty, patience for the one who was impudent among you, and help when one seeks help." Ḍaḥḥāk b. Khalīfa said, "What a morning! I offer my soul as ransom for you! How did you bear the burden of power and splendor, courage and generosity?" He said, Nuʿaym b. Masʿūd al-Ashjaʿī says, "We would sacrifice ourselves for these faces, which are like the lighted lanterns leaving the region of Yathrib. Who is there for the anxious who need help, as guide for the exhausted, and to quench the thirst of the thirsty? Who will provide the fat above the meat? We have no place in Yathrib after you leave." Abū ʿAbs b. Jabr says hearing his words, "Yes, join them so that you may enter hell fire with them." Nuʿaym said, "What is their reward from you? Surely you asked them for help and they helped you against the Khazraj. And surely you asked help from all the Arabs and they refused you!" Abū ʿAbs said, "Islam has destroyed those agreements!"

He said: They passed by, striking tambourines and playing the pipes, the women wearing dyes of saffron and jewelry of gold, all this to show themselves as tough. He said: Jabbār b. Ṣakhr says, "I did not think this glamour of theirs reflected a people who had to leave one home for another." Abū Rāfiʿ Sallām b. Abī l-Ḥuqayq, raising the grip of the camel, cried, "This is that which we reckon as the lowering and rising (for good times and for bad) of the land, if there are palm trees that we have left here, surely we are going to other date palms in Khaybar." Abū Bakr b. Abī Sabra related to me from Rubayḥ b. ʿAbd al-Raḥmān b. Abī Saʿīd al-Khudrī, from his father from his grandfather, who said: Surely, that day, some of their women who passed [Page 376] in those howdas with their faces uncovered. Perhaps I will never see the like of their beauty in women again! I saw al-Shaqrāʾ bt. Kināna, that day, like the pearl of a pearl diver, and al-Ruwāʿ bt. ʿUmayr who was like the sunrise. On their hands were bracelets of gold and around their necks, pearls.

The Hypocrites were greatly saddened on the day they departed. I met Zayd b. Rifāʿa b. al-Tābūt who was with ʿAbdullah b. Ubayy, whispering to him about Banū Ghanm saying, "I am desolate in Yathrib for the loss of the Banū Naḍīr, but they leave for the power and wealth of their confederates and to impenetrable, towering fortresses, on the tops of mountains unlike those here." He said, "I listened to them for a while and every one of them was unfaithful to God and his Messenger."

They said: The exodus included Salmā, the mistress of ʿUrwa b. al-Ward al-ʿAbsī." According to a tradition of theirs, she was a woman of the Banū Ghifār. ʿUrwa captured her from her tribe, and she was a woman of beauty. She delivered to him sons, and she won his good opinion. She said to him when his sons were being reproached about their mother as "sons of the enslaved", "Do you not see your sons being shamed?" He said, "What do you advise?" She said, "Return me to my people until they let you marry me." He agreed. So, she sent to her people asking them to meet him with wine, then to leave him until he drinks and becomes drunk, because when he becomes drunk he will grant everything that one asks of him. They met him and he stayed with the Banū Naḍīr. They gave him wine to drink and when he was intoxicated they asked him for Salmā, and he returned her to them. Later, they gave her in marriage to him.

Others say: Rather, he came with her to the Banū Naḍīr, destitute, looking for loot. They gave him wine to drink. When he was intoxicated they stopped him. There was nothing with him but her. He pawned her and did not stop drinking until she (the pawn) was lost. When he regained consciousness, he said to her, "Leave with me!" They said, "There is no way to that. You forfeited her as ransom. With this she belongs to the B. Naḍīr."

They gave me wine to drink,
And then overwhelmed me,
The enemies of God, from lying and deceit.
They said: After the ransoming of Salmā

You will be neither rich with what you have, nor poor.
No by God, if my situation were as it is today and if I had the circumspection that I now have
I would have opposed them as regards Salmā,
Even if they ascended into the thorny shrubs of Mustaʿūr.

Ibn Abī Zinād recited it to me.

[Page 377] Abū Bakr b. ʿAbdullah related to me from al-Miswar b. Rifāʿa: The Messenger of God seized the wealth and the weapons, and among the latter he found fifty armor plates, fifty helmets, three hundred and forty swords, and it is said that they hid some of their weapons and took them away. Muḥammad b. Maslama was in charge of taking the property and the weapons and disclosing them. ʿUmar said, "O Messenger of God, are you not going to take out one fifth of what you gained from the Banū Naḍīr, the same as the one fifth that you gained from Badr?" The Messenger of God said, "I will not apportion something God most high has given me to the exclusion of the believers." In the words of the highest, *What God bestowed on his Messenger from the people of the Townships*. The verses are like the group of verses that came down about the portions for the Muslims.

ʿUmar used to say, there was for the Messenger of God three leader's portions (the leader was allowed the first pick) of booty: [Page 378] The Banū Naḍīr's property was reserved for unexpected contingencies; Fadak was for the wayfarer; and Khaybar was divided into three parts, two portions for the Muhājirūn, and a portion of it was being paid to the Prophet's family. If there was excess he returned it to the destitute among the Muhājirūn.

Mūsā b. ʿUmar al-Ḥārithī related to me from Abī ʿUfayr, saying: Rather, the Prophet paid for the support of his family from the Banū Naḍīr's booty. It was purely his property. From it he gave out as he wished, and held as he wished. He planted many plants under the date palms. From it food was produced for the Messenger of God and his family, every year, of barley and dates for his wives and the sons of ʿAbd al-Muṭṭalib. Whatever was in excess he allocated to horses and weapons. Indeed, both Abū Bakr and ʿUmar had these weapons that were bought during the time of the Messenger of God. The Messenger of God appointed Abū Rāfiʿ, his *mawlā*, in charge of the property of the Banū Naḍīr. Sometimes Abū Rāfiʿ came to the Messenger of God with the first fruits from it. The Messenger of God's *sadaqa* (alms) was from it and from the property of Mukhayrīq.

There were seven gardens: al-Mīthab, al-Ṣāfiya, al-Dalāl, Husnāʾ, Burqa, al-Aʿwāf, and the water hole of Umm Ibrahīm—the mother of Ibrahīm lived here. The Messenger of God used to visit her there. It is said that when the Messenger of God moved from Banū ʿAmr b. ʿAwf, to Medina, his companions amongst the Muhājirūn also moved. The Anṣār competed to have them live in their homes and they cast lots about it and no one hosted any of them except by the casting of lots.

Maʿmar related to me from al-Zuhrī, from Khārija b. Zayd, from Umm al-ʿAlāʾi. [Page 379] She said, "ʿUthmān b. Mazʿūn came to us by casting lots. He was in our house until he died. The Muhājirūn were in their land and property, but when the Messenger of God took booty from the Banū Naḍīr, he called Thābit b. Qays b. Shāmmās and said, "Call your people for me." Thābit said, "The Khazraj, O Messenger of God?" The Messenger of God said, "The Anṣār, all of them!" So he summoned the Aws and the Khazraj to him. The Messenger of God spoke and he praised God, and he praised Him as is befitting to Him. Then he mentioned the Anṣār and what they did for the Muhājirūn, their hosting of them in their houses, and their preferring the Muhājirūn to themselves. Then he said, "Surely, if you like, I will divide the booty God has given me from the Banū Naḍīr between you and the Muhājirūn, and the Muhājirūn will still be living in your dwellings and your property. Or, if you like, I will give it all to them and they will leave your homes." Saʿd b. ʿUbāda and Saʿd b. Muʿādh spoke, saying, "O Messenger of God, rather you will apportion it all to the Muhājirūn, but they will stay in our homes just as they are." And the Anṣār called out, "We are satisfied and content, O Messenger of God." The Messenger of God said, "May God have compassion on the Anṣār and the sons of the Anṣār." The Messenger of God divided what God had given as booty to him, and he gave the Muhājirūn and he did not give any one of the Anṣār anything from that booty except to two men. They were the two needy: Sahl b. Ḥunayf and Abū Dujāna. He gave Saʿd b. Muʿādh the sword of Ibn Abī l-Ḥuqayq, which was a sword that was renowned among them.

They said: Among the named recipients of the Muhājirūn were Abū Bakr al-Ṣiddīq, who received Bi'r Ḥijr; ʿUmar b. al-Khaṭṭāb was given Bi'r Jaram, ʿAbd al-Raḥmān b. ʿAwf was given Suāla—also called Māl Sulaym, and Ṣuhayb b. [Page 380] Sinān, was given al-Ḍarrāṭa. The Messenger of God gave al-Buwayla to al-Zubayr b. al-Awwām and Abū Salama b. ʿAbd al-Asad. The property of Sahl b. Ḥunayf and Abū Dujāna was well known. It was known as the property of Ibn Kharasha. The Messenger of God was generous to the people as regards that property.

MENTION OF WHAT WAS REVEALED OF THE QUR'ĀN CONCERNING THE BANŪ NAḌĪR

All that is in the heavens and on earth praise God (Q. 59:1): He said, all things praise Him, even the demolished walls give praise. Rabīʿa b. ʿUthmān related to me from Ḥuyayy from Abū Hurayra about that. *It is He who drove the unbelievers, among the people of the book, out of their homes, at the first gathering* (Q. 59:2): meaning the Banū Naḍīr, when the Messenger of God exiled them from Medina to al-Shām; and that was the first gathering in the world to al-Shām. *You did not think that they would leave* (Q. 59:2): God most high said to the believers, You did not think, for they had power and might. *They thought that their fortress would defend them from God* (Q. 59:2): when they were besieged. But the wrath of God came to them from regions that they did not expect (Q. 59:2): He said, the Messenger of God's appearance, and their exile. *He cast terror into their hearts* (Q. 59:2): when the Messenger of God descended to their courtyards, they were fearful and certain of destruction. Fear was in their hearts for him, and they trembled. *They were destroying their homes with their own hands and the hands of the believers* (Q. 59:2): He said when the Muslims besieged them and dug from behind them, looking for what was assigned to them, taking the wood and the lintels. *Take warning then, O you, with eyes to see* (Q. 59:2): He meant, O people with [Page 381] understanding. *Since God had decreed banishment for them* (Q. 59:3): He says, it is written in the mother of the book that they will be exiled. *That is because they resisted God and His messenger* (Q. 59:4): He says they disobeyed God and His messenger and opposed Him. *Whether ye cut down the tender palm trees* (Q. 59:5): He said that the Messenger of God had employed Abū Laylā al-Māzinī and ʿAbdullāh b. Salām to cut their date palm, and Abū Laylā was cutting the ʿAjwa, and Ibn Salām was cutting the lwn. The Banū Naḍīr said to them, "You are Muslims and it is not lawful for you to destroy the palms." The companions of the Prophet disputed about that. Some said that they are to be cut and others that they are not to be cut. God most high revealed about that, *What you cut of the tender palm trees* (Q. 59:5): meaning the various kinds of the palms except the ʿAjwa. *Or you left them standing on their roots* (Q. 59:5): He said, the ʿAjwa. *It was by leave of God in order that he might cover with shame the rebellious transgressors* (Q. 59:5): He means, what was cut of the dates will enrage them. *What God bestowed on His Apostle and taken away from the people of the townships belongs to God and His Apostle and to kindred and orphans and the needy and the wayfarer* (Q. 59:7): God says, For what is for Allah and His messenger is the same. *And to those who possess kinship* (Q. 59:7): meaning the relatives of the Messenger of God. *And the orphans, the poor, and the wayfarer* (Q. 59:7): The share of the Messenger of God is a fifth of the *khums*. The Messenger of God used to give the Banū Hāshim from the *khums* and marry off their widows. ʿUmar had offered them what was required to have their widows married, their families employed, and pay off the debts of the indebted. They refused and demanded that all of the *khums* be submitted, which ʿUmar refused. Muṣʿab b. Thābit related to me from Yazīd b. Rūmān, from ʿUrwa that Abū Bakr, ʿUmar and ʿAlī used to give it to the orphans, the poor and the wayfarer. He says, *in order that it may not (merely) make a circuit between the wealthy among you* (Q. 59:7): He means in order that it does not become a practice [Page 382] that it is given to the rich. *So take what the Apostle assigns to you and deny yourselves that which he withholds from you* (Q. 59:7): He says what comes from the Messenger of God by way of command or prohibition has the status of that which has been revealed. (*Some part is due) to the indigent Muhājirs, those who were expelled from their homes and their property, while seeking grace from God and His good pleasure* (Q. 59:8): that is the first Muhājirūn from the Quraysh who emigrated to Medina before Badr. *But those who before them, had homes (in Medina) and had adopted the faith, show their affection to such as came to them for refuge* (Q. 59:9): meaning the Anṣār. He says the Aws and the Khazraj are the people of the homes. And entertain no desire in their hearts for things given to the latter, but give them preference over themselves, even though poverty was their own lot (Q. 59:9): They did not find in themselves envy for what was given to the rest of them, meaning the Muhājirūn, when the Messenger of God gave them and did not give the Anṣār. This is the preference over themselves, when they said to the Prophet: Give them and do not give us, for they are needy. And those saved from the covetousness of their own souls (Q. 59:9): he said the evil of the people. *And those who came after them* (Q. 59:10): meaning those who embraced Islam; it is incumbent on them to seek forgiveness for the companions of the Prophet. *Hast thou not observed the Hypocrites say to their disbelieving brethren among the people of the book? If you are expelled, we too will go out with you, and we will never hearken to any one in your affair* (Q. 59:11): the words of Ibn Ubayy when he sent Suwayd and Dāʿis to the Banū Naḍīr: stay and do not leave, surely with me and my people and others, are two thousand who will enter with you and die, to the last of them, defending you. God most high says: *But God is witness that they are indeed liars* (Q. 59:11): meaning Ibn Ubayy and his companions. *If they are expelled* (Q. 59:12): when the Messenger of God expelled them, not a single man from the Hypocrites left with them, and when they fought, not one man among them entered [Page 383] their fortress. *And if they do help them they will turn their backs* (Q. 59:12): meaning they will be put to flight from fear. *You are more awful as a terror in their bosoms than Allah* (Q. 59:13): meaning Ibn Ubayy and the Hypocrites who, with him, fear that the Muslims would proceed against them, *That is because they are men devoid of understanding. They will not fight you even together* (Q. 59:14): meaning the Banū Naḍīr and the Hypocrites. *Except in fortified townships* (Q. 59:14): he says in their fortresses. *Their adversity among themselves is very great* (Q. 59:14): for each other. *You would think they were united but their hearts are divided* (Q. 59:14): meaning the Hypocrites and the Banū Naḍīr. *That is because they are a people devoid of wisdom* (Q. 59:14): he says the religion of the Banū Naḍīr is different from the religion of the Hypocrites and they are all united in their enmity towards the Muslim community. *Like those who in the recent past have tasted the evil result of their conduct* (Q. 59:15): meaning the Qaynuqāʿ when the Messenger of God exiled them. *Like the evil one when he says to man, "Deny God," but when (man) denies God (the evil one) says, "I am free of you. I do fear God, the Lord of the Worlds* (Q. 59:16): He said that this is comparable to Ibn Ubayy and his companions who came to the Banū Naḍīr saying, falsly, "Stay in your fortresses for we will fight with you if you are attacked, and we will leave if you leave." They gave them false hope. *O you who believe, fear God and let every soul look to what (provision) he has sent forth for the morrow* (Q. 59:18): he means what you did for the Day of Resurrection. *And be not like those who forgot God. And He made them forget their own souls* (Q. 59:19): He says that they turn away from the remembrance of God, and God leads them astray from doing good for themselves. *The Holy one* (Q. 59:23): the obvious. *The guardian* (Q. 59:23): the one who sees.

[Page 384] **THE RAID OF BADR AL-MAWʿID**

The raid took place in the month of Dhū l-Qaʿda, forty-five months after the Prophet's emigration to Medina. The Messenger of God was absent for sixteen nights. He returned to Medina with fourteen days remaining in the month of Dhū l-Qaʿda. He appointed Ibn Rawāḥa over Medina.

Al-Ḍaḥḥāk b. ʿUthmān, Muḥammad b. ʿAmr al-Anṣārī, Mūsā b. Muḥammad b. Ibrāhīm b. al-Ḥārith, Abū Bakr b. ʿAbdullah b. Muḥammad b. Abī Sabra, Maʿmar b. Rāshid, Abū Maʿshar, ʿAbdullah b. Jaʿfar, Muḥammad b. ʿAbdullah b. Muslim, ʿAbd al-Ḥamīd b. Jaʿfar, Ibn Abī Ḥabība, Muḥammad b. Yaḥyā b. Sahl, as well as others who are not named, related portions of this tradition to me. They said: When Abū Sufyān desired to return on the day of Uḥud, he called out, "Is there an appointment between us and you at Badr al-Ṣafrāʾ in the beginning of the year, so we can meet and fight?" The Messenger of God said to ʿUmar b. al-Khaṭṭāb, "Say, yes, God willing." Some said: Abū Sufyān said at that time, "Your appointment at Badr al-Ṣafrāʾ is in two months." Ibn Wāqid said: The first tradition is confirmed with us. The people dispersed after that.

The Quraysh returned and informed those who were near them of their appointment and they prepared to go out and gathered together. This was for them the greatest of days because they had returned from Uḥud where they had been victorious. They desired a similar victory in the appointment at Badr. Badr al-Ṣafrāʾ was the meeting place of the Bedouin and there was a market held there for eight nights during the month of Dhū l-Qaʿda, and when the eight nights had past, the people dispersed to their land. When the appointment drew near Abū Sufyān hated to go out to the Messenger of God. [Page 385] He began to wish that the Messenger of God and his companions would stay in Medina and not keep the appointment. All those who arrived at Mecca on the way to Medina announced to him, "We desire to attack Muḥammad with a concentrated group." A visitor arrived before the companions of Muḥammad and seeing them prepare said, "I left Abū Sufyān who has gathered a group. He joins with the Bedouin to march to you for your appointment." The Muslims hated it for that frightened them.

Nuʿaym b. Masʿūd al-Ashjaʿī arrived in Mecca, and Abū Sufyān b. Ḥarb came to him with a man from the Quraysh and said, "O Nuʿaym, indeed I promised Muḥammad and his companions on the day of Uḥud, that we would meet, we and he, at Badr al-Ṣafrāʾ in the beginning of the year, which has arrived." Nuʿaym said, "What brought me is what I saw Muḥammad and his companions prepare of weapons and stones. The allies of the Aws from the Baliyy and Juhayna and others have rallied to him. I left Medina yesterday and it was like a pomegranate—full of people." Abū Sufyān said, "Is it true, what you say?" He replied, "Indeed, by God." They rewarded Nuʿaym well, joined with him and helped him. Abū Sufyān said, "I hear what you say, but how have they prepared in this year of drought?" Nuʿaym said, "The earth is like the back of the shield. Nothing on the earth is good for the camel. What would be good for us is a plentiful and fertile year where the cattle and horses graze and we drink the milk." Abū Sufyān said, "I hate it that Muḥammad and his companions are setting out emboldened against us, while I do not go out. A breach on their part is more desirable to me. We will owe you twenty camels, ten portions of five-year-old camels and ten of four-year-old she-camels fit for riding. It will be given to you by [Page 386] Suhayl b. ʿAmr who will guarantee it for you." Nuʿaym said, "I am satisfied." Suhayl was a friend of Nuʿaym, and he went to Suhayl and said, "O Abū Yazīd, will you guarantee that I will receive twenty camels if I go to Medina and persuade the companions of Muḥammad to stay away?" Suhayl said, "Yes." Nuʿaym said, "Indeed, I shall set out." He set out on a camel that they gave him. The journey was quick, and he arrived, with his head shaven as a pilgrim, and found the companions of Muḥammad in preparation.

The companions of Muḥammad said, "From where are you, Nuʿaym?" He replied, "I went as a pilgrim to Mecca." They said, "Do you have information on Abū Sufyān?" He said, "Yes. I left Abū Sufyān collecting a group, and he has gathered the Bedouin to him. He is coming with a force you are incapable of matching. So stay and do not set out, for indeed, they came to you in your land and your dwelling, and none but the fugitive could escape among you. Your leaders were killed and Muḥammad himself was wounded. Now, you desire to go out to meet them in a given location? Miserable is the opinion you have of yourselves. It is the time for people getting together. By God, I do not see one of you escaping." He circulated this among the companions of the Prophet until he frightened them. Going out became hateful to them, and they, or those who spoke from among them, believingly pronounced the words of Nuʿaym.

The Hypocrites and Jews rejoiced over it. They said, "Muḥammad will never escape from this group," and Satan brought his friends to frighten the people until that reached the Messenger of God. The information with him was so widespread that the Prophet feared that no one would go out with him. Abū Bakr b. Quhāfa and ʿUmar b. al-Khaṭṭāb had heard what was going around and they said, "O Messenger of God, surely God will demonstrate His religion and the excellence of His Prophet. The people promised us an appointment and we do not desire to stay [Page 387] away from them. They will consider this cowardice from us. Proceed to the appointment, for by God, it will be for the best." The Messenger of God smiled at that and said, "By Him who holds my soul in His hand, I shall surely set out, even if no one sets out with me!" He said: And when the Prophet spoke, he spoke about what God had revealed to the people, and he removed what Satan frightened them of. The Muslims set out with their merchandise to Badr.

Yazīd, who had learned from Khuṣayfa, informed me that ʿUthmān b. ʿAffān used to say: Surely I remember how fear had been cast into our hearts. I did not think that even one had the intention of setting out, until God opened the eyes of the Muslims and removed the fear of Satan from them. They set out, and indeed I set out with them, to the fair at Badr. I made a profit of a dinar for a dinar, and we returned by the goodness and grace of our Lord. The Messenger of God went with the Muslims, and they set out with merchandise of theirs and money for expenses. When they reached Badr it was a night in the month of Dhu al-Qaʿda.

The market happens at the beginning of the month, and they stayed for eight days while the market was standing. The Messenger of God had set out with a thousand and five hundred of his companions and ten horses. There was a horse for the Messenger of God, and a horse each for Abū Bakr, ʿUmar, Abū Qatāda, Saʿīd b. Zayd, al-Miqdād, Ḥubāb, al-Zubayr and ʿAbbād b. Bishr.

ʿAlī b. Zayd informed me from his father that al-Miqdād said: I witnessed Badr al-Mawʿid on my horse Sabḥa. I rode on its back going and coming. There was no fighting. Then Abū Sufyān said, "O people of the Quraysh, we sent Nuʿaym b. Masʿūd in order to persuade the companions of Muḥammad against setting out, and he tried. So, we will set out and march for a night or two, and then return. If Muḥammad does not set out it will reach him that we set out and returned because he did not set out. This will be for us and against him. If he sets out, we will show that this is a year of drought and that we have not prepared except for a year of pasture."

[Page 388] They said, "Yours is a good plan." So he set out with the Quraysh, and they were a thousand, with fifty horses when they reached Majanna. Then he said, "Return! Only a plentiful year will suit us wherein we can graze our cattle on shrubs and drink the milk. Indeed, this year of yours is a year of drought. Indeed I shall return so you too return." The people of Mecca named that army the army of Barley saying, "They went out drinking barley."

He who carried the greatest flag of the Messenger of God, was ʿAlī b. Abī Ṭālib. A man from the Banū Ḍamra called Makhshī b. ʿAmr approached. He was among those who contracted with the Messenger of God on behalf of his people during the first raid of the Messenger of God to Waddān. He said: The people were gathering in their market. The companions of the Messenger of God were the majority on that pilgrim site. He said, "O Muḥammad, we were informed that not one of you would stay. I did not recognize you except as people of the fair." The Messenger of God said—he said this so that this would be taken to his enemies among the Quraysh—"We have not set out except to the appointment of Abū Sufyān and to battle with our enemies. But if you wish, we will put aside our promise to you and to your people, then we will fight with you before we withdraw from this place of ours." Al-Ḍamrī said, "Rather, we will hold back our hands from you and we will keep your pact." Maʿbad b. Abī Maʿbad al-Khuzāʿī heard that and departed swiftly. He stayed for eight days. He saw the people of the fair and the companions of the Messenger of God. He heard the words of Makhshī and hurried back until he arrived in Mecca. He was the first of those who arrived with news of the fair of Badr. They questioned him and he informed them about the numerous companions of Muḥammad, that they were the majority at the fair, and of what he heard of the words of the Messenger of God to al-Ḍamrī. He said, "Muḥammad appeared with two thousand companions [Page 389] and stayed for eight days until the people of the pilgrim center dispersed."

Ṣafwān b. Umayya said to Abū Sufyān, "By God, I forbade you, on that day, from promising the people. They have become bold against us. They think that we have broken our appointment; indeed, weakness has kept us away from them." They started plotting and spending with regard to fighting the Messenger of God. They summoned those who were around them among the Bedouin, gathered great wealth, and caused the people of Mecca to rise. He imposed a tax on each one of them; no one was exempt. Less than an ounce for the raid of al-Khandaq was not accepted from any one of them. Maʿbad said: What I saw transported me such that I pronounced a poem:

Attached to the ancient customs of her father's property,
At that time she made the water of Qudayd a meeting place.
The water of Ḍajnān will be hers tomorrow noon.
She fled from the two companies of Muḥammad
And from ʿAjwa, which are like black raisins.

They allege that Ḥumām said it.

God most high revealed about that, *Men said to them, "Indeed the people have gathered against you,"* to the end of the verse, meaning Nuʿaym b. Masʿūd. Kaʿb b. Mālik said, al-Wāqidī said, the elders of the family of Kaʿb and our companions all related to me:

Abū Sufyān promised to meet us at Badr
But we did not find him true to his promise.
I swear if you had kept your word and met us
You would have returned disgraced without your nearest kin.
[Page 390] We had left there the limbs of ʿUtba and his son
And ʿAmr Abū Jahl in his grave.
You disobeyed the Messenger of God. Fie to your religion
And your evil affair that was lost.
If you reproach me, I will say
My wealth and people be the Apostle's ransom!
We obey him treating none among us as his equal.
He is our guiding light in the darkness of the night.

Ḥassān b. Thābit al-Anṣārī said, and Ibn Abī Zinād and Ibn Jaʿfar and others have confirmed his saying:

We stayed by the shallow well eight nights
With a large, well equipped and blessed force,
With every red horse its middle half its size,
White camels, tall, of wide shoulders
You could see little trees
Roots being unearthed by the feet of the hastening camels
If they descend the sandy ʿĀlij
Say to them this is not the road.
You can say goodbye to al-Shām's running streams,
For in-between are swords like mouths of pregnant camels that feed on Arak trees.
[Page 391] In the hands of men who have immigrated to their lord,
The helpers of the true who are helped by the angels.

If on our journeys we meet Furāt b. Ḥayyān
He will become death's hostage.
If we meet Qays b. Imrā' l-Qays after,
We will make his black face darker.

Abū Sufyan b. al-Ḥārith b. ʿAbd al-Muṭṭalib answered him, and it was thus.

THE EXPEDITION OF IBN ʿATĪK TO ABŪ RĀFIʿ

They set out on the night of the Monday at daybreak on the fourth of Dhū l-Hijja, forty-six months AH, and they were gone for ten days.

Abū Ayyūb b. al-Nuʿmān related to me from his father from ʿAṭiyya b. ʿAbdullah b. Unays from his father. He said: we set out from Medina until we reached Khaybar. The foster mother of ʿAbdullah b. ʿAtīk, a Jewish woman who had nursed him, was in Khaybar. The Messenger of God had sent five of us: ʿAbdullah b. Atīk, ʿAbdullah b. Unays, Abū Qatāda, al-Aswad b. al-Khuzāʿī and Masʿūd b. Sinān. He said: When we reached Khaybar, ʿAbdullah sent to his mother informing her of his situation. She came out to us with a basket filled with dates, pickles and bread, and we ate of it. Then, he said to her, "Evening is coming upon us, put us up for the night at your place and take us into Khaybar." His mother said, "How will Khaybar be possible when there are four thousand warriors in it? Whom do you want there?" He replied, "Abū Rāfiʿ." She said, "You will not be able to reach him." [Page 392] He said, "By God, I will kill him or be killed instead before that." She said, "Come to me at night."

They entered when the people of Khaybar were sleeping. ʿAbdullah's mother had said to them, "Enter, during the socializing of the people, and when the traffic of feet has subsided, hide." So they did, and they came to her and she said, "Indeed the Jews do not lock their doors upon themselves for fear that a guest may knock on them during the night, so that anyone arriving in the courtyard not having been given hospitality, will find the door open, and may enter and eat."

When the sound of feet had subsided she said, "Go and ask to be admitted to Abū Rāfiʿ, saying 'We have brought Abū Rāfiʿ a gift,' and they will open up for you." So they did, and they did not pass a door of a house of Khaybar but they locked it, until they had locked every house in the entire village, when, finally, they reached the ladder at the castle of Sallām. He said: We ascended and sent ʿAbdullah b. ʿAtīk because he speaks Yahudiyya. Then they asked to be entered to Abū Rāfiʿ, and his wife came out and said, "What is your business?" ʿAbdullah b. ʿAtīk said, speaking Yahudiyya, "I bring Abū Rāfiʿ a gift." She opened for him, but when she saw the weapons she wanted to scream.

ʿAbdullah b. ʿUnays said: We crowded through the door to try to get to him first, and she wanted to shout, so I pointed the sword at her. He said: I hated that my companion overtook me, to him. He said: She was calm for a while. Then I said to her, "Where is Abū Rāfiʿ? Tell me, and I will not strike you with the sword." She said, "He is there in the house." He said: We went to him and we did not know him except for his whiteness, like a piece of cotton clothing. We were upon him with our swords, while his wife shouted. Some of us started to go out to her, and then we remembered that the Messenger of God had forbidden us from killing women. He said: [Page 393] When we reached the point where the ceiling of the house was made too low for us, our swords began to rebound. Ibn Unays said: I was a dim-sighted man and I could not see by night except very weakly. I saw Abū Rāfiʿ as though he were the moon. I pressed with my sword upon his stomach until I heard it enter the bed, and I knew he was dead. He said: The gang began to strike him together. Then we came down, but Abū Qatāda forgot his bow and remembered it only after he came down. His companions said, "Leave the bow," but he refused, and returned and took it. His leg became dislocated and they carried him between them. Abū Rāfiʿ's wife shouted, and the people of the house began to shout after he was killed.

The people of the houses could not release themselves for the long night. The gang hid in some canal of Khaybar. The Jews and al-Ḥārith Abū Zaynab approached, and Abū Rāfiʿ's wife came out to him and said, "The gang has gone now."

Al-Ḥārith set out with three thousand men in our tracks. They hunted us with torches and palm fronds set on fire. Perhaps they walked in the river, but we were inside the canal and they were on its surface and they did not see us. When they set out on the search and did not see anything they returned to his wife and said to her, "Did you recognize one of them?" She said, "I heard the voice of ʿAbdullah b. ʿAtīk among them, and if he is in this land of ours he was with them." So they returned for a second search.

The band said among them selves, "Suppose one of us went to them to see if the man is dead or not." Al-Aswad b. al-Khuzāʿī set out until he entered with the people and mingled with them. He held a firebrand like theirs in his hand. When the people returned a second time to the castle, he returned with them, and found the house was [Page 394] full. He said that they approached together to observe what had happened to Abū Rāfiʿ. He said: His wife approached carrying a torch of fire. She leant over him to see if he were alive or dead. She said, "He is dead, by the God of Moses!" He said: Then I turned to go back and make sure the affair was certain. I entered a second time with them, and not a vein of the man was moving. The Jews came out keening together in one voice. They began preparing him for burial.

I came out with them for I had delayed my companions some moments. I descended to them in the river and informed them. We stayed in our place for two days until the search for us had subsided. Then we set out towards Medina, each of us claiming to have killed him. We arrived before the Prophet, and he was at the pulpit. When he saw us he said, "May your faces prosper!" We replied, "And may your face prosper, Oh Messenger of God." He said, "Did you kill him?" We said, "All of us claim to have killed him." He said, "Hurry and show me your swords." So we brought our swords. Then he said, "This killed him. This is the trace of food on the sword of ʿAbdullah b. Unays."

He said: Ibn Abī l-Ḥuqayq had incited the Ghatafān and the Arab polytheists around him. He offered them great inducements to fight the Messenger of God, so the Prophet sent those men to him.

Ayyūb b. al-Nuʿmān related to me that Khārija b. ʿAbdullah had related to him saying: When they reached Abū Rāfiʿ they disputed about killing him. He said: They drew lots about it, and the arrow came out to ʿAbdullah b. Unays. But he was a weak sighted man and he said to his companions, "Where is his place?" They said, "You will see his whiteness as though he were a moon." He said: He said, "I saw it." ʿAbdullah b. Unays approached, while the group stayed with his wife afraid that she would shout. They pointed their swords at her. [Page 395] ʿAbdullah b. Unays entered. He struck with his sword, and the sword rebounded to him for the ceiling was low. So he leaned upon him, and he was full of wine, until he heard the sword enter in the bed.

Some say that the expedition (*sariyya*) took place in the month of Ramaḍān in the year six.

THE RAID OF DHĀT AL-RIQĀʿ

It was named Dhāt al-Riqāʿ because it was a mountain of red, black and white patches of earth. The Messenger of God set out on the night of the Sabbath, on the tenth of Muḥarram, forty-seven months after the *hijra*. He arrived in Ṣirār on Sunday, five days to the end of Muḥarram, and he was gone for fifteen days.

Al-Ḍaḥḥāk b. ʿUthmān related to me from ʿUbaydullah b. Miqsam, and Hishām b. Saʿd related to me from Zayd b. Aslam, from Jābir, and from ʿAbd al-Karīm b. Abī Ḥafṣa, from Jābir and ʿAbd al-Raḥmān b. Muḥammad b. Abī Bakr from ʿAbdullah b. Abī Bakr and Mālik b. Anas, and ʿAbdullah b. ʿUmar from Wahb b. Kaysān from Jābir b. ʿAbdullah; and some of them have expanded the tradition according to others. And others have related to me about it as well. They said: The newcomer arrived with goods he had purchased in the Nabṭ market. They said, "From where are your goods?" He replied, "I come from Najd. I have seen the Anmār and Thaʿlaba gather together to attack you and I see that you are undisturbed about this."

His words [Page 396] reached the Messenger of God, and he set out with four hundred of his companions—another said that they were seven or eight hundred. The Messenger of God set out from Medina until he came to al-Maḍīq then went to Wadī al-Shuqra and stayed there for a day. He dispatched a raiding party and they returned with the night. They informed him that they did not see anyone, but they had trodden on recent tracks. Then the Messenger of God marched with his companions until he came to a resting site of theirs, and they found a campsite, but there was no one there. The Bedouin had gone to the tops of the mountains and were watching the Prophet. Some of the people feared others among them. The polytheists among them were near. The Muslims feared that they would attack them when they were careless. The Bedouin feared that the Messenger of God would not leave until he had uprooted them.

During this time the Prophet prayed the prayer of fear. Rabīʿa b. ʿUthmān informed me from Abū Nuʿaym from Jābir b. ʿAbdullah that it was the first prayer against fear that was prayed at the time. He feared that they would attack him while they were in prayer, arranged in rows.

ʿAbdullah b. ʿUthmān informed me from his brother from Qāsim b. Muḥammad from Ṣāliḥ b. Khawwāt from his father, who said: I prayed with the Messenger of God, at the time, the prayer of fear. The Messenger of God faced the *qibla*. There was a faction behind him and a faction facing the enemy. He prayed with the faction that was behind him, one bowing and two prostrations. Then he remained standing and they prayed one bowing and two prostrations, and they gave greetings. Then the other faction came and the Prophet prayed a bowing and two prostrations with them while the first faction faced the enemy. When he had prayed with them a bowing he remained seated until they completed for themselves a bowing and two prostrations and then gave greetings.

[Page 397] The Messenger of God had taken women from their settlement. There was with the captives a beautiful girl whose husband loved her. When the Prophet turned to return to Medina, her husband made an oath to seek out Muḥammad. He would not return to his people until he had taken Muḥammad, or shed blood among the Muslims, or he rescued his female companion.

Meanwhile the Messenger of God was marching at nightfall to Dhāt al-Rīḥ. He alighted in the gorge in front of him and said, "Who is the man who will guard us this night?" Two men, ʿAmmār b. Yāsir and ʿAbbād b. Bishr, came forward. They said, "We will protect you." The wind stirred and the two men sat at the mouth of the ravine, and one of them said to his companion, "Which part of the night is more desirable to you? Would you prefer the first part or the latter part?" He replied, "The first part." So ʿAmmār b Yāsir slept while ʿAbbād stayed up praying.

The enemy of God approached seeking a heedless moment when the wind was still. When he saw ʿAbbād's form from close he said, "God knows, indeed this is a guard of the people." He aimed an arrow that pierced ʿAbbād, and ʿAbbād removed it and dropped it. So he aimed another, and it pierced ʿAbbād and ʿAbbād removed it and dropped it. Then he aimed a third arrow at him and pierced him. When the bleeding overpowered ʿAbbād he bowed and touched his forehead to the ground in prayer; then he said to his companion, "Sit up for I am dying." ʿAmmār sat up, and when the Bedouin saw that ʿAmmār had risen he knew that they were aware (guarded) against him. ʿAmmār said, "O my brother, what prevented you arousing me when the first arrow was shot by him?" He replied, "I was in the midst of the verse I was reciting from the chapter al-Kahf. I hated to stop until I had completed it. Not only that, I was very careful to follow what the Messenger of God had ordered me to do, and I would not leave it until I was dead." Some say that the Anṣār was ʿUmāra b. Ḥazm. Ibn Wāqid said: Of the two, ʿAmmār b. Yāsir is more confirmed with us.

[Page 398] Jābir used to say: Indeed we were with the Prophet when one of his companions arrived with a young bird and the Messenger of God looked at it. Its parents or one of them approached until it threw itself in the hands of the man who had taken its young. The people looked and were surprised by that. The Messenger of God said, "Are you surprised by this bird? You took its young, so it threw itself in your hands to save it. But by God, indeed, the Lord is more protective of you than this bird of its young."

Al-Wāqidī said: The Messenger of God used to pray, on his saddle, facing the East during a raid.

Jābir said: During our return the Messenger of God came to us while I was in the shade of a tree. I said, "Would you like some shade, O Messenger of God?" and he drew near the shade for its protection. I wanted to offer him something but I could not find anything but a cucumber in the bottom of the sack. He said: I broke it, and then offered it to him. The Messenger of God said, "From where did you get this?" I said, "It is a thing left from the provisions of Medina." The Messenger of God took some of it.

We appointed a companion of ours who was wearing a torn garment to graze our animals. The Messenger of God said, "Is there nothing else for him?" We said, "Rather, O Messenger of God, there are two new garments in the leather bag." The Messenger of God said, "Put on your two garments." So he took out his garments and wore them, then left. The Messenger of God said, "Is it not better that he wears his clothes when God strikes off his head?" The man heard that and said, "In the way of God, O Messenger of God?" The Messenger of God said, "In the way of God." Jābir said: His head was cut off, after that, in the way of God.

[Page 399] He said: Meanwhile the Messenger of God was speaking to us when ʿUlba b. Zayd al-Ḥārithī arrived with three ostrich eggs. He said, "O Messenger of God I found these eggs in an ostrich nest." The Messenger of God said, "Here you are, O Jābir, make these eggs!" So I jumped up to prepare them, then I came with the eggs in a bowl, and I began to look for bread but I could not find any. He said: The Messenger of God and his companions began to eat the eggs without bread. I saw the Messenger of God take his hand and I thought that he had had his fill. But the egg was in the bowl just as it had been. He said: Then the Messenger of God stood up, and the general public from our companions ate of it. Then we relaxed coolly.

Jābir said: We were traveling, when the Prophet overtook me. He said, "What is the matter with you, O Jābir?" I said, "O Messenger of God, a sickly camel has been granted to me, for the people have passed and left me." He said: The Prophet knelt his camel, and said, "Is there some water with you?" I said, "Yes," and I gave him a bowl of drinking water. He blew on it, then splashed it on my camel's head, back and rump. Then he said, "Give me a stick." so I gave him the stick that was with me, or cut a stick for him from a tree, and he urged it and prodded it with the stick. Then he said, "Ride, O Jābir." He said: And I rode. He said: He set out, and by Him who sent him with the truth, Jābir's camel exceeded its pace and did not fail him.

He said: I was conversing with the Messenger of God, and he said [Page 400] "O Abū ʿAbdullah are you married?" I said, "Yes." He said, "Was she a virgin or not?" I replied, "She was not a virgin." He said, "Was it not a young girl so that you could play with, and she with you?" I said, "O Messenger of God, by my father and my mother, my father was taken on the day of Uḥud and he left nine daughters. I married a community conscious woman who would set them straight and be concerned about them." He said, "You have done well. If we arrive in Ṣirār we will order camels to be slaughtered and stay there for that day. When she hears about us she will shake of the dust from her cushions." He said: I said, "By God, O messenger of God we do not have cushions." He said, "Indeed there will be. When you arrive act wisely." He said: I said, "I will do as much as I can." He said: Then the Prophet said, "Sell me this camel of yours, O Jābir." I said, "Rather, it is for you, O Messenger of God." He said, "No, sell it to me." He said: I said, "Yes. Make me an offer for it." He replied, "Indeed, I will take it for a dirham." He said: I said, "You will be cheating me, O Messenger of God." He said, "No, by my life!" Jābir said: And he continued to increase his price with me dirham by dirham until he reached forty dirhams, and he said, "Are you not satisfied?" I said, "It is yours." He said, "you may ride it until you arrive in Medina." He said: And some say that the Prophet said, "I will take it from you for an Ūqiyya, but you may ride it until then," and he sold it on that condition. He said: When we arrived in Ṣirār he ordered a camel to be slaughtered, so I stayed with him for a day, and then we entered Medina.

Jābir said: I said to my wife, "The Prophet commanded me to act wisely." She said, "Listen and obey the command of the Messenger of God. Beware and act." He said: I rose in the morning and, leading the camel by its head, left until I knelt the camel at the room of the Prophet, and sat until he came out. When the Prophet came out he said, "Is this the camel?" I replied, "Yes, O Messenger of God, you bought it." The Messenger of God called Bilāl and said, "Go and give him an Ūqiyya, and take your camel by its head, O son of my brother, for it is yours." I left with Bilāl and Bilāl said, "Are you the son [Page 401] of the master of the ravine?" I said, "Yes." He said, "By God, indeed I will give you and increase for you," and he increased by about a weight or two. He said: Indeed that profit continued and we prospered, by God, with it and we recognized the place of the camel until it was wounded here, near your place, referring to the camel.

Al-Wāqidī said: Ismāʿīl b. ʿAṭiyya b. ʿAbdullah b. Unays related to me from his father from Jābir b. ʿAbdullah. He said: On our return, when we were in al-Shuqra, the Messenger of God said to me, "O Jābir, what debt did your father leave you?" I said, "O Messenger of God, I hope he clipped the dates." The Messenger of God said, "When you have clipped the dates, call me." He said: I said, "Yes." Then he said, "Who is the master of the debt of your father." I replied, "Abū al-Shaḥm the Jew. My father owes him a load of dates." The Messenger of God said to me, "When do you cut it?" I said, "Tomorrow." He said, "O Jābir, when you cut it, set aside the ʿAjwa separately, and the Alwān separately." He said: And I did, and I separated the Ṣayḥān dates of Medina, and the sources of the two kinds were separated. And the ʿAjwa was separated. Then I proceeded to bring together from the similar selected dates and pods, and separated the rest of the kinds. And these were the least of the dates. I made a single pile of dates, and came to the Prophet and informed him. The Messenger of God left, and the elite of his companions came with him. They entered the enclosure and Abū Shaḥm was present.

He said: [Page 402] When the Messenger of God looked at the dates as they were arranged, he said, "May God bless him." Then he went to the ʿAjwa and handled the variety of dates. Then he sat in the middle of it. Then he said, "Call your creditor," and Abū l-Shaḥm came and said, "Scoop it up." So I scooped up his due, all of it, from the single pile, and it was the ʿAjwa. But the dates remained just as they were. Then Messenger of God said, "O Jābir, is there any thing left against your father?" He said: I said, "No." He said: The rest of the dates remained and we ate from it for a lifetime, and we sold of it until the new crop arrived the following year. Indeed I used to say: If I sold its source it would not reach what my father owed. But God fulfilled my father's debt. Indeed I remember the Prophet saying, "What happened to your father's debt?" I said, "God most high fulfilled it." He said, "O God, forgive Jābir!" and in one night he asked forgiveness for me twenty-five times.

ʿĀʾidh b. Yaḥyā related to me from Abū l-Ḥuwayrith, who said: The Messenger of God appointed ʿUthmān b. ʿAffān over Medina during his absence.

THE RAID OF DŪMAT AL-JANDAL

The Raid of Dūmat al-Jandal took place in Rabīʿ al-Awwal, the forty-ninth month AH. The Messenger of God set out during the last five nights of Rabīʿ al-Awwal and returned with ten remaining in Rabīʿ al-Ākhir.

Ibn Abī Sabra related to me from ʿAbdullah b. Abī Labīd from Abū Salama b. ʿAbd al-Raḥmān. And ʿAbd al-Raḥmān b. ʿAbd al-ʿAzīz related to me from ʿAbdullah b. Abī Bakr. Both of them related to me about this tradition. One of them provided more information. Others also related to us.

[Page 403] They said: The Messenger of God desired to approach the place closest to al-Shām. He was told that Dūmat al-Jandal was on the fringe of the entrance to al-Shām, and that if you drew near to it, this would terrify Caesar. It was mentioned to the Prophet that many gathered in Dūmat al-Jandal and that they ill-treated the Ḍāfiṭ (those who brought goods to the cities—they were Nabatean bringing flour and oil) who passed by them. It had a great market and traders, and many Arab Bedouin had recourse to it, and they desired to approach Medina. The Messenger of God delegated the people, and he set out with a thousand Muslims. He was marching by night and hiding by day. With him was a guide from the Banū ʿUdhra named Madhkūr. He was an experienced guide.

The Messenger of God set out in haste. When the Messenger of God drew near to Dūmat al-Jandal, he deviated from their road. There was between him and it a day's or night's journey for a speedy rider. The guide said to him, "Indeed their cattle are grazing, so stay until I get some information for you." The Messenger of God agreed. The ʿUdhrī set out, ascending, until he found the tracks of cattle and sheep going out. Then he returned to the Prophet and informed him, so he knew their situation. The Messenger of God marched until he attacked their cattle and their shepherd. The Messenger of

God attacked whomever he attacked. Those who escaped fled in every direction. News came to the people of Dūmat al-Jandal and they dispersed. The Messenger of God alighted in their yard, but he did not find anyone there. He stayed there for days and dispatched raids in different directions. They were gone for a day, then they returned. They did not find anyone of them. The raiders returned with a portion of their camels.

[Page 404] Except for Muḥammad b. Maslama who captured one of their men and brought him to the Prophet. The Prophet asked him about his companions. He said, "They fled yesterday when they heard that you had taken their cattle." The Prophet offered him Islam for several days and he converted. The Prophet returned to Medina. The Messenger of God appointed Sibāʿ b. ʿUrfuṭa over Medina during his absence.

THE RAID OF Al-MURAYSĪʿ

It was in the year five that the Messenger of God set out on a Monday, the second of Shaʿbān. He arrived in Medina in the month of Ramaḍān, and he was absent for a month less two nights.

Al-Wāqidī informed us saying: Muḥammad b. ʿAbdullah, ʿAbdullah b. Jaʿfar, Ibn Abī Sabra, Muḥammad b. Ṣāliḥ, ʿAbd al-Ḥamīd b. Jaʿfar and Ibn Abī Ḥabība, Hishām b. Saʿd, Maʿmar b. Rāshid, Abū Maʿshar, Khālid b. Ilyās, ʿĀʾidh b. Yaḥyā, ʿUmar b. ʿUthmān al-Makhzūmī, ʿAbdullah b. Yazīd b. Qusayṭ, ʿAbdullah b. Yazīd al-Hudhalī, all informed me in portions, and others informed me as well. They said: The Balmuṣṭaliq of the Khuzāʿa, allies of the Banū Mudlij, were camping around al-Furʿ. Their leader and master, al-Ḥārith b. Abī Ḍirār, had gone to his people and those who had power over him from the Bedouin, and invited them to fight the Messenger of God, and they bought horses and weapons and prepared to march to the Messenger of God. Riders began to arrive from their region and inform about their march. This reached the Messenger of God, and he sent Burayda b. al-Ḥuṣayb al-Aslamī to learn that information. He sought permission of the Prophet to speak freely, and the Prophet permitted him.

Burayda set out until he arrived [Page 405] upon them at their waters. He found a misled people who had rallied and come together. They said, "Who is the man?" He said, "A man from you; I arrived for what reached me about your gathering for this man. I will march with my people and those who obey me, and our hands will be one until we destroy him." Al-Ḥārith b. Abī Ḍirār said, "We are with you. Hasten to us." Burayda said, "I will ride now and bring you a group of tough men from my people who will obey me." They rejoiced at that from him. Burayda returned to the Messenger of God and informed him about the people.

The Messenger of God summoned his people and informed them with news of the enemy, and the people hastened to set out. They led their rides and there were thirty horses: with the Muhājirūn ten and with the Anṣār twenty. There were two horses for the Messenger of God, and a horse each for ʿAlī, Abū Bakr, ʿUmar, ʿUthmān, al-Zubayr, ʿAbd al-Raḥmān b. ʿAwf, Ṭalḥa b. ʿUbaydullah and al-Miqdād b. ʿAmr. And with the Anṣār, Saʿd b. Muʿādh, Usayd b. Ḥuḍayr, Abū ʿAbs b. Jabr, Qatāda b. Nuʿmān, ʿUwaym b. Sāʿida, Maʿan b. ʿAdī, Saʿd b. Zayd b. Ashhalī, al-Ḥārith b. Ḥazma, Muʿādh b. Jabal, Abū Qatāda, Ubayy b. Kaʿb, al-Ḥubāb b. al-Mundhir, Ziyād b. Labīd, Farwa b. ʿAmr and Muʿādh b. Rifāʿa b. Rāfiʿ.

They said: Many people from the Hypocrites set out with the Messenger of God. They had never set out in a raid like it. They did not desire *jihād* except to take from the goods of the world. The Messenger of God set out until he came to Ḥalāʾiq and alighted there. A man from ʿAbd al-Qays was brought before him, at that time. He greeted the Messenger of God, and the Messenger of God said to him, [Page 406] "Where are your people?" He replied, "At al-Rawhāʾ." The Prophet said, "Where are you going?" He said, "I come to you for I believe in you, and I witness that indeed you come with the truth. I will fight your enemy with you." The Messenger of God said to him, "Praise be to God who guided you to Islam." He said, "O Messenger of God, what deed is most desirable to God?" The Prophet replied, "Prayer as soon as it is time." He said: After that, whenever the sun declined and entered the time of ʿAṣar, and whenever it set, the man did not delay prayer for a later time.

He said: When they alighted in Baqʿāʾ, a spy from the polytheists was captured. They said to him, "What is behind you? Where are the people?" He replied, "I have no information about them." Hishām b. Saʿd related to me from Yaʿqūb, from Zayd b. Ṭalḥa, who said: ʿUmar b. al-Khaṭṭāb said, "Tell the truth, or I will strike off your head." He replied, "I am a man from the Balmuṣṭaliq. I left al-Ḥārith b. Abī Ḍirār who has collected a group against you, and many people have rallied to him. He sent me to you to bring him information about you and whether you were marching from Medina." ʿUmar brought that spy to the Messenger of God and informed him of the news. The Messenger of God called him and offered him Islam. But he refused, saying, "I will not follow your religion until I see what my people do. If they enter your religion I will be one of them, and if they affirm their religion I will be a man among them." ʿUmar said, "O Messenger of God, I will cut off his head." The Messenger of God brought him, and he cut off his head. This news reached the Balmuṣṭaliq.

Juwayriyya, daughter of al-Ḥārith used to say, after she converted to Islam: News of his execution and the march of the Messenger of God reached us before the Prophet arrived before us, and my father and those with him were hollow with a great fear. Those who had gathered to them from unnamed tribes of the Bedouin left them. No one but they remained.

[Page 407] The Messenger of God reached al-Muraysīʿ. He alighted at the water, where a tent of leather was struck up for him. His wives ʿĀʾisha and Umm Salama were with him. They gathered at the water and prepared for battle. The Messenger of God arranged his companions in rows, handed the banner of the Muhājirūn to Abū Bakr, and the banner of the Anṣār to Saʿd b. ʿUbāda. Some say the banner of the Muhājirūn was with ʿAmmār b. Yāsir. Then the Prophet commanded ʿUmar b. al-Khaṭṭāb to call out to the people, "Say, there is no God but Allāh, and protect your souls and your property." ʿUmar did so, but they refused.

The first to aim an arrow was a man from among them, and the Muslims aimed arrows for a while. Then, the Messenger of God commanded his companions to attack. They attacked as a single man and not a man among them escaped. Ten of them were killed and the rest of them were taken captive. The Messenger of God captured men women and children. Cattle and sheep were plundered. Only one man was killed from the Muslims.

Abū Qatāda used to relate saying: The flag of the polytheists was carried by Ṣafwān Dhū l-Shuqr. I was not prepared when I attacked him and it was victory. The battle cry was: O Manṣūr, kill, kill! Ibn ʿUmar used to relate that when the Prophet attacked the Banū Muṣṭaliq they were unaware. Their cattle were quenching their thirst at the water when he killed their warriors and captured their children. The first tradition is confirmed with us.

Hāshim b. Ḍubāba had set out in search of the enemy. He returned with the wind [Page 408] and the swirl of dust. He encountered a man from the band of ʿUbāda b. al-Ṣāmit, named Aws, and thinking that he was from the polytheists, attacked and killed him. He learned later that he was a Muslim. The Messenger of God commanded that he set out his blood money. Others say that a man from the Banū ʿAmr b. ʿAwf killed him. His brother, Miqyas, arrived before the Prophet who ordered that the blood money be paid to him. Miqyas took it, and then attacked the killer of his brother and killed him. Then he set out to the Quraysh, an apostate. He used to say:

> It eased the soul that had stayed the night in the lowland.
> The blood of his neck veins dying his garments.
> I avenged Fihr on him and laid his blood-wit
> On the Chiefs of the Banū Najjār, the Lords of Fāriʿ.
> I gave free vent to my vengeance
> And was the first to return to the idols.

I heard ʿAbd al-Raḥmān say, "My father recited it." The Messenger of God permitted his killing, and Numayla killed him at the Conquest.

Saʿīd b. ʿAbdullah b. Abī l-Abyaḍ, from his father from his grandmother, who was the slave of Juwayrīya, informed me saying: I heard Juwayriyya, daughter of al-Ḥārith, say, "The Messenger of God came to us while we were at al-Muraysīʿ and I heard my father say, 'He came to us with what we had no power over.' " She said: I saw so many people and horses that I have no words to describe it. When I converted to Islam the Messenger of God married me and we returned, and I began to look at the Muslims, and they were not as I thought. I learned that it was the fear that God had thrown [Page 409] in the hearts of the polytheists. A man among them who had converted and practiced the best Islam used to say: Surely we saw white men on piebald horses, and we never saw them before or after.

Ibn Abī Sabra related to me from al-Ḥārith b. al-Fuḍayl saying: Ibn Masʿūd b. Hunayda related to me from his father saying: I met the Messenger of God in Baqʿāʾ, and he said, "Where are you going?" And Hunayda said, "I come to greet you, for Abū Tamīm has set me on the correct path." He said, "May God bless you. Where did you leave your people?" He said, "I left them in a place known as al-Khadhawāt. The people are good. They desired Islam and it spread around us." The Messenger of God said, "Praise God who guided them!" Then Masʿūd said, "O Messenger of God, yesterday I think I met a man from ʿAbd al-Qays and I invited him to Islam and I awakened in him a desire for Islam." The Messenger of God replied, "Surely his conversion through your hands is better for you than whatever he could have had under the sun." Then he said, "Stay with us until we meet our enemy, for indeed I hope that God will grant us their property as spoil."

He said: I went with the Messenger of God when God plundered their property and their children for him. The Messenger of God gave me a portion of camels and a portion of sheep. I said, "O Messenger of God, how can I drive the camels while I hold the sheep? Make it either all sheep or all camels." The Messenger of God smiled and said, "Which of that is more desirable to you?" I replied, "I will take the camels." He said: He gave him ten camels. He said: I was given them. It was said to him, "Was it from the property or the fifth?" He said: And by God, I did not know. I returned to my people, and by God, we continue to prosper from it to this day of ours.

Abū Bakr b. ʿAbdullah b. Abī Sabra related to me from Abū Bakr b. ʿAbdullah b. [Page 410] Abī Jahm, saying: The Messenger of God ordered that the captives be bound and put aside, and he employed Burayda b. al-Ḥuṣayb over them. He ordered that what was found in their saddles of old clothes and weapons be collected, and the cattle and sheep be driven, and he employed his *mawlā*, Shuqrān, over them. He gathered the women and children aside and appointed Maḥmiya b. Jazʿa al-Zubaydī over the apportioning—of the fifth and the portions of the Muslims. The Messenger of God took out a fifth of all the plunder, and Mahmiyya administered it.

Muḥammad b. ʿAbdullah from al-Zuhrī from ʿUrwa b. al-Zubayr, and ʿAbdullah b. ʿAbdullah b. al-Ḥārith b. Nawfal both related to me saying: The Messenger of God appointed Maḥmiyya b. Jazʿa al-Zubaydī over the fifths apportioned by the Muslims. The two men said: He collected the fifths and separated the alms (*ṣadaqa*). The people who received the *faʾi* [plunder taken without force] were kept away from the *ṣadaqa*, and the people of *ṣadaqa* were kept from the *faʾi*. The orphans, the poor, and the weak were given portions from the *ṣadaqa*. When an orphan attained puberty he was transferred to the *fāʾi* and moved out of the *ṣadaqa*, and *jihād* was made incumbent upon him. If he disliked *jihād* and refused it, he was not given anything from the *ṣadaqa*. He became free to earn for himself.

The Messenger of God did not refuse one who asked. Two men came to him and asked him about the apportioning of the fifth. He said, "If you wish I will give you from it, but there is no portion in it for the rich or for those with the ability to be gainfully employed." The two men said: The prisoners were apportioned and dispersed into the hands of men. The old clothes were apportioned and the cattle and sheep were apportioned. One camel equaled ten sheep. The old clothes were sold among those who desired it. The horse was apportioned two portions and its master one. There were two thousand camels and five thousand sheep. The prisoners were two hundred of the people of the House. Juwayriyya, the daughter of al-Ḥārith, arrived as the portion of Thābit b. Qays and his cousin. [Page 411] Thābit contracted to release her for nine ounces of gold.

ʿAbdullah b. Yazīd b. Qusayṭ related to me from his father from Thawbān, from ʿĀʾisha. She said: Juwayriya was a beautiful woman, and as soon as one saw her one was captivated by her. While the Prophet was with me at the water, she came before him and asked about her contract of release. ʿĀʾisha said: By God, as soon as I saw her, I hated her coming to the Prophet, for I knew he would see her as I did. Juwayriya said, "O Messenger of God, indeed I am a Muslim woman and I witness that there is no God but Allah and that you are the Messenger of God. I am Juwayriya, daughter of al-Ḥārith b. Abī Ḍirār, lord of his people. We were captured from the affair that you know of, and I fell in the portion of Thābit b. Qays b. Shammās and his cousin. He released me from his cousin with dates of his from Medina. Thābit wrote a document concerning me over which I have no power. Nothing forced me to it except that I hoped in you, may peace be upon you. So help me with this contract." The Messenger of God said, "Or better than that?" She said, "What is it, O Messenger of God?" He replied, "I will pay for your contract and I will marry you." She said, "Yes, O Messenger of God, I agree." The Messenger of God sent for Thābit and asked for her from him. Thābit said, "By my father and my mother, she is yours." The Messenger of God paid her contract, released her and married her. The news went out to the people. Men of the Banū Muṣṭaliq had been apportioned and become property, and their women taken sexually. They now said, "These are the relatives of the Prophet by marriage!" They set free the prisoners they held. ʿĀʾisha said, "A hundred from her family were released with the marriage of the Messenger of God to her. I do not know a woman who was a greater blessing for her people than her."

Ḥizām b. Hishām related to me from his father, who said: Juwayriya said, "Before the arrival of the Prophet, I dreamed [Page 412] for three nights that the moon came from Yathrib and fell into my lap, and I hated to inform anyone, until the Prophet arrived and we were captured, for I hoped for the dream. By God, when he manumitted me and married me, I did not speak to him about my people until the Muslims sent them back to us. I did not know until a girl from the daughters of my uncle informed me of it, and I praised God." Some say: Indeed the Messenger of God made her bridal contract the release of every prisoner from the Banū Muṣṭaliq, while others say that he made her bridal contract the release of forty of her people.

Ibn Abī Sabra related to me from ʿUmāra b. Ghaziyya that: Some of the prisoners were favored by the Messenger of God and released without a ransom, while others were ransomed. And that was after the prisoners came into the hands of men. The women and children were ransomed with six camels. They had arrived in Medina with some prisoners, and the families of the prisoners came and ransomed them. There did not remain a woman from the Banū Muṣṭaliq, but she returned to her people. This tradition is confirmed.

ʿUmar b. ʿUthmān related to me from ʿAbd al-Malik b. ʿUbayd from ʿAbd al-Raḥmān b. Saʿīd b. Yarbūʿ, from ʿImrān b. Ḥuṣayn, who said: The party arrived in Medina and the prisoners were ransomed after they were apportioned. ʿAbdullah b. Abī l-Abyaḍ, who is knowledgeable in their traditions, related to me from his grandmother, who was the slave (*mawlat*) of Juwayriyya, that: I heard Juwayriyya say, "My father ransomed me from Thābit b. Qays b. Shammās with the ransom of a woman among the prisoners. Then the Prophet asked my father for my hand, and my father gave me in marriage." She said: Her name was Barra but the Prophet named her Juwayriyya for he hated to say that he had set out from the house of Barra. Ibn Wāqid said: The tradition of ʿĀʾisha is confirmed with us, that the Messenger of God paid her contract and freed her and married her.

[Page 413] Isḥāq b. Yaḥyā informed me from al-Zuhrī from Mālik b. Aws b. al-Ḥadathān, from ʿUmar b. al-Khaṭṭāb that the Messenger of God apportioned for Juwayriyya just as he apportioned for his wives, and he made her wear the *ḥijāb*. Al-Ḍaḥḥāk b. ʿUthmān related to me from Muḥammad b. Yaḥyā b. Ḥibbān from Abū Muḥayrīr and Abū Ḍamra from Abū Saʿīd al-Khudrī, who said: We set out with the Messenger of God for the raid of the Banū Muṣṭaliq and we captured prisoners. With us was a desire for women strengthened by our bachelorhood, but we preferred the ransom, so we practiced safe sex, and we said "We will keep the women from impregnation." The Messenger of God was in our midst before we asked him about that. We asked him and he replied, "I do not recommend it. Indeed, a creation that God intended will be to the Day of Judgment."

Abū Saʿīd used to say: Their party arrived upon us and ransomed the children and women. They returned with them to their land. Among the prisoners who were given the choice, all chose to return. Ḍaḥḥāk said: I related this tradition to Abū l-Naḍr and he said: Abū Salama b. ʿAbd al-Raḥmān informed me from Abū Saʿīd al-Khudrī, who said: As I set out to sell a slave girl of mine in the market, one of the Jews said, "O Abū Saʿīd, perhaps you desire to sell her because an infant from you is in her womb!" I said, "No, indeed I had safe sex with her." He replied, "That is akin to a small killing." He said: I came to the Prophet and informed him of that, and he said, "The Jew lies! The Jew lies!"

[VOLUME 2 Page 415] THE AFFAIR OF IBN UBAYY

They said: While the Muslims were at the waters of al-Muraysīʿ and the fighting had stopped, there was little water. Indeed the bucket came out half filled. Sinān b. Wabr al-Juhannī, an ally of the Banū Sālim, approached, and with him were youths from the Banū Sālim coming for water. At the water they found all of the soldiers from the Muhājirūn and the Anṣār. Now, Jahjā b. Saʿīd al-Ghifārī was a hired hand of ʿUmar b. al-Khaṭṭāb, and Sinān let down his bucket at the same time that Jahjā let his bucket down. Jahjā was the water carrier standing closest to Sinān b. Wabar, and the bucket of Sinān was mistaken for the bucket of Jahjā. One of the two buckets was drawn out, and it was the bucket of Sinān b. Wabar. Sinān said: I said, "My bucket!" But Jahjā said, "By God, it is no one's bucket but mine."

They argued about it until Jahjā raised his hand and struck Sinān, and blood flowed. Sinān called out, "O family of the Khazraj," and the men were roused. Sinān said: Jahjā fled, and I could not reach him, nor could my companions. Then, Jahjā began to call out in the camp, "O families of the Quraysh! O families of Kināna!" and the Quraysh approached him swiftly. Sinān said: When I saw that, I called out to the Anṣār. He said: The Aws and Khazraj approached and drew their weapons, until I feared there would be a great civil war. Then the people from the Muhājirūn came to me saying, "Leave your right!"

Sinān said: When Jahjā struck me, he did not injure me. Sinān said: I tried but I could not go against my confederates in forgiveness for the words of the Muhājirūn. My people refused to [Page 416] forgive except with the command of the Messenger of God, or that I retaliate against Jahjā. Then the Muhājirūn spoke to my confederates, and they spoke to ʿUbāda b. al-Ṣāmit and others among my confederates, and my confederates spoke to me, and I left it, and did not raise it before the Messenger of God.

Ibn Ubayy was seated with ten of the Munāfiqūn: Ibn Ubayy, Mālik, Dāʿis, Suwayd, Aws b. Qayẓī, Muʿattib b. Qushayr, Zayd b. al-Luṣayt, and ʿAbdullah b. Nabtal; and with the people was Zayd b. Arqam, a lad who had not reached maturity, or had just reached it. When the shout of Jahjā, "O family of the Quraysh!" reached him, Ibn Ubayy became very angry, which was apparent from his words. It was heard that he said, "By God, I have not seen such a day of humiliation! By God, I was reluctant for this direction, but my people over-ruled me! They did it, they shunned us and they surpassed us in our land, and they denied us our favors. By God, our situation now with those rags of Quraysh is as the sayer said, 'Fatten your dog and it will eat you.' By God, I thought I would be dead before I heard such shouting as the shout of Jahjā, and I present doing nothing; and there can be no anger about that from me! By God, when we return to Medina the stronger will drive out the weaker!" Then he approached those who attended from his people and said, "This is what you have done to yourselves. You permitted them to enter your land, and they have entered your homes. You shared your property with them until they have become rich. Had you kept it in your hands they would have gone elsewhere. They will not be satisfied with what you do until you make yourselves a target for death. You will be killed instead of him, and you will die [Page 417] and your children will become orphans, and you will decrease and they will increase."

Zayd b. Arqam conveyed this news, all of it, to the Messenger of God. He found him with a group of his companions from the Muhājirūn and the Anṣār—Abū Bakr, ʿUthmān, Saʿd, Muḥammad b. Maslama, Aws b. Khawlī, and ʿAbbād b. Bishr, and he informed him of the news. The Messenger of God hated the news and his face changed. Then he said, "O lad, perhaps you are angry with him!" He said, "No, by God, indeed I heard it from him." He said, "Perhaps it was a mistake that you heard!" He replied, "No, O Prophet of God!"

What Ibn Ubayy said spread in the camp, and there was no news with the people but what Ibn Ubayy said. A group of the Anṣār began to blame the lad, saying, "You attend upon the master of your people, and you say what he did not say against him. You have harmed and cut off the relationship." Zayd said, "By God, surely I heard him!" He said, "By God, there was not a single man with the Khazraj that I preferred to ʿAbdullah b. Ubayy. By God, if I had heard these words from my father I would have related them to the Messenger of God. Indeed I hope that it will be revealed by God to his Prophet, that they may learn whether I am a liar or not, or that Muḥammad will see the truth of my words." And Zayd began to say, "O God, reveal to Your Prophet the truth of my news."

Someone said, "O Messenger of God, command ʿAbbād b. Bishr to bring you his head." The Messenger of God detested these words. Others said that he said, "Ask Muḥammad b. Maslama to bring you his head." The Prophet said, while turning away from him, "People will not say that Muḥammad kills his companions."

A group of the Anṣār heard the words of the Prophet and his answer to the lad. They came to Ibn Ubayy and informed him. Aws b. Khawlī said, "O Abū l-Ḥubāb, "If you said it, [Page 418] inform the Prophet and he will forgive you. Do not disclaim it, for your falsehood will be revealed. But if you did not say it, come to the Messenger of God, and explain it to him, and swear to the Messenger of God about what you said." Ibn Ubayy swore by God most high that he did not say that thing. Then Ibn Ubayy came to the Messenger of God, and the Messenger of God said, "O Ibn Ubayy, if the words passed from you, ask for forgiveness." He swore repeatedly, "By God, I did not say what Zayd said. I did not speak about it." And Ibn Ubayy was a noble among his people, and there were those who believed him and those who had a low opinion of him.

Hishām b. Saʿd related to me from Zayd b. Aslam, from his father from ʿUmar b. al-Khaṭṭāb, who said: When there was from the words of Ibn Ubayy what there was, the Messenger of God hastened the journey, and I hastened with him. There was a workman with me and I employed him to stay with my horse. He detained me and I stopped for him on the road and waited until he arrived, and when he came and saw the anger that was in me, he felt concerned that I may quarrel with him. He said, "O man, take it easy." Indeed, there was an affair that was more extensive, and he related to me about the words of Ibn Ubayy. ʿUmar said: I approached until I came to the Messenger of God. He was in the shade of a tree and with him was a young black slave who was palpating his back. I said, "O Messenger of God, do you complain about your back?" He replied, "I was jostled by my camel tonight." I said, "O Messenger of God, permit me to cut off the head of Ibn Ubayy for his words." The Messenger of God said, "And you would do it?" He said, "Yes; By Him who sent you with the truth!" The Messenger of God said, "Many noses tremble for him in Yathrib. If I command them to kill him they will kill him." I said, "O Messenger of God, command Muḥammad b. Maslama to kill him." He said, "The people will not say that Muḥammad kills his companions." He said: So I said, "Then order the people to travel." He said, "Yes," and he called the people to travel.

[Page 419] It was said that the people of the camp did not know other than that the

Messenger of God had got up on his camel al-Qaṣwāʾ. They were in days of great heat, and generally, the Prophet did not go out until it cooled down, but when the news of Ibn Ubayy came to him, he departed within the hour. Saʿd b. ʿUbāda was the first of those who met him, and he said, "Greetings to you, O Prophet," and the Messenger of God replied, "And peace be with you." He said, "O Messenger of God, you depart at a shocking hour, when you usually do not leave." Others said that Usayd b. Ḥuḍayr met him. Ibn Wāqid said, and this is confirmed with us, he said, "O Messenger of God, you set out at a bad hour when you are usually not able to depart." The Messenger of God replied, "And did you not hear what your companion said?" He said, "Which Companion, O Messenger of God?" He replied, "Ibn Ubayy. He believes that if he returns to Medina, the stronger will cast out the weaker!" He said, "You, O Messenger of God, will cast him out if you wish, for he is the weaker, and you, the stronger. The power is with God, you and the believers." Then he said, "O Messenger of God, be gentle with him, for by God, surely God brought you when his people were preparing to crown him, and there does not remain except a single gem with Joshuʿa the Jew, who was accomplished in them. He bargained hard with them since he knew their need for it. But God brought you in the midst of this, and he sees only that you have deprived him of his kingship."

He said: Meanwhile, the Prophet was going about his day, riding his beast, and Zayd b. Arqam did as the Prophet did, riding his beast and keeping the Prophet in view as he journeyed. The Messenger of God urged his camel, going at a quick pace, when all of a sudden a revelation came upon him. Zayd b. Arqam said: Before long, I saw the Messenger of God have a severe fit. His forehead was sweating, and his hand was heavy on his camel. No sooner was it revealed, than I knew that the Messenger of God had been inspired, and I hoped that it would reveal to him [Page 420] the honesty of my news. Zayd b. Arqam said: As soon as the Prophet was released from the fit, he took my ear—and I was on my beast and I was lifted from my seat—and directed it to the heavens, saying, "Your ear is perfect, lad. God confirms your news." God revealed a chapter about Ibn Ubayy, alone, from beginning to end: *When the Hypocrites come to you* . . . (Q. 63:1).

ʿUbaydallah b. al-Hurayr related to me from his father from Rāfiʿ b. Khadīj, who said: I heard ʿUbāda b. Ṣāmit saying, at that time, to Ibn Ubayy, before the Qurʾān was revealed about him, "Come to the Messenger of God, and he will ask for your forgiveness." He said: I saw him turn away his head uncaringly. ʿUbada says, "By God, a Qurʾān will be revealed about the turning of your head with which worship will be performed."

Yūnus b. Muḥammad al-Ẓafarī related to me from his father from ʿUbāda b. al-Walīd b. ʿUbāda al-Ṣāmit saying, ʿUbāda b. al-Ṣāmit passed by ʿAbdullah b. Ubayy, in the same evening that the Prophet went from al-Muraysīʿ, after the chapter on the Munafiqūn was revealed, and he did not greet him. Then Aws b. Khawlī passed by him and he did not greet him. Ibn Ubayy said, "Indeed this is an affair you have conspired about together." They returned to him and blamed him and censured him about what he did, and about what the Qurʾān revealed of the falseness of his information, and Aws b. Khawlī began to say: "I will never say in defense that you have not lied until I know that you have left your ways and turned to God. Indeed, we approached Zayd b. Arqam and blamed him saying, 'You lie about a man from your people.' Until the Qurʾān revealed the truth of Zayd's news and the falseness of yours." Ibn Ubayy said repeatedly, "I will not do it again!"

The words of ʿUmar b. al-Khaṭṭāb to the Messenger of God, "Command Muḥammad

b. Maslama to bring you his head," reached his son, ʿAbdullah b. ʿAbdullah b. Ubayy, so he came to the Messenger of God [Page 421] and said, "If you desire to kill my father for what has reached you, command me, for by God, I could bring you his head before you get up from this seat of yours. By God, the Khazraj know that there is not a man more dutiful to his father than I. Indeed, since thus and thus of time, he does not eat nor drink except by my hand. I fear, O Messenger of God, that you will command another to kill him and my soul will not permit me to look at the murderer of my father walk with the people, and I will kill him, and I will enter the fire. Your kindness is most pleasing, and your forgiveness most wise." The Messenger of God replied, "O ʿAbdullah, I do not desire to kill him, nor will I command you to do so. Let us deal kindly with his companionship when he is among us." ʿAbdullah said, "O Messenger of God, indeed this town had gathered to crown my father when God brought you, and God put him down and He raised us through you. With him is a group who go around him remembering things that God has overpowered." He said: When ʿAbdullah turned from the place of the Prophet, he knew that the Messenger of God had left him and had not ordered him to kill his father.

Indeed, the world is full of events waiting to happen.
And from the most amazing of the traditions is what ʿUmar said
Advising him who possessed the revelation thus.
But he did not seek his advice
About that which one shaves the hair
If there was to Khaṭṭāb a sin like his sin
And I said of him what he said about my father, such evil,
He would growl.
The day when he said: Send Muḥammad to kill him,
Miserable, by your life, was the command.
I said: Messenger of God, if you act,
I will be sufficient for you, against Abdullah,
In the wink of an eye,
A helpful hand and generous soul helped me
And a heart that is harder than stone in times of distress.
In it is what there is and in the other, deficiency,
My eye regarding the other is blinded.
Then he added, may a man not kill, in obedience,
His father, while the Mudar are enraged by it.

[Page 422] Ismāʿīl b. Muṣʿab b. Ismāʿīl b. Zayd b. Thābit recited it to me, saying: I took it from the book, and Ibrāhīm b. Jaʿfar b. Maḥmūd from Muḥammad b. Maslama. ʿUbaydullah b. al-Hurayr related to me from his father, from Rāfiʿ b. Khadīj saying: We left al-Muraysīʿ before noon and we were tired of traveling day and night, for a man did not kneel among us except for a need, or to pray his prayers. The Messenger of God spurred his camel with the whip on the tender part of its belly until it was dawn. We continued until it was midday or nearly. The people stopped speaking of Ibn Ubayy and what happened to him when they were overtaken by sleeplessness and tiredness in the march. When they alighted, the words of Ibn Ubayy were no longer heard. Indeed, the Messenger of God had hastened with the people only to make them stop talking of Ibn Ubayy.

As soon as they alighted and felt the ground, they fell asleep. Then the Messenger of God traveled in the afternoon with the people as it cooled, and alighted the next morning at the water named Baqʿā', above al-Naqīʿ. The people dispatched their animals until a strong wind took them, and the people became concerned about it. They asked the Messenger of God about it. They feared that ʿUyayna b. Ḥiṣn had come to Medina in their absence. They said, "This wind did not flare up except from an incident. Indeed in Medina are our descendants and our youth." And there was between the Messenger of God and ʿUyayna an appointed time. That was when it elapsed and a strong fear entered them. Their fear reached the Messenger of God. He said "There will not be any misery to you because of it. There is not a breach in Medina but an angel is watching over it. An enemy will not enter Medina until you arrive. But a great hypocrite has died [Page 423] in Medina. It is for this that the wind storms. His death was a great irritation to the Hypocrites." It was Zayd b. Rifāʿa b. al-Tābūt who died that day.

Khārija b. al-Ḥārith related to me from ʿAbbās b. Sahl from Jābir b. ʿAbdullah saying: The wind was at that time stronger than ever until the sun set, and it became calm at the end of the day. Jābir said: When I arrived, I asked before I entered my house, "Who died?" They said, "Zayd b. Rifāʿa b. al-Tābūt." The people of Medina mentioned that they too had experienced the strong wind until when the enemy of God was buried, the wind calmed.

ʿAbd al-Hamīd b. Jaʿfar related to me from his father, that ʿUbāda b. al-Ṣāmit said to Ibn Ubayy at that time, "Abū Ḥubāb, your friend has died!" He said, "Which of my friends?" He replied, "The one whose death is an opening for Islam and its people." He said, "Who?" He answered, "Zayd b. Rifāʿa b. al-Tābūt." He said, "Woe unto me, he was thus and thus," and he began remembering him. I said, "You cling to a broken tail." He said, "Who informed you about his death, O Abū Walīd." I said, "The Messenger of God informed us that he just died." He said: Ibn Ubayy was silenced and he turned dejected and saddened. They said: At the end of the day the wind was calm and the people gathered their animals.

ʿAbd al-Ḥamīd b. Jaʿfar related to me from Ibn Rūmān, and Muḥammad b. Ṣāliḥ from ʿAsim b. Umar b. Qatāda, who said: The camel of the Messenger of God, al-Qaswā' was lost from the midst of camels. The Muslims began to look for it in every direction. Zayd b. al-Luṣayt—and he was a hypocrite with the company of people from al-Anṣār, including ʿAbbād b. Bishr b. Waqash, Salama b. Salāma b. Waqash, and Usayd b. Ḥuḍayr—said, "Where are those people going in every direction?" They said, "Seeking the camel of the Messenger of God [Page 424] which is lost." He said, "Will not God inform him of the place of his camel?" The people disapproved of that from him. They said, "May God fight you, O enemy of God, you are being hypocritical!"

Then Usayd b. Ḥuḍayr approached him and said, "By God, if I did not know that the Messenger of God would not approve of it, I would pierce your testicles with my spear, O enemy of God. Why did you set out with us while this was in your heart?" He replied, "I set out to seek the profit of the world. By my life, indeed Muḥammad informs us about greater affairs than a camel. He informs us about the affairs of the heavens." They pounced upon him together and said, "By God, you will never escape from this, and we will never share the same roof. If we knew what was in your heart we would not have associated with you for a moment of the day." Zayd fled, defeated fearing that they would attack him, and the Muslims threw away his possessions. He came to the Messenger of God and sat with him, a fugitive from his companions seeking refuge with him.

News of what he said came to the Messenger of God from the heavens. The Messenger of God said, as the hypocrite listened, "Indeed a man from the Hypocrites laughs at the misfortune that the camel of the Messenger of God is lost. He said, 'Will not God inform him of its place? By my life, indeed Muḥammad informs us of more than the affair of a camel!' But only God knows the hidden. Indeed God most high has informed me about its place. It is in this gorge right in front of you. Its rope is attached to a tree, so go to it." They went and brought it from where the Prophet said it was. When the hypocrite saw it, he went swiftly to his companions who were with him, and lo and behold his saddle and possessions had been cast out, and they were seated, and not a man had left his seat. They said to him, when he came close, "Do not come near us!" He said, "I would speak to you!" And he drew close and said, "I implore you, by God, did one of you go to Muḥammad and inform him of what I said?" They said, "No, by God, we did not leave this seat of ours." He said, "Indeed, I found my words with the people and I did not speak of it, but the Messenger of God spoke about it," and he informed them about what the Messenger of God said. [Page 425] "Indeed, his camel was brought. Surely, I had doubts about the affair of Muḥammad, but I witness that Muḥammad is the Messenger of God! Indeed, I did not accept Islam except today." They said to him, "Go to the Messenger of God and he will ask forgiveness for you." Some said that he continued to be false until he died, and he did something similar during the raid of Tabūk.

Ibn Abī Sabra related to me from Shuʿayb b. Shaddād saying that when the Messenger of God passed by Naqīʿ departing from al-Muraysīʿ, he saw the abundance, the pasture and the many streams flowing down. He was informed of the healthy foods and their purity. He asked about water and it was said, "O Messenger of God, when summer comes the water decreases and the streams are gone." The Messenger of God ordered Ḥāṭib b. Abī Baltaʿa to dig a well, and he commanded that the water that rose in it be protected. He employed Bilāl b. al-Ḥārith al-Muzannī over it. Bilāl said, "O Messenger of God, what is the extent that I must protect?" He replied, "Send a man with a loud voice at the break of dawn to this mountain—referring to the Mount Muqmil—and let the distance to which his voice carries be the extent that shall be preserved for the horses of the Muslims and the camels on which they raid." Bilāl said: "O Messenger of God, do you not consider the roving cattle of the Muslims?" He replied, "Do not permit them." Then I said: "O Messenger of God, do you consider that the weak men and women who have small cattle would be weakened from moving?" He said, "Permit them to graze." And when it was the caliphate of Abū Bakr he protected it as the Prophet had [Page 426] protected it, while ʿUmar increased the extent for the horses and ʿUthmān protected it as well.

At that time the Prophet held a race for the horses and camels. Qaṣwāʾ preceded the camels. And the Prophet's horse won—he had two horses with him, Lizāz, and another named al-Ẓarīb—and on that day the horse that won was Zarīb, and its driver was Abū Usayd al-Sāʿidī, while Bilāl rode his camel.

THE RECORD OF ʿĀʾISHA, AND THE COMPANIONS OF THE LIE

Yaʿqūb b. Yaḥyā b. ʿAbbād related to me from ʿĪsā b. Maʿmar from ʿAbbād b. ʿAbdullah b. al-Zubayr saying: I said to ʿĀʾisha "Tell us your version of the raid of al-Muraysīʿ."

She said, "O son of my brother, when the Messenger of God used to set out on a journey, he used to cast lots between his wives and she whose portion was drawn went out with him, though he did not like to be separated from me whether on a journey or not. When he desired to raid al-Muraysīʿ he cast lots between us and my portion and the portion of Umm Salama were pulled out, so we went with him, and God granted him as plunder their property and their people. Then we left, returning, and the Prophet who had no water with him, alighted at a place, that had no water. A chain of mine fell from my neck, so I informed the Messenger of God, and he stopped with the people until morning. The people raised a hue and cry and said, "ʿĀʾisha kept us!" The people came to Abū Bakr and said, "Did you not see what ʿĀʾisha did? She held back the Messenger of God, and the people were not at the water, nor did they have water with them." Abū Bakr became dejected about that and he came to me angrily and said, "Do you not think of what you do to the people? You hold back [Page 427] the Messenger of God and the people from water while they have no water with them." ʿĀʾisha said: He rebuked me strongly, and he began to hurt me on my hip with his hand. What stopped me from agitating was the place of the Prophet; his head was on my thigh, and he was sleeping. Usayd b. Ḥuḍayr said, "By God, indeed I hope that permission will be revealed to us," when the verse of *tayammum* (Q. 4:43), was revealed. The Messenger of God said, "Those who were before you were not permitted to pray except in churches and synagogues. To me the clean earth is permitted whenever prayer time catches up with me." Usayd b. Ḥuḍayr said, "It is not the first of your blessings, O family of Abū Bakr." She said: And Usayd was a good man with the house of the great Aws.

Then we went with the camp until, lo and behold, we alighted at a place mild, good, and possessing the Arāka (a tree whose roots are used for cleaning teeth). The Prophet said, "O ʿĀʾisha would you like to run a race?" I said, "Yes." I girded up my garment and the Messenger of God did that also, and then we raced and he went ahead of me. He said, "This is in return for the race in which you beat me." He had come to the place of my father and I had something with me. He said, "Give it to me." I had refused, and run ahead, and he followed in my tracks, but I beat him. This raid took place after the *hijāb* was established.

She said: The women at that time were of lighter weight for they used to eat only what was sufficient, and refrained from meat for fear of becoming heavy. There were two men on foot who led my camel. One of them was a freedman of the Messenger of God named Abū Mawhiba. He was a good man, and he used to lead my camel.

When I was seated in the hawda, he would come and carry the hawda and place it on the camel, fix it with ropes and dispatch it. Taking the reins of the camel, he then led the camel that carried me. [Page 428] Umm Salama was also led in this manner. We were kept at the edge of the people, and those who drew near us were driven away. Sometimes the Messenger of God rode on my side and sometimes he rode on Umm Salama's side. When we drew near Medina we alighted and stopped for some nights. Then the Prophet set out at nightfall, and he announced to the people about the departure, and the camp departed.

I had gone for a "need," walking past the camp, wearing the necklace of Ẓafār beads, which was given to me by my mother when she handed me in marriage to the Messenger of God. When I finished my "need" it had slipped from my neck without my knowledge. When I returned to the stop I touched my neck and could not find it. The camp was already moving, except for a few camels, but I thought that even if I stayed a month the camel drivers would not send away my camel until I was in my hawda. So I went back to search for the necklace and found it where I thought it would be. But finding the necklace had kept me, and the two men had come and driven the camel that carried my hawda, thinking that I was in it. They had placed the hawda on the camel having no doubt that I was within. On previous occasions when I was in the hawda, I had not spoken, so they did not suspect anything. They dispatched the camel, leading it by its reins, and departed. I returned to the camp and there was not in it a call or answer and I heard neither voice nor cry. She said: I wrapped myself in my garment and lay down to sleep knowing that indeed I would be missed and returned to. She said: By God, I lay down in my place and sleep overcame me.

Ṣafwān b. Muʿaṭṭil al-Sulamī, that is, al-Dhakwānī was at the rear of the people. He traveled by night and arrived at dawn at my place in the dimness of the dawn. He saw the shadow of a person and came to me. He had seen me before I put on the *ḥijāb*, and though now I was covered, knew and [Page 429] recognized me. I was awakened by his words, "From God do we come and to God do we return," and I concealed my face with my wrap. By God, he did not say a word to me except his words about returning to God, when he knelt his camel. Then he made his hand into a step, looking away from me. I got up on his camel, and he departed leading me until we arrived at the camp at the peak of noon. The camp was disquieted, and the companions of the lie had said what they said. ʿAbdullah b. Ubayy was responsible for most of it. I did not know anything about that but the people became absorbed in the words of the companions of the lie.

After we arrived I did not hesitate to make a strong complaint, but information about the gossip did not reach me. That finally reached my parents, but they did not mention that thing to me, except that I was denied the Messenger of God's gentle attention and graciousness, and I no longer received the gentleness that I knew when I complained. Indeed, he used to come and greet me saying, "How are you?" And when I complained he would be gentle and gracious to me and sit with me.

We were an Arab people and did not have the toilet in our houses. We hated it and were contaminated by it. We used to go out to the toilet between Maghrib and ʿIshāʾ for our needs. I went out at night and with me was Umm Misṭaḥ, covered in a woolen scarf. She tripped on it and said, "May Misṭaḥ stumble!" I said, "Miserable by the life of God is what you say. You say this to a man from the people of Badr?" She responded to my answer saying, "Do you not know what has leaked out about you?" I said, "What are you saying?" She informed me about the talk of the companions of the lie. That destroyed me and I was not able to go for my need. My sickness increased. I could not stop crying night and day. She said: The Messenger of God visited me after that and I said, "Permit me to go to my parents," for I desired to ascertain the news from both of them. He granted permission, and I came to my parents and said to my mother, "May God forgive you. The people talked of what they talked and mentioned what they did, and you said nothing to me of it!" She said, "O my little daughter, take it easy. There was not a beautiful girl married to a man who loves her, but her rival wives gossiped against her, [Page 430] and men do so too." I said, "Praise be to God, the people conversed about all of that?" She said: I cried that night until next morning and my tears did not stop flowing, and I was not refreshed by sleep.

She said: The Messenger of God called ʿAlī and Usāma and asked their advice about leaving his wife. She said: One of the two men had softer words than the other. Usāma said, "O Messenger of God, this is baseless and false. We do not know except good of her. Indeed, Burayra will tell you the truth." ʿAlī said, "God does not restrain you. Women are plentiful, and God will absolve and make agreeable, so separate from her and marry another." She said: When they both departed, the Prophet went to take counsel from Burayra, saying, "O Burayra, what kind of a woman do you know ʿĀʾisha to be?" Burayra replied, "She is better than the best of gold. By God, I know only good of her. By God, O Messenger of God, if she were other than that God most high would have informed you about it. Except that she is a woman who falls asleep over the dough until the sheep come and eat it. I have scolded her more than once about that."

The Messenger of God then asked Zaynab bt. Jaḥsh, and there was not a woman as similar to ʿĀʾisha, in the opinion of the Messenger of God, than her. ʿĀʾisha said of her: I was afraid that she would be destroyed by her jealousy of me. The Prophet said to her, "O Zaynab, what do you know of ʿĀʾisha?" She said, "O Messenger of God, far be it from my hearing and my sight that I should know anything but good of her. By God, I do not speak to her for indeed I moved away from her. I do not say except the truth." ʿĀʾisha said: As for Zaynab, God protected her, while the others were destroyed with those who were destroyed. Then the Messenger of God asked Umm Ayman, and she said, "Far be it from my hearing and my sight that [Page 431] I should ever know or think anything but good of her."

Then the Messenger of God ascended the *minbar*. He praised God and lauded Him. Then he said, "Who will protect me from those who hurt me with my family. They talk about a man, and by God, I do not know anything but good of the man; he has not entered one of my houses except with me. They do not speak the truth about him." Saʿd b. Muʿādh stood up and said, "I will protect you from him, O Messenger of God. If he were from the Aws I would bring you his head. But if he is from among our brothers, the Khazraj, with your command we will depart for your purpose." Then Saʿd b. ʿUbāda stood up, and he was before that a good man but anger had reached him, and that made him a little hypocritical—nothing more than this. He said, "You lie, by the life of God, You will not kill him nor will you be able to kill him. By God, you said these words only because you knew that he is from the Khazraj. If he were from the Aws you would not have spoken thus. You take us with the same resentment that was between us in *jāhiliyya* which God has extinguished." Usayd b. Huḍayr said, "You lie by God, we would surely kill him, despite your reluctance. Indeed you are a hypocrite who defends Hypocrites. By God, if we knew that the Messenger of God desired that in my closest family I would bring him his head before the Messenger of God moves from his place. But I do not know what the Messenger of God desires." Saʿd b. ʿUbāda said, "O family of Aws, you refuse except to use our resentment which was in *jāhiliyya*. By God, there is no need to remember it. Surely you know who was victorious in it. Indeed, God extinguished all of that with Islam." Then, Usayd b. Ḥuḍayr stood up and said, "You saw our stand on the day of Buʿāth!" and they hardened towards each other.

Saʿd b. ʿUbāda was angry and he called out, "O family of the Khazraj!" And all the Khazraj withdrew to [Page 432] Saʿd b. ʿUbāda. And Saʿd b. Muʿādh called out, "O family of the Aws!" and the Aws withdrew to Saʿd b. Muʿādh. Al-Ḥārith b. Ḥazma set out aggressively until he came with the sword saying, "I will strike the head of the hypocrite in his hideout." Usayd b. Ḥuḍayr met him while he was with his group and he said, "Drop it! A weapon is brought only by the command of the Messenger of God. If we knew that the Messenger of God had such a desire or command, then you would not beat us to this." Al-Ḥārith returned, and the Aws and the Khazraj lined up. The

Messenger of God advised the two together to be silent. Then he descended from the pulpit, and calmed and coaxed them until they returned home.

ʿĀ'isha said: The Messenger of God came and visited me and sat with me. He had stayed a month before that, and nothing had been revealed to him about me. She said: The Messenger of God testified to the oneness of God when he sat. Then he said, "As to what happened after, O ʿĀ'isha, thus and thus has reached me. If you are guiltless, God will exonerate you. If you have done something about which the people speak, ask for God's forgiveness. Indeed when the slave recognizes his sin and asks forgiveness from God, God will forgive him."

ʿĀ'isha said: When he finished speaking, my tears stopped until I could not find any. I said to my father, "Answer the Messenger of God." He replied, "By God, I do not know what I will say and what I will reply on your behalf." She said: I said to my mother, "Reply to the Messenger of God on my behalf." She said, "By God, I do not know what to answer on your behalf to the Messenger of God." I was a girl, young in age, and did not read much of the Qur'ān. She said: I said, "Indeed, I, by God, know that you heard this rumor which has come to you and you believe it. If I said to you that I am innocent you will not believe me. But if I acknowledge to you about the affair, and God knows that I am innocent of it, you will believe me. Indeed, [Page 433] and by God, I have not found an example like me except in Jacob (Abū Yusuf) when he said, *Nay, but your minds have made up a tale (that may pass) with you. For me patience is most fitting. To God I turn for help against what you describe* (Q. 12:18)." And, by God, the mentioning of Jacob did not come to me, except for the anger that was in me. Then I withdrew and I lay down on my bed saying, "God knows that I am innocent, and I, by God, trust that God will exonerate me."

Abū Bakr said: "I do not know a family of the house of the Arabs who had the same experience as that which entered upon the family of Abū Bakr. By God, this was not said to us in *jāhiliyya* when we did not worship God or ask anything of him. But it is said to us in Islam!" She said: My father approached me angrily. I wept and I said to myself, "By God, I will not ask for forgiveness of God for what you mention, ever. Woe unto me, I am, by God, more scorned in my heart and too diminished a thing that He should reveal a Qur'ān about me that people would read in their prayers." And yet I hoped that the Messenger of God would see in his sleep something to indicate that God disbelieves them about me for what He knows of my innocence, or that news would reach him. And as for a Qur'ān, no by God, how could I think it!

She said: The Prophet did not leave his seat, nor did anyone go out from the family of the house, when it enveloped him from the command of God, what enveloped him. She said: He was wrapped in his garment and a cushion of leather was placed under his head. As for me when I saw what I saw, by God, I relaxed, for I knew that I was innocent, and that God most high would not be unjust to me. She said: As for my parents, by Him who holds my soul in his hands, until the Prophet was released, both my parents were dying of fear that Allah would reveal the confirmation of the talk of the people.

Then the Messenger of God revealed his face and he was laughing. Indeed perspiration was shed from him like pearls, and he wiped his forehead. The first words he said were: [Page 434] "O ʿĀ'isha, indeed God has revealed your innocence." Fear was dispelled from my parents, and my mother said, "Stand up for the Messenger of God," and I said, "By God, I do not stand except to praise God, and not you." God revealed these verses: *Those who brought forward the lie are a body among yourselves* (Q. 24:11), to the end of the verse.

She said: The Prophet set out to the people happily. He ascended the pulpit and praised God and lauded Him with what was fitting. Then he told them about what was revealed to him of the innocence of ʿĀʾisha. She said: The Messenger of God struck them and established the prescribed boundaries. The most guilty leaders were ʿAbdullah b. Ubayy, Misṭaḥ b. Uthātha and Ḥassān b. Thābit. Abū ʿAbdullah said that it was said that the Messenger of God did not strike them, and this is confirmed with us. Saʿīd b. Jubayr used to say about this verse: Whoever accuses the innocent is cursed by God, in this world and the next. He said: That refers to the mother of the believers especially.

Ibn Abī Ḥabība related to me from Dāwud b. al-Ḥuṣayn from Abū Sufyān from Aflaḥ, the *mawlā* of Abū Ayyūb, that Umm Ayyūb said to Abū Ayyūb, "Do you not hear what the people say about ʿĀʾisha?" He said, "Of course. But that is false. And you, O Umm Ayyūb, would you do that?" She said: "By God, no." He said, "And ʿĀʾisha, by God, is better than you." When the verse came down, it mentioned the people of the lie, and God said: *Why did not the believers men and women, when they heard of the affair, put the best construction on it in their own minds and say: This charge is an obvious lie* (Q. 24:12), referring to Abū Ayyūb and what he said to Umm Ayyūb. Some said: Rather, Ubayy b. Kaʿb said it. Khārija b. ʿAbdullah b. Sulaymān told me from Ibrāhīm b. Yaḥyā from Umm Saʿd bt. Saʿd b. Rabīʿ: Umm al-Ṭufayl said to Ubayy b. Kaʿb, "Do you not hear what the people say about ʿĀʾisha?" He said, "What is that?" She told him what they said. [Page 435] He said, "It is, by God, a lie. Would you do this?" She said, "I seek refuge with God." He said, "She is, by God, better than you." She said, "I testify to this." And this verse was revealed.

They said: The Messenger of God stayed for several days. Then he took Saʿd b. Muʿādh, who was with a group, by the hand, individually, and set out leading him until he came to Saʿd b. ʿUbāda and those who were with him, and they spoke with him for a while. Saʿd b. ʿUbāda offered him some food and the Messenger of God and Saʿd b. Muʿādh and those who were with him took from it. Then the Messenger of God set out and he stayed away for several days. Then the Messenger of God took Saʿd b. ʿUbāda, by the hand, and the group with him, and he departed with him until he entered the house of Saʿd b. Muʿādh. Then they spoke for a while and Saʿd b. Muʿādh offered food, and the Messenger of God and Saʿd b. ʿUbāda and those who were with him took it. Then the Messenger of God set out. The Messenger of God did that in order that the bitterness within their hearts, because of the words that they had both said, may go away.

Maʿmar related to me from al-Zuhrī, from ʿUbaydullah b. ʿAbdullah b. ʿUtba, from Ibn ʿAbbās from ʿAmmār b. Yāsir, who said: We were with the Messenger of God when the soldiers were detained on account of the necklace of ʿĀʾisha, at Dhat al-Jaysh. When dawn rose, or almost, the verse concerning *tayammum* was revealed, and we grabbed the earth with our hands and wiped our hands up to our elbows, above and below. He combined the two prayers during his journey.

ʿAbd al-Ḥamīd b. Jaʿfar related to me from Ibn Rūmān and Muḥammad b. Ṣāliḥ, from ʿĀṣim b. ʿUmar and ʿAbdullah b. Yazīd b. Qusayṭ from his mother, all have related this tradition to me in portions. The source of this tradition is from Ibn Rūmān, ʿĀṣim and others. They said: When Ibn Ubayy said what he said and mentioned Juʿayl b. Surāqa and Jahjā who are among the poor of the Muhājirūn—he said, "Such as these two have increased against my people. [Page 436] We received Muḥammad in the houses of Kināna in its might! By God, indeed Juʿayl was happy to be silent and not speak.

But, today he speaks." Also, the words of Ibn Ubayy, as well, about Ṣafwān b. Muʿaṭṭil and of what he accused him. Ḥassān b. Thābit said:

> Of late, the vagabond-immigrants have become more prosperous and numerous,
> While Ibn al-Furayʿa has become isolated in the land.

When they arrived in Medina, Ṣafwān came to Juʿayl b. Surāqa and said, "Come with us, we will strike Ḥassān, for, by God, he only desires me and you, and indeed, we are closer to the Messenger of God than he." But Juʿayl refused to do so, saying, "I will only do what the Messenger of God commands me to do. And you must not act until the Messenger of God commands you about that." But Ṣafwān refused. He set out with sword drawn until he struck Ḥassān b. Thābit in an assembly of his people. The Anṣār jumped on him and tied him in shackles. Thābit b. Qays b. Shammās was in charge. They captured Ṣafwān in an ugly imprisonment. ʿUmāra b. Ḥazm passed by them and said, "What are you doing? Is this by the command of the Messenger of God and with his approval, or is it from a command of yours?" They said. "The Messenger of God does not know about it." ʿUmāra said, "Indeed, you have been bold. Set him free!" Then he went with him and with Ḥassān to the Messenger of God, driving them. Ḥassān desired to turn back, but ʿUmāra refused until he came to the Messenger of God. Hassān said, "He unsheathed his sword upon me while I was in an assembly of people. Then he struck me in order to kill me. He gave me no alternative except death." The Messenger of God approached Ṣafwān saying, "Why did you strike him and [Page 437] use your weapon against him?" The Messenger of God was angry. Ṣafwān said, "He has hurt me, insulted me, and called me stupid for he envies me my Islam." The Prophet approached Ḥassān and said, "Did you call a people who converted to Islam stupid?" Then the Messenger of God said, "Imprison Ṣafwān, and if Ḥassān dies kill him." So they set out with Ṣafwān.

What Ṣafwān had done reached Saʿd b. ʿUbāda. He set out with his people from the Khazraj until he came to them. He said, "You intended to hurt, and insult with poetry and admonish a man who is one of the companions of the Messenger of God who was angry for what was said of him. Then you take him prisoner in the ugliest way while the Messenger of God is in your midst!" They said, "Indeed the Messenger of God ordered us to take him prisoner. He said, 'If your companion dies kill him for it.'" Saʿd said, "By God, surely, the Messenger of God prefers forgiveness. But the Messenger of God has judged between you rightly. Indeed, the Messenger of God desires that Ṣafwān be left alone. By God, I will not leave until he is set free." Then Ḥassān said, "What was for me by right is for you, Abū Thābit." But his people refused. Then, Qays, his son, became very angry. He said, "How strange you are. I have not seen such a day! Ḥassān has given up his right and you refuse to let him! I did not think that one of the Khazraj would refuse Abū Thābit a command he wishes." The people were embarrassed and set Ṣafwān free and released him from his shackles. Saʿd went with Ṣafwān to his house and dressed him in clothes. Then Ṣafwān set out and entered a mosque to pray. The Messenger of God saw him and said, "Ṣafwān?" They said, "Yes, O Messenger of God." He said, "Who dressed him?" They said, "Saʿd b. ʿUbāda," and he said, "May God dress him in garments of Paradise."

Then Saʿd b. ʿUbāda spoke to Ḥassān b. Thābit saying, "I will not speak to you ever if you will not go to the Messenger of God and say: All rights to me [Page 438] regarding Ṣafwān are for you, O Messenger of God." So Ḥassān approached with his people until he stood before the Prophet and said, "O Messenger of God, every right for me from Ṣafwān b. Muʿaṭṭil is yours." The Messenger of God said, "You have done well and I agree to it." The Messenger of God gave Ḥassān an open (with no trees, etc.) piece of land at Barāḥ called Bayraḥāʾ, including what was around it, and Sīrīn, a Coptic slave girl, and Saʿd b. ʿUbāda gave him a garden of palm trees in excellent condition and very valuable, in exchange for what he dropped of his rights.

Abū ʿAbdullah said: This tradition was related to Ibn Abī Sabra, who said: Sulaymān b. Suḥaym informed me from Nāfiʿ b. Jubayr that Ḥassān b. Thābit imprisoned Ṣafwān. And when Ḥassān was healed, the Messenger of God sent for him and said, "O Ḥassān, be good to him who wounded you." And Ḥassān said, "He is for you, O Messenger of God. The Messenger of God gave him an estate and Sīrīn in exchange. Aflaḥ b. Ḥumayd related to me from his father saying: ʿĀʾisha does not mention Ḥassān except with good words. Indeed, she heard ʿUrwa b. al-Zubayr insult him one day for what he had done and she said, "Do not insult him, son. Is it not he who says: My father and my grand father and my honor is the protection for the honor of Muḥammad among you." Saʿīd b. Abī Zayd al-Anṣārī told me that: One who heard Abū ʿUbayda [Page 439] b. ʿAbdullah b. Zamaʿa al-Asadī related to me that he was informed that Ḥamza b. ʿAbdullah b. ʿUmar heard ʿĀʾisha say: I heard the Messenger of God say, "Ḥassān is a screen between the believers and the Hypocrites. The Hypocrites do not like him and the believers do not hate him." Ḥassān said, praising ʿĀʾisha:

> Chaste and stable, one cannot have misgivings about her, and yet, she becomes the talk the town.
> If I said what was related from me then let not my hands perform their office.

These verses were recited to me by Ibn Abī l-Zinād and Ibn Jaʿfar.

ʿAbdullah b. Jaʿfar b. Muslim related to me from Abū Atīq from Jābir b. ʿAbdullah, who said: I was the companion of ʿAbdullah b. Rawāḥa during the raid of al-Muraysīʿ. We approached until we came to Wādī al-Aqīq in the middle of the night, and the people took a break. We said, "Where is the Messenger of God?" They said, "He sleeps in the front."

ʿAbdullah b. Rawāḥa said to me, "O Jābir, would you agree to go ahead with us and visit our families?" I replied, "O Abū Muḥammad, I do not like to be different from the people. I do not see any one going ahead." Ibn Rawāḥa said, "By God, the Prophet did not forbid us from going ahead." Jābir said: Rather, I would not depart. So he left me and departed to Medina. I watched him on the road and no one was with him. He knocked on his family's door, BalḤārith b. al-Khazraj, and there was a light in the middle of his home and a tall person was with his wife. He thought it was a man. [Page 440] He was shocked, and regretted that he had come ahead. He began to say, "Satan is with the careless," and he burst into the house raising his sword. He had removed it from its sheath desiring to strike them. Then he reflected and remembered. He kicked his wife with his foot, and she awakened and shouted, and she was sleepy. He said, "I am ʿAbdullah, who is this?" She replied, "Rujayla. We heard that you were coming ahead, so I called her to comb my hair, and she spent the night with me."

He spent the night there and when it was morning, he set out at a run to the Messenger of God and met him at the well of Abū ʿUtba. The Messenger of God was walking between Abū Bakr and Bashīr b. Saʿd. The Messenger of God turned and said to Bashīr, "O Abū Nuʿmān." And he said, "What is it?" He said, "Indeed the face of ʿAbdullah informs you that he hated looking up his family."

When ʿAbdullah reached the Messenger of God the Prophet said, "Your news, O Ibn Rawāḥa?" He informed him of how he had gone ahead and what followed. The Messenger of God said, "Do not awaken your wife at night." Jābir said, "That was the first of what the Messenger of God forbade." Jābīr said, "I do not think anything is better than sticking to the camp or staying with the group." Indeed, when we approached from Khaybar, we passed Wādī al-Qurā and reached al-Jurf by night. A herald of the Messenger of God called out, "Do not knock on the doors of your women by night." Jābir said: Two men left, disobeying the Messenger of God, and both saw what they detested.

THE RAID OF AL-KHANDAQ

The Messenger of God gathered an army on Tuesday, the eighth of Dhū l-Qaʿda. They (the Meccans and their allies) besieged him for fifteen days. He turned back on a Wednesday, with seven days remaining in year five AH. [Page 441] He appointed Ibn Umm Maktūm over Medina.

Mūsā b. Muḥammad b. Ibrāhīm b. al-Ḥārith from his father, Rabīʿa b. ʿUthmān, and Muḥammad from al-Zuhrī, and ʿAbd al-Ṣamad b. Muḥammad, Yūnus b. Muḥammad al-Ẓafarī, ʿAbdullah b. Jaʿfar, Yaḥyā b. ʿAbdullah b. Abī Qatāda, Ibn Abī Sabra, ʿAbd al-Ḥamīd b. Jaʿfar, Maʿmar b. Rāshid, Ḥizām b. Hishām, Muḥammad b. Yaḥyā b. Sahl, Ayyūb b. al-Nuʿmān b. ʿAbdullah b. Kaʿb b. Mālik, Mūsā b. ʿUbayda, Qudāma b. Mūsā, ʿĀʾidh b. Yaḥyā al-Zuraqī, Muḥammad b. Ṣāliḥ, ʿAbd al-Raḥmān b. ʿAbd al-ʿAzīz, Hishām b. Saʿd, Mujammiʿ b. Yaʿqūb, Abū Maʿshar, al-Ḍaḥḥāk b. ʿUthmān, ʿAbd al-Raḥmān b. Muḥammad b. Abī Bakr, Ibn Abī Ḥabība, Ibn Abī l-Zinād, and Usāma b. Zayd, all have related portions of this tradition to me.

They said: When the Messenger of God cast out the Banū Naḍīr, they went to Khaybar where there were a number of steadfast people among the Jews. But none of their houses possessed the esteem that had accrued to the Banū Naḍīr. The Banū Naḍīr and the Qurayẓa were the original Jews, from the children of the Kāhin of the Banū Hārūn. When they arrived in Khaybar, Ḥuyayy b. Akhṭab, Kināna b. Abī l-Ḥuqayq, Hawdha b. al-Ḥuqayq, and Hawdha b. Qays al-Wāʾilī from al-Aws of the Banū Khatma, and Abū ʿĀmir, the monk, with some ten men set out for Mecca, and asked the Quraysh and their followers to join them in fighting Muḥammad. They said to the Quraysh, "We will be with you until we destroy Muḥammad." Abū Sufyān said, "Is this what brought you here?" They replied, "Yes. We come as [Page 442] your confederates, in enmity against Muḥammad in order to fight him." Abū Sufyān said, "Greetings. The most loved of the people to us are those who help us against the enmity of Muḥammad." The group said, "Take fifty men, all of them from the tribes of the Quraysh, including yourself. We will enter under the curtains of the Kaʿba with you until we touch our hearts to it. Then we will together swear by God that we will not abandon each other. Our words will be as one against this man as long as one of us remains." And so they did: they swore to that and made an agreement. Then some of the Quraysh said to some, "The heads of the people of Yathrib, the people of knowledge and the first books, have come, so ask them about how we stand against Muḥammad. Which of us is more guided?" The Quraysh agreed; so Abū Sufyān said, "O community of Jews, you are the people of the first books and knowledge, so inform us of what we have become, for we are in dispute with Muḥammad. Is our religion good or is the religion of Muḥammad good? We are the keepers of the house, we slaughter the cattle, we quench the thirst of the pilgrims, and we worship images." The Jews replied, "By God, you are the first in truth about it. Indeed, you magnify this house, you maintain the provision of water, you slaughter the sacrifice, you worship what your forefathers worshiped. You, rather than he, are the first in truth." And God most high revealed about that: *Have you not considered those who were given a portion of the book? They believe in sorcery and evil and say to the unbelievers that they are better guided in the right path than the believers* (Q. 4:51).

They prepared to set an appointed time. Ṣafwān b. Umayya said, "O community of Quraysh, surely you have promised those people this time and they have departed from you on that basis. So fulfill for them. This will not be as it was when we promised Muḥammad to appear at Badr al-Ṣafrā' and did not keep the appointment. He was bold in that against us. Indeed, I detested the promise of Abū Sufyān, at that time."

The Jews set out until they came to Ghaṭafān, while the Quraysh began preparations. They sent to the Bedouin asking for their help. They invited the *Aḥābīsh* (a mixed group of different tribal backgrounds) and those who followed them. Then, the Jews set out until they came to the Banū Sulaym [Page 443] and the latter promised that they would join when the Quraysh marched. They went to the Ghaṭafān and promised them dates of Khaybar for a year, if they would help them and march with the Quraysh to Muḥammad when they marched. The Ghaṭafān agreed to that, and there was not one more swift to that than ʿUyayna b. Ḥiṣn.

The Quraysh, and those who followed them from the *Aḥabish*, set out, four thousand in all. They established their flag in the Dār al-Nadwa. They led three hundred horses, and behind them were one thousand five hundred camels. The Banū Sulaym came forward and joined them at Marr al-Ẓahrān. The Banū Sulaym numbered seven hundred at that time. Leading them was Sufyān b. ʿAbd Shams, the ally of Ḥarb b. Umayya, who was the father of Abū l-Aʿwar—who was later with Muʿāwiya b. Abī Sufyān at Ṣiffīn.

The Quraysh set out, led by Abū Sufyān b. Ḥarb. The Banū Asad set out led by Ṭalḥa b. Khuwaylid al-Asadī, and the Banū Fazāra, all of them, set out, and they numbered a thousand, and they were led by ʿUyayna b. Ḥiṣn. The Ashjaʿ—not all of them, but four hundred, were led by Masʿūd b. Rukhayla. And al-Ḥārith b. ʿAwf set out leading his people, the Banū Murra, and they numbered four hundred.

When the Ghaṭafān gathered for the march, al-Ḥārith b. ʿAwf refused to march with them, saying to his people, "Disperse in your land and do not attack Muḥammad. Indeed I think that Muḥammad will be victorious. Even if those between the east and west oppose him, he will still win." So they dispersed in their land and not one of them was present. Thus al-Zuhrī and the Banū Murra related the tale of the Banū Murra.

ʿAbd al-Raḥmān b. ʿAbd al-ʿAzīz from ʿAbdullah b. Abī Bakr b. ʿAmr b. Ḥazm and ʿĀṣim b. ʿUmar b. Qatāda, both related to me saying that the Banū Murra witnessed al-Khandaq; they numbered four hundred, and their leader was al-Ḥārith b. ʿAwf al-Murrī. Ḥassān insulted them pronouncing poetry, [Page 444] and they mentioned an agreement of the Prophet at that time. This was confirmed with us, that he witnessed al-Khandaq with his people, but he was better at dissimulation than ʿUyayna. They said: The people were all those who appeared at al-Khandaq from the Quraysh, Sulaym, Ghaṭafān and Asad: ten thousand. There were three camps, and the management of the affair was with Abū Sufyān.

The Quraysh approached and alighted in Rūma and Wādī al-ʿAqīq with the Aḥābīsh and those who had recourse to them from the Bedouin. The Ghaṭafān approached with their leader and alighted at al-Zaghāba by the side of Uḥud. The Quraysh began to dispatch its riders to Wādī al-Aqīq with its thorn trees. There was nothing here for the horses except the fodder they had brought with them—namely corn. The Ghaṭafān dispersed their camels to the wild Tamarisk and Athal trees on the slopes. They had arrived at a time when there was no wild or cultivated crop. The people had harvested a month before and brought in the harvest and straw. The Ghaṭafān sent their horses to the remnants of the harvest, and there were three hundred in the valley and it was barely sufficient for them. Their camels were almost destroyed by starvation. The night they arrived there was a drought in the city.

When the Quraysh departed from Mecca to Medina, a group of riders from the Khuzāʿa set out to the Prophet and informed him of the departure of the Quraysh. They went from Mecca to Medina in four days.

That was when the Prophet called and informed them of the news of their enemy. He consulted them about the affair with seriousness and effort, and he promised them help if they were patient and God fearing. He commanded them to obey God and His prophet. [Page 445] The Messenger of God consulted them frequently in matters of war. He said: "Should we go out to them from Medina or should we stay inside and build a ditch around us? Or shall we stay close and keep our backs to the mountain?" And they argued. And a faction said: We will stay close to Buʿāth in Thanniyat al-Wadāʿ, on the slopes. Another said: Let us leave Medina behind. Salmān said, "O Messenger of God, when we were in Persia and feared a cavalry, we built a ditch around us. Do you think we should dig a ditch around us?" Salmān's suggestion pleased the Muslims. They remembered when the Prophet had asked them to stay in Medina on the day of Uḥud and that they had set out. The Muslims hated going out, and desired to stay in Medina. Abū Bakr b. Abī Sabra related to me saying: Abū Bakr b. ʿAbdullah b. Jahm related to me that the Messenger of God went on a horse of his with a group of his companions from the Muhājirūn and the Anṣār, until he came to a place where he alighted. The place that pleased him was that which placed Salʿ to his back, where he could build the trench from al-Madhād to Dhubāb to Rātij.

At the time, the Messenger of God was working in the trench. He called the people and informed them of the approach of their enemy and he gathered the forces at the foot of Salʿ. The Muslims began to work hurriedly to confront the daring of the enemy. The Messenger of God continued to work with them in the trench urging the Muslims. As they worked, they borrowed many tools of iron, hoes and baskets from the Banū Qurayẓa. They dug the trench with him, for they were at that time at peace with the Prophet [Page 446] and they hated the bold daring of the Quraysh. The Messenger of God appointed a group on every side of the trench to dig it. The Muhājirūn dug from Rātij to Dhubāb, and the Anṣār, from Dhubāb to Mount Banū ʿUbayd. The attached buildings protected the rest of Medina.

Muḥammad b. Yaḥyā b. Sahl related to me from his father from his grandfather saying: I observed the Muslims and the youth transport the soil, and the trench grew, more or less, to the height of a man. The Muhājirūn and Anṣār transported the soil in baskets on their heads, and when they returned they brought stones from Mount Salʿ in the baskets. They were taking the soil from near the Prophet and his companions, and arranging the stones there as though they were a pile of dates—and the stones were among their best weapons with which they aimed.

Ibn Abī Sabra related to me from Marwān b. Abī Saʿīd saying: The Messenger of God was at that time carrying soil in the baskets and throwing it, and the people composed a *rajaz* verse about it and the Messenger of God saying:

> This beauty is not the beauty of Khaybar.
> This fulfills the promise to our Lord and purifies.

At that time, the Muslims, when they saw a lazy man, laughed at him. The people competed for Salmān al-Fārisī. The Muhājirūn said, "Salmān is from us! He is strong and informed on digging the trench." The Anṣār said, "He is from us, and we deserve him." Their words reached the Messenger of God and he said, "Salmān is a man from us, the [Page 447] family of the Prophet." Indeed at that time he did the work of ten men, so that Qays b. Abī Ṣaʿṣaʿa gave him the evil eye and he was thrown to the ground by it. They asked the Messenger of God, and he said, "Tell him to take ablutions, wash with that water, and then turn the vessel upside down." He did as told, and was released from the rope of envy. Ibn Abī Sabra related to me from Fuḍayl b. Mubashshir saying: I heard Jābir b. ʿAbdullah say: Indeed I saw Salmān, at that time, and they had made him dig five cubits of land. He did not look around until he had completed it, by himself, saying, "By God, there is no life except in the next world."

Ayyūb b. al-Nuʿmān related to me from his father from his grandfather, from Kaʿb b. Mālik, who said: We began on the day of al-Khandaq, singing *rajaz* and digging, and we were the Banū Salama, on one side. But the Messenger of God bound me not to recite anything. I asked, "Did the Messenger of God bind anyone else?" and they said, "Ḥassān b. Thābit," and I knew that the Messenger of God had prevented us because of our superiority over the others. So I did not say a word until we completed the ditch. The Messenger of God said, "Do not be angry at what your friend says for he does not intend any harm." Except what Kaʿb and Ḥassān said for indeed they hit upon the truth.

Yaḥyā b. ʿAbd al-ʿAzīz related to me from ʿĀṣim b. ʿUmar b. Qatāda, who said: Juʿayl b. Surāqa was a good man. He was very ugly and, at that time, used to work with the Muslims in the ditch. The Messenger of God changed his name and called him ʿAmr. The Muslims composed a verse about that saying:

> [Page 448] His name was changed from Juʿayl to ʿAmr.
> It helped the miserable man that day.

The Messenger of God did not add anything to this, but he joined in at ʿAmr.

While the Muslims were digging, Zayd b. Thābit had been transporting the soil with the Muslims. Saʿd b. Muʿādh looked at him, while he sat with the Prophet, and said, "Praise be to God, O Messenger of God, who kept me alive until I believed in you. Indeed, I had embraced the father of this, Thābit b. al-Ḍaḥḥāk, on the day of Buʿāth—and he threw me to the ground." The Messenger of God said, "Is he not, indeed, a good lad!" Zayd b. Thābit lay asleep in the trench. Sleep had overtaken him so that even when his weapons were taken—his shield, his bow, and his sword—he did not know it. It was very cold, and he was with the Muslims, at the very edge of the trench. The Muslims were exposed, and wanted to go around the ditch and guard it. They left Zayd sleeping, unaware of the situation, when ʿUmāra b. Ḥazm came and took his weapons. Zayd did not realize it until he became afraid when he lost his weapons. This reached the

Messenger of God. He called Zayd and said, "O father of sleep, you slept until your weapons were gone!" Then the Messenger of God said, "Who has knowledge of this lad's weapons?" ʿUmāra b. Ḥazm replied, "I, O Messenger of God, they are with me." He said, "Return them to him." The Messenger of God forbade frightening a Muslim or stealing his property whether in jest or in seriousness.

ʿAlī b. ʿIsā related to me from his father, saying: At that time there was no one among the Muslims who was not either digging in the ditch or transporting the soil. Indeed the Messenger of God was seen with [Page 449] Abū Bakr and ʿUmar—and the latter were not separated in their work, or march, or camp—hurriedly transporting the soil in their garments, when they could not find baskets, because of the haste of the Muslims.

Barāʾ b. ʿĀzib used to say, "I have not seen one who looked better than the Messenger of God in a ruddy dress. He was very fair and had much hair that came down to his shoulders. I saw him at that time carrying the earth on his back until the dust between us moved, and I saw the whiteness of his stomach."

Abū Saʿīd al-Khudrī said: I looked at the Messenger of God and he was digging in the trench with the Muslims, and the dust was on his chest and between the folds of his stomach. He was saying, "If not for You Oh God, we would not have been guided, never given alms, or prayed." He kept repeating that. Ubayy b. ʿAbbās b. Sahl related to me from his father, from his grandfather: We were with the Messenger of God on the day of al-Khandaq. He took a spade and struck a stone, and the stone made a sound. The Messenger of God laughed, and someone said, "O Messenger of God, why are you laughing?" He replied, "I laugh about the people who come from the East in iron chains. They are being driven to Paradise, and they are reluctant!"

ʿĀṣim b. ʿAbdullah al-Ḥakamī related to me from ʿUmar b. al-Ḥakam: ʿUmar b. al-Khaṭṭāb was digging at that time with a hoe, when he struck at a [Page 450] hard stone that he had not expected to find. The Messenger of God took the hoe from ʿUmar, he was at mount ʿUbayd, and struck once, and the first strike brought a spark that went like lightening to Yemen. Then he struck again, and the lightening went towards al-Shām. Then he struck again and the lightening went towards the East, and the stone broke at the third stroke. ʿUmar b. al-Khaṭṭāb used to say: By Him who sent him with the truth, it became like sand.

Wherever he struck, Salmān followed it with his eyes, and he saw with every blow a light. Salmān said, "O Messenger of God, I observed the hoe whenever you struck with it, and it lit up what was under it." And the Prophet said, "Did you see that?" And he said, "Yes." The Prophet said, "Indeed, I saw with the first, the castles of al-Shām; with the second, the castles of al-Yemen. And with the third, the white castles of Khusrau, of the nobility in Madāʾin." He began to describe it to Salmān, who said, "You speak the truth. By Him who sent you with the truth, indeed this is the description. I witness that you are indeed the messenger of God!" The Messenger of God said, "This conquest of God will open for you after me, O Salmān, for al-Shām will be open to you. Heraclius will flee to the most distant kingdom, and you will be victorious over al-Shām and no one will contest you. Yemen will be open to you. The East will be conquered and Khusrau killed after it." Salmān said, "All this did I see." They said: The trench extended from Mount Banū ʿUbayd, in Khurbā to al-Rātij.

The Muhājirūn controlled the area from Dhubāb to Rātij. The Anṣār dug in the region between Dhubāb to Khurbā. All this was what the Messenger of God and the Muslims dug. Medina was inter-locked with buildings in every direction, so that it was like a fortress. The Banū ʿAbd al-Ashhal dug the trench from around Rātij to what came after, until the trench came from behind the mosque; The Banū Dīnār dug [Page 451] from Khurbā to the place where the house of Ibn Abī l-Janūb stands today. The Muslims took the women and children up to the fortresses. The Banū Ḥāritha took their children up to their fortress, which was a forbidding one; ʿĀʾisha was there, at that time. The Banū ʿAmr b. ʿAwf took their women and children up to the fortresses. Some of them dug a ditch around the fortresses of Qubāʾ. The Banū ʿAmr b. ʿAwf together with the Khaṭma, the Banū Umayya, Wāʾil and Wāqif fortified the fortresses. Their children were in their fortresses.

ʿAbd al-Raḥmān b. Abjar related to me from Ṣaliḥ b. Abī Ḥassān, who said: The elders of the Banū Wāqif informed me that they took their women and children to the fortress while they were with the Prophet, but they had promised to meet their families at mid day, with the permission of the Prophet. The Prophet, however, forbade them, but when they begged, he commanded them to take their weapons, for fear that the Banū Qurayẓa might attack them.

Hilāl b. Umayya used to say: I approached with a group of my people and the Banū ʿAmr b. ʿAwf. We had deviated from al-Jasr, and from Ṣafna and we took the road to Qubāʾ. When we reached ʿAwsā, all of a sudden, a group of them (the Banū Qurayẓa), including Nabbāsh b. Qays al-Quraẓī sprayed us with arrows for a while. We aimed back at them, and some of us were wounded. Then they withdrew to their garrison and we returned to our families. We did not see a group of them together after that.

Aflaḥ b. Saʿīd related to me from Muḥammad b. Kaʿb that the trench that the Messenger of God dug was between Mount Banū ʿUbayd and al-Rātij, [Page 452] and this is the strongest tradition with us. They mentioned that the ditch had gates, but we do not know where they were situated. Muḥammad b. Ziyād b. Abī Hunayda related to me from Muḥammad b. Ibrāhīm b. al-Ḥārith from Jābir b. ʿAbdullah who said that the people came to a piece of hard ground, on the day of al-Khandaq, and struck it with their pick-axes until the pick-axes broke. They called the Messenger of God, who asked for water and poured it over the hard ground and reduced it to a sand hill.

Jābir b. ʿAbdullah said: I saw the Messenger of God digging, and I saw the wrinkle in the midst of his belly. His stomach was hollow and I saw dust on the folds of his skin. I went to my wife and informed her of what I saw of the empty stomach of the Messenger of God, and she said, "By God, we do not have anything with us except this lamb and a measure of barley." Jābir said, "Grind it and season it." She said: We cooked some of it and roasted some of it, and the barley was made into bread. Jābir said: Then I went to the Messenger of God, and I stayed until such time that I thought the food would be done. Then, I said, "O Messenger of God, I have made food for you so come with those who you desire from your companions." The Messenger of God intertwined his fingers with mine, and said, "Jābir invites you!" They came forward with him, and I said to myself, "By God, it is indeed a disgrace!" I went to my wife and informed her, and she said, "You called them, or he called them?" I said, "Rather, he called them!" She said, "Let them come. He knows best." He said: The Messenger of God approached leading his companions. They were in groups, tens upon tens. Then he said to us, "Scoop from the pot, then cover it, and take out the bread from the oven, then cover it." We did so. We began to spoon and cover the pot, and when we opened it, we saw no decrease. We took out the bread from the oven and covered it, and we did not see it decrease, either. The people ate until they were full. And we ate and shared with the others.

All the people and the Prophet worked at that time. The Anṣār composed a verse saying, [Page 453] "We are those who acknowledge Muḥammad as long as we live." The

Prophet said, "O God there is no good except the good of the after life, so pardon the Anṣār and the Muhājirūn."

Ibn Abī Sabra related to me from Ṣāliḥ b. Muḥammad b. Zā'ida from Abū Salama b. ʿAbd al-Raḥmān b. ʿAwf from Abū Wāqid al-Laythī, who said: I saw the Messenger of God review the youths. He approved of those he approved and returned those he returned. Those who had not attained puberty and to whom he had not granted permission worked with him. But when the affair intensified he commanded those who had not attained puberty to return to their families in the fortresses with the children. The Muslims at that time were three thousand. Indeed I saw the Messenger of God when he struck once with the pickaxe, once, shoveling the earth with a shovel, and once, carrying the earth in a basket. Indeed I saw him one day overcome by it. The Messenger of God sat, reclined on a stone on his left side, asleep. I saw Abū Bakr and ʿUmar standing at his head and turning aside the passers by for fear of disturbing him. I approached him and he jumped up, saying, "You should wake me up." He took the pickaxe and struck with it saying, "O God, life is life in the hereafter, forgive the Anṣār and the Muhājirūn. O God, curse al-ʿAḍal and al-Qāra for they force me to transport stones." Among those the Prophet approved of at that time were Ibn ʿUmar, Zayd b. Thābit, and al-Barā' b. ʿĀzib, who were each fifteen years of age.

[Page 454] ʿAbd al-Ḥamīd b. Jaʿfar related to me from his father, who said: When the Messenger of God completed the ditch—he had dug for six days—and fortified it, he alighted behind Salʿ. He kept it behind him, and the trench in front of him, and set up camp there. He put up his tent of leather, which was by the place of prayer (*masjid*), at the foot of the mountain—Mount al-Aḥzāb.

The Prophet used to take turns with his wives. It would be ʿĀ'isha one day, then Umm Salama, then Zaynab bt. Jaḥsh. They were the three who took turns between them during al-Khandaq. The rest of his wives were in the fortress of Banū Ḥāritha. Some said: They were in al-Musayr, the fortress of the Banū Zurayq, which was strong. It was also said that some of them were in al-Fāriʿ. We heard all of this.

Abū Ayyūb b. al-Nuʿmān related to me from his father, who said: Ḥuyayy b. Akhṭab used to say to Abū Sufyan b. Ḥarb and to the Quraysh who marched with them, "Indeed my people, the Qurayẓa, are with you. They are the people of abundant coats of mail. They number seven hundred and fifty warriors." When they drew near, Abū Sufyān said to Ḥuyayy b. Akhṭab, "Go to your people until they destroy the contract which is between them and Muḥammad." Ḥuyayy went until he came to the Qurayẓa. The Messenger of God had made a pact with the Qurayẓa, the Naḍīr and those Jews who were in Medina, when he arrived, on condition that they were with him and not against him. It was said: He reconciled them on condition that they helped him against those who attacked him, and they maintained the previous blood price that was between the Aws and the Khazraj. It was said: Indeed, Ḥuyayy [Page 455] turned away from Dhū l-Ḥulayfa and went above al-ʿAsba until he knocked on the door of Kaʿb b. Asad. Kaʿb was the master of the contract of the Banū Qurayẓa and the agreement.

Muḥammad b. Kaʿb al-Quraẓī used to relate saying: Ḥuyayy b. Akhṭab was a man of ill omen. He was the curse of the Banū Nadīr and its people, and the curse of the Qurayẓa until they were killed. He desired to show off his status and his leadership to them. His parallel among the Quraysh was Abū Jahl b. Hishām. When Ḥuyayy came to the Banū Qurayẓa they hated his entering their home. The first among those who met him was Ghazzāl b. Samaw'al. Ḥuyayy said to him, "I bring you that which will relieve you of Muḥammad. These Quraysh have dismounted at Wādī al-ʿAqīq; and the

Ghaṭafān at al-Zaghāba." Ghazāl said, "You come to us, by God, with eternal humiliation!" Ḥuyayy said, "Do not say that." Then he went to the door of Kaʿb b. Asad and knocked on his door. Kaʿb expected it. He said, "What shall I do about Ḥuyayy coming to see me? He is an unlucky man who has brought bad luck to his people. He is now asking me to destroy the agreement." He said: He said: Ḥuyayy knocked on Kaʿb's door. Kaʿb said, "Surely you are a man who brings bad luck. You brought misfortune to your people until you destroyed them. So leave us. Indeed, you desire to destroy me, and my people." But Ḥuyayy refused to turn away. Kaʿb said, "O Ḥuyayy, indeed I made an agreement with Muḥammad, and I contracted with him. We have only seen honesty from him. He has not abandoned his protection of us, nor exposed us to ill. Indeed he is the best of our protectors." Ḥuyayy replied, "Woe unto you. Indeed I bring you an overwhelming sea and an eternal glory. I bring you the Quraysh and their leaders and their nobility. I have brought you the Kināna and have camped them at Ruma. I have brought you the Ghaṭafān and their leadership and nobility and encamped them in al-Zaghāba to Naqmā. They led their horses and rode their camels. They number ten thousand, and a thousand horses, and many weapons. Muḥammad will not escape in this outburst of ours. [Page 456] They have agreed that they will not return until they have destroyed Muḥammad and those who are with him."

Kaʿb said, "Woe unto you! You come to me, by God, with eternal humiliation, and clouds of lightning and thunder, with nothing in them. I am in a bottomless sea. I am not able to leave my home, my wealth is with me and my children and my women. So leave me. Indeed there is no use for me in what you bring." Ḥuyayy said, "Woe unto you! I must speak to you." Kaʿb said, "I will not do it." Ḥuyayy said, "By God, you do not lock me out except for fear that I will eat your porridge. I promise you, I will not put my hand in it." Kaʿb said that this irritated him so he opened his door, and Ḥuyayy entered. He continued to try and win Kaʿb over until finally, he softened to him. Kaʿb said, "Leave me this day of yours, until I consult the leaders of the Jews." But Ḥuyayy said, "They gave you an agreement and a contract so you decide for them," and he kept begging him until he changed his decision. Kaʿb b. Asad said, "O Ḥuyayy, I have entered into what you want detesting it, and I fear that Muḥammad will not be killed, the Quraysh will leave for their land, and you will return to your people, while I remain in the center of my land, and I and those who are with me will be killed." Ḥuyayy replied, "To you is what is in the Torah which was revealed to Moses on Mount Sinai. If Muḥammad is not killed in this outburst, the Quraysh and the Ghaṭafān will return before they are taken by Muḥammad, but I will enter with you in your fortress until what happens to you happens to me."

So Kaʿb destroyed the agreement that was between him and the Messenger of God, and Ḥuyayy called for the document that the Messenger of God had written between them, and tore it. When Ḥuyayy tore it, he knew that the affair had fested and corrupted. He set out to the Banū Qurayẓa and they were encircled around the place of Kaʿb b. Asad, and he informed them of the news. Al-Zabīr b. Bāṭā said, "The Jews will be destroyed. The Quraysh and Ghaṭafān will turn away [Page 457] and leave us in the center of our homes, our property and our children. We will not have strength against Muḥammad. No more Jews will spend the night in prudent resolve, in Yathrib, again." Then Kaʿb b. Asad sent a group of five Jewish leaders—al-Zabīr b. Bāṭā, Nabbāsh b. Qays, Ghazzāl b. Samaw'al, ʿUqba b. Zayd, and Kaʿb b. Zayd and informed them of Ḥuyayy's news, and how Ḥuyayy promised him that he would return with him so that what happens to him will happen to Ḥuyayy. al-Zabir b. Bāṭā said, "Why do you want to be killed and have Ḥuyayy killed with you?" Kaʿb was silent, and the people said, "We detest demeaning your opinion or contradicting you, but Ḥuyayy is one who is known for his misfortune." Kaʿb b. Asad regretted destroying the contract. The affair intensified for what God desired of their fighting and destruction.

While the Messenger of God and the Muslims were in al-Khandaq, ʿUmar b. al-Khaṭṭāb came to the Messenger of God who was in his tent—the tent was made of leather and had been put up beside the masjid, which was at the bottom of the mountain. With the Messenger of God was Abū Bakr. The Muslims at their trench were taking shifts. With them were some thirty horses. The riders of the horses were going around the trench between both ends. They employed men and placed them in positions at the trench, until ʿUmar arrived. He said, "O Messenger of God, it has reached me that the Banū Qurayẓa have destroyed the agreement and are preparing for war." That distressed the Messenger of God and he said, "Whom shall we send to seek out information about them?" ʿUmar said, "al-Zubayr b. al-ʿAwwām."

The first of the people that the Messenger of God sent was al-Zubayr b. al-ʿAwwām. He said, "Go to the Banū Qurayẓa." Zubayr went and observed, then he returned and said, "O Messenger of God, I saw them putting their fortresses in order, and preparing the roads and they have herded their cattle." That was when the Messenger of God said, "Indeed for every Prophet is a disciple. Al-Zubayr is my disciple and the son of my aunt." [Page 458] Then the Messenger of God called for Saʿd b. Muʿādh and Saʿd b. ʿUbāda and Usayd b. Ḥuḍayr. He said, "Indeed it has reached me that the Banū Qurayẓa have destroyed the agreement which was between us, and gone to war. Go and observe if what has reached me is true. If it is baseless, proclaim it aloud. If it is true say it in code and I will know. Do not undermine the support of the Muslims."

When they went to Kaʿb b. Asad they found that the people had destroyed the agreement. They pleaded with them in the name of God for the agreement that had been between them; that they return to what they were before the affair had intensified, and that they do not obey Ḥuyayy b. Akhṭab. But Kaʿb said, "We will not return ever. I have cut it just as I have cut the straps of my sandals." Kaʿb fell on Saʿd b. Muʿādh with insults. Usayd b. Ḥuḍayr said, "Do you insult your patron, O enemy of God? You are not his equal! Is it not so, by God, O son of a Jew? The Quraysh will turn away, if God wishes, defeated, and you will be left in the heart of your homeland. And we will come to you, and you will step out of your hiding upon our judgement. Surely you knew the Naḍīr. They were the most dignified among you, the mightiest in this land. Your blood is half their blood value, and you saw what God did with them. And before that, the Banū Qaynuqāʿ, and they yielded to our judgement."

Kaʿb said, "O Ibn Ḥuḍayr, will you frighten me with your marching to me? By the Torah! Surely your father saw me on the day of Buʿāth. If not for us the Khazraj would have kicked him out. By God you have not met one more skilled in fighting or more knowledgeable of it. We, by God, are the best of your warriors." They defamed the Messenger of God and the Muslims with the ugliest of words. They insulted Saʿd b. ʿUbāda with the most abusive rebuke until they angered him. Saʿd b. Muʿādh said, "Leave them. We did not come for this. That which is between us is more hurtful than abuse—it is the sword!"

[Page 459] It was Nabbāsh b. Qays who insulted Saʿd b. ʿUbāda. He said, "You bit the clitoris of your mother!" Saʿd b. ʿUbāda became violently angry. Saʿd b. Muʿādh said, "Surely I fear that a day similar to the day of the Banū Naḍīr will overtake you. Ghazzāl b. Samaw'al said, "You bit the penis of your father!" Saʿd b. Muʿādh said, "Other words would be better than these." He said: Then they returned to the Prophet.

When they finally reached the Prophet, Saʿd b. ʿUbāda said: "ʿAdal and al-Qāra." The two men were silent. By this—ʿAḍal and Qāra, he referred to the betrayal of Khubayb and the companions of al-Rajīʿ. Then they sat down. The Messenger of God proclaimed *takbīr*. He said, "Rejoice, O Muslims, in God's victory and His help." The news finally reached the Muslims that the Banū Qurayẓa had broken their agreement. Fear intensified and the trial became overwhelming.

It was read on the authority of Ibn Abī Ḥabība and I was listening. He said, "Muḥammad b. al-Thaljī related to us that al-Wāqidī related to us saying: Abd al-Raḥmān b. Muḥammad b. Abī Bakr related to me from ʿAbdullah b. Abī Bakr b. Ḥazm saying, "The Messenger of God sent Saʿd b. ʿUbāda, Saʿd b. Muʿādh, ʿAbdullah b. Rawāḥa, and Khawwāt b. Jubayr to the Banū Qurayẓa. Ibn Wāqid said: The first is confirmed with us. They said: Hypocrisy spread, and the people became disheartened; misery increased, and fear intensified, and there was fear for the children and the women. They were just as God most high said: *When they came on you from above you and below and the sights were dimmed dim, and the hearts came to their mouths* (Q. 33:10).

The Messenger of God and the Muslims were facing the enemy. They could not leave from their places. They took turns keeping watch over the trench. People spoke using ugly words. Muʿattib b. Qushayr said, "Muḥammad promises us the treasures of Khusrau and Ceasar, yet not one of us [Page 460] feels safe to go even for his need. God and His Messenger promise us only deception."

Ṣāliḥ b. Jaʿfar related to me from Ibn Kaʿb, who said: The Messenger of God said: Indeed I hope to circumambulate the ancient house and take the key, for God will destroy Khusrau and Ceasar and their wealth will be paid in the way of God. He was saying that when he saw the suffering of the Muslims, and Muʿattib heard him and repeated what he said. Ibn Abī Sabra related to me from Ḥārith b. al-Fuḍayl saying: The Banū Qurayẓa intended to raid the main part of Medina by night. They sent Ḥuyayy b. Akhṭab to the Quraysh to bring with them a thousand men, and from the Ghaṭafān a thousand, to attack them. News of that great misfortune came to the Messenger of God, so he sent Salama b. Aslam b. Ḥuraysh al-Ashhalī with two hundred men, and Zayd b. Ḥāritha with three hundred, to protect Medina while proclaiming *takbīr*, and with them were the cavalry of the Muslims. When it was morning, they were safe. Abū Bakr al-Ṣiddīq used to say: We feared more for our children in Medina from the Qurayẓa than from the Quraysh and Ghaṭafān. I used to go to the hill of Salʿ and look at the houses of Medina. When I saw them calm, I would praise God.

One of the ways by which God prevented the Qurayẓa from what they intended was by keeping Medina guarded. Ṣāliḥ b. Khawwāt related to me from Ibn Kaʿb saying: Khawwāt b. Jubayr said: The Messenger of God called me while we were fortifying the trench. He said, "Hurry to the Qurayẓa and observe if you see carelessness or weakness in their position and inform me." He said: I set out from his place at sunset, and I slid down the hill of Salʿ. [Page 461] The sun had set so I prayed Maghrib. Then I set out until I arrived in Rātij, then ʿAbd al-Ashhal, then Zuhra, then Buʿāth. When I was close to the people, I said to myself, I shall hide from them, and I hid and watched the fortresses for a while. Then I fell asleep and did not feel anything until a man picked me up while I slept. He placed me over his neck and walked with me. He said: I was alarmed, for a man was walking with me on his shoulder, and I knew that he was a youth from the Qurayẓa. I felt a strong shame at that moment before the Messenger of God for I had lost the watch he had commanded me with. Then I remembered that sleep had over come me. He said: The man trotted with me to their fortress. He spoke in Yehudiyya, a Jewish language, and I understood him. He said, "Rejoice in a fat carrot!" I remember striking with my hands—from my experience with them, one of them would never go out except with a spade in his middle—until I placed my hand on the spade and pulled it out, while he was busy talking to the man above the fortress. I grabbed the spade and struck him in his heart, and he slumped, shouting, "The lion!" The Jews lit the fire on their tower with palm torches. He fell dead and was revealed, but they could not reach me.

I approached the road I had come from, and Gabriel appeared to the Messenger of God. The Messenger of God said, "You succeeded O Khawwāt!" Then he set out and informed his companions saying, "Thus and thus is the affair of Khawwāt." I came to the Messenger of God who was seated with his companions, conversing. When he saw me, he said, "May you prosper!" I said, "You too, O Messenger of God." He said, "Tell me your news," and I informed him. The Prophet said, "Thus did Gabriel inform me." The people said, "Thus did the Messenger of God inform us." Our night in the trench was like a day. Someone other than Sāliḥ said that Khawwāt said: I remember [Page 462] the bad effect my niceness and sincerity had on them. I said, "They will retalliate," when I remembered the spade.

Abū Bakr b. Abī Sabra related to me from ʿAbdullah b. Abī Bakr b. Ḥazm, who said: Nabbāsh b. Qays set out by night from their fortress towards Medina. With him were ten of their strongest Jews, and they were saying, "Perhaps we can take them by surprise." They reached Baqīʿ al-Gharqad and found a group of Muslims who were companions of Salama b. Aslam b. Ḥuraysh, and attacked them, aiming arrows at them for a while. Then the Qurayẓa were exposed turning away. This reached Salama b. Aslam while they were in the region of Banū Ḥāritha. He approached with his companions, until they reached the fortress of the Qurayẓa, and began to go around it until the Jews became afraid, and lit fires on their towers saying, "The inhabitants!" The Muslims destroyed the two poles of a well, and brought it down on them, so the Jews were not able to escape from their fortress and became very afraid.

An old man from the Quraysh related to me that Ibn Abī l-Zinād and Ibn Jaʿfar said, and this is more confirmed than that which was said in Uḥud, that Ḥassān b. Thābit was a coward. He went with the women up to the fortress. Ṣafiyya was in the fortress of Fāriʿ. With her was a group, and Ḥassān was with them. Ten Jews and their leader, Ghazzāl b. Samaw'al from the Banū Qurayẓa, approached by day, and they began to enter while aiming at the fortress. Ṣafiyya said to Ḥassān, "They are yours, O Abū l-Walīd!" He said, "No, by God, I will not expose myself to those Jews." One of them drew near to the gates desiring to enter. Ṣafiyya covered herself with her garments, and then [Page 463] took a piece of wood to him and crushed his head and killed him, while the rest of them fled. The Banū Ḥāritha gathered and sent Aws b. Qayẓī to the Messenger of God. They said, "O Messenger of God, our homes are exposed. There is not a house among the houses of the Anṣār like our home. There is no one between us and the Ghaṭafān who will restrain them from us. Permit us to return to our homes and protect our children and our women." The Messenger of God permitted them to return, and they prepared to depart. This reached Saʿd b. Muʿādh. He came to the Messenger of God and said, "O Messenger of God, do not permit them to leave. Indeed, whenever we have been overtaken by a difficulty, they have done this." Then he approached them, and said to the Banū Ḥāritha, "You do this to us always. We have not been overcome with a difficulty, but you have done this." The Messenger of God brought them back.

ʿĀʾisha, the wife of the Prophet, used to say: I saw Saʿd b. Abī Waqqāṣ at night while we were in the trench, and I will always love him for it. She said: The Messenger of God was frequenting a gap in the trench, keeping watch, until when the cold hurt him, he came to me and I warmed him in my lap, and when he was warmed he set out again to that gap to watch over it, saying, "I do fear only that the people will be attacked from here." While the Messenger of God was in my lap and warmed he says, "Would that there were a good man to watch over me!" She said: Then I heard the sound of weapons and the clash of iron, and the Messenger of God said, "Who is this?" A man replied, "Saʿd b. Abī Waqqāṣ." He said, "Keep watch on this spot." She said: Then the Messenger of God slept until I heard his snore.

Al-Wāqidī said: ʿAbd al-Raḥmān b. Muḥammad b. Abī Bakr related to me from ʿAbdullah [Page 464] b. Abī Bakr b. Ḥazm saying, Umm Salama said: I was with the Messenger of God in the trench, and I did not leave him for his entire stay. He was keeping watch by himself in the trench, and we were in extreme cold. I observed him stand and pray, in his tent, as God wished him to pray. Then he set out and kept watch for a while and I heard him say, "This is the cavalry of the polytheists going around the trench. Who is for them?" Then he called out, "O ʿAbbād b. Bishr." And Abbād said, "Here I am!" He said, "Is anyone with you?" He said, "Yes. I am with a group of my companions and we are around your tent." He said, "Hurry with your companions and go around the trench. This is one of their cavalry going around you desiring to take you by surprise. O God, drive their evil away from us, and help us against them, to overwhelm them. They will not be overcome without You." ʿAbbād b. Bishr set out with his companions, and, lo and behold, Abū Sufyān with his cavalry of polytheists was circumambulating the pass of the trench. The Muslims were warned about them and aimed at them with stones and arrows. We stopped with them and aimed at polytheists until we weakened them with the shots. They were exposed returning to their stations and I returned to the Messenger of God. I found him praying, and I informed him. Umm Salama said: He slept until I heard his deep sleep, and he did not stir until I heard Bilāl's call to pray Subḥ at the light of daybreak. He went out and prayed with the Muslims. She used to say: May God bless ʿAbbād b. Bishr, for surely he was the most committed of the companions of the Messenger of God to the tent of the Messenger of God, keeping watch over him always.

Ayyūb b. al-Nuʿmān related to me from his father that Usayd b. Ḥuḍayr used to watch the trench with his companions. When they reached the place of the trench that the cavalry had leapt over, [Page 465] they were surprised by the vanguard of the polytheists, and a hundred horses or so led by ʿAmr b. al-ʿĀṣ, desiring to attack the Muslims. Usayd b. Ḥuḍayr stood up against them with his companions. He aimed at them with stones and arrows until they departed. That night, Salmān al-Fārisī, who was with the Muslims, said to Usayd, "Surely this place of the trench is narrow. We fear their cavalry will jump over it." The people hastened to dig it. They hurried, staying up the night, to widen it until it became the shape of the trench, and they were safe from the attack of the cavalry. The Muslims took turns guarding it while they were in extreme cold and hunger.

Khārija b. al-Ḥārith related to me from Abū ʿAtīq al-Sulamī from Jābir b. ʿAbdullahsaying: Indeed I remember keeping watch at the trench. The cavalry of the polytheists circumambulated the trench seeking an unexpected narrowing of it to plunge through. ʿAmr b. al-ʿĀṣ and Khālid b. al-Walīd were among those doing that, seeking negligence from the Muslims. We met Khālid b. al-Walīd with a hundred horsemen. He, too, went around with his cavalry seeking a narrowing of the trench desiring to cross with his horsemen. We sprayed them with arrows until he turned back. Ibrāhīm b. Jaʿfar related to me from his father that Muḥammad b. Maslama said that Khālid b. al-Walīd had approached that night with a hundred riders. They approached from al-ʿAqīq until they stood at al-Madhād facing the tent of the Prophet. I knew about the group and I said to ʿAbbād b. Bishr, the watchman of the tent of the Prophet, as he stood up to pray, "You have been visited." He bowed and then prostrated. Khālid approached with three individuals, and he was the fourth. I could hear them say, "This is the tent of the Prophet. Shoot!" And they aimed. But we were diligent against them, until we stood at the edge of the ditch, and they were at the edge of the ditch on the other side [Page 466] aiming at us. Our companions returned to us, and their companions gathered to them. The wounds increased among us and them. Then they followed the trench along the two sides and we followed them, while the Muslims kept watch against them. Whenever we passed a watch-post a faction attacked with us, while a faction stayed until we reached Rātij, when they stopped for a long while. They were expecting the Qurayẓa desiring to raid the center of Medina. We only sensed the cavalry of Salama b. Aslam b. Ḥuraysh who was keeping watch. They came from behind Rātij, and met Khalid b. Walīd. They fought each other and became confused, and soon (in the time it takes to milk a goat) I saw the cavalry of Khālid b. al-Walīd turn away. Salama b. Aslam followed him until he sent him back to where he had come from. In the morning the Quraysh and Ghatafān rebuked Khālid saying, "You did not do anything about those who were in the trench nor about those who came out to you." Khālid said, "I will stay tonight. Send the cavalry until I decide what to do."

Ibn Abī Sabra related to me from ʿAbd al-Wāhid b. Abī ʿAwn from Umm Salama the wife of the Prophet, who said: Indeed, in the middle of the night—and I was in the tent of the Prophet where he slept—I heard the fearful scream of the enemy, and someone say, "O the cavalry of God!" The Messenger of God had established the signal of the Muhājirūn as "O cavalry of God," so the Messenger of God was alarmed by the call and set out from his tent. A group of his companions were at his tent keeping watch, among them ʿAbbād b. Bishr. The Prophet said, "What happened to the people?" ʿAbbād replied, "This is the voice of ʿUmar b. al-Khaṭṭāb. Tonight it is his turn to call out 'O the cavalry of God.' The people are going to him while he is in the direction of Ḥusayka between Dhubāb and the Mosque of al-Fatḥ." The Messenger of God said [Page 467] to ʿAbbād b. Bishr, "Go and observe, then return to me, if God wills, and inform me!" Umm Salama said: I stood at the door of the tent and heard the whole conversation. She said: The Messenger of God continued to stay up until ʿAbbād b. Bishr returned to him and said, "O Messenger of God, this is ʿAmr b. ʿAbd with the cavalry of the polytheists, and with him is Masʿūd b. Rukhya b. Nuwayra b. Ṭarīf b. Suḥma b. ʿAbdullah b. Hilāl b. Khalāwa b. Ashjaʿ b. Rayth b. Ghaṭafān with the cavalry of the Ghaṭafān. The Muslims are shooting arrows and stones at them." She said: The Messenger of God came in and put on his armor and helmet, then rode his horse, setting out with his companions, until he came to that gap. It was not long before he returned. He was content and said, "God has pushed them away and their injuries have increased." She said: He slept until I heard his snore, when I heard the frightening sound of the enemy. The Prophet was alarmed and jumped up shouting: "O ʿAbbād b.

Bishr," and ʿAbbād replied, "I am at your service." The Prophet said, "Go and observe what this is!" ʿAbbād went and then returned and said, "This is Ḍirār b. al-Khaṭṭāb with the cavalry of the polytheists and with him is ʿUyayna b. Ḥiṣn with the cavalry of the Ghatafān at Mount Banū ʿUbayd. The Muslims are aiming at them with stones and arrows." The Messenger of God turned, put on his armor and rode his horse, setting out with his companions to that gap. He did not come to us until it was dawn, when he returned saying, "They turned back defeated and their injuries are many." Then he prayed the Ṣubḥ prayer with his companions and sat down. Umm Salama used to say: I have witnessed with him scenes of fighting and fear at al-Muraysīʿ, Khaybar, as well as in Ḥudaybiyya, al-Fatḥ, and Ḥunayn. But there was not in all of that anything more tiring to the Messenger of God, or more fearful to us, than al-Khandaq. That was because the Muslims were like a tree of many branches—surrounded by enemies—and did not trust the Qurayẓa regarding the children. Medina was guarded until the morning. The *takbīr* of the Muslims was heard until it was morning, for fear [Page 468] until God turned them back in their frustration without gaining any good.

Ibrāhīm b. Jaʿfar related to me from his father from Muḥammad b. Maslama, saying: We were around the tent of the Messenger of God guarding it. The Messenger of God was sleeping and we heard him snoring, when the horses appeared on Salʿ. ʿAbbād b. Bishr saw them and informed us about them. He said, "Go to the cavalry," and ʿAbbād stood at the door of the tent of the Messenger of God, holding the sword while waiting for me. I returned and said, "The cavalry of the Muslims appears led by Salama b. Aslam b. Ḥuraysh," and I returned to our place. Muḥammad b. Maslama added: Our night in the trench was a day until God dispelled it.

Khārija b. al-Ḥārith related to me from Abū ʿAtīq from Jābir, and Ḍaḥḥāk b. ʿUthmān related to me from ʿUbaydullah b. Miqsam, from Jābir b. ʿAbdullah saying: We feared more from the Banū Qurayẓa for our children in Medina than from the Quraysh, until God dispelled that.

They said: The polytheists were taking turns among them. Abū Sufyān with his companions took a turn one day; and similarly, Hubayra b. Abī Wahb, ʿIkrima b. Abī Jahl, Ḍirār b. al-Khaṭṭāb each took a day in turn. They did not stop circulating their cavalry between Mudhād and Rātij. They were in a group of their companions dispersing and coming together later, until it was the greatest trial and the people became very afraid. They put forward their marksmen—and they had two archers: Ḥibbān b. al-ʿAriqa and Abū Usāma al-Jushamī. The rest of them were [Page 469] unknown Bedouin. Once, they challenged each other with arrows for a while. All of them stood in one direction facing the tent of the Prophet. The Messenger of God stood in his armor and helmet, and some added, on his horse. Ḥibān b. al-ʿAriqa shot Saʿd b. Muʿadh with an arrow that struck the vein of his hand. He said, "Take it, and I am Ibn al-ʿAriqa!" The Messenger of God said, "May God strike your face with fire." Some said: Abū Usāma aimed at the Prophet while he was in armor.

ʿĀʾisha the wife of the Prophet used to say: We were in the fortress of the Banū Ḥāritha, before the *ḥijāb*, and with us was Umm Saʿd b. Muʿādh. Saʿd b. Muʿādh passed by us, at that time, wearing a nice perfume, and I had not seen anyone with a perfume like it. He wore armor that revealed his forearms, however, and I feared for him, then, for the shortness of his armor. He passed by juggling a spear in his hands, saying:

> Stay a bit Ḥamal, see the fight.
> How good is death when the time is right.

His mother said, "Catch up with the Messenger of God, my little son, by God, you are late." I said, "By God, O Umm Saʿd, I wish that the armor of Saʿd covered up to his fingers." Umm Saʿd said, "God decides as He fulfills." He deemed that he be taken at that time. Indeed the news came that he had been shot. His mother said, "What a destiny!"

[Page 470] Their leaders gathered together to attack. Abū Sufyān b. Ḥarb, ʿIkrima b. Abī Jahl, Ḍirār b. al-Khaṭṭāb, Khālid b. al-Walīd, ʿAmr b. al-ʿĀṣ, Hubayr b. Abī Wahb, Nawfal b. ʿAbdullah al-Makhzūmī, ʿAmr b. ʿAbd, Nawfal b. Muʿāwiya al-Dīlī as well as a number of others began to go around the trench. With them were the leaders of the Ghaṭafān, ʿUyayna b. Ḥiṣn and Masʿūd b. Rukhayla, and al-Ḥārith b. ʿAwf. From the Sulaym, were their leaders, and from the Banū Asad, Ṭulayḥa b. Khuwaylid. They left the men among them to follow, seeking a pass, and desiring to plunge their cavalry at the Messenger of God and his companions. Finally they reached a place neglected by the Muslims, and tried to force their horses, saying, "This strategy is not an Arab's doing. It is not their strategy." They said, "Indeed with him is a Persian. It is he who has showed them this." They said, "Who is there then?" ʿIkrima b. Abī Jahl, Nawfal b. ʿAbdullah, Ḍirār b. al-Khaṭṭāb, Hubayra b. Abī Wahb, ʿAmr b. ʿAbd crossed, while the rest of the polytheists stayed behind the trench and did not cross. It was said to Abū Sufyān, "Will you not cross?" He replied, "You have crossed, and if you need us, we will cross."

ʿAmr b. ʿAbd began to call for a duel, saying, "I am hoarse with calling to all of you. Is there one who will compete? ʿAmr was at that time furious. He had witnessed Badr and been carried away wounded, but he had not witnessed Uḥud. He had forbidden himself oil until he took revenge on Muḥammad and his companions. He was old, at that time. It was said he had reached ninety years. When he called for the duel, ʿAlī said, "I will duel him, O Messenger of God!" Thrice. At that time the Muslims were pessimistic because of the reputed bravery of ʿAmr. [Page 471] The Messenger of God gave ʿAlī his sword, wrapped his head in a turban, and prayed, "O God, help ʿAlī against him!"

He said: ʿAmr approached, at that time, riding a horse, while ʿAlī was on foot. ʿAlī said to him, "Surely you used to say in *jāhiliyya*, one will not offer me one of three, but I will accept one." He replied, "Yes, indeed!" ʿAlī said, "I invite you to witness that there is no God but Allah and that Muḥammad is his Messenger, and to submit to God the Lord of the worlds." He said, "O son of my brother, other than this is for me." He said, "The other: return to your land, and if Muḥammad speaks the truth you will be the happiest of men about him. If not, he is that which you desired." ʿAmr replied, "This is what the women of the Quraysh will never speak about. I have vowed what I have vowed, and forbade myself oil." He said, "And the third?" ʿAlī replied, "The duel." He said: ʿAmr laughed and said, "Surely this is the challenge that I did not think an Arab would offer me. Indeed, I detest that I kill the likes of you. Your father was my friend. So return! You are a young lad. Rather I would like an older Quraysh, Abū Bakr or ʿUmar." He said: ʿAlī said, "Indeed I invite you to the duel, for I desire to kill you." ʿAmr was saddened. He alighted and tied his horse.

Jābir used to narrate saying: One of them drew near his companion. Dust was raised between them, and we could not see them. Then we heard the *takbīr* under it and we knew that ʿAlī had killed him. His companions who were in the trench were revealed and they fled, their cavalry escaped with them, except for Nawfal b. ʿAbdullah who fell down with his horse in the trench. Stones were aimed at him until he was killed. They had turned fleeing. Al-Zubayr b. al-ʿAwwām and ʿUmar b. al-Khaṭṭāb followed in their tracks. They battled for a while, and Ḍirār b. al-Khaṭṭāb attacked ʿUmar b. al-Khaṭṭāb with a spear. All of a sudden ʿUmar found the touch of his spear and raising it from him said, "This is a happy favour. Keep it in mind, O son of al-Khaṭṭāb. Indeed I have vowed that my hands will not make me take the life of a man from the Quraysh ever." Ḍirār turned and returned to Abū Sufyān and his companions. They stayed on Mount Banū ʿUbayd.

[Page 472] It was said: al-Zubayr attacked Nawfal b. ʿAbdullah b. al-Mughīra with a sword until it broke in two while he cut the *undūj* of the saddle—*al-undūj* is the cloth placed under the saddle—and some say, at the nape of the neck of the horse. Some one said, "O Abū ʿAbdullah, we have not seen a sword such as yours." Another says, "By God, it is not a sword but his forearm." ʿIkrima and Hubayra fled and joined Abū Sufyān. Al-Zubayr attacked Hubayra and struck the back of his horse. The crupper of his horse was cut, and the armor that was behind the horse fell, and al-Zubayr took the armor. ʿIkrima fled and laid down his spear. When they returned to Abū Sufyān, he said, "This is a day in which we will not gain anything, so return!" The Quraysh fled and returned to al-ʿAqīq, and the Ghaṭafān returned to their stations. They agreed to come together in the morning, and not one of them stayed behind. The Quraysh stayed up the night mobilizing their companions, and the Ghaṭafān stayed up the night calling up theirs. They appeared before the Messenger of God at the trench before sunrise. The Messenger of God had prepared his companions and encouraged them to battle. He promised them victory if they would be patient. The polytheists held the Muslims in what was comparable to a fortress of their squadron. They set out in every direction from the trench.

Al-Ḍaḥḥāk b. ʿUthmān related to me from ʿUbaydullah b. Miqsam from Jābir b. ʿAbdullah, who said: They fought us, that day of theirs, and spread out their squadrons. They designated a tenacious squadron against the Messenger of God, which included Khālid b. al-Walīd. He fought them that day of his until a part of the night. Neither the Messenger of God nor any of the Muslims was able to withdraw from their situation. The Messenger of God was not able to pray the Ẓuhr, [Page 473] *ʿAṣar, Maghrib* or *ʿIsha'* prayers. His companions began to say, "O Messenger of God, we did not pray!" And he says, "Nor I, by God, I have not prayed!" until God exposed them and they returned, scattered. The Quraysh returned to their stations, and the Ghaṭafān, to theirs.

The Muslims turned towards the tent of the Messenger of God. Usayd b. Ḥuḍayr stayed with two hundred Muslims in the trench. They were at the edge of the trench when the cavalry of polytheists returned seeking an unguarded moment. Leading them was Khālid b. al-Walīd. They struggled for a while against the polytheists, including Waḥshī. The latter pierced al-Ṭufayl b. al-Nuʿmān with one of his javelins and killed him. He used to say, "God most high honored Ḥamza and Ṭufayl with my javeline; He did not humiliate me with either of theirs."

When the Messenger of God returned to the place of his tent he commanded Bilāl to proclaim the call to prayer. ʿAbdullah b. Masʿūd used to say: The Messenger of God proclaimed the call to prayer, and stood up for the Ẓuhr prayer. He stood up afterwards for every prayer again and again, with an *iqāma*—the reply to the call to prayer—recited before each prayer.

Ibn Abī Dhiʾb related to me, and it is the more confirmed of two traditions that we have, saying: al-Maqburī informed me from ʿAbd al-Raḥmān b. Abī Saʿīd al-Khudrī from his father, who said: We sat on the day of al-Khandaq, until it was after the

Maghrib prayer, and with the fall of night we were safe. That was the saying of God most high: *God is sufficient for the fighting believers. God is powerful, wise* (Q. 33:25). The Messenger of God called Bilāl and commanded him, and he led the Ẓuhr prayer, and it was the best of prayers that was prayed during its time. Then he led the prayer of ʿAṣr and it was the best of what was prayed in its time. Then he led the prayer of *Maghrib* and it was as good as what was prayed in its time. Then he led the prayer of ʿIshāʾ and it was as good as what was prayed in its time. He said: That was before God revealed the prayer of fear: *Whether on foot or riding* (Q. 2:239).

[Page 474] Ibn ʿAbbās used to relate saying: The Messenger of God said at that time, "The polytheists distracted us from midday prayer—meaning ʿAṣar. May God fill their insides and their graves with fire." The Banū Makhzūm sent to the Prophet seeking the corpse of Nawfal b. ʿAbdullah to purchase for blood money. The Messenger of God said, "Surely it is the corpse of a donkey!" He hated to evaluate it. When the polytheists returned that night there was no battle for them, except that they did not relinquish sending a squadron at night seeking an attack. Two squadrons of the Messenger of God set out, after that, by night. They met and some of them did not know some of the others. They did not think except that the other was the enemy. There was between them wounding and killing. We did not know who was killed for they were not named to us. Then they called out with the password of Islam, and some of them resisted fighting. Their password was "*Ḥa* Mīm they will not be victorious!" They came to the Prophet and informed him. The Messenger of God said, "Your wounds were in the path of God, so whoever was killed is a martyr." After that, when some of the Muslims drew near others, they called out their password so that some of them desisted and they did not shoot with arrows or stones. They surrounded the trench by night, taking turns, until it was morning. The polytheists did thus also, going around the trench until it was morning.

Men from the people of al-ʿAwālī looked up their families. The Messenger of God said to them, "Indeed I fear the Banū Qurayẓa will attack you." When they insisted on his permission in greater numbers, he said: "Whoever goes from among you must take his weapon, for indeed I do not trust the Banū Qurayẓa who are on their way to your families. All of those who go among them must take the road to Salʿ until they enter Medina, and from there they can leave for al-ʿĀliya.

[Page 475] Mālik b. Anas related to me from Ṣayfī, the *mawlā* of Ibn Aflaḥ from Abū l-Sāʾib the freedman of Hishām b. Zuhra, that he visited Abū Saʿīd al-Khudrī in his house and found him praying. He said: I sat waiting for him until he finished his prayers. He said: I heard movement under the bed in his house, and, lo and behold, it was a snake. I got up to kill it, but he indicated to me to be seated. When I sat, he greeted, finishing his prayer, and pointed to a room in the house. He said to me, "Do you see this room? I said, "Yes." He said that a youth who had recently contracted a marriage had been using it. Then, we set out with the Messenger of God to the trench. At mid-day the youth asked permission of the Messenger of God to visit his wife, and the Messenger of God gave him a day, and said, "Take your weapon for indeed I fear for you from the Banū Qurayẓa." He said: The man took his weapon and went until he saw his wife standing between the two doors. He prepared to pierce her with his spear for the envy that overtook him, but she said, "Desist from using your spear until you see what is in your bed." So he desisted and entered, and lo and behold, it was a snake curled up on his bed. So he planted his spear in it and killed it. Then he went out with it and displayed it in the land, but the snake stirred at the tip of the spear and the youth fell down dead. We do not know which of them was quicker to die, the youth or the snake.

Abū Saʿīd said: We came to the Messenger of God and mentioned that to him and said, "O Messenger of God, ask God that he lives?" And he said, "Ask for forgiveness for your companion." Then he said, "Indeed, in Medina are Jinn who have converted. When you see among them something, grant it three days, and if it appears to you after that kill it, for surely it is Satan."

Qudāma b. Mūsā related to me from ʿĀʾisha bt. Qudāma from her father, who said: We sent the son of our sister, Ibn ʿUmar, to bring us food and blankets, for hunger and cold had reached us. Ibn ʿUmar set out until when he descended from Salʿ—it was night—sleep overcame him until morning. We were distressed about him so I set out searching and found him sleeping. The sun revealed him. I said, "The prayers. Did you pray today?" He said, "No." I said, "Pray." He went swiftly [Page 476] to the water. I went to our station in Medina and brought dates and a blanket. We all covered ourselves with that blanket together. Those who went from us to keep watch, went into the cold, then returned and entered under the blanket, until God relieved us.

The Messenger of God said, "I was helped by the East Wind, and ʿĀd was destroyed by the West Wind." Ibn ʿAbbās used to say: the South Wind came to the North Wind and said, "Go with me, by the help of God and His Messenger." The North Wind replied, "The free do not leave by night," so God most high sent the East Wind and extinguished their fires and cut the tent rope and attacked them.

ʿUmar b. ʿAbdullah b. Riyāḥ al-Anṣārī related to me from al-Qāsim b. ʿAbd al-Raḥmān b. Rāfiʿ from Banū ʿAdī b. al-Najjār, who said: A severe famine struck the Muslims, and their families sent them what they could. ʿAmra bt. Rawāḥa sent her daughter with a bowl of ʿAjwa dates in her garment. She said, "My little daughter, go to your father, Bashīr b. Saʿd, and your uncle, ʿAbdullah b. Rawāḥa, with their meals." The girl went to the trench and finding the Messenger of God seated with his companions asked for her father and uncle. The Messenger of God said, "Come here, little girl, what do you bring?" She said, "My mother sent me with food for my father and uncle." The Messenger of God said, "Give it!" She said: I gave it, and he took it in his two hands. Then he commanded that a cloth be spread out for it, and he brought the dates and let them fall on the cloth. Juʿāl b. Surāqa said, "Call out to the people at the trench to come forward to the meal." The people of the trench gathered together to eat of it. And when the people of the trench left, the dates continued to flow.

Shuʿayb b. ʿUbāda related to me from ʿAbdullah b. Muʿattib saying: [Page 477] Umm ʿĀmir al-Ashhaliyya sent me with a bowl containing dates mixed in butter to the Messenger of God while he was in his tent with Umm Salama. After Umm Salama ate to her satisfaction, the Messenger of God set out with the bowl, and his herald called out inviting the people for supper. The people of the trench ate their fill, and yet, it appeared to be untouched.

Muḥammad b. ʿAbdullah related to us from al-Zuhrī from Saʿīd b. al-Musayyib, who said: The Messenger of God and about ten of his companions were encircled until the distress was clear to every man among them. The Messenger of God said, "O Lord, I implore you your covenant and your promise. O Lord, if You wish You will not be worshipped." While they were thus, the Messenger of God sent for ʿUyayna b. Ḥiṣn and al-Ḥārith b. ʿAwf. Neither al-Ḥārith b. ʿAwf nor his people were at the trench—though some say that al-Ḥārith b. ʿAwf was there. Ibn Wāqid said: The second saying is more confirmed with us. Indeed the Messenger of God sent for him and for ʿUyayna saying,

"Do you think that if I put away a third of the dates of Medina for you, you will consider returning with those who are with you, and you two will discourage the Bedouin?" They said, "Will you give us half of the dates of Medina?" The Messenger of God refused to give them more than a third. They agreed to that, and they came with ten of their people when the affair drew near. They came, and the Messenger of God brought his companions and he brought paper and pen. ʿUthmān b. ʿAffān was present and the Prophet gave him the paper for he desired that he write the agreement between them. ʿAbbād b. Bishr stood at the head of the Messenger of God dressed in iron. Then, Usayd b. Ḥuḍayr approached the Messenger of God, [Page 478] not knowing what they were talking about.

When Usayd came before the Messenger of God, ʿUyayna entered, stretching his legs in front of the Messenger of God, and Usayd realized what they desired. He said, "O son of a monkey, do you stretch out your legs before the Messenger of God," and he had a spear. "By God, if not for the Messenger of God I would pierce your testicles with this spear!" Then he approached the Messenger of God and said, "O Messenger of God if the affair is from the heavens, fulfill it. But if it is not that, by God, we will not give them other than the sword. When did they covet this from us?" The Messenger of God was silent. Then the Messenger of God called for Saʿd b. Muʿādh and Saʿd b. ʿUbāda and asked for their advice about that, relying on them. The people were seated and he spoke in quiet tones. The Prophet informed them of what he desired from the agreement. They both said, "If this is an affair from the heavens fulfill it. If it is an affair you were not commanded about, but for which you have a desire, then we hear and obey. But if it is an opinion that you seek, then we have only the sword for them." Saʿd b. Muʿādh took the document. The Messenger of God said, "Indeed I thought the Bedouin will shoot you with a single bow, so I said to myself I will satisfy them and not fight them." They both said: "When they ate al-ʿIlhiz in *jāhiliyya* from exhaustion, they never coveted this from us. They shall have the dates only through purchase, or as guests. God brought you to us, honored us and guided us through you, and we give back dishonor! We will not give them anything but the sword!" The Messenger of God said, "Tear the document." Saʿd spat on it and tore it up. He said, "Between us is the sword." ʿUyayna stood up saying, "By God, is not what you left better than the plan you have chosen? [Page 479] You do not have the capability with these people." ʿAbbād b. Bishr said, "O ʿUyayna, do you frighten us with the sword? You know which of us is more worried! Indeed you and your people were eating ʿIlhiz and remnants of animals from hunger when you came over here. You have no hope for these dates from us except as purchase or as guests. We did not worship anything, and now, when God guides us through Muḥammad, you ask this from us? By God, if it were not for the position of the Messenger of God you would never reach your people." The Prophet said, "Return! Between us is the sword."

ʿUyayna and al-Ḥārith returned saying, "By God, we did not think that we would obtain anything from them. Indeed the people have a clear perception. I did not attend, except with dislike, for I was forced. Our stay here is of no value. If the Quraysh learn of what we offered Muḥammad they would know that we have let them down and not helped." ʿUyayna said, "That is indeed true." Ḥārith said, "And we will not get anything by helping the Quraysh against Muḥammad. By God, if the Quraysh overcome Muḥammad everything will go to them and not the rest of the Arabs. Indeed, I consider the affair of Muḥammad a victorious affair. By God, indeed the scholars from the Jews of Khaybar used to relate what they found in their books, that a prophet will be sent from the sanctuary with his description." ʿUyayna said, "Indeed, by God, we did not come to help the Quraysh, and if we ask the Quraysh for help, they will not help us nor will they set out with us from their sanctuary. But I desired to take the dates of Medina so we will be remembered for it, and besides, and what comes to us from the plunder, although we help our allies among the Jews who brought us over here." Al-Ḥārith said, "By God, the Aws and the Khazraj will only accept the sword. By God, they will fight for these palms until there is not a man among them, the [Page 480] surroundings are barren, and camel and sheep destroyed." ʿUyayna said, "There is nothing."

When they both arrived at their campsite, the Ghaṭafān came to them and said, "What happened to you?" They said, "The affair was not completed. We saw a people who have a vision, and who will give themselves for their leader. We and the Quraysh are destroyed. The Quraysh will return and not even speak to Muḥammad. The anger of Muḥammad will fall on the Banū Qurayẓa. If we turn back, he will sit on them and besiege them together until they give him what is before them. Al-Ḥārith said, "May they be destroyed. Muḥammad is more dear to us than the Jews."

A RECORD OF NUʿAYM B. MASʿŪD

ʿAbdullah b. ʿĀṣim al-Ashjaʿī related to us from his father from Nuʿaym b. Masʿūd, who said: The Banū Qurayẓa were a people of nobility and property while we were an Arab people possessing neither dates nor grapevine. Rather we were a people of sheep and camels. I used to go to Kaʿb b. Asad's and stay with them for days, drinking their drink and eating their food. Then they would load dates for me on my beast, and I would return to my family. When the factions marched against the Messenger of God I marched with my people. I had my religion and the Messenger of God was aware of it. The factions stayed until the neighborhood was affected by drought; the sheep, horses and camels were destroyed, and God most high flung Islam into my heart. I concealed my Islam from my people, and set out until I came before the Prophet between Maghrib and ʿIshāʾ and found him praying.

When the Prophet saw me, he sat up and said, "What brings you O Nuʿaym?" I said, "Indeed I came trusting you. I testify that what you have come with is the truth. Command me with what you wish, O Messenger of God, for by God, you will not order me but I will fulfill it. Neither my people nor the others know of my Islam." He said, "If you can hinder the people, hinder them!" He said: I said, "I will do so. But, O Messenger of God, [Page 481] I will speak untruths, so permit me." He said, "You are free to say what you will."

He said: I went until I arrived at the home of the Banū Qurayẓa, and when they saw me they welcomed, honored and greeted me, and attended to me with food and drink. I said, "I am not here for this. Indeed, I have come with a stake in your affairs, and fearing for you, so I will indicate to you an opinion. You know of my liking for you, and the special nature of what is between me and you." They said, "We know that, and we feel the same towards you. We recognize your sincerity." He said, "Keep it secret about me." They said, "We will do so." He said, "Surely, the matter of this man is a trial—referring to the Messenger of God—you saw what he did with the Banū Qaynuqāʿ and the Banū Naḍīr. He expelled them from their land after taking their wealth. Ibn Abī l-Ḥuqayq went with us and we rallied together with him to help you. I see the affair has been prolonged just as you see. Indeed you, the Quraysh and the Ghaṭafān are now in the same position in relation to Muḥammad. As for the Quraysh and the Ghaṭafān, they are a people who came traveling until they alighted where you saw. If they found an opportunity they took advantage of it. If the war, or what they detested overwhelmed them, they would withdraw to their land. You are not able to do that. This land is your land. In it are your wealth and your children and your women. Muḥammad's side was harsh on them. Yesterday they attacked him at night and he killed their leader ʿAmr b. ʿAbd, and they fled from him wounded. They are nothing without you. So do not fight with the Quraysh or Ghaṭafān until you have taken a hostage from them or a guarantee from their nobility, and you are confident that they will fight Muḥammad to the end." They said, "You advise us with a sound opinion and good advice." They thanked him and prayed to God for him, and said, "We will do as you say." He said: "But keep it secret about me." They said, "Yes. We will."

Then Nuʿaym set out to Abū Sufyān b. Ḥarb and men from the Quraysh and said, "O Abū Sufyān, I bring you advice, but you must keep it secret about me." He said, "I will do so." He said, "You know the Qurayẓa have regretted what they did about what was between them [Page 482] and Muḥammad, and they desire to rectify it and return to him. They sent out to him, while I was with them, saying, 'Indeed we will take, from the nobility of the Quraysh and the Ghaṭafān, seventy men and surrender them to you to strike off their heads and you will return our faction that you exiled to their land—meaning the Banū Naḍīr. We will be with you against the Quraysh until we turn them from you.' Indeed the Qurayẓa have sent to you asking for hostages, but do not send them anyone, and be vigilant about your nobility. Conceal about me and do not mention a word of this."

Then Nuʿaym set out until he came to the Ghaṭafān and he said, "O people of the Ghaṭafān, indeed I am a man from among you so conceal about me. Know that the Qurayẓa sent to Muḥammad," and Nuʿaym said to them similar to what he said to the Quraysh. "Be vigilant when you send them one of your men." And he was one of them so they trusted him.

The Jews sent Ghazzāl b. Samaw'al to Abū Sufyān b. Ḥarb and the nobility of the Quraysh, saying, "Indeed your stay was long and you did not do anything, and what you do is not wise. If you will assure us of the day you will march to Muḥammad, and you come from a certain direction, and the Ghaṭafān come from a certain direction, and we set out from another direction, Muḥammad will not escape from some of us. But we will not set out with you until you send us hostages from your nobility, and they are with us. Indeed we fear that if the war touches you, and what you detest overwhelms you, you will escape and leave us in the center of our land, while we have withdrawn from Muḥammad in enmity." The messenger returned to the Banū Qurayẓa, but the Quraysh did not send them anything. Abū Sufyān said, "This is what Nuʿaym told us."

Nuʿaym set out to the Banū Qurayẓa and said, "O people of the Qurayẓa, I was with Abū Sufyān until your messenger came to him seeking a hostage. Abū Sufyān did not give him anything. And when your messenger turned away he said, 'If they asked me for a goat I would not pledge it. I would not pledge the elders of my companions so that they hand them to Muḥammad to be killed.' So consider your decision until you take a hostage. Indeed if you do not fight Muḥammad and Abū Sufyān turns away, you will be at your first agreement." They said, [Page 483] "You expect that, O Nuʿaym?" He replied, "Yes." Kaʿb b. Asad said, "Indeed we will not fight him. By God, surely I detest this; but Ḥuyayy is a man of misfortune." Zabīr b. Bāṭa said, "If the Quraysh and Ghaṭafān withdraw from Muḥammad, Muḥammad will come to us only with the sword." Nuʿaym said, "Do not fear that, O Abū ʿAbd al-Raḥmān." Zabīr said, "By the Torah, if the Jews make the right decision, the matter will intensify and they will set out to Muḥammad and they will not seek a hostage from the Quraysh. Indeed, the Quraysh will never give us a hostage. For what reason will the Quraysh gives us hostages? Their numbers are greater than ours. They have cattle and we have none, and they are able to flee, and we are not able to do so. The Ghaṭafān sought Muḥammad to get some dates of the Aws and turn back. But Muḥammad would give them only the sword. So they turned back without anything."

When it was the night of the Sabbath it was what God did for His Prophet that Abū Sufyān said, "O people of the Quraysh, indeed the region has suffered a drought. The camels and cattle are destroyed. The Jews are treacherous and have lied. This is not the time to stay, so return." The Quraysh said, "Learn the information of the Jews and ascertain their news." So they sent ʿIkrima b. Abī Jahl until he came to the Banū Qurayẓa at sunset on the eve of the night of the Sabbath. ʿIkrima said, "O community of Jews, we have stayed here a long period of time and our livestock is decreasing, and there is a drought in the region. This is not a place to stay in. Let us set out to this man and fight him to the end." They said, "Tomorrow is the Sabbath and we will not fight nor do any work in it. Indeed, we will not fight with you even when our Sabbath is fulfilled unless you give us hostages from your men who will be with us in order that you will not leave until we have battled Muḥammad. Indeed, we fear that if the war overwhelms you, you will flee to your land and leave us with him in our land and we will not be able to confront him. With us are our children and women and property." ʿIkrima returned to Abū Sufyān, and they—the Quraysh—asked, "What happened?" He replied, "I swear by God, indeed, the information that Nuʿaym brought is true. Surely the enemies of God are treacherous."

The Ghaṭafān sent Masʿūd b. Rukhayla and other men to the Banū Qurayẓa [Page 484] with a message similar to that of Abū Sufyān, and they replied with a reply similar to what they gave Abū Sufyān. The Jews said, when they saw what they saw among them, "We swear by God that the news which Nuʿaym related is true." They knew that the Quraysh were not staying and they were at a loss, bewildered. Abū Sufyān came back to them and said, "Indeed we, by God, will not act. If you desire to fight, go out and fight." The Jews said as they first said, and the Jews said repeatedly, "The news is as Nuʿaym said." The Quraysh and the Ghaṭafān began to say, also, "The news is as Nuʿaym said." And those gave up hope in each other.

Their affair was disputed. Nuʿaym used to say: I held back the factions from each other until they dispersed in every direction. I was the trustee of the Messenger of God over his secrets. Nuʿaym was a true Muslim after that.

Mūsā b. Muḥammad b. Ibrāhīm related to me from his father, who said: When the Qurayẓa said what they said to ʿIkrima b. Abī Jahl, Abū Sufyān b. Ḥarb said to Ḥuyayy b. Akhṭab, "Where is what you promised us of help from your people? They have left us desiring treachery for us." Ḥuyayy replied, "No, by the Torah. But the Sabbath has arrived and we will not break the Sabbath. How can we be victorious over Muḥammad if we break the Sabbath? But when it is Sunday they will attack Muḥammad and his companions like a burning flame." Ḥuyayy b. Akhṭab set out until he came to the Banū Qurayẓa and said, "May my father and mother be your ransom, surely, the Quraysh suspect you of treachery, and they suspect me with you. And what is the Sabbath, if you break it for what has arrived from the affair of your enemy?" He said: Kaʿb b. Asad was angry, and he said that even if Muḥammad killed them until not one of them remained,

"We would not break the Sabbath." Ḥuyayy returned to Abū Sufyān, and Abū Sufyān said, "Did I not inform you, O Jew, that your people desire treachery?" Ḥuyayy replied, "No, by God, they do not desire treachery, but they desire to go out on Sunday." Abū Sufyān said, [Page 485] "And not the Sabbath? What is the Sabbath?" He said, "It is one of the days they find painful to fight in. That is because a tribe of ours ate fish on the day of Sabbath and God turned them into monkeys and swine." Abū Sufyān said, "I do not think I need help from the brothers of monkeys and swine." Then he added, "I sent ʿIkrima b. Abī Jahl and his companions to them and they said, 'We will not fight until you send us hostages from your nobility.' And earlier, this message is what Ghazzāl b. Samaw'al came to us with." Abū Sufyān said, "I swear by al-Lāt, it is your treachery! I believe that you have entered into treachery with the people." Ḥuyayy said, "By the Torah that was revealed to Moses on the day of Mount Sinai, I am not treacherous. Indeed I come to you from my people, and they are enemies of Muḥammad and are keen to fight him. What is the significance of one day if they will set out with you!" Abū Sufyān said, "No, by God, there is no time, not even an hour, and I will not stay with the people awaiting your treachery." Until Ḥuyayy b. Akhṭab feared for his life from Abū Sufyān, and he set out with them from fear until he reached al-Rawḥāʾ. He did not return except with reluctance for the promise he had given Kaʿb b. Asad that he would return to him. He entered with the Banū Qurayẓa into their fortress by night, and found the Messenger of God marching to them the moment the factions turned.

Ṣāliḥ b. Jaʿfar related to me from Abū Kaʿb al-Quraẓī, who said: Ḥuyayy b. Akhṭab said to Kaʿb b. Asad, when he went to him and Kaʿb continued to refuse, "Do not fight until you take seventy men from the Quraysh and Ghaṭafān hostage." That was a trick from Ḥuyayy so that he would destroy Kaʿb's agreement—with Muḥammad. He knew that if Kaʿb destroyed the agreement, the affair would be settled. Ḥuyayy did not inform the Quraysh about what he had said to the Banū Qurayẓa. When ʿIkrima came to them and asked them to go out with him on the Sabbath they said, "We will not break the Sabbath, but on Sunday, and we will not set out until you give us hostages." ʿIkrima said, "Which [Pages 486] hostages?" Kaʿb said, "That which you stipulated for us." He said, "Who stipulated it for you?" They said, "Ḥuyayy b. Akhṭab." And ʿIkrima informed Abū Sufyān of that. Abū Sufyān said to Ḥuyayy, "O Jew, did we say to you thus and thus?" He replied, "No, by the Torah, you did not say that." Abū Sufyān said, "Rather it is the treachery of Ḥuyayy," and Ḥuyayy began to swear by the Torah that he had not said that.

Mūsā b. Yaʿqūb related to me from his uncle, who said: Kaʿb said, "O Ḥuyayy, we will not set out until we have taken from each of your companions, from every clan, seventy men as hostages." Ḥuyayy mentioned that to the Quraysh and the Ghaṭafān and the Qays, and they acted and they signed a contract, an agreement, between them; until Kaʿb tore up the document. When the Quraysh sent to Kaʿb seeking help, he demanded hostages. They denied that and disagreed, for that was what God most high desired.

Maʿmar related to me from al-Zuhrī, who said: I heard him say: The Banū Qurayẓa sent to Abū Sufyān to come "And we will attack the heartland of the Muslims from behind them." Nuʿaym b. Masʿūd heard that—and he was a trustee of the Prophet. And Nuʿaym was with ʿUyayna when the Banū Qurayẓa sent that message to Abū Sufyān and his companions. Nuʿaym approached the Prophet and informed him of the news, and what the Qurayẓa sent with ʿUyayna to the factions. The Messenger of God said: "Perhaps we commanded them about that." Nuʿaym set out, with these words of the Messenger of God, from the Messenger of God's home. He said: Nuʿaym was a man who did not hide the news. When he turned from the home of the Prophet, he went to the Ghaṭafān. ʿUmar b. al-Khaṭṭāb said, "O Messenger of God, what is it that you said? If the affair was from God fulfill it. If this is a decision that has come to you of its own accord, then indeed the matter of the Banū Qurayẓa is more despicable than that you say something that will affect you." The Messenger of God said, "Rather it is a decision of mine. [Page 487] War is deceit."

Then the Messenger of God sent for Nuʿaym, and he called him and said, "Did you consider what you heard me say previously? Be silent about it and do not mention it." So Nuʿaym turned away from the Prophet until he came to ʿUyayna b. Ḥiṣn and those who were with him from the Ghaṭfān, and said to them: "Did you know of Muḥammad saying something ever, but it was true?" They said, "No." He said, "Indeed he told me regarding what the Banū Qurayẓa sent you: 'Perhaps we commanded them thus.' Then he forbade me to mention it to you." ʿUyayna rushed off until he met Abū Sufyān b. Ḥarb and he informed him of what Nuʿaym had told him about the Messenger of God. He said to them, "Surely the Banū Qurayẓa have deceived you." Abū Sufyān said, "We will send to them now and ask them for the hostages. If they give us the hostages they have been honest with us. If they refuse, we have been deceived by them."

The messenger of Abū Sufyān came to them (the Banū Qurayẓa) and asked them for hostages on the night of the Sabbath and they said: This is the night of the Sabbath and we do not fulfill in it, or in its day, any affair. So give us time until the Sabbath is over. The messenger set out to Abū Sufyān and Abū Sufyān said, while the leaders of the factions were with him: "This is treachery from the Banū Qurayẓa. Leave, for you have stayed too long." They called out to leave. Then God sent them a wind, and as soon as one of them was guided to the place of his ride, he rode away, fleeing.

It was said: Indeed Ḥuyayy b. Akhṭab said to Abū Sufyān, "I shall take seventy men as hostages from the Banū Qurayẓa to stay with you until they set out to fight. They know more about fighting Muḥammad and his companions." This was he, who said, "Indeed Abū Sufyān seeks hostages." Ibn Wāqid said: The more reliable of these stories, with us, is the first saying of Nuʿaym. ʿAbdullah b. Abī Awfā related that the Messenger of God prayed to God against the factions and said: "O God, who revealed the Book, swift to account, put the factions to flight! O God, defeat them!"

[Page 488] Kuthayyir b. Zayd related to me from ʿAbd al-Raḥmān b. ʿAbdullah b. Kaʿb b. Mālik, from Jābir b. ʿAbdullah, who said: The Messenger of God prayed to God against the factions, in the Masjid al-Aḥzāb on Monday, Tuesday and Wednesday. His prayer was answered for him, between *Ẓuhr* and *ʿAṣar*, on Wednesday. He said: We saw the joy in his face. Jābir said: Whenever I have difficulties, I wait for this hour of that day, and ask God and I find the answer.

Ibn Abī Dhi'b used to relate from a man of the Banū Salama, from Jābir b. ʿAbdullah, who said that the Messenger of God stood on the Mountain on which was the Mosque, and prayed, wearing a waist-wrap, his hands outstretched. Then he came again and prayed and asked God. ʿAbdullah b. ʿUmar used to say: The Messenger of God prayed in al-Kharīq approaching al-Ṣābbi in the land of the Banū Naḍīr. Today, it is the place at the bottom of the Mountain on which the mosque stands. It was said that he prayed at all the places around the mosque, which was on top of the mountain. Ibn Wāqid said: This is the best confirmed of the reports.

They said: When it was the night of Sabbath, God sent the wind, so it took what it took and left what it left behind. The Messenger of God stood praying until a third of the night had gone. Thus did he do on the night of the murder of Ibn al-Ashraf. Whenever an affair distressed him, the Messenger of God, prayed a lot.

They said: The siege of al-Khandaq took place during intense cold and hunger. Ḥudhayfa b. al-Yamān used to say: Indeed I remember us in the trench with the Messenger of God, in a night of great coldness. The cold and hunger and fear had gathered upon us. [Page 489] The Messenger of God said, "Who is the man who will observe what the people of the factions are doing, for God will make him my companion in Paradise?" Ḥudhayfa said: The Messenger of God was stipulating Paradise and return for him, yet not a man among us went forward. The Messenger of God called three times, but not a single man among us came forward because of the strength of the hunger, fear and cold.

When the Messenger of God saw that not a man came forward, he called me and said, "O Ḥudhayfa!" He said: I could find no alternative but to go forward when he mouthed my name, so I went to him, my heart pounding in my chest. The Messenger of God said, "You have heard my words since night and you do not come forward?" I said, "No, by Him who sent you with the truth, I was not able to overcome the hunger and cold within me." He said, "Go and observe what the people are doing, but do not shoot an arrow or stone, nor pierce with a spear, nor strike with a sword until you have returned to me." I said, "O Messenger of God, I do not fear that they will kill me, but rather, that they will mutilate me." The Messenger of God said, "Do not worry about it." And, with the first words of the Messenger of God, I knew that I need not worry. He said, "Go and enter with the people and observe what they are saying." When Ḥudhayfa turned to leave, the Messenger of God said, "O God, protect him from in front and behind, and from his right and from his left, and from above and below."

Ḥudhayfa entered their camp, and lo and behold, they were sitting around the warmth of their fires, while indeed the wind did what it did, leaving no home of theirs unturned. He approached and sat at the fire with the people, and Abū Sufyān stood up and said, "Beware of investigators and spies. Every man should observe who is sitting with him." Ḥudhayfa said: I turned to ʿAmr b. al-ʿĀṣ and said, "Who are you?" He was on my right, and he said, "ʿAmr b. al-ʿĀṣ." And I turned to Muʿāwiya b. Abī Sufyān and said, "Who are you?" and he said, "Muʿāwiya b. Abī Sufyān." Then Abū Sufyān said, [Page 490] "You, by God, are not in a land where one can stay; your livestock is destroyed, the region has suffered drought, and the Banū Qurayẓa have broken their promise to us. That which we detest has reached us about them, while the wind has brought us what you see. By God, there is not a structure that is confirmed for us, nor a kettle that will stand still. Leave, for indeed I am leaving." Abū Sufyān rose and sat upon his camel while it was tied. Then he struck it and it jumped up on its three legs. But he did not loosen its rope until after it stood up. If not for the promise the Messenger of God took from me, I would have killed him. ʿIkrima b. Abī Jahl called out to him, "You are the head of the people and their leader, yet, you disperse and leave the people?" And Abū Sufyān felt shame. He knelt his camel and alighted from it. He took its rein, leading it. Then he said, "Leave!" Ḥudhayfa said: The people began to leave and Abū Sufyān stayed until the camp had departed. Then he said to ʿAmr b. al-ʿĀṣ, "O Abū ʿAbdullah, it is necessary for me and you to stay with a detachment of cavalry to confront Muḥammad and his companions. Indeed we are not safe from being sought out until the camp is depleted." ʿAmr said, "I will stay." Abū Sufyān said to Khālid b. al-Walīd, "What do you think, O Abū Sulaymān?" He replied, "I, too, will stay." So

ʿAmr and Khālid stayed with two hundred horsemen. Except for this detachment on the backs of horses, the camp departed.

They said: Ḥudhayfa left for the Ghaṭafān and found them departing. He returned to the Messenger of God and informed him. The cavalry stayed until it was dawn. Then they left. They caught up with the baggage and the military joined with the rise of the day, at Malal. They arrived at Sayyāla the next morning. When the Ghaṭafān departed, Masʿūd b. Rukhayla stopped with the cavalry of his companions, and al-Ḥārith b. ʿAwf stayed with the cavalry of his companions, and some riders of the Banū Sulaym stayed with their companions. They endured together on the same road. They hated to disperse until [Page 491] they came to al-Marāḍ. Then each tribe dispersed to its place.

ʿAbdullah b. Jaʿfar related to me from ʿUthmān—meaning Ibn Muḥammad al-Akhnasī—who said: When ʿAmr b. al-ʿĀṣ turned away, he said, "All those who possess intelligence know that Muḥammad does not lie." ʿIkrima b. Abī Jahl said, "You are exactly the person who ought not to say this." ʿAmr said, "Why?" He replied, "Because he put down the nobility of your father and killed the lord of your people." Others said that Khālid b. al-Walīd was the one who said this, but we do not know. Perhaps they both spoke about it. Khālid b. al-Walīd said, "All who have brains know that Muḥammad does not lie ever." Abū Sufyān b. Ḥarb said, "You are exactly the person who must not say this." He asked, "Why?" Abū Sufyān replied, "He put down the nobility of your father and killed Abū Jahl the lord of your people."

Muḥammad b. ʿAbdullah related to me from al-Zuhrī from Ibn al-Musayyib, who said: The polytheists besieged the Messenger of God in the trench for some ten days. Al-Ḍaḥḥāk b. ʿUthmān related to me from ʿUbaydullah b. Miqsam from Jābir b. ʿAbdullah, who said that it was twenty days. Others said, fifteen days. This is the most confirmed with us.

When the Messenger of God rose in the trench, that morning, not one of the troops attacked him. They had fled and gone. It was established that they had dispersed to their lands. When the Muslims arose, the Messenger of God permitted them to return to their homes. They set out in haste and swiftly. The Messenger of God detested that the Banū Qurayẓa knew of their return to their homes, so he ordered them to come back. He sent out the heralds in their tracks. But not a single man came back. [Page 492] Among those who went to bring them back was ʿAbdullah b. ʿUmar. The Messenger of God commanded him. ʿAbdullah said: I began to shout in their tracks in every direction, "The Messenger of God commands you to come back." Not a single man among them came back because of the cold and hunger. He used to say: The Messenger of God detested seeing their haste, and he detested that there would be spies from the Quraysh. Jābir b. ʿAbdullah said: The Messenger of God commanded me to bring them back, and I repeatedly shouted to them, but not one of them came back. I hurried in the tracks of the Banū Ḥāritha, but by God, I could not reach them before they entered their homes. Indeed I shouted but not one of those who strove from hunger and cold came out to me. I returned to the Messenger of God and I joined him with the Banū Ḥarām departing. I informed the Messenger of God, and he laughed.

Mūsā b. Muḥammad b. Ibrāhīm related to me from Abū Wajza, who said: The Quraysh are fed up with staying with the drought in the region, and they are depressed by the trench. Abū Sufyān desired to attack the heart of Medina. He wrote a document that said, "In the name of God, I swear by al-Lāt and al-ʿUzzā, surely I came to you with a group, and indeed, we desired not to return until we eliminated you. I saw you and you hated to meet us, and you made the deep trench. I wish I knew who informed you of this! If we return to you, from us will be a day such as the day of Uḥud. The women will be stunned by it." He sent the letter with Abū Usāma al-Jushamī. When he arrived with the document, the Messenger of God called Ubayy b. Kaʿb, and went into his tent with him. He read the letter of Abū Sufyān to him. The Messenger of God wrote to him, "From Muḥammad the Messenger of God to Abū Sufyān b. Ḥarb . . . As for later, for a long time you have attempted to mislead. As for what you mention, that you came to us with all of yours, and that you did not desire [Page 493] to return until you had eliminated us, that is an affair that God will make between you and Him. It will be our turn, until you stop mentioning al-Lāt and al-ʿUzzā. As for your words, 'who informed you of the trench that you made,' indeed God most high inspires me, for what He desires of your anger and the anger of your companions. Surely a day will come when you will push me with your hand, and a day will come when I will break al-Lāt, al-ʿUzzā, Isāf, Nāʾila, and Hubal, and I shall remind you of this letter." Abū ʿAbdullah said: I mentioned that to Ibrāhīm b. Jaʿfar, and he said: My father informed me that the document stated, "Surely, you know that I met your companions in Aḥyāʾ. I was in a caravan of the Quraysh, and your companions did not besiege us. They were content to let the winds push us. Then I approached in the caravan of the Quraysh until I joined my people. You did not intercept us. You attacked my people, but I did not witness the battle. Then I attacked you in the heart of your homeland, and I killed and I burned—referring to the raid of Sawīq. Then I raided with all of us on the day of Uḥud. Our situation with you was similar to your situation with us at Badr. Then we came to you, all of us, and those who banded together with us, on the day of the trench. And you stayed attached to the fortresses and you built trenches."

[Page 494] **WHAT GOD REVEALED OF THE QUR'ĀN ABOUT AL-KHANDAQ TRENCH**

Mūsā b. Muḥammad b. Ibrāhīm related to me from his father from Ibn ʿAbbās, who said: God most high revealed about the affair of the trench, mentioning His blessings and His sufficiency against their enmity and the evil suspicions among them and the words of those who spoke with hypocrisy. He said: *O you who believe, remember the Grace of God bestowed on you when there came down on you hosts to overwhelm you; but We sent a hurricane against them and forces that you did not see* (Q. 33:9). He said: The soldiers who came to the believers were the Quraysh, Ghaṭafān, Asad and Sulaym. The troop that God sent against them was the wind. He mentions: *When they came to you from above you and below you, and behold the eyes became dim and the hearts gaped up to the throats, and you imagined various thoughts about God* (Q. 33:10). There were those who came to them, from above them, the Banū Qurayẓa, and from below them, the Quraysh, the Ghaṭafān, the Asad and the Sulaym. *In that situation were the Believers tried. They were shaken as by a tremendous shaking* (Q. 33:11). *And behold the Hypocrites and those in whose hearts is a disease said: God and His Messenger promised us nothing but delusions* (Q. 33:12). Referring to the words of Muʿattib b. Qushayr and those who had an opinion similar to his. *"Behold, you men of Yathrib," a party among them said, "you cannot stand the attack, therefore go back." A band of them asked for leave saying, "Truly our houses are exposed," though they were not exposed. They only intended to run away* (Q. 33:13): The words of Aws b. Qayẓī, and those of his people who had an opinion similar to his. *If an entry had been forced on them from their quarters (of the city)*

(Q. 33:14). Meaning, from around it. *And they were asked to apostatize, and they would certainly have done so with only a brief delay* (Q. 33:14) . . . referring to the Hypocrites. *They had already covenanted with God not to turn their backs* (Q. 33:15), until God's words: [Page 495] *And even if you do escape, no more than a brief respite will you be allowed to enjoy* (Q. 33:1). Thaʿlaba had promised God on the day of Uḥud that he would never turn back, after Uḥud. Then he mentioned the people of faith, when the factions came to them and besieged them. The Banū Qurayẓa helped them at the trench and the trials strengthened upon them. They said when they saw that: *This is what God and His messenger promised us, and God and His Messenger told us what was true* (Q. 33:22). Those are His words in *al-Baqara: Do you think that you shall enter the garden (of Bliss) without such (trials) as came to those who passed away before you? They encountered suffering and adversity and were so shaken in spirit that even the Apostle and those of faith who were with him cried: When will the help of God come? Ah! Verily the help of God is always near!* (Q. 2:214). And about His words: *Men who have been true to their covenant with God, of them some have completed their vow to the full* (Q. 33:23): He says they were killed or tried. *And some still wait* (Q. 33:23) to be killed or tried. *But they have never changed their determination in the least* (Q. 33:23). Meaning, their intentions have not changed. *That God may reward the men of truth and punish the Hypocrites if that be His will, or turn to them in mercy: For God is oft forgiving, most merciful* (Q. 33:24).

Isḥāq b. Yaḥyā related to me from Mujāhid, who said: The Messenger of God looked at Ṭalḥa b. ʿUbaydullah and said, "This is one who fulfilled his vow completely."

THE RECORD OF THOSE KILLED AMONG THE MUSLIMS IN THE BATTLE OF AL-KHANDAQ TRENCH

From the Banū ʿAbd al-Ashhal: Saʿd b. Muʿādh; Ḥibbān b. ʿAriqa shot him and he died. Others say that Abū Usāma al-Jushamī shot him. And Anas b. Aws b. ʿAtīk b. ʿAmr b. ʿAbd al-Aʿlam b. Zaʿūra b. Jusham b. ʿAbd al-Ashhal; Khālid b. al-Walīd shot him with an arrow and killed him. And ʿAbdullah b. Sahl al-Ashhalī was shot and killed by a man from the Banū ʿUwayf.

[Page 496] From the Banū Salama: Al-Ṭufayl b. al-Nuʿmān was killed by Waḥshī. Wahshī used to say: God was most gracious with my javelin against Ḥamza and al-Ṭufayl. Thaʿlaba b. Ghanama b. ʿAdī b. Nābī was killed by Hubayra b. Abī Wahb al-Makhzūmī. And from the Banū Dīnār: Kaʿb b. Zayd was carried off wounded on the day of Biʾr Maʿūna, but he recovered. Then he was killed in the trench by Ḍirār b. al-Khaṭṭāb. Altogether six individuals were martyred among the Muslims.

THE RECORD OF THOSE KILLED AMONG THE POLYTHEISTS

Those who were killed among the polytheists: ʿAmr b. ʿAbd b. Abī Qays b. ʿAbd Wudd was killed by ʿAlī b. Abī Ṭālib. Nawfal b. ʿAbdullah b. al-Mughīra al-Makhzūmī was killed by al-Zubayr b. al-Awwām, but some say it was ʿAlī b. Abī Ṭālib who killed him.

From the Banū ʿAbd al-Dār: ʿUthmān b. Munabbih b. ʿUbayd b. al-Sabbāq. He died later in Mecca, but was killed by what had been thrown during the Battle of al-Khandaq. Three were killed.

The record of the poetry that was said in the trench

Ḍirār b. al-Khaṭṭāb said: Thus it was . . .

THE RAID OF THE BANŪ QURAYẒA

The Prophet marched to them on a Wednesday with seven days left to the end of Dhū l-Qaʿda. He besieged them for fifteen days, and then turned back, on Thursday, the seventh of Dhū l-Hijja in the year five AH. He appointed Ibn Umm Maktūm to take his place in Medina.

They said: When the polytheists turned away from the trench, the Banū Qurayẓa became very fearful and said, "Muḥammad will march to us." The Messenger of God did not give the order to fight them until [Page 497] Gabriel came to him.

The wife of Nabbāsh b. Qays had a vision when the Muslims were in the siege of the Trench. She said, "I see the trench and there is no one in it. I see the people diverted to us, and we are in our fortresses. We are slaughtered like sheep." She mentioned that to her husband. Her husband set out and mentioned it to al-Zabīr b. Bāṭa. Zabīr said, "What is the matter with her. May she never sleep! The Quraysh will flee, and Muḥammad will besiege us! By the Torah, what is after the siege will be worse than the siege!"

They said: When the Messenger of God returned from al-Khandaq he entered the house of ʿĀʾisha, washed his head and bathed. He called for the coals to be burned and he prayed *Ẓuhr*. Gabriel came to him riding a mule that had a saddle, and on it velvet plush, and on its teeth the dust of battle. He stopped at the place of the funerals and called out, "Who excused you from fighting!" He said: The Messenger of God set out alarmed, and Gabriel said, "Did I not see you put down your helmet, and the angels have not yet put theirs down? Surely we drove them to Ḥamrāʾ al-Asad. Surely, God commands you to march to the Banū Qurayẓa. Indeed, I will approach them and shake their fortresses." It was said that Gabriel came to him on a piebald horse. The Messenger of God called ʿAlī, and gave him the flag, which was still in its place, not taken down since the return from the trench. The Messenger of God sent Bilāl to proclaim to the people, "Indeed, the Messenger of God commands you not to pray *ʿAsar* except in the land of the Banū Qurayẓa." The Messenger of God put on his weapons, head cover, armor, and helmet. He took a spear in his hand, put on a shield, and rode his horse. His companions surrounded him, put on their weapons, and rode their horses. There were thirty-six riders. The Messenger of God led two horses [Page 498] and rode another called Luḥayf; so there were three horses with him. And ʿAlī was a rider, as was Marthad b. Abī Marthad. The riders from the Banū ʿAbd Manāf were ʿUthmān b. ʿAffān, Abū Ḥudhayfa b. ʿUtba b. Rabīʿa, ʿUkkāsha b. Miḥṣan, Sālim the freedman of Abū Ḥudhayfa, and al-Zubayr b. al-ʿAwwām. From the Banū Zuhra the riders were ʿAbd al-Raḥmān b. ʿAwf and Saʿd b. Abī Waqqāṣ. From the Banū Taym: Abū Bakr al-Ṣiddīq and Ṭalḥa b. ʿUbaydullah. From the Banū ʿAdī: ʿUmar b. al-Khaṭṭāb. From the Banū ʿĀmir b. Luayy: ʿAbdulllah b. Makhrama. From the Banū Fihr: Abū ʿUbayda b. al-Jarrāḥ. From al-Aws: Saʿd b. Muʿādh, Usayd b. Ḥuḍayr Muḥammad b. Maslama, Abū Nāʾila and Saʿd b. Zayd. From the Banū Ẓafar: Qatāda b. al-Nuʿmān. From the Banū ʿAmr b. ʿAwf: ʿUwaym b. Sāʿida, and Maʿan b. ʿAdī, Thābit b. Aqram, and ʿAbdullah b. Salama. From the Banū Salama: Al-Ḥubāb b.

al-Mundhir b. al-Jamūḥ, Muʿādh b. Jabal, Quṭba b. ʿĀmir b. Ḥadīda. From the Banū Mālik b. Najjār: Abdullah b. ʿAbdullah b. Ubayy. From the Banū Zurayq: Ruqād b. Labīd, Farwa b. ʿAmr, Abū ʿAyyāsh and Muʿādh b. Rifāʿa. And from the Banū Sāʿida: Saʿd b. ʿUbāda.

Ibn Abī Sabra related to me from Ayyūb b. ʿAbd al-Raḥmān b. Abī Ṣaʿṣaʿa, who said: The Messenger of God marched with his companions, and cavalry, and foot soldiers around him. The Messenger of God passed by a group of Banū Najjār in al-Ṣawrayn, and with them was Ḥāritha b. al-Nuʿmān. They were arranged in line and wearing weapons. He said, "Did anyone pass by you?" They said, "Yes, Diḥya al-Kalbī passed on a mule with a saddle, and on it velvet material. [Page 499] He commanded us to put on our weapons. So we took our weapons and lined up. He said, 'This is the Messenger of God coming to you now.' "

Ḥāritha b. al-Nuʿmān said: We were in two lines and the Messenger of God said to us, "That was Gabriel!" Ḥāritha b. al-Nuʿmān used to say: I saw Gabriel twice in my lifetime: on the day of al-Ṣawrayn, and on the day of the site of the funeral when we returned from Ḥunayn. The Messenger of God reached the Banū Qurayẓa and alighted at our well, below the field of the Banū Qurayẓa. ʿAlī had already arrived with a group of Muhājirūn and Anṣār including Abū Qatāda.

Ibn Abī Sabra related to me from Usayd b. Abī Usayd from Abū Qatāda, who said: We reached them, and when they saw us they were certain of disaster. ʿAlī planted the flag at the foot of the fortress, while they confronted us in their fortresses insulting the Messenger of God and his wives. Abū Qatāda said: We did not answer but said, "The sword is between us and you." The Messenger of God appeared, and when ʿAlī saw him, he went back to him. He commanded me to keep close to the flag, and I stuck with it. ʿAlī detested that the Messenger of God should hear their insults and their scoldings. The Messenger of God marched to them. Usayd b. Ḥuḍayr approached the fortress and said, "O enemies of God we will not leave your fortress until you die of starvation. You in your homes are like foxes in their dens." They said, "O Ibn Ḥuḍayr, we, not the Khazraj, are your allies!" and they were fearful. He said, "There is no agreement between me and you, and no alliance."

The Messenger of God drew near them while we shielded him. He said, [Page 500] "O brothers of monkeys and pigs and worshipers of evil, did you insult me?" He said: They began to swear by the Torah that was revealed to Moses, "We did not!" They said, "O Abū l-Qasim, you are not ignorant." Then the Messenger of God sent forward the marksmen among his companions. Farwa b. Zubayd related to me from ʿĀʾisha bt. Saʿd from her father, who said: The Messenger of God said to me, "O Saʿd, go forward and shoot them." So I went forward where my arrows would reach them. With me were about fifty men, and we shot at them for a while such that our arrows were like the locust. They hid in their den, and not one of them came out. We worried about our arrows that went, and we began to shoot some and keep some. Kaʿb b. ʿAmr al-Māzanī—who was a marksman—used to say: I shot at that time with what was in my quiver, until after an hour into the night we stopped. They shot at us while the Messenger of God stopped on his horse wearing his weapons, and the companions of the cavalry were around him. Then the Messenger of God commanded us, and we turned back to our stations, and spent the night in our camp. Our food was the date. Saʿd b. ʿUbāda sent a load of dates, and we spent the night eating them. Indeed, the Messenger of God, Abū Bakr, and ʿUmar were seen eating from those dates. The Messenger of God used to say, "The best food is the date."

The Muslims gathered at the Messenger of God's for *'Ishā'*. Among them were those who did not pray until they came to the Banū Qurayẓa, and those who had prayed. They mentioned that to the Messenger of God, and he did not blame one who prayed, nor one who did not pray until he reached the Banū Qurayẓa. We reached them before dawn.

[Page 501] The Prophet sent the marksmen forward. He mobilized his companions and they surrounded their fortress from every direction. The Muslims began to aim at them with arrows and stones. They took turns, some of them replacing others. The Messenger of God did not stop shooting at the enemy until he was certain of their destruction.

Al-Ḍaḥḥāk b. ʿUthmān related to me from Nāfiʿ from Ibn ʿUmar, who said: The Banū Qurayẓa were shooting at us with strength from their fortress using arrows and stones. We stayed where our arrows would reach them.

Al-Ḍaḥḥāk b. ʿUthmān related to me from Jaʿfar b. Maḥmūd, who said, Muḥammad b. Maslama said: We besieged them with the strongest of sieges. I remember the day we reached them before dawn. We approached the fortress and aimed at them from a short distance. We attached ourselves to their fortress and we did not disperse until it was twilight. The Messenger of God encouraged us to *jihād* and patience. We spent the night at the fortress and we did not return to our station until they ceased fighting.

The Banū Qurayẓa said, "We want to speak to you." The Messenger of God said, "Yes." They sent Nabbash b. Qays who spoke to the Messenger of God for a while. He said, "O Muḥammad, we will accept what the Banū Naḍīr accepted. To you will be our property and weapons, and in return our blood will be saved. We will set out from your land with our women and children. We will take what the camels can carry except for the weapons." The Messenger of God refused. So they said, "Save our blood and give us our women and children, and we will not load our camels." The Messenger of God said, "No. You will submit only to my judgment." Nabbāsh returned to his companions with the reply of the Messenger of God. Kaʿb b. Asad said, "O people of the Banū Qurayẓa, by God, indeed you know that Muḥammad is a prophet of God. Only our envy of the Arabs has kept us from him since he is not a prophet from the Banū [Page 502] Isrāʾīl. It is how God made it. Indeed I detested destroying the contract and the agreement. But it is the trial and misfortune of this man (Ḥuyayy) upon us. His people were worse than us. Muḥammad will not spare a single man except those who follow him. Do you remember what Ibn Khirāsh said to you when he arrived before you? He said, 'I left the wine, the leavened bread and the authority and I came to the water bag, the dates and the barley.' They said, 'Why is that?' He said, 'A prophet will come out from this village, and if he sets out while I am living, I will follow him and help him. If he appears after me, beware that you may be cheated away from him. Follow him and be his help and his friends. You have believed in the two books, both of them, the first and the last.'" Kaʿb said, "Come, let us follow him, trust him and believe in him, and we will protect our blood, our children, our women and our wealth. We will be in the position of those who are with him." They said, "We will not follow other than ours. We are the people of the book and the prophethood. Shall we follow other than us?" Kaʿb tried to answer them with words of advice. They said, "We will not depart from the Torah nor will we leave what was ours from the command of Moses." He said, "Then let us kill our women and our children, and then set out with swords in our hands to Muḥammad and his companions. If we are killed we are killed and we leave nothing behind us that will worry us. If we succeed, by my life, we shall take women and have children." Huyayy b. Akhṭab laughed sarcastically and said, "What is the crime of those women and children?" The head of the Jews, al-Zabīr b. Bāṭa and his relatives said, "There is no good in life without women and children." He said, "Only one position remains from the opinions. If you do not follow it, you will be the sons of the cursed." They said, "What is it?" He said, "Tonight is the Sabbath and it is logical that Muḥammad and his companions believe that we will not fight in it. But we will set out [Page 503] and perhaps catch him unawares." They said, "We will not corrupt our Sabbath. You know what got to us in it." Ḥuyayy said, "I called you to this while the Quraysh and the Ghaṭafān are attending and you refuse to break the Sabbath. If the Jews obeyed me they would do it." The Jews shouted, "No we will not break the Sabbath."

Nabbāsh b. Qays said, "How will you achieve heedlessness from them when you see that their affairs are stronger every day? In the beginning when they besieged us, indeed they fought us by day and returned at night, and you used to say, 'if we could keep them up at night.' But now, they are staying up the night and standing their ground during the day. So what heedlessness may we achieve from them? It is the catastrophe and trial that was written for us." So they disputed and were at a loss. They regretted what they did, and were tender regarding their women and children. The women and children when they saw their weakness were deeply depressed and cried, so they felt sorry for them.

Ṣāliḥ b. Jaʿfar related to me from Muḥammad b. ʿUqba from Thaʿlaba b. Abī Mālik, who said: Thaʿlaba and Usayd the two sons of Saʿiyya, and Asad b. ʿUbayd their uncle said, "O community of the Banū Qurayẓa, by God, indeed you know that he is the Messenger of God, for his description is with us. Our scholars and the scholars of the Banū Naḍīr have related to us about it. This is the first of them—meaning Ḥuyayy b. Akhṭab—with Jubayr b. al-Hayyibān, the most truthful people with us. He informed us about his description at his death." They said, "We will not depart from the Torah." When those three saw their refusal they came down in the same night in which, in its morning, the Qurayẓa came down and converted to Islam and they secured themselves, their families and their wealth.

Ḍaḥḥāk b. ʿUthmān related to me from Muḥammad b. Yaḥyā b. Ḥibbān, that ʿAmr b. Suʿdā, a man from among them, said, "O Community of Jews surely you entered into an alliance with Muḥammad according to which you agreed that you would not help one of his enemies against him, and that you would help him [Page 504] against those who attacked him. But you destroyed the agreement that was between you and him. I did not enter in it, and I did not associate with you in your treachery. If you refuse to enter with him then confirm Judaism and pay the *jizya*. But by God, I do not know whether he will accept it or not." They said, "We will not be established for the Arab with a tax on our necks. Death is better than that!" He said, "Indeed I am free of you."

He set out in that night with the sons of Saʿiyya and he passed the guard of the Prophet. Over them was Muḥammad b. Maslama. Muḥammad b. Maslama said, "Who is this?" He said, "ʿAmr b. Suʿdā." Muḥammad said, "Pass! O God, do not forbid me the cancellation of the steps of the noble." He went on his way, and he set out until he came to the Mosque of the Messenger of God, where he spent the night until next morning. On the morrow, it was not known where he was until this hour. The Messenger of God was asked about him and he said, "That is a man God rescued for his faithfulness." It was said: Indeed, he was one who did not appear among them and brought no challenge to battle, according to our narration.

Ibrāhīm b. Jaʿfar related to me from his father, who said: ʿAmr b. Suʿda passed by the watch. Muḥammad b. Maslama called out to him, "Who is this?" He replied, "ʿAmr b. Suʿda." Muḥammad said, "We know you." Then he said, "O Lord do not prohibit me from forgiving a mistake of the noble." Al-Thawrī related to me from ʿAbd al-Karīm al-Jazarī, from ʿIkrima, who said: When it was the day of the Banū Qurayẓa a man from the Jews said, "Who will duel?" Al-Zubayr stood up to him and fought him. Ṣafiyya said, "How serious!" The Messenger of God said, "Of the two, the one above his companion will kill the other." Al-Zubayr was above, and he killed his companion. The Messenger of God gave him his booty. [Page 505] Ibn Wāqid said: This tradition of their fighting was not heard. I think this was in Khaybar.

Maʿmar b. Rāshid related to me from al-Zuhrī from Ibn al-Musayyib, who said: The first affair that the Messenger of God blamed Abū Lubāba b. ʿAbd al-Mundhir for was his quarreling with an orphan about a cluster of grapes belonging to him. The Messenger of God had judged the grapes for Abū Lubāba, but the orphan began to howl and complain to the Messenger of God. The Messenger of God said to Abū Lubāba, "Give me the grapes, O Abū Lubāba, in order that I may give it to the orphan." But Abū Lubāba refused to give it to the Messenger of God. The Prophet said, "O Abū Lubāba, I will give it to the orphan, and you will have the same in Paradise." Still, Abū Lubāba refused to give it to him. Al-Zuhrī said: A man from the Anṣār related to me that when he refused to give it, Ibn Daḥdāḥa—a man from the Anṣār—said, "Do you think, O Messenger of God, if I bought these grapes and gave it to the orphan I will have similar to it in Paradise?" The Messenger of God said, "Yes." Abū Daḥdāḥa rushed until he met Abū Lubāba and said, "I will purchase your grapes from you with my gardens"—there was to him a garden of date palm—Abū Lubāba agreed. Ibn Daḥdāḥa purchased the grapes with the garden of date palm, and gave it to the orphan. Ibn Daḥdāḥa had not hesitated to approach the disbelieving Quraysh at Uḥud. Ibn Daḥdāḥa set out and was killed as a martyr. The Messenger of God said, "May the grapes come down to Ibn Daḥdāḥa in Paradise."

They said: When the siege intensified against them they sent to the Messenger of God saying, "Send us Abū Lubāba b. ʿAbd al-Mundhir." [Page 506] Rabīʿa b. al-Ḥārith related to me from ʿAbdullah b. Muḥammad b. ʿAqīl from al-Sāʾib b. Abī Lubāba b. ʿAbd al-Mundhir from his father, who said: When the Banū Qurayẓa sent to the Messenger of God and asked him to send me to them, the Messenger of God called me and said, "Go to your allies, for indeed they sent for you from the Aws." He said, "I entered upon them, and the siege was strengthened against them. They rushed to me saying, "O Abū Lubāba, we are your allies among the people, all of them." Kaʿb b. Asad stood up and said, "Abū Bashīr, you know what we did in your affairs and the affairs of your people on the day of al-Ḥadāʾiq and Buʿāth, and every war you were in. The invasion is strong against us and is destroying us, and Muḥammad refuses to withdraw from our fortress until we yield to his judgment. If he withdraws from us we will go ahead to the land of Syria or Khaybar, and we will never stop close to him nor regroup against him." Abū Lubāba said, "Since 'this' is with you he will never leave your destruction," and pointed to Ḥuyayy b. Akhṭab. Kaʿb said, "He, by God, brought me to this and does not take me out of it." Ḥuyayy said, "What did I do? I was greedy to get to him, and when he escaped me, I shared my destiny with you, and what hurt you, hurt me." Kaʿb said, "What need have I until you and I are killed and our children enslaved." Ḥuyayy said, "Tragedy and catastrophe were written for us." Then Kaʿb said, "Do you not see? Indeed, we chose you above the rest of you. Surely, Muḥammad has refused except that we yield to his judgment. So shall we yield?" He said, "Yes, yield," then indicating his throat, "and it will be slaughter."

Abū Lubāba said: I immediately regretted it, and declared, "To God must we return." Kaʿb said to me, "What is the matter with you, O Abū Lubāba?" I said, "I have betrayed God and His Messenger." I stepped out and indeed my beard was full of tears. [Page 507] The people expected my return to them, until I took another path behind the fortress in order to come to the mosque, and tied myself to a perfumed column called the column of forgiveness. Some say it was not that column, but rather, that I tied myself to the column, which was facing the *minbar* at the door of Umm Salama, the wife of the Prophet. This is the more confirmed of the two sayings. My going and what I did reached the Messenger of God and he said, "Leave him, until God does with him what He wills. If he had come to me, I would have asked for his forgiveness. If he does not come to me, but goes, leave him!"

Abū Lubāba said: I was in a great turmoil for fifteen nights and I recall a vision that I saw. Mūsā b. ʿUbayda related to me from Ayyūb b. Khālid, who said: Abū Lubāba said: I had dreamed, while we were besieging the Banū Qurayẓa, as though I were in stagnant mud. I did not leave from it until I almost died of its stench. Then I saw a river running and I saw myself washing from it until I was purified, and I found a fragrant breeze. Abū Bakr interpreted it and said, "You will enter an affair that will depress you, and then you will be relieved." I used to recall the words of Abū Bakr while I was tied. I hoped that my forgiveness would be revealed.

Maʿmar related to me from al-Zuhrī, who said: The Messenger of God appointed Abū Lubāba over their fighting, but when what happened, happened he dismissed him and appointed Usayd b. Ḥuḍayr. Abū Lubāba was tied for around seven days and nights at the pillar, which was at the door of Umm Salama, in the strong heat. He neither ate nor drank. He said, "I will continue thus until I am separated from the world, or God forgives me." He said: He continued this way until he could no longer hear voices for exhaustion. The Messenger of God looked at him every morning [Page 508] and evening. Then God forgave him and it was proclaimed, "Indeed, God has forgiven you!" The Prophet sent someone to untie his ropes, but he refused to let any one but the Messenger of God untie him. So the Messenger of God came, and released him.

Al-Zuhrī said: Hind bt. al-Ḥārith said to me from Umm Salama the wife of the Prophet: I saw the Messenger of God release him from his ropes. Indeed the Messenger of God raised his voice to speak to him and inform him of his forgiveness. He did not understand much of what was said for the exhaustion and weakness. It was said that he stayed tied for fifteen days. His daughter came to him with dates to break his fast. He chewed some of them and left some, saying, "By God I am not able to stomach it for fear that my forgiveness shall not be revealed." She untied him at the time of every prayer if there was a need for him to perform ablution. If not, she returned the rope. Indeed the rope made cuts on his arms. It was of hair. He was treated for it afterwards for a long time, and a mark remained on his arms after he was healed. We heard another story about his forgiveness, as well.

ʿAbdullah b. Yazīd b. Qusayṭ related to us from his father, from Muḥammad b. ʿAbd al-Raḥmān b. Thawbān from Umm Salama the wife of the Prophet, who said: Indeed the forgiveness of Abū Lubāba was revealed in my house. Umm Salama said: I heard the Messenger of God laugh before dawn and I said, "About what are you laughing, O Messenger of God, may God keep you happy?" He said, "Abū Lubāba is forgiven."

She said: I said, "May I inform him about it?" He said, "If you wish." She said, "I stood at the door of my room, and it was before the veil, and I said, "O Abū Lubāba, rejoice, God has forgiven you." [Page 509] The people clamored to set him free. Abū Lubāba said, "No. When the Messenger of God comes it will be he who sets me free." When the Messenger of God set out for the morning prayer he set him free. God revealed about Abū Lubāba b. ʿAbd al-Mundhir: *Those who have confessed their sins and mixed their good deeds with the bad, may God forgive them* (Q. 9:102) to the end of the verse. Some say, *O you who believe betray not God and His Messenger* (Q. 8:27), was revealed.

Muḥammad b. ʿAbdullah related to me from al-Zuhrī, who said the words, *O Apostle, do not grieve because of those who rush into unbelief among those who say that they believe with their lips . . .* to the end of the verse, were revealed (Q. 5:41). The most confirmed with us are His words: *Those who have confessed their sins and mixed their good deeds*.

Maʿmar related to me from al-Zuhrī from Ibn Kaʿb b. Mālik, who said: Abū Lubāba came to the Messenger of God and said, "I renounce the house of my people in which I committed this sin. I donate my property as charity to God and His Messenger." The Prophet said, "One third is sufficient from you." So he paid one third. Abū Lubāba renounced the house of his people and God forgave him. There was only good in his Islam until he departed the world.

They said: When the siege exhausted them the Banū Qurayẓa yielded to the judgment of the Messenger of God. The Messenger of God commanded their imprisonment and the tying of their wrists. Muḥammad b. Maslama began to tie them. They were taken aside. They took out the women and children from their fortresses and set them aside. The Messenger of God appointed ʿAbdullah b. Salām, and ordered [Page 510] the collection of their belongings including what was found in their fortresses of weapons and furniture and clothing. Ibn Abī Sabra related to me from al-Miswar b. Rifāʿa, who said: one thousand five hundred swords, three hundred armors, one thousand lances, one thousand five hundred shields and *ḥajafa*, i.e. shields made of camel skin were found. They took out much furniture and many utensils; they found wine and jars of alcohol, but all of that was spilled out and the fifth was not taken. They found a number of watering camels among the livestock and collected all of them. ʿUmar b. Muḥammad related to me from Abū Saʿīd from Jābir b. ʿAbdullah, who said: I was among those who broke the jar of alcohol at that time.

Khārija b. ʿAbdullah related to me from Dāwud b. al-Ḥuṣayn from Abū Sufyān from Muḥammad b. Maslama, who said: The Messenger of God leaned and sat down, and the Aws drew near the Messenger of God. They said, "O Messenger of God, these are our confederates to the exclusion of the Khazraj. You remember what you did with the Banū Qaynuqāʿ, the confederates of Ibn Ubayy, yesterday. You gave him three hundred unprotected and four hundred armed men. Our confederates have regretted their destruction of the agreement, so give them to us." The Messenger of God was silent. He did not speak until they pressed him and insisted, and all of the Aws spoke. The Messenger of God said, "Will it satisfy you that a man from among you will judge them?" They said, "But of course." He said, "That will be Saʿd b. Muʿādh." At that time Saʿd was at the Mosque in the tent of Kuʿayba bt. Saʿd b. ʿUtba. She used to treat the wounded and clean up the messy persons. She used to take care of the lost ones and those who did not have anyone to care for them. She had a tent in the mosque and the Messenger of God had placed Saʿd in it. When the Messenger of God gave [Page 511] the judgement to Saʿd b. Muʿādh, the Aws left to meet him. They carried him on a donkey with a saddle of coir; above the saddle a layer of velvet. And its bridle was a rope of coir. They set out around him saying, "O Abū ʿAmr, surely the Messenger of God has appointed you judge over the affair of your confederates that you may judge favorably about them and be good to them. You saw Ibn Ubayy and what he did for his confederates." Al-Ḍaḥḥāk b. Khalīfa said, "Your confederates, your confederates. They have defended you in all your wars. They chose you above everybody else and hope for your protection. They own a number of camels and equipment." Salama b. Salāma b. Waqash said, "O Abū ʿAmr be kind to your freedmen and your confederates. Indeed, the Messenger of God would let them live. They helped you on the day of Buʿāth and Ḥadāʾiq. Do not be more evil than Ibn Ubayy."

Ibrāhīm b. Jaʿfar said, from his father: A sayer of theirs used to say: O Abū ʿAmr, indeed, by God, we fought and killed with them. We needed their support and were strengthened by them. They said: Saʿd did not speak until they pressed him. Then, Saʿd said, "The time has come for Saʿd to fear the blame of God alone." Al-Ḍaḥḥāk b. Khalīfa said, "Stand up for him!" Then Ḍaḥhāk returned to the Aws and announced to them the death of the Banū Qurayẓa. Muʿattib b. Qushayr said, "What a terrible morning it is." Ḥāṭib b. Umayya b. al-Ẓafarī said, "My people have gone to meet their destiny." Saʿd approached the Messenger of God, and the people were seated around the Messenger of God. When Saʿd appeared the Messenger of God said, "Stand up for your master." A man from the Banū ʿAbd al-Ashhal used to say: We stood up on our feet in two lines. Every man among us greeted him until at last it was the turn of the Messenger of God. Someone said, "When the Messenger of God said, 'Stand up for your master,' he meant the Anṣār, not the Quraysh."

[Page 512] The Aws, who stood up with the Messenger of God for Saʿd, said, "O Abū ʿAmr, indeed the Messenger of God has appointed you judge. Be good to them and remember their trials with you." Saʿd said, "Will you be satisfied with my judgment over the Banū Qurayẓa?" They said, "Yes. We agreed to your judgment in your absence. You are chosen from us, so we hope that you will secure for us just as another secured for his confederates from the Qaynuqāʿ. Our traditions with you are our traditions. We are most in need today of your facilitation." Saʿd said, "I will not spare you any effort." They said, "What does he mean by these words?" Then he said, "Do you promise by God and his covenant that the judgment with you is what I judge?" They said, "Yes." Saʿd said in the other direction, which included the Messenger of God, but not looking directly at the Messenger of God out of respect for him, "And to those who are here, similarly?" The Messenger of God and those who were with him said, "Yes." Saʿd said, "Indeed I judge about them, that whoever shaves a beard be killed; their women and children be enslaved; and their property be apportioned." The Messenger of God said, "Surely you judge with the judgment of God above the seven heavens."

Saʿd b. Muʿādh had prayed in the night of the morning the Qurayẓa had yielded to the judgment of the Messenger of God. He had prayed to God and said, "O God, if you have preserved something from the war against the Quraysh, leave me for it. There is not a people I would like to fight more than those who refused to believe in the Messenger of God. They have harmed him and expelled him. If the war has ended between us and them, grant me martyrdom and do not let me die until I satisfy myself regarding the Banū Qurayẓa." So God satisfied him about them.

He commanded that the prisoners be taken to the house of Usāma b. Zayd, and the women and children to the house of the daughter of al-Ḥārith. The Messenger of God [Page 513] commanded the taking of dates and their division among them. That night they ate hungrily like donkeys. They spent the night studying the Torah. Some instructed others on how to affirm their religion and stick to the Torah. The Messenger of God gave instructions about the weapons and the furniture and the chattel and the garments. They were taken to the house of the daughter of al-Ḥārith. He gave instructions concerning the camels and the plunder, and they were taken over there to graze among the trees. They said: The Messenger of God breakfasted at the market and gave instructions for a furrow to be dug there between the house of Abū Jahm al-ʿAdawī and the Aḥjār al-Zayt in the market. His companions were digging there. The Messenger of God sat with the distinguished among his companions. He called for the men of the Banū Qurayẓa, and they came out at a leisurely pace, and their heads were cut off.

They said to Kaʿb b. Asad: "Do you not see what Muḥammad is doing to us?" He said, "What hurts you and what harms you, woe unto you! What ever the case may be, you do not understand. Do you not see that the one who calls does not stop calling, and that he who goes from you does not return? It is, by God, the sword. I invited you to other than this but you refused." They said, "This is not a good time for blame. We regret that we reviled your opinion. We should not have destroyed the covenant that was between us and Muḥammad." Ḥuyayy said, "Leave what you see of blame, for indeed, it does not spare you anything. Be patient for the sword." And they continued to be killed by Muḥammad. Those who did the killing were ʿAlī and al-Zubayr. They brought in Ḥuyayy b. Akhṭab with his hands gathered to his neck. He wore a red garment to be killed in and proceeded to tear it up with his finger-tips in order that one would not take it as plunder. The Messenger of God said to him, "Did not God grant you to us?" He said, [Page 514] "But of course, and by God, I do not blame myself for opposing you. Indeed I sought the power at his place, but God refused except that you overpower me. I have tried every way, but whoever lets God down is forsaken." Then he drew near to the people and said, "O People there is no problem regards God's wishes. By fate and destiny, tragedy was written for the Banū Isrāʾīl." Then Muḥammad commanded that his head be struck off. Then Ghazzāl b. Samawal was brought. He said, "Did not God grant you to us?" He said, "Yes, O Abū l-Qāsim." The Prophet ordered that his head be cut off. Then they brought Nabbāsh b. Qays, and he contended with who came with him when he fought him, and he quarreled with the man who brought him until he had a nose bleed. The Messenger of God said to the man who came with him, "Why are you doing this to him? Is not the sword sufficient?" He replied, "O Messenger of God he contended with me because he wants to get away." And he said, "By the Torah he is lying. If he released me I would not delay from the place where my people are to be killed until I am as one of them." He said: The Messenger of God said, "Be good to your captives. Let them rest; quench their thirst until they are cool. Then, kill those who remain. Do not apply both the heat of the sun and the heat of the weapons." It was a summer's day. They let them rest. They quenched their thirst and fed them. When they were cool the Messenger of God began to kill those who were left.

The Prophet looked at Salmā bt. Qays. She was one of his aunts. She had prayed towards the two *qiblas* and given allegiance to him. Rifāʿa b. Samawʾal was a companion to her and her brother Salīṭ b. Qays and the people of the house. When he was in prison he sent for her, saying, "Talk to Muḥammad so that he will leave me. I have a relationship with you. You are one of his mothers and it will be a favor from you to me until the Day of Judgment." The Messenger of God said, [Page 515] "What is with you O Umm al-Mundhir?" She replied, "O Messenger of God, Rifāʿa b. Samawʾal used to visit us and to him is a protection with us. Give him to me." The Messenger of God had seen him take protection with her, so he said, "Yes. He is for you." Then she said, "O Messenger of God, he will pray with me and eat the flesh of the camel." The Prophet smiled and said, "If he prays it is good for him. But if he stays in his religion it is evil for him." She said, "He converted." He used to be called the *mawlā* of Umm al-Mundhir. That destroyed him and he avoided the house. When that reached Umm al-Mundhir she sent for him saying, "Indeed, and by God, I am not your mistress. But I spoke to the Messenger of God and he gave you to me. I spared your blood and you have your lineage." After that he used to visit her. He returned to the house.

Saʿd b. ʿUbāda and al-Ḥubāb b. al-Mundhir came and they said: O Messenger of God, indeed the Aws detest the killing of the Banū Qurayẓa because of the significance of their confederacy. Saʿd b. Muʿādh said, "O Messenger of God, those who are good among the Aws do not detest it. For those who detest it among the Aws, may God not satisfy him." Usayd b. Ḥuḍayr stood up and said, "O Messenger of God, do not leave one of the houses of the Aws, except you apportion the Jews to it. As for those who are displeased, God will force him. So send to my house first." He sent to the Banū ʿAbd al-Ashhal with two. Usayd b. Ḥuḍayr cut off the head of one of them and Abū Nāʾila killed the other. And he sent to the Banū Ḥāritha with two. Abū Burda b. al-Nīyyār struck off the head of one of them, and Muḥayyiṣa finished him off. Abū ʿAbs b. Jabar killed the other, and Ẓuhayr b. Rāfīʿ finished him off. He sent two prisoners to the Banū Ẓafar. Yaʿqūb b. Muḥammad related to me from ʿĀṣim b. ʿUmar b. Qatāda, who said: [Page 516] Qatāda b. al-Nuʿmān killed one of them and Naḍr b. al-Ḥārith killed the other. ʿAṣim said: Ayyūb b. Bashīr al-Muʿāwiya said: He sent us—the Banū Muʿāwiya—two prisoners. Jabar b. ʿAtīk killed one of them and Nuʿmān b. ʿAṣar killed the other, an ally of theirs from the Baliyy. They said: Send the Banū ʿAmr b. Awf two prisoners, ʿUqba b. Zayd and his brother Wahb b. Zayd. ʿUwaym b. Sāʿida killed one of them and Sālim b. ʿUmayr killed the other. He sent for the Banū Umayya b. Zayd.

Kaʿb b. Asad was brought with his hands tied to his neck. His face was beautiful. The Messenger of God said, "Kaʿb b. Asad?" Kaʿb said, "Yes, O Abū l-Qāsim." He said, "You did not make use of the advice of Ibn Khirāsh, for he believed in me. Did he not command you to follow me, and if you saw me, to convey his greetings?" He said, "But yes, by the Torah, O Abū l-Qāsim. And if the Jews did not reproach me about fearing the sword I would have followed you. But to me is the religion of the Jew." The Messenger of God said, "Send him forward and cut off his head." So they sent him forward and cut off his head.

ʿUtba b. Jabīra related to me from al-Ḥuṣayn b. ʿAbd al-Raḥmān b. ʿAmr b. Saʿd b. Muʿādh, who said: When Ḥuyayy b. Akhṭab, Nabbāsh b. Qays, Ghazzāl b. Samawal, and Kaʿb b. Asad had been killed the Messenger of God stood up and said to Saʿd b. Muʿādh, "Attend to those who remain." Saʿd called them out one by one to be killed.

They said: There was a woman among the Banū Naḍīr called Nubāta. She was married to a man from the Banū Qurayẓa, and he loved her and she loved him. When the siege was strengthened against them, she cried out to him, "Indeed you will be separated from me." He said, "By the Torah, it is as you think. You are a woman so throw down a millstone on them. Indeed, we have not killed one of them yet. You are a woman and if [Page 517] Muḥammad defeats us he will not kill women." In fact, he hated that she should be taken prisoner and wanted her to be killed for the crime. When she was in the fortress of al-Zabīr b. Bāṭā she threw down a millstone from above the fortress. The Muslims would sometimes be seated under the fortress seeking the shade in its shadow. The millstone appeared, and when the people saw it they moved away.

But it reached Khallād b. Suwayd and crushed his head. The Muslims became cautious of the bottom of the fortress.

When it was the day the Messenger of God commanded that they be killed, Nubāta came before ʿĀ'isha and began to laugh hysterically. She said, "The leaders of the Banū Qurayẓa are being killed." All of a sudden she heard the voice of a speaker say, "O Nubāta!" She said, "I am, by God, she who is being called." ʿĀ'isha said, "For what?" She said, "My husband killed me." She was a soft-spoken girl. ʿĀ'isha said, "How did your husband kill you?" She said, "I was in the fortress of al-Zabīr b. Bāṭā, and he commanded me to push the millstone on the companions of Muḥammad. It crushed the head of a man among them to death, and I killed him. And the Messenger of God commanded that I be killed for Khallād b. Suwayd." ʿĀ'isha said, "I shall never forget the good soul of Nabāṭa and her hysterical laughter when she knew that she would be killed." ʿĀ'isha used to say that the Banū Qurayẓa continued to be killed that day until it was night and that they were killed throughout the night with the help of a torch. Ibrāhīm b. Sumāma used to say from al-Miswar b. Rifāʿa from Muḥammad b. Kaʿb al-Quraẓī, who said: They were slaughtered until twilight withdrew. Then they were covered with the dust in the trench. Whoever they doubted had reached puberty they looked into his underwear. If he had grown hair he was killed, and if not he was taken prisoner.

ʿAbd al-Raḥmān b. ʿAbd al-ʿAzīz related to me from ʿAbdullah b. Abī Bakr b. Ḥazm, who said: They were six hundred except for ʿAmr b. Suʿdāʾ whose dead body was found and saved. Ibn Wāqid said: I confirm that he set out from the fortress. [Page 518] Mūsā b. ʿUbayda related to me from Muḥammad b. al-Munkadir, who said: They numbered between six and seven hundred. Ibn ʿAbbās used to say they numbered seven hundred and fifty.

They said: The Women of the Banū Qurayẓa, when they were moved to the house of Ramla bt. al-Ḥārith and the House of Usāma, were saying, "Would that Muḥammad will set the men free and accept a ransom." When it was morning and they learned of the killing of their men they screamed and ripped their clothes from the neckline, tore their hair, and slapped their cheeks for their men. He said: al-Zabīr b. Bāṭā said, "Be silent. Do you think you are the first to be taken prisoners from the women of the Banū Isrā'īl since the beginning of the world? There will be no end to the taking of prisoners until we meet with you at the end of time. If there were good in your men they would have saved you. Stay attached to the religion of Judaism. We shall die with it and live with it."

ʿAbd al-Ḥamīd b. Jaʿfar related to me from Muḥammad b. Yaḥyā b. Ḥibbān and Ibn Abī Ḥabība related to me from Dawūd b. al-Ḥuṣayn. All have related portions of these traditions to me. They said: al-Zabīr b. Bāṭā had done a favor for Thābit b. Qays on the day of Buʿāth. Thābit came to al-Zabīr and said, "O Abū ʿAbd al-Raḥmān, do you know me?" He replied, "Do you think one like me will not know the likes of you?" Thābit said, "You have done me a good deed and I want to repay you." Zabīr replied, "Indeed the noble reward the noble. I am in the greatest need of your help today." Thābit came to the Messenger of God and said, "O Messengr of God, [Page 519] Zabīr helped me when my hopes were cut off on the day of Buʿāth. I mention this good deed to you, for I desire to help him, so give him to me." The Messenger of God said, "He is for you." Then Thābit came to Zabīr and said, "Indeed the Messenger of God has given you to me." Al-Zabīr said, "I am an old man. I have no family or son or wealth in Yathrib. What will I do with life?" So Thābit came to the Messenger of God and said, "O

Messenger of God, give me his son." So he gave him his son. Then he said, "O Messenger of God, give me his property and his family." So the Messenger of God gave Thābit Zabīr's property, son and family. Thābit returned to al-Zabīr and said, "Indeed the Messenger of God has given me your son and your property and your family."

Zabīr said, "O Thābit, you have rewarded me and repaid your debt, but, what has happened to him whose face is like a Chinese mirror, in which the virgins of the neighborhood could see themselves, Kaʿb b. Asad?" He said, "He is killed." Al-Zabīr said, "What happened to the master of the cities and the desert, the lord of the two neighborhoods who carries them in war and feeds them at home, Ḥuyayy b. Akhṭab?" He said, "He is killed." Al-Zabīr said, "What happened to the leader of the vanguard of the Jews at war when they charge, and their protector at the back when they retreat, Ghazzāl b. Samaw'al?" He said, "He is killed." Al-Zabīr said, "What does the charger who does not ever approach a group without dispersing it, and would not attend to a knot without loosening it, Nabbāsh b. Qays?" He said, "He is killed." Al-Zabīr said, "What happened to the carrier of the flag on the day of war, Wahb b. Zayd?" He said, "He is killed." Al-Zabīr said, "What happened to the one who attends to the feeding of the Jews and fathers the parentless and widows, ʿUqba b. Zayd?" He said, "He is killed." Zabīr said, "What happened to the two ʿAmrs who used to meet to study the Torah?" He said, "They are killed." Al-Zabīr said, "O Thābit? What good is life after those? Must I return to the home they were living in to stay after them? I do not desire that. Indeed I ask you in return for my debt to send me forward and kill me with the killing of the nobility of the Banū Qurayẓa. Take my sword for surely it is sharp, and strike me with it, and finish it off. Raise your hand away from the food [Page 520] and bring it closer to the head, lower from the brain. Indeed it is best that the body remain with the neck. O Thābit, I am impatient to find my loved ones." Hearing his words, Abū Bakr said, "Woe unto you, O Ibn Bāṭā, indeed it is not an emptying of the bucket, but an eternal suffering." He replied, "O Thābit, send me forward and kill me." Thābit said, "I will not kill you." Al-Zabīr said, "I do not care who kills me! But, O Thābit, see to my wife and my son for they are anxious about death. Ask your friend to release them and return their property. I will go towards al-Zubayr b. al-ʿAwwām." He approached al-Zubayr and al-Zubayr struck off his head. Thābit asked the Messenger of God about his wife and his property and his son. The Messenger of God returned all of that to his son. He set his wife free, and he returned their property of dates and camels and clothes, but not the weapons, to them. They stayed with the family of Thābit b. Qays b. Shammās.

They said: Rayḥāna, the daughter of Zayd of the Banū Naḍīr, was married to one of the Banū Qurayẓa. The Messenger of God took her for himself as the leader's share. She was beautiful. The Messenger of God suggested that she convert, but she refused except Judaism. The Messenger of God kept away from her and was grieved in his heart. He sent for Ibn Saʿiyya and mentioned that to him. Ibn Saʿiyya said, "May my father and my mother be your ransom! She will convert," and he set out until he came to her. He said to her, "Do not follow your people, you have seen what Ḥuyayy Ibn Akhṭab brought them. So convert to Islam. The Messenger of God will choose you for himself." Meanwhile the Messenger of God was with his companions when he heard the sound of sandals. He said, "Indeed the two sandals of Ibn Saʿiyya who will gladden me with the conversion of Rayḥāna." Ibn Saʿiyya came to him and said, "O Messenger of God, Rayḥāna has converted." The Messenger of God was happy about that.

ʿAbd al-Malik b. Sulaymān related to me from Ayyūb b. ʿAbd al-Raḥmān b. Abī [Page 521] Ṣaʿṣaʿa from Ayyūb b. Bashīr al-Muʿāwī, who said: The Messenger of

God sent her to the house of Salmā bt. Qays Umm Mundhir. She stayed with her until she menstruated. Then she was cleaned of the menstruation and Umm al-Mundhir came and informed the Prophet. The Messenger of God came to her in the house of Umm al-Mundhir, and said, "If you desire that I set you free and marry you, I will do so. If you desire to be my concubine and that I co-habit with you, I will do so." She said, "O Messenger of God, it is easier for you and me that I be your property." So she was the property of the Prophet and he co-habited with her until she died as his property.

Ibn Abī Dhi'b related to me saying: I asked al-Zuhrī about Rayḥāna, and he said: She was the slave of the Messenger of God and he freed her and married her. She concealed herself in her family saying, "No one will see me after the Messenger of God." This is the more confirmed of the two traditions with us. The husband of Rayḥāna before the prophet was al-Ḥakam.

THE RECORD OF THE PORTIONING OF THE BOOTY AND ITS SALE

They said: When the plunder was gathered, the Messenger of God commanded about the property and its sale to those who desired it. And the sale of prisoners to those who desired. The date palms were apportioned. To the Banū ʿAbd al-Ashhal, Ẓafar, and Ḥāritha and Banū Muʿāwiya and those of the Nabīt was a portion. To the Banū ʿAmr b. ʿAwf and those who remained among the Aws was a portion. To the Banū Najjār, Māzin, Mālik, Dhubyān and ʿAdī, a portion. To the Zurayq and Balḥārith b. Khazraj, a portion. The cavalry was thirty-six horses. The first of what was known of the two portions of the horse was on the day of al-Muraysīʿ. Then what was practiced at Muraysīʿ was practiced with the Banū Qurayẓa [Page 522] also. Two portions were granted to each horse and one to its rider, and one portion to a foot soldier. The Messenger of God gave a portion to Khallād b. Suwayd who was killed under the fortress, and another to Abū Sinān b. Miḥṣan, who died while the Messenger of God was besieging them and he was fighting with the Muslims. There were three thousand Muslims. The cavalry consisted of thirty-six riders. The portions numbered three thousand and seventy-two, two portions each for the horses and one for its owner.

Ibrāhīm b. Jaʿfar related to me from his father, who said: The cavalry for the Banū Qurayẓa consisted of thirty-six horses. The Messenger of God led three horses but he took only one portion. The portions numbered three thousand and seventy-two portions. At that time he apportioned the wealth, which was divided into five parts. A portion was written to God. The portions were equal at that time. The portions were set out, and likewise, worn out clothes, camels, sheep, and prisoners. Then he dispersed four portions to the people. He gave from it to the women, who, at that time, attended the battle. He struck a portion for two men, one was killed and the other died. The Messenger of God gave—as a gift to the women who witnessed the Banū Qurayẓa, but he did not apportion booty for them—Ṣafiyya bt. ʿAbd al-Muṭṭalib, Umm ʿUmāra, Umm Salīṭ, Umm al-ʿAlā', al-Sumayrā' bt. Qays, Umm Saʿd b. Muʿādh.

Muḥammad b. ʿAbdullah b. Mālik b. Muḥammad b. Ibrāhīm b. Aslam b. Najra al-Sāʿidī related to me from his grandfather, who said: I attended the Messenger of God who was selling the prisoners of the Banū Qurayẓa. Abū al-Shaḥm al-Yahūdī bought two women, with each one of them [Page 523] three male children, for one hundred and fifty dinars. He kept saying, "Are you not of the Jewish faith?" The two women replied, "We will not depart from the religion of our people until we die!" They were crying.

Ibn Abī Sabra related to me from Yaʿqūb b. Zayd b. Ṭalḥa from his father, who said: When the Banū Qurayẓa—the women and children—were imprisoned, the Messenger of God sold a portion of them to ʿUthmān b. ʿAffān and ʿAbd al-Raḥmān b. ʿAwf. He sent a portion to Najd and another to Syria with Saʿd b. ʿUbāda to sell them and purchase weapons and horses. Some said, the Prophet sold them to ʿUthmān b. ʿAffān and ʿAbd al-Raḥmān b. ʿAwf, and the two men divided between them. ʿUthmān paid much money for his portion. ʿUthmān made something more from each of those prisoners. It was found that much money could be obtained with the old, but not with the young. ʿUthmān made more profit—than the portion of ʿAbd al-Raḥmān—and that was because ʿUthmān had the old in his portion. Some say when he divided, he put the young in one portion and the old in another. Then ʿAbd al-Raḥmān let ʿUthmān choose, and ʿUthmān chose the old people.

ʿAbd al-Ḥamīd b. Jaʿfar related to me from his father, who said: The prisoners included a thousand women and children. The Messenger of God took his fifth before selling the plunder. He apportioned the prisoners into five parts, and he took a fifth and he set free from it, and he gifted from it, and he gave favors from it to those who desired. Thus he did with what he obtained of their old clothes that were divided before they were sold; and thus with the dates. His fifth was set aside and all of it was apportioned by the Prophet into five parts. A portion of it was written to God, and he took out the portion. And wherever his portion occurred he took it and was not selective. [Page 524] A fifth went to Maḥmiyya b. Jazaʿa al-Zubaydī for it was he who apportioned the plunder among the Muslims. ʿAbdullah b. Nāfiʿ related to me from his father from Ibn ʿUmar that the Messenger of God was apportioned a share, and that he did not choose.

ʿAbd al-Ḥamīd b. Jaʿfar related to me from his father, who said: The Messenger of God forbade the separation among the prisoners of the Banū Qurayẓa in the division and sale of the women and children. Ibn Abī Sabra related to me from Isḥāq b. ʿAbdullah that the Messenger of God said at that time, "Do not separate the mother from her children until they have matured." It was said, "O Messenger of God, how will we know that they have matured?" He replied, "The girls will menstruate and the youths will have wet dreams." Ibn Abī Sabra related to me from Yaʿqūb b. Zayd from his father, who said: At that time two sisters were separated when they matured, and a mother from her daughter when she matured. A mother with her little child was sold among the polytheist Arabs, and the Jews of Medina, Tayma, and Khaybar who came out with them. But when there was a little child who was not with his mother, he was not sold among the polytheists or the Jews, but kept with the Muslims.

ʿUtba b. Jabīra related to me from Jaʿfar b. Maḥmūd, who said: Muḥammad b. Maslama said: At that time I bought three prisoners, a woman with her two sons, for forty-five dinars. It was my right and the right of my horse from the prisoners, their land and their clothes. And others did as I did. The portion for the rider was three portions, for him one portion and for his horse, two.

Al-Mughīra b. ʿAbd al-Raḥmān al-Ḥizāmī—his *laqab* was Quṣay—related to me, from Jaʿfar b. Khārija, who said: al-Zubayr b. al-Awwām said: I witnessed the Banū Qurayẓa as a rider, and a portion was given to me and another for my horse. [Page 525] ʿAbd al-Malik b. Yaḥyā related to me from ʿĪsā b. Maʿmar, who said: At that time al-Zubayr had two horses, so the Prophet apportioned five portions for him.

THE RECORD OF SAʿD B. MUʿĀDH

They said: When Saʿd b. Muʿādh judged the Banū Qurayẓa he returned to the tent of Kuʿayba bt. Saʿd al-Aslamiyya for Ḥibban b. al-ʿAriqa had shot him—some say it was Abū Usāma al-Jushamī—and cut his vein. The Messenger of God cauterized it with fire. His hand was swollen and he let the blood drip. So the Prophet did it again and his hand swelled. When Saʿd saw that, he said, "O God, lord of the seven heavens and the seven worlds, indeed there will not be with men a people more desirable for me to fight than a people who lied about Your messenger and threw him out from the Quraysh. Indeed, I think that the war between us and them has ended. If it remains between us, keep me alive to fight them for You, and let me live to fight them in Your name. And if the war has subsided, open this wound and place my death in it since I have satisfied myself with the Banū Qurayẓa for their enmity to You and to Your prophet and Your loved ones (*awliyā*ʾ)!" God split open his wound, and indeed he lay asleep between nightfall and daybreak but did not know of it. The Messenger of God came to visit him leading a group of his companions. They found him shrouded in a white sheet.

Saʿd was a tall white man, and the Messenger of God sat at his head and placed his head in his lap. Then he said, "O God, Saʿd fought for you. He believed in Your messenger and fulfilled his duties. Take his soul in the best way that You take the souls of Your creation." Saʿd opened his eyes when he heard the Prophet and said, "Peace be upon you, O Messenger of God. I witness that you delivered His message." [Page 526] The Messenger of God moved Saʿd's head from his lap and then stood up. He had not yet died, when the Prophet returned to his house. He lived for an hour of the day or more and died after.

When Saʿd died, Gabriel came down to the Messenger of God wearing a turban of velvet. He said, "O Muḥammad, who is this good man who has died among you? The doors of the heavens are opened for him. The throne of the Merciful moved for him." The Messenger of God replied to Gabriel, "My charge is Saʿd b. Muʿādh, and he is dying!" He set out fearfully to the tent of Kuʿayba and tugged at his garments swiftly, but he found Saʿd dead. Men from the Banū ʿAbd al-Ashhal approached and carried him to his house. He said: The Messenger of God set out in his tracks. If one of his sandals were cut he would not have stopped for it; if his outer garment fell he would not have bothered about it; one did not stop for another until they entered upon Saʿd. Abū ʿAbdullah said: We heard that the Prophet attended him when he died.

Muʿādh b. Muḥammad informed me from ʿAṭāʾ b. Abī Muslim from ʿIkrima from Ibn ʿAbbās, who said: When the hand of Saʿd discharged blood, the Messenger of God stood by him and embraced him. The blood splattered the face of the Messenger of God and his beard. The more one desired to keep the blood from the Messenger of God, the more the Messenger of God desired to get closer to Saʿd, until he died.

Sulaymān b. Dāwud related to me from al-Ḥuṣayn from his father from Abū Sufyān from Salama b. Ḥarīsh, who said: I saw the Messenger of God while we were at the gates desiring to enter in his tracks. The Messenger of God entered, and there was no one in the house except Saʿd's shroud. He said: I saw the Prophet leap, and when I saw him leap I stopped. He signalled me to stop. I stopped and drove back whoever was behind me. He sat for a while, then he came out. I said, "O Messenger of God I did not see anyone, yet I saw you leap up!" [Page 527] The Messenger of God said, "I was not able to sit until one of the angels grabbed his wing for me, and then I sat down." The Messenger of God says, "Glad tiding to you, O Abū ʿAmr, glad tidings to you."

Muḥammad b. Ṣāliḥ related to me from Saʿd b. Ibrāhīm from ʿĀmir b. Saʿd from his father, who said: The Messenger of God was done, and the mother of Saʿd was crying, saying: Woe unto the mother of Saʿd.

ʿUmar b. al-Khaṭṭāb said, "Gently, O mother of Saʿd, do not mention Saʿd to me." The Prophet said, "Leave her O ʿUmar, every mourner exaggerates except the mother of Saʿd. Whatever she says of his goodness is no lie." The mother of Saʿd was Kabsha daughter of ʿUbayd b. Muʿāwiya b. ʿUbayd b. al-Abjar b. ʿAwf b. al-Ḥārith b. al-Khazraj. Her sister was al-Fāriʿa daughter of ʿUbayd b. Muʿawiya b. ʿUbayd. She was the mother of Saʿd b. Zurāra.

They said: Then the Messenger of God commanded that he be washed. Al-Ḥārith b. Aws b. Muʿādh, ʿUsayd b. Ḥuḍayr and Salama b. Salāma b. Waqash poured water while the Messenger of God attended. He was washed the first time with water, and second, with water and the lotus, and third, with water and camphor. Then he was wrapped in three Yemenī cloths. A bed was brought from the family of Sabṭ, and the deceased was carried on it. The Messenger of God was seen carrying him between the pillars of the bed when he was raised from his house, until he was taken out.

ʿAbd al-Raḥmān b. ʿAbd al-ʿAzīz related to me from ʿAbdullah b. Abī Bakr b. Ḥazm [Page 528] from Yaḥyā b. ʿAbdullah b. ʿAbd al-Raḥmān, from ʿAmra from ʿĀʾisha, who said: I saw the Messenger of God walking in front of the dead body of Saʿd b. Muʿādh. Saʿīd b. Abī Zayd related to me from Rubayḥ b. ʿAbd al-Raḥmān b. Abī Saʿīd al-Khudrī from his father from his grandfather, who said: We were with the Messenger of God when the news about the death of Saʿd b. Muʿādh reached him. He went out with the people and when he arrived at al-Baqīʿ, he said, "Begin preparations for your companion." Abū Saʿīd said: I was among those who dug his grave. There exuded a pleasant smell of musk, while we dug his grave, from the dust until we finally completed the grave. Rubayḥ said: Indeed Muḥammad b. al-Munkadir informed me from Muḥammad b. Shuraḥbil b. Ḥasana, who said that a man took a hand full of soil from the grave of Saʿd b. Muʿādh and took it away. Then he looked at it later and lo and behold it was musk!

They said: Then he was carried and someone said, "O Messenger of God, surely you cut us off when you ran to Saʿd's place!" The Messenger of God said, "We feared that we had been preceded by angels just as they preceded us to wash Ḥanẓala (b. Abī ʿĀmir)." They said, "O Messenger of God, Saʿd was a heavy man yet we did not see one so light as he." The Messenger of God said, "I saw the angels carry him." They said, "O Messenger of God, indeed the Hypocrites say that he was light because he judged the Banū Qurayẓa." He said, "They lied. He was light because the angels carried him."

Abū Saʿīd al-Khudrī used to say: The Messenger of God appeared to us. We had finished Saʿd's grave and placed brick and water at the grave that we dug for him at the place where the house of ʿUqayl stands today. The Messenger of God appeared to us, and the Messenger of God placed him in the grave, and prayed for him. I saw al-Baqīʿ filled with people.

[Page 529] Al-Wāqidī said: Ibrāhīm b. al-Ḥuṣayn related to me from Dāwud b. al-Ḥuṣayn from ʿAbd al-Raḥmān b. Jābir from his father, who said: When they finally reached his grave, four men alighted in his grave. They were ʿUsayd b. Ḥuḍayr, al-Ḥārith b. Aws b. Muʿādh, Abū Nāʾila and Salama b. Salāma, while the Messenger of God stood at the foot of his grave. When Saʿd was placed and buried, the face of the Messenger of God altered. He glorified God thrice, and the Muslims praised God thrice until al-Baqīʿ was shaking. Then the Messenger of God proclaimed *takbīr* thrice, and his companions proclaimed *takbīr* thrice and al-Baqīʿ was shaking for the *takbīr*. The Messenger of God was questioned about that, saying, "O Messenger of God, we saw your face alter while you praised God thrice." He said, "The grave was narrow for your companion, and he was squeezed in it. If one is delivered from it surely Saʿd will be delivered from it. May God relieve him of it."

Ibrāhīm b. al-Ḥuṣayn related to me from al-Miswar b. Rifāʿa, who said: The mother of Saʿd, Kabsha bt. ʿUbayd, came to look at Saʿd in the grave, but the people returned her. The Messenger of God said, "Let her." So she came forward until she saw him. He was in the grave before it was constructed with bricks and sand. She said, "I hope that God will reward you." The Messenger of God consoled her at Saʿd's grave. He sat at a side, and the Muslims made to return the dust to the grave and smooth it over, and the Messenger of God stepped aside. He sat until it was covered over and water was sprinkled on it. Then he approached and stood by it and prayed for him. Then he left.

A RECORD OF THE MUSLIMS WHO WERE KILLED DURING THE SEIGE OF THE BANŪ QURAYẒA

Khallād b. Suwayd from the Balḥārith b. al-Khazraj: Nubāta pushed a millstone on him and it crushed his head. The Prophet said, "He shall have the recompense of two martyrs." He also had Nubāta executed in retaliation. Abū Sinān b. Miḥṣan died and the Messenger of God buried him there. [Page 530] He lies buried in the graveyard of the Banū Qurayẓa, today.

Al-Wāqidī related to us: he said: Ibrāhīm b. Jaʿfar related to me from his father, who said: When the Banū Qurayẓa were killed, Husayl b. Nuwayra al-Ashjarī arrived at Khaybar—he had gone for two days. The Jews of the Banū Naḍīr—Sallām b. Mishkam, Kināna b. Rabīʿ b. Abī l-Ḥuqayq and the Jews of Khaybar were sitting in council to consider the news of the Qurayẓa. It had reached them that the Messenger of God had besieged the Qurayẓa, and they dreaded what it was. They said, "What brought you?" He said, "Evil. The Qurayẓa warriors were executed by the sword." Kināna said, "What did Ḥuyayy do?" Ḥusayl said, "Ḥuyayy died for he was executed." He began to inform them about their chief Kaʿb b. Asad, and Ghazzāl b. Samaw'al and Nabbāsh b. Qays; that he attended them and that they were killed before Muḥammad. Sallām b. Mishkam said, "This, all of it, is the work of Ḥuyayy b. Akhṭab. He was an ill omen, first, and we disregarded the matter. He took us from our wealth and our nobility, and our brothers were killed. And worse than killing, the youths were taken captive. Judaism will not be established in the Ḥijaz, ever. The Jews have no opinion or decision."

They said: The news reached the women, and they cried out. They tore their dresses and cut their hair, and had a ceremonial mourning. The women of the Arabs joined them. The Jews hurried to Sallām b. Mishkam. They said, "What is your opinion of Abū ʿAmr?" Or "Abū l-Ḥakam?" He said, "What will you do with my opinion? You did not listen to a word I said." Kināna said, "This is not a good time for blame. The affair has come to what you see." He said, "Muḥammad has brought an end to the Jews of Yathrib and is marching to you. He will come over to your field and do with you what he did with the Banū Qurayẓa." They said, "And what is the decision?" He said, "We will march to Muḥammad with those who are with us from the Jews of Khaybar, and they are many. We will call in the Jews of Taymā' and Fadak and Wādī al-Qurā. We will not call for help from a single Arab, for you saw in the raid of al-Khandaq what the

Arabs did with you after you stipulated the dates of Khaybar to them; they destroyed that and forsook you. They asked Muḥammad for dates of the Aws and the Khazraj, and they turned from him, although [Page 531] Nuʿaym b. Masʿūd was the one who duped them with Muḥammad, and they were well aware of it. Then, we will march to the heart of his homeland and we will fight in retalliation, for the past and present." The Jews said, "This is the decision." Kināna said, "Surely I consulted the Bedouin and I saw that they are much opposed to him. These fortresses of ours are not like those that are there. Muḥammad will never come to us, ever." Sallām b. Mishkam said, "This man does not fight until he is provoked. This is, by God, praiseworthy."

He said: Ḥassān b. Thābit said a poem in memory of Saʿd b. Muʿādh.

THE EXPEDITION OF ʿABDULLAH B. UNAYS TO SUFYĀN B. KHĀLID B. NUBAYḤ

ʿAbdullah b. Unays said: I set out from Medina on Monday the fifth of al-Muḥarram, the fifty-fourth month AH. I was absent for twelve nights, and arrived on the Sabbath, with seven days left in al-Muḥarram.

Al-Wāqidī said: Ismāʿīl b. ʿAbdullah b. Jubayr related to us from Mūsā b. Jubayr, who said: It reached the Messenger of God that Sufyān b. Khālid b. Nubayḥ al-Hudhalī, the Liḥyānī, had alighted at ʿUrana and its suburbs with people from his and other tribes: he had gathered a group to attack the Messenger of God. Many people from the exhausted crowds had recourse to him. The Messenger of God called ʿAbdullah b. Unays and sent him, by himself, on an expedition to kill Sufyān. The Messenger of God said to him, [Page 532] "Attach yourself to the Khuzāʿa." And ʿAbdullah b. Unays said, "O Messenger of God, I do not know him. Describe him to me." The Messenger of God said, "Indeed when you see him you will dread him, fear him, and remember Satan." But I did not fear men, so I said, "O Messenger of God, I have not feared anything, ever." The Messenger of God said, "It will be a sign between you and him that you will shudder when you see him." I asked permission of the Prophet to speak freely. He said, "You may say whatever comes to you."

He said: I took my sword and nothing more, and set out to find the Khuzāʿa. I took the road until I reached Qudayd, where I found many Khuzāʿa who offered me beasts to ride on, and escorts, but I did not desire that. I set out until I came to Baṭn Sarif, and then turned until I arrived at ʿUrana. I began to tell those whom I met that I desired Sufyān b. Khālid, for I would be with him, until when I was in Baṭn ʿUrana I met him marching, and behind him were the *Aḥābīsh* and those who were attracted and drawn to him. When I saw him I feared him, and recognized him by the description that the Messenger of God gave me. I saw myself drip with perspiration and I said, "By God, His Messenger said truly!" It was the time of the *ʿAṣar* prayer when I saw him, and I prayed while walking and pointing with my head. When I was near him, he said, "Who is this man?" I said, "A man from the Khuzāʿa. I heard that you were gathering against Muḥammad, and I have come to be with you." He said, "Yes, indeed, I am in the group against him." I walked with him and conversed with him, and he was delighted by my conversation. I recited a poem and I said, "It is wondrous that Muḥammad innovates a new thing with this new religion. He deserts the forefathers and ridicules their values." He said, "Muḥammad has not met anyone like me!" He said: He was supporting himself on a stick striking the ground until he reached his tent.

[Page 533] His companions separated from him to their stations near him for they were around him. He said, "Come forward O brother of the Khuzāʿa!" and I drew near him. He said to his slave girl, "Bring me some milk!" She brought some milk and served it to me. I took a sip and then gave it to him. He gulped it just as a camel until his nose was hidden in the froth. Then he said, "Sit," and I sat with him, until when the people became calm and slept, and he became calm, I took him by surprise, killed him, and took his head. Then I turned, leaving his women crying over him.

I escaped and ascended the mountain and entered a cave. The search of the cavalry and men approached and dispersed in every direction. I was hiding in the cavern of the mountain. The spider built its web over the cavern. A man approached, and he had a water bottle while his sandals were in his hands—I was afraid, but my gravest problem was thirst, and I remembered Tihāma and its heat—He put down his water bottle and sandals and urinated at the mouth of the cavern. Then he said to his companions, "There is no one in this cave," so they turned and went back. I went to the water bottle and drank from it and took the sandals and put them on. I traveled by night, and concealed myself by day until I came to Medina and found the Prophet in the mosque. He said, "May you prosper!" and I said, "May you prosper, O Messenger of God." I placed Sufyān's head before him and informed him of my news. He gave me a stick and said, "Support yourself in Paradise with it. Indeed there are but a few who have such supports in Paradise." That stick stayed with ʿAbdullah b. Unays until he died. He willed that his family insert it in his coffin. He killed Sufyān b. Khālid b. Nubayḥ in Muḥarram, the fifty-fourth month AH.

[Page 534] **THE RAID OF AL-QURṬĀ'**

Khālid b. Ilyās related to me from Jaʿfar b. Maḥmūd, who said: Muḥammad b. Maslama said: I set out on the tenth al-Muḥarram, and I was absent for nineteen days. I arrived with a night left to al-Muḥarram, the fifty-fifth month AH.

Muḥammad b. Anas al-Ẓafarī related to me from his father, and ʿAbd al-ʿAzīz b. Saʿd related to me from Jaʿfar b. Maḥmūd, one of them adding more to the tradition than his companion. They both said: The Messenger of God sent Muḥammad b. Maslama with thirty men, including ʿAbbād b. Bishr and Salama b. Salāma b. Waqash and al-Ḥārith b. Khazama to the Banū Bakr b. Kilāb. He commanded him to march by night and hide by day, and launch an attack against them. Muḥammad marched by night and hid by day until when he was in al-Sharaba, he met a camel-litter and sent one of his companions to ask about it. The messenger went and returned to him and said, "They are a people of war." So they alighted close to them. They disbanded and revived their cattle. Muḥammad granted them respite until when they were departing he attacked them. He killed a few, but the rest of them fled. He did not follow those who fled.

He drove the cattle and sheep and did not obstruct their litter. Then he departed until when he was in a place above the Banū Bakr he sent ʿAbbād b. Bishr to them. ʿAbbād approached the settlement and stayed, and when they were reviving their cattle and milking and roasting, ʿAbbād came to Ibn Maslama and informed him. Muḥammad b. Maslama set out and launched an attack on them. He killed ten of them. They drove the cattle and sheep and descended towards Medina.

[Page 535] He next rose at dawn in Ḍariyya. The march was a night or two nights. Then we brought down the cattle and we feared the search. We drove out the sheep with great effort, and they ran with us as though they were horses until we reached al-ʿAdāsa. The sheep delayed us in al-Rabadha. We left them behind with a group of my companions who went with them. The cattle were driven and arrived in Medina before the Prophet.

Muḥammad b. Maslama used to say: I set out from Ḍariyya, and I did not ride a step until I arrived in Baṭn Nakhl. There arrived with the cattle a hundred and fifty camels and three thousand sheep. When we arrived, the Prophet took his fifth of the booty and distributed what was left to his companions. They equated one camel with ten sheep and every man among them took from it.

THE RAID OF THE BANŪ LIḤYĀN

ʿAbd al-Malik b. Wahb Abū l-Ḥasan al-Aslamī related to me from ʿAṭāʾ b. Abī Marwān, who said: The Messenger of God set out in Rabīʿ al-Awwal, in the year six AH. He reached Ghurān and ʿUsfān. He was gone for fourteen nights.

Maʿmar related to me from al-Zuhrī from Ibn Kaʿb b. Mālik, and Yaḥyā b. ʿAbdullah b. Abī Qatāda related to me from ʿAbdullah b. Abī Bakr b. Ḥazm, as well as others related to me; and one of them added to the information of his companion. They said: The Messenger of God was very grieved [Page 536] about ʿĀṣim b. Thābit and his companions, who were killed at Biʾr Maʿūna. He set out with his companions and alighted at Maḍrib al-Qubba in the direction of al-Jurf. He camped in the beginning of the day claiming that he desired al-Sham. Then refreshed by the cool breeze he went past Ghurāba and then to Bīn until he set out to the rocky tracts of al-Thumām, and joined the road there. The Messenger of God hurried on until he came to the valley of Ghurān where they had been afflicted. He prayed for God's mercy upon them, saying, "May there be happiness for those of you who are martyred."

The Liḥyān heard about it and fled to the mountain tops. We had no power over any one of them. The Prophet stayed a day or two and sent out expeditions in every direction but had no power over any one. Then he set out until he came to ʿUṣfān. The Messenger of God said to Abū Bakr, "Indeed the Quraysh are informed of my expedition and know that I have reached ʿUsfān. They fear that I will come to them. Go out with ten riders." So Abū Bakr set out with them until they came to al-Ghamīm. Then Abū Bakr returned to the Messenger of God for he did not meet anyone. The Messenger of God said, "Surely this will reach the Quraysh and frighten them. They will fear that we will go to them."

Now, Khubayb b. ʿAdī was in the hands of the Quraysh, at that time, and when it reached the Quraysh that the Messenger of God had come to al-Ghamīm, they said, "Muḥammad did not come to al-Ghamīm except to get Khubayb." [Page 537] Khubayb and two of his companions were in iron shackles at that time. They put their heads together and they said, "Muḥammad has reached Ḍajnān and he is coming for us." Māwiyya visited Khubayb and informed him of the news. She said, "This companion of yours has reached Ḍajnān and is coming for you." Khubayb said, "Is it so?" She replied, "Yes." Khubayb said, "God does as He wills." She said, "By God, they wait only until the end of the protected month. Then they will come out to you and kill you. They say, 'Do you see Muḥammad raid us in the protected months when we do not regard it lawful to kill his companion in the protected month?' " He was a prisoner of theirs, and they feared that the Messenger of God would come to them.

The Messenger of God turned towards Medina saying, "Returning repentant, worshipers praising our lord. O God, You are the companion of the journey, the one who takes care of the family behind us. O God I take refuge in You from the hardships of the journey, its unhappy ending, and the evil appearance of family and property. O God, bring us good news that will make us happy, your forgiveness, and satisfaction."

The Messenger of God was absent from Medina for fourteen nights. He appointed Ibn Umm Maktūm to take his place in Medina. This was in al-Muḥarram, of the year six AH. This was the first time that he said this prayer. All our companions mentioned it.

THE RAID OF AL-GHĀBA

ʿAbd al-ʿAzīz b. Uqba b. Salama b. al-Akwaʿ informed me from Iyās b. Salama from his father, who said: ʿUyayna raided on the night of the Wednesday, the third of Rabīʿ al-Ākhir in the year six AH. We marched, with the Messenger of God, in search of him, on Wednesday. We were absent for five nights and returned on the night of the Monday. The Messenger of God appointed Ibn Umm Maktūm [Page 538] to take his place in Medina.

Mūsā b. Muḥammad b. Ibrāhīm related to me from his father, and Yaḥyā b. ʿAbdullah b. Qatāda as well as ʿAlī b. Yazīd and others. All have related portions of this tradition to me. They said: The milk camels of the Messenger of God numbered twenty suckling camels, and they were from different origins. Among them was what he took in Dhāt al-Riqāʿ, and what Muḥammad b. Maslama brought him from Najd. He was grazing them in al-Bayda' and beyond al-Baydā', when a drought overtook them. So he took them to al-Ghāba to feed on the Tamarisk and other trees. Abū ʿAbdullah said: "Al-Ghādīya" refers to their feeding on ʿIḍāh, Umm Ghaylān, and other plants. "Al-Wāḍiʿa" are camels grazing on al-Ḥamḍ. The "Awāriq" graze on al-Arāk. The shepherd returns with its milk every night at sunset. Abū Dharr asked permission of the Messenger of God to go to his milk camels. The Messenger of God said, "Indeed I fear you may be attacked in this neighbourhood. We are not safe from ʿUyayna b. Ḥiṣn and his relatives. The camels are within their borders." Abū Dharr pleaded with him and said, "O Messenger of God grant me permission?" When he pleaded about it the Messenger of God said, "It is as if I have exchanged places with you; your son is killed, your wife is taken, and you come supporting yourself on your staff." Abū Dharr used to say: It was a surprise to me that the Messenger of God should say: "It is as if," when I was pleading about it, and by the lord, what the Prophet said to me came true.

Al-Miqdād b. ʿAmr used to say: When it was the night of the dispatch my horse Sabḥa did not settle down, moving to and fro and neighing. Abū Maʿbad said, "Indeed there is something the matter with her. We observed its place of confinement, and it was filled with fodder. He says it is thirsty, but it was disinclined to water and did not desire it. When it was dawn he saddled it and put on his weapons. He set out until he prayed with the Prophet and he did not see anything. The Prophet entered [Page 539] his house, and al-Miqdād returned to his. But his horse would not settle down. He put down its saddle and his weapons, and lay down. He placed one of his legs over the other. Someone came to him and said, "Surely the horses neigh about it."

Abū Dharr used to say: Indeed we were in our stations, and the camel of the Messenger of God was relaxed and had been milked, and it was getting dark and we slept. When it was night, ʿUyayna encircled us with forty riders. They shouted at us and rose over our heads. My son appeared before them and they killed him. With him were his wife and three individuals and they escaped. I withdrew from them, and the release of the cord of the camel distracted them from me. Then they shouted behind them and it was the last time of the ties with them. I went to the Prophet and informed him, and he smiled.

Salama b. al-Akwaʿ used to say: I rose in the morning desiring al-Ghāba and the camel of the Prophet, for I used to take him its milk, when I met a youth belonging to ʿAbd al-Raḥmān b. ʿAwf who was watching the camels of ʿAbd al-Raḥmān b. ʿAwf. They had missed their place and reached the camels of the Prophet. He informed me that the camels of the Prophet had been attacked by ʿUyayna b. Ḥiṣn with his forty riders, and that later they had seen reinforcements helping ʿUyayna. Salama said: I attended my horse returning to Medina until when I reached Thanniyat al-Wadāʿ, I shouted with my voice raised, "What a dawn!" three times in order that my voice reached those who were between the two borders.

Mūsā b. Muḥammad related to me from ʿĀṣim b. ʿUmar from Maḥmūd b. Labīd, who said: He called out, "The fear, the fear," three times. Then he stopped, standing on his horse until the Messenger of God appeared in his iron helmet, and stood, waiting. The first to approach him was [Page 540] al-Miqdad b. ʿAmr, wearing armor and helmet, and drawing his sword. The Messenger of God handed him the flag fixed to his spear and said, "Go forth until the cavalry meets you. Indeed we will follow in your tracks." Miqdād said: I set out, asking God for martyrdom, when I reached the last of the enemy. A horse of theirs had lagged behind them and its rider had jumped just behind one of his companions. So I took the condemned horse, and lo and behold, it was weak, of reddish complexion, and old. They had ridden upon it from the forest and it was exhausted. I tied a piece of bow-string around its neck and set it free. I said, "If one passes it and takes it I will show him my sign on it." Then I reached Masʿada and I pierced him with the spear that had the flag. The spear missed and Masʿada bent towards me and pierced me. I took the spear in my upper arm and broke it. But he fled and I could not reach him. I planted my flag, saying, "My companions will see it." Abū Qatāda, recognized by his yellow turban, joined me on a horse of his. I walked with him for a while and we observed the rear of Masʿada. Then, Abū Qatāda spurred his horse and went ahead of my horse. His determination was clear and he was faster than my horse until he was lost to me and I could not see him. Then I met him, and he was stripping off his cloak. I shouted, "What are you doing?" He said, "Good. I am doing just as you did with the horse." He had killed Masʿada and was covering him with his cloak. We returned and, lo and behold, there was a horse in the hand of ʿUlba b. Zayd al-Ḥārithī. I said, "My horse! This is my sign on it." He said, "Come to the Prophet," and he made it booty.

Salama b. al-Akwaʿ set out running on his two legs to outstrip the horses like a lion. Salama said: Until I joined the people I tried to shoot at them with arrows, saying as I shot, "Take this from me, and I am Ibn al-Akwaʿ! One of their cavalry attacked me. When [Page 541] he came towards me, I departed, fleeing and outdistanced him. I reached the exposed place and looking down upon him, aimed with arrows when it was possible to shoot, saying:

Take this and I am Ibn al-Akwaʿ.
Today is the day for the wicked.

I continued to fight them while saying, "Stop a little; your lords from the Muhājirūn and Anṣār will join you!" Their anger against me increased and they attacked me. I ran, and they were unable to catch me, until I finally reached Dhū Qarada with them. The Messenger of God and the cavalry joined us in the evening. I said, "O Messenger of God, surely the people are thirsty but there is no water for them other than in little springs. If you send me with a hundred men I will salvage what they hold of the cattle, and take the heads of the people." The Prophet said, "You are able, so be kind." The Prophet said, "Indeed they are established in Ghaṭafān."

Khālid b. Ilyās related to me from Abū Bakr b. ʿAbdullah b. Abī Jahm, who said that eight riders went. They were: al-Miqdād, Abū Qatāda, Muʿādh b. Māʿiṣ, Saʿd b. Zayd, Abū Ayyāsh al-Zuraqī, Muhriz b. Naḍla, ʿUkkāsha b. Miḥṣan and Rabīʿa b. Aktham. Mūsā b. Muḥammad informed me from ʿĀṣim b. ʿUmar b. Qatāda, who said: There were three from the Muhājirūn: Al-Miqdād, Muḥriz b. Naḍla, and ʿUkkāsha b. Miḥṣan. And, from the Anṣār: Saʿd b. Zayd, who was their commander, Abū ʿAyyāsh al-Zuraqī with his horse, Julwa, [Page 542] ʿAbbād b. Bishr, Usayd b. Ḥuḍayr, and Abū Qatāda.

Abū ʿAyyāsh said: I appeared upon a horse of mine, and the Messenger of God said to me, "Perhaps you will give your horse to one who is a better rider than you, and follow the cavalry!" I said, "I, Messenger of God, am the best rider of the people," and I raced it. The horse had not run five measures with me when it threw me to the ground. Abū ʿAyyāsh used to say: What a surprise! Indeed the Messenger of God said, "Perhaps you will give your horse to one who is a better rider than you," and I said, "I am the best rider of the people!"

They said: The cry for help went to the Banū ʿAmr b. ʿAuf, and help arrived. The cavalry continued to arrive, men on foot, and camels, and the people taking turns on the camels and donkeys, until they reached the Messenger of God in Dhū Qarad. They recovered ten milch camels. The people got away with what remained, and that was ten. Muḥriz b. Naḍla was an ally of ʿAbd al-Ashhal, so when there was the call for help, "Terror! Terror!" There was a horse belonging to Muḥammad b. Maslama called Dhū l-limma, which was tied to the wall. When Muḥriz heard the sound of the horses neighing—he became preoccupied with the wall to which the horse was tied. The women said to him, "Are you concerned, oh Muḥriz, about this horse, for indeed it is as you see, good and restored, and you could ride it and reach the flag." He saw the flag of the Messenger of God, al-ʿUqāb, pass by—flying high—as Saʿd carried it. They said: He set out crossing the valley of Qanāʿa and overtook al-Miqdād. Then he came to the people at Hayqa and detained them. They resisted, and they attacked each other for a while with spears. Masʿada [Page 543] attacked Muḥriz and pierced him with a spear and wounded him in his spine. He took the spear of Muḥriz, but Muḥriz' horse escaped and returned to Āriyyih. When the women and the people of the house saw it, they said, "Muḥriz has been killed." Some said that Muḥriz was on a horse of ʿUkkāsha b. Miḥṣan called al-Janāḥ, and that he fought on it. It was said: He who killed Muḥriz b. Naḍla was Awthār. ʿAbbād b. Bishr approached and overtook Awthār. The two detained and fought each other until their spears broke. Then they took their swords and ʿAbbād b. Bishr pounced on him and held him tight and then pierced him with a dagger, and killed him.

ʿUmar b. Abī ʿĀtika related to me from Abū l-Aswad from ʿUrwa, who said: Awthār and ʿAmr b. Awthār were on a horse of theirs called al-Furu, and they rode one behind the other on it. ʿUkkāsha b. Miḥṣan killed both of them.

Zakariyyā b. Zayd related to me from ʿAbdullah b. Abī Sufyān from his father, from Umm ʿĀmir bt. Yazīd b. al-Sakan, who said: I was among those who prodded Muḥriz to stay close to the Messenger of God, for by God we were surely in our fortress observing the rising dust when the horse of Muḥammad b. Maslama, Dhū l-Līma, approached until it reached Āriyyih. I said, "By God, he is taken." We took hold of a rider from the neighborhood, and we said, "Inform us of the Messenger of God; observe if he is well, then return to us swiftly." He said: He set out with the horse until he joined the Messenger of God in Hayqā with the people, then he returned and informed us of the safety of the Messenger of God. We praised God for the safety of the Messenger of God.

Ibn Abī Sabra related to me from Ṣāliḥ b. Kaysān, who said: Muḥriz b. Naḍla said, "One day, [Page 544] before the people arrived, I saw the heavens open to me, and I entered the heaven of the earth until I entered the seventh heaven, and I reached the Lotus at the highest level, and it was said to me, 'This is your station.' I informed Abū Bakr who was among the best interpreters of the people, and he said, 'Rejoice in martyrdom!' " Muḥriz was killed a day later.

Yaḥyā b. ʿAbdullah b. Abī Qatāda related to me from his mother from his father, who said that Abū Qatāda said: I was washing my head, and I had washed one half of it when my horse neighed and kicked with its hoof. I said, "This is war." I stood up and did not wash the other half of my head, but rode, dressed in a robe of mine, when all of a sudden the Messenger of God was heard shouting, "Help! Help." He said: I reached Miqdād b. ʿAmr and accompanied him for a while. Then my horse went ahead of his, for it was a better horse. When he was racing me, al-Miqdād had informed me that Masʿada had killed Muḥriz. Abū Qatāda said to al-Miqdād, "O Abū Maʿbad, I will kill the killer of Muḥriz or die in the attempt." Abū Qatāda struck his horse and joined them. Masʿada stopped for him. Abū Qatāda attacked him with the spear and crushed his spine saying, "Take this and I am the Khazrajī," and Masʿada fell dead. Abū Qatāda alighted and covered him with his cloak. With Masʿada's horse at his side, he set out in the tracks of the people until he joined them. Abū Qatāda said: When the people passed by, they saw the cloak of Abū Qatāda and recognized it. They said, "This is Abū Qatāda's dead body." One of them said, "To God must we return." But the Messenger of God said, "No. It is the victim of Abū Qatāda and he has put his cloak on him so that you know that he killed him. Let Abū Qatāda have his victim and his booty and his horse." So Abū Qatāda took all of it. Saʿd b. Zayd had taken his booty, but the Prophet said, "No by God, Abū Qatāda killed him, so give it to him."

[Page 545] ʿAbdullah b. Abī Qatāda related to me from his father Abū Qatāda, who said: When the Prophet reached me at that time he looked at me and said, "God bless his hair and his skin." He said, "May you prosper!" I said, "And may you prosper, O Messenger of God!" He said, "Did you kill Masʿada?" I said, "Yes." He said, "What is this in your face?" I said, "An arrow aimed by him, O Messenger of God." He said, "Come close to me!" So I went close to him and he spat on it, and it neither hurt nor festered. Abū Qatāda died at the age of seventy and he appeared to be fifteen years of age. He said: At that time, the Prophet gave me Masʿada's horse and weapons, saying, "May God bless you with them!"

Ibn Abī Sabra related to me from Sulayman b. Suḥaym, who said that Saʿd b. Zayd al-Ashhalī said: When it was the day of the departure, the call for help came to us while I was with the Banū ʿAbd al-Ashhal. I put on my armor, took my weapons, and mounting a horse of mine named al-Nakhl that was rested, reached the Messenger of God who was wearing his armor and helmet so that I could only see his eyes. The cavalry had raced in the direction of the canal. The Messenger of God addressed me and said, "Depart, I have appointed you over the cavalry until I meet you, God willing." My horse advanced for a while, then I let it free, and it went on at a trot. I passed a tired horse, and I said, "What is this?" I had passed by Masʿada, the victim of Abū Qatāda. And I passed the body of Muḥriz and it hurt me. Then I joined al-Miqdād b. ʿAmr and Muʿādh b. Māʾiṣ. We trotted along observing the dust of the people. Abū Qatāda was on their tracks. I observed Ibn al-Akwaʿ overtake the cavalry and confront the people pelting them with arrows. They stopped and we joined them and engaged them in a skirmish for a while. I attacked Ḥubayb b. ʿUyayna [Page 546] with the sword and cut his left shoulder. He gave free rein to his horse and fell on his face. I rushed at him and killed him, and took his horse. Our code was "Kill! Kill!" We also heard another story about the killing of Ḥubayb b. ʿUyayna.

Mūsā b. Muḥammad b. Ibrāhīm related to me from his father, who said: Indeed when the Muslims and the enemy pursued each other, Muḥriz b. Naḍla was killed among them. Abū Qatāda set out in his direction and he killed Masʿada. Awthār and ʿAmr b. Awthār were killed by ʿUkkāsha b. Miḥṣan. Indeed, Ḥubayb b. ʿUyayna was riding a horse of his with Faraqa b. Mālik b. Ḥudhayfa b. Badr, and al-Miqdād b. ʿAmr killed them. They said: The people met each other at Dhū Qarad, where the Messenger of God prayed the prayer of fear.

Sufyān b. Saʿīd related to me, and Ibn Abī Sabra related to me from Abū Bakr b. ʿAbdullah b. Abī Jahm from ʿUbaydullah b. ʿUtba from Ibn ʿAbbās, who said: The Messenger of God stood facing the *qibla*, and a faction stood in line behind him, while a faction faced the enemy. He prayed one bowing and two prostrations with the faction that was behind him, then they turned and stood in their companion's place and the others came forward, and the Messenger of God prayed a bowing and two prostrations with them. Thus the Messenger of God prayed two bowings, while the two groups had prayed one bowing each.

Mālik b. Abī l-Rajjāl related to me from ʿAbdullah b. Abī Bakr b. Ḥazm from ʿUmāra b. Maʿmar, who said: The Messenger of God stayed a day and a night in Dhū Qarad taking account of the news. He apportioned for every hundred of his companions a slaughtering beast, which they slaughtered, and they were five hundred in all. Others say they were seven hundred. They said: The Messenger of God appointed [Page 547] Ibn Umm Maktūm over Medina during his absence.

Saʿd b. ʿUbāda, with three hundred of his men (Khazraj), guarded Medina for five nights until the Messenger of God returned. On the first month of the year, he sent the Prophet dates and ten beasts for slaughter in Dhū Qarad. Qays b. Saʿd, on a horse of his named al-Ward, was with the people and it was he who approached the Prophet with the dates and slaughtering animals. The Messenger of God said, "O, your father has sent you on a horse and strengthened the fighters, while he guards Medina from its enemies. May God bless Saʿd and the family of Saʿd." Then the Messenger of God said, "What a good man is Saʿd b. ʿUbāda!" Then the Khazraj spoke, saying, "O Messenger of God, he is of our house, our Master, and the son of our Master. They were providing food during the drought, transporting the weary, greeting the guests, giving during the disaster, and protecting the community." The Prophet said, "The best of the people in

Islam are the best of those in *jāhiliyya* when they understand the religion." When the Messenger of God reached the Well of Hamma, they said, "O Messenger of God, are you poisoning the Well of Hamma?" The Prophet said, "No, but some of you will purchase it and give it in charity." Ṭalḥa b. ʿUbaydullah bought it and gave it as charity.

Mūsā b. Muḥammad related to me from his father, who said: Al-Miqdād was the commander of two riders until the Messenger of God joined them in Dhū Qarada. Muḥammad b. al-Faḍl b. ʿUbaydullah b. Rāfiʿ b. Khadīj related to me from al-Miswar b. Rifāʿa from Thaʿlaba b. Abī Mālik, who said: Saʿīd b. Zayd was the commander of the people [Page 548] and he said to Ḥassān b. Thābit, "Did you see how you made al-Miqdād the head of expedition while you knew that the Messenger of God had appointed me over the expedition? Indeed you knew the herald called, 'Help!' And al-Miqdād was the first of those who rose, and the Messenger of God said, 'Depart until the cavalry joins you,' so he went first. Then later we all gathered with the Prophet, but al-Miqdād was the first of us to have departed, so the Messenger of God appointed me over the raid." Ḥassān said, "O cousin, by God I did not desire except a rhyme when I said, 'The day when the horses of al-Miqdād . . .' " Saʿd b. Zayd swore that he would never speak to Ḥassān. The most confirmed with us is that Saʿd b. Zayd b. Ashhal was their commander.

They said: When the Messenger of God reached Medina, the wife of Abū Dharr approached on the camel of the Prophet, al-Qaṣwā', which was in the courtyard with the camel of Abū Jahl that was among what the Muslims had rescued. She came to the Prophet and informed him of the news of the people. Then she said: "O Messenger of God, I vowed that if God saved me upon it, I would slaughter it and eat of its liver and its hump." The Prophet smiled and said, "Miserable is how you reward what God carried you and saved you on. You slaughter it! Indeed it is a vow that goes against God. Moreover, the camel is not yours. Surely it is one of my female camels, so return to your people with God's blessings." Fā'id, the *mawlā* of ʿAbdullah, related to me from ʿAbdullah b. ʿAlī from his grandmother, Salmā, who said: I observed the milch camel, at the door of the Messenger of God, named al-Samrā', and I recognized it, so I visited the Messenger of God and said [Page 549], "This is surely your camel al-Samrā' at your door." The Messenger of God went out rejoicing, and lo and behold, its head was in the hands of my nephew ʿUyayna. When the Messenger of God saw it he recognized it and said: "What is the matter with you, ʿUyayna?" He said: "O Messenger of God, I gift this milch camel to you." The Messenger of God smiled and took it from him. Then he waited a day or two. Then he ordered three measures of silver for ʿUyayna but he was unhappy. He said: And I said, "O Messenger of God, are you rewarding him for one of your camels?" The Messenger of God said, "Yes, and he does not like it." After the Messenger of God prayed the *Ẓuhr* prayer, he ascended the *minbar* and praised God and commended Him. Then he said, "A man gifted me a mare from my camels, and I recognized it just as I recognize some of my people. Then I paid him for it. Yet he continues to complain to me. Henceforth, I will not accept gifts."

A RECORD OF THOSE WHO WERE KILLED FROM THE MUSLIMS AND THE POLYTHEISTS

From the Muslims, one: Muḥriz b. Naḍla was killed by Masʿada. From the polytheists: Masʿada b. Ḥakama was killed by Abū Qatāda. Awthār and his son ʿAmr b. Awthār were killed by ʿUkkāsha b. Miḥṣan. Ḥubayb b. ʿUyayna was killed by al-Miqdād. Ḥassān b. Thābit said . . .

[Page 550] THE EXPEDITION OF ʿUKKĀSHA B. MIḤṢAN TO AL-GHAMR

Ibn Abī Sabra related to me from ʿAbd Rabbīh b. Saʿīd, who said: I heard a man from the Banū Asad b. Khuzayma narrate to al-Qāsim b. Muḥammad saying: The Messenger of God sent ʿUkkasha b. Miḥṣan with forty men, including Thābit b. Aqram, Shujāʿ b. Wahb and Yazīd b. Ruqaysh. He set out swiftly, speeding along the way. But the people knew of his coming so they fled from their water and alighted on the lofty heights of their lands. ʿUkkāsha finally reached the water and found the settlement they had left behind. He sent observers to seek out information and look for recent tracks. Shujāʿ b. Wahb returned and informed him that he saw traces of sheep close by. They assumed responsibility and set out until they came to one of their guards who had stayed up the night listening to the sounds, but fallen asleep at daybreak. They captured him while he was sleeping, saying, "Give us information about the people!" He said, "Where are the people? They are settled in the upper regions of their land." They said, "And the cattle?" He replied, "With them." One of them struck him with the whip in his hand. He said, "Protect my blood and I will show you the sheep belonging to a cousin of theirs who does not know of your marching to them." They said, "Yes." They departed with him. They set out until he was far out and they became fearful that he would be treacherous. So they drew him close and said, "Tell us the truth or we will cut off your head!" He said, "You will see them from this hillock." He said: They approached the hillock, and all of a sudden a sheep was startled. They attacked it and captured it while the Bedouin fled in every direction. ʿUkkasha restrained them from the search. They drove the two hundred camels down to Medina. Then they set the man free. [Page 551] They arrived before the Prophet. Not one of them was taken, and there was no fighting.

THE EXPEDITION OF MUḤAMMAD B. MASLAMA TO DHŪ L-QAṢṢA

ʿAbdullah b. al-Ḥārith related to me from his father, who said: The Prophet sent Muḥammad b. Maslama with ten others, and they arrived upon them at night. The people hid until Ibn Maslama and his companions fell asleep. Then a hundred men surrounded them, and one did not know it except for the arrows that came to them. Ibn Maslama jumped up with his bow and shouted to his companions, "The weapons!" They jumped up and aimed for an hour of the night. The Bedouin attacked with spears and killed three of them. The companions of Ibn Maslama joined him and killed one of them. Then the people attacked and they killed the rest of Ibn Maslama's companions. Muḥammad b. Maslama fell wounded. His ankle was struck and he could not move. They stripped the dead of their garments and departed. A man passed by the dead and said, "To God may he return." When Ibn Maslama heard him, he knew he was a Muslim and he moved closer to him. The man gave Ibn Maslama food and drink and carried him until they arrived in Medina.

The Prophet sent Abū ʿUbayda b. al-Jarrāḥ with forty men to their death site, but they could not find anyone. He drove the cattle and returned.

Abū ʿAbdullah said: I mentioned this expedition to Ibrāhīm b. Jaʿfar b. Maḥmūd b. Muḥammad b. Maslama and he said, "My father informed me that Muḥammad b. Maslama set out with ten individuals: Abū Nāʾila, al-Ḥārith b. Aws, Abū ʿAbs b. Jabar, Nuʿmān b. ʿAṣar, Muḥayyiṣa b. Masʿūd, Ḥuwayyiṣa, Abū Burda b. Niyār, two men from the Muzayna, and a man from the Ghaṭafān. The two men from Muzayna and the man from Ghaṭafān were killed.

[Page 552] Ibn Maslama collected what was left on the battlefield among the dead. He said: During the raid of Khaybar, I saw one of the individuals who had turned and struck me on the day of Dhū l-Qaṣṣa. When he saw me, he said, "I surrender to God." I said, "It is best!"

THE EXPEDITION LED BY THE COMMANDER ABŪ ʿUBAYDA TO DHŪ L-QAṢṢA

The expedition took place in Rabīʿ al-Ākhir in the year six on the night of the Sabbath. He was gone for two nights. ʿAbd al-Raḥmān b. Ziyād al-Ashjaʿī related to me from ʿĪsā b. ʿUmayla, and ʿAbdullah b. al-Ḥārith b. al-Faḍl related to me from his father; one of them added to the information of his companion. They said: The land of the Banū Thaʿlaba and Anmār was suffering from drought. Clouds of rain came down from al-Marāḍ to Taghlamayn. The Banū Muḥārib and Thaʿlaba and Anmār came to this region. They had decided to attack the cattle of Medina, which were, at that time, grazing in the valley of Hayqā.

The Messenger of God sent Abū ʿUbayda b. al-Jarrāḥ with forty men from the Muslims. They prayed Maghrib, and spent their night marching until they came to Dhū l-Qaṣṣā with the darkness of the dawn. He attacked them and incapacitated them as they fled into the mountains. He captured a man from them and found a group of sheep from their cattle and drove it, and some old utensils, and arrived with them in Medina. The man converted, and the Messenger of God let him live. The Messenger of God took his fifth share, when he arrived, and apportioned the rest to them.

[Page 553] THE EXPEDITION OF ZAYD B. ḤĀRITHA TO AL-ʿĪṢ

Mūsā b. Muḥammad b. Ibrāhīm related to me from his father, who said: When the Messenger of God returned from the Raid of al-Ghāba, it reached him that the caravan of the Quraysh was approaching from al-Shām, so he sent Zayd b Ḥāritha with one hundred and seventy riders and they captured the caravan and what was in it. At that time, they took much silver belonging to Ṣafwān b. Umayya, and prisoners, from men who were in the caravan with them, including Abū l-ʿĀṣ b. al-Rabīʿ, and al-Mughīra b. Muʿāwiya b. Abī l-ʿĀṣ. As for Abū l-ʿĀṣ, he did not delay to come to Medina and visit Zaynab the daughter of the Messenger of God, at dawn, for she was his wife, and ask her to protect him. When the Messenger of God was praying at dawn, Zaynab stood at her door and called out in her high voice, "I have granted protection to Abū l-ʿĀṣ." The

Messenger of God said, "O people, did you hear what I heard?" They said, "Yes." He said, "By Him who holds my soul in His hand, I did not know any thing about this until I heard what you heard. Muslims are one hand against the rest, and the lowest of them can grant protection. So we shall grant protection to who she protects." When the Prophet returned to his house Zaynab went to him and asked him to return the wealth that was taken from Abū l-ʿĀṣ. He did so, but he also commanded that Abū l-Āṣ should not approach her, that she was not free for him as long as he continued to be a polytheist.

Then the Messenger of God spoke to his companions. Abū l-ʿĀṣ had held merchandise belonging to more than one of the Quraysh. They returned every thing to him, even the cleansing bowl and piece of rope [Page 554] until there was nothing left. Abū l-ʿĀṣ returned to Mecca and discharged his debts to all who possessed a claim against him. He said, "O people of the Quraysh, does anything remain for anyone among you?" They replied, "No, by God." Then, he said, "I witness that there is no God but Allah and that Muḥammad is His messenger. Indeed, I converted in Medina, and what prevented me from standing up in Medina was the fear that you would think that I converted because I had left with what was yours." Then he returned to the Prophet and the Prophet returned Zaynab to him in their marriage. Some say that this caravan had taken the road to Irāq. Its guide was al-Furāt b. Ḥayyān al-ʿIjlī.

Muḥammad b. Ibrāhīm said: As for al-Mughīra b. Muʿāwiya, he escaped. He directed himself towards Mecca, taking the same road. Saʿd b. Abī Waqqāṣ met him bringing seven others with him. He who took al-Mughīra prisoner was Khawwāt b. Jubayr. He went with him until they entered Medina after *ʿAṣar*, and the day had turned cool.

Muḥammad b. Ibrāhīm said: Dhakwān, the *mawlā* of ʿĀ'isha related to me from ʿĀ'isha that the Prophet said to her, "Guard this prisoner!" and then went out. ʿĀ'isha said: However I was distracted by a woman I was talking to, and the prisoner set out and I did not know. Then the Prophet entered, and he did not see the prisoner, so he said, "Where is the prisoner?" I replied, "By God, I do not know. I was careless about him, but he was here previously." The Prophet said, "May God cut off your hand!" She said: Then he set out and shouted to the people, and they set out in search of the "prisoner" and found him in al-Ṣawrayn, and brought him before the Prophet.

ʿĀ'isha said: The Prophet came to me, so I turned my hands to him, and he said, "What is the matter with you?" I said, "I consider how my hands will be cut, as you have asked in your prayer about me!" She said: The Prophet turned in the direction of prayer and raising both his hands, said, "O God, surely I am a man. I get angry and I regret it [Page 555] just as any other man would. Whichever one of the believing men or women I pray against, transform my prayer into a blessing."

THE EXPEDITION OF ZAYD B. ḤĀRITHA TO AL-ṬARAF

Usāma b. Zayd al-Laythī related to me from ʿImrān b. Mannāḥ, who said: The Messenger of God sent Zayd b. Ḥāritha to al-Ṭaraf to the Banū Thaʿlaba. He set out with fifteen men until when they were in al-Ṭaraf they took cattle and sheep. The Bedouin fled for they feared that the Messenger of God would march to them. Zayd b. Ḥāritha descended until in the morning he arrived in Medina with the sheep. The Bedouin set out in search of him until they were no longer able.

Zayd arrived with twenty camels, and there was no fighting in this expedition. But they were absent for four nights.

Ibn Abī Sabra related to me from Abū Rushd from Ḥumayd b. Mālik from those who attended the expedition: They took two camels or the equivalent of them in sheep, and there was for every camel ten sheep. The code was Kill! Kill!

THE EXPEDITION OF ZAYD B. ḤĀRITHA TO ḤISMĀ

Mūsā b. Muḥammad b. Ibrāhīm related to me from his father, who said: Diḥya al-Kalbī approached from the place of Ceasar (Heraclius) who had apportioned money and clothes to him. He proceeded until he arrived in Ḥismā where the people from Judhām blocked his path. They took every thing that he had with [Page 556] him, and he arrived in Medina in tatters. He did not enter his house until he had first reached and knocked on the door of the Messenger of God. The Messenger of God said, "Who is this?" and he replied, "Diḥyā al-Kalbī." The Prophet said, "Enter." So he entered, and the Messenger of God asked that he inform him about what Heraclius had said to the end. Then he said, "O Messenger of God, I approached from his presence until I was in Ḥismā when the people of Judhām attacked me, and they did not leave me with anything, so that I arrive in these tattered garments."

Mūsā b. Muḥammad related to me: I heard an old man from Saʿd Hudhaym inform from his father, saying: Indeed, Diḥya when he was taken, was taken by al-Hunayd b. ʿĀriḍ and his son ʿĀriḍ b. al-Hunayd, who were two miserable and unlucky men. They did not leave anything with him. A group of the Banū al-Ḍubayb heard about this and they hastened against al-Hunayd and his son. In that group was al-Nuʿmān b. Abī Juʿāl with ten men. al-Nuʿmān was a man of the *wādī* who possessed physical strength and command of archery. He and Qurra b. Abī Aṣfar al-Ṣalaʿī wrestled with each other, and Qurra shot al-Nuʿmān in his ankle and forced him to the ground. Then Nuʿman rose and aimed at him with a broad headed arrow, saying, "Take this from me, youth." The arrow flew to his knee and he twitched and fell. They set Diḥya free with his belongings, and he returned in safety to Medina.

Mūsā said: I heard another old man say, "One of his companion from the Quḍāʿa released the belongings of Diḥya. It was he who salvaged everything that was taken from Diḥya [Page 557] and returned it to him." Diḥya returned to Medina and mentioned that to the Prophet, and sought the Prophet's permission to shed the blood of al-Hunayd and his son. The Prophet commanded the attack, and Zayd b. Ḥāritha set out with him.

Rifāʿa b. Zayd al-Judhāmī arrived before the Prophet. The Prophet granted him permission to stay in Medina. Then he asked the Prophet to write a document with him. The Prophet wrote with him: In the name of God the Gracious the Merciful, to Rifāʿa b. Zayd, to his people in general and to those who entered with them. He invited them to God and His messenger. And those among them who accepted were of the party of God and the party of His messenger. Whoever rejected it was granted protection for two months. When Rifāʿa arrived before his people with the document of the Prophet, he read it to them, and they answered him swiftly, and arrived at the place where Diḥya al-Kalbī was attacked. They found that his companions had dispersed.

Zayd b. Ḥāritha came, after them, to the Messenger of God who sent him back with five hundred men, and Diḥya al-Kalbi. Zayd had marched by night and hidden by day. With him was a guide from the Banū ʿUdhra. All the Ghaṭafān and the Wāʾil had come together, as well as those who were from Salāmāt and Bahrāʾ, when Rifāʿa b. Zayd came to them with the document of the Prophet and alighted—the men and Rifāʿa—in Kurāʿ of Ruʾayya, not knowing. The ʿUdhrī guide proceeded with Zayd b. Ḥāritha until he suddenly came upon them. They attacked al-Hunayd, his son, and those who were in their camp at dawn. They took what they found and they killed [Page 558] violently. They killed al-Hunayd and his son. They attacked their cattle and their sheep and their women. They took from their cattle a thousand camels, and five thousand of their sheep, and among the prisoners were a hundred women and children. Indeed, the guide had come to them from the tribe of al-Awlāj.

When the Ḍubayb heard about that and about what Zayd b. Ḥāritha did, they rode out. Among those who rode were Ḥibbān b. Milla and his son. They drew near the soldiers, and except for Ḥibbān b. Milla, were advised not to speak. And there was a sign between them that when one of them desired to strike with his sword he would say, "Qawdī!" When they appeared at the camp they found a multitude of slaves and cattle and women and prisoners, approaching together. Ḥibbān b. Milla said, "Indeed, we are a group of Muslims."

The first who met them was a man on a horse, and he displayed his spear. Hibbān approached, driving them, and a man among them said, "Qawdī" (the code word), and Ḥibbān said, "Slow down!" When they stopped before Zayd b. Ḥāritha, Ḥibbān said to him, "Indeed we are Muslims." Zayd said, "Recite the mother of the books!" And Zayd was testing one of them with the mother of the book, but no more. When Ḥibbān recited it, Zayd said to him, "Call off the soldiers, for indeed we are prohibited from those who recite the mother of the book." The people returned and Zayd forbade them to descend to the valley they came from, and they spent the evening with their families. They watched Zayd and his companions, and listened until the companions of Zayd fell asleep, and when they were calm and asleep, they rode to Rifāʿa b. Zayd. Among the riders that night were Abū Zayd b. ʿAmr, Abū Asmāʾ b. ʿAmr, Suwayd b. Zayd and his brother, Bardhaʿaʿ b. Zayd, and Thaʿlaba b. ʿAdī.

[Page 559] They arrived in the morning before Rifāʿa in Kurāʿ Ruʾayya. Ḥibbān said, "Surely you are sitting and milking goats," and he informed them of the news and entered with them, until they arrived before the Prophet at Medina. They marched for three days. Rifāʿa led them, and showed the Prophet the document that he had written with him. When the Prophet read his document he inquired of them, and they informed the Prophet about what Zayd b. Ḥāritha did. He said, "What can I do about the dead?" Rifāʿa replied, "O Messenger of God, you know best. Do not forbid us what is permitted, nor allow us what is forbidden." Abū Zayd said, "Release to us those who are living, O Messenger of God, and as for those who are killed, they are under my two feet." The Messenger of God said, "You speak the truth, Abū Zayd!" The people said, "O Messenger of God, send a man with us to Zayd b. Ḥāritha, so he will release our women and our property to us." The Prophet said, "Go with them, O ʿAlī." ʿAlī replied, "O Messenger of God, Zayd will not obey me." The Messenger of God said, "This is my sword, take it." So ʿAlī took it and said, "I do not have a camel to ride." Some of the people said, "This is a camel!" So he rode one of their camels setting out with them until they met Rāfiʿ b. Makīth, the messenger of Zayd b. Ḥāritha on one of the female camels of the people. ʿAlī returned it to the people, and Rāfiʿ b. Makīth returned with ʿAlī, in the rear, until they met Zayd b. Ḥāritha at al-Faḥlatayn. ʿAlī joined him, and said, “Surely the Messenger of God commands you to return to those people the prisoners or captives and property you hold.” Zayd said, “Show me a sign from the Messenger of God!” ʿAlī replied, “This is his sword!” Zayd knew the sword, so he alighted and shouted, [Page 560] “O people, gather before me. Whoever has something of captives or property, he shall surely return it. This is a command from the Messenger of God.” So he returned to the people all that was taken from them, immediately—even the women who were under the thighs of men.

Usāma b. Zayd b. Aslam informed me from Busr b. Miḥjan al-Dīlī from his father, who said: I was in that expedition. Every man received seven camels and seventy sheep, and a woman or two from the prisoners. A man could have sex with his slave girl after the woman completed her menstrual cycle. Then the Messenger of God returned all of the plunder, even what was separated and sold from it, to its owners and families.

THE EXPEDITION OF ITS COMMANDER ʿABD AL-RAḤMĀN B. ʿAWF TO DŪMAT AL-JANDAL

Saʿīd b. Muslim b. Qamādīn related to me from ʿAṭāʾ b. Abī Rabāḥ from Ibn ʿUmar, who said: The Messenger of God called ʿAbd al-Raḥmān b. ʿAwf and said, “Make preparations, for indeed I am sending you on an expedition from this day of yours, or from tomorrow, God willing.” Ibn ʿUmar said: I heard that and I said, “Surely I shall visit and pray with the Prophet tomorrow, and I will listen to his advice to ʿAbd al-Raḥmān b. ʿAwf.”

He said: I woke up on the morrow and prayed, and, lo and behold, there were Abū Bakr, ʿUmar, people from the Muhājirūn, and with them ʿAbd al-Raḥmān b. ʿAwf. Then the Messenger of God commanded him to march by night to Dūmat al-Jandal and invite them to Islam. The Messenger of God said to ʿAbd al-Raḥmān, “What delayed you from your companions?” Ibn ʿUmar said: His companions had left before dawn. They were encamped in al-Jurf and were seven hundred men. ʿAbd al-Raḥmān said, “I would like, O Messenger of God, that this will be the last of my assignments with you. I am wearing garments of the traveler.” He said: And ʿAbd al-Raḥmān had a turban wrapped around his head. Ibn ʿUmar said: The Prophet called him and made him sit down before him, and removed his turban with his hand, then he draped a black turban [Page 561] which he let fall between his shoulders, saying, “This is how you put on a turban, O Ibn ʿAwf!” He said: Ibn ʿAwf was wearing a sword on a decorated belt. Then the Messenger of God said, “Attack in the name of God, and in the way of God and fight those who disbelieve in God. Do not be an extremist, double cross anyone or kill a boy.” Ibn ʿUmar said: Then he extended his hands and said, “O people, beware of five things before you are taken. Whenever a people are not honest in their measure, God punishes them for years with a shortage of crops, until they repent. Whenever a people violate their agreement, God commands their enemy against them. Whenever a people refuse *zakāt*, God keeps from them the rain of the heavens, and their domestic animals will not be quenched of thirst. Corruption will be punished with plague. And, whenever a people judge against the laws of the Book, God divides them into factions, and each faction will suffer from the other.”

He said: ʿAbd al-Raḥmān set out until he joined his companions, and marched until he arrived in Dūmat al-Jandal. When he dismounted there, he invited the people to

Islam, and stayed there for three days inviting them to Islam. At first they refused all but the sword. When it was the third day, al-Asbagh b. ʿAmr al-Kalbī converted. He was a Christian and their leader. ʿAbd al-Raḥmān wrote to the Prophet and informed him about that. The Prophet sent a man from the Juhayna named Rāfiʿ b. Makīth. Rāfiʿ wrote to the Prophet informing him that he desired to marry one of them. The Prophet wrote asking him to marry the daughter of al-Aṣbagh, Tumāḍir. ʿAbd al-Raḥmān married her and consummated his marriage with her, and returned with her. She was the mother of Abū Salama b. ʿAbd al-Raḥmān b. ʿAwf.

ʿAbdullah b. Jaʿfar informed me from Ibn Abī ʿAwf from Ṣāliḥ b. Ibrāhīm that the Prophet sent ʿAbd al-Raḥmān b. ʿAwf to the Kalb. He said, "Comply with their request to you and marry the daughter of their king or Lord." When he arrived he invited them [Page 562] to Islam and they complied, but he continued the *jizya* payment. He married Tumāḍir the daughter of al-Aṣbagh b. ʿAmr, their king. Then he arrived with her in Medina. She was the mother of Abū Salama.

THE EXPEDITION OFʿ ʿALĪ B. ABĪ ṬĀLIB TO THE BANŪ SAʿD IN FADAK

ʿAbdullah b. Jaʿfar related to me from Yaʿqūb b. ʿUtba, who said: The Messenger of God sent ʿAlī with a hundred men to confront the Banū Saʿd in Fadak for it had reached the Messenger of God that they had a group desiring to help the Jews of Khaybar. ʿAlī marched by night and hid by day until he reached al-Hamaj. He captured a spy and said, "Who are you? Do you have information of what has happened to the group of the Banū Saʿd?" The spy replied, "No, I do not have any information about it." But they were firm with him and he confirmed that he was a spy of the Banū Saʿd sent to Khaybar to propose to the Jews of Khaybar that they would help them if the Jews of Khaybar would provide them dates just as they did for others who helped them. They said to him, "Where are the people?" He replied, "I left them; they had gathered among two hundred men, and their leader is Wabr b. ʿUlaym." They said, "Lead us to them." He replied, "On condition that you protect me!" They said, "If you will take us to them and their cattle, we will protect you. If not, we will not protect you." He said, "So be it!"

He set out guiding them until they became suspicious of him. He passed by deserts and hills and came to low land and behold, there were sheep and cattle. He said, "Release me!" They replied, "Not until we secure our demand!" The shepherds who were grazing the sheep and cattle fled to their group and cautioned them, [Page 563] so they dispersed and fled. The guide said, "Why are you keeping me prisoner? The Bedouin have dispersed and the shepherds have warned them." ʿAlī replied, "We have not reached their camp, yet." He reached it with them but they did not see anyone. So they released the spy and drove the cattle and sheep. The cattle included five hundred camels and a thousand sheep.

Ubayr b. al-ʿAlāʾ related to me from ʿĪsā b. ʿAlayla from his father from his grandfather, who said: Indeed I was at the Wādī al-Hamaj at Badīʿ. I only knew that the Banū Saʿd were carrying their hawdas and fleeing, so I said, "What happened to them today?" I went close to them and met their leader Wabr b. ʿUlaym, and I said to him, "What is this journey?" He replied, "Evil. A group from Muḥammad is marching to us before we can prepare for war, and we do not have power against them. They have captured a messenger of ours that we sent to Khaybar, and he has informed them of us and done what he did." I said, "And who is he?" He replied, "The son of my brother. We did not consider there to be a youth better than him among the Bedouin." I said, "I think Muḥammad commands an affair that has become secure and fixed. He attacked the Quraysh and did with them what he did. Then he attacked the people of the fortresses in Yathrib, the Qaynuqāʿ the Banū Naḍīr and the Qurayẓa, and now he marches to those in Khaybar." Wabar said to me, "Do not fear that! Indeed in it are men and forbidding fortresses, and a source of water. Muḥammad will not draw near them, ever, and it is best for them to attack him in the heart of his home." I said, "Do you think that?" He replied, "It is their decision."

ʿAlī stayed for three days, then he apportioned the plunder and put aside the prescribed fifth of the Prophet, a camel named al-Ḥafida, and arrived with it in Medina.

[Page 564] THE EXPEDITION OF ZAYD B. ḤĀRITHA TO UMM QIRFA

Abū ʿAbdullah Muḥammad b. ʿUmar al-Wāqidī related to me that ʿAbdullah b. Jaʿfar related to us from ʿAbdullah b. al-Ḥusayn b. al-Ḥusayn b. ʿAlī b. Abī Ṭālib, who said: Zayd b. Ḥāritha set out with merchants to al-Shām. He had money from the companions of the Prophet, and he took two testicles from a billygoat, tanned them, and put the goods in them. Then he set out until when he was outside Wādī al-Qurā with people from his companions, groups from the Banū Fazāra of the Banū Badr saw him and struck him and his companions until they thought they were dead, and took what Zayd had brought with him. But, Zayd escaped and arrived in Medina before the Prophet. The Prophet sent him on an expedition, saying, "Hide by day and march by night." One of their guides set out with them.

The Banū Badr were warned about them, so they looked for them in the morning from the top of the mountain overlooking the road, which they believed they were coming from. Observing the determined route by day, he says, "Move freely, there will be no harm to you on this night of yours." When Zayd b. Ḥāritha and his companions were marching to the route at night, the guide mistook the road with them, and he took them on another road until in the evening they knew they were mistaken. Then they waited for them in the night until it dawned on them, but Zayd b. Ḥāritha stopped them as they were far from their goal. He said: Then he advised them not to disperse and said, [Page 565] "When I proclaim *takbīr*, you proclaim *takbīr*." They encircled the residents, then he proclaimed *takbīr* and they proclaimed *takbīr*.

Salama b. al-Akwaʿ set out seeking a man of theirs to kill. He was thorough in his search, and he captured a girl, the daughter of Mālik b. Ḥudhayfa b. Badr, whom he found in one of their houses—her mother was Umm Qirfa. Umm Qirfa was Fāṭima, daughter of Rabīʿa b. Zayd—and they plundered. Zayd b. Ḥāritha came forward, and Salama b. al-Akwaʿ approached with the girl. Zayd mentioned that to the Prophet and he mentioned her beauty to him. The Prophet said, "What girl did you take, O Salama?" He replied, "A girl, O Messenger of God, with whom I hope to ransom a woman of ours from the Banū Fazāra." The Prophet repeated his question a second and a third time, "What girl did you take?" Until Salama knew that he wanted her, so he gave her to him. The Prophet gifted her to Ḥazan b. Abī Wahb. She bore him a daughter, and he did not have another child by her.

Muḥammad related to me from al-Zuhrī from ʿUrwa from ʿĀʾisha, who said: Zayd b. Ḥāritha arrived from his direction while the Messenger of God was in my house. Zayd came and knocked on the door. The Messenger of God went to him naked, pulling his clothes on. I have not seen him naked before that. He embraced him and kissed him, then he questioned him, and Zayd informed him of God's victory.

A RECORD OF THOSE KILLED AT UMM QIRFA

Qays b. al-Muḥassir killed Umm Qirfa—violently. He tied a rope between her legs then tied it between two camels. She was an old lady. ʿAbdullah b. Masʿada was killed as was Qays b. al-Nuʿmān b. Masʿada b. Ḥakama b. Mālik b. Badr.

[Page 566] THE EXPEDITION OF THE COMMANDER ʿABDULLAH B. RAWĀḤA TO USAYR B. ZĀRIM

Al-Wāqidī said: Mūsā b. Yaʿqūb related to me from Abū l-Aswad, who said: I heard ʿUrwa b. al-Zubayr say: ʿAbdullah b. Rawāḥa marched to Khaybar twice. The first time, the Prophet sent him to Khaybar in Ramaḍān with three men to observe Khaybar, the condition of its people, what they desired and what they spoke about. He went forward until he came to the region of Khaybar and tried to enter its fortifications. He dispersed his companions to al-Naṭā, al-Shaqq and al-Katība. They learned what they heard of Usayr and others. Then they set out after a stay of three days and returned to the Messenger of God during the last nights of Ramaḍān. ʿAbdullah informed the Prophet of all that he saw and heard; then he set out to Usayr in Shawwāl.

Ibn Abī Ḥabība related to me from Dāwud b. al-Ḥuṣayn from Abū Sufyān from Ibn ʿAbbās, who said: Usayr was a brave man. When Abū Rāfiʿ was killed Usayr b. Zārim took command of the Jews. He stood up before the Jews and said, "By God, Muḥammad did not attack any one of the Jews, but he sent one of his companions to get whatever he desired from them. I will do what my companions did not do." They said, "What do you seek to do that your companions did not do?" He replied, "I will march to the Ghaṭafān and I will gather them." And he marched to the Ghaṭafān and collected them. Then he said, "O community of Jews, we will march to Muḥammad in the heart of his home, for surely one is not attacked in his home except his enemies will take some of what they desire." They said, "Your opinion is correct," and that reached the Messenger of God.

He said: Khārija b. Ḥusayl al-Ashjaʿī arrived before the Prophet and informed him of what was behind him. Then Khārija said, "I left [Page 567] Usayr b. Zārim marching to you with a contingent of Jews." Ibn ʿAbbās said: The Messenger of God summoned the people, and appointed thirty men. ʿAbdullah b. Unays said: I was with them. The Messenger of God appointed ʿAbdullah b. Rawāḥa over us.

He said: We set out until we arrived at Khaybar, and we sent a message to Usayr, saying, "Are we secure if we come to you and present you with what we bring from the Messenger of God?" He replied, "Yes, and can I expect the same from you?" We said, "Yes." We went before him and said, "The Messenger of God sent us to you that you may go to him and he will appoint you over Khaybar and be good to you." But Usayr was ambitious about that. He consulted the Jews and they opposed him going out. They said, "Muḥammad would not appoint a man from the Banū Isrā'īl." He said, "Of course, but we are tired of war."

He said: Usayr set out with thirty men from the Jews, and each man had a Muslim companion. He said: We marched until all of a sudden we were in Qarqara Thibār. Then, Usayr regretted until we knew the regret in him. ʿAbdullah b. Unays said: He fell down with his hand at my sword and I was alerted to it. So I pushed my camel forward and said, "Treachery is God's enemy." Then I pretended to sleep, and I drew near him and observed what he did. He reached for my sword! I put down my camel and said, "Is there a man who will alight and lead us?" But no one got down. So I got down from my camel and led the people in order to confront Usayr. I struck him with my sword, and I cut the end of his leg, and made most of his thigh and his leg fall, and he fell from his camel. In his hand was a crooked stick from the Shawḥasa tree, and he struck me on the crown of my head with it. We turned on [Page 568] his companions and killed all of them, except for a single man who fought back. Not a single Muslim was killed. Then we approached the Messenger of God.

He said: Meanwhile, the Messenger of God was conversing with his companions, saying to them, "Walk with us to al-Thaniyya, we expect news from our companions." They set out with him and when they looked down on al-Thaniyya, lo and behold two of our companions were hastening towards them. He said: The Messenger of God sat down with his companions. He said: We reached him and informed him of the news, and he said, "God saved you from the people of oppression."

ʿAbdullah b. Unays said: I drew close to the Prophet and he blew on the crown of my head. It did not bleed after that day, nor did it hurt. The bone was already broken. He rubbed on my face and prayed for me. He cut a portion of a stick and said, "Take this with you as a sign between you and me, and on the Day of Judgment I will recognize you by it. Indeed you will arrive on the Day of Judgment bearing a stick." When ʿAbdullah was buried, the stick was placed beside his skin under his clothing.

Khārija b. al-Ḥārith related to me from ʿAṭiyya b. ʿAbdullah b. Unays from his father, who said: I was mending my bow. He said: When I arrived I found my companions were going to Usayr b. Zārim. The Prophet said, "I will not see Usayr b. Zārim," meaning, kill him.

THE EXPEDITION OF THE COMMANDER KURZ B. JĀBIR

The expedition took place when the milch camels of the Prophet were raided in Shawwāl of the year six, in Dhūl-Jadr, which lies eight miles from Medina.

[Page 569] Khārija b. ʿAbdullah related to us from Yazīd b. Rūmān, who said: A group of eight from ʿUrayna came before the Messenger of God and converted. They deemed Medina unhealthy, and the Prophet commanded them to be moved to his milch camels that were in Dhūl-Jadr. The cattle of the Muslims were there in Dhūl-Jadr until they became healthy and put on weight. They asked permission of the Prophet to drink the camels' milk and urine. He permitted them, and in the morning they left with the camels. The *mawlā* of the Prophet overtook them, but there was a group with them that fought him. They captured him and they cut his hand and leg, and pierced his tongue and eyes with a fork until he died. Then they left with the camels.

A woman from the Banū ʿAmr b. Awf approached on a donkey of hers until she passed Yasār under a tree. When she saw him and what happened to him, he was dead. She returned to her people and informed them. They set out towards Yasār until they brought him to Qubā', dead. The Messenger of God sent twenty riders in the tracks of those from ʿUrayna. He appointed Kurz b. Jābir al-Fihrī over them. They set out in search of them until they reached them at night. They spent the night in the district and rose in the morning, but did not know where to go. All of a sudden, they found themselves with a woman carrying the shoulder of a camel. They took her captive, and said, "What do you have with you?" She said, "I passed by a people who had slaughtered a camel and they gave it to me." They said, "Where are they?" She replied, "They are in that wasteland of the district. When you are before them you will see their smoke."

So they left until they came to the men from ʿUrayna when they had finished their food. They surrounded them and asked them to surrender. All of them were captured; not a man escaped. They tied them and seated them behind them on their horses until they arrived with them in Medina. They found the Messenger of God in al-Ghāba and they set out to meet him.

Khārija said: Yazīd b. Rūmān said: Anas b. Mālik related to me, saying: [Page 570]

I set out walking in their tracks with some youths. When the Prophet met them in al-Zaghāba where the waters meet, he commanded that their hands and legs be cut. Their eyes were scooped out and they were crucified there. Anas said: I was standing there and I observed what was done to them.

Al-Wāqidī said: Isḥāq related to me from Ṣāliḥ, *mawlā* of al-Tawama from Abū Hurayra, who said: When the Prophet cut the hands of the companions of the milch camels, and their legs, and gouged out their eyes, these verses were revealed: *The punishment of those who wage war against God and His apostle and strive for corruption in the land, is execution or crucifixion, or the cutting off of hands and feet from opposite sides* . . . (Q. 5:33) to the end of the verse. He said: After that an eye was never gouged.

He said: Abū Jaʿfar related to me from his father from his grandfather, who said: Whenever the Prophet sent a mission after that he forbad mutilation.

Ibn Bilāl related to me from Jaʿfar b. Muḥammad from his father from his grandfather, who said: The Messenger of God did not cut a tongue ever. Nor did he gouge out an eye. Indeed, he did not go beyond cutting hands and feet. Ibn Abī Ḥabība related to me from ʿAbd al-Raḥmān b. ʿAbd al-Raḥmān, who said that the commander of the expedition was Ibn Zayd al-Ashhalī.

Ibn Abī Sabra related to me from Marwān b. Abī Saʿīd b. al-Muʿallā, who said: When they were successful with the milch camels they appointed Salama b. al-Akwaʿ over them. With him was Abū Ruhm al-Ghifārī. There were fifteen milch camels, and they were ample camels. When the Messenger of God approached Medina from Zaghāba he sat in the mosque, and all of a sudden the milch camels were at the door of the mosque. The Messenger of God went out and observed them. He searched for his camel named al-Ḥinā' among them. [Page 571] He said, "O Salama, where is al-Ḥinā'?" He replied, "The people slaughtered it and they slaughtered no other." Then the Messenger of God said, "Look for a place for them to graze." He replied, "There is no better place than where they were in Dhū l-Jadr." He said, "Then, return them to Dhū l-Jadr." They were there. Their milk was brought every night to the Messenger of God. Every night there was a provision of milk.

Ibn Abī Sabra said: Isḥāq b. ʿAbdullah related to me from some boy of Salama b. Akwaʿ that he informed him about roughly twenty horsemen. He said that they included himself, Abū Ruhm al-Ghifārī, Abū Dharr, Burayda b. al-Khuṣayb, Rāfiʿ b. Makīth, Jundub b. Makīth, Bilāl b. al-Ḥārith al-Muzannī, ʿAbdullah b. ʿAmr b. ʿAwf al-Muzannī, Juʿāl b. Surāqa, Ṣafwān b. Muʿāṭṭil, Abū Rawʿā, Maʿbad b. Khālid al-Juhannī, ʿAbdullah b. Badr, Suwayd b. Ṣakhr, and Abū Ḍubays al-Juhannī.

THE RAID OF AL-ḤUDAYBIYYA

He said: Rabīʿa b. ʿUmayr b. ʿAbdullah b. al-Haram, Qudāma b. Mūsā ʿAbdullah b. Yazīd al-Hudhalī, Muḥammad b. ʿAbdullah b. Abī Sabra, Mūsā b. Muḥammad, Usāma b. Zayd al-Laythī, Abū Maʿshar, ʿAbd al-Hamīd b. Jaʿfar, ʿAbd al-Raḥmān b. ʿAbd al-ʿAzīz, Yūnus b. Muḥammad, Yaʿqūb b. Muḥammad b. [Page 572] Abī Ṣaʿṣaʿa, Mujammiʿ b. Yaʿqūb, Saʿīd b. Abī Zayd al-Zuraqī, ʿĀbid b. Yaḥyā, and Muḥammad b. Ṣāliḥ related to us from ʿĀṣim b. ʿUmar, Muḥammad b. Yaḥyā b. Sahl b. Abī Ḥathma, Yaḥyā b. ʿAbdullah b. Abī Qatāda, Muʿādh b. Muḥammad, ʿAbdullah b. Jaʿfar and Ḥizām b. Hishām from his father, all have related to me about this tradition in portions. Some of them are more reliable about this tradition than others. Others who are unnamed, people of trust, have also informed me. I wrote down all that was related to me.

They said: The Messenger of God had seen in his sleep that he entered the "House," his head shaven, taken the key to the "House," and stood at the place of the halting at al-ʿArafat. So, he called his companions to perform the *ʿUmra*. They hastened their preparations to set out.

Busr b. Sufyān al-Kaʿbī arrived before the Prophet on the last night of Shawwāl of the year 6 AH. He had arrived safely before the Messenger of God as a visitor while returning to his family. The Messenger of God said to him, "O Busr, do not leave until you have set out with us, for indeed, if God wills, we shall set out for *ʿUmra*." Busr stayed, and the Messenger of God commanded him to purchase sacrificial camels, so Busr purchased the camels and sent them to Dhū l-Jadr until he set out, when he would command that they be brought to Medina. The Prophet ordered Nājiya b. Jundub al-Aslamī to dispatch the camels to Dhū l-Ḥulayfa and appointed Nājiya b. Jundub over them. The companions of the Messenger of God set out to Mecca, not doubting its opening because of the Prophet's dream. They set out without weapons except for the sword in its scabbard. A group of his companions drove the sacrificial animals. The people of power were Abū Bakr, [Page 573] ʿAbd al-Raḥmān b. ʿAwf, ʿUthmān b. ʿAffān, and Ṭalḥa b. ʿUbaydullah, and they drove the offerings until he stopped at Dhū l-Ḥulayfa. Saʿd b. ʿUbāda drove some animals.

ʿUmar b. al-Khaṭṭāb said, "O Messenger of God, do you not fear that Abū Sufyān b. Ḥarb and his companions might attack us for we have not made preparations for war?" The Messenger of God said, "I do not know. I do not desire to carry weapons as a pilgrim." Saʿd b. ʿUbāda said, "O Messenger of God, if we carry weapons, then, if we see something suspicious among the people, we will be prepared for them." The Messenger of God said, "I will not carry weapons. Surely I am setting out as a pilgrim for *ʿUmra*." The Prophet appointed Ibn Umm Maktūm in charge of Medina during his absence.

The Messenger of God set out from Medina on a Monday in Dhū l-Qaʿda. He washed in his house and put on two garments from the fabric of Ṣuḥār. He rode his camel al-Qaṣwāʾ from the door of his house. The Muslims set out. The Messenger of

God prayed *Ẓuhr* in Dhū l-Ḥulayfa. He then called for the sacrificial camels to be covered and he himself marked some of those on the right side, as they stood facing the Kaʿba. Some say that he marked one camel on the right side, and then commanded Nājiya b. Jundub to mark the rest of them, and hang upon them sandal after sandal.

There were seventy camels including the camel of Abū Jahl, which the Messenger of God had taken as his share from the plunder at Badr. It used to be with the milch camels in Dhū l-Jadr. The Muslims marked their sacrifical animals, and strung sandals on the necks of the animals. The Messenger of God called Busr b. Sufyān from Dhū l-Ḥulayfa and sent him as his spy. He said, "Surely, the Quraysh have learned that I desire to perform *ʿUmra*, so inquire about them and bring me this information." [Page 574] So Busr went ahead.

The Messenger of God called ʿAbbād b. Bishr and sent him ahead as a vanguard with a cavalry of twenty horsemen. There were men from the Muhājirūn and Anṣār among them. Al-Miqdād b. ʿAmr, Abū ʿAyyāsh al-Zuraqī, Ḥubāb b. al-Mundhir, ʿĀmir b. Rabīʿa, Saʿīd b. Zayd, Abū Qatāda, Muḥammad b. Maslama, and a number of others, all rode horses. Some say their commander was Saʿd b. Zayd al-Ashhalī.

The Messenger of God entered the Mosque and prayed two bowings. Then he went out, called for his ride and rode it from the door of the mosque. When it rose with him in the direction of the *qibla*—he declared his state of ritual consecration (*iḥrām*)—and called out four times the words "Here I come to you, O Lord! There is no partner to You. Here I come my Lord! Praise and goodness and possession is Yours. You have no partners." The rest of the Muslims also declared their state of ritual consecration, but there were some who only declared it in al-Juḥfa.

The Messenger of God took the road to al-Baydāʾ. A thousand six hundred Muslims set out with him. Some say a thousand four hundred, and some say a thousand five hundred and twenty-five. A hundred men from the Aslam set out with him, and some say they were seventy. Four women went with him: His wife, Umm Salama, Umm ʿUmāra, Umm Manīʿ and Umm ʿĀmir al-Ashhaliyya. The Prophet passed by the Bedouin who were between Medina and Mecca, and called out to them. But they were too busy for it with their property, their children and their descendants. They included the Banū Bakr, the Muzayna and Juhayna. Talking among themselves, some said, "Does Muḥammad desire to attack, with us, a people destined and confirmed in spear shafts and weapons? Surely Muḥammad and the small group of his companions are camel eaters [foolhardy]! Muḥammad and his companions will never return from this journey of theirs. [Page 575] His is a community with neither weapons, nor numbers. Indeed, he arrives before a people whose experience with those who were taken from them at Badr is recent."

The Messenger of God dispatched the men on horseback. Then he dispatched Nājiya b. Jundub, who had a youth from the Aslam with him, with the sacrificial animals. The Muslims also dispatched their sacrificial animals with Nājiya b. Jundub, the master of the sacrificial animals of the Messenger of God.

The Messenger of God set out at dawn on Wednesday to Malal. He travelled from Malal, ate dinner in Sayyāla, and arrived at dawn in al-Rawhāʾ. There, he met a group from the Banū Nahd who had sheep and cattle. He invited them to Islam, but they did not reply and held back. They sent the Messenger of God milk through a man, but the Messenger of God refused to accept it from them. He said, "I cannot accept a gift from a polytheist." The Messenger of God commanded that it be bought from them. So they purchased it from the Bedouin and the people were happy. They brought three live lizards and offered it, and those who were not in *iḥrām* bought it. They ate some and offered some to the pilgrims, but the latter refused until they asked the Messenger of God about it. He said, "Eat, for all that has not been hunted for you is permitted, when you are in *iḥrām*. But you must avoid what you hunt or what is hunted for you." They said, "O Messenger of God, by God, we did not hunt it, nor was it hunted except for the Bedouin. The Bedouin who gave it to us did not know they would meet us."

The Bedouin are a people who travel by land. When the day dawns on them on the morrow, they are in another land, seeking the rains. They desired the green plains of Malal that had enjoyed rain-clouds in Autumn. The Messenger of God called one of them and asked him, "Where are you going?" He said, "O Muḥammad, a cloud was mentioned to us at this time in the green plains of Malal, a month ago. We sent one of our men, and he explored [Page 576] the land, and returned, and informed us that the cattle were content and the camel walked heavily from the water collected, and that there were many thirst quenching springs. We want to go there."

ʿAbd al-ʿAzīz b. Muḥammad related to me from ʿAmr b. Abī ʿAmr, from Muṭṭalib b. ʿAbdullah b. Ḥanṭab from Abū Qatāda, who said: We set out with the Messenger of God for the *ʿUmra* from al-Ḥudaybiyya accompanied by ordinary travelers as well as pilgrims, until we reached al-Abwāʾ. I, who was not a pilgrim, saw wild donkeys, so I saddled my horse and rode, saying to one of them, "Give me my whip!" He refused to give it. So I said, "Give me my spear!" And he refused again. So I alighted and took my whip and my spear and rode my horse. I attacked a donkey, killed it and brought it to my companions—to those who were pilgrims and those who were not. The pilgrims had doubts about eating it until we reached the Messenger of God and asked him about it. He said, "Do you have some of it with you?" I gave him a leg of donkey and he ate it until he came to the very end of it, and he was a pilgrim. Someone said to Abū Qatāda, "What keeps you from joining the Messenger of God?" He said: We cooked the donkey, and when it was well cooked we joined him.

ʿAbd al-Raḥmān b. ʿAbd al-ʿAzīz related to me from al-Zuhrī from ʿUbaydullah b. ʿAbdullah b. ʿUtba, from Ibn ʿAbbās from al-Ṣaʿb b. Jaththāma, who said that he came to the Messenger of God, at that time, in al-Abwāʾ with a wild donkey and gifted it to him but the Messenger of God returned it. Ṣaʿb said: But when he saw the unhappiness on my face as he returned my gift, he said, "I am only returning it as I am in *iḥrām*." I questioned the Messenger of God at that time and said, "O Messenger of God, what is the opinion when we come upon the enemy and the attack takes place in the darkness of dawn, and we mistakenly strike children hiding under the bellies of the horses?" The Messenger of God said, "They are with their parents." [Page 577] He said: I heard him say, at that time, "There is no protection except for God and his Messenger." It was said: Indeed the donkey was living at that time.

ʿAbd al-Raḥmān b. al-Ḥārith related to me from his grandfather from Abū Ruhm al-Ghifārī, who said: When they alighted at al-Abwāʾ, Īmāʾ b. Raḥḍa gifted a hundred sheep and sent them with his son, Khufāf b. Īmāʾ, along with two camels carrying milk. When Khufāf reached the Messenger of God he said, "My father sends these slaughtering animals and milk to you." The Messenger of God said, "When did you camp over here?" He said, "Recently. Our water had dried up so we drove our cattle to the water here." The Messenger of God said, "How is the land here?" He replied, "It feeds its cattle." As for the sheep, they were not mentioned. The Messenger of God accepted his gift. He ordered the distribution of sheep among his companions. They drank the milk in huge gulps, until it was finished. He said: May God bless you!

Abū Jaʿfar al-Ghifārī related to me from Usayd b. Abī Usayd, who said: At that time I gifted three things from Waddān to the Messenger of God: bread, plants, and cucumber. The Messenger of God began to eat the cucumber with the plants and he liked it. He commanded that the cucumber be taken to his wife Umm Salama. The Messenger of God indicated that the gift pleased him, and he showed its owner that it was unusual.

Sayf b. Sulaymān related to me from Mujāhid from ʿAbd al-Raḥmān b. Abī Laylā from Kaʿb b. ʿUjra, who said: [Page 578] When we were in al-Abwāʾ the Messenger of God stood before me, while I was blowing under a pot of mine. My head was pressed with lice but I was a pilgrim. The Messenger of God said, "Does your head trouble you, O Kaʿb?" I replied, "Yes, O Messenger of God." He said, "Shave your head." These verses were revealed about it: *He should, in compensation, either fast, or feed the poor, or offer a sacrifice* (Q. 2:196). The Messenger of God commanded me to sacrifice a sheep or fast for three days or feed six of the poor, and every poor person a debtor. He said, "Do what is best for you." It was said that Kaʿb b. ʿUjra gifted a young cow that he "garlanded" and marked.

Nājiya b. Jundub said: A camel from my sacrificial animals was injured when I was keeping watch at al-Abwāʾ, so I came to the Messenger of God at al-Abwāʾ and informed him. He said: "Slaughter it and immerse its collar in its blood, and do not eat it or permit anyone of your companions to eat of it. But let the people take from it."

When the Messenger of God alighted in al-Juḥfa, he could not find water there. He sent a man with a water carrying camel to al-Kharrār. The man set out and returned soon after with the camel. He said, "O Messenger of God, I was not able to proceed for fear." The Messenger of God said, "Be seated!" And he sent another man, and he set out with a water-camel until when he was at the place where the first man took fright, he returned. The Messenger of God said, "What is the matter with you?" He replied, "By Him who sent you with the truth, I was not able to proceed for fear!" The Messenger of God said, "Be seated!" Then he sent another man, and when he reached the place from which the two men had recently returned, he became similarly fearful and returned. So the Messenger of God called one of his companions and sent him with a water-camel, and the water carrier set out with him. They did not doubt their return because of what they saw of those who returned. They arrived at al-Kharrār and they drew the water, and returned with it.

Then the Messenger of God commanded [Page 579] that what was under a tree be swept. He spoke to the people and said, "O People, indeed I exist for you as a reward. I leave with you, in your hands, what will not lead you astray, the book of God and its practices." And some say that he said, "I have left with you the Book of God and the practices of His Prophet."

When news of the Messenger of God setting out to Mecca reached the polytheists, it alarmed them. They gathered and consulted the people of opinion—people who mattered. They said: He desires to enter upon us with his forces as pilgrims of *ʿUmra*. The Bedouin have heard about it. He would enter upon us by force, and between us and him is that which is between us from the war. By God, this will never be, as long as we live. So consider your decision. They came to an agreement that the decision would be made by a group of decision makers. They were Ṣafwān b. Umayya, Sahl b. ʿAmr, and ʿIkrima b. Abī Jahl. Ṣafwān said, "We will not carry out an affair until we have consulted you. We hope to dispatch two hundred riders to Kurāʿ al-Ghamīm and we will appoint a strong man over them." The Quraysh said, "What you contemplate is good." So they dispatched their cavalry with ʿIkrima b. Abī Jahl—others say Khālid b.

al-Walīd—and the Quraysh called for help from those who would obey them from among the Aḥābīsh.

The Thaqīf joined them. They dispatched Khālid b. al-Walīd with the cavalry. They placed spies on the mountains until they reached a mountain called Wazar wazaʿ. Their spies were ten men led by al-Ḥakam b. ʿAbd Manāf. Some of them informed others quietly, saying, "Muḥammad does thus and thus," until it finally reached the Quraysh in Baldaḥ. The Quraysh set out to Baldaḥ and put up their tents and buildings. They set out with their women and children and camped there. Busr b. Sufyān entered Mecca and heard their words and saw what he saw among them. Then he returned to the Messenger of God [Page 580] and joined him by the stream of Dhāt al-Ashaṭāṭ from behind ʿUsfān. When the Messenger of God saw him, he said, "O Busr, what did you learn?" He replied, "O Messenger of God, I left your people, Kaʿb b. Luay and ʿĀmir b. Luay. They have heard about your march and they fear and dread that you will enter upon them by force. They have sought the help of the Aḥābīsh and those who obey them. With them are their women and children. They are wearing the skins of leopards in order to turn you from the sacred mosque. They have set out to Baldaḥ and put up their buildings. I left their station where the Aḥābīsh and those who have rallied to them in their land are feeding on their slaughtered animals. They have dispatched a cavalry of two hundred horses led by Khālid b. al-Walīd. This is their cavalry in al-Ghamīm. They have placed spies on the mountains as well as guards."

The Messenger of God said to the people, "This is Khālid b. al-Walīd in al-Ghamīm with the cavalry of the disbelievers." Then the Messenger of God stood with the Muslims, and praised God as He deserved. Then he said, "What do you think, O Muslims, about those who seek help against me, and those who obey them in order to turn us away from the sacred mosque? Do you think we should proceed as we intended to the 'House' and fight those who turn us from it. Or should we go before those who have set out to us, to their families and take them? If they pursue us, we will pursue them and God will cut off their heads. If they stay they remain grief stricken and longing for revenge."

Abū Bakr stood up and said, "God and His messenger know best. We think that we should proceed in the direction of the Kaʿba and fight those who turn us from it." The Messenger of God said, "Surely the cavalry of the Quraysh including Khālid b. al-Walīd is in al-Ghamīm." Abū Hurayra said, "I have not seen any one who consults with his companions more than the Messenger of God. But his consultation with his companions concerns war only." He said: Then al-Miqdād b. ʿAmr stood up and said, [Page 581] "O Messenger of God, we do not say as the Banū Isrāʾīl said to Moses: *Go you and your Lord and fight, while we sit here* (Q. 5:42). But, go you and your Lord and fight and we will fight with you. By God, O Messenger of God, if you go to Birk (the pond) al-Ghimād we will go with you, and not a man among us will stay behind." Usayd b. Ḥuḍayr spoke and said, "O Messenger of God, we think that we should fulfill what we set out to do and fight those who turn us away." The Messenger of God said, "Indeed we did not set out to fight anyone. Surely we set out for the *ʿUmra.*"

Budayl b. Warqāʾ joined him with a group of his companions and said, "O Muḥammad, surely you are deceived about the fighting of your people, the cloaked Arabs. By God, I do not think even one of you has the knowledge. Indeed, I see you as a people without weapons!" Abū Bakr al-Ṣiddīq said, "You bit the clitoris of al-Lāt!" Budayl said, "Surely, by God, if you had not helped me before, I would respond. By God, neither I, nor my people should be accused of not desiring Muḥammad's triumph. Indeed, I see the Quraysh fight you about their descendants and their property. They have set out to Baldaḥa and put up buildings, and with them are their women and children. They take turns offering slaughtering animals to those who come to them. They empower them thereby in their war with you. So, consider your decision!"

Saʿīd b. Muslim b. Qamādīn related to me from ʿUthmān b. Abī Sulaymān, who said: The Quraysh had collected and gathered their property to feed those who gathered to them from the Aḥābīsh. There was provision for food in four places: in the house of Nadwa for all their community, and in the homes of Ṣafwān b. Umayya, Suhayl b. ʿAmr, ʿIkrima b. Abī Jahl, and Ḥuwayṭib b. ʿAbd al-ʿUzzā.

[Page 582] Ibn Abī Ḥabība related to me from Dāwud b. al-Ḥuṣayn, who said: Khālid b. al-Walīd drew near with his cavalry in order to observe the companions of the Messenger of God. He arranged his cavalry in rows in the area between the Messenger of God and the *qibla*, and there were two hundred horses. The Messenger of God commanded ʿAbbād b. Bishr to go forward with his cavalry and he stood confronting al-Walīd and the rows of his companions.

Dāwud said: ʿIkrima related to me from Ibn ʿAbbās, who said: The time for the *Ẓuhr* prayer approached, and Bilāl pronounced the call to prayer and stood up. The Messenger of God faced the *qibla*, and the row of people behind him went down, to their knees and then to the floor, in prayer. Then he gave greetings, and they stood up in the places of those who were ready to fight. Khālid b. al-Walīd said, "They are heedless; if we attack them we will surely take them. Prayer will come in an hour, and prayer is more desirable to them than themselves and their sons." He said: Then, Gabriel came down with this verse between the *Ẓuhr* and *ʿAṣar* prayers: *When thou, O Apostle of God, art with them, and standest to lead them in prayer* . . . (Q. 4:102). The time for the *ʿAṣar* prayer approached and Bilāl called out the call to prayer, and the Messenger of God got up and stood facing in the direction of prayer even as the enemy was before him. The Messenger of God proclaimed *takbīr* and the two rows proclaimed *takbīr* together, then the two rows bent down to their knees together. Then the row, which was next to him, went down in prostration, and the other row stood and kept watch. The Messenger of God fulfilled the *prostration* with the first row, and they stood up with him. Then the row that was immediately behind him stepped back and the rear row came forward. They followed the Messenger of God [Page 583] and all of them stood together. Then, the Messenger of God bowed and all of them bowed together; then he made the prostration and so did the row behind him. The others stood watching over him against the enemy. And when the Messenger of God raised his head from the two prostrations, the rear row completed the two prostrations that remained for them. The Messenger of God sat up and recited the testimony (*shahāda*: that there is but one God and Muḥammad is His prophet), and then he gave them greetings. Ibn ʿAbbās used to say: this was the first prayer the Messenger of God prayed in fear.

Sufyān b. Saʿīd related to me from Manṣūr from Mujāhid from Ibn ʿAyyāsh al-Zuraqī, that he was with the Prophet at that time, and he mentioned that the Prophet prayed thus. Abū ʿAyyāsh mentioned that it was the first prayer of fear that the Prophet prayed. Rabīʿa b. ʿUthmān related to me from Wahb b. Kaysān, from Jābir b. ʿAbdullah, who said: the Messenger of God prayed the first prayer of fear at Dhāt al-Riqāʿ. Then they prayed the prayer of fear at ʿUsfān. Between those two were four years. This is confirmed with us.

They said: When it was evening the Messenger of God said, "Turn right at this bend, for surely the spies of the Quraysh are in Marr al-Ẓahrān or Ḍajnān. Which of you knows Thanniyat Dhāt al-Ḥanẓal?" Burayda b. al-Ḥuṣayb al-Aslamī said, "I know it, O Messenger of God." The Messenger of God said, "Lead us." Burayda took the bend before Jibāl Sirāwiʿ before Maghrib. He went a short distance but the stones turned him away, and the trees hung down on him, [Page 584] and he was confused, as though he had never known it. He said: By God, indeed I had passed by it on many Fridays. When the Messenger of God realized that I did not know the direction, he said, "Ride," and I rode.

The Messenger of God said, "Who is the man who will guide us to Dhāt al-Ḥanẓal?" This time, Ḥamza b. ʿAmr al-Aslamī said, "I, O Messenger of God, will guide you." He walked a little bit. Then he fell at a veiling tree, not knowing where to go. The Prophet said, "Ride!" Then again, the Messenger of God said, "Is there one who can guide us to Dhāt al-Ḥanẓal?" ʿAmr b. ʿAbd Nuḥm al-Aslamī alighted and said, "I will guide you, O Messenger of God." The Prophet said, "Go before us." ʿAmr went before them until the Messenger of God saw the narrow pass, and he said, "Is this the narrow pass Dhāt al-Ḥanẓal?" ʿAmr said, "Yes, O Messenger of God." He stood on the top of it, and slowly descended it with him. ʿAmr said: By God, what helped me was not my striving, but rather it was like a narrow strap which widened for me until it came into view as a passable and large road. Indeed on that night a group of people could walk and turn, talking to each other because of its breadth. The night was illuminated as though we were under a full moon. The Messenger of God said, "By Him who holds my soul in His hands, this pass is like the gate about which God said to the Banū Isarāʾīl: *Enter the gate with humility in posture and words . . .* (Q. 2:58)."

Ibn Abī Ḥabība related to me from Dawud b. al-Ḥuṣayn from al-Aʿraj, from Abū Hurayra, who said: [Page 585] The Messenger of God said: The "word" which was presented to the Banū Isrāʾīl is *There is no God but Allah, so enter the gate in humility*! He said: The gate of Jerusalem. They entered on their backsides, saying: "The seed is in the grain."

ʿAbd al-Raḥmān b. ʿAbd al-ʿAzīz related to me from ʿAbdullah b. Abī Bakr b. Ḥazm, who said: The Messenger of God said, "The words presented to the Banū Isrāʾīl were: We seek God's forgiveness and repent." These two traditions have both been narrated. They said: Then the Messenger of God said, "One does not pass through this narrow pass, but God will forgive him." Abū Saʿīd al-Khudrī said: My brother through my mother, Qatāda b. al-Nuʿmān, was the last of those people. He said: I stood at the pass, and I began to say to the people, "The Messenger of God said that one does not pass through this pass, but God will forgive him," and the people began to hurry until my brother passed at the end of the people. He said: I feared that it would dawn before we all went through.

The Messenger of God said when he alighted, "Whoever has *thaqal* with him, let him cook it." Abū Saʿīd said: The Messenger of God had *thaqal. Thaqal* means flour; most of our provision consisted of dates.

We said: "O Messenger of God, surely we fear the Quraysh are watching us." The Messenger of God said: "Indeed, they will not see you. Surely God will protect you against them. So kindle the fires and let those who want to cook, cook." They ignited more than five hundred fires. When dawn came upon us, the Messenger of God prayed the *Ṣubḥ* prayer. Then he said, "By Him who has my soul in his hands, indeed God will forgive the riders, all of them, except the one on the red camel." Men of the people had encountered him and he was not from them. They looked for him in the camp, and it was thought that he was among the companions of the Prophet. When, all of a sudden, he was seen in the protection of Saʿīd b. Zayd b. ʿAmr b. Nufayl of the Banū Ḍamra, from the [Page 586] people of Sīf al-Baḥr. Someone said to Saʿīd: Surely the Messenger of God said thus and thus. Saʿīd said, "Woe unto you! Go to the Messenger of God and ask for his forgiveness." He replied, "My Camel, by God, is more important to me than that Muḥammad forgive me," and indeed, he had lost a camel of his, and was following the troops, arriving with them, and seeking his camel—"Indeed it is with your troops, so, give me my camel." Saʿīd said, "Keep away from me for God will not grant you life! Desist, for I only see disaster near me, and I do not know about it." So the Bedouin departed seeking his camel. After that he released himself from the camp. Then, while he was in the mountains of Surāwiʿ his shoe slipped, and he fell and died, and no one knew about it until the lions ate him up.

Hishām b. Saʿd related to me from Zayd b. Aslam from ʿAṭāʾ b. Yasār from Abū Saʿīd al-Khudrī, who said: The Messenger of God said, "Indeed there will come a people compared to whose deeds you will consider your own deeds paltry." Someone said, "O Messenger of God, is it the Quraysh?" He said, "No, rather, they are the people of Yemen. Indeed, they have more sensitive and softer hearts." We said, "O Messenger of God, are they better than us?" And he said with his hands thus, and Hishām describes it as if he means the same. Are we not better than those people? The words *Not equal among you are those who spent freely and fought before the conquest of Mecca* (Q. 57:10), were revealed.

Ibn Abī Dhiʾb related to me from Ḥārith b. ʿAbd al-Raḥmān from Muḥammad b. Jubayr b. Muṭʿim from his father, that he heard the Messenger of God say, at that time, "The people of Yemen came to you as though they were a portion of the clouds. They were the best of those on earth." A man from the Anṣār said repeatedly, "Better than us, O Messenger of God?" Thrice, the Messenger of God was silent. The fourth time he said softly, "Except you."

Maʿmar and ʿAbd al-Raḥmān b. ʿAbd al-ʿAzīz related to me from al-Zuhrī, from ʿUrwa from Miswar b. Makhrama [Page 587], who said: The Messenger of God marched and when he was close to al-Ḥudaybiyya, at the pass, a leg of the camel slipped on the excrement of the people. The camel knelt down, and the Muslims said: Ḥal! Ḥal! But the camel refused to be provoked. They said: Al-Qaṣwāʾ knelt down. The Messenger of God said, "Indeed, she generally does not refuse. It is not her custom. What confines her is what confined the elephant. Today, whatever they ask me of a plan regarding the glorification of God's sanctuary, I shall grant it to them." Then we rebuked it and it stood up, turned and returned to the beginning until it alighted with the people at one of the watering places of al-Ḥudaybiyya suspecting that it had a little water. A spring of water came up but the people expressed their doubts to the Messenger of God of the little water. The Messenger of God pulled out an arrow from his quiver and commanded that the watering place be stabbed with it. A rivulet bubbled up for them until they left it soaking. He said: Indeed they filled their utensils sitting on the edge of the well. He who alighted with the arrow was Nājiya b. al-Aʿjam from the Aslam. It was said that a slave girl from the Anṣār said to Nājiya b. Jundub while he was in the well:

O you at the bottom, my pail is near you
I saw the people thank you, praise you well, and glorify you.

Nājiya replied, while he was in the spring:

[Page 588] The Yameni girl knows that I, down below, am Nājiya
Pierced by me splattering—I pierce it under the breasts of the highlands.

A man who was the son of Nājiya b. al-Aʿjam, and some call him ʿAbd al-Malik b. Wahb al-Aslamī, informed me of it. Mūsā b. ʿUbayd related to me from Iyās b. Salama b. al-Akwaʿ from his father, who said: He who alighted with an arrow was Nājiya b. Jundub.

Al-Haytham b. Wāqid related to me from ʿAṭā' b. Abī Marwān from his father, who said: A man from the Aslam related to me from the companions of the Prophet that Nājiya b. al-Aʿjam—and Nājiya b. al-Aʿjam had related—says: The Messenger of God called me when there were complaints about the small quantity of water. He drew out an arrow from his quiver, gave it to me, and asked me for a bucket of well water. I took it to him and he performed ablutions. He said: The Messenger of God washed his mouth, then spat in the bucket. The people were very hot, and indeed it was a single well. Moreover, the polytheists had arrived earlier at Baldaḥ and taken its water. Then, the Messenger of God said, "Alight! Go down into the water and pour it in the well and induce its water with the arrow." So I did. By He who sent him with the truth, I had hardly got out when it overflowed to me. It bubbled just as the pot bubbles until it overflows. It leveled to its edge and then spilled over its sides until they drank to the last of them.

He said: At the water, at that time, were a group of Hypocrites, al-Jadd b. Qays, Aws, and ʿAbdullah b. Ubayy. They were seated observing the water. The well overflowed with fresh water and they were seated at its edge. Aws b. Khawlī said, "Woe unto you O Abū l-Ḥubāb! Do you not now notice what you are against? Is there anything more that you expect? We came to a well with hardly any water: he comes out with a cup containing a mere gulp of water. The Messenger of God took ablutions with the bucket and washed his mouth in it. [Page 589] Then he emptied the bucket in the well, went down with an arrow and stirred it up, and it became agitated with fresh water." He said: Ibn Ubayy said, "I have seen something similar." And Aws said, "May God make you and your vision ugly!"

Ibn Ubayy approached desiring the Messenger of God, and the Messenger of God said, "What is it Abū l-Ḥubāb, where did you see something similar to what you saw today?" And he replied, "I have never seen anything similar." The Messenger of God said, "Then why did you say what you said?" Ibn Ubayy said, "I ask God's forgiveness." His son said, "O Messenger of God, forgive him!" The Messenger of God forgave him.

ʿAbd al-Raḥmān b. al-Ḥārith b. ʿUbayd, from his grandfather ʿUbayd b. Abī ʿUbayd said: I heard Khālid b. ʿAbbād al-Ghiffārī say, "I went down with an arrow, at that time, to the well." Sufyān b. Saʿīd related to me from Abū Isḥāq al-Hamdānī, who said: I heard al-Barā' b. ʿĀzib say, "I went down with an arrow."

They said: The Messenger of God was rained on, in al-Ḥudaybiyya, several times and the water increased. Sufyān b. Saʿīd related to me from Khālid b. al-Ḥadhdhā from Abū Mulayḥ al-Hudhalī from his father, who said: Rain rained on us in al-Ḥudaybiyya, until it wet the bottom of our sandals and a herald of the Messenger of God called out, "Prayer will take place on the saddle." Mālik b. Anas related to me from Ṣāliḥ b. Kaysān from ʿUbaydullah b. ʿUtba from Zayd b. Khālid al-Juhannī, who said: The Messenger of God prayed the dawn prayer with us in al-Ḥudaybiyya soon after the rainfall during the night. When he finished, he approached the people and said, "Do you know what your Lord said?" They said, "God and His messenger are most wise!"

[Page 590] He said, "There has risen among the worshipers a believer in me, and a disbeliever. As for he, who said it rained by the grace of God and His graciousness, he believes in me and does not believe in the stars. As for he who says it rained on us emphasizing the position of such and such a star, thus and thus, that is one who does not believe in me but believes in the stars."

Ibn Abī Sabra related to me from Isḥāq b. ʿAbdullah from Abū Salama al-Ḥaḍramī, who said: I heard Abū Qatāda say, I heard Ibn Ubayy say, "We were in al-Ḥudaybiyya and it rained on us there." And Ibn Ubayy said, "This is typical of Autumn; It rains on us with the rise of Sirius!"

Muḥammad b. al-Ḥijāzī related to me from Usayd b. Abī Usayd from Abū Qatāda, who said: When we alighted at al-Ḥudaybiyya there was little water. I heard al-Jadd b. Qays say, "Our coming to these people has not produced anything. We will die of thirst to the last of us." I said, "Do not say this, O Abū ʿAbdullah, why did you come out?" He said, "I came out with my people." I said, "Did you not come out as a pilgrim?" He said, "No, by God, I am not a pilgrim." Abū Qatāda said, "Did you not intend *ʿUmra*?" He said, "No!" When the Messenger of God called the man who alighted with the arrow, the Messenger of God took ablutions and gargled his mouth in the bucket, then he returned the water in the well. And the well became agitated with fresh water. Abū Qatāda said: I saw al-Jadd stretching out his legs at the mouth of the well containing water and I said, "O Abū ʿAbdullah where is what you said?" He replied, "Surely I was joking with you. Do not mention any of what I said to Muḥammad." Abū Qatāda said: I had already mentioned it before that to the Prophet. He said: Jadd was angry. He said, "We stayed with the youth of our people and they do not recognize our nobility or age. The belly of the earth today is better than its surface!" Abū Qatāda said: [Page 591] I mentioned his words to the Messenger of God and he said, "His son is better than him!" Abū Qatāda said: A group from my people joined me and they began to scold me and blame me for raising his words with the Messenger of God, and I said to them, "Miserable are you people; woe unto you. Are you defending Jadd b. Qays?" They said, "Yes, he is our leader and our lord." I said, "By God, the Messenger of God rejected his power among the Banū Salima and appointed Bishr b. al-Barāʾ b. Maʿrūr as leader over us. We destroyed our sleeping chamber, which was at the door of Jadd, and built it at the gate of Bishr b. al-Barāʾ. He is our leader until the day of resurrection." Abū Qatāda said: When the Messenger of God called for a pledge Jadd b. Qays fled under the stomach of a camel. I came out, ran and took the hand of a man who spoke to me and, together, we dragged him out from under the camel's stomach. I said, "Woe unto you, what brought you here? Are you fleeing from what the Holy spirit revealed?" He replied, "No, but I was afraid, and I heard a loud sound." The man said, "I would never protect you. There is no goodness in you."

Later, when Jadd fell sick and death came to him, Abū Qatāda stayed in his house and did not come out until Jadd died and was buried. This was mentioned to him, and he replied: By God, how was I to pray for him when I had heard him say on the day of al-Ḥudaybiyya, thus and thus, and during the raid of Tabūk, thus and thus. I was embarrassed before my people who saw me going out but did not see him. Some say Abū Qatāda set out to his property in al-Wādayn and he was in it until Jadd was buried. Al-Jadd died during the caliphate of ʿUthmān.

They said: When the Messenger of God alighted at al-Ḥudaybiyya ʿAmr b. [Page 592] Sālim and Busr b. Sufyān the two from the Khuzāʿī gifted him a slaughtering animal, and ʿAmr b. Sālim gave Saʿd b. ʿUbāda a slaughtering animal for he was a friend of his. Saʿd brought the animal to the Messenger of God and informed him that ʿAmr gifted it to him. The Messenger of God said, "ʿAmr has given us what you see, may God bless ʿAmr." Then the Messenger of God ordered its slaughter. It was sacrificed and apportioned among his companions. The Messenger of God divided the meat, all of it, among his companions. Umm Salama, the wife of the Prophet who was with him, said: He sent us some from the meat of the slaughter in the same way as what was sent to any man from the people. We shared the mutton when some of it was brought to us.

One of their lads brought the gift to us. The Messenger of God seated the boy in front of him, and the lad was wearing a worn out cloak. He said, "O youth, where did you leave your family?" He replied, "I left them close by in Ẓajnān and its surrounds." He said, "How did you leave the land?" The lad said, "I left it in good condition. The date had put out tender shoots. I snatched at what was within easy reach. Its branches have sprouted leaves, and its greens have appeared. The earth is moistened and its cattle are satiated at night; the camels are filled with what is gathered from the palm and wet earth, and vegetables. I left the plentiful waters in which the cattle rush. The needs of the cattle at the water were little because of the moistness of the land." He pleased the Messenger of God and his companions with his language. The Messenger of God commanded that a robe be given to the lad. The lad said, "Indeed, I would like to take your hand [Page 593] and seek your blessing." The Messenger of God said, "Come close!" So he went close and he took the hand of the Messenger of God and kissed it. The Messenger of God stroked his head and said, "May God bless you!" He reached a ripe old age and enjoyed grace and happiness with his people until he died in the time of Walīd, the son of ʿAbd al-Malik.

They said: When the Messenger of God had settled in al-Ḥudaybiyya, Budayl b. Waraqāʾ and riders from the Khuzaʿa who were depositories of advice of the Messenger of God in Tihāma came to him. Among them were Muslims as well as those who had a contract. In Tihāma they did not hide anything from the Prophet. They alighted from their riding beasts before the Messenger of God. Then they came and greeted him. Budayl said, "We come to you from those who are with your people, the Quraysh, Kaʿb b. Luʾayy and ʿĀmir b. Luʾayy. The *Ahābīsh*, and others who obey them have mobilized against you. With them are their old and young, their women and children. They swear by God that they (i.e. all the people) will set out between you and the House of God, and block your way even if their people are destroyed." The Messenger of God said, "Indeed we did not come to fight anyone. We only come to circumambulate this House. But we will fight whoever obstructs us from it. The Quraysh are a people injured and exhausted by the war. If they wish, I will grant them a protected period when they will be secure, and free what is between us and the people. And the people are more than them. If I am victorious over the people, then they can join in the pact that the others have entered. Or they will fight when they have gathered! By God I will surely strive over this command of mine until I die or God fulfills His command."

[Page 594] Budayl memorized his message and rode. Then they rode to the Quraysh. Amr b. Sālim was with the riders and he began to say: By God, you will not be victorious over those who oppose this ever, until they descended to the polytheistic Quraysh. People among the Quraysh said: This is Budayl and his companions. Indeed they come desiring to inform you. Do not ask them a single word! When Budayl and his companions saw that, they did not seek information from them. Budayl said, "Indeed we come from Muḥammad. Do you not want us to inform you?" ʿIkrima b. Abī Jahl and al-Ḥakam b. Abīl-ʿĀṣ said, "No, by God, there is no need for you to inform us about him. But rather inform him from us that he will never enter against us this year, as long as there is a man among us." ʿUrwa b. Masʿud said, "By God I have not seen a decision more surprising as on this day. Do not reject hearing from Budayl and his companions. If the affair pleases you, accept it. And if you detest anything, leave it. A people who do this will never be content."

Men from the decision makers and their nobility, Ṣafwān b. Umayya and al-Ḥarith b. Hishām, said, "Inform us about what you saw and what you heard." So they informed them about the letter of the Prophet, and what he offered the Quraysh concerning the time. ʿUrwa said, "O people of the Quraysh, do you not trust me? Are you not the father and I the son? I called upon the people of ʿUkkāz to help you, and when they urged against me, I rushed to you with my soul and my child and those who followed me." They said, "That you did!" He said, "Indeed I am an advisor to you and fond of you. I do not keep advice from you. Indeed Budayl has come to you with a valid affair and anyone who rejects it will only take evil from it. So accept it from him and send me until I bring confirmation from him. I will observe those with him. I will be your eyes, and I will come to you with news of him." So the Quraysh sent him to the Messenger of God.

ʿUrwa b. Masʿud approached until his camel knelt [Page 595] at the Prophet's, then he went forward until he came to him. Then he said, "O Muḥammad, I left your people, Kaʿb b. Luʾayy and ʿĀmir b. Luʾayy at the many waters of al-Ḥudaybiyya with their women and children. They have called upon the *Aḥābīsh* and those who follow them for help against you. They have taken an oath that they will not free your path to the 'House' unless you remove them forcibly. Indeed, you have concerning them one of two possibilities. To destroy your people—the Quraysh—and before you, we have not heard of a man who exterminates his roots; or those who follow you will let you down. Indeed we do not see with you except a confused mix of people, I do not know their faces nor their genealogy." Abū Bakr al-Ṣiddīq became angry. He said, "Suck the clitoris of al-Lāt! Shall we abandon him?" ʿUrwa replied, "By God, if I did not owe you a debt that I have not fulfilled, I would react." ʿUrwa b. Masʿūd had sought help in paying a blood debt. A man had helped him with two portions, and for the third, Abū Bakr had helped with ten camels, and this helping hand of Abū Bakr was not forgotten by ʿUrwa b. Masʿūd. ʿUrwa continued and, as he spoke to the Messenger of God, he now took a hold of the Prophet's beard; Mughīra was standing at the head of the Messenger of God, with the sword, and wearing a helmet over his face, and whenever ʿUrwa touched the beard of the Prophet, Mughīra immediately pushed his hand away saying, "Keep your hand from touching the beard of the Prophet or I shall attack you!" When he persisted in telling him to desist from touching the beard, ʿUrwa became angry and said, "How strange! Who are you, Muḥammad, to deserve what I see from among your companions?" The Messenger of God replied, "This is al-Mughīra b. Shuʿba the son of your brother." ʿUrwa said, "You are with that, O treacherous one? By God, was it not yesterday I washed your stools with water! Indeed, because of you we have acquired the enmity of the Thaqīf to the end of time. [Page 596] O Muḥammad, do you know how he did this? Indeed he set out with a group of camel riders from his people. When they were among us, sleeping, he knocked on them and killed them, plundered them and fled."

Al-Mughīra had set out with a group of the Banū Mālik b. Ḥuṭayṭ b. Jusham b. Qasiyyu, and al-Mughīra was one of the cautious. With al-Mughīra were two of his allies, one named Dammūn, a man from the Kinda, and the last of the fugitives; the other, al-Sharid, or rather, his name was ʿAmr, but when al-Mughīra did what he did with his companions, ʿAmr became a fugitive (*sharrada*) and was therefore named al-Sharīd—the fugitive. They set out to al-Muqawqis, the ruler of Alexandria, and the Banū Mālik came, and he (Muqawqis) valued them over Mughira. Then, the two proceeded to return. When they arrived in Baysān they drank wine. Mughīra desisted from some of the drink and kept to himself. But the Banū Mālik drank until they were intoxicated. Then Mughīra grabbed them and killed them. There were thirteen men. When he killed them, Dammūn observed them and hid from them. He thought that Mughīra would attack him on account of the alcohol. al-Mughīra began searching for Dammūn, shouting for him, but he did not come out. He turned over the dead and could not see for crying. When Dammūn saw that, he went out to him and al-Mughīra said to him, "Where were you hiding?" He replied, "I feared that you would kill me just as you killed the people." al-Mughīra said, "I killed the Banū Mālik for what al-Muqawqis did with them."

He said: al-Mughīra took their goods and their wealth and joined the Prophet. The Prophet said, "I do not want a fifth of it for this is treachery." That was when the Prophet was informed of their news. al-Mughīra converted to Islam. Al-Sharīd arrived in Mecca and informed Abū Sufyān b. Ḥarb about what al-Mughīra did with the Banū Mālik. Abū Sufyān sent Muʿāwiya b. Abī Sufyan [Page 597] to ʿUrwa b. Masʿūd to inform him of the news. That was al-Mughīra b. Shuʿba b. Abī ʿĀmir b. Masʿūd b. Muʿattib. Muʿāwiya said: I set out until when I was in Naʿmān I said to myself, "Where am I going? If I take the road to Dhū Ghifār, it is distant but easy. If I take the road Dhūl-Alaq it is difficult but short." I took Dhū Ghifār and I bumped into ʿUrwa b. Masʿūd b. ʿAmr al-Mālikī. By God I had not spoken to him for ten years, and that night I would speak to him.

He said: We set out to Masʿūd and ʿUrwa called out to him, and he said, "Who is this?" He answered, "ʿUrwa." Masʿūd approached saying, "Do you knock on my door in tranquility or with catastrophe? In fact, you come with catastrophe. Did their cavalry kill ours or did our cavalry kill theirs? If our cavalry killed theirs ʿUrwa b. Masʿūd will not knock me up." ʿUrwa said, "You are right, my cavalry took yours, O Masʿūd. Watch what you do!" Masʿūd said, "I know of the rashness of the Banū Mālik and their swiftness to war, so give me some quiet." So we turned away from him.

When Masʿūd rose the next day he said, "Indeed it is because of the affair of Mughīra b. Shuʿba that he killed your brother, the Banū Mālik. So listen to me and take the blood money. Accept it from the son of your uncle and your people." They replied, "No, that will never be. By God, the allies will never settle with you if you accept it." And he repeated, "Listen to me, and accept what I say to you. For, by God, it is as if I see Kināna b. ʿAbd Yalīl approach, wearing armor down to his feet. He will not embrace a man, except to throw him to [Page 598] the ground. By God, it is as if I am with Jundub b. ʿAmr who approaches like a lord, replacing arrows at the bow-string to the end, and his arrow does not go to one, but he places it where he chooses!"

When they overwhelmed him, he prepared for the battle they chose. Kināna b. ʿAbd Yālīl approached wearing armor down to his feet, saying, "Who wants to wrestle?" Then Jundub b. ʿAmr approached replacing the arrows at the bowstring to the end. Masʿud said, "Obey me, O sons of Mālik." They replied, "The command is yours." He said: Masʿūd b. ʿAmr appeared and he said, "O ʿUrwa b. Masʿūd, come out to me!" So he went out to him and they met between the two lines. He said, "To you are thirteen blood dues, for indeed al-Mughīra killed thirteen men, so carry their debt." ʿUrwa replied, "I accept it. It is on me." He said: The people came to an agreement. Al-Aʿshā the brother of Banū Bakr b. Wā'il said:

ʿUrwa carried the troubles of the allies
When he saw an affair troubling their hearts.
Three hundred and a thousand running,
Thus do the patient and tough endure.

Al-Wāqidī said: When ʿUrwa finished speaking to the Messenger of God, the Messenger of God responded with what he had said to Budayl b. Waraqā' and his companions, and offered them some time.

ʿUrwa b. Masʿūd rode until he came to the Quraysh and said, "O people, I have gone before kings, Kisra, Heraclius, and the Najashī, and by God, I have never seen a king who was obeyed by those he was in the midst of, as Muḥammad is by his companions. By God, they do not look directly at him. They do not raise their voices in his presence. It is sufficient that he only indicates an affair and it is done. He does not clear his throat and spit, but it falls on the hand of a man among them and he rubs it on his skin. He does not make ablution, but they swarm to him, each of them to take something from it. I have assessed the people, so know that if you desire the sword they will exchange blows with you. I have seen a people who do not mind what is done with them when they protect their companion. [Page 599] By God, surely I saw women with him, and they would never surrender under any condition.

They will consider your decision. Do not be weak in your decision. A path has been presented to you, so linger on it. O people, accept what has been presented, for indeed I have advice for you, although I fear that you will not take it. A man comes to this house to glorify it, bringing sacrificial animals to be slaughtered, and he is turned away?" The Quraysh said, "Do not speak of this O Abū Yaʿfur. If anyone other than you had spoken thus, we would have faulted him. We will turn him from the house this year of ours; he may return a year after."

They said: Then Mikraz b. Ḥafṣ b. al-Akhīf arrived and when he appeared, the Messenger of God saw him and said, "Surely this man is treacherous!" When he finally reached the Prophet he spoke to him about what his companions spoke. When he reached the Quraysh he informed them about what the Prophet had replied to him. They sent al-Hulays b. Alqama who was at that time the lord of the *Aḥābīsh*.

When al-Hulays appeared, the Messenger of God said, "This man is from a people who honor the sacrificial animal and respect acts of devotion. So send the sacrificial animals in his direction that he may see them." So they sent the animals, and when he saw the sacrificial animals stream through the wadi wearing necklaces, and having eaten their hair, nostalgia returned. The people set out in his direction shouting the pilgrim's cry—the *talbiya*. They had stayed for half a month and smelled badly and were disheveled. Al-Hulays turned back without meeting the Messenger of God, impressed by what he had seen. He returned to the Quraysh and said, "Indeed I have seen what is not lawful to turn away. I saw the sacrificial animals with their necklaces, having eaten their hair, detained from its abode (for sacrifice). The men who have come to circumambulate this house smell badly and are covered in lice. By God, is it for this that we are your allies? We have not contracted with you [Page 600] in order that you may reject one who comes to venerate the house according to its due, and drives the detained sacrificial animals to reach the place of sacrifice. By Him who keeps my soul in His hand set them free to do what they came for, or I shall surely leave with every single one of the *Aḥābīsh*." They said, "Surely all of what you saw is a trick of Muḥammad and his companions. Desist from us until we take for ourselves what we may find satisfaction in."

The first of those the Messenger of God sent to the Quraysh was Khirash b. Umayya al-Kaʿbī on a camel belonging to the Messenger of God, named al-Thaʿlab, to notify their nobility about the Messenger of God and what he came for. He says, "Indeed we come as pilgrims, we have sacrificial animals with us. We shall circumambulate the house, discharge our duty and turn back." But they wounded the camel of the Prophet. He who discharged the wound was ʿIkrima b. Abī Jahl, and he desired to kill it. And there were from his people those who restrained him, until Khirash was on his way. As soon as he returned to the Prophet, Khirash informed the Prophet of what happened and said, "O Messenger of God, send a man of greater resistance than me." So the Messenger of God called for ʿUmar b. al-Khaṭṭāb to send him to the Quraysh. But ʿUmar said, "O Messenger of God, I fear the Quraysh are against me. They know of my hostility towards them. There is not one from the Banū ʿAdī with them who will protect me. But if you desire it, O Messenger of God, I will go." The Messenger of God did not say anything. Then, ʿUmar said, "But I will indicate to you a man more loved than I in Mecca, has many friends, and is more resistant, ʿUthmān b. ʿAffān." The Messenger of God called ʿUthmān and said, "Go to the Quraysh and inform them that I have not come to fight anyone. Indeed we have come as visitors to the House, venerating its sanctuary. We have with us sacrificial animals that we will slaughter, and then we will turn back."

ʿUthmān went out until he came to Baldaḥ. The Quraysh were found there and they said, "Where are you going?" He replied, "The Messenger of God has sent me to you. He calls you to God and Islam. [Page 601] So enter the religion together, for indeed God elevates His religion, and honors His prophet; an option is that you refrain, and let others fight him. And if they are victorious over Muḥammad that is what you desire, but if Muḥammad is victorious, you will have a choice. Either, you enter what the people enter—[Islam], or you fight while you are plentiful and strong. Indeed war has exhausted you and has removed the exemplary among you. Finally, the Messenger of God informs you that he did not come to fight anyone. Surely he comes as a pilgrim. With him are the sacrificial animals wearing necklaces. He will slaughter them and then turn back." ʿUthmān began to speak to them but he brought them what they did not desire. They said, "We have heard what you say but this will never be. Muḥammad will not enter the Kaʿba against our will. So return to your companion and inform him that he shall not come to us."

Then Abān b. Saʿīd b. al-Āṣ came up to ʿUthmān, made him welcome, and granted him permission and said, "Do not refrain from your need." Then he alighted from the horse he was on, and lifted ʿUthmān onto the saddle, and seated ʿUthmān behind him. ʿUthman entered Mecca, and the noblility came, man by man. Abū Sufyān b. Ḥarb, Ṣafwān b. Umayya and the rest of them. Among them were those he met in Baldaḥ and those he met in Mecca.

Then they began to respond to him. "Indeed, Muḥammad shall never enter upon us." ʿUthmān said: Then I had entered upon a community of believers, men and women, who were oppressed, so I say, "Surely the Messenger of God brings you good news of the opening, and says, 'I will persist until there is no concealment of your faith in Mecca.'" ʿUthmān said: I saw men and women among them weep for joy at what I informed them. They asked about the Messenger of God in a secretive manner. It was difficult for them, and that strengthened them and they said, "Convey our greetings to the Messenger of God. Indeed He who brought him into al-Ḥudaybiyya decrees that He will bring him to the heart of Mecca."

Meanwhile, the Muslims said, "O Messenger of God, ʿUthmān has arrived at the House and circumambulates it!" The Messenger of God said, "I do not think ʿUthmān will circumambulate the house while we are restricted." They said, "O Messenger of God, [Page 602] is he not permitted though he has arrived at the house?" The Messenger of God said, "My opinion is that he will not circumambulate until we circumambulate it." And when ʿUthmān returned to the Prophet, they said, "Were you satisfied with the house, O slave of Allah?" ʿUthman replied, "Miserable is what you think of me. If I were in Mecca for one year, while the Prophet was in Medina, I would not circumambulate it. Indeed the Quraysh invited me to circumambulate it but I refused." The Muslims said, "The Messenger of God is more knowledgeable about God, and better than us in his opinions."

The Messenger of God had commanded his companions in al-Ḥudaybiyya to keep watch at night. One of the men from his companions would stay up the night keeping watch, going around the camp until it dawned. The three companions who took turns at the watch were Aws b. Khawlī, ʿAbbād b. Bishr and Muḥammad b. Maslama. Muḥammad b. Maslama was on a horse belonging to the Prophet the night ʿUthmān left for Mecca. The Quraysh had sent fifty men that night under Mikraz b. Ḥafs. They commanded them to go around the Prophet hoping to capture one of them or to take them by surprise. But Muḥammad b. Maslama and his companions captured them instead, and brought them before the Messenger of God.

ʿUthman stayed in Mecca for three nights to negotiate with the Quraysh, while some of the Muslims entered Mecca, with the permission of the Prophet, to visit their families. Then it reached the Messenger of God that ʿUthmān and his companions had been killed, so he called for negotiations.

The capture of their companions reached the Quraysh. A group of Quraysh came to the Prophet and aimed at him with arrows and stones. At that time the Muslims again took prisoners from the polytheists. Then the Quraysh sent Suhayl b. ʿAmr, Ḥuwayṭib b. ʿAbd al-ʿUzzā and Mikraz b. Ḥafṣ. The Messenger of God set out at that time towards the station of the Banū Māzin b. al-Najjār who had all alighted in the region of al-Ḥudaybiyya.

[Page 603] Umm ʿUmara said: Messengers were exchanged between the Messenger of God and the Quraysh. The Messenger of God passed by us one day in our station. She said: I thought that he had a need, but in fact, it had suddenly reached him that ʿUthman was killed. He sat with our riders, and said, "Surely God has commanded me to negotiate a pact." She said: The people approached and gave him their pledge of allegiance in our camp, until the people overtook each other and there was nothing left but it was trampled upon. Her husband was Ghaziyya b. ʿAmr. Umm ʿUmāra said: The people made a pledge to the Prophet, at that time. She said: It was as though I watched the Muslims put on their weapons and we had few, for indeed, we were going out on *ʿUmra*. I observed Ghaziyya b. ʿAmr as he belted on his sword, and I stood at the column we were shaded by, and took the sword in my hand. I fastened a knife, which I had with me, to my waist, and said, "If any one comes near me I hope that I will kill him."

The Messenger of God was accepting the pledge of the people at that time, and ʿUmar b. al-Khaṭṭāb took his hand for the oath that they would not flee. Someone said that it was an agreement unto death. Another said that the first of the people to give the oath was Sinān b. Abī Sinān b. Miḥṣan. He said, "O Messenger of God, I pledge allegiance to you and to what you desire." The Messenger of God took the pledge from the people in the same manner he did from Sinān.

Ten Muhājirūn visited their families. They were Kurz b. Jābir al-Fihrī, ʿAbdullah b. Suhayl b. ʿAmr, ʿAyyāsh b. Abī Rabīʿa, Hishām b. al-ʿĀṣ b. Wāʾil, Ḥāṭib b. Abī-Baltaʿa, Abū Ḥāṭib b. ʿAmr b. ʿAbd Shams, ʿAbdullah b. Ḥudhāfa, Abū l-Rūm b. ʿUmayr, ʿUmayr b. Wahb al-Jumahī, and ʿAbdullah b. Abī Umayya b. Wahb, an ally of Suhayl in the Banū Asad b. ʿAbd al-ʿUzzā.

When Suhayl b. ʿAmr arrived, the Prophet said that their affair was easy. [Page 604] Suhayl said, "Those who fight you are not among those of us who have esteem, opinion, or rank, nor is he the possessor of more wisdom than us. Rather, we were reluctant to it when it reached us and we did not know of it, and it was from among our simple-minded people. So send us those of our companions whom you captured the first time and the last time. The Messenger of God said, "Indeed I will not send them until you return my companions." Suhayl said, "You have acted justly with us." Suhayl b. ʿAmr and Ḥuwayṭib b. ʿAbd al-ʿUzzā and Mikraz b. Ḥafṣ sent to the Quraysh, al-Shutaym b. ʿAbd Manāf al-Taymī saying, "Surely you imprison men from the companions of Muḥammad and between you is kinship. You did not kill them for we were reluctant for that. Muḥammad has refused to send those whom he captured of your companions until you return his companions. He has acted justly towards us. You know that Muḥammad will set your companions free." So they sent him those who were with them. They were eleven men. And the Messenger of God returned their companions who were taken the first time and the last time. ʿAmr b. Abī Sufyān was among those who were taken the first time.

The people gave a pledge to the Messenger of God under a green tree at that time. Among what God did for the Muslims was that Muḥammad commanded a herald to cry out, "Surely the holy-spirit dwelt in the Messenger when he commanded the pledge, so go out in the name of God and make a pledge." Ibn ʿUmar said: I went out with my father who was a herald for the pledge. When he finished the call, my father sent me to the Messenger of God and I informed him that I had called the people. ʿAbdullah said: When I returned I found the Messenger of God taking the pledge of the people, and I pledged allegiance a second time. ʿAbdullah told ʿUmar that he wanted to return to the Prophet, so ʿUmar granted him permission and he returned. ʿAbdullah took the Prophet by his hand and pledged allegiance. When the Quraysh—Suhayl b. ʿAmr, Ḥuwayṭib b. ʿAbd al-ʿUzzā and others who were with him and spies of the Quraysh—observed what they saw of the haste of the people to acknowledge the Prophet, and their preparedness to fight, their alarm and fear increased and they hastened to act.

[Page 605] When ʿUthmān returned, the Messenger of God brought him to the tree of allegiance. But, before that, when the people gave their pledge, the Prophet said: Indeed ʿUthmān acts in accordance with the needs of God and His messenger, so I shall pledge for him, and he struck his right hand on his left.

Al-Wāqidī said: Jābir b. Sulaym informed me from Ṣafwān b. ʿUthman, who said: The Quraysh sent to ʿAbdullah b. Ubayy saying, "If you desire to enter and circumambulate the house you may do so." But his son was seated with him, and his son said, "I remind you, by God, that you will disgrace us in every region if you circumambulate the house and the Prophet does not." So Ibn Ubayy refused saying, "I will not circumambulate until the Prophet circumambulates." His words reached the Messenger of God and that made him happy.

Ḥuwayṭib b. ʿAbd al-ʿUzzā, Suhayl b. ʿAmr and Mikraz b. Ḥafṣ returned to the Quraysh. They informed them of what they saw, of the speed of the companions of the Prophet to pledge loyalty to him, and what they did for him. The people of opinion said of them: There is nothing better than that we make peace, on condition that Muḥammad turn away from us this year and return later to stay three days, slaughter his sacrifice and go back. Let him stay in our land but not visit us. They agreed on that and when the Quraysh had agreed on the peace and the agreement, they sent for Suhayl b. ʿAmr, Ḥuwayṭib b. ʿAbd al-ʿUzza and Mikraz b. Ḥafṣ, and said, "Go to Muḥammad and contract with him that he will not enter this year. By God, the Bedouin will not say that you entered our city by force. Suhayl came to the Prophet, and when the Prophet saw him appear, he said, "The people desire an agreement." The Messenger of God spoke lengthening the words. They responded and voices were raised and lowered.

Yaʿqūb b. Muḥammad related to me from ʿAbd al-Raḥmān b. ʿAbdullah from al-Ḥārith b. ʿAbdullah b. Kaʿb, who said: I heard Umm ʿUmāra say: At that time, I watched [Page 606] the Messenger of God sitting crosslegged, and ʿAbbād b. Bishr, and Salama b. Aslam b. Harīsh, masked in iron masks, stood by the head of the Prophet. When Suhayl raised his voice, they both said, "Lower your voice to the Prophet." Suhayl was kneeling on his knees and raising his voice and I observed the cleft on his lip and his molars, while the Muslims were seated around their Prophet.

They said: When they became reconciled and nothing remained except to write a document, ʿUmar jumped up before the Prophet and said, "O Messenger of God, are we not Muslims?" The Messenger of God said, "But of course!" He said, "Then for what reason do we give a lower position to the Prophet in our religion?" The Messenger of God said, "I am the slave of God and his messenger. I will never go against God's command, and He will never ruin me." Then ʿUmar went to Abū Bakr and said, "O Abū Bakr, are we not Muslims?" He replied, "Yes, of course!" And ʿUmar said, "Why do we grant what is detrimental to our religion?" Abū Bakr said, "Stick by him. Indeed I witness that he is the Messenger of God and that he commands the truth. We will never differ from the command of God and God will never betray him." But ʿUmar had great difficulty with this matter. He tried to dispute the Messenger of God's words saying, "Why are we granting terms detrimental to our religion?" The Messenger of God said repeatedly, "I am the Messenger of God and God will never ruin me!" He said: And ʿUmar tried to dispute the words of the Messenger of God.

He said: Abū ʿUbayda b. al-Jarrāḥ says, "Do you not hear, O Ibn al-Khaṭṭāb, what the Messenger of God says? Seek refuge in God from the devil and doubt your opinion." ʿUmar said: I began to seek refuge in God from the cursed devil out of shame. Nothing has happened to me since as it did that day. [Page 607] And I continue to fast and give alms for what I did for fear of the words that I spoke at that time. Ibn ʿAbbas used to say: During his caliphate ʿUmar said to me: I was suspicious that day in a manner that I had never been since I converted. If on that day, I had found a group separating from the Muslims because they disliked the contract I would have joined them. Then God made its outcome good and guided. Indeed, the Messenger of God was most knowledgeable.

Abū Saʿīd al-Khudrī said: I sat with ʿUmar b. al-Khaṭṭāb one day, and he mentioned the contract to me and said: Surely doubt entered me at that time. I disputed the Prophet returning answer for answer, and I have not disputed like that with him ever.

I have manumitted slaves because of what I did at that time and fasted for periods of time. I remember what I had done then and it has been my greatest sorrow. Then God made the outcome of the contract good, for it is necessary for the worshiper to question the opinion. By God, doubt surely entered me at that time, until I said to myself: If we were a hundred men who thought like me we would not enter into it ever. When the contract was signed, a greater number converted to Islam during the truce than the number that converted from the very first day of Islam until then. There was not in Islam a victory greater than that of al-Ḥudaybiyya.

The companions of the Prophet detested the agreement. They had set out with certainty about the opening because of the dream of the Prophet that he shaved his head, entered the house, took the key of the Kaʿba, and stood at ʿArafat. So, when they saw the agreement they were so hurt that they were almost destroyed.

While the people considered the agreement being made, and the document was still unwritten, Abū Jandal b. Suhayl approached. He had escaped his shackles, put on a sword and walked free in lower Mecca. He set out from its lower region until he came to the Messenger of God who was dictating to Suhayl. Suhayl raised his head, [Page 608] and lo and behold, there was his son Abū Jandal. Suhayl went up to him and struck his face with a thorny branch and took him by his throat. Abū Jandal shouted, raising his voice, "O Muslim people, would you return me to the polytheists who will tempt me from my religion?" He pressured the Muslims with the fear that they already had, and they began to cry over the words of Abū Jandal. He said: Ḥuwayṭib b. ʿAbd al-ʿUzzā says to Mikraz b. Ḥafṣ: "I have never seen a people showing stronger affection for Muḥammad and each other than the companions of Muḥammad. Indeed, I tell you, you will never receive justice from Muḥammad after this day, until he enters Mecca by force." Mikraz said: "I see that."

Suhayl said, "The first of what I demand of you is about him. Return him!" The Messenger of God said, "We have not yet written the document." Suhayl said, "By God I will not document anything for you until you return him to me." So the Messenger of God returned him. The Messenger of God spoke to Suhayl and asked Suhayl to leave him, but Suhayl refused. Mikraz b. Hafs and Ḥuwayṭib said, "O Muḥammad, we will protect him for you." They kept him in a fortress and protected him, and his father held back from him. Then the Messenger of God raised his voice and said, "O Abū Jandal, be patient and look forward to a reward in the hereafter. Indeed, God is your rewarder, and for those who are with you there is relief and escape. We have agreed to a peace between us and the people. Accordingly, we have given them and they have given us a contract. We will not be treacherous."

ʿUmar turned to the Messenger of God and said, "O Messenger of God, are you not God's messenger?" He replied, "But of course!" He said, "Are we not on the true path?" He replied, "Of course!" He said, "Are not our enemies false?" He replied, "Of course." He said, "Then why do we denigrate our religion?" The Messenger of God said, "Indeed, I am the Messenger of God and I will never reject God, and He will never let me down." So ʿUmar left until he came to Abū Bakr and he said to him something similar to what he had said to the Prophet. Abū Bakr said, "Indeed he is the Messenger of God and God will never let him down. Stop your thoughts O ʿUmar." ʿUmar said, "I jumped at Abū Jandal and walked at his side." Suhayl b. ʿAmr pushed him, and ʿUmar says, "Be patient, [Page 609] O Abū Jandal, surely they are disbelievers and the blood of one of them is the blood of a dog. Surely he is a man, and you are a man, but you have a sword." ʿUmar hoped that Abū Jandal would take the sword and strike his father. But the man withheld from his father. ʿUmar said, "O Abū Jandal, surely a man may kill his father for God. By God, if our fathers attacked us we would surely fight them in God's name, man for man." He said: Abū Jandal approached ʿUmar and said, "Why do you not kill him?" ʿUmar replied, "The Messenger of God forbade me." Abū Jandal said, "Are you more righteous in your obedience to the Messenger of God than I?"

ʿUmar and men with him who were companions of the Prophet said, "O Messenger of God, did you not say to us that you will enter the sacred mosque, take the key of the Kaʿba and stand with those who stand at ʿArafat? Yet neither our sacrificial animals nor we have arrived at the house." The Messenger of God said, "Did I speak to you about this journey of yours?" ʿUmar said, "No." The Messenger of God said, "Indeed, you will not enter it! But I will take the key of the Kaʿba, and I will shave my head and your heads in the heart of Mecca. And I will stand with those who stand at ʿArafat." Then the Prophet approached ʿUmar and said, "Have you forgotten the day of Uḥud, when you ascended and would not wait for anyone, and I called to you about your hereafter? Have you forgotten the day of al-Aḥzāb when they came to you from above and below, and when perception left you and your hearts were in your throats? Have you forgotten such a day?" The Messenger of God began to remind them of the matters: have you forgotten such a day? The Muslims said, "By the mercy of God and His messenger, we have forgotten about that and you have reminded us. Surely you are more knowledgeable of God and His affairs than we are."

And when the Messenger of God entered the year of the fulfillment and shaved his head, he said, "This is what I promised you." When it was the day of the Conquest he took the key and said, "Call ʿUmar b. al-Khaṭṭāb to me!" He said, "This is what I said to you." When it was Ḥajjat al-Wadaʿ at al-ʿArafat he said, "Where is ʿUmar? This is what I said to you!" ʿUmar said, "Indeed, O Messenger of God, there was not a conquest in Islam greater [Page 610] than the truce of al-Ḥudaybiyya!"

Abū Bakr al-Ṣiddīq used to say: There was not a conquest in Islam greater than the conquest of al-Ḥudaybiyya. But the people at that time failed to reach a decision as to what was between Muḥammad and His Lord. Man hastened, but God most high did not hasten as did man, until the affair was as God desired. Indeed, I observed Suhayl b. ʿAmr during his pilgrimage, standing at the slaughtering ground and bringing forward the sacrificial animal of the Messenger of God. The Messenger of God slaughtered it himself. He called for the barber to shave his head and I observed Suhayl pick up his hair and place it on his eyes. And I remembered his refusal on the day of Hudaybiyya to put down in writing, "In the Name of God most gracious most merciful," and his refusal to write "Muḥammad is the Messenger of God." I praised God who brought him to Islam. May the grace of God and His blessings visit the Prophet who brought Islam to us and delivered us from destruction.

Many words and revisions later the inkwell and paper were brought. When the affair was agreed on, the Messenger of God invited a man to write the document between them. He called Aws b. Khawlī to write, but Suhayl said, "Only one of two men, ʿAlī, the son of your uncle, or ʿUthmān b. ʿAffān shall write." So the Prophet commanded ʿAlī to write. He said, "Write: In the name of God, most gracious most merciful." But Suhayl said, "I do not know the 'merciful,' so write as we write: 'In the name of God'." The Muslims became angry with that and said, "He is *Raḥmān*; do not write except *Raḥmān*." Suhayl said, "Then I will not make a peace agreement with you on anything." The Messenger of God said, "Write: In the name of God (*Allahumma*) this is what the Messenger of God has agreed to." But Suhayl said, "If I knew that you were the Messenger of God, I would not differ from you and I would follow you. I prefer your name. Do you then detest your name and the name of your father, Muḥammad b. ʿAbdullah?" The Muslims raised a hue and cry about this, which was greater than the first, and voices were raised. [Page 611] Men from the companions of the Messenger of God came forward saying, "We will only write 'Muḥammad the Messenger of God'."

Ibn Abī Sabra related to me from Isḥāq b. ʿAbdullah, from Abū Farwa, from Wāqid b. ʿAmr, who said: Those who saw Usayd b. Ḥuḍayr and Saʿd b. ʿUbāda related to me that they took the hand of the writer and said, "Do not write other than Muḥammad the Messenger of God, or the sword shall be between us. Why would we permit this insult to our religion?" The Messenger of God tried to calm them and signaled with his hand to them to be silent. Ḥuwayṭib was amazed at what they were doing, and he approached Mikraz b. Ḥafṣ saying, "I have not seen a people more concerned about their religion than those people." The Messenger of God said, "Write in the name of *Allahumma*, this is what is agreed between Muḥammad b. ʿAbdullah and Suhayl b. ʿAmr." The following verse was revealed concerning Suhayl when he insisted on rejecting al-Raḥmān: *Call him Allah or call him al-Raḥmān, whatever you call Him, He has beautiful names* (Q. 4:110). The Messenger of God said, "I am Muḥammad b. ʿAbdullah, write: In the Name of Allah, this is what was agreed between Muḥammad b. ʿAbdullah and Suhayl."

They agreed on not fighting for ten years. The people would be secure and would keep away from each other on condition that there would be no bribery or treachery. Among us there shall be a restrained censure. One who desires to enter into an agreement with Muḥammad and make a promise to him may do so. And one who desires to join the Quraysh and make an agreement with them may do so. One who comes to Muḥammad from them without the permission of his guardian shall be returned, while one who comes to the Quraysh from the companions of Muḥammad, shall not be returned. And that Muḥammad will [Page 612] leave us (the Meccans) this year of his, with his companions, but he may enter upon us later with his companions and stay for three days. He will not enter upon us with weapons except the weapons of the traveler, namely, the sword in its scabbard. Abū Bakr b. Quḥāfa, ʿUmar b. al-Khaṭṭāb, ʿAbd al-Raḥmān b. ʿAwf, Saʿd b. Abī Waqqās, ʿUthmān b. ʿAffān, Abū ʿUbayda b. Jarrāḥ, Muḥammad b. Maslama, Ḥuwayṭib b. ʿAbd al-ʿUzzā, Mikraz b. Ḥafṣ b. al-Akhīf, witnessed, and it was written on the front of the document. When the document was written Suhayl said, "I will keep it with me!" The Messenger of God said, "Rather, with me!" They argued, and a copy was written for him, and the Messenger of God took the first, and Suhayl took the copy, and kept it.

The Khuzāʿa jumped up and said: We will enter with the agreement of Muḥammad and his promise, and we are with those who follow us from our people. The Banū Bakr jumped up and said: We will enter with the Quraysh in their agreement and their promise. We are with those who follow us from our people. Ḥuwayṭib said to Suhayl, "Your uncles displayed their hostility first. They have entered into an agreement with Muḥammad and have contracted with him." Suhayl said, "They are like the rest of them. Those are our relatives and our flesh and they have entered with Muḥammad, and are a people who chose for themselves, so what can we do about it?" Ḥuwayṭib said, "We should get our allies, the Banū Bakr, to fight them." Suhayl said, "Take care that the Banū Bakr do not hear this from you. Indeed they are a people of bad luck. They will put down the Khuzāʿa and Muḥammad will be angry for his allies, and he will destroy the agreement between us and him." Ḥuwayṭib said, "By God you have gained from your uncles in every way."

Suhayl said: Do you think that my uncles are dearer to me than the Banū Bakr? By God, the Quraysh did not do anything except I did it. So if the Quraysh help the Banū Bakr against the Khuzāʿa, I am a man from the Quraysh. But the Banū Bakr are closer to me by lineage even if those people are my uncles. The Banū Bakr are those whom you know, and there are memories from them for us. However, not all of it is good. From them was the day of ʿUkkaẓ.

[Page 613] They said: When the Messenger of God completed the document, and Suhayl b. ʿAmr had departed with his companions, the Messenger of God said to his companions, "Stand up, sacrifice, and shave!" But not a man among them responded. The Messenger of God repeated his command thrice, yet not one among them obeyed. The Messenger of God turned around in great anger, and came to Umm Salama, his wife who was with him on his journey, and lay down. She said, "What is the matter, O Messenger of God?" many times. "Will you not answer me?" The Messenger of God replied, "It is amazing, O Umm Salama! Surely, I said to the people, sacrifice, shave and discharge your oath, several times, yet not one of the people responded, although they heard my words and observed my face." She said: Then I said, "O Messenger of God, go you to your sacrificial animal and slaughter it, and they will do as you do."

She said: The Messenger of God put on his robe leaving his right shoulder exposed, and then set out taking the spear with him to urge on the sacrificial beast. Umm Salama said: Then, as I watched, he pounced with his spear on the animal, crying out, "In the name of God most great." She said: As soon as the people saw him slaughter, they too pounced on the animals, and crowded around him until I feared that some of them would hurt others.

Yaʿqūb b. Muḥammad related to me from ʿAbd al-Raḥmān b. ʿAbdullah, from al-Ḥārith b. ʿAbdullah b. Kaʿb from Umm ʿUmāra, who said: It was as though I saw the Messenger of God, his garment exposing his right shoulder, the spear in his hand, slaughtering the animal. Mālik b. Anas related to me from Abū l-Zubayr from Jābir, who said: The Messenger of God shared the sacrifice with his companions. He cut the animal into seven portions. [Page 614] There were seventy sacrificial animals. The camel of Abū Jahl was the portion allotted to the Messenger of God on the day of Badr. The Muslims had plundered it in a raid. It was assigned with the milch camels of the Messenger of God that ʿUyayna b. Ḥiṣn was herding from Dhū l-Jadr to al-ʿUraniyyūn. The camel of Abū Jahl was a superior Mahrī camel and it was left to pasture with the sacrificial animals. Before the agreement, it fled and did not stop until it reached the house of Abū Jahl, and they recognized it. ʿAmr b. ʿAnama al-Sulamī set out in its tracks. One of the foolish of Mecca refused to return it. Suhayl b. ʿAmr said, "Give it to him"—they offered him a hundred she-camels. The Messenger of God said, "If we had not named it with the sacrificial animals we would have done it." The camel was slaughtered for seven, one of them was Abū Bakr, and another, ʿUmar b. al-Khaṭṭāb. Ibn al-Musayyib, used to say: There were seventy camels and seven hundred people, and every sacrifice was for ten persons. But the first saying is confirmed with us, that there were sixteen hundred.

He said: Ṭalḥa b. ʿUbaydullah sacrificed a camel of his that he brought from Medina, as did ʿAbd al-Raḥmān, and ʿUthmān b. ʿAffān. The Messenger of God struck up his tent outside the sanctuary, but he used to pray in the sanctuary. At that time, poor people looking for flesh of the camel came to him. The Messenger of God gave them from the flesh of the camel and its hide. Umm Kurz al-Kaʿbiyya said: I came to ask the Messenger of God about the meat of the sacrifice [Page 615] when he slaughtered in al-Ḥudaybiyya, and I heard him say, for a boy, two sheep are appropriate, for a girl, one. The Muslims ate from the sacrifice that they slaughtered at that time and they fed the poor among those who attended. The Messenger of God sent twenty animals to be sacrificed at al-Marwa, with a man from the Aslam. He slaughtered them at al-Marwa and apportioned their meat.

Yaʿqūb b. Muḥammad related to me from ʿAbd al-Raḥmān b. ʿAbdullah b. Abī Ṣaʿṣaʿa from al-Ḥārith b. ʿAbdullah from Umm ʿUmāra, who said: I observed the Messenger of God when he finished sacrificing the animal and entered his tent of reddish leather. In it was a barber who shaved his head. I watched as he put his head out of the tent saying, "May God bless those who shave." Someone said, "O Messenger of God, and those who shorten?" He said, "Those who shave," three times. Then he added, "And those who shorten."

Ibrāhīm b. Yazīd related to me from Abū l-Zubayr, from Jābir. He said: I watched him when he shaved his head. He threw his hair under a tree that was at his side—a green Samura. Umm ʿUmāra said: People began to take the hair from above the tree and share it, and I competed for some and took a bunch of hair. It was with her until she died washing for the sick. He said: Some people shaved at that time. Others shortened. Umm Salama the wife of the Prophet said: At that time I shortened the ends of my hair. Umm ʿUmāra used to say: At that time I shortened my hair—whatever was grey—with scissors that I had brought with me. [Page 616] Khirāsh b. Hunayd related to me from his father, who said: He who shaved him was Khirāsh b. Umayya.

They said: The Messenger of God stayed in al-Ḥudaybiyya for some ten days; and some say twenty nights. When he turned back from al-Ḥudaybiyya he stopped at Marr al-Ẓahrān, and then at al-ʿUsfān.

They consumed the provisions, and the people complained to the Messenger of God that they were hungry. But the people had beasts for riding. They said, "We will slaughter, O Messenger of God, annoint with its fat and make shoes from its hide." The Messenger of God granted them permission. ʿUmar b. al-Khaṭṭāb was informed of it and he came to the Messenger of God and said, "Do not do it. If a beast remains with you and the people, it will be better. But ask them about their provisions and pray to God about it." The Messenger of God commanded that the leather mat be spread. Then his herald called out, "Whoever has what remains of his provision, let him disperse it on the mat." Abū Shurayḥ al-Kaʿbī said: Indeed I saw those who came with a single date! Most of them did not bring anything. He had come with sufficient flour and barley, but now all that remained was a little. When they had collected their provisions, the Messenger of God walked up to it and prayed about it with blessings. Then he said, "Bring your containers closer." They came with their receptacles. Abū Shurayḥ said: While I was present, each man came and took what he wished from the provisions until he had taken more than he could carry.

The Messenger of God called out for the departure, and when they departed it rained as they wished it would for they were in Summer. The Messenger of God got down, and they got down with him and drank from the water. Then, the Messenger of God stood up [Page 617] and spoke to them. Three individuals appeared. Two sat with the Messenger of God. One went, turning away. He was ashamed, and God was also embarrassed for him. As for the other, he asked for forgiveness, and God forgave him. As for the third, he turned away, and God turned away from him. Muʿādh b.

Muḥammad related to me saying: I heard Shuʿba the *mawlā* of ʿAbbās say, I heard Ibn ʿAbbās say, ʿUmar b. al-Khaṭṭāb said: I was walking with the Messenger of God during his parting from al-Ḥudaybiyya. I questioned the Messenger of God and he would not answer me. Then I questioned him again and he would not answer me. Then I questioned him a third time and he would not answer me. ʿUmar said: I said to myself, "Your mother has lost you, O ʿUmar! You have been warned by the Messenger of God three times." Each time he did not respond to me, I prodded my camel until I was ahead of the people. I feared that a Qur'ānic verse would be revealed about me. I was overwhelmed for I had disputed the Messenger of God in al-Ḥudaybiyya, as the contract was hateful to me. Troubled, I proceeded ahead of the people. All of a sudden there was the cry of the herald, "O ʿUmar b. al-Khaṭṭāb!" Then I felt what God knows best.

I approached until I reached the Messenger of God and greeted him, and he returned my greeting happily. The Messenger of God said, "A verse has been revealed to me that is dearer to me than what the sun rises over." Then, he recited: *Indeed we have granted you a clear conquest* (Q. 48:1). He gave him glad tidings of his forgiveness, the perfection of his goodness and help, the obedience of those who obey God, and the hypocrisy of those who are hypocritical. God revealed ten verses about that.

Mujammiʿ b. Yaʿqūb related to me from his father from Mujammiʿ son of the slave girl, who said: [Page 618] When we were in Ẓajnān, returning from al-Ḥudaybiyya, I saw the people rush, and they were saying, "A *qur'ān* has been revealed to the Messenger of God." I rushed with the people until we reached the Prophet, and lo and behold, he was reciting: *Indeed We have granted you a clear victory*. When Gabriel revealed it, he said, "May it gladden you, O Messenger of God!" When Gabriel gladdened him, the Muslims gladdened him.

What was revealed about al-Ḥudaybiyya *Verily we have granted thee a manifest victory* (Q. 48:1); He said: we have fulfilled for you a clear fulfillment; the "opening" of the Quraysh and their reconciliation. It is the greatest conquest. *That God forgives thee thy faults in the past and those that follow* (Q. 48:2): He said, what was before the prophethood, and what came after. He said, what was before death until the death of the Messenger of God. *Fulfill His favor to you*: with an agreement with the Quraysh. *And guide you on the straight way*: He said, the truth. *And that God may help you with powerful help* (Q. 48:3): until you prevail and there will be no polytheism. *It is He who sent down tranquility into the hearts of the Believers* (Q. 48:4): He said, the security. *That they may add faith to their faith*: referring to conviction and belief. *The forces of the heavens and the earth belong to God*: God most high said. *That He will admit the men and women who believe to gardens beneath which rivers flow and remove their ills from them*: He said, what they had committed. *And that is in the sight of God the highest achievement*: He said, Success for them is that He forgives them their sins. *He will punish the Hypocrites, men and women, and the polytheists, men and women, who imagine an evil opinion of God. On them is a round of evil* (Q. 48:5): [Page 619] referring to those whom he passed between Mecca and Medina, from the Muzayna, the Juhayna and the Banū Bakr. He had sought their aid at al-Ḥudaybiyya. But they made excuses and were distracted by their families and their wealth. He said, for them is what they favored and assumed, and that was that they said. Surely, Muḥammad set out with a few, approaching a people wronged by the murder of a relative, but they refused to band with him. *We have truly sent thee as a witness and as a bringer of glad tidings* (Q. 48:8). A witness against them, a bringer of good tidings about Paradise, and a warner to them about hell fire. *And to strengthen him* (Q. 48:9): He said, you will help him and respect him and glorify him, and *celebrate His praises morning and evening*: He said, pray to God in the morning and evening. *Verily those who pledge their acceptance to you do no more than pledge their fealty to God. The hand of God is above their hands* (Q. 48:10): When the Messenger of God asked for the oath of fealty under the tree. They contracted with him at that time on condition that they do not flee, it was said, to death. *One who violates his oath does so to the harm of his own soul*: He said, those who alter or change what he had promised the Messenger of God, surely that will be upon his soul. And those who fulfill, indeed for him is Paradise. *The desert Arabs who lagged behind will say to thee, We were engaged in our flocks and our families: Do thou ask forgiveness for us, saying with their tongues what is not in their hearts* (Q. 48:11): He said, they are those whom the Messenger of God passed by, and called on them for help and support in the beginning, but they were busy with their families and their property. And when the Messenger of God was secure and came to Medina, they came to him saying, "Seek forgiveness for us for our refusal to go with you."

God most high said, *They say with their tongues but not with their hearts* [Page 620]: He said, It is the same to them, whether you forgive them or not. *No you thought that the Apostle and the believers will never return to their families* (Q. 48:12): Till God most high said, *You are a people lost (in wickedness)*: He said, Their words when the Messenger of God passed by them, "Surely Muḥammad is with a few, going out to a people wronged by the murder of one in their family—and Muḥammad has no weapons or preparedness," and they refused to hasten. *That was pleasing in your hearts*: He said, There was certainty in their hearts. God says, *You are a people lost in wickedness*: He refers to destruction. His words, *Those who lagged behind will say, When ye march and take booty* (Q. 48:15), to the end of the verse: He said, They are those who stay behind and refuse to hasten with him. Those are the Bedouin Arabs of the Muzayna and Juhayna and Bakr. When the Messenger of God desired to go to Khaybar they said, "We will follow you." God said, *They desire to alter the word of God*: He said, That which God had destined. He had decreed that you will not follow us, and it is the word of God, it is said, His decree. He said, *Say to those who stay behind among the Bedouin*: he refers to those who stayed behind from you in the ʿUmrat al-Ḥudaybiyya. *You shall be summoned to fight against a people given to vehement war* (Q. 48:16): He said, They are the Persians and Byzantines. Some say the Hawāzin, and some say the Banū Ḥanīfa on the day of Yamāma. *Then shall ye fight or they shall submit. Then, if you show obedience, God will show you a goodly reward, but if you turn back as you did before, He will punish you severely*: He said, if you refuse to fight, as you refused to go out with the Messenger of God to the raid of al-Ḥudaybiyya. [Page 621] *There is no blame on the blind or the lame or the ill* (Q. 48:17): He said, when three defects were revealed. Let those whom your right hands possess seek permission (Q. 24:58): The blind and the sick and the lame set out from their homes. God revealed, *There is no blame upon the blind*: He said, this is about the raid.

Muḥammad and Maʿmar related to me from al-Zuhrī, who said: I heard Saʿīd b. al-Musayyib say, This verse was revealed about a community of Muslims who, when they banded together for the raid, put down the keys of their homes with the very sick. God most high revealed about that a measure of leniency and permitted them in this. *Surely God was satisfied about the believers when they pledged to you under the tree*: He said, it was a verdent Samura tree. *What was in their hearts was known*: He said, their intentions were honest. *He sent down tranquility upon them*: referring to the peace of mind during the pledge of acceptance. *A speedy victory*: He said, concerning the agreement of the Quraysh. *And many gains will they acquire*: Until the Day of Judgment. About God's words, *He has hastened these for you*: He said, the conquest of Khaybar. *He has restrained the hands of men from you*: He said, those who went around the Prophet from the polytheists hoped to take the Muslims by surprise. The companions of the Prophet took prisoners from them. *That it may be a sign for the believers*: He said, it was a warning. The peace agreement and judgment of the Quraysh will be without a sword. It was [Page 622] the greatest conquest. *And others that are not within your power* (Q. 48:21): He said, concerning the Persia and Byzantium. Some say Mecca. *If the unbelievers would fight you, they should certainly turn their backs. Then would they find neither protector nor helper* (Q. 48:22): He said, if the Quraysh should fight you, they will be defeated, then God will not be their benefactor or protector, and there will be no help from the Bedouin. *(Such has been) the practice of God already in the past; no change will you find in God's practice* (Q. 48:23): He said, God has fulfilled that which was decreed. There will be no change in God's decree that His prophets will be victorious. *It is He who has restrained their hands from you and your hands from them in the midst of the Mecca valley after which He gave you victory over them* (Q. 48:24): He said, the companions of the Messenger of God had captured prisoners from the polytheists in al-Ḥudaybiyya, but God had stopped the hands of the Muslims from killing them. *And He kept their hands from you*: Referring to those who were imprisoned in Mecca. This was the victory. *They are the ones who denied the revelation and hindered you from the sacred mosque and detained the sacrificial animals from reaching their place of sacrifice*: He said, when they (the sacrificial animals) did not arrive at the House and were kept in al-Ḥudaybiyya. *Had there not been believing men and women whom you did not know that you were trampling down, and on whose account you would have commited a crime without your knowledge, that He may admit in his mercy who He will. If they had been apart, we should certainly have punished the unbelievers among them with a grievous punishment*: He said, if there were no men and women who were deemed weak in Mecca. *That you were trampling them*: He said, that you would have killed them and you would not know them, so there would come to you from that a great misery. When you kill Muslims and you do not know. *If they had been apart*: He said: if they set out away from them. *We have certainly punished those who disbelieve*: He says, He would place you in authority over them by the sword. [Page 623] *When He put into the hearts of those who disbelieve the fire (enthusiasm) of ignorance* (Q. 48:26): Since Suhayl b. ʿAmr refused to write "Muḥammad the Messenger of God," and when he refused to write, "In the name of God Most gracious most merciful." *And God revealed His tranquility on His Apostle and on the believers*: He said, among them. *Their sticking close to the command of self-restraint, and well were they entitled to it and worthy of it*: He who says, there is no God but one, is more correct and more entitled than the disbelievers. *Truly did God fulfill the vision for His Messenger. You shall enter the sacred mosque* (Q. 48:27), until His words, *He granted, besides this, a speedy victory*: The speedy victory is the recent peace of al-Ḥudaybiyya. The Messenger of God entered during the *ʿUmrat al-Qaḍiyya*, and he shaved, and people shaved with him, and others shortened. He entered his pilgrimage, and with him were his trusted companions who feared God alone. *Muḥammad is the Apostle of God, and those who are with him are strong against unbelievers but compassionate amongst each other: You will see them bow and prostrate themselves in prayer seeking grace from God and His good pleasure* (Q. 48:29): He said, those who bow and prostrate anticipate the grace of God and His pleasure. *On their faces are their marks, the traces of their prostration*: He said, traces of humility and modesty. *Their similitude in the Torah and their similitude in the gospel is like a seed which sends forth its blade, then makes it strong; it then becomes thick and it stands on its own stem filling the sowers with wonder and delight*: This is in the gospels, meaning the companions of the Messenger of God were few, then they increased, then they were many. Then they became strong. And He said, *Among those who believe in God and His messenger, they are the sincere* (Q. 57:19): He said that it is what distinguishes them. They believe in God and His messenger, and they speak the truth. And later, *The martyrs with their Lord*, concerning God's words, *But the Unbelievers—never will disaster cease to seize them for their (ill) deeds*: [Page 624] Meaning what was conquered in Islam was greater than the conquest of al-Ḥudaybiyya.

The war had separated the people and stopped the debate. Indeed there was fighting when they met. When there was peace the war put down its burdens. Some people trusted others. There was not one who spoke about Islam understanding something, but he entered Islam. Even braves from the polytheists, who supported polytheism and war, entered that peace—ʿAmr b. al-ʿĀṣ, Khālid b. al-Walīd, and others similar to them. Indeed there was peace for twenty-two months until they destroyed the contract. The number of people who entered Islam was equal to and more than those who had entered Islam previously. Islam spread in every direction in the regions of the Bedouin.

When the Messenger of God arrived in Medina from al-Ḥudaybiyya, Abū Baṣīr, that is ʿUtba b. Usayd b. Jāriya (Ḥāritha), an ally of the Banū Zuhra, came to him as a Muslim. He had escaped from his people, and come walking. Al-Akhnas b. Sharīq and Azhar b. ʿAbd ʿAwf al-Zuhrī wrote a letter to the Messenger of God. They sent a man from the Banū ʿĀmir b. Lu'ayy, having hired him for the price of a camel. Khunays b. Jābir, the ʿĀmirī, set out with a *mawlā* of his named Kawthar. The two had sent Khunays b. Jābir on a camel, with a letter mentioning the peace between them, and requesting the return of Abū Baṣīr to them. When they arrived before the Messenger of God, they arrived three days after Abū Baṣīr. Khunays said, "O Muḥammad, this is a letter." The Messenger of God called Ubayy b. Kaʿb, and he read what was in it. It said: You know what we agreed about and what we witnessed between us and between [Page 625] you regarding the return of those who come to you from our companions, so send us our companion. So the Messenger of God commanded Abū Baṣīr to return with them and he handed him to them. Abū Baṣīr said, "O Messenger of God are you returning me to the polytheists who tempt me from my religion?" The Messenger of God said, "O Abū Baṣīr, indeed we have given those people what you know, and treachery is not fitting for us in our religion. Indeed God will make for you, and for those who are with you from the Muslims, a release from suffering and a way out." Abū Baṣīr said, "O Messenger of God, do you return me to polytheists?" The Messenger of God said, "Go, O Abū Baṣīr, indeed God will provide you a way out," and the Messenger of God handed him to the ʿĀmirī and his companion, and he set out with them." The Muslims tried to cheer up Abū Baṣīr. "O Abū Baṣīr, rejoice! Indeed there is a reward for you and a way out. Perhaps one man will be better than a thousand men. So act, act!" and they commanded him about those who were with him.

They set out until they were in Dhū l-Ḥulayfa, in time for the *Ẓuhr* prayer. Abū Baṣīr entered the mosque of Dhū l-Ḥulayfa and prayed two bowings as a traveler. With him were the provisions he brought of dates. He bent down to the bottom of the wall of the mosque and placed his provisions, and tried to eat. He said to his two companions, "Draw near and eat." They said, "We have no need for your food." He replied, "If you offered me your food, I would respond and eat with you." They felt ashamed, drew near, and put their hands into the dates with him. They presented their own food, and they ate together, and he behaved in a friendly manner towards them. The ʿĀmirī hung up his sword on a stone in the wall. Abū Baṣīr said, "O brother of the Banū ʿĀmir, what is your name?" He said, "Khunays." He said, "The son of?" He replied, "The son of Jābir." Then Abū Baṣīr said, 'O Ibn Jābir, is this sword of yours sharp?' He replied, "Yes." He said, "Hand it to me, let me examine it if you will?" so the ʿĀmirī took it, for he was closer to the sword than Abū Baṣīr, and [Page 626] Abū Baṣīr, standing, took the sword out, while the ʿĀmirī held the scabbard. Then, Abū Baṣīr overwhelmed the ʿĀmirī with it until he was cold. Kawthar set out fleeing, and ran towards Medina, and Abū Baṣīr set out in his tracks, but he was unable to catch him and Kawthar preceded him to the Messenger of God. Abū Baṣīr says, "If I catch him I will lead him on the road of his companion!"

Meanwhile the Messenger of God was sitting with his companions, after the *ʿAṣar* prayer, when the *mawlā* appeared running. When the Messenger of God saw him, he said, "This is a man who is terrified." Kawthar approached until he stood before the Prophet, and the Messenger of God said, "What is the matter with you?" He replied, "Your companion killed mine. I am fleeing from him, and have barely done so." What kept Abū Baṣīr was carrying their booty on their camel. Kawthar did not leave his place until Abū Baṣīr appeared. The camel knelt at the door of the mosque and Abū Baṣīr entered wearing the sword of the ʿĀmirī. He stood before the Messenger of God and said to him, "Your protection is over, God has removed it from you. You handed me to the enemy, and I protected my religion from their obstruction. Do you desire that I lie about the truth?" The Messenger of God said, "Woe is his mother! He would have kindled a war if there were more men with him." Abū Baṣīr arrived with the loot of the Āmirī, Khunays b. Jābir, his ride and his sword and said, "A fifth is for the Messenger of God." The Messenger of God said, "If I take a fifth, they will think that I have not fulfilled my contract with them. The booty is the concern of you and your companion."

Then the Messenger of God said to Kawthar, "Return with Abū Baṣīr to your companions." He replied, "O Muḥammad, he frightens me, and I do not have the power nor help." The Messenger of God said [Page 627] to Abū Baṣīr, "Go where you wish!" So Abū Baṣīr set out until he came to al-ʿĪṣ. Here, he got down from his camel on the seacoast on the route of the Qurayshī caravan to al-Shām. Abū Baṣīr said, "I set out with only a handful of dates, and I ate it for three days. I was coming along the coast so I collected the fish that the sea had thrown out and ate it."

The words of the Messenger of God to Abū Baṣīr, "Woe to his mother. He would have kindled a war if there were more men with him," reached the Muslims who were imprisoned at Mecca and desired to join the Messenger of God. They tried to steal away to Abū Baṣīr. So ʿUmar b. al-Khaṭṭāb wrote to them about what the Messenger of God had said to the Muslims. When the letter of ʿUmar came to them informing them that Abū Baṣīr was at the coast, on the road of the Qurashī caravan, the Meccan Muslims tried to creep away, man by man until they reached Abū Baṣīr and gathered around him. They numbered almost seventy men. They created anxiety among the Quraysh, killing those they overpowered. A caravan did not pass, but they took possession of it, until they hurt the Quraysh. Indeed, riders traveling to al-Shām bringing thirty camels passed by, and this was the last of what the Muslims took possession of. Each one of them took a man. Every man that he took from them was valued at thirty dinars. Some of them said, "Send a fifth to the Messenger of God." Abū Baṣīr said, "The Messenger of God will not accept it. I took him the booty of the ʿĀmirī, and he refused it. He said, 'If I do this, their contract will not be fulfilled for them.' "

They appointed Abū Baṣīr as their commander. He prayed with them and fulfilled what was obligatory for them. He rounded them up and they listened to him and obeyed him.

When Suhayl b. ʿAmr learned that the ʿĀmirī was killed by Abū Baṣīr, he became violent. He said, "By God, has not Muḥammad made an agreement about this?" [Page 628] The Quraysh said, "Muḥammad is completely free of it. Your companion made it possible and he killed him on the road. What has Muḥammad to do with this?" Suhayl said, "By God, I knew that Muḥammad would fulfill. He came to us only because of the two messengers." He said: He leant his back against the Kaʿba and said, "By God, I will not remove my back until this man's blood-wit is paid." Abū Sufyān said, "This is sheer stupidity! By God, it will not be paid!" Three times. "Why should the Quraysh pay it? Did not the Banū Ẓuhra send him?" Suhayl said, "By God, you speak the truth. His debt is only upon the Banū Ẓuhra for they sent him, and nobody else should take out their blood money because the killer is from them." Al-Akhnas said, "By God, we will not pay his blood-wit, we did not kill him, nor did we command someone to kill him. A man who disagrees with our religion and a follower of Muḥammad killed him. Send to Muḥammad for his bloodwit." Abū Sufyān said, "No, Muḥammad does not have to pay it. He is innocent. What more could Muḥammad do than what he did. Indeed, he handed him to the two messengers." Al-Akhnas said, "If the Quraysh pay all of his blood-wit, the Zuhra are a clan of the Quraysh and they will pay it with them. If the Quraysh do not pay the blood-wit, we will never pay it." The blood-wit was not paid to him until the Messenger of God arrived in the Year of the Conquest. Mawhab b. Riyāḥ said, concerning what Suhayl said about the Banū Zuhra and what he desired from them in payment of the bloodwit:

A brief word from Suhayl reached me
And woke me from my sleep.
If you want to reproach me
Then reproach me, for you are not far from me.
If you put me to the test you will not find me
Weak in determination in grave misfortunes.
He elevates the most generous with the best of people
They are the overseeing leaders with humanity.

ʿAbdullah b. Abī ʿUbayda recited it to me, and I heard them confirm it.

[Page 629] Abū Baṣīr made the Quraysh very angry, and the Quraysh sent a man and wrote a letter to the Messenger of God asking him by their kinship, "Will you not admit Abū Baṣīr and his companions, for there is no requirement for us with them?" So the Messenger of God wrote to Abū Baṣīr to come to him with his companions. The letter reached Abū Baṣīr while he was dying, and he kept reading it while he was dying. He died while it was in his hand. His companions buried him there and they prayed over him, and built a mosque over his grave.

His companions went to Medina. They totaled seventy men, including al-Walīd b.

al-Walīd b. al-Mughīra. When he entered the lava field he stumbled and cut his finger. He bandaged it while saying:

> Are you not but a finger bleeding,
> Suffering in the way of God.

He entered Medina and died there. Umm Salama said: O Messenger of God, permit me to cry over al-Walīd. He said, "You may cry for him!" He said: she brought the women together and made food for them. This is what surfaced about her crying.

> O Eye, cry for al-Walīd b. al-Walīd b. al-Mughīra.
> The Parallel of al-Walīd b. al-Walīd father of al-Walīd is sufficient for the tribe.

Ibn Abī l-Zinād related to me from his father, who said: When the Messenger of God heard the repetition of al-Walid, he said, "They do not adopt 'al-Walīd' except with compassion."

They said: We have not learned of a Qurayshi woman setting out from her father as a muslim immigrant to God except Umm Kulthūm bt. ʿUqba b. Abī Muʿayṭ. She used to say: I had set out to the desert to my relatives and I stayed with them three or four days. It was in the direction of Tanʿīm or Ḥaṣḥāṣ. Then I returned to my family and they did not refuse my going when I decided to make the trip. [Page 630] I set out one day from Mecca as though I desired the desert where I had been before, when he who was following me returned. I set out until I reached the road. Suddenly, a man from the Khuzāʿa appeared and said, "Where are you going?" I said: "For a need of mine. Why do you ask, and who are you?" He replied, "One of the Khuzāʿa." When he mentioned the Khuzāʿa I felt at ease and trusted him, for the Khuzāʿa had entered into an agreement with the Messenger of God. I said, "Indeed I am a woman from the Quraysh and I desire to meet the Messenger of God, but have no knowledge of the road." He replied, "I am from the people of the night and day. I shall be your companion until you reach Medina." Then he brought me a camel and I rode it. He led the camel with me riding it, and by God, not a word did he speak to me, until when the camel knelt, he withdrew from me. When I got down, he came to the camel and tied it to the tree, and then withdrew. When it was time for the departure he started the camel and brought it close and turned away from me. When I was on it, he took it by its head and did not turn to look behind until we alighted. It continued thus until we arrived in Medina. May God reward him for being the best companion. She used to say: Blessed is the tribe of the Khuzāʿa!

She said: I visited Umm Salama, the wife of the Prophet, and I was veiled and she did not know me until I traced my ancestry and lifted the veil. She persisted with me and said, "Have you immigrated to God and His Messenger?" I said, "Yes, and I fear the Messenger of God will return me to the polytheists as he returned others from the men, Abū Jandal b. Suhayl, and Abū Baṣīr. But the condition of the men, O Umm Salama, is not the same as the condition of the women. The people will realize my absence in the morning. It is [Page 631] eight days since I left them. They will wait the number of days I usually go away, and then look for me. If they do not find me they will ride looking for me for three days."

The Messenger of God visited Umm Salama and she informed him of the news of Umm Kulthūm. The Messenger of God welcomed her, and Umm Kulthūm said, "O Messenger of God, indeed I fled with my religion to you, so keep me and do not return me to them, they will prevent me and hurt me. I have no patience with pain. I am a woman and women are weak, as you know. I have seen you return two men to the polytheists until one of them refused. But I am a woman!" The Messenger of God said, "Indeed, God has revoked the agreement concerning women. God has revealed *Mumtahina*—the test (Q. 50) about them." He judged about that with wisdom, satisfying all of them.

The Messenger of God returned those who came from the men, but he did not return those who came from the women. Her two brothers, al-Walīd and ʿUmāra the sons of ʿUqba b. Abī Muʿīṭ arrived in the morning. They said, "O Muḥammad, return her to us in accordance with our laws and what you contracted with us." He replied, "God has revoked it." So they returned. Muḥammad b. ʿAbdullah related to me from al-Zuhrī, who said: I visited ʿUrwa b. al-Zubayr and he was writing to Hunayd the companion of al-Walīd b. ʿAbd al-Malik. He wrote asking him about the word of God: *O you who believe, when believing women refugees come to you, examine and test them.* (Q. 60:10). And he wrote to him that indeed the Messenger of God made a peace with the Quraysh at al-Ḥudaybiyya on condition that he return to them those who came without permission from his guardian, and he returned the men. But when the women emigrated, God refused that he return them if he tested them with the test of Islam. She claimed that she came desiring it. [Page 632] God commanded Muḥammad to return their dowries to their husbands if they did not join the women in their *emigration*, and that the men return the same amount that was paid to them if they come to join their women. He said: *They—the unbelievers—ask for what they have spent* (Q. 60:10). Her brothers arrived in the morning on the following day seeking her. The Messenger of God refused to return her to them. So they returned to Mecca. They informed the Quraysh, but they did not send any one about that. They were content that the women were detained. *They ask for what they have spent. Such is the command of God. He judges between you, God is full of knowledge and Wisdom. And if any of your wives deserts you to the unbelievers, and you have an accession—by the coming over of a woman from the other side—Then pay to those whose wives have deserted them* (Q. 60:11). He said: if one of his family escapes to the disbelievers; and if a woman comes to you from them, you gain and reimburse from what you gain from the *mahr* of the women who come to you. The believers obeyed the law of God. The polytheists refused to confirm what was due to the polytheist from the Muslim, the *mahr* of those who emigrated from the polytheists' wives. *Then pay to those whose wives have deserted* (Q. 60:11). The wealth of the polytheists is in your hands. We do not know a woman from the Muslims who left her husband to join the polytheists after their faith, but it is a judgment God judged about the affair. God is knowledgeable and wise. *But hold not to the guardianship of unbelieving women* . . . (Q. 60:10). Referring to those who are not people of the book.

ʿUmar b. al-Khaṭṭāb divorced Zaynab bt. Abī Umayya, and Muʿāwiya b. Abī Sufyān married her. ʿUmar [Page 633] also divorced the daughter of Jarwal al-Khuzāʿiyya and Abū Jahm b. Ḥudhayfa married her. ʿIyāḍ b. Ghanm al-Fihrī divorced Umm al-Ḥakam bt. Abī Sufyān at that time. ʿAbdullah b. ʿUthmān al-Thaqafī married her. She gave birth to ʿAbd al-Raḥmān b. Umm al-Ḥakam.

THE RAID OF KHAYBAR

Abū ʿUmar Muḥammad b. al-ʿAbbās b. Muḥammad b. Zakariyya b. Ḥayyawayh related, in the year three hundred and seventy-seven AH. that Abū l-Qāsim ʿAbd al-Wahāb b. ʿĪsā b. Abī Ḥayya said that Abū ʿAbdullah Muḥammad b. Shujāʿ al-Thaljī said that Abū ʿAbdullah Muḥammad b. ʿUmar b. Wāqid al-Wāqidī related to us saying: Muḥammad b. ʿAbdullah, Mūsā b. Muḥammad b. Ibrāhīm b. al-Ḥārith al-Taymī, ʿAbdullah b. Jaʿfar, Ibn Abī Sabra, Ibn Abī Ḥabība, ʿAbd al-Raḥmān b. ʿAbd al-ʿAzīz, Muḥammad b. Ṣāliḥ, Muḥammad b. Yaḥyā b. Sahl, ʿĀʾidh b. Yaḥyā, ʿAbd al-Ḥamīd b. Jaʿfar, Yaḥyā b. ʿAbdullah b. Abī Qatāda, Usāma b. Zayd al-Laythī, Abū Maʿshar, Muʿādh b. Muḥammad, Ibrāhīm b. Jaʿfar, Yūnus and Yaʿqūb the sons of Muḥammad al-Ẓafarī, Yaʿqūb b. Muḥammad b. Abī Ṣaʿṣaʿa, Saʿīd b. Abī Zayd b. al-Muʿallā al-Zuraqī, Rabīʿa b. ʿUthmān, Muḥammad b. Yaʿqūb, ʿAbdullah b. Yazīd, ʿAbd al-Malik and ʿAbd al-Raḥmān the sons of Muḥammad b. Abī Bakr, Maʿmar b. Rāshid, and Ismāʿīl b. Ibrāhīm b. ʿUqba, all have related portions of this tradition about Khaybar to me. Some were more reliable than others, and others not mentioned have informed me as well. I wrote it as they related it to me.

[Page 634] They said: The Messenger of God arrived in Medina from al-Ḥudaybiyya in Dhū l-Ḥijja at the end of year six AH. He stayed in Medina for the rest of Dhū l-Ḥijja and Muḥarram. He went out in Ṣafar of the year seven—some say it was in the month of Rabīʿ al-Awwal—to Khaybar. The Messenger of God ordered his companions to prepare to raid, and they were diligent in their preparation, and he stirred up those around him to go raiding with him. Those who had stayed behind came to him desiring to go out with him hoping for plunder. They said, "We will go out with you!" They had stayed behind during the raid of al-Ḥudaybiyya spreading falsehood about the Prophet and the Muslims. But now they said, "We will go out with you to Khaybar. Surely it is the countryside of the Ḥijāz with rich food and property." The Messenger of God said, "You will not go out with me unless you desire *jihād*. As for plunder, there will be none." He sent a herald out to cry, "Only those desiring *jihād* will go out with us. And as for plunder there will be none!"

When the people prepared for Khaybar it was unbearable to the Jews of Medina who had an agreement with the Messenger of God. They knew that if the Muslims entered Khaybar, God would destroy Khaybar just as He had destroyed the Banū Qaynuqāʿ, Naḍīr, and Qurayẓa. He said: When we were ready, there did not remain one Jew of Medina who had a claim over one of the Muslims, but he now demanded its return. Abū l-Shahm, the Jew, held a claim against ʿAbdullah b. Abī Ḥadrad al-Islāmī for five dirhams' worth of barley that he had taken to his family. ʿAbdullah clung to it, and said, "Postpone it for me, for I hope to come to you and pay you back, God willing. Indeed, God most high has promised His Prophet Khaybar for plunder." ʿAbdullah b. Abī Ḥadrad was among those who had witnessed al-Ḥudaybiyya. He said, "O, Abū l-Shahm, we are setting out to the countryside of the Ḥijāz where there is food and property." Abū l-Shahm, who was greedy and envious, replied, "Do you think that fighting Khaybar is like fighting among the Arabs? By the Torah, in it are ten thousand warriors!" [Page 635] Ibn Abī Ḥadrad said, "O enemy of God, do you frighten us about our enemies while you are under our protection and live as our neighbours? By God I shall inform the Messenger of God about you." And he said, "O Messenger of God, did you hear what this Jew says?" and he informed him about what Abū l-Shahm said. The Messenger of God was silent and did not say anything to him. But Ibn Abī Ḥadrad saw the Messenger of God mutter to himself though he could not hear him. Then the Jew said, "O Abū l-Qāsim, this has tyranized me and kept my rights from me, and taken my food." The Messenger of God said, "Give him his dues." ʿAbdullah said: I went out and sold one of my garments for three dirhams and I asked what remained of his dues and fulfilled it. I put on the other garment of mine. I had a turban that I wrapped myself with, and Salama b. Aslam gave me another garment. So I set out with the Muslims on two garments. But God's bounty to me was good. I captured a woman who was a relative of Abū l-Shahm as plunder and I sold her to him.

Abū ʿAbs b. Jabr arrived. He said, "O Messenger of God, we do not have funds, provisions, or clothes to set out in." The Messenger of God gave him a garment from Sunbulāniyya. He sold it for eight dirhams, bought dates for two dirhams as his provisions, gave his family two dirhams as funds, and bought a cloak for four dirhams. Later, on a moonlit night, when the Messenger of God was on his way to Khaybar, he saw a man walking in front of him, wearing something glittering in the moonlight as though it were in the sun, and upon him was a "helmet" of iron. The Messenger of God said, "Who is this?" Someone said, "Abū ʿAbs b. Jabr." The Messenger of God said, [Page 636] "Overtake him!" He said: They overtook me and imprisoned me. I became anxious about the consequences of my actions and I thought that something had been revealed from the heavens about me. I tried to remember what I did until the Messenger of God joined me and said, "What is the matter with you that you go ahead of the people and do not go with them?" I replied, "O Messenger of God, surely my camel is superior." He said, "Where is the garment with which I clothed you?" I said, "I sold it for eight dirhams, made a provision of dates for two dirhams, left two dirhams as funds for my family, and bought a cloak for four dirhams." The Messenger of God laughed and said, "O Abū ʿAbs, you and your companions are, by God, poor! By Him who keeps my soul in his hands, if you stay safe and live a little, your provisions will increase, and what you leave to your family will increase; and your land and your slaves and whatever is in your interest will increase, and how good it will be for you!" Abū ʿAbs said: And by God, it was just as the Messenger of God said."

The Messenger of God appointed Sibāʿ b. ʿUrfaṭa al-Ghifārī to take his place in Medina. Abū Hurayra said about it: We arrived in Medina and we were eighty families of Daws. A sayer said, "The Messenger of God is in Khaybar; he has preceded you." I replied, "I have not heard of him alighting in a place, ever, but I have come to it." We traveled until we came to Khaybar and we found he had already taken al-Naṭā, and was besieging al-Katība; we persisted until God conquered it for us. We arrived in Medina and we prayed the *Ṣubḥ* prayer behind Sibāʿ b. ʿUrfaṭa, and during the first bowing he recited the chapter *al-Maryam* (Q. 19) and during the next, the chapter on fraud (*al-Muṭaffifīn*—Q. 83). When he came to the words *When they take from the people a full measure* (Q. 83:2), I said, "I left my uncle at al-Sarā with two measures, one measure [Page 637] was a little less, but one measure was a little more." Some said that the Messenger of God appointed Abū Dharr to take his place in Medina, but we confirm that it was Sibāʿ b. ʿUrfaṭa.

The Jews of Khaybar did not think that the Messenger of God would raid them for they had strengthened their fortresses and their weapons and their numbers. Ten thousand warriors would set out every day in rows, saying, "Will Muḥammad raid us? How preposterous!" While those Jews who were in Medina used to say, when the Prophet prepared for Khaybar, "By God, how much more forbidding is Khaybar for you! If you see Khaybar and its fortresses and its men you will surely return before you reach them. The towering fortresses are on the tops of mountains, and the water in it flows continuously. Indeed, in Khaybar are a thousand men in armor. How were the Asad and the Ghaṭafān protected from all the Bedouin without exception, except by them? And you will conquer Khaybar?" They tried to impress that notion on the companions of the

Prophet. The companions of the Prophet used to say, "God has promised His prophet that he will plunder it."

The Messenger of God set out to them, and God blinded them with doubt about his setting out, until the Messenger of God alighted in their yard at night. They differed among themselves about where they sensed the march of the Messenger of God. Al-Ḥārith Abū Zaynab, the Jew, recommended to them that they should camp outside their fortresses and face him. Indeed, I saw one who went to him from the fortress. There was no existence for them after he attacked them until they submitted to his judgment. Among them were those who were imprisoned and those who were executed.

The Jews said, "These fortresses of ours are not like those. These are forbidding fortresses on the tops [Page 638] of mountains." They opposed him and they stood firm in their fortresses. When the Messenger of God arrived in the morning, they assessed him and were certain of the destruction.

The Messenger of God set out taking the road to Thanniyyat al-Wadāʿ then al-Zaghāba, Naqmā, al-Mustanākh, then he raided al-Waṭīḥ. With them were two guides from the Ashjaʿ, one of them was called Ḥusayl b. Khārija and the other ʿAbdullah b. Nuʿaym. The Messenger of God set out to Mt. ʿAṣar where there was a mosque, then to al-Ṣahbāʾ. When he was on his journey he said to ʿĀmir b. Sinān, "Get down, O Ibn al-Akwaʿ, and begin one of your verses for us." So ʿĀmir got down from his ride and composed a verse (*rajaz*) about the Messenger of God saying:

> By God, without you we would not have seen the right path,
> Nor given charity nor prayed.
> So throw Your tranquility (*sakīna*) upon us, and strengthen our feet when we meet.
> Indeed, when we are called, we answer. They can depend on our help.

The Messenger of God said, "May God be merciful to you." ʿUmar b. al-Khaṭṭāb said, "By God, you have made his death inevitable, O Messenger of God." A man from the people said, "If not, may you grant us enjoyment through him, O Messenger of God." ʿĀmir was martyred on the day of Khaybar.

Salama b. al-Akwaʿ [Page 639] used to say: When we were outside Khaybar, I saw a gazelle lie down in the shade of a tree. I withdrew and aimed an arrow at it. The arrow did nothing, but the gazelle was startled. Then ʿĀmir joined me and he aimed an arrow that fell in its side. The string of his bow snapped and the sinew became attached to his side, and he could not release it except by pulling it. An evil omen came to me at that time, and I hoped for his martyrdom—then I saw a man from the Jews take him and he died.

The Messenger of God said to ʿAbdullah b. Rawāḥa, Will you not stimulate our journey? ʿAbdullah got down from his ride and said:

> O God, without You we would not have seen the right path, nor given charity nor prayed.
> So throw Your tranquility upon us, and strengthen our feet when we meet.
> For the polytheists oppress us.

The Messenger of God said, "May God have mercy upon you!" ʿUmar said, "You have made his death inevitable." Al-Wāqidī said: He was martyred at the battle of Mu'ta.

They said: The Messenger of God reached al-Ṣahbā᾽ and prayed the *ʿAṣar* prayer there. Then he asked for food and only barley and dates were brought. The Messenger of God ate, and they ate with him. Then he stood up to pray *Maghrib* with the people but he did not perform ablutions. Then he prayed *ʿIshā᾽* with the people. Then he called for the guides, and Ḥusayl b. Khārija al-Ashjaʿī and ʿAbdullah b. Nuʿaym al-Ashjaʿī arrived.

He said: The Messenger of God said to Ḥusayl, "Go before us and lead us in front of al-Awdiya until we reach Khaybar from between it and al-Shām, so that I can interpose between them and between al-Shām and their allies from the Ghaṭafān." Ḥusayl said, "I will take the road with you." He brought him to the site of the crossroads and said to him, [Page 640] "O Messenger of God, there are many roads, and all of them come from here." The Messenger of God said, "Name them for me." The Messenger of God liked good signs and good names. He detested treachery and ugly names. The guide said, "Some call this road Ḥazana." The Messenger of God said, "Do not take it." He said, "This road is called Shāsh." The Messenger of God said, "Do not take it." He said, "This road is called Ḥāṭib." The Messenger of God said, "Do not take it." ʿUmar b. al-Khaṭṭāb said, "I have not seen such a night and such ugly names named to the Messenger of God!" He said, "Only one road remains." ʿUmar said, "Name it." He said, "Its name is Marḥab." The Messenger of God said, "Yes, take it." ʿUmar said, "Why did you not name this road first!"

The Messenger of God sent ʿAbbād b. Bishr with some riders ahead. He captured a spy from the Jews of the Ashjaʿ and asked, "Who are you?" He said, "A seeker, for I seek camels lost to me, and I am on their track." ʿAbbād said to him, "Do you have information of Khaybar?" he said, "My acquaintance with it is recent. What is it you want to know? He said, "About the Jews." He said, "Yes, Kināna b. Abī l-Ḥuqayq and Hawdha b. Qays went with their allies of the Ghaṭafān, whom they had called to fight with them, having promised them dates of Khaybar for a year. They came prepared with food and weapons, and leading them was ʿUtba b. Badr. They entered their fortress in which are ten thousand warriors. They are people of unmatched fortresses. They have many weapons, food sufficient for two years in case they are besieged, and flowing water for them to drink within their fortress. I have not seen another with their capacity." ʿAbbād b. Bishr raised his whip and lashed it twice. He said, "You are only a spy of theirs. Tell me the truth or I shall cut off your head." The Bedouin said, "Will you protect me [Page 641] if I speak the truth?" ʿAbbād said, "Yes."

The Bedouin said, "The people are alarmed about you and fearful. They fear what you did with the Jews of Yathrib (Medina). The Jews of Yathrib sent a cousin of mine having found him in Medina. He had arrived with goods to sell. They sent him to Kināna b. Abī l-Ḥuqayq informing him of your small numbers, and the few horses and weapons you possess. They say to them, 'Give them a good beating and they will turn away from you.' Indeed, he has not met a people more suited to battle. The Quraysh and the Bedouin are pleased with Muḥammad's march to you for they know of your possessions, the large numbers of your weapons and the excellence of your fortress. The Quraysh and others who have the same desires, want Muḥammad. The Quraysh say, 'Indeed Khaybar will be victorious,' but others say, 'Muḥammad will be victorious.' If Muḥammad succeeds, it will be timeless humiliation." The Bedouin said, "I heard all this," when Kināna said to me, "Go running to the road for surely they will not deny you your place, and evaluate them for us. Get close to them and plead for help. Throw at them the magnitude of our numbers, our possessions, for indeed they will never ignore you. Then hurry and return to us with their news."

ʿAbbād brought him to the Prophet and informed him of the news. ʿUmar b. al-Khaṭṭab said, "Cut off his head." ʿAbbād said, "I promised him protection." The Messenger of God said, "Keep him with you, O ʿAbbād, and tie him up." When the Messenger of God entered Khaybar, he proposed Islam to him. The Messenger of God said, "Indeed, I invite you," three times. "If you do not convert, he will not take off the rope from your neck except to go up—hang." The Bedouin converted.

The guide went out marching with the Messenger of God taking the path between Ḥayāḍ and al-Sarīr. He followed to the front of al-Awdiyya when he descended to al-Kharaṣa. Then he carried on until he took the road between al-Shiqq [Page 642] and al-Naṭā. When the Messenger of God looked down upon Khaybar, he said to his companions, "Stop!" Then he said, "Say: O God, Lord of the seven heavens and what they protect, Lord of the seven worlds and what they carry, Lord of the wind and what it scatters, we ask You for the good of this village, and the good of its families, and the good of what is in it, and we seek protection with You from its evil and the evil of what is in it." Then he said, "Enter with the blessing of God." He went until he reached al-Manzila, and spent an hour of the night there.

The Jews rose every night before dawn. They put on their weapons and lined up the squadrons. They were ten thousand warriors. Kināna b. Abī l-Ḥuqayq had set out with a ride to the Ghaṭafān, to ask them to help them in exchange for half the dates of Khaybar, for a year. It had reached them that the Messenger of God was marching to them. A man from the Banū Fazāra who was an ally of theirs arrived in Medina to sell his goods. Then he went back to them and said, "I left Muḥammad mobilizing his companions to march against you." So they sent for their allies from the Ghaṭafān. Kināna b. Abī l-Ḥuqayq set out with fourteen men from the Jews to ask them for help, and in return, he promised them half the dates of Khaybar for a year.

When the Messenger of God alighted in their courtyard that night, they did not stir, and not a cock of theirs crowed until the sun rose. They rose with their hearts pounding. They opened their fortresses carrying with them their shovels, and hoes, and baskets. When they saw that the Messenger of God had alighted in their courtyard, they said, "Muḥammad and the army!" and they turned and fled into their fortress.

[Page 643] The Messenger of God said repeatedly, "God is most great. Khaybar is destroyed." When we alighted in the courtyard of the people, the morning was made evil for those who were warned. When the Messenger of God reached al-Manzila, he established a prayer ground and prayed in it from the end of the night, a supererogatory prayer. His ride had become excited so he pulled at its halter. Unexpectedly, it had come before a rock and refused to be ridden. The Messenger of God said, "Leave it for surely it is charged." When it knelt at the rock, the Messenger of God moved to it, and commanded that its saddle be removed. He commanded the people to move to the rock. Then the Messenger of God commanded that a mosque be built at that site. It is their mosque today.

In the morning, al-Ḥubāb b. al-Mundhir came to him and said, "O Messenger of God, surely you have alighted in this station of yours. If it is from a command you have been commanded with, we will not speak about it. But if it is your opinion, let us discuss it." The Messenger of God said, "Rather, it is my opinion." He said, "O Messenger of God, you draw near to the fortress, and you alight between the rear of its dates, and the muddy land. The people of Naṭā are known to me, and there is not a people who can outdistance, or are more accurate in shooting than them, and they are high above us from where it is speedier to send their arrows down to us. Nor do I feel secure from their attack at night for they may hide in between the palm trees. So move, O Messenger of God, to a place away from the muddy land and the infectious areas. Let us put the ḥarra—the lava field—between us, where their arrows will not reach us."

Then the Messenger of God said, "We will fight them this day." The Messenger of God called for [Page 644] Muḥammad b. Maslama and said, "Look for a site far from their fortress and safe from infectious disease, where we will be safe from their nightly attack." Muḥammad b. Maslama walked around until he reached al-Rajīʿ. He returned to the Prophet at night and said, "I found a site for you." The Messenger of God said, "By the grace of God." The Messenger of God fought that day until nightfall against the people of Naṭā. They fought them from below. The Jews became mobilized at that time, and Ḥubāb said to him, "When will you leave, O Messenger of God?" The Messenger of God replied, "When it is evening, God willing, we will leave." The arrows of the Jews reached the camp of the Muslims and outdistanced it. The Muslims began to collect their arrows and aim back at them. When it was evening the Messenger of God departed. He ordered the people to move to al-Rajīʿ.

The next morning the Messenger of God moved out with the Muslims under their banners. Their slogan was: Ya Manṣūr kill! Al-Ḥubāb b. al-Mundhir said to him, "Surely the Jews consider their date palms to be more precious than their first born children. So cut down their date palms." The Messenger of God ordered the cutting down of the date palms. The Muslims began to cut them down in haste. Abū Bakr came to him and said, "O Messenger of God, surely God most high has promised you Khaybar, and He will fulfill what he has promised you. So do not cut down the date palms." The Messenger of God commanded a herald to call out and prevent them from cutting the date palms. Muḥammad b. Yaḥyā related to me from his father from his grandfather, who said, "I saw the date palms of Khaybar, in Naṭā, in pieces, and that was from what the companions of the Messenger of God cut down." [Page 645] Usāma b. Zayd al-Laythī related to me from Jaʿfar b. Maḥmūd b. Muḥammad b. Maslama, who said: The Muslims cut down four hundred date palms of ʿIdhq in al-Naṭā. They were cut only in Naṭā.

Muḥammad b. Maslama observing the date in the pickle said: I cut this date with my own hands until I heard Bilāl call out with resolution from the Messenger of God, "Do not cut the date palm!" and we stopped. He said: Maḥmūd b. Maslama was fighting with the Muslims at that time, and it was a very hot summer's day. It was the first day the Messenger of God fought with the people of Naṭā. When the heat was strongest over Maḥmūd, it was his custom, in all his attire, to sit under the fortress of Nāʿim desiring its shade. It was the first fortress the Messenger of God began with. Maḥmūd did not think that there were any warriors in it. Indeed he thought that there was furniture or goods in it, for Nāʿim was a Jew who possessed a number of fortresses, including this one. Marḥab threw down a millstone and it struck Maḥmūd's head. It struck the helmet of his head until the skin of his forehead fell on his face. He was brought to the Messenger of God and he pushed the skin until it returned just as it was. The Messenger of God bandaged it with a cloth. When it was evening, the Messenger of God moved to al-Rājīʿ for he feared his companions would be attacked. He struck up his tent there and he stayed up the night in it. He stayed in al-Rajīʿ for seven days.

He raided every day with the Muslims under their banner, in armor, leaving the campsite in al-Rajīʿ, appointing ʿUthmān b. ʿAffān to take his place. He fought the people of Naṭā from day to night. When it was evening he returned to al-Rajīʿ. The first day he fought from below al-Naṭā. Then he returned later and fought them from above the fortress, until [Page 646] God conquered it. Those who were wounded among the Muslims were carried to the campsite and treated. If there were an outburst in it, they would depart to the camp of the Prophet. On the first day those who fought among the Muslims and were wounded from their arrows, were fifty. They were treated for their wounds. The people complained to the Messenger of God of the infection of this place and he commanded them to move to al-Rajīʿ. They arrived at Khaybar with its green dates, but it was infected and unhealthy. They ate from that date and the fever infected them. They complained to the Messenger of God about that, and he said: Pour the water in buckets, and when it is between the two calls to prayer, pour the water on yourselves and mention the name of God. They did so and became well again.

Kaʿb b. Mālik used to relate: A man from the Jews of Naṭā called out to us after night, while we were in al-Rajīʿ, "Will you give me protection if I inform you?" We said, "Yes." He said: We hastened to him and I was the first of those who reached him and I said, "Who are you?" He said, "A man from the Jews." We took him to the Messenger of God and the Jew said, "O Abū l-Qāsim, give me and my family protection, and I will guide you to the weakest point of the Jews." The Messenger of God said, "Yes." So he led us to the weak spot of the Jews. He said: The Messenger of God called his companions, at that hour, and encouraged them to *jihād*. He informed them that the Jews and their allies had betrayed them and fled. Indeed they had quarreled, disputing among themselves. [Page 647] Kaʿb said: We went to them in the morning and God gave us victory over them. There were no children in Naṭā but when we reached al-Shiqq, we found children. The Messenger of God handed the Jew his wife who was in al-Shiqq. He handed her to him and I saw him take the hand of a beautiful woman.

The Messenger of God used to appoint his companions successively to keep watch at night during his seven days' stay in al-Rajīʿ. On the sixth of the seven nights he appointed ʿUmar b. al-Khaṭṭāb over the camp. ʿUmar circumambulated the camp with his companions and dispersed them or dispersed some of them. When a man was brought from the Jews in the middle of the night, ʿUmar commanded that he be executed. But the Jew said, "Take me to your Prophet and let me speak to him." So ʿUmar grabbed him and took him to the door of the Prophet, where he found him praying. The Messenger of God heard the words of ʿUmar and he greeted him and let him in. ʿUmar entered with the Jew.

The Messenger of God said to the Jew, "What happened to you, and who are you?" The Jew said, "Will you protect me, O Abū'l Qāsim, if I speak the truth?" The Messenger of God said, "Yes." The Jew said, "I set out from the fortress of Naṭā living with a people who are not organized. I left them sneaking out of the fortress this very night." The Messenger of God asked, "Where are they going?" He replied, "To a place more humiliating than they were in—to al-Shiqq. They were so frightened of you that their hearts were beating. But in this fortress of the Jews are weapons and food and fat, as well as tools of the fortress with which some of them fought others. They have hidden it in a room of their fortress, under the ground." The Messenger of God said, [Page 648] "What are they?" He replied, "A mangonel taken apart; two war machines (made of wood and skins) and weapons, from coats of mail and helmets to swords. And if you go to the fortress tomorrow morning you will enter it." The Messenger of God said, "If God wills." The Jew said, "If God wills, I will tell you how. For indeed, none of the Jews knows of it but I and another." It was said, "What is it?" He said, "You will remove the mangonel and then I will install it in the fortress of al-Shiqq. The men will enter under the war machines and they will dig the fortress, and you will open it in a day." And he did thus with the fortress of al-Katība. ʿUmar said, "Indeed I think he speaks the truth." The Jew said, "O Abū'l Qāsim, spare my blood." The Prophet said, "You are protected." He said, "My wife is in the fortress of al-Nizār, so give her to me." He replied, "She is yours." The Messenger of God said: "What is the matter with the Jews? Did they move their children from al-Naṭā?" He said, "They stripped it in order to fight. They moved their children to al-Shiqq and al-Katība."

They said: Then the Messenger of God invited him to Islam. He replied: Grant me a few days. In the morning the Messenger of God went with the Muslims to al-Naṭā, and God conquered the fortress. He took out what the Jew said was in it, and ordered that the mangonel be put together and erected at al-Shiqq, at the wall of the fortress of al-Nizār. So they set it up, and aimed at al-Shiqq with stones until God conquered it for them. When the Messenger of God reached it he pelted the fortress with pebbles that sank in the ground, until he captured its people. The Jew's wife was brought out, and her name was Nufayla, and he pushed her to the Jew.

When the Messenger of God had conquered Waṭīḥ and Sulālim the Jew converted to Islam. Then he set out from Khaybar and he was not mentioned. His name was Simāk.

When the Messenger of God reached the fortress of Nāʿim in al-Naṭā he arranged his companions in a row, and prohibited them from [Page 649] fighting until he granted them permission, but a man from the Ashjaʿī proceeded to attack the Jews. So Marḥab attacked him and killed him. The People said, "O Messenger of God so and so is martyred!" The Messenger of God said, "Did I not forbid the fighting?" They said, "Yes." The Messenger of God commanded a herald to call out, "There is no place in Paradise for the disobedient." Then the Messenger of God permitted the fighting, and he encouraged it. The Muslims prepared to fight.

Now, Yasār al-Ḥabashī was a black slave belonging to ʿĀmir the Jew and cared for the sheep of his master. When he saw the people of Khaybar fortifying themselves and fighting, he asked them, and they said, "We fight this man who claims that he is a prophet." He said: And that word fell in my soul. And he approached with his sheep and drove them to the Messenger of God. He said, "O Muḥammad, what do you say? What are you calling us to?" He replied, "I am inviting you to Islam, and to witness that there is only one God and that I am His messenger." He said, "And what is for me?" He replied, "Paradise if you affirm it." He said, "I submit." He said, "Indeed these sheep of mine are a debt." The Prophet said, "Take them out of the camp and shout at them, and throw stones at them. Surely God most high will convey them from you and protect you." The slave did so and the sheep went back to their master, and the Jew knew that his slave had converted to Islam.

The Messenger of God preached to the people, and divided the flags among them. There were three flags, and there was not a flag before the day of Khaybar. Rather they were banners. The flag of the Prophet was black, and made from ʿĀ'isha's cloak. It was called ʿUqāb. His banner was white. He handed a flag to ʿAlī, a flag to Ḥubāb b. al-Mundhir, and a flag to Saʿd b. ʿUbāda. ʿAlī set out with the flag. The black slave followed him and fought until he was killed. He was carried and brought into one of the tents in the camp. The Messenger of God examined him [Page 650] in the tent. He said, "Surely God was gracious to this black slave and dispatched him at Khaybar. Islam was truly from his soul. I saw two wives from the Ḥūri at his head."

They said: A man from the Banū Murra called Abū Shuyaym says: I was with the soldiers who were with ʿUyayna of the Ghaṭafān who had come to help the Jews. We alighted in Khaybar but we did not enter a fortress. The Messenger of God sent a message to ʿUyayna b. Ḥiṣn who was the head of the Ghaṭafān and their leader, saying, "Return with those who are with you, and you shall have half the dates of Khaybar this year, for indeed God has promised me Khaybar." ʿUyayna said, "I am neither an ally nor a neighbor of the Muslims." While we were thus standing with ʿUyayna we heard shouting, and we did not know whether it came from the heavens or the earth. "Your poeple, your people in Hayfāʾ." Three shouts. "Surely you should go to them!"

Some say that when Kināna b. Abī l-Ḥuqayq went to them they made a pact with him, for ʿUyayna b. Ḥiṣn was their leader, and they numbered four thousand. They entered with the Jews into the fortress of Naṭā before the Messenger of God arrived three days later. When the Messenger of God arrived in Khaybar, he sent Saʿd b. ʿUbāda to them while they were in the fortress. When Saʿd reached the fortress he called to them saying, "I desire to speak to ʿUyayna b. Ḥiṣn." ʿUyayna desired to bring him into the fortress but Marḥab said, "Do not bring him in for he will see the cracks in our fortress and know from which direction he should come. But go out to him." ʿUyayna said, "Indeed I would like to bring him and show him its fortifications and its many numbers." Marḥab refused to let him enter, so ʿUyayna set out to the gate of the fortress. Saʿd said, "The Messenger of God sent me to you saying: God has surely promised me Khaybar so return and desist. If we are victorious over them, you shall have the dates of Khaybar for a year." But ʿUyayna said, "By God, we will not submit our allies for anything. Indeed we know what you have, and that you are incapable of overpowering us here. [Page 651] These are a community, a people of forbidding fortresses, and numerous men and weapons. If you stay you will destroy those with you. If you desire to fight they will hasten to you with men and weapons. No, by God, these are, unlike the Quraysh, a people who will march to you. If they obtain heedlessness from you, that is what they desire, if not, they will turn back. They will deceive you about the war and lengthen it for you until you become tired of them." Saʿd b. ʿUbāda said, "I testify that he will attend to you in this fortress of yours, until you seek what we offered you, and we will give you only the sword. You saw, O ʿUyayna, who we dissolved in his courtyard among the Jews of Yathrib. How they were destroyed, every shred!" Saʿd returned to the Messenger of God and informed him of what he said. Saʿd said, "O Messenger of God, surely God will fulfill for you what he promised you and make His religion victorious. Do not give these Bedouin a single date, O Messenger of God. When the sword takes him he will flee to his land, just as he did before, on the day of al-Khandaq."

The Messenger of God commanded his companions to march to the fortress in which were the Ghaṭafān. That was late in the evening [*ʿIsha*ʾ] when they were in the fortress of Nāʿim. A herald of the Messenger of God called out, "Appear with your flags at the fortress of Naʿim in which are the Ghaṭafān." He said: They were terrified about that, day and night. And later on, that night, they heard someone shout, they did not know from heaven or from earth, "O people of the Ghaṭafān, your families, your families. Help, help, in Ḥayfāʾ." It shouted thrice—"There is no land nor wealth!" He said: the Ghaṭafān set out to difficult and easy affairs. It was an affair God made for His Prophet.

When they rose, Kināna was informed while he was in al-Katība about their turning back, and he was bewildered and humiliated, and he became convinced of the destruction. He said, "We were deceived by those Bedouin. Indeed we marched with them and they promised us victory, and they deceived us. By my life, if they had not promised us their help we would not have opposed Muḥammad with war. [Page 652] We forgot the words of Sallām b. Abī l-Ḥuqayq when he said: We will never seek assistance from those Bedouin, for surely we have experienced them. He brought them along to help the Banū Qurayẓa but they deceived them. We did not see them show loyalty to us. Ḥuyayy b. Akhṭab had marched with them and they began to seek peace from Muḥammad. Then Muḥammad marched to the Banū Qurayẓa, and the Ghaṭafān were revealed returning to their families."

They said: When the Ghaṭafān reached their families in Ḥayfā' they found their families as before. They said, "Did something frighten you?" They said, "By God, no!" They said, "Surely, we thought that you had captured booty, but we see you have neither plunder nor profit." ʿUyayna said to his companions, "This, by God, is one of the tricks of Muḥammad and his companions. He misled us, by God." Ḥārith b. ʿAwf said to him, "With what thing?" ʿUyayna said, "We were in the fortress of Naṭā after the quiet, when we heard a voice shout, we do not know if it came from the heavens or the earth: 'Your people, your people, in Ḥayfā'—three shouts—there is no property nor wealth.'" Al-Ḥārith b. ʿAwf said, "O ʿUyayna, surely you let slip what you could have taken advantage of. By God, what you heard was surely from the heavens. By God, Muḥammad will be victorious over those who oppose him. Even if the mountains oppose him, he will grasp from them what he desires."

ʿUyayna stayed for several days with his family, then, he called his companions to set out to help the Jews. Al-Ḥārith b. ʿAwf came to him and said, "O ʿUyayna, listen to me and stay in your home, and give up helping the Jews. I do not see you return to Khaybar except Muḥammad will take it and there will be no protection for you." But ʿUyayna refused to listen. He said, "I will not submit my allies for anything."

When ʿUyayna turned back to his family, the Messenger of God attacked the fortresses, fortress by fortress. The Messenger of God reached the fortresses of Nāʿim with the Muslims. The fortresses of Nāʿim were numerous. The Jews aimed at that time with arrows. The companions of the Messenger of God shielded the Messenger of God.

[Page 653] At that time the Messenger of God wore two armors, cap and helmet, and he was on a horse named al-Ẓarib. In his hand was a spear and shield. His companions surrounded him. He gave a flag to a man from the Muhājirūn, and he returned without accomplishing anything. Then he gave the flag to another, and he returned without accomplishing anything. Then, the Messenger of God gave the flag of the Anṣār to one of the Anṣār and he set out and returned without accomplishing anything. The Messenger of God incited the Muslims. A squadron of Jews went by, led by al-Ḥārith Abū Zaynab, and they destroyed the earth badly. The keeper of the Anṣārī flag approached and he continued to drive them until they reached the fortress and entered it. Usayr the Jew set out ahead of his companions taking his runners with him, and he removed the flag of the Anṣār until he reached the Messenger of God in his position.

The Messenger of God felt a sharp anger within himself. He reminded them of what God had promised them. The Messenger of God spent the evening feeling anxious. Saʿd b. ʿUbāda had returned wounded and he made his companions wait. The flag-holder of the Muhājrūn made his companions wait. He says, "You, you." The Messenger of God said, "Indeed, Satan came to the Jews, and said to them, 'Muḥammad is fighting you for your property,' so call out to them. Say, 'There is no God but one,' and protect your wealth and your blood for your reckoning is with God." He called to them thus, and the Jews called out, "We will not act nor leave the covenant of Moses, and the Torah that is among us."

The Messenger of God said, "Tomorrow I will give the flag to someone that God and His messenger loves, and God will conquer through him for he will not flee. Rejoice, O Muḥammad b. Maslama, for tomorrow if God wills, the battle of your brother will be fought and the Jews will flee." [Page 654] In the morning the Messenger of God sent for ʿAlī b. Abī Ṭālib, who had an eye infection. He said, "I cannot see either valley or mountain." He said: The Prophet went to him and said, "Open your eyes." And when he opened them, and the Prophet spat on them ʿAlī said: I have had no eye disease since that time. The Messenger of God handed him the flag, and prayed for him and those who were with him from his companions, to be victorious.

The first of those who set out to them was al-Ḥārith, the brother of Marḥab, with the runners. The Muslims appeared, and ʿAlī jumped and struck hard, and ʿAlī killed him. The companions of al-Ḥārith returned to the fortress, entered and locked themselves in. Then Marḥab came out saying, "Khaybar knows that I am Marḥab with the piercing weapons, a proven brave. I strike occasionally and at other times I am struck." ʿAlī attacked him and pulled at the door and opened it. There were two doors to the fortress. Ibn Abī Sabra related to me from Khālid b. Rabāḥ from an old man of the Banū Sāʿida. They said: Abū Dujāna killed al-Ḥārith Abū Zaynab. He was at that time marked by a red turban. Al-Ḥārith wore a mark above his helmet. Yāsir, ʿĀmir and Usayr were also marked.

Ibn Abī Sabra related to me from ʿAmr b. Abī ʿAmr, who said: I alighted in Arīḥā/Jericho in the time of Sulaymān b. ʿAbd al-Malik, and there was a district for the Jews. There was a man who grumbled about his old age. He said: From where are you? We said: From the Ḥijāz. The Jew said: I long for the Ḥijāz. I am the son of al-Ḥārith the Jew, the knight of Khaybar. A man from the companions of Muḥammad killed him on the day of Khaybar, saying, "I am Abū Dujāna," on the day Muḥammad alighted in Khaybar. We were among those whom ʿUmar b. al-Khaṭṭāb expelled to al-Shām. I said: Did you not convert? He said: Indeed, it would have been better for me if I did. [Page 655] But the Jews would have compared me, saying, "Your father, O son of a leader of the Jews, would never leave Judaism. Your father was killed for it and you will differ from him?"

Abū Rāfiʿ said: We were with ʿAlī when the Prophet sent him with the flag. ʿAlī met a man at the gate of the fortress. The man struck ʿAlī, and ʿAlī protected himself with the shield. Then ʿAlī took a door, which was in the fortress, and shielded himself with it. The door stayed in his hand until God conquered the fortress for him. He sent a man to announce to the Prophet that they had taken the fortress and were entering it. It was the fortress of Marḥab. It was said: Marḥab appeared like a competing stallion reciting rajaz verse:

> Khaybar knows that I am Marḥab of the piercing weapons,
> A proven brave, I will strike sometimes, and sometimes will be struck.

He called for a duel. Muḥammad b. Maslama said, "O Messenger of God, I am a wronged and angry person. My brother was killed yesterday, so permit me to fight Marḥab for he is the killer of my brother." The Messenger of God permitted him to duel. He prayed for him and gave him his sword. Muḥammad went out shouting, "O Marḥab, did you call for a duel?" He said, "Yes." Marḥab came out to him reciting rajaz:

> Khaybar knows that I am Marḥab

And, Muḥammad b. Maslama went out saying:

Khaybar knows that I am sharp,
sweet when I wish, and poisonous to the end.

He says: At that time he composed the rajaz saying:

O my soul, if you do not kill, you will die.
I have no patience left after Abū Nubayt.

It was his brother Maḥmūd who was called Abū Nubayt. He said: Each of them came out to his companion. He said: There was situated between them a group of trees. Its roots were like the roots of the date palm [Page 656] and its branches were strange. Meanwhile one of them struck his companion who was hidden behind the ʿUshar tree until they cut every branch of it, while its roots remained standing like a man. Each one of them reached for his companion and Marḥab surprised Muḥammad, raising his sword to strike him. Muḥammad met him with his shield but his sword stuck fast to its scabbard. Marhab was wearing armor that was rolled up. Muḥammad struck the thighs of Marhab and cut them. It was said: Muḥammad b. Maslama protected himself with the shield—the armor from Marḥab's legs was pulled up when he raised his hand with the sword, and Muḥammad bent with the sword and cut his two legs, and Marḥab fell. Marḥab said, "Finish me off, O Muḥammad!" Muḥammad replied, "Taste death, just as my brother Maḥmūd tasted it!" and he walked past him. Then ʿAlī passed by and struck off his head, and took his booty.

They quarreled before the Messenger of God about his booty. Muḥammad b. Maslama said, "O Messenger of God, surely I cut off his legs and left him only that he may taste the bitterness of the sword and the violence of death just as my brother did, for he stayed three days dying. Nothing prevented me from finishing him off. I could have finished him off after I cut his legs." ʿAlī said, "He is truthful. I cut off his head after his legs had been cut off." The Messenger of God gave Muḥammad b. Maslama Marhab's sword, shield, cap and helmet. The family of Muḥammad b. Maslama has his sword, and with it a document—no one knew what it was until one of the Jews of Tayma read it. It said: This is the sword of Marḥab. Whoever tastes it will die.

Muḥammad b. al-Faḍl related to me from his father from Jābir, and Zakariyya b. Zayd related to me from ʿAbdullah b. Abī Sufyān, from his father, from Salama b. Salāma; and Mujammiʿ [Page 657] b. Yaʿqūb from his father from Mujammiʿ b. Ḥāritha. They all said that Muḥammad b. Maslama killed Marḥab.

They said: Usayr appeared. He was a strong man though he was short, and he began to shout, "Is there anyone for a duel?" Muḥammad b. Maslama went out to him and they exchanged strokes and Muḥammad b. Maslama killed him. Then Yāsir came out. He was among the vigorous. He had a spear to keep back the Muslims. ʿAlī went out to him and al-Zubayr said, "I entreat you leave him to me." So ʿAlī did. Yasir approached with his spear and drove the people with it. Al-Zubayr duelled him. Ṣafiyya said, "O Messenger of God, it makes me sad. My son will be killed, O Messenger of God." He said, "Rather your son will kill him." He said: They fought each other and al-Zubayr killed him. The Messenger of God said to him, "May your ransom be your uncle and aunt." Then he added, "To every prophet is a disciple, and al-Zubayr is my disciple, and the son of my aunt."

When Marḥab and Yasir were killed the Messenger of God said, "Rejoice! Khaybar welcomes and facilitates." Then ʿĀmir came out: He was a tall man. When ʿĀmir appeared, the Messenger of God said, "Do you think he is five arm lengths?" He called for a duel, brandishing his sword. He wore armor covered in iron. He shouted, "Who will contest me?" The people recoiled from him. ʿAlī went out to him and struck him. But all that did nothing until he struck his legs. Then he fell down, and ʿAlī finished him off and took his weapons.

Al-Ḥārith, Marḥab, Usayr, Yāsir, and ʿĀmir were killed with many people from the Jews—[Page 658] but those who were named were mentioned because they were the brave ones. Those were all in the fortress of Nāʿim.

When Maḥmūd b. Maslama was struck in the fortress of Nāʿim he was carried to al-Rajīʿ and he stayed three days dying. He who struck Maḥmūd was Marḥab. Maḥmūd began to say to his brother, "O brother, the daughters of your brother can neither seek booty nor ask the people." Muḥammad b. Maslama says, "If you do not leave property, I have property." Maḥmūd had more property—but inheritance for daughters was not revealed at that time. Maḥmūd died on the third day, and it was the day on which Marḥab was killed.

The Messenger of God said, "Who is the man who will inform Maḥmūd that God has revealed the daughter's right to inheritance, and that Muḥammad b. Maslama has killed his killer?" Juʿāl b. Surāqa set out to inform him and he was happy about that. Maḥmūd commanded him to extend his greetings to the Messenger of God. He said: I conveyed to him greetings from the Messenger of God and Maḥmūd said, "I did not think he would remember me." The Messenger of God was spending the night in a place in al-Rajīʿ, when Maḥmūd died, away from him. When the Messenger of God returned to al-manzila, ʿĀmir b. al-Akwaʿ had hurt himself and was brought to al-Rajīʿ, where he died. ʿĀmir was buried with Maḥmūd in a cave. Muḥammad said, "O Messenger of God, grant me some land by the grave of my brother." He replied, "To you is the extent of a horse's run; and if you work, it shall be doubled."

The fortress of al-Ṣaʿb b. Muʿādh was in al-Naṭā. Within the fortress of the Jew were food, fat, cattle and utensils. There were five hundred soldiers in it. The people (Muslims) had stayed for days fighting, but the only food they ate was al-ʿAlaf. Muʿattib al-Aslamī said: [Page 659] We were a people of the Aslam, destitute when we arrived in Khaybar. We stayed ten days at the fortress of Naṭā and we did not eat any food. The Aslam sent for Asmāʾ b. Ḥaritha and said, "Go to Muḥammad, the Messenger of God, and say that the Aslam extend to you greetings, and inform him that we are exhausted from hunger and weakness." Burayda b. al-Ḥuṣayb said, "By God, I never saw such an affair as today, and Arabs doing this!" Hind bt. Ḥāritha said, "By God, we hoped that a mission to the Messenger of God would be a key for the better." So Asmāʾ b. Ḥāritha came to him and said, "O Messenger of God the Aslam say: Surely we are exhausted from hunger and weakness, so ask God for us." The Messenger of God prayed for them and said, "By God, there is nothing in my hands that I can hand them." Then he shouted with the people and said, "O God, open for them the greatest fortress containing more food and more fat." Then he handed the flag to al-Ḥubāb b. al-Mundhir b. al-Jamūḥ, and he charged the people, and we did not return until God conquered the fortress of al-Ṣaʿb b. Muʿādh for us.

Umm Muṭāʿ al-Aslamiyya, who said that she had witnessed Khaybar with the Messenger of God and other women, said: Indeed I saw the Aslam when they complained to the Messenger of God of the misfortune of their situation. The Messenger of God charged the people and the people rose. I saw the Aslam were the first to reach the fortress of al-Ṣaʿb b. Muʿādh in which were five hundred soldiers. The sun did not set on that day until God conquered it. There was brave fighting. A man from the Jews named Yawshaʿ appeared and called for a duel. Ḥubāb b. al-Mundhir duelled him. They exchanged strokes and Ḥubāb killed him. Another appeared named al-Zayyāl. ʿUmāra b. ʿUqba al-Ghifārī appeared unexpectedly and duelled him. Al-Ghifārī struck him a blow on the crown of his head. He says, "Take this, and I am the youth al-Ghifārī." The People said, "His *jihād* was erased by these words." It reached the Messenger of God [Page 660] and he said, "There is nothing wrong with it. He will be rewarded and praised."

Abū l-Yasar used to narrate that they besieged the fortress of al-Ṣaʿb b. Muʿādh for three days. It was a forbidding fortress. Sheep belonging to a man from the Jews approached to graze behind their fortress, and the Messenger of God said, "Who is the man who will feed us from these sheep?" I said, "I, O Messenger of God." I went out running like a gazelle, and when the Messenger of God saw me turn, he said, "O God, let us enjoy it." I reached the sheep, the first of which had entered the fortress, took two sheep from the rear and clasped them under my arms. Then, I approached, running as though I had nothing with me, and brought them to the Messenger of God. The Messenger of God ordered that they be slaughtered, and then he apportioned them. There did not remain one of the people of the camp who had besieged the fortress with him, but he ate from it. It was said to Abū l-Yasar: How many were there? He replied: There were many. It was said: where are the rest of the people? He says: In al-Rajīʿ in the camp. Abū l-Yasar was heard—he was a very old man—crying about something that angered him about some of his children. He said: By my life, I remain after my companions; they enjoyed with me, but I do not enjoy with them; referring to the words of the Messenger of God, "O God, let us enjoy it." He remains among the last of them.

Abū Ruhm al-Ghifārī used to relate: A great hunger came to us, as we alighted in Khaybar at the time for the dates. The very hot land and dwellings dry them. Meanwhile we were besieging the fortress of al-Saʿb b. Muʿādh. Twenty or thirty donkeys came out, and the Jews were not able to take them back inside. Their fortress was impenetrable. The Muslims took the donkeys and slaughtered them. [Page 661] They lit fires and cooked the meat in pots. The Muslims were starving. The Messenger of God passed by them while they were in that situation, and asked and commanded a herald to announce, "The Messenger of God forbids you from eating domesticated donkeys—He said: So they overturned the pots—from pleasure marriages with women, and from all animals that possess a sharp tooth or claw."

Ibn Abī Sabra related to me from al-Fuḍayl b. Mubashshir. He said: Jābir b. ʿAbdullah used to say, the Messenger of God fed us the flesh of the horse. People from the Muslims slaughtered one of the horses before they took the fortress of al-Ṣaʿb b. Muʿādh. It was said to Jābir, "What about the mules? Have you eaten them?" He said, "No." Ibn Abī Sabra related to me from ʿAbd al-Raḥmān b. ʿAbdullah b. Abī Ṣaʿṣaʿa from al-Ḥārith b. ʿAbdūllah b. Kaʿb from Umm ʿUmāra, who said: We slaughtered two horses in Khaybar for the Banū Māzin b. Najjār. We ate that before we took the fortress of al-Ṣaʿb b. Muʿādh.

Thawr b. Yazīd related to me from Ṣāliḥ b. Yaḥyā b. al-Miqdām, from his father from his grandfather, who said: I heard Khālid b. al-Walīd say: I attended the Messenger of God in Khaybar and he said, "Eating of the domesticated donkey, horse, and mule is forbidden." They said: And all that possess teeth of the beast of prey, and claws of the bird are forbidden. Al-Wāqidī said: I have confirmed among ourselves that Khālid did not witness Khaybar, for he converted just before al-Fatḥ. He and ʿAmr b. al-ʿĀṣ, and ʿUthmān b. Ṭalḥa b. Abī Ṭalḥa, converted on the first day of Ṣafar in the year eight AH.

Ibn al-Akwaʿ used to say: We were at the fortress of al-Ṣaʿb b. Muʿādh, and the Aslam had gathered there. The Muslims besieged the people of the fortress. Indeed, I saw us, and the master of our flag, Saʿd b. ʿUbāda. The Muslims were retreating. Then, Saʿd took the flag and we went with him. In the morning, ʿĀmir b. Sinān met a man from the Jews, and the Jew unexpectedly struck ʿĀmir. ʿĀmir said: [Page 662] I protected myself from him with my shield, for the sword of the Jew bounced off from it. ʿĀmir said: I struck the leg of the Jew and cut it. The Jew returned the sword against ʿĀmir, but its tip cut him (the Jew), and he bled profusely and died. Usayd b. Ḥuḍayr said that ʿĀmir's work was futile. His words reached the Messenger of God, and he said, "Whoever said that, lied. Indeed he will be recompensed. He was a brave warrior, and he will float into Paradise and enter every part of it."

Khālid b. Ilyās related to me from Jaʿfar b. Maḥmūd b. Muḥammad from Muḥammad b. Maslama, who said: I was with those who were shielding the Prophet. I began to shout with his companions, "Aim at the leather shields." They did, and they aimed at us, until I thought they would not give up. Then, I saw the Messenger of God aim with an arrow. He did not miss a man among them. The Messenger of God smiled at me. The Muslims opened, and entered the fortress.

Ibn Abī Sabra related to me from Isḥaq b. ʿAbdullah b. Abī Farwa from ʿAbd al-Raḥmān b. Jābir b. ʿAbdullah from his father. He said: When we reached the fortress of al-Ṣaʿb b. Muʿādh, the Muslims were very hungry, and the food, all of it, was in the fortress. Al-Ḥubāb b. al-Mundhir b. al-Jamūḥ attacked with us, while holding our flag, and the Muslims followed him. We stayed there for two days fighting them fiercely. When it was the third day, the Messenger of God set out to them early in the morning, and one of the Jews came out appearing like a ship's mast, carrying a spear in his hand. He set out with a group of runners and they aimed arrows for a while, swiftly. We shielded the Messenger of God [Page 663] and they rained arrows on us. Their arrows were like the locust, until I thought they would not give up. They attacked us as a single man. The Muslims were retreating until they reached the Messenger of God who was standing. He had alighted from his horse and Midʿam held it, while al-Ḥubāb stayed with the flag. By God, he did not stop shooting at them from his horse. The Messenger of God charged the Muslims, and encouraged them to *jihād*, and excited them with it. He informed them that God had promised him Khaybar and that he would plunder it for them. The people approached together until they returned to the keeper of their flag. Al-Ḥubāb marched with them continuing to draw closer little by little. The Jews returned to their retreat until evil overwhelmed them and they withdrew swiftly. They entered the fortress and locked it upon themselves. They appeared on the walls, and it had a wall outside the wall, and they began to aim at us with stones, throwing many. We moved away from their fortress with the falling of the stones until we returned to the original site of al-Ḥubāb.

Then the Jews began to blame each other among themselves. They said, "Why do we preserve ourselves? The people of determination and patience were killed in the fortress of Nāʿim." They set out seeking death, and we returned to them. We fought each other at the gate of the fortress, fiercely. Three of the companions of the Prophet were killed at the gate of the fortress. There was Abū Ṣayyāḥ who had witnessed Badr. A man from them struck him with the sword and whisked the cap off his head. There was ʿAdī b. Murra b. Surāqa; one of them stabbed him between his breasts with a spear and he died. The third was al-Ḥārith b. Ḥāṭib who had witnessed Badr. A man from above the fortress aimed at him and broke his head.

We killed many of them at the fortress. Whenever we killed one of their men, they carried him back into the fortress. Then the master of the flag attacked and we attacked with him. We entered the Jewish fortress and followed them to its interior. Once we entered their fortress, they were like sheep. We killed those who appeared before us, and took prisoners from them.

[Page 664] They fled in every direction riding the *ḥarra*—the lavas—desiring the fortress castle of al-Zubayr. We let them flee. The Muslims ascended its walls while proclaiming "God is great," many times (*takbīr*s). We weakened the force of the Jews with the *takbīr*. Indeed I saw youths from the Aslam and Ghifār above the fortress proclaim *takbīr*. We found, by God, from the foods, what we did not think was there: barley, and dates, and ghee, honey, oil and fat. The herald of the Messenger of God called out, "Eat and feed your cattle but do not take away." He says: Do not take it to your land. The Muslims were taking food from that fortress for their stay and for their riding beasts. No one was forbidden to take his needs but the food was not apportioned.

They found clothes and glass in the fortress. They were commanded to break the jars of alcohol. They were broke them until the alcohol dripped all over the fortress. The jars were large and it was not possible to carry them. Abū Thaʿlaba al-Khushanī used to say, "We found in it containers of brass and clay." The Jews used to eat and drink with them. We asked the Messenger of God and he said, "Wash it and cook and eat and drink with it." He said, "Heat water in it and cook after. Eat and drink." We took many sheep, cattle and donkeys from there. We also took many tools of war, a mangonel and many wooden vessels. We knew that they thought that the siege would be forever, but God hastened their humiliation.

ʿAbd al-Ḥamīd b. Jaʿfar related to me from his father, who said: There went out from one of the fortresses of al-Ṣaʿb b. Muʿādh, twenty bundles of cloth, packages of coarse goods from Yemen, and one thousand five hundred pieces of velvet. Every man arrived with velvet for his family. They found ten loads of wood. It was commanded that the wood be taken out of the fortress and burnt. [Page 665] They took several days to burn. The jars of alcohol were broken, and the skins of wine, spilled. One of the Muslims came, at that time, and drank from the wine and the issue was raised before the Messenger of God. He detested it—when he was brought before him, he beat him with a sandal, and those who were present beat him with their sandals. He was named ʿAbdullah the Alcoholic. He was a man who could not abstain from drink, and the Prophet struck him several times. ʿUmar b. al-Khaṭṭāb said, "God curse him! How often must he be beaten!" The Messenger of God said, "O ʿUmar, do not say that, for indeed he loves God and His messenger." He said: Then ʿAbdullah relaxed and sat down with them as though he were one of them.

Ibn Abī Sabra related to me from ʿAbd al-Raḥmān b. ʿAbdullah b. Abī Ṣaʿṣaʿa from al-Ḥārith b. ʿAbdullah b. Kaʿb from Umm ʿUmāra. She said: We found in the fortress of al-Ṣaʿb b. Muʿādh, food—I did not think could be there in Khaybar. The Muslims were able to eat during their stay for months and more than that, from the fortress, and feed their animals. No one was prevented, and there was no taking of the fifth. I took out from the cloth many things to sell in al-Miqsam. There were beads from the beads of the Jews. It was said to her, "Who is it that will purchase it in al-Miqsam?" She said,

"The Muslims, the Jews in al-Katība who have converted, and those Bedouin who are present." And all of those bought. As for those Muslims who purchased beads, it was deducted as booty.

Al-Wāqidī said: Ibn Abī Sabra related to me from Isḥāq b. ʿAbdullah. He said: When ʿUyayna b. Ḥiṣn looked at the fortress of al-Ṣaʿb b. Muʿādh, and observed the Muslims transfer the food, fodder and cloth from it, he said, "Not one provided us and our animals and fed us from this perishing food; and its former owners were so generous!" And the Muslims scolded him and said, [Page 666] "For you is what the Prophet provides, obstinate one, so be silent!" Meanwhile the Muslims roamed the fortress of al-Ṣaʿb b. Muʿādh, and it had entrances. They brought out a Jew, and cut off his head, and were surprised at the blackness of his blood. One of them says, "I have never seen such black blood." He said: A speaker says, "One of those shelves holds garlic and broth," and so the Jew was revealed. They brought him forward and cut off his head.

The Jews of the fortress of Nāʿim, all of them, those from the fortress of al-Ṣaʿb b. Muʿādh, and those from every fortress in Naṭā were transferred to a fortress named Qalʿat al-Zubayr. The Messenger of God and the Muslims marched to them. They besieged them and imprisoned them in their fortress, which was inaccessible. Indeed it was on the top of a rock and neither horse nor man could ascend it, for it was inaccessible. The rest stayed, and there is no mention of them, in the fortress of al-Naṭā—but a man or two. The Messenger of God placed men in front of them to keep watch over them. A Jew did not appear before them but they killed him. The Messenger of God stayed besieging those who were in Qalʿat al- Zubayr for three days.

A man from the Jews named Ghazzāl arrived. He said, "Abū Qāsim, grant me protection and I will lead you to what will relieve you from the people of al-Naṭā and you will go out to the people of al-Shiqq, for indeed the people of al-Shiqq are destroyed from fear of you." He said: The Messenger of God granted security to him, his family and his property.

The Jew said, "If you stayed a month they would not care, for they have streams under the earth. They would go out at night, drink there and return to their fortress [Page 667], which is inaccessible to you. But if you cut off their water, they will be distressed." The Messenger of God went to their streams and stopped them. When he stopped their drinking source they were not able to stay thirsty. They set out and fought a strong battle. A few Muslims were killed, at that time, and ten Jews were taken that day. The Messenger of God conquered it and it was the last of the fortresses of Naṭā.

When the Messenger of God finished with Naṭā he commanded that they transfer, and the troops move from their station in al-Rajīʿ back to al-Manzilo. The Messenger of God was protected from night attacks, the war of the Jews, and what he feared from them. The people of Naṭā were the most violent of the Jews and the people of the Najd were among them. Then the Messenger of God moved to the people of al-Shiqq.

Mūsā b. ʿUmar al-Ḥārithī related to me from Abū ʿUfayr Muḥammad b. Sahl b. Abī Ḥathma, who said: when the Messenger of God moved to al-Shiqq, which possessed numerous fortresses, the first fortress he started at was the fortress of Ubayy. The Messenger of God stood before a fortress (*qalʿa*) called Sumrān. He fought a severe battle against the people of the fortress. A man from the Jews named Ghazzāl came out and called for a duel. Al-Ḥubāb b. al-Mundhir duelled with him and they exchanged blows. Then Ḥubāb attacked him and cut off his right hand from the middle of his arm. The sword fell from the hand of Ghazzāl and he was defenseless. He returned defeated to the fortress. Al-Ḥubāb followed him and cut his Achilles tendon. Ghazzāl fell down, and al-Ḥubāb finished him off.

Then another came out shouting, "Who will duel with me?" A man from the Muslims from the family of Jaḥsh dueled him and the Jaḥshī was killed. The Jew stayed in his place inviting another challenger [Page 668] and Abū Dujāna who wore a red band wrapped around his head above his skull cap, answered him with a conceited swagger. Abū Dujāna took the Jew unawares and cut his legs; then he finished him off and took his booty: his armor and his sword. He brought it to the Prophet, and the Messenger of God gave them to him.

After that, they refrained from dueling. The Muslims proclaimed *takbīr*, attacked the fortress and entered it, and Abū Dujāna led them. They found in it furniture, property, cattle and food. The warriors who were in it fled. They jumped the walls like gazelles until they came to the fortress of al-Nizār in al-Shiqq. Those who remained from the highest peaks of al-Naṭā kept coming to the fortress of al-Nizār, and they became attached to it and fortified themselves in it. The Messenger of God marched to them with his companions and fought them. They were the strongest people of al-Shiqq who fought. They aimed at the Muslims with arrows and stones. The Messenger of God was with them until the arrow grabbed the garment of the Messenger of God and hung in it. He took the arrow and gathered it. Then he took a handful of pebbles and threw them at their fortress. It trembled with that and then sank to the ground.

Ibrāhīm b. Jaʿfar said: It was leveled to the ground when the Muslims came, and they took its people completely. In it were Ṣafiyya the daughter of Ḥuyayy and the daughter of her Uncle. ʿUmayr, the *mawlā* of Abū l-Laḥm used to say: I saw Ṣafiyya brought with her cousin [Page 669] and the young girls from the fortress of al-Nizār. When the Messenger of God conquered the fortress of al-Nizār, some fortresses in al-Shiqq remained. The people there fled until they reached the people of al-Katība, Waṭīḥ, and Sulālim. Muḥammad b. Maslama used to say, the Messenger of God looked at the fortress of al-Nizār and said, "This is the last fortress of Khaybar in which there will be fighting." After we took this fortress there was no more fighting until the Messenger of God set out from Khaybar.

ʿAbd al-Raḥman b. Muḥammad b. Abī Bakr related to me, saying: I said to Jaʿfar b. Maḥmūd: How did Ṣafiyya come to be in the fortress of al-Nizār in al-Shiqq, when the fortress of the family of Abū l-Ḥuqayq was in Sulālim? One did not take prisoners from the women and children from the fortress of Naṭā or al-Shiqq. Only from the fortress of al-Nizār. Were there indeed women and children in it? He replied. The Jews of Khaybar sent the women and children out to al-Katība, and emptied the fortress of Naṭā, because of the fighting. No female prisoner was taken from them except for those who were in the fortress of al-Nizār. They were Ṣafiyya, her cousin, and the young girls. Kināna had considered the fortress of al-Nizār to be the most fortified of what was there, so he brought her in the night, on the morning of which the Messenger of God transferred to al-Shiqq, in order that she be imprisoned with her cousin and the children of the Jews. In al-Katība there were more than two thousand Jews, their women and children. When the Messenger of God made peace with the people of al-Katība he granted protection to the men and children, and in return they gave him property, silver, gold, weapons, and garments—other than those worn by the people. Indeed those Jews to whom the Messenger of God granted protection came and went, and sold and bought. Indeed, the people made a profit out of the garments [Page 670] and goods, but they concealed their cash and the source of their wealth.

They said: Then the Messenger of God moved to al-Katība, al-Waṭīḥ, Sulālim, and the fortresses of Ibn Abī l-Ḥuqayq in which the Jews had fortified themselves thoroughly. All who fled and were defeated from al-Naṭā and al-Shiqq came to them, and they were fortified with them in al-Qamūṣ in al-Katība, which was a forbidding fortress, and in al-Waṭīḥ and Sulālim. They did not come out of these fortresses, but locked themselves inside.

The Messenger of God decided to erect the mangonel when he saw that those who locked themselves in would not come out to challenge them. When they were convinced of the destruction, for the Messenger of God had besieged them for fourteen days, they asked the Messenger of God for peace. Abū ʿAbdullah said: I said to Ibrāhīm b. Jaʿfar, "Five hundred Arab bows were found in al-Katība," and he said, "My father informed me from those who saw, that Kināna Ibn Abī l-Ḥuqayq aimed three arrows at three hundred arm lengths," referring to the distance, that entered within a span of their target. And soon it was said, "Here is Muḥammad approaching with his companions from al-Shiqq." The people of Qamūṣ were prepared. They stood at the gate of the fortress with arrows. Kināna rose to his bow, but was not able to string it for trembling. He signaled to the people of the fortress, "Do not shoot," and he stayed in his fortress. Not one among them was seen until the attack strained them and God hurled fear into their hearts. Kināna sent a man from the Jews named Shammākh to the Prophet saying, "May I come to you and speak with you?" When Shammākh arrived, the Muslims brought him to the Prophet and he greeted him and he informed him of the message of Kināna, and he was gracious to him. Kināna arrived with a group of Jews and made a peace with the Prophet in accordance with his agreement, and contracted with him according to his terms. Ibrāhīm said that the bow and weapons belonged to the family of Abū l-Ḥuqayq and they hired them out to the Arabs. Their jewelry was also hired out to [Page 671] the Arabs. They were the most evil of the Jews of Yathrib.

They said: Kināna b. Abī l-Ḥuqayq sent a request to the Messenger of God, "May I come down and speak with you?" The Messenger of God said, "Yes." Ibn Abī l-Ḥuqayq came down and made an agreement with the Messenger of God, that he spare the blood of the soldiers who were in their fortress and leave their children for them. They set out from Khaybar and its land, with their children, and they relinquished all they possessed of property or land to the Messenger of God such as gold, silver, quivers, weapons, and cloth, except for the garments worn by the people.

The Messenger of God said: The protection of God and His messenger is relinquished from you if you conceal anything from me. And Ibn Abī l-Ḥuqayq agreed with him about that. The Messenger of God sent for the wealth and took it one by one. He sent for the chattels and the weapons and he kept them, and he found among the coats of mail a hundred coats, four hundred swords, a thousand spears, and five hundred bows with their quivers. The Messenger of God asked Kināna b. Abī l-Ḥuqayq about the treasure of the family of Abū l-Ḥuqayq, and the jewelry from their jewelry, and what there was of the skin of the camel. Their nobility was known by it. When there was a wedding in Mecca they would approach them; and the jewelry would be loaned to them for a month when it would be with them. That jewelry was with one lord after the other from the family of Abū l-Ḥuqayq. He replied, "O Abū l-Qasim, we spent it during our war and there does not remain anything from it. We saved it for such a day as this. The war and provisions for the warriors left nothing behind." They took an oath about that, and they affirmed their oath, and they strove. The Messenger of God said to him, [Page 672] "The protection of God and His prophet will be denied you if it is discovered with you." And he agreed. Then the Messenger of God said, "All that I took from your property and your blood is released to me, and there will be no protection for you!" He said, "Yes." Then the Messenger of God asked Abū Bakr, ʿUmar, ʿAlī and ten Jews to witness the agreement. A man from the Jews went to Kināna b. Abī l-Ḥuqayq and said, "If you have what Muḥammad is seeking from you or you know of it, inform him, for surely you will protect your blood. If not, by God, it will appear to him. He has come to know about other things we did not know." Ibn Abī l-Ḥuqayq scolded him, and the Jew stepped aside and sat down. Then the Messenger of God asked Thaʿlaba b. Sallām b. Abī l-Ḥuqayq, who was a weak man, about their treasure. He replied, "I only know that I used to see Kināna, every morning, go around these ruins," and he pointed to the ruins, "if there was something and he buried it, it is in there."

Kināna b. Abī l-Ḥuqayq had, when the Messenger of God was successful over Naṭā, ascertained the destruction. The people of Naṭā were taken by fear, and he went with the skin of the camel containing their jewelry, and he dug for it in the ruins by night and no one saw him. Then he leveled it with the dust of al-Katība. These were the ruins that Thaʿlaba saw him go around every morning.

The Prophet sent al-Zubayr b. al-Awwām and a group of Muslims with Thaʿlaba to those ruins. He dug where Thaʿlaba showed him, and he pulled out from it that treasure. Some say: Indeed God most high showed His messenger that treasure. When the treasure was taken out, the Messenger of God commanded al-Zubayr to hurt Kināna b. Abī l-Ḥuqayq until he revealed all that he had with him. Al-Zubayr hurt him: he came to him with a firebrand and pierced him in his chest. Then the Messenger of God commanded that he hand him to Muḥammad b. Maslama [Page 673] to kill him for his brother, and Muḥammad b. Maslama killed him. He commanded that the other Ibn Abī l-Ḥuqayq (the brother of Kināna) also be tortured and then handed over to the care of Bishr b. al-Barāʾ to be killed by him. Some say that he cut off his head. After that the Messenger of God felt he had the right to their property and imprisoned their children.

Khālid b. al-Rabīʿa b. Abī Hilāl related to me from Hilāl b. Usāma from one of those who observed what was in the skin of the camel, which was brought and laid before the Messenger of God. Most of it consisted of bracelets and bangles of gold, anklets, necklaces and earings of gold, a string of gems and emeralds, rings of gold, toe rings of onyx of Ẓafār dappled with gold. The Messenger of God saw an arrangement of jewelry and gave it to some of his family, either to ʿĀʾisha or one of his daughters. She accepted it but did not keep it for more than an hour of the day, when she divided it among the people of need and the widows. Abū al-Shahm bought bits of it. When it was evening the Messenger of God came to his bed and could not sleep. The next morning at breakfast he came to ʿĀʾisha—though it was not her night—or to his daughter, and said, "Return the jewelry for indeed it is not for me, and you have no right to it either." She informed him of what she had done with it. He praised God and went back.

Ṣafiyya bt. Ḥuyayy used to say: That was the necklace for the daughter of Kināna. Ṣafiyya was married to Kināna b. Abī l-Ḥuqayq. The Messenger of God had taken her prisoner before he reached al-Katība. The Messenger of God sent her with Bilāl to his ride. Bilāl passed by the killed with her and her cousin, and her cousin screamed. The Messenger of God detested what Bilāl did. He said, "Has graciousness left you that you take a young girl past the dead?" [Page 674] Bilāl said, "O Messenger of God, I did not think that you would hate that. I wanted her to see the destruction of her people." The Messenger of God said to the girl, "This is only a devil."

Diḥya al-Kalbī had seen Ṣafiyya and asked the Messenger of God for her. It was said that he had promised him a girl from those taken prisoner in Khaybar. He gave him Ṣafiyya's cousin. Ibn Abī Sabra related to me from Abū Ḥarmala, from his sister Umm ʿAbdullah from the daughter of Abū l-Qayn al-Muzannī, who said: Among the wives of the Prophet, I used to visit Ṣafiyya frequently. She told me about her people and what she heard from them. She said: We set out from Medina when the Messenger of God expelled us and we stayed in Khaybar. Kināna b. Abī l-Ḥuqayq married me and he was my husband for some days before the Messenger of God arrived. He moved me to his fortress in Sulālim where I saw in my sleep that the moon had approached from Yathrib and fallen in my lap. I mentioned that to Kināna, my husband, and he struck my eye and it turned green. The Messenger of God looked at it when I came to him and he asked me, and I informed him. She said: The Jews placed their children in al-Katība, and they emptied the fortress of Naṭā of their children.

When the Messenger of God arrived in Khaybar and took the fortresses of Naṭā, Kināna visited me and said, "Muḥammad has finished with Naṭā and there is not a single warrior here." The Jews were killed when the people of Naṭā were killed and the Arabs did not believe us. Then Kināna moved me to the fortress of al-Nizār in al-Shiqq. He said, "It is the most fortified of the fortresses that we still hold." He took me, my cousin, and the young girls, who were with us, and secured us in al-Nizār. The Messenger of God marched to us before al-Katība. I was taken prisoner from al-Nizār before the Prophet reached al-Katība. [Page 675] The Messenger of God sent me to his saddle, then he came to us in the evening and called to me. I came, modestly veiled, and sat before him. He said, "If you persist in your religion, I will not force you from it, but if you choose God and His messenger it will be better for you."

Ṣafiyya said: I chose God and His messenger and Islam, and the Messenger of God set me free, and married me, and he made manumission my bridal price. When the Prophet desired to set out to Medina his companions said, "Today we will know whether she is his wife or concubine. If she is his wife he will cover her; if not she is his concubine." When the Prophet set out, he commanded that I be veiled and it was known that I was his wife. He placed his thigh and I placed my foot on it, and I found it great that I placed my thigh on his, and rode. I suffered his wives who looked down on me saying, "O daughter of a Jew." But I used to see the Messenger of God, and he was gracious and generous to me. One day when he visited me I was crying. He said, "What is the matter with you?" I said, "Your wives look down on me and say, 'O daughter of a Jew.'" She said: I saw that the Messenger of God was angry. He said, "When they speak to you or dismiss you, say, 'My father is Aaron and my uncle, Moses.'"

They said: Abū Shuyaym converted, and his Islam was the best. He related to us saying: When we hastened to their families in Ḥayfāʾ with ʿUyayna, and arrived before them, they were settled and content, not agitated, so ʿUyayna returned with us. When we were outside Khaybar in a place called al-Ḥaṭām we camped for the night and were suddenly woken up. ʿUyayna said, "Rejoice, for I have seen tonight in my sleep, that I was granted Dhū Ruqayba, a mountain in Khaybar, and indeed I took Muḥammad by his neck." He said: When we arrived in Khaybar, ʿUyayna arrived and found the Messenger of God [Page 676] had conquered Khaybar and God had plundered what was in it. ʿUyayna said, "O Muḥammad, give me some of what you plundered from my allies for I have kept away from you and have not fought you, and I abandoned my allies and did not attack you. I retreated with four thousand warriors from you." The Messenger of God said, "You lie, but the shouting you heard hastened you to your people." He said, "Reward me, O Muḥammad." He said, "For you is Dhū Ruqayba." ʿUyayna said, "What is Dhū Ruqayba?" He replied, "The mountain that you took in your dream." ʿUyayna turned and went secretly to the Jews and said, "I have not seen such an affair as today. By God, I thought that you alone could take Muḥammad." I said, "People of fortresses, arms and wealth, did you surrender while you were in this forbidding fortress, and had such an abundance of food—that you could not find sufficient people to eat it—and flowing water?" They said, "We desired the fortification of al-Zubayr, but the tunnels were cut off, and it was hot and we could not survive in thirst." He said, "You turned from the fortresses of Nāʿim, defeated, until you arrived at the fortress of Qalʿat Zubayr?" He began asking about those who were killed among them, and he was informed. He said, "By God, the people of seriousness and endurance are killed. There was no organization to the Jews of the Ḥijāz ever."

Thaʿlaba b. Sallām b. Abī l-Ḥuqayq heard his words. They used to say that he was weak in mind and confused. He said, "O ʿUyayna, you misled them and abandoned them and left them to fight Muḥammad. And, before that, you did the same with the Banū Qurayẓa." ʿUyayna said, "Indeed, Muḥammad duped us about our people and we hastened to them when we heard the scream, for we thought that Muḥammad had clashed with them. But we did not see anything there, so we came back to you to help you." Thaʿlaba said, "Who remains for you to help? Those who were killed were killed and those who remain, stayed and became slaves to Muḥammad who has imprisoned us [Page 677] and grabbed our property." A man from the Ghaṭafān says to ʿUyayna, "You did not help your allies to keep our agreement. Nor did you take the dates of Khaybar for a year from Muḥammad. By God, I see the affair of Muḥammad is successful, for surely he overcomes those who oppose him." ʿUyayna turned to his people twisting his hands. When he returned to his people, al-Ḥārith b. ʿAwf came to him and said, "Did I not say to you, you are rushing about nothing. By God, Muḥammad will surely be victorious over whoever is between the East and the West. The Jews have informed us about this. I was there and I heard Sallām b. Abī l-Ḥuqayq say, 'We envied Muḥammad his prophet hood when it left the Banū Hārūn. He is the Prophet dispatched by God, but the Jews do not agree with me about this. From him we have received two slaughters: The first in Yathrib and the other in Khaybar.'" Al-Ḥārith said: I said to Sallam, "He possesses all the earth." He said, "Yes, by the Torah, which was revealed to Moses, I do not like the Jews to learn of my words about it."

They said: When Muḥammad conquered Khaybar and was confident, Zaynab bt. al-Ḥārith began to ask, "What part of lamb is most desirable to Muḥammad?" They said, "The forearm and the shoulder." She approached a goat of hers and slaughtered it. Then she took some potent poison—she had consulted the Jews about poison and they agreed over this poison specifically. She poisoned the lamb, putting more on the forearms and shoulders.

When the sun went down, the Messenger of God prayed the *Maghrib* prayer and turned back to his house. He found Zaynab sitting in his seat. He inquired about it and she says, "Abū l-Qāsim, it is a gift I bring you." The Messenger of God used to eat gifts, but he would not eat charity. He commanded that the gift be taken from her and placed before him. [Page 678] Then the Messenger of God said to his companions who were attending, or those who attended among them: "Draw near and eat." So they came close and put out their hands. The Messenger of God took the forearm, while Bishr b. al-Barāʾ took the shinbone. The Messenger of God took a bite of it, and Bishr took a bite, and when the Messenger of God swallowed his food, Bishr also swallowed his. The

Messenger of God said: "Stop! Surely this forearm informs me that it is poisoned." Bishr b. al-Barāʾ said: "By God, I found that from the bite I ate, and what prevented me from spitting it out was that I hated to spoil your pleasure at your food, for when you swallowed what was in your hand I would not favor myself over you. I hoped only that you did not eat what was bad in it." Bishr did not move from his place until his color became like a head shawl (*taylāsan*). His pain did not last a year. He did not change, except what was changed, and he died of it. It was said that he did not leave his place until he died.

The Messenger of God lived for three more years. The Messenger of God called Zaynab, and said, "Did you poison the shoulder?" She said, "Who told you?" He replied, "The shoulder." She said, "Yes." He asked, "What persuaded you to do that?" She said, "You killed my father, my uncle and my husband. You took from my people what you took. I said to myself: If he is a prophet he will be informed. The sheep will inform him of what I did. If he is a king, we will be relieved of him." There was disputation among us about her. A sayer said: The Messenger of God commanded about her and she was killed, then crucified. Another said that he had pardoned her. Three individuals put their hands in the food but did not swallow any of it. The Messenger of God commanded his companions to draw blood from the middle of their heads because of the sheep. The Messenger of God cupped blood from under his left arm. It was said he cupped blood from the nape of his neck. Abū Hind removed it with a horn and blade.

[Page 679] They said: The Mother of Bishr b. al-Barāʾ used to say: I visited the Messenger of God during the sickness of which he died. He was feverish and I felt him and said, "I have not found what makes you sick on any other." The Messenger of God said, "Just as rewards are given us, so are trials inflicted on us. People claim that the Messenger of God has pleurisy. God would not inflict it upon me. Rather, it is the touch of Satan caused by eating what I, and your son ate on the day of Khaybar. I will continue to feel pain until the time of death overwhelms me." The Messenger of God died a martyr. It was said that he who died of the lamb was Mubashshir b. al-Barāʾ. But Bishr is better confirmed with us. There is agreement upon it.

ʿAbdullah said: I asked Ibrāhīm b. Jaʿfar about the words of Zaynab, daughter of al-Ḥarith, "You killed my father." He said: Her father al-Ḥārith and her uncle Yasār were killed on the day of Khaybar. He was the most knowledgeable of the people. It was he who was brought down from al-Shiqq. Al-Ḥārith was the bravest of the Jews. His brother, Zabīr, was killed at that time. Her husband was their master, but the bravest of them was Sallām b. Mishkam. He was sick while he was in the fortress of al-Naṭā and it was said to him, "You have no strength to fight, so stay in al-Katība." He replied, "I will never do that." He was killed when he was sick. He is Abū l-Ḥakam. Rabīʿ b. Abī l-Ḥuqayq says of him:

> When they call us with their swords
> And there was stabbing, we called Sallām.
> If we did not call him we would give the leaders of the enemy
> Poison to drink. [page 680]
> He was a master of their war but God troubled him with sickness.

They said: the Messenger of God appointed Farwa b. ʿAmr al-Bayāḍī over the plunder, on the day of Khaybar. He collected the booty of the Muslims in the fortresses of Naṭā, al-Shiqq and al-Katība. He did not leave other than the garment on his/her back for even one of the people of al-Katība among its men, women and children. They gathered much furniture, cloth, velvet, many weapons, sheep, cattle, food, and many camels. The food, camels and fodder were not divided into five portions. The people took what they needed from it. He who needed weapons to fight with took it from the one who possessed plunder, until God conquered for them and that was returned in the plunder. When all of that was collected the Messenger of God commanded that it be apportioned into five portions. One portion was written to God, and the rest of the portions were left anonymous.

The first of what was taken out was the portion of the Prophet, and he did not choose his fifth. Then the Messenger of God commanded the selling of the four-fifths to those who desired, and Farwa began to sell to those who desired. The Prophet asked blessings for it, saying, "O God, let it all be sold." Farwa b. ʿAmr said: Surely I saw the people overtake me and rush to it until it was sold in two days, and I had thought that we could not finish it for there was so much of it.

The fifth, which came to the Prophet, was from the plunder. He gave from it as God desired, from the weapons and clothing. He gave to those of his family clothing, beads, and utensils. He gave to the men and women of the Banū ʿAbd al-Muṭṭalib, and he gave to the orphan and the beggar. Manuscripts of the Torah were also collected with the plunder. The Jews came seeking them and they spoke to the Messenger of God about them [Page 681] pleading that they be returned to them. A herald of the Messenger of God called out: Return even the thread and needle, for indeed the excess taken will bring shame, vice and fire on the day of Judgment.

At that time Farwa sold the goods, he took a band and bandaged his head with it to shade it from the sun. Then he returned to his station while it was still on his head. Then he remembered, and went out and removed it. The Messenger of God was informed about it. He said, "You bandaged your head with a band of fire." A man asked the Messenger of God, at that time, for something from the booty (*fay'*). The Messenger of God said, "Neither a needle nor a thread is permitted to me from the booty (*fay'*). I will not take, nor will I give from it." A man asked the Messenger of God for a band (*ʿiqāl*). The Messenger of God said, "When we apportion the booty then I will give you a cord (*ʿiqāl*), and if you wish, one made of rope."

A black man named Karkara, who was with the Messenger of God holding his riding beast at the battle, was killed at the time, and it was said, "O Messenger of God, was Karkara martyred?" The Messenger of God replied, "He is even now burning in fire for a cloak he took in excess." A man from the people said, "O Messenger of God, I took two thongs at the time of thus and thus." The Messenger of God said, "The thongs are of fire."

A man from the Ashjaʿ died at the time. They mentioned it to the Messenger of God, and he said, "Pray for your companion." At that the faces of the people changed. The Messenger of God said, "Indeed, your companion took more than his due while fighting in the cause of God." Zayd b. Khālid al-Juhannī said, "We examined his goods and we found beads of the Jews valued at less than two dirhams." A group of Muslims had taken some of the Jewish beads. The Muḥaddith said of this tradition, "If the beads were with you today they would not equal two dirhams." These beads were brought to the Messenger of God after he completed the apportioning, and they said, [Page 682] "O Messenger of God, we forgot! These beads are with us!" The Messenger of God said, "Will all of you swear by God that you forgot it?" They said, "Yes," and they all swore by God that they forgot it. The Messenger of God called for the coffin of the dead and they were tied to it. Then he prayed over them the prayer for the dead. When the Messenger of God found more than his due taken from the spoil in the saddle of a man, he did not punish him. It was not heard that he burned the saddle of such a one; but he did treat harshly, blame, hurt, and publicize his guilt.

They said: That on the day of Khaybar, they bought nuggets with gold at random, and the Messenger of God ignored it. Faḍāla b. ʿUbayd said: I acquired at that time a necklace and sold it for eight dinars. I mentioned that to the Messenger of God and he said, "Sell the gold weight for weight." But there was in the necklace gold and other metal so I returned it. The two Saʿds bought nuggets with gold, and one of them was more in weight. The Messenger of God said, "You have committed usury, so return it." At that time a man found two hundred dirhams in the ruins. The Messenger of God took the fifth and returned the rest to him.

At that time the Messenger of God was heard saying, "Who believes in God and the last day, his water shall not irrigate other than his plants. And he will not sell any of his booty until it is assigned to him. And he shall not ride a beast from the plunder until he exhausts it, and then return it. Nor does he wear a garment from the plunder until it is worn out and then return it. Nor does he come among the women prisoners until she menstruates once and is cleansed, and if she is pregnant, until she delivers her child."

The Messenger of God passed [Page 683] a woman who, at that time, was at the end of her term. He said, "To whom does this woman belong?" It was said, "To so and so." He said, "Perhaps he sleeps with her?" They said, "Yes." He said, "How will her son inherit from him when it is not his child? Or will he make him his slave, while he runs under his hearing and his sight? Surely I have in mind to curse him with a curse that will follow him to his grave."

They said: People from two ships arrived from the Negus soon after Khaybar was conquered. When the Prophet saw Jaʿfar he said, "When I saw Jaʿfar I did not know which of the two I should be happy about, the arrival of Jaʿfar or the conquest of Khaybar." Then the Messenger of God embraced him and kissed him between his eyes.

The Daws arrived, and with them was Abū Hurayra, al-Ṭufayl b. ʿAmr and their companions and a group of the Ashjaʿ. The Messenger of God spoke to his companions about sharing the booty with them. They said, "Yes, O Messenger of God." Abān b. Saʿīd b. al-ʿĀṣ looked at Abū Hurayra and said, "But not for you." Abū Huraya said, "O Messenger of God, this is the killer of Ibn Qawqal." Abān b. Saʿīd said, "O how strange; for a hair, let fall upon us from the arrival of sheep, holds against me the killing of a Muslim whom God honored by my hand and did not humiliate me by my opponent's hand."

They said: A fifth was for the Messenger of God from all the plunder that the Muslims took, whether the Messenger of God witnessed it or not. But there was no portion in the plunder for those who were not present, if they did not witness it; except at Badr where he gave to eight who did not witness, and [Page 684] each had a right to it. And Khaybar was for the people of al-Ḥudaybiyya, too, those who witnessed it among them or were absent from it. *God promises you plunder in plenty take it when he hastens this for you* (Q. 48:20): referring to Khaybar. Men who had stayed behind from Khaybar were Murayy b. Sinān, Ayman b. ʿUbayd, and Sibāʿ b. ʿUrfuta al-Ghifārī. He appointed Jābir b. ʿAbdullah and others to take his place in Medina. Two of them died. The Messenger of God apportioned to those who stayed behind and those who died.

He apportioned to those who witnessed Khaybar among people who did not witness al-Ḥudaybiyya. He apportioned to messengers who were appointed to the people of Fadak, Muḥayyiṣa b. Masʿūd al-Ḥārithī, and others. The Messenger of God apportioned to those who attended, but also to three sick people who did not attend the battle: Suwayd b. al-Nuʿmān, ʿAbdullah b. Saʿd b. Khaythama, and a man from the Banū Khuṭāma. And he apportioned to the dead who were killed among the Muslims.

Ibn Abī Sabra related to me from ʿAbd al-Raḥmān b. ʿAbdullah b. ʿAbd al-Raḥmān b. Abī Ṣaʿṣaʿa that a sayer had said: Indeed Khaybar was for the People of Ḥudaybiyya. Others than them did not witness it, and others than them were not given a portion of it. The first saying is confirmed with us, that a people who witnessed Khaybar were given portions even though they had not witnessed al-Ḥudaybiyya.

Ibn Abī Sabra related to me from Quṭayr al-Ḥārithī from Ḥizām b. Saʿd b. Muḥayyiṣa, who said: The Messenger of God set out with ten Jews from Medina, and he attacked Khaybar with them. He apportioned to them as he apportioned to the Muslims. Some said: He gave them but he did not apportion to them. There were slaves with them, including ʿUmayr, the *mawlā* of Abū Laḥm. ʿUmayr said: He did not apportion to me but he gave me furniture and goods. The Messenger of God had gifted it to them.

[Page 685] The Messenger of God set out from Medina with twenty women: Umm Salama his wife, Ṣafiyya bt. ʿAbd al-Muṭṭalib, Umm Ayman, Salmā (the wife of Abū Rāfiʿ, a *mawlā* of the Prophet), the woman of ʿĀṣim b. ʿAdī who delivered Sahla bt. ʿĀṣim in Khaybar, Umm ʿUmāra, Nusayba bt. Kaʿb, and Umm Manīʿ, who was the mother of Shubāth, Kuʿayba bt. Saʿd al-Aslamiyya, Umm Mutāʿ al-Aslamiyya, Umm Sulaym bt. Milḥān, Umm al-Ḍaḥḥāk bt. Masʿūd al-Ḥāritha, Hind bt. ʿAmr b. Ḥizām, Umm al-ʿAlāi al-Anṣāriyya, Umm ʿĀmir al-Ashhaliyya, Umm ʿAṭiyya al-Anṣāriyya, and Umm Salīṭ.

Ibn Abī Sabra related to me from Sulaymān b. Suḥaym from Umm ʿAlī bt. al-Ḥakam, from Umayya bt. Qays b. Abī l-Ṣalt al-Ghifāriyya, who said: I went to the Messenger of God with women from the Banū Ghifār, and we said, "We desire, O Messenger of God, to set out with you in this direction of yours, and we will treat the wounded and help the Muslims in whatever way we can." The Messenger of God said, "May God bless you!"

She said: We set out with him and I was a girl young in years, and the Messenger of God seated me right behind him on the saddle bag of his saddle. He alighted at dawn and made his camel lie down, and lo and behold I saw the blood from me on the saddlebag. It was the first time that I menstruated, and I grabbed at the camel for I was ashamed of myself. When the Messenger of God saw me and saw the blood he said, "Perhaps you are menstruating?" I said, "Yes." He said: "Restore yourself. Then take a vessel of water, throw some salt in it and wash the blood on the saddlebag, and then return to me." I did so.

[Page 686] When God conquered Khaybar, the Prophet gave us gifts from the booty but he did not apportion to us. He took this necklace that you see around my neck and gave it to me, and he hung it with his hand around my neck, and by God I have not removed it ever. It was around her neck when she died. She "willed" that she be buried with it. She did not cleanse except she placed salt in the cleansing water. She willed that salt be used in washing her, when she was washed for her burial.

ʿAbd al-Salām b. Mūsā b. Jubayr related to me from his father, from his grand father, from ʿAbdullah b. Unays, who said: I set out with the Prophet to Khaybar, and with me was my pregnant wife. She was in labour on the road and I informed the Messenger of

God and he said, "Soak some dates for her, and when they are well soaked then let her drink it." I did, and her labor was made easy. When we conquered Khaybar he gave the women gifts but he did not apportion to them. He gave both my wife, and my child who was just born. ʿAbd al-Salām said: I do not know if it was a boy or girl.

Ibn Abī Sabra related to me from Isḥāq b. ʿAbdullah from ʿUmar b. al-Ḥakam from Umm ʿAlā al-Ansāriyya, who said: I acquired three beads, and my female companions acquired the same. Earrings of gold were brought at that time. The Messenger of God said, "These are for the daughters of my brother Saʿd b. Zurāra." He brought the earrings to them, and I have seen them wearing the earrings. That was from his fifth, on the day of Khaybar.

ʿAbdullah b. Abī Yaḥyā related to me from Thubayta bt. Ḥanẓala al-Aslamī from her mother Umm Sinān, who said: When the Messenger of God desired to set out I came to him and said, [Page 687] "O Messenger of God, I will set out with you in this direction of yours. I will string the waterbags, care for the sick and wounded, and if they are wounded—it will not be—I will watch the saddles." The Messenger of God said, "Set out with God's blessings on you and your companions. Your people have spoken to me, and I have permitted to those among your people and the rest of them. If you wish, go with your people and if you wish, with us." I said, "With you!" He said, "Then stay with Umm Salama, my wife." She said: And I was with her.

The Messenger of God raided from al-Rajīʿ every morning wearing his armor. In the evening he returned to us. He continued thus for seven days until God conquered Naṭā for him. When he conquered it he moved to al-Shiqq, and he moved us to al-Manzila. When he conquered Khaybar he gave us gifts from the booty (*fay*ʾ). He gave me beads and jewelry of silver that was acquired in the plunder. He gave me velvet from Fadak, cloth from Yemen, a thick garment, and a pot of brass. Men from his companions were wounded and I tended to them with medicines that came from my family and they recovered. I returned with Umm Salama and when we returned and entered Medina, and I was on one of the camels of the Prophet that he had given me, she said, "The camel, on which you ride, is for you. The Prophet gives it to you." She said: I praised God, and I arrived with the camel and sold it for seven dinars. She said: God granted me happiness in this journey of mine.

They said: He apportioned to the women, and he apportioned for Sahla bt. ʿĀṣim, who was born in Khaybar. A child was born as well to ʿAbdullah b. Unays, in Khaybar. He apportioned to the women and boys. Some said: He gifted to the women and children for he did not regard them as people of *jihād*.

[Page 688] Yaʿqūb b. Muḥammad related to me from ʿAbd al-Raḥmān b. ʿAbdullah b. Abī Ṣaʿṣaʿa from al-Ḥārith b. ʿAbdullah b. Kaʿb, who said: I saw red beads on the neck of Umm ʿUmāra, so I asked her about them. She said that the Muslims acquired beads that had been buried in the grounds of Ṣaʿb b. Muʿādh's fortress. They were brought to the Messenger of God and he commanded that they be shared among the women who were with him. They were counted. We were twenty women and he apportioned those beads among us. And he gifted for us from the *fay*ʾ, velvet, Yemenī cloth, and two dinars. Thus did he give me and my female companions. I said: How many portions were for the men? She said: My husband Ghaziyya b. ʿAmr sold goods worth eleven and a half dinars and he did not ask for anything. We thought that these were portions of the riders—he was a rider—And he sold three portions in al-Shiqq, during the time of ʿUthmān, for thirty dinars.

The Messenger of God led three horses in Khaybar, Lizāz, al-Ẓarib, and al-Sakb.

Al-Zubayr b. al-Awwām also led horses. Khirāsh b. al-Ṣimma led two horses. And al-Barā' b. Aws b. Khālid b. al-Ja'd b. 'Awf (also called Abū Ibrāhīm) the nursing father of Ibrāhīm, the son of the Prophet, led two horses and Abū 'Amr al-Anṣārī led two horses. He said: The Messenger of God apportioned to each one who had two horses five portions. Four for his two horses, and a portion for himself. Where there were more than two horses he did not apportion to him. Others said that he apportioned only to one horse. It is confirmed that he apportioned for one horse. Others said that he classified the horses into Arab horses and the mixed breed on the day of Khaybar, and he apportioned for the Arab horses but neglected the mixed breed. Some said: There were no mixed breeds in the time of the Messenger of God. There were only Arab horses until the time of 'Umar b. al-Khaṭṭāb, when he conquered Iraq and al-Shām.

[Page 689] It was not heard that the Messenger of God struck a portion for the horses that were with him except for one horse, and it was known as the portion of the horse. The portions of the Messenger of God in Naṭā were three portions: for his horse two portions, and for him one portion. The horse was with 'Āṣim b. 'Adī. Ibn Abī Sabra related to me from Isḥāq b. 'Abdullah b. Abī Farwa, from Ḥizām b. Sa'd b. Muḥayyiṣa, who said: Suwayd b. al-Nu'mān set out on a horse. When he saw the houses of Khaybar in the night, he fell with his horse. The horse was destroyed and Suwayd's hand was broken. He did not set out from his camp until the Messenger of God conquered Khaybar. The Messenger of God apportioned to him the portion of his horse.

They said: The cavalry constituted two hundred horses; some said three hundred. Two hundred is confirmed with us. He who was in charge of counting the Muslims was Zayd b. Thābit. The Prophet apportioned between them what they plundered from the goods that were sold. Then he counted them. They numbered one thousand four hundred. There were two hundred horses. There were eighteen portions. They were those that the Messenger of God gave as portions. For the cavalry were fourteen hundred shares. As for the cavalry's two hundred horses, to them were allotted four hundred shares.

The portions of the Muslims that the Messenger of God apportioned in Naṭā or in al-Shiqq were three unregulated portions; it was not according to the agreement of the Messenger of God and it was not limited, nor apportioned. Rather to each of them were named leaders. For every hundred was a known leader who divided among his companions what came out from its revenue. The leaders in al-Shiqq and Naṭā were: 'Āṣim b. 'Adī, 'Alī b. Abī Ṭālib, 'Abd al-Raḥmān b. 'Awf, Ṭalḥa b. 'Ubaydullah, may the grace of God be upon them. And the portion of the Banū Sā'ida and the portion of the Banū al-Najjār had a leader. The portion of [Page 690] Ḥāritha b. al-Ḥārith and the portions of Aslam and Ghifār, and the portion of Banū Salima who were more in number—and their leader was Mu'ādh b. Jabal. And there was a portion to 'Ubayda, a man from the Jews; a portion to the Aws, the Banū Zubayr, Usayd b. Ḥuḍayr, and Balḥārith b. Khazraj; its leader was 'Abdullah b. Rawāḥa. A portion to Bayāḍa, whose chief was Farwa b. 'Amr, and a portion to Nā'im. These were eighteen unregulated portions in al-Shiqq and Naṭā, and their leaders took what was earned and then divided it among them. A man would sell his share and that was lawful. Indeed, the Messenger of God bought, from a man from the Banū Ghifār, his portion in Khaybar, with two camels. Then he said to him, "Know that what I take from you is better than what I give you; and what I give you is less than what I take from you. If you wish take, and if you wish, keep it." The Ghifārī took it.

ʿUmar b. al-Kaṭṭāb bought a share from the Messenger of God. He took from his companions who were a hundred. It was the portion of Aws, named the portion of al-Lafīf, until it came to ʿUmar b. al-Khaṭṭāb. Muḥammad b. Maslama bought from the portion of the Aslam several portions. It was said, the Aslam numbered around seventy and the Ghifār some twenty, and together they numbered a hundred. Some said that the Aslam numbered a hundred and seventy, and at Ghifār around twenty and this was two hundred portions. The first saying is confirmed with us.

When the Messenger of God conquered Khaybar, the Jews questioned him and said, "O Muḥammad, we are lords of the date palms, a people knowledgeable of it." The Messenger of God gave them a contract in Khaybar for half of the dates and the crops that were planted under the dates. The Messenger of God said, "I will establish you over what God established you." [Page 691] They maintained the contract with the Messenger of God until his death, then with Abū Bakr, and in the beginning of the caliphate of ʿUmar.

The Messenger of God used to send ʿAbdullah b. Rawāḥa to estimate their dates. Each time he would evaluate it and say, "If you wish it is for you and you will guarantee half of its value to us, or if you wish it is for us and we will guarantee for you what I estimate." Indeed, he estimated forty thousand barrels for them at one time. They collected the jewelry of their women and said, "This is for you, so sanction the portion." He said, "O community of Jews, by God, to me you are the most loathsome creation of God, but that will not bring me to deal unjustly against you." They said: This is how the heavens and the earth were established. And ʿAbdullah b. Rawāḥa was the valuer for them. When he was killed at the battle of Muʾta the Messenger of God sent Abū l-Haytham b. al-Tayyihān to evaluate for them—and some said Jabbār b. Ṣakhr. He did similar to what ʿAbdullah b. Rawāḥa did with them. Some said that he who evaluated after Ibn Rawāḥa was Farwa b. ʿAmr.

They said: The Muslims began to take from their plantations and their legumes after the contract, and after that half of it was assigned to the Jews. The Jews complained of that to the Messenger of God. So he called Khālid b. al-Walīd, and some say ʿAbd al-Raḥmān b. ʿAwf, and he called out, "Indeed, prayer is for everyone, and only the Muslim who submits will enter Paradise." The people gathered. The Messenger of God stood up and praised God and commended Him. Then he said, "The Jews complain to me that you have taken from their quarter. We have given them protection over their blood and their property and that which is before them of their lands. And we trade with them. Surely one does not dissolve the property of the contractors except in righteousness. The Muslims shall not take from their greens except for a price. May be the Jews say: I will give it for free, but the Muslims must refuse except for a price."

Ibn Wāqid said: It was disputed among us about al-Katība; someone said: [Page 692] It was purely for the Prophet; the Muslims were not troubled about it. Rather, it was for the Prophet. ʿAbdullah b. Nūḥ related to me from Ibn Ghufayr, and Mūsā b. ʿAmr b. ʿAbdullah b. Rāfiʿ from Bashīr b. Yasār, and Ibrāhīm b. Jaʿfar related to me from his father that a sayer said: The fifth of the Messenger of God from Khaybar was from al-Shiqq and al-Naṭā. Qudāma b. Mūsā related to me from Abū Bakr b. Muḥammad b. ʿAmr b. Ḥizām, who said: ʿUmar b. ʿAbdul ʿAzīz wrote to me during his caliphate saying, "Investigate al-Katība for me!" Abū Bakr said: I asked ʿAmra bt. ʿAbd al-Raḥmān and she said: Indeed, when the Messenger of God contracted a peace with the Banū Abī l-Ḥuqayq he divided Naṭā and al-Shiqq and al-Katība into five parts. Al-Katība was a part of it. The Messenger of God made five "droppings", and from it he apportioned one dropping for God. Then the Messenger of God said, "O God, I will make your portion in al-Katība." The first of what came out was that in which it was written al-Katība. So al-Katība was the fifth of the Prophet. The other portions were not marked. They were equal to eighteen shares for the Muslims. Abū Bakr said: I wrote to ʿUmar b. ʿAbd al-ʿAzīz about that.

Abū Bakr b. Abī Sabra related to me from Abū Mālik from Ḥizām b. Saʿd b. Muḥayyiṣa, who said: When the portion of the Prophet was taken out, al-Shiqq and Naṭā constituted four fifths for the Muslims equally. ʿAbdullah b. ʿAwn related to me from Abū Mālik al-Ḥimyarī, from Saʿīd b. al-Musayyib, [Page 693] and Muḥammad related to me from al-Zuhrī. They said: al-Katība was the fifth of the Messenger of God. He said: The Messenger of God ate the food from al-Katība and paid his family from it. Ibn Wāqid said: It is confirmed with us that it was the fifth of the Prophet from Khaybar. The Messenger of God did not eat the food of al-Shiqq and al-Naṭā alone, he made them portions for the Muslims. Al-Katība was what he ate from. Al-Katība was estimated at eight thousand barrels of dates. And there was for the Jews half of it, i.e. four thousand barrels. Barley was planted in al-Katība, and three thousand measures were reaped from there, and half of it was for the Prophet, that is, one thousand five hundred measures of barley. There were date stones and perhaps about a thousand measures were gathered, half of which were for the Messenger of God. The Messenger of God gave from all of this barley and dates, and date-stones to the Muslims.

THE NAMES OF THE PORTIONS OF AL-KATĪBA

A fifth was for the Messenger of God alone; and Sulālim and the two Jāsam. There were two portions for the women, and two portions for the Jew, Miqsam; two portions for ʿAwān; a portion for the Ghirrīth and a portion for Nuʿaym. A total of twelve portions.

A RECORD OF THE PROVISION OF THE PROPHET IN AL-KATĪBA, FOR HIS WIVES AND OTHERS

To each of his wives the Prophet provided eighty *wasq* of dates and twenty *wasq* of barley; to al-ʿAbbās b. ʿAbd al-Muṭṭalib, two hundred *wasq*; and to Fāṭima and ʿAlī, [Page 694] from the barley and dates, three hundred *wasq*: i.e. eighty-five *wasq* of barley. Fāṭima was given two hundred *wasq*. Usāma b. Zayd received hundred and fifty *wasq*, forty of it in barley and fifty of date seeds. Umm Rimtha bt. ʿUmar b. Hāshim b. Muṭṭālib received five *wasq* of barley, and al-Miqdād b. ʿAmr received fifteen *wasq* of barley.

Mūsā b. Yaʿqūb related to me from his aunt from his mother, who said: We bought fifteen *wasq* of barley from the portion allotted to Miqdād b. ʿAmr at Khaybar, from Muʿāwiya b. Abī Sufyān for a hundred thousand dirham.

In the name of God most gracious most merciful: Muḥammad the Messenger of God gave Abū Bakr b. Abī Quḥāfa a hundred *wasq*; ʿAqīl b. Abī Ṭālib a hundred and forty *wasq*; the sons of Jaʿfar b. Abī Ṭālib, fifty *wasq*; Rabīʿa b. al-Ḥārith, a hundred *wasq*; Abū Sufyān b. al-Ḥārith b. ʿAbd al-Muṭṭalib, a hundred *wasq*; al-Ṣalt b. Makhrama b. al-Muṭṭalib thirty *wasq*; Abū Nabqa, fifty *wasq*; Rukāna b. ʿAbd Yazīd, fifty *wasq*;

Qāsim b. Makhrama b. al-Muṭṭalib, fifty *wasq*; Misṭaḥ b. Uthātha b. ʿAbbād and his sister Hind, thirty *wasq*; Ṣafiyya bt. ʿAbd al-Muṭṭalib, forty *wasq*; Buḥayna bt. al-Ḥārith b. al-Muṭṭalib thirty *wasq*; Ḍubāʿa bt. Zubayr b. ʿAbd al-Muṭṭalib forty *wasq*; Ḥuṣayn, Khadīja and Hind b. ʿUbayda b. al-Ḥārith, a hundred *wasq*; Umm al-Ḥakam bt. al-Zubayr b. ʿAbd al-Muṭṭalib, thirty *wasq*; to Umm Hānī bt. Abī Ṭālib, forty *wasq*; Jumāna bt. Abī Ṭālib, thirty *wasq*; Umm Ṭālib bt. Abī Ṭālib, thirty *wasq*; Qays b. [Page 695] Makhrama b. al-Muṭṭalib fifty *wasq*; Abū Arqam fifty *wasq*; ʿAbd al-Raḥmān b. Abī Bakr forty *wasq*; Abū Baṣra forty *wasq*; Ibn Abī Ḥubaysh thirty *wasq*; ʿAbdullah b. Wahb and his two sons, fifty *wasq*; Umm Ḥabība bt. Jaḥsh, thirty *wasq*; Numayla al-Kalbī of the Banū Layth, fifty *wasq*; Umm Ḥabība bt. Jaḥsh, thirty *wasq*; Malakān b. ʿAbda, thirty *wasq*; Muḥayyiṣa b. Masʿūd, thirty *wasq*.

In his last will, the Prophet bequeathed to the Rahāwiyyūn (Yemenī tribe) in portions from the fifth of Khaybar, a hundred *wasq*; to the Dariyyūn, a hundred *wasq*; There were ten Dariyyūn who came to the Prophet from al-Shām, and he left them from the portions a hundred *wasq*. They were Hānī b. Ḥabīb, al-Fākih b. al-Nuʿmān, Jabala b. Mālik, Abū Hind b. Barr and his brother al-Ṭayyib b. Barr—the Messenger of God named him ʿAbdullah—Tamīm b. Aws, Nuʿaym b. Aws, Yazīd b. Qays, ʿAzīz b. Mālik—the Messenger of God named him ʿAbd al-Raḥmān—and his brother Murra b. Mālik. The Prophet left a hundred *wasq* to the Ashʿariyyūn.

ʿAbd al-Wahhāb b. Abī Ḥayya, Ibn al-Thaljī, and al-Wāqidī said, informing us, that: Maʿmar related to each of them from al-Zuhrī from ʿUbaydullah b. ʿAbdullah b. ʿUtba, who said: The Messenger of God only decreed three things in his will: in all earnestness he left 1) to the Dariyyūn a hundred *wasq*, to the Ashʿarīyyūn a hundred *wasq*, and to the Rahhāwiyyūn a hundred *wasq*; and 2) that Usāma b. Zayd goes out with the army. The Messenger of God wanted him to go to the place where [Page 696] his father had been killed. 3) That two religions would not be practiced in the Arab peninsula.

They said: The Messenger of God sought the advice of Gabriel about the apportioning of the fifth of Khaybar and he advised him to apportion among the Banū Hāshim, the Banū Muṭṭalib, and the Banū ʿAbd Yaghūth.

Maʿmar related to me from al-Zuhrī from Saʿīd b. al-Musayyib, who said: Jubayr b. Muṭʿim said: When the Messenger of God apportioned the portions to the relatives in Khaybar among the Banū Hāshim and the Banū Muṭṭalib, I and ʿUthmān b. ʿAffān walked until we entered before the Messenger of God and we said, "O Messenger of God, as for those of our brothers from the Banū Muṭṭalib, we do not deny the importance for your relationship to them that God placed you among them. But did you consider our brothers among the Banū Muṭṭalib? Surely we are in the same position? But you give them and leave us." The Messenger of God said, "Indeed, the Banū Muṭṭalib did not abandon me in *jāhiliyya* and Islām. They entered with us in the pass. Indeed the Banū Hāshim and the Banū Muṭṭalib are the same!" and the Messenger of God intertwined his fingers.

They said: ʿAbd al-Muṭṭalib b. Rabīʿa b. al-Ḥārith said that al-ʿAbbās b. ʿAbd al-Muṭṭālib and Rabīʿa b. al-Ḥārith came together and said, "If we sent two youths of mine and Faḍl b. ʿAbbās to the Messenger of God and they spoke to him and he gave them authority over these charities, they will pay what should be paid to the people, and make what they could of profit." So al-Faḍl and I were sent, and we set out until we came to the Messenger of God and we went before him. He turned to us at *Ẓuhr*, while we stopped for him at lady Zaynab's place. He took hold of their shoulders, and said, "Tell me your secrets?" When he entered, they entered with him and they said,

"O Messenger of God, we come to you to be appointed over these charities, to make what people make of profit." [Page 697] The Prophet was silent. He raised his head to the ceiling of the house, then approached and said, "Surely charity is not permissible for Muḥammad or the family of Muḥammad. Indeed it is the alms of the people. Call Maḥmiyya b. Jaza al-Zubaydī and Abū Sufyān b. al-Ḥārith b. ʿAbd al-Muṭṭalib for me." He said to Maḥmiyya, "Marry this (al-Faḍl) to your daughter." And he said to Abū Sufyān, "Marry this (ʿAbd al-Muṭṭalib b. Rabīʿa b. al-Ḥārith) to your daughter." He said to Maḥmīya, "Give them a bridal dower from what you have of the fifth," for he was appointed over the fifth. Ibn ʿAbbās used to say: ʿUmar appealed to us to give the widows in marriage with this money, and to help the families' providers and fulfill the debts. But we refused. We insisted that all of it be submitted, and he denied that to us.

Muṣʿab b. Thābit related to me from Yazīd b. Rūmān from ʿUrwa b. al-Zubayr that Abū Bakr, ʿUmar and ʿAlī gave these portions to the orphans and the poor. Some of them said that it was used for weapons and equipment in the way of God. Those food provisions were taken as the payment of the Messenger of God during his life, and during the caliphates of Abū Bakr, ʿUmar, ʿUthmān and Muʿāwiya—may God bless them. When it was Yaḥyā b. al-Ḥakam he increased the payment by a sixth of the amount, and he gave the people from the payment that was increased. Then Abān b. ʿUthmān increased it and he gave them with that. Among those who were provided with subsistence were those who died or were killed. During the life of the Prophet and Abū Bakr, one's provision was transfered to one's heirs.

When it was under the guardianship of ʿUmar b. al-Khaṭṭāb he took the provisions from those who died and did not transfer them. He took the provisions of Zayd b. Ḥāritha, and Jaʿfar b. Abī Ṭālib. ʿAlī b. Abī Ṭālib spoke to him [Page 698] about it, but he refused. When he took the provisions of Ṣafīyya bt. ʿAbd al-Muṭṭalib, al-Zubayr spoke to him about that, and was harsh, but he refused to hand it to him. When he insisted, he said, "I will give you some of it." Zubayr said, "No, by God, do not hold back a single date and keep it from me!" ʿUmar refused to submit all of it to him. al-Zubayr said, "I will only take all of it!" ʿUmar refused to return it to the Muhājirūn; and he also took from the provisions of Fāṭima. Someone talked to him about it but he refused to act.

ʿUmar gave the wives of the Prophet according to their actions. Zaynab bt. Jaḥsh died during his caliphate, and he gave a free hand concerning her inheritance. He permitted what they made by sale or gift. He transferred that to all of her heirs but he did not permit that for other than her. He refused to allow the sale of those who sold their provisions. He said, "This thing is not known. When one who was supplied with the provisions dies, his rights become void, so how can their sale be permitted?" Only the wives of the Messenger of God were permitted to do what they did.

When it was the caliphate of ʿUthmān, all of Usāma's portion was returned to Usāma, but not to the others. al-Zubayr spoke to ʿUthmān about the provision of his mother, Ṣafiyya, but he would not return it. He said "I was present with you when you spoke to ʿUmar, and ʿUmar refused you, saying, 'Take some of it.' I will give you some of what ʿUmar turned in to you; I will give you two thirds and keep a third." al-Zubayr said, "No by God, not a single date; submit all of it, or keep it."

Shuʿayb b. Ṭalḥa b. ʿAbdullah b. ʿAbd al-Raḥmān b. Abī Bakr related to me from his father, who said: When Abū Bakr died, his sons were his heirs and they took his provisions from Khaybar—a hundred *wasq* during the caliphate of ʿUmar and ʿUthmān. His wives Umm Rūmān bt. ʿĀmir b. ʿUwaymir al-Kināniyya and Ḥabība bt.

Khārija b. Zayd b. Abī Zuhayr were appointed heirs, [Page 699] and his portion continued to flow to them until it was the time of ʿAbd al-Malik or after him. Then it was stopped.

Abū ʿAbdullah said: I asked Ibrāhīm b. Jaʿfar, "To whom did the Messenger of God give from the fifth of Khaybar?" He said, "Do not ask any one but me about it ever. One who was given from it received the provision until he died. Then it was transferred to those who were his heirs. They sold it and ate it and gave gifts. This was during the time of Abū Bakr and ʿUmar and ʿUthmān." I said, "From whom did you hear that?" He replied, "From my father and others of my people." Abū ʿAbdullah said: I mentioned this tradition to ʿAbd al-Raḥmān b. ʿAbd al-ʿAzīz, and he said, "One whom I trust informed me about the tradition that ʿUmar kept those provisions when they died, during the life of the wives of the Prophet and others of them." Then he said: Zaynab bt. Jaḥsh died in the year twenty during the caliphate of ʿUmar, and he kept her portion, and it was talked about, but he refused to give her heirs. ʿUmar said that indeed there was provision from the Prophet during the person's life; but that when the person died his heirs had no right to it. He said: That was the command about that during the caliphate of ʿUmar until his death. Then ʿUthmān took charge. The Prophet had made provision for Zayd b. Ḥāritha from Khaybar, which was not written for him, and when Zayd died the Prophet gave it to Usāma b. Zayd. I said: Indeed, some who narrate about it say: Usāma b. Zayd spoke to ʿUmar and ʿUthmān about the provision of his father but he was refused. He said: It was not except as I inform you. Abū ʿAbdullah said, "This is the affair."

THOSE WHO WERE MARTYRED AT KHAYBAR UNDER THE MESSENGER OF GOD

From the Banū Umayya and their allies: Rabīʿa b. Aktham was killed in al-Naṭā by al-Ḥārith the Jew. And Thaqif b. ʿAmr b. Sumayṭ was killed by the Jew, Usayr. And Rifāʿa b. Masrūḥ, [Page 700] was killed by the Jew, al-Ḥārith.

Among the Banū Asad ʿAbd al-ʿUzzā: ʿAbdullah b. Abī Umayya b. Wahb was an ally of theirs, and he was the son of their sister. He was killed in al-Naṭā. Among the Anṣār, Maḥmūd b. Maslama was killed when Marḥab let fall a millstone on him from the fortress of Nāʿim in al-Naṭā.

From the Banū ʿAmr b. ʿAwf: Abū l-Ḍayyāḥ b. al-Nuʿmān who witnessed Badr, Ḥārith b. Ḥāṭib who witnessed Badr, and ʿAdī b. Murra b. Surāqā, Aws b. Ḥabīb and Unayf b. Wāʾila were killed on the fortress of Nāʿim.

From the B. Zurayq: Masʿūd b. Saʿd was killed by Marḥab. From the Banū Salima: Bishr b. al-Barāʾ b. Maʿrūr died of the lamb that was poisoned. And, Fuḍayl b. al-Nuʿmān who was from the Bedouin.

From the Aslam. ʿĀmir b. al-Akwāʿ wounded himself at the fortress of Nāʿim where he was buried. He and Maḥmūd b. Maslama were buried in the same cave in al-Rajīʿ.

From the Banū Ghifār: ʿUmāra b. ʿUqba b. ʿAbbād b. Mulayl, and Yasār the black slave, a man from the Ashjaʿ. Altogether those who were martyred totaled fifteen men. There was disagreement about the prayers over them. A sayer said: The Messenger of God prayed over them. Another said: He did not pray over them.

Ninety-three men were killed from the Jews. The Messenger of God gave Jabala b. Jawwāl al-Thaʿlabī all the domesticated animals in Khaybar. It was said: He gave him all the domesticated animals in al-Naṭā. He did not give him anything from al-Katība or al-Shiqq.

[Page 701] A RECORD OF WHAT WAS SAID AMONG THE POETS OF KHAYBAR

Nājiya b. Jundub al-Aslamī said:

> O worshipers of God,
> In what we desire is only what is edible and drinkable
> And the garden with them is peaceful and admirable.

He also said:

> I am for those who see me, Ibn Jundab.
> Many an opponent have I defeated.
> The vulture and the fox attacked him.

ʿAbd al-Malik b. Wahb, the son of Nājiya recited it to me. He said: I always recited it to my father when I was little.

ʿAbd al-Raḥmān b. ʿAbd al-ʿAzīz related to us from ʿAbdullah b. Abī Bakr b. Ḥazm that he was asked about a wager among the Quraysh when the Messenger of God marched to Khaybar. He said: Ḥuwayṭib b. ʿAbd al-ʿUzzā used to say: I turned away from the truce of al-Ḥudaybiyya for though I was certain that Muḥammad would prevail over mankind, yet the perseverance of Satan within me insisted that I stay attached to my religion. Then, ʿAbbās b. Mirdās al-Sulamī appeared before us and informed us that Muḥammad had marched to Khaybar, and that Khaybar had come together and that Muḥammad had no escape. When ʿAbbās b. Mirdās said, "Who wishes to make a wager about him, that Muḥammad has no escape?" I said, "I will risk it." Ṣafwān b. Umayya said, "I am with you, O ʿAbbās." Nawfal b. Muʿāwiya said, [Page 702] "I am with you, O ʿAbbās." A group of Quraysh joined me, and we wagered on a hundred camels, five at a time. My party and I said, "Muḥammad will be victorious," and ʿAbbās said—and he was within his bounds—"The Ghaṭafān will be victorious." There was a restless sound. Abū Sufyān b. Ḥarb said, "By al-Lāt, I fear for ʿAbbās b. Mirdās and his party," and Ṣafwān became angry and said, "May you be bannished!" Abū Sufyān was silent. News came to him about the victory of the Prophet and reached Ḥuwayṭib who won his wager.

They said: Oaths were made on Khaybar. When the Messenger of God faced Khaybar, the people of Mecca had taken a wager about it. Among them were those, who said: The Jews in Khaybar and their two allies, Asad and Ghifār, will be victorious. That was because the Jews mobilized their allies, and sought their help in exchange for the dates of Khaybar, for one year. There was between them about that a great sale.

Al-Ḥajjāj b. ʿIlāṭ al-Sulamī, then al-Bahzī, had set out raiding in some raid of his when it was mentioned to him that the Messenger of God was in Khaybar, and he converted and attended with the Prophet in Khaybar. Umm Shayba bt. ʿUmayr b. Hāshim, the sister of Muṣʿab al-ʿAbdī, was his wife. Al-Ḥajjāj was rich, and had lots of wealth, treasures of gold that were in the land of the Banū Sulaym. He said,

"O Messenger of God, permit me, until I go and take what is mine that is with my wife, for if my Islam is known I will not be able to take anything." The Messenger of God permitted him and he said, "There is no certainty, O Messenger of God, about what I will say." And the Messenger of God permitted him to say what he wished.

Al-Ḥajjāj said: [Page 703] I set out and when I reached the sanctuary I alighted and found them in al-Thanniyat al-Bayḍā', and lo and behold there were men with them from the Quraysh who were seeking news. They had heard that the Messenger of God had marched to Khaybar. They learned that in the village of al-Ḥijāz in the countryside, and it was strong with men and weapons. They were considering the news with what was before them of the wager, when they saw me, and they said, "Al-Ḥajjāj b. ʿIlāṭ? By God, he will have the news! O Ḥajjāj, it has reached us that the Divider has marched to Khaybar, the land of the Jews and the outskirts of the Ḥijāz." I said, "It has reached me that he has marched to Khaybar; and I have news that will gladden you." So, they lay down by the side of me and my ride saying, "O Ḥajjāj, tell us." I said, "Muḥammad and his companions will not meet a people that are better at fighting than the people of Khaybar. The Jews have marched with the Bedouin gathering groups against him and they have brought to him ten thousand. He was defeated in a manner never heard of, and Muḥammad was taken prisoner. They said, 'We shall not kill him until we bring him to the people of Mecca, and we shall kill him, when he appears, before them for those he killed from us and from them.' Thus, they will surely return to you seeking protection with their relatives, and they will return to what they were. Do not accept from them, after what they did to you."

He said: They shouted in Mecca and said, "The news has come to you?" "This Muḥammad is surely expected to arrive in Mecca before you," I said. "Help me to collect my wealth from debtors, for I desire to arrive and take from Muḥammad and his companions before the merchants precede me to what is there." They stood up and collected my wealth for me as an urgent collection, and I heard about it. I came to my female companion, who had wealth of mine with her, and I said to her, "My wealth. Perhaps I will reach Khaybar, and I will acquire from the sale, before the merchants precede me to those who are broken there among the Muslims."

Al-ʿAbbās heard that and he got up, but his back failed him and he could not stand. [Page 704] He was concerned that he would enter his house and be harmed, and he knew that he would be harmed at that home. He commanded the door of his house opened while he ascended. He called his son, Qutham, who resembled the Prophet, and he composed a *rajaz* verse and raised his voice, so that the enemy would not rejoice about him. Among those present at al-ʿAbbās's door, were the angry, the saddened, and the gloating; as well as Muslims, men and women, feeling defeated for the victory of disbelief and oppression. When the Muslims saw al-ʿAbbās himself in good spirits, they were content and their resolve was strengthened. He called a youth named Abū Zubayna and said to him, "Go to al-Ḥajjāj and say, 'Al-ʿAbbās says that what you say is not true, for God is most high and most honorable.'" He came to al-Ḥajjāj, and al-Ḥajjāj said, "Say to Abū l-Faḍl, allow me in some of your houses until I come to you at noon with some of what you desire, but keep it secret."

Abū Zubayna approached and al-ʿAbbās was happy. "Rejoice about what gladdens you," he said, and it was as if he had not kept anything from him. Al-Zubayna came to him, and al-ʿAbbās embraced him and set him free. He informed him of what he said. Al-ʿAbbās said, "By God I will manumit ten slaves." When it was noon, al-Ḥajjāj came to him and implored him, "By God, conceal the information about me for three days," and al-ʿAbbās agreed to that. He said, "I have converted to Islam and I have money with my woman and debts from the people. But if they know about my Islam they will not pay me. I left the Messenger of God and he has conquered Khaybar. The arrows of God and His messenger sped into it. I left him marrying the daughter of Ḥuyayy b. al-Akhṭab, after Ibn Abī l-Ḥuqayq was killed."

He said: When in the evening al-Ḥajjāj set out, the nights seemed longer for al-ʿAbbās. It was said: Indeed al-ʿAbbās waited one day and one night. Then, al-ʿAbbās began to say, "O Ḥajjāj, observe what you say, for indeed I know about Khaybar which is entirely in the outskirts of the Ḥijāz. They are a people of strength and readiness. Is it true what you say?" He said, "Yes, by God. So keep my secret for a day and a night. Until when the time has passed and the people [Page 705] are busy about an affair they will not agree on."

Al-ʿAbbās took a suit of clothing and wore it. Then he put on perfume, and took a rod in his hand. Then he strode proudly forward until he stood at the door of al-Ḥajjāj b. ʿIlāṭ, and he knocked on it and his wife said, "Do not enter, Abū l-Faḍl." He said, "Where is al-Ḥajjāj?" She said, "He went to the plunder of Muḥammad to purchase what the Jews have taken from them before the merchants precede him to it." Al-ʿAbbās said to her, "Surely the man is not a husband to you unless you follow his religion. Indeed he has converted to Islam and attends the conquest with the Messenger of God. He went with his property fleeing from you and your people fearing that you may take it." she said, "Is it true, O Abū l-Faḍl?" He replied, "Yes, by God." She said, "By the shooting stars, you speak the truth." Then she stood up and informed her people.

Al-ʿAbbās turned to the temple and the Quraysh and informed them about the news of al-Ḥajjāj. When they looked at him and his condition, they made signs to one another, and were pleased about his endurance. Then he entered and circumambulated the house and they said, "O Abū l-Faḍl, this is, by God, endurance in the heat of the misfortune. Why did you not appear for three days?" Al-ʿAbbās said, "By no means! By that which you swear, surely he has conquered Khaybar, and was left a bride in the daughter of their king, Ḥuyayy b. Akhṭab. He has struck off the white and curly heads of the sons of Abū l-Ḥuqayq. You saw them, the Lords of the Naḍīr in Yathrib. Al-Ḥajjāj has fled with his wealth which was with his wife." They said, "Who informed you about this?" Al-ʿAbbās said, "The truth in my heart. Send to his family." So they sent and found that al-Ḥajjāj had left with his wealth that was previously with his wife. His family had kept it secret until morning. They asked about all of it and they found it true. The polytheists were crushed and the Muslims rejoiced about that. The Quraysh did not wait five days, when news came to them about that.

[Page 706] **THE AFFAIR OF FADAK**

They said: When the Messenger of God approached Khaybar, he went close to Fadak and sent Muḥayyiṣa b. Masʿūd to invite the people of Fadak to Islam, filling them with fear that they would attack them as they had attacked the people of Khaybar, and descend on their fields. Muḥayyiṣa said: I went to them and stayed with them for two days, and they tried to wait for an opportunity, saying, "In Naṭā are ʿĀmir, Yāsir, Usayr, al-Ḥārith and the lord of the Jews, Marḥab; we do not think Muḥammad would draw near pursuing them. Indeed, in it are ten thousand soldiers." Muḥayyiṣa said: When I saw their evil, I desired to ride back, but then they said, "We will send men with you who will take the peace for us," for they thought that the Jews would resist the Muslims. They continued thus until news arrived of the killing of the people of the fortress of Nāʿim including the people of help. That weakened their strength and they said to Muḥayyiṣa, "Hide about us what we say to you and you shall have this jewelry!" They had collected much of the jewelry of their women. Muḥayyiṣa said, "Rather, I will inform the Messenger of God about what I heard from you," and he informed the Messenger of God of what they said. Muḥayyiṣa said: A man from their leaders, called Nūn b. Yawshaʿ, came with me, with a group of Jews, and made an agreement with the Messenger of God that they would retain their blood, and he would dislodge them, and they would leave what lies between him and their property, and he did. It was said: They proposed to the Prophet that they go out from their land but that the Prophet should not take anything from their property. And when it was harvest time they would come and cut it. The Prophet refused [Page 707] to accept that, and Muḥayyiṣa said to them, "You have neither power nor men nor fortress. If the Messenger of God sent you a hundred men they would drive you to him." The agreement occurred between them, that to them was half of the land with its soil, and half for the Messenger of God. The Messenger of God accepted that. This is the most confirmed. The Messenger of God established them according to that, and he did not attack them.

When it was the caliphate of ʿUmar b. al-Khaṭṭāb, he expelled the Jews of Khaybar. ʿUmar sent those who would evaluate their land to them. He sent Abū l-Haytham b. al-Tayyihān, Farwa b. ʿAmr b. Ḥayyān b. Ṣakhar and Zayd b. Thābit and they evaluated the dates and the land for them. ʿUmar b. al-Khaṭṭāb took it and paid them half of the value of the dates and their soil. That reached fifty thousand dirham or more. That was the money that came to him from Iraq. ʿUmar expelled them to al-Shām. It was said that he sent Abū Khaythama al-Ḥārithī to evaluate it.

THE RETURN OF THE MESSENGER OF GOD FROM KHAYBAR TO MEDINA

Anas said: We turned with the Messenger of God from Khaybar, and he desired to go to Wādī al-Qurā. With him was Umm Sulaym bt. Milḥān. Some people wanted to ask the Messenger of God about Ṣafiyya when he passed with her and threw his cloak upon her. Then he proposed Islam to her and said, "If you will be in your religion, we will not compel you; but if you choose God and His messenger I will take you for myself." She replied, "Rather, I will choose God and His messenger." He manumitted her and he married her, and her freedom was her marriage price—*mahar*.

When they were in al-Ṣaḥbāʾ he said to Umm Sulaym: Watch over this companion of yours and comb her! He desired to marry her there. So Umm Sulaym rose. Anas said: we had neither tents nor canopies. So she took two garments [Page 708] two woolen wraps and hid them with those at a tree. She combed Ṣafiyya and perfumed her, and the Messenger of God married her there.

When he had set out from Khaybar, the Messenger of God had Ṣafiyya's camel brought to her. The Prophet secreted her in his garment; he put out his leg for her foot to be placed on it, but she refused and placed her knee on his leg. When he reached Thibār he desired to marry her there, and when she refused, he was hurt within, until he reached al-Ṣaḥbāʾ and went down to a tree; then she agreed. The Messenger of God said, "What brought you to what you did when I desired to alight in Thibār?"—and

Thibār was six miles, while al-Ṣaḥbā was twelve miles away. She replied, "O Messenger of God, I feared for your proximity to the Jews. When it was later I was secure." It increased his contentment with her, and he knew she had spoken truly. She went to him the eve of that night. The Prophet had a banquet for her at that time with ghee, barley and dates. Their bowl was of leather and spread out. The Messenger of God was seen eating with them on that leather. They said: Abū Ayyūb stayed up the night close to the Prophet's tent, standing with the sword until morning. When the Messenger of God set out next morning Abū Ayyūb pronounced *takbīr* and the Prophet said, "What is the matter, O Abū Ayyūb?" He replied, "O Messenger of God, you entered with this girl, and you had killed her father, brothers, uncle and husband and generally her relatives, and I feared that she would kill you." The Messenger of God laughed and spoke kind words to him.

When the Messenger of God alighted in Medina, Ṣafiyya alighted in the house of al-Ḥāritha b. al-Nuʿmān, and Ḥāritha moved out of it. ʿĀʾisha and Ḥafsa joined hands. [Page 709] ʿĀʾisha sent Barīra to Umm Salama to greet her. Umm Salama was the wife of the Prophet who was with the Prophet when he raided Khaybar. She asked her about Ṣafiyya, if she was beautiful. Umm Salama said, "Who sent you? ʿĀʾisha?" She was silent, and Umm Salama knew that ʿĀʾisha had sent her. Umm Salama said, "By my life, she is indeed beautiful. Indeed the Messenger of God loves her." Barīra came and informed ʿĀʾisha of the news. ʿĀʾisha went out disguised until she entered upon Ṣafiyya, and with her were women from the Anṣār. She looked at her, and ʿĀʾisha was veiled, but the Messenger of God knew her. When she went out the Messenger of God returned to her. He said, "O ʿĀʾisha, how did you like Ṣafiyya?" She said, "I did not see her long. I saw a Jewish woman, among Jewish women—she meant her aunts, paternal and maternal. But I was informed that you loved her, and this is better for her than if she were beautiful." He said, "O ʿĀʾisha, do not say this for surely I proposed Islam to her and she was swift to convert. Her Islam is good." He said: ʿĀʾisha returned and informed Hafsa of her beauty, and Hafsa also went to her and looked at her. Then she returned to ʿĀʾisha and said, "She is beautiful, but she is not as you described."

When the Messenger of God came to al-Ṣaḥbāʾ he went to Birma until he came to Wādī al-Qurā seeking those Jews who lived there. Abū Hurayra related: We set out with the Messenger of God from Khaybar to Wādī al-Qurā. Rifāʿa b. Zayd b. Wahb al-Judhāmī had gifted to the Messenger of God a black slave named Midʿam who would fix the saddle for the Messenger of God. [Page 710] When they alighted in Wādī al-Qurā, we finally reached the Jews and the people from the Bedouin had recourse to them. While Midʿam settled the Messenger of God, the Jews received us with spears where we alighted. There was no preparation and they were shouting in their fortresses. A destitute arrow pierced Midʿam and killed him. The people said: Paradise will delight you. The Messenger of God said, "No. By Him who holds my soul in his hand, the cloak, which he took on the day of Khaybar from the booty that had not been divided as it should, is now burning him in hell." When the people heard that, a man came to the people with a shoelace, or two. The Prophet said that the shoelace was of fire.

The Messenger of God charged his companions to fight. He lined them up and gave a flag to Saʿd b. ʿUbāda, a banner to al-Ḥubāb b. al-Mundhir, another to Sahl b. Ḥunayf, and yet another to ʿAbbād b. Bishr. Then the Messenger of God invited the Jews to Islam. He informed them that if they converted they would keep their property and retain their blood, and God would deal with them according to their accounts. A man among them challenged for a duel and al-Zubayr b. al-Awwām accepted it, and killed him. Then another challenged, and al-Zubayr accepted and killed him as well. Then another challenged, and ʿAlī accepted his challenge and killed him. Then another challenged to a duel and Abū Dujāna went to him and killed him. Then another challenged to a duel, and Abū Dujāna killed him also, until the Messenger of God had killed eleven men from them. Whenever a man was killed he invited those who were remaining to Islam. Indeed prayers were attended at that time. The Messenger of God prayed with his companions at that time. Then he returned and invited them to God and His Prophet.

[Page 711] They fought each other until evening, and it came to the point where the sun did not appear as much as a spear, when they surrendered. He conquered them by force. God plundered their property and they took furniture and goods in plenty. The Messenger of God stayed in Wādī al-Qurā for four days. He apportioned what he took among his companions in Wādī al-Qurā. But he left the dates and land in the hands of the Jews and employed them on it.

When news about the Messenger of God's conquest of Khaybar, Fadak and Wādī al-Qurā, reached the Jews of Taymā' they made peace with the Messenger of God on the *jizya*, and their property was established in their hands. During the caliphate of ʿUmar, he expelled the Jews of Khaybar and Fadak, but he did not expel the Jews of Taymā' and Wādī al-Qurā, because the latter were within the land of al-Shām. It was believed that land from below Wādī al-Qurā to Medina was the Hijāz. And what was north of the Hijāz was part of al-Shām. The Messenger of God turned from Wādī al-Qurā to return, after the completion of his conquest of Khaybar and Wādī al-Qurā, and God plundered it.

When he was close to Medina the Messenger of God traveled by night until, when it was almost dawn, he alighted and rested. He said, "Is there a righteous man who will protect his eyes from sleep, and preserve the prayer of dawn for us? Bilāl said, "I will, O Messenger of God." And the Messenger of God put down his head, and the people put down their heads. Abū Bakr al-Ṣiddīq said to Bilāl: "Watch your eyes." He said: I wrapped myself in my woolen cloak to confront the dawn. And I did not know when I lay down on my side, except when I awakened with the awakening of the people and the heat of the sun. Their tongues attacked me with blame, and the most vehement against me was Abū Bakr.

[Page 712] The Messenger of God completed his prayer, and his blaming was lighter than the people's. The Messenger of God said, "Whoever has a need let him disperse to it," and the people dispersed to the roots of trees. The Messenger of God said, "Proclaim the first call to prayer (*adhān*), O Bilāl." Bilāl said: Thus did I do on his trips. And I called out the call to prayer, and when the people gathered. The Messenger of God said: "Kneel for two bowings (*rakʿa*) of the dawn prayer," and they knelt. Then he said, "Call out the response to the call to prayer (*iqāma*), O Bilāl." And he continued to pray with us until the man was dripping sweat from his side for the heat of the sun. Then he gave greetings (*salām*s). He approached the people and said, *Our souls are in the hands of God, and if He wished He would have taken them, and He is entitled to them* (Q. 39:4). When He returned them (the souls) to us we prayed. Then he approached Bilāl and said, "What happened, O Bilāl." Bilāl said, "By my father and my mother, what took your soul took mine." The Prophet smiled.

When the Messenger of God looked at Uḥud he said, "Uḥud is a mountain that loves us and we love it. O God, indeed I will protect what lies between the two sides of Medina!" He said: The Messenger of God reached al-Jurf by night. He forbade the men from knocking on the door of his family after dark (*ʿIshā'*). Yaʿqūb b. Muḥammad related to me from ʿAbd al-Raḥmān b. ʿAbdullah b. Abī Ṣaʿaṣaʿa from al-Ḥārith b. ʿAbdullah b. Kaʿb from Umm ʿUmāra, who said: I heard the Messenger of God say while he was in al-Jurf, "Do not knock on the doors of women after the prayer of al-ʿIshā." She said: A man from the district visited his family and found what he detested, so he went on his way [Page 713] and did not renounce it. He withheld from divorcing her for he had children by her and loved her. But he disobeyed the Messenger of God and saw what he regretted.

ʿAbdullah b. Nūḥ al-Ḥārithiyya related to me from Muḥammad b. Sahl b. Abī Ḥathma from Saʿd b. Ḥizām b. Muḥayyiṣa from his father, who said: He said: We were in Medina and a famine struck us. We went out to Khaybar and stayed there, then we returned. Some times we went out to Fadak and Taymā'. The Jews were a community who had fruits, which they did not remove or cut down. As for Taymā' it was the source of a spring that went out from the bottom of a mountain and had never stopped since it began. As for Khaybar it had flowing water and the water was covered. As for Fadak, it was like that as well. And that was before Islam.

When the Messenger of God arrived in Medina and conquered Khaybar, I said to my companion, "Is there anything for you in Khaybar," for we were exhausted and famine had reached us. My companion said, "Surely, the land is not as it was. We are a Muslim people and surely we have arrived upon a people of enmity and deceit toward Islam and its people. And before that we were not worshiping anything." They said: We were exhausted and we went out until we reached Khaybar, and we reached a people possessing land, and dates, but not as they used to be. The Messenger of God paid them half. As for the nobility of the Jews, and the people of affluence among them—the sons of Abū l-Ḥuqayq, Sallām b. Mishkam, and Ibn al-Ashraf—had been killed. The remaining people had no wealth and indeed were laborers. We used to be in al-Shiqq for a day, in al-Naṭā for a day and in al-Katība for a day. We saw that al-Katība was the best for us, so we stayed there a few days. Then my companion went to al-Shiqq, away from me, and [Page 714] I had warned him of the Jews.

Later, I followed in his tracks asking about him until I finally reached al-Shiqq. The people from among them in the house said to me, "He passed by us when the sun was setting, desiring al-Naṭā." He said: I approached al-Naṭā until a youth among them said to me, "Let me show you your companion." Finally, he took me to a manhole and when he stood me on it, the flies rose from the man hole, and there was my dead, murdered companion. So I said to the people of al-Shiqq, "You have killed him." They said, "No by God, we had no knowledge of it." He said: A group of Jews helped me to take him out and I wrapped him in a cloth and buried him. Then I hurried out until I arrived at my people in Medina and informed them of the news. We found the Messenger of God desiring to fulfill his *ʿUmra*.

Thirty men came out with me from my people. The oldest was my brother Huwayyisa. The brother of the dead man, ʿAbd al-Raḥmān b. Sahl, came out with us. The dead man was ʿAbdullah b. Sahl; ʿAbd al-Raḥmān b. Sahl was younger than me. He was remembering his brother sadly. There was a softness about him. He knelt before the Messenger of God and we sat around him. The news had reached the Prophet.

ʿAbd al-Raḥmān said, "O Messenger of God, my brother was killed." The Messenger of God said, "Proclaim *takbīr*." Then, I spoke and he said, "Proclaim *takbīr*," and he was silent. My brother Ḥuwayyiṣa spoke, mentioning that we were suspicious of the Jews, and our opinion of them, and he was silent. Then I spoke. I informed the Messenger of God of the news, and the Messenger of God said, "Either they pay the blood money of your brother, or they should be informed of a battle from God and His messenger." The Messenger of God wrote to them about that, and they wrote to him, "We did not kill him." The Messenger of God said to Ḥuwayyisa, Muhayyisa and ʿAbd al-Raḥmān, and those who were with them, "Will you swear fifty oaths that you are entitled to the blood of your companion?" They said, "O Messenger of God, we were not present, and we cannot testify." He said, "But the Jews will swear to you." They said, "O Messenger of God they are not Muslims." [Page 715] The Messenger of God paid the blood money with a hundred camels, twenty-five date palms twenty-five ḥiqqa camels, twenty-five young female labnūn camels, and twenty-five young female makhād camels. Sahl b. Abī Ḥathma said: I saw them haul a hundred camels and a red camel kicked me: I was a youth at that time.

Ibn Abī Dhi'b and Maʿmar related to me from al-Zuhrī, from Saʿīd b. al-Musayyib, who said: The *qasāma* was in *jāhiliyya* and the Messenger of God accepted it in Islam. He judged the Anṣārī, who was found killed in Khaybar in one of the wells of the Jews, according to it. The Messenger of God said to the Anṣār, "The Jews will swear to you, fifty men fifty oaths, 'By God, we did not kill.'" They said, "O Messenger of God, how will you accept the oath of a people who are disbelievers?" The Messenger of God said, "Will you swear, fifty men, fifty oaths, by God, that they killed your companion and that you are entitled to the blood money?" They said, "O Messenger of God, we did not attend and we did not witness." He said: The Messenger of God placed the blood money on the Jews because he was killed in their presence.

Makhrama b. Bukayr related to me from Khālid b. Yazīd from ʿAmr b. Shuʿayb from his father, from his grandfather, He said: The Messenger of God judged his blood money on the Jews. If they did not give it, surely there would be a call to war from God and His messenger. The Messenger of God helped them with some thirty camels. It was the first of what was the *qasāma*. The people continued to attend to their properties in Khaybar according to the contracts of the Messenger of God, Abū Bakr, ʿUmar and ʿUthmān.

ʿAbd al-Raḥmān b. al-Ḥārith related to me from Sālim b. ʿAbdullah from his father (ʿAbdullah b. ʿUmar). [Page 716] He said: We went, I, al-Zubayr, al-Miqdād b. ʿAmr, and Saʿīd b. Zayd b. ʿUmar b. Nufayl, to our properties in Khaybar. We attended to it together. Abū Bakr used to send one who attended to it and saw to it. ʿUmar did that also. When we approached Khaybar we dispersed to our properties. We were attacked in the middle of the night, while I was sleeping on my bed, and my hands got injured. They asked me, "Who did this to you?" I said, "I do not know." They attended to my hands. One other than Sālim said from Ibn ʿUmar: They have charmed him in the night while he was sleeping in his bed. His hand was bent, as if he was tied up, and his friends came and attended to his hands. Ibn ʿUmar arrived in Medina and informed his father about what was done with him.

Muḥammad b. Yaḥyā b. Sahl b. Abī Ḥathma related to me from his father, who said: Muẓahhir b. Rāfiʿ al-Ḥārithī approached from al-Shām with ten infidels who worked for him in his land. He approached until he alighted in al-Khaybar and he stayed there for three days, when a man from the Jews visited them and said, "You are Christians and we are Jews and those people are Arabs who have vanquished us with the sword. And you are ten men, and one of them approached you and drove you from a land of wine and goodness to exhaustion and misery. You will be in deep subservience. So when you leave from our village, kill him." They said, "We do not have weapons with us." So they smuggled two or three knives to them. He said: They set out and when they were in Thibār, Muẓahhir said to one of them, and he was one who served them, "Get me such and such." When they approached him together, they had unsheathed their knives, so Muẓahhir set out running to his sword, which was in a container in his saddle. When he reached the container, he could not open it, and they slit his stomach. Then they turned and fled swiftly until they arrived in Khaybar at the Jews' place and the Jews gave them shelter and supplies, and strength to reach al-Shām.

News of the death of Muẓahhir b. Rāfiʿ, and what the Jews did to him, came to ʿUmar. ʿUmar stayed and spoke to the people. He praised God and extolled Him. Then he said, "O people, [Page 717] indeed the Jews did what they did with ʿAbdullah; and they did with Muẓahhir b. Rāfiʿ as they did with their enemy ʿAbdullah b. Sahl during the time of the Prophet. I do not doubt that they are his companions, and we do not have an enemy here other than them. So whoever has in it property, let him set out with me, for I am leaving to apportion the wealth in it, draw its borders, and define its limits and its features and to expel the Jews from it." Indeed, the Messenger of God said to them, "I establish according to what God establishes you." God permitted their exile, and if a man among them comes with an agreement or evidence that the Messenger of God established him, only then will I establish him. Ṭalḥa b. ʿUbaydullah stood up and said, "By God, you are right, O commander of the believers, I agree with you." Indeed, the Messenger of God said, "I will establish you in the manner God established you," and they did what they did with ʿAbdullah b. Sahl in the time of the Prophet. They incited against Muẓahhir b. Rāfiʿ until his slaves killed him. And they did what they did with ʿAbdullah b. ʿUmar, for they are a people whom we doubt and suspect. ʿUmar said: Who is with you that agrees with you? He said: All the Muhājirūn and the Anṣār. ʿUmar was happy about that.

Maʿmar related to me from al-Zuhrī from ʿUbaydullah b. ʿAbdullah b. ʿUtba, who said: It reached ʿUmar that the Messenger of God said during his sickness of which he died, "Two religions will not gather in the Arab peninsula." ʿUmar inquired about that until he found it confirmed by those whom he did not doubt. So he sent to the Jews of the Ḥijāz and said, "Those among you who have an agreement with the Messenger of God, I exile them. Indeed God most high has permitted their exile." ʿUmar sent out the Jews of the Ḥijāz.

[Page 718] They said: ʿUmar set out four portions: Farwa b. ʿAmr al-Bayāḍī, who had witnessed Badr; Ḥubāb b. Ṣakhr al-Sulamī who had winessed Badr; Abū l-Haytham b. al-Tayyihān who witnessed Badr; and Zayd b. Thābit. They apportioned Khaybar according to eighteen portions, on the heads of those the Prophet had named. He named eighteen portions and the names of its leaders. It was said: ʿUmar b. al-Khaṭṭāb named the heads, then he apportioned al-Shiqq and al-Naṭā. They apportioned it into eighteen portions. They made eighteen dung droppings and placed them in everyone's sight. For every head there was a token in the droppings. When the first dropping was taken out it was said: A portion for so and so. There were thirteen portions in al-Shiqq, and five portions in al-Naṭā. Ḥakīm b. Muḥammad related to me about that from the family of Makhrama from his father. The first portion he took out in al-Naṭā was apportioned to al-Zubayr b. al-Awwām. Then he apportioned to Bayāḍa. Some said its head was Farwa b. ʿAmr. Then it was apportioned to Usayd b. Ḥuḍayr, then, BalḤārith b. al-Khazraj. It was said that its leader was ʿAbdullah b. Rawāḥa. Then the portion of Nāʿim the Jew was apportioned. Then they apportioned in al-Shiqq.

ʿUmar b. al-Khaṭṭāb said: O ʿĀṣim b. ʿAdī, indeed you are a man of boundaries. So apportion to the Messenger of God from your portion. The first portion ʿĀṣim established was in al-Shiqq. It was said: Indeed he apportioned to the Prophet, and it was with the Banū Bayāḍā. And it is confirmed that it was with ʿĀṣim b. ʿAdī. Then he set out a portion for ʿAlī following the portion of ʿĀṣim. Then he apportioned to ʿAbd al-Raḥmān b. ʿAwf, then Ṭalḥa b. ʿUbaydullah, then the Banū Sāʿida. It was said: Their leader was Saʿd b. ʿUbāda. Then he apportioned to the Banū Najjār; then to the Banū Ḥāritha b. al-Ḥārith. Then he apportioned [Page 719] to the Aslam and Ghifār. It was said that their leader was Burayda b. al-Ḥuṣayb. Two portions were given for the Salima together. Then he apportioned to ʿUbayd al-Sihām, to ʿUbayd and to Aws. He came to ʿUmar b. al-Khaṭṭāb about it. Ibn Wāqid said: I asked Ibn Abī Ḥabība why he was named ʿUbayd al-Sihām? He said, "Dāwud b. al-Ḥuṣayn informed me that his name was ʿUbayd. But he began to purchase the *sihām* in Khaybar, so he was called ʿUbayd al-Sihām."

Ismāʿīl b. ʿAbd al-Malik b. Nāfiʿ, the *mawlā* of Banū Hāshim informed me from Yaḥyā b. Shibl from Abū Jaʿfar, who said: The first of what was apportioned in al-Shiqq was the portion of ʿĀṣim b. ʿAdī and in it was a portion for the Messenger of God.

Ibrāhīm b. Jaʿfar informed me from his father, who said, ʿUmar b. al-Khaṭṭāb said: I desired to take out my portion with the portion of the Messenger of God, but when he missed me, I said, "O God, make my portion in a place isolated so there will not be anyone on my path." His portion was isolated, and the Bedouin were his associates. And he extracted from their portions. He exchanged for a horse and other little things until the entire portion of the Aws belonged to him.

ʿAbdullah related to me from Nāfiʿ from Ibn ʿUmar, who said: When ʿUmar apportioned Khaybar he gave the wives of the Prophet a choice: to keep the provisions from al-Katība that the Prophet had apportioned to them, or to exchange it for land and water. ʿĀʾisha and Ḥafṣa were among those [Page 720] who chose land and water. The rest of them were guaranteed measures of dates. Aflaḥ b. Ḥumayd related to me, saying: I heard al-Qāsim b. Muḥammad say, I heard ʿĀʾisha say one day, "May God bless Ibn al-Khaṭṭāb. He let me choose between land and water, and provisions. I chose land and water, and they are in my hands." Those who chose provisions were apportioned once by Marwān, and once they were not given anything; and once it was given to them. It was said: Indeed ʿUmar only permitted the wives of the Prophet to choose.

Ibrāhīm b. Jaʿfar related to me from his father, who said: ʿUmar let all the people choose. Those who wished took a dry measure of provisions and those who wished took water and earth. He permitted all those who wished to sell, to sell; and all those who preferred to keep, he let those people keep it. And among those who sold were the Ashʿarī who took five thousand one hundred *dinar* from ʿUthmān b. ʿAffān, and Ruhāwī who took a similar amount from Muʿāwiya b. Abī Sufyān. Abū ʿAbdullah said: This is confirmed with us, and I saw the people of Medina doing this.

Ayyūb b. al-Nuʿmān related to me from his father, who said: ʿUmar gave the choice, to those who had provisions, between water and land or a guarantee of provisions. Usāma b. Zayd took the guarantee of provisions. When ʿUmar had finished apportioning, he sent out the Jews of Khayābir. ʿUmar went from Khaybar, with the Muhājirūn and the Anṣār, to Wādī al-Qurā. And Muʿāwiya set out with the portion which they apportioned: Jabbār b. Ṣakhr, Abū l-Haytham b. al-Tayyihān, Farwa b. ʿAmr, Zayd b. Thābit, apportioned it according to the number of portions. [Page 721] They knew its extent, and they drew its limits, and they made the portions a reward. What ʿUmar apportioned from Wādī al-Qurā to ʿUthmān b. ʿAffān was a consideration; to ʿAbd al-Raḥmān b. ʿAwf, a consideration; to ʿUmar b. Abī Salama there was a consideration—a consideration was a portion. To ʿĀmir b. Rabīʿa was a consideration; to Muʿayqib, a consideration; to ʿAbdullah b. al-Arqam, a consideration; to the Banū Jaʿfar, a consideration; to ʿAmr b. Surāqa, a consideration; to ʿAbdullah and ʿUbaydullah two portions; to Shuyaym, a portion; to Ibn ʿAbdullah b. Jahsh, a portion; to Ibn Abī Bakr, a portion; to ʿUmar a portion, to Zayd b. Thābit, a portion, to Ubayy b Kaʿb a portion, to Muʿādh b. ʿAfrā, to Abū Ṭalḥa and Jubayr, to Jabbār b. Sakhr, to Jabbār b. ʿAbdullah b. Rabāb, to Mālik b. Ṣaʿṣaʿa and Jābir b. ʿAbdullah b. ʿUmar, to Salama b. Salāma, to ʿAbd al-Raḥmān b. Thābit, and Ibn Abī Shurayq, to Abū ʿAbs b. Jabr and Muḥammad b. Maslama, and ʿAbbād b. Ṭāriq, a portion each. To Jabr b. ʿAtīk and Ibn al-Ḥārith b. Qays half a portion; to Ibn Jarma and al-Ḍaḥḥāk a portion.

ʿAbd al-Raḥmān b. Muḥammad b. Abī Bakr related to me from ʿAbdullah b. Abī Bakr from ʿAbdullah b. Muknif al-Ḥārithī, who said: Surely ʿUmar b. al-Khaṭṭāb set out to survey the land with two men, Jabbār b. Ṣakhr and Zayd b. Thābit. They were the assessors of Medina and its accountants. They surveyed Khaybar and evaluated the date palms of Fadak and its land. ʿUmar paid the Jews of Fadak half its value. The two men surveyed the portions in Wādī al-Qurā, then ʿUmar exiled the Jews of the Ḥijāz from it. Zayd b. Thābit donated as charity what came to him from Wādī al-Qurā with the rest of it.

[Page 722] THE EXPEDITION OF ʿUMAR B. AL-KHAṬṬĀB TO TURBA

Usāma b. Zayd b. Aslam related to us from Abū Bakr b. ʿUmar b. ʿAbd al-Raḥmān, who said: The Messenger of God sent thirty men with ʿUmar to ʿAjuz Hawāzin in Turba. ʿUmar set out with a guide from the Banū Hilāl. They marched by night and hid by day, but news came to the Hawāzin and they fled. ʿUmar came to their locality but did not meet even one of them. He turned to return to Medina, and when he was passing al-Najdiyya, and he was at the wall, the Hilālī said to ʿUmar b. al-Khaṭṭāb, "Would you like to have another group that I have left, from Khathʿam? They came walking, for their land is dry." ʿUmar said, "The Prophet did not command me about them. Indeed, he commanded me to stay and fight the Hawāzīn in Turba." And ʿUmar returned to Medina.

THE EXPEDITION OF ABŪ BAKR TO NAJD

Ḥamza b. ʿAbd al-Wāḥid related to me from ʿIkrima b. ʿAmmār from Iyās b. Salama from his father, who said: The Messenger of God sent Abū Bakr and appointed him commander over us. Our house was populated with Hawāzin. I killed seven of the people from Abyāt with my hands. The code was "Kill! Kill!"

[Page 723] THE EXPEDITION OF BASHĪR B. SAʿD TO FADAK

ʿAbdullah b. al-Ḥārith b. al-Fuḍayl related to me from his father, who said: The Messenger of God sent Bashīr b. Saʿd with thirty men to the Banū Murra in Fadak. He went out and met the shepherds and asked, "Where are the people?" They said, "They are in their wādī," for the people were experiencing winter and were not at the water. So he drove their sheep and the cattle and returned descending towards Medina. The herald came out and informed them, when a large group of Murra overtook him at night. So they spent the night aiming at them with arrows until Bashīr's companions ran out of arrows. In the morning the Murra attacked them and captured Bashīr's companions while those who turned escaped. Bashīr fought hard until his ankle was struck. Some said that he died. The Murra returned with their cattle and their sheep.

The first of those who arrived with news of the expedition and its misfortune was ʿUlba b. Zayd al-Ḥārithī. Bashīr b. Saʿd, who was with the casualties, now proceeded slowly. When it was evening he struggled on his feet until he reached Fadak. He stayed in Fadak with the Jews for several days until he recovered from the wound. Then he returned to Medina.

The Messenger of God armed al-Zubayr b. al-Awwām and said, "Go until you reach the wounded companions of Bashīr. If God grants you success, do not stay with them." He armed and sent two hundred men with al-Zubayr and gave al-Zubayr the flag. Then, Ghālib b. ʿAbdullah arrived from an expedition in which God had granted them success, so the Messenger of God said to Zubayr b. al-Awwām, "Be seated," and he sent Ghālib b. Abdullah with the two hundred men instead. Usāma b. Zayd together with ʿUlba b. Zayd (al-Ḥārithī) set out on [Page 724] the expedition, as well, until they reached the place of the wounded Bashīr and his companions.

Aflaḥ b. Saʿīd related to me from Bashīr b. Muḥammad b. ʿAbdullah b. Zayd, who said: Ghālib was with ʿUqba b. ʿAmr Abū Masʿūd, Kaʿb b. ʿUjra, Usāma b. Zayd, and ʿUlba b. Zayd. When Ghālib drew near them he sent the vanguard, i.e. ʿUlba b. Zayd with ten men, to observe the troops and their location. ʿUlba went close to a group of them and then returned and informed Ghālib. Ghālib now approached marching until all of a sudden he was among them, and visible to the eye by night. So they procured and prepared a place for the animals and came to a halt.

Ghalib stood and praised God and lauded him. Then he said, "As for later, I am decreed your guardian, fearing the One God who has no partner; so obey me, and do not resist nor dispute my command. Indeed, there is no decision for him who is not obeyed." Then Ghālib brought harmony between them, saying, "O so and so, go with so and so; none shall separate from his companion. If one of you should return to me alone, I will say, 'Where is your companion, so and so?' And never shall he answer, 'I do not know.' When I proclaim *takbīr*, you must proclaim *takbīr*." He said: And he proclaimed *takbīr*, and they proclaimed *takbīr*, and they took out their swords.

He said: We came down to where the sheep were settled, but their cattle were settled by the water hole. The men came out to us and we fought for a while. We placed our swords where we wished among them and we shouted out our code "Kill! kill!" Usāma b. Zayd set out in the tracks of a man among them named Nahayk b. Mirdās, and he had gone far. We united against the settled and we killed those who killed us, and with us were women and cattle. Our commander said, "Where is Usāma b. Zayd?" He arrived after a while in the night. Our commander rebuked him with a good scolding, and said, "Did you not understand my command?" [Page 725] He replied, "Indeed, I set out in the tracks of a man who made fun of me until I drew near him and struck him with my sword. Then, he said, 'There is no God but He!'" Our commander said, "And did you sheath your sword?" He said, "No, by God, I did not do so until I brought him to the other life." He said: We said, "By God, miserable is what you did, and how you brought him. You say you killed a man who says 'There is no God but Allah!'" And Usāma repented, and was confused about what he had done. He said: We drove the cattle, the sheep, and the children. Their portions were ten camels for every man, or an equal amount of cattle. A slaughter camel counted for ten sheep.

Shibl b. al-ʿAlāʾi related to me from Ibrāhīm b. Ḥuwayyiṣa from his father from Usāma b. Zayd, who said: Our commander established a brotherhood between me and Abū Saʿīd al-Khudrī. Usāma said: When I hurt him, I found a strong pain in my soul because of that, and I remember I was not able to eat food until I arrived in Medina. I came to the Messenger of God, and he received me and embraced me and I embraced him. Then he said to me, "O Usāma, inform me about your raid."

He said: And Usāma began to inform him of the news until he reached his companion who was killed. The Messenger of God said, "You killed him, O Usāma, when he said, 'There is no God but Allah?'" He said: I began to say, "O Messenger of God, surely he said it as a protection from being killed." The Messenger of God said, "Did you split open his heart to learn whether he was truthful or a liar?" Usama said, "I will not kill one who says there is no God but Allah." Usāma said: I wished that I had not converted except at that time.

Maʿmar b. Rāshid informed me from al-Zuhrī from ʿAṭā b. Yazīd al-Laythī from ʿUbaydullah b. ʿAdī b. al-Jabbār from al-Miqdād b. ʿAmr, who said: I said, "O Messenger of God, do you think if a man from the disbelievers who fought me, who struck one of my hands with the sword and cut it, and [Page 726] then sought protection from me in a tree and said, 'I have converted, by God,' that I could kill him after he said it?" The Messenger of God said, "Do not kill him!" He said, "Indeed, I killed him, so what?" The Messenger of God said, "What if he were in the situation you were in, before you killed him, and you were in his situation before he says the words that he said?"

THE EXPEDITION OF THE BANŪ ʿABD B. THAʿLABA COMMANDED BY GHĀLIB B. ʿABDULLAH TO AL-MAYFAʿA

ʿAbdullah b. Jaʿfar related to me from Ibn Abī ʿAwn from Yaʿqūb b. ʿUtba, who said: When the Messenger of God arrived from the raid of al-Kudra, he stayed several days, as God wished him to stay, and Yasār said to his master, "O Messenger of God, indeed I have known the heedlessness of the Banū ʿAbd b. Thaʿlaba, so send me with troops to them." The Prophet sent Ghālib b. ʿAbdullah and a hundred and thirty men with him. Yasār set out with them, departing on another road, until their provisions ended and they were exhausted and they were apportioning the dates by number.

Meanwhile the people were in the night, and their thoughts of Yasār were evil. The people thought that his Islam was not sound. They reached a place that had been hollowed out by a stream, and when Yasār saw it he proclaimed *takbīr*. He said, "By God, your success is in your need. Let us go along this hollow until it ends." The people went in it for a while, with their feelings concealed, and they did not speak except in whispers until they reached [Page 727] the rock of the Ḥarra.

Yasār said to his companions, "If a man shouted with a strong voice, surely the people will hear him, so make up your minds." Ghālib said. "Let us depart, O Yasār, I and you, and we will leave the people concealed," and so they did. And we set out, until all of a sudden we were among the people, within sight, and we heard the sounds of people, and shepherds and she-camels.

The two returned swiftly and reached their companions. Together they approached until they were close to the neighborhood. Their commander, Ghalib, had preached to them and awakened in them interest in *jihād*. He forbade them from going too far in a quest. He united them and said, "When I proclaim *takbīr*, you proclaim *takbīr*." He proclaimed *takbīr*, and they proclaimed *takbīr* with him. They fell into the middle of their courtyard and drove the cattle and sheep, killing those who opposed them. They met that night at the water named Mayfaʿa. He said: They drove the sheep down to Medina. It was not heard that they brought prisoners.

THE EXPEDITION OF BASHĪR B. SAʿD TO AL-JINĀB

Yaḥyā b. ʿAbd al-ʿAzīz related to me from Bashīr b. Muḥammad b. ʿAbdullah b. Zayd, who said: A man from the Ashjaʿa named Ḥusayl b. Nuwayra, the guide of the Messenger of God to Khaybar, arrived. The Messenger of God said to him, "From where do you come, Ḥusayl?" He said, "I come from al-Jināb." The Messenger of God said, "What is behind you?" He said, "I left a group of Ghaṭafān in al-Jināb. ʿUyayna had sent to them saying, 'If you do not march to us we will march to you.' So they sent to him saying, 'March [Page 728] to us and we will march to Muḥammad together,' for they desire you or some part of you."

He said: The Messenger of God called Abū Bakr and ʿUmar and mentioned that to them, and they both said, "Send Bashīr b. Saʿd." The Messenger of God called Bashīr and handed him the flag and sent three hundred men with him. He commanded them to march by night and hide by day, and Ḥusayl b. Nuwayra the guide set out with them. They marched by night and hid by day until they came to the bottom of Khaybar and they alighted at Salāḥ. Then they set out from Salāḥ until they were close to the people, and the guide said to them, "Between you and the people is two thirds or a half day's journey. If you like, hide, and I will set out ahead of you and bring you news, and if you like we will go together." They said, "Rather, we will send you ahead," and they sent him ahead.

The guide was gone for a while, then returned to them and said, "This is the first cattle of theirs, so would you attack them?" The companions of the Prophet disputed, and some of them said, "If we attack now, the men who are relaxing will be warned of us." The others said, "Let us capture what appears before us, and then we will seek out the people." They were daring about the cattle, and they took many cattle and filled their hands. But the shepherds dispersed, and they set out swiftly. They warned the group and the group dispersed and warned others. They went to a high place in their land. When Bashīr set out with his companions to their center he found no one there.

They returned with the cattle, and when they were in Salāḥ, those returning met a spy of ʿUyayna and killed him. Then, they met the group of ʿUyayna's people and ʿUyayna did not notice them and there was a skirmish. The group of ʿUyayna's people was exposed and the companions of the Prophet followed them. They took a man or two from them as captives and arrived with them before the Messenger of God. But the two converted, and the Messenger of God set them free.

[Page 729] They said: Al-Ḥārith b. ʿAwf al-Murrī was an ally of ʿUyayna and he joined him, fleeing on an excellent horse of his that ran swiftly with him. Al-Ḥārith asked ʿUyayna to stop, but he said, "No, the companions of Muḥammad are seeking me," and he continued galloping. Al-Ḥārith b. ʿAwf said, "Is it not time for you to see what you are doing? Indeed, Muḥammad has taken control of the land and your position is nothing." Al-Ḥarith said, "I step aside from the path of Muḥammad's horse, so that I see them but they do not see me. And I stop when the sun sets until night, and I do not see anyone." In truth, they were not really looking for him, it was only the fear in his heart that made him imagine things.

He said: I met him after that, and al-Ḥārith said, "Surely, I stayed in a place from sun set until night, and I did not see any one looking." ʿUyayna said, "That is it. Indeed, I feared captivity. My history with Muḥammad is, as you know, not perfect." Al-Ḥārith said: O man, you saw, and we saw with you a clear affair with the Banū Naḍīr, and the battle of al-Khandaq and Qurayẓa, and before that the Banū Qaynuqāʿ. And in Khaybar; indeed, they were the most excellent Jews of all al-Ḥijāz. Their bravery and generosity was well established. They were the people of forbidding fortresses, people of the date palm. By God, if the Arabs sought protection with them, they would be sheltered. Indeed Ḥāritha b. al-Aws went to them when there was between them and their people, what there was, and they were protected by them from the people. Then you saw Muḥammad alight with them, and how they lost their authority and were transformed. ʿUyayna said, "It is that, by God. But my heart does not settle me."

Al-Ḥārith said, "Enter with Muḥammad." ʿUyayna said, "I become a follower! The people who joined him earlier reviled those who come after them saying, 'We witnessed Badr and other wars.'" Al-Ḥārith said, "Indeed it is as you say. But if we approach him, we will be prominent companions of his. His people (the Quraysh) are still at peace with him. But he will cause their disaster, when the affair is established for him."

ʿUyayna said, "I see, by God!" They both agreed, [Page 730] desiring to emigrate, and to come before the Prophet, until Farwa b. Hubayra al-Qushayrī passed by them desiring *ʿUmra* and they both talked about it. The two informed him about what they were about and what they desired. Farwa said, "If you hold back until you see what his people (the Quraysh) do about this, for the period in which they are in, I will bring you news of them."

So they delayed meeting the Prophet, and Farwa went to Mecca seeking news of the Quraysh. And he found the people were still in enmity against Muḥammad. They did not desire to enter in obedience, ever. He informed them about what Muḥammad had done with the people of Khayābir. Farwa said, "I left the leaders of the vicinity in a state similar to what you are about enmity to Muḥammad." The Quraysh said, "What is the decision—you are the lord of the Bedouin?" He said, "We will spend this period of truce that is between you and him and we will summon the Bedouin. Then we will attack him in the heart of his homeland."

He stayed for several days occupied with the councils of the Quraysh and Nawfal b Muʿāwiya al-Dīlī heard about it. He came to him from the desert and Farwa informed him about what he said to the Quraysh. Nawfal said, "Then will I find something with you! I have come to meet you since news of your arrival reached me. We have an enemy whose house is close. They are a weak point for they are advisors of Muḥammad, and they do not hide a word of our affairs from him." He said, "Who are they?" Nawfal said, "The Khuzāʿa." He said, "The Khuzāʿa are ugly. May their right side be crippled!" Farwa said, "Then what?" He said, "Ask the Quraysh to help us against them." Farwa said, "I am sufficient for you." He met their leaders, Ṣafwān b. Umayya, ʿAbdullah b. Abī Rabīʿa, and Suhayl b. ʿAmr, and he said, "Do you not see what happened to you! Indeed you will be happy to push aside Muḥammad with ease." They said, "What should we do?" He said, "Help Nawfal b. Muʿāwiya against his enemies and yours." They said, "Then Muḥammad will attack us with what we have no power over, and he will trample us in victory, and his judgment will come down on us. [Page 731] We are now in a period of truce, keeping our faith." He joined Nawfal and said, "The people have nothing." Farwa returned and joined ʿUyayna and al-Ḥārith and he informed them and said, "I saw his people (Quraysh). They have made up their minds against him and come close and prepare the affair. But they advance on one foot and delay with the other in hesitation."

THE RAID OF AL-QAḌIYYA

Muḥammad b. ʿAbdullah related to me from al-Zuhrī and Ibn Abī Ḥabība from Dāwud b. al-Ḥuṣayn and Muʿādh b. Muḥammad from Muḥammad b. Yaḥyā b. Ḥubāb, ʿAbdullah b. Jaʿfar, Ibn Abī Sabra and Abū Maʿshar. Each related to me a portion of this tradition, as well as others whom I have not named. I wrote down all that they related to me.

They said: In Dhū l-Qaʿda of the year seven, the Messenger of God commanded his companions to go on pilgrimage to fulfill their *ʿUmra*. Not one who witnessed al-Ḥudaybiyya should stay behind. None who witnessed al-Ḥudaybiyya stayed behind except those who were martyred at Khaybar and those who had died. A group of Muslims who did not witness the peace of al-Ḥudaybiyya also set out with the Messenger of God as pilgrims. There were two thousand Muslims in the ʿUmrat al-Qaḍiyya.

Khārija b. ʿAbdullah related to me from Dāwud b. al-Ḥuṣayn from ʿIkrima from Ibn ʿAbbās, who said: the Messenger of God set out in Dhū l-Qaʿda in the year seven, four months after his arrival. It was the month in which the polytheists turned him away. For [Page 732] God most High says, *The prohibited month for the prohibited month. And so for all things prohibited* (Q. 2:194): God says, They turned you away from the House, so perform the lesser pilgrimage (*ʿUmra*) in the following holy month. Men from the settlers of Medina among the Bedouin said, "By God, O Messenger of God, we do not have provisions nor do we have those who will feed us." The Messenger of God commanded the Muslims to spend in the way of God, to give charity, and to not hold back their hands and destroy themselves. They said, "O Messenger of God, with what will one of us give charity when he does not find anything." The Messenger of God said, "With anything. Even with half a date, and even with the head of an arrow one of you carries with him in the way of God." God most high revealed about that: *And spend in the cause of God, and make not your own hands contribute to (your) destruction* (Q. 2:195). He said: It was revealed about the omission of spending in the cause of God.

Al-Thawrī related to me from Manṣūr b. al-Muʿtamir from Abū Ṣāliḥ from Ibn ʿAbbās, who said, "Provide in the cause of God even with an arrowhead. Let not your own hands contribute to your destruction." Al-Thawrī related to me from al-Aʿmash from Abū Wāʾil from Ḥudhayfa, who said that these verses were revealed about the omission of spending in the way of God. Ibn Mawhab related to me from Muḥammad b. Ibrāhīm b. al-Ḥārith, who said: The Messenger of God drove sixty sacrificial animals during the pilgrimage of fulfillment.

Ghānim b. Abī Ghānim related to me from ʿUbaydullah b. Yanār, who said: The Messenger of God appointed Najiya b. Jundub al-Aslamī over the sacrificial animals. He went, with the animals before him, seeking pasture in the trees. With him were four youths from the Aslam. [Page 733] ʿAbd al-Raḥmān b. al-Ḥārith related to me from ʿUbayd b. Abī Ruhm, who said: I was among those who drove the sacrificial animals, and I rode upon an animal intended for sacrifice. Muḥammad b. Nuʿaym related to me from his father from Abū Hurayra, who said: I was among those who accompanied the sacrificial animals and I drove them.

Yūnus b. Muḥammad related to me from Shuʿba, *mawlā* of Ibn ʿAbbās, who said: the Messenger of God adorned his sacrificial animal with his own hands, by himself.

Muʿādh b. Muḥammad related to me from ʿĀṣim b. ʿUmar, who said: the Messenger of God carried the weapons, helmet, armor and spear. He led a hundred riders. When he reached Dhū l-Ḥulayfa, he sent the cavalry forward, ahead of him. Leading the hundred riders was Muḥammad b. Maslama. He sent the weapons ahead, and appointed Bashīr b. Saʿd over them. It was said, "O Messenger of God, you carry weapons, but they have prescribed that we must only enter upon them with the weapons of the traveler, the swords sheathed." The Messenger of God said, "Indeed, we will not take the weapons into the sanctuary, but they will be close to us. If a disturbance from the people stirs us, the weapons will be near us." It was said, "O Messenger of God, do you fear the Quraysh about that?" The Messenger of God was silent and he sent the sacrificial animals forward.

Ibn Abī Sabra related to me from Mūsā b. Maysara from Jābir b. ʿAbdullah, who said: The Messenger of God put on his pilgrim's garb (*iḥrām*: two unstitched pieces of white cloth) at the gate of the sanctuary because he took the road of al-Furʿ. Otherwise, he would surely have appeared from al-Baydāʾ.

Ibn Abī Sabra related to me from Mūsā b. Maysara from ʿAbdullah b. Abī Qatāda from his father, who said: For the *ʿUmrat al-Qaḍiyya*, we took the road above al-Furʿ. My companions draped their *iḥrām* without me. I saw a wild donkey, and I desired it and killed it. I brought it to my companions and some of them ate and some of them left it. I asked the Prophet and he said, "Eat!"

[Page 734] Abū Qatāda said that when he performed the farewell pilgrimage, he wore the *iḥrām* from al-Baydāʾ. But this *ʿUmrat al-Qaddiyya* was from the *masjid* because his road was not through al-Baydāʾ. Ibn Wāqid said: The Messenger of God went, proclaiming, "I am at your service Lord," And the Muslims were proclaiming it also. Muḥammad b. Maslama went with the horses to Marr al-Ẓahrān. There, he found a group of the Quraysh who asked Maslama, and he said, "This is the Messenger of God who will arrive in the morning, at this station, tomorrow, God willing." They saw many weapons with Bashīr b. Saʿd and they set out swiftly until they came to the Quraysh and informed them about what they saw of horses and weapons. The Quraysh were afraid and they said, "By God, we did not do anything wrong and we are upon our document and our terms. Why would Muḥammad and his companions attack us?"

The Messenger of God alighted in Marr al-Ẓahrān. The Messenger of God sent the weapons to Baṭn Yaʾjaj where he saw the idols of the sanctuary. The Quraysh sent Mikraz b. Ḥafṣ b. al-Aḥnaf with a group of Quraysh to meet him in Baṭn Yaʾjaj. The Messenger of God was with his companions, his sacrificial animals and his weapons. They joined him and said, "O Muḥammad, by God, when you were little or older, you were never known for treachery. Yet, you enter the sanctuary with weapons against your people. You agreed that you would enter only with weapons of the traveler, and your swords in their scabbards." The Messenger of God said, "We will not enter it except thus," and Mikraz returned swiftly with his companions to Mecca and said, "Indeed, Muḥammad will not enter with weapons. He is following the prescriptions that you prescribed." When Mikraz came with news of the Prophet, the Quraysh set out from Mecca to the tops of the mountains and released Mecca. They said, "We will not observe either him or his companions." The Messenger of God ordered the sacrificial animals to be kept before him until they were moved to Dhū Ṭuwā.

The Messenger of God and his companions set out and God blessed them. The Messenger of God was on his camel [Page 735] al-Qaṣwāʾ, and his companions surrounded the Messenger of God, put on their swords and proclaimed the pilgrims call (*talbiyya*). When they reached Dhū Ṭuwā the Messenger of God stopped on his camel al-Qaṣwāʾ and the Muslims surrounded him. Then he entered from the narrow pass, which raised him above the pilgrims, on his camel Qaswāʾ. Ibn Rawāḥa took the reins of his camel. Saʿīd b. Muslim related to me from Zayd b. Qusayṭ from ʿUbayd b. Khadīj from one of the companions of the Prophet, that the Prophet did not stop the *talbiyya* until he came to the houses of Mecca.

Usāma b. Zayd related to me from ʿAmr b. Shuʿayb from his father from his grandfather that the Prophet called out the *talbiyya* until he touched the corner of the Kaʿba (*rukn*). ʿĀʾidh b. Yaḥyā related to me from Abū Ḥuwayrith, who said: The Messenger of God left behind two hundred men with weapons, under the command of Aws b. Khawlī.

Yaʿqūb b. Muḥammad b. ʿAbd al-Raḥmān b. ʿAbdullah b. Abī Ṣaʿṣaʿa related to me from al-Ḥārith b. ʿAbdullah b. Kaʿb from Umm ʿUmāra, who said: I witnessed *ʿUmrat al-Qadiyya* with the Messenger of God and I had witnessed Ḥudaybiyya. It is as though I see the Prophet as he reaches the house. He is on his camel and Ibn Rawāḥa has taken its reins and the Muslims have lined up for him. Then he draws near the corner until he reaches it. He touches the corner with his staff while he is on his camel, the end of his cloak draped under his right arm and over his left shoulder. [Page 736] The Muslims circumambulated with him, their garments draped similarly. ʿAbdullah b. Rawāḥa says:

> Get out of his way you sons of unbelievers.
> Indeed I witness that he is the Messenger of God.
> Truly, every good thing is in his way.
> We fought you on the basis of his interpretation
> Just as we fought you on his revelation
> With strokes that remove heads from shoulders
> Making friend unmindful of friend.

ʿUmar b. al-Khaṭṭāb said, "O Ibn Rawāḥa!" The Messenger of God said, "O ʿUmar, indeed I can hear!" and he kept ʿUmar quiet. Ismāʿīl b. ʿAbbās related to me from Thābit b. al-ʿAjlān from ʿAṭāʾ b. Abī Rabāḥ, who said: Gabriel came down to the Prophet and said, "Indeed the polytheists are on the mountain and they are observing you, so walk between the Yamani or Southern corner (of the Kaʿba) and the black stone." So they did.

Ibrāhīm b. Ismāʿīl related to me from Dāwud b. al-Ḥuṣayn from ʿIkrima from Ibn ʿAbbās, who said: The Messenger of God circumambulated the house, and then went between al-Ṣafā and al-Marwa on his camel. When it was his seventh arrival at al-Marwa, at its completion, he had the sacrificial animals brought to al-Marwa, and the Messenger of God declared, "This is the slaughtering place, and every wide road of Mecca is a slaughtering place," and he slaughtered at Marwa. Ibn Wāqid said: The people who went on *ʿUmra* with the Messenger of God but did not witness Ḥudaybiyya, did not slaughter. As for those who witnessed Ḥudaybiyya and set out on the *ʿUmra* of fulfillment, they shared the sacrificial animals.

Yaʿqūb b. Muḥammad related to me from ʿAbd al-Raḥmān b. ʿAbdullah b. Abī [Page 737] Ṣaʿṣaʿa from al-Ḥārith b. ʿAbdullah from Umm ʿUmāra, who said: Not one of the people of al-Ḥudaybiyya stayed behind, except those who were killed or had died. I set out with some women, and we did not arrive at the "House" at al-Ḥudaybiyya. They shortened their hair in al-Ḥudaybiyya; then they went on ʿUmra with the Prophet and fulfilled the ʿUmra. The Messenger of God slaughtered between al-Ṣafā and al-Marwa. Those who witnessed al-Ḥudaybiyya but were killed in Khaybar and could not witness the ʿUmrat al-Qaḍiyya were: Rabīʿa b. Aktham, Rifāʿa b. Masrūḥ, Thaqf b. ʿAmr, ʿAbdullah b. Abī Umayya b. Wahb al-Asadī, Abū Ṣayyāḥ, al-Ḥārith b. Ḥāṭib, ʿAdī b. Murra b. Surāqa, Aws b. Ḥabīb, Unayf b. Wāʾila, Masʿūd b. Saʿd al-Zurafī, Bishr b. al-Barā and ʿĀmir b. al-Akwaʿ. Ibn ʿAbbās used to relate that the Messenger of God commanded them to slaughter during the ʿUmrat al-Qaḍīyya. Those who found sacrificial camels slaughtered them. Those who did not find slaughtering camels were permitted to slaughter cows. When someone arrived with a cow, the people bought it from him.

Ḥizām b. Hishām related to me from his father that Khirāsh b. Umayya shaved the head of the Messenger of God at al-Marwa. ʿAbd al-Ḥamīd b. Jaʿfar related to me from Muḥammad b. Yaḥyā b. Ḥibbān that Maʿmar b. ʿAbdullah al-ʿAdawī shaved the Prophet. ʿAlī b. ʿUmar related to me from ʿAbdullah b. Muḥammad b. ʿUqayl from Saʿīd b. al-Musayyib, who said: When the Messenger of God completed the pilgrimage rituals he entered the House. He stayed in it until Bilāl proclaimed the call to prayer for *Ẓuhr*, from above the back of the Kaʿba. The Messenger of God had commanded him about that.

ʿIkrima b. Abī Jahl said, "Indeed God is most generous [Page 738] to Abū l-Ḥakam for he will not hear this slave say what he says." Ṣafwān b. Umayya said, "Praise be to God who removes my father before he sees this! "Khālid b. Asyad said, "Praise be to God who caused the death of my father so that he cannot witness this day when Bilāl, the son of Umm Bilāl, stands braying above the Kaʿba!" As for Suhayl b. ʿAmr and the men with him, when they heard that, they covered their faces.

Ibrāhīm b. Ismāʿīl related to me from Dāwud b. al-Ḥuṣayn, who said: The Messenger of God did not enter the Kaʿba during *al-Qaḍīya*. The Messenger of God sent to the Meccans requesting permission, but they refused. They said, "It is not in your agreement." He commanded Bilāl to proclaim the call to prayer from above the Kaʿba at that time, once, and he did not go back afterwards. It is confirmed.

Ibn Abī Ḥabība related to me from Dāwud b. al-Ḥuṣayn from ʿIkrima from Ibn ʿAbbās that the Prophet proposed to Maymūna while he was a pilgrim. She took her affair to al-ʿAbbās b. ʿAbd al-Muṭṭalib, and al-ʿAbbās gave her in marriage to the Prophet while he was a pilgrim. Hishām b. Saʿd related to me from ʿAṭāʾ al-Khurasānī from Saʿīd b. al-Musayyib, who said: After the Prophet dissolved his *ihram*, he married her.

Ibn Abī Ḥabība related to me from Dāwud b. al-Ḥuṣayn from ʿIkrima from Ibn ʿAbbās, who said: Indeed ʿUmāra bt. Ḥamza b. ʿAbd al-Muṭṭalib and her mother Salmā bt. ʿUmays were in Mecca when the Messenger of God arrived. ʿAlī spoke to the Prophet and said, "Why do we leave the daughter of our uncle, an orphan, in the midst of polytheists?" The Prophet did not forbid ʿAlī from going out to her, and he went to her. Zayd b. Ḥāritha spoke, and he was the trustee of Ḥamza, and the Prophet had established a brotherly bond between them when he fraternized the Muhājirūn—emigrants—and established a brotherly pact between them. [Page 739] And he said: I have a greater right with her, the daughter of my brother. When Jaʿfar heard that, he said, "The aunt is a mother. I have a greater right to her for her aunt, Asmāʾ bt. ʿUmays, is with me." ʿAlī said, "Do not dispute about my cousin, for it was I who set out with her from the midst of the polytheists. You do not have a relationship with her without me, and I am closer to her than you!"

The Messenger of God said, "I will judge between you! As for you, O Zayd, you are the freedman of God and His messenger; You, O ʿAlī, are my brother and my companion, As for you, O Jaʿfar, you bear a resemblance to my outer appearance (*khalq*) and my character (inner appearance). You, O Jaʿfar, have a greater right with her. Her aunt is your wife. A woman should not be married to the husband of her maternal or paternal aunt." And the Messenger of God judged her for Jaʿfar. Ibn Wāqid said: When he judged her for Jaʿfar, Jaʿfar stood up and skipped around the Prophet. The Prophet said, "What is this, O Jaʿfar?" He replied, "O Messenger of God, when the Negus satisfied one from his community, the man would stand up and skip around the Negus." It was said to the Prophet, "Marry her!" He said, "She is the daughter of my foster brother who nursed with me." The Messenger of God married her to Salama b. Abī Salama. The Prophet used to say, "Have I rewarded Salama?"

ʿUbaydullah b. Muḥammad related to me: At noon on Wednesday, Suhayl b. ʿAmr and Ḥuwayṭib b. ʿAbd al-ʿUzzā arrived, while the Messenger of God was in one of the councils with the Anṣār, and Saʿd b. ʿUbāda was talking to him. He said, "Your time is fulfilled, so leave us!" The Prophet said, "Would you allow me to be married in your midst, and I will prepare food for you?" They said, "We have no need [Page 740] for your food. Leave us! We beseech you, by God, O Muḥammad. The agreement between us and you is that you leave our land—for the three days are past." The Messenger of God did not stay at any house. He had struck up a tent of leather in al-Abṭaḥ and he stayed there until he departed. He did not enter under a roof of one of their houses. Saʿd b. ʿUbāda was angry when he saw the rudeness of their words to the Prophet. He said, "O Suhayl, You lie! May you not have a mother! This is neither your land nor the land of your fathers. By God, we do not depart from it except as obedient and satisfied." The Messenger of God smiled. He said, "O Saʿd, do not harm a people who visit us during our journey." He said: The two men were silent before Saʿd. He said: Then the Messenger of God commanded Abū Rāfiʿ about the journey. He said that no Muslim should spend the night in Mecca.

The Messenger of God rode until he alighted in Sarif. The people had fulfilled their pilgrimage. He left Abū Rāfiʿ behind, to bring his wife to him in the evening. Abū Rāfiʿ stayed and set out with Maymūna and those who were with her in the evening. They had trouble from the foolish among the polytheists who harmed the Prophet with their tongues. Abū Rāfiʿ said to her: I expected one of them to attack him, but they did not. I said to them, "What do you wish! These are, by God, the horses and weapons that were in Baṭn Yaʿjaj!" Indeed, the horses had drawn near and stopped for us, over there, with the weapons. The Messenger of God had commanded two hundred of his companions when they had circumambulated the house to go to their companions in Baṭn Yaʾjaj and stay by the weapons, while the others came and fulfilled their devotions, and they did as commanded. When [Page 741] we reached Baṭn Yaʾjaj they marched with us. We did not reach Sarif until most of the night had passed by. Then we came to Sarif. The Messenger of God consummated his marriage with her. Then he set out at nightfall until he arrived in Medina.

THE EXPEDITION OF IBN ABĪ L-ʿAWJĀʾ AL-SULAMĪ IN DHŪ L-ḤIJJA IN THE YEAR SEVEN AH

Muḥammad related to me from al-Zuhrī, who said: When the Messenger of God returned from ʿUmrat al-Qaḍiyya in the year seven—he returned in Dhu al-Ḥijja—he sent Ibn Abī l-ʿAwjāʾ al-Sulamī with fifty men to the Banū Sulaym. There was a spy from the Banū Sulaym with him. When he departed from Medina the spy set out to his people and warned them and informed them, so they gathered many together. When Ibn Abī l-ʿAwjāʾ came to them the people were prepared for him. When the companions of Muḥammad saw them, and they saw all of them, they invited them to Islam. But they pelted them with arrows and did not hear their words. They said, "There is no need for your invitation to Islam," and they aimed at them for a while. Helpers came until they surrounded them from every direction. The people fought a terrible battle until most of them were killed. Ibn Abī l-ʿAwjāʾ, their leader was wounded among the dead. He braced himself until he reached the Messenger of God.

THE CONVERSION OF ʿAMR B. AL-ĀṢ

ʿAbd al-Ḥamīd b. Jaʿfar related to us from his father, who said: ʿAmr b. al-ʿĀṣ said: I was a stranger to Islam and resisted it. I attended Badr with the polytheists, and was saved. I attended Uḥud, and was saved. Then I attended al-Khandaq, and I said to myself, how much [Page 742] must I suffer? By God, Muḥammad will surely be victorious over the Quraysh! And I left my property with my people and fled—meaning from the people. I did not attend al-Ḥudaybiyya or its peace. The Messenger of God turned back with the truce and the Quraysh returned to Mecca. I said repeatedly, Muḥammad will enter Mecca next year with his companions. Mecca and al-Ṭāʾif are not stations. There is nothing better than going out. I am distinct from Islam. I believed that even if all the Quraysh converted, I would not convert. I arrived in Mecca and gathered men from my people, and they used to consider my opinion and listen to me, and they would send me to represent them. I said to them, "How am I with you?" They said, "The possessor of our opinion and our lord, with a lucky soul and a blessed affair." He said, "You know, by God, that I see the affair of Muḥammad is an affair that will rise to unacknowledged heights. Indeed I have an idea." They said, "What is it?" He said, "We will go to the Negus and stay with him. If Muḥammad is victorious we will be with the Negus; and we will be under the hand of the Negus, which is more desirable than that we be under the hand of Muḥammad. If the Quraysh are victorious, we are those whom they know." They said, "This is the decision."

They decided on what to take as a gift for the Negus. The most desirable thing to gift from our land was leather. He said: we collected much leather. Then we set out until we arrived at the Negus' and, by God, we were with him when ʿAmr b. Umayya al-Ḍamrī arrived. The Messenger of God had sent him with a document marrying him to Umm Ḥabība, the daughter of Abū Sufyān. He went before him and then came out from his presence. [Page 743] I said to my companions, "This is ʿAmr b. Umayya, and if I go before the Negus and ask him for ʿAmr, and he hands him to me, I shall cut off his head. If I do that, the Quraysh will be happy, for I would satisfy the Quraysh when I kill the messenger of Muḥammad."

He said: I entered upon the Negus and I bowed down to him just as I used to do. He said, "Greetings to my friend! Do you bring me a gift from your land?" He said: I said, "Yes, O King, I have brought you a gift of many skins." Then I took it close to him and it pleased him. He distributed some of it among the patriarchs and he commanded that the rest of it be stored in a place, and he commanded that it be recorded and protected. When I saw his satisfaction I said, "O King, indeed I saw a man go out from your place. He is the messenger of a man who is an enemy of ours. He has wronged us and killed our nobility and the best of us, so give him to me that I may kill him!" He raised his hand and struck my nose with a blow, I thought he had broken it. My nose began to bleed and I made to receive the blood in my garment. Shame struck me to such an extent that if the earth were cleft I would have entered in it from fear. Then I said to him, "O King, if I thought that you would detest what I did I would not ask you." He said he was embarrassed. He said, "O ʿAmr, you ask me to hand you the messenger of the Messenger of God—to whom the great namus, which came to Moses and to Jesus son of Mary, arrived, so that you may kill him?" ʿAmr said: God changed my heart from what I was about, and I said to myself, the Arabs and non-Arabs knew about this truth but you disagreed? I said, "Did you witness, O King, about this?" He said, "Yes, I witnessed about him with God, O ʿAmr, so obey me and follow him. By God, he is on the truth and he will be victorious over every religion opposing him, just as Moses was victorious over the Pharoah and his soldiers." I said, "Will you take my pledge of allegiance to Islam?" He said, "Yes." He stretched out his hand and I gave him my pledge of allegiance to Islam.

[Page 744] He called for a tub and washed the blood from me and dressed me in garments, for my garments were full of blood and I threw them away. Then I set out to my companions and when they saw the clothes of the king they were happy about that and they said, "Did you take what you desired from your master?" I said to them, "I hated to speak to him in the first visit, and I said I would return to him." They said: The consensus (opinion) is what you see!

I withdrew from them as though I was approaching a need of mine, and I went to the place of the ships. I found a ship loaded with cloths. I rode with them and they pushed it until it reached al-Shuʿayba. Then I set out from al-Shuʿayba. I had some money with me, and I purchased a camel and set out in the direction of Medina until I was close to Marr al-Ẓahrān. Then I continued until I was in al-Hadda, where two men who were just ahead of me had stopped. One of them was in his tent. The other was standing holding their two animals. I looked, and lo and behold, it was Khālid b. al-Walīd. I said, "Abū Sulaymān?" He said, "Yes." I said, "What do you want?" He said, "Muḥammad. People have entered Islam, and none who is ambitious is left out. By God, if we stay he will take our necks just as the neck of the hyaena is taken in its cave." I said, "I, too, by God, desire Muḥammad and Islam." ʿUthmān b. Ṭalḥa came out and he welcomed me and we alighted together in the shelter. Then we were companions until we arrived in Medina. I shall not forget the words of the man whom we joined in Biʾr Abī ʿInaba, shouting, "O profit! O profit." We regarded his words as a good omen, and were happy. Then he looked at us and I heard him say, "Mecca has offered the leaders after these!" I thought he meant me and Khālid b. al-Walīd. Then he turned his back, running to the mosque swiftly, [Page 745] and I thought that he was informing the Messenger of God of our arrival.

It was just as I thought. We stopped at al-Ḥarra and put on some suitable clothes. There was the call for the *ʿAsar* prayer, and we departed together until we appeared before the Prophet, may peace be upon him. Indeed he was happy—his face shone like the moon. The Muslims around him rejoiced in our Islam. Khālid b. al-Walīd went ahead and gave his allegiance. Then ʿUthmān b. Ṭalḥa went and gave his; then I went forward, and by God it was not until I sat down before him—and I was not able to raise my glance to his for shyness of him. I pledged to him, provided that he forgave me my previous sins. To ask for forgiveness of my future sins did not occur to me. He said that Islam cuts off completely what was before it, and that the emigration would cut off what was before it.

The Messenger of God has not turned away from me and Khālid b. al-Walīd for one of his companions about a serious affair of his, since we converted. Indeed we were on the same level with Abū Bakr. And I was on the same level as ʿUmar. But ʿUmar censured Khālid. ʿAbd al-Ḥamīd said: I mentioned this tradition to Yazīd b. Abī Ḥabīb and he said: Rāshid mawlā of Ḥabīb b. Abī Uways from Ḥabīb b. Aws al-Thaqafī from ʿAmr informed me about that. ʿAbd al-Ḥamīd said: I said to Yazīd, "Did he not specify the time for you when ʿAmr and Khālid arrived?" He said, "No, except that it was shortly before the conquest." I said: Indeed. My father informed me that ʿAmr and Khālid and ʿUthmān b. Ṭalḥa arrived in Medina in the beginning of Ṣafar, in the year eight AH.

Abū l-Qāsim ʿAbd al-Wahāb b. Abī Ḥabība informed us saying, Muḥammad b. Shujāʿ informed us that Muḥammad b. ʿUmar al-Wāqidī said: Yaḥyā b. al-Mughīra b. ʿAbd al-Raḥmān b. al-Ḥārith b. Hishām said: I heard my father relate and say, [Page 746] that Khālid b. al-Walīd said: When God desired goodness from me, he cast the love of Islam in my heart. Reason came to me and I said, "I have witnessed these battles all of them against Muḥammad, and from every battle that I witnessed I departed believing that I was on the wrong side and Muḥammad would surely be victorious." When the Messenger of God went to al-Ḥudaybiyya I went out with the cavalry of the polytheists and met the Messenger of God with his companions in ʿUsfān. I stood in front of him resisting him. But he prayed *Ẓuhr* with his companions secure from us even as we planned to attack him—and we could not do it.—There was goodness in him, and he beheld what was in our hearts. He prayed the prayer of *ʿAsar*, in fear, with his companions. This impressed me and I said, "The man is protected." We separated and he deviated from the path of our cavalry and took the road to the right. When he made peace with the Quraysh in al-Ḥudaybiyya the Quraysh pushed him to the latter part of the day—delaying him. I said to myself, "Which thing is for me? What is left? Where is the way to the Negus? He follows Muḥammad, and his companions are safe with him. Shall I set out to Heraclius? Do I leave my religion for Christianity or Judaism and live with non-Arabs, following them, or stay in my homeland with those who remain?" And I was considering that when the Messenger of God entered for the ʿUmrat al-Qadiyya. I, however, was absent and did not witness his entry.

[Page 747] My brother al-Walīd b. al-Walīd had entered Mecca with the Prophet during the *ʿUmrat al-Qaḍiyya*. He looked for me but could not find me, so he wrote a letter to me. It said: "In the name of God most gracious most merciful." And after, "I do not see anything more strange than your staying away from Islam. You have such a good mind. Can anyone miss Islam? The Messenger of God asked me about you. He said, 'Where is Khālid?' I said, 'God will bring him.' He said, 'None like him can be ignorant of Islam. If he placed his intelligence and resoluteness with the Muslims against the polytheists, it would be better for him. We would prefer him over others—or we would make him a leader over others.' So understand, O brother, what is passing you by. Many good opportunities have passed you by."

When his letter came to me I was eager to go out. It increased my appetite for Islam and the words of the Prophet pleased me. Khālid said: I dreamed that I set out from a poor and barren land to a green and spacious one. I said, indeed this is a dream. But when I arrived in Medina I thought, surely I should mention it to Abū Bakr. He said: I mentioned it and he said, "The destination to which God guides you is Islam. Your earlier poverty was due to your polytheism."

When I gathered to go out to the Messenger of God I said: Who will I take with me to the Messenger of God? I met Ṣafwān b. Umayya and I said, "O Abū Wahb, do you not see what we are in? Indeed we are the main fodder. Muḥammad is victorious over the Arabs and non-Arabs. If, however, we go before Muḥammad and follow him, indeed the nobility of Muḥammad will be our nobility." But he refused with great aversion and said, "Even if I were the only Qurayshī alive, I would never follow him." We separated, and I said: This is a man wronged by the murder of a relative who seeks revenge. His father and his brother were killed at Badr. Then I met ʿIkrima b. Abī Jahl and I said to him as I said to Ṣafwān, and he replied in a similar vein. [Page 748] I said, "Keep secret what I said to you." He replied, "I will not mention it." I went to my house and ordered my ride to be brought to me. I set out with it until I met ʿUthmān b. Ṭalḥa. I said to myself: surely, this is a friend. Let me tell him what I desire. Then I mentioned those who were killed among his forefathers though I hated reminding him. Then I said: What will happen to me? I shall leave this minute. I mentioned to him how the affair had affected him, and I said: Surely we are like a fox in a hole. If a bucket of water were poured upon it, it would leave. He said: I repeated to him what I had said to his two companions. He hastened to respond saying, "Surely, you leave today and I desire to leave, but my ride is tied up in Fakh." He said: I came to an understanding with him to meet around Yaʿjaj. If he preceded me he would wait for me, and if I preceded him I would wait for him. He said: We set out at nightfall in the last part of the night, and the dawn did not rise until we met in Yaʿjaj. We departed until at last we reached al-Hadda, and found ʿAmr b. al-ʿĀṣ there. He said, "Greetings to the people." And we said, "And to you too." He said, "Where are you going?" We said, "What brings you out?" He said, "And what is it that takes you out?" We said, "The desire to enter Islam and follow Muḥammad." He said, "That is what brings me out, as well."

He said: We set out together until we reached Medina. There, we stopped our rides on top of al-Ḥarra. The Messenger of God was informed about us and he was happy to hear about us. I put on one of my best garments and approached the Messenger of God. My brother met me. He said, "Hurry, for indeed the Messenger of God has been informed about you and is happy about your arrival and is expecting you." I hurried, walking, and ascended to meet him. He kept smiling until I stopped before him. I greeted him submitting to his prophethood. [Page 749] He returned the greeting with a face of happiness. I said, "I testify that there is no God but Allah and that you are His messenger." He said, "Praise be to God who guided you. I have noticed your intelligence and hope that your Islam is only for the good." I said, "O Messenger of God, you saw what I witnessed from those places against you, stubbornly resisting the truth. Ask God, so that He will pardon me?" The Messenger of God said, "Islām cuts off what was before it." I said, "O Messenger of God, from that? So he said, "O God, forgive Khālid, all that he did to impede others from your path." Khālid said: Then ʿAmr went forward, and then ʿUthmān pledged allegiance to the Messenger of God. We had arrived in Ṣafar, of the year eight. By God, the Messenger of God was on the same footing with me as he was with one of his companions about what happened to him.

Abū ʿAbdullah said: I asked ʿAbdullah b. ʿAmr b. Zuhayr al-Kaʿbī: When did the Messenger of God write his letter to the Khuzāʿa? He said: My father informed me from Qabīṣa b. Dhuayb that he wrote to them in Jamādā l-Ākhira in the year eight AH, and that many of the Bedouin had converted. But there were also those who remained in their polytheism.

When the Messenger of God turned from al-Ḥudaybiyya there did not remain a single Khuzāʿa who was not a Muslim believing in Muḥammad. They came to him in Islam while he was with a few of his companions. Even ʿAlqama b. ʿUlātha and the two sons of Hawdha came forward and emigrated. That was when the Messenger of God wrote to the Khuzāʿa, "In the name of God, most gracious and merciful, from Muḥammad the Messenger of God to Budayl, and to Bishr and Sarawāt, the sons of ʿAmr, peace to you! Indeed, I praise God for you. There is no God except He." Then after, "I did not commit the smallest wrong against you nor did I attack your site. [Page 750] Indeed the most noble of the Tihāma, in my estimation, are you and the closest in relationship are you and those who follow you among the good people. I have taken for those who emigrated among you similar to what I took for myself—even if he emigrated in his land—there is no settling in Mecca except as a pilgrim for the *ʿUmra* and the *Ḥajj*. I will not attack you if I have a truce, and you should not be afraid, nor besieged from my side. Later, ʿAlqama and his two sons converted to Islam. They followed and immigrated with those who followed them from ʿIkrima. I take from those of you who follow me, what I take from myself. We belong to each other forever, during both protected and free times. By the Lord, I do not lie to you, and the Lord loves you."

ʿAbdullah b. Budayl related to me from his father from his grandfather from ʿAbdullah b. Maslama from his father from Budayl b. Waraqāʾ, similarly.

THE EXPEDITION OF ITS COMMANDER GHĀLIB B. ʿABDULLAH IN AL-KADĪD

Al-Wāqidī related to us that ʿAbdullah b. Jaʿfar related to us from ʿAbd al-Wāhid b. Abī ʿAwn from Yaʿqūb b. ʿUtba from Muslim b. ʿAbdullah al-Juhannī from Jundub b. Makīth al-Juhannī, who said: The Messenger of God sent Ghālib b. ʿAbdullahal-Laythī one of the Banū Kalb b. ʿAwf on an expedition, and I was with them. He commanded him to raid the Banū al-Mulawwaḥ in al-Kadayd. They were from the Banū Layth. We set out until all of a sudden we were in Qudayd where al-Ḥārith b. Mālik b. al-Barṣāʾ met us. We took him captive, and he said, [Page 751] "Surely I came desiring Islam." We said, "A knot will not harm you in a night, even if you desired Islam. If it is otherwise, we have made sure of you." We secured him with shackles. One of us, Suwayd b. Ṣakhr, stayed behind with him, and we said, "If he resists you, cut off his head." Then we marched until we came to al-Kadayd at sunset. We hid in the region of the wadi.

My companions sent me as a scout for them. I set out and I came to a hill that rose above the settlement to overlook them. When I ascended it, and I was at its top, I lay down with my face to the ground, and, by God, I observed a man among them come out from his hiding place. He said to his wife, "By God, I see over the hill, a blackness that I did not see over it this forenoon. Look at your vessels and see if the dogs have not taken something from it." She looked and she said, "By God, I have not lost any of my utensils." He said, "Bring me my bow and my arrow!" So she brought his bow and arrows, and he sent an arrow, which by God, it did not escape my side. I pulled it out and placed it firmly beside me. Then he aimed at me again and he struck me with it also. I took it and placed it at my side. He said to his wife, "By God, if it were living, it would surely move after! Surely, two arrows pierced him or may you not have a father! When it is morning go and get the two arrows. The dogs must not chew them." Then he entered his hideout, and let the cattle graze among the community's camel and sheep, and they were milked and made to rest after drinking at the watering place. When they were rested and calm, we launched a raid against them. We killed the warriors and took the children prisoner.

We drove the cattle and set out descending in the direction of Medina until we passed by Abū Barṣā'. [Page 752] We took him and we took our friend. Screams of the people went out to their people and what had never occurred to us came to us. They observed us, and between us and them was a riverbed (*wādī*) and they were facing us. Then God brought water to the *wadi* from where He wished and filled its sides. By God, before that, we had not seen a cloud or rain. And He brought what one was not able to cross. Indeed I saw them standing and observing us. We ascended to al-Mushallal. We went ahead of them and they were not able to reach us. I shall not forget the *rajaz* of our commander Ghālib:

> Abū l-Qāsim refused that you stay,
> And that was a true saying, he did not lie.
> In fields of thick grass with golden yellow tops.

ʿAbd al-ʿAzīz b. ʿUqba related to me about Muḥammad b. Ḥamza b. ʿAmr al-Aslamī from his father, who said: I was with them, and we were about ten men. Our code was, "Kill! Kill!"

THE EXPEDITION OF KAʿB B. ʿUMAYR TO DHĀT AṬLĀḤ

Al-Wāqidī said: Muḥammad b. ʿAbdullah related to me from al-Zuhrī, who said: The Messenger of God sent Kaʿb b. ʿUmayr al-Ghifārī with fifteen men to Dhāt Aṭlāḥ near the land of al-Shām. There they found one of the larger groups [Page 753] and invited them to Islam, but they did not reply, but pelted them with arrows. When the companions of the Prophet saw that, they fought hard until they were killed. A wounded man from among the dead escaped. In the cooling night he struggled until he came to the Messenger of God and informed him of the news. That was unbearable to the Messenger of God and he almost sent a raid against them. But it reached him that they had marched to another place so he left them.

Ibn Abī Sabra related to me from al-Ḥārith b. al-Fuḍayl, who said: Kaʿb used to hide by day and march by night until he was near them. A spy of theirs saw him and informed them about the small number of the companions of the Prophet. They came, riding horses and killed them.

THE EXPEDITION OF SHUJĀʿ B. WAHB TO AL SIYY

Al-Wāqidī related to me saying: Ibn Abī Sabra related to me from Isḥāq b. ʿAbdullah b. Abī Farwa from ʿUmar b. al-Ḥakam, who said: The Messenger of God sent Shujāʿ b. Wahb with twenty-four men to a gathering of the Hawāzin in al-Siyy. The Messenger of God commanded him to attack them. So he set out. He used to march by night and hide by day until he attacked them one morning when they were careless. He had informed his companions before that, that they should not be excessive in the search. They captured many cattle and sheep. They drove all of that until they arrived in Medina. Their portions were fifteen camels for every man. [Page 754] A camel was equal to ten sheep. The expedition lasted fifteen nights.

Ibn Abī Sabra said: I related this tradition to Muḥammad b. ʿAbdullah b. ʿUmar b. ʿUthmān, who said: They had captured women from the settlement and driven them. Among those they captured was a beautiful girl, and they brought her to Medina. Then a party of them who were Muslims arrived in Medina and spoke to the Messenger of God about the prisoner. Then the Prophet spoke to Shujāʿ and his companions about returning the women, and they returned the women to their companions.

Ibn Abī Sabra said: I informed an old man from the Anṣār about that and he said: As for the beautiful girl, Shujāʿ b. Wahb had taken her for himself for a price and had intercourse with her. When the party arrived he let her choose, and she chose to stay with Shujāʿ b. Wahb. Indeed, he was killed on the day of Yamāma while she was still with him. He did not have a child by her. I said to Ibn Abī Sabra, "I have never heard mention of this expedition." Ibn Abī Sabra said, "You have not heard all the information." He said, "You are right, by God."

Ibn Abī Sabra said: Indeed Isḥāq b. ʿAbdullah related to me about another expedition. Isḥāq said: Ibn Kaʿb b. Mālik related to me that the Messenger of God sent Quṭba b. ʿĀmir b. Ḥadīda with twenty men to a community from Khathʿam in the region of Tabāla. He commanded him to attack them, to march by night and hide by day. He commanded him to hasten the march. They set out on ten camels riding one behind the other. They hid the weapons. They took al-Fatq until they reached Baṭn Majab. They captured a man and asked him [Page 755] but he could not understand them. He promptly began to shout. So Quṭba took him and struck off his head. They stayed until it was an hour from night. One of them set out as a scout and found a group of cattle—cattle and sheep. He returned to his companions and informed them. They came crawling, fearing the guards until they reached the settlement, while they slept and were quiet. Then they proclaimed *takbīr* and attacked. Men from the settlement went out to meet them. They fought a fierce battle. There were many wounded in both parties. In the morning many Khathʿam people arrived. A falling flood came between them. Not a single man could cross until Quṭba conquered the people of the settlement. He brought the cattle and sheep and women to Medina. Their portions were four, and four. The camel equals ten sheep after the fifth was taken out. This took place in Ṣafar in the year nine AH.

THE RAID OF MU'TA

Al-Wāqidī related to us saying: Rabīʿa b. ʿUthmān related to me from ʿUmar b. al-Ḥakam, who said: The Messenger of God sent al-Ḥārith b. ʿUmayr al-Azdī, one of the Banū Lihb, to the king of Buṣrā with a document. When he came down to Mu'ta, Shuraḥbīl b. ʿAmr al-Ghassānī confronted him and said, "Where are you going?" He replied, "Al-Shām." He said, "Perhaps you are one of the messengers from the Messenger of God?" He said, "Yes. I am a messenger from the Messenger of God." Then, Shuraḥbīl commanded that he be tied with rope, and executed him. Only he was killed for the Messenger of God.

[Page 756] The news reached the Messenger of God and affected him badly. He summoned the people and informed them of the death of al-Ḥārith and of who killed him. The people hastened and went out and camped at al-Jurf. The Messenger of God did not clarify the affair. When the Messenger of God prayed *Ẓuhr* he sat down with his companions. Al-Nuʿmān b. Funḥuṣ, the Jew, came and stopped before the Messenger of God who was with the people (nās). Then the Messenger of God said, "Zayd b. Ḥāritha is the commander of the people; if Zayd is killed, Jaʿfar b. Abī Ṭālib shall be the commander; and if Jaʿfar is wounded, ʿAbdullah b. Rawāḥa shall take his place. If ʿAbdullah is wounded the Muslims will approve of a man and appoint him over themselves." Then al-Nuʿmān b. Funḥuṣ said, "Abū l-Qāsim, if you are a prophet and you name whom you name, a few or many, they will be wounded all of them. Indeed the prophets of Isrā'īl when they appointed a man over the people and said, if so and so is wounded, and if they named a hundred, they would all be wounded." Then the Jew began to say to Zayd b. Ḥāritha, "Make your testimony, for you will not return to Muḥammad ever, if he is a prophet." Zayd replied, "I testify that Muḥammad is a true and faithful prophet."

When they gathered for the march, Muḥammad made a flag for them and he handed it to Zayd b. Ḥāritha—a white flag. The people walked to the commanders of the Messenger of God and bade them farewell and prayed for them. Some of the Muslims bade farewell to others, and there were three thousand Muslims. When they left their camp, the Muslims called out: May God drive the enemy from you and return you well and successful. [Page 757] Ibn Rawāḥa said:

> But I, I ask the Merciful for forgiveness.
> And a wide open wound discharging blood.

Shuʿayb b. ʿUbāda recited these verses to me.

Ibn Abī Sabra related to me from Isḥāq b. ʿAbdullah b. Abī Ṭalḥa from Rāfiʿ b. Isḥāq from Zayd b. Arqam that the Messenger of God said, "I decree for you fear of God, and for those Muslims who are with you, goodness." Or he said, "Raid, in the name of God and in the path of God, and fight those who disbelieve in God. Do not betray or be extreme or kill children. If you meet your enemy from the polytheists, ask them one of three questions. Whatever each of them answers, accept it from them, and refrain from them. Invite them to enter Islam. If they do, accept them and refrain from them. Then invite them to transfer from their homeland to the homeland of the emigrants. If they do, inform them that to them is what belongs to the emigrants, and upon them is what is upon the emigrants. But if they enter Islam and prefer their homelands, inform them that they will be as the Bedouin of the Muslims. The judgment of God will come upon them, and they shall not receive either *fay'* or portions in anything except when they fight together with the Muslims. If they refuse, invite them to pay the *jizya*, and if they agree to pay the *jizya*, accept them and refrain from them. If they refuse, ask God's help and fight them. If you besiege the people of the fortress or the city and they desire you to invoke the judgment of God, do not invoke God, but bring down your own judgment upon them. Indeed, you do not know if you obtain for them the judgment of God or not. If you besiege the people of the fortress or the people of the city and they desire you to give them a protection of God and a protection of the Messenger of God, do not do so. But grant them a protection from you, and a protection from your father, and a protection [Page 758] from your companions. For surely you may break your agreement, and your father's agreement to protect them, but that is better for you than if you break the protection from God and His prophet."

Abū Ṣafwān related to me from Khālid b. Yazīd, who said: The Prophet went out walking with the people of Mu'ta until he reached Thanniyat al-Wadāʿ, and he stopped, while they stood around him, and said, "Attack in the name of God, and fight the enemy of God and your enemy in al-Shām. You will find men in hermitage cells, withdrawn from the people. Do not attack them. You will find others desiring Satan, their heads seeking out vice. Draw your swords against them. Do not kill a woman or a suckling child, or the old and senile. Do not destroy the date palm, cut down trees, or pull down a house."

Abū l-Qāsim b. ʿUmāra b. Ghaziyya related to me from his father from ʿAṭā' b. Abī Muslim, who said: When the Messenger of God appointed ʿAbdullah b. Rawāḥa, Ibn Rawāḥa said, "O Messenger of God, command me about something that I will learn from you." He said, "Indeed you will arrive in a land tomorrow in which prostration is little, so increase your prostration." ʿAbdullah said, "Tell me more, O Messenger of God." He said, "Remember God. Indeed, He will help you about whatever you ask Him." He stood among those who were with him until when he was leaving on his journey, he returned to him and said, "O Messenger of God, indeed God is single (*witr*) and He loves the odd number (*witr*)." He replied, "O Ibn Rawāḥa, you are not weak, and you will not fail to perfect one, if you miss ten." Ibn Rawāḥā said, "I will not ask you about anything after this."

[Page 759] Abū ʿAbdullah said: Zayd b. Arqam used to say: I was under the protection of ʿAbdullah b. Rawāḥa and I have not seen a guardian of an orphan who was better than him. I went out with him to Mu'ta. He loved me and I, him. He used to seat me behind him on his saddle. One night, while on his horse, seated between the two pieces of wood of the saddle, he quoted some verses of poetry:

> When you have brought me and carried my gear
> A four nights' journey from the swampy ground,
> Then enjoy life and bear no blame.
> May I never return to my people at home.
> And when the Muslims have gone and left me
> In al-Shām where I wish to be,
> There I shall not care for the pollen of the date,
> Nor for the palms whose roots are watered.

When I heard these verses I wept. He flicked me with his hand and said, "O silly one, would that God would grant me martyrdom and release me from this world, its hardship, its anxieties, its sorrows and its misfortunes." He repeated the verse as he sat between the wood of the saddle. Then he descended in the night and prayed two bowings. He followed them with a long prayer. Then he said to me, "O boy!" And I said, "Here I am, at your service." He said, "It is martyrdom, if God wills."

The Muslims went from Medina, and the enemy heard of their marching to them before they reached [Page 760] the place where al-Ḥārith b. ʿUmayr was killed. When the Muslims left Medina, the enemy heard about their marching to them and had gathered together. A man from al-Azd whom the people called Shuraḥbīl led them. The vanguard arrived in front of him. The Muslims alighted in Wādī al-Qurā and stayed a few days. He sent his brother Sadūs and Sadūs was killed. Shuraḥbīl b. ʿAmr was afraid and he fortified himself. Then he sent a brother of his named Wabr b. ʿAmr. The Muslims marched until they alighted on Arḍ Maʿān in Arḍ al-Shām. It reached the people that Heraclius had alighted in Maab of Arḍ al-Balqāʾ in Bahrāʾ Zʾ with the Wāʾil, Bakr, Lahm and Judhām and a hundred thousand men. Their commander was a man from Balī named Mālik.

When that news reached the Muslims, they stayed two nights contemplating with their commander. They said: We will write to the Messenger of God and inform him of the news, and either he will withdraw us or increase our men. While the people were on that from their command, Ibn Rawāḥa came to them and encouraged them, saying, "By God, we have never fought the people with great numbers or with many weapons, or with many horses, but only with this religion that God has blessed us. So leave! By God, surely I remember, on the day of Badr, we only had two horses, and on the day of Uḥud a single horse. Indeed the choice is between two good results. If not victory against them, for that is what God promised us, and what our Prophet promised us, and there is no variance to His promise—martyrdom; and we shall be attached to the brotherhood and we shall accompany them in the gardens." The people were encouraged by similar words from Ibn Rawāḥa.

Rabīʿa b. ʿUthmān related to me from al-Maqburī from Abū Hurayra, who said: I witnessed Mu'ta. When we saw the polytheists we saw what was beyond us in numbers, and weapons and quivers. The brocade, silk, gold and glitter blinded me. Thābit b. Arqam said to me, "O Abū Hurayra, what is the matter with you? It is as though you saw numerous gatherings." I said, "Yes." He said, "You should have seen us at Badr. Indeed, we did not have large numbers then to help us!"

[Page 761] Bukayr b. Mismār related to me from Ibn Kaʿb al-Quraẓī, and Ibn Abī Sabra from ʿUmāra b. Ghaziyya, and one of them was better informed than the other. He said: When the Muslims and the polytheists met, the commanders were at that time fighting on their feet. Zayd b. Ḥāritha held the banner, and the people fought with him. The Muslims were arranged in rows. Then Zayd b. Ḥāritha was killed. Ibn Kaʿb al-Quraẓī said: One who was present at that time informed me that Zayd was killed by the spear. Then Jaʿfar took the banner. He alighted from a horse, red in hue, hamstrung it and fought until he was killed. ʿAbdullah b. Muḥammad related to me from his father, who said: A man from Rūm struck him and cut him in two halves. One half fell on the grape vine, and roughly thirty wounds were found on it. Abū Maʿshar related to me from Nāfiʿ from Ibn ʿUmar, who said: The body of Jaʿfar held seventy-two scars between his shoulders where he had been either struck by a sword or pierced by a spear. Yaḥyā b. ʿAbdullah b. Abī Qatādā related to me from ʿAbdullah b. Abī Bakr b. Ṣāliḥ from ʿĀṣim b. ʿUmar, who said: On the body of Jaʿfar were more than sixty wounds, as well as the stab that pierced him.

Muḥammad b. Ṣāliḥ related to me from ʿĀṣim b. ʿUmar b. Qatāda, and ʿAbd al-Jabbār b. ʿUmāra b. ʿAbdullah b. Abī Bakr related to me, and one of them was more knowledgeable in traditions: They said: While the people met in Mu'ta, the Messenger of God sat on the *minbar* in Medina and there was revealed to him all that occurred between him and al-Shām, and he observed the battle ground.

The Messenger of God said: Zayd b. Ḥāritha took the flag, when Satan came to him, and made [Page 762] life attractive and death detestable to him. Then he made the world attractive to him. Then Zayd said, "Now, when faith is deeply rooted in the hearts of the believers you will make the world attractive to me!" And he went valiantly forward until he was martyred. The Messenger of God prayed over him and said, "I ask for his forgiveness, for he entered Paradise willingly." Then Jaʿfar b. Abī Ṭālib took the banner. And Satan came to him and made life favorable and death detestable to him, and the world became desirable to him. And Jaʿfar said, "Now when faith is rooted in the hearts of men, you will make the world desirable!" And he went forward valiantly until he was martyred. The Messenger of God prayed over him, and asked God for him. Then he said, "I ask for your brother's forgiveness, for indeed he is a martyr. He flies with wings of rubies to wherever he wishes in Paradise." Then ʿAbdullah b. Rawāḥa took the banner and he was martyred. He entered Paradise protesting. That grieved the Anṣār. The Prophet said, "The wound took him." It was said, "O Messenger of God, why did he protest?" He replied, "When he was wounded, he was weakened, and he blamed himself, and he was brave. He was martyred and entered Paradise." His people were relieved.

ʿAbdullah b. Muḥammad b. ʿUmar b. ʿAlī related to me from his father, who said: The Messenger of God said, "I saw Jaʿfar as an angel, flying in Paradise, his foremost feathers stained with blood. And I saw Zayd below him, and I said, "I did not think that Zayd was less than Jaʿfar." Then Gabriel came and said, "Indeed, Zayd is not less than Jaʿfar. But we prefer Jaʿfar because of his relationship to you."

Yaḥyā b. ʿAbdullah b. Abī Qatādā related to me from al-Maqburī from Abū Hurayra, who said: The Messenger of God said, "Abū Qatāda was the best of the knights and Salama b. al-Akwaʿ is the best of the men on foot." Nāfiʿ b. Thābit related to me from Yaḥyā b. ʿAbbād from his father that a man from the [Page 763] Banū Murra was with the soldiers, and someone said to him, "Surely the people say that Khālid fled from the polytheists." He replied, "No, by God, that was not so! When Ibn Rawāḥa was killed, I looked at the banner and it had fallen, and the Muslims were blended with the polytheists. Then I saw the banner in the hand of Khālid, and he was withdrawing. We followed him when there was defeat."

Muḥammad b. Ṣāliḥ related to me from one of the Bedouin from his father, who said: When Ibn Rawāḥa was killed, the Muslims were defeated and it was the worst defeat I ever saw anywhere. Then, indeed, the Muslims withdrew. A man from the Anṣār named Thābit b. Arqam approached. He took the banner and began to shout at the Anṣār, and the people began to return to him from every direction, but they were few. Then he says, "Come to me, O people!" And they gathered to him. He said: Then Thābit looked at Khālid and said, "Abū Sulaymān, take the banner." He replied, "No I will not take it, for you are more deserving of it. You are a man who has seniority, and you witnessed Badr." Thābit said, "Take it, O man, for by God, I did not take it except for you." So Khālid took it and carried it for a while. The polytheists began to attack him, and he stood firm until the polytheists wavered. Then, he attacked with his companions and he broke up one of their groups. Then many men from them surprised him, but the Muslims banded together and they made clear their return.

Ibn Abī Sabra related to me from Isḥāq b. ʿAbdullah from Ibn Kaʿb b. Mālik, who said: A group of my people (*qawm*) who attended at that time related to me, saying: When he took the banner and was exposed with the people (*nās*), there was defeat. The Muslims were killed and the polytheists followed them. Quṭba b. ʿĀmir began to shout, "O people, the man who is killed going forward is better than the man who is killed from behind." He shouted at his companions but none came to him. It was defeat. They followed the keeper of the banner in defeat.

[Page 764] Ismāʿīl b. Muṣʿab related to me from Ibrāhīm b. Yaḥyā b. Zayd, who said: When Thābit b. Arqam took the banner, the people agreed upon Khālid b. al-Walīd. Thābit said, "Have you agreed upon Khālid?" They replied, "Yes." So Khālid took it and was exposed with the people. ʿAṭṭāf b. Khālid related to me, saying: When Ibn Rawāḥā was killed in the evening, Khālid b. al-Walīd stayed up the night, and when the next day dawned he had made the rear guard his front and his front his rear guard. And his right became his left, and his left, his right. And the enemy did not recognize what they knew of their banners and their positions. They said, "Help has come to them!" And they were frightened, and withdrew, defeated. They were killed as never before.

ʿAbdullah b. Fuḍayl related to me from his father, who said: When Khālid took the banner the Messenger of God said, "Now the battle rages!" Abū ʿAbdullah said: The first is confirmed with us: that Khālid withdrew with the people. Ibn Abī l-Zinād said: The blood reached the horses on the spot near the hoof, and the battleground was also thus, and when that place of the riding beast (hoof) is heated, it runs faster.

Dawūd b. Sinān related to me saying: I heard Thaʿlaba b. Abī Mālik say: Khālid withdrew at the time until they were blamed for fleeing; the people regarded him as an ill omen. Khālid b. Ilyās related to me from Ṣāliḥ b. Abī Ḥassān from ʿUbayd b. Ḥunayn from Abū Saʿīd al-Khudrī, who said: Khālid b. al-Walīd came with the people, withdrawing.

[Page 765] When the people of Medina heard about the army of Mu'ta arriving, they received them at al-Jurf; they began to scatter dust in their faces, saying, "O deserters, did you flee from the path of God?" The Messenger of God said, "They are not deserters, but rather those who will return, God willing!"

Khālid b. Ilyās related to me from Abū Bakr b. ʿAbdullah b. ʿUtba saying: No army sent with us received what the companions of Mu'ta received from the people of Medina. The people of Medina met them with evil, to the extent that even when a man knocked on the door of his family, they refused to open to him saying, "Did you not go forward with your companions?" As for those elders from the companions of the Messenger of God, they kept to their homes, ashamed, until the Prophet sent for them man by man, saying, "You are among those who will return in the way of God."

Muṣʿab b. Thābit related to me from ʿĀmir b. ʿAbdullah b. al-Zubayr from Abū Bakr b. ʿAbd al-Raḥmān b. al-Ḥārith b. Hishām, who said: There was in that army Salama b. Hishām b. Mughīra. His wife visited Umm Salama the wife of the Prophet and Umm Salama said, "Why is it that I do not see Salama b. Hishām? Is he complaining of something?" His wife replied, "No, by God. But he is not able to go out. When he goes out they shout at him and his companions, 'O cowards, did you flee from the way of God?' so that he stays in the house." Umm Salama mentioned that to the Messenger of God. The Messenger of God said, "Rather, they are those who will return in the way of God. He must go out!" So he went out.

Khālid b. Ilyās related to me from al-Aʿraj from Abū Hurayra, who said: We were going out and we heard what we detested from the people. Indeed there were words between me and one of my cousins. He said, "Were you not a coward on the day of Mu'ta!" I did not know what to say to him.

[Page 766] Mālik b. Abī l-Rajjāl related to me from ʿAbdullah b. Abū Bakr b. Ḥazm from Umm ʿĪsā b. al-Ḥazzār from Umm Jaʿfar bt. Muḥammad b. Jaʿfar from her grandmother, Asmā' bt. ʿUmays, who said: When I rose on the morning of the day Jaʿfar and his companions were taken, the Prophet came to me. I had prepared forty *mann* [a *mann* weighs roughly 2 ratl] of "dip" and kneaded the dough. I took my two sons and I washed their faces and put oil on them. The Messenger of God came to me and said, "O Asmā' where are the sons of Jaʿfar?" I brought them to him and he embraced them and smelt them, then his eyes welled up and he cried. I said, "Why, Messenger of God, perhaps something has reached you about Jaʿfar?" He replied, "Yes, he was killed today." She said: I stood up and screamed, and the women came to me. The Prophet began to say, "O Asmā', do not speak obscene words or beat your chest!" She said: The Messenger of God went out until he met his daughter Fāṭima, and she said, "O my uncle!" The Messenger of God said, "For the example of Jaʿfar mourners weep!" Then the Messenger of God said, "Prepare food for the family of Jaʿfar for they are preoccupied today."

Muḥammad b. Muslim related to me from Yaḥyā b. Abī Yaʿlā, who said: I heard ʿAbdullah b. Jaʿfar say: I remember when the Messenger of God visited my mother and announced the death of my father to her. I looked at him and he touched me on my head and the head of my brother. His eyes [Page 767] shed tears until they flowed on his beard. Then he said, "O God, indeed Jaʿfar has arrived at the best of rewards. Compensate him through his descendants with the best of what you have granted to one who is your slave among his descendants." Then he said, "O Asmā', will you not rejoice?" She replied, "But of course, for you are most dear to me." He said, "Indeed, God most high has made two wings for Jaʿfar that he may fly with them in Paradise!" She replied, "By my father and my mother, O Messenger of God, inform the people of that!"

The Messenger of God stood up and took my hand [i.e. of ʿAbdullah b. Jaʿfar], and he touched my head with his hand until he mounted the *minbar*. Then he seated me in front of him on the lower step, and his sorrow was obvious. He said that indeed, the man most like his brother was the son of his uncle. That Jaʿfar was martyred, and that God had made two wings for him that he may fly in Paradise. Then the Messenger of God came down, and entered his house and he took me in. He ordered food that was prepared for my family. He sent for my brother and we breakfasted with him, and by God, the food was tasty and good. Salmā his servant attended to the barley and ground it. Then she pulverized it. Then she cooked it well and spiced it with oil. Then she put pepper on it. My brother and I lunched with the Prophet and we stayed three days in his house. We went around with him whenever he went into one of the houses of his wives. Then we returned to our house.

The Messenger of God came while I was bargaining over a sheep belonging to my brother. The Messenger of God said, "O God, bless his transactions." ʿAbdullah said: And I did not sell or purchase anything but there were blessings in it.

ʿUmar b. Abī ʿĀtika related to me from ʿAbd al-Raḥmān b. al-Qāsim from his father from ʿĀ'isha, who said: When news of the death of Jaʿfar arrived we knew of the sorrow of the Messenger of God. She said: In those days it did not harm the people to raise many questions. A man came to the Messenger of God and said, "O Messenger of God, the women have depressed us with their crying." The Messenger of God said,

"Return to them and silence them. If they refuse, scatter dust in their mouths." [Page 768] I said to myself: May God banish you! You will not spare yourself, nor will you obey the Prophet.

Sulaymān b. Bilāl related to me from Yaḥyā b. Saʿīd, from ʿAmra from ʿĀʾisha, who said: I was peeping through the crack of the door when I heard this. ʿAbdullah b. Muḥammad related to me from Ibn ʿAqīl, from Jābir b. ʿAbdullah, who said: The people from the Muslims were wounded in it. The Muslims plundered some things from the polytheists. Among what they plundered was a ring that a man brought to the Messenger of God saying, "I killed its owner, at the time." The Messenger of God gave it to him.

ʿAwf b. Mālik b. Ashjaʿī said: We met them with a group of Quḍāʿa and the rest of them were Christian Arabs. We were arranged in rows, and a man from the Byzantines on a light hued horse made to draw his sword against the Muslims and attack them. He had weapons of gold and a gold bridle. I began to say to myself: Who is this? A man from the helpers of Ḥimyar had accompanied me and was with us during our march. That man did not have a sword. When a man from the people slaughtered a camel, the helper asked him for a portion of its skin, and he gifted it to him. He spread it in the sun and fixed its edge with pegs. When it had dried he took a grab of it and made a shield. When this helper saw what the Byzantine did with the Muslims he concealed himself behind a rock, and when the Byzantine passed by, leapt on him and hamstrung his horse. The horse fell upon its legs and the infidel fell from it. He attacked him, took his sword, raised it above him and killed him.

[Page 769] Bukayr b. Mismār related to me from ʿUmāra b. Ghaziyya from his father, who said: I attended Mu'ta. There, I challenged a man to a duel and killed him. At that time he was wearing a helmet with a ruby on it. I only wanted that ruby so I took it. When we were exposed and defeated I returned with the ruby to Medina and handed it to the Messenger of God who gave it to me. I sold it during the caliphate of ʿUmar b. al-Khaṭṭāb for a hundred dinars and purchased a date orchard in Banū Khatma with it.

A RECORD OF THOSE WHO WERE MARTYRED AT MUʾTA AMONG THE BANŪ HĀSHIM AND OTHERS

The martyred among the Banū Hāshim were: Jaʿfar b. Abī Ṭālib and Zayd b. Ḥaritha. From the Banū ʿAdī b. Kaʿb: Masʿūd b. al-Aswad b. Ḥāritha b. Naḍla was martyred; and from the Banū ʿĀmir b. Luay of the Banū Mālik b. Ḥusayl: Wahb b. Saʿd b. Abī Sarḥ.

Those who were killed among the Anṣār were:

From the Banū Najjār of the Banū Māzin: Surāqa b. ʿAmr b. ʿAṭiyya b. Khanasā. From the Banū Najjār: Al-Ḥārith b. al-Nuʿmān b. Yasāf b. Naḍla b. ʿAmr b. ʿAwf b. Ghanm b. Mālik. From the Banū al-Ḥārith b. al-Khazraj: ʿAbdullah b. Rawāḥa, and ʿUbāda b. Qays. The others returned to Medina.

THE RAID OF DHĀT AL-SALĀSIL

Rabīʿa b. ʿUthmān related to me from Ibn Rūmān; and Aflaḥ b. Saʿd related to me from Saʿīd b. ʿAbd al-Raḥmān b. Ruqaysh from Abū Bakr b. Ḥazm; [Page 770] and

ʿAbd al-Ḥamīd b. Jaʿfar also informed me, each relating portions of the information—some of them were more reliable than others. I collected what was related to me. Some who are not named also informed me. They said: It reached the Messenger of God that a group of Baliyy and Quḍāʿa had come together desiring to draw near the region of the Messenger of God. The Messenger of God called ʿAmr b. al-ʿĀṣ and handed him a white flag of which he made a black flag. He sent him with the best of the Muhājirūn and the Anṣār—three hundred of them, including ʿĀmir b. Rabīʿa, Ṣuhayb b. Sinān, Abū l-Aʿwar Saʿīd b. Zayd b. ʿAmr b. Nufayl, and Saʿd b. Abī Waqqāṣ. And from the Anṣār: Usayd b. Ḥuḍayr, ʿAbbād b. Bishr, Salama b. Salāma, and Saʿd b. ʿUbāda. He commanded him to seek help from those Bedouin whom he would pass by, as he marched to the land of the Baliyy, ʿUdhra and Balqayn. This was because ʿAmr b. al-ʿĀṣ was related to them. Umm al-ʿĀṣ b. Wāʾil was a Balawīy, and the Messenger of God desired to unite them through ʿAmr.

He marched, hiding by day and marching by night. He had thirty horses. When he was near the people, it reached him that they had a large group. He alighted close to them at ʿIshā, and this was in winter. A group of his companions gathered wood desiring to warm themselves—for the land was cold—but he forbade them. It was difficult for them to the extent that some of the Muhājirūn spoke to him about that and opposed him rudely. ʿAmr said, "You were commanded to listen to me and obey me!" He said, "Do so!"

Rāfiʿ b. Makīth sent al-Juhannī to the Messenger of God informing him that they had a large group and asking him for help with more men. The Messenger of God sent Abū ʿUbayda b. al-Jarrāḥ and handed the banner to him, and sent the leaders of the Muhājirūn—Abū Bakr and ʿUmar—and the Anṣār with him. The Messenger of God commanded him to join ʿAmr b. al-ʿĀṣ. Abū ʿUbayda went out with two hundred men. The Messenger of God commanded him that they should work together and not at variance. They marched until they joined [Page 771] ʿAmr b. al-ʿĀṣ. Abū ʿUbayda desired to lead the people and precede ʿAmr. ʿAmr said to him, "Surely you have come to help me. It is not for you to lead me. I am the commander, and indeed the Prophet sent you to help me." But the Muhājirūn said, "No! Rather you are the commander of your companions and he is the commander of his companions." ʿAmr said, "No, rather you are an aid to us." When Abū ʿUbayda noticed their differences, and as he was a good person of gentle character, he said, "Calm down, O ʿAmr, you know that the last thing the Prophet entrusted me with was, 'When you arrive before your companion, you will agree and not dispute.' By God, indeed, even if you oppose me, I will surely obey you." And Abū ʿUbayda submitted.

ʿAmr prayed with the people. All submitted to ʿAmr, and there were five hundred of them. He marched by night and day until he set foot in the land of Baliyy and conquered it. He learned that whenever he wound up at a place, all who were in this place dispersed when they heard of him. When he wound up at the furthest land of Baliyy and ʿUdhra and Balqayn, he met with a small group. They fought for a while and aimed arrows. ʿĀmir b. Rabīʿa was aimed at with an arrow, which wounded his arm. But the Muslims attacked them and they fled. They incapacitated them as they fled and dispersed in the land. ʿAmr conquered what was there and stayed for several days without hearing of a group of them meeting, or of a place they went to. He sent out his cavalry and they returned with sheep and cattle they used to slaughter and sacrifice. There was nothing more than that. No plunder was apportioned except what was mentioned.

Rāfiʿ b. Abī Rāfiʿ al-Ṭāʾī used to say: I was in the group that was with Abū ʿUbayda b. al-Jarrāḥ, and I was a man who had raided the property of the people in *jāhiliyya*. [Page 772] I used to collect water in egg shells—eggs of the Ostrich—and hide them in places I knew. If I was thirsty, and passed by it, I would take it out and drink from it. When I was in that "sending" I said to myself, by God, I will choose a companion for myself whom God will benefit me with, and I chose Abū Bakr al-Ṣiddīq, and accompanied him. He possessed a cloak from Fadak, which, when he rode, he gathered to himself with a pin. When we alighted, he spread it out. When we returned I said, "O Abū Bakr, may God bless you, teach me something that will profit me before God." He replied, "I would do so, even if you did not ask me. Do not associate a partner with God. Establish your prayer. Give *zakāt*, and fast during the month of Ramaḍān, make a pilgrimage to the House and perform the *ʿUmra*, and do not assume command over even two Muslims." He said: So I said, "As for what you command me about prayer and fasting and pilgrimage, I will do it. As for the authority, indeed I have seen that people do not attain this nobility and this wealth and this status with the Messenger of God and the people except because of it." He replied, "You asked for my advice and I did my best for you. Indeed people enter Islam; some in obedience and others with detestation. God grants all of them protection from tyranny, and they are the guests of God, the protected of God and in his protection. He who ignores God's protection violates the covenant of God. Indeed, when the cattle of one, or his camel is lost, the muscles of the owner will swell in irritation for his protected beast. Similarly, God is behind those He protects." He said: When the Messenger of God died and Abū Bakr succeeded him, I went to him and said, "Did you not forbid me to command more than two?" He said, "Of course, and I agree with that." He said, "So what has happened to you that you command the community of Muḥammad?" He replied, "The people disputed, and I feared that [Page 773] they would be destroyed. They asked me, and I could not escape that."

He said: ʿAwf b. Mālik al-Ashjaʿī, a companion of Abū Bakr and ʿUmar was with them during their journey. One day ʿAuf went out in the camp and passed a group of people in whose hands was a camel which they could not slaughter. ʿAuf was knowledgeable about slaughtering camels, and he said, "If you will give me some of it I will apportion it among you. They said, "Yes, we will give you a tenth of it." He slaughtered it and divided it among them. They gave him a portion from it and he brought it to his companions. They cooked it and ate it. When they had finished, Abū Bakr and ʿUmar asked, "From where did you get this meat?" He informed them and they said, "By God, you did not do well to provide us this food. Then they stood up and vomited. And when Abū Bakr and ʿUmar did that, the army did that. Abū Bakr and ʿUmar said to ʿAuf, "You hastened to your reward!" Then Abū ʿUbayda came and said similar words.

When we returned, ʿAmr b. al-ʿĀṣ had a wet dream in a night that was extremely cold. He asked his companion, "What do you think? Indeed I had a wet dream and if I bathe, I will die!" And he called for water to take ablution, and he washed his "penis" and performed *tayammam* (cleaning with dust). Then he came and prayed with them. He was the first who sent ʿAwf b. Mālik as a messenger. ʿAwf b. Mālik said: I arrived before the Messenger of God, at dawn, while he was praying in his house. I greeted him, and the Messenger of God said, "ʿAwf b. Mālik?" I replied, "ʿAwf b. Mālik, O Messenger of God!" He said, "The master of slaughtering camels?" I said, "Yes." And he did not say anything else. Then he said, "Inform me!" I informed him of what happened during our march, and of what happened between Abū ʿUbayda b. al-Jarrāḥ and ʿAmr b. al-ʿĀṣ and the compliance of Abū ʿUbayda. The Messenger of God said,

"May God bless Abū ʿUbayda b. al-Jarrāḥ." Then I informed him that ʿAmr prayed with us while he was in a state of ritual impurity. [Page 774] That even though he had water, he did not exceed over washing his private parts with water and performed *tayammam*. The Messenger of God was silent. When ʿAmr arrived before the Prophet he asked him about his prayer, and ʿAmr informed him and said, "By Him who sent you with the truth, if I had washed, I would have surely died! I have never found anything so cold, and God has said: Do not kill yourselves, indeed God is most merciful!" The Messenger of God laughed. We did not learn that he said anything.

THE EXPEDITION TO AL-KHABAṬ LED BY ABŪ ʿUBAYDA

Al-Wāqidī said: Dāwud b. Qays, Mālik b. Anas, and Ibrāhīm b. Muḥmmad al-Anṣārī related to me from the sons of Thābit b. Qays b. Shammās and Khārija b. al-Ḥārith, and some of them were more knowledgeable. They said: The Messenger of God sent Abū ʿUbayda b. al-Jarrāḥ on a raid, and with him were both the Muhājirūn and the Anṣār. They were three hundred men marching to the seacoast to a community of Juhayna, when they were overtaken by extreme hunger. Abū ʿUbayda commanded that some provisions be brought together, and finally they were left apportioning dates. Someone said to Jābir, "What use is a third of a date?" and he replied that indeed they grieved for its loss. He said that their beasts were not with them, and they were on their feet, while a few camels were carrying the provisions. They ate the mix of camel food, which at that time had thorns, until indeed the mouth of one of them was like the lip of the camel's snout.

We stayed thus [Page 775] until someone said, "If we meet an enemy we will not be able to confront him for the people have no strength." Then, Qays b. Saʿd said, "Who will trade dates from me for a camel, but he will pay me a camel here, and I will pay him dates in Medina." And ʿUmar began to say, "How strange is this youth. He has no money at hand so he purchases with money that he does not possess!" Qays b. Saʿd found a man from Juhayna, and said, "Sell me a camel and I will pay in measures of dates in Medina." The Juhannite said, "By God, I do not know you! Who are you?" He replied, "I am Qays b. Saʿd b. ʿUbāda b. Dulaym." The Juhannite said, "How well I know your genealogy! Indeed, Saʿd and I have a friendship. He is the Lord of the people of Yathrib." The youth bought five camels from them, and each camel was purchased for two measures of dates. As the transaction took place, the Bedouin stipulated his terms—"Dried dates of Dhuakhīra, from the dates of the family of Dulaym." He said: Qays said, "I agree." The Juhannite said, "Witness for me!" A group of Anṣār together with a group of Muhājirūn were willing witnesses for him. Qays said, "Take whom you like for a witness."

Among those whom he called to witness was ʿUmar b. al-Khaṭṭāb. ʿUmar said, "I will not witness. He becomes a debtor and he has no money with him. Rather, the money is his father's." The Juhannite said, "Surely Saʿd will not fail his son for a measure of dates. I see a beautiful face and a noble act." There were words between ʿUmar and Qays, until the words of Qays were most rude. Then Qays took the camels and slaughtered them for them in three places, each day a camel. When it was the fourth day his commander forbade him saying, "You desire to destroy your reputation and you have no money!"

Muḥammad b. Yaḥyā b. Sahl related to me from his father, from Rāfiʿ b. Khadīj, who said: Abū ʿUbayda b. al-Jarrāḥ approached, and with him was ʿUmar b. al-Khaṭṭāb.

Abū ʿUbayda said, [Page 776] "I order you not to slaughter the camel. Do you desire to destroy your reputation when you have no wealth?" Qays replied, "O Abū ʿUbayda, did you see Abū Thābit (*kunya* of Saʿd) while he fulfilled the debt of the people? He helped the needy and fed them during the famine, and you think he would not provide a measure of dates for people who strive in the way of God?" Abū ʿUbayda was on the verge of yielding to him and leaving him, when ʿUmar began to say, "Command him." So, he commanded him and refused to let him slaughter the camels. Two camels were left with him until the people found the fish.

Qays arrived in Medina with the two camels walking one behind the other. News concerning the hunger of the people had reached Saʿd. He said, "If I know Qays, he will slaughter for the people." When Qays arrived, Saʿd met him and said, "What did you do when the famine overtook the people?" He replied, "I slaughtered." He said, "You did right; you slaughtered!" He said: "Then what?" He replied, "I slaughtered." He said, "You did right. You slaughtered." He said, "Then what?" He said, "Then I slaughtered." He said, "You did right; you slaughtered!" He said, "Then what happened?" He said, "I was forbidden." He said, "Who forbade you?" He replied, "Abū ʿUbayda b. al-Jarrāḥ, my commander." He said, "Why?" He said, "He believed it was not my money but rather the money of my father. And I said, 'My father fulfilled the promise of the most distant relatives. He helps the needy and feeds during the famine. And he will not do this for me?'" He said, "For you are four gardens." He said, "He wrote a document for him about that." He said: He brought the document to Abū ʿUbayda and he witnessed it. ʿUmar arrived and he refused to witness it. The smallest among the gardens produced fifty measures. The Bedouin arrived with Qays and he paid him his measures and his ride and his clothes. The actions of Qays reached the Prophet and he said, "Indeed he is from the most generous of families."

Mālik b. Anas related to me from Wahb b. Kaysān from Jābir b. ʿAbdullah, who said: [Page 777] The sea brought us a fish that resembled a small mountain. The army ate of it for twelve nights. Then Abū ʿUbayda ordered one of its ribs to be planted on the ground. He called for his riding animal and it was saddled, and he rode under it but could not touch it. Ibn Abī Dhiʾb related to me from his father from Jābir b. ʿAbdullah, who said: Indeed a man could sit in the hole of its eye! And indeed the rider could pass between two of its ribs upon his horse.

ʿAbdullah b. al-Ḥijāzī related to me from ʿUmar b. ʿUthmān b. Shujāʿ, who said: When the Bedouin arrived before Saʿd b. ʿUbāda he said, "O Abū Thābit! By God, a son such as yours should not be treated this way and left without money. Your son is one of the lords of his people. The commander forbade me to sell to him. I said, 'Why?' and he replied, 'He has no money.' When he traced his ancestry to you, I recognized him and I came forward for I knew that you possess the highest and most noble character. You are not censured even by those who have no knowledge of your position." He said: He gave his son great wealth at that time.

THE EXPEDITION TO KHAḌIRA LED BY ABŪ QATĀDA IN SHAʿBĀN OF THE YEAR EIGHT

Al-Wāqidī related to us saying: Muḥammad b. Sahl b. Abī Ḥathma related to me from his father, who said: ʿAbdullah b. Abī Ḥadrad al-Aslamī said: I am married to the daughter of Surāqa b. Ḥāritha al-Najjārī who was killed at Badr, and there was nothing in the world that was more desirable to me than to be with her. I had promised her a dowry of two hundred dirham but I could not find any part of it to take to her and I said to myself [Page 778] I shall trust in God and His Messenger. I came to the Prophet and informed him. He said, "How much have you promised her?" I said, "Two hundred dirham." He said, "If you scooped up the region of Baṭḥān you would not find so much." I said, "O Messenger of God, help me for I have promised her." The Messenger of God said, "I have not agreed to help you with this. But I have determined to send fourteen men with Abū Qatāda on an expedition. Would you like to go out with them, for, indeed, I hope that God will grant you plunder for your woman's dowry?" I said, "Yes."

We went out and we were sixteen men with Abū Qatāda, who was our commander. The Messenger of God sent us to the Ghaṭafān around Najd, saying, "March by night and hide by day. Make an attack, but do not kill women and children." So we went out until we came to the region of Ghaṭafān, and we attacked a large settlement of theirs. He said: Abū Qatāda spoke to us and urged us on with the fear of God most high. He put together every two men and said, "Each man must not separate from his companion unless he is killed or returns to inform me about his news. A man will not come to me, who, when I ask him about his companion says, 'I have no information about him!' When I proclaim *takbīr*, proclaim *takbīr*; when I attack, attack; do not become excessive in your search for the enemy." We encircled the settlement and I heard a man scream: O Khaḍira! I regarded it as a good omen and I said, "I will surely achieve good and have my wife." We had come to them at night.

He said: Abū Qatāda drew his sword and we drew our swords; He proclaimed *takbīr* and we proclaimed *takbīr* with him; we strengthened against the settlement, and men fought. All of a sudden a tall man drew his shining sword, while he was walking backwards and said, "O Muslim, come forward to Paradise!" So I went after him, and he said, "Surely your companion is a trickster, and his command is the real command," and he says, 'Paradise! Paradise!' and makes fun of us." But I knew that the enemy was ahead, and I went out in his tracks. My companion called out to me, "Do not go far, our commander has forbidden us to be excessive in the search." I reached my enemy and aimed at the middle of the back of his neck. [Page 779] Then he said, "Draw near, O Muslim, to Paradise!" I shot him until I killed him with my arrows. He fell dead and I took his sword. My companion began to call out, "Where have you gone? Indeed and by God, if I go to Abū Qatāda and he asks me about you I will inform him."

He said: I met him, before I met Abū Qatāda, and I inquired, "Did my commander ask about me?" He replied, "Yes, and he was furious with me and you." He informed me that they had collected the booty, and killed those who came out to them. I went to Abū Qatāda and he censured me. I said that I had killed a man, his affair was thus and thus, and I informed him about his words, all of them. Then we drove the cattle and carried the women, the scabbards of the swords hanging with the saddles. In the morning, as my camel lay smeared—I met a woman like a gazelle. She increasingly looked behind her while crying. I said, "What are you looking for?" She said, "By God, I seek a man who, if he were alive, would surely recover us from you." I realized that it was the man I had killed and I said, "Surely I killed him. This sword of his hangs by the saddle at its scabbard." She said, "This, by God, is the scabbard of his sword. So sheath it, if you speak the truth." I sheathed the sword and it was covered. He said: She cried and became resigned. Ibn Abī Hadrad said: We went to the Prophet with sheep and cattle.

Abū Mawdūd related to me from ʿAbd al-Raḥmān b. ʿAbdullah b. Abī Ḥadrad from his father, who said: When I returned from the raid of Khaḍira, and we had taken *fay'*, the [Page 780] portion of every man was twelve camels. I consummated my marriage and God granted me happiness.

ʿAbdullah b. Jaʿfar related to me from Jaʿfar b. ʿAmr, who said: They were gone for fifteen nights. They came with two hundred camels and a thousand sheep. They had taken many prisoners. The fifth was withdrawn. Their portions were twelve camels each. The camel was the equivalent of ten sheep.

Ibn Abī Sabra related to me from Isḥāq b. ʿAbdullah from ʿAbd al-Raḥmān b. ʿAbdullah b. Abī Ḥadrad from his father, who said: We captured four women during our outing; with them was a young girl like a gazelle, an amazing thing of youthfulness and sweetness; and children—boys and girls. They apportioned the prisoners and that beautiful young girl went to Abū Qatāda. Maḥmiyya b. Jaz' al-Zubaydī came and said, "O Messenger of God, indeed Abū Qatāda has taken this beautiful girl. But you promised me a girl from the first *fay'* that God grants you." He said: The Messenger of God sent for Abū Qatāda and said, "What girl came in your portion?" He replied, "A girl from the prisoners, who is the most beautiful of those prisoners. I took her for myself after apportioning the fifth." He said, "Give her to me." He replied, "Yes, O Messenger of God." The Messenger of God took her and gave her to Maḥmiya b. Jaz' al-Zubaydī.

THE RAID OF AL-FATḤ

Muḥammad b. ʿAbdullah, Mūsā b. Muḥammad, ʿAbdullah b. Jaʿfar, ʿAbdullah b. Yazīd, Ibn Abī Ḥabība, Ibn Abī Sabra, ʿAbd al-Ḥamīd b. Jaʿfar, ʿAbd al-Raḥmān b. ʿAbd al-ʿAzīz, Yūnus b. Muḥammad, Muḥammad b. Yaḥyā b. Sahl, [Page 781] Ibn Abī Ḥathma, Muḥammad b. Ṣāliḥ b. Dinār, Nujayḥ, Usāma b. Zayd, Ḥizām b. Hishām, Muʿādh b. Muḥammad b. Yaḥyā b. ʿAbdullah b. Abī Qatāda, and Maʿmar b. Rāshid, all have related the traditions of the "Conquest" in portions to me, and some of them are more reliable than others. And others have related to me also. I wrote all of what I heard from them.

They said: The Khuzāʿa had captured a man from the Banū Bakr in *jāhiliyya* and taken his property. Later, when a man from the Khuzāʿa passed by the Banū al-Dīl, the Banū al-Dīl killed him. A war took place between them. When the sons of al-Aswad b. Razn—Dhuayb, Salmā, and Kulthūm—passed by the Khuzāʿa, the Khuzāʿa killed them in ʿArafat by the idols of the sanctuary.

The people of al-Aswad in *jāhiliyya* used to pay double the blood money because of their standing with the Banū Bakr. But they left this practice behind and they refrained from each other from the time of Islam. Nevertheless, their enmity continued within them, except that Islam had entered upon them and they all held fast.

When it was the Peace of al-Ḥudaybiyya the Khuzāʿa entered into an agreement and a contract with the Messenger of God. The Khuzāʿa had been allies of ʿAbd al-Muṭṭalib, and the Messenger of God was aware of this. Indeed, at that time the Khuzāʿa came to the Prophet with the document of ʿAbd al-Muṭṭālib and read it out. Ibn Wāqid said: It stated: "In your name, O God, this is the pact of ʿAbd al-Muṭṭalib b. Hāshim to the Khuzāʿa." Their leaders and people of opinion came to the Messenger of God, and their absentees were content with what their witnesses agreed to, saying,

"Indeed, between us and you are the promises of God and his agreements that will never be forgotten. It will not bring strong disputes. The hand is one and the help is one, as long as Mt. Thabīr and Mt. Ḥirā stand. As long as the waters of Ṣūfa are wet [i.e. forever], what is between us and you will increase [Page 782] by renewal for ever and ever. Time is eternal." Ubayy b. Kaʿb read it to him and said, "How great is my knowledge about your pact while you are on the pact that you submitted to him! Every pact that was established in *jāhiliyya* was merely strengthened by Islam. A new pact was not made in Islam."

The Aslam came to the Prophet while he was in Ghadīr Ashṭāṭ. Burayda b. al-Ḥuṣayb brought them to him and said: O Messenger of God, this is the Aslam and this is their location. Those who emigrated to you emigrated from here. However, some people among them remained with their cattle and their livelihood. The Messenger of God said, "You are Muhājirūn wherever you are." He called al-ʿAlāʾ b. al-Ḥaḍramī and commanded him to write a document for them, stating: "This is a document from Muḥammad, the Messenger of God, to the Aslam, for those who believe among them in God, and testifies that there is no God but Allah and that Muḥammad is His servant and his messenger. Indeed he is secure in the protection of God, and to him is a *dhimma* from God and His messenger. Indeed your affair and ours is against those who attack, us from the people, with injustice. The hand is one and the help is one. What is for the people of the desert is similar to what is for the people of the settlements. They are Muhājirūn wherever they are." Al-ʿAlāʾ b. al-Ḥaḍramī wrote it down.

Abū Bakr al-Ṣiddīq said, "O Messenger of God, Burayda b. al-Ḥuṣayb is an excellent man to his people. Great are His blessings upon them. We passed by him one night while we were immigrating to Medina. He has embraced Islam with some of his people." The Messenger of God said, "Excellent is the man Burayda both to his people, and to those who are not his people, O Abū Bakr. Indeed the best is one who defends his people as long as he does not sin. Indeed sin has no good in it."

ʿAbdullah b. ʿAmr b. Zuhayr related to me from Mihjan b. Wahb, who said: It was the last of what was between Khuzāʿa and Kināna that Anas b. Zunaym al-Dīlī insulted the Messenger of God. A lad from Khuzāʿa heard him and fell upon him and struck him. He went out [Page 783] to his people and showed them his wounded head and mischief was stirred up with what was among them, and with what the Banū Bakr required of their blood-wit from the Khuzāʿa. When it was Shaʿbān, during the first twenty-two months of the Peace of al-Hudaybiyya, Banū Nufātha of the Banū Bakr spoke to the nobility of the Quraysh—the Banū Mudlij withdrew and did not break the agreement—to help with men and weapons against their enemy among the Khuzāʿa. They reminded them of the dead whom the Khuzāʿa had killed. They indicated to them their relationship and informed them about their entering with them in their contract and agreement, and of the Khuzāʿa going to Muḥammad with his contract and his agreement. The Banū Bakr found the people [Quraysh] hasten to that, except for Abū Sufyān. His advice was not sought about that and he did not know. Some said: Indeed they conferred with him but he refused them. The Banū Nufātha and Bakr began to say: Rather it is us! They helped them with weapons and quivers and men, and they plotted in secret in order that the Khuzāʿa would not know. They were secure and over-confident about the agreement and with what Islam hindered between them.

Then the Quraysh made an appointment at al-Watīr with those who were with them. They appeared for the appointment with elders of the Quraysh disguised and veiled:

Ṣafwān b. Umayya, Mikraz b. Ḥafṣ b. al-Akhīf, and Ḥuwayṭib b. ʿAbd al-ʿUzzā brought their slaves with them. The head of the Banū Bakr was Nawfal b. Muʿāwiya al-Dīlī. The Khuzāʿa stayed up the night, overconfident and feeling safe from their enemy. For if they were fearful of this, surely they would have been on guard and prepared.

The fighting continued until they were at the idols of the sanctuary. They said, "O Nawfal, your gods! your gods! You have entered the sanctuary." He replied, "I have no gods today, O Banū Bakr! You have robbed the pilgrim and you will not take your revenge from your enemy? One of you will not desire to come to his woman until he has asked my permission. One of you will not delay, the day after this day of his, from his revenge." When the Khuzāʿa ended up at the sanctuary, they entered the house of Budayl b. Waraqāʾ and Rāfiʿ the two Khuzāʿa, and the Banū Bakr ended up with them in the darkness of the dawn. The elders of the Quraysh entered their homes hoping [Page 784] that they would not be recognized, and that this would not reach Muḥammad.

ʿAbdullah b. ʿĀmir al-Aslamī related to me from ʿAṭāʾ b. Abī Marwān, who said: The Quraysh and Banū Bakr had killed twenty men among them while the Khuzāʿa were present in the house of Rāfiʿ and Budayl. When it was morning the Khuzāʿa lay killed at the door of Budayl and Rāfiʿ, the *mawlā* of Khuzāʿa. The Quraysh went out, regretting what they did. They knew that what they did broke the agreement that was between them and the Messenger of God for the determined period of time.

ʿAbdullah b. ʿAmr b. Zuhayr related to me from ʿAbdullah b. ʿIkrima b. ʿAbd al-Ḥārith b. Hishām, who said: Al-Ḥārith b. Hishām and Ibn Abī Rabīʿa came to Ṣafwān b. Umayya, Suhayl b. ʿAmr, and ʿIkrima b. Abī Jahl and blamed them for helping the Banū Bakr. Between them and Muḥammad was a fixed period and this was now broken for them. Those people turned and slipped to Nawfal b. Muʿāwiya, and he who led their talk was Suhayl b. ʿAmr, who said, "You saw what we made with you and your companions and how you killed from the people, and attended to them desiring to kill those who remained. This is what we do not agree with you about. Leave them for us." He said, "Yes." He left them and they went out. Ibn Qays al-Ruqayyāt said mentioning Suhayl b. ʿAmr:

> He was good to his uncles of the Khuzāʿa
> When the people of Mecca overpowered them.

And about the same issue Ibn Luʿṭ al-Dīlī said:

> Have not the most distant of the tribe heard that we repulsed the Banū Kaʿb in impotent disgrace.
> [Page 785] We made them keep to the dwelling of the slave Rāfīʿ, and they were confined helpless with Budayl.
> We held them there to the end of a lengthy day, then we charged down on them from every pass
> We slaughtered them like sacrificial goats while we were like lions racing to get our teeth in them.

He said: al-Ḥārith b. Hishām and ʿAbdullah b. Abī Rabīʿa walked up to Abū Sufyān and said, "This matter must surely be rectified. By God, if this affair is not corrected surely Muḥammad and his companions will frighten you!" Abū Sufyān said, "Hind bt. ʿUtba saw this dream, and I detest it, was shocked by it and am fearful of its evil." The people said, "What is it?" He said, "She saw blood come from al-Ḥajūn and flow until it stopped at al-Khandama, for a while, then it disappeared." The people hated this, They said, "This is evil."

Mujammiʿ b. Yaʿqūb related to me from his father, who said: When Abū Sufyān saw what he saw of evil he said, "This, by God, is an affair I have not witnessed, but I was not absent from it. This is a burden only to me. No, by God, I was not consulted, and I did not desire it when it reached me. By God, Muḥammad will surely attack us. If my misgiving is true, and it never fails me, I have no option but to go to Muḥammad and ask him to increase the peace and renew the contract before this affair reaches him." The Quraysh said, "By God, you have arrived at the right decision!" The Quraysh repented for helping the Bakr against the Khuzāʿa. They knew that the Messenger of God would never leave them until he attacked them. Abū Sufyān went out on two rides, taking a *mawlā* of his with him. He hastened his journey believing that he was the first of those who went from Mecca to the Messenger of God.

[Page 786] Abū ʿAbdullah said: We have a version about the affair of the Khuzāʿa; I have not seen people narrate it before us, nor did they know of it. A trustworthy one has transmitted it. Its source is trustworthy and convincing. I do not see one who knows another version of it except that the people before us denied it, saying, "It was not so." I mentioned it to Ibn Jaʿfar and Muḥammad b. Ṣāliḥ, Abū Maʿshar and others among those who knew of Abū Sufyān's journey. But all of them denied knowing any version of it.

The first of the traditions was that one who I trusted related to me that he heard ʿAmr b. Dīnār who related from Ibn ʿUmar, that when a group of camel riders from the Khuzāʿa arrived before the Messenger of God and informed him about who was killed among them, the Messenger of God said, "Whom do you accuse and whom do you suspect?" They said, "The Banū Bakr." He said, "All of them?" They said, "No, but we accuse a few of the Banū Nufātha, and the chief of the people, Nawfal b. Muʿāwiya al-Nufāthī." He said, "This is a clan of the Banū Bakr, and I am sending a message to the people of Mecca to ask them about this affair, giving them different choices." He sent Ḍamra to them and let them choose between one of three: Pay the blood money to the Khuzāʿa; or break their pact with the Nufātha, or that they reject their agreement with them equitably. Ḍamra, the messenger of the Messenger of God, came to them and informed them of what the Messenger of God had sent. He said that he asked them to choose between providing the blood money of the dead Khuzāʿa, or breaking from their pact with the Nufātha; or the rejection of their agreement (by the Messenger of God) equitably. Quraṭa b. ʿAbd ʿAmr al-Aʿjamī said, "As for us paying the blood debt of the dead Khuzāʿa, indeed the Nufātha are a violent people, and we will not pay them (until there are no sheep or cattle with us) ever. As for us breaking from the pact of Nufātha, surely there is not a tribe among the Bedouin who perform pilgrimage to this House and hold a [Page 787] greater reverence for this House than the Nufātha. They are our allies and we will not break from their pact, until we have neither cattle nor sheep. But we reject him (i.e. Muḥammad) equitably." Ḍamra returned to the Messenger of God with those words of theirs. Then the Quraysh sent Abū Sufyān b. Ḥarb to ask the Messenger of God to renew the pact. The Quraysh regretted their reply to the Messenger of God.

Abū ʿAbdullah said: All of our companions deny this tradition. He said: The Messenger of God took the narrow roads through the mountains and the news was obscured, until Muḥammad entered Mecca unexpectedly. When I mentioned this tradition to Ḥizām b. Hishām al-Kaʿbī, he said: He who related this to you did not miss anything. But the affair is according to what I say to you: The Quraysh regretted helping Nufātha, saying, "Muḥammad will attack us!"

ʿAbdullah b. Saʿd b. Abī Sarḥ said, and at that time he was with the Quraysh, a renegade disbeliever, "Indeed I had the opinion that Muḥammad does not attack you until he warns you and gives you many choices. All of them are easier on you than his attack." They said, "What is it?" He said, "He will send, requiring you to pay the blood money of the dead Khuzāʿa, and there were twenty-three killed. Or release from the pact with those who destroyed the pact between us—the Banū Nufātha, or we (the Muslims) shall throw war at you." He said, "What do you think of these choices?" The people said, "The last of what Ibn Abī Sarḥ said." He knew about it. Suhayl b. ʿAmr said, "What is easier upon us than breaking the pact of the Banū Nufātha." Shayba b. ʿUthmān al-ʿAbdarī said, "You will remember your uncles and you will be angry for them." Suhayl said, "Abū Quraysh did not bear the Khuzāʿa." Shayba said, "No, but we will pay the blood money for the dead Khuzāʿa. It is easier for us." [Page 788] Quraṭa b. ʿAbd ʿAmr said, "No, by God, they will not be paid the blood money. And we will not break from the pact of Nufātha who have supported us in our hard times; but we will break with him equitably!" Abū Sufyān said, "This is not wise! The only opinion is to deny that the Quraysh joined in destroying the agreement and cutting the period of time. If the people cut it without our consent and consultation there is no blame upon us." They said, "This is the decision. There is no decision other than to deny all that happened." He said, "Indeed, I did not witness it and there were no commands about it. And I am sincere about that. Surely, I detest what you did, and knew that it would be a day of darkness." The Quraysh said repeatedly to Abū Sufyān, "Go to Muḥammad with that!" until he went out to meet the Prophet.

Abū ʿAbdullah said: I mentioned the tradition of Ḥizām to Ibn Jaʿfar and others of his companions and they did not deny it. They said: This is his version. ʿAbdullah b. Jaʿfar wrote it from me.

ʿAbdullah b. ʿĀmir al-Aslamī related to me from ʿAṭāʾ b. Abī Marwān, who said: The Messenger of God said to ʿĀʾisha, "I am perplexed by the affair of the Khuzāʿa." Ibn Wāqid said: ʿĀʾisha replied, "O Messenger of God, do you think the Quraysh would dare to break the agreement between you and them, when the sword has already exhausted them?" The Messenger of God said, "They destroy the agreement for an affair that God desires for them." ʿĀʾisha said, "Good or evil, O Messenger of God?" He said, "Good."

Ḥizām b. Hishām b. Khālid al-Kaʿbī related to me from his father, who said: ʿAmr [Page 789] b. Sālim al-Khuzāʿa went out with forty riders from the Khuzāʿa to seek the help of the Messenger of God and inform him about what happened to them and how the Quraysh helped the Banū Bakr against the Khuzāʿa, with men and weapons and quivers, while Ṣafwān b. Umayya attended that with men from his people who were disguised; they were killed by their hands. The Messenger of God was seated in the mosque with his companions, when the chief of the Khuzāʿa, ʿAmr b. Sālim, stood up and implored the Messenger of God who permitted him and listened to him. He said:

O Lord, I come to remind Muḥammad

by the ancient pact that existed between our forefathers.
You were like sons and we were the fathers.
Then we converted to Islam and continued our aid.
Indeed the Quraysh have broken their promise to you,
they have violated their pledge.
Help us now, and may God guide you,
And call God's servants to our aid,
Among them the Messenger of God prepared for war
With a great army like the foaming sea,
A lord for a lord, proud like a lion.
It was they who attacked us at night in al-Watīr while we were sleeping.
We recited the Qur'ān and performed sujūd and rukūʿ.
They claim that I do not worship any God
And they are but a miserable few.

When the riders concluded, they said, "O Messenger of God, indeed Anas b. Zunaym al-Dīlī insulted you." The Messenger of God permitted his blood to be taken. It reached Anas b. Zunaym and he arrived [Page 790] before the Messenger of God apologizing because of what had reached him. He said:

Is it you by whose orders Maʿadd was led?
Nay, God guided them and said to you, Testify!
No camel ever carried a purer man,
More true to his promise than Muḥammad;
Swifter to do good, more lavish in giving,
When he went forth like a polished Indian sword,
More generous in giving a rich Yamani robe hardly worn
And the horse that was easily first in the race.
Know, O Apostle of God, that you will get me
And that a threat from you is as good as fulfilled.
Know, O apostle, that you have power
Over them that dwell in highland and plain.
They told the Apostle that I insulted him.
Were it true, may my hand never lift a whip.
I merely said woe to the heroes
Who were slain in unhappy unlucky days!
Those not their equal in blood killed them
And great was my weeping and dismay.
Dhuayb and Kulthūm and Salmā went successively together
If my eye does not weep let me grieve.
There is no one like Salma and his brothers
Are kings like slaves? I have not broken with custom or shed blood.
Consider, you who know the truth, and act!

Ḥizām related this to me. His poem and his apology reached the Messenger of God. Nawfal b. Muʿāwiya al-Dīlī spoke to him and said, "O Messenger of God, you are the first of men in forgiveness. [Page 791] Who among us has not hurt and insulted you? We were in *jāhiliyya* and we did not know what we should take and what we should leave, until God guided us through you from destruction. The riders lied about him and they increased with you. He said, "Leave the riders. Indeed we have not found in Tihāma one who possesses a relationship—near or distant—who has better fulfilled with us than the Khuzāʿa." Nawfal b. Muʿāwiya was silent, and when he was silent the Messenger of God said, "I have forgiven him [i.e. Anas b. Zunaym]." Nawfal said, "For you I would ransom my father and my mother!"

ʿAbd al-Ḥamīd b. Jaʿfar b. ʿImrān b. Abī Anas related to me from Ibn ʿAbbās, who said: The Messenger of God stood up, pulled the tip of his garment and said, "I will not succeed if I do not help the Banū Kaʿb as I help myself." Ḥizām b. Hishām related to me from his father, who said: The Messenger of God said, "It is as if I see you with Abū Sufyān who comes saying, 'Strengthen the pact and increase the peace,' but returns in displeasure." Then the Messenger of God said to ʿAmr b. Sālim and his companions, "Return, and disperse in the valleys." The Messenger of God got up and went to ʿĀʾisha and he was irritated. Then he asked for water and began washing. ʿĀʾisha said: I heard him say while he poured the water on himself, "I will not succeed if I do not help the Banū Kaʿb."

Abū Sufyān went out from Mecca and he feared that ʿAmr b. Sālim and his companions were coming from the Messenger of God. When the people came to al-Abwāʾ they turned and dispersed. A faction went to the coast across the road. Budayl b. Umm Aṣram in a group with him adhered to the road. Abū Sufyān met him. Abū Sufyān was anxious that Budayl was coming from Muḥammad, even certain that he had been with him. He said to the people, "Inform me about Yathrib. [Page 792] How much do you know about it?" They said, "We have no knowledge of it." He knew that they concealed it. He said, "Is it not with dates of Yathrib that you feed us? Surely, the dates of Yathrib are better than the dates of Tihāma." They said, "No." He said: But his heart refused to accept it. He said, "O Budayl, did you go to Muḥammad?" He replied, "No, I did not. But I traveled in the land of Kaʿb and Khuzāʿa from this coast regarding the murder of one of them, and I made peace between them." He said: Abū Sufyān says, "You, by God—I have always known—as a pious conciliator." Then Abū Sufyān gave them to drink until Budayl and his companions left. Then he came to their station and crumbled the dung of their camels and found date seeds in it. And, in their station he found seeds of the dates of ʿAjwa, like the tongue of the bird. Abū Sufyān said, "I swear by God, surely the people came to Muḥammad!" The people—when it happened—were setting out on the morning of that day—they marched for three days to where Abū Sufyān met them.

The Banū Bakr had imprisoned the Khuzāʿa in the house of Budayl and Rāfiʿ for three days and they had not spoken to them. The Quraysh plotted that Abū Sufyān go out, and he stayed for two days and went out. This was five days after the killing of the Khuzāʿa. Abū Sufyān approached until he arrived in Medina. He went before the Prophet, and said, "O Muḥammad, indeed I was absent during the Peace of al-Ḥudaybiyya. Strengthen the agreement and increase for us the term." The Prophet said, "Did anything take place recently?" He said, "God forbid!" The Messenger of God said, "We are in accordance with our term and our peace on the day of al-Ḥudaybiyya. We will not change nor will we alter."

Then Abū Sufyān got up from those with him and went before his daughter Umm Ḥabība [a wife of the Prophet]. When he went to sit on the bed of the Messenger of God she folded it away from him. He said, "Do you dislike this bed for me, or me for it?" She replied, [Page 793] "Rather it is the bed of the Messenger of God, and you are an unclean man and a polytheist." He said, "O my daughter, surely evil has overtaken you and your understanding!" She said, "God has guided me to Islam, and you, O lord of the Quraysh and its elder, refuse it. How did entering Islam fail you, and you worship stones that do not see nor hear?" He said, "O how remarkable! This from you as well! Must I leave what my forefathers worshiped and follow the religion of Muḥammad?" Then he got up from her and met Abū Bakr al-Siddīq, and spoke to him. He said, "Will you speak to Muḥammad so that you may grant protection among the people?" Abū Bakr said, "My protection is in the protection of the Messenger of God." Then he met ʿUmar and spoke to him as he spoke to Abū Bakr. ʿUmar said, "By God, if I should find the red ants attacking you I would help them against you." Then he went to ʿUthmān b. ʿAffān and said, "Indeed there is not one among the community who is dearer to me in relationship than you, so increase the peace and strengthen the pact. Indeed your friend will never reject it from you, ever. By God, I have never seen a man who is more generous to his companion than Muḥammad is to his companions." ʿUthmān said: My protection is in the protection of the Messenger of God."

ʿAbdullah b. Muḥammad related to me from his father, who said: Abū Sufyān visited Fāṭima, the daughter of the Prophet, and spoke to her. He said, "Grant me protection among the people." She said, "Surely, I am a woman." He said, "Your protection is lawful. Your sister protected Abū al-ʿĀṣ b. al-Rabīʿ, and Muḥammad accepted that. Fāṭima said, "That is up to the Messenger of God," and she refused him. He said, "Command one of your sons to give protection to the people!" [Page 794] She replied, "They are children. Such as they cannot give protection." When she refused him, he came to ʿAlī and said, "O Abū Ḥasan, grant protection to the people, and ask Muḥammad to increase the term." ʿAlī replied, "Woe unto you, O Abū Sufyān, indeed the Messenger of God has resolved that he will not do it, and one is not able to speak to the Messenger of God about something he detests." Abū Sufyān said, "Is that the opinion? Make it easy for me. Indeed it has depressed me. Advise me about an affair that you think is useful to me." ʿAlī said, "For you I do not find anything better than that you stand and grant protection among the people, for indeed you are the lord of the Kināna." He said, "Do you think that a dispensation from me is worth something?" ʿAlī replied, "I do not think that, by God, but I do not find anything else." So Abū Sufyān stood in the midst of the people and shouted, "Indeed, I grant protection among the people. I do not think Muḥammad will embarrass me." Then he went to the Prophet and said, "O Muḥammad I did not think that you would refuse my protection!" The Messenger of God said, "You say that, O Abū Sufyān!"

Ibn Abī Ḥabība related to me from Wāqid b. ʿAmr b. Saʿd b. Muʿādh. He said: Abū Sufyān came to Saʿd b. ʿUbāda and said, "O Abū Thābit, indeed you know what was between you and me, and that I was your protector in our sanctuary. You were to me similarly in Yathrib. You are the lord of this land. Grant protection among the people and increase the term." Saʿd said, "O Abū Sufyān, my protection is in the protection of the Messenger of God. One will not grant protection against him." It was said that Abū Sufyān went out on what the Messenger of God said to him: "You say that, O Abū Sufyān!"

[Page 795] It was said: After he shouted, Abū Sufyān did not approach the Prophet but rode his camel and departed to Mecca. He had been detained and his absence was long. The Quraysh accused him when he delayed with severe accusations. They said, "By God, indeed we think he has converted and follows Muḥammad secretly and hides his Islam." When he entered on Hind at night she said, "Surely you were detained until your people suspected you. If with this long stay you brought them success, then indeed, you are the man!" He drew near her and sat in the manner a man would sit with a woman, and she began to say, "What did you do?" He informed her of the news and said, "I did not find except what ʿAlī said to me." She beat him with her legs on his chest and said, "You are a shameful messenger of the people!"

ʿAbdullah b. ʿUthmān b. Abī Sulaymān related to me from his father, who said: When it was morning, and Abū Sufyān shaved his head before the idols of Isāf and Nā'ila, and sacrificed for them, and made to rub blood on their heads while saying, "I will not withdraw from worshiping you until I die as my father died," he was acquitted by the Quraysh of what they accused him. Hizām b. Hishām related to me from his father, who said: The Quraysh said to him, "What happened? Did you bring us a document from Muḥammad, or did you increase the term? We do not believe that they will attack us!" He said, "By God, surely Muḥammad refused me. Indeed I spoke to the distinguished companions and was not able to get anything from them but that they were aiming one word at me. Except for ʿAlī, who said, when I was depressed, 'You are the lord of the Kināna, so grant protection among the people!' I proclaimed protection, then I visited Muḥammad and I said, 'Surely I have granted protection among the people and I do not think that you will refuse my protection.' Muḥammad said, 'You say that, O Abū Sufyān.' He did not say anything more than this." They said, "He only increased his toying with you!" He said, "By God, I did not find other than that."

Muḥammad b. ʿAbdullah related to me from al-Zuhrī from Muḥammad b. Jubayr b. [Page 796] Muṭʿim, who said: When Abū Sufyān turned to return, the Messenger of God said to ʿĀ'isha, "Prepare us and hide your affair!" The Messenger of God said, "O God, seal the information from the Quraysh and their spies until we come to them as a surprise." Some said that he said, "O God, take from the Quraysh their sight and do not let them see me except all of a sudden, nor hear of me except unexpectedly." They said: the Messenger of God held to the passes, and ʿUmar b. al-Khaṭṭāb circumambulated the passes guarding them, and saying, "Do not let anyone pass by you that you do not know except to ward him off—for the passes belonged to the Muslims—except one who has been to Mecca, or in the direction of Mecca. Hold him and question him about it."

They said: Abū Bakr went to ʿĀ'isha while she was preparing the Messenger of God and she packed wheat, barely, flour and date. Abū Bakr came to her and said, "O ʿĀ'isha, does the Messenger of God intend a raid?" She replied, "I do not know." He said, "If the Messenger of God intends to travel informs us, we will prepare for him." She replied, "I do not know." "Perhaps he desires the Banū Sulaym, perhaps the Thaqīfā, perhaps the Hawāzin?" But she was silent about it. When the Prophet entered, Abū Bakr said to him, "O Messenger of God, are you going to travel?" The Messenger of God replied, "Yes." He said, "Shall I make preparations?" The Messenger of God replied, "Yes." Abū Bakr said, "Where are you going?" He replied, "To the Quraysh. But hide that, O Abū Bakr." The Messenger of God ordered preparation. Abū Bakr said, "Is there not between us and them a term?" The Messenger of God replied, "Surely they have attacked and broken the agreement. Indeed, we will attack them." He said to Abū Bakr, "Conceal what I mentioned to you!"

One thought that the Messenger of God desired al-Shām; another thought it was the Thaqīf; another, the Hawāzin. The Messenger of God sent Abū Qatāda b. Ribʿī with eight individuals to the valley of Iḍam in order to make some think, and the news spread, that the Messenger of God was going in that direction.

[Page 797] ʿAbdullah b. Yazīd b. Qusayṭ related to me from his father from Ibn Abī Ḥadrad from his father, who said: The Messenger of God sent us to the valley of Iḍam. Our commander was Abū Qatāda in that expedition. Muḥallim b. Jaththāma al-Laythī and I were with them. While we were in a part of Wādī Iḍam ʿĀmir b. al-Aḍbaṭ al-Ashjaʿī passed by us all of a sudden, and greeted us with the greeting of Islam, so we kept away from him. But Muḥallim b. Jaththāma attacked and killed him. He stole a camel of his, utensils, and a milk skin of milk that was with him. When we joined the Prophet the Qurʾān was revealed about us: *O believers, when you are journeying in the path of God be discriminating, and do not say to him who offers you a greeting, "Thou art not a believer, seeking the chance goods of the present life* (Q. 4:94)." The people turned and did not meet a group until they ended up at Dhū Khushub. It reached them that the Messenger of God was going to Mecca. They went towards Bīn until they met the Prophet in al-Suqyā.

Al-Mundhir b. Saʿd related to me from Yazīd b. Rūmān, who said: When the Messenger of God gathered to march to the Quraysh, the people were informed about that. Ḥāṭib b. Abī Baltaʿa wrote to the Quraysh informing them about what the Messenger of God intended. He gave the document to a woman of the Muzayna, and promised her a reward provided she handed it to the Quraysh. She put it in her head and plaited over it. Then she went out. News of what Ḥātib did came from the heavens to the Messenger of God. He sent for ʿAlī and al-Zubayr [Page 798] and said, "Overtake a woman from Muzayna. She has the document that Ḥāṭib wrote warning the Quraysh." So they went out and overtook her in al-Khulayfa. They made her alight and they searched for it in her saddle, but they could not find anything. They said to her, "We swear by God, the Prophet was not deceived, and we are not deceived. So take out this document or we will surely undress you!" When she saw their seriousness she said, "Turn away from me." They turned away from her, and she untied the plait of her head, took out the document and gave it to the two of them, and they brought it to the Messenger of God. The Messenger of God called Ḥāṭib and said, "What caused you to do this?" He replied, "O Messenger of God, indeed I am a believer in God and His Messenger. I have not altered nor changed! But I am a man with neither lineage nor kinship among the people, and I have, in their [Quraysh] midst, a family and a son, and I did it to flatter and bribe them." ʿUmar b. al-Khaṭṭāb said, "May God fight you! You saw the Messenger of God taking the passes, and you write a document to the Quraysh warning them? Give him to me, O Messenger of God and I will cut off his head. Indeed he is a hypocrite." The Messenger of God said, "How would you know that, O ʿUmar? Perhaps, on the day of Badr, God watched over the people of Badr." Then he said, "Do as you wish for I have pardoned you." God revealed about Ḥāṭib: *O believers take not my enemy and your enemy as benefactors offering them love* (Q. 60:1), to the end of the verse.

Mūsā b. Muḥammad b. Ibrāhīm related to me from his father, who said: Ḥāṭib wrote to three people. Ṣafwān b. Umayya, Suhayl b. ʿAmr, and ʿIkrima b. Abī Jahl, saying, "Indeed the Messenger of God has called the people to attack. I do not see him desire other than you. I wish that this letter of mine will be of help to you." He gave the document to a woman named Kanūd, from Muzayna of the people of ʿArj. He offered her a dinar provided the document reached. He said, [Page 799] "Hide whatever you can, and do not take the road for indeed it is being watched." She did not take the pass, but travelled left of Maḥajja in the cracks until she came to the road in al-ʿAqīq. ʿUtba b. Jabīra related to me from al-Ḥuṣayn b. ʿAbd al-Raḥmān b. ʿAmr b. Saʿd, who said: Her name was Sāra; he gave her ten dinars.

They said: When the Messenger of God revealed the raid, he sent to the people of the desert and to those around it among the Muslims saying to them, "Whoever is a believer in God and the last day will surely attend Ramaḍān in Medina." He sent a messenger in every direction until they arrived before the Messenger of God: the Aslam, the Ghifār, Muzayna, Juhayna, and Ashjaʿ. He sent to the Banū Sulaym, and they joined him in Qudayd. As for the rest of the Bedouin, they set out from Medina.

He said: Saʿīd b. ʿAṭāʾ b. Abī Marwān related to me from his father from his grandfather, who said: The Messenger of God sent Asmāʾ b. Hāritha and Hind b. Hāritha to the Aslam saying to them, "Indeed the Messenger of God commands you to attend Ramaḍān in Medina." The Messenger of God sent Jundub and Rafiʿ, the two sons of Makīth, to Juhayna, commanding them to attend Ramaḍān in al-Medīna. The Messenger of God sent Īmāʾ b. Rahḍa and Abū Ruhm Kulthūm b. al-Ḥuṣayn to the Banū al-Ghifār and Ḍamra. The Messenger of God sent Maʿqil b. Sinān and Nuʿaym b. Masʿūd to Ashjaʿ; he sent Bilāl b. al-Ḥārith and ʿAbdullah b. ʿAmr al-Muzannī to the Muzayna; and he sent al-Ḥajjāj b. ʿIlāṭ al-Sulamī, then al-Bahzī [Page 800] and al-ʿIrbāḍ b. Sāriya to the Banū Sulaym; he sent Bishr b. Sufyān and Budayl b. Waraqāʾ to the Banū Kaʿb Banī ʿAmra. The Banū Kaʿb met the Prophet in Qudayd. Those of the Banū Kaʿb who were with him in Medina, had set out with him from Medina.

The Messenger of God camped in Biʾr Abī ʿInaba where he handed out the flags and banners. The Muhājirūn had three banners—a banner with al-Zubayr, a banner with ʿAlī, and a banner with Saʿd b. Abī Waqqāṣ. There was with the Aws of Banū ʿAbd al-Ashhal a banner with Abū Nāʾila, and in the Banū Ẓafar a banner with Qatāda b. al-Nuʿmān; and in Banū Ḥāritha a banner with Abū Burda b. Niyār; and in the Banū Muʿawiya a banner with Jabar b. ʿAtīk, and in the Banū Khaṭma a banner with Abū Lubāba b. ʿAbd al-Mundhir, and in the Banū Umayya a banner with Mubayyaḍ—Ibn Ḥayawayh said it was Nubayḍ in the book of Abū Ḥayya, but I have left it as it was, "Mubayyaḍ." And in the Banū Sāʿida a banner with Abū Usayd al-Sāʿidī; and in the Banū al-Ḥārith b. al-Khazraj a banner with ʿAbdullah b. Zayd; in the Banū Salima a banner with Quṭba b. ʿĀmir b. Ḥadīda; in the Banū Mālik b. Najjār a banner with ʿUmāra b. Ḥazm; and in the Banū Māzin a banner with Salīṭ b. Qays, and in the Abū Dīnār a banner was carried by __________.

The Muhājirūn were seven hundred. There were three hundred horses with them from the cavalry. The Anṣār were four thousand, and with them from the cavalry were five hundred. The Muzayna numbered a thousand, and held among the cavalry, a hundred horses and a hundred coats of mail: al-Nuʿmān b. Muqarrin, Bilāl b. al-Ḥārith, and ʿAbdullah b. ʿAmr, each held a banner. The Aslam were four hundred, with thirty horses, and two banners: one carried by Burayda b. al-Ḥuṣayb, and the other by Nājiya b. al-Aʿjam. The Juhayna were eight hundred. Among their cavalry were fifty horses and four banners: Suwayd b. Ṣakhr, Ibn Makīth, Abū Zurʿa and ʿAbdullah b. Badr, each held a banner.

[Page 801] The Banū Kaʿb b. ʿAmr numbered five hundred; they had three banners: a banner with Bishr b. Sufyān, Ibn Shurayḥ, and ʿAmr b. Sālim. They did not set out with the Messenger of God from Medina, but joined him in Qudayd.

He said: ʿUtba b. Jabīra related to me from al-Ḥuṣayn b. ʿAbd al-Raḥmān, who said: The Messenger of God did not grant the flags and the banners until he finally reached Qudayd. Then he handed out the banners of the Muhājirūn and the Anṣār according to what we mentioned. He said: The banner of the Ashjaʿ was with ʿAwf b. Mālik. The Messenger of God set out on Wednesday, the tenth of Ramaḍan, after the *ʿAṣar* prayer, and a knot was not untied until he reached al-Ṣulṣul. The Muslims set out leading the horses and mounting the camels, and numbered ten thousand. The Prophet dispatched al-Zubayr b. al-Awwām in front of him with two hundred Muslims. When the Messenger of God reached al-Baydā' he said: (Yaḥyā b. Khālid b. Dīnār related to me from ʿAbdullah b. ʿUmayr from Ibn ʿAbbās, who said: Dāwud b. Khālid related to me from al-Maqburī from Abū Hurayra, who said that the Messenger of God said) "Surely I see the clouds open with the victory of the Banū Kaʿb." The Messenger of God set out from Medina and his herald called out: Whoever desires to fast, let him fast and whoever desires to break the fast let him break it! The Messenger of God fasted.

Mālik b. Anas related to me from Sumā, the *mawlā* of Abū Bakr, from Abū Bakr b. ʿAbd al-Raḥmān b. al-Ḥārith from a man, who said that he saw the Messenger of God [Page 802] in al-ʿArj pour water on his head and on his face for the thirst.

He said: ʿAbd al-Raḥmān b. ʿAbd al-ʿAzīz related to me from Ḥakīm b. Ḥakīm from Abū Jaʿfar from Jābir b. ʿAbdullah, who said: When we were in al-Kadayd, between the *Ẓuhr* and *ʿAṣar* prayers, the Messenger of God held up a vessel of water in his hand until the Muslims saw it, and then broke his fast at that time. It reached the Messenger of God that a community was fasting and he said, "Those are the disobedient!" Abū Saʿīd al-Khudrī said, "The Messenger of God said, "Surely you will meet your enemy in the morning. Breaking the fast is better for you!" He said that in Marr al-Ẓahrān. When the Messenger of God alighted in al-ʿArj, the people did not know where the Messenger of God was going: to the Quraysh, to the Hawāzin, or to Thaqīf! They wanted to know. He sat with his companions in al-ʿArj, talking, when Kaʿb b. Mālik said: I will go to the Messenger of God and learn for you his direction. Kaʿb came and knelt before the Messenger of God on his knees, then he said:

> We fulfilled in Tihāma and Khaybar every suspicion,
> Then we relaxed the swords.
> We asked them, and if they could speak, they would say
> Their blades are for the Daws or Thaqīf.
> I am not for a settlement if you do not see thousands of blades in your yard.
> We pull the tent at the heart of Waj
> And leave their homes empty.

Ayyūb b. al-Nuʿmān related from his father, who said: The Messenger of God smiled but did not add to that. The people began to say: By God, the Messenger of God did not clarify anything for you. We do not know before whom he will appear: the Quraysh, the Thaqīf or the Hawāzin.

[Page 803] He said: Hishām b. Saʿd related to me from Zayd b. Aslam, who said: When the Messenger of God alighted in Qudayd it was said: Do you have a share in white women and brown camels? The Messenger of God replied, "Indeed, God has forbidden them to me for reasons of kinship," as he prodded the camels on their chests. Al-Zubayr b. Mūsā related to me from Abū l-Huwayrith from the Prophet, that he said, "Indeed, God forbade them to me for my duty to the parent," and he prodded the camels on their chests.

He said: Qurrān b. Muḥammad related to me from ʿĪsā b. ʿUmayla al-Fazzārī, who said: ʿUyayna was with his people in Najd when news came to him that the Messenger of God was setting out. The Bedouin had gathered to him. He set out with a group of his community until he arrived in Medina. He found the Messenger of God had set out two days earlier. He went from Rukūba and proceeded to al-ʿArj. The Messenger of God found him in al-ʿArj. When the Messenger of God alighted there, ʿUyayna came to him and said, "O Messenger of God, news came to me of your setting out and of those who gathered to you, and I came promptly, for I did not know. I will gather my people and we will have a large gathering. But, I do not see in you the appearance of war; I do not see flags or banners! Do you desire to make the *ʿUmra*? Yet I do not see in you the appearance of ritual dress! Where are you going, O Messenger of God?" He replied, "Where God wishes," and he continued on his journey, and ʿUyayna went with him. He found al-Aqraʿ b. Ḥābis in al-Suqyā. [Page 804] He had come there with ten of his people, and they marched with him. When he alighted in Qudayd, he granted the flags and gave out the banners. When ʿUyayna saw the tribes take the flags and banners, he bit his fingers, and Abū Bakr said, "What do you regret?" He said, "For my people, that they do not go out with Muḥammad. O Abū Bakr where is Muḥammad going?" He replied, "Where God wishes." The Messenger of God entered Mecca at that time between al-Aqraʿ and ʿUyayna.

He said: ʿAbd al-Raḥmān b. Muḥammad related to me from ʿAbdullah b. Abī Bakr b. Ḥazm, who said: When The Messenger of God marched from al-ʿArj, and he was between al-ʿArj and al-Ṭalūb, he saw a bitch whine over its puppies while they were, around her, suckling. The Prophet commanded a man from his companions called Juʿayl b. Surāqa to stay in front of it so that none of the army would harm it and its puppies.

He said: Muʿādh b. Muḥammad related to me from ʿAbdullah b. Saʿd, who said: When the Messenger of God went from al-ʿArj, a group of the cavalry went ahead of him, so that it was in front of the Muslims. When they were between al-ʿArj and al-Ṭulūb they brought a spy from the Hawāzin to the Messenger of God and said: "O Messenger of God, we saw him when we rose above him. He was on his saddle, hidden away from us in low ground. Then he ascended the high ground and sat there, and we rushed to him while he tried to flee from us, but he had tied his camel below the high ground when he concealed it. We said: 'Who sent you?' He said: 'A man from the Banū Ghifār.' We said: 'They are people from this land.' We said: 'From which clan of the Banū Ghifār are you?' But he was unable to express himself and [Page 805] his genealogy did not come through to us. Our doubts about him increased and the suspicion about him distressed us. We said: 'Where are your people?' He replied: 'Near!' and he motioned with his hand in a direction. We said: 'On which water, and who was with you there?' But we understood nothing. When we saw his confusion, we said: 'Speak the truth or indeed we shall cut off your head!' He replied: 'If I tell you the truth will that profit me with you?' We said: 'Yes.' He replied: 'Indeed, I am a man from the Hawāzin from the Banū Naḍr. The Hawāzin sent me as a spy. They said: "Go to Medina until you reach Muḥammad and inquire for us what he desires in the matter of his allies. Does he send a delegation to the Quraysh or will he raid them himself, for we think that he will attack them. If he goes out marching or sends a mission, then march with him until you reach the Baṭn Sarif. If he desires us first, he will go through the valley of Sarif until he comes out to us; if he desires the Quraysh he will keep to the road".'" The Messenger of God said: "Where are the Hawāzin?" He replied: "I left them in Baqʿāʾ. They have gathered in groups. They have attracted the Bedouin, and sent to the Thaqīf who have responded to them. I left the Thaqīf hastily gathering in groups. They sent to al-Jurash for information on war machines and mangonels. They march to join the Hawāzin and they will be together." The Messenger of God asked, "Who did they appoint as their commander?" He replied, "A youth of theirs, Mālik b. ʿAwf." The Messenger of God asked, "Has every Hawāzin responded to Mālik's call?" He said, "The serious and tough among the Banū ʿĀmir have slowed down." He said, "Who?" He replied, "The Kaʿb and the Kilāb." He asked, "What did the Hilāl do?" He replied, "Only a few of them joined him. I passed your people yesterday in Mecca, and Abū Sufyān b. Ḥarb had come to them, but they were exasperated with what he brought them: fearful and apprehensive."

[Page 806] The Messenger of God said, "God is indeed sufficient for us, and the best of guardians. I think he spoke honestly to me!" The man said, "Will I be rewarded?" The Messenger of God commanded Khālid b. al-Walīd to imprison him. They feared that he would go ahead and warn the people. When the camp alighted at Marr al-Dhahrān the man escaped. Khālid b. al-Walīd sought out and captured him at al-Arāk. He said, "If I had not promised to protect you, I would cut off your head." He informed the Messenger of God and the Messenger of God ordered that he be imprisoned until they entered Mecca. When the Messenger of God entered Mecca and conquered it, he was brought to the Messenger of God who invited him to Islam, and he converted. Then he set out to the Hawāzin and he was killed at Awṭās.

He said: Saʿīd b. Muslim b. Qamādīn related to me from ʿAbd al-Raḥmān b. Sābiṭ and others, who said: Abū Sufyān b. al-Ḥārith b. ʿAbd al-Muṭṭalib was brother in suckling to the Messenger of God, for Ḥalīma nursed him for days. He was on intimate terms with the Messenger of God and a friend of his, but when the Messenger of God attained prophethood, he treated him with enmity as no one before him. He had not entered the agreement. He insulted the Messenger of God and he insulted his companions, and he insulted Ḥassān [b. Thābit] saying:

> Who will deliver a message to Ḥassān from me?
> I think you are one of the most evil of destitute men.
> Your father is the father of evil and your uncle is the same.
> You are not better than your father and your uncle.

The Muslims said to al-Ḥassān, "Insult him!" He replied, "I will not act until I ask permission of the Messenger of God." He asked the Messenger of God, and the Messenger of God said, "How can I permit you concerning the son of my Uncle, the brother of my father?" Ḥassān replied, "I will withdraw you from him as one withdraws a hair from the dough," [Page 807] and Ḥassān recited a poem. The Messenger of God commanded him to repeat some of it to Abū Bakr al-Ṣiddīq, and he repeated it to him. He said: Abū Sufyān stayed an enemy to Islam for twenty years. He insulted the Muslims and they insulted him. He did not stay away from a location the Quraysh went through to fight the Messenger of God. Then God cast Islam in his heart, and Abū Sufyān said: I said to myself, "Whom should I accompany and with whom shall I be?" Indeed, Islam had struck his neighborhood and become established. I went to my wife and child and I said, "Prepare to go out, for Muḥammad's coming is very near." They said, "Finally, you see that the Bedouin and the foreigner have followed Muḥammad, while you stay confirmed in enmity to him. You should have been the first of his people in his help!" I said to my slave, Madhkūr, "Hurry with the camels and horse." He said: Then we marched until we alighted in al-Abwāʾ. Its first part (the vanguard of the army) had alighted at al-Abwāʾ. I was disguised and feared that I would be killed, for my blood was permitted. I set out with my son, Jaʿfar, and I found the Messenger of

God about a mile ahead of me, in the morning of which he rose in al-Abwā'. The people drew near in groups, and I withdrew to a corner fearing Muḥammad's companions. When his ride appeared I confronted him, face to face. When his eyes filled with me, he turned his face away from me and in another direction; I turned to the direction of his face, but he turned away from me repeatedly. I became anxious about the consequences of my actions, and I said: I will be killed before I reach him. I remembered his graciousness and my close relationship with him and this held me up. I had no doubt that the Messenger of God and his companions would rejoice greatly in my Islam because of my relationship to the Messenger of God.

When the Muslims saw him turn away from me, [Page 808] they all turned away from me, and Ibn Abī Quḥāfa who met me, turned away. I saw ʿUmar tempting a man of the Anṣār with me. He attached a man to me, who said, "O enemy of God, you are he who harms the Messenger of God and his companions. Your enmity to him has reached the East and West of the world!" I returned some response about myself. He was arrogant towards me and raised his voice until he put me in what seemed like a thicket of people who were content with what he did with me.

He said: I visited my uncle al-ʿAbbās and said, "O ʿAbbās, I had hoped that the Messenger of God would rejoice in my conversion because of my relationship and my nobility. But what I have received is as you have seen, so speak to him and make him accept me." He replied, "No, by God, I will never speak a word about you to him, after what I saw of him, unless I see a way. Indeed I revere the Messenger of God and am in awe of him." I said, "O, my uncle, to whom will you assign me?" He said, "That is it." He said: I met ʿAlī and spoke to him, and he said similar to that. So I returned to ʿAbbas and said, "O uncle, keep from me the man who insults me." He said, "Describe him to me." I said, "He is a man who is dark, very dark, and short and has a mark between his eyes." He said, "That is Nuʿmān b. al-Ḥārith al-Najjārī." So he sent for him and said, "O Nuʿmān, surely Abū Sufyān is the son of the uncle of the Messenger of God and the son of my brother. If the Messenger of God was annoyed, he will soon be satisfied, so desist from him." Even after much he did not stop. He said, "I will not leave him." Abū Sufyān said: I set out and sat at the door of the station of the Messenger of God until he set out to al-Juḥfa. Still, he did not speak to me, nor did any of the Muslims. [Page 809] I brought it about that he did not alight at a station but I was at its door, and with me my son Jaʿfar, yet, he did not see me except to turn away from me. I set out thus until I witnessed the conquest of Mecca with him. I stayed with a group encircling the Prophet until he descended from Adhākhir until he alighted in al-Abṭaḥ. I drew near to the door of his tent and he gave me a look that was more tender than the first look, and I hoped that he would smile. When women from the Banū Muṭṭalib visited him, my wife entered with them, and she softened him about me. He came out to the Mosque and I was in front of him, and I did not withdraw from him on any condition until he set out to the Hawāzin. I set out with him, and the Bedouin gathered to him as never before. They set out with women and children and cattle. When I met them I said: Today my mark will be seen, if God wills. When I met them they made the attack which God mentions: *Then you turned away fleeing* (Q. 9:25). The Messenger of God stood firm on his grey mule and drew his sword, I went through with my horse while in my hand was a drawn sword. Its scabbard was broken. But by God, I knew that I desired to die for him, while he looked at me. Al-ʿAbbās b. ʿAbd al-Muṭṭalib took the rein of the mare, and I took the other side, and he said, "Who is this?" I removed the helmet, but al-ʿAbbās said, "O Messenger of God, your brother, and the son of your uncle, Abū Sufyān b. al-Ḥārith! so accept him, O Messenger of God!" He said, "I have, and God has forgiven every hostile act he did to me!" I kissed his leg in the stirrup, and he turned to me and said, "By my life, this is my brother!" Then he commanded al-ʿAbbās and said, "Call, 'O companions of the cow, and companions of al-Samura of the day of Ḥudaybiyya! O the Muhājirūn, O the Anṣār, [Page 810] O al-Khazraj!'" They responded, "O caller of God, we answer you!" They attacked as a single man. They destroyed the scabbards and aimed their spears, and lowered the blades. They were as swift as stallions. I saw myself, and indeed, I was fearful of the aim of their spears against the Messenger of God, until they surrounded the Messenger of God. The Messenger of God said to me, "Be bold and fight the people!" I made an attack and I clung to them from their position. The Messenger of God followed me as I went ahead with the slaughter of the people. They took nothing as long as he advanced, until there was not a leg to support them. I drove them the extent of a *farsakh*, and they dispersed in every direction. The Messenger of God sent a group of his companions in search of them. He sent Khālid b. al-Walīd in one direction; ʿAmr b. al-ʿĀṣ in another direction; Abū ʿĀmir al-Ashʿarī to the camp in Awṭās where he was killed, and Abū Mūsā, his killer, was killed.

Abū ʿAbdullah said: I heard another version about the conversion of Abū Sufyān b. al-Ḥārith. Abū Sufyān said: I met the Messenger of God, I and ʿAbdullah b. Abī Umayya in Nīq al-ʿUqāb. We tried to visit the Messenger of God and he refused our visit. Umm Salama, his wife, said, "O Messenger of God, your relative by marriage, the son of your aunt, and the son of your uncle and your milk brother! God has brought them to be Muslims. Do not make them miserable." The Messenger of God said, "I have no need of them. As for my brother and the sayer to me in Mecca of what he said, he will never believe me until I ascend to the heavens." And that is the saying of God most High: *Or you attain a finely decorated house or ascend to the heavens, and we shall not believe in your ascending until you reveal a book that we could read* (Q. 17:93). [Page 811] She said, "O Messenger of God, surely he is from your people, is he not? He spoke and all the Quraysh spoke, and the Qurʾān came down about him in particular. You have forgiven people who are more criminal than him. He is the son of your uncle and related to you. You should be the first to forgive him his crime." The Messenger of God said, "It is he who insulted my honor. I have no need of them."

When the news went out to them, Abū Sufyān b. al-Ḥārith who was with his son, said, "By God, he will receive me or I will take my son by the hand and go out in the land until I am destroyed by thirst and hunger. You are the most patient and generous of people, and I am related to you." His words reached the Messenger of God and he softened to him.

ʿAbdullah b. Abī Umayya said, "Surely I came to tell you the truth. I have ties of blood and marriage to you." And Umm Salama began to speak to him about the two of them. The Messenger of God melted towards them and he permitted them to enter. They converted and they were both the best of Muslims. ʿAbdullah b. Abī Umayya was killed in al-Ṭāʾif. Abū Sufyān b. al-Ḥārith died in Medina during the caliphate of ʿUmar and nothing bad was said about him. The Messenger of God had permitted his blood before he received him. The Messenger of God said to Abū Sufyān b. al-Ḥārith, on the day of Nīq al-ʿUqāb, "You are he who says: You reject me in every way, but, rather God rejects you in every way." Abū Sufyān said, "I said these words in ignorance. But you are the first of men in forgiveness and patience."

As for his words "I claim, even if I am not a relative of Muḥammad," indeed he fled and arrived before Caesar, the King of Byzantium. He said, "And who are you?" and Abū Sufyān b. al-Ḥārith b. ʿAbd al-Muṭṭalib explained his relationship to him. Caesar said, "If you speak the truth you are the son of Muḥammad's uncle." He said: I said, "Yes. I am the son [Page 812] of his uncle." I said: I did not see myself with the King of Rūm, while I had fled from Islam, yet knowing only Muḥammad. Thus Islam entered me, and I realized the error of polytheism. But we were with a community, a people of high mindedness. I saw the excellence of the people who lived with their discernment and opinion. They went through a mountain pass and we followed. Then the people of nobility and age began to break away from Muḥammad, and they helped their gods and defended their forefathers, and we followed them." Al-ʿAbbās b. ʿAbd al-Muṭṭalib and Makhrama b. Nawfal met him in al-Suqyā. Al-ʿAbbās visited him, and he did not go out until the Messenger of God went out. And he alighted with him in every station until he entered Mecca. When it was the night in which he alighted in al-Juḥfa, Abū Bakr al-Ṣiddīq saw that when the Prophet and his companions approached from Mecca, a bitch went out to them whining, and when they drew near, lay down on its back, and lo and behold, its nipples gushed forth milk. Abū Bakr mentioned it, and the Messenger of God said, "Their rabies went away and their success drew near. They will ask you about their relationship. You will meet some of them. If you meet Abū Sufyān do not kill him."

When the Messenger of God alighted in Qudayd, the Sulaym met him. They went out from their land to join him. They were nine hundred cavalry altogether. Every man had his spear and his weapons. The two messengers who were sent to them by the Messenger of God arrived with them. [Page 813] They both mentioned that they were swift to alight upon them. They mobilized—and some say they were a thousand—and the Sulaym said, "O Messenger of God, indeed, you have gone a long way to deceive us, and we are your uncles—the mother of Hāshim b. ʿAbd Manāf was ʿĀtika bt. Murra b. Hilāl b. Fāliḥ b. Dhakwān of the Banū Sulaym—. We arrived, O Messenger of God, so that you see how distressed we are. Indeed we are patient with the war, and truthful at the meeting. Good riders are on the backs of horses." He said, "They have two flags and five banners. The banners are black." The Messenger of God said, "March!" And he made them his vanguard. Khālid b. al-Walīd was in front of the Prophet, when the Banū Sulaym joined him in Qudayd, until they came down to Marr al-Ẓahrān.

He said: Shuʿayb b. Ṭalḥa related to me from ʿAbdullah b. ʿAbd al-Raḥmān b. Abī Bakr from his father, who said: The Banū Sulaym went out, nine hundred on horses, wearing spears and outer armor. They had rolled up their flags and banners, for not a flag or banner of theirs was unfurled. They said, "O Messenger of God, grant us a place for our flag where you think it should be." He said, "He who carried your flag in *jāhiliyya* will carry it today. Where is the handsome and well spoken youth who arrived with your party before me?" They said, "He died recently."

He said: ʿIkrima b. Farrūkh related to me from Muʿāwiya b. Jāhima b. ʿAbbās b. Mirdās al-Sulamī, who said that ʿAbbās said: I met him while he was marching when he descended from al-Mushallal with tools of war. The iron on us was visible, and the horses struggled against us to be free. We were arranged in rows for the Messenger of God, and at his side were Abū Bakr and ʿUmar. Then ʿUyayna called out from behind him, saying, "I am ʿUyayna." The Banū Sulaym have attended with what you see of their numbers [Page 814] and many weapons. Indeed, they adhere to their horses and are men of war, and aim at the target." ʿAbbās b. Mirdās said, "Be brief, O man! For, by God, you know we are the better knights on the backs of horses; we pierce better with the spear, and strike better with the sword than you and your people." ʿUyayna said, "You lie and you are sly. We are the first in what you mention. All the Bedouin have acknowledged us." The Prophet signed to them with his hand until they were both silent. The Muslims gathered in Marr al-Ẓahrān.

Not a word of the Prophet's march to them had reached the Quraysh. They worried and feared that Muḥammad would attack them. When the Messenger of God alighted in Marr al-Ẓahrān at *ʿIshāʾ*, he commanded his companions to light fires, and they lit ten thousand fires. The Quraysh decided to send Abū Sufyān to carefully consider the news. They said, "If you meet Muḥammad, obtain a protection for us from him—unless you see weakness from his companions—then declare war." Abū Sufyān and Ḥakīm b. Ḥizām set out and they met Budayl b. Waraqāʾ and they ordered him to follow them and he set out with them. When they reached al-Arāk from Marr al-Ẓahrān they saw the buildings of the camp and the fires. They heard the neighing of horses and the groan of the camels. That terrified them very much. They said, "Those are the Banū Kaʿb. The war has gathered them." Budayl said, "Those are more than the Banū Kaʿb." They said, "The Hawāzin seek food in our land. By God, we did not know this. Indeed this camp is like the pilgrimage of the people."

[Page 815] They said: The Messenger of God employed ʿUmar b. al-Khaṭṭāb on the watch. Al-ʿAbbās b. ʿAbd al-Muṭṭalib rode Duldul, the mule of the Messenger of God, possibly to reach a messenger to the Quraysh who would inform them that the Messenger of God was coming to them with ten thousand. He heard the voice of Abū Sufyān and said, "Abū Ḥanaẓala!" Abū Sufyān said, "I am all yours Abū al-Faḍl." Al-ʿAbbās said, "Yes!" Abū Sufyān said, "What brings you?" Al-ʿAbbās said, "This is the Messenger of God with ten thousand Muslims. So convert! May your mother and your close relatives lose you!" Then he approached Ḥakīm b. Ḥizām and Budayl b. Warqāʾ and said, "Convert! and indeed I will protect you until you reach the Messenger of God. I fear that you may be cut to pieces before you reach the Messenger of God!" They said, "We are with you." He said: al-ʿAbbās set out with them until he came to the Messenger of God, and he visited him and said, "O Messenger of God, I have granted assylum to Abū Sufyān, Ḥakīm b. Ḥizām and Budayl b. Warqāʾ, and they want to come to you." The Messenger of God said, "Let them enter." So they came before him and they stayed most of the night while he investigated them and invited them to Islam. He said, "Witness that there is but one God and that I am the Messenger of God." As for Ḥakīm and Budayl they witnessed. As for Abū Sufyān, he witnessed that there is no God but Allah, but when the Prophet said, "And that I am the Messenger of God," he said, "By God, O Muḥammad, indeed within me about this thing is a slight gap, so I will postpone it." Then the Prophet said to ʿAbbās, "We have granted them protection. Go with them to your house." When that morning, the call for Subḥ was proclaimed, the entire camp called out, and Abū Sufyān was afraid of their call to prayer. He said, "What are they doing?" Al-ʿAbbās said: I said, "The prayer." Abū Sufyān said, "How many prayers in a day and night?" Al-ʿAbbās said, "They pray five prayers." Abū Sufyān said, "Many, by God!" He said: [Page 816] Then he saw them rush to the ablution of the Messenger of God, and he said, "I have not seen, O Abū l-Faḍl, a ruler thus ever. Neither Kisra and nor the king of Banū al-Aṣfar (Byzantines)!" Al-ʿAbbās said, "Woe unto you, believe!" He said, "Take me before him, O Abū l-Faḍl!" And ʿAbbās took him before Muḥammad, and he said, "O Muḥammad, I asked help of my God, and you asked help of your God. No by God, whenever I confront you, you are victorious over me. And if my God were true and your God false, I would be victorious over you." And Abū Sufyān testified that Muḥammad was the Messenger of God.

Then Abū Sufyān said, "O Muḥammad, you come with a mix of people who are known and not known to your close relatives and your roots." The Messenger of God said, "You are most unjust and corrupt. You broke the agreement of al-Ḥudaybiyya, and you helped against the Banū Kaʿb with sin and enmity in the sanctuary of God while under His protection." Abū Sufyān said, "Woe unto you, O Messenger of God! If only you had made your anger and your shrewd policy against the Hawāzin, for they are more distant in relationship and stronger to you in enmity!" The Messenger of God said, "Indeed, I hope that my Lord will gather them to me, all of them through the conquest of Mecca, and strengthen Islam through them and defeat the Hawāzin. I wish that God would grant me plunder from their wealth and their children. Indeed, I beg that of God!"

He said: ʿAbdullah b. Jaʿfar related to me saying that he heard Yaʿqūb b. ʿUtba who was informed by ʿIkrima from Ibn ʿAbbās, who said: When the Messenger of God alighted in Marr al-Ẓahrān, al-ʿAbbās b. Muṭṭalib said: What a morning for the Quraysh! By God, if the Messenger of God took them by force surely he would destroy the Quraysh to the end of time. He said: I took the mule of the Messenger of God, al-Shahbāʾ, and I rode it. I said: I will find a man and send him to the Quraysh, so that they will meet the Messenger of God before he marches against them.

He said: By God I was in al-Arāk, and I was seeking [Page 817] a man, when I heard someone say, "By God, if you saw such a night of fires!" He said: Budayl said, "These, by God, are the Khuzāʿa gathering for war!" Abū Sufyān said, "The Khuzāʿa are less in number, and too humble to have these fires and that camp." He said: And lo and behold, it was Abū Sufyān, and I said, "Abū Ḥanẓala!" He said, "I am all yours, Abū al-Faḍl—for he knew my voice—what happened to you? May my father and my mother be my ransom." I said, "Woe unto you. This is the Messenger of God with ten thousands." He said, "By my father and my mother, what do you command me. Is there a way?" I said, "Yes. You will ride on the back of this mule to the Messenger of God and I will go with you. And indeed, if you are caught before you reach the Messenger of God, you will be surely killed." Abū Sufyān said, "By God, I see that." He said: And Budayl and Ḥakīm returned.

He rode behind me, and I went forward with him. Whenever I passed one of the Muslim's fires, they said, "Who is this?" And when they saw me, they said, "The uncle of the Messenger of God on his mule;" until I passed the fire of ʿUmar b. al-Khaṭṭāb. When he saw me, he stood up and said, "Who is this?" I said, "Al-ʿAbbās." He went looking and he saw Abū Sufyān behind me, and he said, "Abū Sufyān, the enemy of God! Praise God who makes it possible to reach you without agreement or contract!" Then he went towards the Messenger of God angrily. I raced the mule until we met together at the door of the tent of the Messenger of God. He said: I entered before the Messenger of God and ʿUmar entered immediately after me. ʿUmar said, "O Messenger of God, this is Abū Sufyān, the enemy of God. God has made him available here without agreement or contract. Let me cut off his head." He said: I said, "O Messenger of God, indeed I have given him protection!" He said: I stuck to the Messenger of God and I said, "By God, no one but I shall converse with him tonight." When ʿUmar increased against him, I said, "Slow down, O ʿUmar! For indeed if he was a man from the Banū ʿAdī b. Kaʿb, you would not say this. But he is one of the ʿAbd Manāf." ʿUmar said, "Take it easy, O Abū Faḍl, for by God, your Islam was [Page 818] more desirable to me than the Islam of one from the family of al-Khaṭṭāb if he converted." The Messenger of God said, "Go with him. I hand him over to your protection, so he will spend the night with you until you come to us tomorrow morning." When I rose, I went to him, and when the Messenger of God saw him, he said, "Woe unto you, O Abū Sufyān! Is it not time for you to know that there is no God but One?" He said, "By my father, there is none more patient than you, more generous than you and greater in forgiveness than you! I had believed that if there was with Allah another God, a partner, he has not yet enriched me." He said, "O Abū Sufyān, is there no way for you to know that I am the Messenger of God?" He replied, "You, by my father and my mother, there is not one more patient than you, more generous than you and greater in forgiveness than you! As for this, by God, indeed within me about it is something of doubt." Al-ʿAbbās said: I said, "Woe unto you, testify that there is no God but God, and that Muḥammad is His servant and His Messenger before you are killed!" He said that he witnessed the testimony of truth, and said, "I witness that there is but one God and that Muḥammad is his slave and His messenger." Al-ʿAbbās said, "O Messenger of God, you know Abū Sufyān and how he likes rank and glory. Make for him something!" He said, "Yes. Whoever enters the house of Abū Sufyān, he shall be secure. And whoever locks himself within his house, he is secure." Then the Messenger of God said to al-ʿAbbās after what he set out, "Keep him in a deep valley at Khaṭm al-Jabal until the soldiers pass by him and he sees them."

Al-ʿAbbās said: I took him to the narrow valley at Khaṭm al-Jabal. When I imprisoned Abū Sufyān, he said, "Is this treachery, O Banū Hāshim?" Al-ʿAbbās said, "Surely the people of prophecy are not treacherous. But I have a purpose for you." Abū Sufyān said, "Why not begin with it first and say, 'I have a requirement for you,' and dispel my fear." Al-ʿAbbās said, "I did not think you would do this."

The Messenger of God mobilized his companions. The tribes passed with their leaders, squadrons and flags. The first who arrived before the Messenger of God was Khālid b. al-Walīd with the Banū Sulaym. [Page 819] They were a thousand. With them was a flag carried by ʿAbbās b. Mirdas al-Sulamī, and a flag carried by Khufāf b. Nudba, and a banner carried by al-Ḥajjāj b. ʿIlāṭ. Abū Sufyān said, "Who are those?" Al-ʿAbbās said, "Khālid b. al-Walīd." He said, "The youth?" He replied, "Yes." When Khālid was opposite al-ʿAbbās, and Abū Sufyān was at his side, he proclaimed *takbīr* three times. Then they left. Immediately after him al-Zubayr b. al-Awwām came by with five hundred men (among them were the *Muhājirūn* and unknown Bedouin)—and carrying a black banner. When he was opposite Abū Sufyān, he proclaimed *takbīr* three times with his companions. Abū Sufyān said, "Who is this?" Al-ʿAbbās replied, "al-Zubayr b. al-Awwām." Abū Sufyān said, "The son of your sister?" He said, "Yes." Then, the Banū Ghifār passed by with three hundred, and Abū Dharr al-Ghifārī—some say it was Īmā' b. Raḥḍa—carrying their banner. When they passed by Abū Sufyān they proclaimed *takbīr* three times, and he said, "O Abū l-Faḍl, who are those?" Al-ʿAbbās replied, "The Banū Ghifār." Abū Sufyān said, "What have I to do with the Banū Ghifār!" Then the Aslam went by with four hundred. They had two flags. The first carried by Burayda b. al-Ḥuṣayb and the other by Nājiya b. al-Aʿjam. When they passed by they proclaimed *takbīr* three times, and Abū Sufyān said, "Who are those?" Al-ʿAbbās said, "The Aslam." And he said, "O Abū l-Faḍl, what have I to do with the Aslam! There was never a passing between us and them." Al-ʿAbbās said, "They are a community of Muslims and they have entered Islam." Then the Banū ʿAmr b. Kaʿb passed by with five hundred, and Busr b. Sufyān carrying their flag. He said, "Who are those?" Al-ʿAbbās replied, "The Banū Kaʿb b. ʿAmr." He said, "Yes, those are the allies of Muḥammad!" When they passed they proclaimed *takbīr* [Page 820] three times. Then the Muzayna passed with a thousand men, they had three flags and a hundred horses. Carrying their flags were al-Nuʿmān b. Muqarrin, Bilāl b. al-Ḥārith, and ʿAbdullah b. ʿAmr. When they passed by, they proclaimed *takbīr*. He said, "Who are those?" Al-ʿAbbās replied, "The Muzayna." He said, "O Abū l-Faḍl, what have I to do with the Muzayna! They came to me rattling from their high mountains." Then the Juhayna passed with eight hundred and its leaders. They had four flags carried by Abū Rawʿa Maʿbad b. Khālid, Suwayd b. Ṣakhr, Rāfiʿ b. Makīth and ʿAbdullah b. Badr. He said: When they passed they proclaimed *takbīr* three times. Then the Kināna, Banū al-Layth, Ḍamra and Saʿd b. Bakr passed with two hundred. Carrying their flag was Abū Wāqid al-Laythī, and when they passed they proclaimed *takbīr* three times. Abū Sufyān said, "Who are those?" He replied, "The Banū Bakr." He said, "Yes, the people of ill omen, by God! Muḥammad is attacking us because of them. By God, no one consulted me, and I did not know about it. And I hated it when it reached me. But it is a predetermined affair!" Al-ʿAbbās said, "God has chosen for you an attack by Muḥammad so that all of you will enter Islam."

He said: ʿAbdullah b. ʿĀmir related to me from Abū ʿAmra b. Ḥimās, who said: The Banū Layth passed by alone. They were two hundred and fifty. Carrying their flag was al-Ṣaʿb b. Jaththāma. When they passed they proclaimed *takbīr* three times and Abū Sufyān said, "Who are those?" Al-ʿAbbas said, "The Banū Layth." Then the Ashjaʿ passed by, they were the last to pass by and they numbered three hundred. They had two flags, a flag carried by Maʿqil b. Sinān, and a flag held by Nuʿaym b. Masʿūd. Abū Sufyān said, "Those were the strongest Bedouin against Muḥammad." Al-ʿAbbās said, "God put Islam in their hearts. This was by the grace of God." Abū Sufyān was silent, then he said, "Muḥammad has not yet passed by!" Al-ʿAbbās said, "He has not yet gone by. [Page 821] If you saw the battalion that included Muḥammad, you would have seen iron, and horses and men and one has not the strength for it." He said, "By God, O Abū l-Faḍl, who could have the strength against all those?"

When the green battalion of the Messenger of God appeared, black dust rose from the hooves of the horses, and the people began to pass. All that time he kept repeating, "Muḥammad has not yet passed!" Al-ʿAbbās said, "No." Until the Messenger of God passed by marching on his female camel al-Qaṣwāʾ, between Abū Bakr and Usayd b. Ḥuḍayr, and he was talking to them. Al-ʿAbbās said, "This is the Messenger of God with his green battalion, in it are the Muhājirūn and the Anṣār. They have flags and banners. With every clan of the Anṣār is a flag and a banner. Clad in iron, one sees only their eye balls." To ʿUmar b. al-Khaṭṭāb is a verse (*zajāl*) about it—Upon him the iron—with raised voice—he rouses them. Abū Sufyān said, "O Abū l-Faḍl, who is this speaker?" He said, "ʿUmar b. al-Khaṭṭāb." He said, "Surely the commander of the Banū ʿAdī is in control now, after being few in number and humiliated!" Al-ʿAbbās said, "O Abū Sufyān, surely God raises who He wishes, with what He wishes, and indeed ʿUmar is among those whom Islam raised." It was said: There was with the battalion a thousand plates of armour. The Messenger of God gave his banner to Saʿd b. ʿUbāda and he was at the head of the battalion.

When Saʿd passed by holding the banner of the Messenger of God he called out, "O Abū Sufyān, today is the day of fierce battle! Today what is holy will be re-appropriated! Today God will humiliate the Quraysh!" The Messenger of God approached until when he was in front of him, Abū Sufyān called out to him, "O Messenger of God, did you commanded the killing of your people? Saʿd and those with him claimed when they passed by us saying, "O Abū Sufyān, today is the day of fierce battle. Today what is holy will be reappropriated! Today God will humiliate the Quraysh! Indeed, I implore you by God, about your people. You are the most charitable of people, the most merciful of people, and the most connected of people." ʿAbd al-Raḥmān b. [Page 822] ʿAwf, and ʿUthmān b. ʿAffān said, "O Messenger of God, we do not believe Saʿd will be tyrannical with the Quraysh." The Messenger of God said, "Today is the day of graciousness! Today, God will make the Quraysh mighty."

He said: The Messenger of God sent for Saʿd and dismissed him. He gave the banner to Qays b. Saʿd, for the Messenger of God saw that the banner did not go out from Saʿd when it went to his son. Saʿd refused to submit the banner without a sign from the Prophet, so the Messenger of God sent his turban, and Saʿd recognized it and gave the banner to his son, Qays.

He said: Ibn Abī Sabra related to me from Saʿīd b. ʿAmr b. Shuraḥbīl from his family, who said: By God, Saʿd entered with his flag until he planted it in al-Ḥajūn. Ḍirār b. al-Khaṭṭāb al-Fihrī said that it was said: Indeed the Messenger of God commanded ʿAlī about it, and that ʿAlī took the flag. ʿAlī carried it until he entered Mecca and planted it in al-Rukn (the Southern-corner). Abū Sufyān said, "I have never seen such a battalion, where no informer informed me of it. Praise God, no one has power or strength against this." Then he added, "Surely the property of the son of your brother became mighty this morning." He said: I said, "Woe unto you, O Abū Sufyān, it is not a kingship but prophethood." He said, "Yes!"

He said: ʿAbdullah b. Yazīd informed me from ʿAbdullah b. Sāʿida, who said: Al-ʿAbbās said to him, "Be saved, woe unto you, and overtake your people before he enters upon them." He said: Abū Sufyān set out, and he preceded the people, all of them, until he entered from al-Kadāʾ saying, "Whoever locks his door from within, he has protection!" Until he finally reached Hind bt. ʿUtba. She took him by his head and said, "What has happened?" He replied, "This is Muḥammad with ten thousand, wearing iron. He promised me that [Page 823] whoever enters my house will be protected; and whoever locks his door will be protected; and whoever discards his weapons, is protected." She said, "May God denounce you as a messenger of the people."

He said: And he began to call out in Mecca, "O people of the Quraysh, woe unto you! Indeed he has brought what was out of your reach! This is Muḥammad with ten thousand, wearing iron, so submit!" They said, "May God denounce you as the delegate of the people!" Hind began to say, "Kill this delegate of yours! May God denounce you as the delegate of the people." He said: Abū Sufyān said, "Woe unto you, this woman shall not deceive you from yourselves! I saw what you did not see! I saw the men, the quivers, and the weapons. One has no strength for this!"

They said: The Muslims finally reached Dhū Ṭuwā. They stood looking at the Messenger of God until the Muslims gathered. Ṣafwān b. Umayya, ʿIkrima b. Abī Jahl, Suhayl b. ʿAmr had called out to fight the Messenger of God. People from the Quraysh and from the Banū Bakr and Hudhayl joined them, and put on their weapons and they took an oath by God that Muḥammad would never enter Mecca by force.

There was a man from Banū Dīl named Ḥimās b. Qays b. Khālid al-Dīlī who, when he heard about the Messenger of God, sat down to sharpen his weapons. His wife said to him, "For whom do you prepare this?" He replied, "For Muḥammad and his companions. Indeed I hope to use one of them as a servant, for surely you need one." She said, "Woe unto you, do not do so, nor fight Muḥammad! By God, this will fail you when you see Muḥammad and his companions." He said, "You will see."

He said: The Messenger of God approached with his green battalion on his camel al-Qaṣwā', dressed in a garment, a cloak from Yemen. He said: Muḥammad b. ʿAbdullah related to me from ʿAbbād b. Abī Ṣāliḥ from his father [Page 824] from Abū Hurayra, who said: The Messenger of God entered, at that time, wearing a black turban; his flag and banner were black, and he stopped in Dhu Ṭuwā in the midst of the people, his beard almost touching the middle of the saddle. He inclined himself humbly before God, when he saw what he saw of the conquest and the increase of Muslims. Then he said, "The life is the other life." He said: The horses began to meander in Dhū Ṭuwā in every direction, then settled where the Messenger of God was in their midst.

He said: Yaʿqūb b. Yaḥyā b. ʿAbbād related to me from ʿĪsā b. Maʿmar, from ʿAbbād b. ʿAbdullah from Asmā' bt. Abī Bakr, who said: Abū Quḥāfa ascended at that time with his youngest daughter Qurayba bt. Abī Quḥāfa. She led him until she appeared at Abū Qubays—for his sight had gone. And when she ascended with him on Abū Qubays he said, "O little daughter, what do you see?" She said, "I see a man moving in the midst of the crowd coming and going." He said, "That is the commander. O little daughter, tell me what you see!" She said, "The crowd disperses." He said, "The army has dispersed! The house, the house!" She said: I came down with him. He said: The girl was terrified by what she saw. He said, "Little daughter, do not fear! For by God, indeed your brother ʿAtīq is surely the most preferred of the companions of Muḥammad with Muḥammad."

He said: She was wearing a necklace of silver and someone who entered stole it. They said: When the Messenger of God entered, Abū Bakr spoke of it and said, "I plead, by God, for the necklace of my sister!" thrice. Then he said, "O my little sister, consider that your necklace is with God, for indeed there is little trustworthiness with the people."

[Page 825] They said: Then the Messenger of God turned to a man from the Anṣār at his side and said, "What did Ḥassān b. Thābit say?" And he said:

> If you do not see the horses stirring dust
> from the shoulders of Kadā', may we have no horses!"

Then the Messenger of God commanded al-Zubayr b. al-Awwām to enter from Kudā, Khālid b. al-Walīd to enter from al-Līṭ, and Saʿd b. ʿUbāda to enter from al-Kadā, and the flag held by Saʿd's son Qays. The Messenger of God entered from Adhākhir. The Messenger of God forbade fighting. He ordered the killing of six men and four women: ʿIkrima b. Abī Jahl, Habbār b. al-Aswad, ʿAbdullah b. Saʿd b. Abī Sarḥ, Miqyās b. Ṣubāba al-Laythī, al-Ḥuwayrith b. Nuqaydh, ʿAbdullah b. Hilāl b. Khaṭal al-Adramī, Hind bt. ʿUtba b. Rabīʿa, Sāra, *mawlāt* of ʿAmr b. Hāshim, and the two songstresses of Abū Khaṭal, Qurayna and Qurayba—some said, Fartana and Arnaba. All of the soldiers entered and did not meet a crowd.

When Khālid b. al-Walīd entered, he met a group from the Quraysh and the *Aḥabīsh*—a group of men from several tribes—who gathered to him. With them were Ṣafwān b. Umayya, ʿIkrima b. Abī Jahl, and Suhayl b. ʿAmr. They prevented him from entering, unsheathed their weapons, and aimed arrows. They said, "You will not enter Mecca by force ever!" Khālid b. al-Walīd shouted with his companions and fought them. He killed twenty-four men from the Quraysh, and four from [Page 826] the Hudhayl. They suffered the most shameful defeat until they were killed in al-Ḥazwara.

As they turned in every direction a battalion broke off from them from above the top of the mountain. The Muslims followed them. Abū Sufyān b. Ḥarb and Ḥakīm b. Ḥizām began shouting, "O people of the Quraysh, why are you killing yourselves? Whoever enters his house is protected. Whoever puts down his weapons, is protected." People began to rush to their houses and lock themselves in. They threw the weapons in the streets so that the Muslims could take them. When the Messenger of God appeared at Thanniyat Adhākhir he looked at the gleam of the swords and said, "What is this gleam? Did I not forbid fighting?" Someone said, "O Messenger of God, Khālid b. al-Walīd was attacked; and if he was not attacked he would not have fought!" The Messenger of God said, "God fulfills what is best!"

He said: He began to compare these verses while he fought Khārija b. Khuwaylid al-Kaʿbī. Someone recited it from his father:

When the Messenger of God is among us,
You see us as the roar of the sea reaching its bed.
When we put on the armor and picked up the spears
The deaf could be led by its sounds.
Indeed Muḥammad would help it. It becomes mighty, and its helper mighty too.

Ibn Khaṭal approached from Mecca, wearing iron armor, on a horse with a long tail, and carrying a spear. It had been mentioned to the daughters of Saʿīd b. al-ʿĀṣ that the Messenger of God had arrived, [Page 827] so they set out, their heads revealed, striking the faces of the horses with their scarves. Ibn Khaṭal came upon them, as he arrived from upper Mecca. He said to them, "By God, Muḥammad will not enter it until you see a widespread fighting like the widening of the tip of the *mazād* (a whip which widens at the tip)." Then he went out until he reached al-Khandama and saw the horses of the Muslims, and the fighting. Fear entered him and a shiver seized him until he reached the Kaʿba and alighted from his horse. He discarded his weapons, came to the House and entered between its curtains.

He said: Ḥizām b. Qays b. Hishām related to me from his father, who said: A man from the Banū Kaʿb took his armor, and its undergarment, his helmet and his cap, and his sword. He reached his horse with difficulty and settled on it. He met the Prophet in al-Ḥājūn.

They said: Ḥimās b. Khālid approached fleeing until he reached his house. He knocked and his wife opened to him and he entered. But he had lost his spirit. She said, "Where is the servant that you promised me? I have been waiting for you in order to enslave him!" He said, "Forget it. Lock my door! Indeed, whoever locks his door is secure!" She said, "Woe unto you! Did I not forbid you from fighting Muḥammad? I told you that if he fights you, he would be victorious over you. And what good is our door?" He said, "Indeed, one's door will not be opened against him." Then he said: Ibn Abī l-Zinād recited to me:

If you had seen us in al-Khandama
When Ṣafwān and ʿIkrima fled
And Abū Yazīd was standing like a widower
You would not have uttered a word of blame.
The Muslims struck us with their swords
[Page 828] And there was a roar and the sound of warring.

He said: al-Zubayr b. al-Awwām, together with those Muslims who were with him, approached until he reached al-Ḥajūn. He planted the flag at the station of the Messenger of God. No one was killed among the Muslims except for two of his companions. They mistook his path and went on another and were both killed. They were Kurz b. Jābir al-Fihrī and Khālid al-Ashqar who defended the Prophet—he was the grandfather of Ḥizām b. Khālid—until he was killed. The man who killed Khālid was Ibn Abī l-Jidha' al-Jumaḥī.

He said: Qudāma b. Mūsā related to me from Bashīr, the *mawlā* of Māziniyyīn from Jābir b. ʿAbdullah, who said: I was with those who were attached to the Messenger of God and I entered with him, on the day of the conquest, from Adhākhir. When he ascended on Adhākhir and looked at the houses of Mecca, he stopped before them and praised God; then he looked at the situation of his tent and said, "This was our station, O Jābir, when the Quraysh distributed the property among themselves in their unbelief." Jabir said: I remember a tradition that I heard, before that, from the Messenger of God in Medina. He said, "Our station tomorrow, if God wills, when God conquers Mecca for us, will be at al-Khayf where the disbelievers apportioned among themselves against me." We were in al-Abṭaḥ facing Shiʿb Abū Ṭālib where the Messenger of God and the Banū Hāshim were besieged for three years.

He said: ʿAbdullah b. Zayd informed me from Abū Jaʿfar, who said: Abū Rāfiʿ [Page 829] put up the tent of leather in al-Ḥajūn, and the Messenger of God approached until he reached his tent; with him were Umm Salama and Maymūna. He said: It was said to the Messenger of God, "Did you not descend to your house from al-Shiʿb?" He said, "Did ʿAqīl leave us a house?" ʿAqīl had sold the house of the Messenger of God and the house of his brethren among the men and women of Mecca. It was said to the Messenger of God, "Alight in one of the houses of Mecca, other than your house!" The Messenger of God refused, saying, "I will not enter those houses," and he continued to stay unsettled in al-Ḥajūn, and he never entered a house. He came to the mosque from al-Ḥajūn.

He said: Ibn Khadīj related to me from ʿAṭā', who said: After the Messenger of God immigrated to Medina, he did not enter the houses of Mecca. He stayed unsettled in al-Abṭaḥ during the ʿUmrat al-Qaḍīya, the year of the Conquest, and during his pilgrimage.

He said: Ibn Abī Sabra related to me from Muḥammad b. Jubayr b. Muṭʿim from his father from his grandfather, who said: I saw the Messenger of God unsettled in al-Ḥajūn during the conquest. He came for every prayer.

They said: Umm Hānī bt. Abī Ṭālib was married to Hubayra b. Abī Wahb al-Makhzūmī, and when it was the day of the conquest, her brothers-in-law, ʿAbdullah b. Abī Rabīʿa al-Makhzūmī and al-Ḥārith b. Hishām came to her seeking protection. They said, "We are in your protection?" She said, "Yes, you are in my protection." Umm Hānī said, "They were with me when ʿAlī, wearing armor, entered slowly on a horse. I did not recognize him, so I said to him, 'I am the daughter of the Prophet's uncle.'" [Page 830] She said: He held back from me and revealed his face, and lo and behold, it was ʿAlī! I said, "My brother!" I embraced him and greeted him, but he looked at them, and drew his sword against them. I said, "My brother from among the people does this to me!" She said: I threw a garment over them and he said, "Are you protecting disbelievers?" I stood before them and said, "By God, you will surely begin with me before you attack them!" She said: He went out, and I immediately locked the house upon them and said, "Do not fear!"

He said: Ibn Abī Dhi'b related to me from al-Maqburī from Abū Murra, the *mawlā* of ʿAqīl (b. Abī Ṭālib), from Umm Hānī, who said: I went to the tent of the Messenger of God in al-Baṭḥā' and I did not find him, but I found Fāṭima there and I said, "What did I meet from him who is the son of my mother, ʿAlī? I gave protection to my brothers-in-law who are disbelievers and he seized upon them both to kill them!" She said: And Fāṭima was more violent against me than her husband! She said, "You gave protection to disbelievers?" She said: Until the Messenger of God appeared, with traces of dust upon him, and he said, "Greetings to the esteemed Umm Hānī!" and he was wearing a single garment. I said, "What did I meet from my brother ʿAlī? I barely escaped him! I gave protection to my brothers-in-law, who are disbelievers, and he would sieze them both to kill them!" The Messenger of God said, "This should not be. We granted security to those you sheltered, and protection to those you protected." Then he commanded Fāṭima, and she poured water for him to wash and he took ablutions. Then he prayed eight bowings with a single garment around him. And that was before noon during the Conquest of Mecca.

They said: She said: I returned to them and I informed them and said, "If you wish, stay, and if you wish, return to your homes." She said: They stayed with me for two days in my home, and then they returned to their homes. She said: I was with the Messenger of God in his tent in al-Abṭaḥ until he set out to Ḥunayn. She said: Someone came to the Messenger of God [Page 831] and said, "O Messenger of God, al-Ḥārith b. Hishām and Ibn Abī Rabīʿa are seated in their meeting place wearing garments from Yemen." The Messenger of God said, "There is no way to them; we have granted them protection!"

He said: The Messenger of God stayed in his house an hour of the day and rested and washed. Then he called for his ride al-Qaṣwā' and it was brought close to the door of his tent. He called to put on the weapons, his helmet on his head, and the people lined up for him. He rode on his beast while the horses hurried by between al-Khandama and al-Ḥajūn. The Messenger of God passed by with Abū Bakr at his side, walking and talking to him. He passed the daughters of Abū Uḥayḥa in al-Baṭḥā' facing the house of Abū Uḥayḥa and they revealed their heads, striking the faces of the horses with their scarves. The Messenger of God looked at Abū Bakr and smiled. He mentioned the verse of Ḥassān b. Thābit and Abū Bakr recited it for him:

> Our horses will keep on racing each other
> While the women strike them with scarves.

When the Prophet reached the Kaʿba and saw it, the Muslims were with him. He went forward on his beast, touched the corner with his staff, and proclaimed *takbīr*. The Muslims responded, and returned the *takbīr* until Mecca shook with the *takbīr*, so that the Messenger of God began signing to them to be silent. The polytheists were above the mountain observing. Then the Messenger of God circumambulated the Kaʿba on his camel. Muḥammad b. Maslama took his camel by the reins.

[Page 832] Around the Kaʿba were three hundred idols. Sixty idols were of lead. Hubal was the largest of them. It was facing the Kaʿba at its door. Isāf and Nā'ila stood at the place of slaughter and sacrifice of the sacrificial camels. Whenever the Prophet passed one of the idols he pointed at it with the staff in his hand saying, *Truth came and throttled the false, indeed the false are destroyed* (Q. 17:81), and the idol fell to the ground on its face. He said: Ibn Abī Sabra related to me from Ḥusayn b. ʿAbdullah from ʿIkrima from Ibn ʿAbbās, who said: The Messenger of God no more than pointed at the idol with his staff, and it fell down on its face.

The Messenger of God circumambulated the Kaʿba seven times touching the black corner with his staff with every circumambulation, and when he completed his seventh he alighted from his ride. Maʿmar b. ʿAbdullah b. Naḍla arrived and took the camel out. The Messenger of God reached the "*Maqām* (where Abraham had stood in prayer)." At the time, the *Maqām* was close to the Kaʿba. The Prophet was wearing his armor and helmet and his turban fell between his shoulders. He prayed two bowings, then turned towards Zamzam and observed it. He said, "If it would not appear as though the Banū ʿAbd al-Muṭṭalib were defeated, I would have drawn a bucket of water." Al-ʿAbbās b. ʿAbd al-Muṭṭalib drew out a bucket of water for him and the Prophet drank it. Some said: He who drew out the bucket was Abū Sufyān b. al-Ḥārith b. ʿAbd al-Muṭṭalib. The Prophet commanded that Hubal be destroyed as he watched. al-Zubayr b. al-Awwām said to Abū Sufyān b. Ḥarb, "O Abū Sufyān, Hubal lies broken! Was it not indeed you who on the day of Uḥud, in self-deception, claimed that he bestowed his favours!" Abū Sufyān said, "Forget it, O Ibn Awwām, indeed I see that if there were another associated with the God of Muḥammad, it would not be the same."

They said: Then the Messenger of God turned [Page 833] and sat down in the region of the *Masjid*, while the people were around him. He sent Bilāl to ʿUthmān b. Ṭalḥa to come to him with the key of the Kaʿba. Bilāl went to ʿUthmān and said, "Indeed, the Messenger of God has commanded that you bring the key of the Kaʿba." ʿUthmān agreed, and set out to his mother who was the daughter of Shayba. Bilāl returned to the Prophet and informed him that ʿUthmān had agreed. Then Bilāl sat with the people. ʿUthmān said to his mother, "Give me the key, for indeed the Messenger of God has sent for me and commands me to bring it to him." His mother said, "I seek God's protection for you that you will not be he who hands out the glory of his people." He said, "By God, you will surely give it to me, or someone else will come and take it from you." She placed it in the waistband of her pants, saying, "Which man will put his hand here?" While they were on that, and he was speaking to her, all of a sudden the voices of Abū Bakr and ʿUmar were heard in the house. ʿUmar raised his voice, when he saw ʿUthmān being delayed, saying, "O ʿUthmān, come out to me!" His mother said, "O my little son, take the key, for indeed, you taking it is better than Taym and ʿAdī taking it." ʿUthmān took the key and came and handed it to the Messenger of God. When he handed it, al-ʿAbbās b. ʿAbd al-Muṭṭalib stretched out his hand and said, "O Prophet of God, gather for us the offices of *Ḥijāba* (gatekeeper) and *Siqāya* (thirst quencher)." The Messenger of God said, "I will give you what you will gain from it and not what you will lose from it." I have also heard another tradition about the taking of the key.

He said: Ismāʿīl b. Ibrāḥīm b. Uqba related to me from Nāfiʿ from Ibn ʿUmar, who said: [Page 834] On the day of the Conquest the Messenger of God arrived on a camel belonging to Usāma b. Zayd who was seated behind the Messenger of God. With him were Bilāl and ʿUthmān b. Ṭalḥa, and when he reached the top of al-Thaniya he sent for ʿUthmān who brought him the key and he received him with it. They said: ʿUthmān, who had converted before the conquest, reached the Messenger of God with Khālid b. al-Walīd and ʿAmr b. al-ʿĀṣ. ʿUthmān had set out with us from Medina. Abū ʿAbdullah said this is the most confirmed of the versions.

They said: Indeed the Messenger of God dispatched ʿUmar b. al-Khaṭṭāb with ʿUthmān b. Ṭalḥa from al-Baṭḥā', commanding him to approach and open the House, and to erase all the pictures and leave none. And to leave no images within—except for the portrait of Ibrāhīm. When he entered the Kaʿba he had seen the representation of Abraham as a big old man casting lots with arrows. It was also said: The Messenger of God commanded him to leave no picture within, but to erase it, but that ʿUmar left the picture of Abraham. When the Messenger of God entered, he saw the picture of Abraham and said, "O ʿUmar, did I not command you to erase every picture?" ʿUmar said, "The picture is of Abraham." The Prophet said, "Erase it."

Al-Zuhrī used to say: When the Prophet entered and saw the pictures of angels and others, and the picture of Ibrāhīm he said, "May God fight them, they have represented Ibrāhīm as an old man casting lots!" Then he saw the picture of Maryam and he placed his hand on it and said, "Erase all the pictures, except that of Ibrāhīm."

He said: Ibn Abī Dhiʾb related to me from ʿAbd al-Raḥmān b. Mihrān from ʿUmayr, mawlā of Ibn ʿAbbās, from Usāma b. Zayd, who said: I entered the Kaʿba with the Messenger of God, and he saw a drawing in it and commanded me to bring him a bucket of water. Then he wet the garment and struck off the drawing with it, saying, "May God destroy a people who draw what they cannot create!"

[Page 835] They said: The Messenger of God commanded that the Kaʿba be locked behind him. With him were Usāma b. Zayd, Bilāl b. Rabāḥ, and ʿUthmān b. Ṭalḥa. He stayed in it as God willed. The house stood at that time on six pillars. Ibn ʿUmar said: I asked Bilāl what the Prophet did when he entered the House? He said: He put two pillars to his right and a pillar to his left and three pillars behind him. Then he prayed two bowings. Then the Messenger of God went out with the key in his hand. Khālid b. al-Walīd stood at the door driving away the people from the door until the Messenger of God went out.

He said: ʿAlī b. Muḥammad b. ʿUbaydullah related to me from Manṣūr al-Ḥajabī from his mother, Ṣafiyya bt. Shayba from Barra bt. Abī Tijra, who said: I looked at the Messenger of God when he came out from the House. He stopped at the entrance, held the two doors and looked down on the people, and in his hand was the key. Then he put the key in his sleeve.

They said: When the Messenger of God looked down on the people who were glued to the Kaʿba and seated around it, he said, "Praise God who granted me His promise and helped His servant. He defeated the factions alone. What do you say and what do you expect?" They said, "We say it is good, and expect good. An honorable brother and the son of an honorable brother. You have the power over us!" The Messenger of God said, "Indeed, I say just as my brother Yūsuf said: *No reproach this day shall be upon you; God will forgive you. He is the most merciful of the merciful.* (Q 12:92). Indeed every usurious act in *jāhiliyya*, whether blood, [Page 836] property, or memorable event, is forgotten; except for the custody of the temple and the watering of the pilgrims. Those unintentionally but inevitably killed by club or whip, for him the blood-wit is heavy: a hundred camels, of which forty must be pregnant. Indeed God has removed the arrogance of *jāhiliyya* and its veneration of the forefathers. All of you are from Adam and Adam was from dust. The most honorable of you before God, is the most pious of you. Did not, indeed, God make Mecca sacrosanct the day He created the heavens and the earth, for it is a sanctuary by the grace of God. It was not lawful to one before me and it is not lawful to one who will be after me. It was not lawful to me except for a part of the day, and the Messenger of God indicated a reduction with his hands thus. Do not frighten its game nor prune its shrubs. Its gleanings are not lawful to you except for the needy, and do not cut the herbage." Al-ʿAbbās said, and he was an old experienced man, "Except for the *Idhkhir*, O Messenger of God, for indeed it is necessary for the graves and to purify the houses." He said: The Prophet was silent for a while and then said, "Except for the *Idhkhir, for it is surely permitted.* There is no 'will' for an heir. The child belongs to the bed, and to the adulterer a stone. It is not lawful for a woman to give of her property except with the permission of her husband. The Muslim is the brother of the Muslims. The Muslims are brethren. The Muslims are one hand against those who oppose them. Their blood is equal. The farthest of them is answerable to them and the nearest of them will contract with them. The strong will protect the weak among them, and the active will help the incapable. No Muslim will be killed for a disbeliever, and no possessor of an agreement will be killed for the duration of that agreement. People of two different faiths do not inherit from each other. The one who pays *zakāt* does not bring it to the collector, nor does he meet the collector at some other destination; indeed the charity of Muslims must be collected [Page 837] in their houses and courtyards. The woman will not marry one who is married to her aunt; the claim must be proved, and he who denies it, must take the oath. No woman shall travel for more than three days alone, except with someone who is lawful to her. There is no prayer after *ʿAsar*, or after *Ṣubḥ*, and fasting on two days, on *ʿĪd al-aḍḥā* and *al-fiṭr* is forbidden. I forbid two kinds of clothing—one is that which reveals one's private parts; the other is clothing that has no openings. I do not doubt that you understand my meaning."

He said: Then the Messenger of God alighted, and he had the key with him. He withdrew to the side of the *masjid* and sat down. The Messenger of God had taken the watering from al-ʿAbbās and the key from ʿUthmān. When he sat down he said: "Call ʿUthmān for me!" And ʿUthman b. Abī Ṭalḥa was called. One day while he was inviting him to Islam, and the key was with ʿUthmān, the Messenger of God had said to him, "Perhaps you will see this key in my hand and I will put it where I wish!" And ʿUthmān said: "Surely it will be when the Quraysh are destroyed and laid low." The Messenger of God replied: "Rather they will be prosperous [Page 838] and powerful at that time." When he called me after he took the key, I remembered his words and what he had said, and I approached, and received him with joy, and he received me with joy. Then he said, "Take it, O son of Abū Ṭalḥa, time honored and abiding. Only a tyrant will remove it. O ʿUthmān, surely God grants you protection in His house. Take only what is lawful." ʿUthmān said: And when I turned away he called me and I returned to him, and he said: "Is it not as I said to you?" I remembered his words to me in Mecca and I said, "But of course; I testify that you are the Messenger of God!" The Prophet gave him the key. The Prophet was lying down in his garment, and he said, "Help him!" Then he said, "Guard the door and take what is lawful."

The Messenger of God handed the watering to al-ʿAbbās. Al-ʿAbbās had administered it from among the Banū ʿAbd al-Muṭṭalib in *jāhiliyya* and his children after them. Muḥammad b. al-Ḥanafiyya had spoken about it to Ibn ʿAbbās. Ibn ʿAbbās said: What is your concern for it? We are the most deserving with it in *jāhiliyya*, and your father had spoken to me about it, and I brought the evidence. Ṭalḥa b. ʿUbaydullah, ʿĀmir b. Rabīʿa and Azhar b. ʿAbd ʿAwf and Makhrama b. Nawfal witnessed that al-ʿAbbās used to administer it in *jāhiliyya*, while your father was shepherding his camels in ʿUrana. Moreover, the Messenger of God gave it to al-ʿAbbās on the day of the Conquest and those who were present knew that. It was in the hand of ʿAbdullah b. ʿAbbās after him. There is no disputing them about it, nor any argument about it. Al-ʿAbbās had property in al-Ṭāʾifa. Grape vines whose dried fruit was carried to Mecca and pressed in *jāhiliyya* and Islam. Then, ʿAbdullah b. ʿAbbās did similarly. And ʿAlī b. ʿAbdullah b. ʿAbbās does similarly even today.

He said: Khālid b. al-Walīd came to the Messenger of God and the Messenger of God said: [Page 839] "Why did you fight when you were forbidden from fighting?" He replied, "They, O Messenger of God, started the fighting, and pelted us with arrows, and inserted their weapons in us. I held back as much as I could and invited them to Islam that they may enter with what people entered Islam, but they refused until I had no escape but to fight them. God granted us victory over them and they fled in every direction, O Messenger of God." The Messenger of God said, "God fulfilled well."

The Messenger of God said, "O Muslim people, except the Khuzāʿa from the Banū Bakr, restrain your weapons," at the ʿAṣar prayer. So the Khuzāʿa struck them, and they fought them for an hour, and it was an hour that was permitted to the Messenger of God alone, and not permitted to anyone before him. The Mesenger of God forbade the killing of any of the Khuzāʿa.

Abū l-Yasar said: We entered with Khālid b. al-Walīd from al-Layṭ. There were those who started fighting, and they refused to let us in. Khālid b. al-Walīd spoke to them and pleaded with them but they refused. Khalid said: Attack them! And we attacked, and they could not stand up to us for the time between two milkings of the camels! They fled, but he forbade us from following them. Abū Yasar said: I was bound to my sword, and I swooped down on a man and struck him, but he withdrew to the Khuzāʿa. He had fallen by my hand and I began to ask about him and it was said to me: Indeed he is from al-Ḥayā- the brother of Khuzāʿa, and I praised God that I had not killed one of the Khuzāʿa.

They said: Abū Aḥmad ʿAbdullah b. Jaḥsh stood at the door of the *masjid* seated on [Page 840] a camel of his, and when the Prophet completed his speech, he began to shout: I implore by God, O Banū ʿAbd Manāf, my pact. I implore by God, O Banū ʿAbd Manāf, my house. He said: The Messenger of God called ʿUthmān b. ʿAffān and whispered something to him, and ʿUthmān went to Abū Aḥmad and whispered to him. Abū Aḥmad came down from his camel and sat with the people. And Abū Aḥmad was not heard to mention it until he died. After the death of the Messenger of God, it was said to ʿUthmān, "What did the Messenger of God say to you on the day of the Conquest that you conveyed to Abū Aḥmad?" He replied, "I did not mention it during the life of the Messenger of God, and I will mention it after his death?"

Abū Aḥmad had made an agreement with Ḥarb Ibn Umayya. al-Muṭṭalib b. al-Aswad invited him to make a pact and said, "My blood for yours and my property for yours." Abū Aḥmad contracted with Ḥarb b. Umayya and said about that:

> O Banū Umayya, why do you abandon me, when I am your son and your ally in the ten days?
> Indeed another invited me but I refused him, and I have kept you from the catastrophe of time.

They joined in alliance during the ten days of the month of Ḥajj, standing up, and rubbing hands with each other just as buyers and sellers deal with each other. They had made an appointment with each other before the ten days. Abū Sufyān had bought his house from Ibn ʿAlqama al-ʿĀmarī [Abū Aḥmad] for four hundred dinars. He gave him a hundred dinars and agreed to pay the rest in installments.

[Page 841] He said: The family of Abū Aḥmad related to me that the Messenger of God said: You shall have a house in Paradise instead. Abū Aḥmad said, during the sale of his house to Abū Sufyān, ʿUmar b. ʿUthmān al-Jaḥshī sang verses about it for me:

You broke your agreement with us and the consequences will be regrettable.
Do you not remember the ten nights in which we stood?
My promise and your promise were established.
There was no stopping it nor misdeeds
You sold the house of your cousin.
You used it to pay your creditor.
Take it, take it.
May you be encircled by it like the necklace of the pigeon.
You were swift to refractoriness, your behaviour was the worst.
I took refuge in highland where there was good living and peace.
Your contract was not like that of Ibn ʿAmr to Ibn Māma.

They said: Isāf and Nāʾila were a man and a woman. The man was Isāf b. ʿAmr and the woman was Nāʾila bt. Suhayl from Jurhum. They committed adultery within the Kaʿba, and were transformed into stone, and the Quraysh began to worship them. They sacrificed to them shaving their heads when they became ascetic. From one of them came a woman, grey haired, black, her face scratched, naked, with her hair loose. She called out lamenting. This was related to the Prophet and he said: That is Nāʾila who laments that she was ever worshiped in your land. It was said: Satan cried out three times when [Page 842] he was cursed and his form was changed from the form of an angel. He cried out when he saw the Messenger of God praying in Mecca. And he cried out when the Messenger of God conquered Mecca, and his descendants came together. Satan said, "Do not hope that you may turn the community of Muḥammad back to polytheism after this day of theirs. But spread among them the weeping and poetry."

Abraham was the first who erected the stones of the sanctuary and Gabriel showed it to him. Then it was not disturbed until the time of Ismāʿīl who renewed it. Then it was not disturbed until Quṣay renewed it. Then it was not disturbed until the day of the Conquest. The Messenger of God sent Tamīm b. Asad al-Khuzāʿī and he renewed the stones of the sanctuary. Then it was not disturbed until ʿUmar b. al-Khaṭṭāb. He sent four of the Quraysh who used to move around the outskirts of Mecca: Makhrama b. Nawfal, Azhar b. ʿAbd ʿAwf, Ḥuwayṭib b. ʿAbd al-ʿUzzā and Abū Hūd Saʿīd b. Yarbūʿ al-Makhzūmī. Then there was ʿUthmān b. ʿAffān and he sent those same individuals. Then there was Muʿāwiya who launched the *Ḥajj* and he sent those same individuals.

He said: Ibn Abī Sabra related to me from al-Miswar b. Rifāʿa, who said: When ʿAbd al-Malik b. Marwān pilgrimaged he sent to the oldest leaders he knew of, at the time, from the Khuzāʿa, and the Quraysh, and the Banū Bakr, and commanded them to renew it. Every *wadi* in the sanctuary extends beyond the sanctuary, but not the reverse, except in one place in al-Tanʿīm. It was said: Do not scare away its animals. He said, "Do not chase them from the shade to the sun," and it was said, "Do not frighten them."

He said: ʿAbd al-Malik b. Nāfiʿ related to me from his father, who said: [Page 843] The pigeons used to hover over Ibn ʿUmar, his saddle, his garments and his food, and he never drove them away. Ibn ʿAbbās used to permit shooing them off. As for the Prophet's words, "What falls to the ground is not permitted except to the needy," he says: Do not eat what falls to the ground in Mecca as one does in other lands.

They said: The raiders of Hudhayl went out in *jāhiliyya* and with them was Junaydib b. al-Adlaʿ desiring the tribe of Aḥmar Baʾsā. Aḥamar Baʾsā was a man from the

Aslam, brave and difficult to beat. He did not sleep with his tribe/clan. Rather he slept outside the settlement. When he sleeps he snores loudly, and his place cannot be hidden. Whenever fear came to the settlement they screamed for Aḥmar Ba'sā and he appeared like the lion. When those raiders of Hudhayl came to them, Junaydib b. al-Adlaʿ said, "If Aḥmar Ba'sā is in the settlement there will be no way to them. But he has a snore that cannot be missed, so let me listen." He tracked the sound and heard him and he went to him and he found him sleeping and he killed him. He placed the sword on his chest, leaned on it and killed him. Then they attacked the tribe, and the tribe shouted, "Aḥmar Ba'sā!" But there was nothing. Aḥmar Ba'sā could not come for he had been killed. They took what they needed from the settlement and turned back. And the people were busy with Islam. One day, after the Conquest, Junaydib b. al-Adlaʿ entered Mecca and sought out and observed the people who were secure. Jundub b. al-Aʿjam al-Aslamī saw him and said, "Junaydib b. Adlaʿ the killer of Aḥmar Ba'sā!" And he said, "Yes." Jundub went out and mobilized a group against him, and the first he met was Khirāsh b. Umayya al-Kaʿbī and he informed him about it. Khirāsh put on his sword and then approached Junaydib. The people were around him and he was talking to them about the killing of Aḥmar Ba'sā. While they gathered around him, [Page 844] Khirāsh b. Umayya approached all of a sudden, with his sword and said, "Keep away from the man!" and by God, the people did not doubt except that he wanted to give him space, and they surely turned around from him and were separated from him. Then Khirāsh attacked him with his sword and pierced him in his stomach. Ibn Adlaʿ leaned against one of the walls of Mecca, and what was inside of him began to flow from his stomach, and indeed his eyes were glistening in his head as he said, "You did it, O people of the Khuzāʿa!" And the man fell dead.

The Messenger of God heard about his killing, and he stood up and spoke. This speech was on the following day from the day of the Conquest after *Ẓuhr*. He said, "O people, indeed God made Mecca a sanctuary when he created the heavens and the earth, and the day he created the sun and the moon and put down these two mountains. It is a sanctuary until the day of Judgement. It is not lawful for a believer, by God and the last day, to shed blood in it, or harm its trees. It is not permitted to anyone before me, and it is not permitted to any one after me. It was permitted to me only for a part of the day, and then its holiness was returned as before. Surely you who witness will notify those who are absent among you. If someone says: The Messenger of God fought in the sanctuary, say: Indeed God permitted it to His Messenger, but he does not permit it to you! O People of the Khuzāʿa, remove your hands from killing. Surely, and by God, there has been too much killing even if there were profit in it. You killed this dead one, and by God I will surely pay his blood money! Whoever kills after, my position is this: his family has the choice: if they wish, the blood of the killer, or if they wish, the blood money.

[Page 845] When Abū Shurayḥ entered upon ʿAmr b. Saʿīd b. al-ʿĀṣ who desired to fight Ibn al-Zubayr, he reported this tradition and said, "Indeed the Prophet commanded us as witnesses to inform those who were not present. I was a witness and you were absent. I bring you what the Prophet commanded." ʿAmr b. Saʿīd said, "Return, O elder, for we are better informed of its sanctity than you. Indeed, it does not restrain us from the tyrant, from one who casts off his allegiance, or from one who sheds blood." Abū Shurayḥ said, "I bring you what the Prophet has commanded. Now, its up to you!"

He said: ʿAbdullah b. Nāfiʿ related to me from his father that he informed Ibn ʿUmar of what Abū Shurayḥ said, and that Ibn ʿUmar said, "May God bless you, Abū

Shurayḥ. He fulfilled his duty. I knew that the Messenger of God had spoken at that time with the Khuzāʿa when they killed al-Hudhalī in an affair which I do not remember, except that I heard the Muslims say that the Messenger of God said: 'Inform!' "

He said: ʿAmr b. ʿUmayr b. ʿAbd al-Malik b. ʿUbayd informed me from Juwayriyya bt. al-Ḥusayn, from ʿImrān b. al-Ḥuṣayn, who said: Khirāsh killed him after what the Prophet forbade about killing. And he added, if I were a murderous believer with a disbeliever, I would surely kill Khirāsh for the Hudhalī. Then the Messenger of God commanded the Khuzāʿa to send out his blood debt, and the Khuzāʿa sent out his blood debt. ʿImrān b. al-Ḥuṣayn said: It is as if I see the dusty white cattle that the Banū Mudlij brought in the blood debt. They were their equals in blood-wit during [Page 846] *jāhiliyya*, and Islam strengthened it. It was the first killing in Islam in which the Messenger of God paid its blood debt.

He said: Ibn Abī l-Zinād related to me from ʿAbd al-Raḥmān b. Ḥarmala from Ibn al-Musayyib, who said: The Messenger of God commanded the Banū Kaʿb, and they gave a hundred camels for the killed. *Ẓuhr* came, and the Messenger of God commanded Bilāl to proclaim the call to prayer for *Ẓuhr* from above the Kaʿba. At that time the Quraysh were on the mountain-top. Indeed their nobility had fled, fearing they would be killed. Among them were those seeking protection, and those who had protection. When Bilāl proclaimed the call to prayer he raised his voice as strongly as possible, and when he reached *Ashhadu anna Muḥammad al-rasūl Allah*, Juwayriya bt. Abū Jahl said, "By my life, your fame has been increased! As for prayer, we will pray; but by God, we will never love the man who killed our loved ones. Surely, he who came to Muḥammad from the prophethood came to my father, but he returned it not wanting the disagreement of his people."

Khālid b. Asyad said, "Praise God who was generous to my father so he could not hear this today!" Al-Ḥārith b. Hishām said, "What a loss! Would that I were dead before this day that I hear Bilāl bray above the Kaʿba." al-Ḥakam b. Abī l-ʿĀṣ said, "This, by God, is great news that the slave of Banū Jumaḥ shouts from atop the little building of Abū Ṭalḥa." Suhayl b. ʿAmr said, "If this was the anger of God he will change it; if it satisfied God, he will establish it." Abū Sufyān said, "As for me, I will not say anything. If I said something these stones would inform him of it!" Gabriel came to the Messenger of God and informed him of them.

Mūsā b. Muḥammad related to me from his father, who said: Suhayl b. ʿAmr said: When the Messenger of God entered Mecca, and became victorious, I rushed to my house [Page 847] and locked the door upon me, and I sent to my son ʿAbdullah b. Suhayl to get me protection from Muḥammad, for indeed I believed that I would be killed. I began to remember the past with Muḥammad and his companions, and there was not one who had a more evil past than I. Indeed, I greeted the Messenger of God on the day of al-Ḥudaybiyya, as one never does, and it was I who wrote the document for him. I had opposed him at Badr and Uḥud and whenever the Quraysh made a disturbance I was with them. ʿAbdullah b. Suhayl went to the Messenger of God and said, "O Messenger of God, will you grant him protection?" He replied, "Yes, he is protected and he has the protection of God, so let him appear!" Then the Messenger of God said to those who were around him, "Whoever meets Suhayl b. ʿAmr, do not stare at him. Let him leave, for by my life, Suhayl possesses a mind and nobility. And whoever is like Suhayl cannot ignore Islam. Surely he realized that what he was practicing could not profit him." ʿAbdullah went to his father and informed him about the words of the Messenger of God, and Suhayl said, "He was, by God, righteous, whether young or old!" Suhayl hesitated to approach Islam. He went out to Ḥunayn with the Messenger of God while continuing to practice polytheism, until he converted in al-Jiʿirrāna.

Hubayra b. Abī Wahb fled—he was at that time married to Umm Hānī bt. Abī Ṭālib (Hind)—together with Ibn al-Zibaʿrā, until they reached Najrān, and they did not feel safe until they entered the fortress of Najrān. It was said to them, "What brings you?" They replied, "As for the Quraysh, they are killed, and Muḥammad has entered Mecca. We, by God, think that Muḥammad is marching to this fortress of yours!" The BalḤārith and Kaʿb began to restore what was worn out in their fortress. They gathered their cattle. Ḥassān b. Thābit sent verses meant for Ibn al-Zabaʿrā, and Ibn Abī l-Zinād recited them to me:

May you never lose this man, hatred of whom
Has made you live in Najrān in utmost misery.
[Page 848] Your spear is worn out in the wars
So it was thrown out as weak and faulty
God is angry at al-Zabaʿrā and his son
And they will suffer evil as long as they live.

When the poetry of Ḥassān came to Ibn al-Zibaʿrā he prepared to go out. Hubayra b. Abī Wahb said, "Where are you going, O cousin?" He replied, "By God, I desire Muḥammad." He said, "Do you want to follow him?" He said, "Yes, by God!" He said: Hubayra said, "If only I had accompanied other than you! By God, I did not think that you would follow Muḥammad, ever." Ibn al-Zibaʿrā said, "It is thus. Why do we stay with the Banū al-Ḥārith b. Kaʿb, and leave my cousin and the best of the people, and their kindness and my community, and my house." So Ibn al-Zibaʿrā came down to the Messenger of God who was seated with his companions. When the Messenger of God looked at him he said, "This is Ibn al-Zabaʿrā, and in his face is the light of Islam." And when he stood before the Messenger of God he said, "Peace upon you who are the Messenger of God! I testify that there is no God but Allah and that you are His servant and messenger. Praise God who guided me to Islam. Surely I (Ibn al-Zibaʿrā) was your enemy and I gathered against you. I rode the horse and the camel and walked on my feet with enmity towards you. Then I fled from you to Najrān, and I desired never to draw close to Islam. Then God most high desired me for good, so He threw Islam in my heart and He endeared Islam to me. I recall the error I was in: adhering to what was not profitable to a man of intellect who worships stone and slaughters for it, which does not know who worships it and who does not worship it." The Messenger of God said, "Praise be to God who guided you to Islam. Indeed Islam cancels what was before!"

Hubayra stayed in Najrān, and Umm Hānī converted to Islam. Hubayra said when news of her Islam reached him on the day of the Conquest:

[Page 849] Does Hind long for you or did she forget you?
For separation is the cause of change of heart.
On a high inaccessible fort in Najrān her shadow has banished my sleep.
But I am of a people who if they do their utmost
They attain their end forthwith.
Indeed I am a protector of the rear of my tribe
Even when the braves of the tribe hated to go to their spears.
Indeed words spoken without intent

Are like arrows falling without arrowheads.
If you have followed Muḥammad's religion
And you have cut relationships from you
Stay on a high round brown hill, with dry tops.
Hubayra stayed in Najrān until he died a polytheist.

He said: Ibn Abī Sabra related to me from Mūsā b. ʿUqba from al-Mundhir b. Jahm, who said: When it was the day of the Conquest of Mecca, Ḥuwayṭib b. ʿAbd al-ʿUzza fled until he reached the wall of ʿAwf and entered there, and Abū Dharr had set out for his need while he was entering it. When Abū Dharr saw Ḥuwayṭib flee he called to him, "Come, you are protected!" So he turned to him and greeted him. Then Abū Dharr said, "You are protected. If you wish, I will take you before the Messenger of God, and if you wish, go to your home." He said, "Do I have a way to my home? I will be met and killed before I reach my home, or I will be killed in my house." He replied, "I will come with you [Page 850] to your home." And he went with him to his house. Then he began to call out at his door: "Indeed, Ḥuwayṭib is protected, so do not attack him." Then Abū Dharr returned to the Messenger of God and informed him. He said, "Is there not protection to all the people except those who you ordered to be killed?"

He said: Ibn Abī Sabra related to me from Mūsā b. ʿUqba from Abū Ḥabība, the *mawlā* of al-Zubayr from ʿAbdullah b. al-Zubayr, who said: When it was the day of the Conquest, Hind bt. ʿUtba, Umm Ḥakīm bt. al-Ḥārith b. Hishām the wife of ʿIkrima b. Abī Jahl, and the wife of Ṣafwān b. Umayya, al-Baghūm bt. al-Muʿadhdhal from Kināna, Fāṭima bt. al-Walīd b. al-Mughīra, and Hind bt. Munabbih b. al-Ḥajjāj who was the mother of ʿAbdullah b. ʿAmr b. al-ʿĀṣ converted to Islam with ten women from the Quraysh. They came to the Messenger of God in al-Abṭaḥ, they acknowledged his leadership, and entered upon him. With him were his wife, his daughter, Fāṭima, and women from the Banū ʿAbd al-Muṭṭalib. Hind bt. ʿUtba spoke and said, "O Messenger of God, praise God who makes distinct the religion which He chose for himself, let your grace touch me O Muḥammad. Indeed I am a believing woman attesting before God." Then she removed her veil and said, "Hind bt. ʿUtba," and the Messenger of God said, "Greetings to you." She said, "By God, O Messenger of God, what was most desirable for me was the humiliation of you and the people of your tent; but today I woke up, and there is no one on earth for whom I wish more glory than you and your people." The Messenger of God said, "And still more!" Then the Messenger of God read the Qur'ān to them and acknowledged them. Hind said from among them, "O Mesenger of God, we will shake your hand." The Messenger of God said, "I do not shake the hands of women. [Page 851] Indeed my word to a hundred women is like my word to a single woman." Some said that he put a cloth on his hand, and then the women touched his hand at the time. Another said that a bowl of water was brought and the Prophet immersed his hand in it, and then he handed it to them, that they then immersed their hands in it. The first saying is confirmed with us: "Indeed I do not touch the hands of women."

Then Umm Ḥakīm the wife of ʿIkrima b. Abī Jahl said, "O Messenger of God ʿIkrima fled from you to Yemen, for he feared that you will kill him, so grant him protection." The Messenger of God said, "He is protected." So Umm Ḥakīm set out in search of him. With her was a slave of hers from Rūm. He desired to lie with her and she began to give him hope until they reached a clan of ʿAkka. She asked for their help against him and they tied him with a rope. She overtook ʿIkrima who had reached one of the coasts of Tihāma and was on the sea. The sailor of the ship began to say to him,

"Save yourself!" He said, "What shall I say?" He said, "Say: There is no God but Allah." ʿIkrima said, "I did not flee except from this." Umm Ḥakīm arrived at these words. She began to implore him saying, "O cousin, I come to you from him who reaches for the people, is most kind to the people, and the best of the people. Do not destroy yourself." And he stopped for her until she reached him. She said, "Indeed I have asked Muḥammad to grant you protection." He said, "You did?" She said, "Yes, I spoke to him and he granted your protection." So he returned with her and said, "How was your slave from al-Rūm?" So she informed him of the news and ʿIkrima killed him. And at that time he had not converted. When he drew near to Mecca the Messenger of God said to his companions, "ʿIkrima b. Abī Jahl comes to you a believer and an emigrant so do not insult his father. Indeed insulting the dead hurts the living and does not reach the dead."

He said: ʿIkrima began seeking his wife to have intercourse with her, but she refused him saying, "Indeed you are a disbeliever, and I am a Muslim." So he says, "Surely a matter that keeps you from me is an important matter." When the Prophet saw [Page 852] ʿIkrima, he rushed to him—and he was not wearing an outer wrap—and he was joyous about ʿIkrima. Then the Messenger of God sat down and ʿIkrima stopped before him, and his wife was veiled, and he said, "O Muḥammad, this woman (my wife) informed me that you granted me protection." The Messenger of God said, "She spoke the truth, you are protected." ʿIkrima said, "So what do you ask, O Muḥammad?" He replied, "I ask you to testify that there is no God but Allah and that I am His messenger, that you will get up for prayer, and that you will give *zakāt*;" and he continued until he had enlisted all the characteristics of Islam. ʿIkrima said, "By God, you do not invite except to the truth, and a good and beautiful affair. You were, by God, with us before you invited to what you invite, you are more sincere with us in speech and more kind to us in caring." Then ʿIkrima said, "I witness that there is no God but Allah and that Muḥammad is his servant and messenger." The Messenger of God was happy about that.

Then ʿIkrima said, "O Messenger of God, teach me about the best thing that I can say?" He said: Say, "I testify that there is no God but Allah and that Muḥammad is his servant and his messenger." ʿIkrima said, "Then what?" The Messenger of God said, "Say: I testify to God and I testify to those who are present that I am a Muslim, an emigrant and a striver." ʿIkrima said that, and the Messenger of God said, "Ask any one thing of me today and I will give it to you." ʿIkrima said, "I ask that you forgive me every hostility I returned to you, or journey that I put down in it, or place that I met you in, or words I spoke to you directly, and in your absence." The Messenger of God said, "O God, forgive all the enmity that he returned to me. And every march in which he went into a place desiring with that march to put out your light. Forgive him his insults to my face, or in my absence." ʿIkrima said, "I am satisfied, O Messenger of God." Then ʿIkrima said, "I swear by God, before you, O Messenger of God, that I will never miss an expense. I used to spend to turn away from the path of God but I shall spend twice as much in the way of God. [Page 853] The battle that I used to fight in opposition to the way of God, now, shall I fight doubling my effort in the way of God." Thus he strove in battle until he was killed a martyr. The Messenger of God then returned his wife to him keeping their first marriage.

As for Ṣafwān b. Umayya, he fled until he came to al-Shuʿayba, and he began to say to his slave Yasār, and there was no one else with him, "Woe unto you, look at who you see!" He replied, "This is ʿUmayr b. Wahb." Ṣafwān said, "What should I do with ʿUmayr? By God, he did not come except desiring my death. He helped Muḥammad against me." Then Ṣafwān went up to him and said, "O ʿUmayr, is it not enough, what you have done to me? You made me carry your debt and your children. Then you come desiring to kill me!" He said, "Abū Wahb, I am your ransom! I come to you from the home of the kindest of people, the most affectionate of people." ʿUmayr had said to the Messenger of God, "O Messenger of God, the lord of my people went out fleeing to throw himself into the sea for fear that you would not grant him protection, so grant him protection and your ransom is my father and my mother!" The Messenger of God said, "I grant him protection." So ʿUmayr went out in Ṣafwān's tracks and said to him, "Indeed, the Messenger of God has granted your protection." Ṣafwān said, "No, by God, I will not return until you bring me a sign that I know." So he returned to the Messenger of God and said, "O Messenger of God, I reached Ṣafwān fleeing, desiring to kill himself and I informed him of your protection, but he replied, 'No, I will not return until you bring a sign that I know.'" The Messenger of God said, "Take my turban." He said: ʿUmayr returned to him with it. It was a garment that the Messenger of God, at the time, wound around his head, a garment of Ḥibara. So ʿUmayr went out seeking him a second time [Page 854] until he brought the garment and said, "Abū Wahb, I come to you from the home of the best of people, the most affectionate of people, and the kindest of people, and the most patient of people. His glory is your glory; his might is your might; his power is your power. Son of your mother and your father, I remind you of God for your soul." Ṣafwān said to him, "I fear I will be killed." He said, "He invites you to enter Islam, and if you are not satisfied he will grant you two months, and he is the most faithful of the people, the kindest of them. He sent to you this garment that he wore around his head the day he entered Mecca. Do you recognize it?" He said, "Yes," and he took it out. He said, "Yes, that is it!" So Ṣafwān returned until he reached the Messenger of God. The Messenger of God was praying the *ʿAṣar* prayer with the Muslims in the mosque, and they stood waiting. Ṣafwān said, "How many times do you pray night and day?" He replied, "Five prayers." He said, "Muḥammad prays them?" He replied, "Yes."

When he greeted, Ṣafwān shouted, "O Muḥammad, indeed, ʿUmayr b. Wahb brought me your garment and claims that you invited me to follow you if I am satisfied with the decree, and if not, that you will grant me two months." He said, "Come down, Abū Wahb." He replied, "No, by God, not until you make clear to me." He said, "Rather you will have four months." So Ṣafwān came down.

The Messenger of God went out to the tribes of the Hawāzin, and Ṣafwān went out with him, as a polytheist. And he sent to him requesting his weapons, so he lent him his weapons: A hundred armor plates with its tools. And he said, "willingly or unwillingly?" The Messenger of God replied, "A loan for a period." So he lent it to him. The Messenger of God commanded him and he took the arms to Ḥunayn, so he witnessed Ḥunayn and al-Ṭā'if, then the Messenger of God returned to al-Jiʿirrāna. While the Messenger of God was marching with the plunder and looking at it, Ṣafwān b. Umayya was with him. Ṣafwān began to look at the pass full of cattle, and sheep. He continued looking at it and the Messenger of God observing him said, "Abū Wahb, do you like this pass?" [Page 855] He said, "Yes." He said, "It is yours with everything in it." Ṣafwān said at that, "No one would give this with such satisfaction as one with the heart of a prophet. I witness that there is no God but Allah, and Muḥammad is his messenger." And he converted instantly.

He said: ʿAbd al-Ḥamīd b. Jaʿfar related to me from Yazīd b. Abī Ḥabīb from ʿAṭāʾ b. Abī Rabāḥ, who said: Abū Sufyān b. Ḥarb, Ḥakīm b. Ḥizām, and Makhrama b. Nawfal converted before their wives converted. Then they arrived before their wives during the *ʿidda*—period of waiting—and the Messenger of God returned them to their marriage. The wife of Ṣafwān and the wife of ʿIkrima converted before their husbands converted and the Messenger of God returned their wives to them. That was because their conversion was during their period of waiting.

They said: ʿAbdullah b. Saʿd b. Abī Sarḥ used to write the revelation for the Messenger of God. Maybe the Prophet dictated it as "*samīʿun ʿalīmun*" but he wrote "ʿalī*mun ḥakīmun*," and yet the Prophet established it, saying God established it thus. So he was tempted away from Islam and he said, "Muḥammad does not know what he says! Indeed I wrote for him what I wished. This, which I wrote, was revealed to me just as it was revealed to Muḥammad," and he went out fleeing from Medina to Mecca, an apostate. The Messenger of God permitted the shedding of his blood on the day of the Conquest. At that time Ibn Abī Sarḥ came to ʿUthmān b. ʿAffān who was his milk brother and said: O my brother, indeed I have chosen you, so imprison me here, and go to Muḥammad and speak to him about me, for indeed if Muḥammad saw me he would cut off my head; indeed my crime was the most harmful of crimes, I have come seeking forgiveness. ʿUthmān replied, "Rather, come with me." ʿAbdullah said, "By God, if he saw me he would surely cut off my head without a word. He has permitted my blood and his companions seek me in every place." ʿUthmān said, "Leave with me [Page 856] and he will not kill you, God willing." The Messenger of God was surprised by ʿUthmān when he stood with ʿAbdullah b. Saʿd b. Abī Sarḥ before him. ʿUthmān approached the Prophet and said, "O Messenger of God, indeed his mother carried me, and made him walk; nursed me and cut him off, She was kind to me and neglected him. So gift him to me." And the Messenger of God turned away from him. And every time the Prophet turned his face away, ʿUthmān confronted him and repeated these words to him. Surely the Prophet turned away from him desiring that a man stand and cut off his head because he did not grant him protection. But when he saw that no one stepped forward, ʿUthmān bent over the Prophet and kissed him on his head saying, "O Messenger of God acknowledge him," and he pleaded with him (your ransom is my father and my mother). The Messenger of God said, "Yes." Then he turned to his companions and said, "What prevented one of you from going to this dog and killing him?" Or he said, "the corrupt one." ʿAbbād b. Bishr said, "If only you gave me a sign, O Messenger of God? By Him who sent you with the truth, indeed I followed your eye from every direction hoping that you will indicate to me so I may cut off his head." And some said that Abū al-Yasar said this, and others that ʿUmar b. al-Khaṭṭāb said it. The Messenger of God said, "Indeed I do not kill with signs." A sayer says: The Prophet said at that time: Indeed the Prophet will not have the treachery of the eyes. The Messenger of God acknowledged him, but he began to flee from the Messenger of God whenever he saw him. ʿUthmān said to the Messenger of God, "By my father and mother, have you seen my brother flee from you whenever he sees you!" The Messenger of God smiled and said, "Did I not acknowledge him and grant him protection?" He said, "But of course, O Messenger of God! But he remembers the grievous harm he did to Islam." [Page 857] The Prophet said, "Islam canceled what came before it." So ʿUthmān returned to Abī Sarḥ and informed him. So he came and greeted the Prophet with the people.

As for Ḥuwayrith b. Nuqaydh who was the son of Quṣayy, indeed he used to insult the Messenger of God. So the Prophet permitted the taking of his blood. While he was in his house on the day of the Conquest, he had locked his door upon himself. ʿAlī approached asking about him, and it was said he was in the desert. Ḥuwayrith was informed that he was being sought out. ʿAlī went away from his door. Al-Ḥuwayrith went out desiring to flee from one house to another. But ʿAlī met him and cut off his head.

As for Habbār b. al-Aswad, indeed the Messenger of God, whenever he sent out an expedition, commanded it regarding Habbār that if he were found he should be burned in the fire. Then he changed his mind saying: Surely only, the lord of the hell fire should cause such suffering. Cut off his hands and his legs if you have power over him, then kill him. None had power over him on the day of the Conquest. His crime was that he sought out the daughter of the Messenger of God, Zaynab, and struck her back with a spear until she who was pregnant fell and lost her baby. The Prophet permitted his blood. Meanwhile, the Messenger of God was seated with his companions in Medina when Habbār b. al-Aswad appeared. And he was good with his words. He said: "O Muḥammad! May those who insult you be insulted. Indeed I have come impregnated with Islam. I testify that there is no God but Allāh; He is one and has no partner, and Muḥammad is His slave and His messenger." The Messenger of God accepted that from him. Then Salmā, the mawlāt of the Prophet, came out and said, "May God make you despicable to every eye, you who did and did!" He replied, "Islam has erased that." [Page 858] The Messenger of God forbade insulting him and exposing him to it.

He said: Hishām b. ʿUmāra related to me from Saʿīd b. Muḥammad b. Jubayr b. Muṭʿim from his father from his grandfather, who said: I was seated with the Prophet and his companions in his mosque, departing from al-Jiʿirrāna, and Habbār b. al-Aswad appeared at the door of the Messenger of God. When the people saw him they said, "O Messenger of God, Habbār b. al-Aswad!" The Messenger of God said, "I saw him." Some of the people wanted to stand up to him, and the Prophet indicated that they be seated. Habbār stopped before him and said, "Peace on you, O Messenger of God, indeed I testify that there is no God but Allah and that you are His messenger. Indeed, I fled from you in the lands and I desired to join the foreigners. Then I remembered your attributes, your kindness, your piety, and your forgiveness. We were a people of polytheism, and God guided us through you and saved us from destruction. So forgive my ignorance, and what reached you about me. Indeed I admit my wrong doings." The Messenger of God said, "I have forgiven you. God was gracious to you when he guided you to Islam. And Islam cancels what was before it."

He said: Wāqid b. Abī Yāsir related to me from Yazīd b. Rūmān, who said: al-Zubayr b. al-Awwām said: I have not seen the Messenger of God mention Habbār ever except in anger. I have not seen the Messenger of God send an expedition ever, except he said: If you defeat Habbār cut off his hands and legs and then his head. By God, surely I have sought him and asked about him, and God knows if I defeated him before he came to the Prophet I would certainly have killed him. Then he appeared before the Messenger of God while I was with him, seated, and he began apologizing to the Messenger of God saying, "O Muḥammad, [Page 859] may those who insulted you be insulted, and those who hurt you be hurt. Surely I went too far in hurting you and insulting you. Indeed I was forsaken. Then God helped me and guided me to Islam." Al-Zubayr said: I kept looking at the Prophet as he lowered his head embarrassed by Habbār's apology. The Messenger of God said repeatedly, "I have forgiven you, Islam cancels what was before it." Habbār was good with words. He was insulted until it hurt him, but he did not ask for justice from anyone. His patience and suffering reached the Messenger of God, and he said, "Habbār insult whoever insults you!"

They said: As for Ibn Khaṭal, indeed he set out until he entered between the curtains of the Kaʿba. Yaʿqūb b. ʿAbdullah related to me from Jaʿfar b. Abī l-Mughīra from

Saʿīd b. ʿAbd al-Raḥmān b. Abazā, who said: I heard Abū Barza al-Aslamī say about whom these verses were revealed: *I swear by this land; You are a free inhabitant of this land* (Q. 90:1 and 2). I set out for ʿAbdullah b. Khaṭal while he was attached to the curtains of the Kaʿba, and I cut off his head between the Rukn and the Maqām. It was said: Saʿīd b. Ḥurayth al-Makhzūmī killed him. Others said: ʿAmmār b. Yāsir, and still others said Sharīk b. ʿAbda al-ʿAjlānī. Abū Barza is confirmed with us. Ibn Khaṭal's crime was that he converted and immigrated to Medina and the Prophet sent him walking and he sent a man from the Khuzāʿa with him who used to make his food and serve him. They alighted in Majmaʿ and Ibn Khatal ordered his companion to make him some food while he slept half of the day. But when he woke up, the Khuzaʿa was asleep and had not prepared any food for him. He became angry with him and beat him and did not stop until he had killed him. When he killed him, he said, "By God, Muḥammad would surely kill me for him if I return." So he apostatized from Islam. He carried what he took of charity and fled to Mecca. The people of Mecca said to him, "Why do you return to us?" He replied, "I did not find [Page 860] a better religion than your religion." And he returned to his polytheism. He had two singers. One of them was Fartanā and the other was Arnab. They were both corrupt and used to recite poetry insulting the Messenger of God, and he commanded them to sing about him. The polytheists came upon him and his two singers drinking wine, and the two songstresses sang that defamatory song.

Sāra, the *mawlāt* of ʿAmr b. Hishām was a female singer and mourner in Mecca, and insulting poetry was dictated to her about Messenger of God and she would sing it. She had arrived before the Messenger of God and asked for help claiming she was in need. The Messenger of God said, "Did not your singing and lamenting help you!" She replied, "O Muḥammad, indeed the Quraysh, since those who were killed among them in Badr, have stopped listening to the singers." So the Messenger of God gave and loaded a camel with food for her. She returned to the Quraysh and kept her religion. On the day of the Conquest, the Messenger of God commanded that she be killed, and she was killed at that time. As for the two singing girls, the Messenger of God commanded their killing as well. One of them was killed: Arnab or Fartanā. As for Fartanā, he granted her protection until she believed. She lived until someone broke her ribs in the time of ʿUthmān b. ʿAffān and she died of it. ʿUthmān granted her a judgement of eight thousand dirhams. Six thousand as blood debt and two thousand for the harshness of the crime.

They said: As for Miqyas b. Ṣubāba, he was with his uncles from the Banū Sahm—his mother was a Sahmite—and he was having a morning draught of wine on the day of the Conquest with a companion of his. Numayla b. ʿAbdullah al-Laythī came, knowing of his place, and called him, and he went out to him while he was drunk.

He is represented in these verses that Ibn Jaʿfar and the rest recited:

[Page 861] Let me spend the morning, O Bakr
Surely I have seen death looking for Hishām,
He also looked for your father Abū Yazīd,
He is the brother of the singers and the honorable drinkers.
With them the mountains of Thabīr and Thaur were established
And the slyest is never deaf.
The pigeons are singing to me
As if my people are Khuzaʿa or from Judhām.

Numayla struck Miqyas with the sword until he was cold. Some said: He set out while he was drunk between al-Ṣafā and al-Marwa. The Muslims saw him and knocked him down with their swords until they killed him. Their poet said:

By my life surely Numayla has brought shame to his people
And the people of honor were shocked by Miqyas.
May God protect the eyes of him who saw similar to Miqyas
On that day, the mother after delivery was not granted food.

His crime was that his brother Hāshim b. Ṣubāba had converted and witnessed al-Muraysīʿ with the Messenger of God, when a man from the Banū ʿAmr b. ʿAwf killed him by mistake, not knowing—he thought that he was a polytheist. Miqyas b. Ṣubāba arrived and the Messenger of God fulfilled for him his debt against the Banū ʿAmr b. ʿAwf. He took it and converted, then returned for the killer of his brother, the ʿAmrī, and killed him. Then he fled apostatizing to polytheism and reciting poetry. It was said that Aws b. Thābit killed him. He was from the tribe of ʿUbāda b. al-Ṣāmit, and he did not know it. That was because he was in the dust of the enemy during battle. He had set out seeking them and returned, when Aws met him, and thinking that he was one of the polytheists, killed him. The Messenger of God fulfilled his debt to the tribe of ʿUbāda b. al-Ṣāmit. This is the most confirmed of the two sayings. He said:

[Page 862] My heart was healed that he spent his night at the bottom on a support.
His two garments are stained with the blood from the jugular veins.
I retaliated for Fihr and I made the nobility of the Banū Najjār, the lords of Fāriʿ, carry his blood money.
I took my revenge and achieved my goal.
I was the first to return to the idols.

The Prophet permitted his blood. He said: Al-Wāqidī related to us that Ibn Abī Sabra related to me from Isḥāq b. ʿAbdullah b. Abī Farwā from Ubayy b. Kaʿb b. Mālik, who said: When Miqyas b. Ṣubaba returned to the Quraysh and to Mecca they said, "What brought you back to us when you have followed Muḥammad?" He said: He left for the two idols, shaved his head and said, "I did not find a better religion than your religion nor one more ancient." Then he informed them of what he did and how he killed the killer of his brother.

He said: ʿAbdullah b. Yazīd al-Hudhalī informed me from Abū Ḥuṣayn al-Hudhalī, who said: When the group whose killing was commanded by the Prophet was killed, the lament over them was heard in Mecca, and Abū Sufyān b. Ḥarb came pleading and said, "Your ransom is my father and mother. Let your people live." The Messenger of God said, "The Quraysh will not be executed after today!" He meant for disbelief.

He said: Yazīd b. Firās related to me from ʿIrāk b. Mālik from al-Ḥārith b. al-Barṣāʾ, who said: I heard the Messenger of God say, "The Quraysh will not be raided after today until the day of resurrection." He meant, for disbelief.

He said: Ibn Abī Sabra related to me from Ḥusayn b. ʿAbdullah from ʿIkrima from Ibn ʿAbbās, who said: The Messenger of God commanded the killing of Waḥshī [Page 863] with the group. The Muslims were most greedy to take Waḥshī. Waḥshī fled to al-Ṭāʾif. He stayed there until he reached the place of the Messenger of God with the party of al-Ṭā'if. Then he entered upon him and said, "I witness that there is no God but Allah and that Muḥammad is His messenger." The Messenger of God said, "Waḥshī?" He replied, "Yes." He said, "Sit. Tell me how you killed Ḥamza." So he informed him. The Messenger of God said, "Hide your face from me." He said, "When I saw him I used to hide from him. Then the people set out to Musaylima and I attacked Musaylima and pierced him with my spear. A man from the Anṣār struck him, and God knows which of us killed him."

He said: Ismāʿīl b. Ibrāhīm b. ʿAbdullah b. Abī Rabīʿa related to me from his father, who said: the Messenger of God, in the year of the Conquest, sent requesting a loan from ʿAbdullah b. Abī Rabīʿa of forty thousand dirham, and he gave it to him. When God granted the Muslims success over the Ḥawāzin, and the Prophet had gained their property, he returned the loan, saying, "The return of a loan should be completed with gratitude." He said, "May God bless your property and your children."

He said: ʿAbdullah b. Zayd al-Hudhalī related to me from Abū Ḥuṣayn al-Hudhalī, who said: The Messenger of God asked for a loan from three individuals among the Quraysh: from Ṣafwān b. Umayya, fifty thousand dirham, and he lent it; from ʿAbdullah b. Abī Rabīʿa, forty thousand dirham, and from Ḥuwayṭib b. ʿAbd al-ʿUzza, forty thousand dirham. This totaled a hundred and thirty thousand. The Messenger of God apportioned it among his indigent companions.

He said: A man from the Banū Kināna—and they were with the Messenger of God in the Conquest—informed me that the Messenger of God apportioned dirhams among them. Each man obtained roughly fifty dirhams, [Page 864] and he also sent some of that money to the Banū Jadhīma.

He said: Sufyān b. Saʿīd related to me from al-Kalbī from Ṣāliḥ from Muṭṭalib b. Abī Wadāʿa, who said: The Messenger of God circumambulated the House on a hot day. He was thirsty and asked for a drink. A man said, "O Messenger of God, we are having a drink from this raisin, will you not drink from it?" He replied, "But of course." He said: The man sent to his house and brought a large bowl. The Prophet approached it and he found it had a strong smell, which he detested, so he returned it. He said: The Prophet called for water, then he asked about it. He said: the water of Zamzam was brought and he poured it for him until I saw the water overflow from its side. He drank what he needed from it and then handed it to who was at his right and said, "Whoever is suspicious about his drink let him replace it with water."

He said: Usāma b. Zayd related to me from Aslam and Hishām b. Saʿd from Zayd b. Aslam from Abū Waʿla from Ibn ʿAbbās, who said: A companion of the Messenger of God from Thaqīf granted me a camel bearing wine. The Messenger of God said, "Did you not know that God has forbidden it?" The man whispered to his servant, "Take it to al-Ḥazwara and sell it." The Messenger of God said, "With what do you command him?" He replied, "With selling it?" The Messenger of God said, "Surely He who forbids drinking it also forbids selling it!" It reached me that it was emptied in al-Baṭhā'.

He said: Ibn Abī Dhi'b related to me from al-Zuhrī, who said: On the day of the Conquest the Messenger of God forbade the selling of wine, pork, the meat of the dead, and of idols, and the presenting of money to the Kāhin.

He said: Saʿīd b. Bashīr related to me from ʿAbd al-Karīm b. Abī Umayya from [Page 865] ʿAṭā' b. Abī Rabāḥ from Jābir b. ʿAbdullah, who said: It was said to the Messenger of God on the day of Fatḥ, "What do you think about using the fat of the dead meat for anointing the water bags?" The Messenger of God replied, "May God fight the Jews. He forbad them the fat of the dead, but they sell it and eat from its money."

He said: Maʿmar related to me from al-Zuhrī from Ibn al-Musayyib, who said: The Messenger of God was asked at that time about the money from wine. He replied, "May God fight the Jews. He forbade them from lard, so they sell it and eat with the money they make from it."

He said: Maʿmar and Ibn Abī Dhi'b related to me from al-Zuhrī from al-Rabīʿ b. Sabra from his father, who said: The Messenger of God forbad the temporary marriage of women at that time.

He said: Ibn Abī Dhi'b and Maʿmar related to me from al-Zuhrī from Abū Salama b. ʿAbd al-Raḥmān b. ʿAwf from Abū ʿAmr b. ʿAdī b. al-Ḥamrā', who said: I heard the Messenger of God say on the day of the Conquest while he was in al-Ḥazwara, "By God, indeed you are the best of the land of God and you are the most loved of the land of God to me. If I were not expelled from you I would not depart!"

He said: Saʿīd b. ʿAbdullah related to me from Ibn Abī Mulayka from the Prophet something similar. He said, "If your people had not come out with me, I would not have left."

An old man from the Khuzāʿa related to me from Jābir b. ʿAbdullah, who said: Banū ʿAbd al-Dār had a slave called Jabr who was a Jew. He heard the Messenger of God, before he emigrated, read the chapter of Yūsuf, and recognized what was mentioned in that. He trusted the Prophet and he converted. When ʿAbdullah b. Saʿd b. Abī Sarḥ apostatized from Islam, he returned to Mecca and informed Jabr's family about his Islam. The slave used to conceal [Page 866] his Islam from his family before he entered their house. They tortured him until he said to them what they desired. When the Messenger of God conquered Mecca he went to the Messenger of God and complained to him, and informed him of what he met because of ʿAbdullah b. Saʿd b. Abī Sarḥ. He said: The Messenger of God gave him his price and he purchased his freedom. He became rich and married a woman of nobility.

He said: Ibrāhīm b. Yazīd related to me from ʿAṭā' b. Abī Rabāḥ, who said: A man came to the Messenger of God on the day of the Conquest and said, "Indeed I swear that I will pray in the Bayt al-Maqdis if God conquers Mecca for you." The Messenger of God said, "Here is better." And he said that three times. The Messenger of God said, "By Him who holds my soul in his hands, surely a prayer here is better than a thousand of what is equal to it in other countries." Maymūna, the wife of the Prophet said, "O Messenger of God, indeed I have promised myself that if God conquers Mecca for you I will pray in Bayt al-Maqdis." The Messenger of God said, "You will not able to do that, for the Byzantines obstruct it from you." She replied, "I will take a watchman who will be attentive, and slip through." He said, "You will not be able to do that, but send oil and it will be lit for you in it, as if you had gone there." Every year Maymūna sent money, with which to purchase oil, to the Bayt al-Maqdis, and it was lit in the Bayt al-Maqdis until she died, and she bequeathed that.

He said: Ibn Abī Dhi'b related to me from al-Ḥārith b. ʿAbd al-Raḥmān b. ʿAwf and Ibrāhīm b. ʿAbdullah b. Muḥriz, who said: When the Messenger of God conquered Mecca, ʿAbd al-Raḥmān b. ʿAwf sat in council with the community, and among them was Saʿd b. ʿUbāda. [Page 867] Some women of the Quraysh passed by the council, and Saʿd b. ʿUbāda said, "It was mentioned to us that the women of the Quraysh were lovely and beautiful, but we have not seen them thus!" He said: ʿAbd al-Raḥmān became angry until he almost attacked Saʿd and treated him harshly. Saʿd fled from him until he came to the Messenger of God and said, "O Messenger of God, what did I meet from ʿAbd al-Raḥmān!" The Messenger of God said, "What is the matter with him?" So he informed him about what it was. The Prophet became angry such that his face reddened. Then he said, "You saw them when they were hurt because of their fathers and children and brothers and husbands. The best of the women who ride the camels are the women of the Quraysh! They are the most kind to their children and most generous to their husbands with all they possess."

Abū al-Ṭufayl ʿĀmir b. Wāthila used to say: I saw the Messenger of God on the day of the Conquest of Mecca. He had not forgotten his very whiteness and the black of his hair. Indeed among the men were those who were taller than him, and those who were shorter than him. He was walking and those around him were walking. He said: I said to my mother, "Who is this?" She replied, "The Messenger of God." It was said to him, "What was he wearing?" He replied, "I do not know."

He said: ʿAbdullah b. Yazīd related to me from Rabīʿa b. ʿAbbād, who said: We—I was with my father—entered Mecca a few days after Muḥammad conquered it, and we looked around. I saw the Messenger of God, and the moment I saw him I knew him and I remembered when I saw him in Dhū l-Majāz. Abū Lahab was following in his tracks at that time. The Messenger of God says, "There is no pact in Islam; Islam does not extend the pact of *jāhiliyya* except to strengthen it."

[Page 868] Umm Hānī used to narrate saying, "I have not seen any one with a better smile than the Messenger of God. And, whenever I see the stomach of the Messenger of God, I remember the folded sheets (she was referring to the folds of his skin), and I saw him when he entered on the day of the Conquest, his head was braided with four braids."

He said: ʿAlī b. Yazīd related to me from his father from his uncle from Umm Salama the wife of the Prophet, who said, "I braided the head of the Prophet in Dhū al-Ḥulayfa, with four braids. He did not unbraid it even with the conquest of Mecca and his stay in Mecca. When he desired to go out to Ḥunayn, he took it out and I washed his head with Lotus."

He said: ʿAbdullah b. Yazīd related to me from Abū Ḥuṣayn al-Hudhalī, who said: When Hind bt. ʿUtba converted she sent the Messenger of God a gift of two goats roasted and skinned—he was in al-Abṭaḥ—through one of her slave girls. The slave girl reached the tent of the Messenger of God and greeted and asked permission to enter. He permitted her and she entered before the Messenger of God, and he was among his women, Umm Salama his wife and Maymūna and women from the Banū ʿAbd al-Muṭṭalib. She said, "Indeed, my mistress sent you this gift, and excuses herself to you saying that our sheep today breed little." The Messenger of God said, "May God bless you with your sheep and increase its offspring." [Page 869] The slave girl returned to Hind and informed her of the prayers of the Messenger of God and she was happy about that. The slave girl used to say: Surely we experienced an increase in the number of our sheep and their offspring that we had not seen before that event—or recently. Hind says, "This is because of the prayer of the Messenger of God and his blessing. Praise God who guided us to Islam." Then she added, "Surely, I saw in my sleep that I was always in the sun, standing. The shade was close to me but I was not able to get to it. When the Prophet drew near to us I saw as if I entered the shade."

Abū Ḥuṣayn said: One of the women of the Banū Saʿd b. Bakr—an aunt on the mother's or father's side—arrived with a receptacle of fat and a case of cheese. She came to the Prophet while he was in al-Abṭaḥ. When she entered she traced her relationship to him. The Messenger of God knew her and invited her to Islam. She converted and was sincere. Then the Messenger of God ordered the acceptance of her gift. Then he began to ask her about Ḥalīma and she informed him that she had died in time.

The eyes of the Messenger of God filled with tears. Then he asked her, "Who remains among them?" She replied, "Your brother and your sister. They, by God, require your assistance and your kinship. They used to have an income to rely on but it is gone." The Messenger of God said to her, "Where is your family?" She replied, "In Dhanb Awṭās." The Messenger of God ordered clothing for her and gave her a camel with a sedan seat, and two hundred dinars, and she departed, saying, "You were the best foster child as a baby, and you are the best of men as an adult. You are a great blessing."

He said: ʿAbdullah b. Yazīd related to me from Saʿīd b. ʿAmr al-Hudhalī, who said: [Page 870] When the Messenger of God conquered Mecca he sent out the raiding party. He sent Khālid b. al-Walīd to al-ʿUzzā, and al-Ṭufayl b. ʿAmr al-Dawsī to Dhū l-Kaffayn the idol of ʿAmr b. Ḥumama. He burned it with fire saying:

O Dhū l-Kaffayn I am not among your worshipers.
Our creation was long before yours
I inflamed the fire in your heart.

He sent Saʿd b. Zayd al-Ashhalī to Manāt in al-Mushallal and he pulled it down. And he sent ʿAmr b. al-ʿĀṣ to the idol of Hudhayl—Suwāʿ—and he pulled it down. ʿAmr used to say: I reached the idol and also the gatekeeper. He said, "What do you want?" I said, "To bring down Suwāʿ." He said, "What do you intend with it?" I said, "The Messenger of God commanded me." He said, "You will not be able to bring it down." I said, "Why?" He replied, "It will prevent you." ʿAmr said, "Until now you are in the wrong! Woe unto you. Can it hear or see?" ʿAmr said: I drew close to it and broke it. I commanded my companions and they pulled down the house of its treasury. They did not find anything in it." Then he said to the gate-keeper, "What do you think?" He replied, "I submitted to God."

Then a herald of the Messenger of God called out in Mecca, "Whoever believes in God and His messenger does not leave an idol in his house but breaks it." He said: The Muslims began to break the idols. ʿIkrima b. Abī Jahl when he converted, did not hear about an idol in one of the houses of the Quraysh except he marched to it and destroyed it. Abū Tujra used to make them in *jāhiliyya* and sell them. Saʿd b. ʿAmr said: He informed me that he used to see him make the idol and sell it. There was not a man among the Quraysh in Mecca but he had an idol in his house.

He said: Ibn Abī Sabra related to me from Sulaymān b. Suḥaym from some relatives of Jubayr b. Muṭʿim from Jubayr b. Muṭʿim, who said: When it was the day of the Conquest [Page 871] a herald of the Messenger of God called out: "Whoever is a believer in God will not leave an idol in his house, but will break it or burn it, for its price is forbidden." Jubayr said: The Bedouin used to purchase them and take them to their homes with them. There was not a man from the Quraysh except there was an idol in his house. When he entered he touched it, and when he went out he touched it and was blessed by it.

He said: ʿAbd al-Raḥmān b. Abī l-Zinād related to me from ʿAbd al-Majīd b. Suhayl, who said: When Hind b. ʿUtba converted to Islam she began to break the idol in her house with a hammer, bit by bit, saying, "We were deceived about you!"

He said: Muḥammad related to me from al-Zuhrī from ʿUbaydullah b. ʿUtba, who said: The Messenger of God stayed in Mecca for fifteen days; he prayed two bowings. He said: Makhrama b. Bukayr related to me from his father, ʿArrāk b. Mālik,, who said: The Messenger of God stayed twenty nights. He prayed two bowings.

[VOLUME 3 Pages 873/1123] THE DESTRUCTION OF AL-ʿUZZĀ

He said: ʿAbdullah b. Yazīd related to me from Saʿīd b. ʿAmr al-Hudhalī, who said: The Messenger of God arrived in Mecca on Friday, ten nights before the end of Ramaḍān. The Squadrons spread in every direction. He commanded them to attack those who were not following Islam. Hishām b. al-ʿĀṣ set out with two hundred men in the direction of Yalamlam. Khālid b. Saʿīd b. al-ʿĀṣ set out with three hundred men in the direction of ʿUrana. The Prophet sent Khālid b. al-Walīd to al-ʿUzza to bring it down. Khālid set out with thirty riders from his companions to al-ʿUzza and brought it down. Then he returned to the Prophet, who inquired, "Is it destroyed?" He said, "Yes, O Messenger of God." The Prophet said, "Did you see anything?" He replied, "No." The Prophet said, "Surely, you have not destroyed it. Return and destroy it." So Khālid returned, irritated. When he reached al-ʿUzzā, he drew his sword, and a black woman came out to him, naked, with hair spread out. The gatekeeper of the idol's sanctuary shouted out to her. Khālid said, "A chill went down my spine as he began shouting":

> O ʿUzzā, give me strength and do not be false with me before Khālid,
> throw the head cover and fold up your sleeves
> O ʿUzzā', if you do not kill the man, Khālid,
> come to me with speedy crimes or help me!

[Page 874] He said: Khālid approached her with the sword while saying:

> O ʿUzzā', you will be humiliated, not praised
> Indeed I have found God and will disgrace you.

He said: He struck her with the sword and cut her in two. Then he returned to the Messenger of God and informed him. He said, "Yes, that was al-ʿUzzā who despairs that she will never be worshiped in your land." Then Khālid said, "O Messenger of God, praise God who is generous to us and saves us from destruction! Indeed, I used to see my father come to al-ʿUzzā' with his gifts of a hundred camels and cattle, and slaughter them to al-ʿUzzā'. He would stay with her for three nights and return to us content. I look at what my father died on, believing that vision that overwhelmed their lives. How he was deceived, even came slaughtering to a stone which neither hears nor sees, and is of no harm or use." The Messenger of God said, "Surely this affair belongs to God. Whoever He prepares to guide will be successful, and whoever He leads to error, errs." He destroyed al-ʿUzzā five nights before the end of Ramaḍān in the year eight AH.

The Keeper of al-ʿUzzā was Aflaḥ b. Naḍr al-Shaybānī from the Banū Sulaym. When death besieged him sadness entered upon him and Abū Lahab said to him, "Do not be sad, I will guard al-ʿUzzā after you," and he promised all those he met saying, "If al-ʿUzzā is victorious, I have had a hand in protecting her. But, if Muḥammad is victorious over al-ʿUzzā—and I do not expect it—he is the son of my brother!" God revealed *Perish the hands of the father of flame* (Q. 111:1). Some say that He said this about al-Lāt. Ḥassān b Thābit said . . .

[Page 875] THOSE MUSLIMS WHO WERE KILLED ON THE DAY OF THE CONQUEST

Men who lost their way were Kurz b. Jābir al-Fihrī, Khālid al-Ashʿar, and those of the Banū Kaʿb. Those executed by the sword among the polytheists were Ibn Khaṭal who was killed by Abū Barza; al-Ḥuwayrith b. Nuqaydh, killed by ʿAlī b. Abī Ṭālib; and Miqyas b. Ḍubāba, killed by Numayla. Twenty-four men were killed from the polytheists in al-Khandama.

THE RAID OF THE BANŪ JADHĪMA

He said: ʿAbd al-Raḥmān b. ʿAbd al-ʿAzīz related to me from Ḥakīm b. ʿAbbād b. Ḥunayf from Abū Jaʿfar, who said: When Khālid b. al-Walīd returned from the destruction of al-ʿUzza to the Messenger of God, who was staying in Mecca, the Messenger of God sent him to the Banū Jadhīma, not on a mission of war, but, with an invitation to Islam. Khālid set out with Muslims from the Muhājirūn, the Anṣār, and the Banū Sulaym—numbering three hundred and fifty men—and he reached the Banū Jadhīma at the bottom of Mecca. It was said to the Banū Jadhīma, "This is Khālid b. al-Walīd with the Muslims," and the Banū Jadhīma said, "We are a Muslim community; we bless and trust Muḥammad. We built the mosque and call to prayer in it." Khālid reached them and said, "Submit!" They said, "We are Muslims!" He said, "Then why do you carry weapons? They said, "Indeed, among us and among the community of Bedouin are enemies, and we feared that you were from them. We took the weapons in order to defend ourselves from those who oppose Islam." Khālid said, "Put down your weapons!" A man from them named Jaḥdam said, [Page 876] "O Banū Jadhīma, indeed he is, by God, Khālid. Muḥammad did not seek from anyone more than that he accept Islam. And we have accepted Islam. But he is Khālid, and he does not desire with us what is desired of Muslims. Indeed, what he accepts with weapons are only prisoners, and after the prisoners, the sword!" They said, "We remind you of God and you humiliate us," and Jaḥdam refused to put down his sword until they spoke to him together and he put down his sword. Then they said, "Indeed, we are Muslims and the people have converted. Muḥammad conquered Mecca, so what do we fear from Khālid?" He said, "Is it not, by God, that he will take you by the ancient hatred that was between you." The people put down their weapons. Then Khālid said to them, "Surrender!" And Jaḥdam said, "O community, he does not want a community of Muslims to surrender! Indeed, he desires what he desires. You have disagreed with me and disobeyed my command, By God, it is the sword."

The community surrendered. Some of them were commanded to tie others. When they were tied Khālid pushed to every man among the Muslims one or two men. They spent the night tied up. When it was time to pray, they spoke to the Muslims and prayed, then they were tied, again. When it was dawn, the Muslims disagreed among themselves. A sayer says, "We do not want their imprisonment. We will take them to the Prophet." Another says, "We will observe how they hear or obey. So let us test them." The people were divided between these two speakers. When it was dawn, Khālid b. al-Walīd called out, "Whoever has a prisoner with him dispatch him. Finish him off with the sword." The Banū Sulaym killed all their captives. As for the Muhājirūn and the Anṣār, they released their prisoners.

He said: Mūsā b. ʿUbayda related to me from Iyās b. Salama from his father, who said: I was with Khālid b. al-Walīd and there was a prisoner in my hands. I released him and said, "Go where you wish!" There were prisoners with the Anṣār, and they released them. [Page 877] He said: ʿAbdullah b. Nāfiʿ related to me from his father from Ibn ʿUmar, who said: I released my prisoner. I did not like to kill him, nor that it depended on me whether the sun rose over him or set. My people who were with me from the Anṣār released their prisoners.

He said: Maʿmar related to me from al-Zuhrī from Sālim from Ibn ʿUmar, who said: When Khālid called out, "Who has a prisoner with him, dispatch him," I released my prisoner.

He said: ʿAbdullah b. Yazīd related to me from Ḍamra b. Saʿīd, who said: I heard Abū Bashīr al-Māzinī say, "I had one of the captives with me." He said: When Khālid called out, "Who has with him a prisoner dispatch him," I pulled out my sword to cut off his head, but the prisoner said to me, "O Brother from the Anṣār, indeed, this will not escape you. Observe your community!" He said: So I looked, and lo and behold, the Anṣār without exception had released their prisoners. He said: I said, "Go where you wish!" And he said, "May God bless you. But those who are of closer kinship than you—the Banū Sulaym—have killed us!"

He said: Isḥāq b. ʿAbdullah related to me from Khārija b. Zayd b. Thābit, who said: When Khālid b. al-Walīd called out about dispatching the prisoners, the Banū Sulaym pounced on their prisoners and killed them; as for the Muhājirūn and Anṣār, they released them. Khālid was angry with the Anṣār who released the prisoners. Abū Usayd al-Sāʿidī spoke to him at that time and said, "Fear God, O Khālid, for by God, we may not kill a community of Muslims!" He said, "What is the matter with you?" He said, "We heard their acceptance of Islam. These mosques are in their courtyards."

He said: ʿAbdullah b. Yazīd b. Qusayṭ related to me from his father from ʿAbd al-Raḥmān b. ʿAbdullah b. Abī Ḥadrad from his father, who said: Indeed, we were in the army and the Banū Jadhīma were tied up. Some of them were commanded to tie up some. A man from the prisoners said, "O young man!" [Page 878] And I said, "What do you want?" He replied, "Will you take me by this rope of mine and lead me to the women, then return me and do with me what is done with my companions?" He said: I took him by his rope and reached the women. When he finally reached them he spoke to a woman among them about some of what he desired. He said: Then I turned back with him until I returned him with the prisoners and some of them rose and cut off his head.

It was said: Indeed, the army took a youth from the Banū Jadhīma in the evening. He called to the people to desist from him. Those who wanted him were the Banū Sulaym. They were irritated with him because of previous wars that had taken place in Burza and other places. The Banū Jadhīma had captured them in Burza, and they had suffered death and desired vengeance from them, so they attacked him. When he saw that they would only kill him, he strengthened against them and he killed a man from them. Then he strengthened against them a second time and killed another of them. Then darkness came and obstructed them from each other and the youth found relief. When he rose in the morning he realized that he had killed two men from the community, while the women and children were in the hands of Khālid. So he asked for protection and turned his horse away. When they looked at him they said, "This is he who did what he did yesterday." They attacked him a part of the day, then he weakened them and attacked them. He said, "If you want I will alight, provided that you grant me a contract and an agreement to do with me what you do with the women. If you let them live, I ask that

I live, if you kill them I will be killed." They said, "You shall have that." So he alighted with an agreement from God and a contract. But when he alighted the Banū Sulaym said, "This is our companion who did what he did yesterday." They said, "Leave him with the male captives. If Khālid kills him he is our leader and we are his followers, and if he forgives him, he is like one of them." Some of them said, "Surely we gave him a contract and an agreement that he will be with the women, and you know [Page 879] Khālid will not kill the women. He will either apportion them or forgive them." The youth said, "Since you have done with me what you did, take me to the women there. Then do whatever you wish." He said: They did. He was tied up with a rope when he stood before one of the women. He stayed fixed to the ground and said, "Greetings Ḥubaysh, life is at an end! I have not sinned!" He said a poem:

Reward me with love before distance divides
And the chief goes off with a dear one thus parted.
Is it right for a lover to get what he seeks
Who undertakes journeys by night and by noon?
Did I not seek you and meet you in Ḥalya
Or overtake you in al-Khawāniq?
I was never disloyal to our secret trust
And my eye never looked admiringly at another.
But when the tribe's troubles distracted me from love
Even then the attraction of love was still there.

Ibn Qusayṭ, and Ibn Abī l-Zinād recited it to me.

He said: ʿAbdullah b. Abī Ḥurra related to me from Walīd from Saʿīd from Ḥanẓala b. ʿAlī, who said: A woman came forward at that time, after his head was cut off. He says: [Page 880] She placed her mouth on his and took his mouth in hers. She did not stop kissing him until she died.

He said: ʿAbdullah b. Zayd related to me from Iyās b. Salama from his father, who said: When Khālid b. al-Walīd arrived before the Prophet, ʿAbd al-Raḥmān b. ʿAwf found fault with Khālid for what he did. He said, "O Khālid, you took the authority of *jāhiliyya*! You killed them for your uncle al-Fākih, may God slay you!" He said: ʿUmar b. al-Khaṭṭāb supported him against Khālid, and Khālid said, "I took them for the death of your father." ʿAbd al-Raḥmān said, "You lie, by God. Indeed, I killed the killer of my father with my own hand, and I made ʿUthmān b. ʿAffān witness to his death." And he turned to ʿUthmān and said, "May God be your witness, do you know that I killed the killer of my father?" And ʿUthmān said, "Praise God, yes." Then ʿAbd al-Raḥmān said, "Woe unto you, O Khālid, even if I did not kill the slayer of my father, you have killed a community of Muslims because of my father in *jāhiliyya*?" Khālid said, "Who informed you that they had converted? He said, "The people of the expedition, all of them informed us that you found that they had built mosques and accepted Islam. Yet, you attacked them with the sword." He said, "The Messenger of God came to me to attack them, and I attacked because of the command of the Prophet." ʿAbd al-Raḥmān said, "You lie against the Messenger of God!" And ʿAbd al-Raḥman was harsh.

The Messenger of God turned away from Khālid and was angry with him. What happened with ʿAbd al-Raḥmān reached him, and he said, "O Khālid, leave me my companions! When the nose of a man is struck, he weakens. If Mt. Uḥud were gold, and you spent it ounce by ounce in the way of God, and if you journeyed morning and evening, you could not outweigh ʿAbd al-Raḥmān b. ʿAwf."

He said: ʿAbdullah b. ʿUmar related to me from Nafiʿ from Ibn ʿUmar, who said that ʿUmar said to Khālid, "Woe unto you, O Khālid, you took the Banū Jadhīma with the laws of *jāhiliyya*. Does not Islam erase what was before it, in *jāhiliyya*?" He replied, "O Abū Ḥafṣ, by God, I did not take them except according to the law! I hastened to a community of polytheists and [Page 881] they resisted. It was inevitable when they resisted that I fight them. I captured them, and then attacked them with the sword." ʿUmar said, "What kind of a man do you think ʿAbdullah b. ʿUmar is?" He replied, "By God, he is a good man." ʿUmar said, "And he informed me other than what you inform me. And he was with you in that army." Khālid said, "Indeed I ask God's forgiveness and submit to Him." He said: ʿUmar broke away from him. He said, "Woe unto you. May the Messenger of God ask forgiveness for you!"

He said: Yaḥyā b. ʿAbdullah b. Abī Qatāda related to me from his family from Abū Qatāda while he was with the community that when Khālid called out in the dawn, "Whoever holds a prisoner dispose of him," I released my prisoner and said to Khālid, "Fear God, for surely you will die! Indeed those are a Muslim community!" He replied, "O Abū Qatāda, surely you have no knowledge about these people." Abū Qatāda said, "Indeed, Khālid spoke to me from the hatred in his heart against them."

They said: When the actions of Khālid b. al-Walīd reached the Messenger of God, he raised his hands until the whiteness of his armpits were visible saying, "O God, indeed I disclaim to you what Khālid did!" When Khālid arrived the Prophet censured him.

He said: Maʿmar related to me from al-Zuhrī from Ibrāhīm b. ʿAbd al-Raḥmān b. ʿAwf from his father, who said: There were words between ʿAbd al-Raḥmān b. ʿAwf and Khālid, and ʿAbd al-Raḥmān turned away from him. Khālid walked with ʿUthmān b. ʿAffān to ʿAbd al-Raḥmān and apologized to him until he was satisfied about it and said, "Ask God for my forgiveness, O Abū Muḥammad!"

They said: ʿAmmār entered before the Prophet and said, "O Messenger of God, surely he angered a community who prayed and submitted." Then he criticized Khālid before the Prophet, and Khālid who was seated did not say a word. When ʿAmmār rose, Khālid criticized him and the Prophet said, "Be silent, O Khālid, do not criticize Abū al-Yaqẓān. Indeed he [Page 882] is one whose enemy is God's enemy, and whoever hates him, God hates, and whoever insults him, God insults."

They said: When the Messenger of God conquered Mecca, he asked for a loan of money in Mecca. The Messenger of God called ʿAlī and gave him some money and said, "Hurry to the Banū Jadhīma and decree that the law of *jāhiliyya* is over and pay the blood money to them for those whom Khālid captured." So ʿAlī went to them with that money and paid the blood money for what Khālid had done. He gave them their money and left them what remained of the money as well. Then ʿAlī sent Abū Rāfiʿ to the Messenger of God to ask for more of it. And he increased his money. And ʿAlī paid blood money for all that was taken, even the trough of the dog, until there did not remain anything to ask of him. The money that remained was with ʿAlī, and ʿAlī said, "This remnant of money is for you from the Messenger of God for what Khālid took, and of which he had no knowledge nor understanding," and he gave them that money. Then he turned back to the Prophet and informed him. It was said, indeed, the money that was sent by him with ʿAlī was the loan sought by the Prophet from Ibn Abī Rabīʿa and Ṣafwān b. Umayya and Ḥuwayṭib b. ʿAbd al-ʿUzzā. When ʿAlī returned and came before the Messenger of God, the Messenger of God said, "What did you do, O ʿAlī?"

He informed him and said, "O Messenger of God, we found a community of Muslims who had built mosques in their courtyard. I paid the blood money, for all those who Khālid killed, as well as the dog trough. Then with the rest of the money, I said, "This is from the Messenger of God for what he has no knowledge and does not know of." The Messenger of God said, "You did well! I did not command Khālid to fight. Rather I commanded him to invite them to Islam."

The Messenger of God [Page 883] did not approach Khālid. He turned away from him. Khālid objected before the Messenger of God. He swore he did not kill them for hatred or enmity. But after ʿAlī arrived and paid their blood money, the Messenger of God approached Khālid, and continued keeping him among his prominent companions until his death.

He said: ʿAbdullah b. Jaʿfar related to me from ʿUthmān b. Muḥammad al-Akhnasī from ʿAbd al-Malik b. Abī Bakr b. ʿAbd al-Raḥmān, who said: The Messenger of God said, "Do not curse Khālid b. al-Walīd for surely he is one of the swords of God who drew his sword against the polytheists!"

He said: Muḥammad b. Ḥarb related to me from Abū Bakr b. ʿAbdullah from Abū al-Aḥwaṣ from the Prophet, who said, "Blessed is the slave of God, Khālid b. al-Walīd, the brother of the tribe and one of the swords of God who drew his sword against the disbelievers and the Hypocrites!"

He said: Yūsuf b. Yaʿqūb b. ʿUtba related to me from ʿUthmān b. Muḥammad al-Akhnasī from ʿAbd al-Malik b. ʿAbd al-Raḥmān b. al-Ḥārith, who said: The Messenger of God commanded Khālid b. al-Walīd to raid the Banū Kināna unless he hears the call to prayer or perceives Islam. So he set out until he reached the Banū Jadhīma, and they resisted him with all their might, and they fought and wore their weapons. He waited with them for the prayers of *ʿAṣar* and *Maghrib* and *ʿIshā'*, and he did not hear the call to prayer. Then he attacked them and killed those who were killed and imprisoned those who were imprisoned. And later, they alleged Islam. ʿAbd al-Malik said: The Messenger of God did not censure Khālid about that, for surely he was the military leader until he died. Indeed he set out after that with him as the leader to Ḥunayn and Tabūk. The Messenger of God sent him to Ukaydir and Dūmat al-Jandal. He captured whom he captured, then he reconciled them. Indeed the Messenger of God sent him to Balḥārith b. Kaʿb at Najrān as a commander and [Page 884] missionary to God. Indeed, he set out with the Messenger of God for the Ḥajjat al-Wadāʿ, and when the Messenger of God was shaving his head he gave him a forelock of his. It was kept in the front of his headgear. He did not fight anyone but God defeated his opponent. Indeed, he fought on the day of Yarmūk and his headgear fell down, and he began to say, "The headgear, the headgear!" Later someone said to him, "O Abū Sulaymān, how strange to look for your headgear when you are in the midst of battle!" He said, "Indeed, in it is a forelock of the Prophet, and whoever faces it flees." Khālid died on the day God took him, while striving in the way of God. His grave is in Ḥimṣ. He who washed him and attended his death informed me that he look at what was under his clothes and no part of him was left unmarked by either a blow from a sword, the piercing of a spear or the throw of an arrow head.

Indeed the relationship between Khālid and ʿUmar b. al-Khaṭṭāb was not like that mentioned above. Later ʿUmar remembered him and was gracious about him and forgave him what he did during his command. He used to say: He was one of the swords of God! Indeed the Messenger of God alighted when he (Khālid) came down from Laft during his pilgrimage. With him was a man, and the Messenger of God said, "Who is this?" The man said, "So and so." The Messenger of God said, "Miserable is the slave of God, so and so!" Then another man arose, and he said, "Who is this?" And he said, "So and so." And he said, "Miserable is the slave of God, so and so." Then Khālid rose, and he said, "Who is this?" He replied, "Khālid b. al-Walīd." He said, "Blessed is the slave of God, Khālid b. al-Walīd!" A man from the Banū Jadhīma who was a transcriber said: I heard Khālid b. Ilyās say: It reached us that he killed almost thirty men.

[Page 885] **THE RAID OF ḤUNAYN**

Abū ʿAbdullah Muḥammad b. Shujāʿ al-Thaljī said: Al-Wāqidī related to us that Muḥammad b. ʿAbdullah, ʿAbdullah b. Jaʿfar, Ibn Abī Sabra, Muḥammad b. Ṣāliḥ, Abū Maʿshar, Ibn Abī Ḥabība, Muḥammad b. Yaḥyā b. Sahl, ʿAbd al-Ṣamad b. Muḥammad al-Saʿdī, Muʿādh b. Muḥammad, Bukayr b. Mismār, and Yaḥyā b. ʿAbdullah b. Abī Qatāda, as well as others not named—people of trust—all have related portions of this tradition to us. Some of them are more reliable than others, and I have gathered all that was related to me about it.

They said: When the Messenger of God conquered Mecca, the nobility of the Hawāzin and the Thaqīf came together and they mobilized and rose up and demonstrated and said: By God, Muḥammad has not yet met with a people who are good in battle, so make up your minds and march to him before he marches to you. And the Hawāzin gathered under their commander Mālik b. ʿAwf, who at that time was thirty years of age, a lord of theirs, and wore a long cloak. He acted with his money and was commended for it, and all of the Hawāzin gathered. The two lords of the Thaqīf were at that time Qārib b. al-Aswad b. Masʿūd who commanded the Aḥlāf, while Dhū l-Khimār, Subayʿ b. al-Ḥārith (and others said it was al-Aḥmar b. al-Ḥārith), who was the ally of the Thaqīf, commanded the Banū Mālik.

All of them gathered with the Hawāzin who came together for the expedition against Muḥāmmad, and the Thaqīf were swift to join them. They said: We were about to march to him for we detest that he march to us. [Page 886] Nevertheless, if he came to us he would find an inaccessible fortress that we will fight behind, and much food, until we take him or he turns away. But we do not desire that. We will march with you as one hand. And they set out with them. Ghaylān b. Salama al-Thaqafī said to his sons, and there were ten, "Indeed, I desire a command that has several aspects. Not a man among you will witness it except on a horse." So ten of his children witnessed it on ten horses. And when they were defeated in Awṭās they fled. They entered the fortress of al-Ṭā'if and locked it. Kināna b. ʿAbd al-Yālīl said: O community of Thaqīf, surely you will go out from your fortress, and you will march to a man and you will not know whether he will be for you or against you. So go to your fortress and repair what is not fixed of it, for you do not know whether you will need it. So they went with him and it was repaired. They appointed a man to fix it, and they marched.

People from the Banū Hilāl witnessed it, and they were not many, they did not reach a hundred. Neither the Kaʿb nor the Kilāb attended it from the Hawāzin, and surely the Kilāb were nearby. It was said to some of them: Why did the Kilāb leave and not attend? He said: It was not a matter of them being close, but Ibn Abī l-Barā' forbade them from attending, and they obeyed him. He said, "By God, even if those from the East to the West opposed him, Muḥammad would be victorious over them."

Durayd al-Ṣimma with the Banū Jusham helped them. He was at that time a hundred and sixty years of age, an old man, and there was nothing in him except that he was a good omen and had knowledge of wars. He was old and experienced but had lost his sight at that time. The people gathered—the Thaqīf and others from Hawāzin, to Mālik b. ʿAwf al-Naṣrī. When Mālik gathered the people for the march against the Messenger of God, he ordered the people, and they brought with them their wealth and their women and the children, until they alighted in Awṭās. The people gathered together, and camped, and stayed with him. [Page 887] Help came to them from every direction. Durayd b. al-Ṣimma was at that time in a little hawdah and led on a camel. And he stayed on his camel. When he alighted the old man touched the ground with his hand and said, "In which valley are you?" They said, "In Awṭās." He said, "The field of the horse is good. There are no stony mounds or soft grounds! But I hear the cry of the camel, the bray of the donkey, the sound of the sheep, the moo of the cow, and the crying of little ones." They said, "Mālik brought out the people with their children and their women and their wealth." He said, "O people of the Hawāzin, is there anyone here from the Banū Kilāb b. Rabīʿa?" They said, "No." He said, "Is there anyone here from the Banū Kaʿb b. Rabīʿa with you?" They said, "No." He said, "Is there anyone here from the Banū Hilāl b. ʿĀmir with you?" They said, "No." Durayd said, "If the conditions were good you would not precede them to battle. If there were fame or nobility they would not stay away from it. Obey me, O people of the Hawāzin, and return, and do what they do!" But they refused him. He said, "Who witnesses it among you?" They said, "ʿAmr b. ʿĀmir and ʿAwf b. ʿĀmir." He said, "Those are two weak persons from the ʿĀmir. They are neither harmful nor useful." Then he said, "Where is Mālik?" They said, "This is Mālik." So he called him and said, "O Mālik, indeed you will be fighting a man who is noble. You have become the leader of your people. Indeed, this day is the creator of what follows it from the battles! O Mālik, why do I hear the cry of the camel, the bray of the donkey, the moo of the cows, the crying of children, and the bleeting of sheep?" Mālik said, "I drove the people with their wealth and their children and their wives." Durayd said, "Why?" Mālik said, "I wanted to place behind every man his family, his property, his children and his wives so that [Page 888] he will fight for them." He said: He clapped his hands then, and said, "Watcher of sheep, what is the war to him? Is anything returned to the defeated? Indeed, if you are to be victorious, nothing will help you except he who has his weapons and his spear. If you are defeated, you will be dishonored with your family and your property." Then he said, "What happened to the Kaʿb and Kilāb?" They said, "None of them will witness it." He said, "Seriousness and focus are missing. If the day were significant the Kaʿb and Kilāb would not be absent from it. O Mālik, surely you do nothing useful by dispatching most of the Hawāzīn to slaughter the horses. Even if you did what you did, do not disobey me in this matter. Raise them to the impenetrable regions of their land above their enemy. Then meet the enemy on the backs of horses. If you are victorious, those who are behind you can join you, and you will fear nothing for your family. If you are defeated, your family and your property would be saved."

Mālik became angry at his words and said, "I will not do so, nor will I change a command I have made. Indeed you have grown old and your knowledge is old. After you comes one who is more understanding of war than you!" Durayd said, "O People of the Hawāzin, this is not the right decision for you. This will dishonor you in your weak spot and bring the enemy to you. Reach the fortress of the Thaqīf and stay there." So they turned away and left. Then Mālik drew his sword, turned it towards himself, and said, "O people of the Hawāzin, by God you will obey me or I shall fall upon my sword until it comes out from my back!" Mālik hated that the people still respected Durayd and valued his opinion. The people gathered together and said, "If we disobey Mālik, he is young, and he will surely kill himself [Page 889] and we will stay with Durayd, an old man who cannot fight. He is a hundred and sixty years of age!" So they gathered together with Mālik. When Durayd saw that and that they had opposed him he said:

This is not a day I would not witness nor am I absent from it.
Would that I were a young man
I would ride forward and put down.

Durayd was remembered for his heroic deeds and his bravery. He was barely twenty years when he was lord of the Banū Jusham and the best of them in lineage. But age overtook him until he weakened. He was Durayd b. al-Ṣimma b. Bakar b. ʿAlqama.

He said: Maʿmar related to me from al-Zuhrī, who said: The Messenger of God conquered Mecca on the thirteenth of Ramaḍān, and God revealed: *When comes the help of God and the victory* (Q. 110:1).

They said: The conquest of Mecca was on Friday ten days before the end of Ramaḍān. The Messenger of God stayed in Mecca for fifteen days and prayed two bowings. Then, on the next morning, Saturday, the sixth of Shawwāl, he left, having appointed ʿAttāb b. Asīd in Mecca to pray with them, and Muʿādh b. Jabal to inform them of the practice and jurisprudence of Islam.

They said: The Messenger of God set out with twelve thousand Muslims, ten thousand from the people of Medina, and two thousand from the people of Mecca. When he went out, one of his companions said: If we meet the Banū Shaybān we will not care. One will not defeat us today for our small numbers. God most high revealed about that: *God has already helped you on many fields, and on the day of Hunayn, when your numbers please you* (Q. 9:250).

[Page 890] He said: Ismāʿīl b. Ibrāhīm related to me from Mūsā b. ʿUqba from al-Zuhrī from Saʿīd al-Musayyib, who said: Abū Bakr al-Ṣiddīq said, "O Messenger of God, we will not be defeated to day because of our small numbers." God revealed about that *God has already helped you on many fields*.

He said: Muḥammad b. ʿAbdullah related to me from ʿUbaydullah b. ʿAbdullah b. ʿUtba from Ibn ʿAbbās, who said: The Messenger of God said: The best of the companions are four, and the best of the expeditions are four hundred, and the best of the soldiers are four thousand. Twelve thousand will not be defeated today because of their small numbers. Their word is one.

They said: Many people from the polytheists set out with the Messenger of God, among them, Ṣafwān b. Umayya. The Messenger of God borrowed a hundred armor plates and their tools entirely from him. He said, "O Muḥammad, is it voluntary or by force?" And Muḥammad replied, "A loan to be fulfilled." The Messenger of God said to Ṣafwān, "Help us to transport them." Ṣafwān carried them on his camels until they reached Awṭās, and then handed them to the Messenger of God.

Maʿmar related to us from al-Zuhrī from Sinān b. Abī Sinān al-Dīlī from Abū Wāqid al-Laythī—and some said al-Ḥarith b. Mālik—who said: We set out with the Messenger of God to Ḥunayn. The disbelieving Quraysh and those who were their equals among the Bedouin had a great big green tree named Dhāt Anwāt. They came to it every year and they attached their weapons on it, and they slaughtered before it and devoted a whole day to it. He said: One day, while we were marching with the Prophet we saw a large green tree that concealed us from the [Page 891] side of the street. We said, "O Messenger of God, make for us a Dhāt al-Anwāṭ like their Dhāt al-Anwāṭ." He said: the Messenger of God said, "God is great! God is great! By Him who holds my soul in His hand, you say, just as the people of Moses said, *'Moses, make for us a god as they have gods,' and he said, 'you are surely a people who are ignorant.'* Indeed they are customary practices, customary to those who were before you."

Ibn Abī Ḥabība related to me from Dāwud b. al-Ḥuṣayn from ʿIkrima from Ibn ʿAbbās, who said: Dhāt al-Anwāṭ was a large tree. The people of *jāhiliyya* slaughtered before it and were devoted to it for one day. He who made pilgrimage among them put down his cloak at the tree and entered without his cloak, glorifying it. When the Messenger of God passed to Ḥunayn, a group of his companions said to him—including al-Ḥarith b. Mālik—"O Messenger of God make for us Dhāt Anwāt just like their Dhat al-Anwāṭ." The Messenger of God proclaimed *takbīr* three times. He said, "Thus did the people of Moses act with Moses."

He said: Abū Burda b. Niyār said: When we were below Awṭās we alighted under a tree, and we observed a large tree. The Messenger of God alighted under it, and he hung his sword and bow on it. He said: I was among the closest of the Messenger of God's companions. He said: All of a sudden his voice crying, "O Abū Burda!" startled me: I said, "I obey you!" and approached swiftly, and lo and behold, the Messenger of God was seated with a man. The Messenger of God said, "Indeed, this man arrived while I was sleeping, and he drew his sword and stood with it at my head, and I was startled by his words, 'Who will protect you from me today?' And I said, 'God!'" Abū Burda said: I jumped to my sword and drew it, [Page 892] but the Messenger of God said, "Sheath your sword!" I said, "O Messenger of God, ask me to strike off the head of the enemy. Indeed, this is one of the spies of the polytheists." But he said to me, "Be silent, O Abū Burda." The Messenger of God said nothing to the disbeliever, nor did he punish him. I began shouting about him in the camp and the people witnessed him and someone killed him without the command of the Messenger of God. As for me, indeed, the Messenger of God had stopped me from killing him. The Messenger of God kept saying, "Keep away from the man, O Abū Burda. Indeed, God is my protector and my keeper until His religion is victorious over all other religions."

They said: The Messenger of God reached Ḥunayn in the evening on Tuesday, the tenth of Shawwāl. Mālik b. ʿAwf sent men from the Ḥawāzin to observe Muḥammad and his companions—three men—and he commanded them to disperse in the camp, and they returned to him with their limbs dislocated. He said, "How were you hurt?" They said, "We saw white men on piebald horses. By God, we could not hold ourselves since we took what you see. Surely, we do not fight people of the earth but rather people from the heavens."—And indeed the hearts of his spies were trembling—"If you obeyed us you would return with your people. Indeed the people, if they saw similar to what we saw, would be hurt as we were." He said, "ff! Rather you are a group of the most cowardly people of the military camp," and he imprisoned them fearing that their terror would spread in the camp. Then, he said, "Show me a man who is brave?" So they brought him a man, and he set out; but he returned to him in the same manner as those who went before him among them. He said, "What did you see?" The brave replied, [Page 893] "I saw white men on piebald horses. No one can bear looking at them. I could not hold myself since I took what you see." But that did not weaken his intentions.

They said: The Messenger of God called Ibn Abī Ḥadrad al-Aslamī and said, "Go, and enter in among the people so that you bring news of them, and of what Mālik says." ʿAbdullah set out and walked around their camp. Then he reached Ibn ʿAwf and found the heads of the Hawāzin with him and he heard him say to his companions, "Indeed, Muḥammad did not really fight before this time. Rather, he used to meet an inexperienced community that had no knowledge of war so he would be victorious over them. When it is dawn, line up your cattle and your women and your children behind you and line up yourselves, then you will be the offensive. Then break the scabbards of your swords and meet him with twenty thousand swords with broken scabbard, and attack as one man, and know that the victory is for whoever attacks first." When he understood that, ʿAbdullah b. Abī Hadrad returned to the Prophet and informed him of all that he heard. The Messenger of God called ʿUmar b. al-Khaṭṭāb, and told him what Hadrad said. ʿUmar said, "Ibn Abī Hadrad is a liar." Hadrad said, "If you call me a liar, maybe you do not believe the truth." So ʿUmar said, "O Messenger of God, listen to what Ibn Hadrad says!" The Prophet said, "He speaks the truth. You were astray and God guided you."

They said: Sahl b. Ḥanzaliyya al-Anṣārī said: We marched with the Prophet during the raid of the Hawāzīn. The march was quick until a man came to him and said, [Page 894] "O Messenger of God, those who are behind you are cut off!" So he alighted, and prayed the *ʿAṣar* prayer. The people sought shelter with him and he commanded them to alight. A rider came to him and said, "O Messenger of God, I departed from you to Mount such and such, and lo and behold, there were all the Hawāzin gathered with their virgins and wives and cattle in Wādī Ḥunayn." The Messenger of God smiled and said, "That will be the plunder of the Muslims tomorrow, God willing!"

Then the Messenger of God said, "Are there no riders to guard us this night?" And lo and behold Unays b. Abī Marthad al-Ghanawī approached on his horse and said, "I am he, O Messenger of God." The Messenger of God said, "Depart, until you stop on Mount such and such, and do not alight except to pray or to fulfill a need. Do not endanger those who are behind you!" He said: We stayed up the night until the dawn lightened, and we attended prayer. The Messenger of God came out to us and said, "Did you hear your rider tonight?" We said, "No, by God!" Prayer was announced, and the Prophet prayed with us. As he greeted, I saw the Messenger of God look through the trees and then he said, "Rejoice, your rider comes!" And he came and said, "O Messenger of God, indeed I stopped on the mountain just as you commanded, and I did not alight from my horse except to pray or fulfill a need of mine, until it dawned, and I did not hear anyone." The Messenger of God said, "Leave, depart from your horse, and approach us. This one does no more after such work!"

They said: Men from Mecca went out with the Prophet riding and walking, and not one of them stayed behind—on another faith. They were observing whose turn it would be to [Page 895] take the plunder. They did not detest that the blow could be for Muḥammad and his companions. Abū Sufyān set out in the tracks of the troops, and picked up all that he passed by, of fallen shields, spears or utensils from utensils of the Prophet, and the divining arrowheads in his sack, until it was too heavy for his camel. Ṣafwān, who had not converted, also set out, and he was in a period of protection that Muḥammad made for him. Ṣafwān moved behind the people with Ḥakīm b. Ḥizām, Ḥuwayṭib b. ʿAbd al-ʿUzzā, Suhayl b. ʿAmr, Abū Sufyān b. Ḥarb, al-Ḥārith b. Hishām, and ʿAbdullah b. Abī Rabīʿa and they looked for those who would be successful. They moved behind the people, while the people fought each other. A man passed by Ṣafwān and said, “Rejoice, Abū Wahb! Muḥammad and his companions are defeated!” Ṣafwān said to him, “Indeed, a lord from the Quraysh is more desirable to me than a lord from the Hawāzin, if I must have a lord.”

They said: When it was about night, Mālik b. ʿAwf went to his companions and prepared them in Wādī Ḥunayn—it was an empty hollow, possessing narrow gorges—and he dispersed the people in it. He indicated to the people that they should attack Muḥammad in a single attack.

The Messenger of God prepared his companions and arranged them in rows. At dawn, he placed the banners and flags with its people. The Muhājirūn had a banner carried by ʿAlī, a flag carried by Saʿd b. Abī Waqqāṣ, and another flag carried by ʿUmar b. al-Khaṭṭāb. The Anṣār had flags, too. The Khazrajī banner was carried by al-Ḥubāb b. al-Mundhir, and some said, by Saʿd b. ʿUbāda, and the banner of the Aws was held by Usayd b. Ḥuḍayr. Every clan of the Aws and the Khazraj had a banner or a flag. Abū Nāʾila carried the flag of the Banū ʿAbd al-Ashhal. [Page 896] Abū Burda b. Niyār carried the flag of the Banū Ḥāritha; Qatāda b. al-Nuʿmān carried the flag of the Ẓafar; Jabr b. ʿAtīk carried the flag of the Banū Muʿāwiya. Hilāl b. Umayya carried the flag of the Banū Wāqif; Abū Lubāba b. Mundhir carried the flag of the Banū ʿAmr b. ʿAwf; Abū Usayd al-Sāʿidī carried the flag of the Banū Sāʿida; ʿUmāra b. Ḥazm carried the flag of the Banū Mālik b. Najjār; Abū Salīṭ carried the flag of the Banū ʿAdī b. Najjār; and Salīṭ b. Qays carried the flag of the Banū Māzin.

The flags of the Aws and Khazraj were green and red in *jāhiliyya*, and when Islam arrived, they kept it as before. The flags of the Muhājirūn were black and their banners white. Among the tribes of the Bedouin, the Aslam had two flags: One of them was held by Burayda b. al-Ḥuṣayb, and Jundub b. al-Aʿjam the other; Abū Dharr carried the banner of the Banū Ghifār; The banner of the Banū Ḍamra, Layth, and Saʿd b. Layth were carried by Abū Wāqid al-Laythī and al-Ḥārith b. Mālik. The Kaʿb b. ʿAmr had two banners: Bishr b. Sufyān held one, and Abū Shurayḥ the other. The Banū Muzayna kept three banners: Bilāl b. al-Ḥārith held one, al-Nuʿmān b. Muqarrin, the second, and ʿAbdullah b. ʿAmr b. ʿAwf the third. The Juhayna had four banners: Rāfiʿ b. Makīth held one, ʿAbdullah b. Yazīd held the second, Abū Zurʿa Maʿbad b. Khālid the third, and Suwayd b. Ṣakhr the fourth. The Banū Ashjaʿ had two banners. Nuʿaym b. Masʿūd carried one and Maʿqil b. Sinān the other. The Banū Sulaym had three banners: al-ʿAbbās b. Mirdās held one, Khufāf b. Nudba the second, and al-Ḥajjāj b. ʿIlāṭ the third.

The Messenger of God [Page 897] had dispatched the Sulaym on the day he set out from Mecca and made them the vanguard of the cavalry. The Messenger of God appointed Khālid b. al-Walīd to lead it and he continued to do so until he arrived in Jiʿirrāna.

They said: The Messenger of God came down with his companions. His vanguard had left, while Muḥammad maintained the army in the same form in Wādī Ḥunayn. Then the Messenger of God descended a slope—the wadi was a steep slope—riding his white donkey, Duldul, and wearing his armor, head covering and helmet. He went to meet the rows of soldiers, and he went around them, and some of them were behind some others, and they descended into the wadi. He encouraged them to fight, and announced the good news of the conquest—if they were sincere and patient—to them. Meanwhile they were coming down in the darkness of the dawn.

Anas b. Mālik used to relate saying: When we reached Wādī Ḥunayn—it was one of those valleys of Tihāma with narrow gorges—something came to us from the

Hawāzin—no, by God, I had never, in that time, seen anything like such a dark multitude. They had driven their women, their property and their children, and arranged them in rows. They had placed the women on camels, behind the rows of men. Then they brought camels and cows and sheep and placed them behind that, claiming that they could not run away. And when we saw that dark multitude, we thought it all men, for when we descended into the wadi we were in the darkness of dawn. Suddenly, we felt, nothing but the squadrons that came out to us from the narrow valley and its gorges, and attacked us as one.

The first cavalry to be exposed, the cavalry of Sulaym, turned back, followed by the people of Mecca, followed by the people, defeated running without looking back. Anas said: I heard the Messenger of God looking around to his right and left while the people were fleeing, and he says, "O helpers of God [Page 898] and helpers of His messenger! I am the servant of God and his patient messenger!" He said: Then the Messenger of God came forward with his spear, in front of the people, and by Him who sent him with the truth, not a sword struck us nor a spear pierced us until God defeated them. Then the Prophet returned to the camp and he commanded that those who were caught by the Muslims be killed. The Hawāzin began to flee and those Muslims who had fled came back.

He said: Maʿmar and Muḥammad b. ʿAbdullah related to me from al-Zuhrī, from Kathīr b. al-ʿAbbas b. ʿAbd al-Muṭṭalib from his father, who said: When it was the day of Ḥunayn, the Muslims and the polytheists met, and the Muslims turned away, at that time. And surely, I saw the Messenger of God with none other than Abū Sufyān b. al-Ḥārith b. ʿAbd al-Muṭṭalib taking the mule of the Messenger of God by its crupper [strap]. The Prophet encouraged those who hastened towards the polytheists. He said: I came to him until I took the bit of the bridle of his mule, and he was on his gray mule, and I struck it with the bit. I had a strong voice, and the Messenger of God said, when he saw what he saw among the people and they did not stop for anything, "O ʿAbbās, shout, 'O, people of the Anṣār! O companions of the Samura tree!' " So I called out, "O people of the Anṣār! O companions of the Samura!" He said: They approached like camels when they crave for their young ones, saying, "At your service! At your service!" And the man among them [Page 899] goes to turn his camel, but has no power to do that. He takes his armor and places it on its neck. Then he takes his shield and his sword, and plunges from his camel and sets it free with the people, and goes towards the voice until he reaches the Messenger of God, until all the people returned to him, in a gathering. The call was first: O Anṣār. Then the call was confined to: O al-Khazraj!

He said: They were patient at the meeting, trusting with the war. He said: The Messenger of God looked out, peering over as one who is raised up on his riding animal. Observing the battle he said, "Now there is feverish fighting!" Then he took pebbles in his hand and aimed at them, saying, "Defeat them by the Lord of the Kaʿba!" By God, I continued to see their command go back. Their constraints were weak until God defeated them. As for me, I observed the Messenger of God gallop behind them on his mule. It was said: Indeed, the Messenger of God said to al-ʿAbbās, "Call out: O companions of the Samura," so the Anṣār returned, saying, "The attack after the flight." They bent as the cows bend towards their young and aimed their spears (until, indeed, I feared more for the Messenger of God from their spears than from the spears of the polytheists), leading the lines and saying, "At your service! At your service!" And when they mixed, they struck with the sword. The Messenger of God was standing on his mule fixed on to his stirrups, saying, "O God, I ask you for your promise. Do not raise them to victory." Then he said to al-ʿAbbās, "Get me some pebbles!" So he brought pebbles from the ground. Then he said, "Disgrace them!" and he threw them at the faces of the polytheists. Then he said, "They are defeated by the Lord of the Kaʿba!"

He said: ʿAbd al-Raḥmān b. ʿAbd al-ʿAzīz related to me from ʿĀṣim b. ʿUmar b. Qatāda [Page 900] from ʿAbd al-Raḥmān b. Jābir b. ʿAbdullah from his father, who said: When the people were revealed, and by God, when their defeated returned, they found prisoners tied up with the Prophet. He said: the Messenger of God turned, at that time, to Abū Sufyān b. al-Ḥārith who was masked in iron and one of those who were patient at that time; and he was taking the crupper of the Messenger of God's mule, when the Messenger of God said, "Who is this?" He replied, "The son of your mother, O Messenger of God." And it was said: Indeed, the Prophet said, "Who are you?" and he replied, "Your brother—and your ransom is my father and my mother—Abū Sufyān b. al-Ḥārith." The Messenger of God said, "Yes, my brother, hand me some pebbles from the ground!" He gave them to him, and he threw them in their eyes, all of them, and they were defeated.

They said: When the people were revealed the Messenger of God moved to his right. He stood on his riding beast and did not alight, but drew his sword and threw away the scabbard. The Messenger of God stayed with a group of Muhājirūn and Anṣār and the people of his house: al-ʿAbbās, ʿAlī, al-Faḍl b. ʿAbbās, Abū Sufyān b. al-Ḥārith, and Rabīʿa b. al-Ḥārith, Ayman b. ʿUbayd al-Khazrajī, Usāma b. Zayd, Abū Bakr and ʿUmar. It was said: When the people were revealed, the Messenger of God said to Ḥāritha b. al-Nuʿmān, "O Ḥāritha, how many do you see who hold firm?" He said: When I turned and looked behind me it was limited. I looked on my right and left and estimated them at a hundred. I said, "O Messenger of God, they are a hundred!" Until later in the day I passed the Prophet while he was confiding in the angel Gabriel at the door of the mosque. Gabriel said: [Page 901] "Who is this, O Muḥammad?" The Messenger of God answered, "Ḥāritha b. al-Nuʿmān." Gabriel said, "This was one of the patient hundred on the day of Hunayn." And when he greeted I returned his greeting. I informed the Prophet and said, "I did not think he was other than Diḥya al-Kalbī standing with you."

When the people were exposed around him, and only a hundred enduring ones remained, the Prophet prayed at that time, "O God, to You is praise and to You is my complaint. You are the Helper!" Gabriel said to him, "Surely you understood the words which God taught Moses on the day the sea separated before him, while the Pharaoh was behind him." He said: Maʿmar b. Rāshid related to me from al-Zuhrī from ʿUrwa from ʿĀ'isha, who said: Indeed, Ḥāritha b. al-Nuʿmān passed by the Prophet as he stood, confiding in Gabriel. Ḥāritha greeted them. Later the Messenger of God said, "Did you see that man?" Ḥāritha said, "Yes. But I did not know who he was." The Messenger of God said, "He was Gabriel, and he returns your greetings."

It was said: Indeed, the enduring hundred consisted at that time of thirty-three Muhājirūn, sixty-seven Anṣār, al-ʿAbbās, and Abū Sufyān who was taking the Prophet's mule by the reins. Abū Sufyān was on his right, and around him were the Muhājirūn and the Anṣār. Ibn ʿAbbās used to narrate that Gabriel passed by while Ḥāritha b. Nuʿmān was with the Prophet, standing, and Gabriel said, "Who is this, O Muḥāmmad?" And he replied, "Ḥāritha b. al-Nuʿmān." Gabriel said, "This is one of the eighty enduring. God was responsible for their subsistence and the subsistence of their dependents in Paradise. Ibn ʿAbbās [Page 902] used to say: Abū Sufyān b. al-Ḥārith was among those for whom God would be responsible for their subsistence and the subsistence of their relatives in Paradise.

They said: al-Barāʾ b. ʿĀzib used to say: By God who is the only God, the Messenger of God did not turn back but stood and asked for help. Then he alighted saying, "I am the Prophet, I do not lie; I am the son of ʿAbd al-Muṭṭalib." And God revealed His help to him. His enemy bowed, and his authority prospered.

They said: There was a man from the Hawāzin on a red camel, who held a black flag at the top of a long spear of his. When he overtook anyone he pierced him. He had increased the battle with the Muslims. Abū Dujāna stood up to him and hamstrung his camel. He heard the wail of the camel as it fell down. Then ʿAlī and Abū Dujāna strengthened against him, and ʿAlī cut off his right hand while Abū Dujāna cut off the other. They approached and struck him with their swords, together, until their swords were blunted. One of them desisted, while the other finished him off. Then one of them said to his companion, "Leave, and do not return for his plunder." So they went fighting before the Prophet. Then a rider from the Hawāzin carrying a red flag in his hand confronted them. One of them struck the hand of the rider and he fell to his face. Then they struck him with their swords and they left his booty. Abū Ṭalḥa was passing by, and he took the booty of the first, then, he passed again and took the booty of the last. ʿUthmān b. ʿAffān, ʿAlī, Abū Dujāna, Ayman b. ʿUbayd fought before the Messenger of God.

He said: Sulaymān b. Bilāl related to me from ʿUmāra b. Ghaziyya, who said: Umm ʿUmāra said: When, at that time, the people were defeated in every way, I was with four women, holding a sharp sword in my hand, while Umm Sulaym had a dagger which she had wrapped around her middle—and she was pregnant with ʿAbdullah b. Abī Ṭalḥa. And there was Umm Salīṭ and Umm al-Ḥārith. They said: She tried to draw the sword [Page 903] while shouting at the Anṣār, "What custom is this! Why are you fleeing!" She said: I looked at a man from the Hawāzin on a dark grey camel. He had a flag. He was placing his camel in the tracks of the Muslims. I opposed him and struck the Achilles' tendon of the camel. It was a tall camel, and the man fell on his back. I strengthened against him and I continued to strike him until I killed him. I took his sword and I left the camel groaning as it turned over from its back to its stomach. The Messenger of God stood and raised the sword in his hand. He had thrown his scabbard and was calling out, "O companions of the Chapter of the Cow!" He said: And the Muslims turned around and began to say: O Abū ʿAbd al-Raḥmān! O Banū ʿUbaydullah! O cavalry of God! The Messenger of God had named his cavalry the cavalry of God. He made the code of the Muhājirūn Banū ʿAbd al-Raḥmān; the code of the Aws Banū ʿUbaydullah; Then the Anṣār turned around, and the Hawāzin were paralyzed, and there was the defeat. By God, I have not seen a defeat that was like it. The enemy fled in every direction. And my two sons turned to me—Ḥabīb and ʿAbdullah the sons of Zayd—with prisoners tied up. I went out to them in rage, and I struck off the head of one of them. The people began to arrive with the prisoners. I saw thirty prisoners with the Banū Māzin b. Najjār. The Muslims had reached the furthest of their defeat of Mecca. Then they turned around and returned. The Prophet apportioned to all of them.

Anas b. Mālik used to say: Indeed Umm Sulaym—my mother—the daughter of Milḥān began saying, "O Messenger of God, did you see those who let you down and fled from you and abandoned you! Do not forgive them. [Page 904] When God makes it possible for you among them, kill them just as you killed those disbelievers!"

He replied, "O Umm Sulaym, God is sufficient and ample!" At that time she had a camel of Abū Ṭalḥa of which she feared she would lose control. She drew its head near to her and put her hand in its nose ring along with the nose rein, while she strengthened her waist with her girdle. She had a dagger in her hand and Abū Ṭalḥa said to her, "What is this with you, O Umm Sulaym?" she replied, "A dagger that I took with me. If one of the disbelievers came near me, I would slit him open with it." Abū Ṭalḥa said, "Did you not hear, O Messenger of God, what Umm Sulaym says?"

Umm al-Ḥārith al-Anṣāriyya had taken the bridle of the camel of Abū l-Ḥārith, her husband. His camel was named al-Mijsār. She said, "O Ḥār, are you leaving the Messenger of God!" She took the bridle of the camel—the camel desired to reach the others, and the people were running away defeated—and she did not withdraw from it. Umm al-Ḥarith said that ʿUmar b. al-Khaṭṭāb passed by, and she said, "O ʿUmar, what is this?" ʿUmar replied, "The command of God." Umm al-Ḥārith began to say, "O Messenger of God, whoever passes by my camel I will kill him! By God, I have never seen such a day where those people do with us what they do!" She meant the Banū Sulaym and the people of Mecca who were defeated.

Ibn Abī Sabra related to me and said: Muḥammad b. ʿAbdullah b. Abī Ṣaʿṣaʿa related to me that Saʿd b. ʿUbāda was shouting at that time to the Khazraj, "O al-Khazraj! O al-Khazraj!" And Usayd b. Ḥuḍayr, "O al-Aws," three times. They returned from every region as if they were bees seeking refuge with their leader (Queen). He said: The Muslims were angry at them and killed them until [Page 905] they hastened in killing children of the enemy. That reached the Messenger of God and he said, "What is the matter with people that they go killing even the children! Indeed, children should never be killed!" Three times. Usayd b. Ḥuḍayr said, "O Messenger of God, surely they are the children of polytheists?" The Messenger of God replied, "Are not the best of you children of polytheists? Every living creature has a natural disposition until his tongue can express his intentions. It is their fathers who make them Jews or Christians."

He said: ʿAbdullah b. ʿAlī related to me from Saʿīd b. Muḥammad b. Jubayr b. Muṭʿim from his father from his grandfather, who said: When we and the community looked, we saw black, and we had never seen so much blackness. Indeed that blackness was cattle, and they carried women. He said: The likeness of a black shadow approached from the heavens until it darkened on us and them, and blocked the horizon. Then, all of a sudden I saw Wādī Ḥunayn flow with ants, black ants spread like a carpet and I had no doubt that it was God helping us. And God most high defeated them.

He said: Ibn Abī Sabra related to me saying: ʿAbdullah b. Abī Bakr b. Ḥazm related to me from Yaḥyā b. ʿAbdullah b. ʿAbd al-Raḥmān, from the elders of his community of the Anṣār, who said: We saw, at that time, the likeness of a black garment fall from the heavens in a heap. And we looked and all of a sudden there was a carpet of ants, and indeed we were dusting them off our garments. It was God's help to us.

The mark of the angels on the day of Ḥunayn was a red turban that loosened and dropped between their shoulders. God threw fear in the hearts of the polytheists on the day of Ḥunayn. [Page 906] Suwayd b. ʿĀmir al-Suwāʾ who was present at that time and was asked about fear, used to say that he used to take a pebble and throw it in the basin and it would ring out, and he said: We used to find that it was like this inside us.

Mālik b. Aws b. al-Ḥadathān used to say: A number of my community who witnessed that day related to me: The Messenger of God threw sufficient pebbles, and there was not one among us, but he complained of the dust in his eyes. Indeed, we found a beating in our chests like pebbles in the basin. The beating did not calm down. Surely we saw at that time white men on piebald horses, wearing red turbans that fell down between their shoulders, between the heaven and the earth, squadron upon squadron. They did not hold back anything, and we were not able to fight them for fear.

He said: ʿAbdullah b. ʿAmr b. Zuhayr related to me from ʿUmar b. ʿAbdullah al-ʿAbsī from Rabīʿa, who said: A group of our community who attended, at that time, related to me saying: We hid from them in the narrow passes and gorges, then we attacked them riding at their shoulders until we reached the owner of a gray mule. Around him were white men with beautiful faces. Then he said, "The faces are distorted, turn back!" And they defeated us. The Muslims rode at our shoulders and that was it. We made to turn and look behind us and they were pursuing us, so our group [Page 907] dispersed in all directions. The trembling wore us down until we reached the heights of our land. And if words were related about us we would not know for the terror that was in us. Then, God cast Islam in our hearts.

The flag of the allies of the Thaqīf was held by Qārib b. al-Aswad b. Masʿūd. When the people were defeated he rested the flag against a tree and fled with his cousins from the allies. Only two men were killed from among the Banū Ghiyara: Wahb and al-Lajlāj. When news of the death of al-Lajlāj reached the Prophet, he said: The chief of the young men of the Thaqīf has been killed except for Ibn Hunayda. The flag of the Banū Mālik was with Dhū l-Khimār, and when the Hawāzin were defeated the Muslims followed them. The dead among the Thaqīf in the Banū Mālik numbered almost a hundred of their men, killed under their banner, including ʿUthmān b. ʿAbdullah who fought with them for a long time. He kept urging the Thaqīf and Hawāzin to fight until he was killed. Al-Lajlāj was a man from Banū Kunna. The Messenger of God said to the brother of Banū Kunna: This is the chief of the youth of Banū Kunna, except Ibn Hunayda is al-Ḥārith b. ʿAbdullah b. Yaʿmar b. Iyās b. Aws b. Rabīʿa b. al-Ḥārith, and the Messenger of God was laughing.

Kunna was a woman from Ghāmid, a Yemenite who had given birth in the Bedouin tribes, and she was a slave girl. Al-Ḥārith emancipated all the mamluks of the Banū Kunna. ʿUmar b. al-Khaṭṭāb said to him during his caliphate, "Are you happy that there is a place for the Kunna in both houses of ʿĀmir b. al-Ṭufayl and ʿAlqama b. ʿUlātha?" He replied, "O Commander of the Faithful, I wish that that were so." [Page 908] ʿUmar said, "Would that my mother was Kunna and that God provided me from her charity what He provided you. He was the best of the people to his mother. She would eat food only from his hand. Only he would wash her head, and only he would comb her hair."

They said: The Thaqīf fled. Some elders among them who converted later, and had attended that day said: The Messenger of God continued to seek us according to what we thought. We were turning, when indeed the man among us entered the fortress of al-Ṭāʾif; he thought that the Messenger of God was on his tracks because of his fear of defeat.

Abū Qatāda used to relate: When we met, the Muslims were being defeated. I saw two men fight, a Muslim and a polytheist, and the polytheist was above the Muslim. I went around him until I came to him from behind and struck him on the sinew between his neck and shoulder. He came to me and embraced me such that I smelled on him the breath of death. He almost killed me but that the blood drained from him. He fell, and I killed him and departed, leaving his booty. I met ʿUmar b. al-Khaṭṭāb, and said, "What is the matter with the people?" He replied, "It is the command of God." Then indeed the people returned, and the Messenger of God said, "Whoever kills an enemy and has proof, his booty belongs to him." So I stood up and said, "Who will give evidence for me?" Then I sat down. Then he said, "Whoever makes a killing and he has proof, to him belongs his booty." So I stood up and said, "Who will be my witness?" Then I sat down. Then the Messenger of God said, "Whoever makes a killing and has proof, to him belongs his booty."

ʿAbdullah b. Unays testified for me. Then I met al-Aswad b. al-Khuzāʿī and he testified for me. And all of a sudden, my companion who took the booty no longer denied that I had killed the polytheist. I narrated the story to the Prophet—and he said, "O Messenger of God, the booty of that dead is with me and so I will satisfy him." And Abū Bakr said, "This, by God, will never be. [Page 909] Do not approach one of the lions of God who fight about God and His messenger. He will hand over to you his booty." The Messenger of God said, "He is honest. Give it to him." Abū Qatāda said, "He gave it to me." Ḥāṭib b. Abī Baltaʿa said, "O Abū Qatāda, will you sell me the weapons?" So I sold them to him for seven Awāq. Then I came to Medina and purchased an orchard of date palms from the Banū Salama with it called al-Rudaynī. It was the first property that I obtained in Islam. We continue living from it to this day of ours.

When the Messenger of God went to Ḥunayn, Shayba b. ʿUthmān b. Abī Ṭalḥa promised that he and Ṣafwān b. Umayya—and Umayya b. Khalaf was killed on the day of Badr, and ʿUthmān b. Abī Ṭalha was killed on the day of Uḥud—that if they saw Muḥammad defeated, they would be against him. They followed him. Shayba said: But God entered faith in our hearts. Shayba said: Indeed I was about to kill him, but something came forward until it wrapped my heart and I could not bear that, and I knew that he was protected from me. It was said: He said: Darkness wrapped me until I could not see. So I knew that he was protected from me, and I became convinced of Islam. I have heard another version of this story of Shayba. Shayba b. ʿUthmān used to say: I saw the Messenger of God raid Mecca and be successful, and then set out to the Hawāzin, so I said, "I will set out, and perhaps, take my revenge!" I remembered that my father was killed on the day of Uḥud. Ḥamza had killed him and ʿAlī had killed my uncle. When the Prophet's companions were exposed, I came to him from his right, but all of a sudden al-ʿAbbās stood before me, wearing white armor that appeared silver, and dust was removed from it. I said: His uncle never abandons him. He said: Then I came to him from his left, and lo and behold, there was Abū Sufyān, the son of his uncle. So I said: [Page 910] The son of his uncle will never abandon him! So I came to him from behind him, and it only remained for me to get him with the sword, when all of a sudden a flame was raised between me and him from a fire which looked like lightening. I feared that it would burn me, so I placed my hand on my sight and walked backwards, and the Prophet turned to me and said, "O Shayba, come near me!" Then he put his hand on my chest and said, "O God, take Satan away from him." He said: I raised my head to him, and he was more desirable to me than my hearing or my sight or my heart. Then he said, "O Shayba, fight the disbelievers!" He said: I stepped before him, and I desired by God, to shield him with my soul and with every thing. When the Hawāzin were defeated he returned to his house, and I entered upon him and he said, "Praise God who desired in you better than what you desired for yourself." Then he related to me what I had intended to do with him.

When the defeat was where it was, and the turn was against the Muslims, they spoke about the disbelief and resentment and faithlessness that was in their hearts. Abū Sufyān b. Ḥarb said that their defeat would continue to the seas. He said: A man from the Aslam, who was called Abū Maqīt says, "By God, if I had not heard the Messenger of God forbid your killing, I would have surely killed you!" He said: Kalada b. al-Ḥanbal, the brother of Ṣafwān through his mother, one of the blacks of Mecca, screamed, "Indeed sorcery has become void today." Ṣafwān replied, "Be silent. May God close your mouth! For a lord of the Quraysh is more desirable to me than to be owned by a lord of the Hawāzin." He said: Suhayl b. ʿAmr said, "Muḥammad and his companions will not recover from it!" [Page 911] He said: ʿIkrima says to him, "This is not a saying. Rather the affair is in the hand of God. Muḥammad has nothing of the affair. Indeed, if he is defeated today, to him is the outcome tomorrow." He said: Suhayl says, "Indeed, you follow him but recently!" He said, "O Abū Yazīd, indeed we were, by God, putting down nothing and our minds are our minds. We worship the stones that are neither useful nor harmful."

He said: ʿAbdullah b. Yazīd related to me from Yaʿqūb b. ʿUtba, who said: ʿUthmān b. ʿAbdullah attended it with riders, and he was a slave and a mawla. They were killed at that time with him. Killed with him was also a boy of his, a Christian who was not circumcised. When Ṭalḥa took the booty of the dead from the Thaqīf he passed by him and found him uncircumcised, so he shouted, "O people of the Anṣār, I swear, by God, that the Thaqīf fore skin is not removed!" Mughīra b. Shuʿba said: I heard it and I feared that it would go against us among the Bedouin. So I said, "Do nothing, and your ransom is my father and mother. Surely he is a Christian lad of ours!" Then I began to uncover the dead Thaqīf before him, saying, "Do you think that they are not circumcised?" It was said: Indeed the slave belonged to Dhū l-Khimār and he was a blue-eyed Christian. He was killed with his lord at that time. Abū Ṭalḥa took the booty of the dead. He uncovered him and lo and behold, he was uncircumcised. So he called out in that high voice of his to the Anṣār, and they came to him and he said, "I swear to you, by God, the Thaqīf are not circumcised!" Mughīra b. Shuʿba heard it and became angry within him. He said: And he said, "I will show you, O Abū Ṭalḥa!" and he uncovered ʿUthmān b. ʿAbdullah b. Rabīʿa for him, and said, "This is the lord of the Thaqīf!" Then he came to Dhū l-Khimār, the master of the slave, and lo and behold he was circumcised. Al-Mughīra said: An affair came to me and cut me. I feared that these words against us would be publicized among the Bedouin, unless the community was certain and knew that he was a Christian slave of theirs. He who killed ʿUthmān b. ʿAbdullah was ʿAbdullah b. Abī Umayya. The news reached the Prophet and he said, [Page 912] "May God bless ʿAbdullah b. Abī Umayya! And may God distance ʿUthmān b. ʿAbdullah b. Rabīʿa, for indeed he hated the Quraysh."

He said: the Messenger of God prayed to God to bless ʿAbdullah. It reached him and he said, "Indeed I hope that God will sustain me and make me a martyr in this." He was killed during the siege of al-Ṭāʾif. The Prophet said on the day of Ḥunayn, "If it were not for Ibn Jaththāma the little, the cavalry would be exposed today." A woman from the Khuzāʿa said on the Day of Hunayn:

Indeed the water of Ḥunayn is set free for us.
You may drink from it but never control it.
This the Messenger of God will never control . . .

Ibn Jaʿfar related it to me.

The cavalry of God conquered the cavalry of al-Lāt.
And God best deserves a firm hold.

The Messenger of God dispatched the Sulaym with his vanguard led by Khālid b. al-Walīd. The Messenger of God passed a dead woman, and the people gathered to it. He said, "What is this?" They said, "A woman whom Khālid killed." The Messenger of God commanded a man to overtake Khālid and say, "Surely the Messenger of God forbade you to kill women and old men." The Messenger of God saw another woman and asked about her, and a man said: I killed her, O Messenger of God. I seated her behind me, and she tried to kill me, so I killed her. The Messenger of God commanded that she be buried.

They said: When God defeated the Hawāzin the Muslims followed them and killed them. The Banū Sulaym called out among them, "Stop killing the sons of your mother!" So they raised their spears and desisted from killing (the mother of Sulaym, was Bukma, the daughter of Murra the sister of Tamīm b. Murra). When the Messenger of God saw what they did [Page 913] he said, "See to the sons of Bukma." They did not know that their mother was named Bukma. As for my community, they put down their weapons, and as for their community they raised theirs! The Messenger of God ordered the search for the community. Then he said to his cavalry, "If you catch Bijād do not let him escape! He committed a grave misdeed."

Bijād was from the Banū Saʿd. A Muslim had come to him, and Bijād took him and cut him part by part and burned him in the fire. He knew his crime and he fled. The cavalry caught him attached to Shaymāʾ bt. al-Ḥārith b. ʿAbd al-ʿUzzā, the foster-sister of the Messenger of God. They were rough with her in conversation, and Shaymāʾ bt. al-Ḥārith kept saying, "By God, I am the sister of your master!" But they did not believe her. A group of Anṣār took her and they were the strongest people against the Hawāzin, until they brought her to the Messenger of God. She said, "O Muḥammad, indeed I am your sister!" The Prophet said, "What is the proof of that?" So she showed him a bite mark and said, "You bit me there while I was carrying you on my hip in Wādī al-Sirār. We were at that time with their shepherds. Your father is my father, and your mother, my mother. I competed with you for the breast, do you remember, O Messenger of God?" And the Messenger of God knew the mark. He jumped up and spread his outer garment, and said, "Sit on it!" He welcomed her and his eyes became tearful. He asked her about his foster father and mother. She informed him about their death in the past. Then he said, "If you wish, stay with me for we are loving and generous; but if you like to return [Page 914] to your people and your relatives, return." She said, "I will return to my people." She converted and the Messenger of God gave her three slaves and a slave girl. One of them was called Makḥūl. The slave girl married the slave.

ʿAbd al-Ṣamad said: My father informed me that he reached her children with the Banū Saʿd. Al-Shaymāʾ returned to her home, and the women spoke to her about Bijād. So she returned to the Messenger of God and asked him to gift Bijād to her and to forgive him. He did. Then he ordered a camel or two for her and asked her who was left among them. She informed him about her sister and her brother and their uncle Abū Burqān. She told the Messenger of God about the community. Then the Messenger of God said to her, "Return to al-Jiʿirrāna and you will be with your community, for I am going to al-Ṭāʾif." So she returned to al-Jiʿirrāna. The Messenger of God came to her in al-Jiʿirrāna and gave her cattle and sheep, for herself, and for those who remained from the people of her house.

They said: When the people were defeated, they came to al Ṭāʾif, and a camp was put up in Awṭās. Some of them went towards Nakhla—only the Banū ʿAnaza of the Thaqīf went to Nakhla. The Messenger of God sent cavalry to follow those who went to Nakhla. And he did not follow those who went through al-Thanāya. Rabīʿa b. Rufayʿ b. Uhbān b. Thaʿlaba b. Rabīʿa b. Yarbūʿ b. Sammāl b. ʿAwf b. Imrāʾ l-Qays of the Banū Sulaym caught up with Durayd b. al-Ṣimma. He took the halter of Durayd's camel, for he thought that he was a woman. This was because he was hidden in his hawda. [Page 915] Surprisingly, it was a man, so he knelt his camel. He was an old man of a hundred and sixty years, and he was Durayd. The youth did not know him. The youth said, "I do not desire any other than those who are on the same religion." Durayd said to him, "Who are you?" He replied, "I am Rabīʿa b. Rufayʿ al-Sulamī," and he struck him with his sword to no effect. Durayd said, "Miserable is what your mother armed you with! Take my sword from behind the saddle of the *hawda* and strike with it, above the food and below the brain. Indeed, thus did I kill men. Then, when you get to your mother, inform her that you killed Durayd b. al-Ṣimma, for maybe one day I protected your women." The Banū Sulaym allege that when Rabīʿa struck him, he exposed his perineum and the inside of his thighs were like parchment from riding horses. When Rabīʿa returned to his mother, he informed her of his death, and she said, "By God, he set free three mothers of yours in one evening. And he sheared off the forelock of your father." The youth said, "I did not know."

They said: The Messenger of God sent Abu ʿĀmir al-Ashʿarī on the tracks of those who went to Awṭās. He gave him a flag. With him in that sending was Salama b. al-Akwāʿ, and he used to relate saying: When the Hawāzin were defeated they set up a large camp in Awṭās. Those who dispersed dispersed from them. And those who were killed were killed. And those who were taken prisoner were taken prisoner. We reached their camp, and all of a sudden they were obstructing us. A man challenged to a duel, saying, "Who will fight a duel?" so Abū ʿĀmir fought him. He said: May God be my witness, Abū ʿĀmir killed him and nine others in this manner. When it was his ninth duel a marked man begged for a duel, and Abū ʿĀmir dueled and killed him. When it was the tenth duel, there was a marked man wearing a yellow turban. So Abū ʿĀmir said, [Page 916] "May God be my witness!" He said: And the man says, "May God not witness!" And he struck Abū ʿĀmir and killed him. We carried him while there was a spark of life in him. He appointed Abū Mūsā al-Ashʿarī his successor; Abū ʿĀmir informed Abū Mūsā that the owner of the yellow turban had killed him.

They said: Abū ʿĀmir appointed Abū Mūsā his successor. He gave him the flag and said, "Give my horse and weapons to the Prophet." Abū Mūsā fought them until God conquered for him. He killed the killer of Abū ʿĀmir. He brought his weapons and took them and his horse to the Prophet. He said, "Indeed Abū ʿĀmir commanded me about this. He said, "Say to the Messenger of God, 'Ask God's forgiveness for me.'" The Messenger of God stood up and prayed two bowings. Then he said, "O God, forgive Abū ʿĀmir. Make him among the uppermost of my community in Paradise!" He commanded that the bequest of Abū ʿĀmir be given to his son. He said: Abū Mūsā said, "O Messenger of God, I know that God has forgiven Abū ʿĀmir for he was killed a martyr. But ask God for me." So the Prophet said, "O God, forgive Abū Mūsā and place him with the highest of my companions!" Those who witnessed that called it the day of the two judgments.

They said: the killing of the Banū Naṣr and then of the Banū Ribāb intensified. ʿAbdullah b. Qays—he was a Muslim—began saying, "O Messenger of God, the Banū Ribāb are destroyed." He said: The Messenger of God said, "O God, relieve their misery!"

Mālik b. ʿAwf stood on one of the mountain passes with his riders from among his companions. Then he said, "Wait until your weak go ahead, and then follow at the end." He said, "Observe what you see." They said, "We saw a community on their horses. They had placed their spears on the rumps of the horses." He said, "Those are your brothers the Banū Sulaym. There is no challenge from them. Observe what you see." They said, [Page 917] "We see the backs of men who have placed their spears on the rumps of their horses." He said, "Those are the Khazraj; there is no danger to you from them. Follow the path of your brothers." He said, "Observe what you see." They said, "We see communities like idols on horses." He said, "That is Kaʿb b. Lu'ayy. They will fight you." When the cavalry concealed him [Mālik] he descended from his horse for fear that he would be taken prisoner. Then immediately he sheltered in the trees until he went through Yasūm, a mountain at the top of Nakhla. He fled so they could not reach him. Some said: He said, "What do you see?" They said, "We see a man between two men, marked by a yellow band. He is stamping with his feet on the land. He puts his spear on his shoulder." He said, "That is al-Zubayr, the son of Ṣafiyya. By God, surely he will remove you from your place!" When al-Zubayr saw them he attacked them until he brought them down from the passes. Mālik b. ʿAwf fled and fortified himself in the castle in Liyya (Qasr bi Liyya). It was said that he entered a fortress of the Thaqīf.

It was mentioned to the Prophet that a man who was in Ḥunayn fought a violent battle until he was badly wounded, and the Prophet said, "He is among the people of the fire!" The Muslims were startled by that. Only God knows what occurred to them. When the wound worsened, he took an iron arrowhead from his quiver and killed himself. The Messenger of God commanded Bilal to call out, "Only a believer will enter Paradise," and that God affirms His religion through the sinner.

They said: The Messenger of God ordered that the plunder be collected. His herald called out, [Page 918] "Those who believe in God and the Last day will not be deceitful." The people began to put away their plunder until the Messenger of God was employed over it. ʿAqīl b. Abī Ṭālib came to his wife with his sword soiled with blood. She said, "Indeed, I knew that you fought the polytheists, so what plunder did you take from them?" He said, "This needle. You can sew your garments with it," and he gave it to her. She was Fāṭima bt. al-Walīd b. ʿUtba b. Rabīʿa. The herald of the Messenger of God was heard saying, "Whoever takes something from the plunder, return it." So Aqīl returned it, saying, "By God, I think that your needle is gone," and he threw it in with the plunder.

He said: Ibn Abī Sabra related to me from ʿUmāra b. Ghaziyya that ʿAbdullah b. Zayd al-Māzanī took a bow and shot the polytheists with it. Then he returned it to the plunder. A man came to the Messenger of God with a knot of hair and said, "O Messenger of God, strike me with this," meaning give it to me. The Messenger of God said, "Whatever is for me or the Banū Muṭṭalib, is for you." A man came to him and said, "O Messenger of God, I found this rope when the enemy was defeated and strengthened my saddle with it." He replied, "My share of it is for you. What will you do with the shares of the Muslims?" He said: Mālik b. Anas related to me from Yaḥyā b. Saʿīd from ʿAbdullah b. Mughīra b. Abī Burda that for the battle of Ḥunayn, the Prophet came to the people in their tribes, praying for them. He alighted at one of the tribes, and in a saddle belonging to one of their men they found a necklace of onyx. The Messenger of God came and proclaimed [Page 919] *takbīr* over them, just as he proclaims *takbīr* over the dead. He said: Ibn Abī Sabra related to me from ʿUmāra b. Ghaziyya that the Messenger of God found a chain in the saddle of one of his companions and he blamed him and scolded him, but he did not punish him or destroy his saddle.

They said: The Muslims took two female prisoners at that time. They detested taking them for they were married women. They asked the Prophet about that, and God revealed: *(Forbidden to you) are married women except those whom your right hand possesses*. The Messenger of God said at that time: Pregnant women among the prisoners may not be "trampled" until they are delivered. As for a prisoner who is not pregnant, wait until she menstruates. They asked the Prophet at that time about birth control. He replied, "Pregnancy does not require all the 'water,' and when God desires it, nothing will prevent it."

They said: The Messenger of God prayed *Ẓuhr* at the battle of Ḥunayn. Then he walked away to a tree and sat by it. ʿUyayna b. Ḥiṣn b. Ḥudhayfa b. Badr came to him seeking the blood of ʿĀmir b. al-Aḍbaṭ al-Ashjaʿī—for he was at that time the Lord of the Quraysh. With him was al-Aqraʿ b. Ḥābis. He defended Muḥallim b. Jaththāma for his position among the Khindif, and they quarreled before the Prophet. ʿUyayna says, "O, Messenger of God, by God, I will not leave him until I have brought upon his women the war and sorrow that he brought upon my women." The Messenger of God said, "Take the blood money." But ʿUyayna refused. The voices became raised and the noise increased until a man from the Banū Layth named Mukaytal, who was short and stout, stood up and said, and he had a perfect weapon and shield in his hand, "O Messenger of God, [Page 920] indeed, for what he did to this youth in early Islam I have only found sheep, the first of which have been captured and shot, and the last of which have run away. Enact as today and change tomorrow." The Prophet raised his hand and said, "Accept the blood money of fifty, to be paid immediately, and fifty, when we return to Medina." The Messenger of God continued thus until the people accepted it. Muḥallim b. Jaththama, the killer, was at the edge of the people, and they continued seeing him and saying, "Come to the Messenger of God and ask forgiveness for yourself." So Muḥallim stood up, and he was a tall man reddened with henna and wearing a suit of armor. He had prepared for execution, until he sat before the Messenger of God and his eyes filled with tears. He said, "O Messenger of God, the affair was as it reached you. Indeed I ask God's forgiveness, so pray for my forgiveness." The Messenger of God said, "What is your name?" He replied, "I am Muhallim b. Jaththāma." He said, "You killed him with your weapons in the beginning of Islam! O God, do not forgive Muḥallim!" In a loud voice, seeking the people with it. He said: And he said, "O Messenger of God, it was what has reached you. And I ask forgiveness of God, so pray for my forgiveness." And the Messenger of God replied in a loud voice, seeking the people with his voice, "O God, do not forgive Muḥallim." Until he said it thrice. The Messenger of God returned to his words. Then the Messenger of God said to him, "Stand!" And he stood before the Messenger of God and he let his tears overflow on his cloak. [Page 921] Ḍamra al-Sulamī used to relate, and he was present on that day, saying: We used to talk about what we saw. The Messenger of God moved his lips asking for his forgiveness. But he desired to teach the value of blood with God.

He said: ʿAbd al-Raḥmān b. Abī l-Zinād related to me from ʿAbd al-Raḥmān b. al-Ḥārith from al-Ḥasan al-Baṣrī, who said: When Muḥallim b. Jaththāma died the people buried him and the earth ejected him. They buried him again, and the earth ejected him. Then they buried him again, and the earth ejected him. Then they threw him between two rocks and the lions ate him. He said: Muḥammad b. Ḥarb related to me from Muḥammad b. al-Walīd from Luqmān b. ʿĀmir from Suwayd b. Jabala, who said: When death came to Muḥallim b. Jaththāma, ʿAwf b. Malik al-Ashjaʿī came to him and said, "O Muḥallim, if you are able to return to us you will inform us of what you saw and what you met." He said: He came to him in his sleep a year later, or when God willed, and he said to him, "How are you, O Muḥallim?" He said, "We are well. We found a gracious Lord who forgave us." ʿAwf said, "All of you?" He replied, "All of us except al-Aḥrāḍ." He said, "What is al-Aḥrāḍ?" He replied, "He who is pointed at with the fingers. By God, God did not spend from a thing of mine but it was fully compensated. Indeed, even a cat of my family was destroyed and I was given compensation." ʿAwf said: By God, the confirmation of my dream will come when I go to the family of Muḥallim and ask them about this cat. So he came to them and said, "ʿAwf seeks permission!" So they permitted, and when he entered they said, "You have not been a frequent visitor!" He said, "How are you?" They replied, "We are well. This is the daughter of your brother. Last night she was not sick. And she is this. What is wrong with her is that her father separated from us this night." He said: I said, "Was a cat of yours destroyed?" They said, "Yes. Did you feel sorry for it, O ʿAwf?" [Page 922] He said, "Its information was conveyed and so expect a reward for it in the hereafter."

He said: Usāma b. Zayd related to me from al-Zuhrī from ʿAbd al-Raḥmān b. Azhar, who said: I saw the Prophet in Ḥunayn pass through the men, asking them about the situation of Khālid b. al-Walīd, while I was with him. At that time a youth was brought and the Prophet commanded those who were with him to strike him with whatever was in their hands, and he scattered dust on him.

THE NAMES OF THOSE WHO WERE MARTYRED AT ḤUNAYN

Ayman b. ʿUbayd, who was the son of Umm Ayman, was killed. He was from the Anṣār of the Balḥārith b. al-Khazraj, and a *mawlā* of the Prophet. Also from the Anṣār, Surāqa b. al-Ḥārith and Ruqaym b. Thābit b. Thaʿlaba b. Zayd b. Lawdhān. Abū ʿĀmir al-Ashʿarī was killed in Awṭās. Altogether four were killed.

THE RAID OF AL-ṬĀʾIFA

He said: ʿAbdullah b. Jaʿfar, Ibn Abī Sabra, Ibn Mawhab, ʿAbdullah b. Yazīd, ʿAbd al-Ṣamad b. Muḥammad al-Saʿdī, and Muḥammad b. ʿAbdullah related to me from al-Zuhrī; and also Usāma b. Zayd, Abū Maʿshar, ʿAbd al-Raḥmān b. ʿAbd al-ʿAzīz and Muḥammad b. Yaḥyā b. Sahl, and others who I have not named, people of trust. All have related this tradition to me in portions. I wrote down all that was related to me. They said: When the Messenger of God conquered Ḥunayn, he desired to march to [Page 923] al-Ṭāʾif. He sent al-Ṭufayl b. ʿAmr to Dhū l-Kaffayn—the idol of ʿAmr b. Ḥumama—to destroy it. He commanded him to ask his people to help him and join him in al-Ṭāʾif. Al-Ṭufayl said, "O Messenger of God, advise me." The Messenger of God said, "Spread peace, grant food, be reticent before God, just as an elegant man would be reticent before his family. If you do a bad deed, follow it with a good deed. *For those things that are good remove those that are evil: Be that word of remembrance to those who remember (their Lord)* (Q: 11:114)." He said: So Ṭufayl went out swiftly to his people and destroyed Dhū l-Kaffayn. He stuffed the idol with fire saying:

O Dhū l-Kaffayn we are not your worshipers.
Our birth is more ancient than yours.
Indeed I stuffed your heart with fire.

Al-Ṭufayl hastened and came down with four hundred of his community. They appeared before the Prophet in al-Ṭāʾif after his stay of four days, and he arrived with war machines and mangonels. The Messenger of God said, "O people of al-Azd, who shall carry your banner?" Al-Ṭufayl replied, "He who used to carry it in *jāhiliyya*." The Prophet said, "You are right!" And it was al-Nuʿmān b. al-Zarrāfa al-Lihbī. The Messenger of God dispatched Khālid b. al-Walīd from Ḥunayn to lead the attack. Khālid took some guides to lead him to al-Ṭāʾif. He reached the Messenger of God at al-Ṭāʾif. The Messenger of God commanded that the prisoners be moved to al-Jiʿirrāna. He appointed Budayl b. Warqāʾ al-Khuzāʿī over them. [Page 924] He commanded that the cattle be driven to al-Jiʿirrāna and al-Riththa.

The Messenger of God went to al-Ṭāʾif, and the Thaqīf had repaired their fortress. They had entered it after their defeat at Awṭās and locked themselves in. It was a fortress over their city that had two doors. They trained the skilled to fight and be prepared, and they brought into their fortresses provisions for a year in case they were besieged.

ʿUrwa b. Masʿūd and Ghaylān b. Salama were in al-Jurash to learn the use of the war machines and mangonels. They both desired to aim it against the fortress of al-Ṭāʾif. They were not present at Ḥunayn or at the siege of al-Ṭāʾif. The Messenger of God went from Awṭās and he took the road to Nakhla al-Yamāniyya, then Qarn, then al-Mulayḥ, then Baḥra al-Rughāʾ from Liyya, where he built a mosque and prayed in it.

He said: ʿAbdullah b. Yazīd related to me from Saʿīd b. ʿAmr, who said: One who saw the Messenger of God build a mosque, with his own hands, in Liyya, while his companions transferred the stones to him, related to me that a man from the Banū Layth who had killed a man from Hudhayl was brought before the Prophet. The two litigants applied to the Prophet for a decision, and the Messenger of God handed the Laythī to the Hudhalī, and they took him and cut off his head. It was the first blood stipulated by the Prophet in Islam. The Messenger of God prayed *Ẓuhr* in Liyya, and, at that time, the Messenger of God saw a castle, and he asked about it. They said, "This is the castle of Mālik b. ʿAwf." He said, "Where is Mālik?" They replied, "He observes you now from the fortress of Thaqīf." [Page 925] The Messenger of God said, "Who is in his castle?" They said, "No one is in it." The Messenger of God said, "Burn it!" It burned from the time of the *ʿAṣar* prayer until sun set. The Messenger of God looked at the grave of Abū Uḥayḥa Saʿīd b. al-ʿĀṣ, and the noble grave was in his property. Abū Bakr al-Ṣiddīq said, "May God curse the owner of this grave for surely he was of those who opposed God and His Messenger." His two sons, ʿAmr b. Saʿīd and Abān b. Saʿīd said, and they were with the Messenger of God, "May God curse Abū Quḥāfa (Abū Bakr's father) for he was not hospitable to the guest and did not forbid injustice." The Messenger of God said, "If you curse the dead you harm the living. If you intend polytheists make it general." Then the Messenger of God left Liyya, and took the road that was called al-Ḍayqa—meaning narrow. The Messenger of God said, "Rather, it is *yusra*—easy".

Then he went out to Nakhib until he alighted under a Sidra at the property of a man from Thaqīf. The Prophet sent him a message, saying, "Indeed, you must go out, or we will burn your walls!" But he refused to go out. The Prophet commanded the burning of the walls and whatever was in it.

The Messenger of God proceeded until he alighted close to the walls of the fortress of al-Ṭā'if. He set up his camp there. As soon as the Messenger of God and his companions alighted, al-Ḥubab b. al-Mundhir came to him and said, "O Messenger of God, indeed we are near the fortress. If this decision was due to a command from God, we submit, but if it is an opinion then stay back from the fortress." He said: The Messenger of God was silent.

[Page 926] Amr b. Umayya al-Ḍamrī used to relate saying: As soon as we alighted, we received from their arrows—God only knows how many—as though it was a swarm of locust, and we shielded ourselves from them until the people from the Muslims were wounded. The Messenger of God called al-Ḥubāb and said, "Look for a place raised and at the rear of the people." So al-Ḥubāb set out until he reached the place of the Mosque of al-Ṭā'if, outside the village and he came to the Prophet and informed him. The Messenger of God commanded his companions to move. ʿAmr b. Umayya said: Indeed I saw Abū Miḥjan aim from above the fortress with about ten of his arrow heads as though they were spears, and not an arrow of his fell short of its mark. They said: The Messenger of God ascended to where the masjid al-Ṭā'if stands today. They had sent out a witch, for she received the army in the nude. That was when the Prophet was descending. They defended their fortress with that witch.

When the Messenger of God came down to al-Akama he had two of his wives with him, Umm Salama and Zaynab. The Muslims stormed the fortress. The leader of the people, Yazīd b. Zamaʿa b. al-Aswad came out on his horse and he asked a Thaqīfite for protection desiring to speak to them. They promised him protection but when he came close to them they aimed at him with arrows and killed him. Hudhayl b. Abī l-Ṣalt the brother of Umayya b. Abī l-Ṣalt came out to the gate of the fortress, not thinking that there was anyone with him. It was said that Yaʿqūb b. Zamaʿa had stayed in hiding for him and taken him captive in order to bring him before the Messenger of God. He said, "The killer of my brother, O Messenger of God!" The Messenger of God was happy that he brought him to him. The Prophet [Page 927] gave him the authority, and he cut off his head.

The Messenger of God had struck up two tents for his wives. He used to pray between the two tents, all the time he laid siege to al-Ṭā'if. There was disagreement among us about its siege. Someone said: eighteen days; another, nineteen days; another fifteen days; and all that while he prayed between the two tents two bowings. When the Thaqīf surrendered, Umayya b. ʿAmr b. Wahb b. Muʿattib b. Mālik built a mosque at the place of the Prophet's prayer. In it was a column, and whenever the sun rose over it, since eternity, a sound was heard repeated over ten times. Those who experienced that would say this was the sound of *tasbīḥ* (Glory be to God).

The Prophet established a mangonel. He said: The Messenger of God consulted his companions, and Salmān b. al-Fārisī said to him, "O Messenger of God, I think that you should establish a mangonel against their fortress. Indeed, we in the land of Persia established two mangonels against the fortresses that were established against us. We established mangonels against our enemy and they established mangonels against us. If there were no mangonel, it would be a long stay." The Messenger of God commanded him and he set up a mangonel in front of him. He set it up against the fortress of al-Ṭā'if. It was said: Yazīd b. Zamaʿa brought a mangonel and two war machines. And some said: al-Ṭufayl b. ʿAmr. And some said: Khālid b. Saʿīd arrived from al-Jurash with a mangonel and two war machines. The Prophet spread double-pronged thorns, thorns of the ʿAydān around their fortress. The Muslims entered under the war machine, which was made of cowhide. That day was named al-Shadkha, after it.

[Page 928] Someone asked: What is al-Shadkha? He said: those who were killed among the Muslims—They entered under the war machine, then they crawled with it to the wall of the fortress to breach it, but the Thaqīf sent scraps of iron heated with fire against them and burned the war machine; so the Muslims came out from under it, and among them were those who were wounded. The Thaqīf aimed at them with arrows and some of them were killed.

He said: the Messenger of God ordered them to cut the grape vines and burn them. He said: Who cuts a rope of grapes, for him is a rope in Paradise. ʿUyayna b. Badr said to Yaʿla b. Murra al-Thaqafī, "The cutting of that rewards me?" Yaʿla b. Murra did so. Then Yaʿla came to him and said, "Yes." ʿUyayna said, "For you is the hell-fire." That reached the Messenger of God and he said, "ʿUyayna is more deserving of the fire than Yaʿla." The Muslims began cutting cuttings rapidly.

He said: ʿUmar b. al-Khaṭṭāb called out to Sufyān b. ʿAbdullah al-Thaqafī, "By God, we are surely cutting the provider of your families." Sufyān replied, "Then, you will not destroy the water and soil!" When he saw the cutting, Sufyān called out, "O Muḥammad, why are you cutting our wealth? Indeed you will take it if you are victorious against us. And indeed you will put it down to God and the relatives as you claim!" The Messenger of God said, "Indeed, I can put it down to God and the relatives." So the Messenger of God left it.

Abū Wajza al-Saʿdī narrated: The Messenger of God commanded that every man cut the grapes of five ropes. ʿUmar b. al-Khaṭṭāb came to the Messenger of God and said, "O Messenger of God, [Page 929] surely, it is fully grown and its fruit is not yet harvested." So the Messenger of God commanded that they cut down what was already harvested. He said: So they began to cut the first of the first.

He said: Abū Sufyān b. Ḥarb and al-Mughīra b. Shuʿba proceeded to the Thaqīf and they both said: Grant us protection so that we may speak. So they granted the two protection. They called out to the women from the Quraysh to come to them. But they feared captivity. Among them were the daughter of Abū Sufyān b. Ḥarb, who was married to ʿUrwa b. Masʿūd, and had a son by him, Dāwud b. ʿUrwa, al-Firāsiyya, the daughter of Suwayd b. ʿAmr b. Thaʿlaba, who was married to Qārib b. al-Aswad, and had ʿAbd al-Raḥmān b. Qārib by him, and another woman. When the women refused, the sons of al-Aswad b. Masʿūd said to them, "O Abū Sufyān and Mughīra, can we not lead you to something better than what you have come for. Indeed you know where the property of the Banū al-Aswad is—The Prophet had alighted between them and al-Ṭā'if in a valley called al-ʿAmq—there is no property in al-Ṭā'if that is more significant in ropes (of grapes), nor more significant in provision than that. Nor is there a more significant estate. Indeed, if he cuts it, it will never be restored. So speak to him to take it for himself or leave it to God and the relatives. For indeed between us and him is a relationship of which he is not ignorant." So they spoke to him, and the Messenger of God left it.

A man was standing on the fortress and saying, "Depart, O shepherd of the sheep! Depart, flowing garment of Muḥammad! Depart, slaves of Muḥammad! Do you think we will be miserable over the vine-ropes you take from our vineyards?" The Messenger of God said, "O God, send him to the hell-fire!" Saʿd b. Abī Waqqāṣ said: I aimed at him, and my arrow took his vein, and he fell dead, from the fortress. [Page 930] I saw that the Prophet was happy about that. He said: They began saying about their fortress:

This is the grave of Abū Righāl. He said to ʿAlī, "Do you know, O ʿAlī, what this is? This is the grave of Abū Righāl. They are the community of Thamūd."

They said: Abū Mihjan was on top of the fortress aiming with broad arrow heads and the Muslims were aiming at them. A man from the Muzayna said to his companion, "If we conquer al-Ṭāʾif, you will have women of the Banū Qārib. Indeed, they are the most beautiful women that you will hold, and they will bring a larger ransom if you ransom them." Al-Mughīra b. Shuʿba heard him and said, "O brother of the Muzayna!" He said, "I am at your service!" He said, "Shoot that man," meaning Abū Miḥjan. Indeed, al-Mughīra became zealous when al-Muzannī mentioned the women. He knew that Abū Miḥjan was a marksman, and that an arrow of his did not fail. Al-Muzannī had aimed at him, but his arrow did not do anything. Abū Miḥjan aimed at him with an arrowhead and it fell in his vein and killed him. He said: Al-Mughīra says, "He tempts the men with the women of Banū Qārib." ʿAbdullah b. ʿAmr b. ʿAwf al-Muzannī said to him, and he hears his words, his first and his last, "May God fight you, O Mughīra! You, by God, opposed him for this. Indeed, God has driven him to martyrdom. You, by God, are a hypocrite. By God, if not for Islam I would not leave you until I killed you!" Al-Muzannī kept saying, "Indeed he is very sly and we did not know it. By God, I will never speak to you!" He said: Al-Mughīra asked al-Muzannī to hide that about him. He said. "Never, by God!" He said: This reached ʿUmar b. al-Khaṭṭāb when he was working for ʿUmar in al-Kūfa. And ʿUmar said: By God, al-Mughīra should not be hired for this deed of his!

He said: Abū Miḥjan shot ʿAbdullah b. Abī Bakr, on the day of al-Ṭāʾif, with an arrow. The wound swelled until it became infected. [Page 931] The arrow came out of the wound and Abū Bakr kept it with him. ʿAbdullah b. Abī Bakr died during the caliphate of Abū Bakr. Abū Miḥjan arrived during the caliphate of Abū Bakr and Abū Bakr mentioned the blade and took it out, and said, "O Abū Miḥjan, do you recognize this blade?" He replied, "How could I not recognize it when it was I who sharpened it, and feathered it and arranged it and aimed it at your son? Praise God who honored him with my hand and did not humiliate me with his."

A herald of the Messenger of God called out, "Any slave who comes down from the fortress and comes out to us, is free!" So some ten men set out from the fortress: They were Abū Bakra, al-Munbaʿath—his name was al-Muḍṭajaʿa, but the Messenger of God named him al-Munbaʿath when he converted. He was a slave of ʿUthmān b. ʿAmmār b. Muʿattib; al-Azraq b. ʿUqba b. al-Azraq, who was the slave of Kalada al-Thaqafī of the Banū Mālik—later he became an ally of the Banū Umayyya, and they gave him in marriage; Wardān, the slave of ʿAbdullah b. Rabīʿa al-Thaqafī, the grandfather of al-Furāt b. Zayd b. Wardān; Yuḥannas al-Nabbāl, the slave of Yasār b. Mālik who converted later, and the Prophet returned his rights to him. And they were slaves of al-Ṭāʾif. Ibrāhīm b. Jābir who was the slave of Kharasha al-Thaqafī, and Yasār the slave of ʿUthmān b. ʿAbdullah did not follow him. Abū Bakra Nufaiʿ b. Masrūḥ belonged to al-Ḥārith b. Kalada. He was titled Abū Bakra because he descended from the fortress on a *bakara*—pulley. Nāfiʿ Abū l-Sāʾib was the slave of Ghaylān b Salama. Ghaylan converted [Page 932] later and the Messenger of God returned his rights to him. Marzūq was a youth belonging to ʿUthmān. He did not follow him. The Messenger of God set all of them free.

The Messenger of God handed each man among them to a man from the Muslims to protect and host. Abū Bakra was handed to ʿAmr b. Saʿīd b. al-ʿĀṣ; Al-Azraq to Khālid b. Saʿīd; Wardān to Abān b. Saʿīd; Yuḥannas al-Nabbāl to ʿUthmān b. ʿAffān; Yasār b.

Mālik to Sa'd b. 'Ubāda; and Ibrāhīm b. Jābir to Usayd b. al-Ḥuḍayr. The Messenger of God commanded them to read the Qur'ān to them and teach them the practices.

When the Thaqīf converted, their elders discussed those who were set free—with them was al-Ḥārith b. Kalada—to return them to slavery. The Messenger of God said, "Those whom God set free, cannot be touched." That caused the people of al-Ṭā'if a great hardship. They were very angry about their slaves.

They said: 'Uyayna said, "O Messenger of God, permit me to go to the fortress of al-Ṭā'if and speak to them." So he permitted him, and he went to the fortress and said, "If I come close to you, will I be protected?" They said, "Yes." Abū Miḥjan knew him, and he said, "Draw near." And he went near. And he said, "Enter." And he entered the fortress and said, "Your ransom is my father and mother! By God, surely what I see among you gladdens me. By God, if only the Bedouin had another like you! By God, Muḥammad has not met the likes of you ever. Indeed he grows impatient with your stay, so stand firm in your fortress. Indeed your fortress is inaccessible. Your weapons are many. Your water continues to flow. You do not fear it stopping!" He said: And when he left, the Thaqīf said to Abū Miḥjan, "Indeed we detest his coming in and we fear that he will inform Muḥammad about a fault if he saw it in us or in our fortress." Abū Miḥjan said, "I know 'Uyayna well. There is not from us one more opposed to Muḥammad than he, even if he is with him." When 'Uyayna returned to the Prophet, the Prophet asked him, "What did you say to them?" He said, "I said, [Page 933] 'Enter Islam! By God, Muḥammad will not leave the center of your homes until you come down. So take for yourselves a protection. He has alighted in the courtyards of people of fortresses before you. The Qaynuqā', Naḍīr, Qurayẓa and Khaybar were people of weapons, preparedness, and fortifications.' I persuaded them to abstain, but I was not able." The Messenger of God was silent until he completed his tale, then he said to him, "You lie! You said to them thus and thus!" To which he said: 'Uyayna said, "I ask God's forgiveness." And 'Umar said, "Ask me, and I will dispatch him and cut off his head." The Messenger of God said, "The people will say that I kill my companions." It was said that Abū Bakr was rude to him at that time and said, "Woe unto you, O 'Uyayna! You are always in error. You have done so much of harm to us since the day of the Banū Naḍīr, Qurayẓa and Khaybar. You gathered against us and fought us with your sword. Then you converted just as you claim and you incite our enemies against us!" He said, "I ask God's forgiveness, O Abū Bakr, and repent to Him. I will not repeat it ever!"

They said: The Messenger of God had a *mawlā* belonging to his aunt, Fākhita bt. 'Amr b. 'Āidh b. 'Imrān b. Makhzūm. He was named Māta' and another named Hīt. Māta' used to be in his houses. The Messenger of God did not think that he had an understanding of the affairs of women as men usually do, and he did not think that he had that skill. The Messenger of God heard him say to Khālid b. al-Walīd, and some say to 'Abdullah b. Abī Umayya b. al-Mughīra, "If the Messenger of God conquers al-Ṭā'if tomorrow, do not let Bādiya bt. Ghaylān escape from you."

Indeed she comes in fours and goes in eights.
When she sits, she bends; when she speaks she sings;
When she reclines she weakens.
Between her legs is the likes of a satisfying dish.
Her teeth like the Chamomile
Just as al-Khaṭīm said.
[Page 934] Among the types of Women her creation is established

There is no roughness or fragility
She will make you sink looking at her and she doesn't even notice
Her face is flushed.

The Messenger of God heard his words and said, "I did not know of this harmful understanding of beauty when I set out to al-ʿAqīq! One cannot hold himself when he hears this!" He said, "He shall not enter upon the women of ʿAbd al-Muṭṭalib!" It was said that he said, "Do not let him enter upon one of your women!" And sent both the slaves to the sanctuary—al-Ḥima. They complained of their poverty. So he permitted them to come down every Friday and ask, and then return to their place, until he died. When the Messenger of God died, they both entered with the people. When Abū Bakr became caliph he said, "The Messenger of God expelled you, and you think I will bring you in?" So he expelled them to their places. When Abū Bakr died, they both entered with the people. When ʿUmar became caliph, he said, "The Messenger of God and Abū Bakr expelled you, and you think I will bring you back? Go out to your places!" So they went out to their places. And when ʿUmar was killed they entered with the people.

[Page 935] They said: Abū Miḥjan b. Ḥubayb b. ʿAmr b. ʿUmayr al-Thaqafī said while he was at the fortress of al-Ṭā'if, "O servants of Muḥammad, you, by God, have not met anyone who is better at fighting you than us. You are staying in what you have established, an evil prison. Then you will turn away but you will not reach something that you desire. We are hard hearted (Qasīy) and our father was Qasā. By God, we will not convert as long as you live. We have built an inaccessible fortress!" ʿUmar called out to him, "O Ibn Ḥubayb, we will cut your provisions until you leave this hole of yours. You are a fox in its den and about to leave." Abū Miḥjan said, "O Ibn al-Khaṭṭāb, if you cut the ropes of grapes, surely with water and soil they will be restored." ʿUmar said, "You will not be able to go out to water or soil, for we will never leave from the door of your cave until you die!" He said: Abū Bakr said, "O ʿUmar do not say this. Indeed the Messenger of God is not permitted the conquest of al-Ṭā'if." ʿUmar said, "The Messenger of God said this?" He replied, "Yes." ʿUmar came to the Messenger of God and said, "Is it not permitted to you, O Messenger of God, the conquest of al-Ṭā'if?" He said, "No."

Khawla bt. Ḥakīm b. Umayya b. al-Awqaṣ al-Aslamiyya came, and she was a wife of ʿUthmān b. Maẓʿūn. She said, "O Messenger of God, give me, if God conquers for you, the jewelry of al-Fāriʿa bt. al-Khuzāʿī, or Bādiya bt. Ghaylān. They are among the most beautiful women of Thaqīf." The Messenger of God said to her, "And if it was not permitted to us with the Thaqīf, O Khawla?" He said: Khawla went out and mentioned that to ʿUmar. ʿUmar entered upon the Messenger of God and said, "O Messenger of God did you say to Khawla what she told me you said?" The Messenger of God said, "I said it." ʿUmar said, "O Messenger of God, is it not permitted to you with them?" He replied, "No." He said, "So I should not call [Page 936] the people to depart!" The Messenger of God said, "Of course you should."

ʿUmar called out for the departure. The Muslims began talking to each other. They said, "We will not turn back without conquering al-Ṭā'if! We will not leave until God conquers for us. By God, they are the most low, and least of those whom we met. We met a group of Meccans and a group of Hawāzin. And God dispersed those groups. Rather those are the fox in the den. If we besiege them they will die in this fortress of theirs." The words among them increased and they disputed. They went and spoke to Abū Bakr and Abū Bakr said, "God and His messenger know best. The affair was revealed to him from the heavens." So they spoke to ʿUmar and he refused and said, "We have seen al-Ḥudaybiyya. Only Allah knows the doubt that came to me in al-Ḥudaybiyya. I argued with the Messenger of God with words at that time; would that I did not do so. Rather, that my family and my property were gone! It was good coming to us from God with what He did. There was no conquest better for the people than the peace of al-Ḥudaybīya, without the sword. The people who entered Islam doubled from the day Muḥammad was sent to the day the document was written. Doubt your opinion. The best is what the Messenger of God does. I will never argue with him in this matter, ever. The affair was God's command. He inspires His prophet with what He desires."

The Messenger of God had said to Abū Bakr, "I dreamed that I was given a bowl filled with butter and a cock pecked at it and spilled what was in it." Abū Bakr said, "I do not think that you will get what you desire on this day." The Messenger of God said, "I agree."

He said: Kuthayyir b. Zayd related to me from al-Walīd b. Riyāḥ from Abū Hurayra, who said: When fifteen nights of besieging them had passed, the Messenger of God [Page 937] sought the advice of Nawfal b. Muʿāwiya al-Dīlī and said, "O Nawfal, what do you say or think?" Nawfal said, "O Messenger of God, the fox is in its hole. If you stay over it you will take it. If you leave it nothing will harm you." Abū Hurayra said, "It was not permitted to the Messenger of God to conquer it." He said: The Messenger of God commanded ʿUmar, and he called out for the departure. He said: The people began to clamor about that. The Messenger of God said, "Go in the morning and do battle." So they fought and the Muslims were wounded. The Messenger of God said, "Indeed we will return home if God wills." They rejoiced about that and they obeyed. They began to leave, and the Prophet was laughing. And when the people went in their direction Saʿd b. ʿUbayd b. Asīd b. ʿAmr b. ʿIlāj al-Thaqafī called out, "Is not the tribe established." He said: ʿUyayna b. Ḥiṣn says, "Indeed, by God, a noble glory!" And ʿAmr b. al-ʿĀṣ said, "May God fight you, you praise a polytheistic community calling them undefeatable to the Prophet?" He replied, "I, by God, did not come with you to fight the Thaqīf, but that Muḥammad captures al-Ṭāʾif so that I may take a slave girl from the Thaqīf and impregnate her, and perhaps she will give birth to my son. Indeed the Thaqīf are a fortunate community." ʿUmar informed the Prophet of his words, and the Prophet smiled, and then said, "Such obedient folly!" The Messenger of God said to his companions when they wanted to depart, "Say, there is no God but One. He fulfilled His promise. He helped his servant. He defeated the factions alone." And when they departed, he said: When the Messenger of God departed from al-Ṭāʾif it was said: O Messenger of God, ask God against the Thaqīf, and he said, "O God, guide the Thaqīf and bring them to Islam!"

[Page 938] THE NAMES OF THOSE WHO WERE MARTYRED IN AL-ṬĀʾIF

From the Banū Umayya: Saʿīd b. Saʿīd b. Umayya, and ʿUrfuṭa b. al-Ḥubāb b. Ḥubayb b. ʿAbdManāf b. Saʿd al-Ḥārith b. Kināna b. Khuzayma b. Māzin b. ʿAmr b. ʿĀmir b. Thaʿlaba b. Ḥāritha b. Imrāʾ l-Qays—an ally of theirs.

From the Banū Asad: Yazīd b. Zamaʿa b. al-Aswad, His horse bolted with him—it was called al-Janāḥ—to the fortress of al-Ṭāʾif and they killed him. It was said: He said to them, "Grant me protection until I speak to you." They gave him protection, but then shot at him with arrows until they killed him.

From the Banū Taym: ʿAbdullah b. Abī Bakr b. Abī Quḥāfa; he was shot with an arrow and his wound did not heal. He died in Medina after the death of the Prophet.

From the Banū Makhzūm: ʿAbdullah b. Abī Umayya b. al-Mughīra was shot from the fortress.

From the Banū ʿAdī: ʿAbdullah b. ʿĀmir b. Rabīʿa al-ʿAnazī, an ally of theirs.

From the Banū Sahm: al-Sāʾib b. al-Ḥārith b. Qays, and his brother ʿAbdullah b. al-Ḥārith.

From the Banū Saʿd b. Layth: Julayḥa b. ʿAbdullah b. Muḥārib b. al-Ṣayḥān b. Nāshab b. Saʿd b. Layth.

From al-Anṣār: Thābit b. al-Jadhaʿa; al-Jadhaʿa's name was Thaʿlaba—and al-Ḥārith b. Sahl b. Abī Ṣaʿṣaʿa, and al-Mundhir b. ʿAbdullah b. Nawfal. A total of twelve men.

THE MARCH OF THE PROPHET TO AL-JIʿIRRĀNA, TEN MILES FROM MECCA

[Page 939] They said: The Messenger of God set out from al-Ṭāʾif, and took the road from Daḥnā, passed Qarn al-Manāzil, and Nakhla until he set out to al-Jiʿirrāna. During the march of the Messenger of God, Abū Ruhm al-Ghifārī was at his side on a camel of his wearing two crude sandals on his legs. All of a sudden, his camel shoved the camel of the Messenger of God and the edge of his sandal struck the leg of the Prophet and hurt him. The Messenger of God said, "You hurt me, keep back your leg!" And he rapped Abū Ruhm's leg with his whip. Abū Ruhm said: I was overwhelmed. I feared that the Prophet would reveal a noble Qurʾān about me, and what I did. When we were that morning in Jiʿirrāna, I set out to watch the cattle though it was not my day, fearing that the Prophet might come. The Messenger of God was looking for me. When I had refreshed the camels I asked and they said, "The Messenger of God is looking for you," so I came to him and I waited. He said, "Indeed, you hurt me with your foot which was why I struck you with the whip, so take this sheep in compensation for my striking you." Abū Ruhm said: His satisfaction about me was more desirable to me than the world and what was in it.

ʿAbdullah b. Abī Ḥadrad used to say: I was with the Prophet during his march and he was conversing with me, when my camel began to rub against his camel. My camel was a sturdy camel, and I wanted to turn it away but it would not obey me. It pressed against the camel of the Prophet, and struck the Prophet's leg and he said, "Akh! You hurt me!" And he raised his leg, [Page 940] which was white like the heart of a palm tree, from the stirrup, and pushed my leg with the staff in his hand. He stayed for a while not speaking. By God, I did not alight, for I thought he would reveal suffering about me. He said: When we alighted, I said to my companions, "I will keep watch for you," though that day was not my watch. When I refreshed their camels I said, "Did any one come looking for me?" They said, "The Messenger of God is looking for you." I said to myself, "This, by God, is it!" I said, "Who came?" They said, "A man from the Anṣār." He said: That was most hateful to me for the Anṣār had about them a roughness. He said: Later, a man from the Quraysh came looking for me. He said: I set out fearful until I faced the Messenger of God, and he started to smile at my face. He said, "I hurt you yesterday." Then he said, "Take this portion of sheep." He said: I took it, and I found there to be eight woolly sheep.

Abū Zurʿa al-Juhanī used to relate saying: When the Prophet desired to ride from Qarn on his beast al-Qaṣwā', I would make it kneel before him, and with the halter in my hand restrain it. When he rose to the saddle I handed him the halter and ran behind it. He struck the camel with the whip, and all of that struck me. So he addressed me and said, "The whip struck you?" And I replied, "Yes, by my father and my mother!" He said: When we alighted in al-Jiʿirrāna, lo and behold, there was a pen of cattle in the region of the plunder. He asked about it of the master of the plunder, and he informed him about it something that I do not remember. Then he shouted, "Where is Abū Zurʿa?" He said: I said, "Here I am." He said, "Take these cattle for the whip lash you received yesterday." He said: I counted it and I found a hundred and twenty head. He said: I became rich with the property.

[Page 941] Surāqa b. Juʿsham said: I met the Messenger of God while he was descending from al-Ṭā'if to al-Jiʿirrāna and I stopped in my place. The people went in front of him, in groups, and I fell in with a group of riders from the Anṣār. They began to strike me with their spears, saying, "You! You! What are you?" And they pretended not to know me. Until, when I was near and I knew that he heard my voice, I took the document that Abū Bakr wrote, and I put it between two of my fingers, then I raised my hand and called out, "I am Surāqa b. Juʿsham, and this is my document!" The Messenger of God said, "It is the day of fulfillment, get him close!" And I was drawn close to him such that I could see his leg in the stirrup, like the heart of a palm tree (white). When I reached him, I greeted and handed to him the prescribed tax. I did not remember anything to ask him about except that I said, "O Messenger of God, do you think those camels that have lost their way and descend to my water basin, which I have filled for my camels, will bring me a reward if I quench their thirst?" The Messenger of God said, "Yes. To all who possess a pure heart is a reward."

He said: ʿAbdullah b. ʿAmr b. Zuhayr related to me from al-Maqburī from Abū Hurayra, who said: A man from the Aslam stood before the Messenger of God with his cattle, while the Messenger of God was on his camel, and said, "This is a gift that I give to you." The Prophet said, "Who are you?" He replied, "A man from the Aslam." The Prophet said, "Indeed, I do not accept gifts from polytheists." He said, "O Messenger of God, indeed I believe in One God and His messenger. I have handed the tax to Burayda b. al-Ḥuṣayb [Page 942] the collector for my property. He said: Burayda approached and caught up with the Prophet and said, "He speaks the truth, O Messenger of God. This is a noble from my community and he stays in al-Ṣifāḥ." He said, "And what brings you to Nakhla?" He said, "It is more fertile than al-Ṣifāḥ today." Then the Prophet said, "We are riding on the backs of camels, as you see, so meet us in al-Jiʿirrāna. He said: He set out running in front of the camel of the Messenger of God saying, "O Messenger of God, shall I drive the cattle to al-Jiʿirrāna?" The Messenger of God said, "Do not bring them. But come to us at al-Jiʿirrāna and we will give you other cattle, if God wills!" He said, "O Messenger of God, prayer will overtake me while I am at the resting place of the camels. Shall I pray there?" He said, "No." He said, "It will overtake me while I am in the pasture of the cattle and I should pray in it?" He said, "Yes." He said, "O Messenger of God, perhaps the water will be far from us and the man will approach his wife?" He said, "Yes, and he will perform tayammam." He said, "O Messenger of God, there will be menstrual blood with us." He said, "She will perform tayammam." He said: He joined the Messenger of God in al-Jiʿirrāna and he gave him a hundred sheep.

They said: The Bedouin lay in his path questioning the Messenger of God, and they increased against him until they forced him to the Samura tree, grabbed his cloak and took it out, and he was like a piece of the moon. The Messenger of God stood, saying, "Give me my cloak! Give me my cloak! If the number of these trees (*ʿIḍa*) were cattle I would apportion it among you, and you will find that I am neither stingy nor cowardly nor false."

[Page 943] Then, when he was at the apportioning he said, "Give even the thread and the needle. Never steal. Indeed stealing is a scandal and brings hell-fire and disgrace on the Day of Judgment!" Then he took a hair from the side of a camel and said, "By God, what God grants as booty to you is not permissible to me, not the likeness of this hair; except the fifth. And the fifth I will return to you."

They said: The Messenger of God reached al-Jiʿirrāna, and the prisoners and the plunder with them were put away. The prisoners had used a fence to shade them from the sun, and when the Messenger of God saw that fence, he asked about it and they said, "O Messenger of God, these prisoners from the Hawāzin asked for protection from the sun." The prisoners numbered six thousand and the camels numbered twenty-four thousand. The amount of the plunder was not known. They had said more or less forty thousand. When the Messenger of God arrived he commanded Busr b. Sufyān al-Khuzāʿī to go to Mecca and purchase material for the prisoners to clothe them with the cloth of Muʿaqqad. A man among them should not go out except dressed. Busr purchased clothes and dressed the prisoners, all of them.

We asked permission from the Messenger of God about the prisoners he had distributed and given to other men. A woman from them was with ʿAbd al-Raḥmān b. ʿAwf, who had intercourse with her as his property. The Messenger of God had gifted her to him in Ḥunayn. He resisted her at al-Jiʿirrāna until she menstruated; then, he had intercourse with her. The Messenger of God gave Ṣafwān b. Umayya another. He gave ʿAlī b. Abī Ṭālib a slave girl named [Page 944] Rayṭa bt. Hilāl bt. Ḥayyān b. ʿUmayra; he gave ʿUthmān b. ʿAffān a slave girl named Zaynab b. Ḥayyān b. ʿAmr. ʿUthmān had intercourse with her and she detested him. ʿAlī did not have intercourse. The Messenger of God gave ʿUmar b. al-Khaṭṭāb a slave girl, and ʿUmar gave her to his son, Abdullah b. ʿUmar. Ibn ʿUmar sent her to his uncle in Mecca of the Banū Jumaḥ to improve her until he circumambulated the house and then came to them. She was a slave girl, pure and admirable.

ʿAbdullah b. ʿUmar said: I arrived in Mecca and circumambulated the house, and I set out from the place of prayer desiring to take the slave girl, when I saw an aggressive people, so I said, "What is the matter with you?" They said, "The Messenger of God has returned the women of the Hawāzin and their children." He said: So, I said, "That female companion of yours is with the Banū Juma, go and take her!" And they went and took her.

The Messenger of God gave Jubayr b. Muṭʿim a slave girl from the prisoners of the Hawāzin, and she was not impregnated. The Messenger of God gave Ṭalḥa b. ʿUbaydullah a slave girl and Ṭalḥa had intercourse with her. And he gave Saʿd b. Abī Waqqāṣ a slave girl. The Messenger of God gave Abū ʿUbayda b. al-Jarrāḥ a slave girl and he impregnated her. The Messenger of God gave al-Zubayr b. al-Awwām a slave girl. This was all in Ḥunayn.

When the Messenger of God returned to al-Jiʿirrāna, he waited for the delegation to come to him. He began with the wealth and apportioned it. He gave the first of the people, and their hearts were reconciled (*muallafa Qulubuhum*). The Messenger of God had plundered much silver; four thousand measures. The plunder was gathered in front of the Prophet. Abū Sufyān b. Ḥarb came, and before him was the silver. He said, "O Messenger of God, you have become the most wealthy among the Quraysh!" The Messenger of God smiled. Abū Sufyān said, "Give me from this wealth, O Messenger of God!" The Messenger of God said, "O Bilāl, weigh for Abū Sufyān four measures, [Page 945] and give him a hundred camels." Abū Sufyān said, "Give my son Yazīd!" The Messenger of God said, "Weigh for Yazīd four measures and give him a hundred camels." Abū Sufyān said, "Give my son Muʿāwiya, O Messenger of God!" He said, "Weigh for him, O Bilāl, four measures, and give him a hundred camels." Abū Sufyān said, "Surely you are generous. May your ransom be my father and mother! Surely I fought you and the goodness of the battle was yours. Then I made peace with you and the goodness of the peace is yours. May God reward you well!" And, the Messenger of God gave the Banū Asad.

He said: Maʿmar related to me from al-Zuhrī from Saʿīd b. al-Musayyib and ʿUrwa b. al-Zubayr, who said, Ḥakīm b. Ḥizām related to us: I asked the Messenger of God in Ḥunayn for a hundred camels, and he gave them to me. Then I asked him again for a hundred and he gave them to me. Then I asked him for another hundred and he gave them to me. Then the Messenger of God said, "O Ḥakīm b. Ḥizām indeed this wealth is sweet greenness. Who takes it with generosity of soul will have blessings with it. Who takes it with pride will have no blessings from it, like the one who eats and is not satisfied. The hand above (that gives) is better than the one below (that takes). When you begin start with your dependants!" He said: Ḥakīm said, "By Him who sent you with the truth, I will not take anything from anyone after you!" ʿUmar b. al-Khaṭṭāb used to call him to give him, but he refused to take it, so ʿUmar said, "O People, I testify to you about Ḥakīm that I called him to give him, but he refused to take it." He said: Ibn Abī l-Zinād related to us that: Ḥakīm took the first hundred and then left.

The Banū ʿAbd al-Dār—al-Nuḍayr, who was the brother of al-Naḍr b. al-Ḥārith b. Kalada, [Page 946] had a hundred camels. The Banū Zuhra—Asīd b. Ḥāritha was an ally of theirs—had a hundred camels. He gave al-ʿAlāʾ b. Jāriya fifty camels. He gave Makhrama b. Nawfal fifty camels. I saw ʿAbdullah b. Jaʿfar deny that Makhrama took a share in that. He said, "I did not hear any one of my people mention that he was given something." From the Banū Makhzūm: al-Ḥārith b. Hishām a hundred camels. He gave Saʿīd b. Yarbūʿ fifty camels. He gave the Banū Jumaḥ Ṣafwān b. Umayya a hundred camels. He says that he circumambulated with the Prophet, and the Prophet scrutinized the plunder. When he passed by the ravine of the booty God gave him, filled with plunder and camels and their shepherds. Ṣafwān admired it and began to look at it, and the Messenger of God said, "Does this ravine please you Abū Wahb?" He said, "Yes." The Prophet said, "It is for you, and what is in it." Ṣafwān said, "I testify that no one will give this up, except the Prophet. And I testify that you are the Messenger of God." He gave Qays b. ʿAdī a hundred camels. He gave ʿUthmān b. Wahb fifty camels. And, he gave Suhayl b. ʿAmr, from the Banū ʿĀmir b. Luāyy, a hundred camels. He gave Ḥuwayṭib b. ʿAbd al-ʿUzzā a hundred camels. He gave Hishām b. ʿUmar fifty camels. He gave among the Bedouin; to al-Aqraʿ b. Ḥābis al-Tamīm a hundred camels. He gave ʿUyayna b. Badr al-Fazārī a hundred camels. He gave Mālik b. ʿAwf a hundred camels. He gave al-ʿAbbās b. Mirdas al-Sulamī four camels. Al-ʿAbbās rebuked the Prophet with a poem saying:

It was spoil that I gained when I charged on my horse
The people in the vast plain,
[Page 947] And by inciting the soldiers in order to go loaded.
When they sleep, I stay awake
My spoil and that of ʿUbayd my horse is shared by ʿUyayna and al-Aqraʿ
A few camels given to me the same number as its four legs.
Though I protect my people in battle I was not given anything nor prevented.
Yet neither Ḥiṣn nor Ḥābis are better than Mirdās in the gathering.
I am not inferior to either of them
And he whom you demean today will not be exalted.

Abū Bakr raised his verses before the Prophet, and the Prophet said to al-ʿAbbās, "Are you not he who says, 'My portion and the portion of al-ʿUbayd became the portion of al-Aqraʿ and ʿUyayna?'" And Abū Bakr said about it, "By my father and my mother, O Messenger of God, it is not thus!" He said: The prophet said, "How then?" He said: Abū Bakr related it just as ʿAbbās said it, and the Prophet said, "It is the same thing whether I begin with al-Aqraʿ or ʿUyayna?" Abū Bakr said, "By my father and my mother, you are neither a poet nor a literati. And it is not appropriate for you!" The Messenger of God said, "Cut his tongue from me," meaning silence him. So he gave him a hundred camels, and some said, fifty. The people were alarmed by the words of the Messenger of God. They said that he commanded that ʿAbbās be maimed. It was disputed among us about what the Messenger of God gave the people at that time.

ʿAbdullah b. Jaʿfar related to me from Ibn Abī ʿAwn from Saʿd from [Page 948] Ibrāhīm and Yaʿqūb b. ʿUtba. They said: They were given the surplus of the plunder. He said: Mūsā b. Ibrāhīm related to me from his father, who said: It was from the fifth. Two sayings confirm that it was from the fifth.

He said: Saʿd b. Abī Waqqāṣ said, "O Messenger of God, you gave ʿUyayna b. Ḥiṣn and al-Aqraʿ b. Ḥābis a hundred, and a hundred, and you left Juʿayl b. Surāqa al-Ḍamrī!" The Messenger of God said, "By Him who holds my soul in His hands, to Juʿayl b. Surāqa is better than what is sufficient for the filling of the earth, all of it, like ʿUyayna and al-Aqraʿ. But I reconciled them in order to convert them, and I entrusted Juʿayl b. Surāqa to his Islam."

The Messenger of God sat, and in the garment of Bilāl was silver which he took hold of for the people according to what God showed him. Dhū l-Khuwayṣira al-Tamīm came to him and said, "Be just, O Messenger of God!" The Messenger of God said, "Woe unto you! Who is just if I am not just?" ʿUmar said, "Hand him to me and I will cut off his head!" The Prophet said, "Leave him, for indeed he has followers! One of your prayers and fasting are less in comparison with their prayers and fasting. They read the Qurʾān and do not exaggerate the exaltation. They pierce the religion as an arrow pierces the killed. The marksman looks at its feathers and sees nothing, looks in the arrowhead and sees nothing, then looks at its sinew and sees nothing. It has sped ahead with no trace of entrails or blood. They set out against a group of Muslims. I saw them, indeed, with a black man; [Page 949] one of his hands was like a woman's, the other a piece of shaking flesh." Abū Saʿīd used to say: I testify that I have heard ʿAlī narrate this tradition.

ʿAbdullah Ibn Masʿūd said: I heard a man from the Hypocrites at the time the Messenger of God gave those gifts. He says, "Indeed, they were gifts that God did not desire." I said, "Indeed, by God, I will inform the Messenger of God of what you said." So I came to the Messenger of God and I informed him. His color changed until

I regretted what I did to him, and I wished I had not informed him. Then he said, "May Allah bless my brother Moses. He was harmed by more than this and he was patient." Muʿattib b. Qushayr al-ʿAmrī used to talk about this. Then the Messenger of God commanded Zayd b. Thābit to count the people and the plunder, and then disperse it among the people. Their portions were, for every man four camels or forty sheep. If it was a rider, he took twelve camels or a hundred and twenty sheep. If he had more than one horse with him he did not apportion for him.

A RECORD OF THE PARTY OF HAWĀZIN

They said: The party of Hawāzin arrived, and in the party was the foster uncle of the Prophet, who said at the time, "O Messenger of God, surely in this enclosure are those who were responsible for you from your maternal and paternal aunts, as well as your nursemaids. We nursed you in our rooms, [Page 950] and suckled you at our breast. Surely, I saw you suckling and I did not see one better than you; I saw you weaned, and I did not see one weaned better than you. Then I saw you as a youth, and I did not see a better youth. In you the characteristics of goodness were perfected. We were in your family and your tribe. So give us of your generosity, and may God give you of His generosity!" The Messenger of God said, "I waited for you until I thought you would not come."

The prisoners were apportioned. Two portions went with them. Fourteen men from the Hawāzin became Muslims. They brought Islam to those who followed them from their people. The head of the people and the speaker was Abū Ṣurad Zuhayr b. Ṣurad. He said, "O Messenger of God, surely we are your family and your tribe. We have suffered trials that you know. O Messenger of God, surely in this enclosure are your paternal and maternal aunts and your nursemaids who were responsible for you. If we fostered Ḥārith b. Abī Shimr and al-Nuʿmān b. al-Mundhir, and they reached similar to that which you have reached, we would hope for their kindness and their profit. You are the best of the fostered." It was said: Indeed Abū Ṣurad said at that time, "Surely in this enclosure are your sisters and paternal aunts and the children. The most distant of them are close to you. O Messenger of God, indeed they nursed you in their rooms, and suckled you at their breasts. They seated you on their laps and you were the best of their responsibilities!" And he said:

> Grant us, O Messenger of God, with generosity.
> Indeed you are the man that we hoped for, and rely on.
> Grant women that were crippled by fate,
> Their gathering torn out and their life changed.
> [Page 951] Grant women you used to suckle from.
> Then your mouth filled with their flowing milk,
> Those you as a child used to suckle from.
> Then it beautified you, what you took and what you left.
> Would you not reach those women with blessings that you distribute?
> You who are the most wise even when you are tested.
> Do not make us as those who lose their honor.
> Keep us, indeed we are a good community.
> Indeed we are grateful for gifts even after a long time,
> And with us after this day is a preserving.

The Messenger of God said, "Indeed the best of the traditions is the most trustworthy tradition. With me are those whom you see from the Muslims. Are your children and your women more loved by you than your property?" They said, "O Messenger of God, you let us choose between our relatives and our property? We would not trade anything for our relatives, so return to us our children and our women!" The Prophet said, "As for what is for me and the Banū ʿAbd al-Muṭṭalib, it is for you, and I will ask the people for you. When I pray *Ẓuhr* with the people, say, 'Indeed we ask the Messenger of God to intercede with the Muslims, and for the Muslims to intercede with the Messenger of God!' And, indeed, I will say to you, 'What was for me and for the Banū ʿAbd al-Muṭṭalib is for you.' And I will ask the people for you." And when the Messenger of God prayed *Ẓuhr* with the people, they stood up and spoke about what the Messenger of God commanded them. They said, "Indeed we ask the Messenger of God to intercede with the Muslims and the Muslims to intercede with the Messenger of God!" And the Messenger of God said, "As for what is for me and the ʿAbd al-Muṭṭalib, it is for you." Then, the Muhājirūn said, "What was for us is for the Messenger of God." And the Anṣār said, "What was for us is for the Messenger of God!" Al-Aqraʿ b. Ḥābis said, "As for me and the Banū Tamīm, no!" And ʿUyayna b. Ḥiṣn said, [Page 952] "As for me and the Fazāra, no!" And ʿAbbās b. Mirdās al-Sulamī said, "As for me and the Banū Sulaym, no!" The Banū Sulaym said, "What is for us is for the Messenger of God!" ʿAbbās said, "You put me to shame!"

Then the Messenger of God stood up in the midst of the people and spoke and said, "Indeed, those people come as Muslims. I was hesitant about them, so I let them choose between their women and children, and their property. They do not equate their women and children with anything. He who has with him something from them and is willing to return it, let him return it. And he who refuses among you and holds to his rights, should he return them, there will be for every amount six camels from the first of what God grants us as booty. He said: So command your authorities to hand that to us so we know. They said: O Messenger of God, we are satisfied and we submit!

Zayd b. Thābit used to go around the Anṣār asking them, did you submit with satisfaction. They informed him they submitted and were satisfied. Not a single man disagreed. ʿUmar b. al-Khaṭṭāb sent to the Muhājirūn asking them about that. Not one man among them disagreed. Abū Ruhm used to go around the Bedouin tribes. They gathered the experts, and those trustworthy that the Messenger of God sent. They agreed on one saying: their submission, their satisfaction, and their giving up of the prisoners who were in their hands. The woman who was with ʿAbd al-Raḥmān b. ʿAwf was permitted to choose to stay or return to her people. She chose her people and returned to them. Those who were with ʿAlī, ʿUthmān, Ṭalḥa and Ṣafwān b. Umayya and Ibn ʿUmar were returned to their people. As for she who was with Saʿd b. Abī Waqqāṣ, she chose Saʿd and had a son by him.

ʿUyayna was permitted to choose a prisoner and he took a head from them. He saw a very old woman and he said: This is the mother of the tribe! Perhaps they will pay a high ransom for her. Maybe [Page 953] she has a noble lineage in the tribe! Her son came to ʿUyayna and said, "Would you take a hundred camels?" He said, "No." And he withdrew from him and left him for a while. The Old woman kept saying to her son, "Why would you pay a hundred camels? Leave him, for soon he will leave me without a ransom." When ʿUyayna heard this he said, "I have never seen such a trick as today. Indeed, this woman cheats me. By God, I will send you away." Then her son passed by him, and he said, "Would you take the old woman for the offer you made?" Her son said, "I will not exceed fifty." ʿUyayna said, "I will not do it." He said: He hesitated for a while, and he passed by him another time and ʿUyayna confronted him and said, "Will you take the old woman for your offer?" The youth said, "I will not give you more than twenty-five portions. This is the maximum I can give." ʿUyayna said, "By God, I will not. After a hundred portions, twenty-five!" But when ʿUyayna became fearful that the people would disperse and depart, ʿUyayna came to him and said, "Would you give me what you offered?" The youth said, "If you will take ten portions I will give them to you." ʿUyayna said, "By God, No." But when the people departed, ʿUyayna called out to him, "For you is what you offered me if you wish." The youth said, "Release her and I will give you a beast to ride on." He said, "No, by God, why do I need your beast?" He said: ʿUyayna blamed himself for it saying, "I have not seen such a day!" The youth said, "You did this to yourself. You chose a very old woman, and, by God, her breasts are not rounded, her stomach will not conceive, her mouth is not cooling, and her companion does not care. But you chose her from among those you saw." ʿUyayna said, "Take her. There are no blessings of God in her. Nor do I have a need for her!" He said: The youth says, [Page 954] "O ʿUyayna, indeed the Messenger of God clothed the prisoners, but skipped her, so will you give her clothing?" He said, "No, by God, I have nothing for her with me!" He said, "Don't do it! As you wish!" But he did not depart from him until he took from him a covering garment. Then the youth turned away, saying, "Indeed you lack an awareness of opportunity!" ʿUyayna complained to al-Aqraʿ of what happened, and al-Aqraʿ said, "By God, you neither picked a young virgin nor one plump and middle aged; nor an old woman of nobility. You intended a needy old man in the Hawāzin and imprisoned his wife." ʿUyayna said, "It is so."

The Banū Tamīm with al-Aqraʿ held on to their prisoners. The Messenger of God made the ransom six camels; three camels were four years old, and three, five years. Muʿādh b. Jabal used to say: The Messenger of God said at the time, "If loyalty or slavery were confirmed on one of the Bedouin, it would be affirmed today. But rather, it is captivity and ransom." Abū Ḥudhayfa apportioned the plunder.

The Messenger of God said to the delegation, "What happened to Mālik (b. ʿAwf)?" They said, "He fled and attached himself to the fortress of al-Ṭāʾif with the Thaqīf." The Messenger of God said, "Inform him that if he becomes a Muslim I will return his family and property to him and give him a hundred camels." The Messenger of God commanded [Page 955] the imprisonment of the family of Mālik in Mecca with their aunt Umm ʿAbdullah bt. Abī Umayya. The delegation said, "O Messenger of God, those are our lords, the most dear to us." The Messenger of God said, "Indeed I desire the best for them." He held the property of Mālik and did not apportion it. When the news reached Mālik b. ʿAwf of what Muḥammad did with his people, and what he promised him, and that his family and his property were preserved, Mālik feared the opposition of the Thaqīf against him, that they knew what the Messenger of God said to him, and that they would, therefore, imprison him. He commanded that his riding animal be brought to Daḥnā. Then, he ordered his horse to be brought to him at night, and set out from the fortress by night, and raced until he came to Daḥnā, from where he rode his camel and joined the Messenger of God who caught up with him riding from al-Jiʿirrāna. The Prophet returned his family and his property and gave him a hundred camels, and Mālik converted and his Islam was good. It was also said that he joined the Messenger of God in Mecca.

The Messenger of God appointed him over those who converted among his people, and those tribes around al-Ṭā'if from the Hawāzin and Fahm. A group of Muslims joined him. The Prophet granted him a banner. He used to fight those who were disbelievers. He raided the Thaqīf with them and fought them. The cattle did not leave the Thaqīf, but he attacked them. And he returned when he returned and the people grazed their cattle. They felt secure when they saw the Prophet turn away from them. But they were not able to graze, except Mālik took it. And Mālik did not attack a man except he killed him. He used to send the Prophet the fifth from what he captured: once, a hundred camels; and once a thousand sheep. Indeed he attacked the cattle of the people of al-Ṭā'if and captured a thousand sheep in a single evening. Abū Miḥjan b. Ḥabīb b. ʿAmr b. ʿUmayr al-Thaqafī said about that:

> The enemies fear us
> But the Banū Salima raid us.
> [Page 956] Mālik brought them to us.
> Breaking the agreement and the sacred.
> They came to us in our settlement.
> They were people of revenge.

Mālik b. ʿAwf said:

> I did not see nor hear one like Muḥammad in all the people.
> When asked, he gave generously
> And if you wish he will predict the future
> And when the battalion grinds its teeth and strikes with swords
> At that time he (Muḥammad) is a lion protecting its cubs in the midst of the dust
> Ready to attack.

They said: When the Messenger of God gave the Quraysh and the Bedouin tribes some of the plunder, he did not give the Anṣār anything. This angered the community of Anṣār among themselves, until the words were many and one of them said, "The Messenger of God has found his community. When there is battle, we are his companions; as for when he apportions, it is his community and his tribe. We would like to know from whom this arrived. If it was from God, we will be patient. [Page 957] If this is from the opinion of the Messenger of God, we will solicit him demand an explanation." That reached the Messenger of God and he became very angry. When Saʿd b. ʿUbābda came to him the Messenger of God said to him, "What did your people say about me?" He replied, "What did they say, O Messenger of God?" He said, "They said, 'As for when it is the battle, we are his companions; as for when he apportions, it is his people and his tribe. We desire to know from where this is. If it is from the command of God, we will be patient; if it is from the opinion of the Messenger of God we will solicit him.'" "And where are you about that, Saʿd?" Saʿd replied, "O Messenger of God, what am I except one of them? Indeed we would like to know from where this comes?" The Messenger of God said, "Gather those of the Anṣār over here in this enclosure."

So the Anṣār gathered in that enclosure. Men from the Muhājirūn came, and he let them, and they entered. And others came and he returned them. And when they gathered to him, Saʿd b. ʿUbāda came to him and said, "O Messenger of God I have gathered this community of Anṣār for you." The Messenger of God came to them, and the anger was visible on his face. And he praised God and commended him with what God deserved. Then he said, "O people of the Anṣār, it has reached me that angry words were found among yourselves. I came to you in your error, and has not God guided you? I came to you in your poverty, and did not God enrich you? In enmity, and did not God reconcile you?" They replied, "But, of course. God and his messenger are most kind and most gracious!" He said, "Why do you not answer me, O people of the Anṣār?" They said, "What shall we answer you, O Messenger of God? Kindness and graciousness belong to the Messenger of God." He said, "By God, if you wished you could have said, and you would have spoken truly, You came to us discredited and we trusted you; you were alone, and we helped you. [Page 958] Outcast, and we gave you refuge. In distress, and we comforted you! You are angry amongst yourselves, O people of the Anṣār, about something of this world; that I reconciled a people to bring them to Islam, while I entrusted you to your Islam. Are you not satisfied that the people go with the cattle and camels while you return with the Messenger of God to your saddles? By Him in whose hand is the soul of Muḥammad, if not for the migration I was a man from the Anṣār. If the people of Mecca went to a gorge, and the Anṣār to a gorge, I would go to the gorge of the Anṣār. I will write for you a document about al-Bahrayn, that from after me it will be for you, especially, and not the people of Mecca!" And it was at that time the best of what God made for him from the Anṣār. They said, "What is our need in the world after you, O Messenger of God?" He replied, "Indeed, after me you will see selfishness. Be patient until you meet God and His messenger. Indeed your place of meeting is the basin, which is as large as that between Ṣanʿa and ʿUmān. The bowls are more than the number of stars. O God, bless the Anṣār, the children of the Anṣār, and the children of the children of the Anṣār!" He said: The people cried until they wet their beards. They said, "We are satisfied, O Messenger of God, with a share and a portion." The Messenger of God turned back and they dispersed.

The Messenger of God reached al-Jiʿirrāna on Thursday the fifth of Dhū l-Qaʿda. He stayed in al-Jiʿirrāna thirteen days. When he desired to turn back to Medina, he set out from al-Jiʿirrāna on Wednesday night, twelve nights remaining in Dhū l-Qaʿda. He donned his *iḥrām* at the furthest mosque (al-masjid al-Aqsā), which was below the *wādī* [Page 959] on a remote slope. It was the place of prayer of the Messenger of God when he was in al-Jiʿirrāna. As for the closest mosque, a man from the Quraysh built it and he marked that place with it.

The Messenger of God permitted only those in *iḥrām* to enter the wādī. He did not stop reciting the *labbayka* until he touched the black stone. It was said: When he saw the House [Kaʿba] he stopped reciting the *labbayka.* When he came, he knelt his camel at the gate of Banū Shayba. He entered and circumambulated thrice speedily from corner to corner. Then he set out and circumambulated between al-Ṣafā and al-Marwa on his camel. When he reached al-Marwa on the seventh circumambulation, he shaved his head. Abū Hind ʿAbd Banū Bayāḍa shaved him. Some said that Khirāsh b. Umayya shaved him. The Messenger of God did not drive the sacrificial animals from there. Then the Messenger of God turned towards al-Jiʿirrāna at night as though he were to spend a night in it. When he returned to al-Jiʿirrāna he set out on Thursday and entered Wādī Jiʿirrāna. He kept on this valley until he came to Sarif. Then he took the road until he reached Marr al-Ẓahrān.

The Messenger of God appointed ʿAttāb b. Asīd over Mecca. He appointed Muʿādh b. Jabal and Abū Mūsā al-Ashʿarī to teach the people Qur'ān and Fiqh. He said to him, "Do you know over whom I appoint you?" He replied, "God and His Messenger know better!" He said, "I have appointed you over the people of God. Tell them four things from me: Conditions on sale contracts are not permitted. Borrowing and selling in the same contract is not permitted. There can be no sale without guarantee. Do not eat the profit/usury that is not yours."

ʿAttāb b. Asīd was in charge of the people for the pilgrimage that year—it was the year eight—in the absence of the Messenger of God over the *Ḥajj*. But he was the commander of Mecca [Page 960] and people from the Muslims and the polytheists performed the *Ḥajj* according to their times. Indeed, it was said that the Messenger of God appointed him over the pilgrimage. The Messenger of God arrived on Friday three days from the end of Dhū al-Qaʿda.

THE ARRIVAL OF ʿURWA B. MASʿŪD

They said: When Muḥammad besieged the people of al-Ṭāʾif, ʿUrwa b. Masʿūd was learning to make armored vehicles and Mangonels. Then he returned to al-Ṭāʾif after the Messenger of God turned away. He made armored cars and mangonels and prepared that until God deposited Islam in his heart, and he arrived in Medina before the Prophet and converted. Then he said, "O Messenger of God, grant me permission to go to my people and invite them to Islam, for by God, I do not see one turn away from a religion like this. I will approach my companions and my people with a good approach. A party never arrived upon its people except those who arrived with similar to what I arrive with, and I have precedence in many situations." The Messenger of God said, "Surely they will kill you." He replied, "O Messenger of God, indeed I am more loved by them than the eldest of their children." Then he asked the Messenger of God's permission twice, and the Messenger of God repeated to him his first words. The Messenger of God said, "Surely they will kill you." He said, "O Messenger of God, if they find me sleeping they will not awaken me," and he asked his permission a third time and he said, "If you wish, leave." So he set out to al-Ṭāʾif. He marched to them for five days, arrived before his people at *ʿIshāʾ*, and entered his house. But his people disliked that he entered his house before he visited the goddess. Then they said, "The journey has exhausted him."

[Page 961] They came to his house and greeted him with the greetings of the polytheist, and the first thing ʿUrwa rejected was the greeting of the polytheist. He said, "Upon you are greetings from the people of Paradise." Then he invited them to Islam. He said, "O People, are you suspicious of me? Do you not know that I am the best of your nobility? Your most wealthy in property, the most powerful of you in troops. So what brought me to Islam except that I saw an affair from which no one will turn away? Accept my advice and do not oppose me, for by God, a party did not arrive before a people with something more gracious than what I bring you." They accused him and were suspicious of him. They said, "By al-Lāt, it occurred to us, when you did not approach the goddess or shave your head, that you had apostatized." They attacked him and they hurt him, but he was patient with them. They set out from his place and deliberated about what they should do about him, until when it was dawn, and he went to a room of his and proclaimed the call to prayer, a man from a group of allies called Wahb b. Jābir aimed an arrow at him; and some say Aws b. Mālik from the Banū Mālik aimed at him, and this is more confirmed with us.

ʿUrwa was a man from the allies. He received the arrow in his vein, and his blood did not stop flowing. His people assembled with weapons. The others gathered and mobilized. When ʿUrwa saw what they did, he said, "Do not fight for me. Indeed I have donated my blood to its master (God) to bring peace to you. Martyrdom is a blessing of God, and God favors me with it. God drove me to it. I testify that Muḥammad is the messenger of God. He informed me that you would kill me." Then he said to his group, "Bury me with the martyrs who were killed beside the Messenger of God before he left you." He said: They buried him with them.

His killing reached the Messenger of God and he said, "ʿUrwa is like the hero of Yasīn who invited his people to God and they killed him." Others said, "Indeed ʿUrwa did not come to Medina. He joined the Messenger of God [Page 962] between Mecca and Medina and he converted and then turned back." The first saying is confirmed with us. When ʿUrwa was killed, his son, Abū Mulayḥ b. ʿUrwa b. Masʿūd, and the son of his brother, Qārib b. al-Aswad b. Masʿūd. said to the people of al-Ṭāʾif: We will not join you over anything ever, for you have killed ʿUrwa. Then they joined the Messenger of God and converted. The Messenger of God said to them, "Choose whom you wish as guardian." They said, "We choose God and His Messenger." The Prophet said, "Your uncle is Abū Sufyān b. Ḥarb; make him your ally." So they did. They alighted on al-Mughīra b. Shuʿba and they stayed in Medina until a party of Thaqīf arrived in Ramaḍān in the year nine AH.

They said: ʿAmr b. ʿUmayya was one of the Banū ʿIlāj. He was one of the most cunning of the Bedouin and he renounced them. He was an emigrant to ʿAbd Yālīl b. ʿAmr. He went walking to ʿAbd Yālīl at noon until he entered his locality. Then he sent a message to him, saying: Indeed ʿAmr says come out to me! When the messenger came to ʿAbd Yālīl he said, "Woe unto you! Did ʿAmr send you?" He replied, "Yes, he stands in the locality." ʿAbd Yālīl desired his reconciliation but he hated to go to him. ʿAbd Yālīl said, "Indeed this is something I did not think about ʿAmr. It is not except about an affair that had happened, and it was an affair of evil. It will not be from the region of Muḥammad." So ʿAbd Yālīl set out to him and when he saw him he welcomed him. ʿAmr said, "An affair has alighted on us and there is no escape from it. Indeed it is an affair of this man that I saw. The Bedouin have accepted Islam, all of them, you have no power with them. Indeed we are in this fortress of ours, but what is our stay in the fortress when our borders are attacked? We do not secure one among us to go even one span from this fortress of ours. So think of your affair." ʿAbd Yālīl said, "By God, I saw [Page 963] what you saw. I was unable to proceed in what you proceeded. Indeed the determination and the decision are in your hands."

He said: The Thaqīf deliberated among themselves, and some of them said to the others, "Do you not see that the passes are not secure. One of you will not go out except to be removed." So they deliberated among themselves, and they desired to send a messenger to the Messenger of God, just as ʿUrwa b. Masʿūd had gone out to the Prophet. He said, "Send your leader ʿAbd Yālīl." So they spoke to ʿAbd Yālīl b. ʿAmr b. Ḥubayb. He was the same age as ʿUrwa. He refused to act for he feared that when he returned to his people from the Prophet as a Muslim, they would do with him what was done with ʿUrwa, unless they sent other men with him. So they gathered two men from the allies, and three men from the Banū Mālik. And with ʿAbd Yālīl, they sent al-Ḥakam b. ʿAmr b. Wahb b. Muʿattib, and Shuraḥbīl b. Ghaylān b. Salama b. Muʿattib, from those of the allies of the group of ʿUrwa. And from the Banū Mālik, they sent ʿUthmān b. Abī l-ʿĀṣ, Aws b. ʿAwf, and Numayr b. Kharasha, six in all.

Some said: Indeed the party included some ten men. With them was Sufyān b. ʿAbdullah.

They said: ʿAbd Yālīl set out with them and he was their leader and the master of their affair. But he desired that if they returned they would provide for every man of his band. When they were in Wādī Qanāt around the house of Ḥuruḍ, they alighted and they found a group of camels. One of them said, "If we ask the owner of the camels to whom the camels belong, he will give us news of Muḥammad." So they sent ʿUthmān b. Abī l-ʿĀṣ, and lo and behold it was al-Mughīra b. Shuʿba taking his turn, grazing the camels of the companions of Muḥammad. The companions of the Messenger of God were grazing them in turn.

[Page 964] When al-Mughīra saw them, he left the camels with them and he set out in haste to inform the Prophet of their arrival. When al-Mughīra reached the door of the Mosque, he met Abū Bakr al-Ṣiddīq and he informed him of his people. Abū Bakr said, "I swear by God, you will not precede me to the Messenger of God until I inform him. The Messenger of God is reminding them about some remembrance, so I will inform them of their arrival." And Abū Bakr entered before the Prophet and informed him, while Mughīra was at the door. Then he went out to al-Mughīra and Mughīra went before the Prophet and he was happy. He said, "O Messenger of God, my people arrive, desiring to enter Islam in order that you stipulate to them the laws and you write a document about those who are behind them among their people and their land." The Messenger of God replied, "They do not ask for stipulations, and there is no document that I give to one of the people, but I will give it to them. So inform them of the good news." So al-Mughīra returned and informed them of what the Prophet said. He gave them the good news and he taught them how to greet the Messenger of God. And they did all that Mughīra commanded them except the greeting. Indeed they said, "Have a good morning." They entered the mosque and the people said, "Messenger of God, they have entered the mosque, and they are polytheists?" The Messenger of God replied, "Indeed, nothing pollutes the earth."

Al-Mughīra b. Shuʿba said: "O Messenger of God, come, let my people stay with me and I will be generous with them. Indeed I have a recent crime with them." He said: "I do not trust you to be generous to your people." The crime of Mughīra was that he had set out with thirteen men from the Banū Mālik, but when they arrived before al-Muqawqis, al-Muqawqis greeted the Banū Mālik and was rough with Mughīra and he was from the Allies. Mughīra had two men with him, al-Sharīd and Dammūn. When they were in Sabāq they put down a drink for them, and Mughīra gave them to drink with his hand. [Page 965] He made it light for himself and he gave excessively to the Banū Mālik until they were drunk and fell asleep. When they slept, he jumped at them to kill them. Al-Sharīd fled from them seeking shelter. Dammūn, fearing that he was intoxicated, hid from him. So al-Mughīra began to shout, "O Dammūn!" And there was no Dammūn. So he began to cry. He feared that someone had killed him. Then Dammūn arose and al-Mughīra said: "Where have you been?" He said: "I hid when I saw you do what you did with the Banū Mālik. I feared you had lost your mind." He said: "Rather, I did that with them because al-Muqawqis greeted them and neglected me." Then he approached with their wealth until he came before the Messenger of God and he informed him of the news. He said to the Messenger of God, "Take a fifth of this property." The Messenger of God said, "We are not treacherous. Treachery is not appropriate for us." And he refused the fifth of their property.

Al-Mughīra brought the Thaqīf down to his land in al-Baqīʿ. It was a piece of land that the Prophet had given him. The Prophet commanded that three tents of palm be put up in the mosque. They used to hear the reciting by night while the companions of the Prophet spent the night in prayer. They observed the lines in the prescribed prayer. They returned to the house of al-Mughīra and ate and took ablutions. They stayed with him for as long as they desired, while he went frequently to the mosque. The Prophet used to go to the weak among them in the house of al-Mughīra. They listened to the speech of the Prophet, but they did not hear him mention himself, so they said: He commands us to testify that he is the Messenger of God in his speech, but he does not testify in his own speech. When their words reached the Messenger of God, he said, "I am the first [Page 966] among those who testify that I am the Messenger of God!" Then he stood up and spoke and testified that he was the Messenger of God. They stayed a few days and visited the Prophet every day. They appointed ʿUthmān b. Abī l-ʿĀṣ over their camels, for he was the youngest of them. When they returned they slept until noon.

But ʿUthmān set out to the Prophet and asked him about religion and read the Qur'ān, and greeted his companions happily. He went to the Prophet several times until he was knowledgeable. He heard the Qur'ān, and he read chapters of the Qur'ān from the mouth of the Prophet. If he found the Messenger of God sleeping he went to Abū Bakr and asked him to read to him. Others say, when he found the Prophet sleeping he went to Ubayy b. Kaʿb and asked him to read. He gave his loyalty to the Prophet of Islam, before the party and before the law. ʿUthmān hid that from his companions. The Prophet was pleased with him and loved him. The Party stayed for several days, visiting the Prophet frequently, and the Prophet invited them to Islam. ʿAbd Yālīl said to him, "Are you judging us until we return to our families and our people?" The Messenger of God replied, "Yes, if you establish yourselves in Islam I will judge you. If not, it is no matter, and there is no peace between me and you." ʿAbd Yālīl said, "What do you think of adultery? Indeed, we are single men living far away and adultery is necessary for us." He replied, "It is among what God forbids to Muslims. For God says: *Do not approach Adultery, for indeed it is a corrupt and evil way* (Q. 4:32)." He said, "And what do you think of usurious interest?" He replied, "It is forbidden!" He said, "Indeed all our property is usurious." The Prophet replied, [Page 967] "Only the principal of your property is yours. God says: *O believers fear God and forgo what is still due from usury if you are believers*. (Q. 2:278)." He said, "And what do you think of wine? Indeed. it is the juice of our grapes and we cannot escape from it." The Prophet replied, "Indeed God has forbidden it." Then the Messenger of God recited this verse: *O believers, wine, idols and divining arrows* . . . to the end of the verse.

He said: The people rose, and some retired with others. ʿAbd Yālīl said: Woe unto you, we will return to our people and forbid these three activities. By God, the Thaqīf will not be patient about wine, ever. Nor about adultery ever! Sufyān b. ʿAbdullah said, "Indeed God desires what is best, so be patient about it. Those who are with Muḥammad were like us, but they were patient and left what they used to do (adultery, etc.). Although we fear this man, he has stepped on the earth victorious, and we are in a fortress in a corner of the land. Islam is spreading around us. By God, if he stands over our fortress for a month we will die of hunger, and I do not see except Islam. I fear a day like the Conquest of Mecca!"

Khālid b. Saʿīd b. al-Āṣ was he who walked between them and the Messenger of God until they wrote a document. Khalid wrote it. The Messenger of God used to send them food, but they did not eat any of it unless the Messenger of God ate from it, until they converted. They said, "What do you think of the goddess, what do you see in it?"

He said, "Destroy it." They said, "Never! If the goddess learned that we participated in destroying her, she would kill our families." ʿUmar b. al-Khaṭṭāb said, "Woe unto you, O ʿAbd Yālīl! Surely the goddess is stone and does not know who serves it and who does not." ʿAbd Yālīl said, "We did not come to you, O ʿUmar."

They converted [Page 968] and the peace was completed. Khālid b. Saʿīd wrote that document. When the agreement was completed they spoke to the Prophet to leave the goddess for three years without destroying it, and he refused. They said, "Two years," but he refused. They said, "A year!" and he refused. They said, "One month!" and he refused to give them time. Indeed, they desired to leave the goddess for what they feared from their ignorant and their women and children. They hated that they would frighten their people by destroying her. They asked the Prophet to relieve them of destroying her. The Messenger of God said, "Yes. I will send Abū Sufyān b. Ḥarb and al-Mughīra b. Shuʿba to destroy it." They asked the Messenger of God that they be released from destroying their idols in front of them. He said, "I will order my companions to break them."

Then, they asked the Prophet to relieve them from prayer. The Messenger of God said, "There is no good in a religion that has no prayer in it." So they said, "O Muḥammad, as for prayer, we will worship, as for fasting, we will fast." They learned the compulsories of Islam and its laws. The Messenger of God commanded them to fast in what remained of the month. Bilāl used to bring them their meal to break fast. But they imagined that the sun had not set, saying, "What is this from the Messenger of God but a test of us, he observes our Islam." They said, "O Bilal, the sun has not yet set." And Bilāl says, "I did not come to you until the Messenger of God broke his fast." The party remembered this about the Messenger of God about his immediately breaking fast. Bilāl used to bring them their early morning meal. He said: It was very close to dawn. When they desired to leave, they said, "O Messenger of God, command a man from among us to lead us." He appointed ʿUthmān b. Abī l-ʿĀṣ, who was the youngest of them, for the Messenger of God had seen his keenness about Islam. ʿUthmān said that [Page 969] the last promise he made to the Messenger of God was that he would make the call to prayer and he would not take a reward for it. When you lead the people, evaluate their ability by their weakest. But when you pray by yourself, it is as you wish.

The party went out intending al-Ṭāʾif. When they were close to the Thaqīf, ʿAbd Yālīl said, "I am the most knowledgeable of the people about the Thaqīf so conceal from them the affair. Frighten them with war and battle. Inform them that Muḥammad asked us about affairs that are very hard for us and we refused him. He asked us to forbid adultery and wine, and to cut excessive interest from our property, and that we destroy our goddess." The Thaqīf came out when the party drew near. When the party saw them, they went slowly and gathered their camels. They hid in their garments like the faces of a people who were sad and grieving, and did not return happily. When the Thaqīf saw their faces in sadness and grief, some of them said, "Your party does not come with good news."

The party entered. They began with al-Lāt. The people said, when the party came down to it: They were doing thus. The people entered, they were Muslims, but they observed what they went out for, protecting themselves. The Thaqīf said that it was as though they had never seen her (al-Lāt) before! Then everyone among them returned to his family. Men among them came together from the Thaqīf and asked them, "What did you return with?" The party had asked permission from the Prophet, and that he be indulgent of their loose talk about him. They said, "We come to you from a man who is rough and rude. He takes from his affair what he wishes and conquers with the sword. He subjugated the Bedouin and the people surrendered to him. The sons of cowards were terrified of him in their fortresses. Either he charms with his religion or frightens with the sword. [Page 970] He confronts us with a strong affair and terrifies us with it. We left it with him. He forbade us adultery, and wine, and usury; and ordered that we destroy the goddess." The Thaqīf said, "We will not do this, ever." The party said, "By my life, we hated that he oppressed us. We think he was not fair to us. So prepare your weapons. And repair your fortress, and establish the war machines and mangonels. Take food for a year or two into your fortress. He will not besiege you for more than two years. Dig a trench behind your fortress. Hurry that, for indeed his command remains and we do not trust him."

They held for a day or two desiring battle. Then God placed fear in their hearts and they said, "We have no power against him. He has subjugated the Bedouin, all of them. So return to him and give him what he asks and make peace with him. And write a document between you and him before he marches to us and sends his soldiers."

When the party saw that they had accepted the affair, and were frightened of the Prophet, and desired Islam, and chose security over fear, the party said, "Indeed we have carried it out. He gave us what we loved and stipulated for us what we desired. We found him the most God-fearing of the people; the kindest, the most reaching, the most sincere, trustworthy and most gracious of people. He left us from destroying the goddess for we refused to destroy it, and he said, 'I will send one who will destroy it,' and he will send some one who will destroy it."

He said: An old man from the Thaqīf said that he has some polytheism still remaining in his heart. And that, by God, will prove what is between us and him. If he is able to destroy it then he speaks the truth, and we are worthless. And if al-Lāt resists, then, in my heart from this polytheism (*shirk*) is something left. ʿUthmān b. al-ʿĀṣ said, "Your soul favors you with deception and misleads you. What is the goddess? How does the goddess know who serves her and who does not serve her? Just as al-ʿUzzā did not know who served her and who did not. Khālid b. al-Walīd came to her alone and destroyed her. And thus with Īsāf and Nā'ila and Hubal and Manāt. One man set out to them and destroyed them. And Suwāʿ. One man set out and destroyed it! [Page 971] Did they resist them?" The Thaqafī said, "Surely, the goddess does not resemble any of the gods you mention." ʿUthmān said, "You will see!"

Abū Sufyān and al-Mughīra b. Shuʿba stayed for two or three days. Then they set out, while Abū Mulayḥ b. ʿUrwa and Qārib b. al-Aswad sought a judgment. They desired to march with Abū Sufyān and al-Mughīra to destroy the goddess. Abū Mulayḥ said, "Indeed my father was killed and against him is a debt of a hundred *mithqāl* of gold. If you think that you can fulfill it with the jewelry of the goddess, do so." The Messenger of God said, "Yes." Qārib b. al-Aswad said, "O Messenger of God, what about al-Aswad b. Masʿūd, my father? Indeed, he, too, left a debt like the debt of ʿUrwa." The Messenger of God said, "Al-Aswad is dead and he was a polytheist." Qārib said, "You reach a relationship with it. Indeed the debt is upon me and I am required to fulfill it." The Messenger of God said, "Then I will." And he paid for the debts of ʿUrwa and al-Aswad from the property of the idol.

Abū Sufyān and al-Mughīra and their companions set out to destroy the goddess. When they were close to al-Ṭā'if, al-Mughīra said to Abū Sufyān, "Step forward and enter for the affair of the Prophet." Abū Sufyān said, "Rather, you step forward to your people!" So al-Mughīra went ahead while Abū Sufyan stayed with his property in Dhū l-Harm. Al-Mughīra entered with about ten men to destroy the goddess. When they alighted in al-Ṭā'if, it was *'Ishā'*, so they stayed the night, and went the next morning to destroy the goddess. Al-Mughīra said to his companions who arrived with him, "Today, I will surely make you laugh about the Thaqīf." And he took a pickaxe and settled on the head of the Goddess. And he held a pickaxe, and as he stood, his people, the Banū Muʿattib, stood near him. They had weapons for fear that he would be wounded, just as his uncle, ʿUrwa b. Masʿūd. Abū Sufyān came to him while he was doing that and said, "No! You claim that you have preceded me to the tyrant. Do you think that if I proceeded to destroy it, the Banū Muʿattib [Page 972] would stand near me and protect me?" Al-Mughīra said, "Indeed, the people have gambled about this before you arrived. They desire security over fear. The women of Thaqīf have come out uncovered, crying over the tyrant. The slaves, and the youth, and the men reveal themselves as well. The elders have gone out."

When al-Mughīra struck with the pickax, he fell in a swoon, agitated over it. The people of al-Ṭā'if shouted in one voice, "No! You claim that the goddess does not resist. Rather, by God, she is resisting." Al-Mughīra stayed in that situation for a while. Then he sat up and said, "O people of the Thaqīf, the Bedouin used to say, 'Not a tribe from the tribes of the Bedouin is more intelligent than Thaqīf.' But not a tribe from the tribes of the Bedouin is more stupid than you! Woe unto you! What are al-Lāt and al-ʿUzzā, and the goddess? Are they not stones like this stone? It does not know who worships it and who does not worship it! Woe unto you, did al-Lāt hear or see or benefit or injure?" Then he destroyed her. And the people destroyed with him. The priest began to say, "The priests of al-Lāt from the Thaqīf were the Banū al-ʿIjlān b. ʿAttāb b. Mālik. Its owner among them was ʿAttāb b. Mālik b. Kaʿb, then his sons after him." He says, "You will see what happens when he reaches its foundation, that the foundation will be angry and swallow them." When al-Mughīra heard that, he turned and dug the foundation until he reached as deep as the middle of a man, and he reached al-Ghabghab with its treasures. They pulled its ornaments and its robe and what was in it of perfume and gold and silver. He said: The old woman among them says, "The tricksters took it and they did not fight." The Messenger of God gave from what was found in it to Abū Mulayḥ and Qārib and the people. He put some money in the way of God (charity) and in weapons.

Then the Messenger of God wrote a document for the Thaqīf: [Page 973] In the name of God the Gracious the Merciful. This is a document from the Prophet to the believers. Indeed, the shrubs of Waj and its animals must not be killed. Whoever is found doing that will be whipped on his bare body. If he exceeds that indeed he will be taken to Muḥammad. Indeed, this is the command of the Prophet Muḥammad. Khālid b. Saʿīd wrote: By the command of the Prophet Muḥammad son of ʿAbdullah, one will not exceed it. He was unjust to himself about what Muḥammad commanded. The Prophet forbade cutting the Idāḥ of Wajj and from hunting in it. The man who was found doing that had his clothes torn off. The Messenger of God employed Saʿd b. Abī Waqqāṣ over the Hīma of Wajj.

THE SENDING OF THE MESSENGER OF GOD'S TAX COLLECTORS

He said: Muḥammad b. ʿAbdullah b. Muslim related to us from al-Zuhrī and ʿAbdullah b. Yazīd from Saʿīd b. ʿAmr. They both said: When the Messenger of God returned from al-Jiʿirrāna, he arrived in Medina three nights from the end of Dhū l-Qaʿda. He stayed the rest of Dhū l-Qaʿda and Dhū l-Hijja, and when he saw the moon of al-Muḥarram, he sent out those who collect *ṣadaqa*. He sent Burayda b. al-Ḥuṣayb to the Aslam and Ghifār for their *ṣadaqa* (alms/poortax); and some said that it was Kaʿb b. Mālik. He sent ʿAbbād b. Bishr al-Ashhalī to the Sulaym and Muzayna; Rāfiʿ b. Makīth to the Juhayna; ʿAmr b. al-ʿĀṣ to the Fazāra; Ḍaḥḥāk b. Sufyān al-Kilābī to the Banū Kilāb; Busr b. Sufyān al-Kaʿbī to the Banū Kaʿb. and Ibn al-Lutbiyya al-Azdī to the Banū Zubyān; he sent a man from the Banū Saʿd b. Hudhaym about their *ṣadaqa*.

Bisr b. Sufyān set out about the *ṣadaqa* of the Banū Kaʿb; some said, rather it was Nuʿaym b. ʿAbdullah [Page 974] al-Naḥḥām al-ʿAdawī who went to them. When he arrived, the Banū Juhaym of the Banū Tamīm, and the Banū ʿAmr b. Jundub b. al-ʿUtayr b. ʿAmr b. Tamīm had alighted in their districts, and were drinking with them [Banū Kaʿb] at their pool in Dhāt al-Ashṭāṭ. Some say he found them at ʿUsfān. He ordered the gathering of the cattle of the Khuzāʿa in order to take the *ṣadaqa* from them. He said: The Khuzāʿa collected the *ṣadaqa* from every region, but the Banū Tamīm refused and said, "What is this? Your property is taken from you by force! You mobilize, wear armor, and draw the sword." But the Khuzāʿa said, "We are a people who follow the religion of Islam. This *ṣadaqa* is from our religion." The Tamīm said, "By God, he will never take a camel from it!" When the tax collector saw them, he fled from them and departed turning away, for he was afraid of them. Islam, at that time, had not embraced the Bedouin.

The rest of the Bedouin stayed. They were afraid of the sword because of what the Messenger of God did in Mecca and Ḥunayn. The Messenger of God used to command the tax collectors to take the excess from them and leave the value of their property. The tax collector arrived before the Prophet and informed him of the news. He said, "O Messenger of God, I was with three groups, and the Khuzāʿa jumped on the Tamīm and expelled them from their quarter, saying, 'If not for your relationship you would never reach your land. Misery will surely come to us from the enmity of Muḥammad, and upon yourselves when you confront the messengers of the Messenger of God, pushing them away from collecting the tax (*ṣadaqa*) of our property.' So they set out returning to their land." The Messenger of God said, "Who is for those people who did what they did?" The first of the people he appointed was ʿUyayna b. Ḥiṣn al-Fazārī. He said, "I am, by God, for them. I will follow in their tracks even if they reach Yabrīn, until I bring them to you, God willing, [Page 975] and you will judge them or they will convert." So the Messenger of God sent him with fifty riders from the Bedouin. There was not a single Muhājir or Anṣār with them. He traveled by night and hid from them by day.

He set out from Rakūba until he reached al-ʿArj. He found news of them, that they intended the land of the Banū Sulaym. So he set out in their tracks until he found them turning from al-Suqyā towards the land of Banū Sulaym in Saḥrāʾ. They had alighted and were grazing their cattle. Not one was left behind in the houses except the women and a small group. When they saw the group they turned and took eleven men from them, and they found in the residence of the women, eleven women and thirty youths and they carried them to Medina. The Prophet commanded that they be imprisoned in the house of Ramla bt. al-Ḥārith.

Then ten of their leaders arrived: They were al-ʿUṭārid b. al-Ḥājib b. Zurāra; al-Zabriqān b. Badr; Qays b. ʿĀṣim; Qays b. al-Ḥārith; Nuʿaym b. Saʿd; ʿAmr b. al-Ahtam; al-Aqraʿ b. Ḥābis; Riyāḥ b. al-Ḥārith b. Mujāshaʿ. They entered the mosque before *Ẓuhr* and when they entered they asked about their prisoners and they were informed about them and brought to them. The children and women cried. Then they returned until they entered the mosque a second time.

The Messenger of God was at that time in the house of ʿĀʾisha. Bilāl proclaimed the first call to prayer. The people waited for the Prophet to come out. They urged his coming out. They called out, "O Muḥammad, come out to us!" Bilāl stood before them and said, "Indeed the Messenger of God is coming out now." [Page 976] The people of the mosque raised their voices and began to clap their hands. The Messenger of God came out, and Bilāl rose for prayer. Those who spoke to him clung to him. The Messenger of God stopped with them for some time after Bilal's second call to prayer. They said: We have come to you with our speakers and poets, so hear us out. The Prophet smiled. Then he went and prayed *Ẓuhr* with the people. Then he turned to his house and prayed two bowings. Then he came out and sat in the courtyard of the mosque.

They came before him and introduced al-ʿUṭārid b. Ḥājib al-Tamīmi and he spoke and said, "Praise God who is gracious to us and who made us kings, and gave us property with which to do good. He made us a mighty people of the East, the most wealthy, and largest in numbers. Who compares to us among the people? Are we not the leaders of the people and possessors of their grace? Who boasts such numbers as ours? And if we wish we will increase our words. But we are embarrassed to say more about what God gave us. I say these words of mine in order that words will be brought which are better than our words!"

The Messenger of God said to Thābit b. Qays, "Stand and respond to their speaker!" Thābit stood, and he did not know any thing of that—he had not prepared earlier regarding what to say, He said, "Praise God who created the heavens and the earth, and fulfilled in it His command, and whose knowledge includes everything. You have nothing except by His grace. Then it was from what God established that he made us kings. He chose for us from his creation one who is the noblest of them in genealogy, the most pleasant in features, the most trustworthy in speech. He revealed to him His Book. He trusted him over His creation. He was the best of them among His worshipers. He invited the people to the faith. The emigrants among his people and his family believed. The most beautiful of people in features, he was the most gracious of people in deeds. And we were the first of the people in response, when the Messenger of God called. We are the Anṣār—the helpers—of God and His Messenger. We fight the people until they say, '[Page 977] There is but one God.' The property and blood of those who believe in God and His Messenger are forbidden. Who disbelieves in God, we will fight him about that. His death is easy. I speak these words of mine, and I ask God's forgiveness for the believing men and women." Then he sat.

They said, "O Messenger of God, permit our poet." So he permitted him. They introduced Zabriqān b. Badr, and he said:

We are Kings, no tribe compares to us.
With us are Kings, and with us are places of worship.
How many tribes have we plundered,
For excellence in glory is to be sought after.
We feed in times of drought what they eat
Of camel hump. When there are no rain clouds
We slaughter fat humped camels as a matter of course
Guests when they come are satisfied with food.

The Messenger of God said, "Respond to them, O Ḥassān b. Thābit." So Ḥassān stood up and said:

The leaders of Fihr and their brothers
Made clear the path for the people to follow.
Everyone whose heart is full
With fear of God and the affairs which they legislate,
Such a people when they fight injure their enemies.
Or gain the advantage of their adherents, which they seek.
Such is their nature, no recent habit.
The worst of characteristics is innovation.
Men do not repair what their hands have destroyed in fighting
Nor destroy what they have repaired.
Not mean with their wealth towards the sojourner,
No stain of covetousness touches them.
If after them comes a leader from the people
They won't achieve more than what we have.
[Page 978] The noblest people are partisans of the Messenger of God
At a time when desires and partisanship are dispersed,
Their purity is revealed in the Qur'ān.
They are not greedy, and greed of others does not stop them
Such that they in the midst of battle, facing death,
Are like the Lions of Bīsha with their paws curved.
They do not boast when they nail their enemy.
If they are taken, they are not weak or scared.
When we plot against a tribe we don't crawl to them
As the baby buffalo to its mother.
We rise up when nailed by war
When the mob is yielding from all borders.
Take from them what comes as a bonus when they are angry.
Do not focus on what they forbade.
Indeed their war is fresh poison mixed with calamity
And clinging destruction, so leave it.
A heart that helps him gave them his praise
Which is what his clever tongue desires most.
They are the best of the tribes whether they are serious or joking.

[Page 979] The Messenger of God had ordered a *minbar* to be placed in the mosque and Ḥassān proclaimed from it. He said: Indeed God will surely help Ḥassān with the holy spirit (*rūḥ al-Quds*) as long as he stands for his Prophet. The Messenger of God and the Muslims were happy, at that time, with the place of Thābit and the poetry of Ḥassān. The party withdrew, some of them with others. One of them said, "You must surely know, by God, that this man is supported. People are producing for him. By God, his speaker is better than our speaker. Indeed, their poet is better than ours. They are more reflective than us." Thābit b. Qays was the loudest of the people. God revealed to the Prophet about raising their voices. Allah mentions that they called out to the Prophet from behind the rooms. He said: *O you who believe, do not raise your voices above the voice of the Prophet, till his words—Most of them did not reason* (Q. 49:20)—meaning the *Tamīm* when they called out to the Prophet. It was confirmed when this verse was revealed that Thābit did not raise his voice with the Prophet. The Messenger of God returned the captives.

ʿAmr b. al-Ahtam stood up, at that time, and insulted Qays b. ʿĀṣim. They were both in the party. The Messenger of God had ordered prizes for them. He would award to the party when they arrived before him, the most excellent among them, a gift according to the ability that he saw. After the Messenger of God awarded their prizes to them he said, "Is there one among you who has not been awarded a prize?" They said, "A youth on a horse." The Messenger of God said, "Send him, we will award him." Qays b. ʿĀṣim said: Indeed he is a youth who is not noble. The Messenger of God said, "If he was! Surely he is of the party and he has a right." ʿAmr b. al-Ahtam said a poem aimed at Qays b. al-ʿĀṣim:

> You kept sitting on your tail insulting me in front of the Prophet.
> You did not tell the truth nor were you correct.
> [Page 980] Indeed, we and our power return constantly, but your power is left behind at the level of conceit and of the follower.
> If you hate us, indeed you originate from the Romans
> And the Byzantines cannot help but hate the Arab.

He said: Rabīʿa b. ʿUthmān related to me from an old man; a woman from the Banū Najjār had informed him and said: I observed the party at that time, taking their prizes with Bilāl, twelve weights and a half. I saw a youth that he awarded, at that time, and he was the youngest of them. He was given five weights. I said what is "Nashsh"? She said, "Half a weight."

THE MISSION OF AL-WALĪD B. ʿUQBA TO THE BANŪ AL-MUṢṬALIQ

They said: The Messenger of God sent al-Walīd b. ʿUqba b. Abī Muʿayṭ for the *ṣadaqa* of the Banū Muṣṭaliq. They had converted and built mosques in their courtyards. When al-Walīd came out to them, they heard that he was close to them, and ten of their men went out to meet him with slaughtering camels and sheep, welcoming him. They had never seen one who exacted a tax on camels and sheep. When al-Walīd saw them, he turned and went back to Medina and did not go close to them. He informed the Prophet that when he was close to them they approached him carrying weapons placed between him and the *ṣadaqa*. The Messenger of God was anxious to send them one who would attack them.

That reached the community. The riders who met al-Walīd arrived before the Prophet. They informed the Prophet of the news and said, "O Messenger of God, ask him if he said a word to us or if we spoke?" This verse was revealed as we were with the Messenger of God, talking to him and explaining what happened. The shivering took him, and it was revealed: [Page 981] *O you who believe, if a corrupt man comes to you with news, investigate* . . . (Q. 49:6) to the end of the verse. Then he said, "Who do you want me to send to you?" They said, "Send us ʿAbbād b. Bishr." So he said, "O ʿAbbād go with them and take the *ṣadaqa* of their property, and protect the value of their property." So we set out with ʿAbbād who read the Qurʾān to us and taught us the law of Islam until we alighted with him in the center of our homes. He neither weakened nor increased our rights. The Messenger of God commanded him to stay with us for ten days. Then he returned to the Messenger of God satisfied.

THE EXPEDITION TO QUṬBA B. ʿĀMIR AT AL-KHATHʿAM IN ṢAFAR OF YEAR NINE AH

Ibn Abī Sabra related to us from Isḥāq b. ʿAbdullah, who said: Ibn Kaʿb b. Mālik related to us that the Prophet sent Quṭba b. Āmir b. Ḥadīda with twenty men to the tribe of Khathʿam in the region of Tabāla. He ordered him to raid them and to march by night and hide by day, and to hurry the march. So they set out with ten camels taking turns on them. They hid their weapons. They went along a crack until they reached Baṭn Mashā'. They captured a man and asked him, but could not understand his language, and he immediately began to shout. Information on this expedition is entered with the raid of Shujāʿ b. Wahb.

[Page 982] THE EXPEDITION OF THE BANŪ KILĀB LED BY THEIR LEADER AL-ḌAḤḤĀK B. SUFYĀN AL-KILĀBĪ

He said: Rashīd Abī Mawhūb al-Kilābī related to me from Ḥayyān b. Abī Sulma and ʿAnbasa b. Abī Sulmā and Ḥuṣayn b. ʿAbdullah. They said: The Messenger of God sent an army to al-Quraṭā'; with them was Ḍaḥḥāk b. Sufyān b. ʿAwf b. Abī Bakr al-Kilābī and al-Aṣyad b. Salama b. Qurṭ b. ʿAbd until they met them in Zujj. They invited them to Islam but they refused. So they fought them and defeated them. Then al-Aṣyad met his father, Salama b. Qurṭ, who was on a horse of his at Ghadīr (pool) Zujj, and he invited his father to Islām and gave him protection. But he insulted him and his religion. Al-Aṣyad struck the Achilles' tendon of his horse. When it fell on its heels, Salama leaned on his spear in the water and clung to it until someone other than his son killed him. This expedition was in the month of Rabīʿ al-Awwal in the year nine.

He said: Rashīd Abū Mawhūb related to me from Jābir b. Abī Sulmā and ʿAnbasa b. Abī Sulma who both said: The Messenger of God wrote to Ḥārith b. ʿAmr b. Qurayṭ inviting them to Islam. They took his document and washed it and patched a hole in their leather bucket with it. They refused to answer. Umm Ḥabīb daughter of ʿĀmir b. Khālid b. ʿAmr b. Qurayṭ b. ʿAbd b. Abī Bakra said, and she opposed them in a verse of hers saying:

> O Ibn Saʿīd, don't become a joke.
> Beware and wait for them at Marīr.
> O Ibn Saʿīd, those people are only a community
> Who refused to answer since the religion raised every leader.
> [Page 983] When a sign came to them from Muḥammad they erased it with the water from the well, so it was gone.

They said: When they did what they did with the document, the Messenger of God said, "What is the matter with them. Did God take away their reasoning? They are the people of trembling, of haste, and confused words. A people of stupidity." The man who came to them with the document was from ʿUrayna and he was called ʿAbdullah b. ʿAwsaja. This began in the month of Rabīʿ al-Awwal in the year nine. Al-Wāqidī said: some of them are weak and had no clarity of words.

THE EXPEDITION LED BY ʿALQAMA B. MUJAZZIZ AL-MUDLIJĪ

He said: Mūsā b. Muḥammad related to me from his father; and Ismāʿīl b. Ibrāhīm b. ʿAbd al-Raḥmān from his father: one of them exceeded his companion. They said: It reached the Messenger of God that the people of al-Shuʿayba—on the coast in the region of Mecca—saw the people of al-Ḥabasha (Abyssinia) in boats. And the Messenger of God sent ʿAlqama b. Mujazzaz al-Mudlijī with three hundred men to reach an island in that sea and ʿAlqama went in and those who were there fled. So he turned back.

When he entered some of the houses, some of the soldiers asked permission to go back since there had been no fighting. So he permitted them, and he appointed ʿAbdullah b. Ḥudhāfa al-Sahmī, who had a sense of humor, their commander. We alighted in some street and when the people lit a fire to keep warm before it, and cook the food, the commander said, "I invite you to jump in the fire." Some of the people stood and separated themselves from each other until he thought they would jump in it. So he said, "Sit. Surely I was joking with you." [Page 984] This was mentioned to the Messenger of God, and he said: "Do not obey one who commands you to do what is forbidden."

THE EXPEDITION OF ʿALĪ B. ABĪ ṬĀLIB TO FULS

He said: ʿAbd al-Raḥmān b. ʿAbd al-ʿAzīz related to us, I heard ʿAbdullah b. Abī Bakr b. Ḥazm say to Mūsā b. ʿImrān b. Mannāḥ while they were seated in al-Baqīʿ, "Do you know the Raid of Fuls?" Mūsā replied, "I have not heard about this raid." He said: Then Ibn Ḥazm laughed and said, "The Messenger of God sent ʿAlī with a hundred and fifty men on a hundred camels and fifty horses. Only the Anṣār, and that included the Aws and the Khazraj, participated in the raid. They went alongside the horses and took turns on the camels until they attacked the tribes of the Bedouin. He inquired about the region of the families of Ḥātam, then he alighted upon them. Then they raided them with the dawn. They took prisoners until their hands were full, and cattle and sheep. They attacked al-Fuls, the idol of the Ṭayyiʾ and destroyed it. Then they turned and returned to Medina.

ʿAbd al-Raḥmān b. ʿAbd al-ʿAzīz said: I mentioned this raid to Muḥammad b. ʿUmar b. ʿAlī and he said, "I do not think Ibn Ḥāzm explained the transmission of this expedition or narrated it properly." I said, "Then you bring it!" He said: The Messenger of God sent ʿAlī b. Abī Ṭālib with a hundred and fifty of the Anṣār to destroy al-Fuls. There was not a single Muhājirūn with them, and they had fifty riders and beasts. They mounted the camels and avoided the horses. The Messenger of God commanded him to make a raid.

ʿAlī set out with his companions; he had a black flag and a white banner. They had spears and [Page 985] obvious weapons. He gave his flag to Sahl b. Ḥunayf, and his banner to Jabbār b. Ṣakhr al-Sulamī. He set out with a guide from the Banū Asad called Ḥurayth, and he went with them on the road of Fayd. When he brought them to a certain place he said, "Between you and the tribe you desire is a whole day. If we march to it by day we will reach their extremities and their shepherds, and they will warn the tribe and it will disperse, and you will not take from them your need. So we will stay this day of ours in our position until the evening. Then we will travel by night on the backs of the horses and raid them, and we will greet them in the blind darkness of the dawn." They said, "This is the decision!"

They camped and let the camels graze; they picked, and sent a group of them to penetrate what was around them. They chose Abū Qatāda, al-Ḥubāb b. al-Mundhir, and Abū Nā'ila. They set out on the backs of their horses and went around the camp. They captured a black youth and said, "Who are you?" He replied, "I am looking for what I desire." So they brought him to ʿAlī. He said, "Who are you?" He replied, "One who seeks his desires." So they threatened him. Then he said, "I am the slave of a man from the Ṭayyi' of the Banū Nabhān. They ordered me about this situation. They said, 'If you see horses of Muḥammad, come forth and inform us.' I did not reach any people. When I saw you, I wanted to go to them. Then I said to myself I will not hurry to my companions until I can bring them clear evidence about your numbers, your horses and your beasts. I did not fear you would overtake me and bind me, until your scouts captured me." ʿAlī said, "Tell us the truth, what is behind you?" He replied, "The foremost of the tribe are one long night away. Your cavalry will take them when they leave in the morning." ʿAlī said to his companions, "What do you think?" Jabbār b Sakhr said, "We think that we will depart on our horses at night until we arrive in the morning before the community, [Page 986] and they will be penetrated and we will raid them. We will set out with the black slave by night. We will appoint Ḥārith in charge of the camp, until they follow, God willing." ʿAlī said, "This is the decision!"

They set out with the black slave running with the horses. He was in the rear of some of them for a turn, then he settled in the rear of another for a turn, and he was bound. When it became day, the slave lied and said, "I was wrong about the road and I have left it behind." ʿAlī said, "Then return to where you erred!" So he returned a mile or more, and then he said, "I have made a mistake." ʿAlī said, "Indeed we are deceived about you. You do not desire except to divert us from the tribe. Bring him! Tell us the truth or we shall cut off your head!" He said: He came forward and pointed his sword at the slave's head, and when the slave saw the damage, he said, "Why would I tell you the truth? Will it profit me?" They said, "Yes." He said, "Indeed, I did what you see. It happened to me what happens to people out of timidity. I said to myself, I approach with the community of Muslims, guiding them to the tribe without a trial. Yet, I have no guarantee, so I will protect myself from them. When I saw from you what I saw, I feared that you would kill me, which was to me an excuse. I will take you on the road." They said, "Tell the truth!" He replied, "The tribe is close to you." He set out with them until he was close to the tribe, and they heard the barking of dogs, the movement of the cattle in the pasture, and the sheep. He said: These are the groups and it is one area (*farsakh*). They looked at each other and said, "Where are the people of Ḥātam?" He replied, "They are in the center of these groups." Some of the people said to some, "If we frighten the tribe, they will shout and frighten some of them, and some will hide their faction from us in the darkness of the night. But we will hold back the people until the dawn rises throughout, indeed, its rising is near. Then we will attack. If some of them warn some, it will not be hidden from us where they go. The people do not have horses to flee from them, and we are on horses." [Page 987] They said, "The decision is what you indicate."

He said: When the dawn rose, they raided and killed those who were killed and took prisoners. They drove the children and women and gathered the sheep and cattle. None were hidden or absent, so they were in control. A girl from the tribe who saw the black slave—his name was Aslam—and he was tied up, says, "What is the matter with him, is he crazy! This is the work of your messenger, Aslam. May he never have peace. He brought them to you. Guided them to your weakness." He said: The black one says, "Be brief, O daughter of the nobility, I did not guide them until they threatened to strike off my head!"

The people camped, and they isolated the prisoners, and they were in the region of Nufayr. They isolated the children they took from the family of Ḥātam, the sister of ʿAdī and the women with her, and they isolated them. Aslam said to ʿAlī, "Why do you wait to set me free?" He said, "You will witness that there is no God but Allah, and that Muḥammad is His messenger." He replied, "I follow the religion of my community who are those prisoners. Whatever they do, I do!" He said, "Do you not see them tied up? Shall we put you with them in ropes?" He said, "Yes, to be with those tied up is more desirable to me than that I be with others, free. What holds true about them is true about me." The people of the raid laughed about it. He was tied and thrown in with the prisoners. He said, "I shall be with them until you have judged them." One of the prisoners said to him, "We do not bid you welcome. You brought them to us." Another said, "Welcome to you. You couldn't do more than what you did. If we faced what you faced we would have done the same and worse. So console yourself!"

The soldiers came and gathered. They came close to the prisoners and offered them Islam. Those who converted were left, and those who refused were executed, until they came to al-Aswad. They offered him Islam. He said, "By God, indeed to worry about the sword is ignoble. There is no permanence." A man from the tribe who converted says, "O you are strange. [Page 988] Was this not the place where you were taken, where those who were killed, were killed, and those who were imprisoned, imprisoned. Those who converted among us desired Islam, say whatever you say. Woe unto you, convert and follow the religion of Muḥammad!" He said, "I will convert and follow the religion of Muḥammad!" So he converted and was released. He used to promise and not fulfill until the Ridda. He witnessed al-Yamāma with Khālid b. al-Walīd. His experience was a good one.

He said: ʿAlī went to al-Fuls and attacked and destroyed it. He found three swords in his house: Rasūb, al-Mikhdham, and a sword called Yamānī; and three armors. And there was a garment to wear with it. They gathered the prisoners and employed Abū Qatāda over them. They employed ʿAbdullah b. al-ʿAtīk al-Sulamī over the cattle and chattel (paltry furniture, etc). Then they marched until they alighted at Rakak. They apportioned the prisoners and the plunder. The Prophet isolated his first portion Rasūb and al-Mikhdham. Then later, there came to him another sword. He isolated the fifth, and he isolated the family of Ḥatam. He did not apportion them until he arrived in Medina with them.

Al-Wāqidī said: I narrated this tradition to ʿAbdullah b. Jaʿfar al-Zuhrī and he said: Ibn Abī ʿAwn related to me saying: There was with the prisoners a sister of ʿAdī b. Ḥatam who was not apportioned. She was kept in the house of Ramla bt. al-Ḥārith.

ʿAdī b. Ḥatam had fled when he heard about the movement of ʿAlī. He had a spy in Medina, who warned him, so he set out to al-Shām. [Page 989] The sister of ʿAdī used to say when the Messenger of God passed by, "O Messenger of God, the father is destroyed and the ambassador is absent. So give us from what Allah gave you." At that, the Prophet asked her, "Who is your ambassador?" She said, "ʿAdī b. Ḥatam." And he says, "The fugitive from God and His messenger," so she lost hope. When it was the fourth day, the Prophet went by and she did not talk. A man pointed to her saying, "Rise and talk to him." So she talked and he gave her permission and was kind to her. She asked about the man who pointed to her. It was said, "ʿAlī. He is the man who imprisoned you. Don't you know him?" She said, "No by God, I kept my garment on my face, since the day I was imprisoned, until I came into this house. I have not seen his face or that of any one of his companions."

THE RAID OF TABŪK

It was recited according to Abū l-Qasim b. Abī Ḥayya, who said: Abū ʿAbdullah Muḥammad b. Shujāʿ related to us that al-Wāqidī related to us that ʿUmar b. ʿUthmān b. ʿAbd al-Raḥmān b. Saʿīd, ʿAbdullah b. Jaʿfar al-Zuhrī, Muḥammad b. Yaḥyā, Ibn Abī Ḥabība, Rabīʿa b. ʿUthmān, ʿAbd al-Raḥmān b. ʿAbd al-ʿAzīz b. Abī Qatāda, ʿAbdullah b. ʿAbd al-Raḥmān al-Jumahī, and ʿUmar b. Sulaymān b. Abī Ḥathma, Mūsā b. Muḥammad b. Ibrāhīm, ʿAbd al-Ḥamīd b. Jaʿfar, Abū Maʿshar, Yaʿqūb b. Muḥammad b. Abī Ṣaʿṣaʿa, Ibn Abī Sabra and Ayyūb b. al-Nuʿmān, all of them related portions of this tradition about Tabūk to me. Some of them are more reliable than others, and others not named, who are reliable, informed me as well. I have written all that they related to me.

They said: The Sāqiṭa—they were Nabateans—arrived in Medina with flour [Page 990] and oil in *jahilīyya* and after Islam arrived. Indeed there was news of al-Shām with the Muslims every day. Many of those who came to them were from Nabatea. A group arrived which mentioned that the Byzantines had gathered many groups in al-Shām, and that Heraclius had provisioned his companions for a year. The Lakhmids, Judhām, Ghassān and ʿĀmila had gathered to him. They marched and their leaders led them to al-Balqāʾ where they camped. Heraclius stayed behind in Ḥimṣ. That was not a fact, but rather something that was said to them that they repeated. There was not an enemy more fearful to the Muslims than them. That was because of what they saw of them, when they used to arrive as merchants, of preparedness, and numbers, and sheep.

The Messenger of God did not make a raid except pretending that it was not, lest news should travel that he desired thus and thus, until it was the raid of Tabūk. The Messenger of God raided it when the heat was intense. He assumed a distant journey, and he intended a raid of many numbers. He disclosed to the people their affair in order that they could be better prepared to raid them, and he informed them about the direction that was desired. The Messenger of God sent to the tribes and to Mecca asking them to prepare themselves to go raiding. He sent Burayda b. al-Ḥuṣayb to the Aslam in al-Furʿ. He sent Abū Ruhm al-Ghifārī to his people to find them in their land. Abū Wāqid al-Laythī set out with his people, and Abū Jaʿd al-Ḍamrī set out with his people in the coast. He sent Rāfiʿ b. Makīth and Jundub b. Makīth with the Juhayna. He sent Nuʿaym b. Masʿūd with the Ashjaʿī; he sent Budayl b. Warqāʾ, ʿAmr b. Sālim and Bushr b. Sufyān with the Banū Kaʿb b. ʿAmr. He sent many with the

Sulaym including al-ʿAbbās b. Mirdās. The Messenger of God incited the Muslims [Page 991] to battle and *jihād*, and he excited them about it. He commanded them to pay the *ṣadaqa*, and they collected much *ṣadaqa*. The first of those to convey *ṣadaqa* was Abū Bakr al-Ṣiddīq. He brought his property, all of four thousand dirham. The Messenger of God said, "Have you kept something?" He replied, "God and his Messenger know best!" ʿUmar brought half his property. The Messenger of God said, "Did you keep something?" ʿUmar replied, "Yes. Half of what I brought." When ʿUmar learned of what Abū Bakr brought he said, "Whenever we compete to do good, he beats me to it." ʿAbbās b. ʿAbd al-Muṭṭalib and Ṭalḥa b. ʿUbaydullah brought property to the Messenger of God. ʿAbd al-Raḥmān b. ʿAwf brought the Messenger of God two hundred measures; Saʿd b. ʿUbāda and Muḥammad b. Maslama brought property. ʿĀṣim b. ʿAdī brought ninety measures of dates as *ṣadaqa*. ʿUthmān b. ʿAffān supplied a third of that army. He spent the most, until that army had sufficient supplies, and it was said that every need was met. He even provided the ropes for their water containers. It was said: Indeed the Messenger of God said at that time, "After this, nothing will harm ʿUthmān whatever he does!" The wealthy desired goodness and well being. They estimated their well being for the next life. They strengthened those who were weak among them, until indeed a man brought a camel to the man or two men saying, "Take turns on this camel between you." The man would bring payment and give it to some who were going out. Even the women would offer whatever they could. [Page 992] Umm Sinān al-Aslamī said: Indeed I saw a garment laid out in front of the Messenger of God in the house of ʿĀʾisha and in it were bracelets, bangles, anklets, earrings, rings and thongs from what the women were sending him to offer to the Muslims in their preparations.

The people were in great need, and when the fruit had ripened, and shade was desired, the people wanted to stay, and hated going out in the conditions of that time. The Messenger of God hurried the people and urged seriousness. He put up his tent in Thanniyat al-Wadāʿ. There were many people, and Muḥammad had not put together a document for them. He had departed desiring to send one, but he thought it was kept from him as a revelation did not come down to him about it from God.

The Messenger of God said to al-Jadd b. Qays, "Abū Wahb, when you come out with us for this battle, perhaps you might bring back Byzantine girls with you?" Al-Jadd replied, "You grant me permission but you do not tempt me. Surely my people know there is none with a greater vanity about women than I. But I fear that if I saw a woman of the Byzantines I would not be patient about them." The Messenger of God turned away from him and said, "I grant you permission." His son, ʿAbdullah b. Jadd came to him—he was at Badr, and he was the brother of Muʿādh b. Jabal by his mother, and he said to his father, "Why did you reject the proposition of the Messenger of God? By God, the Banū Salima do not have more property than you, but you will not go out nor will you send anyone!" He replied, "O my little son, why should I go out [Page 993] in the wind and heat and difficulties to the Byzantines? By God, I am not secure from fear of the Byzantines in my own house in Khurbāʿ, so how will I go out to them and raid them? Indeed, my little son, I am knowledgeable about the cycles of life." His son was rude to him. He said, "No, by God, it is hypocrisy! By God, a Qurʾān will be revealed about you to the Messenger of God and they will read it." He said: And he [the father] raised his sandal and struck his son's face with it. And his son turned from him and did not speak to him.

The coward began to discourage his people. He said to Jabbār b. Sakhr and a group with him from the Banū Salama, "O Banū Salama, do not hurry in the heat." He says, "Do not go out in the heat, be moderate in your efforts. There is doubt in the facts and rumors about the Messenger of God." God most high revealed to him about it: *They said: Do not go out in the heat* (Q. 9:81, 82) until His words, *as a reward for what they used to do*. About him was revealed: *And among them were those who say: You permit me, but you do not tempt me* (Q. 9:49). As if he feared the temptation of Byzantine women. But that was not so. Rather, he excused himself with falsehoods. The temptation that he fell in was worse than what he feared. He stayed away from the Messenger of God, and kept himself away. God says: *Hell is filled with disbelievers*. When this verse was revealed the son came to his father and said, "Did I not say to you that a Qur'ān would be revealed about you and the Muslims will read it?" His father says, "Be silent about me, O disgrace! I will never be of use to you. By God, surely you are more severe with me than Muḥammad." He said: The Weepers (Bakkā'ūn) arrived and they asked him for mounts. They numbered seven. They were a people of need. The Messenger of God said, "*I do not find what I can mount you on, so they turned back their eyes overflowing with tears* . . . (Q. 9.92)" to the end of the verse. They were seven of the Banū ʿAmr b. ʿAwf: [Page 994] Sālim b. ʿUmayr had witnessed Badr and there is no dispute about him with us. From the Banū Wāqif, Haramay b. ʿAmr; from the Banū Ḥāritha, ʿUlba b. Zayd; He was one who supplied commodities. And that was because the Messenger of God commanded the *ṣadaqa*. The people began bringing it, and ʿUlba came and said: O Messenger of God, I do not have with me what I could give as *ṣadaqa*, but I will make my goods available. The Messenger of God said, "God accepts your *ṣadaqa*." And from the Banū Māzin b. al-Najjār, Abū Laylā ʿAbd al-Raḥmān b. Kaʿb. From the Banū Salima, ʿAmr b. ʿUtba. From the Banū Zurayq, Salama b. Ṣakhr. From the Banū Sulaym, al-ʿIrbād b. Sāriya al-Sulamī. Those confirmed what we heard.

Some said: ʿAbdullah b. Mughaffal al-Muzannī and ʿAmr b. ʿAwf al-Muzannī, and others said, "They were Banū Muqarrin, from Muzannī." When the weepers, *Bakkā'ūn*, set out from the place of the Messenger of God he informed them that he could not find mounts for them, for they desired beasts. Yāmīn b. ʿUmayr b. Kaʿb b. Shibl al-Naḍrī met Abū Laylā al-Māzinī, and ʿAbdullah b. Mughaffal al-Muzannī and they were crying. He said, "Why are you crying?" They replied, "We came to the Messenger of God for mounts for us, and did not find any. We do not have sufficient money to go out and we detest abandoning a raid with the Messenger of God." So Yāmīn gave them a watering camel of his and they rode it. He supplied every man among them two measures of dates. The two set out with the Messenger of God. Al-ʿAbbās b. Abd al-Muṭṭalib provided a beast for two men. ʿUthmān provided rides for three men, over and above what he provided the army.

The Messenger of God said, "Do not go out with us unless you possess a strong beast." [Page 995] A man went out with a difficult beast and it threw him. The people said: "The martyr! The martyr!" The Messenger of God sent for a herald to call out: "Only a believer, or a soul that believes will enter Paradise. The disobedient will not enter Paradise." The man was thrown from his camel in al-Suwaydā'. They said: People from the Hypocrites came to the Messenger of God and asked permission to be absent without cause, and he permitted them. There were roughly eighty Hypocrites who asked permission.

Those who made excuses among the Bedouin came and made excuses to him but God did not permit them. They were a group from the Banū Ghifār. Among them was Khufāf b. Īmā b. Raḥḍa. They numbered eighty-two men. ʿAbdullah b. Ubayy approached with his army and camped in Thanniyat al-Wadāʿ near al-Dhubāb. With him were his allies from the Jews and Hypocrites from among those who gathered to him. It was said that the camp of Ibn Ubayy was not the lesser of the two camps. He stayed as long as the Messenger of God stayed. The Messenger of God had appointed Abū Bakr al-Ṣiddīq at the camp to lead the people in prayer. When the Messenger of God gathered for the march, he appointed Sibāʿ b. ʿUrfuṭa al-Ghifārī over Medina—some said Muḥammad b. Maslama—and it was the only raid from which he was absent. The Messenger of God said, "Make sure they have sandals. Indeed a man will continue to ride as long as he has sandals."

When the Messenger of God set out, Ibn Ubayy stayed behind with those Hypocrites who stayed behind. He said, "Muḥammad raids the Byzantines despite the strain of the situation and the heat and the distance of the land when he has no power over them! Does Muḥammad consider fighting the Byzantines a game? Those who pretend with him are of a similar opinion." Then Ibn Ubayy said, "By God, tomorrow I will see [Page 996] his companions tied up in ropes." He doubted the Messenger of God and his companions.

When the Messenger of God rode from Thaniyat al-Wadāʿ to Tabūk, he handed out the flags and banners. He handed the biggest flag to Abū Bakr al-Ṣiddīq, and his largest banner to al-Zubayr. He handed the banner of the Aws to Usayd b. al-Ḥuḍayr, and the flag of the Khazraj to Abū Dujāna—some said to al-Ḥubāb b. al-Mundhir b. al-Jamūḥ. They said: All of a sudden a slave belonging to a woman from Banū Ḍamra met him at the top of Thanniyat al-Nūr and the slave was armed. The slave said, "May I fight with you O Messenger of God?" The Messenger of God said, "Who are you?" He replied, "A slave belonging to an evil minded woman from the Banū Ḍamra." The Messenger of God said, "Return to your mistress. Do not fight with me for you will enter the fire." He said: Rifāʿa b. Thaʿlaba b. Abī Mālik related to me from his father from his grandfather, who said: I sat with Zayd b. Thābit and he mentioned the raid of Tabūk. He said that he carried the flag of Mālik b. Najjār in Tabūk, so I said: O Abū Saʿīd, how many Muslims were there? He replied: Thirty thousand. Indeed the people were riding with the setting of the sun. They continued riding, and the rear guard lingered until the troops left. I asked one of those who were in the rear guard and he said: The last of them did not leave except in the evening. Then we rode in their tracks and we did not reach the troops except in the dawn of many people.

They said: A group of Muslims stayed behind. The intention was to slow down from the Messenger of God until they stayed behind from him and were without doubt or suspicion. Among them was Kaʿb b. Mālik. [Page 997] Kaʿb used to say: When I was left behind on the day of Tabūk, my story was that I had never been stronger or had more comforts at the time as when I stayed away from him during that raid. By God, I never gathered to myself two rides until I collected them in that raid! The Messenger of God supplied, and the Muslims supplied with him. I began running to supply with them but I returned and did not fulfill a need. I said to myself, "I am master over that." I continued to persevere by myself until he prepared the people with diligence.

The Messenger of God rose in the morning, a raider with the Muslims. That was a Thursday. The Messenger of God liked going out on Thursdays, but I had not completed any of my preparations. So I said that I will be prepared in a day or two, and that then I would join them and raid. I rose, in the morning after they left, to prepare but I returned and I had not done anything. Then I got up the next morning and did nothing. I continued procrastinating until they hastened and the raid was completed. I said to myself, "I will ride and catch up with them," and I wish I had done, but I did not. When I went out among the people and began to go around them, it saddened me that I only saw men who were despicable in their hypocrisy, or men whom God excused.

The Messenger of God did not remember me until he reached Tabūk. He said, while he was seated with the people, "Where is Kaʿb b. Mālik?" A man from the Banū Salima said, "O Messenger of God, his cloak and his vanity kept him." Muʿādh b. Jabal said to him, "Miserable is what you said. By God, O Messenger of God, we know only good of him." The speaker was ʿAbdullah b. Unays. Some said that he who replied to his words was Abū Qatāda. Muʿādh b. Jabal is the most confirmed with us. Hilāl b. Umayya al-Wāqiffī said, when he stayed back from the Messenger of God [Page 998] in Tabūk: By God, I did not stay back because of doubts or suspicion, but because I was strengthened with property. I said, "I will purchase a camel." Murāra b. al-Rabīʿ met me, and he said, "I am a man of power, I will purchase a camel and depart with it." So I said, "This is a man of property, I will accompany him," and we began to say, "We will raid, and we will purchase two camels and join the Prophet," but that did not happen. We are a people light on the chest of two rides, and in the morning we would leave. And we continued intending that and delaying the days until the Messenger of God was about to take the land. So I said, "This is not the time to go out." I did not see in the house or other houses except excuses and obvious hypocrisy. I returned as one saddened by my situation.

Abū Khaythama had stayed behind with us. There was no suspicion about his Islam nor was it scorned. He intended towards Islam what he intended. Abū Khaythama was named ʿAbdullah b. Khaythama al-Sālamī. He returned, ten days after the Messenger of God had departed, and entered upon his two wives on a hot day, and they were in their huts. Each one of them had sprayed her hut and cooled it with water for him, and prepared food for him in it. When he reached them he stood before the two huts and said, "Praise be to God! The Messenger of God was forgiven his sins, yet he did not delay in the heat of the sun, the wind, and the heat. He carried his weapons on his neck. But Abū Khaythama is in the cool shade and has prepared food, and two beautiful women staying in his property. This is not justice." Then he said, "By God, I will not enter a single hut of yours until I go out and join the Messenger of God." He knelt his camel, tightened its saddle on it, and equipped with provisions, departed. His two wives tried to speak to him, but he would not speak to them. He reached ʿUmayr b. Wahb al-Jumaḥī in Wādī al-Qurā intending the Prophet.

ʿUmayr was his friend, so they accompanied each other, until lo and behold they were before Tabūk. Abū Khaythama said, "O ʿUmayr! Indeed I am guilty of sins, while you are not. Will you not wait [Page 999] until I go ahead of you to the Messenger of God. So ʿUmayr waited. Abū Khaythama went until he was before the Messenger of God, and he was a resident in Tabūk. The people said, "This is a rider of the road." The Messenger of God said, "Is it Abū Khaythama?" The people said, "O Messenger of God, it is Abū Khaythama!" And when he knelt his camel he approached and greeted the Prophet. The Messenger of God said, "You are most deserving, O Abū Khaythama." Then he informed the Messenger of God of the news. The Messenger of God said to him, "Good," and he prayed for him.

The Messenger of God marched from Medina. It dawned in Dhū Khushub and he alighted under a Dawma tree. His guide to Tabūk was ʿAlqama b. al-Faghwā al-Khuzāʿī. The Messenger of God stayed under the Dawma, and departed from there in the evening, when it was cooler. From the day he alighted in Dhu Khushub, he used to group the prayers between the *Ẓuhr* and the *ʿAṣar*. He delayed the *Ẓuhr* prayer until it was cooler, and he advanced the *ʿAṣar*. Then he joined the two prayers. He did all that until he returned from Tabūk. His places of prayer during his journey to Tabūk were well known. He prayed under the Dawma palm in Dhu al-Khushub; the masjid of al-Fayfāʾ, the masjid in al-Suqyā, the masjid in Wādī al-Qurā, the masjid in the Ḥijr, the masjid in al-Dhanb Ḥawṣāʾ, the masjid in Dhū l-Jīfa of Ṣadr Ḥawṣāʾ in Shiq Tārāʾ, and what was next to Jawbar, a masjid in Dhāt al-Khiṭmī, a masjid in Samana, and in al-Akhḍar, in Dhāt al-Zirāb, of al-Midrān, and in Tabūk.

[Page 1000] When the Messenger of God left Thaniyyat al-Wadāʿ he was on foot, and men who lagged behind him were saying, "O Messenger of God, so and so has not come." So he says, "Leave him, and if you are good with him then God will join him to you. If not, then God will relieve you of him!" Many people from the Hypocrites went out with him, and they did not go out except hoping for plunder. Abū Dharr used to say: I delayed during the raid of Tabūk because of my camel. It was thin and emaciated. So I said, "I will feed it for a day and then join the Messenger of God." I fed it for a day and then I set out, but when I was in Dhū l-Marwa, it failed me. I observed it for a day, but I did not see it move. So I took my supplies and put it on my back. Then I set out to follow the Messenger of God, walking in the intense heat. The people were cut off, and I did not see one Muslim join us. I reached the Prophet at mid-day, and I was thirsty. An observer saw me from the road and he said, "O Messenger of God, indeed there is a man walking by himself on the road." The Messenger of God said, "It is Abū Dharr." When the people looked attentively at me, they said, "O Messenger of God, this is Abū Dharr!" The Messenger of God stopped until I was by him, and said, "Greetings, O Abū Dharr! who walks alone, will die alone, and will be raised alone." He said, "What delayed you, O Abū Dharr?" So he informed him about his camel. Then he said, "Indeed you are the most mighty of my people who stayed away from me. God will forgive you a sin for every step it took to reach me." He put down his supplies from his back, then he asked for a drink, and a vessel of water was brought, and he drank it. During the caliphate of ʿUthmān, when ʿUthmān exiled him to al-Rabadha and his appointed time came, no one was with him but his wife and his son. [Page 1001] He commanded them and said, "Wash me and cover me, then place me on the middle of the road when I am dead."

Ibn Masʿūd approached with a group of men from ʿIrāq on pilgrimage (*ʿUmra*). And what surprised them was the bier on the middle of the road. The camels had almost stepped on it. When his son greeted the people and stopped them and said, "This is Abū Dharr, the companion of the Messenger of God. Help me with him." Ibn Masʿūd started to cry, saying, "The Messenger of God spoke truly: Abū Dharr walks alone, will die alone, and will be raised alone." Then he and his companions alighted until they buried him. Then Ibn Masʿūd related to them his tradition, and what the Messenger of God said to him during his march to Tabūk.

Abū Ruhm al-Ghifārī—he was Kulthūm b. al-Huṣayn—had given his oath of allegiance to the Messenger of God under the tree. He said: I raided Tabūk with the Messenger of God. He said: I traveled the whole night with him, and we were in al-Akhḍar, and I was close to the Messenger of God, when I fell asleep. Suddenly I woke up; my beast was by the beast of the Messenger of God, and its closeness alarmed me for I feared that it would strike his leg in the stirrup. I immediately moved my camel away. Until we were on some road in some night, and my beast jostled his, while his leg was in the stirrup, and I was only woken up by his saying, "Ouch!" I said, "O Messenger of God, forgive me!" The Messenger of God said, "Go!" Then the Messenger of God began to ask me about who stayed behind from the Banū Ghifār, [Page 1002] and I informed him. He asked me what happened to the group of red extremely tall men, and I informed him that they had stayed behind. He said, "What happened to the group of short black crinkly chestnut haired people?" I said, "By God, I do not know those." He replied, "Of course. They are those in Shabakat Shadakh." He said: Then I remembered them with the Banū Ghifār and I did not recall who they were. Then I remembered that they were a group from Aslam who were with us, and they were unpacking in Shabakat Shadakh. They had many sheep. So I said, "O Messenger of God, those are a group of Aslam, allies of ours." The Messenger of God said, "What prevented one of those, when he stayed behind, to provide one of his camels to an enthusiastic man in the path of God to go out with us? To him would be a reward similar to the one who goes out. Indeed, the most dear to me of my people to stay behind from me are the Muhājirūn from the Quraysh, the Anṣār, the Ghifār and the Aslam."

They said: While the Messenger of God was marching, he passed a camel from the troops that its owner had left behind because of its thinness and weakness. A passerby stayed with it, fed it for a day, and turned it towards his house. The Camel was usable and he traveled on it. Its previous owner saw it and complained to the Prophet. The Messenger of God said, "Whoever gives life to a mule or sheep in danger from the land, it belongs to him." They said that there were thirty thousand people with the Messenger of God, and ten thousand horses with the cavalry.

The Messenger of God commanded every clan from the Anṣār to take a flag and a banner. The tribes from the Bedouin had banners and flags. [Page 1003] The Messenger of God handed the flag of the Banū Mālik b. al-Najār to ʿUmāra b. Ḥazm, but when Zayd b. Thābit reached him, he gave Zayd the flag. ʿUmāra said, "Perhaps you are angry with me!" The Messenger of God said, "No, by God, but those who have the Qurʾān memorized (the *ḥāfiẓ*) take precedence and Zayd knows more of the Qurʾān than you. The Qurʾān takes precedence even if it were a black slave with a cut off nose." And he commanded the Aws and the Khazraj that the flags should be carried by those who knew more of the Qurʾān.

Abū Zayd carried the flag of the Banū ʿAmr b. ʿAwf, and Muʿādh b. Jabal carried the flag of the Banū Salima. During the journey, the Messenger of God prayed for a day with his companions. He was wearing a cloak of wool, and he took his horse by the reins, or he (the narrator) said, the halter of his horse. While he was praying the horse urinated and wet his cloak, but he did not wash it. He said, "There is nothing wrong with its urine or its saliva or its sweat."

They said: A group of Hypocrites were marching with the Messenger of God in Tabūk. Among them were Wadīʿa b. Thābit, one of the Banū ʿAmr b. ʿAwf, al-Julās b. Suwayd b. al-Ṣāmit, Makhshī b. Ḥumayyir from Ashjaʿ, an ally of the Banū Salima, and Thaʿlaba b. Ḥāṭib. Thaʿlaba said, "Do you think that fighting the Byzantines is like fighting the others? By God, it is as though we will be with you tomorrow bound in ropes!" insulting the Messenger of God and scaring the believers. Wadīʿa b. Thābit said, "Why do I see those companions of ours as the most scared of the clans, the most false in tongue, and the most cowardly in confrontation?" Al-Julās b. Suwayd said—and he was the husband of Umm ʿUmayr whose son ʿUmayr was an orphan in his custody—[Page 1004] "Those are our masters and our lords, the families of graciousness among us. If Muḥammad speaks the truth, surely we are more evil than the donkeys!

By God, indeed I prefer that every man among us is sentenced to a hundred lashes, than that I suffer from a Qur'ān that comes down about us because of what you said!"

The Messenger of God said to ʿAmmār b. Yāsir, "Overtake those people for they are causing harm, and ask them about what they said. If they deny, say, 'Rather, you said thus and thus!'" So ʿAmmār went to them and said that to them, and they came to the Messenger of God and made their excuses to him. Wadīʿa b. Thābit said, while the Messenger of God was on his camel, he took the rope of the camel of the Messenger of God, and his two feet were scattering the stones, and he says, "O Messenger of God, indeed we were discussing playfully!" The Messenger of God did not pay attention to him, and God revealed about it: *If you ask them they will say we were discussing playfully* until His words—*They are sinners* (Q 9:65,66). They said: ʿUmayr answered al-Julās when he said, "Surely we are more evil than the donkeys." He said, "You are more evil than the donkey, and the Messenger of God spoke truly when he called you a liar!" Al-Julās came to the Prophet and he swore that he had not said any of that. God most high revealed about that: *They swear by God that they did not say, but surely they said words of blasphemy* (Q. 9:66). And He revealed about it: *This revenge of theirs was their only return for the bounty with which God and His Apostle had enriched them* . . . to the end of the verse.

He said: Julās had a blood debt from *jāhiliyya* that some of his people owed him, and he was needy. When the Messenger of God arrived in Medina he took it to him, and he was enriched by it. Makhshī b. Ḥumayyir said, "By God, O Messenger of God, my name and the name of my father are a burden to me," for he who was mentioned in this [Page 1005] verse was Makhshī b. Ḥumayyir. The Messenger of God named him ʿAbd al-Raḥmān or ʿAbdullah. He asked God to give him the death of a martyr, and no one knows where he is. He was killed in the battle of Yamāma, and no trace of him was found. Some said about Julās b. Suwayd: Indeed he was one of those Hypocrites who stayed behind during the raid of Tabūk, and discouraged the people from going out. Umm ʿUmayr was married to him. ʿUmayr was an orphan in his custody who had no property so her husband provided for him. He heard him say, "By God, if Muḥammad is truthful, surely we are more evil than the donkey!" ʿUmayr said to him, "O Julās, you are the most loved of people to me, and you left a good impression on me, and you are so dear to me that I cannot see you doing any wrong. But by God, indeed you said words, which if I mention, will expose you, but if I conceal them, I will surely be destroyed. One of these is less painful to me than the other." The words of Julās were mentioned to the Prophet. The Messenger of God had given al-Julās property from the *ṣadaqa* for his needs for he was poor. The Prophet sent for al-Julās and asked him about what ʿUmayr said, and he swore by God that he never spoke about him, and that ʿUmayr was a liar—He was ʿUmayr b. Saʿīd—and he was present with the Prophet, and he stood up and said, "O God, reveal to your messenger, clearly what I said to him!" And God revealed to his Prophet (Q 9:74), *They swear by God, they did not say, and surely they said words of disbelief* . . . until His words: *God and His Prophet made them rich from his favor* (Q. 9:74), for the *ṣadaqa* which the Prophet gave them. Al-Julās said, "Listen! Surely God has offered me forgiveness. By God, indeed I said what ʿUmayr said!" He admitted his sin, and his repentance was good, for he never stopped the provisions that he provided ʿUmayr b. Saʿīd. That was what was known of his repentance.

Abū Ḥumayd al-Sāʿidī said: We set out with the Messenger of God to [Page 1006] Tabūk. When we came to Wādī al-Qurā we passed by a garden belonging to a woman.

The Messenger of God said, "What do you think is the extent of this land?" He gauged it and we gauged with him: ten measures. Then the Messenger of God said, "Keep what comes out from it until we return to you." When, in the evening, we were in al-Ḥijr he said, "Indeed tonight, a strong wind will blow, and let not one among you stand except with his companion. Whoever has a camel let him fasten its cord." He said: A strong wind stirred, and one did not stand except with a companion, except for two men from the Banū Sā῾ida. One of them set out for his need. The other set out in search of his camel. As for he who went for his need, he choked on his way. As for he who went in search of his camel, the wind carried him and threw him between the two mountains of Ṭayyi. The Messenger of God was informed of their news, and he said, "Did I not forbid a man to go out except with a companion of his?" Then he prayed for he who was taken on his way, and he was healed. As for the other who fell between the mountains of Ṭayyi', indeed a man from Ṭayyi gifted him to the Prophet when he arrived in Medina.

When the Messenger of God alighted in Wādī al-Qurā, the sons of the Jew ῾Urayḍ gifted him with a dish of Harīs (a meat dish), and he agreed to provide them forty measures of dates every year as a favor to them. A Jewish woman used to say: This, which Muḥammad made for them, was better than what they inherited from their fathers, because this was a permanent favor to them until the day of judgment. Abū Hurayra used to narrate saying: When we passed al-Ḥijr the people took water [Page 1007] from its well and made bread. A herald of the Messenger of God called out, "Do not drink its water, nor perform ablutions with it for prayer." The dough was fed to the camels.

Sahl b. Sa῾d said: I was the youngest of my companions and I was their prayer reader in Tabūk. When we alighted, I kneaded the dough and left it to rise, and went in search of firewood. All of a sudden the herald of the Messenger of God called out, "The Messenger of God commands you not to drink the water from their well." The people began to throw what was in their waterbags. They said, "O Messenger of God, we have prepared dough." He said, "Feed it to the camels!" Sahl said: I took what I kneaded and fed it to two weak camels of mine, and they were the weakest of our rides. We turned to the well of Ṣāliḥ the prophet. We collected water from the waterbags and washed it. Then we quenched our thirst, and we did not return, at that time, except in the evening.

The Messenger of God said, "Do not ask your prophet for signs! Those people of Ṣāliḥ asked their prophet for signs. There was a she-camel that came to them from this crack. On the day of her turn, she drank from their water and quenched their thirst with her milk. They slaughtered her and were menaced for three days. God's promise (referring to the punishment) was not false. A scream took them, and not one among them remained under the surface of the heavens but he was destroyed. Except for a man in the sanctuary. The sanctuary protected him from the pain of God." They said, "O Prophet of God, who was he?" The Messenger of God said, "Abū Righāl, the father of Thaqīf." They said, "Was he not in the region of Mecca?" He said, "Indeed. Ṣāliḥ had sent Abū Righāl to collect the Ṣadaqa."

Abū Righāl reached a man who had a hundred sheep that had little milk and a sheep that had given birth. The man also had a baby whose mother had died the day before. Abū Righāl said, "Indeed the Messenger of God (Ṣālih) sent me to you." The man said, "Greetings to the Messenger of God and welcome! [Page 1008] Take!" He said: He took the milking sheep, so the man said, "Surely, it is the mother of this little one after its mother; take another ten instead." He said, "No." He said, "Twenty." He said, "No." He said, "Fifty." He said, "No." He said, "Take all of it except this sheep." Abū Righāl refused. The man said, "You like the milk, and I like it," and he scattered his quiver-full, then said, "O God, bare witness!" Then he aimed an arrow at him and killed him. He said: This news will not precede me to the prophet! He came to Ṣāliḥ and he informed him of the news. And Ṣāliḥ raised his hands outstretched and said, "O God, curse Abū Righāl!" thrice. The Messenger of God said, "You will not visit those tormented people without weeping; if you would not weep do not visit them, for what took them will take you."

Abū Saʿīd al-Khudrī said: I saw a man come to the Prophet with a ring, which he found in the houses of the tormented. He said: He turned away from it, and concealed his eyes with his hand to avoid looking at it. He said, "Throw it!" So he threw it, he did not know where it fell. Ibn ʿUmar used to say: Indeed the Messenger of God said to his companions when he faced them, "Surely, this is the Wādī of the troops!" So they rushed their animals there until they departed. He said: Ibn Abī Sabra related to me from Yūnus b. Yūsuf from ʿUbayd b. Jubayr from Abū Saʿīd al-Khudrī, who said: I saw the Messenger of God hurry his beast until he left the *wādī* behind.

He said: the Messenger of God departed in the morning and there was no water with them. They complained about that to the Messenger of God, but the Messenger of God had no water. ʿAbdullah b. Abī Ḥadrad said: I saw the Messenger of God face the *qibla* and pray. And by God, I did not see a cloud in the sky. And he did not stop praying until I saw clouds assemble from every direction. He did not leave his place until the heavens came down upon us [Page 1009] with fresh water. I heard the Messenger of God proclaim God's praises in the rain. Then Allah cleared the sky. Since that time the land is like pools pouring into each other. People brought water and quenched the thirst of the last of them. I heard the Messenger of God say, "I witness that I am the messenger of God." I said to one of the Hypocrites, "Woe unto you, after this have you any more doubts?" He replied, "It is only a passing cloud!" He was Aws b. Qayẓī, and some said, Zayd b. al-Luṣayt.

He said: Yūnus b. Muḥammad related to me from Yaʿqūb b. ʿUmar b. Qatāda who asked Maḥmūd b. Labīd: Did the people know who were the Hypocrites among them? And he replied, "Yes, by God, indeed the man would know even if it were his father and his brother and the sons of his uncle. I heard your grandfather Qatāda b. al-Nuʿmān say: People among us who are Hypocrites follow us in our houses. Later I heard Zayd b. Thābit say about the Banū Najjār, "Those who God will not bless." Someone said, "Who, O Abū Saʿīd?" And he says, "Saʿd b. Zurāra and Qays b. Fihr." Then Zayd says, "Surely you saw us with the Messenger of God during the raid of Tabūk? When it was the affair of the water the Messenger of God prayed and God sent clouds and it rained until the people quenched their thirst." And we said, "Woe unto you, is there some doubt after this?" And he said, "A passing cloud!" He, by God, is a relative of yours, O Maḥmūd b. Labīd! Maḥmūd said, "I know him!"

He said: Then Muḥammad departed towards Tabūk. In the morning in a house, the camel of the Prophet al-Qaṣwāʾ was lost. His companions went out in search of it. With the Messenger of God was ʿUmāra b. Ḥazm who had participated in Aqaba and Badr, and was killed at the battle of Yamāma, a martyr. There was in his company Zayd b. al-Luṣayt, one of the Banū Qaynuqāʿ. [Page 1010] He was a Jew who converted hypocritically. There was in him the deceit of the Jews and their bad faith. He used to support people of hypocrisy. Zayd said, while he was in the company of ʿUmāra, and ʿUmāra was with the Prophet: "Does not Muḥammad claim that he is a Prophet, and inform you about news of the heavens? And he does not know where his camel is?" And the Messenger of God says, "Indeed, a hypocrite says, 'Surely Muḥammad claims he is a Prophet, that informs you of the affairs of the heavens, yet knows not where his camel is!' I, by God, do not know except what God informs me. He has guided me to it. It is in a valley in a pass thus and thus," and he indicated the ravine to them. A tree has caught it by its halter, so go and bring it. So they went and brought it. ʿUmāra b. Ḥazm returned to his company and said: The Messenger of God told us something amazing! Indeed they are the words of someone that God informed him of. He said thus and thus which Zayd said. He said: And a man who was in the company of ʿUmāra, and had not been in the presence of the Messenger of God, said, "Zayd, by God, said these words before you appeared before us!" He said: ʿUmāra approached Zayd b. al-Luṣayt and hit him on his neck saying, "By God, there is a sly person in my company and I did not know it! Leave my company, O enemy of God!" He who informed ʿUmāra about the words of Zayd was his brother, ʿAmr b. Ḥazm. He was in the company with a group of his friends. He who went and brought the camel from the mountain pass was al-Ḥārith b. Khazama al-Ashhalī. He found it, and its stirrup was caught in a tree.

Zayd b. al-Luṣayt said, "It was as if I had not converted until today! I had doubts about Muḥammad. I rose in the morning and I was the possessor of insight. I testify that he is the Messenger of God!" People claim that Zayd asked for forgiveness. Khārija b. Zayd b. Thābit used to deny that he asked for forgiveness saying: He continued to be deceitful until his death.

[Page 1011] When the Messenger of God was in Wādī al-Mushaqaq, he heard a camel driver's song in the middle of the night. He said, "Hurry, let us join him!" The Messenger of God says, "By whom is the camel song, by you, or another?" They said, "Another, of course." The Messenger of God caught up with him and lo and behold, it was a group. He said, "From who are the people?" They said, "From Muḍar." The Messenger of God said, "I am from Muḍar," and he traced his genealogy until he reached Muḍar. The people said, "We are the first of those who drive their camels with a song." The Prophet said, "How is that?" They said, "Of course, some of the people of *jāhiliyya* were attacking some others; we came upon a man who had a boy with him, and his camels had fled. So he commanded the boy to gather them. The boy said, 'I am not able!' So he struck his hand with a stick. The boy began to cry, 'O my hands!' And the camels gathered. His master says, 'Say thus to the camels.'" The Prophet began to laugh.

The Messenger of God said to Bilāl, "Do you want me to make you happy?" They said, "Of course, O Messenger of God!" They were marching on their beasts. He said, "Indeed God has promised me the two treasures of Persia and Byzantium and helps me with the kings of the kings of Himyar. They will strive in the path of God and eat the booty of God."

Al-Mughīra b. al-Shuʿba used to say: We were between al-Ḥijr and Tabūk and the Messenger of God went for a need of his. Whenever he went, he went a distance, and I would follow him with water after the break of dawn. The people were rushing to their prayer—it was the morning prayer—fearful that the sun would rise they proceeded to ʿAbd al-Raḥmān b. ʿAwf and he prayed with them. I went with the Prophet carrying a vessel of water, and when he finished I poured water for him and he washed his face. Then he wanted to wash his hands. The sleeve of his cloak was tight—he was wearing a Byzantine cloak—so he took out his hand from under [Page 1012] the cloak and washed them and stroked his footwear. When we reached ʿAbd al-Raḥmān b. ʿAwf, he had prayed one bowing with the people and they were chanting *subḥanallah* with ʿAbd al-Raḥmān, when they saw the Messenger of God and they were almost distracted. ʿAbd al-Raḥmān wanted to withdraw behind the Prophet but he indicated to him to stay, and the Messenger of God prayed one bowing behind ʿAbd al-Raḥmān. When ʿAbd al-Raḥmān gave the greeting, the people jumped up, but the Messenger of God stayed and prayed the rest of the prayer. Then he greeted after completing it. Then he said, "You are the best! Indeed a prophet will not die until a good man leads from his community."

At that time Yaʿlā b. Munabbih came to him with his servant who had fought a man from the troops, and that man had bitten him. The man pulled his hand from the bite and so pulled out his tooth. The wound persisted and news of it reached the Prophet. He said: I stayed with my servant to observe what he does. He brought them to the Prophet and he said, "One of you took and bit his brother just as a stallion does." The Messenger of God rendered his claim for what he took of his tooth unfounded.

The Messenger of God said: Surely you will arrive tomorrow, God willing, at ʿAyn Tabūk. You will not reach it until forenoon. Whoever comes to it, do not touch any of its water until I arrive. Muʿādh b. Jabal said: When we arrived, two men had preceded us to it. The spring appeared like the white of the egg foam in some of the water, so he asked them, "Did you touch something from the water?" They said, "Yes." The Prophet insulted them and said what God wished him to say. Then he spooned some water out with their help, little by little, until all of it was in a water bag. Then the Prophet washed [Page 1013]; his mouth his face and his hands, and then returned the water to the spring, and the spring filled up with much water and the people quenched their thirst. Then the Prophet said, "This place will soon be filled with gardens, O Muʿādh, and if you live long you will see it."

ʿAbdullah, of the two heavy cloths, (Dhū l-bijādayn) was from Muzayna. He was an orphan who had no wealth. His father had died and he had not inherited anything. But his uncle was rich. He took him and provided for him until he was living well. He had camels and sheep and slaves. When the Messenger of God arrived in Medina, ʿAbdullah began to long for Islam for himself, but he was not able to because of his uncle. Years passed and he observed everything. When the Messenger of God returned from the Conquest of Mecca to Medina, ʿAbdullah said to his uncle, "O Uncle, I waited for your Islam, but I do not think you desire Muḥammad. So permit me Islam!" He replied, "By God, if you follow Muḥammad I will not leave anything in your hands that I was giving you, but I will take it away from you, even your two garments." ʿAbd al-ʿUzza—that was his name at that time—said, "I am by God, a follower of Muḥammad and a Muslim leaving the worship of the stone and idols. These are what are in my hands so take it!" He took back all that he had given him, and even deprived him of his shawl. He went to his mother, and she cut a cloth in two and he covered with one and dressed with the other. Then he went to Medina and he was in Wariqān, a mountain of the sanctuary of Medina, and lay down in the mosque at dawn.

The Messenger of God prayed the *Ṣubḥ* prayer. The Messenger of God used to examine the people when he turned from *Ṣubh*. He looked at ʿAbd al-ʿUzzā and he did not to know him. He said, "Who are you?" So he traced his genealogy for him, and he said, "You are ʿAbdullah the possessor of the two cloths." Then he said, "Stay close to me." He used to be with his guests, and he taught him the Qurʾān, [Page 1014]; until he read the Qurʾān well. The people were preparing for Tabūk, and he was a well known man staying in the mosque, who raised his voice reciting the Qurʾān. ʿUmar said,

"O Messenger of God, do you not hear this Bedouin raise his voice with the Qur'ān even preventing people from reading?" The Prophet said, "Let him, O ʿUmar, for surely he set out as an emigrant to God and His messenger." When they set out to Tabūk, ʿAbdullah said, "O Messenger of God, ask God to grant me martyrdom. He said, "Take me to the bark of the Samura tree," so he took him to the bark of the Samura. The Messenger of God took a piece of bark and tied it on his arm and said, "O God, I forbid his blood to the disbelievers!" He said, "O Messenger of God, I did not want this." The Prophet said, "Indeed, if you set out raiding in the path of God, and a fever takes you and you die, you will be a martyr. And if your 'mount' breaks your neck, even then you will be a martyr. Do not worry about which it will be." When they alighted at Tabūk, they stayed there for several days and ʿAbdullah Dhū l-Bijādayn died. Bilāl b. al-Ḥārith used to say: I attended the Messenger of God, and Bilāl the Muʿadhdhin held a torch of fire at the grave standing by it. And lo and behold the Messenger of God was in the grave. And Abū Bakr and ʿUmar were lowering him to the Prophet while the Prophet was saying, "Get your brother closer to me." When he had prepared him on his side, he said a prayer, "O God, indeed I am this night satisfied about him, so be satisfied with him." He said: ʿAbdullah b. Masʿud said: I wish I were the owner of this grave.

We came to the Messenger of God during his march, and he was riding, while Suhayl b. Bayḍā' was behind him. Suhayl said: The Messenger of God raised his voice and said, "O Suhayl!" And all that Suhayl says is, "I am at your service!" three times, until the people knew that the Messenger of God desired their attention. He [Page 1015] turned and faced him, and those who were behind him among the people joined him. Then the Messenger of God said, "Whoever testifies that there is but one God, and has no partner, God will protect him from the fire."

They said: The people came across a snake during their march. Its might and its ways were mentioned, and the people moved away from it. It approached until it stopped before the Messenger of God, and he stopped on his camel for a long while. The people observed it. Then it curled and moved away from the road and stayed there a while. The People came forward until they joined the Messenger of God, and he said to them, "Do you know who this is?" They replied, "Only God and His messenger know!" He said, "Surely this is one from a group of eight Jinn who desires to hear the Qur'ān. He considered he must—when the Messenger of God settled in his land—greet him. Here is one who extends his greetings to you. So greet him." All the people said, "And peace to you and God's blessings!" The Messenger of God says, "Love worshipers of God whoever they are."

They said: The Messenger of God arrived in Tabūk and stayed there for twenty nights. He prayed two bowings. Heraclius was at that time in Ḥimṣ. ʿUqba b. ʿĀmir used to say: We set out with the Messenger of God to Tabūk, until all of a sudden we were but one night away from it. The Messenger of God went to sleep and did not awake until the sun was reflected in his spear. The Messenger of God said, "O Bilāl, were you not able to keep watch for us tonight?" Bilāl said, "Sleep took me, and what happened to you happened to me!" He said: The Messenger of God departed not far from that place, and then prayed two bowings before dawn. Then he prayed Fajr. Then he hurried during what remained of his day [Page 1016] and night, and was in Tabūk in the morning. He gathered the people, and praised God and commended Him as He deserved. Then he said, "Surely, the most trustworthy of traditions is the Book of God. The word of humility tightens the bond. The best community is the community of Abraham; the best of practices is the practice of Muḥammad. The most noble of the utterances is the remembrance of God. The best of tales is this Qur'ān. The best part of an affair is its outcome. Evil are the innovations; the best guidance is the guidance of the prophets. The noblest death is the death of the martyr. The most blind in error are those who err after guidance. The best works are those that are useful. The best guidance is what is followed. The most evil blindness is the blindness of heart. The [giving] hand above is better than the [taking] hand below. A little that is sufficient is better than a lot that distracts; the most evil of affairs is to ask for forgiveness at death's door. The worst of regrets is on the Day of Judgment. Some people rarely attend *jum'a* and some mention God with ugly words; one of the greatest sins is lying. The best of the wealthy are the rich at heart. The best provision is fear of God. Among the greatest transgressions is the lying tongue. The best wealth is the wealth of the soul/heart. The best provision is the god-fearing provision. The ultimate wisdom is the fear of God. The best of what enters the hearts is certitude in God. Suspicion is from unbelief; lamentation is from pre-Islam; the unfaithful are in the fires of hell. The drunk is at the center of hell fire. Poetry is from Satan. Wine is the gathering of sin; Satan uses women for ensnaring. Youth is a branch of madness; evil are the earnings from usury; evil is the food from the property of the orphan; Happy are those who learn from the experience of others. Miserable is one whose misery begins in the stomach of his mother. Every one of you will end in a little grave of four *adhra'a*; his fate is according to his end; The last deeds decide your fate. Usury is excessive lying; the future is close at hand (life is short). Insulting the believer is corrupt. Killing the believer is disbelief. Eating his flesh (gossiping) is disobeying God; his wealth is forbidden just as his blood is forbidden; he who swears falsely does not believe in God; he who forgives, God forgives him. Who controls his anger, God rewards him; he who is patient in misery, God will compensate him; And who believes rumors, God will have him [Page 1017] maligned. He who is patient God doubles his reward. Who disobeys God, God tortures him. O God forgive me and my people, O God I ask for forgiveness for me and you," three times.

A man from the Banū 'Udhra, who was called 'Adī says: The Messenger of God came to Tabūk and I saw him on a red camel going around the people saying: "O people, the hand of God is above the hand of the giver, and the hand of the giver is the best, and the hand of the receiver is low. O people, be content, even if it is only packing firewood. O God have I conveyed Islam?" Thrice. I said, "O Messenger of God I had two wives. They fought each other, so I aimed and shot one of them with my arrow—" meaning that she died. The Prophet said, "Pay her blood money and do not inherit from her."

The Messenger of God sat in his spot in the mosque in Tabūk and he looked towards the right and raised his hand and pointed towards the people of Yemen and said, "Faith is in Yemen." He looked towards the East and he pointed with his hand and said, "Indeed the roughness and rudeness of the hearts is in the yokes of oxen, and the people of fur from around the East where the two-horned devil will rise.

A man from the Banū Sa'd b. Hudhaym said: I came to the Messenger of God while he was seated in Tabūk with a group of his companions—and he was their seventh. I stood and I greeted, and he said, "Sit!" I said, "O Messenger of God, I witness that there is no God but God and that you are the Messenger of God!" He said, "May you be successful!" Then he said, "O Bilāl, bring us food!" [Page 1018] He said, "Bilāl spread out a mat," then he began to bring out from a leather flask of his, and he pulled out what came out in his hand of dates and dough and fat and cheese. Then the Messenger of God said, "Eat!" And we ate until we were satisfied. I said, "O Messenger of God if I had eaten this alone!" The Messenger of God said, "The disbeliever eats for seven intestines; the believer eats for one." I came to him the next day seeking the time of his meal to be more certain of Islam. And ten individuals were around him. He said, "Feed us O Bilāl." He said: He began taking out from a bag of dates with his hand, hand full after handful. He said, "Take and do not fear stinginess from the possessor of the throne." He brought the bag and scattered it and said. I estimate it to be the Mudayyan date. He said: the Prophet put his hand on the dates. Then he said, "Eat in the name of God!" So the people ate and I ate with them. I loved dates. He said: I ate until I could eat no more. He said: And it remained the same, just as Bilāl brought it, as though we had not eaten a single date from it. He said: Then I returned the next day. And a group had returned in order to stay the night. They were ten or more by one or two men. He said, "O Bilāl, give us food!" He brought that special bag, and I knew it, and he sprinkled it. The Messenger of God put his hand on it and said, "Eat in the name of God," and we ate until we finished. Then he arose as before and poured forth. And he did similarly for three days.

He said: Heraclius had sent a man from the Ghassān to observe the Prophet, his ways, his characteristics, the redness of his eyes, and the seal of prophecy between his shoulders. He asked if he (the Prophet) accepts *ṣadaqa*, and he learned something of the situation of the Prophet. [Page 1019] Then he returned to Heraclius and he mentioned that to him. He invited the people to believe in the Messenger of God, but they refused, until he feared they would go against his authority. He stayed where he was, and did not move or go forward. News that had reached the Prophet, about Heraclius sending his companions and getting close to the South of al-Shām, was false. He did not desire that, nor did he intend it. The Messenger of God consulted about proceeding. ʿUmar b. al-Khaṭṭāb said, "If you were commanded to march, march!" The Messenger of God said, "If I was commanded about it I would not consult you!" He said, "O Messenger of God, the Byzantines have many groups, but there is not one of Muslims. You are close to them as you see, and your closeness frightens them. So return this year until you come to a decision, or God establishes for you in that affair."

A strong wind stirred in Tabūk, and the Messenger of God said: This is for the death of a hypocrite who is famed for his hypocrisy. He said: They arrived in Medina and they found that a hypocrite famed for his hypocrisy had died. Cheese was brought to the Prophet in Tabūk, and they said, "O Messenger of God, surely this is food made by Persians. Indeed we fear that there is death in it." The Messenger of God said, "Put the knife in it and mention the name of God!"

He said: A man form the Quḍāʿa gifted a horse to the Messenger of God, and he gave it to a man from the Anṣār, and commanded him to tie it close by, so he could enjoy its neighing. It continued thus until the Prophet arrived in Medina and he missed the neighing of the horse. He asked its keeper about it, and he said, "I neutered it, O Messenger of God!" The Messenger of God said, "Indeed in the forelocks of the horse are blessings until the day of judgment. Breed horses and boast [Page 1020] about its neigh to the disbelievers. Its mane keeps it warm; its tail is a flywhisk. By Him who has my soul in His hands, surely the martyrs will come with their swords riding on their shoulders, and they will not pass one of the prophets, but the prophets will give way to them; until they pass Abraham al-Khalīl, the friend of the Most Gracious, and he will give way until they sit on a pulpit of light". He says to the people, "These are those who shed their blood for the Lord of the World. It will be thus until God fulfills between his worshipers."

They said: While the Messenger of God was in Tabūk, he came to his horse al-Ẓarib and hung his badge on it. The Prophet began to rub its back with his garment. Someone said, "O Messenger of God, you rub its back with your garment?" He said, "Yes." "How do you know?" "Perhaps Gabriel commanded me about that, although I had stayed up the night. Indeed, the angels blame me for not brushing the horses and stroking them." He added, "My friend Gabriel informed me that for every good deed that I do for my horse, I would be rewarded with good and a sin removed from me." There is not a man among the Muslims who ties his horse in the path of God and feeds it and requests its strength, except God wrote for him, with every seed, a reward and removed evil! It was said, "O Messenger of God, what is a good horse?" He replied, "The most black, with white on its forehead, its nose and a third of its legs, and it is free. And if not black then [Page 1021] chestnut, with this description." He said: It was said, "O Messenger of God, what about fasting in the way of God?" He replied, "He who fasts one day in the way of God, hell shall be distanced from his journey by a hundred years however fast he goes. The women of those who strive are more blessed than those who abstain, like their mothers. There is not one among those who abstain, who frequents a woman from the wives of those who strive, and betrays him with his wife, except he will stand on the Day of Judgment and he will be told: 'This man was disloyal to you with your family, so take what you wish from his good work.' So how would you see it?"

ʿAbdullah b. ʿUmar or ʿAmr b. al-ʿĀṣ used to relate saying: The people were frightened in Tabūk at night. So I set out with my weapons until I sat with Sālim the *Mawlā* of Abū Ḥudhayfa who was wearing his weapons, and I said: I will emulate this good man from the people of Badr! I sat at his side close to the tent of the Prophet. The Messenger of God came out to us angrily and said, "O people, what is this trifling and frivolity? Do you not do what those two good men do?" He was referring to me, and Sālim, the *mawlā* of Abū Ḥudhayfa.

They said: When the Messenger of God reached Tabūk he placed, with his hand, *a stone to indicate the ʿqiblaʾ* at the place of prayer in Tabūk. Then he prayed *Ẓuhr* with the people. Then he approached them and said, "Over there is al-Shām; and over there is Yemen."

ʿAbdullah b. ʿUmar used to say: We were with the Messenger of God in Tabūk. He stayed and prayed through the night, and increased to *tahajjat* of the night. Every time he woke up he cleansed his teeth. When he stood for prayer he prayed in front of his tent. People among the Muslims used to stay and keep watch. On one of those nights when he finished praying he came to those who were around him. When he completed he approached those who were with him and said, "I was given five privileges, no one was given that before me. The first of them was that I was sent to all mankind. Every prophet before me was sent to his own community. The second: that the earth was made a clean place of prayer to me. Wherever the prayer overtakes me [Page 1022] I take *tayammam* and pray. Those who were before me did not pray except in churches or synagogues; plunder was released to me and I use it. Those who were before me were forbidden it; and fifth: what is it? what is it? what is it?. . . He said this thrice! They said, "What is it, O Messenger of God?" The Messenger of God replied, "It was said to me: Ask, for every prophet has asked, and for it is for you and for whoever testifies that there is but one God."

A RECORD OF WHAT WAS REVEALED OF THE QUR'ĀN DURING THE RAID OF TABŪK

The words of God Most High, O you who believe! What is the matter with you that when you are asked to go forth in the cause of God you cling . . . (Q. 9:38): They said that the Prophet raided in extreme heat. The people were exhausted, the fruits were ripe, and shade was desired. People were slow in joining him. The verse of *Barā'a* revealed what they concealed. *Barā'a* also showed the hypocrisy of the Hypocrites among them. *God says: Unless you go forth He will punish you with a grievous penalty* (Q. 9:39): meaning, unless you go forth with the Prophet. *It was not fitting for the people of Medina and the Bedouin Arabs of the neighborhood* (Q. 9:120): He said that there was a community among the companions of the Prophet who set out to the Bedouin teaching them Islam, so the Hypocrites said, a group of the companions of Muḥammad stayed with the Bedouin, and they said, the companions destroyed the Bedouin. It was revealed . . . *The Believers should not go out together*. (Q. 9:122). *Go out whether equipped lightly or heavily* (Q. 9:41): He said, willingly or not. It is said, the light ones are the youth, the heavy are the old. [Page 1023]; *And struggle with your goods and persons in the way of God*: spend your money for your raids and strive. He says *jāhidū* meaning fight. *But the distance was long and weighed on them* (Q. 9:42): Twenty nights. *They would indeed swear by God, If we only could, we should certainly have come out with you*: Allah means the Hypocrites . . . *If there had been immediate gain*: He says, easy plunder. *And the journey were easy, they would have all followed you*. He means that when the Prophet set out to Tabūk they made excuses of hardship and sickness. *They would destroy their own souls*. He means in the other life . . . *For God knows they are certainly lying*: He means that they were certainly powerful and healthy when the prophet accepted their excuses and granted them permission. *May God give you grace! Why did you grant them exemption when you clearly knew who told the truth* (Q. 9:43): Until you test them with the journey and know who is truthful and who is a liar. *Those who believe in God and the last day do not ask your permission* (Q. 9:44): Allah describes the believers who spend their money for this raid. It was cold, a raid of hardship. *Only those who do not believe in God ask you for exemption* (Q. 9:45): He means the Hypocrites. Then he mentions the Hypocrites saying, *Indeed they had plotted sedition before* (Q. 9:48): Before your setting out to Tabūk and before your success. *Their disgust* . . .: Because of your appearance, and because of the people who followed you. *Among them is one who says grant me exemption and draw me not into trial* (Q. 9:49): This was revealed about al-Jadd b. Qays. He was the wealthiest of Banū Salama. He had the most number of animals, and was a man who liked women. The Prophet said to him, "Will you not go and raid the Byzantines, [Page 1024] perhaps you will get a slave girl from them?" He replied, "O Muḥammad, my people know that I like women very much, no one admires women more than me, so do not tempt me with them!" *Have they not fallen into trial* (Q. 9:49): for being absent from the Prophet. *If good befalls you it grieves them* (Q. 9:50): He says: Plunder and good health. Those who were absent and asked permission. But if misfortune befalls you: He means trial and hardship . . . *We took indeed poor precautions beforehand. Say! Nothing will happen to us except what God has decreed for us* (Q. 9:51): He says except what was in the mother of the Books . . . *Say! Can you expect for us other than one of two glorious things* (Q. 9:52): Meaning plunder or martyrdom. *Say! Spend willingly or unwillingly. Not from you will it be accepted* (Q. 9:53): There were powerful men from the Hypocrites who spent money when people were watching, in order that this reaches Muḥammad in order to keep themselves from the battle. *In the words of God Most High: The only reasons why their contributions are not accepted are* (Q. 9:54): *God says, In reality God's plan is to punish them in this life* (Q. 9:55): He says, there will be proof against them, because what they ate from the plunder, was taken in hypocrisy. What they spent was only for good will. *Nor is there blame on those who come to you* (Q. 9:92): These are the weepers, they are seven, Abū Laylā al-Māzinī, Salama b. Ṣakhr al-Māzinī al-Māzini, Thaʿlaba b. Ghanama al-Aslam, ʿUlba b. Zayd al-Ḥārithī, al-Irbāḍ b. Sāriya al-Sulamī from Banū Sulaym, ʿAbdullah b. Amr al-Muzannī, and Sālim b. ʿUmayr al-ʿAmrī. *They prefer to stay with those who stay behind* (Q. 9:93): He means with the women. Al-Jadd b. Qays. *Certain of the desert Arabs around you* [Page 1025] *are Hypocrites* (Q. 9:101): There were men from the Bedouin, among them ʿUyayna b. Ḥiṣn and his community, who used to satisfy Muḥammad and his community and show them that they are with them and satisfy their people . . . *The vanguard—the first of those who had left their homes and those who gave them aid* (Q. 9:100): From those who had prayed facing the two *qiblas*.

THE RAID OF UKAYDIR B. ʿABD AL-MALIK IN DŪMAT AL-JANDAL

He said: Ibn Abī Habība related to me from Dāwnd b. al-Ḥuṣayn, from ʿIkrima, from Ibn ʿAbbās, and Muḥammad b. Ṣāliḥ from ʿĀṣim b. ʿUmar b. Qatāda, and Muʿādh b. Muḥammad from Isḥāq b. ʿAbdullah b. Abī Ṭalḥa, and Ismāʿīl b. Ibrāhīm from Mūsā b. Uqba. All have related portions of this tradition to me, and it is supported by the tradition of Ibn Abī Ḥabība.

They said: the Messenger of God sent Khālid b. al-Walīd from Tabūk with four hundred and twenty horsemen to Ukaydir b. ʿAbd al-Malik in Dūmat al-Jandal. Ukaydir was from Kinda and was their king, and was a Christian. Khālid said, "O Messenger of God, how will it be for me in the middle of the land of the Kalb, for surely I will be with a people of luxury?" The Messenger of God said, "You will find him hunting cows and you will take him." He said: So Khālid went out until all of a sudden the fortress was in his sights in that night of a summer's moon. Ukaydir was on the roof with his wife al-Rabāb, daughter of Unayf b. ʿĀmir from Kinda. He had ascended the roof of the fortress because of the heat. His songstress sang, and he called for a drink and drank it. The cows approached [Page 1026] rubbing their horns on the gate of the fortress. His wife, al-Rabāb, came forward, looked down from the fortress and saw the cows, and said, "I have not seen such a night of meat. Have you ever seen such as this?" He replied, "No!" Then she said, "Who would leave this?" He replied, "No one!" He said: Ukaydir says, "I have not seen such a night when the cattle come to us. Before, I used to prepare the horses, making them lean and light for a month or more, when I wanted to catch them, and I would ride with men and tools."

Ukaydir came down and ordered his horse to be saddled, and a group of people from his house rode with him, including his brother Ḥassān, and two slaves. They set out from their fortress with their hunting spears. When they left the fortress the cavalry of Khālid observed them and not a horse among them either neighed or stirred. The moment Ukaydir departed from the fortress, he was captured by the cavalry of Khālid and taken prisoner, but Ḥassān resisted and fought until he was killed. The two slaves fled, and those who were with him from the people of his house entered the fortress. Ḥassān was wearing a kaftān of brocade embossed with gold and Khālid captured it as plunder and sent it with ʿAmr b. Umayya al-Ḍamrī to the Messenger of God, to arrive before them, and inform the Prophet about the capture of Ukaydir.

Anas b. Mālik and Jābir b ʿAbdullah said: We saw the Kaftān of Ḥassān the brother of Ukaydir when it was taken to the Messenger of God. The Muslims began to touch it with their hands for they were amazed by it. The Messenger of God said, "Does this amaze you? By Him who holds my soul in His hand, the handkerchief of Saʿd b. Muʿādh in Paradise is better than this!"

The Messenger of God had said to Khālid b. al-Walīd, "If you are victorious with Ukaydir, do not kill him, but bring him to me. But if he refuses, kill him." He obeyed him. Bujayr b. Bujara from Tayyi', [Page 1027] mentioning the words of the Prophet to Khālid, "Surely you will find him hunting the cows," said that what the cows did that night at the gate of the fortress confirmed the words of the Messenger of God. He recited a poem:

Blessed is the driver of the cows,
Indeed I see God guide every leader.
Those of you who stayed behind from taking Tabūk,
Indeed we have been ordered to strive/fight in the way of God.

Khālid b. al-Walīd said to Ukaydir, "If I promise to protect you from being killed until you come to the Messenger of God, would you open Dūma for me?" He replied, "Yes, I will do that for you." When Khālid made the agreement with Ukaydir, Ukaydir was in shackles; Khālid departed with him until they were close to the gates of the fortress, and Ukaaydir called out to his family: Open the gate of the fortress! Muḍād the brother of Ukaydir refused them, and Ukaydir said to Khālid, "You know by God, they will not open to me when they see me in shackles. Leave me, and for you by God is the trust that I will open the fortress for you, if you will promise me the security of its people." Khālid said, "Indeed, I do." Ukaydir said, "If you wish I will appoint you arbitrator, and if you wish I will be the arbitrator". Khālid said, "Rather, we will accept whatever you give." So he promised him a thousand camels; eight hundred heads of slaves; four hundred armor plates and four hundred spears on condition that Khālid left with him and his brother to the Messenger of God who would pass judgement over them. Khālid agreed about that and set Ukaydir free, and Ukaydir opened the fortress. Khālid entered it, and his associates shackled Muḍād, the brother of Ukaydir. He took what Ukaydir promised him of camels and slaves and weapons. Then he set out returning to Medina taking Ukaydir and Muḍād with him.

When Ukaydir arrived before the Messenger of God he agreed with him about the *jizya*, and to spare his blood and the blood [Page 1028] of his brother and set them free. The Messenger of God wrote a document about their protection and their peace, and he sealed it at that time with imprint of his nail.

They said: Wāthila b. al-Asqaʿ al-Laythī approached and alighted in the region of Medina in order to come to the Messenger of God and pray the *Ṣubḥ* prayer with him. The Messenger of God, having prayed *Ṣubḥ*, turned to examine the faces of his companions and look at them. When Wāthila came close, he did not recognize him and he said, "Who are you?" So he informed him. He said, "What brings you?" He replied, "I would give you my allegiance." The Messenger of God said, "Are you able?" He said, "Yes," and he gave him his allegiance. The Messenger of God was at that time preparing for Tabūk. The man set out back to his family, and he met his father al-Asqaʿ.

When he saw his condition he said, "You did it!" Wāthila said, "Yes." His father said, "By God, I will never speak to you." So he came to his uncle while he was turning his back to the sun, and he greeted him and he said, "You did it!" He replied, "Yes." He gave him a scolding that was lighter than that of his father. He said, "Did it not occur to you that you should not precede us in such a matter?" The sister of Wāthila heard his words, and she came out to him and greeted him with the greeting of Islam. Wāthila said, "When did this come to you, my little sister?" She replied, "I heard your words and the words of your uncle." Wāthila had mentioned Islam and described it for his uncle. Islam pleased his sister and she converted. Wāthila said, "Surely, God desires your well being little sister! Prepare me, your brother, to go out on a raid. Indeed, the Messenger of God is inclined to march."

So she gave him a measure of flour, and some dough made from flour in a bucket, and she gave him some dates and he took them.

He went to Medina and he found the Messenger of God had already set out to Tabūk. Caravans of people remained and they were about to set out from his house. Indeed the Messenger of God had left two days earlier. He began to call out [Page 1029] in the market of the Banū Qaynuqāʿ: "Whoever will take me, I will give him my portion!" He said: I was a man without a beast. Kaʿb b. ʿUjra called me and said, "I will take you one turn by night and one turn by day; your hand is equal to my hand, and you will give me your portion." Wāthila said, "Yes." After that Wāthila said, "May God reward him well! Indeed he took me twice; he provided me and I ate with him what he brought up for me, until all of a sudden the Messenger of God sent Khālid b. al-Walīd to Ukaydir al-Kindī in Dūmat al-Jandal, and Kaʿb b. ʿUjra set out with the troops of Khālid b. al-Walīd and I went out with him. We took much during the raid, and Khālid b. al-Walīd apportioned it. He apportioned six young she-camels to me, and I approached driving them until I reached the tent of Kaʿb b. ʿUjra and I said, "Take, by God's grace, and look at your camels and keep them." He came out to me smiling and saying, "God has blessed you with them. I did not carry you desiring to take something from you."

Abū Saʿīd al-Khudrī, may God bless him, used to relate saying: We captured Ukaydir, and my portion from the weapons were an armor, a helmet, and a spear; I was also apportioned ten camels. Bilāl b. al-Ḥārith al-Muzannī used to relate saying: We captured Ukaydir and his brother, and we brought them before the Prophet. Before anything was apportioned from the *fay'*, the best part was set aside for the Prophet. Then he apportioned the plunder into five parts and a fifth was for the Prophet. ʿAbdullah b. ʿAmr al-Muzannī used to say: We were forty men from Muzayna with Khālid b. al-Walīd. Our share was five portions. Every man had weapons for armor and spears were apportioned to us.

Yaʿqūb b. Muḥammad al-Ẓafarī related to me from ʿĀṣim b. ʿUmar b. [Page 1030] Qatāda, from ʿAbd al-Raḥmān b. Jābir from his father, who said, "I saw Ukaydir when Khālid brought him. He was wearing a gold cross and silk brocade which was embossed."

Al-Wāqidī said: An old man from the people of Dūma told me that the Messenger of God wrote this document for him:

> In the name of God most gracious most merciful. This is a document from Muḥammad, the Messenger of God, to Ukaydir when he responded to Islam and removed the other Gods and the idols with Khālid b. al-Walīd, the sword of God,

> in Dūmat al-Jandal and its protectorates. Indeed, to us are the outskirts of shallow water, uncultivated land, uninhabited areas and desert lands, coats of mail, weapons, camels and horses and the fortress. For you are the palm trees included within your towns, sources from the cultivated land after the fifth is taken; your camels will not be apportioned, nor will the cattle you set apart for milk be reckoned. Farming is not prohibited to you, nor will the tithe for the utensils of the homes be taken from you. You will stand for prayer when it is time, and will bring the *zakāt* as determined. To you in that is a promise and an agreement. For you with that is truth and fulfillment.

It was witnessed by God and those who attended among the Muslims.

He said: *al-Ḍaḥl* is where there is little water; *al-Būr* is where there are no plants; *al-Maʿāmī* is where there is no fixed boundary known to it as in desert land and waters. *Wa lā tuʿaddu fāradatukum*: he says that sheep and cattle that do not exceed forty will not be counted. *Al-Māʿīn* is surface waters; *al-Ḍāmina min al-nakhl* are palm trees that have roots in the ground. *Wa lā yuḥẓar ʿalaykum al-nabāt* is that you are not forbidden to plant.

They said: He gave him a gift of a robe, and the Messenger of God wrote a document for him granting him protection and peace. He granted his brother protection and put down the *jizya* for him. The Messenger of God did not have his seal with him, so he sealed it with his fingernail.

[Page 1031] Dūma and Ayla and Taymāʾ were afraid of the Prophet when they saw the Bedouin submit. Yuḥanna b. Ruʿba, the king of Ayla, arrived before the Prophet. They were concerned that the Messenger of God would send a force to them just as he had sent one to Ukaydir. The People of Jarbāʾ, and Adhruḥ approached with him. They came to him and he made a peace with them, and he established the *jizya* for them, and the *jizya* was fixed. He wrote a document for them: In the name of God the most gracious the merciful, this is a peace from God and Muḥammad, the prophet and Messenger of God, to Yuḥanna b. Ruʿba and the people of Ayla for their ships and those traveling on land and sea. For them is a protection from God and a protection from Muḥammad, the Messenger of God, and to whoever is with him from the people of al-Shām, the people of Yemen and the people of the sea. Whoever tries to cause mischief, his property will not save him. Indeed it is good to whoever he takes *jizya* from. Indeed it is not permitted to restrain the water they desire or the roads they desire from land or sea. This is the document of Juhaym b. al-Ṣalt and Shuraḥbīl b. Ḥasana by the permission of the Messenger of God. The Messenger of God put down the *jizya* for the people of Ayla at three hundred dinar for every year, and they were three hundred men.

He said: Yaʿqūb b. Muḥammad al-Ẓafarī related to me from ʿĀṣim b. ʿUmar b. Qatāda from ʿAbd al-Raḥmān b. Jābir from his father, who said: I saw Yuḥanna b. Ruʿba on the day he was brought to the Prophet, and he was wearing a cross of gold and he was restrained. When he saw the Prophet he was humble and lowered his head. The Prophet signed to him, "Raise your head!" He made peace with him at that time. The Messenger of God clothed him [Page 1032] in a cloak from Yemen. He ordered a place for him with Bilāl.

The Messenger of God wrote this document for the people of Jarbāʾ and Adhruḥ: From Muḥammad the Prophet and Messenger of God to the people of Adhruḥ. That they are secure in the protection of God and Muḥammad. That from them is due a hundred dinars every Rajab, good and fulfilled. And God is sufficient for them.

Al-Wāqidī said: I copied the document of Adhrūḥ and lo and behold, it said: In the name of God the benificient the merciful. From Muḥammad the Prophet of God to the people of Adhrūḥ: They are guaranteed the protection of God and the protection of Muḥammad. From them is a promise of a hundred dinars every Rajab in good faith. God is sufficient for them in advice and in charity for the Muslims. Whoever seeks refuge with them, from the Muslims, from fear and censure when they fear the Muslims, they are protected until Muḥammad establishes them before his setting out.

They said: He wrote for the people of Maqnā that they are guaranteed the protection of God and the protection of Muḥammad and that for them is a quarter of what they spin and their fruits.

ʿUbayd b. Yāsir b. Numayr, one of the Saʿd Allah, and a man from Judhām, one of the Banū Wāʾil, both arrived before the Prophet in Tabūk and converted to Islam. The Messenger of God gave them both from the income of Maqnā, a fourth of what he took out of the sea and from the fruit, from their dates, and from their spinning. ʿUbayd b. Yāsir was a rider, and the Judhāmī was on foot. The Messenger of God gave for the horse of ʿUbayd b. Yāsir a hundred braids. They continued that with the Banū Saʿd and Wāʿil. The people do this until today.

[Page 1033] Then ʿUbayd b. Yāsir arrived in Maqnā, where there was a Jewess, and she had stayed to take care of his horse. He gave her sixty of the braids that he had received for his horse. This payment continued to be given to the Jewess until it was stopped at the end of the age of the Umayyads. The custom never returned to the descendants of the Jewess or the descendants of ʿUbayd. ʿUbayd had gifted the Prophet an old horse that was called Murāwiḥ. He said, "O Messenger of God, race it!" The Messenger of God made the horse race in Tabūk, and the horse came first. So the Messenger of God took the horse from him. Al-Miqdād b. ʿAmr asked him for the horse. The Messenger of God said, "Where is Sabḥa?" It was the horse of Miqdād on which he had witnessed Badr. He replied, "O Messenger of God, with me; but she is getting old, so I withhold her for the lands that I have witnessed on her. I left her behind because this journey is long and the heat is intense. I want to take this perspiring horse to her so that she will give me a colt." The Prophet said, "So be it!" So al-Miqdād took it. He was informed of its energy. He took it to his horse Sabḥa and it produced a colt for him. It was a leader and they called it al-Dhayyāl. It led during the age of ʿUmar and ʿUthmān. ʿUthmān purchased it from him for thirty thousand.

They said: The Messenger of God passed by Tabūk desiring his need. He saw men gathering and he said, "What is their problem?" It was said, "O Messenger of God, this is a camel of Rāfiʿ b. Makīth al-Juhanna. He slaughtered it and took what he needed, and left the rest for the people and himself to use." The Messenger of God commanded that Rāfiʿ return what he and the people had taken. Then the Messenger of God said, "This is booty, it is not permitted." It was said, "O Messenger of God, surely its owner permitted it." The Messenger of God said, "Even if he permitted it!"

They said: A man came to him and said, "O Messenger of God, which is the best charity? Is it the shade of a tent in the way of God; the service of a servant in the way of God; or the deeds of a stallion/strong man in the path of God?"

[Page 1034] Jābir b. ʿAbdullah used to relate saying: We were with the Messenger of God in Tabūk and he said, "Take off the necklaces of the camel from the camel." It was said, "O Messenger of God, and for the horses?" He replied, "You do not adorn them with cords."

The Messenger of God employed ʿAbbād b. Bishr over the watch in Tabūk, from the day he arrived until his departure from there. ʿAbbād b. Bishr used to go around his companions in the camp. He appeared one morning before the Messenger of God and said, "O Messenger of God, we continuously hear the sound of *takbīr* behind us until morning. Did you appoint one of us to go around the watch?" The Messenger of God said, "I did not. But it could be that some of the Muslims appointed some one over the guard." Then Silkān b. Salāma said, "O Messenger of God, I set out with ten Muslims on our horses to protect the watch." The Messenger of God said, "May God bless those who protect the watch in the way of God!" He said, "To you is a measure of reward for all those whom you watched over from the people in a group, or alone on a beast."

They said: A group from Banū Saʿd Hudhaym arrived before the Prophet and said: O Messenger of God, we have arrived before you while we left our people at our well of little water, for this is the heat of Summer. We fear that we will break up if we disperse because Islam is not yet established around us. So ask God for us about the water for our well? If the water flows in it there will not be a people mightier than us, and not one transgressor will pass us by for our religion. The Messenger of God said, "Bring me some pebbles." So I took three pebbles and gave them to him. He rubbed them with his hand [Page 1035] then he said, "Take these pebbles to your well and throw them one by one and name God." So they turned from the place of the Prophet and did that, and their well bubbled up with water. They expelled those of the disbelievers who were near them, and defeated them. The Messenger of God did not turn back to Medina until they had defeated those around them who were against Islam.

They said: Zayd b. Thābit used to relate saying: We raided Tabūk with the Messenger of God. And we bought and sold. The Messenger of God saw us, and he did not forbid us. He said: Rāfiʿ related saying: We stayed in Tabūk, and ran out of provisions, and we nibbled at the meat for we could not find any. So I came to the Messenger of God and said, "O Messenger of God, surely there is meat here. I have asked the people of the land about hunting and they mentioned to me a hunting ground close by, and they pointed in the direction of the west. So may I go and hunt with a group of my friends?" The Messenger of God said, "If you go, take a number of your companions, and they should be on horses. Indeed you may leave the camp." He said: I departed with ten of the Anṣar, and with them was Abū Qatāda. He was the master of the chase with the spear and I was an archer. We looked for prey and we found it. From his horse, Abū Qatāda killed five donkeys with the spear and I shot almost twenty gazelle. Our companions took two, three and four. We found an Ostrich and chased it on our horses. Then we returned to the camp. We came to them at *ʿIshāʾ*, and the Messenger of God was asking about us. [Page 1036] "Have they not come yet?" We came to him and put down the animals before him. He said, "Divide it among your companions!" I said, "O Messenger of God, order the men to do so." He said: So he ordered Rāfiʿ b. Khadīj and said, "Give the whole tribe the donkey and the gazelle," and he dispersed that, until what came to the Prophet was one slaughtered gazelle, and he ordered that it be cooked. When it was well cooked, he called for it. With him were his guests and they ate. Later he forbade us returning to hunt, saying, "There is no protection," or he said, "I fear for you."

Ibn Abī Sabra related to me from Mūsā b. Saʿīd from al-ʿIrbāḍ b. Sāriya, who said: I was attached to the gate of the Messenger of God during the stopping and the traveling. We were in a night in Tabūk and we had gone for a need. We returned to the station of the Messenger of God and he and the guests who were with him had eaten.

The Messenger of God desired to enter his tent with his wife Umm Salama bt. Abī Umayya, when I appeared before him. He said, "Where were you since night?" So I informed him. Then Juʿāl b. Surāqa and ʿAbdullah b. Mughaffal al-Muzannī appeared, and we were three. And all of us were hungry. Indeed we stayed at the door of the Prophet. The Messenger of God entered the house and looked for something for us to eat but he could not find it. He came out to us and called to Bilāl, "O Bilāl, is there something for those?" He replied, "No, by Him who sent you with the truth, indeed we have depleted our bags and our containers." He said, "Look. Perhaps you will find something." So he took the bags and emptied them, bag by bag. A date and two dates fell out, until I saw between his two hands seven dates. The Messenger of God called for a bowl and put the dates in it. Then he put his hand on the dates and named God and said, "Eat in the name of God!" [Page 1037] I ate, and I counted fifty-four dates as I ate, and I counted their stones in my other hand; and my two companions did what I did. We were satisfied, and each one of us had eaten fifty dates. We raised our hands, and lo and behold there were seven dates just as before." He said, "O Bilāl, raise it in your bag." Indeed one did not eat from it except the date was replaced.

He said: While we were around the tent of the Messenger of God he prayed *tahajjad* of the night. He stood that night praying. When the dawn rose he prayed the two bowings of the dawn prayer. Bilāl called out the call to pray, and the Messenger of God responded and prayed with the people. Then he turned to the space in front of his tent and he sat and we sat around him and he recited ten verses from al-Mu'minūn. He said, "Did you have breakfast?" Al-ʿIrbāḍ said, and I began to say to myself, "What breakfast?" So he asked Bilāl for dates. He placed his hands on it, in the bowl, and said, "Eat in the name of God!" And we ate, by Him who sent him with the truth, until we were full, and indeed we had eaten for ten. Then they raised their hands from it, filled, but lo and behold the dates were just as before. The Messenger of God said: If I were not embarrassed before my Lord, we would surely eat from these dates until we returned to Medina, to the last of us. A youth from the people of the land appeared, and the Messenger of God took the dates in his hand and handed them to him. So the boy went away eating them.

When the Messenger of God gathered for the march from Tabūk, the people hastened. They continued thus until the people came to him and asked his permission to slaughter their beasts and eat them. So he permitted them. ʿUmar b. al-Khaṭṭāb met them while they were about to slaughter, and he asked them to hold their slaughter. Then he entered before the Messenger of God in his tent and said, "Did you permit the people to slaughter their rides and eat them?" The Messenger of God said, "They complained to me about their hunger so I permitted them. The troop will slaughter the camel or two camels, and they will take turns [Page 1038] with what remains of their rides to return home to their people." ʿUmar said, "O Messenger of God, do not do this. If the people had an excess of their rides it will be good, because today the beasts are weak. But call for the excess of their provisions, and gather it and ask God to bless it just as you did during our return from al-Ḥudaybiyya when we were hastening. Indeed, God most high will answer you!" And the herald of the Messenger of God called out, "Whoever has any extra provisions let him bring it!" He ordered a mat of leather to be spread, and the men began to bring measures of flour and barley and dates. It was a handful and a little more of flour and barley and dates. Every kind of that was put down separately. Each of that was a little. All of what was brought of flour and barley and dates were three Afrāq. Then the Messenger of God came and took ablutions and prayed two bowings. Then he asked God most high to bless the food.

Four of the Companions of the Prophet used to narrate together a single tradition, that those who attended and helped him were: Abū Hurayra, Abū Ḥumayd al-Sāʿidī, Abū Zurʿa, al-Juhanna Maʿbad b. Khālid, and Sahl b. Saʿd al-Sāʿadī. They said: Then the Messenger of God turned and his herald called out, "Come to the food, and take from it what you need!" The People approached. Each made to bring a container and fill it. Some of them said: Surely I threw in only a small piece of bread and a handful of dates. And indeed I saw the mat overflow. I brought two bags and I filled one of them with barley and the other with bread, and I took flour in my garment, and that was sufficient for us until we reached Medina. People began to collect the provisions until they were satisfied to the last of them, and until finally the mat was taken and what was on it was dispersed. The Messenger of God began saying, and he was standing, "I testify that there is but one God [Page 1039] and that I am His slave and His messenger. And I testify that only God can protect one who does not say it from his heart."

The Messenger of God set forward on his return when all of a sudden he found himself between Tabūk and a valley called Wādī al-Nāqa, where there was a rock, from the bottom of which water sufficient for two or three riders flowed. The Messenger of God said, "Whoever precedes us to the rock, do not drink from it at all until we arrive." Four of the Hypocrites preceded him. They were: Muʿattib b. Qushayr, al-Ḥārith b. Yazīd al-Ṭāʾī, an ally of the Banū ʿAmr b. ʿAwf, Wadīʿa b. Thābit, and Zayd b. al-Luṣayt. The Messenger of God said, "Did I not forbid you?" And he prayed to God and cursed them. Then he alighted and he placed his hand on the rock, and he touched it with his finger, until he collected a little in the palm of his hand. Then he sprinkled the rock and rubbed it with his hand. Then he prayed, as God wished him to pray, and asked about it, and the water burst out. Muʿādh b. Jabal said, "By Him who holds my soul in His hand, I heard a loud noise issue from it like a thunderbolt! The people drank as they wished and quenched their thirst as they wished." Then the Messenger of God said, "If you stay, or those of you who stay, you will surely hear about this wādī that it is more fertile than what was before or behind it." The people quenched their thirst and drank. Salama b. Salāma b. Waqash said: I said to Wadīʿa b. Thābit, "How much more do you want to see? Will you not consider?" He replied, "Similar to this has been done before." Then the Messenger of God departed.

[Page 1040] He said: ʿUbaydullah b. ʿAbd al-ʿAzīz and his brother ʿAbd al-Raḥmān b. ʿAbd al-ʿAzīz related to me from ʿAbd al-Raḥman b. ʿAbdullah b. Abī Ṣaʿṣaʿa al-Māzanī from Khallād b. Suwayd from Abū Qatāda, who said: While we were with the Messenger of God we marched with the troops by night, and he was returning and I was with him. All of a sudden there was the sound of a knock and the Prophet had fallen on his ride . . . So I went to him and supported him and he awakened. He said, "Who is this?" I replied, "Abū Qatāda, O Messenger of God, I feared that you would fall so I supported you." He said, "May God protect you just as you protected the Messenger of God." Then he went, not much further, and did as before. So I supported him and he woke up. He said, "O Abū Qatāda would you like to rest?" I said, "Whatever you wish, O Messenger of God!" He said, "Look who is behind you!" So I looked, and lo and behold there were two or three men. He said, "Call them!" So I said, "Answer the Messenger of God!" They arrived and we rested. There were five with the Messenger of God. I had a vessel of water and a little copper pot that I drank from. We slept and we did not wake up except for the heat of the sun, and we said, "Indeed, by God, we missed the *Ṣubḥ* prayer." The Messenger of God said, "We will anger Satan just as he angers us." We took ablutions from the water and it overflowed. He said, "O Abū Qatāda, protect what is in the vessel and the pot for indeed they have value." Then he prayed *Fajr* with us after the sun rose and he recited the chapter *al-Mā'ida*. When we turned from prayer he said, "Indeed if they obey Abū Bakr and ʿUmar they will be rightly guided." That was because Abū Bakr and ʿUmar desired to alight at the water with the troops, but the troops refused, and they alighted where there was no water, in a wasteland. The Messenger of God rode and he joined the troops at sunset. We were with him. They had barely stopped, for the men and horses were thirsty. The Messenger of God called for [Page 1041] a pot and emptied what was in the vessel of water into it. Then he placed his fingers on it and the water gushed out from between his fingers. The people approached and quenched their thirst. The water overflowed until they quenched their thirst and the horses and the rides quenched their thirst; indeed there were twelve thousand camels in the camp, and some say fifteen thousand camels. The people numbered thirty thousand, and the horses ten thousand. That was why the Prophet said to Abū Qatāda, protect the copper pot and the vessel of water!

There were in Tabūk four things: while the Messenger of God marched descending to Medina, it was in the strong summer's heat, the thirst of the troops after turning away the thirst on two occasions was very strong, but one could not find water even for his lips. They grumbled about that to the Messenger of God, so he sent for Usayd b. Ḥuḍayr on a summer's day and he was veiled. The Messenger of God said, "Perhaps you will find water for us." So he set out, and when he was between al-Ḥijr and Tabūk, he began to strike in every direction, and he found a camel carrying water with a woman from Baliyy. Usayd spoke to her and informed her about the Messenger of God, and she said, "Take this water to the Messenger of God!" And she placed the water for them between them and the road to Hunayya. When Usayd brought the water, the Messenger of God prayed for it to be blessed. Then he said, "Come and quench your thirst!" And there was not one among them who was thirsty, but his thirst was quenched. Then he called for their riding animals and horses and they drank until their thirst was quenched. It was said: Indeed, the Messenger of God ordered that the water that Usayd brought be poured into the great drinking bowl of the guards of the Bedouin, and he took it in his hand, and he washed his face and his hands and his feet, and prayed two bowings. Then he raised his hands, stretched out, then he turned, and indeed the bowl was bubbling over with water. The Messenger of God said, [Page 1042] "Provide!" And the water increased. The people spread out, until they lined up for it, a hundred, or two hundred, and they drank, and indeed the bowl was bubbling with the flowing water. Then the Messenger of God relaxed and cooled himself with the cool water.

He said: Usāma b. Zayd b. Aslam related to me from Abū Sahl from ʿIkrima, who said: the cavalry set out in every direction seeking water. The first who appeared with it and informed about it was the owner of a light horse. And the second was light, and the third was light. The Messenger of God said, "O God, bless the light skinned horses!" He said: ʿAbdullah b. Abī ʿUbayda, and Saʿd b. Rāshid related to me from Ṣāliḥ b. Kaysān from Abū Murra, the *mawlā* of Aqīl, who said: I heard ʿAbdullah b. ʿAmr b. al-ʿĀṣ say: The Messenger of God said, "The light skinned horses are good."

They said: When the Messenger of God was on some path, some of the Hypocrites deceived him about it and plotted to throw him from a steep incline in the road. When the Messenger of God reached that steep pass, they wanted to take the pass with him, but the Messenger of God was informed about them. He said to the people, "Take the path to Baṭn al-Wādī for indeed it is easier and wider." So the people took the path to Baṭn al-Wādī and the Messenger of God took the path to the pass (ʿAqaba). He commanded ʿAmmār b. Yāsir to take the stirrup of the camel and lead it, and he commanded Ḥudhayfa b. al-Yamān to lead from behind. While the Messenger of God was marching in the pass all of a sudden he heard the noise from people who were hidden. The Messenger of God was angry and he ordered Hudhayfa to return them. Ḥudhayfa returned them, and they saw the anger of the Messenger of God. He began striking the faces of the she-camels with a staff in his hand. Muslim's opponents thought that the Messenger of God had discovered their deceit, and they descended from the pass swiftly until they were mixed with the Muslims. Ḥudhayfa approached until he came to the Messenger of God [Page 1043] and urged him on. When the Messenger of God came out of the pass he came down to the people (*nās*) The Prophet said, "O Ḥudhayfa, did you know any of the riders that you returned?" He replied, "O Messenger of God I knew the beast of so and so, and so and so. But the people were veiled and I did not see them for the darkness of the night."

They had gone forth with the Prophet and some object fell from his saddle. Ḥamza b. ʿAmr al-Aslamī used to say: There was light for me in my five fingers and I searched until we had gathered what fell from the whip and the rope and similar things. Until there did not remain from the object a thing but we had gathered it. He joined the Prophet in the pass.

When it dawned Usayd b. Ḥuḍayr said to him, "O Messenger of God, what prevented you yesterday from the path of the Wādī? Surely it was easier than the pass?" He replied, "O Abū Yaḥyā, do you know what the Hypocrites desired yesterday, and what they worried about? They said: 'We will follow him in the pass, and when the darkness of the night is upon him,' . . . they would cut the thongs of my riding animal and they would prick it until it threw me from my saddle." Usayd said, "O Messenger of God, the people have gathered and come down, so command every family to kill the man who plotted this so that he who kills him will be a man from his own tribe. If you wish, by Him who sent you with the truth, inform me about them, and do not depart until I bring you their heads. Even if they were in al-Nabīt I would be sufficient for you, as when you commanded the Lord of the Khazraj and he was sufficient for you in his region. Surely those should not be left. O Messenger of God, till when shall we keep flattering them? Today they are few in number and humbled, and Islam is established! [Page 1044] So why do we keep them?" The Messenger of God said to Usayd, "Indeed I detest that the people would say, surely, Muḥammad, when he concluded the war between him and the polytheists put his hand to killing his companions." And he said, "O Messenger of God, those are not companions!" The Messenger of God said, "Did they not proclaim and testify that there is but one God?" He replied, "Of course, but there is no evidence for them!" The Messenger of God said, "Did they not proclaim that I am the Messenger of God?" He said, "Of course, but there is no evidence for them!" He replied, "I was forbidden from killing those."

He said: Yaʿqūb b. Muḥammad from Rubayḥ b. ʿAbd al-Raḥmān b. Abī Saʿīd al-Khudrī from his father from his grandfather, who said: The people of the pass who desired the Prophet were thirteen men. The Messenger of God named them to Ḥudhayfa and ʿAmmār.

He said: Ibn Abī Ḥabība related to me from Dāwud b. al-Ḥuṣayn from ʿAbd al-Raḥmān b. Jābir b. ʿAbdullah, from his father, who said: ʿAmmār b. Yāsir and a man from the Muslims contested each other about something, and they insulted each other.

When the man was almost superior to ʿAmmār with insults, ʿAmmār said, "How many were the companions of the pass?" He said, "God knows." ʿAmmār said, "Inform me from your knowledge about them!" And the man was silent. Those who were present said, "Clarify for your companion what he asked you about!" Indeed, ʿAmmār desired something that was concealed from them. The man hated to speak about it. The people were against the man, and the man said, "We used to say that they were fourteen men." ʿAmmār said, "Surely you were among them and they numbered fifteen men!" The man said, "Take it easy; I remind you, by God, do not expose me!" ʿAmmār said, By God, I have not named one, but I testify that there were fifteen men. Twelve of them were enemies of God and His messenger [Page 1045] in the worldly life, and the day of establishing the witnesses; the day when it wil not profit wrong-doers to present excuses, and they will only have the curse and the home of misery."

He said: Maʿmar b Rāshid related to me from al-Zuhrī, who said: The Messenger of God came down from his beast, for there was a revelation to him while his camel was kneeling. The camel stood and tugged at its halter/rope until Ḥudhayfa b. al-Yamān came to it and took its halter and led it where he saw the Messenger of God seated. He knelt the camel and then sat with it until the Prophet stood up and came to him and said, "Who is this?" He replied, "I am Ḥudhayfa." The Prophet said, "Indeed, I trust you with an affair you must not mention. I am forbidden to pray with so and so, and so and so, and so and so," a group who were numbered among the Hypocrites. The Messenger of God did not inform anyone other than Ḥudhayfa about them. When the Prophet died, and it was the caliphate of ʿUmar b. al-Khaṭṭāb, all of a sudden a man who ʿUmar thought was from that group died. So he took Ḥudhayfa by the hand, and led him to pray over him, and if Ḥudhayfa walked with him ʿUmar would pray over him. But if he snatched his hand and refused to go, he would turn back with him. He said: Ibn Abī Sabra related to me from Sulaymān b. Suḥaym from Nāfiʿ b. Jubayr, who said: The Messenger of God did not inform anyone but Ḥudhayfa. They were twelve men and there was not a Quraysh among them. This is confirmed with us.

He said: ʿAbd al-Ḥamīd b. Jaʿfar related to me from Yazīd b. Rūmān, who said: The Messenger of God approached until he alighted in Dhū Awān. Five of the companions of the Mosque of Dissent came to him. They were: Muʿattib b. Qushayr, Thaʿlaba b. Ḥāṭib, Khidhām b. Khālid, Abū Ḥabība b. al-Azʿar, and ʿAbdullah b. Nabtal b. al-Ḥārith. [Page 1046] They said, "Indeed, we are messengers of those of our companions who are behind us. We have built a mosque for the poor and needy as well as for rainy nights and wintry nights, and we would like you to come and pray in it with us!" The Messenger of God was preparing to go to Tabūk. He said, "Indeed, I am about to travel and am very busy. When we arrive we will come and pray in it with you."

But when the Messenger of God came down to Dhū Awān, returning from Tabūk, news of it and its people came to him from the heavens. They were surely its builders, and they said among themselves, "Abū ʿĀmir will come to us and talk with us in it. Indeed, he will say: I am not able to come to the mosque of the Banū ʿAmr b. ʿAwf. Indeed, the companions of the Messenger of God will follow us with their eyes." God says: *[It was built] in preparation for one who warred against God and His Apostle . . .* meaning Abū ʿĀmir. The Messenger of God called ʿĀṣim b. ʿAdī al-ʿAjlānī and Mālik b. al-Dukhshum al-Sālimī and said, "Go to this mosque whose people are evil, and demolish it and burn it!" So they set out swiftly on their feet until they came to Masjid Banī Sālim. Mālik b. Dukhsham said to ʿĀṣim b. ʿAdī, "Wait for me until I come out to you with fire from my people." He visited his people, and took a palm from the date palm and set it on fire. Then they both came out swiftly running until they reached the mosque between the prayers of *Maghrib* and *ʿIshā'* while they were in it. Their imam was at that time Mujammiʿ b. Jāriya. ʿĀṣim said: I shall not forget their coming to us as their call is the call of the wolf. We burned it until it was burned down. He who stayed in it from among them was Zayd b. Jāriya b. ʿĀmir; even his scrotum was burned. We destroyed the mosque until we put it in the ground, and the people dispersed.

[Page 1047] When the Messenger of God arrived in Medina he offered ʿĀṣim b. ʿAdī the mosque for a house which sided the house of Wadīʿa b. Thābit and the house of Abū ʿĀmir that were attached to the mosque, both had burned with it. He said, "I would never take a place such as this for my home. Indeed I am sufficient without it. Rather, Thābit b. Aqram has no house, so give it to him." So he gave it to Thābit.

Abū Lubāba b. ʿAbd al-Mundhir had helped them build it by providing wood. He was not immersed in hypocrisy, but he had done things that were detestable. When the mosque was destroyed Abū Lubāba took its wood and built a house with it beside the place of the mosque. He said that nothing was ever born to him in that house. A pigeon did not stop in it, ever. A hen did not hatch in it, ever.

Those who built the Mosque of Dissent were fifteen. Jāriya b. ʿĀmir b. al-ʿAṭṭāf who was known as Ḥimār al-Dār; his son Mujammiʿ b. Jāriya who was its imām; and his son Zayd b. Jāriya-he whose scrotum were burned so that he refused to come out, and his son Yazīd b. Jāriya, and Wadīʿa b. Thabit (and Khidhām b. Khālid). Those who came out of his house were: ʿAbdullah b. Nabtal, Bijād b. ʿUthmān, Abū Ḥabība b. al-Azʿar, Muʿattib b. Qushayr, ʿAbbād b. Ḥunayf, and Thaʿlaba b. Ḥāṭib.

The Messenger of God said: The nose-rope is better than a nose-ring. The whip is better than the *Bijād*. ʿAbdullah b. Nabtal—whose news was informed—used to come to the Messenger of God and listen to his conversation and then bring it to the Hypocrites. The angel Gabriel said, [Page 1048] "O Muḥammad, indeed a man from the Hypocrites comes to you and listens to your conversation and takes it to the Hypocrites." The Messenger of God said, "Which of them is it?" Gabriel replied, "The black man who possesses much hair, and red eyes like two pots of brass; his liver is the liver of a donkey and he watches with the eye of Satan."

ʿĀṣim b. ʿAdī used to relate saying: we were preparing to go to Tabūk with the Prophet, when I saw ʿAbdullah b. Nabtal and Thaʿlaba b. Ḥāṭib standing in front of the Mosque of Dissent. They had overhauled the drain and were exhausted from it. They said, "O ʿĀṣim, surely the Messenger of God has promised us that he will pray in it when he returns." I said to myself, by God, this mosque was built by Hypocrites, well known for their hypocrisy. Abū Ḥabība b. al-Azʿar established it. I came out of the house of Khidhām b. Khālid and Wadīʿa b. Thābit was in that group. The mosque that the Messenger of God built with his hands was established by Gabriel facing the House (Kaʿba). By God, we had barely returned from our journey when the Qur'ān revealed its faults, and the faults of its people who gathered in its building and helped with it. *Those are they who put up a mosque by way of mischief and infidelity* . . . until His words *God loves those who make themselves pure* (Q. 9:107). They said they were cleansed by the water. *A mosque is established on piety* . . . He said: he means the mosque built by ʿAmr b. ʿAwf in Qubā'. It was said: It affected the mosque of the Prophet in Medina. He said: The Prophet said, "Blessed is the man among them, ʿUwaym b. Sāʿida!" It was said to ʿĀṣim b. ʿAdī: Why did they want to build it? He replied: They were gathering in our mosque, and they were whispering among themselves, and turned to each other, [Page 1049] and the Muslims followed them with their eyes. That was hard on them so they desired a mosque for themselves. No one would visit it except those who had the same opinion. Abū ʿĀmir used to say, "I am not able to enter this enclosure of yours. That is because the companions of Muḥammad follow me and hurt me in a way that I detest." So they said, "We will build a mosque and you will talk with us in it."

They said; Kaʿb b. Mālik said: When it reached me that the Messenger of God was on his way home from Tabūk, it occupied me, and I began to think of a lie, and I said: How will I remove the displeasure of the Messenger of God from me tomorrow? I sought the help of all who possessed an opinion among my family, even perhaps mentioning it to the servant hoping that something would come to me and I would be comforted. When it was said that the Messenger of God was very close to Medina, the falsehood left me, and I knew that I could not be saved except with the truth. That morning the Messenger of God appeared in Medina. When he arrived from a journey, he used to begin from the mosque, pray two bowings, and then sit with the people. When he did that, those who stayed behind began to come to him and make excuses and oaths to him. There were some eighty men. The Messenger of God accepted their announcements and oaths and entrusted their secrets to God.

Another tradition from Kaʿb said: Indeed, when the Messenger of God alighted in Dhū Awān, the ordinary Hypocrites who had stayed behind from him came out. The Messenger of God said, "Do not speak to any one of them who stayed behind from us, and do not sit with them, until I grant you permission." So they did not speak to them. When he arrived in Medina, those who had excuses came to him with oaths, but he turned away from them, and the believers turned away from them, until, indeed, the man was turned away by his father, his brother and his uncle. They began to come to the prophet and make excuses to him about fever [Page 1050] and sickness. The Messenger of God was merciful to them. He accepted their announcements and their oaths. They swore and he believed them and forgave them. He entrusted their secrets to God most High.

They said: Kaʿb b. Mālik said: I came to the Prophet while he was seated in the mosque and greeted him, and he smiled the smile of one who is irritated, and said to me, "Come!" So I approached until I sat before him and he said, "What kept you? Did you not purchase your riding animal?" I replied, "O Messenger of God, if I sat with other than you from the people of this world, I think I could remove the displeasure with an excuse. Indeed, I am given to discussion and debate. But, by God, indeed you know that if I am deceitful with you today so as to make you satisfied about me, God will be displeased with me; and if I have an honest conversation with you today, you will find against me. Yet, I hope the outcome of God is in it. No, by God, I do not have an excuse. By God, I have not been stronger nor more at ease than I was when I stayed away from you!" The Messenger of God said, "Indeed you are truthful. So stand up until God finishes with you!" So I stood up, and a man from the Banū Salima stood with me. They said to me, "By God, we have never learned that you have sinned before this! Are you so weak that you are not able to make excuses to the Messenger of God in the manner those others who stayed behind made excuses? It should be enough for you that the Messenger of God forgives you your sins." They did not stop coming to me again and again, until I wanted to return to the Prophet and lie myself. But I met Muʿādh b. Jabal and Abū Qatāda and they both said to me, "Do not obey your companions, but stay on the truth. Indeed God will make for you a comfort and an outlet if God wills! As for those who make excuses, if they were sincere, God will be satisfied with that and he will inform his Prophet. And if not, he will censure them with the ugliest censure, and he will disbelieve their tales." I said to them, "Did anyone other than I meet this?" They replied, "Yes, two men said similar to what you said, [Page 1051] and the Prophet's response to them was similar to what he said to you." I said, "Who are they?" They replied, "Murāra b. al-Rabīʿ and Hilāl b. Umayya al-Wāqifī." They had mentioned two good men who were role models and examples.

The Messenger of God forbade the people from speaking to three of us among those who stayed behind. People kept away from us, and changed towards us, until I had doubts about myself and the land. The place was not the place that I had known. We lingered on that for fifty nights. As for my two companions they were seated in their homes. As for myself, I was the strongest of the people and the most injured of them. I used to go out and observe the prayers with the Muslims and I would go around the markets, and not one would speak to me. Until I came to the Messenger of God while he was in council after prayer and I greeted him while saying to myself: will he move his lips and return the greeting to me or not; then I prayed close to him and glanced furtively at him. When I approached my prayer he looked at me, but when I turned towards him, he turned away from me. Until when the alienation of the Muslims was too long for me, I walked until I scaled the wall of Abū Qatāda. He was my cousin and the most beloved of the people to me, and I greeted him, and by God, he did not return my greeting. I said to him, "O Abū Qatada, I implore you, do you know that I love God and His messenger?" And he was silent. And I repeated and said to him, "O Abū Qatāda, I implore you by God! Do you know that I love God and His messenger?" and he was silent. And I returned and implored him a third time, and he said, "By God and his messenger, I know!" My eyes overflowed; I jumped up and scaled the wall, and went to the market.

On my way to the market, I was surprised by a Nabatean from Nabatea in al-Shām who had arrived with food to sell in the market, and was asking about me, saying, "Who will take me to Kaʿb b. Mālik?" and the people began to point at me. He handed me a document from al-Ḥārith b. Abī Shamir, King of Ghassān, or, he said from Jabala b. al-Ayham, enclosed in a piece of silk. [Page 1052] His document said: As for what follows, it has reached me that your master was harsh to you and God did not put you in a place of lowliness or disrepute, so join us and we will comfort you. Kaʿb said: I said when I read it, "This is a trial also. What I did affects me to the point that even people of polytheism make me their target." So I took it to the oven and stoked the fire with it.

We stayed with that until forty of the fifty nights had passed and lo and behold a messenger from the Messenger of God came to me and said, "Indeed the Messenger of God commands you to withdraw from your wife." and I said, "To divorce her or what?" He replied, "Rather separate from her and do not be near her." The messenger to me and Hilāl b. Umayya and Murāra b. al-Rabīʿ was Khuzayma b. Thābit. Kaʿb said: I said to my wife, "Go to your people and be with them until God finishes with this affair." As for Hilāl b. Umayya, he was a good man, and he cried until indeed it was seen that he was dying from crying. He kept away from food; indeed he fasted for two or three days without food, except that he drank water or milk, and he prayed the night and sat in his house without leaving because none would speak to him and even if it was a little child they kept him away from him in obedience to the Messenger of God. His wife came to the Messenger of God and said, "O Messenger of God, Hilāl b. Umayya is an old and weak elder, who has no servant, and I am more attached to him than anyone else. If you saw that, you would let me serve him and I will do so." He said, "Yes. But don't let him reach you." She said, "O Messenger of God, he has no desire for me. By God, he continues crying since the day it happened to this day. Indeed his beard flows with tears by night and day. Surely the white of his eyes appear until I fear that he will lose his sight."

Kaʿb said: [Page 1053] Some of my people said to me, "Ask permission of the Messenger of God for your wife, for surely he permitted the wife of Hilāl b. Umayya to serve him." I said, "By God, I will not ask permission about her. I do not know what the Messenger of God will say about that if she asked his permission. I am a young man, and by God, I will not ask his permission." Then we lingered for ten nights, and it completed fifty nights since the Messenger of God forbade the Muslims from speaking to us. Then I prayed the *Ṣubḥ* prayer on the top of one of my houses according to the conditions that God had mentioned. The earth became restricted for me in what was spacious, and I became depressed. A tent was built at the back of Mount Salʿ and I was in it, when I heard a crier call above Salʿ, in a loud voice, "O Kaʿb b. Mālik, rejoice!" I sank to the ground in prostration. I knew that relief had come. The Messenger of God announced God's forgiveness to us when he prayed the *Ṣubḥ* prayer.

Umm Salama the wife of the Prophet used to say: The Messenger of God said to me that night, "O Umm Salama, the forgiveness of Kaʿb b. Mālik and his two companions has been revealed." And I said, "O Messenger of God, can I not take the message to them and make them rejoice?" The Messenger of God replied, "Sleep at the end of the night will prevent you. And they will not be seen until they rise in the morning." He said: When the Messenger of God prayed the *Ṣubḥ* prayer he informed the people of God's forgiveness of those individuals, Kaʿb b. Mālik, Murāra b. al-Rabīʿ and Hilāl b. Umayya. Abū Bakr went out above Salʿ and shouted: God forgave Kaʿb! He made him joyful about that. Al-Zubayr had set out on his horse in Baṭn al-Wādī and he heard the voice of Abū Bakr before he reached Al-Zubayr.

Abū l-Aʿwar Saʿīd b. Zayd b. ʿAmr b. Nufayl set out to Hilāl in the Banū Wāqif to give him the good news. When he informed him, he prostrated. [Page 1054] Saʿīd said: I thought that he would not raise his head until he dies. His happiness was more tearful than his sorrow until people worried about him. People who met him congratulated him. He was not able to walk to the Messenger of God from the weakness and the sadness and the crying, until he rode a donkey. Those who gave the good news to Murāra b. al-Rabīʿ were Silkān b. Salāma Abū Nāila, and Salama b. Salāma b. Waqash. They both prayed the *Ṣubḥ* prayer with the Prophet among the Banū ʿAbd al-Ashhal and departed to Murāra and informed him. Murāra approached until they redeemed him with the Prophet.

Kaʿb said: the sound that I heard at Salʿ arrived more swiftly than the rider who galloped through the valley, al-Zubayr b. al-Awwām. He who shouted above Salʿ, Kaʿb says, was a man from the Aslam called Ḥamza b. ʿAmr, and it was he who gave me the good news. He said: When I heard his voice I removed my two garments and draped them on him for his good news, and, by God I did not possess any other garments at that time, so I borrowed two garments from Abū Qatāda and wore them. Then I departed and went to the Messenger of God. The people met me and were delighted about my being forgiven saying, "God's forgiveness makes us happy for you!" until I entered the mosque and the Messenger of God sat and the people were around him. Ṭalḥa b. Abī Ṭalḥa came and greeted me and congratulated me, and he was the only Muhājir who came to me. Kaʿb never forgot Ṭalḥa for it. Kaʿb said: When I greeted the Messenger of God he said to me, and his face was bursting with smiles, "You have not known a more joyful day since the day your mother gave birth to you!" It was said: He said to him, "Come to the best day you have ever had!" Kaʿb said: I said, "Is it from you O Messenger of God, or from God?" He replied, "From God!"

[Page 1055] He said: When the Messenger of God was happy his face lit up until it was like the half moon. That was known about him. When I sat before him I said, "O Messenger of God, because of my repentance to God and his messenger I will forfeit my property to God and His messenger." The Messenger of God said, "Keep some property for yourself, it will be better for you." He said: I said, "I will keep my portion in Khaybar!" Another tradition was: The Messenger of God said, "No!" I said, "Half!" He said, "No!" I said, "A third." He said, "Yes." He said, "Indeed I, O Messenger of God, will keep my portion, which is in Khaybar." Kaʿb said: I said, "O Messenger of God, indeed God most high rescued me with the truth. My repentance to God is that I will not speak except the truth as long as I live." Kaʿb said: By God, I do not know one of the people God has tested in truthfulness of conversation, since I told the Messenger of God, more than He tested me. By God I have not intended a lie since I told that to the Messenger of God to this day of mine. I hope that God preserves me in what remains. Al-Wāqidī said that Ayyūb b. al-Nuʿmān b. ʿAbdullah b. Kaʿb recited:

Praise my Lord if he does not forgive my mistake.
I had suffered a loss and my words and deeds were miserable.

He said: God revealed: *God turned with favor to the Prophet the Muhājir and the Anṣār who followed him in a time of distress* . . . until his words . . . *with those who are true* (Q. 9:117–19).

Kaʿb said: By God, God did not favor me when he guided me to Islam better than with my truthfulness to the Messenger of God. If I lied to him at that time [Page 1056] I would have perished as those who lie perish. God said about those who lied when he sent down the revelation . . . *They will swear to you by God when you return to them that you may leave them, so leave them* . . . until his words: *Those who disobey* (Q. 9:95–96).

Kaʿb said: We three were kept back from the affair of those from whom the Prophet accepted an apology when they swore and excused themselves and asked for forgiveness. The Prophet postponed our affair until God gave His judgment. God said about that: *And to the three who were left behind* (Q. 9:122): He said, Not from the raid, but His holding us back. He postponed our affair from those who swore to him and made excuses to him and they were accepted.

Kaʿb said, when he built the tent on Salʿ in the mountains, according to what Ayyūb informed me from al-Nuʿmān b. ʿAbdullah b. Kaʿb b. Abī l-Qayn:

Is it after the houses of the honorable Banū al-Qayn
And what they established over the house out of palm leaves.

They said: The Messenger of God arrived in Medina during Ramaḍān in the year nine and said: Praise God who provided us during this journey of ours with a good reward and those of our partners after us. ʿĀʾisha said: O Messenger of God, the journey took you, and it was a difficult journey, and who are your partners after you in it? The Messenger of God said: Indeed in Medina are people who whenever we marched or came down a valley were with us. Sickness kept them. Did not God say in His book: *Nor should the Believers all go forth together* (Q. 9:122).

[Page 1057] We are their raiders, and they are the sitters. By Him who holds my soul in his hand, indeed their prayer is more effective with our enemy than our weapons. The Muslims began to sell their weapons saying: Surely the battle has stopped!

The strong began to purchase them for more strength. That reached the Messenger of God and he forbade them from that. He said, "A group from my community will continue to strive for the truth until Dajjāl arrives."

They said: ʿAbdullah b. Ubayy was sick during the remaining nights of Shawwāl. He died in Dhū l-Qaʿda, and his sickness lasted for twenty nights. The Messenger of God visited him during his sickness, and when it was the day of his death, the Messenger of God visited him while he was dying. He said, "I forbade you from the love of the Jews." ʿAbdullah b. Ubayy replied, "The most detestable of them was Saʿd b. Zurāra and he was not useful." Then Ibn Ubayy said, "O Messenger of God, it is not the right time for blame. It is death. If I die be present and wash me and give me your shirt to be wrapped in." The Prophet gave him the one on top, for he was wearing two shirts, but Ibn Ubayy said, "The one next to your skin." So the Prophet took off the shirt next to his skin and gave it to him. Then Ibn Ubayy said, "Pray for me and ask for my forgiveness!"

He said: Jābir b. ʿAbdullah narrates a different account. He says: After the death of Ibn Ubayy, the Messenger of God arrived at his grave and commanded that he be taken out. He revealed his face, and he sprayed his spit on him. Then he supported himself on his knees and dressed him in his shirt—he was wearing two shirts and he dressed him in what had been next to his skin. The first tradition is confirmed with us: that the Messenger of God attended his washing and his wrapping up. Then he was carried to the place of his funeral and the Messenger of God came forward and prayed for him. When he stood up, ʿUmar b. al-Khaṭṭāb jumped up and said, "O Messenger of God are you praying for Ibn Ubayy, when he had said on this day such and such and on this day such and such?" And he repeated to him his words. The Prophet smiled [Page 1058] and said, "Keep behind me, O ʿUmar!" And when ʿUmar increased against him, he said, "Indeed I had a choice, and I have chosen. If I knew that more than seventy pleas for his forgiveness would secure his forgiveness, I would exceed it because of God's words: *Whether you ask for their forgiveness or not; if you ask seventy times for their forgiveness, God will not forgive them* (Q. 9:80)." It was said: Indeed he said, "I will exceed seventy." The Messenger of God prayed and shortly after he turned away, the verses of Barāʾa were revealed: *You will not pray for one of them that dies nor stand at his grave* (Q. 9:84). Some say that he continued to take a step when these verses were revealed. The Messenger of God knew these verses about the Hypocrites (*Munāfiqūn*). He did not pray over those who were dead.

Mujammiʿ b. Jāriya used to relate saying: I did not see the Messenger of God extend the funeral ever; he did not go beyond the time. Then they set out until they reached Ibn Ubayy's grave. He was carried on a bier upon which the dead are carried in the family of Nubayṭ. Anas b. Mālik used to relate: I saw Ibn Ubayy on the bier and his legs were sticking out from the bier because of his height. Umm ʿUmāra used to relate saying: We saw the funeral of Ubayy, and not a woman from the Aws and Khazraj stayed away from the house of ʿAbdullah b. Ubayy's daughter, Jamīla. She kept saying, "*Wa jabalāh!*" One does not forbid it nor find fault with her over it. "My mountain of support, my corner of support." They said: Indeed it would have reached him in his grave.

ʿAmr b. Umayya al-Ḍamrī used to say: Surely we tried to get near his bier, but were unable. Those Hypocrites took possession of him, and they [Page 1059] proclaimed Islam. They were Hypocrites from the Banū Qaynuqāʿ and others of them: Saʿd b. Ḥunayf, Zayd b. al-Luṣayt, Salāma b. al-Ḥumām, Nuʿmān b. Abī ʿĀmir, Rāfiʿ b. Ḥarmala, Mālik b. Abī Nawfal, Dāʿis and Suwayd. They were the worst of the Hypocrites. They were those who ran him down. His son ʿAbdullah detested nothing more than seeing them. He had a sickness in his belly, so his son locked them out. Ibn Ubayy says, "Do not take me close to them," adding, "You are, by God, more dear to me than water to the thirsty." While they say, "Would that we ransomed you with our souls and the children and the property!"

When they stopped before his grave, the Messenger of God stood looking at them. They crowded to descend into his grave, their voices raised until Dāʿis' nose was hurt. ʿUbāda b. al-Ṣāmit tried to drive them away, saying, "Lower your voices before the Messenger of God!" until Dāʿis' nose began to bleed. Dāʿis wanted to descend into the grave, but he was pushed away. Then men from his group, people of grace and Islam, descended when they saw the Messenger of God pray and attend to him while standing over him. His son, ʿAbdullah, descended in his grave, and Saʿd b. ʿUbāda b. al-Ṣāmit and Aws b. Khawlī also descended until they were on the same level as ʿAbdullah. The prominent companions of the Prophet and the elders of the Aws and Khazraj lowered the body of Ibn Ubayy into the grave while they stood with the Prophet. Mujammiʿ b. Jāriya claimed that he saw the Messenger of God lower him with his hand to them. Then he stood at the grave until he was buried. He comforted his son, and departed. ʿAmr b. Umayya used to say: Those Hypocrites did not join him and his companions. They were those who urged the dusty burial saying, "Would that we had ransomed you with ourselves [Page 1060] while we were before you." And they hurried the dust on their heads. They were those who made good of his affair saying, "There was a group of poor people, and he was good to them."

A RECORD OF WHAT WAS REVEALED OF THE QUR'ĀN ABOUT THE RAID OF TABŪK

O believers, what is amiss with you that when it is said to you, Go forth in the way of God you sink down heavily to the ground? . . . (Q. 9:38) to the end of the verse: He said that the Messenger of God raided in the strong heat and strove among the people, and when the fruit ripened and shade was desired, the people held back. The chapter *Barā'a* revealed what was hidden about them. Their malice was revealed as well as the hypocrisy of the Hypocrites among them. *If you go not forth He will chastise you with a painful chastisement* (Q. 9:39): He says, except for those who go out with the Prophet. *A painful chastisement*: He says, at the end of time. *And instead of you He will substitute another people and you will not hurt Him with anything*: it was said, O Messenger of God, who are those people? *It was not for the people of the city and for the Bedouin, who dwell around them, to stay behind from God's Messenger* . . . (Q. 9:120) to the end of the verse: He said that the people were from the companions who went out to the desert to teach their people Islam. The Hypocrites said that people from the companions of Muḥammad remained in the valley. They said that the companions of the desert are destroyed. So it was revealed: *It is not for the believers to go forth totally, but why should not a party of every section of them go forth* . . . (Q. 9:122) to the end of the verse. He revealed about them: *Those who argue concerning God, after that answer has been made to him, their argument is null and void* . . . (Q. 42:16) to the end of the verse. The verse, *If you do not help him God has helped him* (Q. 9:40): [Page 1061] refers to the Hypocrites from the Aws and the Khazraj. *When the unbelievers drove him forth*: refers to the polytheists from the Quraysh. *The second of two*: He means the Prophet and Abū Bakr. *When the two were in the cave*: He means during the emigration of the Messenger of God. *When he said to his companion, Do not be sad; Surely God is with us. Then God sent down on him His sakīna*: He says, peace of mind. *And confirmed him with legions you did not see*: He means the angels. *He made the word of the unbelievers the lowest and God's word the uppermost*: He made the idols that the Quraysh brought false, and what Muḥammad brought of Monotheism victorious. *He says: Go forth, light and heavy* (Q. 9:41): He says, willingly or not, and it is said that the light ones are the youth, the heavy are the old.

He says: Struggle in God's way with your possessions and yourselves: He says spend your money for your raid and strive in the way of God. *Fight . . . were it gain near at hand*: He means a plunder close by. *And an easy journey*: He means a short journey. *They would have followed you . . .*: He means the Hypocrites. *But the distance was difficult for them*: the journey of Tabūk was twenty nights: *Still they swear by God, Had we been able we would have gone out with you*: He means the Hypocrites, at the time of Tabūk, who made excuses with hardship and sickness. *So destroying their souls*: He means in the next world. *God knows that they are truly liars*: meaning they are strong and healthy, and the Prophet accepted their excuses and granted them permission. *May God pardon you. Why did you permit them when* [Page 1062] *it was clear to you?* (Q. 9:43): until you try them with the journey and know who is false and who is true. *Those who spoke the truth and you knew the liars*: you knew who has strength and who has no strength because some men with strength got your permission. *Those who believe in God and the Last day ask not leave of you, that they may struggle with their possessions and themselves* (Q. 9:44): He describes the believers who spend their money for this raid. It was called the raid of hardship. *They only ask leave of you who believe not in God and the Last Day, so that in their doubt they go this way and that . . .* (Q. 9:45): He means the Hypocrites in their doubts. *If they desired to go forth they would have made some preparation for it. But God was averse that they should be aroused so He made them pause . . .* (Q. 9:44): He says that they were strong in their bodies and wealth, but hated their setting out, so he failed them. *It was said to them: Tarry you with the tarriers*: meaning with the women. *Had they gone forth among you they would only have increased you in trouble* (Q. 9:47): meaning Ibn Ubayy and ʿAbdullah b. Nabtal, and Jadd b. Qays, and all those who asked permission and returned. And it was said: If they were among you *they would only have increased you in trouble*: only evil. *Hurrying to and fro in your midst*: He says the hypocrite will go in between two beasts and be rejected by both of them. *Sowing sedition among you*: those few, he says, they will show hypocrisy and speak it. *And some of you would listen to them*: He says among the Hypocrites, and others who bring the news who are their leaders. *God knows the evildoers*: He mentions the Hypocrites. *They sought to stir up sedition already before and turned things upside down for you* (Q. 9:48): He says, before your setting out, they consulted [Page 1063] about all that would confuse you and your companions. *Until the truth came*: meaning the truth was revealed. *The command of God appeared*: He means, your affair, O Muḥammad. *And they were averse to it*: for you are victorious and have followers. *Among them are those who say, Permit me, but do not tempt me. Have not such men fallen into temptation?* (Q. 9:44): this was revealed about Jadd b. Qays. He was the wealthiest of the Banū Salama and had the largest number of animals and loved women. So the Prophet said, "Will you raid the Byzantines? Perhaps you will win one of their women." He replied, "Muḥammad, my people know that I love women; do not tempt me with them." God says, *Have not such men fallen into temptation?* By his staying away, and his hypocrisy. *Indeed, Hell surrounds the Unbelievers*: meaning him and others like him. *If good befalls you* (Q. 9:50): He means plunder and peace. *It grieves them*: meaning those who stayed behind and asked your permission. *If a misfortune befalls you*: meaning trial and hardship. *They say, indeed we took our precautions*: we took care. *From before*: meaning those who asked his leave, Ibn Ubayy and the others, al-Jadd b. Qays, and those who were on their decision. *And they turn away rejoicing*: about this catastrophe that hit you. God says, *Say: Nothing will happen to us except what God has decreed for us* (Q. 9:51): He says, except what is in the mother of the book. *He is our protector, and on God let us put our trust.* God says to his prophet, *Say, Can you expect for us one of two glorious things? Martyrdom or victory* (Q. 9:52): plunder or martyrdom. *But we can expect for you either that God will send His punishment himself*: meaning the stroke will hit you, *or by our hands*: we are permitted to kill you. *So wait*: He says, wait for us, and we wait for the promise of God. [Page 1064] *Say, spend willingly or unwillingly, not from you will it be accepted: for you are indeed rebellious and corrupt* (Q. 9:53): there were powerful people among the Hypocrites who would display charity and payment when people are watching. This reached the Prophet, and they protected themselves from being sentenced. *The only reasons why their contributions are not accepted are: that they reject God and His Apostle, and that they come to prayer without earnestness*: that means they are pretending to pray. *And that they offer contributions unwillingly* (Q. 9:54): they desire to display their payment. *Let not their wealth dazzle you . . .* (Q. 9:55): meaning what God gave them. *Nor their children*: those to whom God gave them. *In reality God's plan is to punish them with these things in this life*: He says that it is proof about them, because what they used out of it was used in hypocrisy, and what they paid, they paid to show off. *And that their souls may perish in their denial of God*: they will meet the Lord on their hypocrisy. *They swear by God that they are indeed of you; but they are not of you* (Q. 9:56): meaning their leaders and the powerful people among them like Ibn Ubayy and Jadd b. Qays and his family used to come to the Prophet and swear that they were with him, but when they left they broke their word. He says that they are afraid they might be killed for they are few in number. *If they could find a place to flee to, or caves, or a place of concealment, they would turn straight away thereto* (Q. 9:57): He says, if they could find a group or were capable of fleeing from their foe they would go swiftly. *Among them are men who slander you about the alms. If they are given a part of it they are pleased, but if not, they are indignant* (Q. 9:58): this was revealed about Thaʿlaba b. Ḥāṭib. [Page 1065] He was saying that Muḥammad gives *ṣadaqa* to whom he pleases. This reached Muḥammad, so he gave him and he was satisfied. Then he came to him again and he did not give him, so he was displeased. God says . . . *If only they had been content with what God and His messenger gave them* (Q. 9:59): He said if they were not displeased when Muḥammad refused them or gave them a little, equal to what he had in hand, *and had said, Sufficient unto us is God! God and His Apostle will soon give us of His bounty. To God do we turn our hopes!* He says, enough for His prophet. He says that Allah will provide for us when the Prophet receives property. *Alms are for the poor and the needy and those employed to administer the (funds), for those whose hearts have been reconciled; for those in bondage and in debt, in the cause of God and for the wayfarer* (Q. 9:60). It was told that someone asked the Prophet, so the Messenger of God replied that indeed, God did not trust the treasure to a nearby King or Prophet sent, before he apportioned it into eight portions. "If one portion is yours I will give it to you, but if you are rich it is only a headache and a stomachache." The poor are the poor from the Muhajirūn; those who did not ask. The miserable who sought shade in the mosque . . . *and those employed to administer the (funds)*: they are given as much as their duties and their expenses during their journey. *Those whose hearts have been reconciled*: not among the people of our time. Muḥammad used to give communities to reconcile them to Islam. *To those in bondage*: meaning slaves. *Those in debt*: meaning those in debt. *In the way of God*: meaning the warrior. *The wayfarer*: the traveler who is helped and carried even if he is wealthy back home. These charities are [Page 1066] looked at. If people of poverty and need are in one group, and they are given charity, God will reward him. *Among them are men who molest the Prophet and say, He is all ears*: it is better for you. It was revealed about ʿAbdullah b. Nabtal who used to say, I get what ever I wish from Muḥammad, meaning I hurt Muḥammad as much as I wish with words, then I come to him and swear to him and he accepts me. *Say, he listens to what is best for you* (Q. 9:61); *he believes in God and has faith in the Believers*: meaning he accepts from the believers, *and is a mercy to those of you who believe. But those who molest the Apostle*: meaning Ibn Nabtal. *For them is a grievous penalty. To you they swear by God* (Q. 9:62): He swears to the Prophet that he did not say it . . . *In order to please you*: meaning the Prophet and his companion. *But it is more fitting that they should please God and His Apostle, if they are Believers*: do not harass the Prophet and do not say except good of him. *Know they not that for those who oppose God and His Apostle . . .* (Q. 9:63): meaning ʿAbdullah b. Nabtal. *The Hypocrites are afraid lest a chapter should be sent down about them, showing them what is really passing in their hearts* (Q. 9:64): He said, the Hypocrites used to talk against the book and the truth, and when something was revealed they were scared that it was about what they had talked of. *Verily God will bring to light all that you fear*, meaning all that you talk of. A group of them was in Tabūk. Wadīʿa b. Thābit, Julās b. Suwayd, Makhshi b. Ḥumayyir, al-Ashjaʿī, the ally of Banū Salima, Thaʿlaba b. Ḥātib. Thaʿlaba said: Do you consider the fighting of the Byzantine similar to the fighting of others? Tomorrow they will be tied in ropes. [Page 1067] Wadīʿa said: Those companions of ours are the most frightened, and most recent in relationship; they are cowards on confrontation. The Prophet said to ʿAmmār b. Yāsir, "Get to them. Indeed, they are burned." *If you question them, they declare, we were only talking idly and in play* (Q. 9:65) . . . to His words *They are in sin* (Q. 9:66): he who was forgiven by this verse was Makhshi b. Ḥumayyir. He who said we were playing was Wadīʿa b Thābit. He came to the Prophet to apologize. It was revealed, *You have rejected faith after you had accepted it*: He who said the words of disbelief was Julās b. Suwayd b. al-Ṣāmit. He who was forgiven by this verse is Makhshi b Ḥumayyir. The prophet named him ʿAbd al-Raḥmān. He asked him to let him die a martyr no one knows where. He was killed at the battle of Yamāma as a martyr.

The Hypocrites, men and women have an understanding with each other; they enjoin evil . . . (Q. 9:67): He said there were Hypocrites, both men and women; and his words *with each other* meaning they support each other. *They enjoin evil*: referring to their hurting the Prophet and disbelieving him. *And forbid what is just*: they forbid following him. *And close with their hands*: meaning they don't give charity to the poor Muslims. *They have forgotten God so He has forgotten them*: He said that they deserted God, so God deserted them.

God has promised the Hypocrites, men and women, and the rejecters of faith the hell fire. There shall they dwell. Sufficient is it for them (Q. 9:68): He says, it is their reward. *For them is the curse of God*: meaning in this world. *For them is an enduring punishment*: meaning in the next world . . . to the end. *As in the case of those before you: they were mightier than you in power, and more flourishing in wealth and children. They had their enjoyment of their portion; and you have yours, as did those before you . . .* (Q. 9:69):

meaning those who were before you among nations, who disbelieved the prophets and picked on them. God provided them with wealth and many children. [Page 1068] He mentioned that they enjoyed their portion. Then he mentioned those Hypocrites, who enjoyed their portion similarly, and He said, *and you indulge in idle talk just as they did*: they were poking fun at him as the others did. *Those! Their works are fruitless in this world and in the hereafter and those are they who will lose . . .*: meaning the nations who came before them who were Hypocrites.

The Believers men and women are protectors of each other. They enjoin what is just and forbid what is evil (Q. 9:61): He says, command Islam and forbid disbelief. *They observe regular prayers and practice regular charity*: they give charity to the poor. *And obey God and His messenger. He says, O Prophet, strive hard against the unbelievers* (Q. 9:73): meaning the polytheist with the sword. *And the Hypocrites and be firm against them*: He commanded him to be firm in his words against the Hypocrites. *Their abode is hell*: meaning the disbeliever and Hypocrites. *They swear by God that they said nothing, but indeed they uttered blasphemy and they did so after accepting Islam* (Q. 9:74): Referring to Wadīʿa b. Thābit. *They meditated a plot, which they were unable to carry out*: they said, We will crown ʿAbdullah b. Ubayy when we return. It was said they plotted against Muḥammad in al-Aqaba. *This revenge of theirs was only in return for the bounty with which God and His Apostle had enriched them. If they repent it will be best for them*: this was revealed about Julās b. Suwayd. He had blood money during *Jāhiliyya* so when he reached the Prophet, the Prophet collected it for him who needed it.

Among them are men who made a covenant with God that if He bestowed on them of His bounty, they would give in charity, and be truly amongst those who are righteous (Q. 9:75) . . . *But when he did bestow of His bounty* (Q. 9:76) . . . to his words, *because they were liars* (Q. 9:77): this was revealed about [Page 1069] Thaʿlaba b. Ḥāṭib who was needy, and had nothing to give in charity. He said, By God, if I receive money I will give charity and be a good man, but when he received the blood money of twelve thousand dirham, he did not give charity, and was never a good man. *Those who slander believers, who give of themselves freely* (Q. 9:78): He said Zayd b. Aslam al-ʿAjlānī brought *ṣadaqa* out of his property. Muʿattib b. Qushayr and ʿAbdullah b. Nabtal said: Indeed he desires to show off. *As well as, such as can find nothing to give except the fruits of their labour—and throw ridicule on them, God will throw back their ridicule on them, and they shall have a grievous penalty* (Q. 9:79): it was revealed about ʿUlba b. Zayd al-Ḥārithī. He saw the Prophet with an empty stomach. So he came to a Jew and said, I will work for you drawing your bucket for a measure of dates, all cleaned and fresh without rot. He agreed. He worked for him until afternoon and took the dates and brought it to the Prophet. ʿAbdullah b. Nabtal said, "Look at this man and what he does. Is not God sufficient for the Prophet?" *Whether you ask for their forgiveness or not* (Q. 9:80) . . . to the end of the verse: He said that the Prophet was invited to pray over ʿAbdullah b. Ubayy, and that the Prophet said, If I knew that if I asked more than seventy times he would be forgiven, I would ask. I was given the choice and I chose.

Those who were left behind rejoiced in their inaction . . . (Q. 9:81) . . . until his words *a recompense for the (evil) that they do* (Q. 9:82): He said that it was revealed about Jadd b. Qays. *God most high says*, [Page 1070] *If God returns you to a faction among them*: meaning, returns him from the journey to Tabūk. *And they ask you permission for going out*, referring to the Hypocrites who asked your permission to stay. *Say, Never shall you come out with me nor fight an enemy with me. You were satisfied with staying behind the first time*: on my first journey when I set out. *Then sit with those who lag behind*: with the women. *And do not pray for any of them that dies, nor stand at his grave* (Q. 9:84): He said that when Ibn Ubayy died and was prepared for burial, the Prophet stood up to pray over him. ʿUmar said, "O Messenger of God are you praying over him?" He replied, "O ʿUmar I was given the choice and I chose. If I knew that praying more than seventy times would bring him forgiveness, I would." This was for the words of God. *Whether you ask for their forgiveness or not* (Q. 9:80): the Prophet Muḥammad prayed over him and buried him. After the burial he barely moved when this verse was revealed, *Never pray for one of them who died* . . . to the end of the verse.

When a chapter comes down enjoining them to believe in God and to strive and fight with His Apostle, those with wealth and influence among them ask you for exemption (Q. 9:86) . . . until his words . . . *that they will be with those who stay behind* (Q. 9:87): that is with the women. *Their hearts are sealed so they understand not*: this was revealed about Jadd b. Qays. He was wealthy and deflected—not straight. *There were among the desert Arabs men who made excuses . . . and came*: meaning the people who ask for forgiveness. They numbered eighty-one from Ghifar. *To seek permission for them . . .*: to stay behind. He says that they make excuses not to go out. *Those who were false to God and His messenger and sat inactive* (Q. 9:90): He says the Hypocrites stayed behind. They said: stay behind whether he permits you or not. [Page 1071] God most high says, *There is no blame on those who are infirm* (Q. 9:91): referring to people of chronic illness, and old people. *Or ill, or who find no resources to spend*, meaning people in difficulty. *If they are sincere to God and His Apostle, no ground can there be against such as do right, for God is oft forgiving most merciful*: if they were thus. God most high says, *Nor is there blame on those who came to you to be provided with mounts and you said: I can find no mounts for you, and they turned back, eyes streaming with tears of grief that they had no resources with which to provide the expenses* (Q. 9:92): those weepers were seven: Abū Laylā al-Māzinī, Salama b. Ṣakhr al-Zuraqī, Thaʿlaba b. ʿAnama al-Sulamī, ʿAbdullah b. ʿAmr al-Muzannī, and Sālim b. ʿUmayr. God most high says, *The ground of complaint is against such as claim exemption while they are rich. They prefer to stay with those who stay behind* (Q. 9:93): that is with the women, meaning Jadd b. Qays. God most high says, *They will present their excuses to you when you return to them. Say, present no excuses; we shall not believe you* (Q. 9:94): meaning, we will never trust you. *God has already informed us of you*: meaning what He informed him of their stories. *It is your actions that God and His messenger will observe*: Meaning the Hypocrites . . . until his words, *They will swear to you by God, when you return to them, that you may leave them alone* (Q. 9:95): meaning you will not blame them. *So leave them alone*: meaning leave them. *Indeed they are an abomination and hell is their abode because they are evil. They will swear to you that you may be pleased with them* . . . [Page 1072] (Q. 9:96) to the end of the verse. God most high says, *The Arabs of the desert are worst in unbelief and hypocrisy and more suited to be in ignorance of the command which God has sent down to His Apostle* (Q. 9:97) . . . to the end of the verse: He said, he means the Bedouin. *Some of the desert Arabs look upon their payments as a fine* (Q. 9:98), . . . until his words, *the prayers of the Apostle* (Q. 9:99): meaning the prayers of the Messenger asking God. *Indeed they bring them nearer to Him; soon will God admit them to His mercy*. God most high says, *The vanguard of Islam—the first of those who forsook their homes and of those who gave them aid* (Q. 9:100): referring to those who have prayed in two directions. *Those who follow them in good deeds*, to the end of the verse: meaning those who converted before the Conquest of Mecca. During the Conquest God most high says, *Certain of the desert Arabs around you are Hypocrites* (Q. 9:101): there were men from the Bedouin among them ʿUyayna b. Ḥiṣn and his people, who were pleasing the companions of the Prophet and showing them that they are with them, and at the same time pleasing those who were polytheists from their community. *The Medina folk*: meaning the Hypocrites of Medina. *They are obstinate in hypocrisy*: he says they were stubborn in hypocrisy. *You do not know them; We know them*: God most high informed his prophet of them later. *Twice shall we punish them*: meaning the Bedouin. He means the hunger and pain of the grave. *In addition they shall be sent to grievous penalty*: He says, to the fire. *Others have acknowledged their wrong doing* (Q. 9:102) . . . to the end of the verse: It was revealed about Abū Lubāba b. ʿAbd al-Mundhir when he indicated to the Banū Qurayẓa that it would be slaughter. *Take from their wealth voluntary alms so you might purify and sanctify them; and pray for them, indeed your prayers are a source of security for them* (Q. 9:103): meaning the Muslims. The charities of their properties, meaning you will purify them. [Page 1073] *Pray for them*: ask forgiveness for them.

God most high says, *Know they not that God accepts repentance from his worshipers and receives their gifts of charity* (Q. 9:104): He says those who approach and repent and offer charity, desiring the face of God. God says, *Say, Know that God, His messenger and the believers will observe your work* (Q. 9:105), to the end of the verse. *There are others held in suspense for the command of God* (Q. 9:106), to the end of the verse: referring to three: Kaʿb b. Mālik, Hilāl b. Umayya and Murāra b. al-Rabīʿ. *Those who put up a mosque of dissent and infidelity to disunite the believers in preparation for one who opposed God and His messenger* (Q. 9:107): meaning Abū ʿĀmir. *Disuniting the believers*: meaning he separated the Banū ʿAmr b. ʿAwf and some of them prayed in it. *In preparation for one who opposed God and His messenger*: refers to Abū ʿĀmir. He says: He approached us from al-Shām and will speak to us in it! He will not enter the mosque of the Banū ʿĀmr b. ʿAwf. God most high says, *Indeed they swear that their intention is nothing but good*, to the end of the verse. *Never stand forth therein. There is a mosque whose foundation was laid from the first day on piety, it is more worthy that you stand in it*, to his words, *God guideth not people who do wrong* (Q. 9:108): He says, do not pray in this mosque, but pray in the mosque of Banū ʿAmr b. ʿAwf. He said that the Messenger of God said: Indeed, I established it with my hands as Gabriel was leading us to the house. As for God's words, *In it are men who love to be purified*: there were men who cleaned with water, among them ʿUwaym b. Sāʿida. God most high says, *Which then is best? He that lays his foundation on piety to God and His pleasure, or he who lays his foundation on an undermined sand cliff ready to crumble to pieces? And it crumbles to pieces* [Page 1074] *with him in the fire of hell* (Q. 9:109). God most high says, *The foundation of those who build is never free from suspicion in their hearts* (Q. 9:110): He says there is doubt in their hearts. *Until their hearts are cut to pieces*: until they die. He said: Ibn Abī l-Zinād related to us from Shayba b. Niṣāḥ from al-Aʿraj, who said: Surely he meant the two men, rather than the mosque, referring to His words, *Who better established his buildings,* and his words, *Indeed God has purchased from the believers their persons and their goods*, until His words, *That is the achievement supreme* (Q. 9:111): He says, those who purchase from those who strive in the way of God and spend their property in it, to them is Paradise. God's words, *It is not fitting for the Prophet and those who believe that they should pray for the forgiveness of unbelievers even though they be of kin*, until his words, *Companions of the fire* (Q. 9:113): He said, When Abū Ṭālib died, the Messenger of God asked forgiveness for him and said, "Indeed I will ask for forgiveness for you until I am done." And the Muslims asked for forgiveness for the dead among the disbelievers, so this verse was revealed. *After it is clear to them that they are companions of the fire*: He says, they died disbelieving and they did not repent. God most high says that *Abraham prayed for his father's forgiveness only because of a promise he had made to him* (Q. 9:114): He said, he promised he would submit. *But when it became clear to him that he was an enemy of God he dissassociated from him*: When he died in his disbelief, he disassociated himself from him. *For Abraham was most tender hearted, forbearing*: He said, *al-Awāh* means in constant prayer. The words of the most high, *God will never turn them down after he guided them*, to the end of the verse. *God turned with favor to the Prophet, the Muhājir, and the Anṣār who followed him in a time of distress* (Q. 9:117): referring to the raids of distress. It was the raid of Tabūk, which was in the time of great heat. *After that* [Page 1075] *the hearts of a part of them had nearly swerved*: He says, Abū Khaythama and what he related about staying behind from the Prophet because of the strong heat and long journey. Then he resolved to himself to go out. *Then he forgave them for He is kind and most merciful. And to the three who were left behind; until (they felt guilty) to such a degree that the earth seemed constrained to them for all its spaciousness* (Q. 9:118) . . . until his words, *oft-returning most merciful*: referring to Kaʿb b. Mālik, Hilāl b. Umayya and Murāra b. al-Rabīʿ. As for his words: *Those who stayed behind*: He means those who made excuses to the Messenger of God that were accepted from them. *It was not fitting for the people of Medina and the Bedouin Arabs* (Q. 9:120): He means the Ghifār, Aslam, Juhayna, Muzayna and Ashjaʿ. *That they stayed behind from the Messenger of God*: during the raid of Tabūk. *Nor to prefer their own lives to his; because they would never suffer thirst*: meaning be thirsty. *Nor tire*: meaning to labor. *Nor hunger*: starving. *Or tread paths*: in the land of the disbelievers. *Nor did they obtain anything from the enemy except to add to the books of theirs containing good works*. God's words. *Nor could they spend anything, small or big* (Q. 9:121), to the end of the verse. *Nor should the believers go forth together*, to the end of the verse: He says, Nor did the believers, all of them, when the Messenger of God set out in a raid, go forth, and leave the city leaving the children behind. But rather a group from each tribe set out. He says that in order to observe the march of the Prophet with the disbelievers and understand what they hear from him. *They warned their people when they returned to them perhaps that they may be aware* (Q. 9:122): meaning that they fear God.

[Page 1076] He says: *O those who believe, fight those who are near you from the unbelievers* (Q. 9:123), to the end of the verse. God most high says: *When a chapter is revealed, and among them are those who say, which of you has increased his faith* ?(Q. 9:124) meaning with certainty and submission. And the believer will say that it increases with certainty and submission. As for the Hypocrites it increased them with suspicion and doubts. It was said about the polytheists, it increased suspicion in them and certainty about their faith. They died on their disbelief. God most high says about them, *Do they not see that they are tried once or twice every year* (Q. 9:126)? As for he who put them with the Hypocrites, He says, they mislead once or twice a year; as for he who claims they are polytheists, He says, they went on a raid once or twice a year. *Then they do not repent*: He says, they do not submit. *And when a chapter was revealed they looked at each other* (Q. 9:127), to the end of the verse: ʿAbdullah b. Nabtal was sitting with the Prophet, and with him were his hypocrite companions, and when the prophet left, some of them left with others. *Does anyone see you?* They mean the Muslims. He says, *Then they turn*: meaning, they ridicule and disbelieve the truth: *God turned their hearts from it*. God most high says, as he mentions his prophet, *Surely, a messenger came to you from among yourselves* (Q. 9:128): He says about you. *Grievous to Him is your suffering*: He says, whatever your mistakes. *He cares for you and is kind and merciful to the believers. But if they turn away, Say, God is sufficient for me; there is no God but He. I trust Him. He is the Lord of he glorious throne* (Q. 9:129).

ABŪ BAKR'S PILGRIMAGE

He said: Maʿmar related to me from Muḥammad b. ʿAbdullah, Ibn Abī Ḥabība, Ibn Abī [Page 1077] Sabra, Usāma b. Zayd, Ḥāritha b. Abī ʿImrān and ʿAbd al-Ḥamīd b. Jaʿfar, and each one, as well as others, related portions of this tradition to me. They said: It took place before the Qur'ānic chapter *Barā'a* was revealed. The Messenger of God had made an agreement with people among the polytheists. The Messenger of God appointed Abū Bakr over the pilgrimage. Abū Bakr set out with three hundred men from Medina. The Messenger of God sent twenty sacrificial animals with him as well. He adorned them with sandals and marked them with his hand on the right side. He appointed Nājiya b. Jundub al-Aslamī over them. Abū Bakr drove five sacrificial animals. ʿAbd al-Raḥmān b. ʿAwf went on ḥaj, as well, with sacrifical animals, and a group of people of power pilgrimaged with them. Abū Bakr appeared in Dhū l-Ḥulayfa, and marched until he was at al-ʿArj at dawn, when all of a sudden he heard the bray of the Messenger of God's camel, al-Qaṣwā'. He said, "This is al-Qaṣwā'!" and he looked, and lo and behold there was ʿAlī b. Abī Ṭālib on her. He said, "Has the Messenger of God appointed you over the pilgrimage?" ʿAlī replied, "No, but he sent me to recite the *Barā'a* to the people, and to dissolve his agreement with all those who possess an agreement with him." The Messenger of God had promised Abū Bakr that he would oppose the polytheists, and that he would stop at ʿArafa on the day of ʿArafa and that he would not stop in Jamʿ.

Abū Bakr did not push forward from ʿArafa until the sun had set, and he left Jamʿ before sunrise. Abū Bakr set out until he arrived in Mecca and he, alone, led the pilgrimage. He spoke to the people before *tarwiyya*, after *Ẓuhr*, one day. When it was the day of tarwiyya and the sun had declined from the meridian, he circumambulated the house seven times. Then he rode on his beast from the gate of Banū Shayba. He prayed *Ẓuhr, ʿAṣar, Maghrib, ʿIshā'* and *Ṣubḥ* in Minā. Then he rode on, after the sun rose over Thabīr, until he reached Namira. Here he alighted and stopped in a tent of hair. When the sun declined from the meridian, he rode his camel and gave a speech in Baṭn ʿUrana. Then, he knelt his camel and prayed the *Ẓuhr* and *ʿAṣar* prayers with one call to prayer and two responses. [Page 1078] Then, he rode his camel and he stopped in al-Hiḍāb. Al-Hiḍāb is ʿArafa, the place of prayer in ʿArafa. When those who were fasting broke fast, he continued on. He went at a quick pace until he reached Jamʿ. He alighted close to the fire in al-Quzaḥ. At the rise of dawn he prayed Fajr. Then he rose at the break of dawn and began saying, while he stood, "O people, rise for the dawn prayer! O people, rise for the dawn prayer!" Then he pushed forward before the sun, traveling at a quick pace until he reached Muḥassir. There, he hurried his ride, and when he had gone through Wādī Muḥassir, returned to his original pace, until he threw seven stones at al-Jamra, as he rode by. Then he returned to the slaughtering place and slaughtered. Then he shaved.

On the day of the slaughter, at al-Jamra, ʿAlī recited the chapter *Barā'a*, and withdrew the agreement from all who possessed an agreement. He said, "Indeed, the Messenger of God said that a polytheist will not be permitted to make the *Ḥajj* pilgrimage to Mecca after this year, nor will he be permitted to circumambulate the house, naked."

Abū Hurayra used to say: I was present that day—and he used to say: It was the day of the greater pilgrimage—and Abū Bakr spoke on the day of slaughter after *Ẓuhr*, on his camel. Abū Bakr had spoken during his pilgrimage on three days and he did not exceed it: One day before *tarwīyya*, in Mecca after *Ẓuhr*; at ʿArafa, before *Ẓuhr*; and in Minā, on the day of the slaughter, after *Ẓuhr*. Abū Bakr stayed and threw pebbles on foot, going and coming, when it was the fourth day after the slaughter (al-Ṣadr). They said: He threw while walking. When he went past al-ʿAqaba he rode. Others said: He threw, at that time, while riding. When he reached al-Abṭaḥ he prayed *Ẓuhr*. He entered Mecca and prayed *Maghrib* and *ʿIshāʾ*. Then he set out at night returning to Medina.

[Page 1079] **THE EXPEDITION OF ʿALĪ B. ABĪ ṬĀLIB TO YEMEN**

They said: The Messenger of God sent ʿAlī during Ramaḍān in the year ten AH. The Messenger of God commanded him to camp in Qubāʾ, so ʿAlī camped there until his companions arrived. At that time the Messenger of God offered ʿAlī a turban, which he folded in four and fixed on the top of his spear, for a banner and handed it to him. He said, "This is the banner." He draped a turban, rolled thrice, on ʿAlī, placing an arm length between his hands and a span length on his back, saying, "Thus is the turban!"

He said: Usāma b. Zayd related to me from his father from ʿAṭāʾ b. Yasār from Abū Rāfiʿ, who said: When the Messenger of God faced him, he said, "Depart and do not turn back." ʿAlī said, "O Messenger of God, what shall I do?" The Prophet said, "When you alight in their courtyard, do not fight them until they fight you; if they attack you, do not fight them until they kill one of you. If they kill one of you, do not fight them or blame them, but show them patience. Say to them, 'Will you say that there is but one God?' And if they say, 'Yes,' say, 'Will you pray?' And if they say 'Yes,' say, 'Will you take from your property and give charity to your poor?' And if they say 'Yes,' do not desire anything else. By God, may God guide a man by your hand, it is better for you than whatever the sun rises or sets on!"

He said: He set out with three hundred riders, and their cavalry was the first to enter that land. When he reached near the land that he desired—which was the land of Madhḥij—he dispersed [Page 1080] his companions, and they brought plunder and prisoners and women and children and cattle and sheep and other things, by force. ʿAlī appointed Burayda b. al-Ḥuṣayb in charge of the plunder. He gathered what was taken before meeting any group. Then he met a group and invited them to Islam and enticed them with it. But they refused and aimed at his companions. ʿAlī handed the banner to Masʿūd b. Sinān al-Sulamī and he went forward with it. A man from the Madhḥij invited him to a duel, so al-Aswad b. al-Khuzāʿī al-Sulamī dueled him. They attacked one another for a while on horseback. Then al-Aswad killed him and took his booty. Then ʿAlī attacked them with his companions and killed twenty of their men, and they dispersed defeated and left their flag standing. ʿAlī refrained from seeking them out; he invited them to Islam, and they hastened and responded. A group of their leaders approached and granted allegiance to Islam. They said, "We stand for those who are behind us from our people. This is our *ṣadaqa* so take what is due to God from it."

He said: ʿUmar b. Muḥammad b. ʿUmar b. ʿAlī related to me from his father, who said: ʿAlī collected what was taken in plunder and apportioned it into five parts and picked one; he wrote a portion of it, for God. He took out the first of the portions, the portion of the fifth, and he did not give anything extra to anyone. Those who were before him used to give their companions—those present, not others—from the fifth. The Messenger of God was informed about that and he did not oppose it against them. So they requested that from ʿAlī, but he refused. He said, "I will take the fifth to the Messenger of God and he will consider his opinion about it. This is the Messenger of God approaching the festivities. We will meet him and he will do with it what God shows him," and ʿAlī turned to return. He carried the fifth and drove what animals he could. When he was in al-Futuq he hastened. He appointed Abū Rāfiʿ over his companions and the fifth. Included with the fifth were some Yemenī garments.

[Page 1081] The loads were packed up and the cattle were driven with what they plundered. And there were cattle from the *ṣadaqa*—charity—from their property. Abū Saʿīd al-Khudrī, who was with him during that raid, said: Alī forbade us from riding the camels obtained as *ṣadaqa*. The companions of ʿAlī asked Abū Rāfiʿ to dress them in the plundered clothes, and he gave each of them two garments. When they were in al-Sidra at the entrance of Mecca, ʿAlī came out to meet them, and he brought them and settled them, and he saw two garments on every man, and he recognized the garments and said to Abū Rāfiʿ, "What is this?" He replied, "They spoke to me, and I feared their complaints and I thought that this would be easy on you for those who were before you have done this." ʿAlī said, "You saw me refuse them, yet you gave them. Indeed I commanded you to keep what I left with you, and yet you gave them!" He said: ʿAlī refused to do that until some of them removed the two garments. When they arrived before the Messenger of God, they complained, so the Prophet called ʿAlī and said, "Why are your companions complaining about you?" He replied, "I did not cause their complaints! I apportioned to them what I plundered, and I kept the fifth for until I arrived before you, so that you may make a decision about it. The leaders before me used to do differently. They gave extra to whomever they wished out of the fifth. So I thought to bring it to you for you to consider your opinion." The Prophet was silent.

He said: Sālim the *Mawlā* of Thābit related to me from Sālim, the *mawlā* of Abū Jaʿfar, who said: When ʿAlī was victorious over his enemy and they entered Islam, he collected what he plundered and appointed Burayda b. al-Ḥuṣayb over it, and he established in their midst, and he wrote a document to the Messenger of God [Page 1082] with ʿAbdullah b. ʿAmr b. ʿAwf al-Muzannī informing him that he met a group from Zabīd, and others, and that he invited them to Islam and informed them that if they converted he would refrain from them. But they refused that and so he fought them. ʿAlī said: And God provided me with victory over them, until some of them were killed. Then, they responded to what was offered them and they entered Islam, and were obedient about the *ṣadaqa*. Men among them entered the faith and ʿAlī taught them to recite the Qurʾān. The Messenger of God commanded him to meet him during the festivities, and ʿAbdullah b. ʿAmr b. ʿAwf turned back to ʿAlī about that.

He said: Saʿīd b. ʿAbd al-Azīz al-Tanūkhī related to me about Yūnus b. Maysara b. Ḥulays, who said: When ʿAlī b. Abī Ṭālib arrived in Yemen he spoke in Yemen. It reached Kaʿb al-Aḥbār who supported him in his speech. He approached on his beast, wearing a robe, with a learned man from the Jews, until they listened to him and stood with him. He says, "Surely among the people are those who see by night but cannot see by day." Kaʿb said, "It is true!" ʿAlī said, "There are some who cannot see at night or day," and Kaʿb said, "This is true." ʿAlī said, "And those who give little are given generously." And Kaʿb said, "This is true!" The learned Jew said, "How can you confirm it?" He said, "As for his words, 'people who see by night and do not see by day,' it is the believer in the first book who does not believe in the last book. As for his words, 'Among them are those who do not see by night and do not see by day,' it is he who does not believe in the first book or the last book. As for his words 'Those who give a little but are given generously, it is what God accepts from the *ṣadaqa*,' he said, it is an illustration, and I saw him make it clearly." They said: A beggar came to Kaʿb and he gave him his garment and the learned Jew departed angrily. A woman stood at the hand of Kaʿb saying, "Who will exchange a beast for a beast? Kaʿb said, "And a provision of clothes?" She said, "Yes!" Kaʿb took and gave, and he rode the beast and wore the garment. [Page 1083] He hastened his journey until he reached the learned Jew who says, "He who gives little is given generously!"

He said: Isḥāq b. ʿAbdullah b. Nisṭās related to me from ʿAmr b. ʿAbdullah al-ʿAbsī, who said: Kaʿb al-Aḥbār said: When ʿAlī arrived in Yemen, I met him and I said, "Inform me about the ways of Muḥammad?" So he began to inform me about him, and I began to smile, so he said, "Why are you smiling?" I replied, "About what is agreed of what we know of his characteristics." And he said, "What does he permit and what does he forbid?" I said, "It is with us just as you describe! You speak the truth about the Messenger of God and I believe in him." I invited those who were before us among our learned. I brought out a scripture to them and I said, "My father sealed this from me saying, 'Do not open it until you hear of a prophet coming out to Yathrib.'" He said: I stayed in Yemen practicing Islam until the death of the Messenger of God and the death of Abū Bakr. I have arrived during the caliphate of ʿUmar b. al-Khaṭṭāb. Would that I had emigrated during the *hijra*!

[Page 1084] **A CHAPTER ON WHAT WAS RELATED ABOUT THE TAKING OF THE *ṢADAQA***

Ibn Abī Ḥayya informed us that: Abū ʿAbdullah Muḥammad b. Shujāʿ al-Thaljī said: al-Wāqidī related to us that Sālim, the *mawlā* of Thābit, related to me from Yaḥyā b. Shibli, who said: I read a document that was with Abū Jaʿfar; it said: In the name of God the Merciful the Benificient, this is what Muḥammad the Messenger of God commanded about what was taken from the *ṣadaqa* of the Muslims from their grazing cattle: From every forty sheep, one sheep, until a hundred and twenty sheep. And if it were more, another one until it reached two hundred sheep. When the sheep increased to three hundred, three. And, when the sheep were more numerous, for every hundred sheep, an additional sheep.

And in the *ṣadaqa* of the camel: for every twenty-four or less camels, a sheep for every five camels; and when it reached twenty-five you give a young—one-year-old—female camel, and if it was not found, a young—two-year-old—male. And when it reached thirty-six, a two-year-old female; when it reaches forty-six—a three-year-old female; If it is sixty-one, a four-year-old female camel. Till it reaches seventy-six. Then it is two two-year-old female camels until it reaches ninety-one; then you pay two three-year-olds at the age of mating.

Do not take as *ṣadaqa* an old female or a male goat, or one that is flawed, unless the collector wishes it. Do not separate a group nor bring together two groups. Those who provide *ṣadaqa* from a mix of two communities should reconcile. When the camels increase above a hundred and twenty, for every fifty, a three-year-old female camel and for every forty, a two-year-old female camel. There is no *ṣadaqa* for less than thirty cows. For every thirty, a mature (year-old) male or female. [Page 1085] For every forty, a three-year-old cow. Whatever crop is watered by rain or natural sources including the well, one twentieth should be taken. Whoever is Jewish or Christian and refuses to convert from it, one dinar from every adult male or the equivalent in clothes.

He said: Ibrāhīm b. Abī Bakr b. al-Mukaydir related to us from Ḥusayn b. Abī Bashīr al-Māzanī from his father from Abū Saʿīd al-Khudrī, who said: we were with ʿAlī in Yemen, and I saw him take the grain from the grain; camel from camels; sheep from sheep; cows from cows; raisins from raisins; he did not assign the people to toil. He used to come to them in their exhaustion; their cattle were taxed, and he commands those who are near that. He did not actively separate the cattle, but used to sit and whatever was brought to him from the cattle as payment, he accepted. He commanded the collectors to do the same, and it was apportioned to their poor who were near; he pursues them and takes the charity from over here and over here, knowing them [the tax payers].

He said: Al-Ḥārith b. Muḥammad al-Fihrī related to us from Isḥāq b. ʿAbdullah b. Abī Farwa, from Rajāʾ b. Ḥaywa, who said: The Messenger of God sent Khālid b. Saʿīd b. al-ʿĀṣ with the messengers of Ḥimyar, and he sent ʿAlī. The Messenger of God said, "If you two meet an attack, ʿAlī is commander over the people. If the two of you are separated, each one of you is on his own." Rajāʾ said: He made a judgment about a conflict in Ḥimyar. The blood money of a person is a hundred camels for people of the camel; a thousand sheep for people of cattle; and two hundred two-year-old sheep. Then secondly, two hundred cows, half of it male calves under a year old and half of it three-year-old cows. For the people of clothing two thousand Yemenī garments.

[Page 1086] They said: The people dug a well in Yemen. In the morning a lion fell into it and when the people arose they saw it. A man fell in the well, and he clung to another, and he clung to another, and another until there were four in the well. The Lion was enraged and it killed them. A man aimed at it with his spear and killed it. The people said: The first owes the blood money for he killed them. ʿAlī passed by and he said, "I will judge between you. Whoever is satisfied, he is to fulfill it; whoever forgoes it for another, he has no right to it until the Prophet passes judgement with you. So gather those who attended the well among the people!" So all who were present at the well gathered. Then he said, "A fourth of the blood money, a third of the blood money, half of the blood money, and all of the blood money to be paid. To the lowest is a fourth of the blood money because he destroyed the three who were above him; to the second is a third of the blood money because he destroyed two; to the third is half of the blood money because he destroyed the one above him. And to the highest is the complete blood money. If you are satisfied, it is fulfilled between you. If you are not satisfied, you have no right until the Messenger of God comes and judges between you."

The Messenger of God arrived during his pilgrimage and there were ten individuals. They sat before him and related their news to him. He said, "I will judge between you, God willing." One individual stood up and said, "O Messenger of God, indeed ʿAlī has already judged between us." He said, "How did he judge between you?" So they informed him of ʿAlī's judgment. The Prophet said, "It is as he judged," so the people stood up and said, "This is a judgement from the Messenger of God." He fixed the judgment over them and asked them about the lions. "Is it in your land?" They replied,

"O Messenger of God, there are many that attack our cattle." The Messenger of God said, "Did I not inform you about the Lion?" They said, "But, no, O Messenger of God." He said, "Indeed it feasted on the son of Eve. So Eve approached it and said, 'Woe unto you, you ate my son!' It replied, 'Nothing prevents me from eating what God drives in my direction.' Then Adam approached and said, [Page 1087] 'Woe unto to you, you speak to her and you have eaten her son. Shame!' So it lowered its head, and thus it is that it does not walk except with a lowered head." Then the Messenger of God said, "If you wish I will appoint for it a place and it will not run to another. Or if you wish I will leave it to accompany you and you will be on guard against it." Some retired with others and they said, "Appoint for it a place." Others said, "We fear that our people will not carry it and they will not obey it. So we will be in a position where we have promised the Messenger of God, but cannot fulfill it." They said, "O Messenger of God, let it accompany us and we will be on guard against it." He replied, "Thus it is." The people turned and returned to their community. When they approached their people, they informed them, and they said, "By God, you were not guided to your choice. If you accepted what the Messenger of God appointed for it, you will be secure from it. So choose a man and send him to the Messenger of God about that." But the Messenger of God died before he met him.

He said: Abū Bakr b. ʿAbdullah and Ḥātim b. Ismāʿīl *mawlā* of the family of al-Ḥārith b. Kaʿb related to me from Jaʿfar b. Muḥammad from his father from Jābir b. ʿAbdullah, who said: ʿAlī arrived from Yemen and he found Fāṭima free from *iḥrām*, wearing a colored dress and kohl in her eyes. ʿAlī hated that for her but she said, "My father commanded me!" ʿAlī said later, when he was in al-ʿIraq: I went to the Messenger of God exasperated about what Fāṭima had done to ask for a legal opinion from him about what Fāṭima had said about it, and I informed him that I refused that to her and that she said, "My father ordered me about that." The Messenger of God said, "She speaks the truth! What did you say when you intended the *Ḥajj*?" He said, "I said, O God, I proclaim what Your messenger proclaimed." He said, [Page 1088] "Indeed, with me is the sacrificial animal so do not release your *iḥrām*. All the sacrificial animals which ʿAlī brought and which the Prophet drove from Medina numbered a hundred animals. The people who did not have a sacrificial animal removed their *iḥrām* and cut their hair and nails. Then the Messenger of God slaughtered his beast and shared his sacrifice with ʿAlī.

ḤAJJAT AL-WADĀʿ [THE FAREWELL PILGRIMAGE]

He said: Maʿmar b. Rāshid, Ibn Abī Sabra, Usāma b. Zayd, Mūsā b. Muḥammad, Ibn Abī Dhiʾb, Abū Ḥamza ʿAbd al-Wāḥid b. Maymūn, Ḥizām b. Hishām, Ibn Jurayj and ʿAbdullah b. ʿĀmir, all related portions of this tradition to me, and some of them were more reliable than others. Some who are not named also related to us.

They said: The Messenger of God arrived on Monday the twelfth of Rabīʿ al-Awwal. He established the sacrifice in Medina every year, though he did not shave or shorten his hair, and made his raids. He did not perform the *Ḥajj* until he was in Dhū l-Qaʿda, of the year ten, after his immigration to Medina. He proclaimed his intention to go out on *Ḥajj* and many people arrived in Medina, all of them desiring to follow the Prophet's lead, and do as he did.

The Messenger of God had performed *ʿUmra* thrice. The first was the *ʿUmrat al-Hudaybiyya*, when the Prophet slaughtered at al-Ḥudaybiyya and shaved in the month of Dhū l-Qaʿda in the year six. The *ʿUmrat al-Qadiyya* took place in the year seven, in the month of Dhū l-Qaʿda, when the Prophet slaughtered sixty camels, and sacrificed and shaved at al-Marwa. The Prophet performed the *ʿUmrat al-Jiʿirrāna* in Dhū l-Qaʿda in the year eight AH.

He said: Ibn Abī Sabra related to me from al-Ḥārith b. al-Fuḍayl, who said: I asked Saʿīd b. al-Musayyib: How many times did the Prophet perform the *Ḥajj* from the inception of his prophethood until his death? [Page 1089] He said: Only one *Ḥajj* from Medina. Al-Ḥārith said: I asked Abū Ḥāshim ʿAbdullah b. Muḥammad b. al-Ḥanafīyya he said: He performed one *Ḥajj* pilgrimage from Mecca before the *hijra*, soon after his prophethood. And one *Ḥajj* from Medina. Mujāhid used to say, two pilgrimages before his emigration; but the affair that is known among us and that the people of our land agree upon is, indeed, that he performed the pilgrimage once from Medina, and it is the *Ḥajj* which people call the farewell pilgrimage.

He said: Al-Thawrī related to me from Layth from Ṭāwus from Ibn ʿAbbās, who said: The term farewell pilgrimage—*ḥajjat al-Wadāʿ*—was detested so it was called *ḥajjat al-Islām*? He said: Yes.

He said: Ibn Abī Sabra related to me from Saʿīd b. Muḥammad b. Jubayr b. Muṭʿim from his father, who said: The Messenger of God went out from Medina on the Sabbath, five nights before the end of Dhū l-Qaʿda. He prayed *Ẓuhr* at Dhū l-Ḥulayfa—in two bowings—and he put on his *iḥrām* on that day. This is confirmed among us. He said: ʿĀṣim b. ʿAbdullah informed us from ʿUmar b. al-Ḥakam that the Messenger of God reached Dhū l-Ḥulayfa at *Ẓuhr*. He spent the night in order that his companions and their sacrificial animals would gather to him until he put on his *iḥrām* on the following day. He said: Ismāʿīl b. Ibrāhīm b. ʿUqba related to me from his father from Kurayb, from Ibn ʿAbbās, who said: The Messenger of God set out from his house oiled and combed and wearing a light cloth until he came to Dhū l-Ḥulayfa.

He said: Ibn Abī Sabra related to me from Yaʿqūb b. Zayd from his father [Page 1090] that the Messenger of God wore an *iḥrām* of two Suḥāriyyīn garments, a shawl and a waist wrap. He exchanged them in al-Tanʿīm for two similar garments.

They said: When he gathered his wives to him he pilgrimaged with all of them in hawdas. When his companions and the sacrificial animals reached the Messenger of God he entered the mosque of Dhū l-Ḥulayfa after he prayed the *Ẓuhr* prayer; then he prayed two bowings. Then he went out, called for the sacrificial animals and marked them on the right side, and adorned them with two sandals. Then he rode on his she-camel. When he ascended al-Bayda' he put on his *iḥrām*.

He said: Khālid b. Ilyās related to me from Yaḥyā b. ʿAbd al-Raḥmān from Abū Salama b. ʿAbd al-Raḥmān from Umm Salama, who said: We reached the Messenger of God in Dhū l-Ḥulayfa by night. With us was ʿAbd al-Raḥmān b. ʿAwf and ʿUthmān b. ʿAffān, and we spent the night at Dhū l-Ḥulayfa. On the following morning I saw the sacrificial animals displayed before the Messenger of God. When the Messenger of God prayed *Ẓuhr* he marked them and adorned them before he put on his *iḥrām*. The first saying, that he did not spend the night, is confirmed among us.

Muḥammad b. Nuʿaym al-Mujmir said that his father said that he heard a man from the companions of the Prophet say, "When the Messenger of God desired to mark his sacrificial animals, he brought an animal and marked it and adorned it himself." Ibn ʿAbbās used to say: He marked it while he directed his face towards the *qibla*. He drove a hundred sacrificial animals. Some said that the Messenger of God commanded

Nājiya b. Jundub, whom the Messenger of God employed to look after the sacrificial animals, to mark the rest of the animals.

He said: Al-Haytham b. Wāqid related to me from ʿAṭāʾ b. Abī Marwān from his father [Page 1091] from Nājiya b. Jundub, who said: I was on a sacrificial animal of the Messenger of God during his pilgrimage, and there was a youth with me from the Aslam. We were driving the animals in search of pasture—and on them were cloths for protection, I said, "O Messenger of God, what do you think I should do if an animal is wounded badly?" He replied, "Slaughter it and put its neck rope in its blood and mark it with that blood on its right hand side, and do not eat from it or let your companions eat from it."

He said: Then we arrived in Mecca the next day. On the day of *tarwīyya* we went to ʿArafa with the sacrificial animals. Then we descended from ʿArafa until we reached Jamʿ. Then from Jamʿ we reached a station of the Prophet in Minā where he struck up his tent. The Messenger of God directed that the sacrificial animals be taken to slaughter. I saw the Messenger of God slaughter the animals with his own hands, as I brought them to him each with one leg tied.

They said: The Messenger of God passed by a man driving a sacrificial animal and he said, "Ride it, shame on you." The man said, "It is a sacrificial animal." The Messenger of God repeated, "Ride it." The Messenger of God used to command the pedestrian to ride his sacrificial animal.

They said: ʿĀʾisha used to say: I perfumed the *iḥrām* of the Messenger of God with my hand. She used to say: I put on the *iḥrām* with the Messenger of God and I used perfume. When we were in Qāḥa the saffron spilled on my face, and the Messenger of God said, "How beautiful is your color now, Oh blonde one." The Messenger of God prayed two bowings between Mecca and Medina, feeling secure, and fearing only God. When he arrived in [Page 1092] Mecca he prayed only two bowings with them; then he greeted. Then he said, "Complete your prayer, O people of Mecca, we are travelers." What the Prophet proclaimed is disputed among us.

He said: Ibn Abī Ṭawāla related to me from Ḥabīb b. ʿAbd al-Raḥmān from Maḥmūd b. Labīd from Abū Ṭalḥa: The Messenger of God combined the *ʿUmra* with the *Ḥajj*. He said: Mālik b. Anas related to me from Nāfiʿ from Ibn ʿUmar from Hafṣa the wife of the Prophet, who said: I said, "O Messenger of God, you command the people to remove their *iḥrām* and yet you do not release from your *ʿUmra*? He replied: I have gummed my hair, and adorned my sacrificial animals, and I will not remove my *iḥrām* until I have slaughtered my sacrificial animals.

Maʿmar related to me from al-Zuhrī from Muḥammad b. ʿAbdullah b. Nawfal b. al-Ḥārith from Saʿd b. Abī Waqqāṣ; and Maʿmar from al-Zuhrī from Sālim from Ibn ʿUmar who both said: The Prophet proclaimed *ʿUmra* and drove his sacrificial animals. He said: Mālik b. Anas related to me from ʿAbd al-Raḥmān b. al-Qāsim from his father from ʿA'isha, who said: The Messenger of God performed the rights of the *Ḥajj* himself. This practice was adopted by the people of Medina and confirmed by them.

ʿĀʾisha said: The Prophet went on Sunday morning to Malal. Then he went to the top of Sayyāla and dined there, and prayed *Maghrib* and *ʿIshaʾ*. He prayed *Subḥ* at Irq al-Ẓabya between al-Rawḥāʾ and Sayyāla—that is before he reached al-Rawḥāʾ—in a mosque, which was on the right side of the road. The Prophet alighted at al-Rawḥāʾ where the people saw a wounded donkey. It was mentioned to the Prophet, saying, "O Messenger of God, this is a wounded donkey." He said, "Leave it until its master comes." Al-Nahdī arrived, and he was the owner of the donkey and he gifted it to the Messenger of God. [Page 1093] The Messenger of God commanded Abū Bakr to apportion it between his companions. He said, "The wild animal is permitted to you except what you hunt or what is hunted for you." The Prophet left al-Rawḥāʾ and prayed *ʿAṣar* in Munṣarif. There he prayed *Maghrib* and *ʿIshāʾ* and dined. He prayed the *Ṣubḥ* prayer at al-Athāya. He arrived on Tuesday morning at al-ʿArj.

He said: Abū Ḥamza ʿAbd al-Wāḥid b. Maṣūn related to me from ʿUrwa b. al-Zubayr from Asmāʾ bt. Abī Bakr, who said: Abū Bakr said to the Messenger of God in Medina, "I have a camel on which we can carry our provisions." The Messenger of God said, "Let it be so." She said: Thus the she camel of the Messenger of God and that of Abū Bakr was the same. The Prophet commanded that provisions of wheat and barely be placed on the camel of Abū Bakr, and his slave used to ride on it from time to time. When they were at al-Athāya, the slave alighted and made the camel kneel down. Then sleep overcame him. The camel, however, rose, its halter sweeping the ground, and commenced to follow the mountain path. When the slave awoke he followed the path thinking that he would catch up with the camel. He called out to it but could not hear any trace of it. Meanwhile, the Messenger of God had alighted in one of his houses in ʿArj. When the slave arrived at noon, Abū Bakr asked him, "Where is the camel?" He replied, "It is lost." Abū Bakr said, "Woe unto you. If it were only mine it would have been easy for me. But the Messenger of God and his family are involved." It was not long before Ṣafwān b. al-Muʿaṭṭil appeared behind the group of people leading the camel. He knelt the camel at the door of the Prophet and said to Abū Bakr, "See if you have lost anything from your goods." Abū Bakr said, "We have not lost anything except a drinking bowl we used to drink with." [Page 1094] The slave said, "This bowl is with me." Abū Bakr said, "May God deliver whatever is entrusted to you."

He said: Yaʿqūb b. Yaḥya b. ʿAbbād b. ʿAbdullah b. al-Zubayr related to me from ʿĪsā b. Maʿmar from ʿAbbād b. ʿAbdullah from Asmāʾ bt. Abī Bakr: That when the Messenger of God alighted in al-ʿArj, he sat in front of his house. Then Abū Bakr came and sat at his side and ʿĀʾisha sat at his other side, and Asmāʾ came and sat beside Abū Bakr. Then the slave of Abū Bakr approached in a state of confusion. Abū Bakr said to him, "Where is the camel?" He replied, "I have lost it." So Abū Bakr went to him and struck him saying, "One camel and it is lost from you?" The Prophet began to smile saying, "Do you not see this pilgrim and what he is doing?" The Messenger of God did not instruct Abū Bakr to stop.

He said: Abū Ḥamza related to me from ʿAbdullah b. Saʿd al-Aslamī from the family of Naḍla al-Aslamī, that they were informed that the camel of the Messenger of God was lost, so they brought a bowl of curd and placed it in the Messenger of God's hands. The Prophet said, "Come Abū Bakr, God has sent you a good meal." But Abū Bakr was angry with the slave. So the Prophet said, "Take it easy. Surely this matter is neither yours nor ours along with you. Indeed the slave was watching that he does not loose the camel. This is what is left from what he had." [Page 1095] The Messenger of God and his family ate, as did Abū Bakr and all who were with the Prophet, until they were satisfied.

He said: Saʿd b. ʿUbāda and his son Qays b. Saʿd came with a camel carrying provisions. They looked for the Prophet until they found him standing at the door of his house where God had brought his camel. Saʿd said, "O Messenger of God, it has reached us that your camel was lost with the slave, so this is a camel in its place." The Messenger of God said, "God has brought our camel, so we return your camel.

May God bless you. Is it not enough, O Abū Thabit, is it not enough what you have done for us in your hospitality since we alighted in Medina?" Saʿd said, "O Messenger of God, by the grace of God and His messenger, what you take from our wealth is more precious to us than what you do not take." The Prophet replied, "You spoke truly, O Abū Thābit. Rejoice, for you have prospered. Surely kindness is in the hand of God, and God provides gentle ways to whomever he wills. Indeed God has bestowed a good nature upon you." Saʿd said, "Praise be to God who did that." Thābit b. Qays said, "Indeed, O Messenger of God, the family of Saʿd in *jāhiliyya* were our masters who provided us food in barren times." The Messenger of God said, "People remain what they were originally. The best of them in *jāhilīyya* are the best of them in Islam when the understanding of Islam comes to them."

Ibn Abī l-Zinād said: It was said of him, "his remembrance is beautiful!" He said: The Messenger of God was cupped (bled) in Laḥyā Jamal while he was in *iḥrām*, in the middle of his head. He said: Muḥammad, ʿAbd al-Raḥmān b. Abī l-Zinād, and Sulaymān b. Bilāl related to me about that from [Page 1096] ʿAlqama b. Abī ʿAlqama, from al-ʿAʿraj from Ibn Buḥayna, who said: The Messenger of God alighted in al-Suqyā on Wednessday. He rose the next morning in al-Abwāʾ. Ṣaʿb b. Jaththāma gifted him a piece of upper leg from a donkey trickling blood. The Prophet returned it to him saying, "I am in *iḥrām*." Muʿāwiya used to say: I saw the Messenger of God eat peeled grain that was brought to him from Waddān. Then he stood up and prayed and he did not take ablution. He prayed in a mosque, which faced Wādī al-Abwāʾ on your left hand side if you were facing Mecca. Then he left al-Abwāʾ and he prayed at Talaʿāt Yemen. There was a Samura tree there. Ibn ʿUmar used to inform that the Prophet sat under it. Ibn ʿUmar used to pour water from a leather container under that tree whenever he passed by it.

He said: Aflaḥ b. Ḥumayd related to me from his father, who said: Ibn ʿUmar used to relate that the Prophet sat under it. And Ibn ʿUmar used to pour the bag full of water under it to preserve it. He said: Aflaḥ b. Ḥumayd related to me from his father from Ibn ʿUmar, who said: The Messenger of God prayed in the mosque, which was there when he descended from Thaniyyat Arāk over al-Juḥfa. He alighted at al-Juḥfa on Friday. He went from there and prayed in the mosque where people put on their *iḥrām* in the outskirts, east of al-Juḥfa. The mosque was beyond Khumm on the left side of the street. On Saturday he was in Qudayd and he prayed in the mosque of al-Mashallal, [Page 1097] and he prayed in a mosque below Lafat.

He said: Ismāʿīl b. Ibrāhīm related to me from his father from Kurayb from Ibn ʿAbbās, who said: The Prophet passed a woman riding bareback on a camel and carrying her little son. She said to the Messenger of God, "Is there a reward for this one for performing the *Ḥajj*?" He replied, "And for you, in the hereafter."

On Sunday the Prophet was in ʿUsfān; then he left. When he was in al-Ghamīm he met with pedestrians who were arranged in rows. They complained to him of their walk. He said: Help yourselves by walking quickly. They did so and found comfort in that. On Monday they were at Marr al-Ẓahrān. They did not leave until evening when the sun had set. He did not pray *Maghrib* until he entered Mecca. He spent the night between the two heights of Kudā and al-Kadāʾ. The next morning he washed and entered Mecca by daylight.

He said: Ibn Abī Sabra related to me from Mūsā b. Saʿd from ʿIkrima from Ibn ʿAbbās, that the Messenger of God entered Mecca by day from Kudā on his beast al-Qaṣwāʾ. He entered Mecca from above until he reached the gate, which is called the gate of Banū Shayba. When he saw the House (Kaʿba) he raised his hand; the reins of the camel fell down and he gathered them in his left hand. They said that when he saw the House he said, "O God, increase this House with nobility and wisdom and generosity and respect and piety."

He said: Muḥammad b. ʿAbdullah related to me from al-Zuhrī from Sālim from Ibn ʿUmar that the Messenger of God when he entered the mosque, started to circumambulate it before prayer. They said: When he reached the al-Rukn he touched it and kissed it, and he had draped his garment under his right armpit and over his left shoulder. [Page 1098] He said, "In the name of God, God is greatest!" Then he swiftly walked three times around the Kaʿba. He commanded that whoever touches al-Rukn should proclaim, "In the name of God, God is greatest," thus displaying faith in God and sincere belief in the message that Muḥammad had delivered.

He said: Ibn Jurayj related to me from Yaḥyā b. ʿAbdullah from his father from ʿAbdullah b. al-Sā'ib al-Makhzūmī, that he heard the Messenger of God say as he paced between the southern corner and the Black stone, *O Lord give us happiness in both this world and the next, and save us from the pain of hell fire* (Q. 102). He said: ʿAbdullah b. Jaʿfar related to me from ʿĀṣim b. ʿAbdullah from ʿAbdullah b. ʿĀmir b. Rabīʿa from his father, who said: I looked at the Prophet and he only touched the Yemenī corner (al-Rukn) and the Black stone; and he walked four times. They said: When he arrived behind the *maqām* Ibrāhīm he prayed two bowings and recited two chapters: *Say O unbelievers* (Q. 109), and *Say, God is One* (Q. 112). Then he returned to al-Rukn and touched it. He said to ʿUmar, "You are a man of strength. If you find the corner free, then touch it. If not, do not push the people against it for you will hurt people and get hurt yourself." He asked ʿAbd al-Raḥmān b. ʿAwf, "How did you do at the corner, Abū Muḥammad?" He replied, "Sometimes I touched it and sometimes I left it." The Prophet said, "You did right." Then he went out to al-Ṣafā through the Gate of the Banū Makhzūm. He said: "I begin with what God began."

He said: ʿAbdullah b. Wafdān related to me from ʿImrān b. Abī Anas from ʿAbdullah b. Thaʿlaba: that the Messenger of God ran between al-Ṣafā and al-Marwa on his camel soon after that. [Page 1099] He said: al-Thawrī related to me from Ḥammād from Saʿīd b. Jubayr that the Messenger of God arrived and he was calm. He circumambulated between al-Ṣafā and al-Marwa on his camel. He said: Ibn Abī Jurayj related to me from Mujāhid, who said: At that time the Prophet circumambulated between al-Ṣafā and al-Marwa on his mule. The first is confirmed among us and it is recognized that he went on his camel.

They said: The Prophet ascended al-Ṣafā and proclaimed seven *takbīrs*. He said, "There is but one God; He has no partner; To Him is Kingship, and to Him is praise. He has power over all things. God keeps His promise, helps His slave, and defeated the factions alone." The Messenger of God alighted at al-Marwa, and as soon as his feet touched the ground he set off at a trot.

He said: ʿAlī b. Muḥammad related to me from ʿUbaydullah b. ʿAbdullah b. ʿUmar b. al-Khaṭṭāb from Manṣūr b. ʿAbd al-Raḥmān from his mother from Barra bt. Abī Tijrā, who said: When the Prophet reached al-Masʿā he said, "O People, God wrote for you to run, so run," and he ran until I saw his waist cloth reveal his thighs. They said: He said in al-Wādī, "O Lord, forgive and be merciful. You are the highest and most generous." When he reached al-Marwa he did there as he had done in al-Ṣafā. What he began at al-Ṣafā he concluded at al-Marwa. The Messenger of God struck up his tent at al-Abṭaḥ.

He said: Burd related to me that Ibrāhīm b. Abī l-Naḍr related to him from his father from Abū Murra *mawlā* of ʿUqayl from Umm Hānī, who said: I said, "O Messenger of God, will you not alight at the houses of Mecca?" But he refused and struck up his tent at al-Abṭaḥ until he set out on the day of *tarwiyya* (eighth of Dhū l-Ḥijja). Then he returned [Page 1100] from Minā and alighted in al-Abṭaḥ until he set out to Medina. He did not alight in a house or take shelter in one. He said: The Messenger of God entered the Kaʿba, and when he reached its door he removed his sandals. He entered with ʿUthmān b. Abī Ṭalḥa, Bilāl and Usāma b. Zayd. They locked the door on themselves for a long time then they opened it. Ibn ʿUmar said: I was the first of the people to reach him. I asked Bilāl, "Did the Messenger of God pray in it?" He said, "Yes. Two bowings between the two front columns; and there were six columns." Ibn Jurayj related to me from ʿAṭāʾ from Ibn ʿAbbās from Usāma b. Zayd that the Prophet proclaimed *takbīr* in several directions but he did not pray.

They said: ʿĀʾisha used to say: The Prophet entered sadly so I said, "What is the matter, O Messenger of God?" He replied, "Today, I did something that I wish I had not done! I entered the House, and a man from among my followers wished to do so but he was not able to enter it and it will be a grievance in his heart. Surely, we were commanded to circumambulate it not to enter it." The Messenger of God draped the Kaʿba.

He said: Ibn Abī Sabra related to me from Khālid b. Rabāḥ from al-Muṭṭalib b. ʿAbdullah b. Mūsā, who said: I heard al-ʿAbbās b. ʿAbd al-Muṭṭalib say: The Messenger of God draped the house, during his pilgrimage, with a cloth from Yemen. They said: During the age of the Prophet, the Kaʿba was eighteen *dhirāʿa*.

They said: The Messenger of God arrived on Tuesday, Wednesday, Thursday and Friday (and this was the day of *tarwiyya* according to what we gathered of this story). The Messenger of God spoke one day, before *tarwiyya*, after *Ẓuhr* in Mecca.

[Page 1101] He said: Hishām b. ʿUmāra related to me from ʿAbd al-Raḥmān b. Abī Saʿīd from ʿUmāra b. Ḥāritha al-Ẓafarī from ʿAmr b. Yathribī al-Ḍamrī, who said: I saw the Messenger of God speak one day before *tarwiyya* after *Ẓuhr*, and on the day of *ʿArafa* in ʿArafa when the Sun was declining, on his camel before prayer; and on the day following the day of slaughter at Minā after *Ẓuhr*. Al-Wāqidī said: This agreed matter is recognized. It was said: The day of *jumʿa* was the day of *tarwiyya*. The Prophet stood between the corner and the *maqām*. He spoke to the people and said: Who among you is able to pray *Ẓuhr* in Minā, let him do so. He rode while the sun was settting, after he had circumambulated the Kaʿba seven times. He prayed the *Ẓuhr, ʿAṣar, Maghrib, ʿIshāʾ* and *Ṣubḥ* prayers at Minā where he alighted at a place named Dār al-Imāra. ʿĀʾisha said, "O Prophet, may we not build a place for you?" The Prophet refused. He said, "Minā is a stop for those who come earlier."

Ibn Jurayj related to me from Muḥammad b. Qays b. Makhrama that the Messenger of God did not ride from Mina until he saw the sun rise. Then he rode until he came to ʿArafa and alighted in Namira, where he put up his tent of hair. It was said: Rather it was in the shade of a rock. Maymūna his wife stayed in its shade until he departed. His wives remained in tents—or in a tent—around him. When the sun came down from the meridian, the Prophet asked for his camel Qaswāʾ and rode to the interior of the valley of Baṭn ʿUrana.

[Page 1102] They said: The Quraysh were certain that the Prophet did not pass through al-Muzdalifa but stayed there. Nawfal b. Muʿāwiya al-Dīlī, who stood at his left, said to him, "O Messenger of God, your people think that you stayed in Jamʿ."

The Messenger of God said, "I stayed in ʿArafa before my Prophethood in disagreement with the Quraysh." Jubayr b. Muṭʿim said, "I saw the Messenger of God stand in ʿArafa before his prophethood." The Quraysh, all of them, used to stand in Jamʿ, except for Shayba b. Rabīʿa. Indeed Mūsā b. Yaʿqūb related to me from his uncle from ʿAbdullah b. al-Walīd b. ʿUthmān b. ʿAffān from Asmāʾ bt. Abī Bakr, who said: Shayba b. Rabīʿa was the only one from the Quraysh who stayed at ʿArafa. He wore two black garments, and the nose rope of the camel was made of hair between two layers of black leather. He stayed with the people in ʿArafa doing what ever they did. Indeed we did not speak with the people—that is the Bedouin—who had stopped in ʿArafa. The Quraysh in Jamʿ used to say, "We are the people of God!"

He said: Ibn Abī Sabra related to me from Yaʿqūb b. Zayd from his father, who said: When the sun set in Baṭn ʿArafa, the Messenger of God spoke from his camel al-Qaṣwāʾ. When it was the end of his speech, and the Prophet was silent from his words, Bilāl proclaimed the call to prayer. When Bilāl completed his call to prayer the Messenger of God said some words and knelt his camel. Bilāl called out the *iqāma* and the Prophet prayed *Ẓuhr*; then the *iqāma* was announced again, and he prayed *ʿAṣar*. Altogether there was the *adhān* and two *iqāma*.

Usāma b. Zayd related to me from ʿAmr b. Shuʿayb from his father from his grandfather, that he saw the Messenger of God speak, at the time, in Wādī ʿArafa. Then he rode. He said: I saw the Messenger of God indicate with his hand to the people that they should stand.

[Page 1103] **THE SERMON OF THE PROPHET AT ʿARAFAT BEFORE THE PRAYERS**

This was from his speech at that time:

"O people, indeed, by God, I do not know, but perhaps I will not meet you at this place of mine after this day of yours! By the grace of God, may a man who hears my speech retain it. Many a bearer of *fiqh*/jurisprudence has no understanding of it; many a bearer of *fiqh* should go to one who has a better understanding! Know that your property and your blood are sacrosanct to you as the sacredness of this day of yours, in this month of yours, in this land of yours! And know that the hearts will not betray three things: the sincerity of Godly acts; the advising of those with authority; and the attachment to the community of Muslims. Verily their prayers surround and protect them from behind. All things from the affairs of *jāhiliyya* are abolished, under my feet. The first blood of *jāhiliyya* that I abolish is the blood of Iyās b. Rabīʿa b. al-Ḥārith who was nursed among the Banū Saʿd; Hudhayl killed him. And the usury of *jāhiliyya* is abolished as well. The first usury that I abolish is that of al-ʿAbbās b. ʿAbd al-Muṭṭalib.

Fear God with regard to women, for you took possession of them under God's protection. You have rights over their private parts according to the word of God. Surely, you have rights over them: that they do not bring to your bed one you detest. If they do, strike them without hurting them. To them from you is the responsibility for food and clothing in all fairness. I have left you the book of God, which will never lead you astray if you keep to it. You will be asked about me, so what will you reply?"

They said: "We testify that you have delivered, informed and given us advice." Then he said, pointing his finger to the sky and raising it and putting it down three times, "O God, bear witness that I have delivered!"

He said: Muḥammad b. ʿAbdullah related to me from his uncle al-Zuhrī from Abū Salama b. ʿAbd al-Raḥmān, from Ibn ʿAbbās that the Messenger of God stood in the mountains of ʿArafa and said: All of ʿArafa is a station except Baṭn ʿUrana. [Page 1104] All of al-Muzdalifa is a station except Baṭn Muḥassir. All of Minā is a slaughtering place except behind al-ʿAqaba.

They said: The Messenger of God sent someone to the borders of ʿArafa and said: Keep to the ritual practices. Indeed your inheritance is according to the rituals of Abraham. He said: Isḥāq b. Ḥāzm related to me from Abū Najīḥ from Mujāhid from Ibn ʿAbbās, who said: ʿArafa is from the beginning of the mountains around ʿUrana to Mount ʿArafa: all of it is the place of ʿArafa. Ibn ʿAbbās said: I saw the Prophet standing at ʿArafat and his hands were outstretched with his palms directed to his face.

They said: The Messenger of God said: Surely the best of my prayers are the prayers of those prophets before me. There is but one God; He has no partner; To him is Kingship and to him is praise; In His hands is our betterment, life and death; He has power over all things.

He said: Ibn Abī Dhiʾb related to me from Ṣāliḥ *mawlā* of al-Tawama from Ibn ʿAbbās, that people disputed about the fasting of the Prophet on the day of ʿArafa. Umm al-Faḍl said: I am informing you about that. She sent him a large bowl of milk, and he drank as he spoke: They said: The Messenger of God stopped on his ride and prayed a *duʿa* until the sun set. The people of *jāhiliyya* pushed towards ʿArafa when the sun was above the tops of the mountains like turbans arranged on the heads of men. The Quraysh doubted that the Messenger of God would press forward like that. The Messenger of God delayed going forward until the sun set. Thus did the Messenger of God go forward.

He said: ʿAbd al-Raḥmān b. Abī l-Zinād related to me from his father from ʿUrwa b. al-Zubayr [Page 1105] from Usāma b. Zayd, who said: I heard him ask about the march of the Prophet on the eve of ʿArafa. He replied: He used to go at a quick pace, and when he found a hole in the ground he strode over it with a large stride. He said: Ibrāhīm b. Yazīd related to me from ʿAmr b. Dīnār from Ṭāwus from Ibn ʿAbbās, who said that the Messenger of God said, "O people, slow down, and keep your calm. Restrain your strong from your weak."

He said: Maʿmar related to me from Ibn Ṭāwus from his father, who said: The camel of the Prophet did not move its forelegs from where it stood until he threw the stone. He said: Muḥammad b. Muslim al-Juhannī related to me from ʿUyayna b. Jubayr b. Kulayb al-Juhannī from his father from his grandfather, who said: I saw the Messenger of God push from ʿArafa to Jamʿ. The fire was ignited in al-Muzdalifa and he moved towards it until he alighted close to it. He said: Isḥāq b. ʿAbdullah b. Khārija related to me from his father, who said: When Sulaymān b. ʿAbd al-Malik noticed the fire, he said to Khārija b. Zayd, "Since when is this fire, O Abū Yazīd?" He said, "It was in *jāhiliyya* when the Quraysh placed it. Quraysh would not go out from the sanctuary to ʿArafa without saying, 'We are the people of God!' Indeed, Ḥassān b. Thābit, and others in a group of my community informed me that even when they were pilgrims in *jāhiliyya* they would see that fire."

He said: Ibrāhīm b. Yazīd related to me from ʿAmr b. Dīnār from Ibn [Page 1106] ʿAbbās, who said: The Messenger of God said, "To the mountain path!" He said: The mountain path, Shiʿb al-Idhkhir is on the left side of the road between the two mountains. He did not pray.

He said: Ibn Abī Dhiʾb related to me from al-Zuhrī from Sālim from Ibn ʿUmar that the Messenger of God prayed *Maghrib* and *ʿIshā*ʾ in al-Muzdalifa with a single *iqāma*. He did not praise God between the two prayers, nor at the end of each prayer. He said: Ibn Abī Sabra related to me from Yaḥyā b. Shibl from Abū Jaʿfar, who said the Messenger of God prayed both prayers with one *adhān* and two *iqāmas*.

They said: The Messenger of God alighted close to the fire. The fire was on Mount Quzaḥ, which was a sacred precinct. Just before dawn he granted permission to leave [for the ritual stoning] to those who asked him among the people of weakness, children, and women. He said: Aflaḥ b. Ḥumayd related to me from al-Qāsim from ʿĀʾisha, that Sawda bt. Rabīʿa asked permission of the Prophet about approaching from Jamʿ before the people gathered. She was a heavy woman. He granted her permission and kept his wives until she went forward in the morning. ʿĀʾisha said: Would that I had asked permission of the Messenger of God just as Sawda; it would have been more pleasing to me than being imprisoned with him. He said: Ibn Abī Sabra related to me from Isḥāq b. ʿAbdullah from ʿImrān b. Abī Anas from his mother, who said: I approached with Sawda, the wife of the Prophet, during his pilgrimage and we threw stones before dawn.

He said: Ibn Abī Dhiʾb related to me from Shuʿba from Ibn ʿAbbās, that he used to say: [Page 1107] The Messenger of God sent me with his family and they threw stones with the dawn. He said: Jubayr b. Zayd related to me from Abū Jaʿfar, who said: When the dawn lit up, the Prophet prayed the *Ṣubḥ* prayer. Then he rode on al-Qaswāʾ until he stopped at Quzaḥ. The people of *jāhiliyya* did not go forth until the sun rose over Thabīr. They used to say: May it light up Thabīr in order that we may go forth. The Messenger of God said, "Surely the Quraysh opposed the order of Abraham, and went forth before sunrise." He said, "This place is a station and all of al-Muzdalifa is a station!"

He said: Ibn Abī Sabra related to me from ʿUmar b. ʿAṭāʾ from ʿIkrima from Ibn ʿAbbās, who said: Jamʿ is the farthest of the two passes at Qarn which is behind Wādī Muḥassir. He said: Al-Thawrī related to me from Ibn al-Zubayr from Jābir that the Messenger of God stayed in Wādī Muḥassir.

He said: Abū Marwān related to me from Isḥāq b. ʿAbdullah from Abān b. Ṣāliḥ, that the Messenger of God brought pebbles to al-ʿAqaba from al-Muzdalifa. He said: Al-Thawrī related to me from Ayman b. Nāʾil, who said: I heard Qudama b. ʿAbdullah al-Kilābī say: I saw the Messenger of God throw stones of al-ʿAqaba on the day of slaughter, at a white spotted camel, without moving.

He said: Ibn Abī Sabra related to me from al-Ḥārith b. ʿAbd al-Raḥmān from Mujāhid from Abū Maʿmar ʿAbdullah b. Shakhīra from Ibn Masʿūd: the Prophet [Page 1108] did not stop the *talbiyya* until he threw the stones. He said: Ibn Abī Dhiʾb related to me from Shuʿba from Ibn ʿAbbās that the Prophet did not stop the *talbiyya* until he threw the stones. He said: When the Messenger of God reached the slaughtering place he said, "This is the slaughtering place. All of Minā is a slaughtering place. Every road of Mecca is a road and a slaughtering place." He slaughtered sixty-three animals with his hand using a long knife. Then he gave the knife to a man who slaughtered what remained. Then he ordered from every sacrificial animal, including the animal that he slaughtered, a portion. It was put in a pot and cooked and he ate of its meat and sipped its gravy.

He said: Maʿmar related to me from ʿAbd al-Karīm al-Jazarī from Mujāhid from ʿAbd al-Raḥmān b. Abī Laylā from ʿAlī, who said: The Messenger of God commanded me to give charity with the bulk of his sacrificial animal, its skin and its meat. I was not given anything from it after its slaughter.

SHAVING OF THE MESSENGER OF GOD'S HAIR

They said: When the Messenger of God slaughtered the sacrificial animals he called for a barber, and the Muslims attended seeking some hair of the Messenger of God. The Messenger of God gave the barber some hair from the right side of his head, then he gave Abū Ṭalḥa al-Anṣārī. Khālid b. al-Walīd spoke to him about his fore lock, so when he shaved it he gave it to him. Khālid placed it in the front of his cap, and he did not confront a group of the enemy but he dispersed it. Abū Bakr said: I looked at Khālid b. al-Walīd and what we received from him in Uḥud, in Khandaq and in al-Ḥudaybiyya and every situation that he met us in, then I observed him on the day of the sacrifice when he came before the Prophet and his animal which had its leg tied. Then I observed him while the Messenger of God was shaving his head, and he was saying, "O Messenger of God, your forelock! [Page 1109] Do not pass it to anyone but me. I will ransom my father and my mother for you!" And I observed him take the forelock of the Messenger of God and place it on his mouth and eyes.

He said: I asked ʿĀ'isha, from where is this hair that is with you? She replied, "Indeed the Messenger of God, when he shaved his head during the pilgrimage, dispersed his hair among the people, and we took what the people took." When the Messenger of God shaved his head, he cut his moustache and beard, and shortened his nails. He ordered that his hair and his nails be buried. People among his companions cut their hair) short and others shaved. The Messenger of God said, "May God bless the shavers!" Three times. All of them said, "And those who cut their hair, O Messenger of God!" The Messenger of God said, "And those who cut their hair, the fourth time."

They said: The Messenger of God used perfume after he shaved and put on his shirt. He sat with the people. Not a question was asked at that time about anything now or later, but he said, "Do it, and do not hesitate!"

He said: Usāma b. Zayd related to me from ʿAṭā' from Jābir b. ʿAbdullah that a man came and said, "O Messenger of God, I shaved before I slaughtered." He replied, "Slaughter and do not hesitate!" He said, "O Messenger of God, I slaughtered before I threw the stones." He replied, "Throw your stones and do not hesitate."

He said: Ibn Abī Dhi'b related to me from al-Zuhrī, who said: The Messenger of God sent ʿAbdullah b. Ḥudhāfa al-Sahmī to proclaim to the people, "O people, indeed the Messenger of God says that these are the days of eating and drinking and remembering God." He said: The Muslims kept from fasting if not detained by the pilgrimage, or proceeding to the pilgrimage. Indeed they sought permission of the Messenger of God to fast in Minā. The Messenger of God set out on the day of slaughter. Some said that he returned to his wives [Page 1110] at night on the eve of the day of sacrifice. He commanded his companions to return in the day. He came to Zamzam and ordered a bucket to be filled for him. He drank from it and poured it on his head. He said, "If not for the fear that you would lose your position, O son of ʿAbd al-Muṭṭalib, surely I would have filled from it."

He said: Ibn Abī Jurayj related to us from ʿAṭā', who said: The Prophet filled a bucket for himself from Zamzam. ʿAṭā' said: I used to draw water for myself. When I grew old and became weak I commanded those who filled to fill it for me. And he threw the pebbles, when the sun came down from the meridian, before the prayer. Then, he threw two pebbles at the two of them. He threw the pebbles of al-ʿAqaba from Baṭn al-Wādī. He did not stop with the first pebble, any more than that he stopped with the second. Nor did he stop at the third. When he had thrown them he turned back.

He said: Maʿmar related to me from al-Zuhrī, who said: The Messenger of God when he had thrown two pebbles stopped with them, and raised his hands. He did not do that during the throwing of al-ʿAqaba. Then he threw them and turned back. The Messenger of God permitted the herdsmen to spend the night outside Mina, and whoever came could throw at night. The Messenger of God granted permission for that.

He said: ʿAbd al-Raḥmān b. ʿAbd al-ʿAzīz related to me from Abū Bakr b. Ḥazm from Abū l-Badāḥ b. ʿĀṣim b. ʿAdī from his father: The Messenger of God permitted the shepherds to spend the night at Mina. They said: The Messenger of God said, "Throw the pebbles with your fingers!" His wives threw at night.

THE SERMON OF THE PROPHET ON THE DAY OF THE SLAUGHTER

He said: Hishām b. ʿUmāra related to me from ʿAbd al-Raḥmān b. Abī Saʿīd [Page 1111] from ʿUmāra b. Ḥāritha from ʿAmr b. Yathribī, who said: Ibn Abī Dhiʾb related to us from ʿAmr b. Abī ʿAmr from ʿIkrima from Ibn ʿAbbās who both said: The Messenger of God spoke on the day following the day of slaughter, after *Ẓuhr*, while on his camel al-Qaṣwāʾ. One of them added to the story of his companion. They both said: The Messenger of God said, "O People listen to what I say and understand it, for indeed I do not know, perhaps I will not meet you after this year of mine in this station. O people, which month is this?" He said: And the people were silent. The Messenger of God said, "This is a holy month! And what land is this?" And they were silent, and he said, "A holy land." Then he said, "What day is this?" And they were silent, and he said, "A holy day." Then the Messenger of God said, "God has declared your blood unlawful, and your property and your reputation are as sacred as this holy month of yours, in this land of yours, in this day of yours, until you meet your lord. Have I not informed you?" They said, "Yes!" He said, "O God, bare witness!" Then he said, "Surely you will meet your lord, and He will ask you about your deeds. Have I not informed you?" They said, "Yes!" He said, "O God, bare witness! Will not he who has a pledge return it to the one who entrusted him with it. Indeed, all usury in *jāhiliyya* has no place, and all blood in *jāhiliyya* has no place. The first of your blood that I revoke is the blood of Iyās b. Rabīʿa b. al-Ḥārith. He was suckled by the Banū Saʿd b. Layth, and the Hudhayl killed him. Have I not informed?" They replied, "O God, Yes!" He said, "O God, bare witness! The witnesses shall inform those who are not present! All Muslims are unlawful to every Muslim, and no Muslim rights to the property of a fellow Muslim except when it is given from the goodness of his heart."

ʿAmr b. Yathribī said: I said, "O Messenger of God, do you think that I will meet the cattle of [Page 1112] my cousin? Can I slaughter a sheep from them?" And he informed me, "Indeed, you will meet an ewe and attack it with a flint knife in Khabt al-Jamīsh. Al-Jamīsh is a valley that has many trees and the Messenger of God knew that it was on the coast. It is a valley of the Banū Ḍamra. It is the station of ʿAmr b. Yathribī. Some said: Khabt al-Jamīsh is a place in the desert. Others, that it is on the side of al-Kadāʾ, so do not disturb it!"

Then the Messenger of God said, "O people, *Verily the transposing of a prohibited month is an addition to unbelief. The unbelievers are led to wrong thereby for they make it lawful one year and forbidden another year in order to adjust the number of months forbidden by God* (Q. 9:37). Indeed, time has completed its cycle as it was on the day that God created the heavens and the earth. The number of the months is twelve in the Book of God. Of them four are sacred, three consecutive months of Dhū l-Qaʿda, Dhū l-Ḥijja and Muḥarram, and Rajab, which is called the month of Muḍar. It is between Jamādā l-Ākhira and Shaʿbān. And the month has twenty-nine days or thirty. Have I not informed you?" And the people said, "Yes!" He said, "O God, bare witness!" Then, he said, "O People, to the women over you is a right, and indeed, to you over them is a right. You have the right that they should not cause anyone to tread your beds, and that they should not bring in anyone whom you dislike into your houses, except with your permission. If they do, then God permits you to desert them in their beds and to beat them but not severely. If they abstain from evil they have the right to their food and clothing in accordance with custom. Treat women well for they are bound to you and are dependent on you. You have taken them only as a trust from God, and you have made the enjoyment of their persons lawful by the word of God. So fear God [Page 1113] regarding women and intend their good. Have I not informed you?" The people said, "Yes!" He said, "O God, bare witness! Indeed, Satan despairs that he will be worshiped in this land of yours. But he is satisfied that he is followed in any minor act of evil. That would satisfy him (Satan). Indeed, every Muslim is the brother of a Muslim. All Muslims are brethren. It is not lawful for a Muslim to take from his brother except that which he has given him willingly, so do not wrong yourselves. Indeed I was commanded to fight people until they say there is but one God, and when they say it, their blood and their property is protected and they are answerable to God. Do not make tyrants of yourselves and return as disbelievers to kill each other. Indeed, I have left with you the book of God, which will not lead you astray. Have I not informed you?" The people said, "Yes!" He said, "O God, bare witness!" Then he turned back to his station.

According to Ibn Jurayj, ʿAṭāʾ was asked: How would you strike lightly? He replied: With a small stick (tooth-brush) and a sandal. ʿAṭāʾ said that Ibn ʿAbbās was asked about the words of God: *And they have taken from you a solemn covenant* (Q. 4:21). He said: Words of marriage. He said: The Messenger of God forbade that one spends the nights of Minā in any other place. Sulaymān b. Bilāl related to me from ʿAmr b. Abī ʿAmr from ʿIkrima from Ibn ʿAbbās that the Messenger of God prayed the *Ẓuhr* and *ʿAṣar* prayers on the day of Ṣadar in al-Abṭaḥ.

He said: Sufyān b. ʿUyayna related to me from Ṣāliḥ b. Kaysān from Sulaymān b. Yasār from Abū Rāfiʿ, who said: The Messenger of God did not command me to alight in a station. I came to al-Abṭaḥ and struck up his tent, and he came and stayed there. He said: ʿĀʾisha used to say: Indeed he stopped in al-Muḥaṣṣab because it was easiest to go out from there.

[Page 1114] He said: Ibn Aflaḥ b. Ḥumayd related to me from al-Qāsim from ʿĀʾisha, that the Prophet mentioned Ṣafiyya bt. Ḥuyayy. It was said to him, "She has menstruated!" He said, "Is she going to keep us here?" Someone said, "O Messenger of God, indeed she has fulfilled!" He said, "Then she will not keep us!" When ʿĀʾisha came from al-Tanʿīm she had completed her *ʿUmra*, so the Prophet commanded the departure. The Messenger of God passed the House and circumambulated it before dawn. Then he turned and returned to Medina.

They said: The Messenger of God said: The Muhājir will stay three days after *al-Ṣadr*. Someone asked to stay in Mecca, but he did not authorize his stay except for three days. He said, "Indeed it is not a place of residence, and there is no staying!"

He said: Khālid b. Ilyās related to me from Saʿīd b. Abī Saʿīd from ʿUbayd b. Jurayj, that the Prophet, when he took leave of the House at the end of the seventh circumambulation, was behind the House to the right of the door, and he touched it with his stomach and forehead.

They said: The Messenger of God, when he returned from *Ḥajj* or *ʿUmra*, or a raid, ascended over Thaniyya or Fadfad and proclaimed *takbīr* three times, and then said, "There is but one God, He has no partner; to Him is all authority; to Him is all praise. He lives, gives life and death, and He does not die. Good is in His hands. He has power over all things. We are returners, repenting, prostrating worshiping, and we are thankful to the Lord. God has fulfilled his promise. He has made his servant victorious, and He, alone, defeated the factions. O God, we ask your protection from the hardship of traveling, the distress of return, [Page 1115] and the bad image of property and family. O God, let us achieve goodness through which we will achieve your forgiveness and acceptance."

They said: When the Messenger of God alighted in al-Muʿarras he forbade his companions from visiting their wives at night. But two men knocked on their families, and each one of them found what he detested. The Messenger of God knelt his camel in al-Baṭḥāʾ. When he set out for *Ḥajj* he went before al-Shajara. When he returned from Mecca he entered Medina from the resting place of al-Abṭaḥ. The Messenger of God was in his resting place in Baṭn al-Wādī. The people were with him at night. And it was said to him, "Surely you are blessed in Baṭḥāʾ!" The Messenger of God said to his wives, "This is the *Ḥajj*, then the back of the carpet"—meaning stick to your homes. But they continued to make pilgrimage; except for Zaynab bt. Jaḥsh and Sawda bt. Zamaʿa. They both said: An animal will not transport us after the Prophet.

THE VISIT OF THE PROPHET TO SAʿD B. ABĪ WAQQĀṢ AFTER THE FAREWELL PILGRIMAGE

He said: Maʿmar related to me from Muḥammad b. ʿAbdullah and Mālik from al-Zuhrī from ʿĀmir b. Saʿd from his father, who said: The Messenger of God came to me in the year of the farewell pilgrimage, when I got sick and pain overwhelmed me. I said, "O Messenger of God, you see the pain I am in; I am the owner of property but I have no heir except for a daughter of mine. Shall I give a third of my property in charity?" He said, "No!" I said, "Half?" He said, "No!" Then he said, "A third. A third is a lot! It is better that you leave your heir wealthy than that you leave her needy, and begging. Indeed you will never [Page 1116] pay a price desiring to please God with it but you will be rewarded, even if you were to feed your wife." So I said, "O Messenger of God, will I be left behind after my companions?" He replied, "Indeed if you stay behind you will do good works and you will achieve good and a high rank. Perhaps you will stay behind in order that some people benefit, while others are harmed by you. O God, leave to my companions their emigration and do not return them at their end! Miserable is Saʿd b. Khawla."—He lamented that he died in Mecca.

He said: Sufyān b. ʿUyayna related to me from Ismāʿīl b. Muḥammad b. al-Aʿraj, who said: The Messenger of God left a man to watch over Saʿd saying, "If Saʿd dies in Mecca do not bury him there."

He said: Sufyān related to me from Muḥammad b. Qays from Abū Burda b. Abī Mūsā, who said: Saʿd b. Abī Waqqāṣ said to the Prophet, "Is it hateful that the man dies in the land from which he emigrated?" He replied, "Yes!" He said: Sufyān b. ʿUyayna related to me from Ibn Abī Nujayḥ from Mujāhid from Saʿd, who said: I was sick and the Messenger of God came to me and and visited me. He placed his hand between my breast and I found it cooling over my heart. Then he said, "You are a man with chest pain—maf'ūd means an afflicted heart. So bring al-Ḥārith b. Kalada the brother of Thaqīf. He is a medicine man. Ask him to take seven dates from the dates of Medina and grind it with its seeds, and massage you with it."

THE RAID OF USĀMA B. ZAYD TO MU'TA

[Page 1117] They said: The Messenger of God continued to mention the death of Zayd b. Ḥāritha, Jaʿfar, and his companions and he was extremely agitated over them. When it was Monday, four days from the month of Ṣafar in the year eleven AH, the Messenger of God commanded the people to prepare to raid the Byzantines, and he ordered them to hasten in raiding them. The Muslims departed from the place of the Messenger of God and they were diligent in their effort. When the Messenger of God rose the next morning, it was Tuesday three days from Ṣafar, He called Usāma b. Zayd and said, "O Usāma, go in the name of God, and with His blessings until you reach the place where your father was killed, and attack them with the horses, for I have appointed you over this army. Attack the people of Ubnā in the morning and be aggressive. And hasten the march so that you arrive ahead of the information. If God grants you success, shorten your stay with them. Take a guide with you. Send the spies and the foot soldiers to arrive ahead of you."

When it was the fourth day, two nights before Ṣafar, the Messenger of God began a headache and a fever. When it dawned on the Thursday, a night from Ṣafar, the Messenger of God handed a banner to Usāma and said, "O Usāma, attack in the name of God and in the path of God, and fight those who do not believe in God. Attack, but do not act treacherously. Do not kill a new born or a woman, and do not desire to meet the enemy, for indeed you do not know whether you would be destroyed by them, but say, 'O God, protect us from them, and keep their strength from us!' Indeed, they will find you and confront you with screams, and may God inspired tranquility and quiet come upon you. Do not fight each other nor be cowardly, for your power will leave, but say, 'O God, we are your slaves, and they [Page 1118] are your slaves. Our fate and their fate are in your hands. Surely you will conquer them.' Know that Paradise is under the flashing gleam."

He said: Yaḥyā b. Hishām b. ʿĀṣim al-Aslamī related to me from al-Mundhir b. Jahm, who said: The Messenger of God said, "O Usāma engage the troops against the people of Ubnā!"

He said: ʿAbdullah b. Jaʿfar b. ʿAbd al-Raḥmān b. Azhar b. ʿAwf related to me from al-Zuhrī from ʿUrwa from Usāma b. Zayd that the Messenger of God commanded him to attack Ubnā in the morning and to be aggressive. They said: Then the Messenger of God said to Usāma, "Go in the name of God!" He set out with his banner tied and handed it to Burayda b. al-Ḥuṣayb al-Aslamī, and Burayda went with him to Usāma's house. The Messenger of God commanded Usāma to camp in al-Jurf, and put up his troops in Siqāya Sulaymān that day. The people began to prepare to join the troops: He who had completed his needs went out to his camp. He who had not fulfilled his needs was completing them.

One of the first Muhājirūn did not remain but he was present at that raid, including, ʿUmar b. al-Khaṭṭāb, Abū ʿUbayda b. al-Jarrāḥ, Saʿd b. Abī Waqqāṣ, Abū l-Aʿwar, Saʿīd b. Zayd b. ʿAmr b. Nufayl. With the men from the Muhājirūn were a number of Anṣār: Qatāda b. al-Nuʿmān, Salama b. Aslam b. Ḥarīsh. Men from the Muhājirūn, and the harshest of them in that saying was ʿAyyāsh b. Abī Rabīʿa, who said, "Is this youth appointed over the first Muhājirūn?" Many words were said about that. ʿUmar b. al-Khaṭṭāb heard some of those words. He rejected [Page 1119] those who spoke to him and came to the Messenger of God and informed him of the group, who said it. The Messenger of God was deeply angered. He set out with a band on his head and a cover of velvet. He ascended the pulpit and he praised God and commended him. Then he said, "What of these words that I hear from some of you regarding my appointment of Usāma b. Zayd as commander? By God, if you doubt my appointment of Usāma surely you doubted my appointment of his father before him. By God, surely he was one worthy of the authority just as his son, after him, is worthy of the authority. Indeed, he was one of the most beloved of the people to me, and this is one of the most loved of the people to me. Indeed they are both worthy of every goodness. Take care of him, for indeed he is one of your best." Then he got down and went to his house. That day was the Sabbath, ten nights from Rabīʿ al-Awwal.

The Muslims who set out with Usāma came and bade farewell to the Messenger of God, and ʿUmar b. al-Khaṭṭāb was with them, and the Messenger of God says, "Carry out the mission of Usāma!" Umm Ayman entered at that time and said, "O Messenger of God, what if you let Usāma stay in his camp until you get better. Indeed, if Usāma sets out from this situation of his he will not benefit himself." The Messenger of God said, "Carry out the mission of Usāma." The people went to the camp on the eve of Sunday and spent the night. Usāma alighted on Sunday and the Messenger of God was slow and overwhelmed as he had been medicated that day. Usāma entered before the Messenger of God and the Messenger of God's eyes were wondering. With him were al-ʿAbbās and his wives around him. Usāma bowed his head and kissed him. The Messenger of God did not speak. [Page 1120] He began to raise his hand to the heavens, and then placed it on Usāma. Usāma said: I knew that he was praying for me.

Usāma said: I returned to my camp. When it dawned the next morning Usāma returned from his camp to visit the Messenger of God. The Messenger of God rose in the morning feeling better. Usāma came to the Prophet and the Prophet said, "Leave in the early morning with the blessings of God," and Usāma bade him farewell. The Messenger of God's strength improved. His wives began to comb his hair happily and make him comfortable. Abū Bakr visited him and said, "O Messenger of God, you have risen recovering, may God be praised. Today is the day of Ibnat Khārija so grant me leave!" The Prophet permitted him, and Abū Bakr went to al-Sunḥ.

Usāma rode to his camp. He shouted among the people and his companions to follow the troops. When he reached his camp he alighted. He commanded the people to depart, and the day had advanced. Meanwhile Usāma desired to ride from al-Jurf when the messenger of Umm Ayman—she was his mother—informed him that the Messenger of God was dying. Usāma approached Medina, and with him were ʿUmar and Abū ʿUbayda b. al-Jarrāḥ. They reached the Messenger of God who was dying.

The Messenger of God died when the sun declined from the meridian, on Monday the twelfth of Rabīʿ al-Awwal. The Muslims who had camped in al-Jurf entered Medina. Burayda b. al-Ḥuṣayb entered with the banner that Usāma had tied, until he came with it to the door of the Messenger of God and planted it there.

When Abū Bakr was appointed caliph he commanded Burayda to go with the banner to the house of Usāma, and say that he would never discharge Usāma until he raided the Byzantines. Burayda said: I set out with the banner until I brought it to the house of Usāma. Then I set out with it tied, to al-Shām. Then I returned with it to the house of Usāma. And the flag has stayed in the house of Usāma [Page 1121] until Usāma's death.

When news of the death of the Messenger of God reached the Bedouin, those who apostatized left Islam and Abū Bakr said to Usāma, "Complete the mission that the Messenger of God directed you towards." The people prepared to leave and they camped in their first station. Burayda set out with the banner until he reached their first camp and it was hard on the elders of the first Muhājirūn: ʿUmar, ʿUthmān, Saʿd b. Abī Waqqāṣ, Abū ʿUbayda b. al-Jarrāḥ and Saʿīd b. Zayd. So they came to Abū Bakr and said, "O *Khalīfat rasūl Allāh*, indeed the Bedouin have left you from every direction. Indeed you will not achieve anything by commanding the army to leave now. Make them prepare for the people of apostasy and aim them at their throat, otherwise we will not be able to protect the people of Medina that are raided, including the children and the women. Delay the attack on the Byzantines until Islam is established and the apostates return to what they detested (Islam) or they will be killed by the sword. Then, at that moment, send Usāma and we will prevent the Byzantines that march to us." When Abū Bakr understood their words he said, "Does one of you desire to say something?" They said, "No, you have heard our words." Abū Bakr said, "By Him who holds my soul in His hands, even if I thought the lion would eat me in Medina, I would surely carry out this mission. I did not start the first of it. A revelation came down from the heavens to the Messenger of God saying: Dispatch the troops of Usāma! But one thing; I will speak to Usāma about ʿUmar, to leave him behind in Medina, for indeed, we need him. By God, I do not know if Usāma will do it or not. By God, if he refuses I will not force him!" The People knew that Abū Bakr had resolved to dispatch the mission of Usāma.

Abū Bakr walked to Usama in his house, and asked him to leave ʿUmar behind, and Usāma [Page 1122] agreed. Abū Bakr said to him, "Are you pleased?" And Usāma said, "Yes!" So Abū Bakr went out and commanded a herald to proclaim, "I have made the decision that Usāma will not stay behind from the mission of those who departed with him during the life of the Messenger of God. Indeed one who is delayed from departing with him will not be brought to me but I will return him to it even walking." He sent word to a group of Muhājirūn who were disputing about the command of Usāma, and he was rude to them and forced them to leave, and not one man stayed behind from the mission.

Abū Bakr set out to escort Usāma and the Muslims, when Usāma rode from al-Jurf with his companions. They were three thousand men with a thousand horses. Abū Bakr walked beside Usāma for a while, then he said, "I leave your religion and your honesty and the completion of your work in God's hands. Indeed, I heard the Messenger of God advise you, so fulfill the command of the Messenger of God. Indeed, I will not command you nor forbid you. Rather I execute the command that the Messenger of God commanded. So set out swiftly; go through lands that have not apostatized from Islam—Juhayna, and others of the Quḍāʿa."

When Usāma alighted in Wādī al-Qurā, he sent forward a spy of his from the Banū ʿUdhra named Ḥurayth, and he set out on the chest of his horse ahead of him, quickly, until he reached Ubnā. He observed what was there and took the road. Then he returned swiftly until he met Usāma at a distance of two nights from Ubnā, and he informed him that the people were attacking, but had not as yet come together. So Usāma commanded him to hasten the march before the Byzantines gathered together, and to attack them with force.

He said: Hishām b. ʿĀṣim related to me from al-Mundhir b. Jahm, who said: Burayda said to Usāma, "O Abū Muḥammad, indeed, I witnessed the Messenger of God advise your [Page 1123] father to invite them to Islam, and if they obeyed him to let them choose—that if they preferred to stay in their land, they will be as the Bedouin Muslims, and there would be nothing for them from the *fay'* or the plunder, unless they struggled with the Muslims; but if they transferred to the land of Islam there would be for them as there was for the Muhājirūn." Usāma said, "Thus did the Messenger of God advise my father. But the Messenger of God commanded me and this was his last command to me: To hasten the march and to be ahead of the news. And to raid them, without inviting them, and to destroy and burn." Burayda said: Listen and obey the command of the Messenger of God.

When Usāma reached Ubnā and could see it with his eyes, he mobilized his companions and said, "Go and raid, but do not be obsessive with seeking out, and do not disperse. Hold together, and be quiet. Remember God in your hearts and draw your sword and place it in whoever confronts you." Then he pushed them into the raid. A dog did not bark, and no one moved. The enemy did not know except when the army attacked them calling out their slogan, "O Manṣūr, Kill!" He killed those who confronted him and took prisoner those he defeated. He set the borders on fire and their houses and fields and date palm on fire. There arose clouds of smoke, and he went around the courtyard with the horses. They were not obsessive in the search. They attacked what was in their reach, and spent the day packing what they took as plunder. Usāma rode the horse on which his father was killed named Sabḥa, and killed the killer of his father in the raid. Some of the prisoners informed him about the killer. He apportioned two portions to the horse, and one for its master. He took for himself the same. When it was night he commanded the people to depart. The guide went ahead of him. He was Ḥurayth al-ʿUdhrī. They took the same road from which they came. They approached during the night until they reached a distant land. Then he went through the lands until he reached Wādī al-Qurā in nine nights. Then he proceeded immediately to Medina. None of the Muslims was wounded.

The news reached Heraclius who was in Ḥimṣ. He called his commanders and said, "This is what I warned you of, and you refused to accept my warning. The Bedouin come raiding in a month's march to you, then they leave in a while without being hurt." His brother said, "I will send a band of knights to stay in al-Balqā'." He sent the band having appointed one of his companions over them, and he continued to stay over there until the missions of al-Shām were sent during the caliphates of Abū Bakr and ʿUmar.

They said: Opposing Usāma during his departure was a group from the people of Kathkath, one of the villages there. They had opposed his father when he began and attacked the borders of his army. Usāma had defied them with those who were with him. He had succeeded in scaring them away. He drove away some of their cattle and took two of them captive and tied them up while the rest fled. He arrived with the two of them in Medina and executed them.

He said: Abū Bakr b. Yaḥyā b. al-Naḍr related to me from his father that Usāma b. Zayd sent his messenger from Wādī al-Qurā with news of the success of the Muslims. They had attacked the enemy and taken them. When the Muslims heard about their arrival Abū Bakr set out with the Muhājirūn. The people of Medina set out, overcome with joy because of the success of Usāma and [Page 1125] those Muslims who were with him. He had set out, at that time, on a horse of his named Sabḥa from Dhū Khushub wearing armor. The banner was carried in front of him by Burayda until he reached the mosque. He entered and prayed two bowings, then he turned to his house with his banner. His exit from al-Jurf was in the month of Rabīʿ al-Ākhir in the year eleven. He was absent for thirty-five days, twenty when he began and fifteen when he went back.

He said: Muḥammad b. al-Ḥasan b. Usāma b. Zayd related from his family saying: The Messenger of God died when Usāma was nineteen. When he was fifteen years old, the Messenger of God had married him to a woman from Ṭayyiʾ. Then, he separated him from her and married him to another. A child was born to him during the time of the Messenger of God and the Messenger of God provided the wedding feast for him.

He said: Abū l-Ḥurr ʿAbd al-Raḥmān b. al-Ḥurr al-Waqifī related to me from the son of al-Sāʾib from Yazīd b. Ḥuṣayfa that a son of Usama b. Zayd b. Ḥāritha was brought with him before the Messenger of God in the house of Umm Salama. He was black and Umm Salama said, "O Messenger of God if this was a girl no one will ask for her hand in marriage." The Messenger of God said to her, "No, by the will of God, she will have bracelets of silver and earings and may God provide the Muslims with rings of gold."

He said: Muḥammad b. Ḥawṭ related to me from Ṣafwān b. Sulaym from ʿAṭāʾ b. Yasār, who said: Usāma b. Zayd was the first to be attacked by smallpox when it came to Medina while he was a youth. His life/mucus flowed over his mouth and ʿĀʾisha was disgusted by it. [Page 1126] The Messenger of God entered and immediately washed his face and kissed him. ʿĀʾisha said, "By God, after this I will not push him away ever." From Muḥammad b. al-Ḥasan from Ḥusayn b. Abī Ḥusayn al-Māzanī from Ibn Quṣayṭ from Muḥammad b. Zayd, who said: When Usāma fell and his face was injured by a deep wound, the Messenger of God sucked his blood and spat it out. From Ibn Jurayj and Sufyān b. ʿUyayna from ʿAmr b. Dīnār, from Yaḥyā b. Jaʿda: The Messenger of God said to Fāṭima who was wiping something from the face of Usāma, as though she were disgusted by him. The Messenger of God drew him close and scolded her. She said, "I will never be disgusted by him."

He said: Maʿmar related to me from al-Zuhrī from ʿUrwa from ʿĀʾisha that Mujazziz al-Mudlijī looked at Zayd and Usāma who were wearing velvet and were lying down with their heads and feet covered, and said, "Indeed these feet belong to each other." The Messenger of God smiled at the resemblance between Usāma and Zayd b. Ḥaritha. From Muḥammad from al-Zuhrī, from ʿUrwa, from ʿĀʾisha, who said, "I have never seen the Messenger of God naked except once, when Zayd b. Ḥāritha arrived from a raid desiring assistance against the enemy. The Messenger of God heard his voice, and stood up naked—for his garment fell—and kissed him.

He said: Mūsā b. Yaʿqūb related to me from Abū l-Huwayrith and Makhrama b. Bukayr from his father from Urwa b. al-Zubayr, who both said: Indeed the Messenger of God said to Umm Kulthūm bt. ʿUqba, "Will you marry Zayd b. Ḥāritha for indeed he is good for you." [Page 1127] And she hated that. God most high revealed: *It is not fitting for a Believer, man or woman, when a matter has been decided by God and His Apostle to have any option about their decision. If anyone disobeys God and His Apostle, he is indeed on a clearly wrong path* (Q. 33:36).

Index

GH

H

Ḥ

R

Ṣ